STUDENT'S SOLUTIONS MANUAL

to accompany

Precalculus with Limits

Margaret L. Lial
American River College
John Hornsby
University of New Orleans
David I. Schneider
University of Maryland

Addison
Wesley

Boston San Francisco New York
London Toronto Sydney Tokyo Singapore Madrid
Mexico City Munich Paris Cape Town Hong Kong Montreal

Reproduced by Addison-Wesley from camera-ready copy supplied by Laurel Technical Services.

Copyright © 2001 Addison-Wesley.

ISBN   0-321-07702-4

1 2 3 4 5 6 7 8 9 10 VG 03 02 01 00

7 APPLICATIONS OF TRIGONOMETRY

8 SYSTEMS OF EQUATIONS AND INEQUALITIES

9 ANALYTIC GEOMETRY

10 FURTHER TOPICS IN ALGEBRA

11 AN INTRODUCTION TO CALCULUS: LIMITS AND DERIVATIVES

R REFERENCE: ALGEBRAIC EXPRESSIONS

CONTENTS

4 EXPONENTIAL AND LOGARITHMIC FUNCTIONS

5 TRIGONOMETRIC FUNCTIONS

6 TRIGONOMETRIC IDENTITIES AND EQUATIONS

CHAPTER 1 EQUATIONS AND INEQUALITIES

Section 1.1

Exercises

1. The solution set of $2x + 3 = x - 5$ is $\{-8\}$.
Replacing x with -8 gives
$$2(-8) + 3 = -8 - 5$$
$$-13 = -13,$$
so the given statement is true.

3. The equations $x^2 = 9$ and $x = 3$ are equivalent equations. The solution set for $x = 3$ is $\{3\}$, while the solution set for $x^2 = 9$ is $\{3, -3\}$. Since the equations do not have the same solution set, they are not equivalent. The given statement is false.

7. $x^2 + 6x = x(x + 6)$
Since the product of x and $x + 6$ is $x^2 + 6x$, the given equation is true for every value of x, and is an identity. The solution set is {all real numbers}.

9. $3t + 4 = 5(t - 2)$
Replacing t with 7 gives
$$3 \cdot 7 + 4 = 5(7 - 2)$$
$$25 = 25,$$
a true statement. However, using $t = 1$ gives
$3 \cdot 1 + 4 = 5(1 - 2)$, which is false.
$$7 = -5$$
The equation is true for some values of t only, and is a conditional equation. The solution set is $\{7\}$.

11. $2x - 4 = 2(x + 2)$
Applying the distributive property on the right side gives $2x + 4$, so the equation becomes
$2x - 4 = 2x + 4$.
Since this equation is false for all values of x, the equation is a contradiction.
The solution set is $\emptyset$.

13. $\dfrac{5x}{x - 2} = \dfrac{20}{x - 2}$
Solution set: $\{4\}$
$5x = 20$
Solution set: $\{4\}$
Since the solution sets are equal, the equations are equivalent.

15. $\dfrac{x + 3}{x + 1} = \dfrac{2}{x + 1}$
Solution set: $\emptyset$.
$x = -1$.
Solution set: $\{-1\}$
Since the solution sets are not equal the equations are not equivalent.

17. (B) $8x^2 - 4x + 3 = 0$
Because of the x^2 that appears, this equation cannot be written in the form $ax + b = 0$. It is not a linear equation. All of the other choices are equations that can be written in the form $ax + b = 0$ and therefore are linear equations.

19.
$$2m - 5 = m + 7$$
$$2m - 5 - m = m + 7 - m$$
Subtract m from both sides.

$$m - 5 = 7 \quad \text{Add 5 to both sides.}$$
$$m - 5 + 5 = 7 + 5$$
$$m = 12$$
Solution set: $\{12\}$

21. $\dfrac{5}{6}k - 2k + \dfrac{1}{3} = \dfrac{2}{3}$
Multiply both sides of the equation by the least common denominator, 6.
$$6\left(\dfrac{5}{6}k - 2k + \dfrac{1}{3}\right) = 6\left(\dfrac{2}{3}\right)$$
$$5k - 12k + 2 = 4 \quad \text{Distributive property}$$
$$-7k + 2 = 4$$
$$-7k = 2 \quad \text{Subtract 2.}$$
$$k = -\dfrac{2}{7} \quad \text{Divide by 7.}$$
Solution set: $\left\{-\dfrac{2}{7}\right\}$

23. $3r + 2 - 5(r + 1) = 6r + 4$
$$3r + 2 - 5r - 5 = 6r + 4 \quad \text{Distributive Property}$$
$$-2r - 3 = 6r + 4$$
$$-3 = 8r + 4 \quad \text{Add } 2r.$$
$$-7 = 8r \quad \text{Subtract 4.}$$
$$r = -\dfrac{7}{8} \quad \text{Divide by 8.}$$
Solution set: $\left\{-\dfrac{7}{8}\right\}$

25. $2[m - (4 + 2m) + 3] = 2m + 2$
$$2[m - 4 - 2m + 3] = 2m + 2$$
$$2[-m - 1] = 2m + 2$$
$$-2m - 2 = 2m + 2$$
$$-2m - 2 + 2m = 2m + 2 + 2m$$
$$-2 = 4m + 2$$
$$-2 - 2 = 4m + 2 - 2$$
$$-4 = 4m$$
$$-1 = m$$
Solution set: $\{-1\}$

27. $\dfrac{3x - 2}{7} = \dfrac{x + 2}{5}$
Multiply both sides of the equation by the least common denominator, 35.

$$35\left(\frac{3x-2}{7}\right) = 35\left(\frac{x+2}{5}\right)$$
$$5(3x-2) = 7(x+2)$$
$$15x-10 = 7x+14$$
$$15x-10-7x = 7x+14-7x$$
$$8x-10 = 14$$
$$8x-10+10 = 14+10$$
$$8x = 24$$
$$x = 3$$

Solution set: {3}

29. (a) $r = .08, P = 1575, t = \frac{6}{12} = \frac{1}{2}$

$$I = Prt = 1575(.08)\left(\frac{1}{2}\right) = 63$$

The interest is $63.

   (b) The amount Miguel must pay Julio at the end of the six months is $1575 + $63 = $1638.

31. 20°C

$$F = \frac{9}{5}C + 32$$
$$= \frac{9}{5}(20) + 32$$
$$= 36 + 32$$
$$= 68$$

Therefore, 20°C = 68°F.

33. 59°F

$$C = \frac{5(F-32)}{9}$$
$$= \frac{5(59-32)}{9}$$
$$= \frac{5(27)}{9}$$
$$= 15$$

Therefore, 59°F = 15°C.

35. 100°F

$$C = \frac{5(F-32)}{9}$$
$$= \frac{5(100-32)}{9}$$
$$= \frac{5}{9}(68)$$
$$= \frac{340}{9}$$
$$\approx 37.8$$

Therefore, 100°F ≈ 37.8°C.

37. 865°F

$$C = \frac{5}{9}(F-32)$$
$$= \frac{5}{9}(865-32)$$
$$\approx 462.8$$

Therefore, 865°F ≈ 462.8°C.

39. $V = lwh$ for l (volume of a rectangular box)

$$\frac{1}{wh} \cdot V = \frac{1}{wh} \cdot lwh$$
$$\frac{V}{wh} = l$$

41. $P = a+b+c$ for c (perimeter of a triangle)

$P - a = b + c$ Subtract a.
$P - a - b = c$ Subtract b.

43. $A = \frac{1}{2}(B+b)h$ for B (area of a trapezoid)

$2A = (B+b)h$ Multiply by 2.
$2A = Bh + bh$ Distributive property
$2A - bh = Bh$ Subtract bh.
$\dfrac{2A-bh}{h} = B$ Divide by h.

or $\dfrac{2A}{h} - b = B$

45. $S = 2\pi rh + 2\pi r^2$ for h (surface area of a right circular cylinder)

$S - 2\pi r^2 = 2\pi rh$ Subtract $2\pi r^2$.
$\dfrac{S-2\pi r^2}{2\pi r} = h$ Divide by $2\pi r$.

or $\dfrac{S}{2\pi r} - r = h$

47. $S = 2lw + 2wh + 2hl$ for h (surface area of a rectangular box)

$S - 2lw = 2wh + 2hl$ Subtract lw.
$S - 2lw = h(2w + 2l)$ Factor out h.
$\dfrac{S-2lw}{2w+2l} = h$ Divide by $2w + 2l$.

49. (a) $T = 1033.3x + 100$

$$= 1033.3\left(\frac{3}{4}\right) + 100$$
$$\approx 875$$

The temperature at $\frac{3}{4}$ hour is 875°F.

   (b)
$$T = -1033.3x + 3975$$
$$875 = -1033.3x + 3975$$
$$-3100 = -1033.3x$$
$$3 \approx x$$

The cooling cycle begins at about 3 hours.

(c) The cleaning process takes about
3 hours $- \frac{3}{4}$ hours $= 2\frac{1}{4}$ hours.

(d) Using the graph, the thermal door lock goes
on at about .45 hours and off at about
3.30 hours.

(e) On:
$$T = 1033.3x + 100$$
$$= 1033.3(.45) + 100$$
$$\approx 565°F$$
Off:
$$T = -1033.3x + 3975$$
$$= -1033.3(3.30) + 3975$$
$$\approx 565°F$$

51. (a) $9 + 12 + 21 = 42$
The bag measures 42 linear inches. All the
airlines will allow it as a carry-on.

(b) $10 + 14 + 22 = 46$
The bag measures 46 linear inches.
It qualifies as a carry-on on airlines
American, Southwest, Trans World Airlines,
and U.S. Airways.

53. Using the equation solving feature to solve the
equation $2x + 7 - 3(x + 3) + 8 = 0$ gives $x = 6$.
The solution set is $\{6\}$.

55. Using the equation solving feature to solve the
equation $5x - 2(x + 4) - 6x - 3 = 0$ gives $x = -3.\overline{6}$.
The solution set is $\{-3.\overline{6}\}$.

57. Using the equation solving feature to solve the
equation $4 + (.23x + \sqrt{5}) - \sqrt{2}x - 1 = 0$ gives
$x = 16.07$, to the nearest hundredth. The solution
set is $\{16.07\}$.

59. Using the equation solving feature to solve the
equation $2\pi x + \sqrt[3]{4} - .5\pi x + \sqrt{28} = 0$ gives
$x = -1.46$, to the nearest hundredth. The solution
set is $\{-1.46\}$.

Section 1.2

Connections *(page 16)*

Steps 1–3 compare to Polya's first step, while steps 4, 5,
6 compare to Polya's 2nd, 3rd and 4th steps respectively.

Exercises

1. 15 minutes is $\dfrac{1}{4}$ of an hour, so multiply 80 miles
per hour by $\dfrac{1}{4}$ to get a distance of 20 miles.

3. 4% is .04 so, multiply \$100 by .04 and by 2 years
to get interest of \$8.

7. Let w = the width of the rectangle.
Then $2w - 2.5$ = the length.

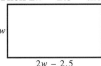

Use the formula for the perimeter of a rectangle.
$$P = 2l + 2w$$
$$40.6 = 2(2w - 2.5) + 2w$$
$$40.6 = 4w - 5 + 2w$$
$$45.6 = 6w$$
$$7.6 = w$$
The width is 7.6 cm.

9. Let w = the width of the tablecloth.
Then $w + 11,757.6$ = the length.
Use the formula for the perimeter of a rectangle.
$$P = 2l + 2w$$
$$23,803.2 = 2(w + 11,757.6) + 2w$$
$$23,803.2 = 2w + 23,515.2 + 2w$$
$$288 = 4w$$
$$72 = w$$
$$w + 11,757.6 = 11,829.6$$
The length is 11,829.6 inches or 328.6 yd.

11. Let h = the height of the cylinder. Use the formula
for the volume of a right circular cylinder.
$$V = \pi r^2 h$$
$$144\pi = \pi \cdot 6^2 \cdot h \quad \text{Let } V = 144\pi, \ r = 6.$$
$$144\pi = 36\pi h$$
$$4 = h$$
The height of the cylinder is 4 in.

13. (B) and (C) cannot be correct equations.
In (B),
$$-2x + 7(5 - x) = 62$$
$$-2x + 35 - 7x = 62$$
$$35 - 9x = 62$$
$$-9x = 27$$
$$x = -3,$$
but the length of a rectangle cannot be negative.
In (C),
$$4(x + 2) + 4x = 8$$
$$4x + 8 + 4x = 8$$
$$8 + 8x = 8$$
$$8x = 0$$
$$x = 0,$$
but the length of a rectangle cannot be zero.

15. Let x = the person's IQ.

$$x = \frac{100 \cdot 20}{16}$$
$$= \frac{2000}{16}$$
$$= 125$$

The IQ is 125.

17. Let x = biking speed;
$x + 4.5$ = driving speed.
Set up a chart, using $d = rt$.

	d	r	t
Car	$\frac{1}{3}(x+4.5)$	$x+4.5$	$\frac{1}{3}$
Bike	$\frac{3}{4}x$	x	$\frac{3}{4}$

Since the speeds are given in miles per hour, the times must be changed from minutes to hours.

$$\frac{\text{Distance}}{\text{driving}} = \frac{\text{Distance}}{\text{biking}}$$
$$\frac{1}{3}(x+4.5) = \frac{3}{4}x$$
$$12 \cdot \frac{1}{3}(x+4.5) = 12 \cdot \frac{3}{4}x$$
$$4(x+4.5) = 9x$$
$$4x+18 = 9x$$
$$18 = 5x$$
$$\frac{18}{5} = x$$

To find the distance use,
$$d = \frac{3}{4}x = \frac{3}{4}\left(\frac{18}{5}\right) = \frac{27}{10} = 2.7.$$
Johnny travels 2.7 mi to work.

19. Let x = time on trip from Denver to Minneapolis.
Set up a chart, using the relationship $d = rt$.

	d	r	t
Denver to Minneapolis	$50x$	50	x
Minneapolis to Denver	$55(32-x)$	55	$32-x$

Distance to Minneapolis	=	Return distance
$50x$	=	$55(32-x)$
$50x$	=	$1760-55x$
$105x$	=	1760
x	=	16.76
d	=	rt
	=	$50(16.76)$
	$\approx$	840

The distance between the two cities is about 840 mi.

21. Let d = distance Janet runs.

Then $d + \frac{1}{2}$ = distance Russ runs.

Set up a chart, using $d = rt$.
This is equivalent to $t = d/r$.

	d	r	t
Russ	$d+\frac{1}{2}$	7	$\frac{d+\frac{1}{2}}{7}$
Janet	d	5	$\frac{d}{5}$

Since they both traveled for the same time, we have the equation

$$\frac{d+\frac{1}{2}}{7} = \frac{d}{5}.$$

Multiply both sides by the least common denominator, 35.

$$35\left(\frac{d+\frac{1}{2}}{7}\right) = 35\left(\frac{d}{5}\right)$$
$$5\left(d+\frac{1}{2}\right) = 35\left(\frac{d}{5}\right)$$
$$5d+\frac{5}{2} = 7d$$
$$\frac{5}{2} = 2d$$
$$\frac{5}{4} = d$$

To find t, use either
$$t = \frac{d+\frac{1}{2}}{7} \text{ or } t = \frac{d}{5}.$$

Then $t = \frac{d}{5} = \frac{\frac{5}{4}}{5} = \frac{1}{4}.$

It will take $\frac{1}{4}$ hr or 15 min until they are $\frac{1}{2}$ mi apart.

23. Let x = the number of hours it takes Plant A to produce the maximum amount of pollutant. Then $2x$ = the number of hours it takes Plant B to produce the maximum of pollutant.

	Rate	Time	Part of the job accomplished
Plant B	$\frac{1}{2x}$	26	$\frac{1}{2x}(26) = \frac{13}{x}$
Plant A	$\frac{1}{x}$	26	$\frac{1}{x}(26) = \frac{26}{x}$

Part done by Plant B	+	Part done by Plant A	=	1 whole job
↓	↓	↓	↓	↓
$\frac{13}{x}$	+	$\frac{26}{x}$	=	1

Multiply both sides by the least common denominator, x.

$$x\left(\frac{13}{x} + \frac{26}{x}\right) = x \cdot 1$$
$$13 + 26 = x$$
$$39 = x$$
$$78 = 2x$$

It will take plant B 78 hr to produce the maximum pollutant alone.

25. Let x = the number of hours to fill the pool with both pipes open.

	Rate	Time	Part of the job accomplished
Inlet pipe	$\frac{1}{5}$	x	$\frac{1}{5}x$
Outlet pipe	$\frac{1}{8}$	x	$\frac{1}{8}x$

Part done by inlet pipe	−	Part done by outlet pipe	=	Full pool
↓	↓	↓	↓	↓
$\frac{1}{5}x$	−	$\frac{1}{8}x$	=	1

Multiply both sides by the least common denominator, 40.

$$40\left(\frac{1}{5}x - \frac{1}{8}x\right) = 40 \cdot 1$$
$$8x - 5x = 40$$
$$3x = 40$$
$$x = \frac{40}{3}$$

It took $\frac{40}{3}$ hr to fill the pool.

27. Let x = number of liters of pure alcohol to be added.

Strength	Liters of solution	Liters of pure alcohol
10%	7	$.10(7)$
100%	x	$1(x)$
30%	$7 + x$	$.30(7 + x)$

Liters of alcohol in 10% solution	+	Liters of alcohol in 100% solution	=	Liters of alcohol in 30% solution
↓	↓	↓	↓	↓
$.10(7)$	+	$1(x)$	=	$.30(7 + x)$

$$.10(7) + 1(x) = .30(7 + x)$$
$$.7 + x = 2.1 + .3x$$
$$.7x = 1.4$$
$$x = 2$$

He should add 2 liters of pure alcohol.

29. Let x = number of liters of pure acid to be added.

Strength	Liters of solution	Liters of pure acid
30%	6	$.30(6)$
100%	x	$1(x)$
50%	$6 + x$	$.50(6 + x)$

Liters of acid in 30% solution	+	Liters of acid in 100% solution	=	Liters of acid in 30% solution
↓	↓	↓	↓	↓
$.30(6)$	+	$1(x)$	=	$.50(6 + x)$

$$.30(6) + 1(x) = .50(6 + x)$$
$$1.8 + x = 3 + .5x$$
$$.5x = 1.2$$
$$x = 2.4$$

2.4 liters of pure acid should be added.

31. Let x = the number of liters of 94 octane gasoline.

Strength	Liters of solution	Amount of pure isooctane
94%	x	$.94x$
99%	200	$.99(200)$
97%	$x + 200$	$.97(x + 200)$

$$.94x + .99(220) = .97(x + 200)$$
$$.94x + 198 = .97x + 194$$
$$4 = .03x$$
$$133\tfrac{1}{3} = x$$

$133\tfrac{1}{3}\left(\text{or } \dfrac{400}{3}\right)$ liters of 94-octane gasoline should be used in the mixture.

33. Let x = amount of short-term note.
Then $125{,}000 - x$ = amount of long-term note.
$$.12x + .10(125{,}000 - x) = 13{,}700$$
$$12x + 10(125{,}000 - x) = 1{,}370{,}000$$
$$\text{Multiply by } 100$$
$$12x + 1{,}250{,}000 - 10x = 1{,}370{,}000$$
$$2x = 120{,}000$$
$$x = 60{,}000$$
The amount of the short-term note is $60,000 and the amount of the long-term note is $125{,}000 - \$50{,}000 = \$65{,}000$.

35. Let x = amount invested at 7%.
Then $4x$ = amount invested at 11%.
$$.07x + .11(4x) = 7650$$
Multiply by 100.
$$7x + 11(4x) = 765{,}000$$
$$7x + 44x = 765{,}000$$
$$51x = 765{,}000$$
$$x = 15{,}000$$
$$4x = 60{,}000$$
The church invested $15,000 at 7% and $60,000 at 11%.

37. 28% of $48,000 is $13,440, so after paying her income tax, Latasha had $34,560 left to invest.
Let x = amount invested at 6.5%.
Then $34{,}560 - x$ = amount invested at 6.25%.
$$.065x + .0625(34{,}560 - x) = 2210$$
Multiply by 10,000 to clear decimals.
$$650x + 625(34{,}560 - x) = 22{,}100{,}000$$
$$650x + 21{,}600{,}000 - 625x = 22{,}100{,}000$$
$$25x = 500{,}000$$
$$x = 20{,}000$$
Latasha invested $20,000 at 6.5% and $34{,}560 - \$20{,}000 = \$14{,}560$ at 6.25%.

39. **(a)** Since each student needs 15 cu ft each minute and there are 60 minutes in an hour, the ventilation required by x students per hour would be
$$V = 60(15x) = 900x.$$

(b) The number of air exchanges per hour would be
$$A = \frac{900x}{15{,}000} = \frac{3}{50}x.$$

(c) If $x = 40$, then
$$A = \frac{3}{50}(40) = 2.4\,\text{ach}.$$

(d) It should be increased by $\dfrac{50}{15} = 3\tfrac{1}{3}$ times.
Smoking areas require more than triple the ventilation.

41. **(a)** The risk for one year would be
$$\frac{R}{72} = \frac{1.5 \times 10^{-3}}{72} \approx .000021 \text{ for each}$$
individual.

(b) $C = .000021x$

(c) $C = .000021(100{,}000)$
$C = 2.1$
There are approximately 2.1 cancer cases in every 100,000 passive smokers.

(d) $C = \dfrac{.44(260{,}000{,}000)(.26)}{72}$
$C \approx 413{,}111$
There are approximately 413,000 excess deaths caused by smoking each year.

43. **(a)** In 2004, $x = 4$.
$y = 36.27x + 124.27$
$y = 36.27(4) + 124.27$
$y = 269.35$
The projected budget surplus for 2004 is $269.35 billion.

(b) $\quad y = 36.27x + 124.27$
$\quad 162 = 36.27x + 124.27$
$\quad 37.73 = 36.27x$
$\quad 1.0 \approx x$
The surplus should reach $162 billion in 2001.

(c) The answers are reasonably close. The answers in parts (a) and (b) are both a little high.

(d) In 1997, $x = -3$.

$y = 36.27x + 124.27$

$y = 36.27(-3) + 124.27$

$y = 15.46$

The surplus would be \$15.46 billion in 1997.

45. Let x be the number of new shares he is issued.

$$\underset{\downarrow}{\underset{\text{Shares}}{\text{Old}}} + \underset{\downarrow}{\underset{\text{Shares}}{\text{New}}} = \underset{\downarrow}{\underset{\text{Shares}}{\text{Total}}}$$

$(.05)(900,000) + x = (.10)(900,000 + x)$

$45,000 + x = 90,000 + .10x$

$.90x = 45,000$

$x = 50,000$

He is issued 50,000 new shares.

Section 1.3

Exercises

3. -5 is a real number.

5. $i\sqrt{6}$ is an imaginary number.

7. $2 + 5i$ is an imaginary number.

9. $\sqrt{-100} = i\sqrt{100} = 10i$

11. $-\sqrt{-400} = -i\sqrt{400} = -20i$

13. $-\sqrt{-39} = -i\sqrt{39}$

15. $5 + \sqrt{-4} = 5 + i\sqrt{4} = 5 + 2i$

17. $9 - \sqrt{-50} = 9 - i\sqrt{50} = 9 - 5i\sqrt{2}$

19. $\sqrt{-5} \cdot \sqrt{-5} = i\sqrt{5} \cdot i\sqrt{5}$

$= i^2 \cdot (\sqrt{5})^2$

$= (-1)(5) \quad i^2 = -1$

$= -5$

21. $\dfrac{\sqrt{-40}}{\sqrt{-10}} = \dfrac{i\sqrt{40}}{i\sqrt{10}}$

$= \sqrt{\dfrac{40}{10}}$

$= \sqrt{4}$

$= 2$

23. $(3 + 2i) + (4 - 3i) = (3 + 4) + [2 + (-3)]i$

$= 7 - i$

25. $(-2 + 3i) - (-4 + 3i) = [(-2) - (-4)] + (3 - 3)i$

$= 2$

27. $(2 - 5i) - (3 + 4i) - (-2 + i)$

$= [2 - 3 - (-2)] + [-5 - 4 - 1]i$

$= 1 - 10i$

29. $(2 + 4i)(-1 + 3i) = 2(-1) + 2(3i) + 4i(-1) + 4i(3i)$

$= -2 + 6i - 4i + 12i^2$

$= -2 + 2i + 12(-1) \qquad i^2 = -1$

$= -14 + 2i$

31. $(-3 + 2i)^2 = (-3)^2 + 2(-3)(2i) + (2i)^2$

Square of a binomial

$= 9 - 12i + 4i^2$

$= 9 - 12i + 4(-1) \quad i^2 = -1$

$= 5 - 12i$

33. $(2 + 3i)(2 - 3i) = 2^2 - (3i)^2$ Difference of

two squares

$= 4 - 9i^2$

$= 4 - 9(-1) \quad i^2 = -1$

$= 13$

35. $(\sqrt{6} + i)(\sqrt{6} - i) = (\sqrt{6})^2 - 1^2$ Difference of

two squares

$= 6 - i^2$

$= 6 - (-1) \qquad i^2 = -1$

$= 7$

37. $i(3 - 4i)(3 + 4i) = i[3^2 - (4i)^2]$ Difference of

two squares

$= i[9 - (-16)]$

$= 25i$

39. $i^5 = i^4 \cdot i = 1 \cdot i = i$

41. $i^9 = i^8 \cdot i$

$= (i^4)^2 \cdot i$

$= 1^2 \cdot i$

$= i$

43. $i^{12} = (i^4)^3 = 1^3 = 1$

45. $i^{43} = i^{40} \cdot i^3$

$= (i^4)^{10} \cdot i^3$

$= 1^{10} \cdot i^3$

$= -i$

47. $\dfrac{1}{i^{12}} = \dfrac{1}{(i^4)^3} = \dfrac{1}{1^3} = 1$

49.
$$i^{-15} = i^{-16} \cdot i$$
$$= (i^4)^{-4} \cdot i$$
$$= 1^{-4} \cdot i$$
$$= i$$

53. $\dfrac{1+i}{1-i}$

Multiply numerator and denominator by $1 + i$, the conjugate of the denominator.

$$\frac{1+i}{1-i} = \frac{(1+i)(1+i)}{(1-i)(1+i)}$$

$$= \frac{1+2i+i^2}{1-i^2} \quad \text{Multiply.}$$

$$= \frac{1+2i-1}{1+1} \quad i^2 = -1$$

$$= \frac{2i}{2}$$

$$= i$$

55. $\dfrac{4-3i}{4+3i}$

Multiply numerator and denominator by $4 - 3i$, the conjugate of the denominator.

$$\frac{4-3i}{4+3i} = \frac{(4-3i)(4-3i)}{(4+3i)(4-3i)}$$

$$= \frac{16-24i+9i^2}{16-9i^2} \quad \text{Multiply.}$$

$$= \frac{16-24i-9}{16+9} \quad i^2 = -1$$

$$\frac{7-24i}{25}$$

$$= \frac{7}{25} - \frac{24}{25} \quad \text{Standard form}$$

57.
$$\frac{3-4i}{2-5i} = \frac{(3-4i)(2+5i)}{(2-5i)(2+5i)}$$

$$= \frac{6+15i-8i-20i^2}{4-25i^2} \quad \text{Multiply.}$$

$$= \frac{26+7i}{29}$$

$$= \frac{26}{29} + \frac{7}{29}i \qquad \text{Standard form}$$

59.
$$\frac{-3+4i}{2-i} = \frac{(-3+4i)(2+i)}{(2-i)(2+i)}$$

$$= \frac{-6-3i+8i+4i^2}{4-i^2}$$

$$= \frac{-10+5i}{5}$$

$$= \frac{10}{5} + \frac{5}{5}i$$

$$= -2+i \qquad \text{Lowest terms}$$

61.
$$\frac{2}{i} = \frac{2(-i)}{i(-i)} \qquad -i \text{ is the conjugate of } i.$$

$$= \frac{-2i}{-i^2}$$

$$= \frac{-2i}{1}$$

$$= -2i$$

65. Evaluate $3z - z^2$ if $z = 3 - 2i$.

$$3z - z^2 = 3(3-2i) - (3-2i)^2$$
$$= 9 - 6i - (9 - 12i + 4i^2)$$
$$= 9 - 6i - (9 - 12i - 4)$$
$$= 9 - 6i - (5 - 12i)$$
$$= 9 - 6i - 5 + 12i$$
$$= 4 + 6i$$

67. $(2+i)^3 = (2+i)^2(2+i)$ is a true statement because the product rule for exponents says that $a^{m+n} = a^m \cdot a^n$, so $a^3 = a^2 \cdot a$.

68.
$$(2+i)^2 = (2+i)(2+i)$$
$$= 4 + 2i + 2i + i^2$$
$$= 4 + 4i - 1$$
$$= 3 + 4i$$

69.
$$(2+i)^2 = (2+i)^2(2+i)$$
$$= (3+4i)(2+i)$$
$$= 6 + 3i + 8i + 4i^2$$
$$= 6 + 11i - 4$$
$$= 2 + 11i$$

Yes, this product agrees with the one found by expanding a binomial using Pascal's triangle.

70. Use the coefficients from the sixth row of Pascal's triangle.

$$(x+y)^6 = x^6 + 6x^5y + 15x^4y^2 + 20x^3y^3$$
$$+ 15x^2y^4 + 6xy^5 + y^6$$
$$(1+i)^6 = 1^6 + 6(1)^5i + 15(1)^4i^2 + 20(1)^3i^3$$
$$+ 15(1)^2i^4 + 6(1)i^5 + i^6$$

Let $x = 1$ and $y = i$
$$= 1 + 6i + 15(-1) + 20(-i) + 15(1) + 6 - 1$$
$$= 1 + 6i - 15 - 20i + 15 + 6i - 1$$
$$= -8i$$

Section 1.4

Exercises

1. D is the only one set up for direct use of the zero-factor property.
$$(3x + 1)(x - 7) = 0$$
$$3x + 1 = 0 \quad \text{or} \quad x - 7 = 0$$
$$x = -\frac{1}{3} \quad \text{or} \quad x = 7$$

Solution set: $\left\{ -\frac{1}{3},\ 7 \right\}$

3. C is the only one that does not require Step 1 of the method of completing the square.
$$x^2 + x = 12$$
$$x^2 + x + \frac{1}{4} = 12 + \frac{1}{4}$$
$$\left(x + \frac{1}{2} \right)^2 = \frac{49}{4}$$
$$x + \frac{1}{2} = \pm\sqrt{\frac{49}{4}}$$
$$x = -\frac{1}{2} + \frac{7}{2}$$
$$x = -\frac{1}{2} + \frac{7}{2} \quad \text{or} \quad x = -\frac{1}{2} - \frac{7}{2}$$
$$x = 3 \quad \text{or} \quad x = -4$$
Solution set: $\{3, -4\}$

5. $p^2 = 16$
$$p = \sqrt{16} \quad \text{or} \quad p = -\sqrt{16}$$
$$\qquad\qquad \text{Square root property}$$
$$p = 4 \quad \text{or} \quad p = -4$$
Solution set: $\{\pm 4\}$

7. $x^2 = 27$
$$x = \sqrt{27} \quad \text{or} \quad x = -\sqrt{27}$$
$$\qquad\qquad \text{Square root property}$$
$$x = 3\sqrt{3} \quad \text{or} \quad x = -3\sqrt{3}$$
Solution set: $\{\pm 3\sqrt{3}\}$

9. $t^2 = -16$
$$t = \sqrt{-16} \quad \text{or} \quad t = -\sqrt{-16}$$
$$\qquad\qquad \text{Square root property}$$
$$t = 4i \quad \text{or} \quad t = -4i$$
Solution set: $\{\pm 4i\}$

11. $(3k - 1)^2 = 12$
$$3k - 1 = \pm\sqrt{12}$$
$$3k - 1 = \pm 2\sqrt{3}$$
$$3k = 1 \pm 2\sqrt{3}$$
$$k = \frac{1 \pm 2\sqrt{3}}{3}$$

Solution set: $\left\{ \dfrac{1 \pm 2\sqrt{3}}{3} \right\}$

13. $p^2 - 5p + 6 = 0$
$$(p - 2)(p - 3) = 0 \quad \text{Factor.}$$
$$p - 2 = 0 \text{ or } p - 3 = 0$$
$$\qquad\qquad \text{Zero-factor property}$$
$$p = 2 \quad \text{or } p = 3$$
Solution set: $\{2, 3\}$

15. $(5r - 3)^2 = -3$
$$5r - 3 = \pm\sqrt{-3}$$
$$5r - 3 = \pm i\sqrt{3}$$
$$5r = 3 \pm i\sqrt{3}$$
$$r = \frac{3 \pm i\sqrt{3}}{5}$$
$$= \frac{3}{5} \pm \frac{\sqrt{3}}{5}i \quad \text{Standard form}$$

Solution set: $\left\{ \dfrac{3}{5} \pm \dfrac{\sqrt{3}}{5}i \right\}$

17. $p^2 - 8p + 15 = 0$
$$p^2 - 8p = -15$$
Half the coefficient of p is -4, and $(-4)^2 = 16$.
Add 16 to both sides.
$$p^2 - 8p + 16 = -15 + 16$$
Factor on the left and combine terms on the right.
$$(p - 4)^2 = 1$$
Use the square root property to complete the solution.
$$p - 4 = \pm 1$$
$$p = 4 + 1 = 5 \text{ or } p = 4 - 1 = 3$$
Solution set: $\{5, 3\}$

19. $x^2 - 2x - 4 = 0$

$$x^2 - 2x = 4$$
$$x^2 - 2x + 1 = 4 + 1$$
$$(x - 1)^2 = 5$$
$$x - 1 = \pm\sqrt{5}$$
$$x = 1 \pm \sqrt{5}$$

Solution set: $\{1 \pm \sqrt{5}\}$

21. $2p^2 + 2p + 1 = 0$

$$p^2 + p + \frac{1}{2} = 0 \qquad \text{Multiply by } \frac{1}{2}.$$
$$p^2 + p = -\frac{1}{2} \qquad \text{Subtract } \frac{1}{2}.$$

Half the coefficient of p is $\frac{1}{2}$ and $\left(\frac{1}{2}\right)^2 = \frac{1}{4}$.

Add $\frac{1}{4}$ to both sides.

$$p^2 + p + \frac{1}{4} = -\frac{1}{2} + \frac{1}{4}$$
$$\left(p + \frac{1}{2}\right)^2 = -\frac{1}{4}$$
$$p + \frac{1}{2} = \pm\sqrt{-\frac{1}{4}}$$
$$p + \frac{1}{2} = \pm\frac{1}{2}i$$
$$p = -\frac{1}{2} \pm \frac{1}{2}i$$

Solution set: $\left\{-\frac{1}{2} \pm \frac{1}{2}i\right\}$

23. He is incorrect. If the constant term is missing from the equation, $c = 0$.

25. $m^2 - m - 1 = 0$
Here $a = 1$, $b = -1$, and $c = 1$.
Substitute these values into the quadratic formula.

$$m = \frac{-b \pm \sqrt{b^2 - 4ac}}{2a}$$
$$= \frac{-(-1) \pm \sqrt{(-1)^2 - 4(1)(-1)}}{2(1)}$$
$$= \frac{1 \pm \sqrt{1 + 4}}{2}$$
$$m = \frac{1 \pm \sqrt{5}}{2}$$

Solution set: $\left\{\dfrac{1 \pm \sqrt{5}}{2}\right\}$

27. $x^2 - 6x + 7 = 0$
Here $a = 1$, $b = -6$, and $c = 7$.

Substitute these values into the quadratic formula.

$$x = \frac{-b \pm \sqrt{b^2 - 4ac}}{2a}$$
$$= \frac{-(-6) \pm \sqrt{(-6)^2 - 4(1)(7)}}{2(1)}$$
$$= \frac{6 \pm \sqrt{36 - 28}}{2} = \frac{6 \pm \sqrt{8}}{2}$$
$$= \frac{6 \pm 2\sqrt{2}}{2}$$
$$= \frac{2(3 \pm \sqrt{2})}{2} \qquad \text{Factor numerator.}$$
$$x = 3 \pm \sqrt{2} \qquad \text{Lowest terms}$$

Solution set: $\{3 \pm \sqrt{2}\}$

29. $4z^2 - 12z + 11 = 0$
Here $a = 4$, $b = -12$, and $c = 11$.
Substitute these values into the quadratic formula.

$$z = \frac{-(-12) \pm \sqrt{(-12)^2 - 4(4)(11)}}{2(4)}$$
$$= \frac{12 \pm \sqrt{144 - 176}}{8}$$
$$= \frac{12 \pm \sqrt{-32}}{8}$$
$$= \frac{12 \pm i\sqrt{32}}{8}$$
$$= \frac{12 \pm 4i\sqrt{2}}{8}$$
$$= \frac{4(3 \pm i\sqrt{2})}{8}$$
$$z = \frac{3}{2} \pm \frac{\sqrt{2}}{2}i$$

Solution set: $\left\{\dfrac{3}{2} \pm \dfrac{\sqrt{2}}{2}i\right\}$

31. $\dfrac{1}{2}t^2 + \dfrac{1}{4}t - 3 = 0$

Multiply both sides by the least common denominator, 4.

$$4\left(\frac{1}{2}t^2 + \frac{1}{4}t - 3\right) = 4(0)$$
$$2t^2 + t - 12 = 0$$

Substitute $a = 2$, $b = 1$, and $c = -12$ into the quadratic formula.

$$t = \frac{-1 \pm \sqrt{1^2 - 4(2)(-12)}}{2(2)}$$

$$= \frac{-1 \pm \sqrt{1 + 96}}{4}$$

$$t = \frac{-1 \pm \sqrt{97}}{4}$$

Solution set: $\left\{ \dfrac{-1 \pm \sqrt{97}}{4} \right\}$

33. $4 + \dfrac{3}{x} - \dfrac{2}{x^2} = 0$

Multiply both sides of the equation by the least common denominator, x^2.

$4x^2 + 3x - 2 = 0$
Here $a = 4$, $b = 3$, and $c = -2$.
Substitute these values into the quadratic formula.

$$x = \frac{-(3) \pm \sqrt{3^2 - 4(4)(-2)}}{2(4)}$$

$$= \frac{-3 \pm \sqrt{9 + 32}}{8}$$

$$x = \frac{-3 \pm \sqrt{41}}{8}$$

Solution set: $\left\{ \dfrac{-3 \pm \sqrt{41}}{8} \right\}$

35. $x^3 - 8 = 0$

Factor the left side as the difference of two cubes.
$(x - 2)(x^2 + 2x + 4) = 0$
Set each factor to zero.
$x - 2 = 0$ or $x^2 + 2x + 4 = 0$
$\qquad x = 2$
Use the quadratic formula to solve
$x^2 + 2x + 4 = 0$.
Here $a = 1$, $b = 2$, and $c = 4$.

$$x = \frac{-2 \pm \sqrt{4 - 16}}{2}$$

$$= \frac{-2 \pm \sqrt{-12}}{2}$$

$$= \frac{-2 \pm 2i\sqrt{3}}{2}$$

$$x = -1 \pm i\sqrt{3}$$

Solution set: $\{2, \ -1 \pm i\sqrt{3}\}$

37. $\qquad x^3 + 27 = 0$

$(x + 3)(x^2 - 3x + 9) = 0$

$x + 3 = 0$ or $x^2 - 3x + 9 = 0$

$\quad x = -3$ or $\qquad x = \dfrac{3 \pm \sqrt{9 - 36}}{2}$

$$= \frac{3 \pm \sqrt{-27}}{2}$$

$$= \frac{3 \pm 3i\sqrt{3}}{2}$$

$x = -3$ or $\qquad x = \dfrac{3}{2} \pm \dfrac{3\sqrt{3}}{2} i$

Solution set: $\left\{ -3, \ \dfrac{3}{2} \pm \dfrac{3\sqrt{3}}{2} i \right\}$

39. $8p^3 + 125 = 0$

Factor the left side as the sum of two cubes.
$(2p + 5)(4p^2 - 10p + 25) = 0$

$2p + 5 = 0$ or $4p^2 - 10p + 25 = 0$

$p = -\dfrac{5}{2}$ or $p = \dfrac{10 \pm \sqrt{100 - 400}}{8}$

$\qquad\qquad\qquad$ Quadratic formula

$$= \frac{10 \pm \sqrt{-300}}{8}$$

$$= \frac{10 \pm 10i\sqrt{3}}{8}$$

$$= \frac{2(5 \pm 5i\sqrt{3})}{2(4)}$$

$$= \frac{5 \pm 5i\sqrt{3}}{4}$$

$p = \dfrac{5}{4} \pm \dfrac{5\sqrt{3}}{4} i$ Standard form

Solution set: $\left\{ -\dfrac{5}{2}, \ \dfrac{5}{4} \pm \dfrac{5\sqrt{3}}{4} i \right\}$

41. $(m - 3)^2 = 5$

$m - 3 = \pm\sqrt{5}$ Square root property

$\qquad m = 3 \pm \sqrt{5}$

Solution set: $\{3 \pm \sqrt{5}\}$

43. $(3y + 1)^2 = -7$

Use the square root property.

$$3y + 1 = \pm i\sqrt{7}$$
$$3y = -1 \pm i\sqrt{7}$$
$$y = \frac{-1 \pm i\sqrt{7}}{3}$$
$$= -\frac{1}{3} + \frac{\sqrt{7}}{3} i \quad \text{Standard form}$$

Solution set: $\left\{ -\frac{1}{3} \pm \frac{\sqrt{7}}{3} i \right\}$

Note for Exercises 45 and 47: The answers given here show all decimal places which are displayed at the bottom of the screen when the graphing method is used. However, the internal memory of the calculator holds more decimal places. To see these extra decimal places, call up X from the home screen after the graphing routine is completed.

45. $\sqrt{2}x^2 - 3x = -\sqrt{2}$

Rewrite as $\sqrt{2}x^2 - 3x + \sqrt{2} = 0$.
Enter: $y_1 = \sqrt{2}x^2 - 3x + \sqrt{2}$
Roots: $x = .7071067812$, $x = 1.414213562$
Solution set: $\{.7071067812, 1.414213562\}$

47. $x(x + \sqrt{5}) = -1$

Simplify and rewrite as
$$x^2 + \sqrt{5}x = -1$$
$$x^2 + \sqrt{5}x + 1 = 0.$$
Enter: $y_1 = x^2 + \sqrt{5}x + 1$
Roots: $x = -1.618013989$, $x = -.6180339887$
Solution set: $\{-1.618033989, -.6180339887\}$

49. $\sqrt{6}x^2 + 5x = -\sqrt{10}$

Rewrite as $\sqrt{6}x^2 + 5x + \sqrt{10} = 0$.
Enter: $a = \sqrt{6}$, $b = 5$, $c = \sqrt{10}$
Solution set: $\{-1.020620726 \pm .4993273296i\}$

51. $8.4x(x - 1) = -8$

Simplify and rewrite as
$$8.4x^2 - 8.4x = -8.$$
$$8.4x^2 - 8.4x + 8 = 0$$

Enter: $a = 8.4$, $b = -8.4$, $c = 8$
Solution set: $\{.5 \pm .8380817098i\}$

53. $2x^2 - 13x - 7 = 0$

Using the SOLVE feature of the graphing calculator, the results are
Guess: -5 Root: $-.5$
Guess: 5 Root: 7.
Solution set: $\{-.5, 7\}$

55. $\sqrt{6}x^2 - 2x - 1.4 = 0$

Guess: -1 Root: $-.4509456768$
Guess: 2 Root: 1.267442258
Solution set: $\{-.4509456768, 1.267442258\}$

57. $s = \frac{1}{2}gt^2$ for t

First, multiply both sides by 2.
$$2s = gt^2$$
Now divide by g.
$$\frac{2s}{g} = t^2$$
Use the square root property and rationalize the denominator on the right.
$$t = \pm\frac{2s}{g} = \pm\frac{\sqrt{2s}}{\sqrt{g}} \cdot \frac{\sqrt{g}}{\sqrt{g}} = \pm\frac{\sqrt{2sg}}{g}$$

59. $F = \frac{kMv^2}{r}$ for v

First, multiply both sides by r.
$$Fr = kMv^2$$
Next, divide both sides by kM.
$$\frac{Fr}{kM} = v^2$$
Now take the square root of both sides.
$$v = \pm\sqrt{\frac{F}{kM}}$$
Finally, rationalize the denominator on the right.
$$v = \pm\frac{\sqrt{Fr}}{\sqrt{kM}} \cdot \frac{\sqrt{kM}}{\sqrt{kM}}$$
$$v = \frac{\pm\sqrt{FrkM}}{kM}$$

61. $P(r + R)^2 = E^2R$ for R
$$P(r^2 + 2rR + R^2) = E^2R$$
$$Pr^2 + 2PrR + PR^2 = E^2R$$
$$PR^2 - E^2R + 2PrR + Pr^2 = 0$$
$$PR^2 + (2Pr - E^2)R + Pr^2 = 0$$
To find R, use the quadratic formula with
$a = P$, $b = 2Pr - E^2$, and $c = Pr^2$.

$$R = \frac{-(2Pr - E^2) \pm \sqrt{(2Pr - E^2)^2 - 4(P)(Pr^2)}}{2(P)}$$

$$= \frac{-2Pr + E^2 \pm \sqrt{4P^2r^2 - 4PrE^2 + E^4 - 4P^2r^2}}{2P}$$

$$= \frac{-2Pr + E^2 \pm \sqrt{E^4 - 4PrE^2}}{2P}$$

$$= \frac{-2Pr + E^2 \pm \sqrt{E^2(E^2 - 4Pr)}}{2P}$$

$$R = \frac{E^2 - 2Pr \pm E\sqrt{E^2 - 4Pr}}{2P}$$

63. $4x^2 - 2xy + 3y^2 = 2$

(a) Solve for x in terms of y.

$$4x^2 - 2yx + 3y^2 - 2 = 0$$

$a = 4, b = -2y, c = 3y^2 - 2$

$$x = \frac{2y \pm \sqrt{4y^2 - 16(3y^2 - 2)}}{8}$$

$$= \frac{2y \pm \sqrt{4y^2 - 48y^2 + 32}}{8}$$

$$= \frac{2y \pm \sqrt{32 - 44y^2}}{8}$$

$$= \frac{2y \pm \sqrt{4(8 - 11y^2)}}{8}$$

$$= \frac{2y \pm 2\sqrt{8 - 11y^2}}{8}$$

$$x = \frac{y \pm \sqrt{8 - 11y^2}}{4}$$

(b) Solve for y in terms of x.

$$3y^2 - 2xy + 4x^2 - 2 = 0$$

$a = 3, b = -2x, c = 4x^2 - 2$

$$y = \frac{2x \pm \sqrt{4x^2 - 12(4x^2 - 2)}}{6}$$

$$= \frac{2x \pm \sqrt{4x^2 - 48x^2 + 24}}{6}$$

$$= \frac{2x \pm \sqrt{24 - 44x^2}}{6}$$

$$= \frac{2x \pm \sqrt{4(6 - 11x^2)}}{6}$$

$$= \frac{2x \pm 2\sqrt{6 - 11x^2}}{6}$$

$$y = \frac{x \pm \sqrt{6 - 11x^2}}{3}$$

65. $x^2 + 8x + 16 = 0$

$a = 1, b = 8, c = 16$

$$b^2 - 4ac = 8^2 - 4(1)(16)$$
$$= 64 - 64$$
$$= 0$$

The equation has one rational solution since the discriminant is 0.

67. $3m^2 - 5m + 2 = 0$

$a = 3, b = -5, c = 2$

$$b^2 - 4ac = (-5)^2 - 4(3)(2)$$
$$= 25 - 24$$
$$= 1$$

The equation has two different rational solutions since the discriminant is a positive perfect square.

69. $4p^2 = 6p + 3$

$$4p^2 - 6p - 3 = 0$$

$a = 4, b = -6, c = -3$

$$b^2 - 4ac = (-6)^2 - 4(4)(-3)$$
$$= 36 + 48$$
$$= 84$$

The equation has two different irrational solutions since the discriminant is positive but not a perfect square.

71. $9k^2 + 11k + 4 = 0$

$a = 9, b = 11, c = 4$

$$b^2 - 4ac = 11^2 - 4(9)(4)$$
$$= 121 - 144$$
$$= -23$$

The equation has two different imaginary solutions since the discriminant is negative.

73. $8x^2 - 72 = 0$

$a = 8, b = 0, c = -72$

$$b^2 - 4ac = 0^2 - 4(8)(-72)$$
$$= 0 + 2304$$
$$= 2304 = 48^2$$

The equation has two different rational solutions since the discriminant is a positive perfect square.

77. $x = 4$ or $x = 5$

$x - 4 = 0$ $x - 5 = 0$

$$(x - 4)(x - 5) = 0$$
$$x^2 - 9x + 20 = 0$$

$a = 1, b = -9, c = 20$

79. $x = 1 + \sqrt{2}$ or $x = 1 - \sqrt{2}$

$x - 1 - \sqrt{2} = 0$ $x - 1 + \sqrt{2} = 0$

$$(x - 1 - \sqrt{2})(x - 1 + \sqrt{2}) = 0$$
$$x^2 - 2x - 1 = 0$$
$$a = 1, b = -2, c = -1$$

Section 1.5

Connections *(page 42)*

1. (a) $d = 16t^2$
    $$= 16(5)^2$$
    $$= 400$$
    It will fall 400 feet in 5 seconds.

    (b) $d = 16t^2$
    $$= 16(10)^2$$
    $$= 1600$$
    It will fall 1600 feet in 10 seconds.

    No, the second answer is $2^2 = 4$ times the first because the number of seconds is squared in the formula.

2. Both formulas involve the number 16 times the square of time. However, in the formula for the distance an object falls, 16 is positive, while in the formula for a propelled object, it is preceded by a negative sign. Also in the formula for a propelled object, the initial velocity and height affect the distance.

Exercises

1. The length of the parking area is $2x + 200$, while the width is x, so the area is $(2x + 200)x$.
    Set the area equal to 40,000.
    $(2x + 200)x = 40,000$.
    The correct choice is A.

3. Use the Pythagorean theorem with $a = x$, $b = 2x - 2$, and $c = x + 4$.
    $$x^2 + (2x - 2)^2 = (x + 4)^2$$
    The correct choice is D.

5. (a) Use the figure and equation A from Exercise 1.
    $$x(2x + 200) = 40,000$$

    (b) $x > 0$

    (c)
    $$2x^2 + 200x = 40,000$$
    $$2x^2 + 200x - 40,000 = 0$$
    $$x^2 + 100x - 20,000 = 0$$
    $$(x - 100)(x + 200) = 0$$
    $$x = 100 \text{ or } x = -200$$

    A rectangle cannot have a negative width, so reject -200 as a solution. If $x = 100$, then

$2x + 200 = 400$. The dimensions of the lot are 100 yd by 400 yd.

7. (a) Let h = height and r = radius.
    Area of side = $2\pi rh$
    Area of circle = πr^2
    Total area = area of side + area of top + area of bottom
    Total area = $2\pi rh + \pi r^2 + \pi r^2$
    $$600 = 2\pi r(4.25) + 2\pi r^2$$

    (b) $r > 0$

    (c)
    $$300 = 4.25\pi r + \pi r^2$$
    $$0 = \pi r^2 + 4.25\pi r - 300$$

    $a = \pi, b = 4.25\pi, c = -300$
    $$r = \frac{-b \pm \sqrt{b^2 - 4ac}}{2a}$$
    $$r = \frac{-4.25\pi \pm \sqrt{(4.25\pi)^2 - 4(\pi)(-300)}}{2\pi}$$
    $$r \approx 7.875 \text{ or } r \approx -12.125$$
    A circle cannot have a negative radius, so reject -12.125 as a solution. The radius is approximately 7.875 inches.

9. (a) Let x = the width of the strip of floor around the rug.

    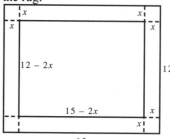

    The dimensions of the carpet are $15 - 2x$ by $12 - 2x$.
    Since $LW = A$, the equation for the carpet area is $(15 - 2x)(12 - 2x) = 108$.

    (b) $0 < x < 6$

    (c) Put this equation in standard form and solve by factoring.

    $$180 - 54x + 4x^2 = 108$$
    $$4x^2 - 54x + 72 = 0$$
    $$2x^2 - 17x + 36 = 0$$
    $$(2x - 3)(x - 12) = 0$$
    $$2x - 3 = 0 \quad \text{or} \quad x - 12 = 0$$
    $$x = \frac{3}{2} \qquad\qquad x = 12$$

    The solutions of the quadratic equation are

$\frac{3}{2}$ and 12.

We eliminate 12 as meaningless in this problem. If $x = \frac{3}{2}$, then $15 - 2x = 12$ and $12 - 2x = 9$.

The dimensions of the carpet are 9 ft by 12 ft.

11. (a) Let x = length of side of square.

Area = x^2

Perimeter = $4x$

$x^2 = 4x$

(b) $x > 0$

(c) $x^2 - 4x = 0$

$x(x - 4) = 0$

$x = 0$ or $x = 4$

We reject 0 since x must be greater than 0.

The side of the square measures 4 units.

13. Let x = the height of the kite.

Apply the Pythagorean theorem to the right triangle shown in the text.

$$a^2 + b^2 = c^2$$

$$x^2 + (x - 10)^2 = 50^2$$

$$x^2 + x^2 - 20x + 100 = 2500$$

$$2x^2 - 20x - 2400 = 0$$

$$x^2 - 10x - 1200 = 0$$

$$(x - 40)(x + 30) = 0$$

$x = 40$ or $x = -30$

Reject the negative solution.

The kite is 40 ft above the ground.

15. Let x = length of short leg,

$x + 700$ = length of long leg,

$x + 700 + 100$ or $x + 800$ = length of hypotenuse.

Apply the Pythagorean theorem.

$$c^2 = a^2 + b^2$$

$$(x + 800)^2 = x^2 + (x + 700)^2$$

$$x^2 + 1600x + 640,000 = x^2 + x^2 + 1400x + 490,000$$

$$0 = x^2 - 200x - 150,000$$

$$0 = (x + 300)(x - 500)$$

$x + 300 = 0$ or $x - 500 = 0$

$x = -300$ or $x = 500$

Discard the negative solution, since measurements cannot be negative.

500 = length of short leg

500 + 700 = 1200 = length of long leg

1200 + 100 = 1300 = length of hypotenuse

500 + 1200 + 1300 = 3000 = length of walkway.

The total length is 3000 yards.

17. Let x = length of ladder

Distance from building to ladder = 8 + 2 = 10

Distance from ground to window = 13

Apply the Pythagorean theorem.

$$a^2 + b^2 = c^2$$

$$10^2 + 13^2 = x^2$$

$$100 + 169 = x^2$$

$$269 = x^2$$

$$\pm\sqrt{269} = x$$

$x \approx -16.4$ or $x \approx 16.4$

Discard the negative solution since measurements cannot be negative. Rounding up to the nearest foot, the thief will need a 17-foot ladder.

19. The height of the rocket is given by

$h = -16t^2 + 128t$.

Set $h = 80$, and solve for t.

$$80 = -16t^2 + 128t$$

$$16t^2 - 128t + 80 = 0$$

Divide by 16.

$$t^2 - 8t + 5 = 0$$

Use the quadratic formula.

$$t = \frac{8 \pm \sqrt{64 - 20}}{2}$$

$$= \frac{8 \pm \sqrt{44}}{2}$$

$$= \frac{8 \pm 2\sqrt{11}}{2}$$

$$t = 4 \pm \sqrt{11}$$

$4 + \sqrt{11} \approx 7.32$

$4 - \sqrt{11} \approx .68$

The rocket will reach a height of 80 ft after .68 sec (on the way up) and after 7.32 sec (on the way down).

21. The height of the ball is given by

$h = -2.7t^2 + 30t + 6.5$.

When the ball is 12 ft above the moon's surface, $h = 12$.

Set $h = 12$ and solve for t.

$$12 = -2.7t^2 + 30t + 6.5$$

$$2.7t^2 - 30t + 5.5 = 0$$

Use the quadratic formula with $a = 2.7$, $b = -30$, and $c = 5.5$

$$t = \frac{30 \pm \sqrt{900 - 4(2.7)(5.5)}}{2(2.7)}$$

$$= \frac{30 \pm \sqrt{840.6}}{5.4}$$

$$\frac{30 + \sqrt{840.6}}{5.4} \approx 10.92$$

$$\frac{30 - \sqrt{840.6}}{5.4} \approx .19$$

Therefore, the ball reaches 12 ft first after .19 sec (on the way up), then again after 10.92 sec (on the way down).

When the ball returns to the surface, $h = 0$.

$0 = -2.7t^2 + 30t + 6.5$

Use the quadratic formula with $a = -2.7$, $b = 30$, and $c = 6.5$.

$$t = \frac{-30 \pm \sqrt{900 - 4(-2.7)(6.5)}}{2(-2.7)}$$

$$= \frac{-30 \pm \sqrt{970.2}}{-5.4}$$

$$\frac{-30 + \sqrt{970.2}}{-5.4} \approx -2.1$$

$$\frac{-30 - \sqrt{970.2}}{-5.4} \approx 11.32$$

Reject the first solution because time cannot be negative. Therefore, the ball returns to the surface after 11.32 sec.

23. Let $x = 50$.

$T = .00787(50)^2 - 1.528(50) + 75.89$

≈ 19.2

The exposure time when $x = 50$ ppm is approximately 19.2 hr.

25. Let $x = 600$ and solve for T.

$T = .0002x^2 - .316x + 127.9$

$= .0002(600)^2 - .316(600) + 127.9$

$= 10.3$

The exposure time when $x = 600$ ppm is 10.3 hr.

27. **(a)** Sales went down in 1991.

(b) From the graph, sales in 1994 were approximately 1.5 million.

$x = 4$ represents 1994.

$S = .016x^2 + .124x + .787$

$= .016(4)^2 + .124(4) + .787$

≈ 1.5

From the equation, sales in 1994 were approximately 1.5 million.
The results are the same.

(c) $x = 11$ represents 2001.

$S = .016x^2 + .124x + .787$

$= .016(11)^2 + .124(11) + .787$

≈ 4.1

From the equation, sales in 2001 will be approximately 4.1 million.

(d) $3 = .016x^2 + .124x + .787$

$0 = .016x^2 + .124x - 2.213$

$a = .016,\ b = .124,\ c = -2.213$

$$x = \frac{-b \pm \sqrt{b^2 - 4ac}}{2a}$$

$$x = \frac{-.124 \pm \sqrt{(.124)^2 - 4(.016)(-2.213)}}{2(.016)}$$

$x \approx -16.3$ or $x \approx 8.51$

Reject the negative solution.

$1990 + 8.51 = 1998.51$

In 1998, sales will reach 3 million.

29. For each \$20 increase in rent over \$300, one unit will remain vacant. Therefore, for x \$20 increases, x units will remain vacant. Therefore, the number of rented units will be $80 - x$.

30. x is the number of \$20 increases in rent. Therefore, the rent will be $300 + 20x$ dollars.

31. $300 + 20x$ is the rent for each apartment, and $80 - x$ is the number of apartments that will be rented at that cost. The revenue generated will then be the product of $80 - x$ and $300 + 20x$, so the correct expression is

$(80 - x)(300 + 20x)$ or $24,000 + 1300x - 20x^2$.

32. Set the revenue equal to \$35,000.
This gives the equation

$35,000 = 24,000 + 1300x - 20x^2$.

Rewrite this equation in standard form.

$20x^2 - 1300x + 11,000 = 0$

33. $20x^2 - 1300x + 11,000 = 0$

$x^2 - 65x + 550 = 0$

$(x - 10)(x - 55) = 0$

$x - 10 = 0$ or $x - 55 = 0$

$x = 10$ or $x = 55$

Solution set: $\{10, 55\}$

If $x = 10$, $80 - x = 70$.

If $x = 55$, $80 - x = 25$.

Because of the restriction that at least 30 units must be rented, only $x = 10$ is valid here, and the number of units rented is 70.

34. Let $x =$ number of passengers in excess of 75.
Then $225 - 5x =$ the cost per passenger
(in dollars);
$75 + x =$ the number of passengers.

Cost per passenger	·	Number of passengers	=	Revenue
↓	↓	↓	↓	↓
$(225 - 5x)$	·	$(75 + x)$	=	16,000

$$16,875 - 150x - 5x^2 = 16,000$$
$$0 = 5x^2 + 150x - 875$$
$$0 = x^2 + 30x - 175$$
$$0 = (x + 35)(x - 5)$$

$x = -35$ or $x = 5$

Reject the negative solution. Since there are 5 passengers in excess of 75, the total number of passengers is 80.

35.
$$L = -41.9x^2 + 350x + 3270$$
$$3000 = -41.9x^2 + 350x + 3270$$
$$0 = -41.9x^2 + 350x + 270$$
$$x \approx 9$$

In 1999, lead emissions will reach 3000 thousand tons.

Section 1.6

Exercises

1. $\dfrac{1}{4p} + \dfrac{2}{p} = 3$

Multiply both sides of the equation by the least common denominator, $4p$, assuming $p \neq 0$.

$$4p\left(\frac{1}{4p} + \frac{2}{p}\right) = 4p(3)$$
$$1 + 8 = 12p$$
$$9 = 12p$$
$$\frac{9}{12} = p$$
$$\frac{3}{4} = p$$

Solution set: $\left\{\dfrac{3}{4}\right\}$

3. $\dfrac{5}{2a+3} + \dfrac{1}{a-6} = 0$

Multiply both sides of the equation by the least common denominator, $(2a + 3)(a - 6)$, assuming $2a + 3 \neq 0$, or $a \neq -\dfrac{3}{2}$ and $a - 6 \neq 0$ or $a \neq 6$.

$$(2a+3)(a-6)\left(\frac{5}{2a+3} + \frac{1}{a-6}\right) =$$
$$(2a+3)(a-6)(0)$$
$$5(a-6) + 1(2a+3) = 0$$
$$5a - 30 + 2a + 3 = 0$$
$$7a - 27 = 0$$
$$7a = 27$$
$$a = \frac{27}{7}$$

Solution set: $\left\{\dfrac{27}{7}\right\}$

5. $\dfrac{3}{y-2} + \dfrac{1}{y+1} = \dfrac{1}{y^2 - y - 2}$

or $\dfrac{3}{y-2} + \dfrac{1}{y+1} = \dfrac{1}{(y-2)(y+1)}$

Multiply both sides of the equation by the least common denominator $(y - 2)(y + 1)$, assuming $y \neq 2$ and $y \neq -1$.

$$(y-2)(y+1)\left(\frac{3}{y-2} + \frac{1}{y+1}\right) =$$
$$(y-2)(y+1)\left(\frac{1}{(y-2)(y+1)}\right)$$
$$3(y+1) + 1(y-2) = 1$$
$$3y + 3 + y - 2 = 1$$
$$4y = 0$$
$$y = 0$$

Solution set: $\{0\}$

7. $\dfrac{2x-5}{x} = \dfrac{x-2}{3}$

Multiply each term in the equation by the least common denominator, $3x$, assuming $x \neq 0$.

$$3x\left(\frac{2x-5}{x}\right) = 3x\left(\frac{x-2}{3}\right)$$
$$6x - 15 = x^2 - 2x$$
$$0 = x^2 - 8x + 15$$
$$0 = (x-5)(x-3)$$
$$x - 5 = 0 \quad \text{or} \quad x - 3 = 0$$
$$x = 5 \quad \text{or} \quad x = 3$$

Solution set: $\{3, 5\}$

9. $\dfrac{2p}{p-2} = 5 + \dfrac{4p^2}{p-2}$

Multiply each term in the equation by the least common denominator, $p - 2$, assuming $p \neq 2$.

$$(p-2)\left(\frac{2p}{p-2}\right) = (p-2)5 + (p-2)\left(\frac{4p^2}{p-2}\right)$$

$$2p = 5p - 10 + 4p^2$$

$$0 = 4p^2 + 3p - 10$$

$$0 = (4p - 5)(p + 2)$$

$$4p - 5 = 0 \quad \text{or} \quad p + 2 = 0$$

$$p = \frac{5}{4} \quad \text{or} \quad p = -2$$

Solution set: $\left\{-2, \frac{5}{4}\right\}$

11. For an equation to be solved by the method of substitution, the highest power of the variable must be twice the next highest power. The correct choice is D.

15. $m^4 + 2m^2 - 15 = 0$

Let $x = m^2$; then $x^2 = m^4$. With this substitution, the equation becomes
$x^2 + 2x - 15 = 0$.
Solve this equation by factoring.
$(x - 3)(x + 5) = 0$
$x = 3$ or $x = -5$
To find m, replace x with m^2.
$$m^2 = 3 \qquad m^2 = -5$$
$$m = \pm\sqrt{3} \qquad m = \pm i\sqrt{5}$$
Solution set: $\left\{\pm\sqrt{3},\ \pm i\sqrt{5}\right\}$

17. $2r^4 - 7r^2 + 5 = 0$

Let $x = r^2$; then $x^2 = r^4$. With this substitution, the equation becomes $2x^2 - 7x + 5 = 0$.
Solve this equation by factoring.
$(x - 1)(2x - 5) = 0$
$$x = 1 \text{ or } x = \frac{5}{2}$$
To find r, replace x with r^2.
$$r^2 = 1 \quad \text{or} \quad r^2 = \frac{5}{2}$$
$$r = \pm\sqrt{\frac{5}{2}}$$
$$r = \pm 1 \text{ or } \quad r = \pm\frac{\sqrt{10}}{2}$$
Solution set: $\left\{\pm 1,\ \pm\frac{\sqrt{10}}{2}\right\}$

19. $(g - 2)^2 - 6(g - 2) + 8 = 0$
Let $x = g - 2$. Solve the resulting equation by factoring.

$$x^2 - 6x + 8 = 0$$
$$(x - 2)(x - 4) = 0$$
$$x = 2 \text{ or } x = 4$$
To find g, replace x with $g - 2$.
$$g - 2 = 2 \quad \text{or} \quad g - 2 = 4$$
$$g = 4 \quad \text{or} \qquad g = 6$$
Solution set: $\{4, 6\}$

21. $6(k + 2)^4 - 11(k + 2)^2 + 4 = 0$

Let $x = (k + 2)^2$. Solve the resulting equation by factoring.
$$6x^2 - 11x + 4 = 0$$
$$(3x - 4)(2x - 1) = 0$$
$$x = \frac{4}{3} \text{ or } x = \frac{1}{2}$$
To find k, replace x with $(k + 2)^2$.
$$(k + 2)^2 = \frac{4}{3}$$
$$k + 2 = \pm\sqrt{\frac{4}{3}}$$
$$= \pm\frac{2\sqrt{3}}{3}$$
$$k = -2 \pm \frac{2\sqrt{3}}{3}$$
$$= -\frac{6}{3} \pm \frac{2\sqrt{3}}{3}$$
$$= \frac{-6 \pm 2\sqrt{3}}{3}$$

or

$$(k + 2)^2 = \frac{1}{2}$$
$$k + 2 = \pm\sqrt{\frac{1}{2}}$$
$$= \pm\frac{\sqrt{2}}{2}$$
$$k = -2 \pm \frac{\sqrt{2}}{2}$$
$$= -\frac{4}{2} \pm \frac{\sqrt{2}}{2}$$
$$= \frac{-4 \pm \sqrt{2}}{2}$$

Solution set: $\left\{\dfrac{-6 \pm 2\sqrt{3}}{3},\ \dfrac{-4 \pm \sqrt{2}}{3}\right\}$

23. $7p^{-2} + 19p^{-1} = 6$

Let $x = p^{-1}$; then $x^2 = p^{-2}$. Solve the resulting equation by factoring.

$7x^2 + 19x - 6 = 0$

$(7x - 2)(x + 3) = 0$

$x = \dfrac{2}{7}$ or $x = -3$

To find p, replace x with p^{-1}.

$p^{-1} = \dfrac{2}{7}$ or $p^{-1} = -3$

$p = \dfrac{7}{2}$ or $p = -\dfrac{1}{3}$

Solution set: $\left\{ \dfrac{7}{2},\ -\dfrac{1}{3} \right\}$

25. $(r - 1)^{2/3} + (r - 1)^{1/3} = 12$

Let $u = (r - 1)^{1/3}$.

Then $u^2 = [(r - 1)^{1/3}]^2 = (r - 1)^{2/3}$.

Solve the resulting equation by factoring.

$u^2 + u = 12$

$u^2 + u - 12 = 0$

$(u + 4)(u - 3) = 0$

$u = -4$ or $u = 3$

To find r, replace u with $(r - 1)^{1/3}$.

$(r - 1)^{1/3} = -4$ or $(r - 1)^{1/3} = 3$

Cube both sides in each equation.

$[(r - 1)^{1/3}]^3 = (-4)^3$

$r - 1 = -64$

$r = -63$

or

$[(r - 1)^{1/3}]^3 = 3^3$

$r - 1 = 27$

$r = 28$

Because the original equation contained rational exponents, both solutions must be checked.
Solution set: $\{-63, 28\}$

27. $\sqrt{3z + 7} = 3z + 5$

$(\sqrt{3z + 7})^2 = (3x + 5)^2$

           Square both sides.

$3z + 7 = 9z^2 + 30z + 25$

           Square of a binomial

$0 = 9z^2 + 27z + 18$

$0 = z^2 + 3z + 2$

           Divide by 2.

$0 = (z + 2)(z + 1)$ Factor.

$z = -2$ or $z = -1$

Check each proposed solution in the original equation.
Let $z = -2$.

$\sqrt{3z + 7} = 3z + 5$

$\sqrt{3(-2) + 7} = 3(-2) + 5$?

$\sqrt{-6 + 7} = -6 + 5$?

$\sqrt{1} = -1$?

$1 = -1$ False

Let $z = -1$.

$\sqrt{3z + 7} = 3z + 5$

$\sqrt{3(-1) + 7} = 3(-1) + 5$?

$\sqrt{-3 + 7} = -3 + 5$?

$\sqrt{4} = 2$?

$2 = 2$ True

These checks show that only -1 is a solution.
Solution set: $\{-1\}$

29. $\sqrt{4x} - x + 3 = 0$

$\sqrt{4x} = x - 3$

$(\sqrt{4x})^2 = (x - 3)^2$

           Square both sides.

$4x = x^2 - 6x + 9$

           Square of a binomial

$0 = x^2 - 10x + 9$

$0 = (x - 1)(x - 9)$

$x = 1$ or $x = 9$

Check each proposed solution in the original equation.
Let $x = 1$.

$\sqrt{4 \cdot 1} - 1 + 3 = 0$?

$\sqrt{4} - 1 + 3 = 0$?

$2 - 1 + 3 = 0$?

$4 = 0$ False

Let $x = 9$.

$\sqrt{4 \cdot 9} - 9 + 3 = 0$?

$\sqrt{36} - 9 + 3 = 0$?

$6 - 9 + 3 = 0$?

$0 = 0$ True

Solution set: $\{9\}$

33.
$$\sqrt{m+7}+3 = \sqrt{m-4}$$
$$(\sqrt{m+7}+3)^2 = (\sqrt{m-4})^2$$

Square both sides.

$$m+7+6\sqrt{m+7}+9 = m-4$$

Square of a binomial

$$6\sqrt{m+7} = -20 \text{ Simplify.}$$
$$3\sqrt{m+7} = -10$$
$$(3\sqrt{m+7})^2 = (-10)^2$$

Square both sides.

$$9(m+7) = 100$$
$$9m+63 = 100$$
$$9m = 37$$
$$m = \frac{37}{9}$$

Check $\dfrac{37}{9}$ in the original equation.

$$\sqrt{\frac{37}{9}+7}+3 = \sqrt{\frac{37}{9}-4} \quad ?$$
$$\sqrt{\frac{100}{9}}+3 = \sqrt{\frac{1}{9}} \quad ?$$
$$\frac{19}{3} = \frac{1}{3} \quad \text{False}$$

Solution set: $\emptyset$

35.
$$\sqrt{2z} = \sqrt{3z+12}-2$$
$$(\sqrt{2z})^2 = (\sqrt{3z+12}-2)^2$$

Square both sides.

$$2z = 3z+12-4\sqrt{3z+12}+4$$

Square of a binomial

$$4\sqrt{3z+12} = z+16$$
$$(4\sqrt{3z+12})^2 = (z+16)^2$$

Square both sides.

$$16(3z+12) = z^2+32z+256$$

Square of a binomial

$$48z+192 = z^2+32z+256$$

Distributive property

$$0 = z^2-16z+64$$
$$0 = (z-8)^2 \text{ Factor.}$$
$$z-8 = 0$$
$$z = 8$$

Check this proposed solution in the original equation.
Solution set: $\{8\}$

37.
$$\sqrt{r+2} = 1-\sqrt{3r+7}$$
$$(\sqrt{r+2})^2 = (1-\sqrt{3r+7})^2$$
$$r+2 = 1-2\sqrt{3r+7}+3r+7$$
$$2\sqrt{3r+7} = 2r+6$$
$$2\sqrt{3r+7} = 2(r+3)$$
$$\sqrt{3r+7} = r+3$$
$$(\sqrt{3r+7})^2 = (r+3)^2$$
$$3r+7 = r^2+6r+9$$
$$0 = r^2+3r+2$$
$$0 = (r+1)(r+2)$$

$r = -1$ or $r = -2$

Check $r = -1$.
$$\sqrt{-1+2} = 1-\sqrt{-3+7} \quad ?$$
$$\sqrt{1} = 1-\sqrt{4} \quad ?$$
$$1 = 1-2 \quad ?$$
$$1 = -1 \quad \text{False}$$

Check $r = -2$.
$$\sqrt{-2+2} = 1-\sqrt{-6+7} \quad ?$$
$$0 = 1-\sqrt{1} \quad ?$$
$$0 = 1-1 \quad ?$$
$$0 = 0 \quad \text{True}$$

Solution set: $\{-2\}$

39.
$$\sqrt[3]{4n+3} = \sqrt[3]{2n-1}$$
$$(\sqrt[3]{4n+3})^3 = (\sqrt[3]{2n-1})^3$$

Cube both sides.

$$4n+3 = 2n-1$$
$$2n = -4$$
$$n = -2$$

Check this proposed solution in the original equation.
$$\sqrt[3]{4(-2)+3} = \sqrt[3]{2(-2)-1} \quad ?$$
$$\sqrt[3]{-5} = \sqrt[3]{-5} \quad \text{True}$$

Solution set: $\{-2\}$

41.
$$(z^2+24z)^{1/4} = 3$$
$$[(z^2+24z)^{1/4}]^4 = 3^4$$

Raise both sides to 4th power.

$$z^2+24z = 81$$
$$z^2+24z-81 = 0$$
$$(z+27)(z-3) = 0$$

$z = -27$ or $z = 3$

Checking will show that both of these proposed solutions are solutions of the original equation.
Solution set: $\{-27, 3\}$

43. $(2r-1)^{2/3} = r^{1/3}$

$[(2r-1)^{2/3}]^3 = (r^{1/3})^3$

　　　　　Cube both sides.

$(2r-1)^2 = r$

$4r^2 - 4r + 1 = r$

$4r^2 - 5r + 1 = 0$

$(4r-1)(r-1) = 0$

$r = \dfrac{1}{4}$ or $r = 1$

Checking will show that both of these proposed solutions are solutions of the original equation.

Solution set: $\left\{ \dfrac{1}{4}, 1 \right\}$

45. $x - \sqrt{x} - 12 = 0$

Let $u = \sqrt{x}$; then $u^2 = x$. Solve the resulting equation by factoring.

$u^2 - u - 12 = 0$

$(u-4)(u+3) = 0$

$u = 4$ or $u = -3$

To find x, replace u with $\sqrt{x}$.

$\sqrt{x} = 4$

$x = 16$

or

$\sqrt{x} = -3$

When $u = -3$, there is no solution for x.

Solution set: $\{16\}$

46. $x - \sqrt{x} - 12 = 0$

Solve by isolating $\sqrt{x}$, then squaring both sides.

$x - 12 = \sqrt{x}$

$(x-12)^2 = (\sqrt{x})^2$

$x^2 - 24x + 144 = x$

$x^2 - 25x + 144 = 0$

$(x-16)(x-9) = 0$

$x = 16$ or $x = 9$

Check $x = 16$.

$16 - \sqrt{16} - 12 = 0$?

$16 - 4 - 12 = 0$?

　　　　$0 = 0$　True

Check $x = 9$.

$9 - \sqrt{9} - 12 = 0$?

$9 - 3 - 12 = 0$?

　　　　$-6 = 0$　False

The checks show that 16 satisfies the equation but 9 does not satisfy the equation.

Solution set: $\{16\}$

48. $3x - 2\sqrt{x} - 8 = 0$

Solve by substitution. Let $u = \sqrt{x}$ and solve the resulting equation by factoring.

$3u^2 - 2u - 8 = 0$

$(3u+4)(u-2) = 0$

$3u + 4 = 0$ 　or　 $u - 2 = 0$

$u = -\dfrac{4}{3}$ 　　　 $u = 2$

To find x, replace u with $\sqrt{x}$.

$\sqrt{x} = -\dfrac{4}{3}$ has no solutions.

$\sqrt{x} = 2$

$x = 4$

Solution set: $\{4\}$

49. $2\sqrt{x} - \sqrt{3x+4} = 0$

Using the SOLVE feature of the graphing calculator yields the value 4.

Solution set: $\{4\}$

51. $\sqrt{x^2 - \sqrt{5}x + 6} = x + \pi$

Rewrite as

$\sqrt{x^2 - \sqrt{5}x + 6} - x - \pi = 0$.

Solution set: $\{-.4542187292\}$

55. $x^{2/3} + y^{2/3} = a^{2/3}$ for y

$y^{2/3} = a^{2/3} - x^{2/3}$

$(y^{2/3})^3 = (a^{2/3} - x^{2/3})^3$

　　　　Cube both sides.

$y^2 = (a^{2/3} - x^{2/3})^3$

$y = \sqrt{(a^{2/3} - x^{2/3})^3}$

$y = (a^{2/3} - x^{2/3})^{3/2}$

57. $\dfrac{1}{R} = \dfrac{1}{r_1} + \dfrac{1}{r_2}$ for R

$Rr_1r_2 \left(\dfrac{1}{R} \right) = Rr_1r_2 \left(\dfrac{1}{r_1} \right) + Rr_1r_2 \left(\dfrac{1}{r_2} \right)$

　　　Multiply both sides by Rr_1r_2.

$r_1r_2 = Rr_2 + Rr_1$

$r_1r_2 = R(r_2 + r_1)$

$\dfrac{r_1r_2}{r_2 + r_1} = R$ or $R = \dfrac{r_1r_2}{r_1 + r_2}$

59. **(a)** If the fluoride level $x = 1$ ppm, find the DMF level.

$$DMF = 200 + \frac{100}{x}$$

$$= 200 + \frac{100}{1}$$

$$= 300$$

There are 300 incidences per 100 examinees.

(b) Find the fluoride level when DMF = 250.

$$DMF = 200 + \frac{100}{x}$$

$$250 = 200 + \frac{100}{x}$$

$$50 = \frac{100}{x}$$

$$x = \frac{100}{50}$$

$$x = 2$$

The fluoride level is 2 ppm.

Section 1.7

Exercises

1. $x < -4$

The interval includes all real numbers less than -4, not including -4. The correct interval notation is $(-\infty, -4)$, so the correct choice is F.

3. $-2 < x \le 6$

The interval includes all real numbers from -2 to 6, not including -2, but including 6. The correct interval notation is $(-2, 6]$, so the correct choice is A.

5. $x \ge -3$

The interval includes all real numbers greater than or equal to -3, so it includes -3. The correct interval notation is $[-3, \infty)$, so the correct choice is I.

7. The interval shown on the number line includes all real numbers between -2 and 6, including -2, but not including 6. The correct interval notation is $[-2, 6)$, so the correct choice is B.

9. The interval shown on the number line includes all real numbers greater than 3, not including 3. The correct interval notation is $(3, \infty)$, so the correct choice is E.

13. $-3p - 2 \le 1$

Add 2 to both sides of the inequality.

$$-3p - 2 + 2 \le 1 + 2$$

$$-3p \le 3$$

Multiply both sides of the inequality by $-\frac{1}{3}$ and reverse the direction of the inequality symbol.

$$\left(-\frac{1}{3}\right)(-3p) \ge \left(-\frac{1}{3}\right)(3)$$

$$p \ge -1$$

Solution set: $[-1, \infty)$

15. $2(m + 5) - 3m + 1 \ge 5$

$$2m + 10 - 3m + 1 \ge 5$$

    Distributive property

$$-m + 11 \ge 5 \quad \text{Combine terms.}$$

$$-m \ge -6 \quad \text{Subtract 11.}$$

$$-1(-m) \le -1(-6)$$

    Multiply by -1; reverse inequality symbol.

$$m \le 6$$

Solution set: $(-\infty, 6]$

17. $\dfrac{4x + 7}{-3} \le 2x + 5$

$$(-3)\left(\frac{4x + 7}{-3}\right) \ge (-3)(2x + 5)$$

    Multiply by -3; reverse inequality symbol.

$$4x + 7 \ge -6x - 15$$

$$4x + 7 + 6x \ge -6x - 15 + 6x$$

    Add $6x$.

$$10x + 7 \ge -15$$

$$10x + 7 - 7 \ge -15 - 7 \quad \text{Subtract 7.}$$

$$10x \ge -22$$

$$\frac{1}{10}(10x) \ge \frac{1}{10}(-22) \quad \text{Multiply by } \frac{1}{10}.$$

$$x \ge -\frac{11}{5}$$

Solution set: $\left[-\dfrac{11}{5}, \infty\right)$

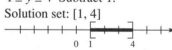

19. $2 \le y + 1 \le 5$

$$1 \le y \le 4 \quad \text{Subtract 1.}$$

Solution set: $[1, 4]$

21. $-10 > 3r + 2 > -16$

$$-10 - 2 > 3r + 2 - 2 > -16 - 2$$

    Subtract 2.

$$-12 > 3r > -18$$

$\frac{1}{3}(-12) > \frac{1}{3}(3r) > \frac{1}{3}(-18)$ Multiply by $\frac{1}{3}$.

$-4 > r > -6$ or $-6 < r < -4$

Solution set: $(-6, -4)$

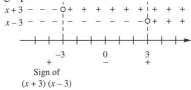

23. $W = 1.98x + 15.6$

$20 < 1.98x + 15.6$

$4.4 < 1.98x$

$2.\overline{2} < x$

In 1992, the percent of waste recovered exceeded 20%.

$20 < 1.98x + 15.6 < 25$

$4.4 < 1.98x < 9.4$

$2.\overline{2} < x < 4.\overline{74}$

Between 1992 and 1994, the percent was between 20% and 25%.

The graph shows that the percent of waste first exceeded 20% in 1993 and was between 20% and 25% in 1993 and 1994.

25. $C = 50x + 5000; R = 60x$

The product will at least break even when $R \geq C$.

Set $R \geq C$ and solve for x.

$60x \geq 50x + 5000$

$10x \geq 5000$

$x \geq 500$

The break-even point is at $x = 500$.

This product will at least break even if the number of units produced is in the interval $[500, \infty)$.

27. $x^2 \leq 9$

$x^2 - 9 \leq 0$

Solve the corresponding quadratic equation by factoring.

$x^2 - 9 = 0$

$(x + 3)(x - 3) = 0$

$x = -3$ or $x = 3$

These two points, –3 and 3, divide a number line into the three regions shown on the following sign graph.

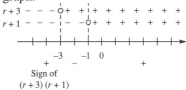

The factor $x + 3$ is positive when $x > -3$, and $x - 3$ is positive when $x > 3$.

We want the product to be negative, which happens if the two factors have opposite signs. As the sign graph shows, this happens when x is between –3 and 3.

The endpoints of the interval are included in the solution because the product is zero (and therefore "less than or equal to zero") when $x = -3$ or $x = 3$.

Solution set: $[-3, 3]$

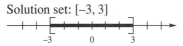

29. $r^2 + 4r + 6 \geq 3$

$r^2 + 4r + 3 \geq 0$

Solve the corresponding quadratic equation.

$r^2 + 4r + 3 = 0$

$(r + 3)(r + 1) = 0$

$r = -3$ or $r = -1$

These two points, –3 and –1, divide a number line into the three regions shown on the following graph.

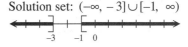

The factor $r + 3$ is positive when $r > -3$, and $r + 1$ is positive when $r > -1$.

We want the product to be positive, which happens if both factors have the same sign. As the sign graph shows, this happens when $r < -3$ or when $r > -1$.

The inequality is also satisfied when $r = -3$ and when $r = -1$ because of the $\leq$ sign, so square brackets should be used at these endpoints.

Solution set: $(-\infty, -3] \cup [-1, \infty)$

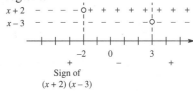

31. $x^2 - x \leq 6$

$x^2 - x - 6 \leq 0$

Solve the corresponding quadratic equation.

$x^2 - x - 6 = 0$

$(x + 2)(x - 3) = 0$

$x + 2 = 0$ or $x - 3 = 0$

$x = -2$ or $x = 3$

These two points divide a number line into three regions.

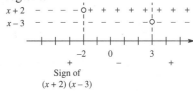

The factor $x - 3$ is positive when $x > 3$ and $x + 2$ is positive when $x > -2$.

The product is negative if the two factors have opposite signs, which happens when x is between

–2 and 3. Use square brackets since the original inequality is ≤, which means that both –2 and 3 are part of the solution set.
Solution set: [–2, 3]

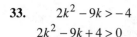

33. $2k^2 - 9k > -4$

$2k^2 - 9k + 4 > 0$

Solve the corresponding quadratic equation.

$2k^2 - 9k + 4 = 0$

$(2k-1)(k-4) = 0$

$k = \dfrac{1}{2}$ or $k = 4$

```
2k – 1   – – – – – – ○+ + + +  + +
k – 4    – – – – – – ○ – – – ○+ +
        ├──┼──┼──┼──┼──┼──┼──┼──┼──→
                 0  1        4
                    2
          +         –        +
        Sign of
        (2k – 1) (k – 4)
```

The product is positive when $k < \dfrac{1}{2}$ or when $k > 4$. No endpoints are included since the inequality symbol is >.

Solution set: $\left(-\infty, \dfrac{1}{2}\right) \cup (4, \infty)$

```
←──┼──┼──┼──)──┼──┼──(──┼──→
             0  1       4
                2
```

35. $x^2 > 0$ is true for all values of x except 0, so that the solution is $(-\infty, 0) \cup (0, \infty)$.

```
←──┼──┼──┼──╳──┼──┼──→
          –1  0  1
```

37. $x - 2$ is negative for $x < 2$ and positive for $x > 2$; D.

39. $(x-2)^2$ is always positive or zero; B.

41. One example is $(x-3)(x-5) > 0$ or $x^2 - 8x + 15 > 0$. Many answers are possible.

43. $\dfrac{m-3}{m+5} \le 0$

To draw a sign graph, first solve the equations $m - 3 = 0$ and $m + 5 = 0$, getting the solutions $m = 3$ and $m = -5$.
Use the values –5 and 3 to divide the number line into three regions.

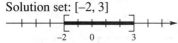

```
m – 3  – – ○– – – – – – – –  + + +
m + 5  – – + + + + + + + +○+ + +
       ├──┼──┼──┼──┼──┼──┼──┼──┼──→
              –5        0    3
          +              –      +
        Sign of
         m – 3
        ─────
         m + 5
```

The quotient is negative when the factors have different signs or when m is between –5 and 3. Since the inequality symbol is ≤, we must check each endpoint separately. Here, –5 gives a 0 denominator, but 3 satisfies the inequality.
Solution set: (–5, 3]

45. $\dfrac{k-1}{k+2} > 1$

$\dfrac{k-1}{k+2} - 1 > 0$ Subtract 1.

$\dfrac{k-1}{k+2} - \dfrac{k+2}{k+2} > 0$ Common denominator

$\qquad\qquad\qquad$ is $3(k+2)$.

$\dfrac{k-1-(k+2)}{k+2} > 0$

$\dfrac{k-1-k-2}{k+2} > 0$

$\dfrac{-3}{k+2} > 0$ Combine terms.

Since –3 is negative, this inequality is true when $k + 2$ is negative, or when $k < -2$.
Solution set: $(-\infty, -2)$

47. $\dfrac{1}{m-1} < \dfrac{5}{4}$

$\dfrac{1}{m-1} - \dfrac{5}{4} < 0$

$\dfrac{4 - 5(m-1)}{4(m-1)} < 0$

$\dfrac{4 - 5m + 5}{4(m-1)} < 0$

$\dfrac{9 - 5m}{4(m-1)} < 0$

Solve the equations $9 - 5m = 0$ and $4(m - 1) = 0$, getting the solutions $m = \dfrac{9}{5}$ and $m = 1$.
Draw a sign graph.

```
9 – 5m   + + + + + +○+ + + +  + – –
4(m – 1) – – – – – – ┊ + + + +○+ +
         ├──┼──┼──┼──┼──┼──┼──┼──┼──→
                 0        1      9
                                 5
              –          +       –
        Sign of
         9 – 5m
        ───────
        4(m – 1)
```

The quotient is negative when $m < 1$ or $m > \dfrac{9}{5}$.

There is no need to check the endpoints, since the original inequality symbol is <. The solution set is

$(-\infty,\ 1) \cup \left(\dfrac{9}{5},\ \infty\right)$.

49. $\dfrac{7}{k+2} \geq \dfrac{1}{k+2}$

Subtract $\dfrac{1}{k+2}$ from both sides.

$\dfrac{7}{k+2} - \dfrac{1}{k+2} \geq 0$

$\dfrac{6}{k+2} \geq 0$

Since 6 is positive, this inequality is true whenever $k + 2$ is positive, or when $k > -2$. Solution set: $(-2, \infty)$

51. $\dfrac{3}{2r-1} > -\dfrac{4}{r}$

Add $\dfrac{4}{r}$ to both sides.

$\dfrac{3}{2r-1} + \dfrac{4}{r} > 0$ Add $\dfrac{4}{r}$.

$\dfrac{3r+4(2r-1)}{r(2r-1)} > 0$ Common denominator is $r(2r-1)$.

$\dfrac{3r+8r-4}{r(2r-1)} > 0$

$\dfrac{11r-4}{r(2r-1)} > 0$

Make a sign graph showing the three factors $11r - 4$, $2r - 1$, and r.

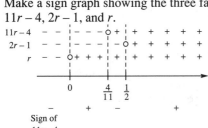

The quotient is positive when $0 < r < \dfrac{4}{11}$ or $r > \dfrac{1}{2}$.

Neither endpoint satisfies the inequality since the inequality symbol is >. The solution set is

$\left(0,\ \dfrac{4}{11}\right) \cup \left(\dfrac{1}{2},\ \infty\right)$

53. $\dfrac{y+3}{y-5} \leq 1$

$\dfrac{y+3}{y-5} - 1 \leq 0$

$\dfrac{y+3-(y-5)}{y-5} \leq 0$

$\dfrac{y+3-y+5}{y-5} \geq 0$

$\dfrac{8}{y-5} \leq 0$

Since 8 is positive, this inequality is true whenever $y - 5$ is negative, that is, when $y < 5$. $y = 5$ cannot be used since it makes the denominator 0. Thus, the solution set is $(-\infty, 5)$.

55. $(3x - 4)(x + 2)(x + 6) = 0$
Set each factor to zero and solve.

$3x - 4 = 0$ or $x + 2 = 0$ or $x + 6 = 0$

$x = \dfrac{4}{3}$ or $x = -2$ or $x = -6$

Solution set: $\left\{\dfrac{4}{3},\ -2,\ -6\right\}$

56. Plot the solutions -6, -3, and $\dfrac{4}{3}$ on a number line.

57. In the region where $x < -6$, choose $x = -10$, for example. It satisfies the original inequality. In the region $-6 < x < -2$, choose $x = -4$, for example. It does not satisfy the inequality. In the region $-2 < x < \dfrac{4}{3}$, choose $x = 0$, for example. It satisfies the original inequality. In the region $x > \dfrac{4}{3}$, choose $x = 4$, for example. It does not satisfy the original inequality.

58. The solution includes all real numbers to the left of -6, including -6, and all real numbers between -2 and $\dfrac{4}{3}$, including -2 and $\dfrac{4}{3}$. Plot the regions of the solution on a number line.

59. $x^3 + 4x^2 - 9x - 36 > 0$

Solve the associated equation.

$x^3 + 4x^2 - 9x - 36 = 0$

$x^2(x+4) - 9(x+4) = 0$

$(x^2 - 9)(x+4) = 0$

$(x+3)(x-3)(x+4) = 0$

$x = -3$ or $x = 3$ or $x = -4$

Plot these points on a number line.

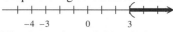

Choose points from each of the four regions, and substitute in the original inequality.

$x = -5$:

$(-5)^3 + 4(-5)^2 - 9(-5) - 36 > 0$?

$-16 > 0$ False

Do not graph the region farthest to the left.

$x = -3.5$:

$(-3.5)^3 + 4(-3.5)^2 - 9(-3.5) - 36 > 0$?

$1.625 > 0$ True

Graph the second region from the left.

$x = 0$:

$(0)^3 + 4(0)^2 - 9(0) - 36 > 0$?

$-36 > 0$ False

Do not graph the third region from the left.

$x = 4$:

$(4)^3 + 4(4)^2 - 9(4) - 36 > 0$?

$56 > 0$ True

Graph the region farthest to the right.

Plot the regions of the solution on a number line.

61. D and F

D $(8p - 7)^2$ is never negative, so $(8p - 7)^2 < 0$ has solution set $\emptyset$.

F $\dfrac{2x^2 + 8}{x^2 + 9}$ is never smaller than $\dfrac{8}{9}$. This means

that $\dfrac{2x^2 + 8}{x^2 + 9}$ is never negative, so $\dfrac{2x^2 + 8}{x^2 + 9} < 0$

has solution set $\emptyset$.

D and F are the only inequalities that have solution set $\emptyset$.

63. $-2(x + 4) \le 6x + 8$

We will use the intersection-of-graphs method.

Graph $y_1 = -2(x + 4)$ and $y_2 = 6x + 8$.

The graphs intersect at $x = -2$, and y_1 is less than y_2 for values of x greater than -2. The solution set is $[-2, \infty)$.

65. $x^2 - x - 12 > 0$

Graph $y_1 = x^2 - x - 12$. The graph intersects the x-axis at $x = -3$ and $x = 4$, and is greater than 0 for values of x less than -3 or greater than 4. The solution set is $(-\infty, -3) \cup (4, \infty)$.

67. $\dfrac{x}{x + 2} \ge 2$

We will use the intersection-of-sets method.

Graph $y_1 = \dfrac{x}{x + 2}$ and $y_2 = 2$.

The graphs intersect at $x = -4$, and y_1 has a vertical asymptote of $x = -2$. y_1 is greater than y_2 for values of x between -4 and -2. The solution is $[-4, -2)$.

71. $(x - 2)(x - 5) > 0$ or $x^2 - 7x + 10 > 0$

73. $(x + 4)(x - 3) \le 0$ or $x^2 + x - 12 \le 0$

75. $\dfrac{x + 3}{x} \ge 0$

77. $\dfrac{x - 9}{x - 4} \le 0$

79. **(a)** Look for places where the graphs intersect: 1978, 1981, 1987, and 1991.

(b) Look for places where the graph of total presidential campaign spending lies above or intersects the graph of congressional campaigns spending: 1972–1981, and 1987–1991. The intervals are [1972, 1981] and [1987, 1991].

Section 1.8

Exercises

1. $|x| = 4$

The solution set includes any value of x whose absolute value is 4; thus $x = 4$ or $x = -4$ are both solutions. The correct graph is F.

3. $|x| > -4$

The solution set is all real numbers, since the absolute value of any real number is always greater than -4. The correct graph is D, which shows the entire number line.

5. $|x| < 4$

The solution set includes any value of x whose absolute value is less than 4; thus x must be between -4 and 4, not including -4 or 4. The correct graph is G.

7. $|x| \leq 4$

The solution set includes any value of x whose absolute value is less than or equal to 4; thus x must be between -4 and 4, including -4 and 4. The correct graph is C.

9. $|3m - 1| = 2$

$$3m - 1 = 2 \quad \text{or} \quad 3m - 1 = -2$$
$$3m = 3 \qquad\qquad 3m = -1$$
$$m = 1 \quad \text{or} \qquad m = -\frac{1}{3}$$

Solution set: $\left\{ -\frac{1}{3}, 1 \right\}$

11. $|5 - 3x| = 3$

$$5 - 3x = 3 \quad \text{or} \quad 5 - 3x = -3$$
$$2 = 3x \qquad\qquad 8 = 3x$$
$$\frac{2}{3} = x \quad \text{or} \qquad \frac{8}{3} = x$$

Solution set: $\left\{ \frac{2}{3}, \frac{8}{3} \right\}$

13. $\left| \dfrac{z - 4}{2} \right| = 5$

$$\frac{z - 4}{2} = 5 \quad \text{or} \quad \frac{z - 4}{2} = -5$$
$$z - 4 = 10 \qquad\qquad z - 4 = -10$$
$$z = 14 \quad \text{or} \qquad z = -6$$

Solution set: $\{-6, 14\}$

15. $\left| \dfrac{5}{r - 3} \right| = 10$

$$\frac{5}{r - 3} = 10$$
$$5 = 10(r - 3)$$
$$5 = 10r - 30$$
$$35 = 10r$$
$$\frac{7}{2} = r$$

or

$$\frac{5}{r - 3} = -10$$
$$5 = -10(r - 3)$$
$$5 = -10r + 30$$
$$-25 = -10r$$
$$\frac{5}{2} = r$$

Solution set: $\left\{ \dfrac{5}{2}, \dfrac{7}{2} \right\}$

17. $|4w + 3| - 2 = 7$

$$|4w + 3| = 9$$
$$4w + 3 = 9 \quad \text{or} \quad 4w + 3 = -9$$
$$4w = 6 \qquad\qquad 4w = -12$$
$$w = \frac{3}{2} \qquad\qquad w = -3$$

Solution set: $\left\{ -3, \dfrac{3}{2} \right\}$

19. $|6x + 9| = 0$

This absolute value equation has only one case.

$$6x + 9 = 0$$
$$6x = -9$$
$$x = -\frac{9}{6}$$
$$= -\frac{3}{2}$$

Solution set: $\left\{ -\dfrac{3}{2} \right\}$

21. $\left| \dfrac{6y + 1}{y - 1} \right| = 3$

$$\frac{6y + 1}{y - 1} = 3$$
$$6y + 1 = 3(y - 1)$$
$$6y + 1 = 3y - 3$$
$$3y = -4$$
$$y = -\frac{4}{3}$$

or

$$\frac{6y + 1}{y - 1} = -3$$
$$6y + 1 = -3(y - 1)$$
$$6y + 1 = -3y + 3$$
$$9y = 2$$
$$y = \frac{2}{9}$$

Solution set: $\left\{ -\dfrac{4}{3}, \dfrac{2}{9} \right\}$

23. $|2k-3|=|5k+4|$

$2k-3=5k+4$

$-7=3k$

$-\dfrac{7}{3}=k$

or

$2k-3=-(5k+4)$

$2k-3=-5k-4$

$7k=-1$

$k=-\dfrac{1}{7}$

Solution set: $\left\{-\dfrac{7}{3},\ -\dfrac{1}{7}\right\}$

25. $|4-3y|=|2-3y|$

$4-3y=2-3y$

$0=-2$ False

or

$4-3y=-(2-3y)$

$4-3y=-2+3y$

$-6y=-6$

$y=1$

Solution set: $\{1\}$

29. $|2x+7|=5$

Graph $y_1=|2x+7|-5$.

The graph intersects the x-axis at -6 and -1. The solution set is $\{-6,-1\}$.

31. $|2+5x|=|4-6x|$

Graph $y_1=|2+5x|-|4-6x|$.

The graph intersects the x-axis at $\dfrac{2}{11}$ and 6. The

solution set is $\left\{\dfrac{2}{11},\ 6\right\}$.

33. $|2x+5|<3$

$-3<2x+5<3$

$-8<2x<-2$

$-4<x<-1$

Solution set: $(-4,-1)$

35. $4|x-3|>12$

$4(x-3)>12$ or $4(x-3)<-12$

$4x-12>12$ $4x-12<-12$

$4x>24$ $4x<0$

$x>6$ or $x<0$

Solution set: $(-\infty,\ 0)\cup(6,\infty)$

37. $|3z+1|\ge 7$

$3z+1\le -7$ or $3z+1\ge 7$

$3z\le -8$ $3z\ge 6$

$z\le -\dfrac{8}{3}$ or $z\ge 2$

Solution set: $\left(-\infty,\ -\dfrac{8}{3}\right]\cup[2,\ \infty)$

39. $\left|\dfrac{2}{3}t+\dfrac{1}{2}\right|\le\dfrac{1}{6}$

$-\dfrac{1}{6}\le\dfrac{2}{3}t+\dfrac{1}{2}\le\dfrac{1}{6}$

Multiply by the least common denominator, 6, to clear fractions.

$-1\le 4t+3\le 1$

$-4\le 4t\le -2$

$-1\le t\le -\dfrac{1}{2}$

Solution set: $\left[-1,\ \dfrac{1}{2}\right]$

41. $\left|5x+\dfrac{1}{2}\right|-2<5$

$\left|5x+\dfrac{1}{2}\right|<7$ Add 2.

$-7<5x+\dfrac{1}{2}<7$

$-\dfrac{15}{2}<5x<\dfrac{13}{2}$ Subtract $\dfrac{1}{2}$.

$-\dfrac{3}{2}<x<\dfrac{13}{10}$ Divide by 5.

Solution set: $\left(-\dfrac{3}{2},\ \dfrac{13}{10}\right)$

43. $|6x+3|\ge -2$

Since the absolute value of a number is always nonnegative, $|6x+3|\ge -2$ is always true.

Solution set: $(-\infty,\infty)$

45. $\left|\dfrac{1}{2}x+6\right|>0$

The absolute value of a number will be positive so long as the number is negative or positive (but not zero).

$\dfrac{1}{2}x+6<0$ or $\dfrac{1}{2}x+6>0$

$\dfrac{1}{2}x<-6$ $\dfrac{1}{2}x>-6$

$x<-12$ or $x>-12$

Solution set: $(-\infty,\ -12)\cup(-12,\ \infty)$

47. $|p - q| = 5$, which is equivalent to $|q - p| = 5$, indicates that the distance between p and q is 5 units.

49. "m is no more than 8 units from 9" is written $|m - 9| \le 8$

51. "p is at least 5 units from 9" is written $|p - 9| \ge 5$.

53. For $x^2 - x$ to have an absolute value equal to 6, the expression must equal –6 or 6.

54. For $x^2 - x$ to equal 6, the equation is
$x^2 - x = 6$.
$x^2 - x - 6 = 0$ Factor.
$(x - 3)(x + 2) = 0$
$x - 3 = 0$ or $x + 2 = 0$
    $x = 3$ or $x = -2$
Solution set: $\{-2, 3\}$

55. For $x^2 - x$ to equal – 6, the equation is
$x^2 - x = -6$.
$x^2 - x = -6$
$x^2 - x + 6 = 0$
Use the quadratic formula with $a = 1$, $b = -1$, and $c = 6$.
$$x = \frac{1 \pm \sqrt{1 - (1)(6)}}{2}$$
$$x = \frac{1 \pm \sqrt{-23}}{2}$$
$$x = \frac{1 \pm i\sqrt{23}}{2}$$
$$= \frac{1}{2} \pm \frac{\sqrt{23}}{2}i$$
Solution set: $\left\{ \dfrac{1}{2} \pm \dfrac{\sqrt{23}}{2}i \right\}$

56. The complete solution set of
$|x^2 - x| = 6$ is
$\left\{ -2, \ 3, \ \dfrac{1}{2} \pm \dfrac{\sqrt{23}}{2}i \right\}$.

57. $|R_L - 26.75| \le 1.42$
$-1.42 \le R_L - 26.75 \le 1.42$
$25.33 \le R_L \le 28.17$
$|R_E - 38.75| \le 2.17$
$-2.17 \le R_E - 38.75 \le 2.17$
$36.58 \le R_E \le 40.92$

61. $|C + 84| \le 56$
$-56 \le C + 84 \le 56$
$-140 \le C \le -28$
In degrees Celsius, the range of temperature is the interval $[-140, -28]$.

63. Let x = the speed of the kite. 148 is 25 more than 123, and 98 is 25 less than 123, so all the speeds are within 25 ft per sec of 123 ft per sec, that is, $|x - 123| \le 25$.
Let x = speed of the wind. 26 is 5 more than 21, and 16 is 5 less than 21, so all the speeds are within 5 ft per sec of 21 ft per sec, that is, $|x - 21| \le 5$.

Chapter 1 Review Exercises

1. $2m + 7 = 3m + 1$
$7 = m + 1$ Subtract $2m$.
$6 = m$ Subtract 1.
Solution set: $\{6\}$

3. $5y - 2(y + 4) = 3(2y + 1)$
$5y - 2y - 8 = 6y + 3$
           Distributive property
$3y - 8 = 6y + 3$
           Combine like terms.
$-8 = 3y + 3$ Subtract $3y$.
$-11 = 3y$ Subtract 3.
$\dfrac{1}{3}(-11) = \dfrac{1}{3}(3y)$ Multiply by $\dfrac{1}{3}$.
$-\dfrac{11}{3} = y$

Solution set: $\left\{ -\dfrac{11}{3} \right\}$

5. $A = \dfrac{24f}{B(p+1)}$ for f (approximate annual interest rate)

$$AB(p+1) = \dfrac{24f}{B(p+1)} \cdot B(p+1)$$

Multiply by $B(p+1)$.

$$AB(p+1) = 24f$$

$$\dfrac{AB(p+1)}{24} = f \quad \text{Divide by 24.}$$

7. Let x = rate biking to library.
Then $x - 8$ = rate biking home.
Set up a chart, using $d = rt$.

	d	r	t
To library	$\dfrac{1}{3}x$	x	$\dfrac{1}{3}$
Return	$\dfrac{1}{2}(x-8)$	$x-8$	$\dfrac{1}{2}$

The times must be changed from minutes to hours, since rates are given in miles per hour.

$$\frac{\text{Distance to library}}{} = \frac{\text{Return distance}}{}$$

$$\dfrac{1}{3}x = \dfrac{1}{2}(x-8)$$

Multiply both sides by the least common denominator, 6.

$$6\left(\dfrac{1}{3}x\right) = 6\left[\dfrac{1}{2}(x-8)\right]$$

$$2x = 3(x-8)$$
$$2x = 3x - 24$$
$$-x = -24$$
$$x = 24$$

To find the distance, substitute $x = 24$ into $d = \dfrac{1}{3}x$.

$$d = \dfrac{1}{3}(24) = 8$$

Alison lives 8 mi from the library.

9. Let x = Lynn's gross weekly pay.
Then $.26x$ = Lynn's weekly deductions.

$$x - .26x = 925$$
$$.74x = 925$$
$$x = 1250$$

Lynn's weekly pay is $1250 before deductions.

11. Let x = average speed upriver.
Then $x + 5$ = average speed on return trip.

	d	r	t
Upstream	$1.2x$	x	1.2
Downstream	$.9(x+5)$	$x+5$	$.9$

$$1.2x = .9(x+5)$$
$$1.2x = .9x + 4.5$$
$$.3x = 4.5$$
$$x = 15$$

The average speed of the boat upriver is 15 mph.

13. **(a)** In one year, the maximum amount of lead ingested would be
.05 mg/liter $\times$ 2 liters/day $\times$ 365.25 days/year = 36.525 mg/year.
The maximum amount A of lead (in milligrams) ingested in x years would be $A = 36.525x$.

   (b) If $x = 72$, then
$A = 36.525(72) = 2629.8$ mg.
The EPA maximum lead intake from water over a lifetime is 2629.8 mg.

15. **(a)** $x = 1985$
$y = .100725x - 196.54$
$y = .100725(1985) - 196.54$
$y \approx 3.40$
The minimum wage in 1985 was $3.40 according to the model. Compared to the table value of $3.35, it is quite close; they differ by just $.05.

   (b) $y = .100725x - 196.54$
$3.80 = .100725x - 196.54$
$200.34 = .100725x$
$1989 \approx x$
In 1989, the model predicts the minimum wage to be $3.80. It is fairly close to the table value of $3.35. The table value for 1990 would be exact.

17. $(6 - i) + (4 - 2i) = 10 - 3i$

19. $(4 - 3i)^2$

$$= 4^2 - 2(4)(3i) + (3i)^2$$

Square of a binomial

$$= 16 - 24i - 9$$
$$= 7 - 24i$$

21. $(b + 7)^2 = 5$
Use the square root property.

$b + 7 = \pm\sqrt{5}$

$b = -7 \pm \sqrt{5}$

Solution set: $\{-7 \pm \sqrt{5}\}$

23. $12x^2 = 8x - 1$

$12x^2 - 8x + 1 = 0$

$(2x - 1)(6x - 1) = 0$ Factor.

$x = \dfrac{1}{2}$ or $x = \dfrac{1}{6}$ Zero-factor property

Solution set: $\left\{\dfrac{1}{2}, \dfrac{1}{6}\right\}$

25. D $(7x + 4)^2 = 11$

This equation has two real, distinct solutions since the positive number 11 has a positive square root and a negative square root.

27. A $(3x - 4)^2 = -4$

This equation has two imaginary solutions since the negative number -4 has two imaginary square roots.

29. $8y^2 = 2y - 6$

$8y^2 - 2y + 6 = 0$

$a = 8, b = -2, c = 6$

$b^2 - 4ac = (-2)^2 - 4(8)(6)$

$= 4 - 192$

$= -188$

The equation has two different imaginary solutions since the discriminant is negative.

31. $16r^2 + 3 = 26r$

$16r^2 - 26r + 3 = 0$

$a = 16, b = -26, c = 3$

$b^2 - 4ac = (-26)^2 - 4(16)(3)$

$= 676 - 192$

$= 484 = 22^2$

The equation has two different rational solutions since the discriminant is a positive perfect square.

33. The projectile will be 624 ft above the ground whenever $220t - 16t^2 = 624$.

Solve this equation for t.

$220t - 16t^2 = 624$

$-16t^2 + 220t - 624 = 0$

Simplify by dividing by -4.

$4t^2 - 55t + 156 = 0$

$(t - 4)(4t - 39) = 0$

$t - 4 = 0$ or $4t - 39 = 0$

$t = 4$ or $t = \dfrac{39}{4} = 9.75$

The projectile will be 624 ft high at 4 sec and at 9.75 sec.

35. Let x = height. Then

$x + 2$ = width, and

14 = length.

A volume reduced by 5% (or .05) is equal to 95% (or .95) the original volume.

$.95[x(x + 2)(14)] = 319.2$

$.95(14x^2 + 28x) = 319.2$

$14x^2 + 28x = 336$

$14x^2 + 28x - 336 = 0$

$x^2 + 2x - 24 = 0$

$(x - 4)(x + 6) = 0$

$x - 4 = 0$ or $x + 6 = 0$

$x = 4$ or $x = -6$

(disregard a negative height)

The height is 4 inches and the width is $4 + 2 = 6$ inches. The present dimensions of the box are 4 in. by 6 in. by 14 in.

37. Let x = the length of the middle side.

Then $x - 7$ = the length of the shorter side and $x + 1$ = the length of the hypotenuse. Use the Pythagorean theorem.

$x^2 + (x - 7)^2 = (x + 1)^2$

$x^2 + x^2 - 14x + 49 = x^2 + 2x + 1$

$x^2 - 16x + 48 = 0$

$(x - 12)(x - 4) = 0$

$x = 12$ or $x = 4$

If $x = 12$, then $x - 7 = 5$

and $x + 1 = 13$.

If $x = 4$, then $x - 7 = -3$,

which is not possible.

The sides are 5 inches, 12 inches, and 13 inches long.

39. $\dfrac{2}{p} - \dfrac{4}{3p} = 8 + \dfrac{3}{p}$

Multiply both sides by the least common denominator, $3p$.

$$3p\left(\frac{2}{p} - \frac{4}{3p}\right) = 3p\left(8 + \frac{3}{p}\right)$$
$$6 - 4 = 24p + 9$$
$$2 = 24p + 9$$
$$-7 = 24p$$
$$p = -\frac{7}{24}$$

Solution set: $\left\{-\dfrac{7}{24}\right\}$

41. $\dfrac{10}{4z - 4} = \dfrac{1}{1 - z}$

Multiply both sides by the common denominator $(4z - 4)(1 - z)$, assuming $z \neq 1$.

$10(1 - z) = 1(4z - 4)$

$10 - 10z = 4z - 4$

$14 = 14z$

$1 = z$

However, substituting 1 for z in the original equation would result in a denominator of 0, so 1 is not a solution.

Solution set: $\emptyset$

43. $4a^4 + 3a^{23} - 1 = 0$

Let $u = a^2$; then $u^2 = a^4$.

With this substitution, the equation becomes

$4u^2 + 3u - 1 = 0$.

Solve this equation by factoring.

$(u + 1)(4u - 1) = 0$

$u + 1 = 0$ or $4u - 1 = 0$

$u = -1$ or $u = \dfrac{1}{4}$

To find a, replace u with a^2.

$a^2 = -1$ or $a^2 = \dfrac{1}{4}$

$a = \pm\sqrt{-1}$ or $a = \pm\sqrt{\dfrac{1}{4}}$

$a = \pm i$ or $a = \pm\dfrac{1}{2}$

Solution set: $\left\{\pm i,\ \pm\dfrac{1}{2}\right\}$

45. $\sqrt{4y - 2} = \sqrt{3y + 1}$

$(\sqrt{4y - 2})^2 = (\sqrt{3y + 1})^2$

Square both sides.

$4y - 2 = 3y + 1$

$y = 3$

Check this proposed solution in the original equation.

$\sqrt{4(3) - 2} = \sqrt{3(3) + 1}$?

$\sqrt{10} = \sqrt{10}$ True

Solution set: {3}

47. $\sqrt{k} = \sqrt{k + 3} - 1$

$(\sqrt{k})^2 = (\sqrt{k + 3} - 1)^2$

Square both sides.

$k = k + 3 - 2\sqrt{k + 3} + 1$

Square of a binomial

$2 = \sqrt{k + 3}$ Divide by -2.

$2^2 = (\sqrt{k + 3})^2$ Square both sides.

$4 = k + 3$

$1 = k$

Checking this proposed solution will show that it satisfies the original equation.

Solution set: {1}

49. $\sqrt[3]{6y + 2} = \sqrt[3]{4y}$

$(\sqrt[3]{6y + 2})^3 = (\sqrt[3]{4y})^3$ Cube both sides.

$6y + 2 = 4y$

$2y = -2$

$y = -1$

A check will show that this proposed solution satisfies the original equation.

Solution set: {−1}

51. $-9x < 4x + 7$

$0 < 13x + 7$

$-7 < 13x$

$-\dfrac{7}{13} < x$

Solution set: $\left(-\dfrac{7}{13},\ \infty\right)$

53. $-5z - 4 \geq 3(2x - 5)$

$-5x - 4 \geq 6z - 15$

$-5z - 4 + 5z \geq 6z - 15 + 5z$

$-4 \geq 11z - 15$

$-4 + 15 \geq 11z - 15 + 15$

$11 \geq 11z$

$1 \geq z$

Solution set: $(-\infty, 1]$

55. $5 \leq 2x - 3 \leq 7$

$8 \leq 2x \leq 10$

$4 \leq x \leq 5$

Solution set: [4, 5]

57. $p^2 + 4p > 21$

$p^2 + 4p - 21 > 0$

Solve the corresponding equation by factoring.

$$p^2 + 4p - 21 = 0$$
$$(p + 7)(p - 3) = 0$$
$$p = -7 \text{ or } p = 3$$

These two points, –7 and 3, divide a number line into the three regions shown on the following sign graph.

```
p + 7  – – –○+ + + + + +│+ + +
p – 3  – – –│– – – – – –○+ + +
      ───┼┼┼┼┼┼┼┼┼┼┼───→
          –7        0  3
        +        –        +
      Sign of
     (p + 7) (p – 3)
```

The product is positive in the intervals $(-\infty, -7)$ and $(3, \infty)$. The endpoints are not included because the inequality symbol is >.
Solution set: $(-\infty, -7) \cup (3, \infty)$

59. $x^2 - 6x + 9 \le 0$
First, solve the corresponding quadratic equation.
$$x^2 - 6x + 9 = 0$$
$$(x - 3)^2 = 0$$
$$x - 3 = 0$$
$$x = 3$$

This point, 3, divides a number line into the region to the left of 3 and the region to the right of 3. Testing any number from either region will result in $(x - 3)^2$ being positive and therefore not less than or equal to zero. The point 3 causes $(x - 3)^2$ to equal 0, so $x = 3$ is the only solution of $x^2 - 6x + 9 \le 0$.
Solution set: $\{3\}$

61. $\dfrac{5p + 2}{p} < -1$

$$\dfrac{5p + 2}{p} + 1 < 0$$

$$\dfrac{5p + 2}{p} + \dfrac{p}{p} < 0$$

$$\dfrac{6p + 2}{p} < 0$$

```
6p + 2  – – – – – –○+ +│+ + + + +
p       – – – – – –│– –○+ + + + +
       ──┼────┼────┼────┼──→
         –1   –⅓   0
          +        –        +
        Sign of
         6p + 2
         ──────
           p
```

The quotient is negative in the interval $\left(-\dfrac{1}{3}, 0\right)$.

Solution set: $\left(-\dfrac{1}{3}, 0\right)$

63. $\dfrac{3}{x + 2} > \dfrac{2}{x - 4}$

$$\dfrac{3}{x + 2} - \dfrac{2}{x - 4} > 0$$

$$\dfrac{3(x - 4) - 2(x + 2)}{(x + 2)(x - 4)} > 0$$

Common denominator is $(x + 2)(x + 4)$.

$$\dfrac{3x - 12 - 2x - 4}{(x + 2)(x - 4)} > 0$$

$$\dfrac{x - 16}{(x + 2)(x - 4)} > 0$$

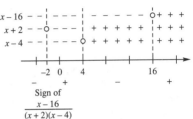

```
x – 16  – –│– – –│– – – – – –○+ + +
x + 2   – –○– – –│+ + + + + │+ + +
x – 4   – –│– – –○+ + + + + │+ + +
       ──┼──┼────┼─────────┼──→
         –2 0    4          16
         –        +          –        +
       Sign of
        x – 16
       ────────
      (x + 2)(x – 4)
```

The quotient is positive in the interval $(-2, 4)$ and $(16, \infty)$. None of the endpoints are included.
Solution set: $(-2, 4) \cup (16, \infty)$

65. $(x - a)^2$ is always greater than or equal to 0.
Therefore, $(x - a)^2$ is positive on $(-\infty, a) \cup (a, \infty)$, and never negative, and zero at $x = a$.

69. "up to 35" means 35 or less; $w \le 35$
"up to 45" means 45 or less; $L \le 45$

71. "fewer than 2000" means less than 2000; $p < 2000$.

73. The industries that released between 200,000,000 and 500,000,000 pounds are Primary Metals and Paper.

75. Let $x = $ the maximum initial concentration of ozone.
$$x - .43x \le 50$$
$$.57x \le 50$$
$$x \le 87.7$$
The filter will reduce ozone concentrations that do not exceed 87.7 ppb.

77. $s = 320 - 16t^2$

(a) When $s = 0$, the projectile will be at ground level.

$$0 = 320t - 16t^2$$
$$16t^2 - 320t = 0$$
$$t^2 - 20t = 0 \quad \text{Divide by 16.}$$
$$t(t - 20) = 0$$
$$t = 0 \text{ or } t = 20$$

The projectile will return to the ground after 20 sec.

(b) Solve $s > 576$ for t.

$$320t - 16t^2 > 576$$
$$-16t^2 + 320t - 576 > 0$$
$$-16(t^2 - 20t + 36) > 0$$
$$t^2 - 20t + 36 < 0$$

Divide by −16; reverse inequality symbol.
$$(t - 2)(t - 18) < 0$$

Draw a sign graph to see that this product is negative only between 2 and 18.
The projectile will be more than 576 ft above the ground between 2 and 18 sec.

79. $|a + 4| = 7$

$$a + 4 = 7 \quad \text{or} \quad a + 4 = -7$$
$$a = 3 \quad \text{or} \qquad a = -11$$

Solution set: $\{-11, 3\}$

81. $\left| \dfrac{7}{2 - 3a} \right| = 9$

$$\dfrac{7}{2 - 3a} = 9$$
$$7 = 9(2 - 3a)$$
$$7 = 18 - 27a$$
$$27a = 11$$
$$a = \dfrac{11}{27}$$

or

$$\dfrac{7}{2 - 3a} = -9$$
$$7 = -9(2 - 3a)$$
$$7 = -18 + 27a$$
$$25 = 27a$$
$$a = \dfrac{25}{27}$$

Solution set: $\left\{ \dfrac{11}{27}, \dfrac{25}{27} \right\}$

83. $|5r - 1| = |2r + 3|$

$$5r - 1 = 2r + 3$$
$$3r = 4$$
$$r = \dfrac{4}{3}$$

or

$$5r - 1 = -(2r + 3)$$
$$5r - 1 = -2r - 3$$
$$7r = -2$$
$$r = -\dfrac{2}{7}$$

Solution set: $\left\{ -\dfrac{2}{7}, \dfrac{4}{3} \right\}$

85. $\qquad |m| \leq 7$
$$-7 \leq m \leq 7$$
Solution set: $[-7, 7]$

87. $|2z + 9| \leq 3$
$$-3 \leq 2z + 9 \leq 3$$
$$-12 \leq 2z \leq -6$$
$$-6 \leq z \leq -3$$
Solution set: $[-6, -3]$

89. $|3r + 7| - 5 > 0$
$$|3r + 7| > 5$$
$$3r + 7 < -5 \quad \text{or} \quad 3r + 7 > 5$$
$$3r < -12 \qquad\qquad 3r > -2$$
$$r < -4 \quad \text{or} \quad r > -\dfrac{2}{3}$$

Solution set: $(-\infty, -4) \cup \left(-\dfrac{2}{3}, \infty \right)$

Chapter 1 Test Exercises

1. $3(x - 4) - 5(x + 1) = 2 - (x + 24)$
$$3x - 12 - 5x - 10 = 2 - x - 24$$
$$-2x - 22 = -x - 22$$
$$-x = 0$$
$$x = 0$$
Solution set: $\{0\}$

2. $\dfrac{2}{t - 3} - \dfrac{3}{t + 3} = \dfrac{12}{t^2 - 9}$

$$\dfrac{2}{t - 3} - \dfrac{3}{t + 3} = \dfrac{12}{(t + 3)(t - 3)}$$

Multiply both sides by the common denominator, $(t + 3)(t - 3)$, assuming $t \neq -3$ and $t \neq 3$.

$$2(t + 3) - 3(t - 3) = 12$$
$$2t + 6 - 3t + 9 = 12$$
$$-t = -3$$
$$t = 3$$

However, substituting 3 for t in the original equation would result in a denominator of 0, so 3 is not a solution.

Solution set: $\emptyset$

3. $\qquad S = 2HW + 2LW + 2LH$ for W(width)

$S - 2LH = 2HW + 2LW$

$S - 2LH = W(2H + 2L)$

$\dfrac{S - 2LH}{2H + 2L} = W$

$\qquad W = \dfrac{S - 2LH}{2H + 2L}$

4. Substituting $q = 3.1 \times 10^{-13}$ and $T = 20$ into the equation we have

$C = \dfrac{5.48 \times 10^3 (3.1 \times 10^{-13})^{.571}(20 + 273)^{-1}}{[2.10 \times 10^{-11} - 6.58 \times 10^{-14}(20 + 273)]^{.571}}$

≈ 7.029 pCi.

Since the level is above 4 pCi/L, it is unsafe.

6. Let x = number of quarts of 60% alcohol solution.

Strength	Quarts of solution	Quarts of pure alcohol
60%	x	$.60x$
20%	40	$.20(40)$
30%	$x + 40$	$.30(x + 40)$

$.60x + .20(40) = .30(x + 4)$

$.60x + 8 = .30x + 12$

$.30x = 4$

$x = \dfrac{4}{.30}$

$= 13\frac{1}{3}$

$13\frac{1}{3}$ quarts of 60% alcohol must be added.

7. Let x = time Fred travels.

Then $x - 3$ = time Wilma travels.

	d	r	t
Fred	$30x$	30	x
Wilma	$50(x-3)$	50	$x - 3$

They both travel the same distance, so

$30x = 50(x - 3)$

$30x = 50x - 150$

$-20x = -150$

$x = 7.5$

and $d = 30(7.5) = 225$.

They travel 225 mi before meeting.

8. $\qquad 3x^3 - 5x = -2$

$3x^2 - 5x + 2 = 0$

Solve by factoring.

$(3x - 2)(x - 1) = 0$

$3x - 2 = 0 \quad$ or $\quad x - 1 = 0$

$x = \dfrac{2}{3} \quad$ or $\qquad x = 1$

Solution set: $\left\{\dfrac{2}{3},\ 1\right\}$

9. $(5t - 3)^2 = 17$

Use the square root property.

$5t - 3 = \pm\sqrt{17}$

$5t = 3 \pm \sqrt{17}$

$t = \dfrac{3 \pm \sqrt{17}}{5}$

Solution set: $\left\{\dfrac{3 \pm \sqrt{17}}{5}\right\}$

10. $\quad 6s(2 - s) = 7$

$12x - 6s^2 = 7$

$0 = 6s^2 - 12s + 7$

Use the quadratic formula with

$a = 6$, $b = -12$, and $c = 7$.

$s = \dfrac{12 \pm \sqrt{144 - 4(6)(7)}}{12}$

$= \dfrac{12 \pm \sqrt{-24}}{12}$

$= \dfrac{12 \pm 2i\sqrt{6}}{12}$

$s = 1 \pm \dfrac{\sqrt{6}}{6} i$

Solution set: $\left\{1 \pm \dfrac{\sqrt{6}}{6} i\right\}$

11. The table shows each equation evaluated at the years 1975, 1994, and 2006. Equation B best models the data.

12. $h = -16t^2 + 96t$

(a) Let $h = 80$ and solve for t.

$\qquad 80 = -16t^2 + 96t$

$16t^2 - 96t + 80 = 0$

Divide by 16.

$t^2 - 6t + 5 = 0$

$(t - 1)(t - 5) = 0$

$t = 1$ or $t = 5$

The projectile will reach a height of 80 ft at 1 sec and 5 sec.

(b) Let $h = 0$ and solve for t.

$0 = -16t^2 + 96t$

$0 = -16t(t - 6)$

$t = 0$ or $t = 6$

The projectile will return to the ground at 6 sec.

13. (a) $(7 - 3i) - (2 + 5i) = (7 - 2) + (-3 - 5)i$
$$= 5 - 8i$$

(b) $(4 + 3i)(-5 + 3i) = -20 + 12i - 15i + 9i^2$
$$= -20 + 12i - 15i - 9$$
$$= -29 - 3i$$

(c) $\dfrac{5 - 5i}{1 - 3i} = \dfrac{(5 - 5i)(1 + 3i)}{(1 - 3i)(1 + 3i)}$

$\qquad = \dfrac{5 + 15i - 5i - 15i^2}{1 - 9i^2}$

$\qquad = \dfrac{20 + 10i}{10}$

$\qquad = 2 + i$

14. $\sqrt{5 + 2x} - x = 1$

$\qquad \sqrt{5 + 2x} = x + 1$

$\qquad (\sqrt{5 + 2x})^2 = (x + 1)^2$

$\qquad 5 + 2x = x^2 + 2x + 1$

$\qquad 0 = x^2 - 4$

$\qquad 0 = (x + 2)(x - 2)$

$x = -2$ or $x = 2$

Check $x = -2$.

$\sqrt{5 + 2(-2)} - (-2) = 1$?

$\qquad \sqrt{1} + 2 = 1$?

$\qquad\qquad 3 = 1$ False

Check $x = 2$.

$\sqrt{5 + 2(2)} - 2 = 1$?

$\qquad \sqrt{9} - 2 = 1$?

$\qquad\qquad 1 = 1$ True

The checks show that 2 satisfies the equation but -2 does not.

Solution set: $\{2\}$

15. $x^4 + 6x^2 - 40 = 0$

Let $u = x^2$, and solve the resulting equation for u.

$u^2 + 6u - 40 = 0$

$(u + 10)(u - 4) = 0$

$u = -10$ or $u = 4$

Replace $u = x^2$ and solve for x.

If $u = -10$, then

$x^2 = -10$

$x = \pm\sqrt{-10}$

$x = \pm i\sqrt{10}$

If $u = 4$, then

$x^2 = 4$

$x = \pm 2.$

Solution set: $\left\{ \pm 2,\ \pm i\sqrt{10} \right\}$

16. $\sqrt[3]{3x - 8} = \sqrt[3]{9x + 4}$

$(\sqrt[3]{3x - 8})^3 = (\sqrt[3]{9x + 4})^3$

$\qquad 3x - 8 = 9x + 4$

$\qquad -6x = 12$

$\qquad x = -2$

Solution set: $\{-2\}$

17. $6 = \dfrac{7}{2y - 3} + \dfrac{3}{(2y - 3)^3}$

Multiply by the common denominator, $(2y - 3)^2$, assuming $y \neq \dfrac{3}{2}$.

$6(2y - 3)^2 = 7(2y - 3) + 3$

$6(4y^2 - 12y + 9) = 14y - 21 + 3$

$24y^2 - 72y + 54 = 14y - 18$

$24y^2 - 86y + 72 = 0$

Divide by 2.

$12y^2 - 43y + 36 = 0$

$(3y - 4)(4y - 9) = 0$

$3y - 4 = 0$ or $4y - 9 = 0$

$y = \dfrac{4}{3}$ or $\qquad y = \dfrac{9}{4}$

Solution set: $\left\{ \dfrac{4}{3},\ \dfrac{9}{4} \right\}$

18. Since Dobson units are linear, we can use proportions. Let x be the thickness of the Antarctic ozone layer. Then,

$\dfrac{x}{110} = \dfrac{3}{300}$

$300x = 330$

$\qquad x = 1.1$

The thickness of the ozone layer in 1991 at the Antarctic ozone hole was 1.1 mm.

19. $-2(x - 1) - 10 < 2(2 + x)$

$-2x + 2 - 10 < 4 + 2x$

$\qquad -2x - 8 < 4 + 2x$

$\qquad\qquad -4x < 12$

$\left(-\dfrac{1}{4}\right)(-4x) > \left(-\dfrac{1}{4}\right)(12)$

Multiply by $-\dfrac{1}{4}$; reverse inequality symbol.

$\qquad\qquad x > -3$

Solution set: $(-3, \infty)$

20. $-2 \le \dfrac{1}{2}x + 3 \le 4$

Multiply all parts by 2.

$-4 \le x + 6 \le 8$

$--10 \le x \le 2$

Solution set: $[-10, 2]$

21. $2x^2 - x - 3 \ge 0$

Solve the corresponding quadratic equation by factoring.

$$2x^2 - x - 3 = 0$$

$$(x+1)(2x-3) = 0$$

$x = -1$ or $x = \dfrac{3}{2}$

These two points divide the number line into three regions.

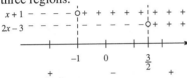

Sign of
$(x+1)(2x-3)$

The sign graph shows that the product is positive in the intervals $(-\infty, -1)$ and $\left(\dfrac{3}{2}, \infty\right)$. The endpoints satisfy the inequality since the inequality symbol is $\ge$.

Solution set: $(-\infty, -1] \cup \left[\dfrac{3}{2}, \infty\right)$

22.

$$\dfrac{x+1}{x-3} < 5$$

$$\dfrac{x+1}{x-3} - 5 < 0$$

$$\dfrac{x+1-5(x-3)}{x-3} < 0$$

$$\dfrac{x+1-5x+15}{x-3} < 0$$

$$\dfrac{-4x+16}{x-3} < 0$$

$-4x+16$ + + + + + + | + + o − − − −
$x-3$ − − − − − − o+ + | + + + +

          0   3   4
                  −   +   −
        Sign of
        $\dfrac{-4x+16}{x-3}$

The quotient is negative in the intervals $(-\infty, 3)$ and $(4, \infty)$. None of the endpoints are included.

Solution set: $(-\infty, 3) \cup (4, \infty)$

23. $|3x + 5| = 4$

$3x + 5 = 4$ or $3x + 5 = -4$

$\quad 3x = -1 \qquad\qquad 3x = -9$

$\quad\; x = -\dfrac{1}{3}$ or $\quad x = -3$

Solution set: $\left\{-3, -\dfrac{1}{3}\right\}$

24. $|2x - 5| < 9$

$-9 < 2x - 5 < 9$

$-4 < 2x < 14$

$-2 < x < 7$

Solution set: $(-2, 7)$

25. $|2x + 1| \ge 11$

$2x + 1 \le -11$ or $2x + 1 \ge 11$

$\quad 2x \le -12 \qquad\qquad 2x \ge 10$

$\quad\;\; x \le -6$ or $\qquad x \ge 5$

Solution set: $(-\infty, -6] \cup [5, \infty)$

CHAPTER 2 RELATIONS, FUNCTIONS, AND GRAPHS

Section 2.1

Connections (*page 86*)

1. Answers will vary.

2. Latitude and longitude values pinpoint distances north or south of the equator and east or west of the prime meridian. Similarly on a Cartesian coordinate system, x- and y-values give distances and directions from the origin.

Exercises

1. True; the origin has coordinates (0, 0). So, the distance from (0, 0) to (a, b) is
$$d = \sqrt{(b-0)^2 + (a-0)^2}$$
$$= \sqrt{b^2 + a^2}$$
$$= \sqrt{a^2 + b^2}$$
$$\left(\frac{a+3a}{2}, \frac{b-3b}{2}\right) = \left(\frac{4a}{2}, \frac{-2b}{2}\right) = (2a, -b)$$

3. False; the relation should be $x^2 + y^2 = 9$ to satisfy these conditions.

5. $\{(-4, 6), (3, 2), (5, 7)\}$
Three ordered pairs which belong to the relation are $(-4, 6)$, $(3, 2)$, and $(5, 7)$.
The domain is the set of first elements, $\{-4, 3, 5\}$.
The range is the set of second elements, $\{6, 2, 7\}$.

In Exercises 7–13, there are other possible answers for the three ordered pairs.

7. $y = 9x - 3$
If $x = -1$, $y = 9(-1) - 3 = -12$.
If $x = 1$, $y = 9(1) - 3 = 6$.
If $x = 2$, $y = 9(2) - 3 = 15$.
Three ordered pairs which belong to the relation are $(-1, -12)$, $(1, 6)$, and $(2, 15)$.
The domain is $(-\infty, \infty)$.
The range is $(-\infty, \infty)$.

9. $y = -\sqrt{x}$
If $x = 0$, $y = -\sqrt{0} = 0$.
If $x = 1$, $y = -\sqrt{1} = -1$.
If $x = 4$, $y = -\sqrt{4} = -2$.
Three ordered pairs which belong to the relation are $(0, 0)$, $(1, -1)$, and $(4, -2)$.
In order for $\sqrt{x}$ to be a real number, $x \geq 0$.
Therefore, the domain is $[0, \infty)$.

Since $y = -\sqrt{x}$, y will never be positive, so the range is $(-\infty, 0]$.

11. $y = |x + 2|$
If $x = 0$, $y = |0 + 2| = 2$.
If $x = 1$, $y = |1 + 2| = 3$.
If $x = -1$, $y = |-1 + 2| = 1$.
Three ordered pairs which belong to the relation are $(0, 2)$, $(1, 3)$, and $(-1, 1)$.
Since we can substitute any real number for x in $|x + 2|$, the domain is $(-\infty, \infty)$.
Since absolute value is never negative, the range is $[0, \infty)$.

13. Annual New Business Incorporations

Year	Number
1990	647,366
1991	628,604
1992	666,800
1993	706,537
1994	741,657

Three ordered pairs which belong to the relation are (1990, 647,366), (1991, 628,604), and (1992, 666,800).
The domain is the set of years, {1990, 1991, 1992, 1993, 1994}.
The range is the set of numbers of new business incorporations, {647,366, 628,604, 666,800, 706,537, 741,657}.

15. Three ordered pairs which belong to the relation shown in the calculator-generated table are $(2, -5)$, $(-1, 7)$, and $(3, -9)$.
The domain is $\{2, -1, 3, 5, 6\}$.
The range is $\{-5, 7, -9, -17, -21\}$.

17. $P(-5, -7)$, $Q(-13, 1)$

(a) $d(P, Q) = \sqrt{[1-(-7)]^2 + [-13-(-5)]^2}$
$$= \sqrt{8^2 + (-8)^2}$$
$$= \sqrt{128}$$
$$= 8\sqrt{2}$$

(b) The midpoint M of the segment joining points P and Q has coordinates
$$\left(\frac{-5+(-13)}{2}, \frac{-7+1}{2}\right) \text{ or } (-9, -3).$$

19. $P(8, 2)$, $Q(3, 5)$

(a) $d(P, Q) = \sqrt{(5-2)^2 + (3-8)^2}$

$= \sqrt{3^2 + (-5)^2}$

$= \sqrt{34}$

(b) The midpoint M of the segment joining points P and Q has coordinates $\left(\dfrac{8+3}{2}, \dfrac{2+5}{2}\right)$ or $\left(\dfrac{11}{2}, \dfrac{7}{2}\right)$.

21. $P(3\sqrt{2}, \ 4\sqrt{5}), \ Q(\sqrt{2}, -\sqrt{5})$

(a) $d(P, Q) = \sqrt{(\sqrt{2} - 3\sqrt{2})^2 + (-\sqrt{5} - 4\sqrt{5})^2}$

$= \sqrt{(-2\sqrt{2})^2 + (-5\sqrt{5})^2}$

$= \sqrt{8 + 125}$

$= \sqrt{133}$

(b) The midpoint M of the segment joining points P and Q has coordinates $\left(\dfrac{3\sqrt{2} + \sqrt{2}}{2}, \dfrac{4\sqrt{5} + (-\sqrt{5})}{2}\right)$ or $\left(2\sqrt{2}, \dfrac{3\sqrt{5}}{2}\right)$.

23. $P(-8, 4), \ Q(3, -5)$

(a) $d(P, Q) = \sqrt{[3 - (-8)]^2 + (-5 - 4)^2}$

$= \sqrt{11^2 + (-9)^2}$

$= \sqrt{121 + 81}$

$= \sqrt{202}$

(b) The midpoint M of the segment joining points P and Q has coordinates $\left(\dfrac{-8+3}{2}, \dfrac{4+(-5)}{2}\right)$ or $\left(-\dfrac{5}{2}, -\dfrac{1}{2}\right)$.

25. Label the points $A(-6, -4)$, $B(0, -2)$, and $C(-10, 8)$.
Use the distance formula to find the length of each side of the triangle.

$d(A, B) = \sqrt{[0 - (-6)]^2 + [-2 - (-4)]^2}$

$= \sqrt{6^2 + 2^2}$

$= \sqrt{40}$

$d(B, C) = \sqrt{(-10 - 0)^2 + [8 - (-2)]^2}$

$= \sqrt{10^2 + 10^2}$

$= \sqrt{200}$

$d(A, C) = \sqrt{[-10 - (-6)]^2 + [8 - (-4)]^2}$

$= \sqrt{(-4)^2 + 12^2}$

$= \sqrt{160}$

Since

$\left(\sqrt{40}\right)^2 + \left(\sqrt{160}\right)^2 = \left(\sqrt{200}\right)^2$,

triangle ABC is a right triangle.

27. Label the points $A(-4, 1)$, $B(1, 4)$, and $C(-6, -1)$.

$d(A, B) = \sqrt{[1 - (-4)]^2 + (4 - 1)^2}$

$= \sqrt{5^2 + 3^2}$

$= \sqrt{34}$

$d(B, C) = \sqrt{(-6 - 1)^2 + (-1 - 4)^2}$

$= \sqrt{(-7)^2 + (-5)^2}$

$= \sqrt{74}$

$d(A, C) = \sqrt{[-6 - (-4)]^2 + (-1 - 1)^2}$

$= \sqrt{(-2)^2 + (-2)^2}$

$= \sqrt{8}$

Since $(\sqrt{8})^2 + (\sqrt{34})^2 \neq (\sqrt{74})^2$, triangle ABC is not a right triangle.

29. Label the given points $M(0, -7)$, $N(-3, 5)$, and $P(2, -15)$. Find the distance between each pair of points.

$d(M, N) = \sqrt{(-3 - 0)^2 + [5 - (-7)]^2}$

$= \sqrt{(-3)^2 + 12^2}$

$= \sqrt{153}$

$= 3\sqrt{17}$

$d(N, P) = \sqrt{[2 - (-3)]^2 + (-15 - 5)^2}$

$= \sqrt{5^2 + (-20)^2}$

$= \sqrt{425}$

$= 5\sqrt{17}$

$d(M, P) = \sqrt{(2 - 0)^2 + [-15 - (-7)]^2}$

$= \sqrt{2^2 + (-8)^2}$

$= \sqrt{68}$

$= 2\sqrt{17}$

Since

$d(M, N) + d(M, P) = d(N, P)$

or $3\sqrt{17} + 2\sqrt{17} = 5\sqrt{17}$,

the given points lie on a straight line.

31. Label the points $A(0, 9)$, $B(-3, -7)$, and $C(2, 19)$.

$$d(A, B) = \sqrt{(-3-0)^2 + (-7-9)^2}$$
$$= \sqrt{(-3)^2 + (-16)^2}$$
$$= \sqrt{265}$$
$$\approx 16.279$$

$$d(B, C) = \sqrt{[2-(-3)]^2 + [19-(-7)]^2}$$
$$= \sqrt{5^2 + 26^2}$$
$$= \sqrt{701}$$
$$\approx 26.476$$

$$d(A, C) = \sqrt{(2-0)^2 + (19-9)^2}$$
$$= \sqrt{2^2 + 10^2}$$
$$= \sqrt{1104}$$
$$\approx 10.198$$

Since
$$d(A, B) + d(A, C) \neq d(B, C)$$
or $$\sqrt{265} + \sqrt{104} \neq \sqrt{701}$$
$$16.279 + 10.198 \neq 26.479,$$
the three given points are not collinear. (Note, however, that these points are very close to lying on a straight line and may appear to lie on a straight line when graphed.)

33. Center $(0, 0)$, radius 6
$$x^2 + y^2 = r^2$$
$$x^2 + y^2 = 6^2$$
$$x^2 + y^2 = 36$$

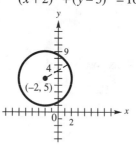

$$x^2 + y^2 = 36$$
From the graph, we see that the domain is $[-6, 6]$ and the range is $[-6, 6]$.

35. Center $(2, 0)$, radius 6
$$(x-h)^2 + (y-k)^2 = r^2$$
$$(x-2)^2 + (y-0)^2 = 6^2$$
$$(x-2)^2 + y^2 = 36$$

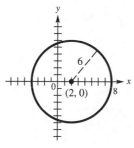

$$(x-2)^2 + y^2 = 36$$
From the graph, we see that the domain is $[-4, 8]$ and the range is $[-6, 6]$.

37. Center $(-2, 5)$, radius 4
$$[x-(-2)]^2 + (y-5)^2 = 4^2$$
$$(x+2)^2 + (y-5)^2 = 16$$

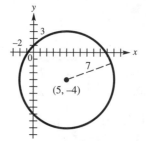

$$(x+2)^2 + (y-5)^2 = 16$$
From the graph, we see that the domain is $[-6, 2]$ and the range is $[1, 9]$.

39. Center $(5, -4)$, radius 7
$$(x-5)^2 + [y-(-4)]^2 = 7^2$$
$$(x-5)^2 + (y+4)^2 = 49$$

$$(x-5)^2 + (y+4)^2 = 49$$
From the graph, we see that the domain is $[-2, 12]$ and the range is $[-11, 3]$.

41. The radius of the circle is the distance from the center $C(3, 2)$ to the x-axis. This distance is 2, so $r = 2$.
$$(x-3)^2 + (y-2)^2 = 2^2$$
$$(x-3)^2 + (y-2)^2 = 4$$

43. $(x+4)^2 + (y-2)^2 = 25$

$$(y-2)^2 = 25 - (x+4)^2$$
$$y - 2 = \pm\sqrt{25 - (x+4)^2}$$
$$y = 2 \pm \sqrt{25 - (x+4)^2}$$
$$Y_1 = 2 + \sqrt{25 - (x+4)^2}$$
$$Y_2 = 2 - \sqrt{25 - (x+4)^2}$$

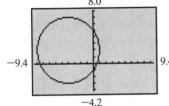

45.
$$x^2 + 6x + y^2 + 8y + 9 = 0$$
Complete the square on x and y separately.
$$(x^2 + 6x) + (y^2 + 8y) = -9$$
$$(x^2 + 6x + 9) + (y^2 + 8y + 16) = -9 + 9 + 16$$
$$(x+3)^2 + (y+4)^2 = 16$$
Yes, it is a circle.
The circle has its center at $(-3, -4)$ and radius 4.

47.
$$x^2 - 4x + y^2 + 12y = -4$$
$$(x^2 - 4x) + (y^2 + 12y) = -4$$
$$(x^2 - 4x + 4) + (y^2 + 12y + 36) = -4 + 4 + 36$$
$$(x-2)^2 + (y+6)^2 = 36$$
Yes, it is a circle.
The circle has its center at $(2, -6)$ and radius 6.

49.
$$4x^2 + 4x + 4y^2 - 16y - 19 = 0$$
$$4(x^2 + x + y^2 - 4y) = 19$$
$$x^2 + x + y^2 - 4y = \frac{19}{4}$$
$$\left(x^2 + x + \frac{1}{4}\right) + (y^2 - 4y + 4) = \frac{19}{4} + \frac{1}{4} + 4$$
$$\left(x + \frac{1}{2}\right)^2 + (y-2)^2 = 9$$
Yes, it is a circle.

The circle has its center at $\left(-\frac{1}{2}, 2\right)$ and radius 3.

51.
$$x^2 + 2x + y^2 - 6y + 14 = 0$$
$$(x^2 + 2x) + (y^2 - 6y) = -14$$
$$(x^2 + 2x + 1) + (y^2 - 6y + 9) = -14 + 1 + 9$$
$$(x+1)^2 + (y-3)^2 = -4$$
No, it is not a circle.

53. The midpoint M has coordinates
$$\left(\frac{-1+5}{2}, \frac{3+(-9)}{2}\right) \text{ or } (2, -3).$$

54. Use points $C(2, -3)$ and $P(-1, 3)$.
$$d(C, P) = \sqrt{(-1-2)^2 + [3-(-3)]^2}$$
$$= \sqrt{(-3)^2 + 6^2}$$
$$= \sqrt{45}$$
$$= 3\sqrt{5}$$
The radius is $3\sqrt{5}$.

55. Use points $C(2, -3)$ and $Q(5, -9)$.
$$d(C, Q) = \sqrt{(5-2)^2 + [-9-(-3)]^2}$$
$$= \sqrt{3^2 + (-6)^2}$$
$$= \sqrt{45}$$
$$= 3\sqrt{5}$$
The radius is $3\sqrt{5}$.

56. Use the points $P(-1, 3)$ and $Q(5, -9)$.
$$d(P, Q) = \sqrt{[5-(-1)]^2 + (-9-3)^2}$$
$$= \sqrt{6^2 + (-12)^2}$$
$$= \sqrt{180}$$
$$= 6\sqrt{5}$$
The radius is $\frac{1}{2} d(P, Q)$.
$$r = \frac{1}{2}(6\sqrt{5}) = 3\sqrt{5}$$

57. The center-radius form for this circle is
$$(x-2)^2 + (y+3)^2 = (3\sqrt{5})^2$$
$$(x-2)^2 + (y+3)^2 = 45.$$

58. Label the endpoints of the diameter $P(3, -5)$ and $Q(-7, 3)$.
The midpoint M of the segment joining P and Q
has coordinates $\left(\frac{3+(-7)}{2}, \frac{-5+3}{2}\right)$ or $(-2, -1)$.
The center is $C(-2, -1)$.
$$d(C, P) = \sqrt{[3-(-2)]^2 + [-5-(-1)]^2}$$
$$= \sqrt{5^2 + (-4)^2}$$
$$= \sqrt{41}$$
The radius is $r = \sqrt{41}$.
The center-radius form of the equation of the circle is
$$[x-(-2)]^2 + [y-(-1)]^2 = (\sqrt{41})^2$$
$$(x+2)^2 + (y+1)^2 = 41.$$

59. The coordinates of the midpoint of the line segment joining (1990, 13,500) and (1994, 15,300) are

$$\left(\frac{1990+1994}{2}, \frac{13,500+15,300}{2}\right) = (1992, 14,400).$$

The revenue in 1992 was $14,400 million.

61. The points to use would be (1960, 3022) and (1970, 3968). Their midpoint is

$$\left(\frac{1960+1970}{2}, \frac{3022+3968}{2}\right) = (1965, \ 3495).$$

In 1965 it was approximately $3495.

63. Midpoint (5, 8), endpoint (13, 10).
Let the unknown endpoint have coordinates (x_2, y_2). Then,

$$\frac{13+x_2}{2} = 5 \quad \text{and} \quad \frac{10+y_2}{2} = 8$$
$$13 + x_2 = 10 \quad \text{and} \quad 16 + y_2 = 12$$
$$x_2 = -3 \quad \text{and} \quad y_2 = 6.$$

The other endpoint has coordinates (–3, 6).

65. Midpoint (12, 6), endpoint (19, 16).
Let the unknown endpoint have coordinates (x_2, y_2). Then,

$$\frac{19+x_2}{2} = 12 \quad \text{and} \quad \frac{16+y_2}{2} = 6$$
$$19 + x_2 = 24 \quad \text{and} \quad 16 + y_2 = 12$$
$$x_2 = 5 \quad \text{and} \quad y_2 = -4.$$

The other endpoint has coordinates (5, –4).

69. To show algebraically that the epicenter lies at (–3, 4), determine the equation for each circle and substitute $x = -3$ and $y = 4$.

Station 1:
Center   (1, 4), r = 4
$$(x-1)^2 + (y-4)^2 = 16$$
$$(-3-1)^2 + (4-4)^2 = 16$$
$$(-4)^2 + 0^2 = 16$$
$$16 + 0 = 16$$
$$16 = 16$$

Station 2:
Center   (–6, 0), $r = 5$
$$(x+6)^2 + y^2 = 25$$
$$(-3+6)^2 + 4^2 = 25$$
$$3^2 + 4^2 = 25$$
$$9 + 16 = 25$$
$$25 = 25$$

Station 3:

Center $(5, -2), \ r = 10$
$$(x-5)^2 + (y+2)^2 = 100$$
$$(-3-5)^2 + (4+2)^2 = 100$$
$$(-8)^2 + 6^2 = 100$$
$$64 + 36 = 100$$
$$100 = 100$$

We have shown that the point (–3, 4) lies on all three circles, so the epicenter lies at (–3, 4).

71. Points in the x-axis have y-coordinates equal to 0. The point on the x-axis will have the same x-coordinate as point (4, 3). Therefore, the line will intersect the x-axis at (4, 0).

73. Since (a, b) is in the second quadrant, a is negative and b is positive.
Therefore, $(a, -b)$ will have a negative x-coordinate and a negative y-coordinate and will lie in quadrant III.
Also, $(-a, b)$ will have a positive x-coordinate and a positive y-coordinate and will lie in quadrant I.
Also, $(-a, -b)$ will have a positive x-coordinate and a negative y-coordinate and will lie in quadrant IV.
Finally, (b, a) will have a positive x-coordinate and a negative y-coordinate and will lie in quadrant IV.

75. Use the distance formula to find the length of each side.

$$d(A, \ B) = \sqrt{(5-1)^2 + (2-1)^2}$$
$$= \sqrt{4^2 + 1^2}$$
$$= \sqrt{17}$$

$$d(B, \ C) = \sqrt{(3-5)^2 + (4-2)^2}$$
$$= \sqrt{(-2)^2 + 2^2}$$
$$= \sqrt{8}$$

$$d(C, \ D) = \sqrt{(-1-3)^2 + (3-4)^2}$$
$$= \sqrt{(-4)^2 + (-1)^2}$$
$$= \sqrt{17}$$

$$d(D, \ A) = \sqrt{(-1-1)^2 + (3-1)^2}$$
$$= \sqrt{(-2)^2 + 2^2}$$
$$= \sqrt{8}$$

Since $d(A, B) = d(C, D)$ and $d(B, C) = d(D, A)$, the points are the vertices of a parallelogram. Since $d(A, B) \neq d(B, C)$, the points are not the vertices of a rhombus.

77. Label the points $P(x, y)$ and $Q(1, 3)$.
If $d(P, \ Q) = 4$,

$$\sqrt{(1-x)^2 + (3-y)^2} = 4$$

$$(1-x)^2 + (3-y)^2 = 16.$$

If $x = y$, then

$$(1-y)^2 + (3-y)^2 = 16$$

$$1 - 2y + y^2 + 9 - 6y + y^2 = 16$$

$$2y^2 - 8y - 6 = 0$$

$$y^2 - 4y - 3 = 0.$$

To solve this equation, use the quadratic formula with $a = 1$, $b = -4$, and $c = -3$.

$$y = \frac{4 \pm \sqrt{(-4)^2 - 4(1)(-3)}}{2}$$

$$= \frac{4 \pm \sqrt{28}}{2}$$

$$= \frac{4 \pm 2\sqrt{7}}{2}$$

$$y = 2 \pm \sqrt{7}$$

Since $x = y$, the points are
$(2 + \sqrt{7},\ 2 + \sqrt{7})$ and
$(2 - \sqrt{7},\ 2 - \sqrt{7})$.

79. Let $P(x, y)$ be a point whose distance from $A(1, 0)$ is $\sqrt{10}$ and whose distance from $B(5, 4)$ is $\sqrt{10}$.

$d(P, A) = \sqrt{10}$, so

$$\sqrt{(1-x)^2 + (0-y)^2} = \sqrt{10}$$

$$(1-x)^2 + y^2 = 10.$$

$d(P, B) = \sqrt{10}$, so

$$\sqrt{(5-x)^2 + (4-y)^2} = \sqrt{10}$$

$$(5-x)^2 + (4-y)^2 = 10.$$

Thus,

$$(1-x)^2 + y^2 = (5-x)^2 + (4-y)^2$$

$$1 - 2x + x^2 + y^2 = 25 - 10x + x^2 + 16 - 8y + y^2$$

$$8x = -8y + 40$$

$$x = -y + 5$$

or $\qquad\quad y = 5 - x.$

Substitute $5 - x$ for y in the equation $(1-x)^2 + y^2 = 10$ and solve for x.

$$(1-x)^2 + (5-x)^2 = 10$$

$$1 - 2x + x^2 + 25 - 10x + x^2 = 10$$

$$2x^2 - 12x + 26 = 10$$

$$2x^2 - 12x + 16 = 0$$

$$x^2 - 6x + 8 = 0$$

$$(x-2)(x-4) = 0$$

$x - 2 = 0$ or $x - 4 = 0$

$x = 2$ or $\quad\;\; x = 4$

To find the corresponding values of y use the equation $y = 5 - x$.
If $x = 2$, $y = 5 - 2 = 3$.
If $x = 4$, $y = 5 - 4 = 1$.
The points are $(2, 3)$ and $(4, 1)$.

81. Label the points $A(3, y)$ and $B(-2, 9)$.
If $d(A, B) = 12$,

$$\sqrt{(-2-3)^2 + (9-y)^2} = 12$$

$$(-5)^2 + (9-y)^2 = 12^2$$

$$25 + 81 - 18y + y^2 = 144$$

$$y^2 - 18y - 38 = 0.$$

Solve this equation by using the quadratic formula with $a = 1$, $b = -18$, and $c = -38$.

$$y = \frac{-(-18) \pm \sqrt{(-18)^2 - 4(1)(-38)}}{2(1)}$$

$$y = \frac{18 \pm \sqrt{476}}{2}$$

$$y = \frac{18 \pm 2\sqrt{119}}{2}$$

$$y = 9 \pm \sqrt{119}$$

The values of y are $9 + \sqrt{119}$ and $9 - \sqrt{119}$.

83. (a) The exact date of "Black Friday" was October 19, 1987. The average at the end of the day on "Black Friday" was 1738.74. So the ordered pair is (October 19, 1987, 1738.74).

(b) The average at the end of the day on October 18, 1987 was 508 points higher than at the end of the day on October 19, 1987. Thus the ordered pair is (October 18, 1987, 2246.74).

Section 2.2

Exercises

1. Growth of Investment Clubs

Year (x)	Number of Clubs (y)
1994	12,429
1995	16,054
1996	25,409
1997	34,618

Since each element in the domain corresponds to exactly one element in the range, the set represents y as a function of x.

3. $\{(1, 3), (2, 4), (3, 5)\}$
Since each element in the domain corresponds to

exactly one element in the range, the set represents y as a function of x.

5. $\{(x,\ y)\,|\,x=y^2\}$

Since the domain element $x=4$ corresponds to the two range elements $y=2$ and $y=-2$, the set does not represent y as a function of x.

7. $\{(x,\ y)\,|\,y=3x-y\}$

Since every domain element x corresponds to exactly one range element y, the set represents y as a function of x.

9. The calculator screen shows some points from $y=x^2$. Since every domain element x corresponds to exactly one range element y, the set represents y as a function of x.

11. Since each vertical line intersects the graph at no more than one point, the graph is the graph of a function. The domain is $(-\infty,\ \infty)$; the range is $(-\infty,\ \infty)$.

13. Since some vertical lines intersect the graph at two points, the graph is not the graph of a function. The domain is $[3,\ \infty)$; the range is $(-\infty,\ \infty)$.

15. Since some vertical lines intersect the graph at two points, the graph is not the graph of a function. The domain is $[-4,\ 4]$; the range is $[-3,\ 3]$.

17. Since each vertical line intersects the graph at no more than one point, the graph is the graph of a function.

19. Since some vertical lines intersect the graph at two points, the graph is not the graph of a function.

21. $f(x)=3x-7$
$f(-6)=3(-6)-7$
$\qquad =-18-7$
$\qquad =-25$

23. $g(x)=x^2-1$
$g(10)=10^2-1$
$\qquad =100-1$
$\qquad =99$

25. $f(x)-g(x)=(3x-7)-(x^2-1)$
$f(0)-g(0)=(3(0)-7)-(0^2-1)$
$\qquad\qquad =(-7)-(-1)$
$\qquad\qquad =-7+1$
$\qquad\qquad =-6$

27. $g(x+h)=(x+h)^2-1$
$\qquad\quad =x^2+2xh+h^2-1$

29. $Y_1=8x-15,\ \ Y_2=-.5x+2$
Using the calculator,
$Y_1(0)+Y_2(2)=-14$

31. $Y_1=8X-15$
Using the calculator,

X	Y_1
3	9
6	33
-2	-31
4	17

33. $Y_1=Y_2$ when $x=2$, as can be seen from the calculator check:
$Y_1=8x-15 \quad Y_2=-.5x+2$
$\quad =8(2)-15 \quad\ =-.5(2)+2$
$\quad =16-15 \qquad =-1+2$
$\quad =1 \qquad\qquad =1$

39. Since $x=3$ and $y=-4,\ f(3)=-4$.

41. **(a)** $f(-2)=0$ since, when $x=-2,\ y=0$.

(b) $f(0)=4$ since, when $x=0,\ y=4$.

(c) $f(1)=2$ since, when $x=1,\ y=2$.

(d) $f(4)=4$ since, when $x=4,\ y=4$.

43. **(a)** $f(-2)=-3$ since, when $x=-2,\ y=-3$.

(b) $f(0)=-2$ since, when $x=0,\ y=-2$.

(c) $f(1)=0$ since, when $x=1,\ y=0$.

(d) $f(4)=2$ since, when $x=4,\ y=2$.

45. The domain is $[-5,\ 4]$, since x takes all values from -5 to 4 inclusive. The range is $[-2,\ 6]$, since y takes all values from -2 to 6 inclusive.

47. The domain is $(-\infty,\ \infty)$, since x can be any real number. The range is $(-\infty,\ 12]$ since y never takes values greater than 12.

49. The domain is [–3, 4], since x takes all values from –3 to 4 inclusive. The range is [–6, 8], since y takes all values from –6 to 8 inclusive.

51. The function graphed in Exercise 41
The domain is [–2, 4], since x takes all values from –2 to 4 inclusive. The range is [0, 4], since y takes on values from 0 to 4 inclusive.

53. $f(x) = 3x - 9$
Since x can be any real-number, the domain is $(-\infty, \infty)$. As x takes on all real-number values, $3x - 9$ will also take on all real number values, so the range is also $(-\infty, \infty)$.

55. $f(x) = x^6$
Since x can be any real number, the domain is $(-\infty, \infty)$. Since x^6 is never negative (it is zero or positive), the range is $[0, \infty)$.

57. $h(x) = \sqrt{9 + x}$
Since $9 + x \geq 0$, $x \geq -9$, and the domain is $[-9, \infty)$. The expression $\sqrt{9 + x}$ means the positive square root, so $\sqrt{9 + x}$ is never negative (it is zero or positive). The range is $[0, \infty)$.

59. $f(x) = -\sqrt{4 - x^2}$
Since $4 - x^2$ must be nonnegative, $4 - x^2 \geq 0$ and $(2 + x)(2 - x) \geq 0$.
Using a sign graph, we see that $-2 \leq x \leq 2$. The domain is [–2, 2]. $f(-2) = 0$ and $f(2) = 0$. When we let $x = 0$, $f(0) = -2$. The largest function value is 0, and the smallest function value is –2. Thus, the range is [–2, 0].

61. $g(x) = \dfrac{3}{7 + x}$
Since denominators can never be zero, x cannot be –7. The domain is $(-\infty, -7) \cup (-7, \infty)$. As x takes on all real-number values except –7, $\dfrac{3}{7 + x}$ will take on all real-number values except zero. The range is $(-\infty, 0) \cup (0, \infty)$.

63. $f(x) = \sqrt[3]{x + 2}$
Unlike square roots, cube roots of negative real numbers are real numbers, and the cube root of a negative real number is also a negative real number. Therefore, the domain of the function is $(-\infty, \infty)$, and the range is also $(-\infty, \infty)$.

65. (a) As x is getting larger on the interval $[4, \infty)$, the value of y is increasing.

(b) As x is getting larger on the interval $(-\infty, -1]$, the value of y is decreasing.

(c) As x is getting larger on the interval $[-1, 4]$, the value of y is constant.

67. (a) As x is getting larger on the interval $(-\infty, 4]$, the value of y is increasing.

(b) As x is getting larger on the interval $[4, \infty)$, the value of y is decreasing.

(c) There is no interval where the value of y is constant.

69. (a) There is no interval where the value of y is increasing.

(b) As x is getting larger on the intervals $(-\infty, -2]$ and $[3, \infty)$, the value of y is decreasing.

(c) As x is getting larger on the interval $(-2, 3)$, the value of y is constant.

71. (a) The function is increasing over the interval [0, 25].

(b) The function is decreasing over the interval [50, 75].

(c) The function is constant over the intervals [25, 50] and [75, 100].

73. (a) At $t = 2$, $y = 240$ from the graph. Therefore, after 2 seconds, the ball is 240 feet high.

(b) At $y = 192$, $x = 1$ and $x = 5$ from the graph. Therefore, after 1 second and after 5 seconds, the height will be 192 feet.

(c) The coordinates of the highest point are (3, 256). Therefore, it reaches a maximum height of 256 feet after 3 seconds.

(d) At $x = 7$, $y = 0$. Therefore, after 7 seconds, the ball hits the ground.

75. (a) At $t = 8$, $y = 24$ from the graph. Therefore, there are 24 units of the drug in the bloodstream after 8 hours.

(b) The coordinates of the highest point are (2, 64). Therefore, after 2 hours, the level of the drug in the bloodstream reaches its greatest value of 64 units.

(c) After the peak, $y = 16$ at $t = 10$.
10 hours – 2 hours = 8 hours after the peak.
8 additional hours are required for the level
to drop to 16 units.

77. (a) Since the cost function is linear, it will have
the form $C(x) = mx + b$, with $m = 10$ and
$b = 500$. That is, $C(x) = 10x + 500$.

(b) Since each item sells for $35, the revenue
function is $R(x) = px = 35x$.

(c) The profit function is given by
$$P(x) = R(x) - C(x)$$
$$= 35x - (10x + 500)$$
$$= 35x - 10x - 500$$
$$= 25x - 500.$$

(d)
$$C(x) = R(x)$$
$$10x + 500 = 35x$$
$$500 = 25x$$
$$20 = x$$
The break-even point is 20 units. Do not
produce the product, since it is possible to
sell only 18 units and no profit is made until
after the 20th unit is sold.

79. (a) $C(x) = mx + b$, with $m = 150$ and $b = 2700$.
$$C(x) = 150x + 2700$$

(b) $R(x) = 280x$

(c)
$$P(x) = R(x) - C(x)$$
$$= 280x - (150x + 2700)$$
$$= 280x - 150x - 2700$$
$$= 130x - 2700$$

(d)
$$C(x) = R(x)$$
$$150x + 2700 = 280x$$
$$2700 = 130x$$
$$x \approx 20.77$$
The break-even point is 21 units. Produce the
product, since it is possible to sell up to
25 units and a profit will be realized starting
with the 21st unit.

81. $C(x) = 200x + 1000$
$R(x) = 240x$

(a)
$$C(x) = R(x)$$
$$200x + 1000 = 240x$$
$$1000 = 40x$$
$$25 = x$$
The break-even point is 25 units.

(b)
$$C(25) = 200(25) + 1000$$
$$= 5000 + 1000$$
$$= 6000$$
$$R(25) = 240(25)$$
$$= 6000$$
At the break-even point of 25 units, the cost
and the revenue are each $6000.

83. (a) The left endpoint of the graph is at
May 26, 1896, and the right endpoint of the
graph is at June 30, 1999. In interval
notation, the domain is
[May 26, 1896, June 30, 1999].

(b) The highest y-coordinate of any x-value in
the domain is at the right endpoint of the
graph: 10,970.8.

(c) Answers will vary.

Section 2.3

Exercises

1. F; $f(x) = 3x + 7$ is a linear function with slope 3.

3. H; $x = 3$ is a vertical line.

5. G; $2x - y = -4$ or $y = 2x + 4$ is a linear equation
with x-intercept –2 and y-intercept 4.

7. E; $x + y = 4$ or $y = -x + 4$ or $y = -1\,x + 4$ is a line
with a negative slope, –1.

9. $f(x) = x - 4$
Use the intercepts.
$$f(0) = 0 - 4$$
$$= -4 \quad y\text{-intercept}$$
$$0 = x - 4$$
$$x = 4 \qquad x\text{-intercept}$$
Graph the line through (0, −4) and (4, 0). The
domain and range are both $(-\infty, \infty)$.

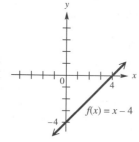

11. $f(x) = \frac{1}{2}x - 6$

Use the intercepts.

$f(0) = \frac{1}{2}0 - 6$

$\qquad = -6 \qquad$ y-intercept

$0 = \frac{1}{2}x - 6$

$6 = \frac{1}{2}x$

$12 = x \qquad$ x-intercept

Graph the line through (0, −6) and (12, 0).
The domain and range are both (−∞, ∞).

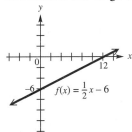

13. $f(x) = 3x$

The x- and y-intercepts are both 0. (1, 3) is one
other point on the line. Graph the line through
(0, 0) and (1, 3). The domain and range are both
(−∞, ∞).

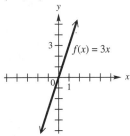

15. $f(x) = -4$ is a constant function.

The graph of $f(x) = -4$ is a horizontal line with
a y-intercept of −4. The domain is (−∞, ∞), and
the range is {−4}.

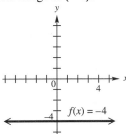

17. $x = 3$

This is a vertical line, intersecting the x-axis at
(3, 0). The domain is {3} and the range is

(−∞, ∞).

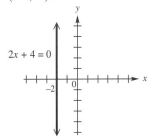

19. $2x + 4 = 0$

$2x = -4$

$x = -2$

This is a vertical line intersecting the x-axis at
(−2, 0). The domain is {−2} and the range is
(−∞, ∞).

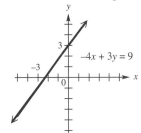

21. $-4x + 3y = 9$

Use the intercepts.

$-4(0) + 3y = 9$

$\qquad\qquad y = 3 \qquad$ y-intercept

$-4x + 3(0) = 9$

$\qquad\qquad x = -\frac{9}{4} \qquad$ x-intercept

Graph the line through (0, 3) and $\left(-\frac{9}{4}, 0\right)$.

The domain and range are both (−∞, ∞).

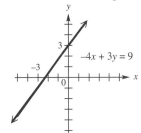

23. $y = 4x + 2$

Use the intercepts.

$y = 4(0) + 2$

$y = 2 \qquad\qquad$ y-intercept

$0 = 4x + 2$

$x = -\frac{1}{2} \qquad\qquad$ x-intercept

Graph the line through (0, 2) and $\left(-\frac{1}{2}, 0\right)$.

The domain and range are both $(-\infty, \infty)$.

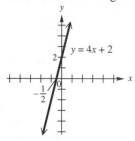

25. $y = 2$ is a horizontal line with y-intercept 2. Choice A resembles this.

27. $x = 2$ is a vertical line with x-intercept 2. Choice D resembles this.

29. $y = 3x + 4$
Use $Y_1 = 3x + 4.$

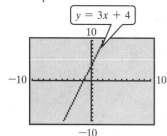

31. $3x + 4y = 6$
Solve for y
$$4y = -3x + 6$$
$$y = -\frac{3}{4}x + \frac{3}{2}$$
Use $Y_1 = \left(\frac{-3}{4}\right)x + \left(\frac{3}{2}\right).$

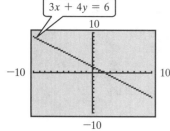

33. The rise is 2.5 feet while the run is 10 feet so the slope is $\frac{2.5}{10} = .25 = 25\% = \frac{1}{4}$. So $A = .25,$
$C = \frac{2.5}{10}, D = 25\%,$ and $E = \frac{1}{4}$ are all expressions of the slope.

35. Through $(2, -1)$ and $(-3, -3)$
Let $x_1 = 2,\ y_1 = -1,\ x_2 = -3,$ and $y_2 = -3.$ Then $\Delta y = -3 - (-1) = -2$ and

$\Delta x = -3 - 2 = -5.$ The slope is
$$m = \frac{\Delta y}{\Delta x} = \frac{-2}{-5} = \frac{2}{5}.$$

37. Through $(5, 9)$ and $(-2, 9)$
$$m = \frac{\Delta y}{\Delta x} = \frac{9 - 9}{-2 - 5} = \frac{0}{-7} = 0$$

39. Horizontal, through $(3, -7)$
The slope of every horizontal line is zero, so $m = 0.$

41. Vertical, through $(3, -7)$
The slope of every vertical line is undefined; m is undefined.

43. Two points in the table are $(0, -6)$ and $(1, -2).$
$$m = \frac{\Delta y}{\Delta x} = \frac{-2 - (-6)}{1 - 0} = \frac{4}{1} = 4.$$

45. Two points on the line are $(0, 2)$ and $(6, -2).$ Use these two points in the slope formula.
$$m = \frac{\Delta y}{\Delta x} = \frac{-2 - 2}{6 - 0} = \frac{-4}{6} = -\frac{2}{3}$$

49. Through $(-1, 3),\ m = \frac{3}{2}$
First locate the point $(-1, 3).$
Since the slope is $\frac{3}{2},$ a change of 2 units horizontally (2 units to the right) produces a change of 3 units vertically (3 units up). This gives a second point, $(1, 6),$ which can be used to complete the graph.

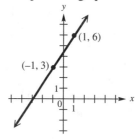

51. Through $(3, -4), m = -\frac{1}{3}$
First locate the point $(3, -4).$
Since the slope is $-\frac{1}{3},$ a change of 3 units horizontally (3 units to the right) produces a change of -1 unit vertically (1 unit down). This gives a second point, $(6, -5),$ which can be used

to complete the graph.

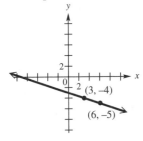

53. Through $\left(-\dfrac{1}{2}, 4\right)$, $m = 0$

The graph is the horizontal line through $\left(-\dfrac{1}{2}, 4\right)$

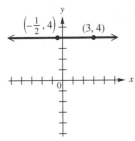

55. **(a)** The slope of $-.0221$ indicates that, on the average, from 1912 to 1992 the 5000 meter run is being run $.0221$ second faster every Olympic Games. It is negative because the times are generally decreasing as time progresses.

(b) World War II (1939–1945) included the years 1940 and 1944.

(c) $y = -.0221\,(1996) + 57.14 = 13.03$ minutes. The times differ by .1 minute.

57. $m = \dfrac{1}{2}$, matches graph D because the line rising gradually as x increases.

59. $m = 0$ matches graph A because horizontal lines have slopes of 0.

61. $m = 2$ matches graph E because the line rises rapidly as x increases.

63. The first two points are $(0, -6)$ and $(1, -3)$.
$$m = \frac{-3 - (-6)}{1 - 0} = \frac{3}{1} = 3$$

64. The second and third points are $(1, -3)$ and $(2, 0)$.
$$m = \frac{0 - (-3)}{2 - 1} = \frac{3}{1} = 3$$

65. If we use any two points on a line to find its slope, we find that the slope is the same in all cases.

66. The first two points are $A(0, -6)$ and $B(1, -3)$.
$$\begin{aligned} d(A, B) &= \sqrt{[-3 - (-6)]^2 + (1 - 0)^2} \\ &= \sqrt{3^2 + 1^2} \\ &= \sqrt{10} \end{aligned}$$

67. The second and fourth points are $B(1, -3)$ and $D(3, 3)$.
$$\begin{aligned} d(B, D) &= \sqrt{[3 - (-3)]^2 + (3 - 1)^2} \\ &= \sqrt{6^2 + 2^2} \\ &= \sqrt{40} \\ &= 2\sqrt{10} \end{aligned}$$

68. The first and fourth points are $A(0, -6)$ and $D(3, 3)$.
$$\begin{aligned} d(A, D) &= \sqrt{[3 - (-6)]^2 + (3 - 0)^2} \\ &= \sqrt{9^2 + 3^2} \\ &= \sqrt{90} \\ &= 3\sqrt{10} \end{aligned}$$

69. $\sqrt{10} + 2\sqrt{10} = 3\sqrt{10}$
The sum is $3\sqrt{10}$, which is equal to the answer in Exercise 68.

70. If points A, B, and C lie on a line in that order, then the distance between A and B added to the distance between B and C is equal to the distance between A and C. (The order of the last two may be reversed.)

71. The midpoint of the segment joining $A(0, -6)$ and $G(6, 12)$ has coordinates $M\left(\dfrac{0+6}{2}, \dfrac{-6+12}{2}\right)$ or $M(3, 3)$.
The midpoint is $M(3, 3)$, which is the same as the middle entry in the table.

72. The midpoint of the segment joining $E(4, 6)$ and $F(5, 9)$ has coordinates $M\left(\dfrac{4+5}{2}, \dfrac{6+9}{2}\right)$ or $M(4.5, 7.5)$. If the x-value 4.5 were in the table, the corresponding y-value would be 7.5.

73. $2(x - 5) + 3x = x + 6$
$2x - 10 + 3x = x + 6$
$5x - 10 = x + 6$
$4x = 16$
$x = 4$
The solution set is $\{4\}$.

(a) $Y_1 = 2(x - 5) + 3x$
$Y_2 = x + 6$

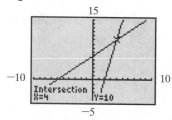

(b) $Y_1 = 2(x - 5) + 3x - (x + 6)$

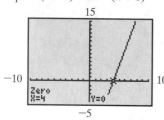

75. $4x - 3(4 - 3x) = 2(x - 3) + 6x + 2$
$4x - 12 + 9x = 2x - 6 + 6x + 2$
$13x - 12 = 8x - 4$
$5x = 8$
$x = 1.6$
The solution set is $\{1.6\}$.

(a) $Y_1 = 4x - 3(4 - 3x)$
$Y_2 = 2(x - 3) + 6x + 2$

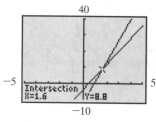

(b) $Y_1 = 4x - 3(4 - 3x) - 2(x - 3) - 6x - 2$

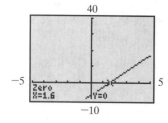

77. $\dfrac{x}{2} = 5 - \dfrac{x}{3}$

$6\left(\dfrac{x}{2}\right) = 6\left(5 - \dfrac{x}{3}\right)$

$3x = 30 - 2x$
$5x = 30$
$x = 6$
The solution set is $\{6\}$.

(a) $Y_1 = \dfrac{x}{2}$

$Y_2 = 5 - \dfrac{x}{3}$

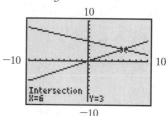

(b) $Y_1 = \dfrac{x}{2} - 5 + \dfrac{x}{3}$

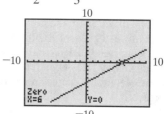

79. $2\pi x + \sqrt[3]{4} = .5\pi x - \sqrt{28}$
$Y_1 = 2\pi x + \sqrt[3]{4}$
$Y_2 = .5\pi x - \sqrt{28}$

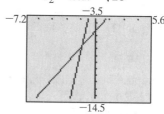

The solution set is $\{-1.459748697\}$.

81. $.23(\sqrt{3} + 4x) - .82(\pi x + 2.3) = 5$

$Y_1 = .23(\sqrt{3} + 4x) - .82(\pi x + 2.3)$

$Y_2 = 5$

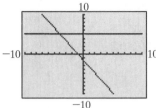

The solution set is $\{-3.917399254\}$.

83. (a) It means that the average remained virtually the same during that period.

(b) The first decrease is seen beginning on October 28, 1929, the date of the stock market crash. A linear approximation for the few years that follow would exhibit a negative slope, meaning that the average declined during that period.

(c) Its slope would be positive, indicating that the average was on the increase during this interval.

Section 2.4

Exercises

1. $y = \dfrac{1}{4}x + 2$ is graphed in D.

The slope is $\dfrac{1}{4}$ and the y-intercept is 2.

3. $y - (-1) = \dfrac{3}{2}[x - (-1)]$ is graphed in C.

The slope is $\dfrac{3}{2}$ and a point on the graph is $(-1, -1)$.

5. Through $(1, 3)$, $m = -2$

Write the equation in point-slope form.

$y - y_1 = m(x - x_1)$

$y - 3 = -2(x - 1)$

Then, change to standard form.

$y - 3 = -2x + 2$

$2x + y = 5$

7. Through $(-5, 4)$, $m = -\dfrac{3}{2}$

Write the equation in point-slope form.

$y - 4 = -\dfrac{3}{2}(x + 5)$

Change to standard form.

$2(y - 4) = -3(x + 5)$

$2y - 8 = -3x - 15$

$3x + 2y = -7$

9. Through $(-8, 4)$, undefined slope

Since undefined slope indicates a vertical line, the equation will have the form $x = k$. The equation of the line is $x = -8$.

11. Through $(-1, 3)$ and $(3, 4)$

First find m.

$m = \dfrac{4 - 3}{3 - (-1)} = \dfrac{1}{4}$

Use either point and the point-slope form.

$y - 4 = \dfrac{1}{4}(x - 3)$

Change to slope-intercept form.

$y - 4 = \dfrac{1}{4}x - \dfrac{3}{4}$

$y = \dfrac{1}{4}x - \dfrac{3}{4} + \dfrac{16}{4}$

$y = \dfrac{1}{4}x + \dfrac{13}{4}$

13. x-intercept 3, y-intercept -2

The line passes through $(3, 0)$ and $(0, -2)$. Use these points to find m.

$m = \dfrac{-2 - 0}{0 - 3} = \dfrac{2}{3}$

Then use point-slope form.

$y - 0 = \dfrac{2}{3}(x - 3)$

Change to slope-intercept form.

$y = \dfrac{2}{3}x - 2$

15. Vertical, through $(-6, 4)$

The equation of a vertical line has an equation of the form $x = k$. Since the line passes through $(-6, 4)$, the equation is $x = -6$. (Since this slope of a vertical line is undefined, this equation cannot be written in slope-intercept form.)

17. The line $x + 2 = 0$ has x-intercept -2. It does not have a y-intercept. The slope of this line is undefined. The line $4y = 2$ has y-intercept $\dfrac{1}{2}$.

It does not have an x-intercept. The slope of this line is zero.

19. (a) The graph of $y = 2x + 3$ has a positive slope and a positive y-intercept. These conditions match graph B.

(b) The graph of $y = -2x + 3$ has a negative slope and a positive y-intercept. These conditions match graph D.

(c) The graph of $y = 2x - 3$ has a positive slope and a negative y-intercept. These conditions match graph A.

(d) The graph of $y = -2x - 3$ has a negative slope and a negative y-intercept. These conditions match graph C.

21. $y = 3x - 1$

This equation is in the slope-intercept form, $y = mx + b$. The slope is $m = 3$ and the y-intercept is $b = -1$.

23. $4x - y = 7$

Solve for y to write the equation in slope-intercept form.
$$-y = -4x + 7$$
$$y = 4x - 7$$
The slope is 4 and the y-intercept is -7.

25. $4y = -3x$
$$y = -\frac{3}{4}x \text{ or } y = -\frac{3}{4}x + 0$$
The slope is $-\frac{3}{4}$ and the y-intercept is 0.

27. (a) Through $(-1, 4)$, parallel to $x + 3y = 5$

First, find the slope of the line $x + 3y = 5$ by writing this equation in slope-intercept form.
$$x + 3y = 5$$
$$3y = -x + 5$$
$$y = -\frac{1}{3}x + \frac{5}{3}$$
The slope is $-\frac{1}{3}$. Since the lines are parallel, $-\frac{1}{3}$. is also the slope of the line whose equation is to be found. Substitute $m = -\frac{1}{3}$, $x_1 = -1$, and $y_1 = 4$ into the point-slope form.
$$y - y_1 = m(x - x_1)$$
$$y - 4 = -\frac{1}{3}[x - (-1)]$$
$$y - 4 = -\frac{1}{3}(x + 1)$$
$$3(y - 4) = -1(x + 1)$$
$$3y - 12 = -x - 1$$
$$x + 3y = 11$$

(b) Solve for y. $3y = -x + 11$
$$y = -\frac{x}{3} + \frac{11}{3}$$
The slope-intercept for m is $y = -\frac{1}{3}x + \frac{11}{3}$.

29. (a) Through $(1, 6)$, perpendicular to $3x + 5y = 1$
First, find the slope of the line $3x + 5y = 1$ by writing this equation in slope-intercept form.
$$3x + 5y = 1$$
$$5y = -3x + 1$$
$$y = -\frac{3}{5}x + \frac{1}{5}$$
This line has a slope of $-\frac{3}{5}$.

Call the line whose equation is to be found L. Since line L is perpendicular to the line $3x + 5y = 1$, the product of their slopes is -1. If line L has slope m, then
$$-\frac{3}{5}m = -1$$
$$m = \frac{5}{3}.$$
To find the equation of the line L, substitute $m = \frac{5}{3}$, $x_1 = 1$, and $y_1 = 6$ into the point-slope form.
$$y - 6 = \frac{5}{3}(x - 1)$$
$$3(y - 6) = 5(x - 1)$$
$$3y - 18 = 5x - 5$$
$$-13 = 5x - 3y$$
or $5x - 3y = -13$

(b) Solve for y. $3y = 5x + 13$
$$y = \frac{5x}{3} + \frac{13}{3}$$
The slope-intercept form is $y = \frac{5}{3}x + \frac{13}{3}$.

31. (a) Through $(-5, 6)$, perpendicular to $x = -2$.
Since $x = -2$ is a vertical line, any line perpendicular to this line will be horizontal and have an equation of the form $y = k$. Since the line passes through $(-5, 6)$, the equation is $y = 6$ or $y - 6 = 0$.

(b) The slope-intercept form is $y = 6$.

33. (a) Find the slope of the line $3y + 2x = 6$.

$$3y + 2x = 6$$
$$3y = -2x + 6$$
$$y = -\frac{2}{3}x + 2$$
$$m = -\frac{2}{3}$$

A line parallel to $3y + 2x = 6$ also has slope $-\frac{2}{3}$.

$$-\frac{2}{3} = \frac{-1-2}{4-k}$$

Solve for k using the slope formula.

$$\frac{-2}{3} = \frac{-3}{4-k}$$
$$-9 = -8 + 2k$$
$$-\frac{1}{2} = k$$

(b) Find the slope of the line $2x - 5y = 1$.

$$2y - 5x = 1$$
$$2y = 5x + 1$$
$$y = \frac{5}{2}x + \frac{1}{2}$$
$$m = \frac{5}{2}$$

A line perpendicular to $2y - 5x = 1$ has slope $-\frac{2}{5}$, since $\frac{5}{2}\left(-\frac{2}{5}\right) = -1$.

Solve for k using the slope formula.

$$-\frac{2}{5} = \frac{-1-2}{4-k}$$
$$\frac{-2}{5} = \frac{-3}{4-k}$$
$$-15 = -8 + 2k$$
$$k = -\frac{7}{2}$$

35. (a) Use the points $(6650, 3839)$ and $(4215, 5494)$ to find a linear equation that models the data.

$$m = \frac{5494 - 3839}{4215 - 6650} = \frac{1655}{-2435} \approx -.680$$

Now use either point, say $(6650, 3839)$, and the point-slope form to find the equation.

$$y - 3839 = -.680(x - 6650)$$
$$y - 3839 = -.680x + 4522$$
$$y = -.680x + 8361$$
$$\text{or} \quad C = -.680I + 8361$$

(b) The slope is $-.680$.
Therefore, the marginal propensity to consume is $-.680$.

37. $(1970, 43.3), (1995, 58.9)$

$$m = \frac{58.9 - 43.3}{1995 - 1970} = \frac{15.6}{25} = .624$$

Now use either point, say $(1970, 433.3)$, and the point-slope form to find the equation.

$$y - 43.3 = .624(x - 1970)$$
$$y - 43.3 = .624x - 1229.28$$
$$y = .624x - 1185.98$$

Let $x = 1996$.

$$y = .624\,(1996) - 1185.98 \approx 59.5$$

The percent of women in the civilian labor force is predicted to be 59.5%
This figure is very close to the actual figure.

39. (a) $(1, 6121), (15, 15{,}380)$

$$m = \frac{15{,}380 - 6121}{15 - 1} = \frac{9259}{14} \approx 661.4$$

Now use either point, say $(1, 6121)$, and the point-slope form to find the equation.

$$y - 6121 = 661.4(x - 1)$$
$$y - 6121 = 661.4x - 661.4$$
$$y = 661.4x + 5459.6$$
$$\text{or} \quad f(x) \approx 661.4x + 5459.6$$

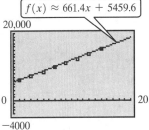

The average tuition increase is about \$661 per year for the period, because this is the slope of the line.

(b) 1990 corresponds to $x = 6$.
$$f(6) = 661.4(6) + 5459.6 \approx 9427.8$$
This is a fairly good approximation.

(c) From the calculator,
$$f(x) \approx 661.45x + 5248.63$$

41. (a) See the graph in the answer to part (b).
While not exactly linear, these data could be approximated by a linear function.

(b) $(1, 1318), (15, 3356)$

$$m = \frac{3356 - 1318}{15 - 1} = \frac{2038}{14} \approx 145.57$$

Now use either point, say $(1, 1318)$, and the point-slope form to find the equation.

$$y - 1318 = 145.57(x - 1)$$
$$y - 1318 = 145.57x - 145.57$$
$$y = 145.57x + 1172.43$$
$$\text{or} \quad f(x) \approx 145.57x + 1172.43$$

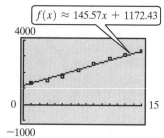

$$f(x) \approx 145.57x + 1172.43$$

The slope represents the average annual change in tuition and fees.

(c) $x = 0$ corresponds to 1984:
$f(0) = 145.57(0) + 1172.43 = 1172.43$
This is slightly less than the actual value, but a fairly close approximation.

(d) $f(x) \approx 153.35x + 1101.57$

(e) Because 1974 and 2010 are so far away from the data used to compute f, it would not be reliable to predict those costs using this function.

43. (a) The ordered pairs are $(0, 32)$ and $(100, 212)$.
The slope is $m = \dfrac{212 - 32}{100 - 0} = \dfrac{180}{100} = \dfrac{9}{5}$.

Use $(x_1, \; y_1) = (0, 32)$ and $m = \dfrac{9}{5}$ in the point-slope form.
$y - y_1 = m(x - x_1)$
$y - 32 = \dfrac{9}{5}(x - 0)$
$y - 32 = \dfrac{9}{5}x$
$y = \dfrac{9}{5}x + 32$
or $F = \dfrac{9}{5}C + 32$

(b) $F = \dfrac{9}{5}C + 32$
$5F = 9C + 160$
$9C = 5F - 160$
$9C = 5(F - 32)$
$C = \dfrac{5}{9}(F - 32)$

(c) If $F = C$,
$F = \dfrac{5}{9}(F - 32)$
$9F = 5(F - 32)$
$9F = 5F - 160$
$4F = -160$
$F = -40$.
$F = C$ when F is $-40°$.

45. The Pythagorean Theorem and its converse assure us that in triangle OPQ, angle POQ is a right angle if and only if
$$[d(O, P)]^2 + [d(O, Q)]^2 = [d(P, Q)]^2.$$

46. $d(O, P) = \sqrt{(x_1 - 0)^2 + (m_1 x_1 - 0)^2}$
$= \sqrt{x_1^2 + m_1^2 x_1^2}$

47. $d(O, Q) = \sqrt{(x_2 - 0)^2 + (m_2 x_2 - 0)^2}$
$= \sqrt{x_2^2 + m_2^2 x_2^2}$

48. $d(P, Q) = \sqrt{(x_2 - x_1)^2 + (m_2 x_2 - m_1 x_1)^2}$

50. $-2m_1 m_2 x_1 x_2 - 2x_1 x_2 = 0$
$-2x_1 x_2 (m_1 m_2 + 1) = 0$

51. $-2x_1 x_2 (m_1 m_2 + 1) = 0$
Since $x_1 \neq 0$ and $x_2 \neq 0$, $-2x_1 x_2 \neq 0$.
By the zero-factor property,
$m_1 m_2 + 1 = 0$
$m_1 m_2 = -1$.

52. The product of the slopes of these lines is -1, and they are perpendicular.

55. $(x_1, \; y_1), (x_2, \; y_2)$
$m = \dfrac{y_2 - y_1}{x_2 - x_1}$
$y - y_1 = \left(\dfrac{y_2 - y_1}{x_2 - x_1}\right)(x - x_1)$

59. $A(-1, 4), B(-2, -1), C(1, 14)$
For A and B, $m = \dfrac{-1 - 4}{-2 - (-1)} = \dfrac{-5}{-1} = 5$
For B and C, $m = \dfrac{14 - (-1)}{1 - (-2)} = \dfrac{15}{3} = 5$
For A and C, $m = \dfrac{14 - 4}{1 - (-1)} = \dfrac{10}{2} = 5$
Since all three slopes are the same, the point are collinear.

61. (a) The period does not show a linear increase. To fit a linear equation to these data would be misleading.

(b) Find the slope.
$$m = \dfrac{11,000 - 3000}{9 - 0} = \dfrac{8000}{9} = 888.\overline{8}$$
The y-intercept is 3000. Use the slope-intercept form to find an equation.
$y = mx + b$

$$y = 888.\overline{8}x + 3000$$
In 1997, $x = 7$ so
$$y = (888.\overline{8})(7) + 3000 = 9222.\overline{2}.$$

Section 2.5

Exercises

1. The function is continuous over the entire domain of real numbers $(-\infty, \infty)$.

3. The function is continuous over the interval $[0, \infty)$.

5. The function has a vertical asymptote at $x = -3$, as indicated by the dashed line. It is continuous over the interval $(-\infty, -3)$ and the interval $(-3, \infty)$.

7. The equation $y = x^2$ matches graph E. The domain is $(-\infty, \infty)$.

9. The equation $y = x^3$ matches graph A. The range is $(-\infty, \infty)$.

11. Graph F is the graph of the identity function. Its equation is $y = x$.

13. The equation $y = \sqrt[3]{x}$ matches graph H.
No, there is no interval over which the function is decreasing.

15. $y = 3x - 2$
Since x and y can take any real number values, both the domain and the range are the set of all real numbers, $(-\infty, \infty)$.
To graph the relation, find several ordered pairs by selecting values for x and finding the corresponding values for y.

x	-3	-2	0	1	4
y	-11	-8	-2	1	10

Use these points to draw the graph, which is a straight line.

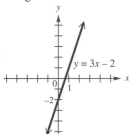

17. $3x = y^2$
Since y^2 cannot be negative, $x = \left(\frac{1}{3}\right)y^2$ cannot be negative, so the domain is $[0, \infty)$. Since y can

have any value, the range is $(-\infty, \infty)$.
Find several ordered pairs by selecting values for y and finding the corresponding x-values.

x	12	3	0	3	12
y	-6	-3	0	3	6

Use these points to draw the graph.

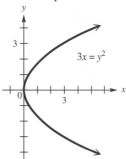

19. $16x^2 = -y$
Rewrite this equation as $y = -16x^2$.
Since x can have any value, the domain is $(-\infty, \infty)$. Since x^2 cannot be negative, $y = -16x^2$ cannot be positive, so the range is $(-\infty, 0]$.
Find several ordered pairs by choosing values for x.

x	-2	-1	0	1	2
y	-64	-16	0	-16	-64

Use these points to draw the graph.

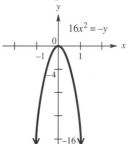

21. $y = |x| + 4$
Find several ordered pairs by selecting values for x.

x	-3	-1	0	1	3
y	7	5	4	5	7

Use these points to draw the graph.

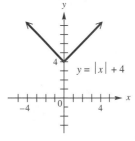

From the graph, we see that the domain is $(-\infty, \infty)$ and the range is $[4, \infty)$.

23. $y = -|x + 1|$

Find several ordered pairs by selecting values for x.

x	-5	-3	-1	1	3
y	-4	-2	0	-2	-4

Use these points to draw the graph.

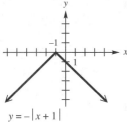

From the graph, we see that the domain is $(-\infty, \infty)$ and the range is $(-\infty, 0]$.

25. $x = \sqrt{y} - 2$

Find several ordered pairs by selecting values for y.

x	-2	-1	0	1	2
y	0	1	4	9	16

Use these points to draw the graph.

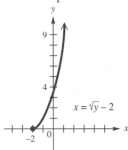

From the graph, we see that the domain is $[-2, \infty)$, and the range is $[0, \infty)$.

27. $x = -\sqrt{y} - 2$

Find several ordered pairs by selecting values for y.

x	0	-1	-2	-3	-4
y	2	3	6	11	18

Use these points to draw the graph.

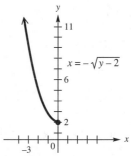

From the graph, we see that the domain is $(-\infty, 0]$, and the range is $[2, \infty)$.

29. $y = \sqrt{2x + 4}$

Find several ordered pairs by selecting values for x.

x	-2	$-\frac{3}{2}$	0	$\frac{5}{2}$	6
y	0	1	2	3	4

Use these points to draw the graph.

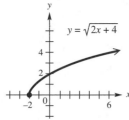

From the graph, we see that the domain is $[-2, \infty)$, and the range is $[0, \infty)$.

31. $y = -2\sqrt{x}$

Find several ordered pairs by selecting convenient values for x. Note that x must be nonnegative.

x	0	1	4	9	16
y	0	-2	-4	-6	-8

Use these points to draw the graph.

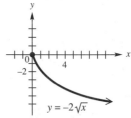

From the graph, we see that the domain is $[0, \infty)$ and the range is $(-\infty, 0]$.

33. To graph $f(x) = x$, enter $Y_1 = X$.

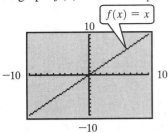

35. To graph $f(x) = x^3$, enter $Y_1 = X \wedge 3$.

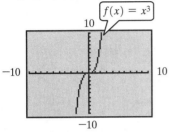

37. To graph $f(x) = \sqrt[3]{x}$, enter $Y_1 = X \wedge (1/3)$

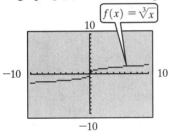

39. If $x = y^2$, then $y = \pm\sqrt{x}$.
To graph
$x = y^2$, enter $Y_1 = \sqrt{X}$ and $Y_2 = -\sqrt{X}$.

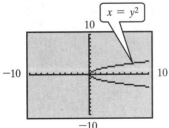

41. $f(x) = \begin{cases} 2x & \text{if } x \le -1 \\ x - 1 & \text{if } x > -1 \end{cases}$

   (a) $f(-5) = 2(-5) = -10$

   (b) $f(-1) = 2(-1) = -2$

   (c) $f(0) = 0 - 1 = -1$

   (d) $f(3) = 3 - 1 = 2$

43. $f(x) = \begin{cases} 2 + x & \text{if } x < -4 \\ -x & \text{if } -4 \le x \le 2 \\ 3x & \text{if } x > 2 \end{cases}$

   (a) $f(-5) = 2 + (-5) = -3$

   (b) $f(-1) = -(-1) = 1$

   (c) $f(0) = -0 = 0$

   (d) $f(3) = 3 \cdot 3 = 9$

45. $f(x) = \begin{cases} x - 1 & \text{if } x \le 3 \\ 2 & \text{if } x > 3 \end{cases}$

Draw the graph of $y = x - 1$ to the left of $x = 3$, including the endpoint at $x = 3$. Draw the graph of $y = 2$ to the right of $x = 3$, but do not include the endpoint at $x = 3$.

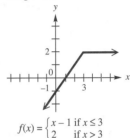

$f(x) = \begin{cases} x - 1 & \text{if } x \le 3 \\ 2 & \text{if } x > 3 \end{cases}$

47. $f(x) = \begin{cases} 4 - x & \text{if } x < 2 \\ 1 + 2x & \text{if } x \ge 2 \end{cases}$

Draw the graph of $y = 4 - x$ to the left of $x = 2$, but do not include the endpoint. Draw the graph of $y = 1 + 2x$ to the right of $x = 2$, including the endpoint.

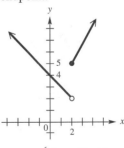

$f(x) = \begin{cases} 4 - x & \text{if } x < 2 \\ 1 + 2x & \text{if } x \ge 2 \end{cases}$

49. $f(x) = \begin{cases} 2 + x & \text{if } x < -4 \\ -x & \text{if } -4 \le x \le 5 \\ 3x & \text{if } x > 5 \end{cases}$

Draw the graph of $y = 2 + x$ to the left of -4, but do not include the endpoint at $x = 4$. Draw the graph of $y = -x$ between -4 and 5, including both endpoints. Draw the graph of $y = 3x$ to the right of

5, but do not include the endpoint at $x = 5$.

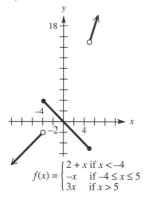

$$f(x) = \begin{cases} 2 + x & \text{if } x < -4 \\ -x & \text{if } -4 \leq x \leq 5 \\ 3x & \text{if } x > 5 \end{cases}$$

51. The solid circle on the graph shows that the endpoint $(0, -1)$ is part of the graph, while the open circle shows that the endpoint $(0, 1)$ is not part of the graph. The graph is made up of parts of two horizontal lines. The function which fits this graph is

$$f(x) = \begin{cases} -1 & \text{if } x \leq 0 \\ 1 & \text{if } x > 0. \end{cases}$$

The domain of this function is $(-\infty, \infty)$, and the range is $\{-1, 1\}$.

53. The graph is made up of parts of two horizontal lines. The solid circle shows that the endpoint $(0, 2)$ of the one on the left belongs to the graph while the open circle shows that the endpoint $(0, -1)$ of the one on the right does not belong to the graph. The function that fits this graph is

$$f(x) = \begin{cases} 2 & \text{if } x \leq 0 \\ -1 & \text{if } x > 1. \end{cases}$$

The domain of this function is $(-\infty, 0] \cup (1, \infty)$, and the range is $\{-1, 2\}$.

55. $f(x) = \left[\!\left[-x\right]\!\right]$
Plot points.

x	$-x$	$f(x) = \left[\!\left[-x\right]\!\right]$
-2	2	2
-1.5	1.5	1
-1	1	1
$-.5$	.5	0
0	0	0
.5	$-.5$	-1
1	-1	-1
1.5	-1.5	-2
2	-2	2

More generally, to get $y = 0$, we need
$$0 \leq -x < 1$$
$$0 \geq x > -1 \text{ or}$$
$$-1 < x \leq 0.$$
To get $y = 1$, we need
$$1 \leq -x < 2$$
$$-1 \geq x > -2 \text{ or}$$
$$-2 < x \leq -1.$$
Follow this pattern to graph the step function. The domain of this function is $(-\infty, \infty)$ and the range is $\{..., -2, -1, 0, 1, 2, ...\}$.

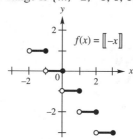

57. $f(x) = \left[\!\left[2x - 1\right]\!\right]$
To get $y = 0$, we need
$$0 \leq 2x - 1 < 1$$
$$1 \leq 2x < 2$$
$$\frac{1}{2} \leq x < 1.$$
To get $y = 1$, we need
$$1 \leq 2x - 1 < 2$$
$$2 \leq 2x < 3$$
$$1 \leq x < \frac{3}{2}.$$
Follow this pattern to graph the step function. The domain of this function is $(-\infty, \infty)$, and the range is $\{..., 2, -1, 0, 1, 2, ...\}$.

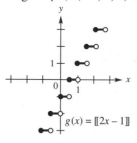

59. The cost of mailing a letter that weighs more than 1 ounce and less than 2 ounces is the same as the cost of a 2-ounce letter, and the cost of mailing a letter that weighs more than 2 ounces and less than 3 ounces is the same as the cost of a 3-ounce letter, etc.
$$f(x) = 11 - 22\left[\!\left[-x\right]\!\right]$$

61. $f(x) = \begin{cases} x^2 - 4 \text{ if } x \geq 0 \\ -x + 5 \text{ if } x < 0 \end{cases}$

The graph is a line with negative slope for $x < 0$ and a parabola opening upward for $x \geq 0$. This matches graph B.

63. $f(x) = \begin{cases} 6 \text{ if } x \geq 0 \\ -6 \text{ if } x < 0 \end{cases}$

The graph is the horizontal line $y = -6$ for $x < 0$ and the horizontal line $y = 6$ for $x \geq 0$. This matches graph D.

65. $C(x) = 100x + 1500$

$C(x) = \begin{cases} 100x + 1500 \text{ if } \quad 0 \leq x \leq 200 \\ 100x + 2000 \text{ if } 200 < x \leq 400 \end{cases}$

67. (a) From 1988 to 1990, the number of rabies cases increased by 100 each year. Then, from 1990 to 1992, they increased by 1700 each year.

(b) If we let $x = 0$ correspond to the year 1988, then we have the following points.

x	y
0	4800
1	4900
2	5000

A line passing through these points has a slope of 100 and a y-intercept of 4800. Thus, for $0 \leq x \leq 2$, $y = 100x + 4800$.
We also have the following points.

x	y
3	6700
4	8400

Using these points, for $2 < x \leq 4$, $m = 1700$ and
$y - 6700 = 1700(x - 3)$
$y - 6700 = 1700x - 5100$
$y = 1700x + 1600.$
Therefore, we have the piecewise-defined function

$f(x) = \begin{cases} 100x + 4800 \text{ if } 0 \leq x \leq 2 \\ 1700x + 1600 \text{ if } 2 < x \leq 4. \end{cases}$

69. (a) $f(x) = \begin{cases} 6.5x \quad\quad \text{if } 0 \leq x \leq 4 \\ -5.5x + 48 \text{ if } 4 < x \leq 6 \\ -30x + 195 \text{ if } 6 < x \leq 6.5 \end{cases}$

Draw a graph of $y = 6.5x$ between 0 and 4, including the endpoints. Draw the graph of $y = -5.5x + 48$ between 4 and 6, including the endpoint at 6 but not the one at 4. Draw

the graph of $y = -30x + 195$, including the endpoint at 6.5 but not the one at 6. Notice that the endpoints of the three pieces coincide.

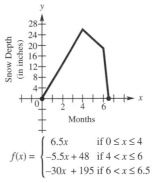

$f(x) = \begin{cases} 6.5x \quad\quad \text{if } 0 \leq x \leq 4 \\ -5.5x + 48 \text{ if } 4 < x \leq 6 \\ -30x + 195 \text{ if } 6 < x \leq 6.5 \end{cases}$

(b) From the graph, observe that the snow depth y reaches its deepest level (26 in.) when $x = 4$, $x = 4$ represents 4 months after the beginning of October, which is the beginning of February.

(c) From the graph, the snow depth y is nonzero when x is between 0 and 6.5. Snow begins at the beginning of October and ends 6.5 months later, in the middle of April.

70. (a)

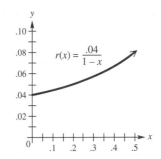

This is not a linear function. The $1 - x$ in the denominator prevents writing it in $y = ax + b$ form.

(b) A tax bracket of 31% has $x = .31$
$r = \dfrac{.04}{1 - .31} \approx .0579 \approx 5.8\%$

(c) A one-year treasury bond pays 6.26% so $r = .0626$. To find the tax bracket,
$r = \dfrac{.04}{1 - x}$
$.0626 = \dfrac{.04}{1 - x}$
$1 - x = \dfrac{.04}{.0626}$
$x = 1 - \dfrac{.04}{.0626}$
$x \approx .36$

You need to be in a 36% tax bracket before the municipal bond is more attractive.

Section 2.6

Exercises

1. (a) B; $y = (x-7)^2$ is a shift of $y = x^2$ 7 units to the right.

(b) D; $y = x^2 - 7$ is a shift of $y = x^2$ 7 units downward.

(c) E; $y = 7x^2$ is a vertical stretch of $y = x^2$ by a factor of 7.

(d) A; $y = (x+7)^2$ is a shift of $y = x^2$ 7 units to the left.

(e) C; $y = x^2 + 7$ is a shift of $y = x^2$ 7 units upward.

3. (a) B; $y = x^2 + 2$ is a shift of $y = x^2$ 2 units upward.

(b) A; $y = x^2 - 2$ is a shift of $y = x^2$ 2 units downward.

(c) G; $y = (x+2)^2$ is a shift of $y = x^2$ 2 units to the left.

(d) C; $y = (x-2)^2$ is a shift of $y = x^2$ 2 units to the right.

(e) F; $y = 2x^2$ is a vertical stretch of $y = x^2$ by a factor of 2.

(f) D; $y = -x^2$ is a reflection of $y = x^2$ across the x-axis.

(g) H; $y = (x-2)^2 + 1$ is a shift of $y = x^2$ 2 units to the right and 1 unit upward.

(h) E; $y = (x+2)^2 + 1$ is a shift of $y = x^2$ 2 units to the left and 1 unit upward.

5. The reflection of the point $(5, -1)$ across the y-axis has coordinates $(-5, -1)$.

7. (a) The point that is symmetric to $(5, -3)$ with respect to the x-axis is $(5, 3)$.

(b) The point that is symmetric to $(5, -3)$ with respect to the y-axis is $(-5, -3)$.

(c) The point that is symmetric to $(5, -3)$ with respect to the origin is $(-5, 3)$.

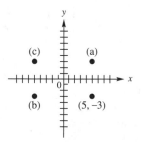

9. (a) The point that is symmetric to $(-4, -2)$ with respect to the x-axis is $(-4, 2)$.

(b) The point that is symmetric to $(-4, -2)$ with respect to the y-axis is $(4, -2)$.

(c) The point that is symmetric to $(-4, -2)$ with respect to the origin is $(4, 2)$.

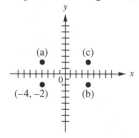

11. (a) $y = g(-x) + 1$

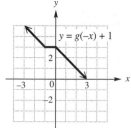

The graph of $g(x)$ is reflected across the y-axis and translated 1 unit upward to obtain the graph of $y = g(-x) + 1$.

(b) $y = g(x - 2)$

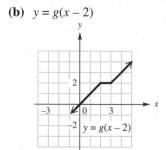

The graph of $g(x)$ is translated to the right 2 units to obtain the graph of $y = g(x - 2)$.

(c) $y = g(x + 1) - 2$

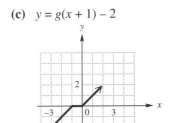

The graph of $g(x)$ is translated to the left 1 unit and downward 2 units to obtain the graph of $y = g(x + 1) - 2$.

(d) $y = -g(x) + 2$

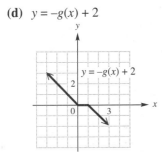

The graph of $g(x)$ is reflected across the x-axis and translated 2 units upward to obtain the graph of $y = -g(x) + 2$.

13. $y = x^2 + 2$

Replace x with $-x$ to obtain
$$y = (-x)^2 + 2 = x^2 + 2.$$
The result is the same as the original equation, so the graph is symmetric with respect to the y-axis. Since y is a function of x, the graph cannot be symmetric with respect to the x-axis.
Replace x with $-x$ and y with $-y$ to obtain
$$-y = (-x)^2 + 2$$
$$-y = x^2 + 2$$
$$y = -x^2 - 2.$$
The result is not the same as the original equation, so the graph is not symmetric with respect to the origin.
Therefore, the graph is symmetric with respect to the y-axis only.

15. $x^2 + y^2 = 10$

Replace x with $-x$ to obtain
$$(-x)^2 + y^2 = 10$$
$$x^2 + y^2 = 10.$$
The result is the same as the original equation, so the graph is symmetric with respect to the y-axis.
Replace y with $-y$ to obtain

$$x^2 + (-y)^2 = 10$$
$$x^2 + y^2 = 10.$$
The result is the same as the original equation, so the graph is symmetric with respect to the x-axis. Since the graph is symmetric with respect to the x-axis and y-axis, it is also symmetric with respect to the origin.

17. $y = -3x^3$

Replace x with $-x$ to obtain
$$y = -3(-x)^3$$
$$y = -3(-x^3)$$
$$y = 3x^3.$$
The result is not the same as the original equation, so the graph is not symmetric with respect to the y-axis.
Replace y with $-y$ to obtain
$$-y = -3x^3$$
$$y = 3x^3.$$
The result is not the same as the original equation, so the graph is not symmetric with respect to the x-axis.
Replace x with $-x$ and y with $-y$ to obtain
$$-y = -3(-x)^3$$
$$-y = -3(-x^3)$$
$$-y = 3x^3$$
$$y = -3x^3.$$
The result is the same as the original equation, so the graph is symmetric with respect to the origin. Therefore, the graph is symmetric with respect to the origin only.

19. $y = x^2 - x + 7$

Replace x with $-x$ to obtain
$$y = (-x)^2 - (-x) + 7$$
$$y = x^2 + x + 7.$$
The result is not the same as the original equation, so the graph is not symmetric with respect to the y-axis.
Since y is a function of x, the graph cannot be symmetric with respect to the x-axis.
Replace x with $-x$ and y with $-y$ to obtain
$$-y = (-x)^2 - (-x) + 7$$
$$-y = x^2 + x + 7$$
$$y = -x^2 - x - 7.$$
The result is not the same as the original equation, so the graph is not symmetric with respect to the origin.

Therefore, the graph has none of the listed symmetries.

21. It is the graph of $f(x) = |x|$ shifted 1 unit to the left, reflected across the x-axis, and shifted 3 units upward. The equation is $y = -|x+1| + 3$.

23. It is the graph of $g(x) = \sqrt{x}$ shifted 4 units to the left, stretched vertically by a factor of 2 and shifted 4 units downward. The equation is $y = 2\sqrt{x+4} - 4$.

25. $y = |x| - 1$
The graph is obtained by translating the graph of $y = |x|$ 1 unit downward.

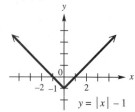

27. $y = -(x+1)^3$
This graph may be obtained by translating it 1 unit to the left and then reflecting it about the x-axis.

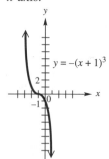

29. $y = 2x^2 - 1$
If $f(x) = x^2$, $y = 2f(x) - 1$.
We start with the familiar graph of $f(x) = x^2$.
The graph of $y = 2f(x)$ stretches the graph of $f(x) = x^2$ vertically.
The graph of $y = 2f(x) - 1$ translates the graph of $y = 2f(x)$ 1 unit downward.

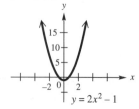

31. Since $f(3) = 6$, the point $(3, 6)$ is on the graph. Since the graph is symmetric with respect to the origin, the point $(-3, -6)$ is on the graph. Therefore, $f(-3) = -6$.

33. Since $f(3) = 6$, the point $(3, 6)$ is on the graph. Since the graph is symmetric with respect to the line $x = 6$ and since the point $(3, 6)$ is 3 units to the left of the line $x = 6$, the image point of $(3, 6)$, 3 units to the right of the line $x = 6$, is $(9, 6)$. Therefore, $f(9) = 6$.

35. An odd function is a function whose graph is symmetric with respect to the origin. Since $(3, 6)$ is on the graph, $(-3, -6)$ must also be on the graph. Therefore, $f(-3) = -6$.

37. If the graph of $f(x) = 2x + 5$ is translated up 2 units, the new graph will correspond to the function
$t(x) = (2x+5) + 2$
$\quad = 2x + 7$.
Now translate the graph of $t(x) = 2x + 7$ to the left 3 units. The final graph will correspond to the function
$g(x) = 2(x+3) + 7$
$\quad = 2x + 13$.
(Note that if the original graph is first translated to the left 3 units and then up 2 units, the final result will be the same.)

39. (a) Since $f(-x) = f(x)$, the graph is symmetric with respect to the y-axis.

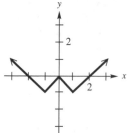

(b) Since $f(-x) = -f(x)$, the graph is symmetric with respect to the origin.

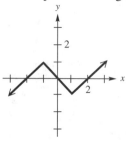

43. The graph of $Y_2 = -Y_1$ is the graph of Y_1 reflected about the x-axis. This is graph F.

45. The graph of $Y_4 = 2Y_1$ is the graph of Y_1 stretched vertically by a factor of 2. This is graph D.

47. The graph of $Y_6 = Y_1 - 2$ is the graph of Y_1 translated 2 units down. This is graph B.

49.

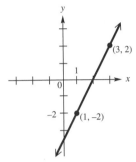

50. $m = \dfrac{2 - (-2)}{3 - 1} = \dfrac{4}{2} = 2$

51. Use the point-slope form; then rewrite the equation in the form $y_1 = mx + b$.

$$y - 2 = 2(x - 3)$$
$$y - 2 = 2x - 6$$
$$y = 2x - 4$$
$$y_1 = 2x - 4$$

52. $(1, -2)$ becomes $(1, 4)$.
$(3, 2)$ becomes $(3, 8)$.

53. $m = \dfrac{8 - 4}{3 - 1} = \dfrac{4}{2} = 2$

54. Use the point-slope form; then rewrite the equation in the form $y_2 = mx + b$.

$$y - 8 = 2(x - 3)$$
$$y - 8 = 2x - 6$$
$$y = 2x + 2$$
$$y_2 = 2x + 2$$

55.

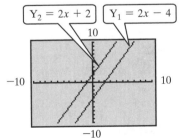

The graph of Y_2 is obtained by shifting the graph of Y_1 6 units upward. The constant, 6, comes from the 6 added in Exercise 52.

56. If the points (x_1, y_1) and (x_2, y_2) lie on a line, then when we add the positive constant c to each y-value, we obtain the points $(x_1, y_1 + c)$ and $(x_2, y_2 + c)$. The slope of the new line is *the same as* the slope of the original line. The graph of the new line can be obtained by shifting the graph of the original line c units in the *upward* direction.

57. (a) The y-intercept for $f(x)$ is $(0, 0)$ while for $g(x)$ it is $(0, 2)$ so $g(x) = f(x) + 2$.

   (b) Find points on $f(x)$ and $g(x)$ with the same y-value. For example $(4, 2)$ is on $f(x)$ while $(0, 2)$ is on $g(x)$ so $g(x)$ is shifted 4 units left from $f(x)$ or $g(x) = f(x + 4)$.

59. The general trend was a gradual decrease in carbon monoxide levels from about 9.0 to 7.4 parts per million.

Section 2.7

Exercises

1. $(f + g)(x) = f(x) + g(x)$
$$= x^2 + 2x - 5$$
$$= 2x - 5 + x^2$$
   C

3. $(fg)(x) = f(x) - g(x)$
$$= x^2(2x - 5)$$
$$= 2x^3 - 5x^2$$
   D

5. $f(x) = 3x + 4, \ g(x) = 2x - 5$
$$(f + g)(x) = f(x) + g(x)$$
$$= (3x + 4) + (2x - 5)$$
$$= 5x - 1$$
$$(f - g)(x) = f(x) - g(x)$$
$$= (3x + 4) - (2x - 5)$$
$$= x + 9$$
$$(fg)(x) = f(x) \cdot g(x)$$
$$= (3x + 4)(2x - 5)$$
$$= 6x^2 - 7x - 20$$
$$\left(\frac{f}{g}\right)(x) = \frac{f(x)}{g(x)}$$
$$= \frac{3x + 4}{2x - 5}$$
The domains of $f + g$, $f - g$, and fg are all $(-\infty, \infty)$.

The domain of $\dfrac{f}{g}$ is $\left(-\infty, \dfrac{5}{2}\right) \cup \left(\dfrac{5}{2}, \infty\right)$ since the denominator cannot be zero.

7. $f(x) = 2x^2 - 3x, \ g(x) = x^2 - x + 3$

$(f + g)(x) = f(x) + g(x)$

$\qquad = (2x^2 - 3x) + (x^2 - x + 3)$

$\qquad = 3x^2 - 4x + 3$

$(f - g)(x) = f(x) - g(x)$

$\qquad = (2x^2 - 3x) - (x^2 - x + 3)$

$\qquad = x^2 - 2x - 3$

$(fg)(x) = f(x) \cdot f(x)$

$\qquad = (2x^2 - 3x)(x^2 - x + 3)$

$\qquad = 2x^4 - 2x^3 + 6x^2 - 3x^3 + 3x^2 - 9x$

$\qquad = 2x^4 - 5x^3 + 9x^2 - 9x$

$\left(\dfrac{f}{g}\right)(x) = \dfrac{f(x)}{g(x)}$

$\qquad = \dfrac{2x^2 - 3x}{x^2 - x + 3}$

If $x^2 - x + 3 = 0$, then by the quadratic formula $x = \dfrac{1 \pm \sqrt{-11}}{2}$.

The equation has no real solutions. There are no real numbers which make the denominator zero. All of the domains are $(-\infty, \infty)$.

9. $f(x) = \sqrt{4x - 1}, \ g(x) = \dfrac{1}{x}$

$(f + g)(x) = f(x) + g(x)$

$\qquad = \sqrt{4x - 1} + \dfrac{1}{x}$

$(f - g)(x) = f(x) - g(x)$

$\qquad = \sqrt{4x - 1} - \dfrac{1}{x}$

$(fg)(x) = f(x) \cdot g(x)$

$\qquad = \sqrt{4x - 1}\left(\dfrac{1}{x}\right)$

$\qquad = \dfrac{\sqrt{4x - 1}}{x}$

$\left(\dfrac{f}{g}\right)(x) = \dfrac{f(x)}{g(x)}$

$\qquad = \dfrac{\sqrt{4x - 1}}{\dfrac{1}{x}}$

$\qquad = x\sqrt{4x - 1}$

All of the domains are $\left[\dfrac{1}{4}, \infty\right)$ because $4x - 1$ must be greater than or equal to 0.

In Exercises 11–21, $f(x) = 5x^2 - 2x$ and $g(x) = 6x + 4$.

11. $(f + g)(3) = f(3) + g(3)$

$\qquad = 5(3)^2 - 2(3) + 6(3) + 4$

$\qquad = 45 - 6 + 18 + 4$

$\qquad = 61$

13. $(fg)(4) = f(4) \cdot g(4)$

$\qquad = [5(4)^2 - 2(4)] \cdot [6(4) + 4]$

$\qquad = 72(28)$

$\qquad = 2016$

15. $\left(\dfrac{f}{g}\right)(-1) = \dfrac{f(-1)}{g(-1)}$

$\qquad = \dfrac{5(-1)^2 - 2(-1)}{6(-1) + 4}$

$\qquad = \dfrac{5 + 2}{-2}$

$\qquad = -\dfrac{7}{2}$

17. $(f - g)(m) = f(m) - g(m)$

$\qquad = (5m^2 - 2m) - (6m + 4)$

$\qquad = 5m^2 - 2m - 6m - 4$

$\qquad = 5m^2 - 8m - 4$

19. $(f \circ g)(2) = f[g(2)]$

$\qquad = f(6 \cdot 2 + 4)$

$\qquad = f(16)$

$\qquad = 5 \cdot (16)^2 - 2(16)$

$\qquad = 1280 - 32 = 1248$

21. $(g \circ f)(2) = g[f(2)]$

$\qquad = g[5(2)^2 - 2(2)]$

$\qquad = g(16)$

$\qquad = 6(16) + 4 = 100$

23. $f(1) + g(1) = 2 + 3 = 5$

25. $f(-2) \cdot g(4) = 0(2) = 0$

27. $(f \circ g)(2) = f[g(2)]$

$\qquad = f(2) = 3$

29. $(g \circ f)(-4) = g[f(-4)]$
$= g(2) = 2$

31. $g[f(2)] = g(1) = 2$
$g[f(3)] = g(2) = 5$
Since $g[f(1)] = 7$, $g(3) = 7$.

x	$f(x)$	$g(x)$	$g[f(x)]$
1	3	2	7
2	1	5	2
3	2	7	5

33. $(f \circ g)(2) = f[g(2)]$
$= f(3) = 1$

35. $(g \circ f)(3) = g[f(3)]$
$= g(1) = 9$

37. $(f \circ f)(4) = f[f(4)]$
$= f(3) = 1$

39. $(f \circ g)(1) = f[g(1)]$
$= f(9)$
However, $f(9)$ cannot be determined from the table given.

41. $f(x) = -6x = 9$, $g(x) = 5x + 7$
$(f \circ g)(x) = f[g(x)]$
$= f(5x + 7)$
$= -6(5x + 7) + 9$
$= -30x - 42 + 9$
$= -30x - 33$
$(g \circ f)(x) = g[f(x)]$
$= g(-6x + 9)$
$= 5(-6x + 9) + 7$
$= -30x + 45 + 7$
$= -30x + 52$

43. $f(x) = 4x^2 + 2x + 8$, $g(x) = x + 5$
$(f \circ g)(x) = f[g(x)]$
$= f(x + 5)$
$= 4(x + 5)^2 + 2(x + 5) + 8$
$= 4(x^2 + 10x + 25) + 2x + 10 + 8$
$= 4x^2 + 40x + 100 + 2x + 18$
$= 4x^2 + 42x + 118$
$(g \circ f)(x) = g[f(x)]$
$= g(4x^2 + 2x + 8)$
$= (4x^2 + 2x + 8) + 5$
$= 4x^2 + 2x + 13$

45. $f(x) = \dfrac{2}{x^4}$, $g(x) = 2 - x$
$(f \circ g)(x) = f[g(x)]$
$= f(2 - x)$
$= \dfrac{2}{(2 - x)^4}$
$(g \circ f)(x) = g[f(x)]$
$= g\left(\dfrac{2}{x^4}\right)$
$= 2 - \dfrac{2}{x^4}$

47. $f(x) = 9x^2 - 11x$, $g(x) = 2\sqrt{x + 2}$
$(f \circ g)(x) = g[g(x)]$
$= f(2\sqrt{x + 2})$
$= 9(2\sqrt{x + 2})^2 - 11(2\sqrt{x + 2})$
$= 9[4(x + 2)] - 22\sqrt{x + 2}$
$= 36x + 72 - 22\sqrt{x + 2}$
$(g \circ f)(x) = g[f(x)]$
$= g(9x^2 - 11x)$
$= 2\sqrt{(9x^2 - 11x) + 2}$
$= 2\sqrt{9x^2 - 11x + 2}$

In Exercises 57–61, we give only one of many possible ways.

57. $h(x) = (6x - 2)^2$
Let $f(x) = x^2$ and $g(x) = 6x - 2$.
Then $(f \circ g)(x) = f(6x - 2)$
$= (6x - 2)^2 = h(x)$.

59. $h(x) = \sqrt{x^2 - 1}$
Let $f(x) = \sqrt{x}$ and $g(x) = x^2 - 1$.
Then $(f \circ g)(x) = f(x^2 - 1)$
$= \sqrt{x^2 - 1}$
$= \sqrt{x^2 - 1} = h(x)$.

61. $h(x) = \sqrt{6x} + 12$
Let $f(x) = \sqrt{x} + 12$ and $g(x) = 6x$.
Then $(f \circ g)(x) = f(6x)$
$= \sqrt{6x} + 12 = h(x)$.

63. $Y_1 = 2x - 5$, $Y_2 = x^2$

(a) $X = 0$

$$(Y_1 \circ Y_2)(0) = Y_1[Y_2(0)]$$
$$= Y_1(0)$$
$$= 2(0) - 5$$
$$= -5$$

(b) $X = 1$

$$(Y_1 \circ Y_2)(1) = Y_1[Y_2(1)]$$
$$= Y_1(1)$$
$$= 2(1) - 5$$
$$= -3$$

(c) $X = 2$

$$(Y_1 \circ Y_2)(2) = Y_1[Y_2(2)]$$
$$= Y_1(4)$$
$$= 2(4) - 5$$
$$= 3$$

(d) $X = 3$

$$(Y_2 \circ Y_2)(3) = Y_1[Y_2(3)]$$
$$= Y_1(9)$$
$$= 2(9) - 5$$
$$= 13$$

65. $f(x) = 6x + 2$

(a) $f(x + h) = 6(x + h) + 2$
$$= 6x + 6h + 2$$

(b) $f(x + h) - f(x) = (6x + 6h + 2) - (6x + 2)$
$$= 6x + 6h + 2 - 6x - 2$$
$$= 6h$$

(c) $\dfrac{f(x + h) - f(x)}{h} = \dfrac{6h}{h}$
$$= 6$$

67. $f(x) = -2x + 5$

(a) $f(x + h) = -2(x + h) + 5$
$$= -2x - 2h + 5$$

(b) $f(x + h) - f(x) = (-2x - 2h + 5) - (-2x + 5)$
$$= -2x - 2h + 5 + 2x - 5$$
$$= -2h$$

(c) $\dfrac{f(x + h) - f(x)}{h} = \dfrac{-2h}{h}$
$$= -2$$

69. $f(x) = x^2 - 4$

(a) $f(x + h) = (x + h)^2 - 4$
$$= x^2 + 2xh + h^2 - 4$$

(b) $f(x + h) - f(x)$
$$= (x^2 + 2xh + h^2 - 4) - (x^2 - 4)$$
$$= x^2 + 2xh + h^2 - 4 - x^2 + 4$$
$$= 2xh + h^2$$

(c) $\dfrac{f(x + h) - f(x)}{h} = \dfrac{2xh + h^2}{h}$
$$= 2x + h$$

71. $f(x) = 12x, \ g(x) = 5280x$

$$(f \circ g)(x) = f[g(x)]$$
$$= f(5280x)$$
$$= 12(5280x)$$
$$= 63,360x$$

The function $f \circ g$ computes the number of inches in x miles.

73. $A(x) = \dfrac{\sqrt{3}}{4} x^2$

(a) $A(2x) = \dfrac{\sqrt{3}}{4}(2x)^2$
$$= \dfrac{\sqrt{3}}{4}(4x^2)$$
$$= \sqrt{3}x^2$$

(b) $A(16) = A(2 \cdot 8)$
$$= \sqrt{3}(8)^2 \quad x = 8$$
$$= 64\sqrt{3} \text{ square units}$$

75. (a)

$$r(t) = 4t$$
$$A(r) = \pi r^2$$
$$(A \circ r)(t) = A[r(t)]$$
$$= A(4t)$$
$$= \pi(4t)^2$$
$$= 16\pi t^2$$

(b) $(A \circ f)(t)$ defines the area of the leak in terms of the time t, in minutes.

(c) $A(3) = 16\pi(3)^2$
$$= 144\pi$$

The area is 144π sq ft

77. Let x = the number of people less than 100 people that attend.

(a) x people fewer than 100 attend, so $100 - x$ people do attend
$$N(x) = 100 - x$$

(b) The cost per person starts at $20 and increases by $5 for each of the x people that do not attend. The total increase is $5x$, and the cost per person increases to $20 + $5x$.
$$G(x) = 20 + 5x$$

(c) $C(x) = N(x) \cdot G(x)$
$$= (100 - x)(20 + 5x)$$

(d) If 40 people attend,
$$x = 100 - 40 = 60.$$
$$C(60) = (100 - 60)[20 + 5(60)]$$
$$= (40)(320)$$
$$= 12,800$$

The total cost is $12,800.

Chapter 2 Review Exercises

1. $\{(-3, 6), (-1, 4), (8, 5)\}$
The domain is $\{-3, -1, 8\}$, the set of first elements. The range is $\{6, 4, 5\}$, the set of second elements.

3. $P(3, -1), Q(-4, 5)$
$$d(P, Q) = \sqrt{(-4 - 3)^2 + [5 - (-1)]^2}$$
$$= \sqrt{(-7)^2 + 6^2}$$
$$= \sqrt{49 + 36}$$
$$= \sqrt{85}$$
Midpoint:
$$\left(\frac{3 + (-4)}{2}, \frac{-1 + 5}{2}\right) = \left(-\frac{1}{2}, 2\right)$$

5. $A(-6, 3), B(-6, 8)$
$$d(A, B) = \sqrt{[-6 - (-6)]^2 + (8 - 3)^2}$$
$$= \sqrt{25}$$
$$= 5$$
Midpoint:
$$\left(\frac{-6 + (-6)}{2}, \frac{3 + 8}{2}\right) = \left(-6, \frac{11}{2}\right)$$

7. $A(-1, 2), B(-10, 5), C(-4, k)$
$$d(A, B) = \sqrt{[-1 - (-10)]^2 + (2 - 5)^2}$$
$$= \sqrt{90}$$

$$d(A, C) = \sqrt{[-4 - (-1)]^2 + (k - 2)^2}$$
$$= \sqrt{9 + (k - 2)^2}$$
$$d(B, C) = \sqrt{[-10 - (-4)]^2 + (5 - k)^2}$$
$$= \sqrt{36 + (k - 5)^2}$$
If segment AB is the hypotenuse,
$$(\sqrt{90})^2 = \left[\sqrt{9 + (k - 2)^2}\right]^2 + \left[\sqrt{36 + (k - 5)^2}\right]^2$$
$$90 = 9 + k^2 - 4k + 4 + 36 + k^2 - 10k + 25$$
$$0 = 2k^2 - 14k - 16$$
$$0 = k^2 - 7k - 8$$
$$0 = (k - 8)(k + 1)$$
$$k = 8 \text{ or } k = -1.$$
If segment AC is the hypotenuse, the product of the slopes of lines AB and BC is -1 since the product of slopes of perpendicular lines is -1.
$$\left(\frac{5 - 2}{-10 + 1}\right) \cdot \left(\frac{k - 5}{-4 + 10}\right) = -1$$
$$\left(\frac{3}{-9}\right) \cdot \left(\frac{k - 5}{6}\right) = -1$$
$$\frac{k - 5}{-18} = -1$$
$$k - 5 = 18$$
$$k = 23$$
If segment BC is the hypotenuse, the product of the slopes of lines AB and AC is -1.
$$\left(\frac{3}{-9}\right) \cdot \left(\frac{k - 2}{-4 + 1}\right) = -1$$
$$\left(\frac{-1}{3}\right) \cdot \left(\frac{k - 2}{-3}\right) = -1$$
$$\frac{k - 2}{9} = -1$$
$$k - 2 = -9$$
$$k = -7$$
The possible values of k are $-7, 23, 8,$ and -1.

9. Center $(-2, 3)$, radius 15
$$(x - h)^2 + (y - k)^2 = r^2$$
$$[x - (-2)]^2 + (y - 3)^2 = 15^2$$
$$(x + 2)^2 + (y - 3)^2 = 225$$

11. Center $(-8, 1)$, passing through $(0, 16)$
The radius is the distance from the center to any point on the circle. The distance between $(-8, 1)$ and $(0, 16)$ is

$$r = \sqrt{(-8-0)^2 + (1-16)^2}$$
$$= \sqrt{8^2 + 15^2}$$
$$= \sqrt{289}$$
$$= 17.$$

The equation of the circle is
$$[x - (-8)]^2 + (y-1)^2 = 17^2$$
$$(x+8)^2 + (y-1)^2 = 289.$$

13. $x^2 - 4x + y^2 = 6y + 12 = 0$

Complete the square on x and y to put the equation in center-radius form.
$$(x^2 - 4x + \ ) + (y^2 + 6y + \ ) = -12$$
$$(x^2 - 4x + 4) + (y^2 + 6y + 9) = -12 + 4 + 9$$
$$(x-2)^2 + (y+3)^2 = 1$$

The circle has center $(2, -3)$ and radius 1.

15.
$$2x^2 + 14x + 2y^2 + 6y + 2 = 0$$
$$x^2 + 7x + y^2 + 3y + 1 = 0$$
$$(x^2 + 7x \quad) + (y^2 + 3y \quad) = -1$$
$$\left(x^2 + 7x + \frac{49}{4}\right) + \left(y^2 + 3y + \frac{9}{4}\right) = -1 + \frac{49}{4} + \frac{9}{4}$$
$$\left(x + \frac{7}{2}\right)^2 + \left(y + \frac{3}{2}\right)^2 = \frac{54}{4}$$

The circle has center $\left(-\dfrac{7}{2}, -\dfrac{3}{2}\right)$ and radius
$$\sqrt{\frac{54}{4}} = \frac{\sqrt{54}}{\sqrt{4}} = \frac{3\sqrt{6}}{2}.$$

17. Find all possible values of x so that the distance between $(x, -9)$ and $(3, -6)$ is 6.

$$\sqrt{(3-x)^2 + (-5+9)^2} = 6$$
$$\sqrt{9 - 6x + x^2 + 16} = 6$$
$$\sqrt{x^2 - 6x + 25} = 6$$
$$x^2 - 6x + 25 = 36$$
$$x^2 - 6x - 11 = 0$$
$$x = \frac{6 \pm \sqrt{36 - 4(1)(-11)}}{2}$$
$$= \frac{6 \pm \sqrt{36 + 44}}{2}$$
$$= \frac{6 \pm \sqrt{80}}{2}$$
$$-\frac{6 \pm 4\sqrt{5}}{2} = \frac{2(3 \pm 2\sqrt{5})}{2}$$
$$x = 3 + 2\sqrt{5} \text{ or } x = 3 - 2\sqrt{5}$$

19. Find all points (x, y) with $x + y = 0$ so that (x, y) is 6 units from $(-2, 3)$.

$$6 = \sqrt{(x+2)^2 + (y-3)^2}$$
$$6 = \sqrt{(x+2)^2 + (-x-3)^2} \quad y = -x$$
$$36 = (x+2)^2 + (-x-3)^2$$
$$36 = x^2 + 4x + 4 + x^2 + 6x + 9$$
$$0 = 2x^2 + 10x - 23$$
$$x = \frac{-10 \pm \sqrt{100 - 4(2)(-23)}\,4}{4}$$
$$= \frac{-10 \pm \sqrt{100 + 184}}{4}$$
$$= \frac{-10 \pm \sqrt{284}}{4}$$
$$= \frac{-10 \pm 2\sqrt{71}}{4}$$
$$x = \frac{-5 \pm \sqrt{71}}{2}$$

Since $x + y = 0$ or $y = -x$,

if $x = \dfrac{-5 + \sqrt{71}}{2}$, then $y = \dfrac{5 - \sqrt{71}}{2}$;

if $x = \dfrac{-5 - \sqrt{71}}{2}$, then $y = \dfrac{5 + \sqrt{71}}{21}$.

The points are
$$\left(\frac{-5 + \sqrt{71}}{2}, \frac{5 - \sqrt{71}}{2}\right),$$

and $\left(\dfrac{-5 - \sqrt{71}}{2}, \dfrac{5 + \sqrt{71}}{2}\right)$.

21. This is not the graph of a function because a vertical line can intersect it in two points. The domain of the relation is $(-\infty, \infty)$. The range is $[0, \infty)$.

23. This is the graph of a function. No vertical line will intersect the graph in more than one point. The domain of the function is $(-\infty, -2]\cup[2, \infty)$. The range is $[0, \infty)$.

25. This is the graph of a function. No vertical line will intersect the graph in more than one point. The domain of the function is $(-\infty, \infty)$. The range is $(-\infty, \infty)$.

27. The equation $x = \frac{1}{2}y^2$ does not define y as a function of x. For some values of x, there will be more than one value of y. For example, if $x = 8$,
$$8 = \frac{1}{2}y^2$$
$$y^2 = 16$$
$$y = \pm 4.$$
Therefore, the ordered pairs $(8, 4)$ and $(8, -4)$ would belong to the relation and the relation would not be a function.

29. The equation $y = -\frac{8}{x}$ defines y as a function of x because for every x in the domain, which is $(-\infty, 0)\cup(0, \infty)$, there will be exactly one value of y.

31. In the function $y = -4 + |x|$, we may use any real number for x. The domain is $(-\infty, \infty)$.

33. In the function $y = -\sqrt{\frac{5}{x^2 + 9}}$, we must have $\frac{5}{x^2 + 9} \geq 0$. However, this will be true for every real value of x. The domain is $(-\infty, \infty)$.

35. (a) As x is getting larger on the interval $[2, \infty)$, the value of y is increasing.

(b) As x is getting larger on the interval $(-\infty, -2]$, the value of y is decreasing.

37. (a) This is the graph of a function since no vertical line intersects the graph in more than one point.

(b) The lowest point on the graph occurs in December, so the most jobs lost occurred in December. The highest point on the graph

occurs in January, so the most jobs gained occurred in January.

(c) The number of jobs lost in December is approximately 6000. The number of jobs gained in January is approximately 2000.

(d) These data show a slight downward trend.

39. Find the slope of the line through $(8, 7)$ and $\left(\frac{1}{2}, 2\right)$.
$$m = \frac{y_2 - y_1}{x_2 - x_1}$$
$$= \frac{-2 - 7}{\frac{1}{2} - 8}$$
$$= \frac{-9}{-\frac{115}{2}}$$
$$= -9\left(-\frac{2}{15}\right)$$
$$= \frac{18}{15} = \frac{6}{5}$$

41. Find the slope of the line through $(5, 6)$ and $(5, -21)$.
$$m = \frac{y_2 - y_1}{x_2 - x_1}$$
$$= \frac{-2 - 6}{5 - 5} = \frac{-8}{0}$$
The slope is undefined.

43. Find the slope of the line $9x - 4y = 2$. Solve for y to put the equation in slope-intercept form.
$$-4y = -9x + 2$$
$$y = \frac{9}{4}x - \frac{1}{2}$$
$$m = \frac{9}{4}$$
(The slope can also be found by choosing two points on the line and using $m = \frac{y_2 - y_1}{x_2 - x_1}$.)

45. Find the slope of the line $x - 5y = 0$. Solve for y to put the equation in slope-intercept form.
$$-5y = -x$$
$$y = \frac{1}{5}x$$
$$m = \frac{1}{5}$$

47. Two points on the graph are $(2, -4)$ and $(3, -7)$.

$$m = \frac{-7-(-4)}{3-2}$$

$$= \frac{-3}{1} = -3$$

49. $3x + 7y = 14$

$$7y = -3x + 14$$

$$y = -\frac{3}{7}x + 2$$

The graph is the line with slope of $-\frac{3}{7}$ and y-intercept 2. It may also be graphed using the x-intercept $\frac{14}{3}$ and y-intercept 2. The domain and range are both $(-\infty, \infty)$.

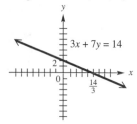

51. $3y = x$

$$y = \frac{1}{3}x$$

The graph is the line with slope $\frac{1}{3}$ and y-intercept 0, which means that it passes through the origin. Use another point such as $(3, 1)$ to complete the graph. The domain and range are both $(-\infty, \infty)$.

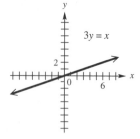

53. $x = -5$

The graph is the vertical line through $(-5, 0)$. The domain is $\{-5\}$ and the range is $(-\infty, \infty)$.

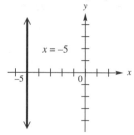

55. Line through $(-2, 4)$ and $(1, 3)$

First find the slope.

$$m = \frac{3-4}{1-(-2)} = \frac{-1}{3}$$

Now use the point-slope form with $(x_1, y_1) = (1, 3)$ and $m = -\frac{1}{3}$.

$$y - 3 = \frac{1}{3}(x - 1)$$

$$3(y - 3) = -1(x - 1)$$

$$3y - 9 = -x + 1$$

$$x + 3y = 10 \quad \text{Standard form}$$

57. x-intercept -3, y-intercept 5

Two points of the line are $(-3, 0)$ and $(0, 5)$.

First, find the slope.

$$m = \frac{5-0}{0+3} = \frac{5}{3}$$

The slope is $\frac{5}{3}$ and the y-intercept is 5. Write the equation in slope-intercept form.

$$y = \frac{5}{3}x + 5$$

Now rewrite the equation in standard form.

$$3y = 5x + 15$$

$$5x - 3y = -15$$

59. Line through $(0, 5)$, perpendicular to $8x + 5y = 3$

Find the slope of $8x + 5y = 3$.

$$8x + 5y = 3$$

$$5y = -8x + 3$$

$$y = -\frac{8}{5}x + \frac{3}{5}$$

Since the slope of $8x + 5y = 3$ is $-\frac{8}{5}$, the slope of a line perpendicular to it is $\frac{5}{8}$. Since $m = \frac{5}{8}$ and $b = 5$, the equation is

$$y = \frac{5}{8}x + 5$$

$$8y = 5x + 40$$

$$-40 = 5x - 8y$$

$$\text{or } 5x - 8y = -40. \quad \text{Standard form}$$

61. Line through $(3, -5)$, parallel to $y = 4$

This will be a horizontal line through $(3, -5)$. Since y has the same value of all points on the line, $b = -5$. The equation is $y = -5$.

63. Line through $(2, -4)$, $m = \frac{3}{4}$

First locate the point $(2, -4)$.

Since the slope is $\frac{3}{4}$ a change of 4 units horizontally(4 units to the right) produces a change of 3 units vertically (3 units up). This gives a second point, $(6, -1)$, which can be used to complete the graph.

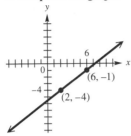

65. (a) $(1995, 157)$, $(2000, 247)$
$$m = \frac{247 - 157}{2000 - 1995} = \frac{90}{5} = 18$$
The approximate slope is 18.

(b) Use any point, say $(1995, 157)$ and the point-slope form to find the equation.
$$y - 157 = 18(x - 1995)$$
$$y - 157 = 18x - 35910$$
$$y = 18x - 35753$$
or $f(x) = 18x - 35,753$

(c) $f(2002) = 18(2002) - 35,753$
$$= 283$$
In 2002, the Medicare cost is predicted to be $283 billion dollars.

67. $f(x) = -|x|$
The graph of $f(x) = -|x|$ is the reflection of the graph of $f(x) = |x|$ about the x-axis.

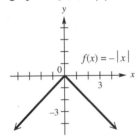

69. $f(x) = -|x| - 2$
Translate the graph in Exercise 67 down 2 units.

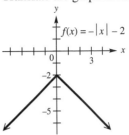

71. $f(x) = 2|x - 3| - 4$
Start with the graph of $f(x) = |x|$.
Stretch the graph vertically by a factor of 2, translate it 3 units to the right and translate it 4 units down.

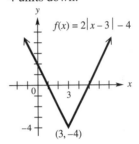

73. $f(x) = \left[\!\left[\frac{1}{2}x - 2 \right]\!\right]$
For y to be 0, we need
$$0 \le \frac{1}{2}x - 2 < 1$$
$$2 \le \frac{1}{2}x < 3$$
$$4 \le x < 6.$$
Follow this pattern to graph the step function.

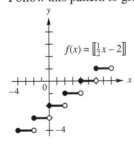

75. $f(x) = \begin{cases} 3x + 1 \text{ if } x < 2 \\ -x + 4 \text{ if } x > 2 \end{cases}$
Graph the line $y = 3x + 1$ to the left of $x = 2$, and graph the line $y = -x + 4$ to the right of $x = 2$.
The graph has an open circle at $(2, 7)$ and a closed

circle at (2, 2).

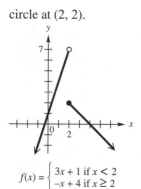

$$f(x) = \begin{cases} 3x + 1 \text{ if } x < 2 \\ -x + 4 \text{ if } x \geq 2 \end{cases}$$

77. The graph of a nonzero function cannot be symmetric with respect to the x-axis.
Such a graph would fail the vertical line test, so the statement is true.

79. The graph of an odd function is symmetric with respect to the origin.
This statement is true.

81. If (a, b) is on the graph of an odd function, so is $(-a, b)$.
This statement is false. For example, $f(x) = x^3$ is odd, and $(2, 8)$ is on the graph but $(-2, 8)$ is not.

83. $3y^2 - 5x^2 = 15$
Replace x with $-x$ to obtain
$$3y^2 - 5(-x)^2 = 15$$
$$3y^2 - 5x^2 = 15.$$
The result is the same as the original equation, so the graph is symmetric with respect to the y-axis.
Replace y with $-y$ to obtain
$$3(-y)^2 - 5x^2 = 15$$
$$3y^2 - 5x^2 = 15.$$
The result is the same as the original equation, so the graph is symmetric with respect to the x-axis.
Since the graph is symmetric with respect to the y-axis and x-axis, it must also be symmetric with respect to the origin.

85. $y^3 = x + 1$
Replace x with $-x$ to obtain
$$y^3 = -x + 1.$$
The result is not the same as the original equation, so the graph is not symmetric with respect to the y-axis.
Replace y with $-y$ to obtain
$$(-y)^3 = x + 1$$
$$-y^3 = x + 1$$
$$y^3 = -x - 1$$

The result is not the same as the original equation, so the graph is not symmetric with respect to the x-axis.
Replace x with $-x$ and y with $-y$ to obtain
$$(-y)^3 = (-x) + 1$$
$$-y^3 = -x + 1$$
$$y^3 = x - 1.$$
The result is not the same as the original equation, so the graph is not symmetric with respect to the origin.
Therefore, the graph has none of the listed symmetries.

87. $|y| = -x$
Replace x with $-x$ to obtain
$$|y| = -(-x)$$
$$|y| = x.$$
The result is not the same as the original equation, so the graph is not symmetric with respect to the y-axis.
Replace y with $-y$ to obtain
$$|-y| = -(-x)$$
$$|y| = x.$$
The result is the same as the original equation, so the graph is symmetric with respect to the x-axis.
Replace x with $-x$ and y with $-y$ to obtain
$$|-y| = -(-x)$$
$$|y| = x.$$
The result is the same as the original equation, so the graph is symmetric with respect to the x-axis.
Replace x with $-x$ and y with $-y$ to obtain
$$|-y| = -(-x)$$
$$|y| = x.$$
The result is not the same as the original equation, so the graph is not symmetric with respect to the origin.
Therefore, the graph is symmetric with respect to the x-axis only.

89. $|x| = |y|$
Replace x with $-x$ to obtain
$$|-x| = |y|$$
$$|x| = |y|.$$
The result is the same as the original equation, so the graph is symmetric with respect to the y-axis.
Replace y with $-y$ to obtain
$$|x| = |-y|$$
$$|x| = |y|.$$
The result is the same as s the original equation, so the graph is symmetric with respect to the

x-axis.
Since the graph is symmetric with respect to the x-axis and with respect to the y-axis, it must also by symmetric with respect to the origin.

91. To obtain the graph of $h(x) = |x| - 2$, translate the graph of $f(x) = |x|$ down 2 units.

93. If the graph of $f(x) = 3x - 4$ is reflected about the x-axis, we obtain a graph whose equation is
$$y = -(3x - 4)$$
$$= -3x + 4.$$

95. If the graph of $f(x) = 3x - 4$ is reflected about the origin, every point (x, y) will be replaced by the point $(-x, -y)$. The equation for the graph will change from $y = 3x - 4$ to
$$-y = 3(-x) - 4$$
$$-y = -3x - 4$$
$$y = 3x + 4.$$

For Exercises 97–105, $f(x) = 3x^2 - 4$ and $g(x) = x^2 - 3x - 4$.

97. $(f + g)(x) = f(x) + g(x)$
$$= (3x^2 - 4) + (x^2 - 3x - 4)$$
$$= 4x^2 - 3x - 8$$

99. $(f - g)(4) = f(4) - g(4)$
$$= (3 \cdot 4^2 - 4) - (4^2 - 3 \cdot 4 - 4)$$
$$= (48 - 4) - (16 - 12 - 4)$$
$$= 44$$

101. $(f + g)(2k) = f(2k) + g(2k)$
$$= [3(2k)^2 - 3(2k) - 4]$$
$$= (12k^2 - 4) + (4k^2 - 6k - 4)$$
$$= 16k^2 - 6k - 8$$

103. $\left(\dfrac{f}{g}\right)(x) = \dfrac{3x^2 - 4}{x^2 - 3x - 4}$
Since $x^2 - 3x - 4 = 0$ when $x = -1$ and division by 0 is undefined, $\left(\dfrac{f}{g}\right)(-1)$ is undefined.

105. $\left(\dfrac{f}{g}\right)(x) = \dfrac{3x^2 - 4}{x^2 - 3x - 4}$
$$= \dfrac{3x^2 - 4}{(x + 1)(x - 4)}$$
The expression is not undefined if $(x + 1)(x - 4) = 0$, that is, if $x = -1$, or $x = 4$. Thus, the domain is the set of all real numbers except $x = -1$ and $x = 4$, or $(-\infty, -1) \cup (-1, 4) \cup (4, \infty)$.

For Exercises 107–109, $f(x) = \sqrt{x - 2}$ and $g(x) = x^2$.

107. $(f \circ g)(x) = f[g(x)]$
$$= f(x^2)$$
$$= \sqrt{x^2 - 2}$$

109. $(f \circ g)(-6) = f[g(-6)]$
$$= \sqrt{(-6)^2 - 2}$$
$$= \sqrt{34}$$

111. $(f \circ g)(x) = f[g(2)]$
$$= f(2)$$
$$= 1$$

113. $f(x) = 2x + 9$
$f(x + h) = 2(x + h) + 9$
$$\dfrac{f(x + h) - f(x)}{h} = \dfrac{2(x + h) + 9 - (2x + 9)}{h}$$
$$= \dfrac{2x + 2h + 9 - 2x - 9}{h}$$
$$= \dfrac{2h}{h}$$
$$= 2$$

115. Let x = number of yards
$f(x) = 36x$ where $f(x)$ is the number of inches
$g(x) = 1760x$ where $g(x)$ is the number of miles
Then
$(g \circ f)(x) = g(f(x)) = 1760(36x) = 63,360x$.
There are $63,360x$ inches in x miles.

117. Use the definition for the perimeter of a rectangle.
P = length + width + length + width
$P(x) = 2x + x + 2x + x$
$P(x) = 6x$
This is a linear function.

Chapter 2 Test Exercises

1. {(1993, 6310), (1994, 7575), (1995, 9117), (1996, 10,346), (1997, 11,128)}

2. $m = \dfrac{4-1}{3-(-2)} = \dfrac{3}{5}$

3. We label the points $A(-2, 1)$ and $B(3, 4)$.

$$d(A, \; B) = \sqrt{[3-(-2)]^2 + (4-1)^2}$$
$$= \sqrt{5^2 + 3^2}$$
$$= \sqrt{34}$$

4. The midpoint has coordinates

$$M\!\left(\dfrac{-2+3}{2}, \; \dfrac{1+4}{2}\right) \text{ or } \left(\dfrac{1}{2}, \dfrac{5}{2}\right).$$

5. Use the point-slope form with $m = \dfrac{3}{5}$,
$x_1 = -2,$ and $y_1 = 1.$

$$y - 1 = \dfrac{3}{5}[x - (-2)]$$
$$y - 1 = \dfrac{3}{5}(x + 2)$$
$$5y - 5 = 3(x + 2)$$
$$5y - 5 = 3x + 6$$
$$-11 = 3x - 5y$$
$$3x - 5y = -11$$

6. Solve $3x - 5y = -11$ for y
$$-5y = -3x - 11$$
$$y = \dfrac{3}{5}x + \dfrac{11}{5}$$
Therefore, the linear function is
$$f(x) = \dfrac{3}{5}x + \dfrac{11}{5}.$$

7. Point A has coordinates $(5, -3)$.

  (a) The equation of a vertical line through A is
  $x = 5$.

  (b) The equation of a horizontal line through A is
  $y = -3$.

8. The slope of the graph of $y = -3x + 2$ is -3.

  (a) A line parallel to the graph of $y = -3x + 2$ has
  a slope of -3.
  $$y - 3 = -3(x - 2)$$
  $$y - 3 = -3x + 6$$
  $$y = -3x + 9$$

  (b) A line perpendicular to the graph of
  $y = -3x + 2$ has a slope of $\dfrac{1}{3}$.
  $$y - 3 = \dfrac{1}{3}(x - 2)$$
  $$y - 3 = \dfrac{1}{3}x - \dfrac{2}{3}$$
  $$y = \dfrac{1}{3}x + \dfrac{7}{3}$$

9. Use the two points $(0, 3)$ and $(4, -13)$.
$$m = \dfrac{-13-3}{4-0} = \dfrac{-16}{4} = -4$$
From the point $(0, 3)$, we see that $b = 3$.
The equation that defines this function is
$y = -4x + 3$.

10. **(a)** This is not the graph of a function because
  some vertical lines intersect it in more than
  one point. The domain of the relation is
  $[0, 4]$. The range is $[-4, 4]$.

  (b) This is the graph of a function because no
  vertical line intersects the graph in more than
  one point. The domain of the function is
  $(-\infty, -1) \cup (-1, \infty)$. The range is
  $(-\infty, 0) \cup (0, \infty)$. As x is getting larger on
  the intervals $(-\infty, -1)$ and $(-1, \infty)$, the value
  of y is decreasing, so the function is
  decreasing, on the intervals $(-\infty, -1)$ and
  $(-1, \infty)$. (The function is never increasing or
  constant.)

11. To graph $y = |x - 2| - 1$, we translate the graph of
  $y = |x|$ 2 units to the right and 1 unit down.

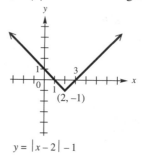

$$y = |x - 2| - 1$$

12. $f(x) = [[x + 1]]$
  To get $y = 0$, we need
  $0 \le x + 1 < 1$
  $-1 \le x < 0.$
  To get $y = 1$, we need
  $1 \le x + 1 < 2$
  $0 \le x < 1.$

Follow this pattern to graph the step function.

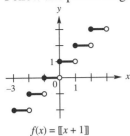

$$f(x) = [\![x + 1]\!]$$

13. $f(x) = \begin{cases} 3 & \text{if } x < -2 \\ 2 - \dfrac{1}{2}x & \text{if } x \geq -2 \end{cases}$

For values of x with $x < -2$, we graph the horizontal line $y = 3$. For values of x with $x \geq -2$, we graph the line with a slope of $-\dfrac{1}{2}$ and a y-intercept of 2. Two points on this line are $(-2, 3)$ and $(0, 2)$.

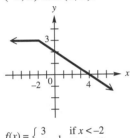

$$f(x) = \begin{cases} 3 & \text{if } x < -2 \\ 2 - \frac{1}{2}x & \text{if } x \geq -2 \end{cases}$$

14. (a) Shift $f(x)$ 2 units vertically upward.

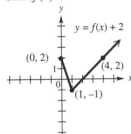

(b) Shift $f(x)$ 2 units horizontally to the left.

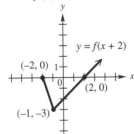

(c) Reflect $f(x)$ across the x-axis.

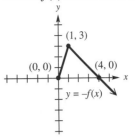

(d) Reflect $f(x)$ across the y-axis.

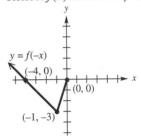

(e) Stretch $f(x)$ by a factor of 2.

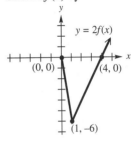

16. $3x^2 - y^2 = 3$

(a) Replace y with $-y$ to obtain
$$3x^2 - (-y)^2 = 3$$
$$3x^2 - y^2 = 3.$$
The result is the same as the original equation, so the graph is symmetric with respect to the x-axis.

(b) Replace x with $-x$ to obtain
$$3(-x)^2 - y^2 = 3$$
$$3x^2 - y^2 = 3.$$
The result is the same as the original equation, so the graph is symmetric with respect to the y-axis.

(c) Since the graph is symmetric with respect to the x-axis and with respect to the y-axis, it must also be symmetric with respect to the origin.

17. $f(x) = 2x^2 - 3x + 2, \quad g(x) = -2x + 1$

(a) $(f - g)(x) = f(x) - g(x)$

$$= 2x^2 - 3x + 2 - (-2x + 1)$$

$$= 2x^2 - 3x + 2 + 2x - 1$$

$$= 2x^2 - x + 1$$

(b) $\dfrac{f}{g}(x) = \dfrac{f(x)}{g(x)}$

$$= \dfrac{2x^2 - 3x + 2}{-2x + 1}$$

(c) $-2x + 1 \neq 0$

Therefore, $-2x \neq -1$

$$x \neq \dfrac{1}{2}$$

The domain is $\left(-\infty, \dfrac{1}{2}\right) \cup \left(\dfrac{1}{2}, \infty\right)$.

(d) $(f \circ g)(x) = f[g(x)]$

$$= f(-2x + 1)$$

$$= 2(-2x + 1)^2 - 3(-2x + 1) + 2$$

$$= 2(4x^2 - 4x + 1) + 6x - 3 + 2$$

$$= 8x^2 - 8x + 2 + 6x - 1$$

$$= 8x^2 - 2x + 1$$

(e) $\dfrac{f(x + h) - f(x)}{h} = \dfrac{[2(x + h)^2 - 3(x + h) + 2] - (2x^2 - 3x + 2)}{h}$

$$= \dfrac{2(x^2 + 2xh + h^2) - 3x - 3h + 2 - 2x^2 + 3x - 2}{h}$$

$$= \dfrac{2x^2 + 4xh + 2h^2 - 3x - 3h + 2 - 2x^{2q} + 3x - 2}{h}$$

$$= \dfrac{4xh + 2h^2 - 3h}{h}$$

$$= \dfrac{h(4x + 2h - 3)}{h}$$

$$= 4x + 2h - 3$$

18. (a) If $x = 0$ represents 1986 and $x = 10$ represents 1996, then we have the two points $(0, 12{,}436)$ and $(10, 24{,}496)$.

$$m = \frac{24{,}496 - 12{,}436}{10 - 0}$$

$$= \frac{12{,}060}{10}$$

$$= 1206$$

Since the y-intercept is 12,436,
$f(x) = 1206x + 12{,}436$.

(b) For 1994, $x = 8$.
If $x = 8$,

$$f(8) = 1206(8) + 12{,}436$$

$$= 22{,}084.$$

The predicted number of new packaged goods in 1994 based on the model is 22,084. This is slightly more than the actual number of 21,986.

19.
$$f(x) + .4[[x]] + .75$$

$$f(5.5) = .4[[5.5]] + .75$$

$$= .4(5) + .75$$

$$= 2 + .75$$

$$= 2.75$$

The call will cost \$2.75.

20. (a) $C(x) = 3300 + 4.50x$

(b) $R(x) = 10.50x$

(c)
$$P(x) = R(x) - C(x)$$

$$= 10.50x - (3300 + 4.50x)$$

$$= 6.00x - 3300$$

(d)
$$P(x) > 0$$

$$6.00x - 3300 > 0$$

$$6.00x > 3300$$

$$x > 550$$

She must produce and sell 551 items before she earns a profit.

CHAPTER 3 POLYNOMIAL AND RATIONAL FUNCTIONS

Section 3.1

Exercises

1. $f(x) = (x+3)^2 - 4$

    (a) Domain: $(-\infty, \infty)$
        Range: $[-4, \infty)$

    (b) Vertex: $(h, k) = (-3, -4)$

    (c) Axis: $x = -3$

    (d) To find the y-intercept, let $x = 0$.
        $y = (0+3)^2 - 4$
        $y = 9 - 4$
        $y = 5$
        y-intercept: 5

    (e) To find the x-intercepts, let $y = 0$.
        $0 = (x+3)^2 - 4$
        $(x+3)^2 = 4$
        $x + 3 = \pm\sqrt{4} = \pm 2$
        $x = -3 \pm 2$
        $x = -5$ or $x = -1$
        x-intercepts: -5 and -1

3. $f(x) = -2(x+3)^2 + 2$

    (a) Domain: $(-\infty, \infty)$
        Range: $(-\infty, 2]$

    (b) Vertex: $(h, k) = (-3, 2)$

    (c) Axis: $x = -3$

    (d) To find the y-intercept, let $x = 0$.
        $y = -2(0+3)^2 + 2$
        $y = -18 + 2$
        $y = -16$
        y-intercept: -16

    (e) To find the x-intercepts, let $y = 0$.
        $0 = -2(x+3)^2 + 2 \!\mid$
        $(x+3)^2 = 1$
        $x + 3 = \pm\sqrt{1} = \pm 1$
        $x = -3 \pm 1$
        $x = -4$ or $x = -2$
        x-intercepts: -4 and -2

5. $f(x) = (x-4)^2 - 3$
    Since $a > 0$, the parabola opens upward. The
    vertex is at $(4, -3)$. The correct graph, therefore,
    is B.

7. $f(x) = (x+4)^2 - 3$
    Since $a > 0$, the parabola opens upward. The
    vertex is at $(-4, -3)$. The correct graph, therefore,
    is D.

9. For parts (a), (b), (c), and (d), see the following
    graph.

    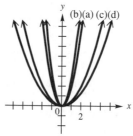

    (e) If the absolute value of the coefficient is
        greater than 1, it causes the graph to be
        stretched vertically, so it is narrower. If the
        absolute value of the coefficient is between 0
        and 1, it causes the graph to shrink vertically,
        so it is broader.

11.   For parts (a), (b), (c), and (d), see the
        following graph.

    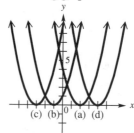

    (e) The graph of $(x-h)^2$ is translated h units to
        the right if h is positive and $|h|$ units to the
        left if h is negative.

13. $f(x) = (x-2)^2$
    This equation is of the form $y = (x-h)^2$, with
    $h = 2$. The graph opens upward and has the same
    shape as that of $y = x^2$. It is a horizontal
    translation of the graph of $y = x^2$ 2 units to the
    right. The vertex is $(2, 0)$ and the axis is the
    vertical line $x = 2$. The domain and range can be
    seen on the graph. The domain is $(-\infty, \infty)$.
    Since the smallest value of y is 0 and the graph

opens upward, the range is $[0, \infty)$.

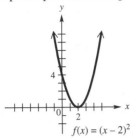

$f(x) = (x-2)^2$

15. $f(x) = (x+3)^2 - 4$

$y = [x - (-3)]^2 + (-4)$

This equation is of the form $y = (x-h)^2 + k$, with $h = -3$ and $k = -4$. The vertex is $(-3, -4)$. The graph opens upward and has the same shape as $y = x^2$. It is a translation of $y = x^2$ 3 units to the left and 4 units down. The axis is the vertical line $x = -3$. The domain is $(-\infty, \infty)$. Since the smallest value of y is -4 and the graph opens upward, the range is $[-4, \infty)$.

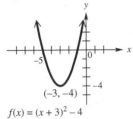

$f(x) = (x+3)^2 - 4$

17. $y = -\frac{1}{2}(x+1)^2 - 3$

The vertex is $(-1, -3)$. The graph opens downward and is wider than $y = x^2$. It is a translation of the graph $y = -\frac{1}{2}x^2$ 1 unit to the left and 3 units down. The axis is the vertical line $x = -1$. The domain is $(-\infty, \infty)$. Since the largest value of y is -3, the range is $(-\infty, -3]$.

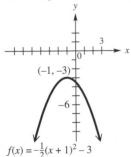

$f(x) = -\frac{1}{2}(x+1)^2 - 3$

19. $f(x) = x^2 - 2x + 3$

Rewrite in the form $y = a(x-h)^2 + k$ by completing the square on x.

$y = (x^2 - 2x + 1) - 1 + 3$

$\quad = (x-1)^2 + 2$

The vertex is $(1, 2)$. The graph opens upward and has the same shape as $y = x^2$. It is a translation of the graph of $y = x^2$ 1 unit to the right and 2 units up. The axis is the vertical line $x = 1$. The domain is $(-\infty, \infty)$. Since the smallest value of y is 2, the range is $[2, \infty)$.

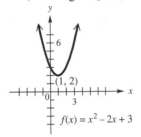

$f(x) = x^2 - 2x + 3$

21. $f(x) = 2x^2 - 4x + 5$

$\quad = 2(x^2 - 2x) + 5$

$\quad = 2(x^2 - 2x + 1 - 1) + 5$

$\quad = 2(x^2 - 2x + 1) - 2 + 5$

$\quad = 2(x-1)^2 + 3$

The vertex is $(1, 3)$. The graph opens upward and has the same shape as $y = 2x^2$. It is a translation of the graph of $y = 2x^2$ 1 unit to the right and 3 units up. The axis is the vertical line $x = 1$. The domain is $(-\infty, \infty)$. Since the smallest value of y is 3, the range is $[3, \infty)$.

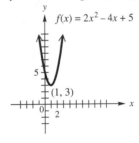

$f(x) = 2x^2 - 4x + 5$

23. The minimum value of $f(x)$ is $f(-3) = 3$.

25. There are no real solutions to the equation $f(x) = 1$ since the value of $f(x)$ is never less than 3.

27. Graph the functions $y = 3x^2 - 2$ and $y = 3(x^2 - 2)$ on the same screen

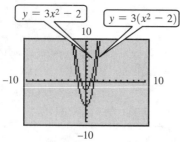

We see that the graphs are two different parabolas. Since the graphs are not the same, the expressions $3x^2 - 2$ and $3(x^2 - 2)$ are not equivalent. This result can be confirmed algebraically:

$3(x^2 - 2) = 3x^2 - 6 \neq 3x^2 - 2$.

29. $a < 0$, $b^2 - 4ac = 0$

The correct choice is E. $a < 0$ indicates that the parabola opens downward, while $b^2 - 4ac = 0$ indicates that the graph has exactly one x-intercept.

31. $a < 0$, $b^2 - 4ac < 0$

The correct choice is D. $a < 0$ indicates that the parabola opens downward, while $b^2 - 4ac < 0$ indicates that the graph has no x-intercepts.

33. $a > 0$, $b^2 - 4ac > 0$

The correct choice is C. $a > 0$ indicates that the parabola opens upward, while $b^2 - 4ac > 0$ indicates that the graph has two x-intercepts.

35. Graph the function $f(x) = x^2 + 2x - 8$.

From the vertex formula, the vertex is $(-1, -9)$ and the axis is $x = -1$. Use a table of values to find points on the graph. From the graph, we see that the x-intercepts are -4 and 2.

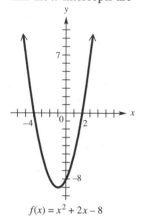

$f(x) = x^2 + 2x - 8$

36. The solution set of the inequality $x^2 + 2x - 8 < 0$ consists of all x-values for which the graph of f

lies below the x-axis. By examining the graph of $f(x) = x^2 + 2x - 8$ from Exercise 35, we see that the graph lies below the x-axis when x is between the -4 and 2. Thus, the solution set is the open interval $(-4, 2)$.

37. Graph $g(x) = -f(x) = -x^2 - 2x + 8$.

The graph of g is obtained by reflecting the graph of f across the x-axis.

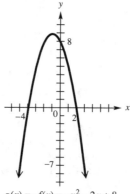

$g(x) = -f(x) = -x^2 - 2x + 8$

38. The solution set of the inequality $-x^2 - 2x - 8 > 0$ consists of all x values for which the graph of g lies above the x-axis. By examining the graph of $g(x) = -x^2 - 2x + 8$ from Exercise 37, we see that the graph lies above the x-axis when x is between -4 and 2. Thus, the solution set is the open interval $(-4, 2)$.

39. The two solution sets are the same, the open interval $(-4, 2)$.

41. The vertex of the parabola in the figure is $(1, 4)$ and the y-intercept is 2. The equation takes the form $f(x) = a(x - 1)^2 + 4$.

When $x = 0$, $f(x) = 2$,

so $2 = a(0 - 1)^2 + 4$

$2 = a + 4$

$a = -2$.

The equation is $f(x) = -2(x - 1)^2 + 4$.

This function may also be written as

$f(x) = -2(x^2 - 2x + 1) + 4$

$= -2x^2 + 4x - 2 + 4$

$f(x) = -2x^2 + 4x + 2$.

Graphing this function on a graphing calculator

shows that the graph matches the equation.

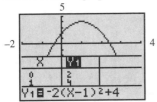

43. The points would lie in a pattern that suggests a parabola opening upward because driving fatality rates are higher for young people and old people and lower for middle-aged people. Therefore, a quadratic function with $a > 0$ would best fit the data.

45. The points would lie in a linear pattern. Therefore, a linear function would best fit the data.

47. Quadratic; the points lie in a pattern that suggests a parabola opening downward, so $a < 0$.

49. Quadratic; the points lie in a pattern suggesting a parabola opening upward, so $a > 0$.

51. The points lie in a linear pattern.

53. $x = 10$ represents 2000
$$f(x) = -.120x^2 + 1.475x + 28.0$$
$$f(10) = -.120(10)^2 + 1.475(10) + 28.0$$
$$f(10) = 30.75$$
The prediction for the percent of births in 2000 is 30.75%.
If we remove the data point for 1994, the graph would be linear and increasing. The data point for 2000, (10, 30.75), would not fit this model. The quadratic model is better because it appears that birth rates are declining after 1994.

55. $f(x) = -.2369x^2 + 1.425x + 6.905$

Maximum at $x = -\dfrac{b}{2a}$
$$x = -\frac{1.425}{2(-.2369)}$$
$$x \approx 3$$
$x = 3$ corresponds to 1995.
The domain of $f(x)$ is [0, 6] because values of x outside of this interval give negative values for the number of students.

57. (a) Plot the 12 points (2, 1563), (3, 4647), … (16, 584,394) on the same calculator screen.

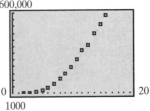

(c) Let the point (2, 1563) be the vertex. Then,
$$f(x) = a(x - 2)^2 + 1563.$$
Next let the point (13, 361,509) lie on the graph of the function.
Solving for a results in
$$f(13) = a(13 - 2)^2 + 1563$$
$$= 361,509$$
$$a = \frac{359,946}{121} \approx 2974.76.$$
Thus, $f(x) = 2974.76(x - 2)^2 + 1563$.
(Other choices will lead to other models.)

(d) Plotting the points together with $f(x)$, we see that there is a relatively good fit.

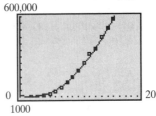

(e) $x = 19$ corresponds to the year 1999, and $x = 20$ corresponds to the year 2000.
$f(19) \approx 861,269$ and $f(20) \approx 965,385$.
In the year 2000, nearly 1 million people will have been diagnosed with AIDS since 1981.

(f) The number of new cases in the year 2000 will be approximately
$$f(20) - f(19) \approx 965,835 - 861,269$$
$$= 104,116.$$

59. $h(x) = -.5x^2 + 1.25x + 3$

(a) Find $h(x)$ when $x = 2$.
$$h(x) = -.5x^2 + 1.25x + 3$$
$$h(2) = -.5(2)^2 + 1.25(2) + 3$$
$$= 3.5.$$
When the distance from the base of the stump was 2 ft, the frog was 3.5 ft high.

(b) Find x when $h(x) = 3.25$.

$$3.25 = -0.5x^2 + 1.25x + 3$$

$$0 = -0.5x^2 + 1.25x - 0.25$$

Multiply by 100 to clear decimals.

$$0 = 50x^2 + 125x - 25$$

Divide by 25.

$$0 = -2x^2 + 5x - 1$$

Use the quadratic formula with $a = -2$, $b = 5$, and $c = -1$.

$$x = \frac{-5 \pm \sqrt{5^2 - 4(-2)(-1)}}{2(-2)}$$

$$= \frac{-5 \pm \sqrt{17}}{-4}$$

$$x = \frac{-5 + \sqrt{17}}{-4}$$

$$\approx .21922 \text{ or } x = \frac{-5 - \sqrt{17}}{-4}$$

$$\approx 2.2808$$

The frog was 3.25 ft above the ground when he was approximately .2 ft from the stump (on the way up) and 2.3 ft from the stump (on the way down).

(c) Since the parabola opens downward, the vertex is the maximum point. Use the vertex formula to find the x-coordinate of the vertex of

$$h(x) = -0.5x^2 + 1.25x + 3.$$

$$x = -\frac{b}{2a} = -\frac{1.25}{2(-0.5)} = 1.25$$

The frog reached its highest point at 1.25 ft from the stump.

(d) The maximum height is the y-coordinate of the vertex.

$$h(x) = -.5x^2 + 1.25x + 3$$

$$y = h(1.25)$$

$$= -.5(1.25)^2 + 1.25(1.25) + 3$$

$$= 3.78125$$

The maximum height reached by the frog was approximately 3.78 ft.

61. (a) $R(x) = (100 - x)(200 + 4x)$

$$= 20,000 + 200x - 4x^2$$

$$= -4x^2 + 200x + 20,000$$

(b)

x	0	10	20	25
$R(x)$	20,000	21,600	22,400	22,500

x	30	40
$R(x)$	22,400	21,600

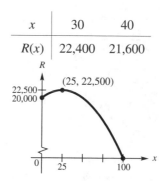

(c) $R = -4(x^2 - 50x) + 20,000$

$$= -4(x^2 - 50x + 2500 - 2500) + 20,000$$

$$= -4(x^2 - 50x + 625) + 20,000 + 2500$$

$$= -4(x - 25)^2 + 22,500$$

The number of unsold seats that will produce the maximum revenue is 25.

(d) The maximum revenue is $22,500.

63. $s(t) = -16t^2 + 80t + 100$

$$= -16(t^2 - 5t) + 100$$

$$= -16(t^2 - 5t + 6.25) + 100 + 100$$

$$= -16(t - 2.5)^2 + 200$$

The vertex of the parabola is $(2.5, 200)$. Since $a = -16 < 0$, this is the maximum point.

(a) The ball will reach its maximum height after 2.5 sec.

(b) The maximum height is 200 ft.

65. Use the formula $s(t) = -16t^2 + v_0 t + s_0$ with $v_0 = 90$ and $s_0 = 0$ (since the rock is thrown from ground level).

$$s(t) = -16t^2 + 90t$$

$$= -16(t^2 - 5.625t)$$

$$= 16(t^2 - 5.625t + 7.91) + 126.5625$$

$$= -16(t - 2.8125)^2 + 126.5625$$

(a) The rock reached a maximum height after 2.8125 sec.

(b) The maximum height reached by the rock was 126.5625 ft.

67. $y = x^2 - 10x + c$

An x-intercept occurs where $y = 0$, or $0 = x^2 - 10x + c$. There will be exactly one x-intercept if this equation has exactly one solution, or if the discriminant is zero.

$$b^2 - 4ac = 0$$

$$(-10)^2 - 4(1)c = 0$$

$$100 = 4c$$

$$c = 25$$

69. x-intercepts 2 and 5, and y-intercept 5
Every quadratic function may be written as

$$f(x) = ax^2 + bx + c.$$

Since the y-intercept is 5, $f(0) = 5$.

$$5 = a(0)^2 + b(0) + c$$

$$c = 5$$

Since 2 and 5 are x-intercepts,
$f(2) = 0$ and $f(5) = 0$. First,

$$0 = a(2)^2 + b(2) + 5 \qquad (1)$$

$$0 = 4a + 2b + 5$$

Then,

$$0 = a(5)^2 + b(5) + 5 \quad (2)$$

$$0 = 25a + 5b + 5$$

$$0 = 5a + b + 1$$

$$-5a - 1 = b.$$

Substitute $-5a - 1$ for b in equation
(1) and solve for a.

$$0 = 4a + 2(-5a - 1) + 5$$

$$0 = 4a - 10a - 2 + 5$$

$$6a = 3$$

$$a = \frac{1}{2}$$

To find the value of b, substitute $\frac{1}{2}$ for a in

equation (2).

$$b = -5\left(\frac{1}{2}\right) - 1$$

$$= -\frac{5}{2} - \frac{2}{2}$$

$$= -\frac{7}{2}.$$

The required quadratic function is

$$f(x) = \frac{1}{2}x^2 - \frac{7}{2}x + 5.$$

71. $y = -(x - 2)^2 + 9$
The graph of this equation is a parabola with
vertex $(2, 9)$ that opens downward. The largest
possible value of y is the value of y at the vertex,
or $y = 9$.

(a) As a number increases, its square root
increases. Since the largest possible value of

$-(x-2)^2 + 9$ is 9, the largest possible value

of $\sqrt{-(x-2)^2 + 9}$ is $\sqrt{9} = 3$.

(b) As a number increases, its reciprocal
decreases. Since the largest possible value of
$-(x-2)^2 + 9$ is 9, the smallest *positive*

value of $\dfrac{1}{-(x-2)^2 + 9}$ is $\dfrac{1}{9}$.

73. Use the distance formula to find the distance
between the points $P(x, 2x)$ and $R(1, 7)$, where P
is any point on the line $y = 2x$.

$$d(P, R)$$

$$= \sqrt{(x_1 - x_2)^2 + (y_1 - y_2)^2}$$

$$= \sqrt{(x - 1)^2 + (2x - 7)^2}$$

$$= \sqrt{(x^2 - 2x + 1) + (4x^2 - 28x + 49)}$$

$$= \sqrt{5x^2 - 30x + 50}$$

Consider the equation $y = 5x^2 - 30x + 50$.
This is the equation of a parabola opening
upward, so the expression $5x^2 - 30x + 50$ has a
minimum value, which is the y-value of the
vertex. Complete the square to find the vertex.

$$y = 5x^2 - 30x + 50$$

$$= 5(x^2 - 6x) + 50$$

$$= 5(x^2 - 6x + 9 - 9) + 50$$

$$= 5(x^2 - 6x + 9) - 45 + 50$$

$$y = 5(x - 3)^2 + 5$$

The vertex is $(3, 5)$ so the minimum value of
$5x^2 - 30x + 50$ is 5 when $x = 3$. Thus, the

minimum value of $\sqrt{5x^2 - 30x + 50}$ is $\sqrt{5}$ when
$x = 3$. The point on the line $y = 2x$ for which $x = 3$
is $(3, 6)$. Thus the closest point on the line $y = 2x$
to the point $(1, 7)$ is the point $(3, 6)$.

75. $f(x) = (x - 5)(x - 9)$ or $f(x) = -(x - 5)(x - 9)$
Any function of the form $f(x) = k(x - 5)(x - 9)$
will do.

77. (a) The years 1977, 1979, and 1981 correspond
to $x = 7$, $x = 9$, and $x = 11$, respectively. The
y-coordinates for 1977, 1979, and 1981 are
$y = 1000$, $y = 965$, and $y = 1000$. The ordered
pairs are $(7, 1000)$, $(9, 965)$, and $(11, 1000)$.

(b)

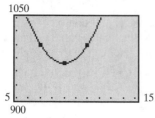

(c) $y = a(x - h)^2 + k$

Since vertex is (9, 965), we have

$y = a(x - 9)^2 + 965$.

To find a, substitute the point (7, 1000) and solve for a.

$1000 = a(7 - 9)^2 + 965$

$1000 = a(-2)^2 + 965$

$1000 = 4a + 965$

$35 = 4a$

$\dfrac{35}{4} = a$

$8.75 = a$

The equation is $y = 8.75(x - 9)^2 + 965$.

(d) For 1981, $x = 11$.

$y = 8.75(11 - 9)^2 + 965$

$= 8.75 \cdot 2^2 + 965 = 1000$

Yes, the equation agrees with the ordered pair.

For 1978, $x = 8$.

$y = 8.75(8 - 9)^2 + 965$

$= 8.75 \cdot (-1)^2 + 965 = 973.75$

For 1980, $x = 10$.

$y = 8.75(10 - 9)^2 + 965$

$= 8.75 \cdot 1^2 + 965 = 973.75$

The values are reasonably close to the actual values.

Section 3.2

Connections (*page 208*)

1. To find $f(-2 + i)$ use synthetic division with

$f(x) = x^3 - 4x^2 + 2x - 29i$

$$
\begin{array}{r|rrrr}
-2+i & 1 & -4 & 2 & -29i \\
 & & -2+i & 11-8i & -18+29i \\
\hline
 & 1 & -6+i & 13-8i & -18
\end{array}
$$

The remainder is -18 so by the remainder theorem $f(-2 + i) = -18$.

2. Use synthetic division to check if i is a zero of

$f(x) = x^3 + 2ix^2 + 2x + i$

$$
\begin{array}{r|rrrr}
i & 1 & 2i & 2 & i \\
 & & i & -3 & -i \\
\hline
 & 1 & 3i & -1 & 0
\end{array}
$$

Since the remainder is 0, $f(i) = 0$ and i is a zero of $f(x)$.

To check $-i$, perform synthetic division

$$
\begin{array}{r|rrrr}
-i & 1 & 2i & 2 & i \\
 & & -i & 1 & -3i \\
\hline
 & 1 & i & 3 & -2i
\end{array}
$$

Since the remainder is $-2i$, $f(-i) = -2i$ and $-i$ is not a zero of $f(x)$.

3. One example is the function $f(x) = x^2 + 1$.

Exercises

1. When the polynomial $f(x)$ is divided by $x - r$, the remainder is $f(r)$. The remainder theorem states if the polynomial $f(x)$ is divided by $x - k$, the remainder is $f(k)$. Therefore, this statement is true.

3. If $x^3 - 1$ is divided by $x + 1$, the remainder is 0.

$\dfrac{x^3 - 1}{x + 1}$

Use $x = -1$ since $x + 1 = x - (-1)$.

$$
\begin{array}{r|rrrr}
-1 & 1 & 0 & 0 & -1 \\
 & & -1 & 1 & -1 \\
\hline
 & 1 & -1 & 1 & -2
\end{array}
$$

The remainder is -2, not 0. Therefore, the statement is false.

5. $\dfrac{x^3 + 4x^2 - 5x + 42}{x + 6}$

$$
\begin{array}{r|rrrr}
-6 & 1 & 4 & -5 & 42 \\
 & & -6 & 1 & -42 \\
\hline
 & 1 & -2 & 7 & 0
\end{array}
$$

Thus,

$\dfrac{x^3 + 4x^2 - 5x + 42}{x + 6} = x^2 - 2x + 7$.

7. $\dfrac{4x^3 - 3x - 2}{x + 1}$

Remember to write 0 for the coefficient of the x^2 term in the synthetic division.

$$-1\overline{)\,4 \quad 0 \quad -3 \quad -2}$$
$$ \quad -4 \quad 4 \quad -1$$
$$\overline{ \,4 \quad -4 \quad 1 \quad -3}$$

Thus,

$$4x^3 - 3x - 2 = 4x^2 - 4x + 1 + \dfrac{-3}{x + 1}.$$

9. $\dfrac{x^4 - 3x^3 - 4x^2 + 12x}{x - 3}$

$$3\overline{)\,1 \quad -3 \quad -4 \quad 12 \quad 0}$$
$$ \quad \;\; 3 \quad \;\; 0 \quad -12 \quad 0$$
$$\overline{ \,1 \quad \;\; 0 \quad -4 \quad \;\; 0 \quad 0}$$

Thus,

$$\dfrac{x^4 - 3x^3 - 4x^2 + 12x}{x - 3} = x^3 - 4x.$$

11. $\dfrac{x^5 + 3x^4 + 2x^3 + 2x^2 + 3x + 1}{x + 2}$

$$-2\overline{)\,1 \quad 3 \quad \;\; 2 \quad 2 \quad \;\; 3 \quad 1}$$
$$ \quad -2 \quad -2 \quad 0 \quad -4 \quad 2$$
$$\overline{ \,1 \quad 1 \quad \;\; 0 \quad 2 \quad -1 \quad 3}$$

Thus,

$$\dfrac{x^5 + 3x^4 + 2x^3 + 2x^2 + 3x + 1}{x + 2}$$
$$= x^4 + x^3 + 2x - 1 + \dfrac{3}{x + 2}.$$

13. $f(x) = 2x^3 + x^2 + x - 8;\ k = -1$

Use synthetic division to write the polynomial in the form $f(x) = (x - k)q(x) + r$.

$$-1\overline{)\,2 \quad 1 \quad 1 \quad -8}$$
$$ \quad -2 \quad 1 \quad -2$$
$$\overline{ \,2 \quad -1 \quad 2 \quad -10}$$

$$f(x) = (x + 1)(2x^2 - x + 2) - 10$$

15. $f(x) = -x^3 + 2x^2 + 4;\ k = -2$

$$-2\overline{)\,-1 \quad 2 \quad \;\; 0 \quad 4}$$
$$ \quad \;\;\;\; 2 \quad -8 \quad 16$$
$$\overline{ \,-1 \quad 4 \quad -8 \quad 20}$$

$$f(x) = (x + 2)(-x^2 + 4x - 8) + 20$$

17. $f(x) = 4x^4 - 3x^3 - 20x^2 - x;\ k = 3$

$$3\overline{)\,4 \quad -3 \quad -20 \quad -1 \quad 0}$$
$$ \quad \;\; 12 \quad \;\; 27 \quad 21 \quad 60$$
$$\overline{ \,4 \quad \;\; 9 \quad \;\;\; 7 \quad 20 \quad 60}$$

$$f(x) = (x - 3)(4x^3 + 9x^2 + 7x + 20) + 60$$

19. $k = 3;\ f(x) = x^2 - 4x + 5$

$$3\overline{)\,1 \quad -4 \quad 5}$$
$$ \quad \;\; 3 \quad -3$$
$$\overline{ \,1 \quad -1 \quad 2}$$

$$f(3) = 2$$

21. $k = 2;\ f(x) = 2x^2 - 3x - 3$

$$2\overline{)\,2 \quad -3 \quad -3}$$
$$ \quad \;\; 4 \quad \;\; 2$$
$$\overline{ \,2 \quad \;\; 1 \quad -1}$$

$$f(2) = -1$$

23. $k = -1;\ f(x) = x^3 - 4x^2 + 2x + 1$

$$-1\overline{)\,1 \quad -4 \quad 2 \quad \;\; 1}$$
$$ \quad \;\; -1 \quad 5 \quad -7$$
$$\overline{ \,1 \quad -5 \quad 7 \quad -6}$$

$$f(-1) = -6$$

25. $k = 3;\ f(x) = 2x^5 - 10x^3 - 19x^2 - 45$

$$3\overline{)\,2 \quad 0 \quad -10 \quad -19 \quad \;\; 0 \quad -45}$$
$$ \quad \;\;\; 6 \quad \;\; 18 \quad \;\; 24 \quad 15 \quad 45$$
$$\overline{ \,2 \quad 6 \quad \;\;\; 8 \quad \;\;\; 5 \quad 15 \quad \;\; 0}$$

$$f(3) = 0$$

27. $k = -8;\ f(x) = x^6 - 7x^5 - 5x^4 + 22x^3 - 16x^2 + x + 19$

$$-8\overline{)\,1 \quad \;\; 7 \quad -5 \quad \;\; 22 \quad -16 \quad 1 \quad 19}$$
$$ \quad \;\; -8 \quad \;\; 8 \quad -24 \quad \;\; 16 \quad 0 \quad -8$$
$$\overline{ \,1 \quad -1 \quad \;\; 3 \quad -2 \quad \;\;\; 0 \quad 1 \quad 11}$$

$$f(-8) = 11$$

29. $k = 2 + i;\ f(x) = x^2 - 5x + 1$

$$2+i\overline{)\,1 \quad -5 \quad \quad\;\; 1}$$
$$ \quad \;\; 2+i \quad -7-i$$
$$\overline{ \,1 \quad -3+i \quad -6-i}$$

$$f(2 + i) = -6 - i$$

31. To determine if 3 is a zero of
$f(x) = 2x^3 - 6x^2 - 9x + 4$, divide synthetically.

$$3\overline{)\,2\quad -6\quad -9\quad\quad 4}$$
$$\underline{\quad\;\; 6\quad\;\; 0\;\; -27}$$
$$\;\; 2\quad\;\; 0\;\; -9\;\; -23$$

No, 3 is not a zero of $f(x)$ because $f(3) = -23$.

33. To determine if -5 is a zero of
$f(x) = x^3 + 7x^2 + 10x$, divide synthetically.

$$-5\overline{)\,1\quad 7\quad 10\quad 0}$$
$$\underline{\;\; -5\;\; -10\;\; 0}$$
$$\;\; 1\quad 2\quad\;\;\; 0\quad 0$$

Yes, -5 is a zero of $f(x)$ because $f(-5) = 0$.

35. To determine if $\dfrac{2}{5}$ is a zero of

$f(x) = 5x^4 + 2x^3 - x + 15$, divide synthetically.

$$\tfrac{2}{5}\overline{)\,5\quad 2\quad 0\quad\;\; -1\quad\quad 15}$$
$$\underline{\phantom{\tfrac{2}{5})}\quad\; 2\quad \tfrac{8}{5}\quad \tfrac{16}{25}\;\; -\tfrac{18}{125}}$$
$$\phantom{\tfrac{2}{5})}\;\; 5\quad 4\quad \tfrac{8}{5}\;\; -\tfrac{9}{25}\quad \tfrac{1857}{125}$$

No, $\dfrac{2}{5}$ is not a zero of $f(x)$ because

$f\!\left(\dfrac{2}{5}\right) = \dfrac{1857}{125}$.

37. To determine if $2 - i$ is a zero of
$f(x) = x^2 + 3x + 4$, divide synthetically.

$$2-i\overline{)\,1\quad\; 3\quad\quad\; 4}$$
$$\underline{\quad 2-i\quad 9-7i}$$
$$\; 1\;\; 5-i\quad 13-7i$$

No, $2 - i$ is not a zero of $f(x)$ because
$f(2 - i) = 13 - 7i$.

39. 1 raised to *any* power is 1.

40. The result from Exercise 39 is 1. If we multiply 1 by a real number, the result is the real number. It is equal to the real number because 1 is the identity element for multiplication.

41. We can evaluate $f(1)$ by adding the coefficients of f.

42. $f(x) = x^3 - 4x^2 + 9x - 6$

$f(1) = (1)^3 - 4(1)^2 + 9(1) - 6$
$\quad\;\; = 1 - 4 + 9 - 6$
$\quad\;\; = 0$

The sum of the coefficients of f is
$1 + (-4) + 9 + (-6) = 0$.
The answers agree.

43. $f(x) = x^3 - 4x^2 + 9x - 6$
$f(-x) = (-x)^3 - 4(-x)^2 + 9(-x) - 6$
$\quad\quad\;\; = -x^3 - 4x^2 - 9x - 6$
$f(-1) = (-1)^3 - 4(-1)^2 + 9(-1) - 6$
$\quad\quad\; = -1 - 4 - 9 - 6$
$\quad\quad\; = -20$

44. $f(-x) = -x^3 - 4x^2 - 9x - 6$
The sum of the coefficients of
$f(-x)$ is $-1 + (-4) + (-9) + (-6) = -20$.
$f(-1) = -20$
They are both -20. Our conjecture is, to find $f(-1)$, add the coefficients of $f(-x)$.

Section 3.3

Connections *(page 217)*

$$x = \sqrt[3]{\frac{n}{2} + \sqrt{\left(\frac{n}{2}\right)^2 + \left(\frac{m}{3}\right)^3}} - \sqrt[3]{\frac{-n}{2} + \sqrt{\left(\frac{n}{2}\right)^2 + \left(\frac{m}{3}\right)^3}}$$

can be used to solve a cubic equation $x^3 + mx = n$.
For $x^3 + 9x = 26$, $m = 9$ and $n = 26$.
Substitute

$$x = \sqrt[3]{\frac{26}{2} + \sqrt{\left(\frac{26}{2}\right)^2 + \left(\frac{9}{3}\right)^3}} - \sqrt[3]{-\frac{26}{2} + \sqrt{\left(\frac{26}{2}\right)^2 + \left(\frac{9}{3}\right)^3}}$$

$$= \sqrt[3]{13 + \sqrt{169 + 27}} - \sqrt[3]{-13 + \sqrt{169 + 27}}$$
$$= \sqrt[3]{13 + 14} - \sqrt[3]{-13 + 14}$$
$$= \sqrt[3]{27} - \sqrt[3]{1}$$
$$= 3 - 1$$
$$= 2$$

Exercises

1. If $x - 1$ is a factor of
$f(x) = x^6 - x^4 + 2x^2 - 2$,
we are assured that $f(1) = 0$.
This statement is justified by the factor theorem; therefore, it is true.

3. For the function
$f(x) = (x + 2)^4 (x - 3)$, 2 is a zero of multiplicity 4. To find the zero, set the factor equal to 0.
$x + 2 = 0$
$\quad\;\; x = -2$
2 is not a zero of the function; therefore, the statement is false. (It would be true to say that -2 is a zero of multiplicity 4.)

5. $4x^2 + 2x + 54;\; x - 4$

Let $f(x) = 4x^2 + 2x + 54$. By the factor theorem, $x - 4$ will be a factor of $f(x)$ only if $f(4) = 0$. Use synthetic division and the remainder theorem.

$$4{\overline{\smash{\big)}\,4\quad 2\quad 54}}$$
$$\underline{16\quad 72}$$
$$4\quad 18\quad 126$$

Since the remainder is 126, $f(4) = 126$, so $x - 4$ is not a factor of $f(x)$.

7. $x^3 + 2x^2 - 3;\ x - 1$

Let $f(x) = x^3 + 2x^2 - 1$. By the factor theorem, $x - 1$ will be a factor of $f(x)$ only if $f(1) = 0$. Use synthetic division and the remainder theorem.

$$1{\overline{\smash{\big)}\,1\quad 2\quad 0\quad -3}}$$
$$\underline{\quad 1\quad 3\quad 3}$$
$$1\quad 3\quad 3\quad 0$$

Since $f(1) = 0$, $x - 1$ is a factor of $f(x)$.

9. $2x^4 + 5x^3 - 2x^2 + 5x + 6;\ x + 3$

Let $f(x) = 2x^4 + 5x^3 - 2x^2 + 5x + 6$. By the factor theorem, $x + 3$ will be a factor of $f(x)$ only if $f(-3) = 0$. Use synthetic division and the remainder theorem.

$$-3{\overline{\smash{\big)}\,2\quad 5\quad -2\quad 5\quad 6}}$$
$$\underline{\quad -6\quad 3\quad -3\quad -6}$$
$$2\quad -1\quad 1\quad 2\quad 0$$

Since $f(-3) = 0$, $x + 3$ is a factor of $f(x)$.

11. $f(x) = 2x^3 - 3x^2 - 17x + 30;\ k = 2$

Since 2 is a zero of $f(x)$, $x - 2$ is a factor.

Divide $f(x)$ by $x - 2$.

$$2{\overline{\smash{\big)}\,2\quad -3\quad -17\quad 30}}$$
$$\underline{\quad 4\quad 2\quad -30}$$
$$2\quad 1\quad -15\quad 0$$

Thus, $f(x) = (x - 2)(2x^2 + x - 15)$
$ = (x - 2)(2x - 5)(x + 3)$.

13. $f(x) = 6x^3 + 13x^2 - 14x + 3;\ k = -3$

Since -3 is a zero of $f(x)$, $x + 3$ is a factor.

Divide $f(x)$ by $x + 3$.

$$-3{\overline{\smash{\big)}\,6\quad 13\quad -14\quad 3}}$$
$$\underline{\quad -18\quad 15\quad -3}$$
$$6\quad -5\quad 1\quad 0$$

Thus, $f(x) = (x + 3)(6x^2 - 5x + 1)$
$ = (x + 3)(3x - 1)(2x - 1)$.

15. $f(x) = x^3 - x^2 - 4x - 6;\ 3$

Since 3 is a zero, first divide $f(x)$ by $x - 3$.

$$3{\overline{\smash{\big)}\,1\quad -1\quad -4\quad -6}}$$
$$\underline{\quad 3\quad 6\quad 6}$$
$$1\quad 2\quad 2\quad 0$$

This gives $f(x) = (x - 3)(x^2 + 2x + 2)$.

Use the quadratic formula with $a = 1$, $b = 2$, and $c = 2$ to find the remaining two zeros.

$$x = \frac{-2 \pm \sqrt{4 - 4(1)(2)}}{2(1)}$$
$$= \frac{-2 \pm \sqrt{-4}}{2} = \frac{-2 \pm 2i}{2}$$
$$= \frac{2(-1 \pm i)}{2} = -1 \pm i$$

The remaining zeros are $-1 \pm i$.

17. $f(x) = 4x^3 + 6x^2 - 2x - 1;\ \dfrac{1}{2}$

Since $\dfrac{1}{2}$ is a zero, first divide $f(x)$ by $x - \dfrac{1}{2}$.

$$\tfrac{1}{2}{\overline{\smash{\big)}\,4\quad 6\quad -2\quad -1}}$$
$$\underline{\phantom{\tfrac{1}{2}}\quad 2\quad 4\quad 1}$$
$$\phantom{\tfrac{1}{2}}4\quad 8\quad 2\quad 0$$

This gives

$$f(x) = \left(x - \frac{1}{2}\right)\!\left(4x^2 + 8x + 2\right)$$
$$= \left(x - \frac{1}{2}\right) \cdot 2(2x^2 + 4x + 1)$$
$$= (2x - 1)(2x^2 + 4x + 1).$$

Use the quadratic formula with $a = 2$, $b = 4$, and $c = 1$ to find the other two zeros.

$$x = \frac{-4 \pm \sqrt{16 - 4(2)(1)}}{2(2)}$$
$$= \frac{-4 \pm \sqrt{8}}{4}$$
$$= \frac{-4 \pm 2\sqrt{2}}{4} = \frac{-2 \pm \sqrt{2}}{2}$$

The remaining zeros are $\dfrac{-2 \pm \sqrt{2}}{2}$.

19. $f(x) = x^4 + 5x^2 + 4;\ -i$

Since $-i$ is a zero, first divide $f(x)$ by $x + i$.

$$-i{\overline{\smash{\big)}\,1\quad 0\quad 5\quad 0\quad 4}}$$
$$\underline{\quad -i\quad -1\quad -4i\quad -4}$$
$$1\quad -i\quad 4\quad -4i\quad 0$$

By the conjugate zeros theorem, i is also a zero, so divide the quotient polynomial from the first synthetic division by $x - i$.

$$i{\overline{\smash{\big)}\,1\quad -i\quad 4\quad -4i}}$$
$$\underline{\quad i\quad 0\quad 4i}$$
$$1\quad 0\quad 4\quad 0$$

The remaining zeros will be zeros of the new quotient polynomial, $x^2 + 4$. Find the remaining zeros by using the square root property.

$$x^2 + 4 = 0$$
$$x^2 = -4$$
$$x = \pm 2i.$$

The other zeros are i and $\pm 2i$.

21. (a) $f(x) = x^3 - 2x^2 - 13x - 10$

p must be a factor of $a_0 = -10$ and q must be a factor of $a_3 = 1$. Thus, p can be $\pm 1, \pm 2, \pm 5, \pm 10$ and q can be ± 1. The possible rational zeros, $\dfrac{p}{q}$, are $\pm 1, \pm 2, \pm 5, \pm 10$.

(b) The remainder theorem shows that -1 is a zero.

$$-1\overline{)1 - 2 - 13 - 10}$$
$$\underline{-1 \quad 3 \quad 10}$$
$$1 - 3 - 10 \quad 0$$

The new quotient polynomial is $x^2 - 3x - 10$. The remainder theorem shows that -2 is a zero.

$$-2\overline{)1 - 3 - 10}$$
$$\underline{-2 \quad 10}$$
$$1 - 5 \quad 0$$

The new quotient polynomial is $x - 5$. The rational zeros are $-1, -2,$ and 5.

(c) Since the three zeros are $-1, -2,$ and 5, the factors are $x + 1, x + 2,$ and $x - 5$.
$$f(x) = (x + 1)(x + 2)(x - 5)$$

23. (a) $f(x) = x^3 + 6x^2 - x - 30$

p must be a factor of $a_0 = -30$ and 2 must be a factor of $a_3 = 1$. Thus, p can be $\pm 1, \pm 2, \pm 3, \pm 5, \pm 6, \pm 10, \pm 15, \pm 30$ and q can be ± 1. The possible zeros, $\dfrac{p}{q}$, are $\pm 1, \pm 2, \pm 3, \pm 5, \pm 6, \pm 10, \pm 15, \pm 30$.

(b) The remainder theorem shows that -5 is a zero.

$$-5\overline{)1 \quad 6 - 1 - 30}$$
$$\underline{-5 - 5 \quad 30}$$
$$1 \quad 1 - 6 \quad 0$$

The new quotient polynomial is $x^2 + x - 6$. The remainder theorem shows that -3 is a zero.

$$-3\overline{)1 \quad 1 - 6}$$
$$\underline{-3 \quad 6}$$
$$1 - 2 \quad 0$$

The new quotient polynomial is $x - 2$. The rational zeros are $-5, -3,$ and 2.

(c) Since the three zeros are $-5, -3,$ and 2, the factors are $x + 5, x + 3,$ and $x - 2$.
$$f(x) = (x + 5)(x + 3)(x - 2)$$

25. (a) $f(x) = 6x^3 + 17x^2 - 31x - 12$

p must be a factor of $a_0 = -12$ and q must be a factor of $a_3 = 6$. Thus, p can be $\pm 1, \pm 2, \pm 3, \pm 4, \pm 6, \pm 12$ and q can be $\pm 1, \pm 2, \pm 3, \pm 6$. The possible zeros, $\dfrac{p}{q}$ are $\pm 1, \pm 2, \pm 3, \pm 4, \pm 6, 12,$
$$\pm \frac{1}{2}, \pm \frac{3}{2}, \pm \frac{1}{3}, \pm \frac{2}{3}, \pm \frac{4}{3}, \pm \frac{1}{6}.$$

(b) The remainder theorem shows that -4 is a zero.

$$-4\overline{)6 \quad 17 \quad -31 \quad -12}$$
$$\underline{-24 \quad 28 \quad 12}$$
$$6 \quad -7 \quad -3 \quad 0$$

The new quotient polynomial is $6x^2 - 7x - 3$.

$$6x^2 - 7x - 3 = 0$$
$$(3x + 1)(2x - 3) = 0$$
$$3x + 1 = 0 \text{ or } 2x - 3 = 0$$
$$x = -\frac{1}{3} \qquad x = \frac{3}{2}$$

The rational zeros are $-4, -\dfrac{1}{3},$ and $\dfrac{3}{2}$.

(c) Since the three zeros are $-4, -\dfrac{1}{3},$ and $\dfrac{3}{2}$, the factors are $x + 4, 3x + 1,$ and $2x - 3$.
$$f(x) = (x + 4)(3x + 1)(2x - 3)$$

27. (a) $f(x) = 12x^3 + 20x^2 - x - 6$

p must be a factor of $a_0 = -6$ and q must be a factor of $a_3 = 12$. Thus, p can be $\pm 1, \pm 2, \pm 3, \pm 6$, and q can be $\pm 1, \pm 2, \pm 3, \pm 4, \pm 6, \pm 12$. The possible zeros, $\dfrac{p}{q}$ are $\pm 1, \pm 2, \pm 3, \pm 6,$
$$\pm \frac{1}{2}, \pm \frac{3}{2}, \pm \frac{1}{3}, \pm \frac{2}{3}, \pm \frac{1}{4}, \pm \frac{3}{4}, \pm \frac{1}{6}, \pm \frac{1}{12}.$$

(b) The remainder theorem shows that $\dfrac{1}{2}$ is a zero.

$$\tfrac{1}{2}\overline{)\;12\quad 20\quad -1\quad -6}$$
$$\phantom{\tfrac{1}{2})12}\;6\quad 13\quad 6$$
$$\overline{12\quad 26\quad 12\quad 0}$$

The new quotient polynomial is
$12x^2 + 26x + 12.$

$12x^2 + 26x + 12 = 0$

$2(6x^2 + 13x + 6) = 0$

$2(2x + 3)(3x + 2) = 0$

$2x + 3 = 0$ or $3x + 2 = 0$

$$x = -\frac{3}{2} \qquad x = -\frac{2}{3}$$

The rational zeros are $\frac{1}{2}$, $-\frac{3}{2}$, and $-\frac{2}{3}$.

(c) Since the three rational zeros are $\frac{1}{2}$, $-\frac{3}{2}$,

and $-\frac{2}{3}$, the factors are $2x - 1$, $2x + 3$, and

$3x + 2$.
$$f(x) = (2x - 1)(2x + 3)(3x + 2)$$

29. $f(x) = 7x^3 + x$

To find the zeros, let $f(x) = 0$ and factor the binomial.

Set each factor equal to zero and solve for x.

$7x^3 + x = 0$ or $7x^2 + 1 = 0$

$x(7x^2 + 1) = 0$ $7x^2 = -1$

$x = 0$ $x^2 = -\dfrac{1}{7}$

$$x = \pm\sqrt{-\frac{1}{7}}$$

$$= \pm\frac{\sqrt{7}}{7}i$$

The zeros are 0 and $\pm\dfrac{\sqrt{7}}{7}i$.

31. $f(x) = 3(x - 2)(x + 3)(x^2 - 1)$

To find the zeros, let $f(x) = 0$.

Set each factor equal to zero and solve for x.

$x - 2 = 0$ or $x + 3 = 0$ or $x^2 - 1 = 0$

$x = 2$ $x = -3$ $x^2 = 1$

$x = \pm 1$

The zeros are 2, -3, 1, and -1.

33. $f(x) = (x^2 + x - 2)^5(x - 1 + \sqrt{3})^2$

To find the zeros, let $f(x) = 0$.

Set each factor equal to zero and solve for x.

$(x^2 + x - 2)^5 = 0$

$x^2 + x - 2 = 0$

$(x + 2)(x - 1) = 0$

$x + 2 = 0$ or $x - 1 = 0$

$x = -2$, multiplicity 5;

$x = 1$, multiplicity 5

$(x - 1 + \sqrt{3})^2 = 0$

$x - 1 + \sqrt{3} = 0$

$x = 1 - \sqrt{3}$, multiplicity 2

The zeros are -2 (multiplicity 5),
1 (multiplicity 5) and $1 - \sqrt{3}$ (multiplicity 2).

In Exercises 35–43, find a polynomial of lowest degree with real coefficients having the given zeros. For each of these exercises, other answers are possible.

35. $3 + i$ and $3 - i$
$$f(x) = [x - (3 + i)][x - (3 - i)]$$
$$= (x - 3 - i)(x - 3 + i)$$
$$= [(x - 3) - i][(x - 3) + i]$$
$$= (x - 3)^2 - (i)^2$$
$$= x^2 - 6x + 9 - i^2$$
$$= x^2 - 6x + 9 + 1$$
$$= x^2 - 6x + 10$$

37. $1 + \sqrt{2}$, $1 - \sqrt{2}$, and 3
$$f(x) = [x - (1 + \sqrt{2})][x - (1 - \sqrt{2})](x - 3)$$
$$= (x - 1 - \sqrt{2})(x - 1 + \sqrt{2})(x - 3)$$
$$= [(x - 1) - \sqrt{2}][(x - 1) + \sqrt{2}](x - 3)$$
$$= [(x - 1)^2 - (\sqrt{2})^2](x - 3)$$
$$= (x^2 - 2x + 1 - 2)(x - 3)$$
$$= (x^2 - 2x - 1)(x - 3)$$
$$= x^3 - 5x^2 + 5x + 3$$

39. $-2 + i$, $-2 - i$, 3, and -3
$$f(x) = [x - (-2 + i)][x - (-2 - i)] \cdot (x - 3)(x + 3)$$
$$= [(x + 2) - i][(x + 2) + i] \cdot (x - 3)(x + 3)$$
$$= [(x + 2)^2 - (i)^2](x - 3)(x + 3)$$
$$= (x^2 + 4x + 4 + 1)(x - 3)(x + 3)$$
$$= (x^2 + 4x + 5)(x^2 - 9)$$
$$= x^4 + 4x^3 - 4x^2 - 36x - 45$$

41. 2 and $3i$

By the conjugate zeros theorem, $-3i$ must also be a zero.
$$f(x) = (x - 2)(x - 3i)[x - (-3i)]$$
$$= (x - 2)(x - 3i)(x + 3i)$$
$$= (x - 2)(x^2 + 9)$$
$$= x^3 - 2x^2 + 9x - 18$$

43. $1 + 2i$, 2 (multiplicity 2).

By the conjugate zeros theorem, $1 - 2i$ must also be a zero.

$$f(x) = (x-2)^2[x-(1+2i)][x-(1-2i)]$$
$$= (x^2 - 4x + 4)[(x-1)-2i][(x-1)+2i]$$
$$= (x^2 - 4x + 4)[(x-1)^2 - (2i)^2]$$
$$= (x^2 - 4x + 4)(x^2 - 2x + 1 + 4)$$
$$= (x^2 - 4x + 4)(x^2 - 2x + 5)$$
$$= x^4 - 6x^3 + 17x^2 - 28x + 20$$

45. Zeros of -3, 1, and 4, $f(2) = 30$

The polynomial function has the form
$f(x) = a(x+3)(x-1)(x-4)$ for some real
number a. To find a, use the fact that $f(2) = 30$.

$$f(2) = a(2+3)(2-1)(2-4) = 30$$
$$a(5)(1)(-2) = 30$$
$$-10a = 30$$
$$a = -3$$

Thus,

$$f(x) = -3(x+3)(x-1)(x-4)$$
$$= -3(x^2 + 2x - 3)(x-4)$$
$$= -3(x^3 - 2x^2 - 11x + 12)$$
$$= -3x^3 + 6x^2 + 33x - 36.$$

47. Zeros of -2, 1, and 0; $f(-1) = -1$

The polynomial function has the form
$f(x) = a(x+2)(x-1)(x-0)$ for some real
number a. To find a, use the fact that $f(-1) = -1$.

$$f(-1) = a(-1+2)(-1-1)(-1-0) = -1$$
$$a(1)(-2)(-1) = -1$$
$$2a = -1$$
$$a = -\frac{1}{2}$$

Thus,

$$f(x) = -\frac{1}{2}(x+2)(x-1)x$$
$$= -\frac{1}{2}(x^2 + x - 2)x$$
$$= -\frac{1}{2}x^3 - \frac{1}{2}x^2 + x.$$

49. Zeros of 5, i, and $-i$; $f(2) = 5$

The polynomial function has the form
$f(x) = a(x-5)(x-i)(x+i)$ for some real number
a. To find a, use the fact that $f(2) = 5$.

$$f(2) = a(2-5)(2-i)(2+i) = 5$$
$$a(-3)(5) = 5$$
$$-15a = 5$$
$$a = -\frac{1}{3}$$

Thus,

$$f(x) = -\frac{1}{3}(x-5)(x-i)(x+i)$$
$$= -\frac{1}{3}(x-5)(x^2 + 1)$$
$$= -\frac{1}{3}(x^3 - 5x^2 + x - 5)$$
$$= -\frac{1}{3}x^3 + \frac{5}{3}x^2 - \frac{1}{3}x + \frac{5}{3}.$$

51. $f(x) = x^3 - 21x - 20$

Find the quotient

$$\frac{x^3 - 21x - 20}{x + 4}$$

$$\begin{array}{r} -4)\overline{1 \quad\ 0 \ -21 \ -20} \\ \underline{-4 \quad 16 \quad 20} \\ 1 \ -4 \ -5 \quad\ \ 0 \end{array}$$

$$g(x) = x^2 - 4x - 5$$

52.

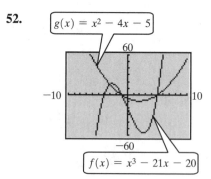

The function g is a quadratic function. The
x-intercepts of g are also x-intercepts of f.

53. $\dfrac{x^2 - 4x - 5}{x - 5}$

$$\begin{array}{r} 5)\overline{1 \ -4 \ -5} \\ \underline{5 \quad\ 5} \\ 1 \quad 1 \quad\ 0 \end{array}$$

$$h(x) = x + 1$$

54.

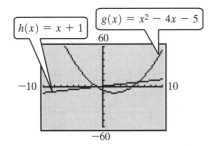

The function h is a linear function. The x-intercept of h is also an x-intercept of g.

55. (a) Let $(3x - 2)(x + 7)(x - 1)^2 = 0$ and solve for x to find x-intercepts.

$3x - 2 = 0$ or $x + 7 = 0$ or $(x - 1)^2 = 0$

$x = \dfrac{2}{3}$ or $x = -7$ or $x = 1$

The x-intercepts are $-7, \dfrac{2}{3}, 1$.

Let $x = 0$ and evaluate to find y-intercept.

$$(3 \cdot 0 - 2)(0 + 7)(0 - 1)^2 = (-2)(7)(-1)^2$$
$$= (-2)(7)(1)$$
$$= -14$$

The y-intercept is -14.

(b) Let $(x + 2)^3(4x + 5)(x - 10) = 0$ and solve for x to find x-intercepts.

$(x + 2)^3 = 0$ or $4x + 5 = 0$ or $x - 10 = 0$

$x = -2$ or $x = -\dfrac{5}{4}$ or $x = 10$

The x-intercepts are $-2, -\dfrac{5}{4}, 10$.

Let $x = 0$ and evaluate to find y-intercept.

$$(0 + 2)^3(4 \cdot 0 + 5)(0 - 10) = 2^3(5)(-10)$$
$$= 8(5)(-10)$$
$$= -400$$

The y-intercept is -400.

57. If -2 is a zero of multiplicity 2, then $f(x) = x^4 + 2x^3 - 7x^2 - 20x - 12$ can be divided by $x + 2$, and the resulting quotient polynomial can be divided by $x + 2$ again. Each time the remainder should be 0. This is demonstrated in the following.

$$
\begin{array}{r|rrrrr}
-2 & 1 & 2 & -7 & -20 & -12 \\
   &   & -2 & 0 & 14 & 12 \\
\hline
   & 1 & 0 & -7 & -6 & 0
\end{array}
$$

Divide the quotient polynomial by $x + 2$.

$$
\begin{array}{r|rrrr}
-2 & 1 & 0 & -7 & -6 \\
   &   & -2 & 4 & 6 \\
\hline
   & 1 & -2 & -3 & 0
\end{array}
$$

Factor the quotient polynomial.

$x^2 - 2x - 3 = (x + 1)(x - 3)$

The remaining zeros are -1 and 3, and $f(x) = (x + 2)^2(x + 1)(x - 3)$.

63. $f(x) = 2.45x^4 - 3.22x^3 + .47x^2 - 6.54x + 3$

Enter this function into the calculator as
$Y_1 = 2.45 * X^\wedge 4 - 3.22 * X^\wedge 3 + .47 * X^\wedge 2$
$\qquad - 6.54 * X + 3.$

Solve $(Y_1, X, 1)$
$\qquad\qquad .44$

Solve $(Y_1, X, 2)$
$\qquad\qquad 1.81$

The real zeros are .44 and 1.81.

65. $f(x) = -\sqrt{7}x^3 + \sqrt{5}x + \sqrt{17}$

Enter this function into the calculator as
$Y_1 = -\sqrt{7} * X^\wedge 3 + \sqrt{5} * X + \sqrt{17}$

Solve $(Y_1, X, 1)$
$\qquad\qquad 1.4$

The only real zero is 1.40.

67. $f(x) = 2x^3 - 4x^2 + 2x + 7$

$f(x)$ has 2 variations in sign. Therefore, f has either 2 or $2 - 2 = 0$ positive real zeros.

$f(-x) = -2x^3 - 4x^2 - 2x + 7$

$f(-x)$ has 1 variation in sign. Therefore, f has 1 negative real zero.

69. $f(x) = 5x^4 + 3x^2 + 2x - 9$

$f(x)$ has 1 variation in sign. Therefore, f has 1 positive real zero.

$f(-x) = 5x^4 + 3x^2 - 2x - 9$

$f(-x)$ has 1 variation in sign. Therefore, f has 1 negative real zero.

71. $f(x) = x^5 + 3x^4 - x^3 + 2x + 3$

$f(x)$ has 2 variations in sign. Therefore, f has 2 or $2 - 2 = 0$ positive real zeros.

$f(-x) = -x^5 + 3x^4 + x^3 - 2x + 3$

$f(-x)$ has 3 variations in sign. Therefore, f has 3 or $3 - 2 = 1$ negative real zeros.

Section 3.4

Exercises

1. $y = x^3 - 3x^2 - 6x + 8$

The range of an odd-degree polynomial is $(-\infty, \infty)$. The y-intercept of the graph is 8. The graph fitting these criteria is A.

3. Since graph C crosses the x-axis at one point the graph has one real zero.

5. A polynomial of degree 3 can have at most 2 turning points. Graphs B and D have more than 2 turning points, so they cannot be graphs of cubic polynomial functions.

7. Since graph B touches the x-axis at –5, the function has 2 real zeros of –5. The two other real zeros are where the graph crosses the x-axis, at 0 and 3.
$$f(x) = x^4 + 7x^3 - 5x^2 - 75x = x(x+5)^2(x-3)$$

9. $f(x) = 2x^4$ is in the form $f(x) = ax^n$.
$|a| = 2 > 1$, so the graph is narrower than $f(x) = x^4$.

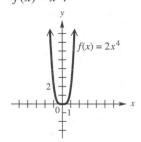

11. $f(x) = -\dfrac{2}{3}x^5$ is in the form $f(x) = ax^n$.

$|a| = \dfrac{2}{3} < 1$, so the graph is broader than that of $f(x) = x^5$.

Since $a = -\dfrac{2}{3}$ is a negative, the graph is the reflection of $f(x) = \dfrac{2}{3}x^5$ about the x-axis.

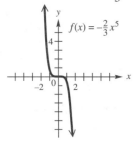

13. $f(x) = \dfrac{1}{2}x^3 + 1$

The graph of $f(x) = \dfrac{1}{2}x^3 + 1$ looks like $y = x^3$ but is broader and is translated 1 unit up. The graph includes the points $(-2, -3)$,

$\left(-1, \dfrac{1}{2}\right)$, $(0, 1)$, $\left(1, \dfrac{3}{2}\right)$, and $(2, 5)$.

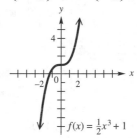

15. $f(x) = -(x+1)^3$
The graph can be obtained by reflecting the graph of $f(x) = x^3$ about the x-axis and then translating it 1 unit to the left.

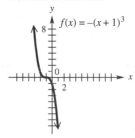

17. $f(x) = (x-1)^4 + 2$
This graph has the same shape as $y = x^4$, but is translated 1 unit to the right and 2 units up.

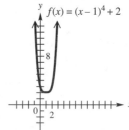

19. C
$f(x) = \dfrac{1}{x}$ does not define a polynomial function since polynomials never have variables in a denominator.

21. $f(x) = 2x(x-3)(x+2)$
First set each of the factors equal to 0 and solve the resulting equations to find the zeros of the function.
$2x = 0$ or $x - 3 = 0$ or $x + 2 = 0$
  $x = 0$ or $x = 3$ or $x = -2$
The three zeros, 0, 3, and –2, divide the x-axis into four regions. Test a point in each region to find the sign of $f(x)$ in that region.

Region	Test Point	Value of $f(x)$	Sign of $f(x)$
$(-\infty, -2)$	-3	-36	Negative
$(-2, 0)$	-1	8	Positive
$(0, 3)$	1	-12	Negative
$(3, \infty)$	4	48	Positive

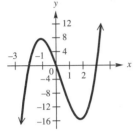

$f(x) = 2x(x-3)(x+2)$

23. $f(x) = x^2(x-2)(x+3)^2$

First set each of the factors equal to 0 and solve the resulting equations to find the zeros of the function.

$x^2 = 0$ or $x - 2 = 0$ or $x + 3 = 0$

$x = 0$ $x = 2$ $x = -3$

The zeros are 0, 2, and -3, which divide the x-axis into four regions. Test a point in each region to find the sign of $f(x)$ in that region.

Region	Test Point	Value of $f(x)$	Sign of $f(x)$
$(-\infty, -3)$	-4	-96	Negative
$(-3, 0)$	-1	-12	Negative
$(0, 2)$	1	-16	Negative
$(2, \infty)$	3	324	Positive

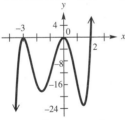

$f(x) = x^2(x-2)(x+3)^2$

25. $f(x) = (3x-1)(x+2)^2$

First set each of the factors equal to 0 and solve the resulting equations to find the zeros of the function.

$3x - 1 = 0$ or $x + 2 = 0$

$x = \dfrac{1}{3}$ $x = -2$

The zeros are $\dfrac{1}{3}$ and -2, which divide the x-axis into three regions. Test a point in each region to find the sign of $f(x)$ in that region.

Region	Test Point	Value of $f(x)$	Sign of $f(x)$
$(-\infty, -2)$	-3	-10	Negative
$\left(-2, \dfrac{1}{3}\right)$	0	-4	Negative
$\left(\dfrac{1}{3}, \infty\right)$	1	18	Positive

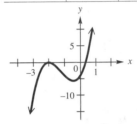

$f(x) = (3x-1)(x+2)^2$

27. $f(x) = x^3 + 5x^2 - x - 5$

$= x^2(x+5) - 1(x+5)$

$= (x+5)(x^2 - 1)$

$= (x+5)(x+1)(x-1)$

First set each of the factors equal to 0 and solve the resulting equations to find the zeros of the function.

$x + 5 = 0$ or $x + 1 = 0$ or $x - 1 = 0$

$x = -5$ $x = -1$ $x = 1$

The zeros are -5, -1, and 1, which divide the x-axis into four regions. Test a point in each region to find the sign of $f(x)$ in that region.

Region	Test Point	Value of $f(x)$	Sign of $f(x)$
$(-\infty, -5)$	-6	-35	Negative
$(-5, -1)$	-2	9	Positive
$(-1, 1)$	0	-5	Negative
$(1, \infty)$	2	21	Positive

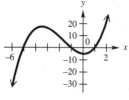

$$f(x) = x^3 + 5x^2 - x - 5$$

29. | $f(x) = 2x(x - 3)(x + 2)$ |

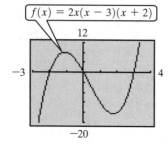

The graph from Exercise 21 is the same as this one.

31. | $f(x) = (3x - 1)(x + 2)^2$ |

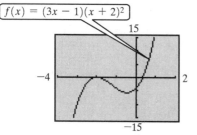

The graph from Exercise 25 is the same as this one.

33. $f(x) = 2x^2 - 7x + 4$; 2 and 3

Use synthetic division to find $f(2)$ and $f(3)$.

```
2)2  -7   4
       4  -6
   ───────────
   2  -3  -2
3)2  -7   4
       6  -3
   ───────────
   2  -1   1
```

Since $f(2) = -2$ is negative and $f(3) = 1$ is positive, there is a zero between 2 and 3.

35. $f(x) = 2x^3 - 5x^2 - 5x + 7$; 0 and 1

Use synthetic division to find $f(0)$ and $f(1)$.

```
0)2  -5  -5   7
      0   0   0
  ──────────────
  2  -5  -5   7
1)2  -5  -5   7
      2  -3  -8
  ──────────────
  2  -3  -8  -1
```

Since $f(0) = 7$ is positive and $f(1) = -1$ is negative, there is a zero between 0 and 1.

37. $f(x) = 2x^4 - 4x^2 + 4x - 8$; 1 and 2

Use synthetic division to find $f(1)$ and $f(2)$.

```
1)2   0  -4   4  -8
      2   2  -2   2
  ───────────────────
  2   2  -2   2  -6
2)2   0  -4   4  -8
      4   8   8  24
  ───────────────────
  2   4   4  12  16
```

Since $f(1) = -6$ is negative and $f(2) = 16$ is positive, there is a zero between 1 and 2.

39. The graph shows that the zeros are -6, 2, and 5. The polynomial function has the form
$$f(x) = a(x + 6)(x - 2)(x - 5).$$
Since $(0, 30)$ is on the graph, $f(0) = 30$.
$$f(0) = a(0 + 6)(0 - 2)(0 - 5)$$
$$30 = 60a$$
$$\frac{1}{2} = a$$
$$a = .5$$
A cubic polynomial that has the graph shown is
$$f(x) = .5(x + 6)(x - 2)(x - 5).$$

45. $f(x) = 2x^2 - 7x + 4$

Enter $f(x)$ as Y_1; then use the "solver" feature.
Solve $(Y_1, X, 2)$
                2.7807764
The real zero between 2 and 3 is approximately 2.7807764.

47. $f(x) = 2x^3 - 9x^2 + x + 20$

Enter $f(x)$ as Y_1; then use the "solver" feature.
Solve $(Y_1, X, 2)$
                2.1933250
The real zero between 2 and 2.5 is approximately 2.1933250.

49. $f(x) = x^3 + 3x^2 - 2x - 6$

The highest degree term is x^3, so the graph will have end behavior similar to the graph of $f(x) = x^3$, which is downward at the left and upward at the right. There is at least one real zero because the polynomial is of odd degree. There are at most three real zeros because the polynomial is third-degree. A graphing calculator can be used to approximate each zero.

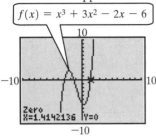

The graph shows that the positive zero is approximately 1.4. Similarly, the other zeros are found to be –3.0 and –1.4.

51. $f(x) = -2x^4 - x^2 + x + 5$

The highest degree term is $-2x^4$ so the graph will have the same end behavior as the graph of $f(x) = -x^4$, which is downward at both the left and the right. Since $f(0) = 5 > 0$, the end behavior and the intermediate value theorem tell us that there must be at least one zero on each side of the y-axis, that is, at least one negative and one positive zero. A graphing calculator can be used to approximate each zero.

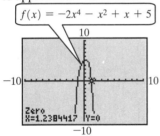

The graph shows that the only positive zero is approximately 1.2. Similarly, the other zero is found to be –1.1.

55.

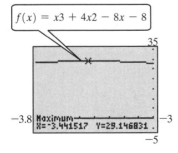

The turning point is (–3.44, 26.15).

57.

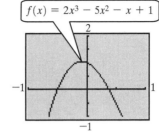

The turning point is (–.09, 1.05).

59.

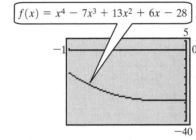

The turning point is (–.20, –28.62).

61. (a) Using $x = t$, graph

$f(t) = .0028t^3 - .011t^2 + .23t + .93$ and

$g(t) = 30$ on the same calculator screen.

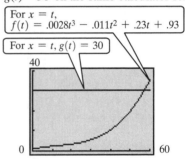

(b) The graphs intersect at $t \approx 56.9$. Since $t = 0$ corresponds to 1930, this would be during 1986.

(c) Because the data consisted of one function value for each year the domain is {1930, 1931, ..., 1990}.

63. $g(x) = -.066x^4 + .14x^3 - .05x^2 + .02x$

(a)

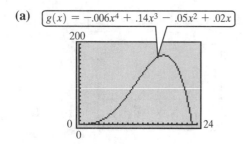

$$g(x) = -.006x^4 + .14x^3 - .05x^2 + .02x$$

(b) By using "maximum" in th CALC menu, we find that the greatest concentration is at 17.3 hours.

(c) Graph $h(x) = 100$ on the same screen as the graph of $g(x)$. We want to determine the values of x for which $g(x) > h(x)$.
Using "intersect" in the CALC menu, we find that the graphs intersect at $x \approx 11.4$ and $x \approx 21.2$. From the graph, we see that the graph of $g(x)$ is above the graph of $h(x)$ between the intersection points. Therefore, the river is polluted from 11.4 to 21.2 hours.

65. (a)   **(i)** $f(x) = .2(x - 1990)^2 + 12.6$
(ii) $f(x) = .55(x - 1990) + 12.6$
(iii) $f(x) = 1.1\sqrt{x - 1990} + 12.6$

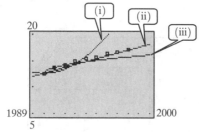

(b) All three approximate the data up to 1994, but only function (ii), the linear function, approximates the data for 1995 – 2000.

67. $f(x) = .05\overline{3}x - .04\overline{3}$

(a) Let $x = 10$.
$f(10) = .05\overline{3}(10) - .04\overline{3}$
$\qquad = .49$
Assuming the function continues to model the situation, 49% of the patients will have AIDS after 10 years.

(b) Let $f(x) = .5$.
$.5 = .05\overline{3}x - .043$
$x \approx 10.2$
After approximately 10.2 years half the patients will have AIDS.

69. (a) If the length of a pendulum increases, so does the period of oscillation, T.

(c) $k = \dfrac{L}{T^n}$ $k = \dfrac{L}{T^n}$

$k = \dfrac{1.0}{1.11^n}$ $k = \dfrac{2.0}{1.57^n}$

Try different values of n.

For $n = 2$, $k = \dfrac{1.0}{1.11^2} \approx .81$

and $k = \dfrac{2.0}{1.57^2} \approx .81$.

When $n = 2$, k is constant. $k \approx .81$

(d) $k \approx .81$, $n = 2$, $L = 5$
$5 = .81T^2$
$6.1728 = T^2$
$\quad T \approx 2.48$
For a pendulum with length 5 ft, the value of T is 2.48 sec.

(e) If $L = 2L$, then $2L = kT^2$

$$\sqrt{\frac{2L}{k}} = T.$$

T increases by a factor of $\sqrt{2} \approx 1.414$.

71. (a) Let $x =$ the length;
$20 - 2x =$ the width.
Both length and width must be positive, so
$x > 0$ and $20 - 2x > 0$
$\qquad\qquad\quad -2x > -20$
$\qquad\qquad\qquad x < 10$.
The restrictions on x are given by the inequality $0 < x < 10$.

(b) $A(x) = x(20 - 2x)$
or $A(x) = -2x^2 + 20x$

(c) The x-value of the vertex of the graph of this quadratic function is the maximum value of x.
Use the vertex formula with $a = -2$ and $b = 20$.
$x = \dfrac{-b}{2a}$
$\quad = \dfrac{-20}{2(-2)}$
$\quad = 5$
The y-value of the vertex gives the maximum area.

$$A(x) = -2x^2 + 20x$$
$$A(5) = -2(5)^2 + 20(5)$$
$$= 50$$

The maximum cross-sectional area is 50 sq in.

(d) We must solve the quadratic inequality
$$-2x^2 + 20x < 40$$
or $-2x^2 + 20x - 40 < 0.$
Solve the corresponding quadratic equation
$$-2x^2 + 20x - 40 = 0$$
or $x^2 - 10x + 20 = 0.$
Use the quadratic formula with $a = 1$, $b = -10$, and $c = 20$.
$$x = \frac{10 \pm \sqrt{10^2 - 4(20)}}{2}$$
$$\approx \frac{10 \pm 4.47}{2}$$
$$x \approx 2.76 \quad \text{or} \quad x \approx 7.24$$

The values 2.76 and 7.24 divide the number line into three intervals: $(-\infty, 2.76)$ and $(2.76, 7.24)$, and $(7.24, \infty)$. However, in part (a), we saw that in this problem x is restricted to $0 < x < 10$, that is, the open interval $(0, 10)$. Therefore, we need to consider the intervals $(0, 2.76)$, $(2.76, 7.24)$, and $(7.24, 10)$. Use a test point in each interval to determine where the expression $-2x^2 + 20x - 40$ is negative. We find that it is negative in the intervals $(0, 2.76)$ and $(7.24, 10)$. Therefore, the area of a cross section will be less than 40 square inches when x is between 0 and 2.76 or between 7.24 and 10.

73. Let $x = $ the length of the hypotenuse.

(a) length of the leg $= x - 1$. The domain is $x - 1 > 0$ or $x > 1$: $(1, \infty)$.

(b) By the Pythagorean theorem,
$$a^2 + b^2 = c^2$$
$$a^2 + (x-1)^2 = x^2$$
$$a^2 = x^2 - (x-1)^2$$
$$a = \sqrt{x^2 - (x-1)^2}$$
length of other leg $= \sqrt{x^2 - (x-1)^2}$

(c) $A = \dfrac{1}{2}bh$
$$84 = \frac{1}{2}(x-1)\left(\sqrt{x^2 - (x-1)^2}\right)$$
Multiply by 2.
$$168 = (x-1)\left(\sqrt{x^2 - (x-1)^2}\right)$$
Square both sides.
$$28,224 = (x-1)^2\left[x^2 - (x-1)^2\right]$$
$$28,224 = (x^2 - 2x + 1)\cdot\left[x^2 - (x^2 - 2x + 1)\right]$$
$$28,224 = (x^2 - 2x + 1)(2x - 1)$$
$$28,224 = 2x^3 - 5x^2 + 4x - 1$$
$$2x^3 - 5x^2 + 4x - 28,225 = 0$$

(d) Solving this cubic equation graphically, we obtain $x = 25$. If $x = 25$, $x - 1 = 24$, and
$$\sqrt{x^2 - (x-1)^2} = \sqrt{625 - 576} = \sqrt{49} = 7.$$
The hypotenuse is 25 inches; the legs are 24 inches and 7 inches.

75. (a)

x	0	15	21	29
y	40	49	51	57

Using a calculator, the quadratic model is:
$$f(x) = .0018x^2 + .5218x + 40.09$$

(b) Using a calculator, the cubic polynomial model is:
$$f(x) = .0015x^3 - .0654x^2 + 1.252x + 40.00$$

(c)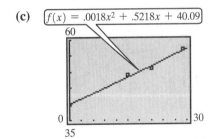

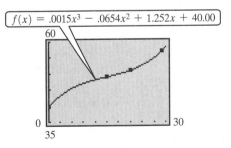

(d) The cubic polynomial model is closest to all four points, although both give reasonable approximations of the data.

77. (a) The maximum value is approximately 1000 which occurred in 1966 and in 1969. The minimum value is approximately 600 which occurred in 1962.

(b) Domain: [61.167, 70]; Range [600, 1000]

Section 3.5

Exercises

1. Graphs A, B, and C have a domain of $(-\infty, 3) \cup (3, \infty)$.

3. Graph A has a range of $(-\infty, 0) \cup (0, \infty)$.

5. Graph A has a single solution to the equation $f(x) = 3$.

7. Graphs A, C, and D have the x-axis as a horizontal asymptote.

9. $f(x) = \dfrac{2}{x}$

Since $\dfrac{2}{x} = 2 \cdot \dfrac{1}{x}$, the graph o $fx = \dfrac{2}{x}$ will be similar to the graph o $f(x) = \dfrac{1}{x}$, except that each point will be twice as far from the x-axis. Just as with the graph of $f(x) = \dfrac{1}{x}$, $y = 0$ is the horizontal asymptote and $x = 0$ is the vertical asymptote.

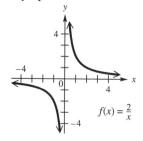

$f(x) = \dfrac{2}{x}$

11. $f(x) = \dfrac{1}{x+2}$

Since $\dfrac{1}{x+2} = \dfrac{1}{x-(-2)}$, the graph of $f(x) = \dfrac{1}{x+2}$ will be similar to the graph of $f(x) = \dfrac{1}{x}$, except that each point will be translated 2 units to the left. Just as with $f(x) = \dfrac{1}{x}$, $y = 0$ is the horizontal asymptote, but

this graph has $x = -2$ as its vertical asymptote.

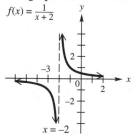

$f(x) = \dfrac{1}{x+2}$

13. $f(x) = \dfrac{1}{x} + 1$

The graph of this function will be similar to the graph of $f(x) = \dfrac{1}{x}$, except that each point will be translated 1 unit upward. Just as with $f(x) = \dfrac{1}{x}$, $x = 0$ is the vertical asymptote, but this graph has $y = 1$ as its horizontal asymptote.

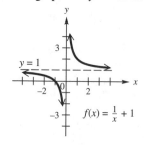

$f(x) = \dfrac{1}{x} + 1$

15. $f(x) = \dfrac{3}{x-5}$

To find the vertical asymptote, set the denominator equal to zero.

$x - 5 = 0$

$x = 5$

The equation of the vertical asymptote is $x = 5$. To find the horizontal asymptote, divide each term by the largest power of x in the expression.

$$f(x) = \dfrac{\frac{3}{x}}{\frac{x}{x} - \frac{5}{x}} = \dfrac{\frac{3}{x}}{1 - \frac{5}{x}}$$

As $|x| \to \infty$, $\dfrac{1}{x}$ approaches 0, $f(x)$ approaches $\dfrac{0}{1-0} = 0$, so the equation of the horizontal asymptote is $y = 0$.

17. $f(x) = \dfrac{4 - 3x}{2x + 1}$

To find the vertical asymptote, set the denominator equal to zero.

$2x + 1 = 0$

$x = -\dfrac{1}{2}$

The equation of the vertical asymptote is

$x = -\dfrac{1}{2}.$

To find the horizontal asymptote, divide each term by the largest power of x in the expression.

$$f(x) = \dfrac{\frac{4}{x} - \frac{3x}{x}}{\frac{2x}{x} + \frac{1}{x}} = \dfrac{\frac{4}{x} - 3}{2 + \frac{1}{x}}$$

As $|x| \to \infty$, $\dfrac{1}{x}$ approaches 0, so $f(x)$ approaches

$\dfrac{0-3}{2+0} = -\dfrac{3}{2}$. The equation of the horizontal

asymptote is $y = -\dfrac{3}{2}$.

19. $f(x) = \dfrac{x^2 - 1}{x + 3}$

The vertical asymptote is $x = -3$, found by solving $x + 3 = 0$. Since the numerator is of degree exactly one more than the denominator, there is no horizontal asymptote, but there may be an oblique asymptote. To find it, divide the numerator by the denominator and disregard any remainder.

$$-3\overline{)\begin{array}{rrr} 1 & 0 & -1 \\ & -3 & 9 \\ \hline 1 & -3 & 8 \end{array}}$$

Thus, $f(x) = \dfrac{x^2 - 1}{x + 3} = x - 3 + \dfrac{8}{x + 3}$.

The oblique asymptote is the line $y = x - 3$.

21. $f(x) = \dfrac{(x-3)(x+1)}{(x+2)(2x-5)}$

The vertical asymptotes are $x = -2$ and $x = \dfrac{5}{2}$,

since these values make the denominator equal to 0.

Multiply the factors in the numerator and

denominator to get $f(x) = \dfrac{x^2 - 2x - 3}{2x^2 - x - 10}$.

Thus, the horizontal asymptote, found by dividing

the numerator and denominator by x^2, is $y = \dfrac{1}{2}$.

23. (a) Translating $y = \dfrac{1}{x}$ three units to the right

gives $y = \dfrac{1}{x-3}$.

Translating $y = \dfrac{1}{x-3}$ two units up yields

$$y = \dfrac{1}{x-3} + 2 = \dfrac{1}{x-3} + \dfrac{2x-6}{x-3} = \dfrac{2x-5}{x-3}$$

So $f(x) = \dfrac{2x-5}{x-3}$.

(b) $f(x) = \dfrac{2x-5}{x-3}$ has a zero when $2x - 5 = 0$

or $x = \dfrac{5}{2}$.

(c) $f(x) = \dfrac{2x-5}{x-3}$ has a horizontal asymptote at $y = 2$ and a vertical asymptote at $x = 3$.

25. (a) $f(x) = \dfrac{1}{(x-2)^2}$

Notice that no matter what value x takes on $(x \neq 2)$, $(x-2)^2$ will be greater than zero. That means $f(x) > 0$, which is graph C.

(b) $f(x) = \dfrac{1}{x-2}$

Notice if $x > 2$, $f(x) > 0$. If $x < 2$, $x - 2 < 0$, and $f(x) < 0$. This is graph A.

(c) $f(x) = \dfrac{-1}{x-2}$

Notice if $x > 2$, $f(x) < 0$. If $x < 2$, $f(x) > 0$. This is graph B.

(d) $f(x) = \dfrac{-1}{(x-2)^2}$

Notice that no matter what value x takes on $(x \neq 2)$, $(x-2)^2$ will be greater than zero. Thus, $f(x) < 0$. This is graph D.

27. $f(x) = \dfrac{x+1}{x-4}$

The graph has a vertical asymptote where $x - 4 = 0$.

$x - 4 = 0$

$x = 4$

Since the degree of the numerator equals the degree of the denominator, the graph has a

horizontal asymptote at $y = \dfrac{1}{1} = 1$.

The y-intercept is $f(0) = -\dfrac{1}{4}$.

Any x-intercepts are found by solving $f(x) = 0$.

$$\frac{x+1}{x-4} = 0$$

$$x + 1 = 0$$

$$x = -1$$

The only x-intercept is -1. Find some additional points.

x	-3	-2	1	3	5	7
y	$\frac{2}{7}$	$\frac{1}{6}$	$-\frac{2}{3}$	-4	7	$\frac{8}{3}$

Use the asymptotes, intercepts, and these points to sketch the graph.

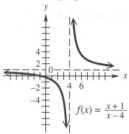

$f(x) = \frac{x+1}{x-4}$

29. $f(x) = \dfrac{3x}{(x+1)(x-2)}$

The graph has vertical asymptotes when $(x+1)(x-2) = 0$, that is, when $x = -1$ and $x = 2$. Since the degree of the numerator is less than the degree of the denominator, the graph has a horizontal asymptote at $y = 0$ (the x-axis). The y-intercept is 0. The only x-intercept is also 0. Find some additional points.

x	-3	-2	$-\frac{1}{2}$	$\frac{1}{2}$	1	3	4
y	$-\frac{9}{10}$	$-\frac{3}{2}$	$\frac{6}{5}$	$-\frac{2}{3}$	$-\frac{3}{2}$	$\frac{9}{4}$	$\frac{6}{5}$

Sketch the graph.

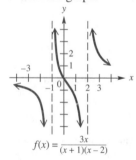

$f(x) = \frac{3x}{(x+1)(x-2)}$

31. $f(x) = \dfrac{5x}{x^2 - 1}$

The graph has vertical asymptotes where $x^2 - 1 = 0$.

$$x^2 - 1 = 0$$

$$(x+1)(x-1) = 0$$

$$x + 1 = 0 \quad \text{or} \quad x - 1 = 0$$

$$x = -1 \quad \text{or} \quad x = 1$$

Since the degree of the numerator is less than the degree of the denominator, the graph has a horizontal asymptote at $y = 0$ (the x-axis). The y-intercept is 0. The only x-intercept is also 0. Find some additional points.

x	-3	-2	$-\frac{1}{2}$	$\frac{1}{2}$	2	3
y	$-\frac{15}{8}$	$-\frac{10}{3}$	$\frac{10}{3}$	$-\frac{10}{3}$	$\frac{10}{3}$	$\frac{15}{8}$

Sketch the graph.

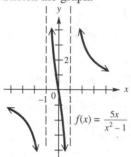

$f(x) = \frac{5x}{x^2 - 1}$

33. $f(x) = \dfrac{(x-3)(x+1)}{(x-1)^2}$

The graph has a vertical asymptote where $(x-1)^2 = 0$.

$$(x-1)^2 = 0$$

$$x - 1 = 0$$

$$x = 1$$

Since the degree of the numerator is the same as the degree of the denominator

$$\left(f(x) = \frac{x^2 - 2x - 3}{x^2 - 2x + 1} \right),$$

the graph has a horizontal asymptote at $y = \dfrac{1}{1} = 1$.

$f(0) = \dfrac{(0-3)(0+1)}{(0-1)^2} = \dfrac{-3}{1} = -3$, so the y-intercept is -3.

The numerator $(x-3)(x+1) = 0$ when $x = 3$ or $x = -1$, so the x-intercepts are 3 and -1.

Using the asymptotes, the intercepts, and a few additional points, we sketch the graph.

x	-2	-1	0	2	3	4
y	$\frac{5}{9}$	0	-3	-3	0	$\frac{5}{9}$

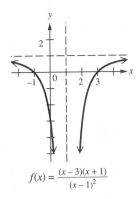

$$f(x) = \frac{(x-3)(x+1)}{(x-1)^2}$$

35. $f(x) = \dfrac{x}{x^2 - 9}$

The graph has a vertical asymptote where $x^2 - 9 = 0$.
$$x^2 - 9 = 0$$
$$(x+3)(x-3) = 0$$
$$x + 3 = 0 \quad \text{or} \quad x - 3 = 0$$
$$x = -3 \quad \text{or} \quad x = 3$$

Since the degree of the numerator is less than the degree of the denominator, the graph has a horizontal asymptote at $y = 0$ (the x-axis). The y-intercept is 0 and the only x-intercept is also zero. Use the asymptotes, the intercepts, and some additional points to sketch the graph.

x	-5	-4	-2	-1	1	2	4	5
y	$-\frac{5}{16}$	$-\frac{4}{7}$	$\frac{2}{5}$	$\frac{1}{8}$	$-\frac{1}{8}$	$-\frac{2}{5}$	$\frac{4}{7}$	$\frac{5}{16}$

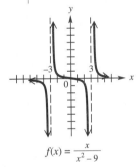

$$f(x) = \frac{x}{x^2 - 9}$$

37. $f(x) = \dfrac{x^2 + 2x}{2x - 1}$

$f(x)$ has a vertical asymptote where $2x - 1 = 0$.
$$2x - 1 = 0$$
$$2x = 1$$
$$x = \frac{1}{2}$$

Since the degree of the numerator is one more than the degree of the denominator, $f(x)$ has an oblique asymptote. Divide $x^2 + 2x$ by $2x - 1$.

$$
\begin{array}{r}
\frac{1}{2}x + \frac{5}{4} \\
2x - 1 \overline{)\, x^2 + 2x } \\
\underline{x^2 - \frac{1}{2}x } \\
\frac{5}{2}x \\
\underline{\frac{5}{2}x - \frac{5}{4}} \\
\frac{5}{4}
\end{array}
$$

$$f(x) = \frac{x^2 + 2x}{2x - 1} = \frac{1}{2}x + \frac{5}{4} + \frac{\frac{5}{4}}{2x - 1}$$

The oblique asymptote is $y = \dfrac{1}{2}x + \dfrac{5}{4}$.

If $x = 0$, $f(x) = 0$, so the y-intercept is 0.

The numerator, $x^2 + 2x$, is equal to 0 when $x = 0$ or $x = -2$. Thus, the graph has two x-intercepts, 0 and -2.

Use asymptotes, the intercepts, and a few additional points to sketch the graph.

x	-2	-1	0	1	2	3	4
y	0	$\frac{1}{3}$	0	3	$\frac{8}{3}$	3	$3\frac{3}{7}$

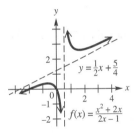

$$y = \frac{1}{2}x + \frac{5}{4}$$
$$f(x) = \frac{x^2 + 2x}{2x - 1}$$

39. $f(x) = \dfrac{x^2 - 9}{x + 3}$

Since $x^2 - 9 = (x + 3)(x - 3)$,
$$f(x) = \frac{(x + 3)(x - 3)}{x + 3}$$
$$= x - 3 \quad (x \neq -3).$$

The graph of this function will be the same as the graph of $y = x - 3$ (a straight line), with the exception of the point with x-value -3. A "hole" appears in the graph at $(-3, -6)$.

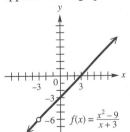

$$f(x) = \frac{x^2 - 9}{x + 3}$$

41. The graph has a vertical asymptote, $x = 2$, so $x - 2$ is the denominator of the function. There is a "hole" in the graph at $x = -2$, so $x + 2$ is in the denominator and numerator also. The x-intercept is 3, so that when $f(x) = 0$, $x = 3$. This condition exists if $x - 3$ is a factor of the numerator. Putting these conditions together, we have a possible function
$$f(x) = \frac{(x-3)(x+2)}{(x-2)(x+2)}$$
or $f(x) = \dfrac{x^2 - x - 6}{x^2 - 4}$.

43. The graph has vertical asymptotes at $x = 4$ and $x = 0$, so $x - 4$ and x are factors in the denominator of the function. The only x-intercept is 2, so that when $f(x) = 0$, $x = 2$. This condition exists if $x - 2$ is a factor of the numerator. The graph has a horizontal asymptote $y = 0$, so the degree of the denominator is larger than the degree of the numerator.
Putting these conditions together, we have a possible function
$$f(x) = \frac{x-2}{x(x-4)} \text{ or } f(x) = \frac{x-2}{x^2 - 4x}.$$

45. Several answers are possible. One answer is
$$f(x) = \frac{(x-3)(x+1)}{(x-1)^2}.$$

47.

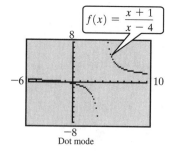

Dot mode

This graph resembles the hand-drawn graph for the same function in Exercise 27, but the calculator graph does not show the asymptotes.

49.

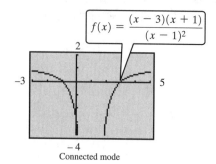

Connected mode

This graph resembles the hand-drawn graph for the same function in Exercise 33, but the calculator graph does not show the asymptotes.

53. (a) The domain of x is $x > 1$.

(b) The vertical asymptote of $P(x) = \dfrac{x-1}{x}$ is found by dividing each term by the largest power of x.
$$P(x) = \frac{\frac{x}{x} - \frac{1}{x}}{\frac{x}{x}} = \frac{1 - \frac{1}{x}}{1}$$
As $|x| \to \infty$, $\dfrac{1}{x}$ approaches 0, so $P(x)$ approaches $\dfrac{1-0}{1} = 1$.
As x increases, the value of $P(x)$ approaches 1.

55. (a) Graph
$$y = d(x) = \frac{8710x^2 - 69,400x + 470,000}{1.08x^2 - 324x + 82,200}$$
and $y = 300$ on the same calculator screen. The graphs intersect when $x \approx 52.1$ miles per hour.

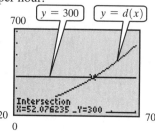

(b)

x	$d(x)$
20	34
25	56
30	85
35	121
40	164
45	215
50	273
55	340
60	415
65	499
70	591

57. **(a)** $R(x) = \dfrac{80x - 8000}{x - 110}$

(i) If $x = 55$,
$$R(x) = \frac{80(55) - 8000}{55 - 110}$$
$$\approx \$65.5 \text{ tens of millions.}$$

(ii) If $x = 60$,
$$R(x) = \frac{80(60) - 8000}{60 - 110}$$
$$= \$64 \text{ tens of millions.}$$

(iii) If $x = 70$,
$$R(x) = \frac{80(70) - 8000}{70 - 110}$$
$$= \$60 \text{ tens of millions.}$$

(iv) If $x = 90$,
$$R(x) = \frac{80(90) - 8000}{90 - 110}$$
$$= \$40 \text{ tens of millions.}$$

(v) If $x = 100$,
$$R(x) = \frac{80(100) - 8000}{100 - 110}$$
$$= \$0.$$

(vi)

$R(x) = \dfrac{80x - 8000}{x - 110}$

(b) $R(x) = \dfrac{60x - 6000}{x - 120}$

(i) If $x = 50$,
$$R(x) = \frac{60(50) - 6000}{50 - 120}$$
$$\approx \$42.9 \text{ tens of millions.}$$

(ii) If $x = 60$,
$$R(x) = \frac{60(60) - 6000}{60 - 120}$$
$$= \$40 \text{ tens of millions.}$$

(iii) If $x = 80$,
$$R(x) = \frac{60(80) - 6000}{80 - 120}$$
$$= \$30 \text{ tens of millions.}$$

(iv) If $x = 100$,
$$R(x) = \frac{60(100) - 6000}{100 - 120}$$
$$= \$0.$$

(v)

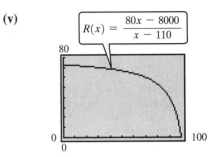

$R(x) = \dfrac{80x - 8000}{x - 110}$

58. **(a)** If the average number of people served is less than 9, the graph of $f(x)$ will be below the x-axis. This would correspond to a negative average waiting time, which is meaningless.

(b) If the average time to serve a customer is 5 minutes, then $\dfrac{60}{5} = 12$ customers can be served in an hour.

(c) If $x = 12$, $f(x) = \dfrac{9}{12(12 - 9)}$

$f(x) = \dfrac{1}{4}$ or 15 minutes

A customer will have to wait 15 minutes on average.

(d) Let $f(x) = \dfrac{1}{8}$

$$\frac{1}{8} = \frac{9}{(x)(x - 9)}$$

Multiply by LCD

$$x(x - 9)(8)\left(\frac{1}{8}\right) = \left[\frac{9}{x(x - 9)}\right](x)(x - 9)(8)$$
$$x^2 - 9x = 72$$
$$x^2 - 9x - 72 = 0$$

Solve for x using the quadratic formula.

$$x = \frac{9 \pm \sqrt{81 - 4(1)(-72)}}{2}$$
$$= \frac{9 \pm \sqrt{369}}{2} \approx 4.25 \text{ min.}$$

The employee must serve each customer in 4.25 minutes to cut the waiting time in half. An assistant could be hired to handle menial tasks, or a more efficient register system could be installed.

Section 3.6

Exercises

1. $c = 2\pi r$, where c is the circumference of a circle of radius c. The circumference of a circle varies directly as (or is proportional to) its radius.

3. $v = \dfrac{d}{t}$, where v is the average speed when traveling d miles in t hours.
   The average speed varies directly as (or is proportional to) the distance traveled and varies inversely as the time.

5. $s = kx^3$, where s is the strength of a muscle of length x. The strength of a muscle varies directly as (or is proportional to) the cube of its length.

7. y varies directly as x, $y = kx$, is a straight-line model.
   It matches graph C.

9. y varies directly as the second power of x, $y = kx^2$, matches graph A.

11. $m = kxy$
    Substitute $m = 10$, $x = 4$, and $y = 7$ to find k.
    $$10 = k \cdot 4 \cdot 7$$
    $$10 = 28k$$
    $$\frac{5}{14} = k$$
    Thus, the relationship between m, x, and y is given by $m = \dfrac{5}{14}xy$.
    Now find m when $x = 11$ and $y = 8$.
    $$m = \frac{5}{14} \cdot 11 \cdot 8$$
    $$= \frac{440}{14}$$
    $$= \frac{220}{7}$$

13. $r = \dfrac{km^2}{s}$
    Substitute $r = 12$, $m = 6$, and $s = 4$ to find k.
    $$12 = \frac{k \cdot 6^2}{4}$$
    $$12 = 9k$$
    $$k = \frac{4}{3}$$
    Thus, the relationship between r, m, and s, is

given by $r = \dfrac{4}{3} \cdot \dfrac{m^2}{s}$.
Now find r when $m = 4$ and $s = 10$.
$$r = \frac{4}{3} \cdot \frac{4^2}{10}$$
$$= \frac{32}{15}$$

15. $a = \dfrac{kmn^2}{y^3}$
    Substitute $a = 9$, $m = 4$, $n = 9$, and $y = 3$ to find k.
    $$9 = \frac{k \cdot 4 \cdot 9^2}{3^3}$$
    $$9 = 12k$$
    $$k = \frac{3}{4}$$

    Thus, $a = \dfrac{3}{4} \cdot \dfrac{mn^2}{y^3}$.
    If $m = 6$, $n = 2$, and $y = 5$, then
    $$a = \frac{3}{4} \cdot \frac{6 \cdot 2^2}{5^3}$$
    $$= \frac{18}{125}$$

17. For $k > 0$, if y varies directly as x, when x increases, y *increases*, and when x decreases, y *decreases*.

19. $y = \dfrac{k}{x}$
    If x is doubled, the right side is divided by 2, or equivalently, multiplied by $\dfrac{1}{2}$. Thus, y is half as large as it was before.

21. $y = kx$
    If x is replaced by $\left(\dfrac{1}{3}\right)x$, the right side is multiplied by $\dfrac{1}{3}$, so y is one-third as large as it was before.

23. $p = \dfrac{kr^3}{t^2}$
    If r is halved, the right side will be multiplied by $\left(\dfrac{1}{2}\right)^3 = \dfrac{1}{8}$.
    If t is doubled, the right side will be divided by

$2^2 = 4$, or, equivalently, multiplied by $\frac{1}{4}$. Thus, the right side is multiplied by $\left(\frac{1}{8}\right)\left(\frac{1}{4}\right) = \frac{1}{32}$, so p is $\frac{1}{32}$ as large as it was before.

25. Let e = weight on earth;
$\quad\quad m$ = weight on moon.
$$e = km$$
Substitute $e = 200$ and $m = 32$ to find k.
$$200 = k \cdot 32$$
$$\frac{200}{32} = k$$
$$6.25 = k$$
Thus, $e = 6.25m$
If $e = 50$, then
$$50 = 6.25m$$
$$\frac{50}{6.25} = m$$
$$8 = m$$
The dog would weigh 8 pounds on the moon.

27. Let d = distance the spring stretches;
$\quad\quad f$ = force applied.
$$d = kf$$
Substitute $d = 8$ and $f = 15$ to find k.
$$8 = k \cdot 15$$
$$\frac{8}{15} = k$$
Thus, $d = \frac{8}{15} \cdot f$.
If $f = 30$, then
$$d = \frac{8}{15} \cdot 30$$
$$d = 16.$$
The spring will stretch 16 in.

29. Let I = illumination;
$\quad\quad d$ = distance from source.
$$I = \frac{k}{d^2}$$
Substitute $I = 70$ and $d = 5$ to find k.
$$70 = \frac{k}{5^2}$$
$$25 \cdot 70 = k$$
$$1750 = k$$
Thus, $I = \frac{1750}{d^2}$.

If $d = 12$, then
$$I = \frac{1750}{12^2}$$
$$= \frac{1750}{144}$$
$$= \frac{875}{72}.$$
The illumination is $\frac{875}{72}$ candela.

31. Let V = volume;
$\quad\quad P$ = pressure;
$\quad\quad T$ = temperature.
$$V = \frac{kT}{P}$$
Substitute $V = 1.3$, $T = 300$, and $P = 18$ to find k.
$$1.3 = \frac{k(300)}{18}$$
$$k = \frac{23.4}{300} = .078$$
Thus, $V = .078\frac{T}{P}$
If $T = 340$ and $P = 24$, then
$$V = .078 \times \frac{340}{24}$$
$$= 1.105.$$
The volume is 1.105 liters.

33. Let V = volume of right circular cylinder;
$\quad\quad r$ = radius of the base;
$\quad\quad h$ = height of the cylinder.
$$V = kr^2h$$
Substitute $V = 300$, $r = 3$, and $h = 10.62$ to find k.
$$300 = k \cdot 3^2 \cdot 10.62$$
$$300 = 95.58k$$
$$3.1387 \approx k$$
Thus, $V = 3.1387r^2h$.
If $h = 15.92$ and $r = 4$, then
$$V = 3.1387 \cdot 4^2 \cdot 15.92$$
$$= 3.1387 \cdot 16 \cdot 15.92$$
$$\approx 799.5.$$
The volume is 799.5 cu cm.

35. Let L = load;
$\quad\quad w$ = width;
$\quad\quad h$ = height;
$\quad\quad l$ = length between supports.
$$L = \frac{kwh^2}{l}$$
Substitute $L = 400$, $w = 12$, $h = 15$, and $l = 8$ to find k.

$$400 = \frac{k \cdot 12 \cdot 15^2}{8}$$

$$400 = \frac{675}{2} \cdot k$$

$$\frac{2}{675} \cdot 400 = k$$

$$\frac{32}{27} = k$$

Thus, $L = \frac{\frac{32}{27} wh^2}{l}$.

If $w = 24$, $h = 8$, and $l = 16$, then

$$L = \frac{\frac{32}{27} \cdot 24 \cdot 8^2}{16}$$

$$= \frac{32 \cdot 24 \cdot 64}{27 \cdot 16}$$

$$= \frac{1024}{9}.$$

The maximum load is $\frac{1024}{9}$ kg.

37. Let $B = $ BMI;
   $w = $ weight;
   $h = $ height.

$$B = \frac{wk}{h^2}$$

Substitute $w = 177$, $B = 24$, and $h = 72$ (6 feet) to find k.

$$24 = \frac{177k}{(72)^2}$$

$$24 = \frac{177k}{5184}$$

$$124,416 = 177k$$

$$\frac{124,416}{177} = k$$

Thus, $B = \frac{124,416w}{177h^2}$.

If $w = 130$ and $h = 66$, then

$$B = \frac{124,416(130)}{177(66)^2}$$

$$B \approx 21.$$

The BMI would be approximately 21.

39. $R = \frac{kl}{r^4}$

Substitute $R = 25$, $l = 12$, and $r = .2$ to find k.

$$25 = \frac{k(12)}{.0016}$$

$$k = \frac{1}{300}$$

Thus, $R = \frac{1}{300} \cdot \frac{l}{r^4}$.

If $r = .3$ and $l = 12$, then

$$R = \frac{1}{300} \cdot \frac{12}{(.3)^4}$$

$$\approx 4.94.$$

The resistance would be 4.94.

41. Let $D = $ distance;
   $Y = $ yield.

$$D = k\sqrt[3]{y}$$

Substitute $Y = 100$ and $D = 3$ to find k.

$$3 = k\sqrt[3]{100}$$

$$k = \frac{3}{\sqrt[3]{100}}.$$

Thus, $D = \frac{3}{\sqrt[3]{100}} \cdot \sqrt[3]{Y}$.

If $Y = 1500$, then

$$D = \frac{3}{\sqrt[3]{100}} \cdot \sqrt[3]{1500}$$

$$= 3\sqrt[3]{15}$$

$$\approx 7.4$$

The distance is 7.4 km.

43. $L = \frac{25F^2}{st}$

Here, $L = 500$, $s = 200$, and $t = \frac{1}{250}$.

Substitute these values into the formula and solve for F.

$$500 = \frac{25F^2}{200 \cdot \frac{1}{250}}$$

$$400 = 25F^2$$

$$16 = F^2$$

$$\pm 4 = F$$

A negative value of F is not meaningful in this problem. The appropriate F-stop is 4.

Chapter 3 Review Exercises

1. $f(x) = 3(x+4)^2 - 5$

The function has the form

$$f(x) = a(x-h)^2 + k$$

with $a = 3$, $h = -4$, and $k = -5$.

The graph is a parabola that opens upward.

Vertex: $(h, k) = (-4, -5)$

Axis: $x = -4$

Find the x-intercepts by letting $f(x) = 0$.

$$3(x+4)^2 - 5 = 0$$
$$3(x+4)^2 = 5$$
$$(x+4)^2 = \frac{5}{3}$$
$$x+4 = \pm\sqrt{\frac{5}{3}}$$
$$x = -4 \pm \sqrt{\frac{5}{3}} = -4 \pm \frac{\sqrt{15}}{3}$$
$$= \frac{-12 \pm \sqrt{15}}{3}$$

x-intercepts: $\dfrac{-12 \pm \sqrt{15}}{3}$

Find the y-intercept by letting $x = 0$.
$$f(0) = 3(0+4)^2 - 5$$
$$= 3(16) - 5$$
$$= 43$$
y-intercept: 43

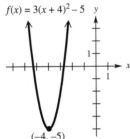

$f(x) = 3(x+4)^2 - 5$

$(-4, -5)$

The domain is $(-\infty, \infty)$. The lowest point on the graph is $(-4, -5)$, so the range is $[-5, \infty)$.

3. $f(x) = -3^2 - 12x - 1$

Complete the square to find the vertex.
$$f(x) = -3(x^2 + 4x) - 1$$
$$= -3(x^2 + 4x + 4) + 12 - 1$$
$$= -3(x+2)^2 + 11$$
The graph is a parabola that opens downward.
Vertex: $(h, k) = (-2, 11)$
Axis: $x = -2$
Find the x-intercepts by letting $f(x) = 0$.
$$-3(x+2)^2 + 11 = 0$$
$$-3(x+2)^2 = -11$$
$$(x+2)^2 = \frac{11}{3}$$
$$x+2 = \pm\sqrt{\frac{11}{3}}$$
$$x = -2 \pm \sqrt{\frac{11}{3}}$$
$$= -2 \pm \frac{\sqrt{33}}{3}$$
$$= \frac{-6 \pm \sqrt{33}}{3}$$

x-intercepts: $\dfrac{-6 \pm \sqrt{33}}{3}$

Find the y-intercept by letting $x = 0$.
$$f(0) = -3(0)^2 - 12(0) - 1 = -1$$
Thus, the y-intercept is -1.

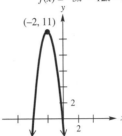

$f(x) = -3x^2 - 12x - 1$

$(-2, 11)$

The domain is $(-\infty, \infty)$. The vertex $(-2, 11)$ is the highest point on the graph, so the range is $(-\infty, 11]$.

5. $f(x) = a(x-h)^2 + k;\ a > 0$

The graph is a parabola that opens upward. The coordinates of the lowest point of the graph are coordinates of the vertex, (h, k).

7. For the graph to have one or more x-intercepts, $f(x) = 0$ must have real number solutions.
$$a(x-h)^2 + k = 0$$
$$a(x-h)^2 = -k$$
$$(x-h)^2 = \frac{-k}{a}$$
$$x - h = \pm\sqrt{\frac{-k}{a}}$$
$$x = h \pm \sqrt{\frac{-k}{a}}$$

These solutions are real only if $\dfrac{-k}{a} \geq 0$.

Since $a > 0$, this condition is equivalent to $-k \geq 0$ or $k \leq 0$.

The x-intercepts for these conditions are given by $\left(h \pm \sqrt{\frac{-k}{a}},\ 0 \right)$.

9. Let $x =$ the width of the rectangular region and $L =$ the length of the region.
Then $x + x + L = 180$, so $L = 180 - 2x$

$180 - 2x$

x x

No fence

Use $A = LW$.

$$A(x) = x(180 - 2x)$$
$$= -2(x^2 - 90x)$$
$$= -2(x^2 - 90x + 2025) + 4050$$
$$= -2(x - 45)^2 + 4050$$

Since the graph of $A(x)$ is a parabola that opens downward, the maximum area is the y-coordinate of the vertex. The x-coordinate of the vertex is the width that gives the maximum area.

$$x = 45$$
$$L = 180 - 2(45) = 90$$

The dimensions of the region are 90 m × 45 m.

11. (a) For 1998, $x = 98$.

$$G(x) = -.115x^2 + 20.47x - 853.8$$
$$G(98) = -.115(98)^2 + 20.47(98) - 853.8$$
$$G(98) = 47.8$$

In 1998, the percent of drug users was 47.8%.

(b)

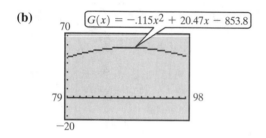

(c) The x-coordinate of the vertex is

$$x = -\frac{b}{2a} = -\frac{20.47}{2(-.115)} = 89$$

$x = 89$ corresponds to 1989.

$$G(89) = -.115(89)^2 + 20.47(89) - 853.8$$
$$G(89) = 57.115$$

The maximum of approximately 57.1% was reached in 1989.

13. $f(x) = -2.64x^2 + 5.47x + 3.54$

Graph this function as Y_1 in the standard viewing window. The graph is a parabola opening downward with two x-intercepts, one negative and one positive. Using the "root" or "zero" option in the CALC menu, we can approximate the two solutions of the equation.

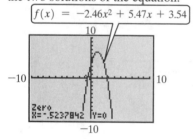

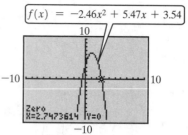

From the preceding calculator screens, we see that (approximating to the nearest hundredth) the solution set is $\{-.52, 2.59\}$.

15. Use TRACE to locate the vertex of the parabola. Use "maximum" from the CALC menu to find the coordinates of the vertex.

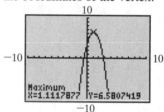

From this screen, we see that the coordinates of the vertex, to the nearest hundredth, are (1.04, 6.37).

17. $\dfrac{3x^3 + 8x^2 + 5x + 10}{x + 2}$

$$-2)\overline{\begin{array}{cccc} 3 & 8 & 5 & 10 \\ & -6 & -4 & -2 \\ \hline 3 & 2 & 1 & 8 \end{array}}$$

The synthetic division shows that $q(x) = 3x^2 + 2x + 1$ and $r = 8$.

19. $f(x) = 2x^3 - 3x^2 + 7x - 12$; find $f(2)$.

$$2)\overline{\begin{array}{cccc} 2 & -3 & 7 & -12 \\ & 4 & 2 & 18 \\ \hline 2 & 1 & 9 & 6 \end{array}}$$

The synthetic division shows that $f(2) = 6$.

21. $f(x) = x^5 + 4x^2 - 2x - 4$; find $f(2)$.

$$2)\overline{\begin{array}{cccccc} 1 & 0 & 0 & 4 & -2 & -4 \\ & 2 & 4 & 8 & 24 & 44 \\ \hline 1 & 2 & 4 & 12 & 22 & 40 \end{array}}$$

The synthetic division shows that $f(2) = 40$.

23. If $f(x)$ has a zero at $x = 3$, then 3 is an x-intercept of the graph of $f(x)$ and $x - 3$ is a factor of $f(x)$. A and C are true.

In Exercises 25 and 27, other answers are possible.

25. Zeros: 8, 2, 3
$$f(x) = (x-8)(x-2)(x-3)$$
$$= (x^2 - 10x + 16)(x-3)$$
$$= x^3 - 13x^2 + 46x - 48$$

27. Zeros: $-2 + \sqrt{5}, -2 - \sqrt{5}, -2, 1$

$$f(x) = [x - (-2 + \sqrt{5})][x - (-2 - \sqrt{5})][x - (-2)](x-1)$$
$$= [(x+2) - \sqrt{5}][(x+2) + \sqrt{5}](x+2)(x-1)$$
$$= [(x+2)^2 - 5](x+2)(x-1)$$
$$= (x^2 + 4x - 1)(x^2 + x - 2)$$
$$= x^4 + 5x^3 + x^2 - 9x + 2$$

29. $f(x) = 8x^4 - 14x^3 - 29x^2 - 4x + 3$

p must be a factor of $a_0 = 3$ and q must be a factor of $a_4 = 8$. Thus, p can be ± 1, ± 3, and q can be $\pm 1, \pm 2, \pm 4, \pm 8$. The possible zeros, $\dfrac{p}{q}$,

are $\pm 1, \pm 3, \pm\dfrac{1}{2}, \pm\dfrac{1}{4}, \pm\dfrac{1}{8}, \pm\dfrac{3}{2}, \pm\dfrac{3}{4}, \pm\dfrac{3}{8}$.

The remainder theorem shows that 3 is a zero.

$$
\begin{array}{r|rrrrr}
3 & 8 & -14 & -29 & -4 & 3 \\
  &   & 24 & 30 & 3 & -3 \\
\hline
  & 8 & 10 & 1 & -1 & 0
\end{array}
$$

The new quotient polynomial is
$8x^3 + 10x^2 + x - 1$.
The remainder theorem shows that -1 is a zero.

$$
\begin{array}{r|rrrr}
-1 & 8 & 10 & 1 & -1 \\
   &   & -8 & -2 & 1 \\
\hline
   & 8 & 2 & -1 & 0
\end{array}
$$

The new quotient polynomial is $8x^2 + 2x - 1$.
$$8x^2 + 2x - 1 = 0$$
$$(4x - 1)(2x + 1) = 0$$
$$4x - 1 = 0 \text{ or } 2x + 1 = 0$$
$$x = \frac{1}{4} \qquad x = -\frac{1}{2}$$

The rational zeros are $3, -1, \dfrac{1}{4}$, and $-\dfrac{1}{2}$.

31.
$$
\begin{array}{r|rrrr}
-1 & 1 & 2 & 3 & 2 \\
   &   & -1 & -1 & -2 \\
\hline
   & 1 & 1 & 2 & 0
\end{array}
$$
Since $f(-1) = 0$, $x + 1$ is a factor of $f(x)$.

33. $f(x) = a(x+2)(x-1)(x-4)$
$$f(2) = 16$$
$$16 = a(2+2)(2-1)(2-4)$$
$$16 = -8a$$
$$a = -2$$
The polynomial function is
$$f(x) = -2(x+2)(x-1)(x-4)$$
$$= -2(x^2 + x - 2)(x-4)$$
$$= -2(x^3 - 3x^2 - 6x + 8)$$
$$= -2x^3 + 6x^2 + 12x - 16.$$

35. Any polynomial that can be factored as $a(x-b)^3$, where a and b are real numbers, will be a cubic polynomial function having exactly one real zero. One example is $f(x) = 2(x-1)^3$.

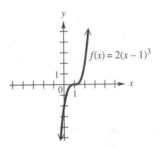

37. $f(x) = 2x^4 - x^3 + 7x^2 - 4x - 4$; 1 and $2i$ are zeros.
Since $2i$ is a zero, $-2i$ is also a zero.
$$(x - 2i)(x + 2i) = x^2 + 4$$
Find $\dfrac{2x^4 - x^3 + 7x^2 - 4x - 4}{x^2 + 4}$ by long division.

The quotient is $2x^2 - x - 1 = (2x + 1)(x - 1)$, so all the zeros are $1, -\dfrac{1}{2}$ and $\pm 2i$.

39. Find a value of s such that when the polynomial $x^3 - 3x^2 + sx - 4$ is divided by $x - 2$, the remainder is 5.

$$
\begin{array}{r|rrrr}
2 & 1 & -3 & s & -4 \\
  &   & 2 & -2 & 2s-4 \\
\hline
  & 1 & -1 & s-2 & 2s-8
\end{array}
$$
$$2s - 8 = 5$$
$$2s = 13$$
$$s = \frac{13}{2}$$

41. $f(x) = 4x^4 - 6x^2 + 2$ has a maximum of three turning points.

43. $f(x) = -(x-2)^2(x-5)$ is the vertical reflection of graph C, so it matches graph D.

45. $f(x) = (x-2)(x-5)$ is a quadratic polynomial that opens up, so it matches graph A.

47. $f(x) = -(x-2)^2(x-5)^2$ is the vertical reflection of graph E, so it matches graph F.

49. The polynomial has a leading coefficient of $-7x^6$.

    (a) The domain is $(-\infty, \infty)$.

    (b) The range is $(-\infty, M]$, where M is the greatest value assumed by the function.

    (c) As $x \to \pm\infty$, $f(x) \to -\infty$.

    (d) There are at most 6 zeros.

    (e) There are at most 5 turning points.

51. Refer to the figure in the textbook.
$L = 3x$, $W = x + 11$, and $H = x$
Write an equation using $V = LWH$.
$$720 = 3x(x+11)x$$
$$= 3x^3 + 33x^2$$
$$3x^3 + 33x^2 - 720 = 0$$
$$x^3 + 11x^2 - 240 = 0$$
Graph $Y_1 = x^3 + 11x^2 - 240$ with a graphing calculator. The graph shows that there is only one x-intercept, which appears to be 4.
The root-finding capability or synthetic division can be used to confirm that 4 is the exact solution of the equation $x^3 + 11x^2 - 240 = 0$.
(The other two solutions of the equation are imaginary.)
Thus, the dimensions of the box are 4 inches by $3(4) = 12$ inches by $4 + 11 = 15$ inches.

53.
$$\begin{array}{r|rrrrr} 1) & 6 & 13 & -11 & -3 & 5 \\ & & 6 & 19 & 8 & 5 \\ \hline & 6 & 19 & 8 & 5 & 10 \end{array}$$

Since $1 > 0$ and all numbers in the bottom row of the synthetic division are nonnegative, the boundedness theorem tells us that $f(x)$ has no real zero greater than 1.

$$\begin{array}{r|rrrrr} -3) & 6 & 13 & -11 & -3 & 5 \\ & & -18 & 15 & -12 & 45 \\ \hline & 6 & -5 & 4 & -15 & 50 \end{array}$$

Since $-3 < 0$ and the numbers in the bottom row of the synthetic division alternate in sign, the boundedness theorem tells us that $f(x)$ has no real zero less than -3.

55.

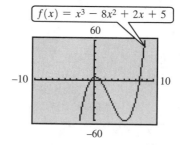

Using the root-find capabilities of the calculator, we find that the real zeros are 7.6533119, 1, and $-.6533119$.

57. $f(x) = 2x^3 + x^2 - x$
$$= x(2x^2 + x - 1)$$
$$= x(2x-1)(x+1)$$
The zeros are 0, $\dfrac{1}{2}$, and -1, which divide the x-axis into four regions. Choose a test point in each region.

Region	Test Point	Value of $f(x)$	Sign of $f(x)$
$(-\infty, -1)$	-2	-10	Negative
$(-1, 0)$	$-\frac{1}{2}$	$\frac{1}{2}$	Positive
$\left(0, \frac{1}{2}\right)$	$\frac{1}{4}$	$-\frac{5}{32}$	Negative
$\left(\frac{1}{2}, \infty\right)$	1	3	Positive

Plot the zeros and the test points. Connect them with a smooth curve.

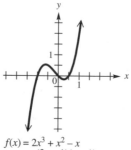

$f(x) = 2x^3 + x^2 - x$
$= x(2x-1)(x+1)$

59. (a)

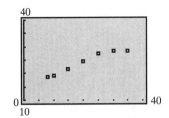

(b) $f(x) = -.011x^2 + .869x + 11.9$

(c) $f(x) = -.00087x^3 + .0456x^2 - .219x + 17.8$

(d)

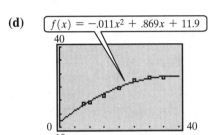

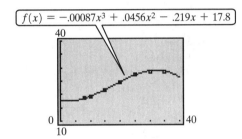

(e) Both functions approximate the data well. The quadratic function is probably better for prediction, because it is unlikely that the percent of out-of-pocket spending would decrease after 2025 (as the cubic function shows) unless changes were made in Medicare law.

61. $f(x) = \dfrac{4x - 2}{3x + 1}$

Find the vertical asymptote by solving $3x + 1 = 0$.

There is one vertical asymptote, $x = -\dfrac{1}{3}$.

Since the numerator and denominator have the same degree, find the horizontal asymptote by dividing numerator and denominator by x and letting $|x| \to \infty$.

The horizontal asymptote is $y = \dfrac{4}{3}$.

$f(0) = \dfrac{4 \cdot 0 - 2}{3 \cdot 0 + 1} = -2$, so the y-intercept is -2.

Any x-intercepts will be the zeros of the numerator.

$4x - 2 = 0$

$4x = 2$

$x = \dfrac{1}{2}$

There is one x-intercept, $\dfrac{1}{2}$.

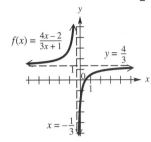

63. $f(x) = \dfrac{2x}{x^2 - 1}$

$f(x) = \dfrac{2x}{(x + 1)(x - 1)}$

The vertical asymptotes are $x = 1$ and $x = -1$, since 1 and -1 are the zeros of the denominator. Since the numerator has lower degree than the denominator, the horizontal asymptote is $y = 0$. Applying the tests for symmetry to the equation

$y = \dfrac{2x}{(x + 1)(x - 1)}$ will show that the graph is

symmetric with respect to the origin. The x- and y-intercepts are both 0.

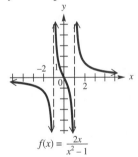

65. $f(x) = \dfrac{x^2 - 1}{x}$

There is one vertical asymptote, $x = 0$. Since the numerator is of degree exactly one more than the denominator, there is no horizontal asymptote, but there may be an oblique asymptote.

$f(x) = \dfrac{x^2 - 1}{x} = x - \dfrac{1}{x}$. Thus, the line $y = x$ is an oblique asymptote. There is no y-intercept because $f(0)$ is undefined.

The zeros of the numerator are -1 and 1, so the

graph has two x-intercepts, -1 and 1.

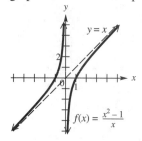

67. $f(x) = \dfrac{4x^2 - 9}{2x + 3}$

$= \dfrac{(2x + 3)(2x - 3)}{2x + 3}$

$= 2x - 3 \left(x \neq -\dfrac{3}{2} \right)$

The graph is the same as that of $f(x) = 2x - 3$, the line with slope 2 and y-intercept -3, except the point with x-value $-\dfrac{3}{2}$ is missing. This is shown by graphing the line $y = 2x - 3$ with an open circle at $\left(-\dfrac{3}{2}, -6 \right)$ to indicate the missing point.

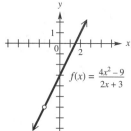

69. (a)

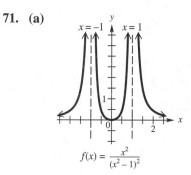

$C(x) = \dfrac{6.7x}{100 - x}$

(b) $C(x) = \dfrac{6.7x}{100 - x}$

$C(95) = \dfrac{6.7(95)}{100 - 95}$

≈ 127.3

It would cost approximately \$127.3 thousand to remove 95% of the pollutant.

71. (a)

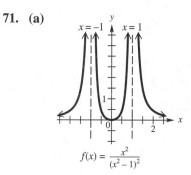

$f(x) = \dfrac{x^2}{(x^2 - 1)^2}$

(b) If $x = -1$ and $x = 1$ are vertical asymptotes, $(x - 1)(x + 1) = x^2 - 1$ is a factor of the denominator. If the x-axis is a horizontal asymptote, the numerator has a lower degree than the denominator. If 0 is an x-intercept, $f(0) = 0$, so the denominator must be 0 if $x = 0$. The function is never negative, so only even-numbered powers of x should appear.

Putting these conditions together, we get a possible function $f(x) = \dfrac{x^2}{(x^2 - 1)^2}$.

73. Let P = pressure;
     D = distance.
     $P = kD$
   Substitute $D = 4$ and $P = 60$ to find k.
     $60 = k(4)$
     $k = 15$
   Thus, $P = 15D$.
   If $D = 10$, then $P = 15 \cdot 10$
                    $= 150$.
   The pressure is 150 kg per sq m.

75. Let p = power;
     v = wind velocity.
     $p = kv^3$
   Substitute $p = 10{,}000$ and $v = 10$ to find k.
     $10{,}000 = k \cdot 10^3$
     $\dfrac{10{,}000}{1000} = k$
     $10 = k$
   Thus, $p = 10v^3$.
   If $v = 15$,
     $p = 10 \cdot 15^3$
       $\approx 33{,}750$
   33,750 units of power are produced.

Chapter 3 Test Exercises

1. $f(x) = -2x^2 + 6x - 3$

$= -2(x^2 - 3x) - 3$

$= -2\left(x^2 - 3x + \dfrac{9}{4}\right) + \dfrac{9}{2} - 3$

$= -2\left(x - \dfrac{3}{2}\right)^2 + \dfrac{3}{2}$

Vertex: $(h, k) = \left(\dfrac{3}{2}, \dfrac{3}{2}\right)$

Axis: $x = \dfrac{3}{2}$

To find the x-intercepts let $f(x) = 0$.

$0 = -2\left(x - \dfrac{3}{2}\right)^2 + \dfrac{3}{2}$

$-\dfrac{3}{2} = -2\left(x - \dfrac{3}{2}\right)^2$

$\dfrac{3}{4} = \left(x - \dfrac{3}{2}\right)^2$

$\pm\sqrt{\dfrac{3}{4}} = x - \dfrac{3}{2}$

$x = \dfrac{3}{2} \pm \sqrt{\dfrac{3}{4}} = \dfrac{3}{2} \pm \dfrac{\sqrt{3}}{2}$

x-intercepts: $\dfrac{3 \pm \sqrt{3}}{2}$

To find the y-intercept, let $x = 0$.

$f(0) = -2(0)^2 + 6(0) - 3$

$= -3$

y-intercept: -3

Domain: $(-\infty, \infty)$

Range: $\left(-\infty, \dfrac{3}{2}\right]$

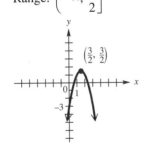

$f(x) = -2x^2 + 6x - 3$

2. $f(x) = 1242x^2 - 707.3x + 428,634$

(a) In 1995, $x = 10$.

$f(10) = 1242(10)^2 - 707.3(10) = 428,634$

$= 545,761$

In 1995, 545,761 degrees were earned.

(b) The minimum is at the vertex.

$x = -\dfrac{b}{2a}$

$= \dfrac{(-707.3)}{2(1242)}$

≈ 0

$f(0) = 1242(0)^2 - 707.3(0) + 428,634$

$= 428,634$

The number of degrees was at a minimum in 1985, when the number of degrees was 428,634.

(c) A positive coefficient of x^2 indicates the graph opens up, so according to the function, the number of degrees is always increasing from 1985 on, because 1985 is the minimum.

3. $\dfrac{3x^3 + 4x^2 - 9x + 6}{x + 2}$

$$
\begin{array}{r|rrrr}
-2) & 3 & 4 & -9 & 6 \\
 & & -6 & 4 & 10 \\
\hline
 & 3 & -2 & -5 & 16 \\
\end{array}
$$

$q(x) = 3x^2 - 2x - 5; \ r = 16$

4. $\dfrac{2x^3 - 11x^2 + 28}{x - 5}$

$$
\begin{array}{r|rrrr}
5) & 2 & -11 & 0 & 28 \\
 & & 10 & -5 & -25 \\
\hline
 & 2 & -1 & -5 & 3 \\
\end{array}
$$

$q(x) = 2x^2 - x - 5; \ r = 3$

5. $f(x) = 2x^3 - 9x^2 + 4x + 8; \ k = 5$

$$
\begin{array}{r|rrrr}
5) & 2 & -9 & 4 & 8 \\
 & & 10 & 5 & 45 \\
\hline
 & 2 & 1 & 9 & 53 \\
\end{array}
$$

$f(5) = 53$

6. $6x^4 - 11x^3 - 35x^2 + 34x + 24; \ x - 3$

Let $f(x) = 6x^4 - 11x^3 - 35x^2 + 34x + 24$.

By the factor theorem, $x - 3$ will be a factor of $f(x)$ only if $f(3) = 0$.

$$
\begin{array}{r|rrrrr}
3) & 6 & -11 & -35 & 34 & 24 \\
 & & 18 & 21 & -42 & -24 \\
\hline
 & 6 & 7 & -14 & -8 & 0 \\
\end{array}
$$

Since $f(3) = 0$, $x - 3$ is a factor of $f(x)$. The other factor is $6x^3 + 7x^2 - 14x - 8$.

7. Since -2 is a zero, first divide $f(x)$ by $x + 2$.

$$
\begin{array}{r|rrrr}
-2) & 2 & -1 & -13 & -6 \\
 & & -4 & 10 & 6 \\
\hline
 & 2 & -5 & -3 & 0 \\
\end{array}
$$

This gives $2x^2 - 5x - 3 = (2x+1)(x-3)$.

The zeros of $f(x)$ are -2, $-\dfrac{1}{2}$, and 3.

8. Zeros of -1, 2 and i; $f(3) = 80$

By the conjugate zeros theorem, $-i$ is also a zero. The polynomial has the form
$f(x) = a(x+1)(x-2)(x-i)(x+i)$.
Use the condition $f(3) = 80$ to find a.

$80 = a(3+1)(3-2)(3-i)(3+i)$

$80 = a(4)(1)(10)$

$80 = 40a$

$a = 2$

Thus,

$f(x) = 2(x+1)(x-2)(x-i)(x+i)$

$\quad = 2(x^2 - x - 2)(x^2 + 1)$

$\quad = 2(x^4 - x^3 - x^2 - x - 2)$

$\quad = 2x^4 - 2x^3 - 2x^2 - 2x - 4.$

9. Because $f(x) > 0$ for all x, the graph never crosses or touches the x-axis, so $f(x)$ has no real zeros.

10. (a) $f(x) = x^3 - 5x^2 + 2x + 7$; 1 and 2

$$1\overline{)1 \quad -5 \quad 2 \quad 7}$$
$$\underline{\quad\quad 1 \quad -4 \quad -2}$$
$$1 \quad -4 \quad -2 \quad 5$$

$$2\overline{)1 \quad -5 \quad 2 \quad 7}$$
$$\underline{\quad\quad 2 \quad -6 \quad -8}$$
$$1 \quad -3 \quad -4 \quad -1$$

By the intermediate value theorem, since $f(1) = 5 > 0$ and $f(2) = -1 < 0$, there must be at least one real zero between 1 and 2.

(b) The real zeros of $f(x) = x^3 - 5x^2 + 2x + 7$ are 4.0937635, 1.8370381, and $-.9308016$.

11.

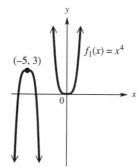

$f_2(x) = -2(x+5)^4 + 3$

To obtain the graph of f_2, shift the graph of f_1 5 units to the left, stretch by a factor of 2, reflect across the x-axis, and shift 3 units up.

12. $f(x) = -x^7 + x - 4$

Since $f(x)$ is of odd degree and the sign of a_n is negative, the left arrow points up and the right arrow points down. The correct graph is C.

13. $f(x) = (3 - x)(x+2)(x+5)$

To find the zeros, set each factor equal to 0 and solve the resulting equations. We obtain the zeros -5, -2, and 3. The zeros divide the x-axis into four regions: $(-\infty, -5)$, $(-5, -2)$, $(-2, 3)$, and $(3, 0)$. Test a point in each region to find the sign of $f(x)$ in that region.

Region	Test Point	Value of $f(x)$	Sign of $f(x)$
$(-\infty, -5)$	-6	36	Positive
$(-5, -2)$	-3	-12	Negative
$(-2, 3)$	0	30	Positive
$(3, 0)$	4	-54	Negative

Use the zeros and the points from the table to sketch the graph.

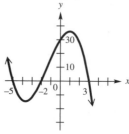

$f(x) = (3 - x)(x + 2)(x + 5)$

14. $f(x) = 2x^4 - 8x^3 + 8x^2$

$\quad = 2x^2(x^2 - 4x + 4)$

$f(x) = 2x^2(x-2)^2$

By setting each factor equal to zero and solving the resulting equations, we see that the zeros are 0 and 2 (each of multiplicity two). The zeros divide the x-axis into three regions: $(-\infty, 0)$, $(0, 2)$, and $(2, \infty)$. Test a point in each region.

Region	Test Point	Value of $f(x)$	Sign of $f(x)$
$(-\infty, 0)$	-1	18	Positive
$(0, 2)$	1	2	Positive
$(2, \infty)$	3	18	Positive

(We can also see from the equation that $f(x)$ can never be negative.) Use the zeros and the points from the table to sketch the graph.

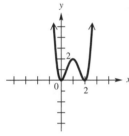

$f(x) = 2x^4 - 8x^3 + 8x^2$

15. The zeros are -3 and 2; $f(0) = 24$.

$\quad f(x) = a(x-2)^2(x+3)$

$\quad 24 = a(0-2)^2(0+3)$

$\quad 24 = 12a$

$\quad a = 2$

The polynomial function is

$\quad f(x) = 2(x-2)^2(x+3)$.

16. (a) $f(t) = 1.06t^3 - 24.6t^2 + 180t$

Let $t = 2$.

$\quad f(2) = 1.06(2)^3 - 24.6(2)^2 + 180(2)$

$\quad\quad = 270.08$

(b)

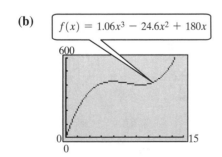

From the graph we see that the amount of change is increasing from $t = 0$ to $t = 5.9$ and from $t = 9.5$ to $t = 15$ and decreasing from $t = 5.9$ to $t = 9.5$.

17. $f(x) = \dfrac{3x-1}{x-2}$

To find any vertical asymptotes, solve the equation $x - 2 = 0$.

There is one vertical asymptote, $x = 2$.

$f(x) = \dfrac{3x-1}{x-2} = \dfrac{3 - \frac{1}{x}}{1 - \frac{5}{x}},$

so as $|x| \to \infty$, $f(x) \to 3$.

The horizontal asymptote is $y = 3$.

$f(0) = \dfrac{3 \cdot 0 - 1}{0 - 2} = \dfrac{1}{2}$, so the y-intercept is $\dfrac{1}{2}$.

The only zero of the numerator is $\dfrac{1}{3}$, so $\dfrac{1}{3}$ is the only x-intercept.

Sketch the graph.

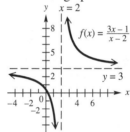

18. $f(x) = \dfrac{x^2 - 1}{x^2 - 9}$

$\quad = \dfrac{(x+1)(x-1)}{(x+3)(x-3)}$

There are vertical asymptotes at $x = -3$ and $x = 3$. Since the numerator and denominator have the same degree, divide by x^2 to find the horizontal asymptote.

$f(x) = \dfrac{1 - \frac{1}{x^2}}{1 - \frac{9}{x^2}} \to \dfrac{1}{1}$ as $|x| \to \infty$,

so $y = 1$ is a horizontal asymptote.

The y-intercept is $\dfrac{1}{9}$.

The x-intercepts are -1 and 1.

Sketch the graph.

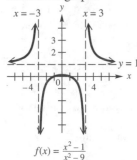

$$f(x) = \frac{x^2 - 1}{x^2 - 9}$$

19. $f(x) = \dfrac{2x^2 + x - 6}{x - 1}$

(a) To find the oblique asymptote, divide:

$$\frac{2x^2 + x - 6}{x - 1} = 2x + 3 - \frac{3}{x - 1}.$$

For very large values of $|x|$, $\dfrac{3}{x-1}$ is close to 0, so the line $y = 2x + 3$ is the oblique asymptote.

(b) To find the x-intercepts, let $f(x) = 0$.

$$0 = \frac{2x^2 + x - 6}{x - 1}$$

$$2x^2 + x - 6 = 0$$

$$(2x - 3)(x + 2) = 0$$

$$x = \frac{3}{2} \text{ or } x = -2$$

x-intercepts: $-2, \dfrac{3}{2}$

(c) To find the y-intercept, let $x = 0$.

$$f(x) = \frac{2(0)^2 + 0 - 6}{0 - 1} = 6$$

y-intercept: 6

(d) To find the vertical asymptote, set the denominator equal to zero and solve for x.

$$x - 1 = 0$$

$$x = 1$$

The equation of the vertical asymptote is $x = 1$.

(e) Use the information from (a)–(d) and a few additional points to graph the function.

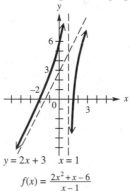

$$y = 2x + 3 \quad x = 1$$

$$f(x) = \frac{2x^2 + x - 6}{x - 1}$$

20. Let D = number of days to ripen;

t = average maximum temperature.

$$D = \frac{k}{t}$$

Substitute $D = 25$ and $t = 80$ to find k.

$$25 = \frac{k}{80}$$

$$80 \cdot 25 = k$$

$$2000 = k$$

Thus, $D = \dfrac{2000}{k}$.

If $t = 75$, $D = \dfrac{2000}{75} = \dfrac{80}{3}$ or $26\dfrac{2}{3}$.

It would take $26\dfrac{2}{3}$ days for the fruit to ripen.

CHAPTER 4   EXPONENTIAL AND LOGARITHMIC FUNCTIONS

Section 4.1

Connections *(page 270)*

1. Decode the message with $f^{-1}(x)$.

$$x = 2y + 5$$
$$x - 5 = 2y$$
$$\frac{x-5}{2} = y$$
$$f^{-1}(x) = \frac{x-5}{2}$$

21; $f^{-1}(21) = \frac{21-5}{2} = 8$; *H*

7; $f^{-1}(7) = \frac{7-5}{2} = 1$; *A*

37; $f^{-1}(37) = \frac{37-5}{2} = 16$: *P*

37; $f^{-1}(37) = \frac{37-5}{2} = 16$: *P*

23; $f^{-1}(23) = \frac{23-5}{2} = 9$; *I*

33: $f^{-1}(33) = \frac{33-5}{2} = 14$; *N*

15; $f^{-1}(15) = \frac{15-5}{2} = 5$; *E*

43; $f^{-1}(43) = \frac{43-5}{2} = 19$; *S*

43; $f^{-1}(43) = \frac{43-5}{2} = 19$; *S*

23; $f^{-1}(23) = \frac{23-5}{2} = 9$; *I*

43; $f^{-1}(43) = \frac{43-5}{2} = 19$; *S*

43; $f^{-1}(43) = \frac{43-5}{2} = 19$; *S*

45; $f^{-1}(45) = \frac{45-5}{2} = 20$; *T*

7; $f^{-1}(7) = \frac{7-5}{2} = 1$; *A*

55; $f^{-1}(55) = \frac{55-5}{2} = 25$; *Y*

23; $f^{-1}(23) = \frac{23-5}{2} = 9$; *I*

33: $f^{-1}(33) = \frac{33-5}{2} = 14$; *N*

19: $f^{-1}(19) = \frac{19-5}{2} = 7$; *G*

35; $f^{-1}(35) = \frac{35-5}{2} = 15$; *O*

47; $f^{-1}(47) = \frac{47-5}{2} = 21$; *U*

45; $f^{-1}(45) = \frac{45-5}{2} = 20$; *T*

35; $f^{-1}(35) = \frac{35-5}{2} = 15$; *O*

17; $f^{-1}(17) = \frac{17-5}{2} = 6$; *F*

21; $f^{-1}(21) = \frac{21-5}{2} = 8$; *H*

35; $f^{-1}(35) = \frac{35-5}{2} = 15$; *O*

43; $f^{-1}(43) = \frac{43-5}{2} = 19$; *S*

37; $f^{-1}(37) = \frac{37-5}{2} = 16$: *P*

23; $f^{-1}(23) = \frac{23-5}{2} = 9$; *I*

45; $f^{-1}(45) = \frac{45-5}{2} = 20$; *T*

7; $f^{-1}(7) = \frac{7-5}{2} = 1$; *A*

29; $f^{-1}(29) = \frac{29-5}{2} = 12$; *L*

43; $f^{-1}(43) = \frac{43-5}{2} = 19$; *S*

7; $f^{-1}(7) = \frac{7-5}{2} = 1$; *A*

33: $f^{-1}(33) = \frac{33-5}{2} = 14$; *N*

13; $f^{-1}(13) = \frac{13-5}{2} = 4$; *D*

11: $f^{-1}(11) = \frac{11-5}{2} = 3$; *C*

35; $f^{-1}(35) = \frac{35-5}{2} = 15$; *O*

47; $f^{-1}(47) = \frac{47-5}{2} = 21$; *U*

41; $f^{-1}(41) = \frac{41-5}{2} = 18$; *R*

45; $f^{-1}(45) = \frac{45-5}{2} = 20$; *T*

41; $f^{-1}(41) = \frac{41-5}{2} = 18$; *R*

$35;\ f^{-1}(35) = \dfrac{35 - 5}{2} = 15;\ O$

$35;\ f^{-1}(35) = \dfrac{35 - 5}{2} = 15;\ O$

$31;\ f^{-1}(31) = \dfrac{31 - 5}{2} = 13;\ M$

$43;\ f^{-1}(43) = \dfrac{43 - 5}{2} = 19;\ S$

The message is HAPPINESS IS STAYING OUT OF HOSPITALS AND COURTROOMS.

2. $B = 2;\ f(2) = 2^3 - 1 = 7$

$I = 9;\ f(9) = 9^3 - 1 = 728$

$G = 7;\ f(7) = 7^3 - 1 = 342$

$G = 7;\ f(7) = 7^3 - 1 = 342$

$I = 9;\ f(9) = 9^3 - 1 = 728$

$R = 18;\ f(18) = 18^3 - 1 = 5,831$

$L = 12;\ f(12) = 12^3 - 1 = 1,727$

$S = 19;\ f(19) = 19^3 - 1 = 6,858$

$D = 4;\ f(4) = 4^3 - 1 = 63$

$O = 15;\ f(15) = 15^3 - 1 = 3,374$

$N = 14;\ f(14) = 14^3 - 1 = 2,743$

$T = 20;\ f(20) = 20^3 - 1 = 7,999$

$C = 3;\ f(3) = 3^3 - 1 = 26$

$R = 18;\ f(18) = 18^3 - 1 = 5,831$

$Y = 25;\ f(25) = 25^3 - 1 = 15,624$

$f^{-1}(x) = \sqrt[3]{x^3 + 1}$

Connections *(page 272)*

1. "radar"

2. "A man, a plan, a canal, Panama"

3. Answers will vary.

Exercises

1. **(a)** The sketch of the inverse of $f(x) = \sqrt{x + 3}$ matches graph C.

   (b) The sketch of the inverse of $f(x) = (x + 4)^3$ matches graph A.

   (c) The sketch of the inverse of $f(x) = \sqrt[3]{x} + 2$ matches graph B.

   (d) The sketch of the inverse of $f(x) = x^2,\ x \ge 0$ matches graph D.

3. The point $(-2, -8)$ is on $f(x)$ but the point $(-8, -2)$ is not on $g(x)$ so the functions are not inverses of each other.

5. In order for a function to have an inverse, it must be one-to-one.

7. If f and g are inverses, then $(f \circ g)(x) = x$, and $(g \circ f)(x) = x$.

9. If the point (a, b) lies on the graph of f, and f has an inverse, then the point (b, a) lies on the graph of f^{-1}.

11. If the function f has an inverse, then the graph of f^{-1} may be obtained by reflecting the graph of f across the line with equation $y = x$.

13. This is a one-to-one function since every horizontal line intersects the graph in no more than one point.

15. This is a one-to-one function since every horizontal line intersects the graph in no more than one point.

17. This is not a one-to-one function since there is a horizontal line that intersects the graph in more than one point. (Here it intersects the curve at an infinite number of points.)

19. $y = (x - 2)^2$

    If $x = 0$, $y = 4$.

    If $x = 4$, $y = 4$.

    Thus, there exist two distinct x-values that lead to the same y-value. Thus, the function is not one-to-one.

21. $y = \sqrt{36 - x^2}$

    Both $x = 6$ and $x = -6$ lead to the same y-value, 0. Thus, the function is not one-to-one.

23. $y = 2x^3 + 1$

    If $x_1 \ne x_2$, then

    $$x_1^3 \ne x_2^3$$
    $$2x_1^3 \ne 2x_2^3$$
    $$2x_1^3 + 1 \ne 2x_2^3 + 1$$
    $$f(x_1) \ne f(x_2),$$

    so the function is one-to-one.

25. $y = \dfrac{1}{x+2}$

If $x_1 \neq x_2$, then
$$x_1 + 2 \neq x_2 + 2,$$
$$\frac{1}{x_1 + 2} \neq \frac{1}{x_2 + 2}$$
$$f(x_1) \neq f(x_2),$$
so the function is one-to-one.

29. The inverse operation of tying your shoelaces would be untying your shoelaces, since untying "undoes" tying.

31. The inverse operation of entering a room would be leaving a room, since leaving "undoes" entering.

33. The inverse operation of taking off in an airplane would be landing in an airplane, since landing "undoes" taking off.

35. These functions are inverses since their graphs are symmetric with respect to the line $y = x$.

37. These functions are not inverses since their graphs are not symmetric with respect to the line $y = x$.

39. $f(x) = 2x + 4$, $g(x) = \dfrac{1}{2}x - 2$

$(f \circ g)(x) = f[g(x)]$
$$= 2\left(\frac{1}{2}x - 2\right) + 4$$
$$= x - 4 + 4$$
$$= x$$
$(g \circ f)(x) = g[f(x)]$
$$\frac{1}{2}(2x + 4) - 2$$
$$= x + 2 - 2$$
$$= x$$
Since $(f \circ g)(x) = x$ and $(g \circ f)(x) = x$, these functions are inverses.

41. $f(x) = \dfrac{2}{x+6}$, $g(x) = \dfrac{6x+2}{x}$

$(f \circ g)(x) = f[g(x)]$
$$= f\left(\frac{6x+2}{x}\right)$$
$$= \frac{2}{\frac{6x+2}{x} + 6}$$
$$= \frac{2}{\frac{6x+2+6x}{x}}$$
$$= \frac{2}{1} \cdot \frac{x}{12x+2}$$
$$= \frac{2x}{12x+2}$$
$$= \frac{x}{6x+1} \neq x$$
Since $(f \circ g)(x) \neq x$, the functions are not inverses. It is not necessary to check $(g \circ f)(x)$.

43. $f(x) = x^2 + 3$, domain $[0, \infty)$,
$g(x) = \sqrt{x-3}$, domain $[3, \infty)$
$(f \circ g) = f[g(x)]$
$$= f\left(\sqrt{x-3}\right)$$
$$= \left(\sqrt{x-3}\right)^2 + 3$$
$$= x$$
$(g \circ f)(x) = g[f(x)]$
$$= g(x^2 + 3)$$
$$= \sqrt{x^2 + 3 - 3}$$
$$= \sqrt{x^2}$$
$$= |x|$$
$$= x, \text{ since } x \geq 0$$
Thus, these functions are inverses.

45. Draw the mirror image of the original graph across the line $y = x$.

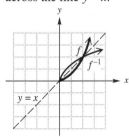

47. Carefully draw the mirror image of the original graph across the line $y = x$.

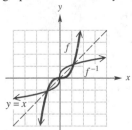

49. To graph the inverse, first draw the line $y = x$. and then draw the mirror image of the graph of the original functions across $y = x$. The graph of the inverse will be another line that also passes through $(0, 0)$.

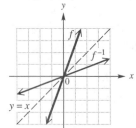

51. To find $f^{-1}(4)$, find the point with y-coordinate equal to 4. That point is $(4, 4)$. The graph of f^{-1} contains $(4, 4)$. Hence $f^{-1}(4) = 4$.

53. To find $f^{-1}(0)$, find the point with y-coordinate equal to 0. That point is $(2, 0)$. The graph of f^{-1} contains $(0, 2)$. Hence $f^{-1}(0) = 2$.

55. $f^{-1}(-3) = -2$, since the point on the graph of f that has y-coordinate equal to -3 is -2.

57.
$$S = 19; \ f(19) = 19^3 - 1 = 6858$$
$$A = 1; \ f(1) = 1^3 - 1 = 0$$
$$I = 9; \ f(9) = 9^3 - 1 = 728$$
$$L = 12; \ f(12) = 12^3 - 1 = 1727$$
$$O = 15; \ f(15) = 15^3 - 1 = 3374$$
$$R = 18; \ f(18) = 18^3 - 1 = 5831$$
$$B = 2; \ f(2) = 2^3 - 1 = 7$$
$$E = 5; \ f(5) = 5^3 - 1 = 124$$
$$W = 23; \ f(23) = 23^3 - 1 = 12,166$$
$$A = 1; \ f(1) = 1^3 - 1 = 0$$
$$R = 18; \ f(18) = 18^3 - 1 = 5831$$
$$E = 5; \ f(5) = 5^3 - 1 = 124$$

59. Decode the message with $f^{-1}(x)$.
$$x = 3y - 2$$
$$x + 2 = 3y$$
$$\frac{x+2}{3} = y$$
$$f^{-1}(x) = \frac{x+2}{3}$$

$$37; \ f^{-1}(37) = \frac{37+2}{3} = 13; \ M$$
$$25; \ f^{-1}(25) = \frac{25+2}{3} = 9; \ I$$
$$19; \ f^{-1}(19) = \frac{19+2}{3} = 7; \ G$$
$$61; \ f^{-1}(61) = \frac{61+2}{3} = 21; \ U$$
$$13; \ f^{-1}(13) = \frac{13+2}{3} = 5; \ E$$
$$34; \ f^{-1}(34) = \frac{34+2}{3} = 12; \ L$$
$$22; \ f^{-1}(22) = \frac{22+2}{3} = 8; \ H$$
$$1; \ f^{-1}(1) = \frac{1+2}{3} = 1; \ A$$
$$55; \ f^{-1}(55) = \frac{55+2}{3} = 19; \ S$$
$$1; \ f^{-1}(1) = \frac{1+2}{3} = 1; \ A$$
$$52; \ f^{-1}(52) = \frac{52+2}{3} = 18; \ R$$
$$52; \ f^{-1}(52) = \frac{52+2}{3} = 18; \ R$$
$$25; \ f^{-1}(25) = \frac{25+2}{3} = 9; \ I$$
$$64; \ f^{-1}(64) = \frac{64+2}{3} = 22; \ V$$
$$13; \ f^{-1}(13) = \frac{13+2}{3} = 5; \ E$$
$$10; \ f^{-1}(10) = \frac{10+2}{3} = 4; \ D$$

The message is MIGUEL HAS ARRIVED.

61. $y = 3x - 4$
Solve for x.
$$y + 4 = 3x$$
$$\frac{y+4}{3} = x = f^{-1}(y)$$
Exchange x and y.
$$\frac{x+4}{3} = y$$
$$f^{-1}(x) = \frac{x+4}{3}$$

The graph of the original function is a line with slope 3 and y-intercept -4. Since $f^{-1}(x) = \dfrac{x+4}{3} = \dfrac{1}{3}x + \dfrac{4}{3}$, the graph of the inverse function is a line with slope $\dfrac{1}{3}$ and y-intercept $\dfrac{4}{3}$.

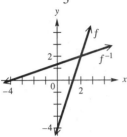

For both $f(x)$ and $f^{-1}(x)$, the domain is $(-\infty, \infty)$ and the range is $(-\infty, \infty)$.

63. $y = x^3 + 1$

$y - 1 = x^3$

$\sqrt[3]{y-1} = x = f^{-1}(y)$

Exchange x and y.

$\sqrt[3]{x-1} = y$

$f^{-1}(x) = \sqrt[3]{x-1}$

Plot points to graph these functions.

x	-1	0	1
$f(x)$	0	1	2

x	0	1	2
$f^{-1}(x)$	-1	0	1

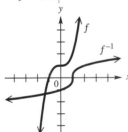

Domains and ranges of both f and f^{-1} are $(-\infty, \infty)$.

65. $y = x^2$

This is not a one-to-one function since $(2)^2 = 4$ and $(-2)^2 = 4$. Thus, the function has no inverse function.

67. $y = \dfrac{1}{x}$

$xy = 1$

$x = \dfrac{1}{y}$

Exchange x and y.

$y = \dfrac{1}{x}$

$f^{-1}(x) = \dfrac{1}{x}$

Observe that this function is its own inverse. Plot points to draw the graph.

x	-2	-1	$-\dfrac{1}{2}$	$\dfrac{1}{2}$	1	2
y	$-\dfrac{1}{2}$	-1	-2	2	1	$\dfrac{1}{2}$

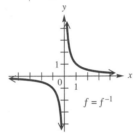

Domains and ranges of both f and f^{-1} are $(-\infty, 0) \cup (0, \infty)$.

69. $f(x) = \sqrt{6+x}$

$y = f(x)$ is one-to-one, so it has an inverse function. Solve for x.

$y = \sqrt{6+x}$

$y^2 = 6 + x, \ y \ge 0$

$y^2 - 6 = x, \ y \ge 0$

Exchange x and y.

$y = x^2 - 6, \ x \ge 0$

$f^{-1}(x) = x^2 - 6, \ x \ge 0$

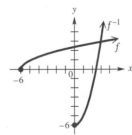

Domain of f = range of f^{-1} = $[-6, \infty)$

Range of f = domain of f^{-1} = $[0, \infty)$

71. $f^{-1}(1000)$ represents the number of dollars required to build 1000 cars.

73. If a line has slope a, the slope of its reflection in the line $y = x$ will be reciprocal of a, which is $\dfrac{1}{a}$.

75. Use a graphing calculator to graph $f(x) = 6x^3 + 11x^2 - x - 6$ using the window $[-3, 2]$ by $[-10, 10]$. The horizontal line test will show that this function is not one-to-one.

77. Use a graphing calculator to graph $f(x) = \dfrac{x-5}{x+3}$ using the window $[-8, 8]$ by $[-6, 8]$. The horizontal line test will show that this function is one-to-one. Find the equation of f^{-1}.

$$y = \frac{x-5}{x+3}$$
$$y(x+3) = x-5$$
$$yx + 3y = x-5$$
$$yx - x = -5 - 3y$$
$$x(y-1) = -5 - 3y$$
$$x = \frac{-5-3y}{y-1} = f^{-1}(y)$$
$$f^{-1}(x) = \frac{-5-3x}{x-1}$$

Graph $f^{-1}(x)$ on the same screen where you have graphed $f(x)$. Note that the two graphs are symmetric with respect to the line $y = x$.

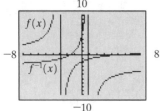

81. (a) No; if the closing average is the same for two different dates, then there is a horizontal line that intersects the graph at two points, so the function is not one-to-one.

(b) Yes; if a curve is increasing on its domain, then every horizontal line that intersects the graph only intersects it at one point, so the model function would be one-to-one.

(c) An inverse function is obtained by interchanging the components of the ordered pairs of a function:
(260.64, October 28, 1929).

Section 4.2

Connections *(page 286)*

1. $e^1 \approx 1 + 1 + \dfrac{1^2}{2 \cdot 1} + \dfrac{1^3}{3 \cdot 2 \cdot 1} + \dfrac{1^4}{4 \cdot 3 \cdot 2 \cdot 1} + \dfrac{1^5}{5 \cdot 4 \cdot 3 \cdot 2 \cdot 1}$

$= 1 + 1 + \dfrac{1}{2} + \dfrac{1}{6} + \dfrac{1}{24} + \dfrac{1}{120}$

≈ 2.717

2. $e^{-.05} \approx 1 + (-.05) + \dfrac{(-.05)^2}{2 \cdot 1} + \dfrac{(-.05)^3}{3 \cdot 2 \cdot 1}$

$+ \dfrac{(-.05)^4}{4 \cdot 3 \cdot 2 \cdot 1} + \dfrac{(-.05)^5}{5 \cdot 4 \cdot 3 \cdot 2 \cdot 1}$

$= 1 - .05 + \dfrac{.0025}{2} - \dfrac{.000125}{6}$

$+ \dfrac{.00000625}{24} - \dfrac{.0000003125}{120}$

$\approx .9512$

3. $\dfrac{x^6}{6 \cdot 5 \cdot 4 \cdot 3 \cdot 2 \cdot 1}$

Exercises

1. $f(x) = 3^x$

$f(2) = 3^2 = 9$

3. $f(x) = 3^x$

$f(-2) = 3^{-2} = \dfrac{1}{9}$

5. $g(x) = \left(\dfrac{1}{4}\right)^x$

$g(2) = \left(\dfrac{1}{4}\right)^2 = \dfrac{1}{16}$

7. $g(x) = \left(\dfrac{1}{4}\right)^x$

$g(-2) = \left(\dfrac{1}{4}\right)^{-2} = 4^2 = 16$

9. $f(x) = 3^x$

$f(1.5) = 3^{1.5} \approx 5.196152423$

11. $g(x) = \left(\dfrac{1}{4}\right)^x$

$g(2.34) = \left(\dfrac{1}{4}\right)^{2.34}$

$\approx .0390103297$

13. Yes; $f(x) = a^x$ is a one-to-one function. Therefore, an inverse function exists for f.

14. Since $f(x) = a^x$ has an inverse, the graph of $f^{-1}(x)$ will be the reflection of f across the line $y = x$.

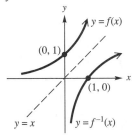

15. Since $f(x) = a^x$ has an inverse, we find it as follows.

$$y = a^x$$
$$x = a^y$$

16. If $a = 10$, the equation for $f^{-1}(x)$ will be given by $x = 10^y$.

17. If $a = e$, the equation for $f^{-1}(x)$ will be given by $x = e^y$.

18. If the point (p, q) is on the graph of f, then the point (q, p) is in the graph of f^{-1}.

19. $f(x) = 3^x$

Make a table of values.

x	–2	–1	0	1	2
y	$\frac{1}{9}$	$\frac{1}{3}$	1	3	9

Plot these points and draw a smooth curve through them. This is an increasing function. The domain is $(-\infty, \infty)$ and the range is $(0, \infty)$. The x-axis is a horizontal asymptote.

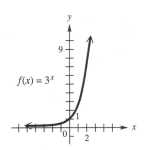

21. $f(x) = \left(\frac{1}{3}\right)^x$

Make a table of values.

x	–2	–1	0	1	2
y	9	3	1	$\frac{1}{3}$	$\frac{1}{9}$

Plot these points and draw a smooth curve through them. This is a decreasing function. The domain is $(-\infty, \infty)$ and the range is $(0, \infty)$. The x-axis is a horizontal asymptote.

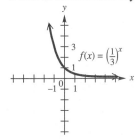

23. $f(x) = \left(\frac{3}{2}\right)^x$

The domain is $(-\infty, \infty)$ and the range is $(0, \infty)$. Make a table of values.

x	–2	–1	0	1	2
y	$\frac{4}{9}$	$\frac{2}{3}$	1	$\frac{3}{2}$	$\frac{9}{4}$

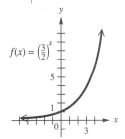

25. $f(x) = e^x$

The domain is $(-\infty, \infty)$ and the range is $(0, \infty)$. Use a calculator to find approximate values of y.

x	1	0	–1
y	2	1	.36

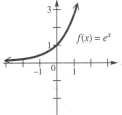

27. $f(x) = e^{-x}$

Use a calculator to find approximate values of y.

x	−2	−1	0	1	2
y	7.39	2.72	1	.368	.135

The graph of $f(x) = e^{-x}$ is the reflection of the graph $f(x) = e^x$ about the y-axis.

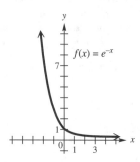

29. $f(x) = 2^{|x|}$

Make a table of values.

x	−3	−2	−1	0	1	2	3
y	8	4	2	1	2	4	8

Notice that for $x < 0$, $|x| = -x$, so the graph is the same as that of $f(x) = 2^{-x}$. For $x \geq 0$, $|x| = x$, so the graph is the same as that of $f(x) = 2^x$. Since $|-x| = |x|$, the graph is symmetric with respect to the y-axis.

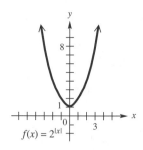

31. $f(x) = 2^x + 1$

This graph is obtained by translating the graph of $f(x) = 2^x$ up 1 unit.

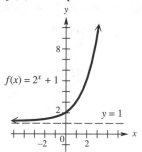

33. $f(x) = 2^{x+1}$

This graph is obtained by translating the graph of $f(x) = 2^x$ to the left 1 unit.

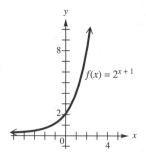

35. $f(x) = \left(\dfrac{1}{3}\right)^x - 2$

This graph is obtained by translating the graph of $f(x) = \left(\dfrac{1}{3}\right)^x$ down 2 units.

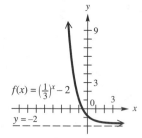

37. $f(x) = \left(\dfrac{1}{3}\right)^{x+2}$

The graph is obtained by translating the graph of

$f(x) = \left(\dfrac{1}{3}\right)^{x}$ 2 units to the left.

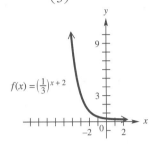

39. $a = 2.3$

Since graph A is increasing, $a > 1$. Since graph A is the middle of the three increasing graphs, the value of a must be the middle of the three values of a greater than 1.

41. $a = .75$

Since graph C is decreasing, $0 < a < 1$. Since graph C decreases at the slowest rate of the three decreasing graphs, the value of a must be the closest to 1 of the three values of less than 1.

43. $a = .31$

Since graph E is decreasing, $0 < a < 1$. Since graph E decreases at the fastest rate of the three decreasing graphs, the value of a must be the closest to 0 of the three values of a less than 1.

45. $f(x) = \dfrac{e^{x} - e^{-x}}{2}$

Graph this function in the standard viewing window.

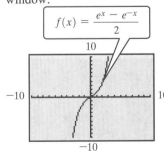

47. $f(x) = x \cdot 2^{x}$

Although this function can be graphed in the standard viewing window, a better picture of the graph is obtained by using window $[-5, 5]$ by $[-2, 5]$.

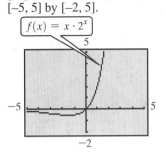

49. $4^{x} = 2$

Write both sides as powers of 2.

$(2^{2})^{x} = 2^{1}$

$2^{2x} = 2^{1}$

$2x = 1$ \qquad Property (b)

$x = \dfrac{1}{2}$

Solution set: $\left\{\dfrac{1}{2}\right\}$

51. $\left(\dfrac{1}{2}\right)^{k} = 4$

$(2^{-1})^{k} = 2^{2}$ \qquad $\dfrac{1}{2} = 2^{-1}$

$2^{-k} = 2$

$-k = 2$ \qquad Property (b)

$k = -2$

Solution set: $\{-2\}$

53. $2^{3-y} = 8$

$2^{3-y} = 2^{3}$

$3 - y = 3$ \qquad Property (b)

$-y = 0$

$y = 0$

Solution set $\{0\}$

55.
$$\frac{1}{27} = b^{-3}$$
$$\left(\frac{1}{27}\right)^{-1/3} = (b^{-3})^{-1/3}$$
$$\frac{1}{\frac{1}{27}^{1/3}} = b^1$$
$$\frac{1}{\sqrt[3]{\frac{1}{27}}} = b^1$$
$$\frac{1}{\frac{1}{3}} = b$$
$$3 = b$$

Solution set: {3}

57. $4 = r^{2/3}$

Raise both sides of the equation to the $\frac{3}{2}$ power,

since $\left(r^{2/3}\right)^{3/2} = r^1 = r$.

$$4^{3/2} = \left(r^{2/3}\right)^{3/2}$$
$$\left(\pm\sqrt{4}\right)^3 = r^1$$
$$(\pm 2)^3 = r$$
$$\pm 8 = r$$

Since raising both sides of an equation to the same power may result in false "solutions," it is necessary to check all proposed solutions in the original equation.

$$4 = 8^{2/3} \qquad\qquad 4 = (-8)^{2/3}$$
$$= \left(\sqrt[3]{8}\right)^2 \qquad\qquad = \left(\sqrt[3]{-8}\right)^2$$
$$= 2^2 \qquad\qquad = (-2)^2$$
$$= 4 \qquad\qquad = 4$$

Both proposed solutions check.
Solution set: {−8, 8}

59.
$$27^{4z} = 9^z + 1$$
$$(3^3)^{4z} = (3^2)^{z+1}$$
$$3^{12z} = 3^{2z+2}$$
$$12z = 2z + 2$$
$$10z = 2$$
$$z = \frac{1}{5}$$

Solution set: $\left\{\dfrac{1}{5}\right\}$

61.
$$\left(\frac{1}{2}\right)^{-x} = \left(\frac{1}{4}\right)^{x+1}$$
$$\left(\frac{1}{2}\right)^{-x} = \left[\left(\frac{1}{2}\right)^2\right]^{x+1}$$
$$\left(\frac{1}{2}\right)^{-x} = \left(\frac{1}{2}\right)^{2x+2}$$
$$-x = 2x + 2$$
$$-3x = 2$$
$$x = -\frac{2}{3}$$

Solution set: $\left\{-\dfrac{2}{3}\right\}$

63. Use the compound interest formula to find the future amount A if the present amount $P = 8906.54$, $r = .05$, $m = 2$, and $t = 9$

$$A = P\left(1 + \frac{r}{m}\right)^{tm}$$
$$= (8906.54)\left(1 + \frac{.05}{2}\right)^{9(2)}$$
$$= (8906.54)(1.025)^{18}$$
$$= (8906.54)(1.5596)$$
$$= 13,891.16$$

The future value is $13,891.16.

65. Use the compound interest formula to find P if $A = 25,000$, $t = \dfrac{11}{4}$, $m = 4$, and $r = .06$.

$$A = P\left(1 + \frac{r}{m}\right)^{tm}$$
$$25,000 = P\left(1 + \frac{.06}{4}\right)^{(11/4)(4)}$$
$$25,000 = P(1.015)^{11}$$
$$\frac{25,000}{(1.105)^{11}} = P$$
$$21,223.34 = P$$

The present value is $21,223.34.

67. Use the compound interest formula to find r if $A = 65{,}325$, $P = 65{,}000$, $t = \dfrac{1}{2}$, and $m = 12$.

$$65{,}325 = 65{,}000\left(1+\frac{r}{12}\right)^{(1/12)(12)}$$

$$65{,}325 = 65{,}000\left(1+\frac{r}{12}\right)^{6}$$

$$1.005 = \left(1+\frac{r}{12}\right)^{6}$$

Next, take the sixth root of both sides (or raise both sides to the 1/6 power) using the exponential key on a calculator.

$$(1.005)^{\frac{1}{6}} = 1+\frac{r}{12}$$

$$1.000832 = 1+\frac{r}{12}$$

$$.000832 = \frac{r}{12}$$

$$.00998 = r$$

$$.010 \approx r$$

The interest rate, to the nearest tenth, is 1.0%.

69. (a)

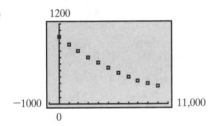

(b) From the graph above, we can see that the data are not linear but exponentially decreasing.

(c)

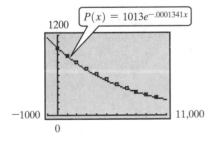

(d)
$$P(x) = 1013e^{-.0001341x}$$
$$P(1500) = 1013e^{-0001341(1500)}$$
$$\approx 828$$
$$P(11{,}000) = 1013e^{-.0001341(11000)}$$
$$\approx 232$$

When the altitude is 1500 m, the function P gives a pressure of 828 mb, which is less than the actual value of 846 mb. When the altitude is 11,000 m, the function P gives a pressure of 232 mb, which is more than the actual value of 227 mb.

71. $y = 4481e^{.0156x}$

(a) 1990 is 10 years after 1980, so use $t = 10$.
$$A(10) = 4481e^{.0156(10)}$$
$$= 4481e^{.156}$$
$$\approx 4481(1.168826)$$
$$\approx 5238$$

The function gives a population of about 5238 million, which differs from the actual value by 82 million.

(b) For 1995, use $t = 1995 - 1980 = 15$.
$$A(15) = 4481e^{.0156(15)}$$
$$= 4481e^{.234}$$
$$\approx 4481(1.2636445)$$
$$\approx 5662$$

The function gives a population of about 5662 million.

(c) For 2005, use $t = 25$.
$$A(25) = 4481e^{.0156(25)}$$
$$= 4481e^{.39}$$
$$\approx 4481^{(1.476991)}$$
$$\approx 6618$$

The function gives a population of about 6618 million.

73. $p(t) = 250 - 120(2.8)^{-.5t}$

(a)
$$p(2) = 250 - 120(2.8)^{-.5(2)}$$
$$= 250 - 120(2.8)^{-1}$$
$$\approx 207$$

After 2 months, a person will type about 207 symbols per minute.

(b) $p(4) = 250 - 120(2.8)^{-.5(4)}$
$= 250 - 120(2.8)^{-2}$
≈ 235
After 4 months, a person will type about 235 symbols per minute.

(c) $p(10) = 250 - 120(2.8)^{-.5(10)}$
$= 250 - 120(2.8)^{-5}$
≈ 249
After 10 months, a person will type about 249 symbols per minute.

75. $5e^{3x} = 75$

$e^{3x} = 15$

Use a graphing calculator to graph the exponential function $f(x) = e^{3x}$ and the horizontal line $g(x) = 15$ on the same screen. There is only one point where these two graphs intersect. Using TRACE or the "intersect" option in the CALC menu to estimate the x-coordinate of this point, we find that the only solution of the given equation is $x \approx .9$.
Solution set: $\{.9\}$

77. $3x + 2 = 4^x$
Use a graphing calculator to graph line $f(x) = 3x + 2$ and the exponential function $g(x) = 4^x$ on the same screen. These two graphs intersect in two points. The x-coordinates of these intersection points are the solutions of the given equation: $x = -.5$ and $x \approx 1.3$.
Solution set: $\{-.5, 1.3\}$

78. $x = 2^x$
Use a graphing calculator to graph the line $f(x) = x$ and the exponential function $g(x) = 2^x$ on the same screen. These two graphs do not intersect, so the given equation has no solution.
Solution set: $\emptyset$

80. $f(x) = a^x$ and $f(3) = 27$
$f(3) = a^3$ and $f(3) = 27$ together imply that $a^3 = 27$, so $a = 3$ and $f(x) = 3^x$.

(a) $f(1) = 3^1 = 3$

(b) $f(-1) = 3^{-1} = \dfrac{1}{3}$

(c) $f(2) = 3^2 = 9$

(d) $f(0) = 3^0 = 1$

81. If the graph of the exponential function $f(x) = a^x$ contains the point (3, 8), we have
$a^3 = 8$
$(a^3)^{\frac{1}{3}} = 8^{\frac{1}{3}}$
$a = 2.$
Thus, the equation which satisfies the given condition is $f(x) = 2^x$.

82. If the graph of the exponential function $f(x) = a^x$ contains the point (–3, 64), we have
$a^{-3} = 64$
$(a^{-3})^{-1/3} = 64^{-1/3}$
$a^1 = \dfrac{1}{\sqrt[3]{64}}$
$a = \dfrac{1}{4}.$
Thus, the equation which satisfies the given condition is $f(x) = \left(\dfrac{1}{4}\right)^x$.

83. $f(t) = 3^{2t+3}$
$= 3^{2t}3^3$
$= 27 \cdot (3^2)^t$
$= (27)9^t$

87. It would be greater than 1, since the graph should be increasing.

89. An exponential function either always increases or always decreases, so the graph that most closely resembles an exponential curve is the one for total all federal campaigns (hard and soft money).

Section 4.3

Connections *(page 299)*

1. $\log_{10} 458.3 \approx 2.661149857$
$+ \ \log_{10} 294.6 \approx 2.469232743$
$\overline{ \approx 5.130382600}$
$10^{5.130382600} \approx 135,015.18$

2. Answers will vary.

Exercises

1. E; $\log_2 16 = 4$ because $2^4 = 16$.

3. G; $\log_{10} .1 = -1$ because $10^{-1} = .1$.

5. C; $\log_{10} 10^5 = 5$ because $10^5 = 10^5$.

7. F; $\log_{1/2} 8 = -3$ because $\left(\dfrac{1}{2}\right)^{-3} = 8$.

9. $3^4 = 81$ is equivalent to $\log_3 81 = 4$.

11. $\left(\dfrac{2}{3}\right)^{-3} = \dfrac{27}{8}$ is equivalent to $\log_{2/3}\left(\dfrac{27}{8}\right) = -3$.

13. $\log_6 36 = 2$ is equivalent to $6^2 = 36$.

15. $\log_{\sqrt{3}} 81 = 8$ is equivalent to $\left(\sqrt{3}\right)^8 = 81$.

19. $x = \log_5\left(\dfrac{1}{625}\right)$

$5^x = \dfrac{1}{625}$

$5^x = \dfrac{1}{5^4}$

$5^x = 5^{-4}$

$x = -4$

Solution set: $\{-4\}$

21. $x = \log_{10} .001$

$10^x = .001$

$10^x = 10^{-3}$

$x = -3$

Solution set: $\{-3\}$

23. $x = 2^{\log_2 9}$

$x = 9$

Solution set: $\{9\}$

25. $\log_x 25 = -2$

$x^{-2} = 25$

$x^{-2} = 5^2$

$\left(x^{-2}\right)^{-1/2} = \left(5^2\right)^{-1/2}$

$x = 5^{-1}$

$x = \dfrac{1}{5}$

Solution set: $\left\{\dfrac{1}{5}\right\}$

27. $\log_4 x = 3$

$4^3 = x$

$64 = x$

Solution set: $\{64\}$

29. $x = \log_4 \sqrt[3]{16}$

$4^x = \sqrt[3]{16}$

$4^x = (16)^{1/3}$

$4^x = (4^2)^{1/3}$

$4^x = 4^{2/3}$

$x = \dfrac{2}{3}$

Solution set: $\left\{\dfrac{2}{3}\right\}$

33. $f(x) = \left(\log_2 x\right) + 3$

This graph is obtained by translating the graph of $f(x) = \log_2 x$ up 3 units.

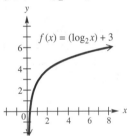

35. $f(x) = \left|\log_2(x+3)\right|$

First, translate the graph of $f(x) = \log_2 x$ to the left 3 units to obtain the graph of $\log_2(x+3)$. (See Exercise 34.) For the portion of the graph where $f(x) \geq 0$, that is, where $x \geq -2$, use the same graph as in 35. For the portion of the graph in 35 where $f(x) < 0$, $x < -2$, reflect the graph about the x-axis. In this way, each negative value of $f(x)$ on the graph in 35 is replaced by its opposite, which is positive. The graph has a vertical asymptote at $x = -3$.

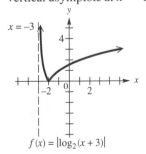

37. $f(x) = \log_{1/2}(x - 2)$

This is the graph of $f(x) = \log_{1/2} x$ translated to the right 2 units. The graph has a vertical asymptote at $x = 2$.

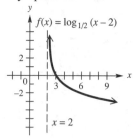

39. $f(x) = \log_3 x$

Write $y = \log_3 x$ in exponential form as $x = 3^y$ to find ordered pairs that satisfy the equation. It is easier to choose values for y and find the corresponding values of x. Make a table of values.

x	$\frac{1}{9}$	$\frac{1}{3}$	1	3	9
y	-2	-1	0	1	2

The graph can also be found by reflecting the graph of $f(x) = 3^x$ about the line $y = x$. The graph has the y-axis as a vertical asymptote.

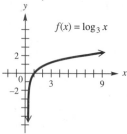

41. $f(x) = \log_{1/2}(1 - x)$

Make a table of values.

x	-7	-3	-1	0	$\frac{1}{2}$	$\frac{3}{4}$	$\frac{7}{8}$
$1 - x$	8	4	2	1	$\frac{1}{2}$	$\frac{1}{4}$	$\frac{1}{8}$
y	-3	-2	-1	0	1	2	3

The graph has a vertical asymptote at $x = 1$.

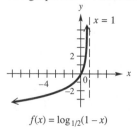

43. $f(x) = \log_3(x - 1)$

To graph the function, translate the graph of $f(x) = \log_3 x$ (from Exercise 39) 1 unit to the right. The vertical asymptote will be $x = 1$.

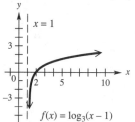

45. $f(x) = \log_2 x$

The x-intercept is 1, and the graph increases. The correct graph is E.

47. $f(x) = \log_2\left(\frac{1}{x}\right) = \log_2 x^{-1} = -\log_2 x$

The graph will be similar to that of $f(x) = \log_2 x$, but will be reflected across the x-axis. The x-intercept is 1. The correct graph is B.

49. $f(x) = \log_2(x - 1)$

The graph will be similar to that of $f(x) = \log_2 x$, but will be shifted 1 unit to the right. The x-intercept is 2 since $\log_2(2 - 1) = \log_2 1 = 0$. The correct graph is F.

51. $f(x) = x \log_{10} x$

Using a graphing calculator, enter $x \log x$ for Y_1. The graph is as shown.

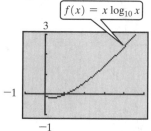

53. If x and y are positive numbers,
$$\log_a \frac{x}{y} = \log_a x - \log_a y.$$

54. Since $\log_2\left(\frac{x}{4}\right) = \log_2 x - \log_2 4$ by the quotient rule, the graph of $y = \log_2\left(\frac{x}{4}\right)$ can be obtained by shifting the graph of $y = \log_2 x$ down $\log_2 4 = 2$ units.

55. Graph $f(x) = \log_2\left(\dfrac{x}{4}\right)$ and $g(x) = \log_2 x$ on the same axes. The graph of f is 2 units below the graph of g. This supports the answer in Exercise 54.

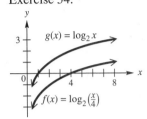

56. If $x = 4$, $\log_2 \dfrac{x}{4} = 0$; since $\log_2 x = 2$ and

$\log_2 4 = 2$, $\log_2 x - \log_2 4 = 0$.

By the quotient rule,

$\log_2\left(\dfrac{x}{4}\right) = \log_2 x - \log_2 4$.

Both sides should equal 0. Since $2 - 2 = 0$, they do.

57. $\log_2\left(\dfrac{6x}{y}\right)$

$= \log_2 6x - \log_2 y$
     Logarithm of a quotient

$= \log_2 6 + \log_2 x - \log_2 y$
     Logarithm of a product

59. $\log_5\left(\dfrac{5\sqrt{7}}{3}\right)$

$= \log_5\left(5\sqrt{7}\right) - \log_5 3$
          Logarithm of a quotient

$= \log_5 5 + \log_5 \sqrt{7} - \log_5 3$
          Logarithm of a product

$= 1 + \log_5 \sqrt{7} - \log_5 3 \qquad \log_b b = 1$

$= 1 + \log_5 7^{1/2} - \log_5 3 \qquad \sqrt{7} = 7^{1/2}$

$= 1 + \dfrac{1}{2}\log_5 7 - \log_5 3$

          Logarithm of a power

61. $\log_4(2x + 5y)$
Since this is a sum, none of the logarithm properties apply, so this expression cannot be simplified.

63. $\log_m \sqrt{\dfrac{5r^3}{z^5}}$

$= \log_m\left(\dfrac{5r^3}{z^2}\right)^{1/2}$

$= \dfrac{1}{2}\log_m \dfrac{5r^3}{z^5}$
          Logarithm of a power

$= \dfrac{1}{2}(\log_m 5r^3 - \log_m z^5)$
          Logarithm of a quotient

$= \dfrac{1}{2}(\log_m 5 + \log_m r^3 - \log_m z^5)$
          Logarithm of a product

$= \dfrac{1}{2}(\log_m 5 + 3\ \log_m r - 5\log_m z)$
          Logarithm of a power

65. $\log_a x + \log_a y - \log_a m$
$= \log_a xy - \log_a m$
          Logarithm of a product

$= \log_a\left(\dfrac{xy}{m}\right)$ Logarithm of a quotient

67. $2\log_m a - 3\log_m(b^2)$
$= \log_m a^2 - \log_m(b^2)^3$
          Logarithm of a power

$= \log_m a^2 - \log_m b^6$

$= \log_m\left(\dfrac{a^2}{b^6}\right)$ Logarithm of a quotient

69. $2\log_a(z - 1) + \log_a(3z + 2)$
$= \log_a(z - 1)^2 + \log_a(3z + 2)$
          Logarithm of a power

$= \log_a[(z - 1)^2(3z + 2)]$
          Logarithhm of a product

71. $\log_{10} 6 = \log_{10}(2 \cdot 3)$
$= \log_{10} 2 + \log_{10} 3$
$= .3010 + .4771$
$= .7781$

73. $\log_{10} \dfrac{9}{4} = \log_{10} 9 - \log_{10} 4$

$= \log_{10} 3^2 - \log_{10} 2^2$
$= 2\log_{10} 3 - 2\log_{10} 2$
$\approx 2(.4771) - 2(.3010)$
$= .9542 - .6020$
$= .3522$

75. (a)

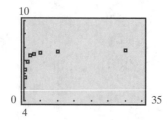

(b) The interest rates increase with time, but not at a constant rate. Therefore, a linear function would not model the data well. The interest rates gradually level off. This resembles a shifted logarithmic function. An (increasing) exponential function does not level off, but rather continues to increase at an even faster rate.

77. $f(3) = 2$
$$f(x) = \log_a x$$
$$2 = \log_a 3$$
$$a^2 = 3$$
$$(a^2)^{1/2} = 3^{1/2}$$
$$a = \sqrt{3}$$

(a) $f(x) = \log_a x$
$$f(x) = \log_{\sqrt{3}} x$$
$$f\left(\frac{1}{9}\right) = \log_{\sqrt{3}}\left(\frac{1}{9}\right)$$
$$y = \log_{\sqrt{3}} \frac{1}{9}$$
$$\left(\sqrt{3}\right)^y = \frac{1}{9}$$
$$(3^{1/2})^y = \frac{1}{3^2}$$
$$3^{y/2} = 3^{-2}$$
$$\frac{y}{2} = -2$$
$$y = -4$$

(b) $f(x) = \log_a x$
$$f(x) = \log_{\sqrt{3}} x$$
$$f(27) = \log_{\sqrt{3}} 27$$
$$y = \log_{\sqrt{3}} 27$$
$$\left(\sqrt{3}\right)^y = 27$$
$$(3^{1/2})^y = 3^3$$
$$3^{y/2} = 3^3$$
$$\frac{y}{2} = 3$$
$$y = 6$$

81. $\log_{10} x = x - 2$
Graph $Y_1 = \log_{10} x$ and $Y_2 = x - 2$ on a graphing calculator. The x-coordinates of the intersection points will be the solutions to the given equation. The solutions are $x \approx .01$ and $x \approx 2.38$.
Solution set: $\{.01, 2.38\}$

83.   Prove: $\log_a \dfrac{x}{y} = \log_a x - \log_a y$.
Let $m = \log_a x$ and $n = \log_a y$.
Changing to exponential form, $a^m = x$ and $a^n = y$.
Then,
$$\frac{x}{y} = \frac{a^m}{a^n}$$
$$\frac{x}{y} = a^{m-n}.$$

Changing to logarithmic form,
$$\log_a \frac{x}{y} = m - n$$
$$\log_a \frac{x}{y} = \log_a x - \log_a y.$$

Section 4.4

Exercises

1. For $f(x) = a^x$, where $a > 0$, the function is *increasing* over its entire domain.

3. $f(x) = 5^x$
$$y = 5^x$$
$$x = 5^y \quad \text{Exchange } x \text{ and } y \text{ to find the inverse.}$$
or $\log_5 x = y$
If $f(x) = 5^x$, then $f^{-1}(x) = \log_5 x$.

5. A base e logarithm is called a *natural* logarithm, while a base 10 logarithm is called a *common* logarithm.

7. $\log_2 0$ is undefined because there is no power of 2 that yields a result of 0.

9. The graph of $y = \log x$ has coordinates $x = 8$, $y = .90308999$. Thus, $\log 8 \approx .90308999$.

11. $\log 36 = 1.5563$

13. $\log .042 = -1.3768$

15. $\log(2 \times 10^4) = 4.3010$

17. $\ln 36 = 3.5835$

19. $\ln .042 = 3.1701$

21. $\ln(2 \times e^4) = 4.6931$

23. Grapefruit, 6.3×10^{-4}

$$pH = -\log[H_3O^+]$$
$$= -\log(6.3 \times 10^{-4})$$
$$= -(\log 6.3 + \log 10^{-4})$$
$$= -(.7793 - 4)$$
$$= -.7993 + 4$$
$$pH = 3.2$$

The answer is rounded to the nearest tenth because it is customary to round pH values to the nearest tenth. The pH of grapefruit is 3.2.

25. Limes, 1.6×10^{-2}

$$pH = -\log[H_3O^+]$$
$$= -\log(1.6 \times 10^{-2})$$
$$= -(\log 1.6 + \log 10^{-2})$$
$$= -(.2041 - 2)$$
$$= -(-1.7959)$$
$$pH = 1.8$$

The pH of limes is 1.8.

27. Soda pop, 2.7

$$pH = -\log[H_3O^+]$$
$$2.7 = -\log[H_3O^+]$$
$$-2.7 = \log[H_3O^+]$$
$$[H_3O^+] = 2.0 \times 10^{-3}$$

29. Beer, 4.8

$$pH = -\log[H_3O^+]$$
$$4.8 = -\log[H_3O^+]$$
$$-4.8 = \log[H_3O^+]$$
$$[H_3O^+] = 10^{-4.8}$$
$$[H_3O^+] = 1.6 \times 10^{-5}$$

31. Wetland, 2.49×10^{-5}

$$pH = -\log(2.49 \times 10^{-5})$$
$$= -(\log 2.49 + \log 10^{-5})$$
$$= -\log 2.49 - (-5)$$
$$= -\log 2.49 + 5$$
$$\approx 4.6$$

Since the pH is between 4.0 and 6.0, it is a poor fen.

33. Wetland, 2.49×10^{-7}

$$pH = -\log(2.49 \times 10^{-7})$$
$$= -(\log 2.49 + \log 10^{-7})$$
$$= -\log 2.49 - (-7)$$
$$= -\log 2.49 + 7$$
$$\approx 6.6$$

Since the pH is greater than 6.0, it is a rich fen.

35. $\log_2 5 = \dfrac{\ln 5}{\ln 2}$

$$\approx \dfrac{1.6094}{.6931}$$
$$\approx 2.3219$$

37. $\log_8 .59 = \dfrac{\log .59}{\log 8}$

$$\approx \dfrac{-.2291}{.9031}$$
$$\approx -.2537$$

39. $\log_{\sqrt{13}} 12 = \dfrac{\ln 12}{\ln \sqrt{13}}$

$$\approx \dfrac{2.4849}{1.2825}$$
$$\approx 1.9376$$

41. $\log_{.32} 5 = \dfrac{\log 5}{\log .32}$

$$\approx \dfrac{.6990}{-.4949}$$
$$\approx -1.4125$$

43. $2 \ln 3x = \ln(3x)^2$

$$= \ln 3^2 x^2$$
$$= \ln 9x^2$$

It is the same as D.

45. $\ln\left(b^4 \sqrt{a}\right) = \ln\left(b^4 a^{1/2}\right)$

$$= \ln b^4 + \ln a^{1/2}$$
$$= 4 \ln b + \frac{1}{2} \ln a$$
$$= 4v + \frac{1}{2}u$$

47. $\ln \sqrt{\dfrac{a^3}{b^5}} = \ln \left(\dfrac{a^3}{b^5} \right)^{1/2}$

$\qquad = \ln \left(\dfrac{a^{3/2}}{b^{5/2}} \right)$

$\qquad = \ln a^{3/2} - \ln b^{5/2}$

$\qquad = \dfrac{3}{2} \ln a - \dfrac{5}{2} \ln b$

$\qquad = \dfrac{3}{2} u - \dfrac{5}{2} v$

49. $g(x) = e^x$

   (a) By the theorem on inverses,

   $\qquad g(\ln 3) = e^{\ln 3}$

   $\qquad \qquad = 3.$

   (b) By the theorem on inverses,

   $\qquad g[\ln (5^2)] = e^{\ln 5^2}$

   $\qquad \qquad = 5^2 = 25$

   (c) By the theorem on inverses,

   $\qquad g\left[\ln \left(\dfrac{1}{e} \right) \right] = e^{\ln(1/e)}$

   $\qquad \qquad = \dfrac{1}{e}.$

51. $f(x) = \ln x$

   (a) By the theorem on inverses,

   $\qquad f(e^5) = \ln e^5$

   $\qquad \qquad = 5.$

   (b) By the theorem on inverses,

   $\qquad f(e^{\ln 3}) = \ln e^{\ln 3}$

   $\qquad \qquad = \ln 3.$

   (c) By the theorem on inverses,

   $\qquad f(e^{2\ln 3}) = \ln e^{2\ln 3}$

   $\qquad \qquad = 2\ln 3$

   $\qquad \qquad \text{or } \ln 9.$

53. $f(x) = \ln |x|$
   The domain is $(-\infty, 0) \cup (0, \infty)$.
   The range is $(-\infty, \infty)$.
   It is symmetric with respect to the y-axis.

55. The table for $Y_1 = \log_3(4 - x)$ shows "ERROR"
   for $x \ge 4$. This is because the function is
   undefined for $x \ge 4$. The domain of $y = \log_a x$ is
   $x > 0$, which means that for Y_1, the domain is
   $4 - x > 0$, or $x < 4$.

57. $f(x) = \ln e^2 x$
   $f(x) = \ln e^2 + \ln x$
   $f(x) = 2 + \ln x$, so it is a vertical shift of the
   graph of $f(x) = \ln x$ upward 2 units.

59. Let $r =$ the decibel rating of a sound.
   $$r = 10 \cdot \log_{10} \dfrac{I}{I_0}$$

   (a) $r = 10 \cdot \log_{10} \dfrac{100 \cdot I_0}{I_0}$

   $\qquad = 10 \cdot \log_{10} 100$

   $\qquad = 10 \cdot 2$

   $\qquad = 20$

   (b) $r = 10 \cdot \log_{10} \dfrac{1000 \cdot I_0}{I_0}$

   $\qquad = 10 \cdot \log_{10} 1000$

   $\qquad = 10 \cdot 3$

   $\qquad = 30$

   (c) $r = 10 \cdot \log_{10} \dfrac{100,000 \cdot I_0}{I_0}$

   $\qquad = 10 \cdot 5$

   $\qquad = 50$

   (d) $r = 10 \cdot \log_{10} \dfrac{1,000,000 \cdot I_0}{I_0}$

   $\qquad = 10 \cdot 6$

   $\qquad = 60$

   (e) $I = 2I_0$

   $\qquad r = 10 \cdot \log_{10} \dfrac{2I_0}{I_0}$

   $\qquad r = 10 \cdot \log_{10} 2$

   $\qquad r = 3.0103$

   The described rating is increased by 3.0103.

61. Let $r =$ the Richter scale rating of an earthquake.
   $$r = \log_{10} \left(\dfrac{I}{I_0} \right)$$

   (a) $r = \log_{10} \dfrac{1000 \cdot I}{I_0}$

   $\qquad = \log_{10} 1000$

   $\qquad = 3$

   (b) $r = \log_{10} \dfrac{1,000,000 \cdot I}{I_0}$

   $\qquad = \log_{10} 1,000,000$

   $\qquad = 6$

(c) $r = \log_{10} \dfrac{100,000,000 \cdot I_0}{I_0}$

$= \log_{10} 100,000,000$

$= 8$

63. $r = \log_{10}\left(\dfrac{I}{I_0}\right)$

$8.1 = \log_{10}\left(\dfrac{I}{I_0}\right)$

$10^{8.1} = \dfrac{I}{I_0}$

$I_0 10^{8.1} = I$

$I \approx 125,892,541 I_0$

65. $f(x) = -273 + 74\ln x$

In the year 2000, $x = 100$.

$f(100) = -273 + 74\ln 100$

≈ 68

Thus, the number of visitors in the year 2000 will be about 68 million. Beyond 1997, we must assume that the rate of increase continues to be logarithmic.

67. $S_n = a\ln\left(l + \dfrac{n}{a}\right)$

$= .36\ln\left(1 + \dfrac{n}{.36}\right)$

(a) $S(100) = .36\ln\left(1 + \dfrac{100}{.36}\right)$

$= .36\ln 278.77$

$= (.36)(5.6304)$

≈ 2

(b) $S(200) = .36\ln\left(1 + \dfrac{200}{.36}\right)$

$= .36\ln(556.555)$

$= .36(6.322)$

≈ 2

(c) $S(150) = .36\ln\left(1 + \dfrac{150}{.36}\right)$

$= .36\ln 417.666$

$= .36(6.0347)$

≈ 2

(d) $S(10) = .36\ln\left(1 + \dfrac{10}{.36}\right)$

$= .36\ln 28.777$

$= .36(3.3596)$

≈ 1

69. The index of diversity H for 2 species is given by

$H = -[P_1 \log_2 P_1 + P_2 \log_2 P_2]$

$P_1 = \dfrac{50}{100}$

$= .5$

$P_2 = \dfrac{50}{100}$

$= .5$

Substituting into the formula gives

$H = -[.5\log_2 .5 + .5\log_2 .5].$

Since $\log_2 .5 = \log_2 \dfrac{1}{2} = -1$, we have

$H = -[.5(-1) + .5(-1)]$

$= -(-1)$

$= 1$

The index of diversity is 1.

71. From Example 5,

$T(R) = 1.03R$

and $R = k\ln\left(\dfrac{C}{C_0}\right).$

By substitution, we have

$T(k) = 1.03k\ln\left(\dfrac{C}{C_0}\right).$

Since $10 \le k \le 16$ and $\left(\dfrac{C}{C_0}\right) = 2$, the range for

$T = 1.03k\ln\left(\dfrac{C}{C_0}\right)$ will be between

$T = 1.03(10)\ln 2 \approx 7.1$

and $T = 1.03(16)\ln 2 \approx 11.4.$

The predicted increased global temperature due to the greenhouse effect from a doubling of the carbon dioxide in the atmosphere is between $7°F$ and $11°F$.

73. (a) The table of natural logarithms takes the following form. Let $x = \ln D$ and $y = \ln P$ for each planet.

Planet	$\ln D$	$\ln P$
Mercury	$-.94$	-1.43
Venus	$-.33$	$-.48$
Earth	0	0
Mars	$.42$	$.64$
Jupiter	1.65	2.48
Saturn	2.26	3.38
Uranus	2.95	4.43
Neptune	3.40	5.10

Plot this data in the window $[-2, 4]$ by $[-2, 6]$.

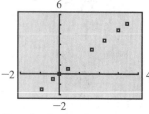

Yes, the data points appear to be linear.

(b) Choose two points from the table showing $\ln D$ and $\ln P$ and find the equation through them. If we use $(0, 0)$, representing Earth and $(3.40, 5.10)$ representing Neptune, we obtain

$$m = \frac{5.10 - 0}{3.40 - 0} = 1.5.$$

Since the y-intercept is 0, the equation is
$$y = 1.5x$$
or $\ln P = 1.5 \ln D$.

Since the points lie approximately but not exactly on a line, a slightly different equation will be found if a different pair of points is used.

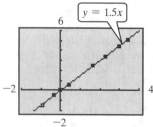

(c) For Pluto, $D = 39.5$, so
$$\ln P = 1.5 \ln D$$
$$= 1.5 \ln 39.5$$
Then
$$P = e^{1.5 \ln 39.5}$$
$$= e^{\ln 39.5^{1.5}}$$
$$= (39.5)^{1.5}$$
$$\approx 248.3.$$
The linear equation predicts that the period of the planet Pluto is 248.3 years, which is very close to the true value of 248.5 years.

Section 4.5

Exercises

1. Since x is the exponent to which 7 must be raised in order to obtain 19, the solution is
$$\log_7 19 \quad \text{or} \quad \frac{\log 19}{\log 7} \quad \text{or} \quad \frac{\ln 19}{\ln 7}.$$

2. Since x is the exponent to which 3 must be raised in order to obtain 10, the solution is
$$\log_3 10 \quad \text{or} \quad \frac{\log 10}{\log 3} \quad \text{or} \quad \frac{\ln 10}{\ln 3}.$$

3. Since x is the exponent to which $\dfrac{1}{2}$ must be raised in order to obtain 12, the solution is
$$\log_{1/2} 12 \quad \text{or} \quad \frac{\log 12}{\log\left(\frac{1}{2}\right)} \quad \text{or} \quad \frac{\ln 12}{\ln\left(\frac{1}{2}\right)}.$$

5. $3^x = 6$
Take base e (natural) logarithms of both sides.
$$\ln 3^x = \ln 6$$
$$x \ln 3 = \ln 6 \quad \text{Logarithm of a power}$$
$$x = \frac{\ln 6}{\ln 3}$$
$$\approx \frac{1.7918}{1.0986}$$
$$\approx 1.6309$$
Solution set: $\{1.6309\}$

7. $6^{1-2x} = 8$

Take base 10 (common) logarithms of both sides. (This exercise can also be done using natural logarithms.)

$$\log 6^{1-2x} = \log 8$$
$$(1-2x)\log 6 = \log 8$$
$$1 - 2x = \frac{\log 8}{\log 6}$$
$$2x = 1 - \frac{\log 8}{\log 6}$$
$$x = \frac{1}{2}\left(1 - \frac{\log 8}{\log 6}\right)$$
$$\approx \frac{1}{2}\left(1 - \frac{.9031}{.7782}\right)$$
$$\approx -.0803$$

Solution set: $\{-.0803\}$

9.
$$2^{x+3} = 5^x$$
$$\log 2^{x+3} = \log 5^x$$
$$(x+3)\log 2 = x\log 5$$
$$x\log 2 + 3\log 2 = x\log 5$$
$$x\log 2 - x\log 5 = -3\log 2$$
$$x(\log 2 - \log 5) = -3\log 2$$
$$x = \frac{-3\log 2}{\log 2 - \log 5}$$
$$x \approx 2.2694$$

Solution set: $\{2.2694\}$

11.
$$e^{x-1} = 4$$
$$\ln e^{x-1} = \ln 4$$
$$x - 1 = \ln 4$$
$$x = \ln 4 + 1$$
$$= 1.3863 + 1$$
$$= 2.3863$$

Solution set: $\{2.3863\}$

13.
$$2e^{5x+2} = 8$$
$$e^{5x+2} = 4$$
$$\ln e^{5x+2} = \ln 4$$
$$5x + 2 = \ln 4$$
$$5x = \ln 4 - 2$$
$$x = \frac{1}{5}(\ln 4 - 2)$$
$$\approx \frac{1}{5}(1.3863 - 2)$$
$$\approx -.1227$$

Solution set: $\{-.1227\}$

15. $2^x = -3$ has no solution since 2 raised to any power is positive.

Solution set: $\emptyset$

17. $e^{8x} \cdot e^{2x} = e^{20}$
$$e^{10x} = e^{20}$$
$$10x = 20$$
$$x = 2$$

Solution set: $\{2\}$

19. $100(1.02)^{x/4} = 200$
$$(1.02)^{x/4} = 2$$
$$\left(\frac{x}{4}\right)\log 1.02 = \log 2$$
$$\frac{x}{4} = \frac{\log 2}{\log 1.02}$$
$$x = 4\frac{\log 2}{\log 1.02}$$
$$x \approx 140.0112$$

Solution set: $\{140.0112\}$

21. $\log x + \log(x - 21) = 2$
$$\log[x(x-21)] = 2$$
$$10^2 = x(x-21)$$
$$100 = x^2 - 21x$$
$$0 = x^2 - 21x - 100$$
$$0 = (x-25)(x+4)$$
$$x - 25 = 0 \quad \text{or} \quad x + 4 = 0$$
$$x = 25 \quad \text{or} \quad x = -4$$

Since $x = -4$ is not in the domain of $\log x$ or $\log(x - 21)$, it cannot be used.

Solution set: $\{25\}$

23. $\ln(5 + 4x) - \ln(3 + x) = \ln 3$
$$\ln\frac{5 + 4x}{3 + x} = \ln 3$$
$$\frac{5 + 4x}{3 + x} = 3$$
$$5 + 4x = 3(3 + x)$$
$$5 + 4x = 9 + 3x$$
$$x = 4$$

Solution set: $\{4\}$

25. $\log_6 4x - \log_6(x - 3) = \log_6 12$
$$\log_6 \frac{4x}{x-3} = \log_6 12$$
$$\frac{4x}{x-3} = 12$$
$$4x = 12(x - 3)$$
$$4x = 12x - 36$$
$$36 = 8x$$
$$\frac{36}{8} = x$$
$$4.5 = x$$

Solution set: $\{4.5\}$

27.
$$5^{x+2} = 2^{2x-1}$$
$$\log 5^{x+2} = \log 2^{2x-1}$$
$$(x+2)\log 5 = (2x-1)\log 2$$
$$x\log 5 + 2\log 5 = 2x\log 2 - \log 2$$
$$x\log 5 - 2x\log 2 = -2\log 5 - \log 2$$
$$x(\log 5 - 2\log 2) = -2\log 5 - \log 2$$
$$x = \frac{-2\log 5 - \log 2}{\log 5 - 2\log 2}$$
$$x \approx -17.5314$$
Solution set: $\{-17.5314\}$

29.
$$\ln e^x - \ln e^3 = \ln e^5$$
$$x - 3 = 5$$
$$x = 8$$
Solution set: $\{8\}$

31.
$$\log_2(\log_2 x) = 1$$
$$\log_2(\log_2 x) = \log_2 2 \quad \text{since } \log_2 2 = 1$$
$$\log_2 x = 2$$
$$x = 4$$
Solution set: $\{4\}$

33.
$$\log x^2 = (\log x)^2$$
$$2\log x = (\log x)^2$$
Let $w = \log x$.
$$2w = w^2$$
$$0 = w^2 - 2w$$
$$0 = w(w-2)$$
$$w = 0 \quad \text{or} \quad w = 2$$
Replace w with $\log x$ to find the values for x.
$$0 = \log x \quad \text{or} \quad 2 = \log x$$
$$1 = x \quad \text{ or } \quad 100 = x$$
Solution set: $\{1, 100\}$

37.
$$I = \frac{E}{R}\left(1 - e^{-Rt/2}\right) \text{ for } t$$
$$I = \frac{E}{R} - \frac{Ee^{-Rt/2}}{R}$$
$$I - \frac{E}{R} = -\frac{Ee^{-Rt/2}}{R}$$
$$\frac{RI - E}{R}\left(-\frac{R}{E}\right) = e^{-Rt/2}$$
$$\frac{E - RI}{E} = e^{-Rt/2}$$
$$\ln\left(\frac{E - RI}{E}\right) = \ln e^{-Rt/2}$$
$$\ln\left(\frac{E - RI}{E}\right) = -\frac{Rt}{2}$$
$$t = -\frac{2}{R}\ln\left(1 - \frac{RI}{E}\right)$$

39.
$$p = a + \frac{k}{\ln x} \text{ for } x$$
$$p - a = \frac{k}{\ln x}$$
$$(p-a)\ln x = k$$
$$\ln x = k/(p-a)$$
To solve for x, change this equation from logarithmic to exponential form.
$$x = e^{k/(p-a)}$$

42.
$$(e^x)^2 - 4e^x + 3 = 0$$
$$(e^x - 1)(e^x - 3) = 0$$

43.
$$(e^x - 1)(e^x - 3) = 0$$
Set each factor to 0 and solve.
$$e^x - 1 = 0 \quad \text{or} \quad e^x - 3 = 0$$
$$e^x = 1 \qquad\qquad e^x = 3$$
$$\ln e^x = \ln 1 \qquad \ln e^x = \ln 3$$
$$x = 0 \quad \text{or} \qquad x = \ln 3$$
Solution set: $\{0, \ln 3\}$

44. Graph $y = e^{2x} - 4e^x + 3$ on a graphing calculator, using the window $[-5, 5]$ by $[-5, 10]$.

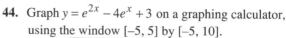

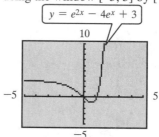

The graph intersects the x-axis at 0 and $1.099 \approx \ln 3$.

45. From the graph, we see that the intervals where $y > 0$ are $(-\infty, 0)$ and $(\ln 3, \infty)$, so the solution set of the inequality
$$e^{2x} - 4e^x + 3 > 0$$
is $(-\infty, 0) \cup (\ln 3, \infty)$.

46. From the graph we see that $y < 0$ on the interval $(0, \ln 3)$, so the solution set of the inequality
$$e^{2x} = 4e^x + 3 < 0 \text{ is } (0, \ln 3).$$

47.
$$f(x) = e^{x+1} - 4$$
$$y = e^{x+1} - 4$$
$$x = e^{y+1} - 4 \qquad \text{Exchange } x \text{ and } y.$$
$$x + 4 = e^{y+1}$$
$$\ln(x+4) = \ln e^{y+1}$$
$$\ln(x+4) = y + 1$$
$$\ln(x+4) - 1 = y$$
$$f^{-1}(x) = \ln(x+4) - 1$$
Domain: $(-4, \infty)$
Range: $(-\infty, \infty)$

49. $\log_3 x > 3$
$\log_3 x - 3 > 0$
Graph $Y_1 = \log_3 x - 3$. Using change of base,
graph $Y_1 = \dfrac{\log x}{\log 3} - 3$.
The graph is positive in the interval $(27, \infty)$, so the solution to the original inequality is $(27, \infty)$.

51. $e^x + \ln x = 5$
Graph $Y_1 = e^x + \ln x$ and $Y_2 = 5$ on the same screen.
Using the "intersect" option in the CALC menu, we find that the two graphs intersect at approximately $(1.52, 5)$. The x-coordinate of this point is the solution of the equation.
Solution set: $\{1.52\}$

53. $2e^x + 1 = 3e^{-x}$
Graph $Y_1 = 2e^x + 1$ and $Y_2 = 3e^{-x}$ on the same screen. The two curves intersect at the point $(0, 3)$. The x-coordinate of this point is the solution of the equation.
Solution set: $\{0\}$

55. $\log x = x^2 - 8x + 14$
Graph $Y_1 = \log x$ and $Y_2 = x^2 - 8x + 14$.
The intersection points are at $x = 2.45$ and $x = 5.66$.
Solution set: $\{2.45, 5.66\}$

57. Double the 1998 value is $2(97.3) = 194.6$.
$$f(x) = 23 \cdot 1.2^x$$
$$194.6 = 23 \cdot 1.2^x$$
$$\frac{194.6}{23} = 1.2^x$$
$$\log \frac{194.6}{23} = \log 1.2^x$$
$$\log \frac{194.6}{23} = x \log 1.2$$
$$\frac{\log \frac{194.6}{23}}{\log 1.2} = x$$
$$x \approx 11.7$$
$1990 + 11.7 = 2001.7$
During 2001, the worldwide shipments will be double their 1998 value.

59. $f(x) = \dfrac{25}{1 + 1364.3e^{x/9.316}}$
In 1997, $x = 97$.
$$f(97) = \frac{25}{1 + 1364.3e^{-97/9.316}}$$
$$f(97) \approx 24$$
In 1997, about 24% of U.S. children lived in a home without a father.

61.   (a) $\ln(1 - P) = -.0034 - .0053T$
Change this equation to exponential form
$$1 - P = e^{-.0034 - .0053T}$$
$$P(T) = 1 - e^{-.0034 - .0034T}$$

(b)

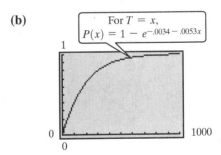

From the graph one can see that initially there is a rapid reduction of carbon dioxide emissions. However, after a while there is little benefit in raising taxes further.

(c) $P(T) = 1 - e^{-.0034 - .0053T}$
$$P(60) = 1 - e^{-.0034 0.0053(60)}$$
$$\approx .275 \text{ or } 27.5\%$$
The reduction in carbon emissions from a tax of \$60 per ton of carbon is 27.5%.

(d) We must determine T when $P = .5$.

$$P(T) = 1 - e^{-.0034 - .0053T} = .5$$
$$.5 = 1 - e^{-.0034 - .0053T}$$
$$.5 = e^{-.0034 - .0053T}$$
$$\ln .5 = -.0034 - .0053T$$
$$T = \frac{\ln .5 + .0034}{-.0053} \approx 130.14$$

The value $T = \$130.14$ will give a 50% reduction in carbon emissions.

63. $A = P\left(1 + \dfrac{r}{m}\right)^{tm}$

To solve to t, substitute
$A = 30,000$, $P = 27,000$, $r = .06$, and $m = 4$.

$$30,000 = 27,000\left(1 + \frac{.06}{4}\right)^{(t)(4)}$$
$$1.1111 \approx (1.015)^{4t}$$
$$\ln 1.1111 = \ln(1.015^{4t})$$
$$\ln 1.1111 = 4t \ln 1.015$$
$$\frac{\ln 1.1111}{4 \ln 1.015} = t$$
$$1.8 \approx t$$

To the nearest tenth of a year, Tom will be ready to buy a car in 1.8 yr.

65.

$$A = P\left(1 + \frac{r}{m}\right)^{tm}$$
$$2500 = 2000\left(1 + \frac{r}{2}\right)^{(3.5)(2)}$$
$$2500 = 2000\left(1 + \frac{r}{2}\right)^{7}$$
$$1.25 = \left(1 + \frac{r}{2}\right)^{7}$$
$$\sqrt[7]{1.25} = 1 + \frac{r}{2}$$
$$2\left(\sqrt[7]{1.25} - 1\right) = r$$
$$.0648 = r$$

The interest rate is about 6.48%.

Section 4.6

Exercises

1. B

3. C

5. $A(t) = 500e^{-.032t}$

(a) $t = 4$
$$A(4) = 500e^{-.032(4)}$$
$$\approx 440$$
After 4 years, about 440 g remain.

(b) $t = 8$
$$A(8) = 500e^{-.032(8)}$$
$$\approx 387$$
After 8 years, about 387 g remain.

(c) $t = 20$
$$A(20) = 500e^{-.032(20)}$$
$$\approx 264$$
After 20 years, about 264 g remain.

(d) Find t when $A(t) = 250$.
$$250 = 500e^{-.032t}$$
$$.5 = e^{-.032t}$$
$$\ln .5 = \ln e^{-.032t}$$
$$-.6931 = -.032t$$
$$21.66 \approx t$$
The half-life is about 21.66 yr.

7. $A(t) = A_0 e^{-.00043t}$
Find t when $A(t) = .5A_0$.
$$.5 A_0 = A_0 e^{-.00043t}$$
$$.5 = e^{-.00043t}$$
$$\ln .5 = \ln e^{-.00043t}$$
$$-.6931 = -.00043t$$
$$1611.97 \approx t$$
The half-life is about 1611.97 yr.

9. $p(h) = 86.3 \ln h - 680$

(a) $h = 3000$
$$p(3000) = 86.3 \ln 3000 - 680$$
$$\approx 11$$
At 3000 ft, about 11% of moisture falls as snow.

(b) $h = 4000$
$$p(4000) = 86.3 \ln 4000 - 680$$
$$\approx 36$$
At 4000 ft, about 36% of moisture falls as snow.

(c) $h = 7000$
$$p(7000) = 86.3 \ln 7000 - 680$$
$$\approx 84$$
At 7000 ft, about 84% of moisture falls as snow.

11. $A(t) = A_0 e^{kt}$

$$k \approx -(\ln 2)\left(\frac{1}{5700}\right)$$

Solve $A(t) = \frac{1}{3}A_0$ for t.

$$\frac{1}{3}A_0 = A_0 e^{-(\ln 2)(1/5700)t}$$

$$\frac{1}{3} = e^{-(\ln 2)(1/5700)t}$$

$$.3333 \approx e^{-(\ln 2)(1/5700)t}$$

$$\ln .3333 \approx -(\ln 2)\left(\frac{1}{5700}\right)t$$

$$-1.0986 \approx -.0001t$$

$$9000 \approx t$$

The Egyptian died about 9000 yr ago.

13. $y = y_0 e^{-(\ln 2)(1/5700)t}$
or
$y \approx y_0 e^{-.0001216t}$

Find t when $y = .15y_0$.

$$.15y_0 = y_0^{-.0001216t}$$

$$.15 = e^{-.0001216t}$$

$$\ln .15 = -.0001216t$$

$$\frac{\ln .15}{-.0001216} = t$$

$$15,600 \approx t$$

The paintings are about 15,600 yr old.

15. $A(t) = T_0 + Ce^{-kt}$

Substitute $T_0 = 20$, $C = 75$, and $k = .1$ into the formula, and solve $A(t) = 25$ for t.

$$25 = 20 + 75e^{-.1t}$$

$$5 = 75e^{-.1t}$$

$$\frac{1}{15} = e^{-.1t}$$

$$\ln \frac{1}{15} = -.1t$$

$$-2.7081 \approx -.1t$$

$$27 \approx t$$

It will take about 27 min.

17. $t = T\dfrac{\ln\left[1 + 8.33\left(\frac{A}{K}\right)\right]}{\ln 2}$

Find t for $\dfrac{A}{K} = .103$ and $T = 1.26 \times 10^9$.

$$t = 1.26 \times 10^9 \cdot \frac{\ln[1 + 8.33(.103)]}{\ln 2}$$

$$\approx 1.126 \times 10^9$$

The rock sample is about 1.126 billion yr old.

19. (a) $A = P\left(1 + \dfrac{r}{m}\right)^{tm}$

$$5000 = 1000\left(1 + \frac{.035}{4}\right)^{4t}$$

$$5 = (1 + .00875)^{4t}$$

$$\ln 5 = 4t \ln 1.00875$$

$$46.2 \approx t$$

It will take about 46.2 yr if interest is compounded quarterly.

(b) $A = Pe^{rt}$

$$5000 = 1000e^{.035t}$$

$$5 = e^{.035t}$$

$$\ln 5 = .035t$$

$$46.0 \approx t$$

It will take about 46.0 yr if interest is compounded continuously.

21. (a) $A = P\left(1 + \dfrac{r}{m}\right)^{tm}$

$$2P = P\left(1 + \frac{.025}{4}\right)^{4t}$$

$$2 = (1.00625)^{4t}$$

$$\ln 2 = 4t \ln 1.00625$$

$$27.81 \approx t$$

The doubling time is about 27.81 yr if interest is compounded quarterly.

(b) $A = Pe^{rt}$

$$2P = Pe^{.025t}$$

$$2 = e^{.025t}$$

$$\ln 2 = .025t$$

$$27.73 \approx t$$

The doubling time is about 27.73 yr if interest is compounded continuously.

23. $A = Pe^{rt}$

$A = 80,000$, $P = 60,000$, $r = .0675$

$$80,000 = 60,000e^{.0675t}$$

$$1.333 \approx e^{.0675t}$$

Take natural logarithms of both sides.

$$\ln 1.3333 \approx .0675t$$

$$4.3 \approx t$$

With the continuous compounding plan, it will take about 4.3 yr for Mrs. Blanchard's $60,000 to grow to $80,000.

25.
$$A = Pe^{rt}$$
$$3P = Pe^{.05t}$$
$$3 = e^{.05t}$$
$$\ln 3 = \ln e^{.05t}$$
$$\ln e = .05t$$
$$\frac{\ln 3}{.05} = t$$
$$t \approx 21.97$$
It will take about 21.97 years for the investment to triple.

27. $f(t) = 6e^{.0121t}$
On July 18, 2005, $t = 6$.
$$f(6) = 6e^{.0121(6)}$$
$$f(6) \approx 6.45$$
On July 18, 2005, the population will be 6.45 billion.
Let $f(t) = 7$ and solve for t.
$$7 = 6e^{.0121t}$$
$$\frac{7}{6} = e^{.0121t}$$
$$\ln \frac{7}{6} = .0121t$$
$$\frac{\ln \frac{7}{2}}{.0121} = t$$
$$t \approx 12.7$$
$1999 + 12.7 = 2011.7$
During 2011, the population will reach 7 billion.

29. $A(t) = 274e^{.075t}$
In 1996, $t = 6$.
$$A(6) = 274e^{.075(6)}$$
$$\approx 429$$
In 1996, personal consumption expenditures will be about 429 billion dollars.

31. $P = P_0 e^{-.04t}$

(a) $t = 1$
$$P = 1,000,000e^{-.04(1)} \approx 961,000$$
The population after 1 year is about 961,000.

(b) Find t when $P = 750,000$.
$$750,000 = 1,000,000e^{-.04t}$$
$$.75 = e^{-.04t}$$
$$\ln .75 = -.04t$$
$$7.2 \approx t$$
It takes about 7.2 yr for the population to be reduced to 750,000.

(c) Find t when $P = .5P_0$.
$$.5P_0 = P_0 e^{-.04t}$$
$$.5 = e^{-.04t}$$
$$\ln .5 = -.04t$$
$$17.3 \approx t$$
It will take about 17.3 yr for the population to decline to half the initial number.

33. $f(t) = 200(.90)^{t-1}$
Find t when $f(t) = 50$.
$$50 = 200(.90)^{t-1}$$
$$.25 = (.90)^{t-1}$$
$$\ln .25 = (t-1)\ln .90$$
$$t - 1 = \frac{\ln .25}{\ln .90} \approx 13.2$$
$$t \approx 14.2$$
The dose will reach a level of 50 mg in about 14.2 hr.

35. $A(t) = 2144e^{.0092t}$
1999 corresponds to $t = 9$
$$A(9) = 2144e^{.0092(9)}$$
$$A(9) \approx 2329$$
About 2329 million books will be sold in 1999.

37. $S(t) = S_0 e^{-at}$

(a) $S(t) = 50,000e^{-.10t}$
$$S(1) = 50,000e^{-.10(1)} \approx 45,200$$
$$S(3) = 50,000e^{-.10(3)} \approx 37,000$$

(b) $S(t) = 80,000e^{-.05t}$
$$S(2) = 80,000e^{-.05(2)} \approx 72,400$$
$$S(10) = 80,000e^{-.05(10)} \approx 48,500$$

39. Use the formula for continuous compounding with $r = .06$.
$$A = Pe^{rt}$$
$$A = 2e^{.06t}$$
Find t when $A = 6$.
$$6 = 2e^{.06t}$$
$$3 = e^{.06t}$$
$$\ln 3 = .06t$$
$$18.3 \approx t$$
The cost will triple in about 18.3 yr.

41. $A = Pe^{rt}$
Let $A = 2P$ and $r = .02$.
$2P = Pe^{.02t}$
$2 = e^{.02t}$
Take natural logarithms of both sides.
$\ln 2 = .02t$
$\dfrac{\ln 2}{.02} = t$
$34.657 = t$
It would take about 34.7 yr.

43. (a) At the age of 60 your investment of $2000 has earned interest for 35 years. Your investment has grown to

$$A = P\left(1 + \frac{r}{m}\right)^{mt}$$

$$A = 2000\left(1 + \frac{.08}{1}\right)^{(1)(35)}$$

$$= 29,570.69$$

The tax is 40% of this, or
$(.40)(29,570.69) = 11,828.28$
So you have $17,742.41 left.

(b) $A = P\left(1 + \dfrac{r}{m}\right)^{mt}$ and $r = .048$, $P = 1200$,
$A = 1200(1 + .048)^{(1)(35)} = \$6191.93$

(c) With the IRA you earn
$17,742.41 - 6191.93 = \$11,550.48$ more.
(d) If you pay taxes on the original $2000, then you have $1200 to invest.

$$A = P\left(1 + \frac{r}{m}\right)^{mt}$$

$$A = 1200\left(1 + \frac{.08}{1}\right)^{(1)(35)}$$

$$= 17,742.41$$

This is the same as with the IRA.

Chapter 4 Review Exercises

1. B has an inverse, because it is one-to-one. It passes the horizontal line test.

3. $f(x) = \sqrt{25 - x^2}$
If $a = 4$ and $b = -4$, then $a \neq b$, but
$$f(a) = \sqrt{25 - 4^2} = \sqrt{25 - 16} = 9$$
and $f(b) = \sqrt{25 - (-4)^2} = \sqrt{25 - 16}$
$$= 9.$$
Since $a \neq b$, but $f(a) = f(b)$, that is, two different x-values correspond to the same y-value, f is not a one-to-one function. Thus, f has no inverse function.

5. The two graphs are reflections of each other across the line $y = x$; thus, they are inverses of each other.

7. $f(x) = \log_{2/3} x$ defines a decreasing function since the base, $\dfrac{2}{3}$, is between 0 and 1.

9. $y = \log_{.3} x$
The point $(1, 0)$ is on the graph of every function of the form $y = \log_a x$, so the correct choice must be either B or C.
Since the base is $a = .3$ and $0 < .3 < 1$, $y = \log_{.3} x$ is a decreasing function, and so the correct choice must be B.

11. $y = \ln x$
or
$y = \log_e x$
The point $(1, 0)$ is on the graph of every function of the form $y = \log_a x$, so the correct choice must be either B or C.
Since the base is $a = e$ and $e > 1$, $y = \ln x$ is an increasing function, and so the correct choice must be C.

13. $2^5 = 32$ is written in logarithmic form as
$\log_2 32 = 5$.

15. $\left(\dfrac{3}{4}\right)^{-1} = \dfrac{4}{3}$ is written in logarithmic form as
$\log_{3/4}\left(\dfrac{4}{3}\right) = -1$.

17.

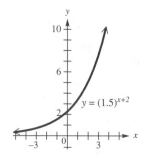

$y = (1.5)^{x+2}$

19. The exact value of $\log_3 9$ is 2 since $3^2 = 9$.

20. The exact value of $\log_3 27$ is 3 since $3^3 = 27$.

21. $\log_3 16$ must lie between 2 and 3. Because the function defined by $y = \log_3 x$ is increasing and $9 < 16 < 27$, we have $\log_3 9 < \log_3 16 < \log_3 27$.

22. By the change-of-base theorem,
$$\log_3 16 = \frac{\log 16}{\log 3} = \frac{\ln 16}{\ln 3}$$
$$\approx 2.523719014.$$
This value is between 2 and 3, as predicted in Exercise 21.

23. The exact value of $\log_5\left(\frac{1}{5}\right)$ is -1 since $5^{-1} = \frac{1}{5}$.

The exact value of $\log_5 1$ is 0 since $5^0 = 1$.

24. $\log_5 .68$ must lie between -1 and 0. Since the function defined by $y = \log_5 x$ is increasing and
$$\frac{1}{5} = .2 < .68 < 1, \text{ we must have}$$
$\log_5 .2 < \log_5 .68 < \log_5 1$.
By the change-of-base theorem,
$$\log_5 .68 = \frac{\log .68}{\log 5} = \frac{\ln .68}{\ln 5}$$
$$\approx -.239625573.$$
This value is between -1 and 0, as predicted above.

25. $\log_9 27 = \frac{3}{2}$
$$9^{3/2} = 27$$

27. $\ln 45 \approx 3.8067$
$$e^{3.8067} \approx 45$$

29. Let $f(x) = a^x$ be the required function. Then
$$f(-4) = \frac{1}{16}$$
$$a^{-4} = \frac{1}{16}$$
$$a^{-4} = 2^{-4}$$
$$a = 2.$$
The base is 2.

31.
$$\log_5\left(x^2 y^4 \sqrt[5]{m^3 p}\right)$$
$$= \log_5 x^2 y^4 (m^3 p)^{1/5}$$
$$= \log_5 x^2 + \log_5 y^4 + \log_5 (m^3 p)^{1/5}$$
Logarithm of a product
$$= 2\log_5 x + 4\log_5 y + \frac{1}{5}(\log_5 m^3 p)$$
Logarithm of a power
$$= 2\log_5 x + 4\log_5 y + \frac{1}{5}(\log_5 m^3 + \log_5 p)$$
Logarithm of a product
$$= 2\log_5 x + 4\log_5 y + \frac{1}{5}(3\log_5 m + \log_5 p)$$
Logarithm of a power

33. $\log 45.6 = 1.6590$

35. $\ln 470 = 6.1527$

37. To find $\log_3 769$, use the change-of-base theorem.
$$\log_3 769 = \frac{\ln 769}{\ln 3}$$
$$\approx 6.0486$$

39. $8^x = 32$
$$(2^3)^x = 2^5$$
$$2^{3x} = 2^5$$
$$3x = 5$$
$$x = \frac{5}{3}$$
Solution set: $\left\{\dfrac{5}{3}\right\}$

41. $10^{2x-3} = 17$
Take common logarithms of both sides.
$$\log 10^{2x-3} = \log 17$$
$$(2x - 3)\log 10 = \log 17$$
$$2x - 3 = \log 17$$
$$2x = \log 17 + 3$$
$$x = \frac{\log 17 + 3}{2}$$
$$x \approx 2.1152$$
Solution set: $\{2.1152\}$

43.
$$e^{x+1} = 10$$
$$\ln e^{x+1} = \ln 10$$
$$(x+1)\ln e = \ln 10$$
$$x+1 = \ln 10$$
$$x = \ln 10 - 1$$
$$= 2.3026 - 1$$
$$= 1.3026$$
Solution set: $\{1.3026\}$

45. $\ln(6x) - \ln(x+1) = \ln 4$
$$\ln\left(\frac{6x}{x+1}\right) = \ln 4$$

Logarithm of a quotient
$$\frac{6x}{x+1} = 4$$
$$4x + 4 = 6x$$
$$4 = 2x$$
$$2 = x$$
Solution set: $\{2\}$

47. $\ln x + 3\ln 2 = \ln \dfrac{2}{x}$

$\ln x + \ln 2^3 = \ln \dfrac{2}{x}$ Logarithm of a power

$\ln(x \cdot 2^3) = \ln \dfrac{2}{x}$ Logarithm of a product

$\ln 8x = \ln \dfrac{2}{x}$

Thus,
$$8x = \frac{2}{x}$$
$$8x^2 = 2$$
$$x^2 = \frac{1}{4}$$
$$x = \pm\frac{1}{2}.$$

$-\dfrac{1}{2}$ is not in the domain of $\ln x$ and $\ln \dfrac{2}{x}$, so it is not a solution.

Solution set: $\left\{\dfrac{1}{2}\right\}$

49. $\ln[\ln(e^{-x})] = \ln 3$

$\ln(-x) = \ln 3$ $\ln e^{-x} = -x$

by theorem on inverses

$$-x = 3$$
$$x = -3$$
Solution set: $\{-3\}$

51. (a) $6.6 = \log_{10} \dfrac{I}{I_0}$
$$\frac{I}{I_0} = 10^{6.6}$$
$$\frac{I}{I_0} \approx 4{,}000{,}000$$
$$I \approx 4{,}000{,}000 \cdot I_0$$
The magnitude was about $4{,}000{,}000 I_0$.

(b) $6.5 = \log_{10} \dfrac{I}{I_0}$
$$\frac{I}{I_0} = 10^{6.5}$$
$$\frac{I}{I_0} \approx 3{,}200{,}000$$
$$I \approx 3{,}200{,}000 \cdot I_0$$
The magnitude was about $3{,}200{,}000 I_0$.

(c) Consider the ratio of the magnitudes.
$$\frac{4{,}000{,}000 \, I_0}{3{,}200{,}000 \, I_0} = \frac{40}{32} = \frac{5}{4} = 1.25$$
The earthquake with a measure of 6.6 was about 1.25 times as great.

53. For 89 decibels, we have
$$89 = 10 \log \frac{I}{I_0}$$
$$8.9 = \log \frac{I}{I_0}.$$
Change this equation to exponential form.
$$\frac{I}{I_0} = 10^{8.9}$$
$$I = 10^{8.9} I_0$$
For 86 decibels, we have
$$86 = 10 \log \frac{I}{I_0}$$
$$\frac{I}{I_0} = 10^{8.6}$$
$$I = 10^{8.6} I_0.$$
To compare these intensities, find their ratio.
$$\frac{10^{8.9} I_0}{10^{8.6} I_0} = \frac{10^{8.9}}{10^{8.6}} \approx 2$$

From this calculation, we see that 89 decibels is about twice as loud as 86 decibels, for a 100% increase.

55. Substitute $P = 48,000$, $A = 58,344$, $r = .05$, and $m = 2$ into the formula.

$$A = P\left(1 + \frac{r}{m}\right)^{tm}$$

$$58,344 = 48,000\left(1 + \frac{.05}{2}\right)^{(t)(2)}$$

$$58,344 = 48,000(1.025)^{2t}$$

$$1.2155 = (1.025)^{2t}$$

$$\ln 1.2155 = \ln(1.025)^{2t}$$

$$\ln 1.2155 = 2t \ln 1.025$$

$$\frac{\ln 1.2155}{2 \ln 1.025} = t$$

$$4.0 \approx t$$

$48,000 will increase to $58,344 in about 4.0 yr.

57. $A = P\left(1 + \dfrac{r}{m}\right)^{tm}$

First, substitute $P = 12,000$, $r = .05$, $t = 8$, and $m = 1$ into the formula.

$$A = 12,000\left(1 + \frac{.05}{1}\right)^{8(1)}$$

$$= 12,000(1.05)^8$$

$$\approx 12,000(1.4775)$$

$$\approx 17,729.47$$

After the first 8 yr, there would be $17,729.47 in the account. To finish off the 14-year period, substitute $P = 17,729.47$, $r = .06$, $t = 6$, and $m = 1$ into the original formula.

$$A = 17,729.47\left(1 + \frac{.06}{1}\right)^{6(1)}$$

$$= 17,729.47(1.06)^6$$

$$\approx 17,729.47(1.4185)$$

$$\approx 25,149.59$$

At the end of the 14-year period, $25,149.59 would be in the account.

59. $f(x) = 6.2(10)^{-12}(1.4)^x$

Find x when $f(x) = 2000$.

$$2000 = 6.2(10)^{-12}(1.4)^x$$

$$322.6 \times 10^{12} = (1.4)^x$$

$$\log(322.6 \times 10^{12}) = x \log 1.4$$

$$99 \approx x$$

Software exports will double their 1997 value in 1999.

61. (a) Compute the natural logarithm of P for each value of P given in the table in the textbook.

x	$\ln P$
0	6.921
1000	6.801
2000	6.678
3000	6.553
4000	6.425
5000	6.293
6000	6.157
7000	6.019
8000	5.878
9000	5.730
10,000	5.580

Plot this data on a graphing calculator using the window $[-100, 11,000]$ by $[5, 7]$ with Xscl = 1000 and Yscl = 1.

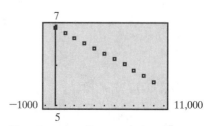

Yes, there is a linear relationship.

(b) $P = Ce^{kx}$

Take natural logarithms on both sides.

$$\ln P = \ln Ce^{kx}$$

$$\ln P = \ln C + \ln e^{kx}$$

$$\ln P = kx + \ln C$$

Thus, $y = \ln P = ax + b$ where $a = k$ and $b = \ln C$, which is a linear function.

63. (a) $A(t) = t^2 - t + 350$

For $t = x$, $A(x) = x^2 - x + 350$

(b) $A(t) = 350 \log(t + 1)$

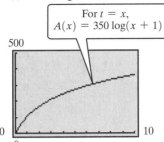

For $t = x$,
$A(x) = 350 \log(x + 1)$

(c)

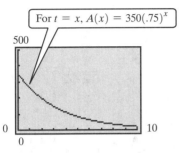

For $t = x$, $A(x) = 350(.75)^x$

(d)

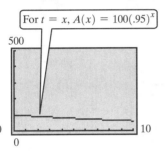

For $t = x$, $A(x) = 100(.95)^x$

Function (c) best describes $A(t)$.

65. $f(x) = \log_4(2x^2 - x)$

(a) Use the change-of-base theorem with base e to write the function as

$$f(x) = \frac{\ln(2x^2 - x)}{\ln 4}.$$

(b) Graph the function.

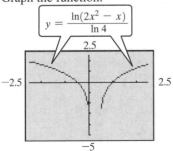

$y = \dfrac{\ln(2x^2 - x)}{\ln 4}$

(c) From the graph, the x-intercepts are $-\dfrac{1}{2}$ and 1.

(d) From the graph, the vertical asymptotes are $x = 0$ and $x = \dfrac{1}{2}$.

(e) To make a y-intercept, $x = 0$ must be in the domain, which is not the case here.

Chapter 4 Test Exercises

1. (a) $f(x) = \sqrt[3]{2x - 7}$
Since it is a cube root, $2x - 7$ may be any real number.
Domain: $(-\infty, \infty)$

(b) $f(x) = \sqrt[3]{2x - 7}$
The cube root of any real number is also any real number.
Range: $(-\infty, \infty)$

(c) $f(x) = \sqrt[3]{2x - 7}$
The graph of f passes the horizontal line test, and thus is a one-to-one function.

(d)
$$y = \sqrt[3]{2x - 7}$$
$$x = \sqrt[3]{2y - 7} \quad \text{Exchange } x \text{ and } y.$$
$$x^3 = \left(\sqrt[3]{2y - 7}\right)^3$$
$$x^3 = 2y - 7$$
$$x^3 + 7 = 2y$$
$$\frac{x^3 + 7}{2} = y$$
$$f^{-1}(x) = \frac{x^3 + 7}{2}$$

(e)

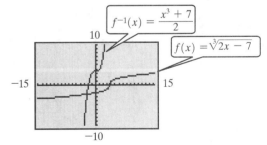

$f^{-1}(x) = \dfrac{x^3 + 7}{2}$

$f(x) = \sqrt[3]{2x - 7}$

These graphs are reflections of each other across the line $y = x$.

2. (a) $y = \log_{1/3} x$

The point $(1, 0)$ is on the graph of every function of the form $y = \log_a x$, so the correct choice must be either B or C.

Since the base is $a = \dfrac{1}{3}$ and

$0 < \dfrac{1}{3} < 1$, $y = \log_{1/3} x$ is a decreasing function, and so the correct choice must be B.

(b) $y = e^x$

The point $(0, 1)$ is on the graph since $e^0 = 1$, so the correct choice must be either A or D. Since the base is e and $e > 1$, $y = e^x$ is an increasing function, and so the correct choice must be A.

(c) $y = \ln x$ or $y = \log_e x$

The point $(1, 0)$ is on the graph of every function of the form $y = \log_a x$, so the correct choice must be B or C. Since the base is $a = e$ and $e > 1$, $y = \ln x$ is an increasing function, and the correct choice must be C.

(d) $y = \left(\dfrac{1}{3}\right)^x$

The point $(0, 1)$ is on the graph since $\left(\dfrac{1}{3}\right)^0 = 1$, so the correct choice must be either A or D.

Since the base is $\dfrac{1}{3}$ and $0 < \dfrac{1}{3} < 1$, $y = \left(\dfrac{1}{3}\right)^x$ is a decreasing function, and so the correct choice must be D.

3. $\left(\dfrac{1}{8}\right)^{2x-3} = 16^{x+1}$

$(2^{-3})^{2x-3} = (2^4)^{x+1}$

$2^{-3(2x-3)} = 2^{4(x+1)}$

$2^{-6x+9} = 2^{4x+4}$

$-6x + 9 = 4x + 4$

$-6x - 4x = 4 - 9$

$-10x = -5$

$x = \dfrac{1}{2}$

Solution set: $\left\{\dfrac{1}{2}\right\}$

4. (a) $4^{3/2} = 8$ is written in logarithmic form as

$$\log_4 8 = \frac{3}{2}$$

(b) $\log_8 4 = \dfrac{2}{3}$ is written in exponential form as

$$8^{2/3} = 4$$

5. $f(x) = \left(\dfrac{1}{2}\right)^x$ and $g(x) = \log_{1/2} x$

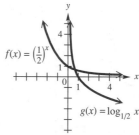

They are inverses of each other.

6. $\log_7 \left(\dfrac{x^2 \sqrt[4]{y}}{z^3}\right)$

$= \log_7 x^2 + \log_7 \sqrt[4]{y} - \log_7 z^3$

$= 2\log_7 x + \dfrac{1}{4}\log_7 y - 3\log_7 z$

7. $\log 237.4 = 2.3755$

8. $\ln .0467 = -3.0640$

9. $\log_9 13 = \dfrac{\ln 13}{\ln 9} = 1.1674$

10. $\log(2.49 \times 10^{-3}) = -2.6038$

11. $\log_x 25 = 2$

$x^2 = 25$

$x^2 = 5^2$

$x = 5$

Solution set: $\{5\}$

12. $\log_4 32 = x$

$4^x = 32$

$2^{2x} = 2^5$

$2x = 5$

$x = \dfrac{5}{2}$

Solution set: $\left\{\dfrac{5}{2}\right\}$

13. $\log_2 x + \log_2(x+2) = 3$
$$\log_2 x(x+2) = 3$$
$$2^3 = x(x+2)$$
$$8 = x^2 + 2x$$
$$0 = x^2 + 2x - 8$$
$$0 = (x+4)(x-2)$$

$x + 4 = 0 \quad$ or $\quad x - 2 = 0$
$\quad x = -4 \quad$ or $\qquad x = 2$

$x = -4$ is not in the domain of $\log_2 x$ or $\log_2(x+2)$, so it is not a solution.
Solution set: $\{2\}$

14. $\qquad 5^{x+1} = 7^x$
$$\ln 5^{x+1} = \ln 7^x$$
$$(x+1)\ln 5 = x \ln 7$$
$$x \ln 5 + \ln 5 = x \ln 7$$
$$\ln 5 = x \ln 7 - x \ln 5$$
$$\ln 5 = x(\ln 7 - \ln 5)$$
$$\frac{\ln 5}{\ln 7 - \ln 5} = x$$
$$4.7833 \approx x$$
Solution set: $\{4.7833\}$

15. $\ln x - 4\ln 3 = \ln\left(\dfrac{5}{x}\right)$
$$\ln\left(\frac{x}{3^4}\right) = \ln\left(\frac{5}{x}\right)$$
$$\frac{x}{81} = \frac{5}{x}$$
$$x^2 = 405$$
$$x \approx 20.1246$$

(Since the domain of $\ln x$ is $(0, \infty)$, only the positive square root of 405 can be a solution.)
Solution set: $\{20.1246\}$

16. $\log_5 27$ is the exponent to which 5 must be raised in order to obtain 27.
To approximate $\log_5 27$ on your calculator use the change-of-base formula;
$$\log_5 27 = \frac{\log 27}{\log 5}$$
$$= \frac{1.43136}{.69897}$$
$$= 2.048.$$

17. $v(t) = 176(1 - e^{-.18t})$
Find the time t at which $v(t) = 147$.
$$147 = 176(1 - e^{-.18t})$$
$$\frac{147}{176} = 1 - e^{-.18t}$$
$$e^{-.18t} = \frac{176}{176} - \frac{147}{176}$$
$$e^{-.18t} = \frac{29}{176}$$

$$\ln e^{-.18t} = \ln \frac{29}{176}$$
$$-.18t \approx \ln .16477$$
$$t \approx \frac{\ln .16477}{-.18}$$
$$\approx \frac{-1.8}{-.18} = 10$$
It will take the skydiver about 10 sec to attain the speed of 147 ft per sec (100 mph).

18. (a) $\qquad A = P\left(1 + \dfrac{r}{m}\right)^{tm}$
$$18,000 = 5000\left(1 + \frac{.068}{12}\right)^{12t}$$
$$3.6 = \left(1 + \frac{.068}{12}\right)^{12t}$$
$$\log 3.6 = 12t \log\left(1 + \frac{.068}{12}\right)$$
$$t = \frac{\log 3.6}{12 \log\left(1 + \frac{.068}{12}\right)}$$
$$t \approx 18.9$$

It will take about 18.9 years.

(b) $\qquad A = Pe^{rt}$
$$18,000 = 5000e^{.068t}$$
$$\frac{18,000}{5000} = e^{.068t}$$
$$\ln \frac{18,000}{5000} = .068t$$
$$\frac{\ln \frac{18,000}{5000}}{.068} = t$$
$$t \approx 18.8$$
It will take about 18.8 years.

19. $A(t) = 600e^{-.05t}$

(a) $A(12) = 600e^{-.05(12)}$

$\qquad = 600e^{-.6}$

$\qquad \approx 600(.5488)$

$\qquad \approx 329.3$

The amount of radioactive material present after 12 days is about 329.3 g.

(b) Solve $A(t) = \dfrac{1}{2}A_0$ for t.

Note that $\dfrac{1}{2}A_0 = \dfrac{1}{2}A(0) = \dfrac{1}{2}(600) = 300.$

$\qquad 300 = 600e^{-.05t}$

$\qquad .5 = e^{-.05t}$

$\qquad \ln .5 = -.05t$

$\qquad -.691 \approx -.05t$

$\qquad 13.9 \approx t$

The half-life of the material is about 13.9 days.

20. Let $x = 0$ correspond to the year 2000. The population of New York (in millions) can be approximated by $y = 18.15e^{.0021x}$.

The population of Florida (in millions) can be approximated by $y = 15.23e^{.0131x}$.

Graph the two functions on the same screen and use the "intersect" option to find the coordinates of the intersection.

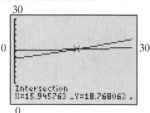

$x \approx 15.9$ corresponds to the end of the year 2015. Near the end of 2015 the populations will be equal.

CHAPTER 5 TRIGONOMETRIC FUNCTIONS

Section 5.1

Exercises

1. Let x = the measure of the angle.
   If the angle is its own complement,
   $$x + x = 90$$
   $$2x = 90$$
   $$x = 45.$$
   A 45° angle is its own complement.

3. $\dfrac{25 \text{ minutes}}{60 \text{ minutes}} = \dfrac{x \text{ degrees}}{360 \text{ degrees}}; x = 150°$

5. $7x + 11x = 180$
   $$18x = 180$$
   $$x = 10$$
   The measures of the two angles are
   $(7x)° = 7(10°) = 70°$ and $(11x)° = 11(10°) = 110°$.

7. $6x - 4 + 8x - 12 = 180$
   $$14x - 16 = 180$$
   $$14x = 196$$
   $$x = 14$$
   The measures of the two angles are
   $(6x - 4)° = 6(14°) - 4° = 80°$ and
   $(8x - 12)° = 8(14°) - 12° = 100°$.

9. If an angle measures x degrees, and two angles are complementary if their sum is 90°, then the complement of an angle of $x°$ is $(90 - x)°$.

11. $62°18' + 21°41' = 83°59'$

13. $71°18' - 47°29' = 70°78' - 47°29'$
    $$= 23°49'$$

15. $90° - 72°58'11'' = 89°59'60'' - 72°58'11''$
    $$= 17°1'49''$$

17. $20°54' = 20° + \dfrac{54°}{60}$
    $$= 20° + .900°$$
    $$= 20.900°$$

19. $91°35'54'' = 91° + \dfrac{35°}{60} + \dfrac{54°}{3600}$
    $$= 91.598°$$

21. $31.4296° = 31° + (.4296)60'$
    $$= 31° + 25.776$$
    $$= 31° + 25' + (.776)(60'')$$
    $$= 31°25'47''$$

23. $89.9004° = 89° + (.9004)(60')$
    $$= 89° + 54.024'$$
    $$= 89° + 54' + (.024)(60'')$$
    $$= 89°54'1''$$

25. $-40°$ is coterminal with $-40° + 360° = 320°$.

27. $539°$ is coterminal with $539° - 360° = 179°$.

29. $30°$
    A coterminal angle can be obtained by adding an integer multiple of 360°.
    $30° + n \cdot 360°$

31. $-90°$
    A coterminal angle can be obtained by adding an integer multiple of 360°.
    $-90° + n \cdot 360°$

33. $Y_1 = 360\left(\left(\dfrac{X}{360}\right) - \text{int}\left(\dfrac{X}{360}\right)\right)$
    $X = -40°$
    $Y_1 = 360\left(\left(-\dfrac{40}{360}\right) - \text{int}\left(-\dfrac{40}{360}\right)\right)$
    $$= 320°$$

For Exercises 35–41 angles other than those given are possible.

35.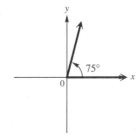

    $75°$ is coterminal with $75° + 360° = 435°$ and $75° - 360° = -285°$. These angles are in quadrant I.

37.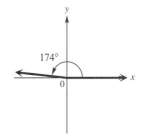

    $174°$ is coterminal with $174° + 360° = 534°$ and $174° - 360° = -186°$. These angles are in quadrant II.

39.

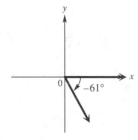

-61° is coterminal with -61° + 360° = 299° and -61° - 360° = -421°. These angles are in quadrant IV.

41. $60° = 60\left(\dfrac{\pi}{180} \text{ radian}\right) = \dfrac{\pi}{3}$ radians

43. $150° = 150\left(\dfrac{\pi}{180} \text{ radian}\right) = \dfrac{5\pi}{6}$ radians

45. $\dfrac{\pi}{3} = \dfrac{\pi}{3}\left(\dfrac{180°}{\pi}\right) = 60°$

47. $\dfrac{7\pi}{4} = \dfrac{7\pi}{4}\left(\dfrac{180°}{\pi}\right) = 315°$

49. $\dfrac{11\pi}{6} = \dfrac{11\pi}{6}\left(\dfrac{180°}{\pi}\right) = 330°$

51. $39° = 39\left(\dfrac{\pi}{180} \text{ radian}\right) = .68$ radian

53. $139°10' = 139\dfrac{1}{6}\left(\dfrac{\pi}{180} \text{ radian}\right) = 2.43$ radians

55. $64.29° = 64.29\left(\dfrac{\pi}{180} \text{ radian}\right)$
$= 1.122$ radians

57. $2 \text{ radians} = 2\left(\dfrac{180°}{\pi}\right)$
$= 114.5916°$
$= 114° + (.5916)(60')$
$= 114°35'$

59. $1.74 \text{ radians} = 1.74\left(\dfrac{180°}{\pi}\right)$
$= 99.6947°$
$= 99° + (.6947)(60')$
$= 99°42'$

61. Answers start at 30° and proceed counterclockwise around circle.

$$30° = 30\left(\dfrac{\pi}{180} \text{ radian}\right) = \dfrac{\pi}{6} \text{ radian}$$

$$\dfrac{\pi}{4} \text{ radian} = \dfrac{\pi}{4}\left(\dfrac{180°}{\pi}\right) = 45°$$

$$60° = 60\left(\dfrac{\pi}{180} \text{ radian}\right) = \dfrac{\pi}{3} \text{ radians}$$

$$\dfrac{2\pi}{3} \text{ radians} = \dfrac{2\pi}{3}\left(\dfrac{180°}{\pi}\right) = 120°$$

$$\dfrac{3\pi}{4} \text{ radians} = \dfrac{3\pi}{4}\left(\dfrac{180°}{\pi}\right) = 135°$$

$$150° = 150\left(\dfrac{\pi}{180} \text{ radian}\right) = \dfrac{5\pi}{6} \text{ radians}$$

$$180° = 180\left(\dfrac{\pi}{180} \text{ radian}\right) = \pi \text{ radians}$$

$$210° = 210\left(\dfrac{\pi}{180} \text{ radian}\right) = \dfrac{7\pi}{6} \text{ radians}$$

$$225° = 225\left(\dfrac{\pi}{180} \text{ radian}\right) = \dfrac{5\pi}{4} \text{ radians}$$

$$\dfrac{4\pi}{3} \text{ radians} = \dfrac{4\pi}{3}\left(\dfrac{180°}{\pi}\right) = 240°$$

$$\dfrac{5\pi}{3} \text{ radians} = \dfrac{5\pi}{3}\left(\dfrac{180°}{\pi}\right) = 300°$$

$$315° = 315\left(\dfrac{\pi}{180} \text{ radian}\right) = \dfrac{7\pi}{4} \text{ radians}$$

$$330° = 330\left(\dfrac{\pi}{180} \text{ radian}\right) = \dfrac{11\pi}{6} \text{ radians}$$

63. $r = 4,\ \theta = \dfrac{\pi}{2}$
$s = r\theta = 4\left(\dfrac{\pi}{2}\right) = 2\pi$

65. $s = 6\pi,\ \theta = \dfrac{3\pi}{4}$
$s = r\theta$
$r = \dfrac{s}{\theta} = \dfrac{6\pi}{\frac{3\pi}{4}}$
$= 6\pi \cdot \dfrac{4}{3\pi}$
$= 8$

67. $r = 3,\ s = 3$
$s = r\theta$
$\theta = \dfrac{s}{r} = \dfrac{3}{3} = 1$ radian

69. $r = 12.3$ cm, $\theta = \dfrac{2\pi}{3}$ radians

$$s = r\theta = 12.3\left(\dfrac{2\pi}{3}\right) \text{ cm}$$
$$= 8.2\pi \text{ cm}$$
$$\approx 25.8 \text{ cm}$$

71. $r = 4.82$ m, $\theta = 60°$
Convert θ to radians.

$$\theta = 60° = \dfrac{\pi}{3}$$
$$s = r\theta = 4.82\left(\dfrac{\pi}{3}\right)$$
$$\approx 1.61\pi$$
$$\approx 5.05 \text{ m}$$

For Exercises 73–77, note that since 6400 has two significant digits and the angles are given to the nearest degree, we can have only two significant digits in the answers.

73. 9° N, 40° N
$$\theta = 40° - 9° = 31°$$
$$= 31\left(\dfrac{\pi}{180} \text{ radian}\right)$$
$$= \dfrac{31\pi}{180} \text{ radian}$$
$$s = r\theta$$
$$= 6400\left(\dfrac{31\pi}{180}\right)$$
$$\approx 3500 \text{ km}$$

75. 41° N, 12° S
$$12° \text{ S} = -12° \text{ N}$$
$$\theta = 41° - (-12°) = 53°$$
$$= 53\left(\dfrac{\pi}{180} \text{ radian}\right)$$
$$= \dfrac{53\pi}{180} \text{ radian}$$
$$s = r\theta = 6400\left(\dfrac{53\pi}{180}\right)$$
$$\approx 5900 \text{ km}$$

77. $r = 6400$ km, $s = 1200$ km
$$s = r\theta$$
$$1200 = 6400\theta$$
$$\theta = \dfrac{3}{16}$$
Convert $\dfrac{3}{16}$ radian to degrees.
$$\theta = \dfrac{3}{16}\left(\dfrac{180°}{\pi}\right) \approx 11°$$
The north-south distance between the two cities is 11°.

Let x = the latitude of Madison.
$$x - 33° = 11°$$
$$x = 44° \text{ N}$$

79. (a) The number of inches lifted is the arc length in a circle with
$r = 9.27$ in. and $\theta = 71°50'$.

$$71°50' = \left(71° + \dfrac{50}{60}^{\circ}\right)\left(\dfrac{\pi}{180°}\right)$$
$$s = r\theta$$
$$= 9.27\left(71° + \dfrac{50}{60}^{\circ}\right)\left(\dfrac{\pi}{180°}\right)$$
$$\approx 11.6$$
The weight will rise 11.6 in.

(b) When the weight is raised 6 in.,
$$s = r\theta$$
$$\theta = \dfrac{s}{r}$$
$$= \dfrac{6}{9.27}\left(\dfrac{180°}{\pi}\right)$$
$$= 37.085° = 37° + (.085)(60')$$
$$= 37°5'.$$
The pulley must be rotated through $37°5'$.

81. A rotation of $\theta = 60.0° = \dfrac{\pi}{3}$ on the smaller wheel moves through an arc length of
$$s = r\theta = 5.23\left(\dfrac{\pi}{3}\right) \approx 5.48 \text{ cm.}$$
Since both wheels move together, the larger wheel moves 5.48 cm, which rotates it through an angle θ, where $5.48 = 8.16\theta$. Thus,
$$\theta = \dfrac{5.48}{8.16} = .671 \text{ radian} = .671\left(\dfrac{180°}{\pi}\right) \approx 38.5°.$$
The larger wheel rotates through 38.5°.

83. The chain moves a distance equal to half the arc length of the larger gear. So, for the large gear and pedal,
$$s = r\theta$$
$$= 4.72(180)\dfrac{\pi}{180}$$
$$= 4.72\pi.$$
Thus, the chain moves 4.72π in. The small gear rotates through an angle
$$\theta = \dfrac{s}{r}$$
$$= \dfrac{4.72\pi}{1.38}$$
$$\approx 3.42\pi.$$

θ for the wheel and θ for the small gear are the same, or 3.42π. So, for the wheel,

$$s = r\theta$$
$$= 13.6(3.42\pi)$$
$$\approx 146 \text{ in.}$$

The bicycle will move 146 in.

85. Let t = the length of the train. t is approximately the arc length subtended by $3°\ 20'$.

$$\theta = 3°20' = 3\frac{1}{3}^{\circ}$$

$$\theta = \left(3\frac{1}{3}\right)\left(\frac{\pi}{180}\right) = \frac{\pi}{54}$$

$$t \approx r\theta = 3.5\left(\frac{\pi}{54}\right) \approx .20 \text{ km}$$

The train is about .20 km long.

87. $r = 6,\ \theta = \dfrac{\pi}{3}$

$$A = \frac{1}{2}r^2\theta$$

$$= \frac{1}{2}(6)^2\left(\frac{\pi}{3}\right)$$

$$= 6\pi$$

89. $A = 3$ units^2, $r = 2$

$$A = \frac{1}{2}r^2\theta$$

$$3 = \frac{1}{2}(2)^2\theta$$

$$3 = 2\theta$$

$$\theta = \frac{3}{2} \text{ or } 1.5 \text{ radians}$$

91. $r = 29.2$ m, $\theta = \dfrac{5\pi}{6}$

$$A = \frac{1}{2}r^2\theta$$

$$= \frac{1}{2}(29.2)^2\left(\frac{5\pi}{6}\right)$$

$$= 355.27\pi$$

$$\approx 1120 \text{ m}^2$$

93. $r = 12.7$ cm, $\theta = 81°$

The formula $A = \dfrac{1}{2}r^2\theta$ requires that θ be measured in radians. Convert $81°$ to radians by multiplying by $\dfrac{\pi}{180}$.

$$\theta = 81\left(\frac{\pi}{180}\right) = \frac{9\pi}{20}$$

$$A = \frac{1}{2}(12.7)^2\left(\frac{9\pi}{20}\right)$$

$$= 36.29\pi$$

$$\approx 114 \text{ cm}^2$$

95. $A = 16$ in.^{2}, $r = 3.0$ in.

$$A = \frac{1}{2}r^2\theta$$

$$16 = \frac{1}{2}(3)^2\theta$$

$$16 = \frac{9}{2}\theta$$

$$\theta \approx 3.6 \text{ radians}$$

97. $A = \dfrac{1}{2}r^2\theta$

Substituting $\theta = 2\pi$,

$$A = \frac{1}{2}r^2(2\pi) = \pi r^2.$$

The area of a circle of radius r is πr^2.

99. $x^2 + y^2 = 4$ is the equation of a circle of radius 2.

$y = \left(\dfrac{\sqrt{3}}{3}\right)x$ is the equation of a line with slope

$\dfrac{\sqrt{3}}{3}$. Therefore, $\tan\theta = \dfrac{\sqrt{3}}{3}$, and so $\theta = \dfrac{\pi}{6}$.

Substitute $r = 2$ and $\theta = \dfrac{\pi}{6}$ in the formula for the area of a sector.

$$A = \frac{1}{2}r^2\theta$$

$$= \frac{1}{2}(2)^2\left(\frac{\pi}{6}\right)$$

$$= \frac{\pi}{3}$$

101. (a)

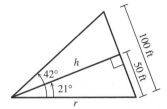

The triangle formed by the central angle and the chord is isoceles. Therefore, the bisector of the central angle is also the perpendicular bisector of the chord.

$$\sin 21° = \frac{50}{r}$$

$$r = \frac{50}{\sin 21°}$$

$$\approx 140 \text{ ft}$$

(b) $r = \dfrac{50}{\sin 21°}$; $\theta = 42°$

Convert θ to radians:

$$42\left(\frac{\pi}{180} \text{ radian}\right) = \frac{7\pi}{30} \text{ radians}$$

$$s = r\theta$$

$$= \frac{50}{\sin 21°} \cdot \frac{7\pi}{30}$$

$$= \frac{35\pi}{3\sin 21°}$$

$$\approx 102 \text{ ft}$$

(c)

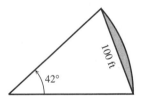

$$A_{\text{sector}} = \frac{1}{2}\left(\frac{50}{\sin 21°}\right)^2\left(\frac{7\pi}{30}\right)$$

$$\approx 7135 \text{ ft}^2$$

Since $\tan 21° = \dfrac{50}{h}$, then $h = \dfrac{50}{\tan 2p}$.

$$A_{\text{triangle}} = \frac{1}{2}bh$$

$$= \frac{1}{2}(100)\left(\frac{50}{\tan 21°}\right)$$

$$\approx 6513 \text{ ft}^2$$

The area bounded by the arc and the chord is $7135 - 6513 = 622 \text{ ft}^2$.

103. Use the Pythagorean Theorem to find the hypotenuse of the triangle, which is also the radius of the sector of the circle.

$$r^2 = 30^2 + 40^2$$

$$r = \sqrt{900 + 1600}$$

$$= \sqrt{2500}$$

$$= 50$$

The total area of the lot is the sum of the areas of the triangle and the sector.

$$A_{\text{triangle}} = \frac{1}{2}bh = \frac{1}{2}(30)(40)$$

$$= 600 \text{ yd}^2$$

$$A_{\text{sector}} = \frac{1}{2}r^2\theta = \frac{1}{2}(50)^2\left(60 \cdot \frac{\pi}{180}\right) = \frac{1250\pi}{3} \text{ yd}^2$$

$$\text{Total area} = \frac{1250\pi}{3} + 600 \approx 1900 \text{ yd}^2$$

Section 5.2

Exercises

For exercises 1–3, since Figure 26 is of the unit circle, then the $\sin\theta$ value and $\cos\theta$ value for an angle θ corresponds to the y-coordinate and x-coordinate, respectively, of the point where the terminal side of the angle intersects the circle. Thus, by Figure 26,

1. $\sin\dfrac{\pi}{2} = 1$

3. $\cos\dfrac{3\pi}{2} = 0$

5. $\cos .8 \approx .7$

7. $x = -.65$
  when $\theta = 4$ radians

9. (a) Since $1.57 < 2 < 3.14$, $\dfrac{\pi}{2} < 2 < \pi$,
  2 radians is in quadrant II. Therefore, $\cos 2$ is negative.

(b) Since $-1.57 < -1 < 0$, $-\dfrac{\pi}{2} < -1 < 0$,
  -1 radian is in quadrant IV. Therefore, $\tan -1$ is negative.

(c) Since $4.71 < 5 < 6.28$, $\dfrac{3\pi}{2} < 5 < 2\pi$,
  5 is in quadrant IV. Therefore, $\sin 5$ is negative.

(d) Since $4.71 < 6 < 6.28$, $\frac{3\pi}{2} < 6 < 2\pi$,

6 is in quadrant IV. Therefore, cos 6 is positive.

11. Find $\cos\frac{5\pi}{3}$.

In radians, the reference angle for $\frac{5\pi}{3}$ is

$2\pi - \frac{5\pi}{3} = \frac{\pi}{3}$.

$\frac{5\pi}{3}$ is in quadrant IV, where the cosine is positive.

$\cos\frac{5\pi}{3} = \cos\frac{\pi}{3} = \frac{1}{2}$

Or, convert to degrees.

$\frac{5\pi}{3} = \frac{5}{3}(180°) = 300°$

$\cos\frac{5\pi}{3} = \cos 300° = \frac{1}{2}$

13. Find $\sec\frac{2\pi}{3}$.

The reference angle for $\frac{2\pi}{3}$ is $\pi - \frac{2\pi}{3} = \frac{\pi}{3}$.

$\frac{2\pi}{3}$ is in quadrant II, where the secant is negative.

$\sec\frac{2\pi}{3} = -\sec\frac{\pi}{3} = -2$

Or, convert to degrees.

$\frac{2\pi}{3} = \frac{2}{3}(180°) = 120°$

$\sec\frac{2\pi}{3} = \sec 120° = -2$

15. Find $\cot\frac{5\pi}{6}$.

The reference angle for $\frac{5\pi}{6}$ is $\pi - \frac{5\pi}{6} = \frac{\pi}{6}$.

$\frac{5\pi}{6}$ is in quadrant II, where the cotangent is negative.

$\cot\frac{5\pi}{6} = -\cot\frac{\pi}{6} = -\sqrt{3}$

Or, convert to degrees.

$\frac{5\pi}{6} = \frac{5}{6}(180°) = 150°$

$\cot\frac{5\pi}{6} = \cot 150° = -\sqrt{3}$

17. Find $\tan\frac{17\pi}{3}$.

$\frac{17\pi}{3}$ is not between 0 and 2π. Subtract 2π twice, that is, 4π.

$\frac{17\pi}{3} - 4\pi = \frac{17\pi}{3} - \frac{12\pi}{3} = \frac{5\pi}{3}$

$\frac{17\pi}{3}$ is coterminal with $\frac{5\pi}{3}$.

The reference angle for $\frac{5\pi}{3}$ is $2\pi - \frac{5\pi}{3} = \frac{\pi}{3}$.

$\frac{5\pi}{3}$ is in quadrant IV, where the tangent is negative.

$\tan\frac{17\pi}{3} = \tan\frac{5\pi}{3} = -\tan\frac{\pi}{3} = -\sqrt{3}$.

Or, converting to degrees,

$\frac{5\pi}{3} = \frac{5}{3}(180°) = 300°$

$\tan\frac{5\pi}{3} = \tan 300° = -\sqrt{3}$.

For Exercises 19–31, your calculator must be set in radian mode. Keystroke sequences may vary based on the type and/or model of calculator being used.

19. cos .6429
Enter: .6429 [COS]
or [COS] .6429 [ENTER]
cos .6429 = .80036052

21. csc 1.3875
Enter: 1.3875 [SIN] [1/x]
or ([SIN] 1.3875) [x⁻¹] [ENTER]
csc 1.3875 = 1.0170372

23. tan 4.0230
Enter: 4.0230 [TAN]
or [TAN] 4.0230 [ENTER]
tan 4.0230 = 1.2131367

25. cos(−3.0602)
Enter: 3.0602 [+/−] [COS]
or [COS] [(−)] 3.0602 [ENTER]
cos(−3.0602) = −.99668945

27. cos s = .78269876
Enter: .78269876 [INV] [COS]
or [2nd] [COS] .78269876 [ENTER]
Display: .67180620
s = .67180620

29. cot s = .29949853
Enter: .29949853 [1/x] [INV] [TAN]
or [2nd] [TAN] .29949853 [x⁻¹] [ENTER]
Display: 1.2797997
s = 1.2797997

31. csc $s = 1.0219553$
Enter: 1.0219553 [1/x] [INV] [SIN]
or [2nd] [SIN] 1.0219553 [x⁻¹] [ENTER]
Display: 1.3631380
$s = 1.3631380$

33. $\left[\dfrac{\pi}{2}, \pi\right]$; $\cos s = -\dfrac{1}{2}$

Because $\cos s = -\dfrac{1}{2}$, the reference angle for s

must be $\dfrac{\pi}{3}$ since $\cos \dfrac{\pi}{3} = \dfrac{1}{2}$. For s to be in the

interval $\left[\dfrac{\pi}{2}, \pi\right]$, we must subtract the reference

angle from π. Therefore, $s = \pi - \dfrac{\pi}{3} = \dfrac{2\pi}{3}$.

35. $\left[\pi, \dfrac{3\pi}{2}\right]$; $\sin s = -\dfrac{1}{2}$

Because $\sin s = -\dfrac{1}{2}$, the reference angle for s

must be $\dfrac{\pi}{6}$ since $\sin \dfrac{\pi}{6} = \dfrac{1}{2}$. For s to be in the

interval $\left[\pi, \dfrac{3\pi}{2}\right]$, we must add the reference angle

to π. Therefore, $s = \pi + \dfrac{\pi}{6} = \dfrac{7\pi}{6}$.

37. $\left[\dfrac{3\pi}{2}, 2\pi\right]$; $\cos s = \dfrac{\sqrt{3}}{2}$

Because $\cos s = \dfrac{\sqrt{3}}{2}$, the reference angle for s

must be $\dfrac{\pi}{6}$ since $\cos \dfrac{\pi}{6} = \dfrac{\sqrt{3}}{2}$. For s to be in the

interval $\left[\dfrac{3\pi}{2}, 2\pi\right]$, we must subtract the

reference angle from 2π. Therefore,

$s = 2\pi - \dfrac{\pi}{6} = \dfrac{11\pi}{6}$.

39. Since $X = \cos s$,
$\cos s = .55319149$
Use radian mode.
Enter .55319149 [INV] [COS]
or [2nd] [COS] .55319149 [ENTER]
Display: .984605869
$s \approx .9846$

For Exercises 41–47, have calculator in radian mode.

41. $s =$ the length of an arc on the unit circle $= 2.5$
$x = \cos s$ $\qquad y = \sin s$
$x = \cos 2.5$ $\qquad y = \sin 2.5$
$x = -.80114362$ $\quad y = .59847214$
$\quad (-.80114362, .59847214)$

43. $s = -7.4$
$x = \cos s$ $\qquad y = \sin s$
$x = \cos (-7.4)$ $\quad y = \sin (-7.4)$
$x = .43854733$ $\quad y = -.89870810$
$\quad (.43854733, -.89870810)$

45. $s = 51$
$\cos 51 = .74215420$
$\sin 51 = .67022918$
Since cosine and sine are both positive, an angle
of 51 radians lies in quadrant I.

47. $s = 65$
$\cos 65 = -.56245385$
$\sin 65 = .82682868$
Since cosine is negative and sine is positive, an
angle of 65 radians lies in quadrant II.

49. $\sin x = \sin (x + 2)$
If x is in quadrant I, then $x + 2$ is in quadrant II.
Therefore,
$x + 2 = \pi - x$
$\quad 2x = \pi - 2$
$\quad\; x = \dfrac{\pi}{2} - 1$.
On the interval $0 \le x \le 2\pi$, this would also be true
if we use an angle of $3\pi - x$ which is coterminal
to $\pi - x$. Therefore,
$2 + x = 3\pi - x$
$\quad 2x = 3\pi - 2$
$\quad\; x = \dfrac{3\pi}{2} - 1$.
For the statement $\sin x = \sin (x + 2)$ to be true
$x = \dfrac{\pi}{2} - 1$ or $x = \dfrac{3\pi}{2} - 1$.

51. $\theta = \dfrac{3\pi}{4}$ radians, $t = 8$ sec

$\omega = \dfrac{\theta}{t} = \dfrac{\frac{3\pi}{4}}{8}$

$\quad = \dfrac{3\pi}{32}$ radian per sec

53. $\theta = \dfrac{2\pi}{9}$ radian, $\omega = \dfrac{5\pi}{27}$ radian per min

$$\omega = \frac{\theta}{t}$$

$$\frac{5\pi}{27} = \frac{\frac{2\pi}{9}}{t}$$

$$t = \frac{2\pi}{9} \cdot \frac{27}{5\pi} = \frac{6}{5} \text{ min}$$

55. $\theta = 3.871142$ radians, $t = 21.4693 \text{ sec}$

$$\omega = \frac{\theta}{t}$$

$$\omega = \frac{3.871142}{21.4693}$$

$$= .180311 \text{ radian per sec}$$

57. The circumference of the unit circle is 2π.
$\omega = 1$ unit per sec, $\theta = 2\pi$ radians

$$\omega = \frac{\theta}{t}$$

$$t = \frac{\theta}{\omega}$$

$$= \frac{2\pi}{1} = 2\pi \text{ sec}$$

61. $v = 18$ ft per sec, $r = 3$ ft
$$v = r\omega$$
$$18 = 3\omega$$
$$\omega = \frac{18}{3}$$
$$= 6 \text{ radians per sec}$$

63. $r = 24.93215$ cm, $\omega = .372914$ radian per sec
$$v = r\omega$$
$$v = (24.93215)(.372914)$$
$$\approx 9.29755 \text{ cm per sec}$$

65. $r = 9$ yd, $\omega = \dfrac{2\pi}{5}$ radians per sec, $t = 12$ sec

$$s = r\omega t$$

$$s = 9\left(\frac{2\pi}{5}\right)(12)$$

$$= \frac{216\pi}{5} \text{ yd}$$

67. $s = \dfrac{3\pi}{4}$ km, $r = 2$ km, $t = 4$ sec

$$s = r\omega t$$

$$\frac{3\pi}{4} = 2(\omega)4$$

$$\omega = \frac{\frac{3\pi}{4}}{8}$$

$$= \frac{3\pi}{32} \text{ radian per sec}$$

71. The line makes 300 revolutions per minute. Each revolution is 2π radians, so
$$\omega = 2\pi(300)$$
$$= 600\pi \text{ radians per min}$$

73. The point on the tread of the tire is rotating 35 times per min. Each rotation is 2π radians.
$$\omega = 35(2\pi) = 70\pi \text{ radians per min}$$
$$v = r\omega, \; r = 18 \text{ cm}$$
$$v = 18(70\pi) = 1260\pi \text{ cm per min}$$

75. The point on the edge of the gyroscope is rotating 680 times per min. Each rotation is 2π radians.
$$\omega = 680(2\pi) = 1360\pi \text{ radians per min}$$
$$v = r\omega, \; r = 83 \text{ cm}$$
$$v = 83(1360\pi)$$
$$= 112,880\pi \text{ cm per min}$$

77. $T(x) = 37\sin\left[\dfrac{2\pi}{365}(x - 101)\right] + 25$

(a) March 1 (day 60)
$$T(60) = 37\sin\left[\frac{2\pi}{365}(60 - 101)\right] + 25$$
$$\approx 1°F$$

(b) April 1 (day 91)
$$T(91) = 37\sin\left[\frac{2\pi}{365}(91 - 101)\right] + 25$$
$$\approx 19°F$$

(c) Day 150
$$T(150) \approx 53°F$$

(d) June 15 is day 166.
$$T(166) \approx 58°F$$

(e) September 1 is day 244.
$$T(244) \approx 48°F$$

(f) October 31 is day 304.
$$T(304) \approx 12°F.$$

79. Mars will make one full rotation (of 2π radians) during the course of one day.
$$2\pi \text{ radians}\left(\frac{1 \text{ hr}}{0.2552 \text{ radians}}\right) \approx 24.62 \text{ hr}$$

81. Since $s = 56$ cm of belt go around in $t = 18$ sec, the linear velocity is

$$v = \frac{s}{t}$$
$$= \frac{56}{18}$$
$$= \frac{28}{9} \text{ cm per sec.}$$
$$v = r\omega, \ r = 12.96 \text{ cm}$$
$$\frac{28}{9} = (12.96)\omega$$
$$\omega = \frac{\frac{28}{9}}{12.96}$$
$$\approx .24 \text{ radian per sec.}$$

Section 5.3

Connections *(page 372)*

1. From the figure, we see that $\triangle QOP$ and $\triangle AOB$ are similar.

$$PQ = y = \frac{y}{1} = \frac{y}{r} = \sin\theta \ (\text{since } r = 1)$$
$$OQ = x = \frac{x}{1} = \frac{x}{r} = \cos\theta \ (\text{since } r = 1)$$
$$\frac{AB}{y} = \frac{OA}{x}$$

Since $OA = 1$, $\frac{AB}{y} = \frac{1}{x}$, so $AB = \frac{y}{x} = \tan\theta$.

2.

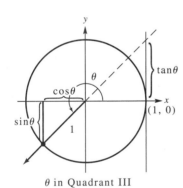

θ in Quadrant III

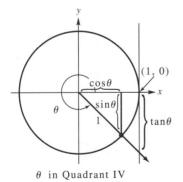

θ in Quadrant IV

Exercises

1.

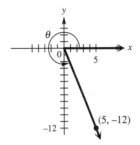

3. $(-3, 4)$
$$x = -3, y = 4$$
$$r = \sqrt{(-3)^2 + 4^2}$$
$$= \sqrt{9 + 16}$$
$$= \sqrt{25}$$
$$= 5$$
$$\sin\theta = \frac{y}{r} = \frac{4}{5}$$
$$\cos\theta = \frac{x}{r} = -\frac{3}{5}$$
$$\tan\theta = \frac{y}{x} = -\frac{4}{3}$$
$$\cot\theta = \frac{x}{y} = -\frac{3}{4}$$
$$\sec\theta = \frac{r}{x} = -\frac{5}{3}$$
$$\csc\theta = \frac{r}{y} = \frac{5}{4}$$

5. $(0, 2)$
$$x = 0, y = 2$$
$$r = \sqrt{0^2 + 2^2}$$
$$= \sqrt{0 + 4}$$
$$= \sqrt{4}$$
$$= 2$$
$$\sin\theta = \frac{2}{2} = 1$$
$$\cos\theta = \frac{0}{2} = 0$$
$$\tan\theta = \frac{2}{0} \text{ undefined}$$
$$\cot\theta = \frac{0}{2} = 0$$
$$\sec\theta = \frac{2}{0} \text{ undefined}$$
$$\csc\theta = \frac{2}{2} = 1$$

7. $\left(1, \sqrt{3}\right)$

$x = 1, \ y = \sqrt{3}$

$r = \sqrt{1^2 + \left(\sqrt{3}\right)^2}$

$\quad = \sqrt{1+3}$

$\quad = \sqrt{4}$

$\quad = 2$

$\sin \theta = \dfrac{\sqrt{3}}{2}$

$\cos \theta = \dfrac{1}{2}$

$\tan \theta = \dfrac{\sqrt{3}}{1} = \sqrt{3}$

$\cot \theta = \dfrac{1}{\sqrt{3}} = \dfrac{1}{\sqrt{3}} \cdot \dfrac{\sqrt{3}}{\sqrt{3}} = \dfrac{\sqrt{3}}{3}$

$\sec \theta = \dfrac{2}{1} = 2$

$\csc \theta = \dfrac{2}{\sqrt{3}} = \dfrac{2}{\sqrt{3}} \cdot \dfrac{\sqrt{3}}{\sqrt{3}} = \dfrac{2\sqrt{3}}{3}$

In Exercises 11–17, $r = \sqrt{x^2 + y^2}$, which is positive.

11. In quadrant II, x is negative so $\dfrac{x}{r}$ is negative.

13. In quadrant IV, x is positive and y is negative so $\dfrac{y}{x}$ is negative.

15. Since $x \geq 0$, the graph of the line $2x + y = 0$ is shown to the right of the y-axis. A point on this line is $(1, -2)$ since $2(1) + (-2) = 0$.

$r = \sqrt{1^2 + (-2)^2} = \sqrt{1+4} = \sqrt{5}$

$2x + y = 0, \ x \geq 0$

$(1, -2)$

$\sin \theta = -\dfrac{2\sqrt{5}}{5}$

$\cos \theta = \dfrac{\sqrt{5}}{5}$

$\tan \theta = -2$

$\cot \theta = -\dfrac{1}{2}$

$\sec \theta = \sqrt{5}$

$\csc \theta = -\dfrac{\sqrt{5}}{2}$

17. Since $x \leq 0$, the graph of the line $-6x - y = 0$ is shown to the left of the y-axis. A point on this graph is $(-1, 6)$ since $-6(-1) - 6 = 0$.

$r = \sqrt{(-1)^2 + 6^2} = \sqrt{1 + 36} = \sqrt{37}$

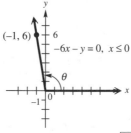

$(-1, 6)$

$-6x - y = 0, \ x \leq 0$

$\sin \theta = \dfrac{y}{r} = \dfrac{6}{\sqrt{37}} = \dfrac{6\sqrt{37}}{37}$

$\cos \theta = \dfrac{x}{r} = \dfrac{-1}{\sqrt{37}} = -\dfrac{\sqrt{37}}{37}$

$\tan \theta = \dfrac{y}{x} = \dfrac{6}{-1} = -6$

$\cot \theta = \dfrac{x}{y} = \dfrac{-1}{6} = -\dfrac{1}{6}$

$\sec \theta = \dfrac{r}{s} = \dfrac{\sqrt{37}}{-1} = -\sqrt{37}$

$\csc \theta = \dfrac{r}{y} = \dfrac{\sqrt{37}}{6}$

21. $4 \csc 270° + 3 \cos 180°$

$= 4(-1) + 3(-1)$

$= -7$

23. $2 \sec 0° + 4 \cot^2 90° + \cos 360°$

$= 2(1) + 4(0)^2 + 1$

$= 3$

25. $\sin^2 360° + \cos^2 360° = 0^2 + 1^2 = 1$

27. $\tan [n \cdot 180°]$

The angle is a quadrantal angle whose terminal side lies on either the positive part of the x-axis or the negative part of the x-axis. Any point on these terminal sides would have the form $(k, 0)$, where k is any real number, $k \neq 0$.

$\tan n \cdot 180 = \dfrac{y}{k} = \dfrac{0}{k} = 0$

29. Using a calculator, $\tan 25° = .466307658$ and
$\cot 65° = .466307658$.
We can conjecture that the tangent and cotangent of complementary angles are equal. Try another pair of complementary angles.
$\tan 45° = .\cot 45°$
$\quad 1 = 1$
Therefore, our conjecture appears to be true.

31. Using a calculator, $\cos 20° = .93969262$ and
$\cos(-20°) = .93969262$.
We can conjecture that the cosines of an angle and its negative are equal. Using a circle, and angle θ having the point (x, y) on its terminal side has a corresponding angle $-\theta$ with point $(x, -y)$ on its terminal side. From the definition of cosine,
$$\cos(-\theta) = \frac{x}{r} \text{ and } \cos\theta = \frac{x}{r}.$$
The cosines are equal.

35. Use the TRACE feature to move around the circle in quadrant I.
$\cos 40° \approx .766$ so $T = 40°$.

37. Use the TRACE feature to move around the circle in quadrant I.
$\cos 45° = \sin 45°$ so $T = 45°$.

39. As T increases from $90°$ to $180°$, the cosine decreases and the sine decreases.

41. -1 is its own reciprocal.
$\cos\theta = \sec\theta = -1$
$\cos 180° = \sec 180° = -1$

43. $\tan\beta = -\frac{1}{5}$
$\cot\beta = \frac{1}{\tan\beta}$
$= \frac{1}{-\frac{1}{5}}$
$= -5$

45. $\cot\theta = -\frac{\sqrt{5}}{3}$
$\tan\theta = \frac{1}{\cot\theta}$
$= \frac{1}{-\frac{\sqrt{5}}{3}}$
$= -\frac{3}{\sqrt{5}} \cdot \frac{\sqrt{5}}{\sqrt{5}}$
$= -\frac{3\sqrt{5}}{5}$

47. $\cos\alpha = \frac{1}{\sec\alpha} = \frac{1}{9.80425133} = .10199657$

51. $\cot\omega = \frac{\sqrt{3}}{3}$
$\tan\omega = \frac{1}{\cot\omega}$
$= \frac{1}{\frac{\sqrt{3}}{3}}$
$= \frac{3}{\sqrt{3}}$
$= \sqrt{3}$

53. $\tan(3B - 4°) = \frac{1}{\cot(5B - 8°)}$
$\tan(3B - 4°) = \tan(5B - 8°)$
$3B - 4° = 5B - 8°$
$4° = 2B$
$B = 2°$

55. $\sin\alpha > 0$ implies α is in quadrant I or II. $\cos\alpha < 0$ implies α is in quadrant II or III. α is in quadrant II.

57. $\tan\gamma > 0$ implies γ is in quadrant I or III. $\cot\gamma > 0$ implies γ is in quadrant I or III. γ is in quadrant I or III.

59. $129°$ is in quadrant II.
$+; -; -$

61. $298°$, is in quadrant IV.
$-; +; -$

63. $-82°$ is in quadrant IV.
$-; +; -$

65. $\tan 30° = \frac{\sin 30°}{\cos 30°}$
$\cos 30° < 1$, so $\sin 30° \div \cos 30° > \sin 30°$.
Therefore, $\tan 30°$ is greater.

67. $\sec 33° = \frac{1}{\cos 33°}$; since
$\cos 33° < 1$, $\frac{1}{\cos 33°} > \cos 33°$.
$\sin 33° < \cos 33° < \sec 33°$.
Therefore, $\sec 33°$ is greater.

69. $\cos\alpha = -1.001$ is impossible since $-1 \le \cos\alpha \le 1$.

71. $\cot\omega = -12.1$ is possible since $\cot\omega$ can be any real number.

73. $\tan\theta$ can take on all values. $\tan\theta = 1$ is possible.

75. $\tan \beta = 2$ is possible, but when $\tan \beta = 2$,

$$\cot \beta = \frac{1}{\tan \beta} = \frac{1}{2}.$$

$\tan \beta = 2$ and $\cot \beta = -2$ is impossible.

77. Find $\sin \alpha$ if $\cos \alpha = -\frac{1}{4}$, with α in quadrant II.

Start with the identity $\sin^2 \alpha + \cos^2 \alpha = 1$, and replace $\cos \alpha$ with $-\frac{1}{4}$.

$$\sin^2 \alpha + \left(-\frac{1}{4}\right)^2 = 1$$

$$\sin^2 \alpha + \frac{1}{16} = 1$$

$$\sin^2 \alpha = \frac{15}{16}$$

$$\sin \alpha = \pm\sqrt{\frac{15}{16}} = \pm\frac{\sqrt{15}}{4}$$

Since α is in quadrant II, $\sin \alpha > 0$, so

$$\sin \alpha = \frac{\sqrt{15}}{4}.$$

79. Find $\sec \theta$ if $\tan \theta = \frac{\sqrt{7}}{3}$ and θ is in quadrant III.

$$\tan^2 \theta + 1 = \sec^2 \theta$$

$$\sec^2 \theta = \left(\frac{\sqrt{7}}{3}\right)^2 + 1$$

$$= \frac{7}{9} + \frac{9}{9}$$

$$= \frac{16}{9}$$

$$\sec \theta = \pm\sqrt{\frac{16}{9}}$$

$$= \pm\frac{4}{3}$$

θ is in quadrant III so $\sec \theta = -\frac{4}{3}$.

81. Find $\sin \theta$, if $\sec \theta = 2$, with θ in quadrant IV.

Since $\sec \theta = 2$ and $\cos \theta = \frac{1}{\sec \theta}$, $\cos \theta = \frac{1}{2}$.

Since $\sin^2 \theta + \cos^2 \theta = 1$, and $\cos \theta = \frac{1}{2}$.

$$\sin^2 \theta + \left(\frac{1}{2}\right)^2 = 1$$

$$\sin^2 \theta + \frac{1}{4} = 1$$

$$\sin^2 \theta = \frac{3}{4}$$

$$\sin \theta = \pm\sqrt{\frac{3}{4}} = \pm\frac{\sqrt{3}}{2}$$

Since θ is in quadrant IV, and $\sin \theta$ is negative in quadrant IV, $\sin \theta = -\frac{\sqrt{3}}{2}$.

83. Find $\tan \beta$, if $\sin \beta = .49268329$, with β in quadrant II.

$$\sin^2 \beta + \cos^2 \beta = 1$$

$$\cos^2 \beta = 1 - \sin^2 \beta$$

$$\cos \beta = \pm\sqrt{1 - \sin^2 \beta}$$

$\cos \beta$ is in quadrant II, and the cosine is negative in quadrant II,

$$\cos \beta = -\sqrt{1 - \sin^2 \beta}$$

$$= -\sqrt{1 - (.49268329)^2}$$

$$= -\sqrt{1 - .24273682}$$

$$= -\sqrt{.75726318}$$

$$= -.87020870$$

$$\tan \beta = \frac{\sin \theta}{\cos \theta}$$

$$= \frac{.49268329}{-.87020870}$$

$$= -.56616682$$

85. $\tan X = 2$

$$\tan^2 X + 1 = \sec^2 X$$

$$\tan^2 X + 1 = \left(\frac{1}{\cos^2 X}\right)$$

$$(2)^2 + 1 = \left(\frac{1}{\cos X}\right)^2$$

$$5 = \left(\frac{1}{\cos X}\right)^2$$

For Exercises 87–91, remember that r is always positive.

87. $\tan \alpha = -\frac{15}{8}$

$\tan \alpha = \frac{y}{x}$ and α is in quadrant II, so let $y = 15$ and $x = -8$.

$$x^2 + y^2 = r^2$$

$$(-8)^2 + 15^2 = r^2$$

$$64 + 225 = r^2$$

$$289 = r^2$$

$$17 = r$$

$$\sin \alpha = \frac{y}{r} = \frac{15}{17}$$

$$\cos \alpha = \frac{x}{r} = \frac{-8}{17} = -\frac{8}{17}$$

$$\tan \alpha = \frac{y}{x} = \frac{15}{-8} = -\frac{15}{8}$$

$$\cot \alpha = \frac{x}{y} = \frac{-8}{15} = -\frac{8}{15}$$

$$\sec \alpha = \frac{r}{x} = \frac{17}{-8} = -\frac{17}{8}$$

$$\csc \alpha = \frac{r}{y} = \frac{17}{15}$$

89. $\tan \beta = \sqrt{3}$

$\tan \beta = \frac{y}{x}$ and β is in quadrant III, so let $y = -\sqrt{3}$
and $x = -1$.

$$x^2 + y^2 = r^2$$

$$(-1)^2 + \left(-\sqrt{3}\right)^2 = r^2$$

$$1 + 3 = r^2$$

$$4 = r^2$$

$$2 = r$$

$$\sin \beta = \frac{y}{r} = \frac{-\sqrt{3}}{2} = -\frac{\sqrt{3}}{2}$$

$$\cos \beta = \frac{x}{r} = \frac{-1}{2} = -\frac{1}{2}$$

$$\tan \beta = \frac{y}{x} = \frac{-\sqrt{3}}{-1} = \sqrt{3}$$

$$\cot \beta = \frac{x}{y} = \frac{-1}{-\sqrt{3}} = \frac{1}{\sqrt{3}} = \frac{\sqrt{3}}{3}$$

$$\sec \beta = \frac{r}{x} = \frac{2}{-1} = -2$$

$$\csc \beta = \frac{r}{y} = \frac{2}{-\sqrt{3}} = -\frac{2\sqrt{3}}{3}$$

91. $\cot \theta = -1.49586$ with θ in quadrant IV.

Since $\cot \theta = \frac{x}{y}$ and θ is in quadrant IV, let
$x = 1.49586$ and $y = -1$.

$$x^2 + y^2 = r^2$$

$$(1.49586)^2 + (-1)^2 = r^2$$

$$2.23760 + 1 = r^2$$

$$3.23760 = r^2$$

$$1.79933 = r$$

$$\sin \theta = \frac{y}{r} = \frac{-1}{1.79933} = -.555762$$

$$\cos \theta = \frac{x}{r} = \frac{1.49586}{1.79933} = .831343$$

$$\tan \theta = \frac{y}{x} = \frac{-1}{1.49586} = -.668512$$

$$\cot \theta = \frac{x}{y} = \frac{1.49586}{-1} = -1.49586$$

$$\sec \theta = \frac{r}{x} = \frac{1.79933}{1.49586} = 1.20287$$

$$\csc \theta = \frac{r}{y} = \frac{1.79933}{-1} = -1.79933$$

95. The statement is false.

$$\sin 30° + \cos 30° \overset{?}{=} 1$$

$$.5 + .8660 \overset{?}{=} 1$$

$$1.3660 \neq 1$$

Since $1.3660 \neq 1$, the given statement is false.

97. Let h = the height of the tree.

$$\cos 70° = \frac{50 \text{ ft}}{h}$$

$$h \cos 70° = 50$$

$$h = \frac{50}{\cos 70°} = \frac{50}{0.3420} \approx 146 \text{ feet}$$

99. (a) From the figure in the text and the definition
of $\tan \theta$, we can see that $\tan \theta = \frac{y}{x}$.

(b) Solve for x.

$$\tan \theta = \frac{y}{x}$$

$$x \tan \theta = y$$

$$x = \frac{y}{\tan \theta}$$

Section 5.4

Exercises

For Exercises 1–5, refer to the Special Angles chart.

1. C; $\sin 30° = \frac{1}{2}$

3. B; $\tan 45° = 1$

5. E; $\csc 60° = \frac{1}{\sin 60°} = \frac{1}{\frac{\sqrt{3}}{2}} = \frac{2}{\sqrt{3}} = \frac{\sqrt{3}}{\sqrt{3}} = \frac{2\sqrt{3}}{3}$

7.

$$\sin A = \frac{\text{side opposite}}{\text{hypotenuse}} = \frac{n}{p}$$

$$\cos A = \frac{\text{side adjacent}}{\text{hypotenuse}} = \frac{m}{p}$$

$$\tan A = \frac{\text{side opposite}}{\text{side adjacent}} = \frac{n}{m}$$

$$\cot A = \frac{\text{side adjacent}}{\text{side opposite}} = \frac{m}{n}$$

$$\sec A = \frac{\text{hypotenuse}}{\text{side adjacent}} = \frac{p}{m}$$

$$\csc A = \frac{\text{hypotenuse}}{\text{side opposite}} = \frac{p}{n}$$

9. $a = 5, \ b = 12$

$c^2 = a^2 + b^2$

$c^2 = 5^2 + 12^2$

$c^2 = 25 + 144$

$c^2 = 169$

$c = 13$

$$\sin B = \frac{\text{side opposite}}{\text{hypotenuse}} = \frac{12}{13}$$

$$\cos B = \frac{\text{side adjacent}}{\text{hypotenuse}} = \frac{5}{13}$$

$$\tan B = \frac{\text{side opposite}}{\text{side adjacent}} = \frac{12}{5}$$

$$\cot B = \frac{\text{side adjacent}}{\text{side opposite}} = \frac{5}{12}$$

$$\sec B = \frac{\text{hypotenuse}}{\text{side adjacent}} = \frac{13}{5}$$

$$\csc B = \frac{\text{hypotenuse}}{\text{side opposite}} = \frac{13}{12}$$

11. $a = 6, \ c = 7$

$c^2 = a^2 + b^2$

$7^2 = 6^2 + b^2$

$49 = 36 + b^2$

$13 = b^2$

$\sqrt{13} = b$

$$\sin B = \frac{\text{side opposite}}{\text{hypotenuse}} = \frac{\sqrt{13}}{7}$$

$$\cos B = \frac{\text{side adjacent}}{\text{hypotenuse}} = \frac{6}{7}$$

$$\tan B = \frac{\text{side opposite}}{\text{side adjacent}} = \frac{\sqrt{13}}{6}$$

$$\cot B = \frac{\text{side adjacent}}{\text{side opposite}} = \frac{6}{\sqrt{13}} = \frac{6\sqrt{13}}{13}$$

$$\sec B = \frac{\text{hypotenuse}}{\text{side adjacent}} = \frac{7}{6}$$

$$\csc B = \frac{\text{hypotenuse}}{\text{side opposite}} = \frac{7}{\sqrt{13}} = \frac{7\sqrt{13}}{13}$$

13.

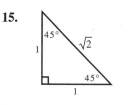

$$\tan 30° = \frac{\text{side opposite}}{\text{side adjacent}}$$

$$= \frac{1}{\sqrt{3}}$$

$$= \frac{\sqrt{3}}{3}$$

15.

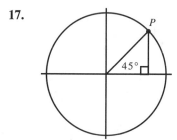

$$\sec 45° = \frac{\text{hypotenuse}}{\text{side adjacent}}$$

$$= \frac{\sqrt{2}}{1}$$

$$= \sqrt{2}$$

17.

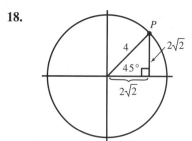

18.

$$\sin 45° = \frac{y}{4} \qquad\qquad \cos 45° = \frac{x}{4}$$

$$y = 4\sin 45° \qquad\qquad x = 4\cos 45°$$

$$= 4 \cdot \frac{\sqrt{2}}{2} \qquad\qquad x = 4 \cdot \frac{\sqrt{2}}{2}$$

$$= 2\sqrt{2} \qquad\qquad\quad = 2\sqrt{2}$$

19. The legs of the right triangle provide the coordinates of P.

P is $(2\sqrt{2}, \ 2\sqrt{2})$.

20. Steps 1 & 2:

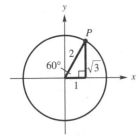

Step 3: $\sin 60° = \dfrac{y}{2}$ $\qquad \cos 60° = \dfrac{x}{2}$

$\qquad\quad y = 2 \sin 60° \qquad x = 2 \cos 60°$

$\qquad\qquad = 2 \cdot \dfrac{\sqrt{3}}{2} \qquad\qquad = 2 \cdot \dfrac{1}{2}$

$\qquad\qquad = \sqrt{3} \qquad\qquad\quad = 1$

Thus the coordinates of P are $(1, \sqrt{3})$.

21. $\quad \sin 0° = 0$

$\quad \sin 45° = .70711$

$\quad \sin 90° = 1$

$\quad\ \tan 0° = 0$

$\quad \tan 45° = 1$

$\quad \tan 90°$ is undefined.

$\quad Y_1$ is $\sin x$ and Y_2 is $\tan x$.

23. $\sin 60° = .8660$ for A between $0°$ and $90°$. Therefore, $a = 60°$.

25. Graph $Y_1 = x$ and $Y_2 = \sqrt{1 - x^2}$ in a window such as $-2 \le x \le 2$, $-2 \le y \le 2$. Use the intersection function to see that the point of intersection is $(.70710678, .70710678)$. This is the point $\left(\dfrac{\sqrt{2}}{2}, \dfrac{\sqrt{2}}{2} \right)$.

$Y_1 = \sqrt{1 - x^2}$ $\qquad$ $Y_2 = x$

These coordinates are the sine and cosine of $45°$.

27.

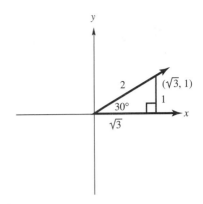

The line passes through $(0, 0)$ and $(\sqrt{3}, 1)$. The slope is $\dfrac{\sqrt{3}}{3}$. The equation of the line is

$y = \dfrac{\sqrt{3}}{3} x.$

29. The slope of a line is the change in y over the change in x, or $\tan \theta$. Since $y = \sqrt{3}x$, $m = \sqrt{3} = \tan \theta$. Since $\tan 60° = \sqrt{3}$, the line $y = \sqrt{3}x$ makes a $60°$ angle with the positive x-axis. (See Exercise 26.)

31. $\quad y = \dfrac{1}{2}(9)$, so $y = \dfrac{9}{2}$.

$\quad x = y\sqrt{3}$, so $x = \dfrac{9}{2}\sqrt{3}$.

$\quad y = z\sqrt{3}$, so

$\quad z = \dfrac{y}{\sqrt{3}} = \dfrac{\frac{9}{2}}{\sqrt{3}} = \dfrac{9\sqrt{3}}{6} = \dfrac{3\sqrt{3}}{2}.$

$\quad w = 2z$, so $w = 2\left(\dfrac{3\sqrt{3}}{2} \right) = 3\sqrt{3}.$

33. $\quad p = 15$

$\quad r = p\sqrt{2}$, so $r = 15\sqrt{2}.$

$\quad r = q\sqrt{3}$, so $q = \dfrac{r}{\sqrt{3}} = \dfrac{15\sqrt{2}}{\sqrt{3}} = 5\sqrt{6}.$

$\quad t = 2q$, so $t = 2\left(5\sqrt{6} \right) = 10\sqrt{6}.$

35. Area $= \dfrac{1}{2}$ base $\cdot$ height

$\qquad = \dfrac{1}{2} \cdot s \cdot s = \dfrac{1}{2} s^2$ or $\dfrac{s^2}{2}$

37. F; $212 - 180 = 32°$

$\quad (212°$ is in quadrant III$)$

39. B; $-60 + 360 = 300°$
$360 - 300 = 60°$
($300°$ is in quadrant IV)

41. B; $480 - 360 = 120°$
$180 - 120 = 60°$
($120°$ is in quadrant II)

47. $45°$:

$$\sin 45° = \frac{\sqrt{2}}{2}$$

$$\cos 45° = \frac{\sqrt{2}}{2}$$

$$\sec 45° = \sqrt{2}$$

$$\csc 45° = \sqrt{2}$$

49. $120°$:

$$\cos 120° = -\cos 60° = -\frac{1}{2}$$

$$\cot 120° = -\cot 60° = -\frac{\sqrt{3}}{3}$$

$$\sec 120° = -\sec 60° = -2$$

51. $150°$:

$$\sin 150° = \sin 30° = \frac{1}{2}$$

$$\cot 150° = -\cot 30° = -\sqrt{3}$$

$$\sec 150° = -\sec 30° = -\frac{2\sqrt{3}}{3}$$

53. $240°$:

$$\tan 240° = \tan 60° = \sqrt{3}$$

$$\cot 240° = \cot 60° = \frac{\sqrt{3}}{3}$$

55. $315°$
Use the method illustrated in Example 3.

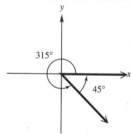

The reference angle is $45°$ Since $315°$ is in quadrant IV, the sine, tangent, cotangent, and cosecant are negative.

$$\sin 315° = -\sin 45° = -\frac{\sqrt{2}}{2}$$

$$\cos 315° = \cos 45° = \frac{\sqrt{2}}{2}$$

$$\tan 315° = -\tan 45° = -1$$

$$\cot 315° = -\cot 45° = -1$$

$$\sec 315° = \sec 45° = \sqrt{2}$$

$$\csc 315° = -\csc 45° = -\sqrt{2}$$

59. $750°$ is coterminal with
$750° - 2(360°) = 750° - 720°$
$= 30°.$

$$\sin 750° = \sin 30° = \frac{1}{2}$$

$$\cos 750° = \cos 30° = \frac{\sqrt{3}}{2}$$

$$\tan 750° = \tan 30° = \frac{\sqrt{3}}{3}$$

$$\cot 750° = \cot 30° = \sqrt{3}$$

$$\sec 750° = -\sec 30° = \frac{2\sqrt{3}}{3}$$

$$\csc 750° = \csc 30° = 2$$

61. $1500°$ is coterminal with
$1500° - 4(360°) = 1500° - 1440°$
$= 60°.$

$$\sin 1500° = \sin 60° = \frac{\sqrt{3}}{2}$$

$$\cos 1500° = \cos 60° = \frac{1}{2}$$

$$\tan 1500° = \tan 60° = \sqrt{3}$$

$$\cot 1500° = \cot 60° = \frac{\sqrt{3}}{3}$$

$$\sec 1500° = \sec 60° = 2$$

$$\csc 1500° = \csc 60° = \frac{2\sqrt{3}}{3}$$

63. $-1020°$ is coterminal with
$-1020° - (-3)(360°) = -1020° + 1080°$
$= 60°.$

$$\sin(-1020°) = \sin 60° = \frac{\sqrt{3}}{2}$$

$$\cos(-1020°) = \cos 60° = \frac{1}{2}$$

$$\tan(-1020°) = \tan 60° = \sqrt{3}$$

$$\cot(-1020°) = \cot 60° = \frac{\sqrt{3}}{3}$$

$$\sec(-1020°) = \sec 60° = 2$$

$$\csc(-1020°) = \csc 60° = \frac{2\sqrt{3}}{3}$$

65. $\sin(30° + 60°) \overset{?}{=} \sin 30° \cdot \cos 60°$
$\qquad + \sin 60° \cdot \cos 30°$
Evaluate each side to determine whether this equation is true or false.
$\sin(30° + 60°) = \sin 90° = 1$
$\sin 30° \cdot \cos 60° + \sin 60° \cdot \cos 30°$
$= \dfrac{1}{2} \cdot \dfrac{1}{2} + \dfrac{\sqrt{3}}{2} \cdot \dfrac{\sqrt{3}}{2}$
$= \dfrac{1}{4} + \dfrac{3}{4} = 1$
Since, $1 = 1$, the statement is true.

67. $\cos 60° \overset{?}{=} 2 \cos 30°$
Evaluate each side to determine whether this statement is true or false.
$\cos 60° = \dfrac{1}{2}$
$2 \cos 30° = 2\left(\dfrac{\sqrt{3}}{2}\right) = \sqrt{3}$
Since $\dfrac{1}{2} \neq \sqrt{3}$, the statement is false.

69. $\sin 120° \overset{?}{=} \sin 180° \cdot \cos 60° - \sin 60° \cdot \cos 180°$
Evaluate each side to determine whether this statement is true or false.
$\sin 120° = \dfrac{\sqrt{3}}{2}$
$\sin 180° \cdot \cos 60° - \sin 60° \cdot \cos 180°$
$= 0\left(\dfrac{1}{2}\right) - \left(\dfrac{\sqrt{3}}{2}\right)(-1)$
$= 0 - \left(-\dfrac{\sqrt{3}}{2}\right) = \dfrac{\sqrt{3}}{2}$
Since $\dfrac{\sqrt{3}}{2} = \dfrac{\sqrt{3}}{2}$, the statement is true.

For the following exercises, be sure your calculator is in degree mode. If your calculator accepts angles in degrees, minutes, and seconds, it is not necessary to change angles to decimal degrees. Keystroke sequences may vary on the type and/or model of calculator being used.

71. $\sin 38° \; 42'$
$38°42' = \left(38 + \dfrac{42}{60}\right)°$
$\qquad = 38.7°$
Enter: 38.7 [SIN]
or [SIN] 38.7 [ENTER]
Display: .6252427

73. $\sec 13° \; 15'$
$13°15' = \left(13 + \dfrac{15}{60}\right)°$
$\qquad = 13.25°$
Enter: 13.25 [COS] [1/x]
or ([COS] 13.25) [x⁻¹] [ENTER]
Display: 1.0273488

75. $\cot 183° \; 48'$
$183°48' = \left(183 + \dfrac{48}{60}\right)°$
$\qquad = 183.8°$
Enter: 183.8 [TAN] [1/x]
or ([TAN] 183.8) [x⁻¹] [ENTER]
Display: 15.055723

77. $\sec 312° \; 12'$
$312°12' = \left(312 + \dfrac{12}{60}\right)°$
$\qquad = 312.2°$
Enter: 312.2 [COS] [1/x]
or ([COS] 312.2) [x⁻¹] [ENTER]
Display: 1.4887142

79. $\sin(-317° \; 36')$
$-317°36' = -\left(317 + \dfrac{36}{60}\right)°$
$\qquad = -317.6°$
Enter: 317.6 [+/−] [SIN]
or [SIN] [(−)] 317.6 [ENTER]
Display: .6743024

81. $\cos(-15')$
$-15' = -\left(\dfrac{15}{60}\right)°$
$\qquad = -.25°$
Enter: .25 [+/−] [COS]
or [COS] [(−)] .25 [ENTER]
Display: .9999905

83. $\dfrac{1}{\cot 23.4°} = \tan 23.4°$
Enter: 23.4 [TAN]
or [TAN] 23.4 [ENTER]
Display: .4327386

85. $\dfrac{\cos 77°}{\sin 77°} = \cot 77°$
Enter: 77 [TAN] [1/x]
or ([TAN] 77) [x⁻¹] [ENTER]
Display: .2308682

87. $\tan \theta = 1.4739716$

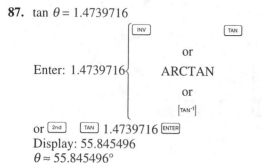

Enter: 1.4739716

or $\boxed{\text{2nd}}$ $\boxed{\text{TAN}}$ 1.4739716 $\boxed{\text{ENTER}}$
Display: 55.845496
$\theta \approx 55.845496°$

89. $\cot \theta = 1.2575516$

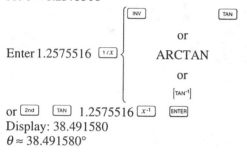

Enter 1.2575516 $\boxed{1/x}$

or $\boxed{\text{2nd}}$ $\boxed{\text{TAN}}$ 1.2575516 $\boxed{x^{-1}}$ $\boxed{\text{ENTER}}$
Display: 38.491580
$\theta \approx 38.491580°$

91. $\sec \theta = 2.7496222$

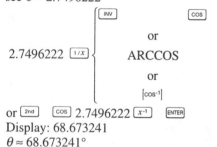

2.7496222 $\boxed{1/x}$

or $\boxed{\text{2nd}}$ $\boxed{\text{COS}}$ 2.7496222 $\boxed{x^{-1}}$ $\boxed{\text{ENTER}}$
Display: 68.673241
$\theta \approx 68.673241°$

93. $A = \sin 22°$
Enter: 22 $\boxed{\text{SIN}}$
or $\boxed{\text{SIN}}$ 22 $\boxed{\text{ENTER}}$
Display: .3746065934
$A \approx .3746065934°$

95. $\theta_1 = 39°$, $\theta_2 = 28°$
$$\frac{c_1}{c_2} = \frac{\sin \theta_1}{\sin \theta_2}$$
$$c_2 = \frac{c_1 \sin \theta_2}{\sin \theta_1}$$
$$c_2 = \frac{3 \times 10^8 (\sin 28°)}{\sin 39°}$$
$$c_2 \approx 2 \times 10^8$$
Since c_1 is only given to one significant digit, c_2 can only be given to one significant digit.
The speed of light in the second medium is about 2×10^8 m per sec.

97. $\theta_1 = 62°$, $c_2 = 2.6 \times 10^8$ m per sec
$$\frac{c_1}{c_2} = \frac{\sin \theta_1}{\sin \theta_2}$$
$$\sin \theta_2 = \frac{2.6 \times 10^8 (\sin 62°)}{3 \times 10^8}$$
$$\theta_2 \approx 50°$$

99. $c_1 = 3 \times 10^8$ m per sec,
$c_2 = 2.254 \times 10^8$ m per sec
$\theta_1 = 90° - 29.6° = 60.4°$
$$\sin \theta_2 = \frac{2.254 \times 10^8 (\sin 60.4°)}{3 \times 10^8}$$
$$\theta_2 \approx 40.8°$$
Light from the object is refracted at an angle of 40.8° from the vertical. Light from the horizon is refracted at an angle of 48.7° from the vertical. Therefore, the fish thinks the object lies at an angle of $48.7° - 40.8° = 7.9°$ above the horizon.

101. Using the values for K_1 and K_2 from Exercise 100, determine V_2 when $D = 200$ and $V_1 = 90$ mph $= 132$ ft/sec.
$$D = \frac{1.05(V_1^2 - V_2^2)}{64.4(K_1 + K_2 + \sin \theta)}$$
$$200 = \frac{1.05(132^2 - V_2^2)}{64.4(.4 + .02 + \sin(-3.5°))}$$
$$200 = \frac{18,295.2 - 1.05V_2^2}{23.12}$$
$$V_2^2 = \frac{23.12(200) - 18,295.2}{-1.05}$$
$$V_2 \approx 114 \text{ ft/sec}$$
$$V_2 \approx 78 \text{ mph}$$

103. $F = W \sin \theta$
$F = 2100 \sin 1.8°$
≈ 65.96 lb

105. $F = W \sin \theta$
$-130 = 2600 \sin \theta$
$$\frac{-130}{2600} = \sin \theta$$
$-.05 = \sin \theta$
$\theta \approx -2.87°$

107. For parts (a) and (b), $\alpha = 3°$, $g = 32.2$, and $f = .14$.

(a) Since 45 mi/hr = 66 ft/sec,

$$R = \frac{V^2}{g(f + \tan\alpha)}$$

$$\approx \frac{66^2}{32.2(.14 + \tan 3°)}$$

$$\approx 703 \text{ ft}$$

(b) Since 70 mi/hr = 102 2/3 ft/sec,

$$R = \frac{V^2}{g(f + \tan\alpha)}$$

$$\approx \frac{102.67^2}{32.2(.14 + \tan 3°)}$$

$$\approx 1701 \text{ ft}$$

(c) Intuitively, increasing α would make it easier to negotiate the curve at a higher speed much like is done at a race track. Mathematically, a larger value of α (acute) will lead to a larger value for $\tan\alpha$. If $\tan\alpha$ increases, then the ratio determining R will *decrease*. Thus, the radius can be smaller and the curve sharper if α is increased.

$$R = \frac{V^2}{g(f + \tan\alpha)}$$

$$\approx \frac{66^2}{32.2(.14 + \tan 4°)}$$

$$\approx 644 \text{ ft}$$

$$R = \frac{V^2}{g(f + \tan\alpha)}$$

$$\approx \frac{102.67^2}{32.2(.14 + \tan 4°)}$$

$$\approx 1559 \text{ ft}$$

As predicted, both values are less.

109. (a) $D = \dfrac{v^2 \sin\theta\cos\theta + v\cos\theta\sqrt{(v\sin\theta)^2 + 64h}}{32}$

Let $v = 44$ ft/sec and $h = 7$ ft.
For $\theta = 40°$,

$$D = \frac{44^2 \sin 40°\cos 40° + 44\cos 40°\sqrt{(44\sin 40°)^2 + 64(7)}}{32}$$

$$\approx 67.00 \text{ ft}$$

For $\theta = 42°$,

$$D = \frac{44^2 \sin 42°\cos 42° + 44\cos 42°\sqrt{(44\sin 42°)^2 + 64(7)}}{32}$$

$$\approx 67.14 \text{ ft}$$

For $\theta = 45°$,

$$D = \frac{44^2 \sin 45°\cos 45° + 44\cos 45°\sqrt{(44\sin 45°)^2 + 64(7)}}{32}$$

$$\approx 66.84 \text{ ft}$$

D increases and then decreases.

(b) Let $h = 7$ ft and $\theta = 42°$.
For $v = 43$ ft/sec,

$$D = \frac{43^2 \sin 42° \cos 42° + 43 \cos 42° \sqrt{(43 \sin 42°)^2 + 64(7)}}{32}$$

≈ 64.40 ft
For $v = 44$ ft/sec,

$$D = \frac{44^2 \sin 42° \cos 42° + 44 \cos 42° \sqrt{(44 \sin 42°)^2 + 64(7)}}{32}$$

≈ 67.14 ft
For $v = 45$ ft/sec,

$$D = \frac{45^2 \sin 42° \cos 42° + 45 \cos 42° \sqrt{(45 \sin 42°)^2 + 64(7)}}{32}$$

≈ 69.93 ft
D increases.

(c) v; the shotputter should concentrate on achieving as large a value of v as possible.

Section 5.5

Exercises

1. 16,454.5 to 16,455.5

3. 8958.5 to 8959.5

7. If h is the actual height of a building and the height is measured as 58.6 ft, then $|h - 58.6| \le .05$.

9. $A = 36°20'$, $c = 964$ m
$A + B = 90°$
$\quad B = 90° - A$
$\quad B = 90° - 36°20'$
$\quad\quad = 89°60' - 36°20'$
$\quad B = 53°40'$
$\sin A = \dfrac{a}{c}$
$\quad a = c \sin A$
$\quad a = 964 \sin 36°20'$
Use a calculator and round answer to three significant digits.
$\quad a = 571$ m
$\cos A = \dfrac{b}{c}$
$\quad b = c \cos A$
$\quad b = 964 \cos 36°20'$
Use a calculator and round answer to three significant digits.
$b = 777$ m

11. $N = 51.2°$, $m = 124$ m
$M + N = 90°$
$\quad M = 90° - N$
$\quad M = 90° - 51.2°$
$\quad M = 38.8°$

$\tan N = \dfrac{n}{m}$
$\quad n = m \tan N$
$\quad n = 124 \cdot \tan 51.2°$
$\quad n = 154$ m

$\cos N = \dfrac{m}{p}$

$\quad p = \dfrac{m}{\cos N}$
$\quad p = \dfrac{124}{\cos 51.2°}$
$\quad p = 198$ m

13.

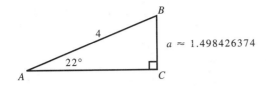

$a \approx 1.498426374$

19. $A = 28.00°$, $c = 17.4$ ft

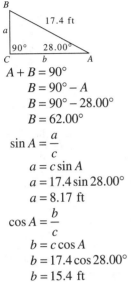

$A + B = 90°$
$B = 90° - A$
$B = 90° - 28.00°$
$B = 62.00°$

$\sin A = \dfrac{a}{c}$
$a = c \sin A$
$a = 17.4 \sin 28.00°$
$a = 8.17$ ft

$\cos A = \dfrac{b}{c}$
$b = c \cos A$
$b = 17.4 \cos 28.00°$
$b = 15.4$ ft

21. $B = 73.00°$, $b = 128$ in.

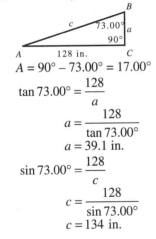

$A = 90° - 73.00° = 17.00°$

$\tan 73.00° = \dfrac{128}{a}$

$a = \dfrac{128}{\tan 73.00°}$
$a = 39.1$ in.

$\sin 73.00° = \dfrac{128}{c}$

$c = \dfrac{128}{\sin 73.00°}$
$c = 134$ in.

23. $a = 76.4$ yd, $b = 39.3$ yd

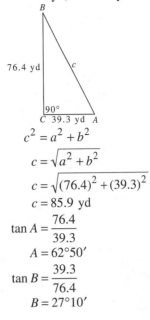

$c^2 = a^2 + b^2$
$c = \sqrt{a^2 + b^2}$
$c = \sqrt{(76.4)^2 + (39.3)^2}$
$c = 85.9$ yd

$\tan A = \dfrac{76.4}{39.3}$
$A = 62°50'$

$\tan B = \dfrac{39.3}{76.4}$
$B = 27°10'$

25. The angle of elevation from X to Y is $90°$ whenever Y is directly above X.

29. It should be shown as an angle measured from due north.

31.

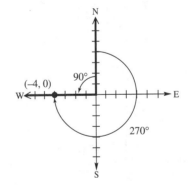

The bearing of the airplane measured in a clockwise direction from due north is $270°$. The bearing can also be expressed as N $90°$ W, or S $90°$ W.

33. Let θ = the angle the guy wire makes with the ground.

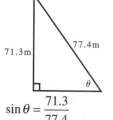

$$\sin \theta = \frac{71.3}{77.4}$$
$$\theta \approx 67.100475°$$
$$\theta \approx 67° + (.100475)(60')$$
$$\theta \approx 67°10'$$

The guy wire makes an angle of 67° 10′ with the ground.

35. The two right triangles are congruent. So corresponding sides are congruent. Since the sides that compose the base of the isosceles triangle are congruent, each side is $\frac{42.36}{2}$, or 21.18 in. Let x = the length of each of the two equal sides of the isosceles triangle.

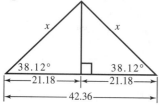

$$\cos 38.12° = \frac{21.18}{x}$$
$$x \cos 38.12° = 21.18$$
$$x = \frac{21.18}{\cos 38.12°}$$
$$x \approx 26.921918$$

The length of each of the two equal sides of the triangle is 26.92 in.

37. $\tan 30.0° = \dfrac{y}{1000}$
$$y = 1000 \cdot \tan 30.0°$$
$$\approx 577$$

However, the observer's eye-height is 6 feet from the ground, so the cloud ceiling is $577 + 6 = 583$ ft.

39. Let θ = the angle of elevation of the sun.

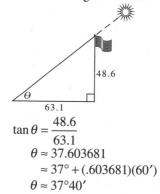

$$\tan \theta = \frac{48.6}{63.1}$$
$$\theta \approx 37.603681$$
$$\approx 37° + (.603681)(60')$$
$$\theta \approx 37°40'$$

The angle of elevation of the sun is 37°40′.

41. Let x = the horizontal distance that the plan must fly to be directly over the tree.
$$\tan 13°50' = \frac{10,500}{x}$$
$$x \tan 13°50' = 10,500$$
$$x = \frac{10,500}{\tan 13°50'}$$
$$x \approx 42,600$$

The horizontal distance that the plan must fly to be directly over the tree is 42,600 ft.

43. Let θ = the angle of depression.
$$\tan \theta = \frac{39.82}{51.74}$$
$$\theta = 37.58° = 37°35'$$

45. Let x = the distance from the assigned target.

In triangle ABC,
$$\tan 0°0'30'' = \frac{x}{234,000}$$
$$x = 234,000 \tan 0°0'30''$$
$$x \approx 34.0$$

The distance from the assigned target is 34.0 mi.

47. Let x = the distance the plane is from its starting point. In the figure, the measure of angle ACB is $40° + (180° - 130°)$ or $90°$. Therefore, triangle ACB is a right triangle.

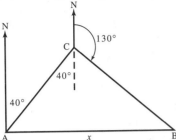

Distance traveled in 1.5 hr:
(1.5 hr)(110 mph) = 165 mi
Distance traveled in 1.3 hr:
(1.3 hr)(110 mph) = 143 mi
Using the Pythagorean theorem, we have
$$x^2 = 165^2 + 143^2$$
$$x^2 = 47,674$$
$$x \approx 220.$$
The plane is 220 mi from its starting point.

49. Let x = distance the ships are apart.
(1.5 hr)(18 knots) = 27 nautical mi
(1.5 hr)(26 knots) = 39 nautical mi
Since $130° - 40° = 90°$, we have a right triangle.
Applying the Pythagorean theorem,
$$x^2 = 27^2 + 39^2$$
$$x^2 = 2250$$
$$x \approx 47.$$
The ships are 47 nautical mi apart.

51. Let x = the distance from Atlanta to Augusta.

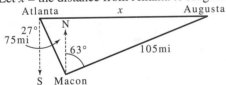

Note that the line from Atlanta to Macon makes an angle of $27° + 63°$, or $90°$, with the line from Macon to Augusta.
Distance from Atlanta to Macon:
$$60\left(1\frac{1}{4}\right) = 75 \text{ mi}$$
Distance from Macon to Augusta:
$$60\left(1\frac{3}{4}\right) = 105 \text{ mi}$$
Use the Pythagorean theorem to find x.
$$x^2 = 75^2 + 105^2$$
$$= 16,650$$
$$x \approx 130 \text{ mi}$$
The distance from Atlanta to Augusta is 130 mi.

53. Let C = the location of the transmitter and a = the distance of the transmitter from B.
angle $CBA = 90° - 53°40'$
$= 36°20'$
angle $CAB = 90 - 36°20'$
$= 53°40'$
$A + B = 90°$, so $C = 90°$.
$$\frac{a}{2.50} = \sin A = \sin 53°40'$$
$$a = 2.50 \sin 53°40'$$
$$\approx 2.01$$
The distance of the transmitter from B is 2.01 mi.

55. Let x = the side adjacent to 52.5° in the smaller triangle.
In the larger triangle:
$$\tan 41.2° = \frac{h}{168 + x}$$
$$h = (168 + x)\tan 41.2°.$$
In the smaller triangle:
$$\tan 52.5° = \frac{h}{x}$$
$$h = x \tan 52.5°.$$
Substitute for h in this equation and solve for x.
$$(168 + x)\tan 41.2° = x \tan 52.5°$$
$$168 \tan 41.2° + x \tan 41.2° = x \tan 52.5°$$
$$168 \tan 41.2° = x \tan 52.5° - x \tan 41.2°$$
$$168 \tan 41.2° = x(\tan 52.5° - \tan 41.2°)$$
$$\frac{168 \tan 41.2°}{\tan 52.5° - \tan 41.2°} = x$$
Then substitute for x in the equation for the smaller triangle.
$$h = x \tan 52.5°$$
$$h = \frac{168 \tan 41.2°(\tan 52.5°)}{\tan 52.5° - \tan 41.2°}$$
$$h \approx 448$$
The height of the triangle is 448 m.

57. Let x = the height of the antenna and h = the height of the house.

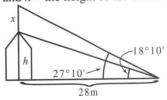

In the smaller right triangle:
$$\tan 18°10' = \frac{h}{28}$$
$$h = 28(\tan 18°10').$$

In the larger right triangle:

$$\tan 27°10' = \frac{x+h}{28}$$
$$x + h = 28(\tan 27°10')$$
$$x = 28(\tan 27°10') - 28(\tan 18°10')$$
$$x \approx 5.18.$$

The height of the antenna is 5.18 m.

59. Let $x =$ the minimum distance that a plant needing full sun can be placed from the fence.

$$\tan 23°20' = \frac{4.65}{x}$$
$$x \tan 23°20' = 4.65$$
$$x = \frac{4.65}{\tan 23°20'}$$
$$x \approx 10.8$$

The minimum distance is 10.8 ft.

61. Let $y =$ the common hypotenuse of the two right triangles.

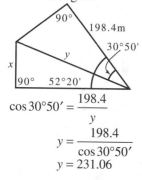

$$\cos 30°50' = \frac{198.4}{y}$$
$$y = \frac{198.4}{\cos 30°50'}$$
$$y = 231.06$$

To find x, first find the angle opposite x in the right triangle by subtracting.

$$52°20' - 30°50' = 51°80' - 30°50'$$
$$= 21°30'$$
$$\sin 21°30' = \frac{x}{y} = \frac{x}{231.06}$$
$$x = 231.06(\sin 21°30')$$
$$x \approx 84.7 \text{ m}$$

63. (a) Let d be the distance between P and Q. Triangle PQC is a right triangle with

$$\tan \frac{\theta}{2} = \frac{d}{R}$$
$$d = R \tan \frac{\theta}{2}$$
$$= 965 \tan \frac{37°}{2}$$
$$= 965 \tan 18.5°$$
$$\approx 323 \text{ ft.}$$

(b) From right triangle CPN,

$$\cos \frac{\theta}{2} = \frac{NC}{R}$$
$$NC = R \cos \frac{\theta}{2}.$$

Now,

$$MN + NC = R$$
$$MN = R - NC$$
$$= R - R \cos \frac{\theta}{2}$$
$$= R\left(1 - \cos \frac{\theta}{2}\right).$$

Section 5.6

Exercises

1. $y = -\sin x$

The graph is a sinusoidal curve with an amplitude of 1 and a period of 2π. Because $a = -1$, the graph is a reflection of $y = \sin x$ in the x-axis. This matches with graph D.

3. $y = \sin 2x$

The graph is a sinusoidal curve with a period of π and an amplitude of 1. Since $\sin 2(0) = 0$, the point $(0, 0)$ is on the graph. This matches with graph A.

5. $y = 2 \cos x$

Amplitude: $|2| = 2$

x	0	$\frac{\pi}{2}$	π	$\frac{3\pi}{2}$	2π
$2 \cos x$	2	0	-2	0	2

This table gives five values for graphing one period of the function.
Repeat this cycle for the interval $[-2\pi, 0]$.

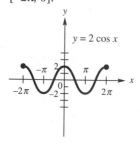

7. $y = \dfrac{2}{3}\sin\ x$

Amplitude: $\left|\dfrac{2}{3}\right| = \dfrac{2}{3}$

x	0	$\dfrac{\pi}{2}$	π	$\dfrac{3\pi}{2}$	2π
$\dfrac{2}{3}\sin\ x$	0	.7	0.	−.7	0

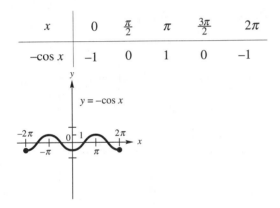

9. $y = -\cos\ x$

Amplitude: $\left|-1\right| = 1$

x	0	$\dfrac{\pi}{2}$	π	$\dfrac{3\pi}{2}$	2π
$-\cos\ x$	−1	0	1	0	−1

11. $y = -2\sin\ x$

Amplitude: $\left|-2\right| = 2$

x	0	$\dfrac{\pi}{2}$	π	$\dfrac{3\pi}{2}$	2π
$-2\sin\ x$	0	−2	0	2	0

13. $y = \sin\dfrac{1}{2}x$

Period: $\dfrac{2\pi}{\frac{1}{2}} = 4\pi$

Amplitude: $\left|1\right| = 1$

Divide the interval $[0, 4\pi]$ into four equal parts to get x-values that will yield minimum and maximum points and x-intercepts. Then make a table.

x	0	π	2π	3π	4π
$\dfrac{1}{2}x$	0	$\dfrac{\pi}{2}$	π	$\dfrac{3\pi}{2}$	2π
$\sin\dfrac{1}{2}x$	0	1	0	−1	0

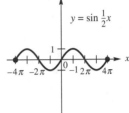

15. $y = \cos\dfrac{3}{4}x$

Period: $\dfrac{2\pi}{\frac{3}{4}} = \dfrac{8\pi}{3}$

Amplitude: 1

x	0	$\dfrac{2\pi}{3}$	$\dfrac{4\pi}{3}$	2π	$\dfrac{8\pi}{3}$
$\dfrac{3}{4}x$	0	$\dfrac{\pi}{2}$	π	$\dfrac{3\pi}{2}$	2π
$\cos\dfrac{3}{4}x$	1	0	−1	0	1

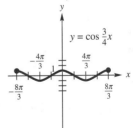

17. $y = 2 \sin \frac{1}{4} x$

Period: $\frac{2\pi}{\frac{1}{4}} = 8\pi$

Amplitude: 2

x	0	2π	4π	6π	8π
$\frac{1}{4} x$	0	$\frac{\pi}{2}$	π	$\frac{3\pi}{2}$	2π
$2 \sin \frac{1}{4} x$	0	2	0	-2	0

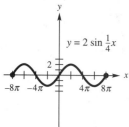

19. $y = -2 \cos 3x$

Period: $\frac{2\pi}{3}$

Amplitude: 2

x	0	$\frac{\pi}{6}$	$\frac{\pi}{3}$	$\frac{\pi}{2}$	$\frac{2\pi}{3}$
$3x$	0	$\frac{\pi}{2}$	π	$\frac{3\pi}{2}$	2π
$-2 \cos 3x$	-2	0	2	0	-2

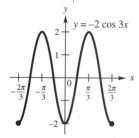

In Exercise 21, there are other correct answers.

21. The graph has an amplitude of 4 and a period of 4π. Then $y = a \sin bx$ where $a = 4$ and $b = \frac{1}{2}$, so

$y = 4 \sin \frac{1}{2} x$.

23. B; amplitude = 3, period = $\frac{2\pi}{2} = \pi$,

phase shift = $\frac{4}{2} = 2$

25. C; amplitude = 4, period = $\frac{2\pi}{3}$, phase shift = $\frac{2}{3}$

27. $y = \sin\left(x - \frac{\pi}{4} \right)$

The graph is a sinusoidal curve $y = \sin x$ shifted $\frac{\pi}{4}$ units to the right. This matches graph D.

29. $y = 1 + \sin x$

The graph is a sinusoidal curve $y = \sin x$ translated vertically 1 unit up. This matches graph B.

31. $y = 2 \sin (x - \pi)$

The amplitude is $|2|$, which is 2.

The period is $\frac{2\pi}{1}$, which is 2π.

There is no vertical translation.

The phase shift is π units to the right.

33. $y = 4 \cos\left(\frac{x}{2} + \frac{\pi}{2} \right)$

$y = 4 \cos \frac{1}{2} (x + \pi)$

The amplitude is $|4|$, which is 4.

The period is $\frac{2\pi}{\frac{1}{2}}$, which is 4π.

There is no vertical translation.

The phase shift is π units to the left.

35. $y = 2 - \sin\left(3x - \frac{\pi}{5} \right)$

$y = -1 \sin 3\left(x - \frac{\pi}{15} \right) + 2$

The amplitude is $|-1|$, which is 1.

The period is $\frac{2\pi}{3}$.

The vertical translation is 2 units up.

The phase shift is $\frac{\pi}{15}$ units to the right.

37. $y = \sin\left(x - \dfrac{\pi}{4}\right)$

The amplitude is 1.
The period is 2π.
There is no vertical translation.

The phase shift is $\dfrac{\pi}{4}$ units to the right.

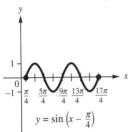

$y = \sin\left(x - \frac{\pi}{4}\right)$

39. $y = 2\cos\left(x - \dfrac{\pi}{3}\right)$

The amplitude is 2.
The period is 2π.
There is no vertical translation.

The phase shift is $\dfrac{\pi}{3}$ units to the right.

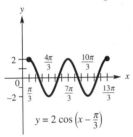

$y = 2\cos\left(x - \frac{\pi}{3}\right)$

41. $y = -4\sin(2x - \pi)$

$y = -4\sin 2\left(x - \dfrac{\pi}{2}\right)$

The amplitude is $|-4|$, which is 4.

The period is $\dfrac{2\pi}{2}$, which is π.

There is no vertical translation.

The phase shift is $\dfrac{\pi}{2}$ units to the right.

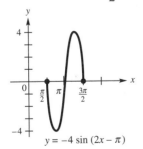

$y = -4\sin(2x - \pi)$

43. $y = \dfrac{1}{2}\cos\left(\dfrac{1}{2}x - \dfrac{\pi}{4}\right)$

$y = \dfrac{1}{2}\cos\dfrac{1}{2}\left(x - \dfrac{\pi}{2}\right)$

The amplitude is $\dfrac{1}{2}$.

The period is $\dfrac{2\pi}{\frac{1}{2}}$, which is 4π.

This is no vertical translation.

The phase shift is $\dfrac{\pi}{2}$ units to the right.

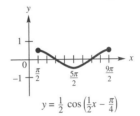

$y = \frac{1}{2}\cos\left(\frac{1}{2}x - \frac{\pi}{4}\right)$

45. $y = 1 - \dfrac{2}{3}\sin\dfrac{3}{4}x$

The amplitude is $\left|-\dfrac{2}{3}\right|$, which is $\dfrac{2}{3}$.

The period is $\dfrac{2\pi}{\frac{3}{4}}$, which is $\dfrac{8\pi}{3}$.

The vertical translation is 1 unit up.
There is no phase shift.

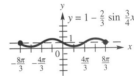

$y = 1 - \frac{2}{3}\sin\frac{3}{4}x$

47. $y = 1 - 2\cos\dfrac{1}{2}x$

The amplitude is $|-2|$, which is 2.

The period is $\dfrac{2\pi}{\frac{1}{2}}$, which is 4π.

The vertical translation is 1 unit up.
There is no phase shift.

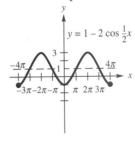

$y = 1 - 2\cos\frac{1}{2}x$

49. $y = -3 + 2\sin\left(x + \dfrac{\pi}{2}\right)$

The amplitude is 2.

The period is 2π.

The vertical translation is 3 units down.

The phase shift is $\dfrac{\pi}{2}$ units to the left.

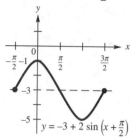

51. $y = \dfrac{1}{2} + \sin 2\left(x + \dfrac{\pi}{4}\right)$

The amplitude is 1.

The period is $\dfrac{2\pi}{2}$. which is π.

The vertical translation is $\dfrac{1}{2}$ unit up.

The phase shift is $\dfrac{\pi}{4}$ units to the left.

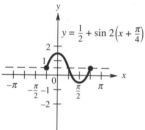

In Exercise 53, there are other correct answers.

53. The graph has an amplitude of 3, a period of π, and a phase shift of $\dfrac{\pi}{4}$ units to the right. In the equation $y = a\sin b(x - d)$, $a = 3$, $b = 2$, and $d = \dfrac{\pi}{4}$; therefore, $y = 3\sin 2\left(x - \dfrac{\pi}{4}\right)$.

55. The graph repeats each day, so the period is 24 hours.

57. Approximately 6 P.M., approximately .2 feet.

59. Approximately 2 A.M.; approximately 2.6 feet.

61. (a) The highest temperature is 80°; the lowest is 50°.

(b) The amplitude is $\dfrac{1}{2}(80° - 50°) = 15°$.

(c) The period is about 35,000 yr.

(d) The trend of the temperature now is downward.

63. (a) The latest time that the animals begin their evening activity is 8:00 P.M., the earliest time is 4:00 P.M.

$4{:}00 \le y \le 8{:}00$

Since there is a difference of 4 hr in these times, the amplitude is $\dfrac{1}{2}(4) = 2$ hr.

(b) The length of this period is 1 yr.

65. $-1 \le y \le 1$

Amplitude: 1

Period: 8 squares $= 8(30°)$

$$= 240° \text{ or } \dfrac{4\pi}{3}$$

67. $E = 5\cos 120\pi r$

(a) Amplitude: $|5| = 5$

Period: $\dfrac{2\pi}{120\pi} = \dfrac{1}{60}$ sec

(b) Number of cycles per second

$$= \dfrac{1}{\text{period}} = \dfrac{1}{\frac{1}{60}} = 60$$

(c) $t = 0$

$E = 5\cos 120\pi(0) = 5$

$t = .03$

$E = 5\cos 120\pi(.03) \approx 1.545$

$t = .06$

$E = 5\cos 120\pi(.06) \approx -4.045$

$t = .09$

$E = 5\cos 120\pi(.09) \approx -4.045$

$t = .12$

$E = 5\cos 120\pi(.12) \approx 1.545$

(d)

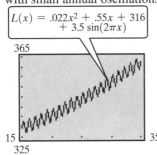

$E = 5 \cos 120\pi t$

(b) The seasonal variations are caused by the term $3.5 \sin (2\pi x)$. The maximums will occur when

$$x = \frac{1}{4}, \ \frac{5}{4}, \ \frac{9}{4}, \ \ldots \ .$$

Since x is in years, $x = \frac{1}{4}$ corresponds to April when the seasonal carbon dioxide levels are maximum. The minimum levels will occur when

$$x = \frac{3}{4}, \ \frac{7}{4}, \ \frac{11}{4}, \ \ldots \ .$$

This is $\frac{1}{2}$ yr later which corresponds to October.

69. (a) The graph has a general upward trend along with small annual oscillations.

$$L(x) = .022x^2 + .55x + 316 + 3.5 \sin(2\pi x)$$

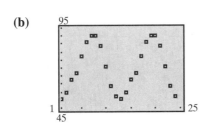

73. $\cos 0 = 1$ and $\cos \pi = -1$, so $\left| \cos \pi \right| = \left| -1 \right| = 1$. Thus, $x = 0$ and $x = \pi$.

75. (a) We can predict the average yearly temperature by finding the mean of the average monthy temperatures:
$$\frac{51 + 55 + 63 + 67 + 77 + 86 + 50 + 90 + 84 + 71 + 59 + 52}{12} = \frac{845}{12} \approx 70.4°F \, , \text{ which is very close to the actual}$$
value of 70°F.

(b)

95

45   1 ·············· 25

(c) Let the amplitude a be $\dfrac{90 - 51}{2} = 19.5.$ Since the period is 12, let $b = \dfrac{\pi}{6}$. Let

$c = \dfrac{90 + 51}{2} = 70.5.$ The minimum temperature occurs in January. Thus, when $x = 1$, $b(x - d)$ must equal an odd multiple of π since the cosine function is minimum at these values. Solving for d

$$\frac{\pi}{6}(1 - d) = -\pi$$
$$d = 7$$

d can be adjusted slightly to give a better visual fit. Try $d = 7.2$. Thus,
$$f(x) = a \cos b(x - d) + c$$
$$= 19.5 \cos \left[\frac{\pi}{6}(x - 7.2) \right] + 70.5.$$

(d) Plotting the data with

$$f(x) = 19.5 \cos\left[\frac{\pi}{6}(x - 7.2)\right] + 70.5$$

on the same coordinate axes give a good fit.

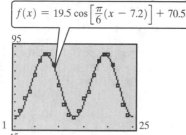

(e)

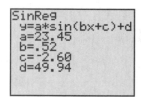

TI-83 fixed to the
nearest hundredth

From the sine regression we get
$$y = 19.72 \sin(.52x - 2.17) + 70.47$$
$$= 19.72 \sin[.52(x - 4.17)] + 70.47.$$

76. (a)

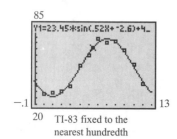

TI-83 fixed to the
nearest hundredth

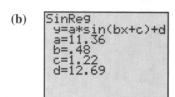

TI-83 fixed to the
nearest hundredth

(b)

SinReg
y=a*sin(bx+c)+d
a=11.36
b=.48
c=1.22
d=12.69

TI-83 fixed to the
nearest hundredth

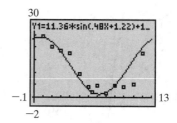

Section 5.7

Exercises

1. (a) $a = 2, \omega = |2| = 2$

$s(t) = a \sin \omega t$

$s(t) = 2 \sin 2t$

amplitude $= |a| = |2| = 2$

period $= \dfrac{2\pi}{\omega} = \dfrac{2\pi}{2} = \pi$

frequency $= \dfrac{\omega}{2\pi} = \dfrac{1}{\pi}$

(b) $a = 2, \omega = 4$

$s(t) = a \sin \omega t$

$s(t) = 2 \sin 4t$

amplitude $= |a| = |2| = 2$

period $= \dfrac{2\pi}{\omega} = \dfrac{2\pi}{4} = \dfrac{\pi}{2}$

frequency $\dfrac{\omega}{2\pi} = \dfrac{4}{2\pi} = \dfrac{2}{\pi}$

3. period $= 1$

$$\frac{2\pi}{\omega} = 1$$

$$2\pi = \omega$$

$$\omega = \sqrt{\frac{g}{l}}$$

$$2\pi = \sqrt{\frac{32}{l}}$$

$$4\pi^2 = \frac{32}{l}$$

$$l = \frac{32}{4\pi^2} = \frac{8}{\pi^2}$$

5. $k = 2$, $m = 1$

(a) $a = \dfrac{1}{2}$

$\omega = \sqrt{\dfrac{k}{m}} = \sqrt{\dfrac{2}{1}} = \sqrt{2}$

amplitude $= a = \dfrac{1}{2}$

period $= \dfrac{2\pi}{\omega} = \dfrac{2\pi}{\sqrt{2}} = \sqrt{2}\,\pi$

frequency $= \dfrac{\omega}{2\pi} = \dfrac{\sqrt{2}}{2\pi}$

(b) $s(t) = a \sin \omega t$

$s(t) = \dfrac{1}{2} \sin \sqrt{2}\, t$

7. $a = -4$, $\omega = 10$

(a) maximum height = amplitude = 4 in.

(b) frequency $= \dfrac{\omega}{2\pi}$

$= \dfrac{10}{2\pi}$

$= \dfrac{5}{\pi}$ cycles per sec

period $= \dfrac{2\pi}{\omega} = \dfrac{\pi}{5}$ sec

(c) $s(t) = -4 \cos 10t = 4$

$\cos 10t = -1$

$10t = \pi$

$t = \dfrac{\pi}{10}$

The weight first reaches its maximum height after $\dfrac{\pi}{10}$ sec.

(d) $s(1.466) = -4 \cos(10 \cdot 1.466) \approx 2$

After 1.466 sec, the weight is about 2 in. above the equilibrium position.

9. $a = -2$

(a) period: $\dfrac{2\pi}{\omega} = \dfrac{1}{3}$

$6\pi = \omega$

$s(t) = a \cos \omega t$

$s(t) = -2 \cos 6\pi t$

(b) frequency $= \dfrac{\omega}{2\pi}$

$= \dfrac{6\pi}{2\pi}$

$= 3$ cycles per sec

Section 5.8

Exercises

1. True; since $\cos \dfrac{\pi}{2} = 0$, $\tan \dfrac{\pi}{2}$ is undefined.

3. True; since $\tan x = \dfrac{\sin x}{\cos x}$ and $\sec x = \dfrac{1}{\cos x}$, the tangent and secant functions will be undefined at the same values.

5. False; $\tan(-x) = \dfrac{\sin(-x)}{\cos(-x)} = \dfrac{-\sin x}{\cos x} = -\tan x$
(since $\sin x$ is odd and $\cos x$ is even) for all x in the domain.

7. $y = \csc x$
The graph is the reflection of the graph of $y = \csc x$ about the x-axis. This matches with graph B.

9. $y = -\tan x$
The graph is the reflection of the graph of $y = \tan x$ about the x-axis. This matches with graph E.

11. $y = \tan\left(x - \dfrac{\pi}{4}\right)$
The graph is the graph of $y = \tan x$ shifted $\dfrac{\pi}{4}$ units to the right. This matches with graph D.

13. $y = \csc\left(x - \dfrac{\pi}{4}\right)$
We graph this function by first graphing the corresponding reciprocal function $y = \sin\left(x - \dfrac{\pi}{4}\right)$. The period is 2π.

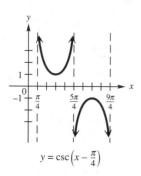

$$y = \csc\left(x - \frac{\pi}{4}\right)$$

15. $y = \sec\left(x + \frac{\pi}{4}\right)$

We graph this function by first graphing the corresponding reciprocal function

$y = \cos\left(x + \frac{\pi}{4}\right)$. The period is 2π.

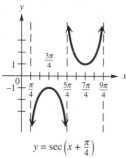

$$y = \sec\left(x + \frac{\pi}{4}\right)$$

17. $y = \sec\left(\frac{1}{2}x + \frac{\pi}{3}\right)$

$y = \sec\frac{1}{2}\left(x + \frac{2\pi}{3}\right)$

We graph this function by first graphing the corresponding reciprocal function

$y = \cos\frac{1}{2}\left(x + \frac{2\pi}{3}\right)$. The period is 4π.

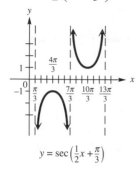

$$y = \sec\left(\frac{1}{2}x + \frac{\pi}{3}\right)$$

19. $y = 2 + 3\sec(2x - \pi)$

$y = 2 + 3\sec 2\left(x - \frac{\pi}{2}\right)$

We graph this function by first graphing the corresponding reciprocal function

$y = 2 + 3\cos 2\left(x - \frac{\pi}{2}\right)$. The period is π.

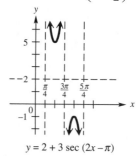

$$y = 2 + 3\sec\ (2x - \pi)$$

21. $y = 1 - \frac{1}{2}\csc\left(x - \frac{3\pi}{4}\right)$

We graph this function by first graphing the corresponding reciprocal function

$y = 1 - \frac{1}{2}\sin\left(x - \frac{3\pi}{4}\right)$. The period is 2π.

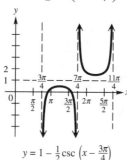

$$y = 1 - \tfrac{1}{2}\csc\ \left(x - \tfrac{3\pi}{4}\right)$$

23. $y = 2\tan x$

Two adjacent vertical asymptotes are $x = -\frac{\pi}{2}$ and $x = \frac{\pi}{2}$. The graph is "stretched" because $a = 2$ and $|2| > 1$.

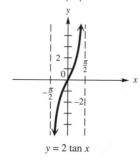

$$y = 2\tan x$$

25. $y = \dfrac{1}{2}\cot x$

Two adjacent vertical asymptotes are $x = 0$ and $x = \pi$. The graph is "compressed" because $a = \dfrac{1}{2}$ and $\left|\dfrac{1}{2}\right| < 1$.

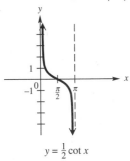

$y = \frac{1}{2}\cot x$

27. $y = \cot 3x$

Two adjacent vertical asymptotes are
$$3x = 0 \quad \text{and} \quad 3x = \pi$$
or $\quad x = 0 \quad$ and $\quad x = \dfrac{\pi}{3}$.

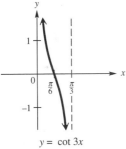

$y = \cot 3x$

29. $y = \tan(2x - \pi)$

$$y = \tan 2\left(x - \dfrac{\pi}{2}\right)$$

The period is $\dfrac{\pi}{2}$.

Two adjacent vertical asymptotes are
$$2\left(x - \dfrac{\pi}{2}\right) = -\dfrac{\pi}{2} \quad \text{and} \quad 2\left(x - \dfrac{\pi}{2}\right) = \dfrac{\pi}{2}$$
or $\quad x - \dfrac{\pi}{2} = -\dfrac{\pi}{4} \quad$ and $\quad x - \dfrac{\pi}{2} = \dfrac{\pi}{4}$
or $\qquad x = \dfrac{\pi}{4} \quad$ and $\qquad x = \dfrac{3\pi}{4}$.

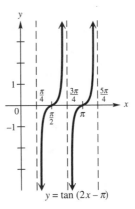

$y = \tan(2x - \pi)$

31. $y = \cot\left(3x + \dfrac{\pi}{4}\right)$

$$y = \cot 3\left(x + \dfrac{\pi}{12}\right)$$

The period is $\dfrac{\pi}{3}$.

Two adjacent vertical asymptotes are
$$3\left(x + \dfrac{\pi}{12}\right) = 0 \quad \text{and} \quad 3\left(x + \dfrac{\pi}{12}\right) = \pi$$
or $\qquad x + \dfrac{\pi}{12} = 0 \quad$ and $\qquad x + \dfrac{\pi}{12} = \dfrac{\pi}{3}$
or $\qquad x = -\dfrac{\pi}{12} \quad$ and $\qquad x = \dfrac{\pi}{4}$.

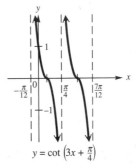

$y = \cot\left(3x + \frac{\pi}{4}\right)$

33. $y = 1 + \tan x$
This is the graph of $y = \tan x$ translated vertically 1 unit up.

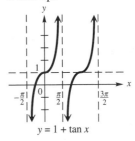

$y = 1 + \tan x$

35. $y = 1 - \cot x$

This is the graph of $y = \cot x$ reflected about the x-axis and then translated vertically 1 unit up.

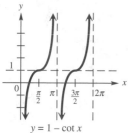

$y = 1 - \cot x$

37. $y = -1 + 2 \tan x$

This is the graph of $y = 2 \tan x$ translated vertically 1 unit down.

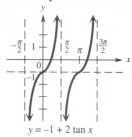

$y = -1 + 2 \tan x$

39. $y = -1 + \dfrac{1}{2} \cot(2x - 3\pi)$

$y = -1 + \dfrac{1}{2} \cot 2\left(x - \dfrac{3\pi}{2}\right)$

The period is $\dfrac{\pi}{2}$.

Two adjacent vertical asymptotes are

$2\left(x - \dfrac{3\pi}{2}\right) = 0$ and $2\left(x - \dfrac{3\pi}{2}\right) = \pi$

or $x - \dfrac{3\pi}{2} = 0$ and $x - \dfrac{3\pi}{2} = \dfrac{\pi}{2}$

or $x = \dfrac{3\pi}{2}$ and $x = 2\pi$.

This is the graph of $y = \dfrac{1}{2} \cot 2x$ translated vertically 1 unit down.

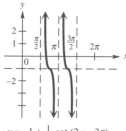

$y = -1 + \frac{1}{2} \cot (2x - 3\pi)$

41. $y = \dfrac{2}{3} \tan\left(\dfrac{3}{4}x - \pi\right) - 2$

$y = -2 + \dfrac{2}{3} \tan \dfrac{3}{4}\left(x - \dfrac{4\pi}{3}\right)$

The period is $\dfrac{\pi}{\frac{3}{4}} = \dfrac{4\pi}{3}$.

Two adjacent vertical asymptotes are

$\dfrac{3}{4}\left(x - \dfrac{4\pi}{3}\right) = -\dfrac{\pi}{2}$ and $\dfrac{3}{4}\left(x - \dfrac{4\pi}{3}\right) = \dfrac{\pi}{2}$

or $x - \dfrac{4\pi}{3} = -\dfrac{2\pi}{3}$ and $x - \dfrac{4\pi}{3} = \dfrac{2\pi}{3}$

or $x = \dfrac{2\pi}{3}$ and $x = 2\pi$.

This is the graph of $y = \dfrac{2}{3} \tan\left(\dfrac{3}{4}x - \pi\right)$ translated vertically 2 units down.

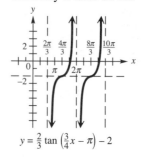

$y = \frac{2}{3} \tan \left(\frac{3}{4}x - \pi\right) - 2$

43. The domain of the tangent function is

$\left\{x \,\middle|\, x \neq \dfrac{\pi}{2} + n\pi, \text{ where } n \text{ is any integer}\right\}$,

and the range is $(-\infty, \infty)$. For the function $f(x) = -4 \tan(2x + \pi)$

$= -4 \tan 2\left(x + \dfrac{\pi}{2}\right)$,

the period is $\dfrac{\pi}{2}$. Therefore, the domain is

$\left\{x \,\middle|\, x \neq \dfrac{\pi}{4} + \dfrac{\pi}{2}n, \text{ where } n \text{ is any integer}\right\}$.

This can also be written as

$\left\{x \,\middle|\, x \neq (2n+1)\dfrac{\pi}{4}, \text{ where } n \text{ is any integer}\right\}$.

The range remains $(-\infty, \infty)$.

45. The function $\tan x$ has a period of π, so it repeats four times over the interval $(-2\pi, 2\pi]$. Since its range is $(-\infty, \infty)$, $\tan x = c$ has four solutions for every value of c.

47. $d = 4 \tan 2\pi t$

   (a) $d = 4 \tan 2\pi(1) = 4 \tan 2\pi = 0$ m

(b) $d = 4 \tan 2\pi(.4)$
$= 4 \tan .8\pi$
$\approx 4(-.7265) \approx -2.9$ m

(c) $d = 4 \tan 2\pi(.8)$
$= 4 \tan 1.6\pi$
$\approx 4(-3.0782) \approx -12.3$ m

(d) $d = 4 \tan 2\pi(1.2)$
$= 4 \tan 2.4\pi$
$\approx 4(3.0774) \approx 12.3$ m

(e) $t = .25$ leads to $\tan \dfrac{\pi}{2}$, which is undefined.

51.

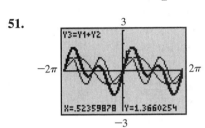

$\sin\left(\dfrac{\pi}{6}\right) + \sin\left(\dfrac{2\pi}{6}\right) = \dfrac{1}{2} + \dfrac{\sqrt{3}}{2} = \dfrac{1+\sqrt{3}}{2}$

53. π

54. $\pi = x - \dfrac{\pi}{4}$
$x = \pi + \dfrac{\pi}{4} = \dfrac{5\pi}{4}$

55. $y = \dfrac{5\pi}{4} + n\pi$

56. approximately .3217505544

57. $.3217505544 + \pi \approx 3.463343208$

58. $.3217505544 + n\pi$

Chapter 5 Review Exercises

1. $-174° + 360° = 186°$

3. 320 rotations per minute
$= 320(360°)$ per minute
$= 115,200°$ per minute
$= \dfrac{115,200°}{60}$ per second
$= 1920°$ per second
$= 1920°\left(\dfrac{2}{3}\right)$ per $\dfrac{2}{3}$ second
$= 1280°$ per $\dfrac{2}{3}$ second

7. $120° = 120\left(\dfrac{\pi}{180}\right) = \dfrac{2\pi}{3}$

9. $\dfrac{5\pi}{4} = \dfrac{5\pi}{4}\left(\dfrac{180°}{\pi}\right) = 225°$

11. $\dfrac{20}{60} = \dfrac{1}{3}$ rotation
$\theta = \dfrac{1}{3}(2\pi) = \dfrac{2\pi}{3}$
$s = r\theta = 2\left(\dfrac{2\pi}{3}\right) = \dfrac{4\pi}{3}$ in.

13. $r = 15.2$ cm, $\theta = \dfrac{3\pi}{4}$
$s = r\theta = 15.2\left(\dfrac{3\pi}{4}\right)$
$= 11.4\pi$
≈ 35.8 cm

15. Because the central angle is very small, the arc length is approximately equal to the length of the inscribed chord. (See directions for Exercises 31–34 in Section 3.2)
Let h = height of tree, $r = 2000$, $\theta = 1° \ 10'$.
$h \approx r\theta$
$= 2000\left(1 + \dfrac{10}{60}\right)\left(\dfrac{\pi}{180}\right)$
≈ 41 yd

17. $\cos \dfrac{2\pi}{3} = \cos 120° = -\dfrac{1}{2}$

19. $\csc\left(-\dfrac{11\pi}{6}\right) = \csc\left(-\dfrac{11}{6} \cdot 180°\right)$
$= \csc(-330°)$
$= \csc(-330° + 360°)$
$= \csc 30°$
$= 2$

21. cot 3.0543
Enter: 3.0543 [TAN] [1/x]
or ([TAN] 3.0543) [x⁻¹]   [ENTER]
cot 3.0543 = −11.426605

23. $\left[\dfrac{\pi}{2}, \pi\right]$, $\tan s = -\sqrt{3}$

Because $\tan s = -\sqrt{3}$, the reference angle for s must be $\dfrac{\pi}{3}$ since $\tan\dfrac{\pi}{3} = \sqrt{3}$. For s to be in the interval $\left[\dfrac{\pi}{2}, \pi\right]$, we must subtract the reference angle from π. Therefore, $s = \pi - \dfrac{\pi}{3} = \dfrac{2\pi}{3}$.

25. $\theta = \dfrac{5\pi}{12}$, $\omega = \dfrac{8\pi}{9}$ radians per sec

$$\omega = \dfrac{\theta}{t}$$
$$\dfrac{8\pi}{9} = \dfrac{\frac{5\pi}{12}}{t}$$
$$t = \dfrac{5\pi}{12} \cdot \dfrac{9}{8\pi}$$
$$= \dfrac{45}{96} = \dfrac{15}{32} \text{ sec}$$

27. The flywheel is rotating 90 times per sec or $90 \cdot 2\pi$ radians per sec,
$r = 7$ m
$v = r\omega$
$= 7(90 \cdot 2\pi)$
$= 1260\pi$ m per sec

29. $\cos\gamma = -\dfrac{5}{8}$, with γ in quadrant III.

$\cos\gamma = \dfrac{x}{r}$, so $x = -5$ and $r = 8$.
$$x^2 + y^2 = r^2$$
$$(-5)^2 + y^2 = (8)^2$$
$$25 + y^2 = 64$$
$$y^2 = 39$$
$$y = \pm\sqrt{39}$$
Since γ is in quadrant III, $y = -\sqrt{39}$.

$$\sin\gamma = \dfrac{y}{r} = \dfrac{-\sqrt{39}}{8} = -\dfrac{\sqrt{39}}{8}$$
$$\cos\gamma = \dfrac{x}{r} = -\dfrac{5}{8}$$
$$\tan\gamma = \dfrac{y}{x} = \dfrac{-\sqrt{39}}{-5} = \dfrac{\sqrt{39}}{5}$$

$$\cot\gamma = \dfrac{x}{y} = \dfrac{-5}{-\sqrt{39}} = \dfrac{5\sqrt{39}}{39}$$
$$\sec\gamma = \dfrac{r}{x} = \dfrac{8}{-5} = -\dfrac{8}{5}$$
$$\csc\gamma = \dfrac{r}{y} = \dfrac{8}{-\sqrt{39}} = -\dfrac{8\sqrt{39}}{39}$$

33.
$$\sin A = \dfrac{\text{side opposite}}{\text{hypotenuse}} = \dfrac{40}{58} = \dfrac{20}{29}$$
$$\cos A = \dfrac{\text{side adjacent}}{\text{hypotenuse}} = \dfrac{42}{58} = \dfrac{21}{29}$$
$$\tan A = \dfrac{\text{side opposite}}{\text{side adjacent}} = \dfrac{40}{42} = \dfrac{20}{21}$$
$$\cot A = \dfrac{\text{side adjacent}}{\text{side opposite}} = \dfrac{42}{40} = \dfrac{21}{20}$$
$$\sec A = \dfrac{\text{hypotenuse}}{\text{side adjacent}} = \dfrac{58}{42} = \dfrac{29}{21}$$
$$\csc A = \dfrac{\text{hypotenuse}}{\text{side opposite}} = \dfrac{58}{40} = \dfrac{29}{20}$$

35. 300°
This angle is in quadrant IV, so the reference angle is $360° - 300° = 60°$.
Since 300° is in quadrant IV, the sine, tangent, cotangent and cosecant are negative.

$$\sin 300° = -\sin 60° = -\dfrac{\sqrt{3}}{2}$$
$$\cos 300° = \cos 60° = \dfrac{1}{2}$$
$$\tan 300° = -\tan 60° = -\sqrt{3}$$
$$\cot 300° = -\cot 60° = -\dfrac{\sqrt{3}}{3}$$
$$\sec 300° = \sec 60° = 2$$
$$\csc 300° = -\csc 60° = -\dfrac{2\sqrt{3}}{3}$$

37. −390° is an angle in quadrant IV with a reference angle $\theta' = 30°$.

$$\sin(-390°) = -\sin 30° = -\dfrac{1}{2}$$
$$\cos(-390°) = \cos 30° = \dfrac{\sqrt{3}}{2}$$
$$\tan(-390°) = -\tan 30° = -\dfrac{\sqrt{3}}{3}$$
$$\cot(-390°) = -\cot 30° = -\sqrt{3}$$
$$\sec(-390°) = \sec 30° = \dfrac{2\sqrt{3}}{3}$$
$$\csc(-390°) = -\csc 30° = -2$$

In Exercises 39–41, be sure that your calculator is in degree mode. Keystroke sequences may vary based on the type and/or model of calculator being used.

39. sec 222° 30′

$$222°\,30' = \left(222 + \frac{30}{60}\right)^{\circ} = 222.5°$$

Enter: 222.5 [COS] [1/X]
or ([COS] 222.5) [x⁻¹] [ENTER]
Display: −1.3563417

41. tan 11.7689°
Enter: 11.7689 [TAN]
or [TAN] 11.7689 [ENTER]
Display: .20834446

In Exercises 43–49, be sure that your calculator is in degree mode. Keystroke sequences may vary based on the type and/or model of calculator being used.

43. sin θ = .8254121

Enter: .82584121 {
[INV]   [SIN]
or
ARCSIN
or
[SIN⁻¹]
}

or [2nd] [SIN] .82584121 [ENTER]
Display: 55.673870
θ = 55.673870°

47. $A = 58°\,30'$, $c = 748$

$$A + B = 90°$$
$$B = 90° - A$$
$$B = 90° - 58°30'$$
$$B = 31°30'$$
$$\sin A = \frac{a}{c}$$
$$a = c \sin A$$
$$a = 748 \sin 58°30'$$
$$a = 638$$
$$\cos A = \frac{b}{c}$$
$$b = c \cos A$$
$$b = 748 \cos 58°30'$$
$$b = 391$$

49. Let x = height of the tower.

$$\tan 38°20' = \frac{x}{93.2}$$
$$x = 93.2 \tan 38°20'$$
$$x \approx 73.693005$$

The height of the tower is 73.7 ft.

51. Draw triangle ABC and extend the north-south lines to a point X south of A and S to a point Y, north of C.

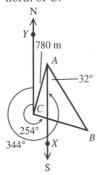

Angle $ACB = 344° - 254° = 90°$, so ABC is a right triangle.
Angle $BAX = 32°$ since it is an alternate interior angle to $32°$.
Angle $YCA = 360° - 344° = 16°$
Angle $XAC = 16°$ since it is an alternate interior angle to angle YCA.
Angle $BAC = 32° + 16° = 48°$
In triangle ABC,

$$\cos A = \frac{AC}{AB}$$
$$AB = \frac{AC}{\cos A}$$
$$AB = \frac{780}{\cos 48°}$$
$$\approx 1200.$$

The distance from A to B is 1200 m.

53. (a) Let $R = 3955$, $T = 25$, $P = 140$.

$$h = R\left(\frac{1}{\cos\left(\frac{180T}{P}\right)} - 1\right)$$
$$= 3955\left(\frac{1}{\cos\left(\frac{180\cdot 25}{140}\right)} - 1\right)$$
$$\approx 716 \text{ mi}$$

(b) Now let $T = 30$.

$$h = R\left(\frac{1}{\cos\left(\frac{180T}{P}\right)} - 1\right)$$
$$= 3955\left(\frac{1}{\cos\left(\frac{180\cdot 30}{140}\right)} - 1\right)$$
$$\approx 1104 \text{ mi}$$

In order to increase the communication time T, the satellite must have a higher orbit.

55. (b) $\csc\theta = 2$

$\sin\theta = \dfrac{1}{2}$

$\theta = \dfrac{\pi}{6}$

d is double h when the sun is 30° above the horizon.

(c) $\csc\dfrac{\pi}{2} = 1$ and $\csc\dfrac{\pi}{3} \approx 1.15$

When the sun is lower in the sky $\left(\theta = \dfrac{\pi}{3}\right)$, sunlight is filtered by more atmosphere. There is less ultraviolet light reaching the earth's surface, and therefore, there is less likelihood of becoming sunburned. In this case, sunlight passes through 15% more atmosphere.

57. Let $|s|$ = the length of the arc.

$\tan s = \dfrac{Y}{X}$

$= \dfrac{-.5250622}{.85106383}$

$\approx -.6170.$

Use radian mode.
Enter: .6170 ‰ i
or b i .6170 r
Display: −.5528258
$s \approx -.5528$
The length of the shortest arc of the circle from (1, 0) to (.85106383, −.5250622) is .5528.

59. $y = 2\sin x$
Amplitude: 2
Period: 2π
Vertical translation: none
Phase shift: none

61. $y = -\dfrac{1}{2}\cos 3x$

Amplitude: $\dfrac{1}{2}$

Period: $\dfrac{2\pi}{3}$

Vertical translation: none
Phase shift: none

63. $y = 1 + 2\sin\dfrac{1}{4}x$

Amplitude: 2

Period: $\dfrac{2\pi}{\frac{1}{4}} = 8\pi$

Vertical translation: up 1 unit
Phase shift: none

65. $y = 3\cos\left(x + \dfrac{\pi}{2}\right)$

Amplitude: 3
Period: 2π
Vertical translation: none

Phase shift: $\dfrac{\pi}{2}$ units to the left

67. $y = \dfrac{1}{2}\csc\left(2x - \dfrac{\pi}{4}\right)$

Amplitude: not applicable

Period: $\dfrac{2\pi}{2} = \pi$

Vertical translation: none

Phase shift: $\dfrac{\pi}{8}$ units to the right

69. The sine function has a period of 2π and passes through the origin.

73. $y = \dfrac{1}{2}\cot 3x$

Period: $\dfrac{\pi}{3}$

Asymptotes: $x = 0,\ x = \dfrac{\pi}{3}$

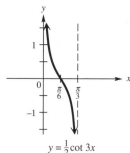

$y = \frac{1}{2}\cot 3x$

75. $y = \tan\left(x - \dfrac{\pi}{2}\right)$

Period: π
Asymptotes: $x = 0,\ x = \pi$

Phase shift: $\dfrac{\pi}{2}$ units to the right

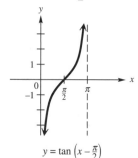

$y = \tan\left(x - \frac{\pi}{2}\right)$

77. $y = -1 - 3 \sin 2x$
Amplitude: 3
Period: $\dfrac{2\pi}{2} = \pi$
Vertical translation: down 1 unit

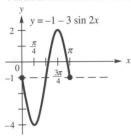

79. $a = 4$, $\omega = \pi$

$\text{amplitude} = |a| = 4$

$\text{period} = \dfrac{2\pi}{\omega} = \dfrac{2\pi}{\pi} = 2$

$\text{frequency} = \dfrac{\omega}{2\pi} = \dfrac{\pi}{2\pi} = \dfrac{1}{2}$

81. The frequency is the number of cycles in one unit of time.
$s(1.5) = 4 \sin 1.5\pi = 4(-1) = -4$
$s(2) = 4 \sin 2\pi = 4(0) = 0$
$s(3.25) = 4 \sin 3.25\pi = 4\left(-\dfrac{\sqrt{2}}{2}\right) = -2\sqrt{2}$

83. The shorter leg of the right triangle has length $h_2 - h_1$.

(b) When $h_2 = 55$ and $h_1 = 5$,
$d = (55 - 5)\cot\theta = 50\cot\theta$.
The period is π, but the graph wanted is d for
$0 < \theta < \dfrac{\pi}{2}$.
The asymptote is the line $\theta = 0$.
When $\theta = \dfrac{\pi}{4}$, $d = 50(1) = 50$.

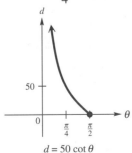

$d = 50\cot\theta$

Chapter 5 Test Exercises

1. $360° + (-157°) = 203°$

2. $450\,\dfrac{\text{rev}}{\text{min}} \cdot \dfrac{1\,\text{min}}{60\,\text{sec}} = 7.5\,\dfrac{\text{rev}}{\text{sec}}$
$7.5\,\text{rev} = 7.5(360°) = 2700°$
The point on the edge of the tire moves $2700°$ in one second.

3. $120° = 120\left(\dfrac{\pi}{180}\,\text{radian}\right) = \dfrac{2\pi}{3}\,\text{radians}$

4. $\dfrac{9\pi}{10} = \dfrac{9\pi}{10}\left(\dfrac{180°}{\pi}\right) = 162°$

5. (a) $r = 150$ cm, $s = 200$ cm
$s = r\theta$
$\theta = \dfrac{s}{r}$
$ = \dfrac{200}{150}$
$ = \dfrac{4}{3}$

(b) $r = 150$ cm, $s = 200$ cm, $\theta = \dfrac{4}{3}$
$A = \dfrac{1}{2}r^2\theta$
$ = \dfrac{1}{2}(150)^2\left(\dfrac{4}{3}\right)$
$ = 15{,}000\ \text{cm}^2$

6. $\sin s = .82584121$
Enter: .82584121 [2nd] [SIN]
or [2nd] [SIN] .82584121 [ENTER]
$s \approx .97169234$

7. If the person travels π radians, then he or she is at the top of the Ferris wheel, so he or she is 50 ft off the ground. The person is $\dfrac{\pi}{6}$ radians short of π radians if he or she travels $\dfrac{5\pi}{6}$ radians.

$\text{distance} = 50\,\text{ft} - \left(25 - 25\sin\dfrac{\pi}{3}\right)$
$\phantom{\text{distance}} \approx 46.65\,\text{ft}$

8. $t = 30$ sec, $\theta = \dfrac{5\pi}{6}$ radians

$$\omega = \dfrac{\theta}{t}$$

$$= \dfrac{\dfrac{5\pi}{6}}{30}$$

$$= \dfrac{\pi}{36} \text{ radian per sec}$$

9. If $\cos\theta < 0$, then θ is in quadrant II or III. If $\cot\theta > 0$, then θ is in quadrant I or III. Therefore θ terminates in quadrant III.

10. $(2, -5), x = 2, y = -5$

$$r = \sqrt{x^2 + y^2}$$

$$r = \sqrt{2^2 + (-5)^2}$$

$$r = \sqrt{29}$$

$$\sin\theta = \frac{y}{r} = \frac{-5}{\sqrt{29}} \cdot \frac{\sqrt{29}}{\sqrt{29}} = -\frac{5\sqrt{29}}{29}$$

$$\cos\theta = \frac{x}{r} = \frac{2}{\sqrt{29}} \cdot \frac{\sqrt{29}}{\sqrt{29}} = \frac{2\sqrt{29}}{29}$$

$$\tan\theta = \frac{y}{x} = \frac{-5}{2} = -\frac{5}{2}$$

11. If $\cos\theta = \dfrac{4}{5} = \dfrac{x}{r}$, let $x = 4$ and $r = 5$.

$$x^2 + y^2 = r^2$$

$$4^2 + y^2 = 5^2$$

$$y^2 = 25 - 16$$

$$y = \pm\sqrt{9}$$

$$y = \pm 3$$

Since θ is in quadrant IV, y is negative, so $y = -3$.

$$\sin\theta = \frac{y}{r} = \frac{-3}{5} = -\frac{3}{5}$$

$$\tan\theta = \frac{y}{x} = \frac{-3}{4} = -\frac{3}{4}$$

$$\cot\theta = \frac{x}{y} = \frac{4}{-3} = -\frac{4}{3}$$

$$\sec\theta = \frac{r}{x} = \frac{5}{4}$$

$$\csc\theta = \frac{r}{y} = \frac{5}{-3} = -\frac{5}{3}$$

12. To find w:

$$\sin 30° = \frac{4}{w}$$

$$w = \frac{4}{\sin 30°}$$

$$w = \frac{4}{\left(\dfrac{1}{2}\right)}$$

$$w = 8$$

To find x:

$$\tan 45° = \frac{4}{x}$$

$$x = \frac{4}{\tan 45°}$$

$$x = \frac{4}{1}$$

$$x = 4$$

To find y:

$$\cos 30° = \frac{y}{w}$$

$$\cos 30° = \frac{y}{8}$$

$$8\cos 30° = y$$

$$8 \cdot \frac{\sqrt{3}}{2} = y$$

$$4\sqrt{3} = y$$

To find z:

$$\sin 45° = \frac{4}{z}$$

$$z = \frac{4}{\sin 45°}$$

$$z = \frac{2}{\left(\dfrac{\sqrt{2}}{2}\right)}$$

$$z = 4\sqrt{2}$$

13. $\cot(-750°)$

$-750° - (-3 \cdot 360°) = 330°$

$-750°$ is coterminal with $330°$, which is in quadrant IV. The cotangent is negative in quadrant IV.

The reference angle is $360° - 330° = 30°$.

$\cot(-750°) = -\cot 30° = -\sqrt{3}$

14. (a) $\sin 78°\,21'$

$$78°\,21' = \left(78 + \frac{21}{60}\right)° = 78.35°$$

Enter: 78.35 [SIN]

or sin 78.35 [ENTER]
Display: .97939940
$\sin 78°\ 21' \approx .97939940$

(b) tan 11.7689°
Enter: 11.7689 [TAN]
or [TAN] 11.7689 [ENTER]
Display: .20834446
tan 11.7689° ≈ .20834446

(c) sec 58.9041°
Enter: 58.9041 cos [1/x]
or [(] cos 58.9041 [)] [x⁻¹] [ENTER]
Display: 1.9362132
sec 58.9041° ≈ 1.9362132

15. $A = 58°30'$, $c = 748$, $C = 90°$

$$\cos A = \frac{b}{c}$$
$$b = c \cdot \cos A$$
$$b = (748)\cos 58°30'$$
$$b \approx 391$$
$$\sin A = \frac{a}{c}$$
$$a = c \cdot \sin A$$
$$a = (748)\sin 58°30'$$
$$a \approx 638$$
$$A + B = 90°$$
$$B = 90° - A$$
$$B = 90° - 58°30'$$
$$B = 31°30'$$

16.

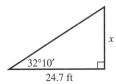

Let x be the height of the flag pole.

$$\tan 32°10' = \frac{x}{24.7}$$
$$x = 24.7\tan 32°10'$$
$$x \approx 15.5 \text{ ft}$$

17.

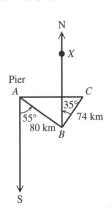

Angle ABX is 55° (alternate interior angles of parallel lines cut by a transversal are congruent). Angle ABC is 55° + 35° = 90°, therefore triangle ABC is a right triangle.

$$AC^2 = 80^2 + 74^2$$
$$AC = \sqrt{80^2 + 74^2}$$
$$AC \approx 110 \text{ km}$$

18. (a) $\dfrac{2\pi}{2} = \pi$

(b) 6

(c) [–3, 9]

(d) $-6\sin\left(2\cdot 0 + \dfrac{\pi}{2}\right) + 3 = -6\sin\left(\dfrac{\pi}{2}\right) + 3$
$$= -6 + 3$$
$$= -3$$

(e) $\dfrac{\pi}{2}\cdot\dfrac{1}{2} = \dfrac{\pi}{4}$ units to the left $\left(\text{that is, } -\dfrac{\pi}{4}\right)$

19. $y = 2\sin(x + \pi) - 1$
Period: 2π
Amplitude: $|2| = 2$
Vertical translation: down 1 unit
Phase shift: π units to the left

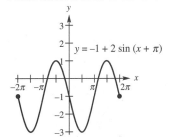

20. $y = -\cos 2x$
Period: π
Amplitude: $|-1| = 1$
Vertical translation: none
Phase shift: none

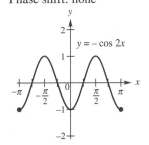

21. $y = \tan\left(x - \dfrac{\pi}{2}\right)$

Period: π

Amplitude: not applicable

Asymptotes: $x = -\pi$, $x = 0$, $x = \pi$

Vertical translation: none

Phase shift: $\dfrac{\pi}{2}$ units to the right

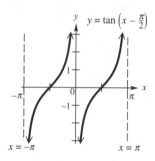

22. (a)

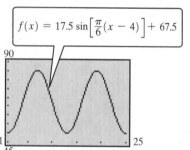

(b) Amplitude: 17.5

Period: $\dfrac{2\pi}{\frac{\pi}{6}} = 2\pi \cdot \dfrac{6}{\pi} = 12$

Phase shift: 4 units to the right

Vertical translation: 67.5 units up

(c) Approximately 52°F

(d) 50°F January; 85°F in July

(e) Approximately 67.5°; this is the vertical translation.

CHAPTER 6 TRIGONOMETRIC IDENTITIES AND EQUATIONS

Section 6.1

Exercises

1. By a negative-angle identity, $\tan(-x) = -\tan x$.
   Since $\tan x = 2.6$, $\tan(-x) = -\tan x = -2.6$.

3. By a reciprocal identity, $\cot x = \dfrac{1}{\tan x}$.

   Since $\tan x = 1.6$, $\cot x = \dfrac{1}{1.6} = .625$.

5. $\cos s = \dfrac{3}{4}$, s is in quadrant I.

   $\sin^2 s + \cos^2 s = 1$

   $\sin^2 s + \left(\dfrac{3}{4}\right)^2 = 1$

   $\sin^2 s = 1 - \dfrac{9}{16} = \dfrac{7}{16}$

   $\sin s = \pm\dfrac{\sqrt{7}}{4}$

   Since s is in quadrant I, $\sin s = \dfrac{\sqrt{7}}{4}$.

7. $\cos s = \dfrac{\sqrt{5}}{5}$, $\tan s < 0$ implies s is in quadrant IV.

   $\sin^2 s + \cos^2 s = 1$

   $\sin^2 s + \left(\dfrac{\sqrt{5}}{5}\right)^2 = 1$

   $\sin^2 s = 1 - \dfrac{5}{25} = \dfrac{20}{25}$

   $= \dfrac{4}{5}$

   $\sin s = \pm\dfrac{2}{\sqrt{5}}$

   Since s is in quadrant IV,

   $\sin s = -\dfrac{2}{\sqrt{5}} = -\dfrac{2\sqrt{5}}{5}$.

9. $\sec s = \dfrac{11}{4}$, $\tan s < 0$ implies s is in quadrant IV.

   Since $\sec s = \dfrac{1}{\cos s}$

   $\dfrac{11}{4} = \dfrac{1}{\cos s}$

   $\dfrac{4}{11} = \cos s$.

   $\sin^2 s + \cos^2 s = 1$

   $\sin^2 s + \left(\dfrac{4}{11}\right)^2 = 1$

   $\sin^2 s + \dfrac{16}{121} = 1$

   $\sin s = \dfrac{105}{12}$

   $\sin s = \pm\dfrac{\sqrt{105}}{11}$

   Since s is in quadrant IV, $\sin s = -\dfrac{\sqrt{105}}{11}$.

13. This is the graph of $f(x) = \csc x$.
    Since $f(-x) = \csc(-x)$

    $= \dfrac{1}{\sin(-x)}$

    $= \dfrac{1}{-\sin(x)}$

    $= -\sec(x)$

    $= -f(x)$,

    $f(-x) = -f(x)$.

15. $\sin\theta = \dfrac{2}{3}$, θ in quadrant II

    $\sin^2\theta + \cos^2\theta = 1$

    $\cos^2\theta = 1 - \sin^2\theta$

    $= 1 - \left(\dfrac{2}{3}\right)^2 = \dfrac{5}{9}$

    $\cos\theta = \pm\dfrac{\sqrt{5}}{3}$

    Since θ is in quadrant II, $\cos\theta = -\dfrac{\sqrt{5}}{3}$.

    $\tan\theta = \dfrac{\sin\theta}{\cos\theta} = \dfrac{\frac{2}{3}}{-\frac{\sqrt{5}}{3}} = -\dfrac{2}{\sqrt{5}} = -\dfrac{2\sqrt{5}}{5}$

    $\cot\theta = \dfrac{1}{\tan\theta} = \dfrac{1}{-\frac{2}{\sqrt{5}}} = -\dfrac{\sqrt{5}}{2}$

    $\sec\theta = \dfrac{1}{\cos\theta} = \dfrac{1}{-\frac{\sqrt{5}}{3}} = -\dfrac{3}{\sqrt{5}} = -\dfrac{3\sqrt{5}}{5}$

    $\csc\theta = \dfrac{1}{\sin\theta} = \dfrac{1}{\frac{2}{3}} = \dfrac{3}{2}$

17. $\tan\theta = -\dfrac{1}{4}$, θ in quadrant IV

$\sec^2\theta = 1 + \tan^2\theta$

$\qquad = 1 + \left(-\dfrac{1}{4}\right)^2$

$\qquad = \dfrac{17}{16}$

Since θ is in quadrant IV, $\sec\theta = \dfrac{\sqrt{17}}{4}$.

$\cos\theta = \dfrac{1}{\sec\theta}$

$\qquad = \dfrac{1}{\frac{\sqrt{17}}{4}} = \dfrac{4}{\sqrt{17}} = \dfrac{4\sqrt{17}}{17}$

$\sin\theta = \tan\theta \cdot \cos\theta$

$\qquad = -\dfrac{1}{4} \cdot \dfrac{4}{\sqrt{17}} = -\dfrac{1}{\sqrt{17}} = -\dfrac{\sqrt{17}}{17}$

$\csc\theta = \dfrac{1}{\sin\theta} = \dfrac{1}{-\frac{1}{\sqrt{17}}} = -\sqrt{17}$

$\cot\theta = \dfrac{1}{\tan\theta} = \dfrac{1}{-\frac{1}{4}} = -4$

19. $\cot\theta = \dfrac{4}{3}$, $\sin\theta > 0$

Since $\cot\theta > 0$ and $\sin\theta > 0$, θ is in quadrant I and all the functions are positive.

$\tan = \dfrac{1}{\cot\theta} = \dfrac{1}{\frac{4}{3}} = \dfrac{3}{4}$

$\sec^2\theta = 1 + \tan^2\theta = 1 + \left(\dfrac{3}{4}\right)^2 = \dfrac{25}{16}$

$\sec\theta = \dfrac{5}{4}$

$\cos\theta = \dfrac{1}{\sec\theta} = \dfrac{1}{\frac{5}{4}} = \dfrac{4}{5}$

$\sin^2\theta = 1 - \cos^2\theta = 1 - \left(\dfrac{4}{5}\right)^2 = \dfrac{9}{25}$

$\sin\theta = \dfrac{3}{5}$

$\csc\theta = \dfrac{1}{\sin\theta} = \dfrac{5}{3}$

21. $\sec\theta = \dfrac{4}{3}$, $\sin\theta < 0$

Since $\sec\theta > 0$ and $\sin\theta < 0$, θ is in quadrant IV.

$\cos\theta = \dfrac{1}{\sec\theta} = \dfrac{1}{\frac{4}{3}} = \dfrac{3}{4}$

$\sin^2\theta = 1 - \cos^2\theta = 1 - \left(\dfrac{3}{4}\right)^2 = \dfrac{7}{16}$

Since $\sin\theta < 0$, $\sin\theta = -\dfrac{\sqrt{7}}{4}$.

$\tan\theta = \dfrac{\sin\theta}{\cos\theta} = \dfrac{-\frac{\sqrt{7}}{4}}{\frac{3}{4}} = -\dfrac{\sqrt{7}}{3}$

$\cot\theta = \dfrac{1}{\tan\theta} = -\dfrac{1}{\frac{\sqrt{7}}{3}} = -\dfrac{3\sqrt{7}}{7}$

$\csc\theta = \dfrac{1}{\sin\theta} = \dfrac{1}{-\frac{\sqrt{7}}{4}} = -\dfrac{4\sqrt{7}}{7}$

23. $\dfrac{\cos x}{\sin x} = \cot x$

Choose expression B.

25. $\cos(-x) = \cos x$

Choose expression E.

27. $1 = \sin^2 x + \cos^2 x$

Choose expression A.

29. $\sec^2 x - 1 = \tan^2 x = \dfrac{\sin^2 x}{\cos^2 x}$

Choose expression A.

31. $1 + \sin^2 x = \csc^2 x - \cot^2 x + \sin^2 x$

Choose expression D.

35. Find $\sin\theta$ if $\cos\theta = \dfrac{x}{(x+1)}$.

$$\cos\theta = \frac{x}{x+1}$$

Since $\sin^2\theta + \cos^2\theta = 1$,

$$\sin^2\theta = 1 - \cos^2\theta$$

$$\sin^2\theta = 1 - \left(\frac{x}{x+1}\right)^2$$

$$= \frac{(x+1)^2 - x^2}{(x+1)^2}$$

$$= \frac{x^2 + 2x + 1 - x^2}{(x+1)^2}$$

$$= \frac{2x+1}{(x+1)^2}$$

$$\sin\theta = \frac{\pm\sqrt{2x+1}}{x+1}.$$

37. $\cot\theta\sin\theta = \dfrac{\cos\theta}{\sin\theta}\cdot\sin\theta = \cos\theta$

39. $\cos\theta\csc\theta = \cos\theta\cdot\dfrac{1}{\sin\theta}$

$$= \frac{\cos\theta}{\sin\theta}$$

$$= \cot\theta$$

41. $\sin^2\theta\left(\csc^2\theta - 1\right) = \sin^2\theta\left(\dfrac{1}{\sin^2\theta} - 1\right)$

$$= \frac{\sin^2\theta}{\sin^2\theta} - \sin^2\theta$$

$$= 1 - \sin^2\theta$$

$$= \cos^2\theta$$

43. $(1 - \cos\theta)(1 + \sec\theta)$

$$= 1 + \sec\theta - \cos\theta - \cos\theta\sec\theta$$

$$= 1 + \sec\theta - \cos\theta - \cos\theta\left(\frac{1}{\cos\theta}\right)$$

$$= 1 + \sec\theta - \cos\theta - 1$$

$$= \sec\theta - \cos\theta$$

45. $\dfrac{\cos^2\theta - \sin^2\theta}{\sin\theta\cos\theta}$

$$= \frac{\cos^2\theta}{\sin\theta\cos\theta} - \frac{\sin^2\theta}{\sin\theta\cos\theta}$$

$$= \frac{\cos\theta}{\sin\theta} - \frac{\sin\theta}{\cos\theta}$$

$$= \cot\theta - \tan\theta$$

47. $\tan\theta + \cot\theta = \dfrac{\sin\theta}{\cos\theta} + \dfrac{\cos\theta}{\sin\theta}$

$$= \frac{\sin^2\theta + \cos^2\theta}{\cos\theta\,\sin\theta}$$

$$= \frac{1}{\cos\theta\sin\theta}$$

$$= \frac{1}{\cos\theta}\cdot\frac{1}{\sin\theta}$$

$$= \sec\theta\csc\theta$$

49. $\sin\theta(\csc\theta - \sin\theta) = \sin\theta\csc\theta - \sin^2\theta$

$$= 1 - \sin^2\theta$$

$$= \cos^2\theta$$

51. $\sin^2\theta + \tan^2\theta + \cos^2\theta$

$$= (\sin^2\theta + \cos^2\theta) + \tan^2\theta$$

$$= 1 + \tan^2\theta$$

$$= \sec^2\theta$$

53. Express $\sin\theta$ in terms of $\cot\theta$ and in terms of $\sec\theta$.

$$\sin\theta = \frac{1}{\csc\theta} = \frac{1}{\pm\sqrt{1 + \cot^2\theta}}$$

$$= \frac{\pm\sqrt{1 + \cot^2\theta}}{1 + \cot^2\theta}$$

$$\sin\theta = \cos\theta\tan\theta$$

$$= \frac{1}{\sec\theta}\cdot\pm\sqrt{\sec^2\theta - 1}$$

$$= \frac{\pm\sqrt{\sec^2\theta - 1}}{\sec\theta}$$

55. Express $\tan\theta$ in terms of $\sin\theta$, $\cos\theta$, $\sec\theta$, and $\csc\theta$.

$$\tan\theta = \frac{\sin\theta}{\cos\theta}$$

$$= \frac{\sin\theta}{\pm\sqrt{1 - \sin^2\theta}}$$

$$= \frac{\pm\sin\theta}{\sqrt{1 - \sin^2\theta}}$$

$$= \frac{\pm\sin\theta\sqrt{1 - \sin^2\theta}}{1 - \sin^2\theta}$$

$$\tan\theta = \frac{\sin\theta}{\cos\theta}$$

$$= \frac{\pm\sqrt{1-\cos^2\theta}}{\cos\theta}$$

$$\tan\theta = \pm\sqrt{\sec^2\theta - 1}$$

$$\tan\theta = \frac{1}{\cot\theta}$$

$$= \frac{1}{\pm\sqrt{\csc^2\theta - 1}}$$

$$= \frac{\pm\sqrt{\csc^2\theta - 1}}{\csc^2\theta - 1}$$

57. Express $\sec\theta$ in terms of $\sin\theta$, $\tan\theta$, $\cot\theta$, and $\csc\theta$.

$$\sec\theta = \frac{1}{\cos\theta}$$

$$= \frac{1}{\pm\sqrt{1-\sin^2\theta}}$$

$$= \frac{\pm\sqrt{1-\sin^2\theta}}{1-\sin^2\theta}$$

$$\sec\theta = \pm\sqrt{\tan^2\theta + 1}$$

Since $\tan\theta = \frac{1}{\cot\theta}$,

$$\sec\theta = \pm\sqrt{\tan^2\theta + 1}$$

$$= \pm\sqrt{\left(\frac{1}{\cot^2\theta}\right) + 1}$$

$$= \frac{\pm\sqrt{1+\cot^2\theta}}{\cot\theta}.$$

$$\sec\theta = \frac{1}{\cos\theta}$$

$$= \frac{1}{\pm\sqrt{1-\sin^2\theta}}$$

$$= \frac{1}{+\sqrt{1-\frac{1}{\csc^2\theta}}}$$

$$= \frac{\sqrt{\csc^2\theta}}{\pm\sqrt{\csc^2\theta - 1}}$$

$$= \frac{\pm\csc\theta\sqrt{\csc^2\theta - 1}}{\csc^2\theta - 1}$$

59. Let $\cos x = \frac{1}{5}$. Then x is in quadrant I or quadrant IV. Then,

$$\sin x = \pm\sqrt{1-\cos^2 x}$$

$$= \pm\sqrt{1-\left(\frac{1}{5}\right)^2}$$

$$= \pm\sqrt{\frac{24}{25}} = \pm\frac{2\sqrt{6}}{5}.$$

$$\tan x = \frac{\sin x}{\cos x} = \frac{\pm\frac{2\sqrt{6}}{5}}{\frac{1}{5}} = \pm 2\sqrt{6}$$

$$\sec x = \frac{1}{\cos x} = 5$$

Quadrant I:

$$\frac{\sec x - \tan x}{\sin x} = \frac{5-2\sqrt{6}}{\frac{2\sqrt{6}}{5}}$$

$$= \frac{25-10\sqrt{6}}{2\sqrt{6}}$$

$$= \frac{25\sqrt{6} - 60}{12}$$

Quadrant IV:

$$\frac{\sec x - \tan x}{\sin x} = \frac{5-(-2\sqrt{6})}{-\frac{2\sqrt{6}}{5}}$$

$$= \frac{25+10\sqrt{6}}{-2\sqrt{6}}$$

$$= \frac{-25\sqrt{6} - 60}{12}$$

61. $y = \sin(-2x)$
$y = -\sin(2x)$

62. It is the negative of $\sin(2x)$.

63. $y = \cos(-4x)$
$y = \cos(4x)$

64. It is the same function.

65. (a) $y = \sin(-4x)$
$y = -\sin(4x)$

(b) $y = \cos(-2x)$
$y = \cos(2x)$

(c) $y = -5\sin(-3x)$
$y = -5[-\sin(3x)]$
$y = 5\sin(3x)$

67.

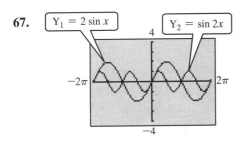

not an identity

69.

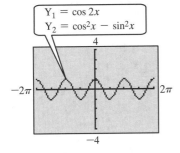

identity

Section 6.2

Connections *(page 466)*

$$\sqrt{(1-x^2)^3} = \sqrt{(1-(\cos\theta)^2)^3}$$
$$= \sqrt{(\sin^2\theta)^3}$$
$$= \sqrt{\sin^6\theta}$$
$$= \sin^3\theta$$

$\cos\theta$ is an appropriate choice since
$\cos^2\theta + \sin^2\theta = 1$.

Exercises

1. $\cot\theta + \dfrac{1}{\cot\theta} = \dfrac{\cos\theta}{\sin\theta} + \dfrac{\sin\theta}{\cos\theta}$

$$= \dfrac{\cos^2\theta + \sin^2\theta}{\sin\theta\cos\theta}$$

$$= \dfrac{1}{\sin\theta\cos\theta} \quad \text{or} \quad \csc\theta\sec\theta$$

3. $\tan s\,(\cot s + \csc s) = \dfrac{\sin s}{\cos s}\left(\dfrac{\cos s}{\sin s} + \dfrac{1}{\sin s}\right)$

$$= 1 + \dfrac{1}{\cos s}$$

$$= 1 + \sec s$$

5. $\dfrac{1}{\csc^2\theta} + \dfrac{1}{\sec^2\theta} = \sin^2\theta + \cos^2\theta = 1$

7. $\dfrac{\cos x}{\sec x} + \dfrac{\sin x}{\csc x} = \cos x(\cos x) + \sin x(\sin x)$

$$= \cos^2 x + \sin^2 x$$
$$= 1$$

9. $(1+\sin t)^2 + \cos^2 t = 1 + 2\sin t + \sin^2 t + \cos^2 t$
$$= 2 + 2\sin t$$

11. $\dfrac{1}{1+\cos x} - \dfrac{1}{1-\cos x} = \dfrac{1-\cos x - 1 - \cos x}{1-\cos^2 x}$

$$= -\dfrac{2\cos x}{\sin^2 x}$$

$$= -2\left(\dfrac{\cos x}{\sin x}\right)\left(\dfrac{1}{\sin x}\right)$$

$$= -2\cot x\csc x$$

13. $\sin^2\gamma - 1 = (\sin\gamma - 1)(\sin\gamma + 1)$

15. $(\sin x + 1)^2 - (\sin x - 1)^2$
Let $a = \sin x + 1$ and $b = \sin x - 1$.
$(\sin x + 1)^2 - (\sin x - 1)^2$
$$= a^2 - b^2$$
$$= (a - b)(a + b)$$
$$= [(\sin x + 1) - (\sin x - 1)][(\sin x + 1) + (\sin x - 1)]$$
$$= 2(2\sin x)$$
$$= 4\sin x$$

17. $2\sin^2 x + 3\sin x + 1$
Let $a = \sin x$.
$2\sin^2 x + 3\sin x + 1 = 2a^2 + 3a + 1$
$$= (2a + 1)(a + 1)$$
$$= (2\sin x + 1)(\sin x + 1)$$

19. $\cos^4 x + 2\cos^2 x + 1$
Let $\cos^2 x = a$.
$\cos^4 x + 2\cos^2 x + 1 = a^2 + 2a + 1$
$$= (a + 1)^2$$
$$= (\cos^2 x + 1)^2$$

21. $\sin^3 x - \cos^3 x$
Let $\sin x = a$ and $\cos x = b$.
$\sin^3 x - \cos^3 x$
$$= a^3 - b^3$$
$$= (a - b)(a^2 + ab + b^2)$$
$$= (\sin x - \cos x)(\sin^2 x + \sin x \cos x + \cos^2 x)$$
$$= (\sin x - \cos x)(1 + \sin x \cos x)$$

23. $\tan\theta\cos\theta = \dfrac{\sin\theta}{\cos\theta}\cos\theta = \sin\theta$

25. $\sec r \cos r = \dfrac{1}{\cos r} \cdot \cos r = 1$

27. $\dfrac{\sin \beta \tan \beta}{\cos \beta} = \tan \beta \tan \beta = \tan^2 \beta$

29. $\sec^2 x - 1 = \dfrac{1}{\cos^2 x} - 1$

$\qquad = \dfrac{1 - \cos^2 x}{\cos^2 x}$

$\qquad = \dfrac{\sin^2 x}{\cos^2 x} = \tan^2 x$

31. $\dfrac{\sin^2 x}{\cos^2 x} + \sin x \csc x = \tan^2 x + \sin x \dfrac{1}{\sin x}$

$\qquad\qquad\qquad = \tan^2 x + 1$

$\qquad\qquad\qquad = \sec^2 x$

33. Verify $\dfrac{\cot \theta}{\csc \theta} = \cos \theta.$

$\dfrac{\cot \theta}{\csc \theta} = \dfrac{\frac{\cos \theta}{\sin \theta}}{\frac{1}{\sin \theta}} = \cos \theta$

35. Verify $\dfrac{1 - \sin^2 \beta}{\cos \beta} = \cos \beta.$

$\dfrac{1 - \sin^2 \beta}{\cos \beta} = \dfrac{\cos^2 \beta}{\cos \beta} = \cos \beta$

37. Verify $\cos^2 \theta (\tan^2 \theta + 1) = 1.$

$\cos^2 \theta (\tan^2 \theta + 1) = \cos^2 \theta \left(\dfrac{\sin^2 \theta}{\cos^2 \theta} + 1 \right)$

$\qquad\qquad = \cos^2 \theta \left(\dfrac{\sin^2 \theta + \cos^2 \theta}{\cos^2 \theta} \right)$

$\qquad\qquad = 1$

39. Verify $\cot s + \tan s = \sec s \csc s.$

$\cot s + \tan s = \dfrac{\cos s}{\sin s} + \dfrac{\sin s}{\cos s}$

$\qquad = \dfrac{\cos^2 s + \sin^2 s}{\sin s \cos s}$

$\qquad = \dfrac{1}{\sin s \cos s}$

$\qquad = \sec s \csc s$

41. Verify $\dfrac{\cos \alpha}{\sec \alpha} + \dfrac{\sin \alpha}{\csc \alpha} = \sec^2 \alpha - \tan^2 \alpha.$
Work with the left side.

$\dfrac{\cos \alpha}{\sec \alpha} + \dfrac{\sin \alpha}{\csc \alpha} = \dfrac{\cos \alpha}{\frac{1}{\cos \alpha}} + \dfrac{\sin \alpha}{\frac{1}{\sin \alpha}}$

$\qquad\qquad = \cos^2 \alpha + \sin^2 \alpha$

$\qquad\qquad = 1$

Now work with the right side.

$\sec^2 \alpha - \tan^2 \alpha = 1$

43. Verify $\sin^4 \theta - \cos^4 \theta = 2 \sin^2 \theta - 1.$

$\sin^4 \theta - \cos^4 \theta$

$= (\sin^2 \theta - \cos^2 \theta)(\sin^2 \theta + \cos^2 \theta)$

$= \sin^2 \theta - \cos^2 \theta$

$= \sin^2 \theta - (1 - \sin^2 \theta)$

$= 2 \sin^2 \theta - 1$

45. Verify

$(1 - \cos^2 \alpha)(1 + \cos^2 \alpha) = 2 \sin^2 \alpha - \sin^4 \alpha.$

$(1 - \cos^2 \alpha)(1 + \cos^2 \alpha) = \sin^2 \alpha (1 + \cos^2 \alpha)$

$\qquad\qquad = \sin^2 \alpha (2 - \sin^2 \alpha)$

$\qquad\qquad = 2 \sin^2 \alpha - \sin^4 \alpha$

47. Verify $\dfrac{\cos \theta + 1}{\tan^2 \theta} = \dfrac{\cos \theta}{\sec \theta - 1}.$
Work with the left side.

$\dfrac{\cos \theta + 1}{\tan^2 \theta} = \dfrac{\cos \theta + 1}{\sec^2 \theta - 1}$

$\qquad = \dfrac{\cos \theta + 1}{\frac{1}{\cos^2 \theta} - 1}$

$\qquad = \dfrac{\cos \theta + 1}{\frac{1 - \cos^2 \theta}{\cos^2 \theta}}$

$\qquad = \dfrac{\cos^2 \theta (\cos \theta + 1)}{(1 - \cos \theta)(1 + \cos \theta)}$

$\qquad = \dfrac{\cos^2 \theta}{1 - \cos \theta}$

Now work with the right side.

$\dfrac{\cos \theta}{\sec \theta - 1} = \dfrac{\cos \theta}{\frac{1}{\cos \theta} - 1} = \dfrac{\cos \theta}{\frac{1 - \cos \theta}{\cos \theta}} = \dfrac{\cos^2 \theta}{1 - \cos \theta}$

49. Verify $\dfrac{1}{1-\sin\theta}+\dfrac{1}{1+\sin\theta}=2\sec^2\theta.$

$$\dfrac{1}{1-\sin\theta}+\dfrac{1}{1+\sin\theta}=\dfrac{(1+\sin\theta)+(1-\sin\theta)}{(1-\sin\theta)(1+\sin\theta)}$$

$$=\dfrac{2}{1-\sin^2\theta}$$

$$=\dfrac{2}{\cos^2\theta}$$

$$=2\sec^2\theta$$

51. Verify $\dfrac{\tan s}{1+\cos s}+\dfrac{\sin s}{1-\cos s}=\cot s+\sec s\csc s.$

$$\dfrac{\tan s}{1+\cos s}+\dfrac{\sin s}{1-\cos s}=\dfrac{\tan s(1-\cos s)+\sin s(1+\cos s)}{1-\cos^2 s}$$

$$=\dfrac{\tan s-\sin s+\sin s+\sin s\cos s}{\sin^2 s}$$

$$=\dfrac{\tan s}{\sin^2 s}+\dfrac{\cos s}{\sin s}$$

$$=\dfrac{\sin s}{\cos s}\cdot\dfrac{1}{\sin^2 s}+\cot s$$

$$=\dfrac{1}{\cos s}\cdot\dfrac{1}{\sin s}+\cot s$$

$$=\sec s\csc s+\cot s$$

53. Verify $\dfrac{\cot\alpha+1}{\cot\alpha-1}=\dfrac{1+\tan\alpha}{1-\tan\alpha}.$

$$\dfrac{\cot\alpha+1}{\cot\alpha-1}=\dfrac{\frac{1}{\tan\alpha}+1}{\frac{1}{\tan\alpha}-1}=\dfrac{\frac{1+\tan\alpha}{\tan\alpha}}{\frac{1-\tan\alpha}{\tan\alpha}}=\dfrac{1+\tan\alpha}{1-\tan\alpha}$$

55. Verify $\sin^2\alpha\sec^2\alpha+\sin^2\alpha\csc^2\alpha=\sec^2\alpha.$

$$\sin^2\alpha\sec^2\alpha+\sin^2\alpha\csc^2\alpha=\dfrac{\sin^2\alpha}{\cos^2\alpha}+1$$

$$=\tan^2\alpha+1$$

$$=\sec^2\alpha$$

57. Verify $\sec^4 x-\sec^2 x=\tan^4 x+\tan^2 x.$

Simplify left side.

$$\sec^4 x-\sec^2 x=\sec^2 x\left(\sec^2 x-1\right)$$

$$=\sec^2 x\tan^2 x$$

Simplify right side.

$$\tan^4 x+\tan^2 x=\tan^2 x\left(\tan^2 x+1\right)$$

$$=\tan^2 x\sec^2 x$$

59. Verify $\sin\theta+\cos\theta=\dfrac{\sin\theta}{1-\frac{\cos\theta}{\sin\theta}}+\dfrac{\cos\theta}{1-\frac{\sin\theta}{\cos\theta}}.$

Work with the right side.

$$\dfrac{\sin\theta}{1-\frac{\cos\theta}{\sin\theta}}+\dfrac{\cos\theta}{1-\frac{\sin\theta}{\cos\theta}}=\dfrac{\sin^2\theta}{\sin\theta-\cos\theta}+\dfrac{\cos^2\theta}{\cos\theta-\sin\theta}$$

$$=\dfrac{\sin^2\theta}{\sin\theta-\cos\theta}+\dfrac{\cos^2\theta}{-(\sin\theta-\cos\theta)}$$

$$=\dfrac{\sin^2\theta-\cos^2\theta}{\sin\theta-\cos\theta}$$

$$=\dfrac{(\sin\theta+\cos\theta)(\sin\theta-\cos\theta)}{(\sin\theta-\cos\theta)}$$

$$=\sin\theta+\cos\theta$$

61. Verify $\dfrac{\sec^4 s-\tan^4 s}{\sec^2 s+\tan^2 s}=\sec^2 s-\tan^2 s.$

$$\dfrac{\sec^4 s-\tan^4 s}{\sec^2 s+\tan^2 s}=\dfrac{\left(\sec^2 s-\tan^2 s\right)\left(\sec^2 s+\tan^2 s\right)}{\sec^2 s+\tan^2 s}$$

$$=\sec^2 s-\tan^2 s$$

63. Verify $\dfrac{\tan^2 t-1}{\sec^2 t}=\dfrac{\tan t-\cot t}{\tan t+\cot t}.$

Work with the right side.

$$\dfrac{\tan t-\cot t}{\tan t+\cot t}=\dfrac{\tan t-\frac{1}{\tan t}}{\tan t+\frac{1}{\tan t}}$$

$$=\dfrac{\frac{\tan^2 t-1}{\tan t}}{\frac{\tan^2 t+1}{\tan t}}$$

$$=\dfrac{\tan^2 t-1}{\tan^2 t+1}$$

$$=\dfrac{\tan^2 t-1}{\sec^2 t}$$

65. Verify $\dfrac{1+\cos x}{1-\cos x}-\dfrac{1-\cos x}{1+\cos x}=4\cot x\csc x.$

$$\dfrac{1+\cos x}{1-\cos x}-\dfrac{1-\cos x}{1+\cos x}$$

$$=\dfrac{1+\cos^2 x+2\cos x-1-\cos^2 x+2\cos x}{1-\cos^2 x}$$

$$=\dfrac{4\cos x}{\sin^2 x}$$

$$=4\cot x\csc x$$

67. Verify $(\sec\alpha+\csc\alpha)(\cos\alpha-\sin\alpha)=\cot\alpha-\tan\alpha.$

$$(\sec\alpha+\csc\alpha)(\cos\alpha-\sin\alpha)$$

$$=\left(\dfrac{1}{\cos\alpha}+\dfrac{1}{\sin\alpha}\right)(\cos\alpha-\sin\alpha)$$

$$=1+\cot\alpha-\tan\alpha-1$$

$$=\cot\alpha-\tan\alpha$$

71.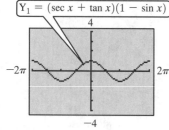

The graph of $y = (\sec x + \tan x)(1 - \sin x)$ appears to be the same as the graph of $y = \cos x$.

$$(\sec\theta + \tan\theta)(1 - \sin\theta) = \left(\frac{1}{\cos\theta} + \frac{\sin\theta}{\cos\theta}\right)(1 - \sin\theta)$$

$$= \frac{(1 + \sin\theta)(1 - \sin\theta)}{\cos\theta}$$

$$= \frac{1 - \sin^2\theta}{\cos\theta}$$

$$= \frac{\cos^2\theta}{\cos\theta}$$

$$= \cos\theta$$

73.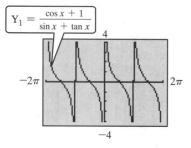

The graph of $y = \dfrac{\cos x + 1}{\sin x + \tan x}$ appears to be the same as the graph of $y = \cot x$.

$$\frac{\cos\theta + 1}{\sin\theta + \tan\theta} = \frac{1 + \cos\theta}{\sin\theta + \frac{\sin\theta}{\cos\theta}}$$

$$= \frac{1 + \cos\theta}{\sin\theta\left(1 + \frac{1}{\cos\theta}\right)}$$

$$= \frac{(1 + \cos\theta)\cos\theta}{\sin\theta\left(1 + \frac{1}{\cos\theta}\right)\cos\theta}$$

$$= \frac{(1 + \cos\theta)\cos\theta}{\sin\theta(\cos\theta + 1)}$$

$$= \frac{\cos\theta}{\sin\theta}$$

$$= \cot\theta$$

75. Is $\dfrac{2 + 5\cos s}{\sin s} = 2\csc s + 5\cot s$ an identity? Graph each side of the equation.

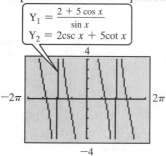

The graphs of $y = \dfrac{2 + 5\cos x}{\sin x}$ and $y = 2\csc x + 5\cot x$ appear to be the same. The given equation may be an identity. Verify it.

$$\frac{2 + 5\cos s}{\sin s} = \frac{2}{\sin s} + \frac{5\cos s}{\sin s}$$

$$= 2\csc s + 5\cot s$$

The given statement is an identity.

77. Is $\dfrac{\tan s - \cot s}{\tan s + \cot s} = 2\sin^2 s$ an identity? Graph each side of the equation.

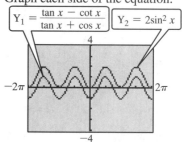

The graphs of $y = \dfrac{\tan x - \cot x}{\tan x + \cot x}$ and $y = 2\sin^2 x$ are not the same. The given statement is not an identity.

79. Is $\dfrac{1-\tan^2 s}{1+\tan^2 s} = \cos^2 s - \sin s$ an identity?

Graph each side of the equation.

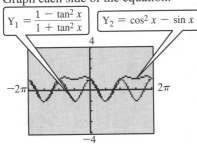

$$Y_1 = \frac{1 - \tan^2 x}{1 + \tan^2 x} \qquad Y_2 = \cos^2 x - \sin x$$

The graphs of $y = \dfrac{1-\tan^2 x}{1+\tan^2 x}$ and $y = \cos^2 x - \sin x$ are not the same. The given statement is not an identity.

81. Is $\sin^2 s + \cos^2 s = \dfrac{1}{2}(1-\cos 4s)$ an identity?

Evaluate each side of the equation using a table of values. Let $Y_1 = \sin^2 s + \cos^2 s$ and $Y_2 = \dfrac{1}{2}(1-\cos 4s)$.

X	Y1	Y2
0	1	0
1.0472	1	.75
2.0944	1	.75
3.1416	1	0
4.1888	1	.75
5.236	1	.75
6.2832	1	0

X=0

The table values are not the same. The given statement is not an identity.

83. Is $\tan^2 x - \sin^2 x = (\tan x \sin x)^2$ an identity?

Evaluate each side of the equation using a table of values. Let $Y_1 = \tan^2 x - \sin^2 x$ and $Y_2 = (\tan x \sin x)^2$.

X	Y1	Y2
0	0	0
1.0472	2.25	2.25
2.0944	2.25	2.25
3.1416	0	0
4.1888	2.25	2.25
5.236	2.25	2.25
6.2832	0	0

X=0

The table values appear to be the same. The given equation may be an identity. Verify it.

$$\tan^2 x - \sin^2 x = \frac{\sin^2 x}{\cos^2 x} - \frac{\sin^2 x \cos^2 x}{\cos^2 x}$$
$$= \frac{\sin^2 x \left(1 - \cos^2 x\right)}{\cos^2 x}$$
$$= \frac{\sin^2 x}{\cos^2 x}\left(1 - \cos^2 x\right)$$
$$= \tan^2 x \sin^2 x$$
$$= (\tan x \sin x)^2$$

The given statement is an identity.

85. Show that $\sin(\csc s) = 1$ is not an identity.
Let $s = 2$.
$\sin(\csc 2) \approx .89109401$
Thus, $\sin(\csc s) \neq 1$ for all real numbers s, so this statement is not an identity.

87. Show that $\csc t = \sqrt{1 + \cot^2 t}$ is not an identity.
Let $t = 1$.
$$\csc \approx 1.1883951$$
$$\sqrt{1 + \cot^2 1} \approx 1.1883951$$
But let $t = 4$.
$$\csc 4 \approx -1.3213487$$
$$\sqrt{1 + \cot^2 1} \approx 1.3213487$$
Recall that $\sqrt{a}$ denotes the positive square root of a.

Thus, $\csc t \neq \sqrt{1 + \cos^2 t}$ for all real numbers t, so this statement is not an identity.

Section 6.3

Exercises

1. $\cos 75°$

$= \cos(30° + 45°)$

$= \cos 30° \cos 45° - \sin 30° \sin 45°$

$= \dfrac{\sqrt{3}}{2} \cdot \dfrac{\sqrt{2}}{2} - \dfrac{1}{2} \cdot \dfrac{\sqrt{2}}{2}$

$= \dfrac{\sqrt{6} - \sqrt{2}}{4}$

3. $\cos(105°)$

$= \cos(60° + 45°)$

$= \cos(60°)\cos(45°) - \sin(60°)\sin(45°)$

$= \dfrac{1}{2} \cdot \dfrac{\sqrt{2}}{2} - \left(\dfrac{\sqrt{3}}{2}\right)\left(\dfrac{\sqrt{2}}{2}\right)$

$= \dfrac{\sqrt{2}}{4} - \dfrac{\sqrt{6}}{4}$

$= \dfrac{\sqrt{2} - \sqrt{6}}{4}$

5. $\cos\left(\dfrac{7\pi}{12}\right) = \cos\left(\dfrac{\pi}{3} + \dfrac{\pi}{4}\right)$

$= \cos\dfrac{\pi}{3} \cos\dfrac{\pi}{4} - \sin\dfrac{\pi}{3} \sin\dfrac{\pi}{4}$

$= \dfrac{1}{2} \cdot \dfrac{\sqrt{2}}{2} - \dfrac{\sqrt{3}}{2} \cdot \dfrac{\sqrt{2}}{2}$

$= \dfrac{\sqrt{2}}{4} - \dfrac{\sqrt{6}}{4}$

$= \dfrac{\sqrt{2} - \sqrt{6}}{4}$

7. $\cos 40° \cos 50° - \sin 40° \sin 50° = \cos(40° + 50°)$

$= \cos 90°$

$= 0$

9. $\tan 87° = \cot(90° - 87°) = \cot 3°$

11. $\cos\dfrac{\pi}{12} = \sin\left(\dfrac{\pi}{2} - \dfrac{\pi}{12}\right) = \sin\dfrac{5\pi}{12}$

13. $\sin\dfrac{5\pi}{8} = \cos\left(\dfrac{\pi}{2} - \dfrac{5\pi}{8}\right) = \cos\left(-\dfrac{\pi}{8}\right)$

15. $\sec 146° 42' = \csc(90° - 146° 42') = \csc(-56° 42')$

17. $\cot\dfrac{\pi}{3} = \underline{\hspace{1cm}} \dfrac{\pi}{6}$

Since $\dfrac{\pi}{6} = \dfrac{\pi}{2} - \dfrac{\pi}{3}$, $\cot\dfrac{\pi}{3} = \tan\dfrac{\pi}{6}$.

Answer: tan

19. $\underline{\hspace{1cm}} 33° = \sin 57°$

$\sin 57° = \cos(90° - 57°)$

$= \cos 33°$

Answer: cos

21. $\tan\theta = \cot(45° + 2\theta)$

Since $\tan\theta = \cot(90° - \theta)$,

$90° - \theta = 45° + 2\theta$

$3\theta = 45°$

$\theta = 15°$.

23. $\sin(3\theta - 15°) = (\cos\theta + 25°)$

Since $\sin\theta = \cos(90° - \theta)$,

$\sin(3\theta - 15°) = \cos\left[90° - (3\theta - 15°)\right]$.

$90° - (3\theta - 15°) = \theta + 25°$

$105° - 3\theta = \theta + 25°$

$80° = 4\theta$

$20° = \theta$

25. $\cos(90° - \theta) = \cos 90° \cos\theta + \sin 90° \sin\theta$

$= 0\cos\theta + 1\sin\theta$

$= \sin\theta$

27. $\cos(270° - \theta) = \cos 270° \cos\theta + \sin 270° \sin\theta$

$= 0\cos\theta + (-1)\sin\theta$

$= -\sin\theta$

29. $\cos s = -\dfrac{1}{5}$ and $\sin t = \dfrac{3}{5}$.

s and t are in quadrant II.

Solve $\sin^2 s + \cos^2 s = 1$ for $\sin s$. Since s is in quadrant II, $\sin s > 0$.

$\sin s = \sqrt{1 - \left(-\dfrac{1}{5}\right)^2} = \dfrac{\sqrt{24}}{5}$

Solve $\sin^2 t + \cos^2 t = 1$ for $\cos t$. Since t is in quadrant II, $\cos t < 0$.

$\cos t = -\sqrt{1 - \left(\dfrac{3}{5}\right)^2} = -\dfrac{4}{5}$

$\cos(s + t) = \cos s \cos t - \sin s \sin t$

$= \left(-\dfrac{1}{5}\right)\left(-\dfrac{4}{5}\right) - \left(\dfrac{\sqrt{24}}{5}\right)\left(\dfrac{3}{5}\right)$

$= \dfrac{4}{25} - \dfrac{3\sqrt{24}}{25}$

$= \dfrac{4 - 6\sqrt{6}}{25}$

$\cos(s - t) = \cos s \cos t + \sin s \sin t$

$$= \left(-\frac{1}{5}\right)\left(-\frac{4}{5}\right) + \left(\frac{\sqrt{24}}{5}\right)\left(\frac{3}{5}\right)$$

$$= \frac{4}{25} + \frac{3\sqrt{24}}{25}$$

$$= \frac{4 + 6\sqrt{6}}{25}$$

31. $\sin s = \dfrac{3}{5}$ and $\sin t = -\dfrac{12}{13}$.

s is in quadrant I and t is in quadrant III

$\cos s > 0$ and $\cos t < 0$.

$$\cos s = \sqrt{1 - \left(\frac{3}{5}\right)^2} = \frac{4}{5}$$

$$\cos t = -\sqrt{1 - \left(-\frac{12}{13}\right)^2} = -\frac{5}{13}$$

$\cos(s + t) = \cos s \cos t - \sin s \sin t$

$$= \left(\frac{4}{5}\right)\left(-\frac{5}{13}\right) - \left(\frac{3}{5}\right)\left(-\frac{12}{13}\right)$$

$$= \frac{16}{65}$$

$\cos(s - t) = \cos s \cos t + \sin s \sin t$

$$= \left(\frac{4}{5}\right)\left(-\frac{5}{13}\right) + \left(\frac{3}{5}\right)\left(-\frac{12}{13}\right)$$

$$= -\frac{56}{65}$$

34. $-\cos 15° = -\cos(45° - 30°)$

$$= -(\cos 45° \cos 30° + \sin 45° \sin 30°)$$

$$= -\left(\frac{\sqrt{2}}{2} \cdot \frac{\sqrt{3}}{2} + \frac{\sqrt{2}}{2} \cdot \frac{1}{2}\right)$$

$$= -\frac{\sqrt{6} + \sqrt{2}}{4}$$

35. $\cos 195° = -\cos 15° = -\dfrac{\sqrt{6} + \sqrt{2}}{4}$

36. (a) $\cos 255° = \cos(180° + 75°)$

$$= \cos 180° \cos 75° - \sin 180° \sin 75°$$

$$= (-1)\cos 75° - (0)\sin 75°$$

$$= -\cos 75°$$

$$= -\cos(45° + 30°)$$

$$= -(\cos 45° \cos 30° - \sin 45° \sin 30°)$$

$$= -\left(\frac{\sqrt{2}}{2} \cdot \frac{\sqrt{3}}{2} - \frac{\sqrt{2}}{2} \cdot \frac{1}{2}\right)$$

$$= -\frac{\sqrt{6} - \sqrt{2}}{4}$$

$$= \frac{\sqrt{2} - \sqrt{6}}{4}$$

(b) $\cos \dfrac{11\pi}{12} = \cos\left(\pi - \dfrac{\pi}{12}\right)$

$$= \cos \pi \cos \frac{\pi}{12} + \sin \pi \sin \frac{\pi}{12}$$

$$= (-1)\cos \frac{\pi}{12} + (0)\sin \frac{\pi}{12}$$

$$= -\cos\left(\frac{\pi}{3} - \frac{\pi}{4}\right)$$

$$= -\left(\cos \frac{\pi}{3} \cos \frac{\pi}{4} + \sin \frac{\pi}{3} \sin \frac{\pi}{4}\right)$$

$$= -\left(\frac{1}{2} \cdot \frac{\sqrt{2}}{2} + \frac{\sqrt{3}}{2} \cdot \frac{\sqrt{2}}{2}\right)$$

$$= -\frac{\sqrt{2} + \sqrt{6}}{4}$$

39. $\sin \dfrac{5\pi}{12} = \sin\left(\dfrac{\pi}{4} + \dfrac{\pi}{6}\right)$

$$= \sin \frac{\pi}{4} \cos \frac{\pi}{6} + \cos \frac{\pi}{4} \sin \frac{\pi}{6}$$

$$= \frac{\sqrt{2}}{2} \cdot \frac{\sqrt{3}}{2} + \frac{\sqrt{2}}{2} \cdot \frac{1}{2}$$

$$= \frac{\sqrt{6}}{4} + \frac{\sqrt{2}}{4}$$

$$= \frac{\sqrt{6} + \sqrt{2}}{4}$$

41. $\tan \dfrac{\pi}{12} = \tan\left(\dfrac{\pi}{4} - \dfrac{\pi}{6}\right)$

$= \dfrac{\tan \frac{\pi}{4} - \tan \frac{\pi}{6}}{1 + \tan \frac{\pi}{4} \tan \frac{\pi}{6}}$

$= \dfrac{1 - \frac{\sqrt{3}}{3}}{1 + (1)\frac{\sqrt{3}}{3}} = \dfrac{1 - \frac{\sqrt{3}}{3}}{1 + \frac{\sqrt{3}}{3}}$

$= \dfrac{3 - \sqrt{3}}{3 + \sqrt{3}}$

$= \dfrac{3 - \sqrt{3}}{3 + \sqrt{3}} \cdot \dfrac{3 - \sqrt{3}}{3 - \sqrt{3}}$

$= \dfrac{12 - 6\sqrt{3}}{6}$

$= 2 - \sqrt{3}$

43. $\sin\left(-\dfrac{7\pi}{12}\right) = \sin\left(-\dfrac{\pi}{4} - \dfrac{\pi}{3}\right)$

$= \sin\left(-\dfrac{\pi}{4}\right)\cos\dfrac{\pi}{3} - \cos\left(-\dfrac{\pi}{4}\right)\sin\dfrac{\pi}{3}$

$= -\sin\dfrac{\pi}{4}\cos\dfrac{\pi}{3} - \cos\dfrac{\pi}{4}\sin\dfrac{\pi}{3}$

$= -\dfrac{\sqrt{2}}{2}\cdot\dfrac{1}{2} - \dfrac{\sqrt{2}}{2}\cdot\dfrac{\sqrt{3}}{2} = -\dfrac{\sqrt{2}}{4} - \dfrac{\sqrt{6}}{4}$

$= \dfrac{-\sqrt{2} - \sqrt{6}}{4}$

45. $\sin 76° \cos 31° - \cos 76° \sin 31°$

$= \sin(76° - 31°)$

$= \sin 45°$

$= \dfrac{\sqrt{2}}{2}$

47. $\dfrac{\tan 80° + \tan 55°}{1 - \tan 80° \tan 55°} = \tan(80° + 55°)$

$= \tan 135°$

$= -1$

49. $\cos(60° + \theta) = \cos 60° \cos\theta - \sin 60° \sin\theta$

$= \dfrac{1}{2}\cos\theta - \dfrac{\sqrt{3}}{2}\sin\theta$

$= \dfrac{1}{2}\left(\cos\theta - \sqrt{3}\sin\theta\right)$

$= \dfrac{\cos\theta - \sqrt{3}\sin\theta}{2}$

51. $\cos\left(\dfrac{3\pi}{4} - x\right) = \cos\dfrac{3\pi}{4}\cos x + \sin\dfrac{3\pi}{4}\sin x$

$= -\dfrac{\sqrt{2}}{2}\cos x + \dfrac{\sqrt{2}}{2}\sin x$

$= \dfrac{\sqrt{2}}{2}\left(-\cos x + \sin x\right)$

$= \dfrac{\sqrt{2}\left(\sin x - \cos x\right)}{2}$

53. $\tan(\theta + 30°) = \dfrac{\tan\theta + \tan 30°}{1 - \tan\theta \tan 30°}$

$= \dfrac{\tan\theta + \frac{1}{\sqrt{3}}}{1 - \frac{1}{\sqrt{3}}\tan\theta}$

$= \dfrac{\sqrt{3}\tan\theta + 1}{\sqrt{3} - \tan\theta}$

55. $\sin\left(\dfrac{\pi}{4} + x\right) = \sin\dfrac{\pi}{4}\cos x + \cos\dfrac{\pi}{4}\sin x$

$= \dfrac{\sqrt{2}}{2}\cos x + \dfrac{\sqrt{2}}{2}\sin x$

$= \dfrac{\sqrt{2}\left(\cos x + \sin x\right)}{2}$

59. $\cos s = \dfrac{3}{5}$, $\sin t = \dfrac{5}{13}$, and s and t are in quadrant I. First, find $\sin s$, $\tan s$, $\cos t$, and $\tan t$. Since s and t are in quadrant I, all are positive.

$\sin s = \sqrt{1 - \left(\dfrac{3}{5}\right)^2} = \dfrac{4}{5}$

$\tan s = \dfrac{\sin s}{\cos s} = \dfrac{\frac{4}{5}}{\frac{3}{5}} = \dfrac{4}{3}$

$\cos t = \sqrt{1 - \left(\dfrac{5}{13}\right)^2} = \dfrac{12}{13}$

$\tan t = \dfrac{\frac{5}{13}}{\frac{12}{13}} = \dfrac{5}{12}$

$$\sin(s+t) = \frac{4}{5} \cdot \frac{12}{13} + \frac{5}{13} \cdot \frac{3}{5} = \frac{63}{65}$$

$$\sin(s-t) = \frac{4}{5} \cdot \frac{12}{13} - \frac{5}{13} \cdot \frac{3}{5} = \frac{33}{65}$$

$$\tan(s+t) = \frac{\tan s + \tan t}{1 - \tan s \tan t}$$

$$= \frac{\frac{4}{3} + \frac{5}{12}}{1 - \left(\frac{4}{3}\right)\left(\frac{5}{12}\right)}$$

$$= \frac{63}{16}$$

$$\tan(s-t) = \frac{\frac{4}{3} - \frac{5}{12}}{1 + \left(\frac{4}{3}\right)\left(\frac{5}{12}\right)}$$

$$= \frac{33}{56}$$

To find the quadrant of $s + t$, notice that $\sin(s + t) > 0$, which implies $s + t$ is in quadrant I or II. $\tan(s + t) > 0$, which implies $s + t$ is in quadrant I or III. Therefore, $s + t$ is in quadrant I. Then, $\sin(s - t) > 0$ and $\tan(s - t) > 0$. From the preceding, $s - t$ must also be in quadrant I.

61. $\sin s = \dfrac{2}{3}$, $\sin t = -\dfrac{1}{3}$, s is in quadrant II, and t is in quadrant IV. Since s is in quadrant II, $\cos s < 0$.

$$\cos s = -\sqrt{1 - \left(\frac{2}{3}\right)^2} = -\frac{\sqrt{5}}{3}$$

Since t is in quadrant IV, $\cos t > 0$.

$$\cos t = \sqrt{1 - \left(-\frac{1}{3}\right)^2} = \frac{\sqrt{8}}{3} = \frac{2\sqrt{2}}{3}$$

$$\tan s = \frac{\frac{2}{3}}{-\frac{\sqrt{5}}{3}} = -\frac{2}{\sqrt{5}} = -\frac{2\sqrt{5}}{5}$$

$$\tan t = \frac{-\frac{1}{3}}{\frac{2\sqrt{2}}{3}} = -\frac{1}{2\sqrt{2}} = -\frac{\sqrt{2}}{4}$$

$$\sin(s+t) = \frac{2}{3}\left(\frac{2\sqrt{2}}{3}\right) + \left(-\frac{\sqrt{5}}{3}\right)\left(-\frac{1}{3}\right)$$

$$= \frac{4\sqrt{2}}{9} + \frac{\sqrt{5}}{9}$$

$$= \frac{4\sqrt{2} + \sqrt{5}}{9}$$

$$\sin(s-t) = \frac{2}{3}\left(\frac{2\sqrt{2}}{3}\right) - \left(-\frac{\sqrt{5}}{3}\right)\left(-\frac{1}{3}\right)$$

$$= \frac{4\sqrt{2}}{9} - \frac{\sqrt{5}}{9}$$

$$= \frac{4\sqrt{2} - \sqrt{5}}{9}$$

Different forms of $\tan(s + t)$ and $\tan(s - t)$ will be obtained depending on whether $\tan s$ and $\tan t$ are written with rationalized denominators.

$$\tan(s+t) = \frac{-\frac{2\sqrt{5}}{5} + \left(-\frac{\sqrt{2}}{4}\right)}{1 - \left(-\frac{2\sqrt{5}}{5}\right)\left(-\frac{\sqrt{2}}{4}\right)}$$

$$= \frac{-8\sqrt{5} - 5\sqrt{2}}{20 - 2\sqrt{10}}$$

or

$$\tan(s+t) = \frac{-\frac{2}{\sqrt{5}} + \left(-\frac{1}{2\sqrt{2}}\right)}{1 - \left(-\frac{2}{\sqrt{5}}\right)\left(-\frac{1}{2\sqrt{2}}\right)}$$

$$= \frac{-4\sqrt{2} - \sqrt{5}}{2\sqrt{10} - 2}$$

$$= \frac{4\sqrt{2} + \sqrt{5}}{2 - 2\sqrt{10}}$$

$$\tan(s-t) = \frac{-\frac{2\sqrt{5}}{5} - \left(-\frac{\sqrt{2}}{4}\right)}{1 + \left(-\frac{2\sqrt{5}}{5}\right)\left(-\frac{\sqrt{2}}{4}\right)}$$

$$= \frac{-8\sqrt{5} + 5\sqrt{2}}{20 + 2\sqrt{10}}$$

or

$$\tan(s-t) = \frac{-\frac{2}{\sqrt{5}} - \left(-\frac{1}{2\sqrt{2}}\right)}{1 + \left(-\frac{2}{\sqrt{5}}\right)\left(-\frac{2}{2\sqrt{2}}\right)}$$

$$= \frac{-4\sqrt{2} + \sqrt{5}}{2\sqrt{10} + 2}$$

To find the quadrant of $s + t$, notice that $\sin(s + t) > 0$, which implies $s + t$ is in quadrant I or II. $\tan(s + t) < 0$, which implies $s + t$ is in quadrant II or IV. Therefore, $s + t$ is in quadrant II. Also notice that $\sin(s - t) > 0$, which implies $s - t$ is in quadrant I or II, and $\tan(s - t) < 0$, which implies $s - t$ is in quadrant II or IV. Therefore, $s - t$ is in quadrant II.

63. $\cos s = -\dfrac{8}{17}$, $\cos t = -\dfrac{3}{5}$, and s and t are in quadrant III.

Since s is in quadrant III, $\sin s < 0$.

$$\sin s = -\sqrt{1 - \left(-\dfrac{8}{17}\right)^2} = -\dfrac{15}{17}$$

Since t is in quadrant III, $\sin t < 0$.

$$\sin t = -\sqrt{1 - \left(-\dfrac{3}{5}\right)^2} = -\dfrac{4}{5}$$

$$\tan s = \dfrac{-\frac{15}{17}}{-\frac{8}{17}} = \dfrac{15}{8}$$

$$\tan t = \dfrac{-\frac{4}{5}}{-\frac{3}{5}} = \dfrac{4}{3}$$

$$\sin(s + t) = \left(-\dfrac{15}{17}\right)\left(-\dfrac{3}{5}\right) + \left(-\dfrac{4}{5}\right)\left(-\dfrac{8}{17}\right) = \dfrac{77}{85}$$

$$\sin(s - t) = \left(-\dfrac{15}{17}\right)\left(-\dfrac{3}{5}\right) - \left(-\dfrac{4}{5}\right)\left(-\dfrac{8}{17}\right) = \dfrac{13}{85}$$

$$\tan(s + t) = \dfrac{\frac{15}{8} + \frac{4}{3}}{1 - \left(\frac{15}{8}\right)\left(\frac{4}{3}\right)} = \dfrac{\frac{77}{24}}{-\frac{36}{24}} = -\dfrac{77}{36}$$

$$\tan(s - t) = \dfrac{\frac{15}{8} - \frac{4}{3}}{1 + \left(\frac{15}{8}\right)\left(\frac{4}{3}\right)} = \dfrac{13}{84}$$

To find the quadrant of $s + t$, notice that $\sin(s + t) > 0$, which implies $s + t$ is in quadrant I or II, and $\tan(s + t) < 0$, which implies $s + t$ is in quadrant II or IV. Therefore, $s + t$ is in quadrant II. Also notice that $\sin(s - t) > 0$, which implies $s - t$ is in quadrant I or II, and $\tan(s - t) > 0$, which implies $s - t$ is in quadrant I or III. Therefore, $s - t$ is in quadrant I.

65.

The graph of $y = \sin\left(\dfrac{\pi}{2} + x\right)$ appears to be the same as the graph of $y = \cos x$. Verify $\sin\left(\dfrac{\pi}{2} + x\right) = \cos x$.

$$\sin\left(\dfrac{\pi}{2} + x\right) = \sin\dfrac{\pi}{2}\cos x + \sin x \cos\dfrac{\pi}{2}$$
$$= 1 \cdot \cos x + \sin x \cdot 0$$
$$= \cos x$$

73. $\sin 165° = \sin(180° - 15°)$
$$= \sin 180° \cos 15° - \cos 180° \sin 15°$$
$$= \sin 15°$$
$$= \sin(45° - 30°)$$
$$= \sin 45° \cos 30° - \cos 45° \sin 30°$$
$$= \dfrac{\sqrt{2}}{2}\cdot\dfrac{\sqrt{3}}{2} - \dfrac{\sqrt{2}}{2}\cdot\dfrac{1}{2}$$
$$= \dfrac{\sqrt{6} - \sqrt{2}}{4}$$

75. $\sin 255° = \sin(270° - 15°)$
$$= \sin 270° \cos 15° - \cos 270° \sin 15°$$
$$= -\cos 15°$$
$$= -\cos(45° - 30°)$$
$$= -(\cos 45° \cos 30° + \sin 45° \sin 30°)$$
$$= -\left(\dfrac{\sqrt{2}}{2}\cdot\dfrac{\sqrt{3}}{2} + \dfrac{\sqrt{2}}{2}\cdot\dfrac{1}{2}\right)$$
$$= -\left(\dfrac{\sqrt{6}}{4} + \dfrac{\sqrt{2}}{4}\right)$$
$$= \dfrac{-\sqrt{6} - \sqrt{2}}{4}$$

77. $\tan\dfrac{11\pi}{12} = \tan\left(\pi - \dfrac{\pi}{12}\right)$
$$= \dfrac{\tan\pi - \tan\frac{\pi}{12}}{1 + \tan\pi\tan\frac{\pi}{12}}$$
$$= -\tan\dfrac{\pi}{12}$$
$$= -\tan\left(\dfrac{\pi}{4} - \dfrac{\pi}{6}\right)$$
$$= -\dfrac{\tan\frac{\pi}{4} - \tan\frac{\pi}{6}}{1 + \tan\frac{\pi}{4}\tan\frac{\pi}{6}}$$
$$= -\dfrac{3 - \sqrt{3}}{3 + \sqrt{3}}\cdot\dfrac{3 - \sqrt{3}}{3 - \sqrt{3}}$$
$$= -\dfrac{12 - 6\sqrt{3}}{6}$$
$$= -2 + \sqrt{3}$$

81. Since $V = 163 \sin \omega t$ and the maximum value of $\sin \omega t$ is 1, the maximum voltage is 163.
Since $V = 163 \sin \omega t$ and the minimum value of $\sin \omega t$ is -1, the minimum voltage is -163.
Therefore, the voltage is not always equal to 115.

83. $e = 20 \sin\left(\dfrac{\pi t}{4} - \dfrac{\pi}{2}\right)$

$= 20\left[\sin\left(\dfrac{\pi t}{4}\right)\cos\left(\dfrac{\pi}{2}\right) - \cos\left(\dfrac{\pi t}{4}\right)\sin\left(\dfrac{\pi}{2}\right)\right]$

$= 20\left[\sin\left(\dfrac{\pi t}{4}\right)(0) - \cos\left(\dfrac{\pi t}{4}\right)(1)\right]$

$= -20\cos\left(\dfrac{\pi t}{4}\right)$

85. (a) $F = \dfrac{.6W\sin(\theta + 90)°}{\sin 12°}$

$= \dfrac{.6(170)\sin(30 + 90)°}{\sin 12°}$

≈ 425 lb

(This is a good reason why people frequently have back problems.)

(b) $F = \dfrac{.6W\sin(\theta + 90)°}{\sin 12°}$

$= \dfrac{.6W(\sin\theta°\cos 90° + \sin 90°\cos\theta°)}{\sin 12°}$

$= \dfrac{.6}{\sin 12°}W\cos\theta$

$\approx 2.9W\cos\theta$

(c) F will be maximum when $\cos\theta = 1$ or $\theta = 0°$. ($\theta = 0°$ corresponds to the back being horizontal which gives a maximum force on the back muscles. This agrees with intuition since stress on the back increases as one bends farther until the back is parallel with the ground.)

Section 6.4

Exercises

1. $\cos 2\theta = \dfrac{3}{5}$, θ is in quadrant I.

$\cos 2\theta = 2\cos^2\theta - 1$

$\dfrac{3}{5} = 2\cos^2\theta - 1$

$2\cos^2\theta = \dfrac{3}{5} + 1 = \dfrac{8}{5}$

$\cos^2\theta = \dfrac{8}{10} = \dfrac{4}{5}$

Since θ is in quadrant I, $\cos\theta > 0$.

$\cos\theta = \dfrac{2}{\sqrt{5}} = \dfrac{2\sqrt{5}}{5}$

Since θ is in quadrant I, $\sin\theta > 0$.

$\sin\theta = \sqrt{1 - \cos^2\theta}$

$= \sqrt{1 - \left(\dfrac{2\sqrt{5}}{5}\right)^2}$

$= \sqrt{\dfrac{1}{5}}$

$= \dfrac{1}{\sqrt{5}}$

$= \dfrac{\sqrt{5}}{5}$

$\tan\theta = \dfrac{\sin\theta}{\cos\theta} = \dfrac{\frac{\sqrt{5}}{5}}{\frac{2\sqrt{5}}{5}} = \dfrac{1}{2}$

$\cot\theta = \dfrac{1}{\tan\theta} = \dfrac{1}{\frac{1}{2}} = 2$

$\sec\theta = \dfrac{1}{\cos\theta} = \dfrac{1}{\frac{2\sqrt{5}}{5}} = \dfrac{5}{2\sqrt{5}} = \dfrac{\sqrt{5}}{2}$

$\csc\theta = \dfrac{1}{\sin\theta} = \dfrac{1}{\frac{\sqrt{5}}{5}} = \sqrt{5}$

3. $\cos 2x = -\dfrac{5}{12}$, $\dfrac{\pi}{2} < x < \pi$

$\cos 2x = 2\cos^2 x - 1$

$2\cos^2 x = \cos 2x + 1$

$= -\dfrac{5}{12} + 1$

$= \dfrac{7}{12}$

$\cos^2 x = \dfrac{7}{24}$

Since $\frac{\pi}{2} < x < \pi$, $\cos x < 0$.

$\cos x = -\sqrt{\frac{7}{24}} = -\frac{\sqrt{7}}{2\sqrt{6}} = -\frac{\sqrt{42}}{12}$

$\sin^2 x = 1 - \cos^2 x = 1 - \frac{7}{24} = \frac{17}{24}$

Since $\frac{\pi}{2} < x < \pi$, $\sin x > 0$.

$\sin x = \frac{\sqrt{17}}{2\sqrt{6}} = \frac{\sqrt{102}}{12}$

$\tan x = \frac{\frac{\sqrt{17}}{2\sqrt{6}}}{-\frac{\sqrt{7}}{2\sqrt{6}}} = -\frac{\sqrt{17}}{\sqrt{7}} = -\frac{\sqrt{119}}{7}$

$\cot x = -\frac{\sqrt{7}}{\sqrt{17}} = -\frac{\sqrt{119}}{17}$

$\sec x = -\frac{2\sqrt{6}}{\sqrt{7}} = -\frac{2\sqrt{42}}{7}$

$\csc x = \frac{2\sqrt{6}}{\sqrt{17}} = \frac{2\sqrt{102}}{17}$

5. $\sin\theta = \frac{2}{5}$, $\cos\theta < 0$

$\cos 2\theta = 1 - 2\sin^2\theta$

$= 1 - 2\left(\frac{2}{5}\right)^2$

$= 1 - \frac{8}{25}$

$= \frac{17}{25}$

$\cos^2 2\theta + \sin^2 2\theta = 1$

$\sin^2 2\theta = 1 - \cos^2 2\theta = 1 - \left(\frac{17}{25}\right)^2 = \frac{336}{625}$

Since $\cos\theta < 0$, $\sin 2\theta < 0$ because $\sin 2\theta = 2\sin\theta\cos\theta < 0$.

$\sin 2\theta = -\sqrt{\frac{336}{625}} = -\frac{4\sqrt{21}}{25}$

$\tan 2\theta = \frac{\sin 2\theta}{\cos 2\theta} = \frac{-\frac{4\sqrt{21}}{25}}{\frac{17}{25}} = -\frac{4\sqrt{21}}{17}$

$\cot 2\theta = -\frac{17}{4\sqrt{21}} = -\frac{17\sqrt{21}}{84}$

$\sec 2\theta = \frac{25}{17}$

$\csc 2\theta = -\frac{25}{4\sqrt{21}} = -\frac{25\sqrt{21}}{84}$

7. $\tan x = 2$, $\cos x > 0$

$\tan 2x = \frac{2\tan x}{1 - \tan^2 x}$

$= \frac{2(2)}{1 - (2)^2} = -\frac{4}{3}$

Since both $\tan x$ and $\cos x$ are positive, x must be in quadrant I. Thus, $2x$ must be in quadrant II.

$\sec^2 2x = 1 + \tan^2 2x = 1 + \frac{16}{9} = \frac{25}{9}$

$\sec 2x = -\frac{5}{3}$

$\cos 2x = \frac{1}{\sec 2x} = -\frac{3}{5}$

$\cot 2x = \frac{1}{\tan 2x} = -\frac{3}{4}$

$\sin 2x = \tan 2x\cos 2x = \left(-\frac{4}{3}\right)\left(-\frac{3}{5}\right) = \frac{4}{5}$

$\csc 2x = \frac{1}{\sin 2x} = \frac{5}{4}$

9. $\sin\alpha = -\frac{\sqrt{5}}{7}$, $\cos\alpha > 0$

$\cos^2\alpha = 1 - \sin^2 a = 1 - \left(-\frac{\sqrt{5}}{7}\right)^2 = \frac{44}{49}$

Since $\cos\alpha > 0$,

$\cos\alpha = \sqrt{\frac{44}{49}} = \frac{\sqrt{44}}{7} = \frac{2\sqrt{11}}{7}$.

$\cos 2\alpha = 1 - 2\sin^2\alpha = 1 - 2\left(\frac{\sqrt{5}}{7}\right)^2 = \frac{39}{49}$

$\sin 2\alpha = 2\sin\alpha\cos\alpha = 2\left(-\frac{\sqrt{5}}{7}\right)\left(\frac{2\sqrt{11}}{7}\right) = -\frac{4\sqrt{55}}{49}$

$\tan 2\alpha = \frac{\sin 2\alpha}{\cos 2\alpha} = \frac{-\frac{4\sqrt{55}}{49}}{\frac{39}{49}} = -\frac{4\sqrt{55}}{39}$

$\cot 2\alpha = \frac{1}{\tan 2\alpha} = -\frac{39\sqrt{55}}{220}$

$\sec 2\alpha = \frac{1}{\cos 2\alpha} = \frac{49}{39}$

$\csc 2\alpha = \frac{1}{\sin 2\alpha} = -\frac{49\sqrt{55}}{220}$

11. $\sin 2X = 2\sin X\cos X$

$\sin X\cos X = \frac{1}{2}\sin 2X$

If $\sin 2X = .4$, then $\sin X\cos X = \frac{1}{2}(.4) = .2$.

Therefore, the screen will display .2 for the final expression.

13. $\cos^2 15° - \sin^2 15° = \cos 30° = \dfrac{\sqrt{3}}{2}$

15. $1 - 2\sin^2 15° = \cos 30° = \dfrac{\sqrt{3}}{2}$

17. $2\cos^2 67\dfrac{1}{2}° - 1 = \cos^2 67\dfrac{1}{2}° - \sin^2 67\dfrac{1}{2}°$

$\qquad\qquad = \cos 2\left(67\dfrac{1}{2}°\right)$

$\qquad\qquad = \cos 135°$

$\qquad\qquad = -\dfrac{\sqrt{2}}{2}$

19. $\dfrac{\tan 51°}{1 - \tan^2 51°}$

Since $\dfrac{2\tan A}{1 - \tan^2 A} = \tan 2A$, then

$\dfrac{1}{2}\left(\dfrac{2\tan A}{1 - \tan^2 A}\right) = \dfrac{1}{2}\tan 2A$

$\dfrac{\tan A}{1 - \tan^2 A} = \dfrac{1}{2}\tan 2A.$

$\dfrac{\tan 51°}{1 - \tan^2 51°} = \dfrac{1}{2}\tan 2(51°)$

$\qquad\qquad = \dfrac{1}{2}\tan 102°$

21. $\dfrac{1}{4} - \dfrac{1}{2}\sin^2 47.1° = \dfrac{1}{4}\left(1 - 2\sin^2 47.1°\right)$

Since $\cos 2A = 1 - 2\sin^2 A$,

$\dfrac{1}{4}\left(1 - 2\sin^2 47.1°\right) = \dfrac{1}{4}\cos 2(47.1°)$

$\qquad\qquad\qquad = \dfrac{1}{4}\cos 94.2°.$

23.

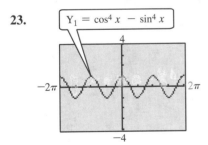

$Y_1 = \cos^4 x - \sin^4 x$

The graph of $y = \cos^4 x - \sin^4 x$ appears to be the same as the graph of $y = \cos 2x$.

$\cos^4 x - \sin^4 x = \left(\cos^2 x + \sin^2 x\right)\left(\cos^2 x - \sin^2 x\right)$

$\qquad\qquad = 1 \cdot \cos 2x$

$\qquad\qquad = \cos 2x$

25. Verify $\left(\sin \gamma + \cos \gamma\right)^2 = \sin 2\gamma + 1.$

$\left(\sin \gamma + \cos \gamma\right)^2 = \sin^2 \gamma + \cos^2 \gamma + 2\sin \gamma \cos \gamma$

$\qquad\qquad = 1 + \sin 2\gamma$

27. Verify $\sin 4\alpha = 4\sin \alpha \cos \alpha \cos 2\alpha.$
Work with the right side.

$4\sin \alpha \cos \alpha \cos 2\alpha = 2(2\sin \alpha \cos \alpha)\cos 2\alpha$

$\qquad\qquad = 2\sin 2\alpha \cos 2\alpha$

$\qquad\qquad = \sin 2(2\alpha)$

$\qquad\qquad = \sin 4\alpha$

29. Verify $\dfrac{2\cos 2\alpha}{\sin 2\alpha} = \cot \alpha - \tan \alpha.$
Work with the right side.

$\cot \alpha - \tan \alpha = \dfrac{\cos \alpha}{\sin \alpha} - \dfrac{\sin \alpha}{\cos \alpha}$

$\qquad\qquad = \dfrac{\cos^2 \alpha - \sin^2 \alpha}{\sin \alpha \cos \alpha}$

$\qquad\qquad = \dfrac{2\left(\cos^2 \alpha - \sin^2 \alpha\right)}{2\sin \alpha \cos \alpha}$

$\qquad\qquad = \dfrac{2\cos 2\alpha}{\sin 2\alpha}$

31. Verify $\sin 2\alpha \cos 2\alpha = \sin 2\alpha - 4\sin^3 \alpha \cos \alpha.$

$\sin 2\alpha \cos 2\alpha = (2\sin \alpha \cos \alpha)\left(1 - 2\sin^2 \alpha\right)$

$\qquad\qquad = 2\sin \alpha \cos \alpha - 4\sin^3 \alpha \cos \alpha$

$\qquad\qquad = \sin 2\alpha - 4\sin^3 \alpha \cos \alpha$

33. Verify $\tan s + \cot s = 2\csc 2s.$

$\tan s + \cot s = \dfrac{\sin s}{\cos s} + \dfrac{\cos s}{\sin s}$

$\qquad\qquad = \dfrac{\sin^2 s + \cos^2 s}{\cos s \sin s}$

$\qquad\qquad = \dfrac{1}{\cos s \sin s}$

$\qquad\qquad = \dfrac{2}{2\cos s \sin s}$

$\qquad\qquad = \dfrac{2}{\sin 2s}$

$\qquad\qquad = 2\csc 2s$

35. Verify $\sec^2 \dfrac{x}{2} = \dfrac{2}{1+\cos x}$.

$$\sec^2 \frac{x}{2} = \frac{1}{\cos^2 \frac{x}{2}}$$

$$= \frac{1}{\left(\pm\sqrt{\frac{1+\cos x}{2}}\right)^2}$$

$$= \frac{1}{\frac{1+\cos x}{2}}$$

$$= \frac{2}{1+\cos x}$$

37. Verify $\sin^2 \dfrac{x}{2} = \dfrac{\tan x - \sin x}{2\tan x}$.

Work with the left side.

$$\sin^2 \frac{x}{2} = \left(\pm\sqrt{\frac{1-\cos x}{2}}\right)^2$$

$$= \frac{1-\cos x}{2}$$

Work with the right side.

$$\frac{\tan x - \sin x}{2\tan x} = \frac{\frac{\sin x}{\cos x} - \sin x}{2\frac{\sin x}{\cos x}}$$

$$= \frac{\sin x - \cos x \sin x}{2\sin x}$$

$$= \frac{1-\cos x}{2}$$

39. $\cos 3x = \cos(2x + x)$

$$= \cos 2x \cos x - \sin 2x \sin x$$

$$= (1 - 2\sin^2 x)\cos x - (2\sin x \cos x)\sin x$$

$$= \cos x - 2\sin^2 x \cos x - 2\sin^2 x \cos x$$

$$= \cos x - 4\sin^2 x \cos x$$

$$= \cos x(1 - 4\sin^2 x)$$

$$= \cos x[1 - 4(1 - \cos^2 x)]$$

$$= \cos x[-3 + 4\cos^2 x]$$

$$= -3\cos x + 4\cos^3 x$$

41. $\tan 3x = \tan(2x + x)$

$$= \frac{\tan 2x + \tan x}{1 - \tan 2x \tan x}$$

$$= \frac{\frac{2\tan x}{1-\tan^2 x} + \tan x}{1 - \frac{2\tan x}{1-\tan^2 x}\tan x}$$

$$= \frac{2\tan x + \tan x - \tan^3 x}{1 - \tan^2 x - 2\tan^2 x}$$

$$= \frac{3\tan x - \tan^3 x}{1 - 3\tan^2 x}$$

43. $2\sin 58° \cos 102°$

$$= 2\left(\frac{1}{2}[\sin(58° + 102°) + \sin(58° - 102°)]\right)$$

$$= \sin 160° + \sin(-44°)$$

$$= \sin 160° - \sin 44°$$

45. $2\cos 85° \sin 140°$

$$= 2\left(\frac{1}{2}[\sin(85° + 140°) - \sin(85° - 140°)]\right)$$

$$= \sin 225° - \sin(-55°)$$

$$= \sin 225° + \sin 55°$$

47. $\cos 4x - \cos 2x = -2\sin\left(\dfrac{4x + 2x}{2}\right)\sin\left(\dfrac{4x - 2x}{2}\right)$

$$= -2\sin\frac{6x}{2}\sin\frac{2x}{2}$$

$$= -2\sin 3x \sin x$$

49. $\sin 25° + \sin(-48°)$

$$= 2\sin\left(\frac{25° + (-48°)}{2}\right)\cos\left(\frac{25° - (-48°)}{2}\right)$$

$$= 2\sin\frac{-23°}{2}\cos\frac{73°}{2}$$

$$= 2\sin{-11.5°}\cos 36.5°$$

$$= -2\sin 11.5° \cos 36.5°$$

51. $\cos 4x + \cos 8x = 2\cos\left(\dfrac{4x + 8x}{2}\right)\cos\left(\dfrac{4x - 8x}{2}\right)$

$$= 2\cos\frac{12x}{2}\cos\frac{-4x}{2}$$

$$= 2\cos 6x \cos(-2x)$$

$$= 2\cos 6x \cos 2x$$

53. $\dfrac{1}{2}\sin x + \dfrac{\sqrt{3}}{2}\cos x$

$$a = \frac{1}{2}, \ b = \frac{\sqrt{3}}{2}$$

$$\sqrt{a^2 + b^2} = \sqrt{\left(\frac{1}{2}\right)^2 + \left(\frac{\sqrt{3}}{2}\right)^2}$$

$$= \sqrt{\frac{1}{4} + \frac{3}{4}}$$

$$= \sqrt{1}$$

$$= 1$$

$$\sin \alpha = \frac{b}{\sqrt{a^2 + b^2}}$$

$$= \frac{\frac{\sqrt{3}}{2}}{1}$$

$$= \frac{\sqrt{3}}{2}$$

$$\cos\alpha = \frac{a}{\sqrt{a^2+b^2}}$$

$$= \frac{\frac{1}{2}}{1}$$

$$= \frac{1}{2}$$

Since $\sin\alpha = \frac{\sqrt{3}}{2}$ and $\cos\alpha = \frac{1}{2}$, $\alpha = 60°$.

$$\frac{1}{2}\sin x + \frac{\sqrt{3}}{2}\cos x = \sqrt{a^2+b^2}\,\sin(x+\alpha)$$

$$= 1\cdot\sin(x+60°)$$

$$= \sin(x+60°)$$

55. $7\cos x - 24\cos x$

$a = 7,\ b = -24$

$$\sqrt{a^2+b^2} = \sqrt{7^2+(-24)^2}$$

$$= \sqrt{49+576}$$

$$= \sqrt{625}$$

$$= 25$$

$$\sin\alpha = \frac{b}{\sqrt{a^2+b^2}}$$

$$= \frac{-24}{25}$$

$$= -\frac{24}{25}$$

$$\cos\alpha = \frac{a}{\sqrt{a^2+b^2}}$$

$$= \frac{7}{25}$$

Since $\sin\alpha = -\frac{24}{25}$ and $\cos\alpha = \frac{7}{25}$, $\alpha \approx 286°$.

$$7\cos x - 24\cos x = \sqrt{a^2+b^2}\,\sin(x+\alpha)$$

$$= 25\sin(x+286°)$$

57. $\sin 67.5° = \sin\left(\dfrac{135°}{2}\right)$

Since $67.5°$ is in quadrant I, $\sin 67.5° > 0$.

$$\sin 67.5° = \sqrt{\frac{1-\cos 135°}{2}}$$

$$= \sqrt{\frac{1+\cos 45°}{2}}$$

$$= \sqrt{\frac{1+\frac{\sqrt{2}}{2}}{2}}$$

$$= \sqrt{\frac{2+\sqrt{2}}{4}}$$

$$= \frac{\sqrt{2+\sqrt{2}}}{2}$$

59. $\cos 195° = \cos\left(\dfrac{390°}{2}\right)$

Since $195°$ is in quadrant III, $\cos 195° < 0$.

$$\cos 195° = -\sqrt{\frac{1+\cos 390°}{2}}$$

$$= -\sqrt{\frac{1+\cos 30°}{2}}$$

$$= -\sqrt{\frac{1+\frac{\sqrt{3}}{2}}{2}}$$

$$= -\sqrt{\frac{2+\sqrt{3}}{4}}$$

$$= \frac{-\sqrt{2+\sqrt{3}}}{2}$$

61. $\cos 165° = \cos\left(\dfrac{330°}{2}\right)$

Since $165°$ is in quadrant II, $\cos 165° < 0$.

$$\cos 165° = -\sqrt{\frac{1+\cos 330°}{2}}$$

$$= -\sqrt{\frac{1+\cos 30°}{2}}$$

$$= -\sqrt{\frac{1+\frac{\sqrt{3}}{2}}{2}}$$

$$= -\sqrt{\frac{2+\sqrt{3}}{4}}$$

$$= \frac{-\sqrt{2+\sqrt{3}}}{2}$$

65. Find $\cos\dfrac{\theta}{2}$, given $\cos\theta = \dfrac{1}{4}$, with $0 < \theta < \dfrac{\pi}{2}$.

$$0 < \theta < \frac{\pi}{2}$$

$$0 < \frac{\theta}{2} < \frac{\pi}{4}$$

Thus, $\cos\dfrac{\theta}{2} > 0$.

$$\cos\frac{\theta}{2} = \sqrt{\frac{1+\cos\theta}{2}}$$

$$= \sqrt{\frac{1+\frac{1}{4}}{2}}$$

$$= \sqrt{\frac{5}{8}}$$

$$= \frac{\sqrt{10}}{4}$$

67. Find $\tan\dfrac{\theta}{2}$, given $\sin\theta=\dfrac{3}{5}$, with $90°<\theta<180°$.

Since $90°<\theta<180°$, $\cos\theta<0$.

$$\cos\theta=-\sqrt{1-\left(\dfrac{3}{5}\right)^2}=-\dfrac{4}{5}$$

$$\tan\dfrac{\theta}{2}=\dfrac{1-\cos\theta}{\sin\theta}=\dfrac{1-\left(-\frac{4}{5}\right)}{\frac{3}{5}}=3$$

69. Find $\sin\dfrac{\alpha}{2}$, given $\tan\alpha=2$, with $0<\alpha<\dfrac{\pi}{2}$.

Since α is in quadrant I, $\sec\alpha>0$.

$$\sec^2\alpha=\tan^2\alpha+1$$
$$=(2)^2+1$$
$$=5$$
$$\sec\alpha=\sqrt{5}$$
$$\cos\alpha=\dfrac{1}{\sec\alpha}=\dfrac{1}{\sqrt{5}}=\dfrac{\sqrt{5}}{5}$$

$0<\alpha<\dfrac{\pi}{2}$ so $0<\dfrac{\alpha}{2}<\dfrac{\pi}{4}$.

Thus, $\sin\dfrac{\alpha}{2}>0$.

$$\sin\dfrac{\alpha}{2}=\sqrt{\dfrac{1-\cos\alpha}{2}}$$
$$=\sqrt{\dfrac{1-\frac{\sqrt{5}}{5}}{2}}$$
$$=\dfrac{\sqrt{50-10\sqrt{5}}}{10}$$

71. Find $\tan\dfrac{\beta}{2}$, given $\tan\beta=\dfrac{\sqrt{7}}{3}$, with $180°<\beta<270°$.

$$\sec^2\beta=\tan^2\beta+1=\left(\dfrac{\sqrt{7}}{3}\right)^2+1=\dfrac{16}{9}$$

Since β is in quadrant III, $\sec\beta<0$ and $\sin\beta<0$.

$$\sec\beta=-\sqrt{\dfrac{16}{9}}=-\dfrac{4}{3}$$
$$\cos\beta=\dfrac{1}{\sec\beta}=\dfrac{1}{-\frac{4}{3}}=-\dfrac{3}{4}$$
$$\sin\beta=-\sqrt{1-\cos^2\beta}=-\sqrt{1-\dfrac{9}{16}}=-\dfrac{\sqrt{7}}{4}$$
$$\tan\dfrac{\beta}{2}=\dfrac{\sin\beta}{1+\cos\beta}=\dfrac{-\frac{\sqrt{7}}{4}}{1+\left(-\frac{3}{4}\right)}=-\sqrt{7}$$

73. $\sqrt{\dfrac{1-\cos40°}{2}}=\sin\dfrac{40°}{2}=\sin20°$

75. $\sqrt{\dfrac{1-\cos147°}{1+\cos147°}}=\tan\dfrac{147°}{2}=\tan73.5°$

77. $\dfrac{1-\cos59.74°}{\sin59.74°}=\tan\dfrac{59.74°}{2}=\tan29.87°$

81. $m=\dfrac{5}{4}$

$$\sin\dfrac{\alpha}{2}=\dfrac{1}{m}=\dfrac{4}{5}=.8$$
$$\dfrac{\alpha}{2}\approx53°$$
$$\alpha\approx106°$$

83. $\alpha=60°$

$$\sin\dfrac{\alpha}{2}=\dfrac{1}{m}$$
$$\dfrac{1}{m}=\sin30°=\dfrac{1}{2}$$
$$m=2$$

85. $\phi=68°47'=68.78333°$, $h=1145$ ft

Use a calculator and substitute these values in

$g=978.0542\left(1+.005297\sin^2\phi\right.$

$\left.-.0000059\sin^2 2\phi\right)-.000094h.$

$g=978.0524\left[1+.005297\sin^2 68.78333°\right.$

$\left.-.0000059\sin^2(2\cdot68.78333°)\right]$

$-.000094(1145)$

$=982.444$ cm per sec^2

87. (a) When $h=0$

$$D=\dfrac{v^2\sin\theta\cos\theta+v\cos\theta\sqrt{(v\sin\theta)^2+64\cdot0}}{32}$$
$$=\dfrac{v^2\sin\theta\cos\theta+v\cos\theta\sqrt{v^2\sin^2\theta}}{32}$$
$$=\dfrac{v^2\sin\theta\cos\theta+(v\cos\theta)(v\sin\theta)}{32}$$
$$=\dfrac{v^2\sin\theta\cos\theta+v^2\sin\theta\cos\theta}{32}$$
$$=\dfrac{2v^2\sin\theta\cos\theta}{32}$$
$$=\dfrac{v^2\sin(2\theta)}{32}$$

Which is dependent on both the velocity and angle at which the object is thrown.

(b) $D = \dfrac{(36)^2 \sin(2 \cdot 30)}{32}$

$= \dfrac{(1296)(0.866)}{32}$

$\approx 35 \text{ ft}$

89. (a) Graph $W = VI = \left[163\sin(120\pi t)\right]$
$\left[1.23\sin(120\pi t)\right]$ over the interval
$0 \le t \le .05$.

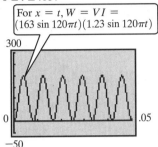

(b) The minimum wattage is 0 and the maximum wattage occurs whenever $\sin(120\pi t) = 1$.
This would be
$163(1.23) = 200.49$ watts.

(c) $\left[163\sin(120\pi t)\right]\!\left[1.23\sin(120\pi t)\right]$

$= 200.49\sin^2(120\pi t)$

$= 200.49\left[\dfrac{1}{2}\left(1 - \cos 240\pi t\right)\right]$

$= -100.245\cos 240\pi t + 100.245$
Then $a = -100.245$, $\omega = 240\pi$, and
$c = 100.245$.

(d) The graphs of
$W = \left[163\sin(120\pi t)\right]\!\left[1.23\sin(120\pi t)\right]$ and
$W = -100.245\cos 240\pi t + 100.245$ are the same.

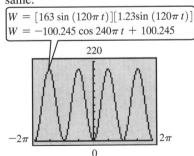

(e) The graph of W is vertically centered about the line $y = 100.245$. An estimate for the average wattage consumed is 100.245 watts. (For sinusoidal current, the average wattage consumed by an electrical device will be equal to half of the peak wattage.)

Section 6.5

Exercises

1. (a) $[-1, 1]$

   (b) $\left[-\dfrac{\pi}{2}, \dfrac{\pi}{2}\right]$

   (c) increasing

   (d) -2 is not in the domain.

3. (a) $(-\infty, \infty)$

   (b) $\left(-\dfrac{\pi}{2}, \dfrac{\pi}{2}\right)$

   (c) increasing

   (d) no

5. $y = \arcsin\left(-\dfrac{1}{2}\right)$

$\sin y = -\dfrac{1}{2}, \ -\dfrac{\pi}{2} \le y \le \dfrac{\pi}{2}$

y is in quadrant IV. The reference angle is $\dfrac{\pi}{6}$.

$y = -\dfrac{\pi}{6}$

7. $y = \tan^{-1} 1$

$\tan y = 1, \ -\dfrac{\pi}{2} < y < \dfrac{\pi}{2}$

y is in quadrant I.

$y = \dfrac{\pi}{4}$

9. $y = \cos^{-1}(-1)$

$\cos y = -1, \ 0 \le y \le \pi$

$y = \pi$

11. $y = \sin^{-1}(-1)$

$\sin y = -1, \ \dfrac{\pi}{2} \le y \le \dfrac{\pi}{2}$

Since $\sin \dfrac{\pi}{2} = 1, \ y = -\dfrac{\pi}{2}$.

13. $y = \arctan 0$

$\tan y = 0, \ -\dfrac{\pi}{2} < y < \dfrac{\pi}{2}$

Since $\tan 0 = 0, \ y = 0.$

15. $y = \arccos 0$

$\cos y = 0, \ 0 \le y \le \pi$

$y = \dfrac{\pi}{2}$

17. $y = \sin^{-1}\left(\dfrac{\sqrt{2}}{2}\right)$

$\sin y = \dfrac{\sqrt{2}}{2}, \ -\dfrac{\pi}{2} \le y \le \dfrac{\pi}{2}$

Since $\sin \dfrac{\pi}{4} = \dfrac{\sqrt{2}}{2}, \ y = \dfrac{\pi}{4}.$

19. $y = \arccos\left(-\dfrac{\sqrt{3}}{2}\right)$

$\cos y = -\dfrac{\sqrt{3}}{2}, \ 0 \le y \le \pi$

Since $\cos \dfrac{5\pi}{6} = -\dfrac{\sqrt{3}}{2}, \ y = \dfrac{5\pi}{6}.$

21. $y = \cot^{-1}(-1)$

$\cot y = -1, \ 0 < y < \pi$

y is in quadrant II. The reference angle is $\dfrac{\pi}{4}.$

$y = \dfrac{3\pi}{4}$

23. $y = \csc^{-1}(-2)$

$\csc y = -2, \ -\dfrac{\pi}{2} \le y \le \dfrac{\pi}{2}, \ y \ne 0$

y is in quadrant IV. The reference angle is $\dfrac{\pi}{6}.$

$y = -\dfrac{\pi}{6}$

25. $y = \text{arc sec}\left(\dfrac{2\sqrt{3}}{3}\right)$

$\sec y = \dfrac{2\sqrt{3}}{3}, \ 0 \le y \le \pi, \ y \ne \dfrac{\pi}{2}$

Since $\sec \dfrac{\pi}{6} = \dfrac{2\sqrt{3}}{3}, \ y = \dfrac{\pi}{6}.$

27. $y = \text{arccot}\left(\dfrac{\sqrt{3}}{3}\right)$

$\cot y = \dfrac{\sqrt{3}}{3}, \ -\dfrac{\pi}{2} \le y \le \dfrac{\pi}{2}, \ y \ne 0$

Since $\cot \dfrac{\pi}{3} = \dfrac{\sqrt{3}}{3}, \ y = \dfrac{\pi}{3}.$

29. $\theta = \arctan(-1)$

$\tan \theta = -1, \ -90° < \theta < 90°$

θ is in quadrant IV. The reference angle is $45°$.
Thus, $\theta = -45°.$

31. $\theta = \arcsin\left(-\dfrac{\sqrt{3}}{2}\right)$

$\sin \theta = -\dfrac{\sqrt{3}}{2}, -90° \le \theta \le 90°$

θ is in quadrant IV. The reference angle is $60°$.
$\theta = -60°.$

33. $\theta = \cot^{-1}\left(-\dfrac{\sqrt{3}}{3}\right)$

$\cot \theta = -\dfrac{\sqrt{3}}{3}, \ 0° < \theta < 180°$

θ is in quadrant II. The reference angle is $60°$.
$\theta = 180° - 60° = 120°$

35. $\theta = \csc^{-1}(-2)$

$\csc \theta = -2$ and $-90° < \theta < 90°, \ \theta \ne 0°$

θ is in quadrant IV. The reference angle is $30°$.
$\theta = -30°$

For Exercises 37–41, be sure that your calculator is in degree mode. Keystroke sequences may vary based on the type and/or model of calculator being used.

37. $\theta = \sin^{-1}(-.13349122)$

Enter: 1.3349122 $\boxed{+/-}$ $\boxed{\text{INV}}$ $\boxed{\text{SIN}}$
or $\boxed{\text{2nd}}$ $\boxed{\text{SIN}}$ $\boxed{(-)}$ .13349122 $\boxed{\text{ENTER}}$
Display: -7.6713835

$\sin^{-1}(-.13349122) = -7.6713835°$

39. $\theta = \arccos(-.39876459)$

Enter: .39876459 $\boxed{+/-}$ $\boxed{\text{INV}}$ $\boxed{\text{COS}}$
or $\boxed{\text{2nd}}$ $\boxed{\text{COS}}$ $\boxed{(-)}$ .39876459 $\boxed{\text{ENTER}}$
Display: 113.50097

$\arccos(-.39876459) = 113.50097°$

41. $\theta = \csc^{-1} 1.9422833$

Enter: 1.9422833 $\boxed{1/x}$ $\boxed{\text{INV}}$ $\boxed{\text{SIN}}$
or $\boxed{\text{2nd}}$ $\boxed{\text{SIN}}$ 1.9422833 $\boxed{x^{-1}}$ $\boxed{\text{ENTER}}$
Display: 30.987961

$\csc^{-1} 1.9422833 = 30.987961°$

For Exercises 43–47, be sure that your calculator is in radian mode. Keystroke sequences may vary based on the type and/or model of calculator being used.

43. $y = \arctan 1.1111111$
Enter 1.1111111 [INV] [TAN]
or [2nd] [TAN] 1.1111111 [ENTER]
Display: .83798122
$\arctan 1.1111111 = .83798122$

45. $y = \cot^{-1}(-.92170128)$
Enter:
.92170128 [+/−] [1/x] [INV] [TAN] [+] [π]
or
[2nd] [TAN] [(−)] .92170128 [x⁻¹] [+] [π] [ENTER]
Display: 2.3154725
$\cot^{-1}(-.91270128) = 2.3154725$

47. $y = \arcsin .92837781$
Enter: .92837781 [INV] [SIN]
or [2nd] [SIN] .92837781 [ENTER]
Display: 1.1900238
$\arcsin .92837781 = 1.1900238$

49.
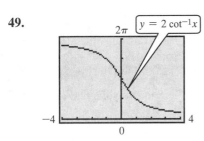
Domain: $(-\infty, \infty)$
Range: $(0, 2\pi)$

51.
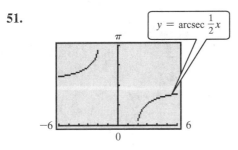
Domain: $(-\infty, -2] \cup [2, \infty)$
Range: $\left[0, \dfrac{\pi}{2}\right) \cup \left(\dfrac{\pi}{2}, \pi\right]$

52.
$$f[f^{-1}(x)] = f\left[\frac{x+2}{3}\right]$$
$$= 3\left(\frac{x+2}{3}\right) - 2$$
$$= x + 2 - 2$$
$$= x$$
$$f^{-1}[f(x)] = f^{-1}[3x - 2]$$
$$= \frac{(3x-2)+2}{3}$$
$$= \frac{3x}{3}$$
$$= x$$

In each case the result is x. The graph is a straight line bisecting the first and third quadrants ($y = x$).

53.
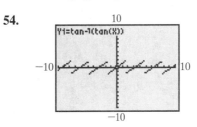

It is the graph of $y = x$.

54.
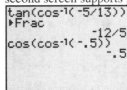

It does not agree because the range of the inverse tangent function is $\left(-\dfrac{\pi}{2}, \dfrac{\pi}{2}\right)$, not $(-\infty, \infty)$, as was the case in Exercise 53.

55. The first screen supports parts (b) and (c) and the second screen supports part (d).

```
tan(cos-1(-5/13))
▶Frac
               -12/5
cos(cos-1(-.5))
                  .5
```

```
cos-1(cos(5π/4))
         2.35619449
3π/4
         2.35619449
```

57. $\tan\left(\arccos\dfrac{3}{4}\right)$

Let $\omega = \arccos\dfrac{3}{4}$, so that $\cos\omega = \dfrac{3}{4}$. Since arccos is defined only in quadrants I and II, and $\dfrac{3}{4}$ is positive, ω is in quadrant I. Sketch ω and label a triangle with the side opposite ω equal to $\sqrt{4^2 - 3^2} = \sqrt{7}$.

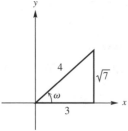

$\tan\left(\arccos\dfrac{3}{4}\right) = \tan\omega = \dfrac{\sqrt{7}}{3}$

59. $\cos(\tan^{-1}(-2))$

Let $\omega = \tan^{-1}(-2)$, so that $\tan w = -2$. Since $\tan^{-1}$ is defined only in quadrants I and IV, and -2 is negative, w is in quadrant IV. Sketch w and label a triangle with the hypotenuse equal to $\sqrt{(-2)^2 + 1} = \sqrt{5}$.

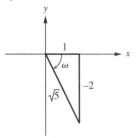

$\cos(\tan^{-1}(-2)) = \cos\omega = \dfrac{\sqrt{5}}{5}$

61. $\cot\left(\arcsin\left(-\dfrac{2}{3}\right)\right)$

Let $\omega = \arcsin\left(-\dfrac{2}{3}\right)$, so that $\sin\omega = -\dfrac{2}{3}$. Since arcsin is defined only in quadrants I and IV, and $-\dfrac{2}{3}$ is negative, w is in quadrant IV. Sketch w and label a triangle with the side adjacent to w equal to $\sqrt{3^2 - (-2)^2} = \sqrt{5}$.

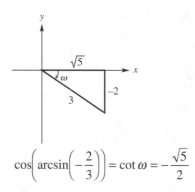

$\cos\left(\arcsin\left(-\dfrac{2}{3}\right)\right) = \cot\omega = -\dfrac{\sqrt{5}}{2}$

63. $\sec(\sec^{-1} 2)$

Since secant and inverse secant are inverse functions, $\sec(\sec^{-1} 2) = 2$.

65. $\arccos\left(\cos\dfrac{\pi}{4}\right) = \arccos\dfrac{\sqrt{2}}{2} = \dfrac{\pi}{4}$

67. $\arcsin\left(\sin\dfrac{\pi}{3}\right) = \arcsin\dfrac{\sqrt{3}}{2} = \dfrac{\pi}{3}$

69. $\sin\left(2\tan^{-1}\dfrac{12}{5}\right)$

Let $\omega = \tan^{-1}\dfrac{12}{5}$, so that $\tan\omega = \dfrac{12}{5}$. Since $\tan^{-1}$ is defined only in quadrants I and IV, and $\dfrac{12}{5}$ is positive, ω is in quadrant I. Sketch w and label a right triangle with the hypotenuse equal to $\sqrt{12^2 + 5^2} = 13$.

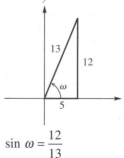

$\sin\omega = \dfrac{12}{13}$

$\cos\omega = \dfrac{5}{13}$

$\sin\left(2\tan^{-1}\dfrac{12}{5}\right) = \sin(2\omega)$

$= 2\sin\omega\cos\omega$

$= 2\left(\dfrac{12}{13}\right)\left(\dfrac{5}{13}\right)$

$= \dfrac{120}{169}$

71. $\cos\left(2\arctan\dfrac{4}{3}\right)$

Let $\omega = \arctan\dfrac{4}{3}$, so that $\tan\omega = \dfrac{4}{3}$. Since arctan is defined only in quadrants I and IV, and $\dfrac{4}{3}$ is positive, w is in quadrant I. Sketch w and label a triangle with the hypotenuse equal to $\sqrt{4^2 + 3^2} = 5$.

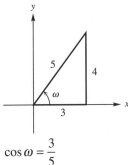

$\cos\omega = \dfrac{3}{5}$

$\sin\omega = \dfrac{4}{5}$

$\cos\left(2\arctan\dfrac{4}{3}\right) = \cos(2\omega)$

$\phantom{\cos\left(2\arctan\dfrac{4}{3}\right)} = \cos^2\omega - \sin^2\omega$

$\phantom{\cos\left(2\arctan\dfrac{4}{3}\right)} = \left(\dfrac{3}{5}\right)^2 - \left(\dfrac{4}{5}\right)^2$

$\phantom{\cos\left(2\arctan\dfrac{4}{3}\right)} = \dfrac{9}{25} - \dfrac{16}{25}$

$\phantom{\cos\left(2\arctan\dfrac{4}{3}\right)} = -\dfrac{7}{25}$

73. $\sin\left(2\cos^{-1}\dfrac{1}{5}\right)$

Let $\omega = \cos^{-1}\dfrac{1}{5}$, so that $\cos\omega = \dfrac{1}{5}$. Since $\cos^{-1}$ is defined only in quadrants I and II, and $\dfrac{1}{5}$ is positive, w is in quadrant I. Sketch w and label a triangle with the side opposite w equal to $\sqrt{5^2 - 1^2} = \sqrt{24} = 2\sqrt{6}$.

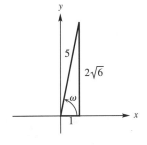

$\sin\omega = \dfrac{2\sqrt{6}}{5}$

$\cos\omega = \dfrac{1}{5}$

$\sin\left(2\cos^{-1}\dfrac{1}{5}\right) = \sin 2\omega$

$\phantom{\sin\left(2\cos^{-1}\dfrac{1}{5}\right)} = 2\sin\omega\cos\omega$

$\phantom{\sin\left(2\cos^{-1}\dfrac{1}{5}\right)} = 2\left(\dfrac{2\sqrt{6}}{5}\right)\left(\dfrac{1}{5}\right)$

$\phantom{\sin\left(2\cos^{-1}\dfrac{1}{5}\right)} = \dfrac{4\sqrt{6}}{25}$

75. $\tan\left(2\arcsin\left(-\dfrac{3}{5}\right)\right)$

Let $\omega = \arcsin\left(-\dfrac{3}{5}\right)$, so that $\sin\omega = -\dfrac{3}{5}$. Since arcsin is defined only in quadrants I and IV, and $-\dfrac{3}{5}$ is negative, w is in quadrant IV. Sketch w and label a triangle with the side adjacent to w equal to $\sqrt{5^2 - (-3)^2} = 4$.

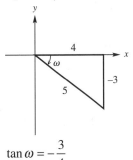

$\tan\omega = -\dfrac{3}{4}$

$\tan\left(2\arcsin\left(-\dfrac{3}{5}\right)\right) = \tan(2\omega)$

$\phantom{\tan\left(2\arcsin\left(-\dfrac{3}{5}\right)\right)} = \dfrac{2\tan\omega}{1 - \tan^2\omega}$

$\phantom{\tan\left(2\arcsin\left(-\dfrac{3}{5}\right)\right)} = \dfrac{2\left(-\frac{3}{4}\right)}{1 - \left(-\frac{3}{4}\right)^2}$

$\phantom{\tan\left(2\arcsin\left(-\dfrac{3}{5}\right)\right)} = \dfrac{-\frac{3}{2}}{1 - \frac{9}{16}} \cdot \dfrac{16}{16}$

$\phantom{\tan\left(2\arcsin\left(-\dfrac{3}{5}\right)\right)} = \dfrac{-24}{16 - 9}$

$\phantom{\tan\left(2\arcsin\left(-\dfrac{3}{5}\right)\right)} = -\dfrac{24}{7}$

77. $\sin\left(\sin^{-1}\dfrac{1}{2}+\tan^{-1}(-3)\right)$

Let $\omega_1 = \sin^{-1}\dfrac{1}{2}$, $-\dfrac{\pi}{2}\le\omega_1\le\dfrac{\pi}{2}$.

$\sin\omega_1 = \dfrac{1}{2}$; ω_1 is in quadrant I.

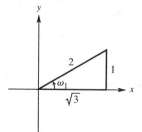

$\cos\omega_1 = \dfrac{\sqrt{3}}{2}$, $\sin\omega_1 = \dfrac{1}{2}$

Let $\omega_2 = \tan^{-1}(-3)$, $-\dfrac{\pi}{2}<\omega_2<\dfrac{\pi}{2}$.

$\tan\omega_2 = -3 = -\dfrac{3}{1}$. ω_2 is in quadrant IV.

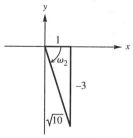

$\cos\omega_2 = \dfrac{1}{\sqrt{10}} = \dfrac{\sqrt{10}}{10}$

$\sin\omega_2 = \dfrac{-3}{\sqrt{10}} = -\dfrac{3\sqrt{10}}{10}$

$\sin\left(\sin^{-1}\dfrac{1}{2}+\tan^{-1}(-3)\right)$

$=\sin(\omega_1+\omega_2)$

$=\sin\omega_1\cos\omega_2+\cos\omega_1\sin\omega_2$

$=\left(\dfrac{1}{2}\right)\left(\dfrac{\sqrt{10}}{10}\right)+\left(\dfrac{\sqrt{3}}{2}\right)\left(\dfrac{-3\sqrt{10}}{10}\right)$

$=\dfrac{\sqrt{10}}{20}-\dfrac{3\sqrt{30}}{20}$

$=\dfrac{\sqrt{10}-3\sqrt{30}}{20}$

79. $\cos\left(\arcsin\dfrac{3}{5}+\arccos\dfrac{5}{13}\right)$

Let $\omega_1 = \arcsin\dfrac{3}{5}$, $-\dfrac{\pi}{2}\le\omega_1\le\dfrac{\pi}{2}$.

$\sin\omega_1 = \dfrac{3}{5}$, ω_1 is in quadrant I.

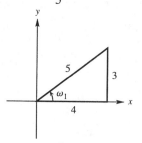

$\cos\omega_1 = \dfrac{4}{5}$

$\sin\omega_1 = \dfrac{3}{5}$

Let $\omega_2 = \arccos\dfrac{5}{13}$, $0\le\omega\le\pi$.

$\cos\omega_2 = \dfrac{5}{13}$, ω_2 is in quadrant I.

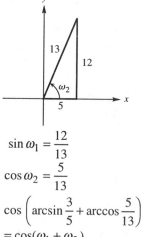

$\sin\omega_1 = \dfrac{12}{13}$

$\cos\omega_2 = \dfrac{5}{13}$

$\cos\left(\arcsin\dfrac{3}{5}+\arccos\dfrac{5}{13}\right)$

$=\cos(\omega_1+\omega_2)$

$=\cos\omega_1\cos\omega_2-\sin\omega_1\sin\omega_2$

$=\left(\dfrac{4}{5}\right)\left(\dfrac{5}{13}\right)-\left(\dfrac{3}{5}\right)\left(\dfrac{12}{13}\right)$

$=\dfrac{20}{65}-\dfrac{36}{65}=-\dfrac{16}{65}$

For Exercises 81–83, be sure that your calculator is in degree mode. Keystroke sequences may vary based on the type and/or model of calculator being used.

81. $\cos(\tan^{-1}.5)$

Enter: .5 [INV] [TAN] [COS]

or [COS] [2nd] [TAN] .5 [ENTER]

$\cos(\tan^{-1}.5) = .894427191$

83. tan (arcsin .12251014)

Enter: .12251014 [INV] [SIN] [TAN]

or [TAN] [2nd] [SIN] .12251014 [ENTER]

tan (arcsin .12251014) = .1234399811

85. sin (arccos u)

Let $w = \arccos u,\ 0 \le w \le \pi$.

$$\cos \omega = u = \frac{u}{1}$$

If $u > 0$, then w is in quadrant I.

If $u < 0$, then w is in quadrant II.

In either quadrant, sin $w > 0$.

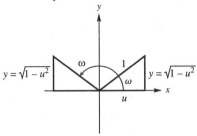

Since $y > 0$, from the Pythagorean theorem,

$$y = \sqrt{1-u^2}\,.$$

$$\sin \omega = \frac{\sqrt{1-u^2}}{1} = \sqrt{1-u^2}$$

Then $\sin(\arccos u) = \sin \omega = \sqrt{1-u^2}$.

87. cot (arcsin u)

Let $\omega = \arcsin u,\ -\dfrac{\pi}{2} \le \omega \le \dfrac{\pi}{2},\ \omega \ne 0$.

Then $\sin \omega = u = \dfrac{u}{1}$.

If $u > 0$, then w is in quadrant I and cot $w > 0$.

If $u < 0$, then w is in quadrant IV and cot $w < 0$.

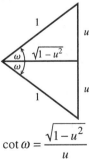

$$\cot \omega = \frac{\sqrt{1-u^2}}{u}$$

Then $\cot(\arcsin u) = \cot \omega = \dfrac{\sqrt{1-u^2}}{u}$.

89. $\sin\left(\sec^{-1}\dfrac{u}{2}\right)$

Let $\omega = \sec^{-1}\dfrac{u}{2},\ 0 \le \omega \le \pi,\ \omega \ne \dfrac{\pi}{2}$.

Since w is in quadrant I or II, sin $w > 0$.

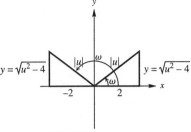

$$\sin \omega = \frac{\sqrt{u^2-4}}{|u|}$$

Then $\sin\left(\sec^{-1}\dfrac{u}{2}\right) = \sin \omega = \dfrac{\sqrt{u^2-4}}{|u|}$.

91. $\tan\left(\arcsin \dfrac{u}{\sqrt{u^2+2}}\right)$

Let $\omega = \arcsin \dfrac{u}{\sqrt{u^2+2}},\ -\dfrac{\pi}{2} \le \omega \le \dfrac{\pi}{2}$.

Then $\sin \omega = \dfrac{u}{\sqrt{u^2+2}}$.

If $u > 0$, then w is in quadrant I and tan $w > 0$.

If $u < 0$, then w is in quadrant IV and $w < 0$.

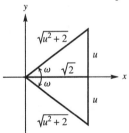

$$\tan \omega = \frac{u}{\sqrt{2}} = \frac{u\sqrt{2}}{2}$$

$$\tan\left(\arcsin \frac{u}{\sqrt{u^2+2}}\right) = \tan \omega = \frac{u}{\sqrt{2}} = \frac{u\sqrt{2}}{2}$$

93. All values in the interval $[0,\ \pi]$

95. (a) $\theta = \arcsin \sqrt{\dfrac{42^2}{2(42^2) + 64(0)}}$

$= \arcsin \dfrac{1}{\sqrt{2}}$

$= \arcsin \dfrac{\sqrt{2}}{2}$

$= 45°$

(b) $\theta = \arcsin \sqrt{\dfrac{v^2}{2v^2 + 64(6)}}$

$= \arcsin \sqrt{\dfrac{v^2}{2v^2 + 384}}$

As v approaches ∞,

$\sqrt{\dfrac{v^2}{2v^2 + 384}} \approx \sqrt{\dfrac{1}{2}} = \dfrac{\sqrt{2}}{2}.$

Thus, $\theta \approx \arcsin \dfrac{\sqrt{2}}{2} = 45°.$

The equation of the asymptote is $\theta = 45°$.

97. $\alpha = 2 \arcsin \dfrac{1}{m}$

(a) $m = 1.2$

$\alpha = 2 \arcsin \left(\dfrac{1}{1.2} \right) = 113°$

(b) $m = 1.5$

$\alpha = 2 \arcsin \left(\dfrac{1}{1.5} \right) = 84°$

(c) $m = 2$

$\alpha = 2 \arcsin \left(\dfrac{1}{2} \right) = 60°$

(d) $m = 2.5$

$\alpha = 2 \arcsin \left(\dfrac{1}{2.5} \right) = 47°$

99. Since the diameter of the earth is 7927 miles at the equator, the radius of the earth is 3963.5 miles. Then

$\cos \theta = \dfrac{3963.5}{20,000 + 3963.5} = \dfrac{3963.5}{23,963.5}$ and

$\theta = \arccos \left(\dfrac{3963.5}{23,963.5} \right) \approx 80.48°$

The percent of the equator that can be seen by the satellite is $\dfrac{2\theta}{360} \cdot 100 = \dfrac{2(80.48)}{360} \approx 44.7\%$

100. The amount of oil in the tank is 20 times the area shaded in the cross-sectional representation. The shaded area is the area of the sector of the circle defined by 2θ (let 2θ be the measure of the angle depicted in the figure) minus the area of the triangles.

Since $\tan \theta = \dfrac{\sqrt{8}}{1} = \sqrt{8}$, $\theta = \arctan \sqrt{8}$

Using the Pythagorean theorem, we see that

$b^2 + 1^2 = 3^2$

$b^2 + 1 = 9$

$b^2 = 9 - 1 = 8$

$b = \sqrt{8}$, where b is the base of one triangle.

The area of both triangles is

$A_\triangle = 2 \cdot \dfrac{1}{2} bh = 2 \cdot \dfrac{1}{2} \left(\sqrt{8} \right)(1) = \sqrt{8}.$

Then the sector area is

$A_s = \dfrac{1}{2}(2\theta)r^2 = (\arctan \sqrt{8})(3)^2$ (with θ in

radians). Thus, the volume of oil in the tank is

$V_{\text{oil}} = 20(A_s - A_\triangle)$

$= 20 \left(9 \arctan(\sqrt{8}) - \sqrt{8} \right)$

$\approx 20(11.08 - 2.83)$

$\approx 165 \text{ cubic ft}$

Section 6.6

Exercises

1. $2 \cot x + 1 = -1$

$2 \cot x = -2$

$\cot x = -1$

$x = \dfrac{3\pi}{4}, \dfrac{7\pi}{4}$

3. $2 \sin x + 3 = 4$

$2 \sin x = 1$

$\sin x = \dfrac{1}{2}$

$x = \dfrac{\pi}{6}, \dfrac{5\pi}{6}$

5. $\tan^2 x + 3 = 0$

$\tan^2 x = -3$

$\tan x = \pm\sqrt{-3}$

The square root of a negative number is not a real number.

No solution.

7. $(\cot x - 1)(\sqrt{3}\cot x + 1) = 0$

$\cot x - 1 = 0$ or $\sqrt{3}\cot x + 1 = 0$

$\cot x = 1$ $\qquad$ $\sqrt{3}\cot x = -1$

$x = \dfrac{\pi}{4}, \dfrac{5\pi}{4}$ $\qquad$ $\cot x = -\dfrac{1}{\sqrt{3}}$

$\qquad\qquad\qquad\qquad \cot x = -\dfrac{\sqrt{3}}{3}$

$\qquad\qquad\qquad\qquad x = \dfrac{2\pi}{3}, \dfrac{5\pi}{3}$

$x = \dfrac{\pi}{4}, \dfrac{2\pi}{3}, \dfrac{5\pi}{4}, \dfrac{5\pi}{3}$

9. $\cos^2 x + 2\cos x + 1 = 0$

$(\cos x + 1)^2 = 0$

$\cos x + 1 = 0$

$\cos x = -1$

$x = \pi$

11. $\qquad -2\sin^2 x = 3\sin x + 1$

$2\sin^2 x + 3\sin x + 1 = 0$

$(2\sin x + 1)(\sin x + 1) = 0$

$2\sin x + 1 = 0$ or $\sin x + 1 = 0$

$\sin x = -\dfrac{1}{2}$ $\qquad$ $\sin x = -1$

$x = \dfrac{7\pi}{6}, \dfrac{11\pi}{6}$ $\qquad$ $x = \dfrac{3\pi}{2}$

$x = \dfrac{7\pi}{6}, \dfrac{3\pi}{2}, \dfrac{11\pi}{6}$

13. $(\cot\theta - \sqrt{3})(2\sin\theta + \sqrt{3}) = 0$

$\cot\theta - \sqrt{3} = 0$ or $2\sin\theta + \sqrt{3} = 0$

$\cot\theta = \sqrt{3}$ $\qquad\qquad$ $\sin\theta = -\dfrac{\sqrt{3}}{2}$

$\theta = 30°, 210°$ $\qquad$ $\theta = 240°, 300°$

$\theta = 30°, 210°, 240°, 300°$

15. $\qquad 2\sin\theta - 1 = \csc\theta$

$2\sin\theta - 1 = \dfrac{1}{\sin\theta}$

$2\sin^2\theta - \sin\theta = 1$

$2\sin^2\theta - \sin\theta - 1 = 0$

$(2\sin\theta + 1)(\sin\theta - 1) = 0$

$2\sin\theta + 1 = 0$ or $\sin\theta - 1 = 0$

$\sin\theta = -\dfrac{1}{2}$ $\qquad$ $\sin\theta = 1$

$\theta = 210°, 330°$ $\qquad$ $\theta = 90°$

$\theta = 90°, 210°, 330°$

17. $\tan\theta - \cot\theta = 0$

$\tan\theta - \dfrac{1}{\tan\theta} = 0$

$\tan^2\theta - 1 = 0$

$\tan^2\theta = 1$

$\tan\theta = \pm 1$

If $\tan\theta = 1$, $\theta = 45°, 225°$.

If $\tan\theta = -1$, $\theta = 135°, 315°$.

$\theta = 45°, 135°, 225°, 315°$

19. $\qquad \csc^2\theta - 2\cot\theta = 0$

$(1 + \cot^2\theta) - 2\cot\theta = 0$

$\cot^2\theta - 2\cot\theta + 1 = 0$

$(\cot\theta - 1)^2 = 0$

$\cot\theta = 1$

$\theta = 45°, \ 225°$

21. $2\tan^2\theta\sin\theta - \tan^2\theta = 0$

$\tan^2\theta(2\sin\theta - 1) = 0$

$\tan^2\theta = 0$ or $2\sin\theta - 1 = 0$

$\tan\theta = 0$ $\qquad\qquad$ $\sin\theta = \dfrac{1}{2}$

$\theta = 0°, 180°$ $\qquad$ $\theta = 30°, 150°$

$\theta = 0°, 30°, 150°, 180°$

23. $\qquad \sec^2\theta\tan\theta = 2\tan\theta$

$\sec^2\theta\tan\theta - 2\tan\theta = 0$

$\tan\theta(\sec^2\theta - 2) = 0$

$\tan\theta = 0$ or $\sec^2\theta = 2$

$\qquad\qquad\qquad\qquad \sec\theta = \pm\sqrt{2}$

$\theta = 0°, 180°$ $\qquad$ $\theta = 45°, 135°, 225°, 315°$

$\theta = 0°, 45°, 135°, 180°, 225°, 315°$

25. $\qquad 3\sin^2\theta - \sin\theta = 2$

$3\sin^2\theta - \sin\theta - 2 = 0$

$(3\sin\theta + 2)(\sin\theta - 1) = 0$

$3\sin\theta + 2 = 0$ or $\sin\theta - 1 = 0$

$\sin\theta = -\dfrac{2}{3}$ $\qquad$ $\sin\theta = 1$

$\theta = 221.8°, 318.2°$ $\qquad$ $\theta = 90°$

$\theta = 90°, 221.8°, 318.2°$

27.
$$\sec^2\theta = 2\tan\theta + 4$$
$$\tan^2\theta + 1 = 2\tan\theta + 4$$
$$\tan^2\theta - 2\tan\theta - 3 = 0$$
$$(\tan\theta - 3)(\tan\theta + 1) = 0$$

$$\tan\theta - 3 = 0 \qquad \text{or} \quad \tan\theta + 1 = 0$$
$$\tan\theta = 3 \qquad\qquad \tan\theta = -1$$
$$\theta = 71.6°, 251.6° \qquad \theta = 135°, 315°$$
$$\theta = 71.6°, 135°, 251.6°, 315°$$

29.
$$9\sin^2\theta - 6\sin\theta = 1$$
$$9\sin^2\theta - 6\sin\theta - 1 = 0$$
We use the quadratic formula with $a = 9$, $b = -6$, and $c = -1$.
$$\sin\theta = \frac{6 \pm \sqrt{36 - [4 \cdot 9(-1)]}}{2 \cdot 9}$$
$$= \frac{6 \pm \sqrt{72}}{18}$$
$$= \frac{1 \pm \sqrt{2}}{3}$$
If $\sin\theta = \dfrac{1 + \sqrt{2}}{3} = .80473787$, $\theta = 53.6°, 126.4°$.

If $\sin\theta = \dfrac{1 - \sqrt{2}}{3} = -.13807119$, $\theta = -7.9°$.

Since this solution is not in the interval $[0°, 360°)$, we must use it as a reference angle to find angles in the interval.
$$\theta = 180° + \left| -7.9° \right| = 187.9° \text{ or}$$
$$\theta = (-7.9°) + 360° = 352.1°$$
$$\theta = 53.6°, 126.4°, 187.9°, 352.1°$$

31. $\tan^2\theta + 4\tan\theta + 2 = 0$
We use the quadratic formula with $a = 1$, $b = 4$, and $c = 2$.
$$\tan\theta = \frac{-4 \pm \sqrt{16 - 4 \cdot 1 \cdot 2}}{2 \cdot 1}$$
$$= \frac{-4 \pm \sqrt{8}}{2}$$
$$= \frac{-4 \pm 2\sqrt{2}}{2}$$
$$= -2 \pm \sqrt{2}$$
If $\tan\theta = -2 + \sqrt{2} = -.5857864$,
$\theta = 149.6°, 329.6°$.

If $\tan\theta = -2 - \sqrt{2} = -3.4142136$,
$\theta = 106.3°, 286.3°$.
$$\theta = 106.3°, 149.6°, 286.3°, 329.6°$$

33. $\sin^2\theta - 2\sin\theta + 3 = 0$
We use the quadratic formula with $a = 1$, $b = -2$, and $c = 3$.
$$\sin\theta = \frac{2 \pm \sqrt{4 - (4 \cdot 1 \cdot 3)}}{2 \cdot 1}$$
$$= \frac{2 \pm \sqrt{-8}}{2}$$
Since $\sqrt{-8}$ is not a real number, the equation has no real number solution.

35.
$$\cot\theta + 2\csc\theta = 3$$
$$\frac{\cos\theta}{\sin\theta} + \frac{2}{\sin\theta} = 3$$
$$\cos\theta + 2 = 3\sin\theta$$
$$(\cos\theta + 2)^2 = (3\sin\theta)^2$$
$$\cos^2\theta + 4\cos\theta + 4 = 9\sin^2\theta$$
$$\cos^2\theta + 4\cos\theta + 4 = 9(1 - \cos^2\theta)$$
$$\cos^2\theta + 4\cos\theta + 4 = 9 - 9\cos^2\theta$$
$$10\cos^2\theta + 4\cos\theta - 5 = 0$$
We use the quadratic formula with $a = 10$, $b = 4$, and $c = -5$.
$$\cos\theta = \frac{-4 \pm \sqrt{4^2 - 4(10)(-5)}}{2(10)}$$
$$= \frac{-4 \pm \sqrt{216}}{20}$$
$$= \frac{-4 \pm 6\sqrt{6}}{20}$$
$$= \frac{-2 \pm 3\sqrt{6}}{10}$$
If $\cos\theta = \dfrac{-2 + 3\sqrt{6}}{10} = .53484692$,
$\theta = 57.7°, 302.3°$.

If $\cos\theta = \dfrac{-2 - 3\sqrt{6}}{10} = -.93484692$,
$\theta = 159.2°, 200.8°$.

Since the solution was found by squaring an equation, we must check that each proposed solution is a solution of the original equation. $302.3°$ and $200.8°$ do not check.
$$\theta = 57.7°, 159.2°$$

37. $2\sin^2 x - \sin x - 1 = 0$
$(2\sin x + 1)(\sin x - 1) = 0$
$2\sin x + 1 = 0$ or $\sin x - 1 = 0$
$\sin x = -\dfrac{1}{2}$ $\sin x = 1$
$x = \dfrac{7\pi}{6}, \dfrac{11\pi}{6}$ $x = \dfrac{\pi}{2}$
$x = \dfrac{\pi}{2} + 2n\pi, \ \dfrac{7\pi}{6} + 2n\pi, \ \dfrac{11\pi}{6} + 2n\pi$, where n is an integer.

39. $4\cos^2 x - 1 = 0$
$\cos^2 x = \dfrac{1}{4}$
$\cos x = \pm \dfrac{1}{2}$
$x = \dfrac{\pi}{3} + 2n\pi, \ \dfrac{2\pi}{3} + 2n\pi, \ \dfrac{4\pi}{3} + 2n\pi,$
$\dfrac{5\pi}{3} + 2n\pi$, where n is an integer.

41. The x-intercept method is shown on the window.

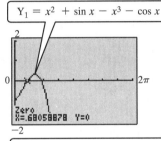

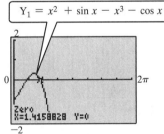

$x = .68058878, \ 1.4158828$

43. $x = \dfrac{2\pi}{6}, \dfrac{2\pi}{2}, \dfrac{8\pi}{6}$
$x = \dfrac{\pi}{3}, \ \pi, \ \dfrac{4\pi}{3}$

45. $\cos 2x = \dfrac{\sqrt{3}}{2}$
Since $0 \le x < 2\pi, \ 0 \le 2x < 4\pi$.
$2x = \dfrac{\pi}{6}, \dfrac{11\pi}{6}, \dfrac{13\pi}{6}, \dfrac{23\pi}{6}$
$x = \dfrac{\pi}{12}, \dfrac{11\pi}{12}, \dfrac{13\pi}{12}, \dfrac{23\pi}{12}$

47. $\sin 3x = -1,$
Since $0 \le x < 2\pi, \ 0 \le 3x < 6\pi$.
$3x = \dfrac{3\pi}{2}, \dfrac{7\pi}{2}, \dfrac{11\pi}{2}$
$x = \dfrac{\pi}{2}, \dfrac{7\pi}{6}, \dfrac{11\pi}{6}$

49. $3\tan 3x = \sqrt{3}, \ \ 0 \le 3x < 6\pi$
$\tan 3x = \dfrac{\sqrt{3}}{3}$
$3x = \dfrac{\pi}{6}, \dfrac{7\pi}{6}, \dfrac{13\pi}{6}, \dfrac{19\pi}{6}, \dfrac{25\pi}{6}, \dfrac{31\pi}{6}$
$x = \dfrac{\pi}{18}, \dfrac{7\pi}{18}, \dfrac{13\pi}{18}, \dfrac{19\pi}{18}, \dfrac{25\pi}{18}, \dfrac{31\pi}{18}$

51. $\sqrt{2}\cos 2x = -1, \ \ 0 \le 2x < 4\pi$
$\cos 2x = \dfrac{-1}{\sqrt{2}} = -\dfrac{\sqrt{2}}{2}$
$2x = \dfrac{3\pi}{4}, \dfrac{5\pi}{4}, \dfrac{11\pi}{4}, \dfrac{13\pi}{4}$
$x = \dfrac{3\pi}{8}, \dfrac{5\pi}{8}, \dfrac{11\pi}{8}, \dfrac{13\pi}{8}$

53. $\sin \dfrac{x}{2} = \sqrt{2} - \sin \dfrac{x}{2}, \ \ 0 \le \dfrac{x}{2} < \pi$
$\sin \dfrac{x}{2} + \sin \dfrac{x}{2} = \sqrt{2}$
$2\sin \dfrac{x}{2} = \sqrt{2}$
$\sin \dfrac{x}{2} = \dfrac{\sqrt{2}}{2}$
$\dfrac{x}{2} = \dfrac{\pi}{4}, \dfrac{3\pi}{4}$
$x = \dfrac{\pi}{2}, \dfrac{3\pi}{2}$

55. $\tan 4x = 0, \ \ 0 \le 4x < 8\pi$
$4x = 0, \ \pi, \ 2\pi, \ 3\pi, \ 4\pi, \ 5\pi, \ 6\pi, \ 7\pi$
$x = 0, \ \dfrac{\pi}{4}, \dfrac{\pi}{2}, \dfrac{3\pi}{4}, \ \pi, \ \dfrac{5\pi}{4}, \dfrac{3\pi}{2}, \dfrac{7\pi}{4}$

57. $8\sec^2 \dfrac{x}{2} = 4$
$\sec^2 \dfrac{x}{2} = \dfrac{1}{2}$
$\sec \dfrac{x}{2} = \pm \dfrac{\sqrt{2}}{2}$
No solution.

59. $\sin\dfrac{x}{2}=\cos\dfrac{x}{2},\ \ 0\le\dfrac{x}{2}<\pi$

$$\sin^2\dfrac{x}{2}=\cos^2\dfrac{x}{2}$$

$$\sin^2\dfrac{x}{2}=1-\sin^2\dfrac{x}{2}$$

$$2\sin^2\dfrac{x}{2}=1$$

$$\sin^2\dfrac{x}{2}=\dfrac{1}{2}$$

$$\sin\dfrac{x}{2}=\pm\sqrt{\dfrac{1}{2}}=\pm\dfrac{\sqrt2}{2}$$

If $\sin\dfrac{x}{2}=\dfrac{\sqrt2}{2},\ \dfrac{x}{2}=\dfrac{\pi}{4},\ \dfrac{3\pi}{4},$ and $x=\dfrac{\pi}{2},\ \dfrac{3\pi}{2}.$

If $\sin\dfrac{x}{2}=-\dfrac{\sqrt2}{2}$, there are no solutions in the interval $[0,\pi)$.

$$x=\dfrac{\pi}{2},\ \dfrac{3\pi}{2}$$

Since the solution was found by squaring an equation, the proposed solutions must be checked.

$x=\dfrac{\pi}{2}$:

$$\sin\dfrac{x}{2}=\sin\dfrac{\pi}{4}=\dfrac{\sqrt2}{2}$$

$$\cos\dfrac{x}{2}=\cos\dfrac{\pi}{4}=\dfrac{\sqrt2}{2}$$

$x=\dfrac{3\pi}{2}$:

$$\sin\dfrac{x}{2}=\sin\dfrac{3\pi}{4}=\dfrac{\sqrt2}{2}$$

$$\cos\dfrac{x}{2}=\cos\dfrac{3\pi}{4}=-\dfrac{\sqrt2}{2}$$

The only solution is $\dfrac{\pi}{2}$.

61. $\sqrt2\sin3\theta-1=0,\ \ 0°\le3\theta<1080°$

$$\sqrt2\sin3\theta=1$$

$$\sin3\theta=\dfrac{1}{\sqrt2}$$

$$=\dfrac{\sqrt2}{2}$$

In quadrant I and II, sine is positive.
$3\theta=45°,\ 135°,\ 405°,\ 495°,\ 765°,\ 855°$
$\theta=15°,\ 45°,\ 135°,\ 165°,\ 255°,\ 285°$

63. $\cos\dfrac{\theta}{2}=1,\ \ 0°\le\dfrac{\theta}{2}<180°$

$$\dfrac{\theta}{2}=0°$$

$$\theta=0°$$

65. $2\sqrt3\sin\dfrac{\theta}{2}=3,\ \ 0\le\dfrac{\theta}{2}<180°$

$$\sin\dfrac{\theta}{2}=\dfrac{3}{2\sqrt3}=\dfrac{3\sqrt3}{6}=\dfrac{\sqrt3}{2}$$

$$\dfrac{\theta}{2}=60°,\ 120°$$

$$\theta=120°,\ 240°$$

67.
$$2\sin\theta=2\cos2\theta$$
$$\sin\theta=\cos2\theta$$
$$\sin\theta=1-2\sin^2\theta$$
$$2\sin^2\theta+\sin\theta-1=0$$
$$(2\sin\theta-1)(\sin\theta+1)=0$$
$2\sin\theta-1=0\quad$ or $\quad\sin\theta+1=0$
$$\sin\theta=\dfrac{1}{2}\qquad\qquad\sin\theta=-1$$
$\theta=30°,\ 150°\qquad\theta=270°$
$\theta=30°,\ 150°,\ 270°$

69.
$$1-\sin\theta=\cos2\theta$$
$$1-\sin\theta=1-2\sin^2\theta$$
$$2\sin^2\theta-\sin\theta=0$$
$$\sin\theta(2\sin\theta-1)=0$$
$\sin\theta=0\quad$ or $\quad2\sin\theta-1=0$
$\theta=0°,\ 180°\qquad\quad\sin\theta=\dfrac{1}{2}$
$$\theta=30°,\ 150°$$
$\theta=0°,\ 30°,\ 150°,\ 180°$

71.
$$\csc^2\dfrac{\theta}{2}=2\sec\theta$$
$$\dfrac{1}{\sin^2\frac{\theta}{2}}=\dfrac{2}{\cos\theta}$$
$$2\sin^2\dfrac{\theta}{2}=\cos\theta$$
$$2\left(\dfrac{1-\cos\theta}{2}\right)=\cos\theta$$
$$1-\cos\theta=\cos\theta$$
$$1=2\cos\theta$$
$$\dfrac{1}{2}=\cos\theta$$
$\theta=60°,\ 300°$

73. $2 - \sin 2\theta = 4 \sin 2\theta$, $0° \le 2\theta < 720°$
$$2 = 5 \sin 2\theta$$
$$\sin 2\theta = \frac{2}{5} = .4$$
$$2\theta = 23.6°, \; 156.4°, \; 383.6°, \; 516.4°$$
$$\theta = 11.8°, \; 78.2°, \; 191.8°, \; 258.2°$$

75. $0° \le 2\theta < 720°$,
$$2 \cos^2 2\theta = 1 - \cos 2\theta$$
$$2 \cos^2 2\theta + \cos 2\theta - 1 = 0$$
$$(2 \cos 2\theta - 1)(\cos 2\theta + 1) = 0$$
$2 \cos 2\theta - 1 = 0$ or $\cos 2\theta + 1 = 0$
$\cos 2\theta = \dfrac{1}{2}$ $\cos 2\theta = -1$
$2\theta = 60°, \; 300°, \; 420°, \; 660°$ $2\theta = 180°, \; 540°$
$\theta = 30°, \; 150°, \; 210°, \; 330°$ $\theta = 90°, \; 270°$
$\theta = 30°, \; 90°, \; 150°, \; 210°, \; 270°, \; 330°$

77.

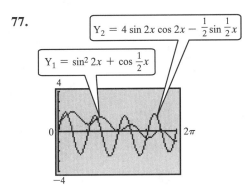

78. In both cases, the value is approximately .7621.

79. $P = A \sin(2\pi f t + \phi)$

   (a) Let $f = 261.63$, $A = .004$, and $\phi = \dfrac{\pi}{7}$.

       Graph $P = .004 \sin\left[2\pi(261.63)t + \dfrac{\pi}{7}\right]$ on the interval $[0, .005]$.

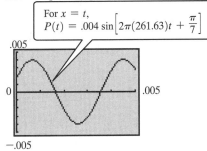

   (b) $0 = .004 \sin\left[2\pi(261.63)t + \dfrac{\pi}{7}\right]$
$$0 = \sin(1643.87t + .45)$$
       $1643.87t + .45 = n\pi$, where n is an integer.
$$t = \frac{n\pi - .45}{1643.87}$$
       If $n = 0$, then $t = .000274$.
       If $n = 1$, then $t = .00164$.
       If $n = 2$, then $t = .00355$.
       If $n = 3$, then $t = .00546$.
       The only solutions for t in the interval $[0, .005]$ are .00164 and .00355.

   (c) We must solve the trigonometric equation $P = 0$ to determine when $P \le 0$. From the graph we can estimate that $P \le 0$ on the interval $[.00164, .00355]$.

   (d) $P \le 0$ implies that there is a decrease in pressure so an eardrum would be vibrating outward.

81. (a) 3 beats per sec

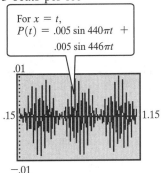

   (b) 4 beats per sec

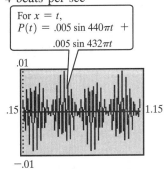

   (c) The number of beats is equal to the absolute value of the difference in the frequencies of the two tones.

83. $h = \dfrac{35}{3} + \dfrac{7}{3} \sin \dfrac{2\pi x}{365}$

(a) Find x such that $h = 14$.

$$14 = \frac{35}{3} + \frac{7}{3}\sin\frac{2\pi x}{365}$$

$$14 - \frac{35}{3} = \frac{7}{3}\sin\frac{2\pi x}{365}$$

$$\frac{7}{3} = \frac{7}{3}\sin\frac{2\pi x}{365}$$

$$\sin\frac{2\pi x}{365} = 1$$

$$\frac{2\pi x}{365} = \frac{\pi}{2} \pm 2\pi n, \; n \text{ is an integer.}$$

$$x = \left(\frac{\pi}{2} \pm 2\pi n\right)\left(\frac{365}{2\pi}\right)$$

$$= \frac{365}{4} \pm 365n$$

$$= 91.25 \pm 365n$$

$x = 91.25$ means about 91.3 days after March 21, on June 20.

(b) h assumes its least value when $\sin\dfrac{2\pi x}{365}$ takes on its least value, which is -1.

$$\sin\frac{2\pi x}{365} = -1$$

$$\frac{2\pi x}{365} = \frac{3\pi}{2} \pm 2\pi n, \; n \text{ is an integer.}$$

$$x = \left(\frac{3\pi}{2} \pm 2\pi n\right)\left(\frac{365}{2\pi}\right)$$

$$= \frac{3(365)}{4} \pm 365n$$

$$= 273.75 \pm 365$$

$x = 273.75$ means about 273.8 days after March 21, on December 19.

(c) Let $h = 10$.

$$10 = \frac{35}{3} + \frac{7}{3}\sin\frac{2\pi x}{365}$$

$$30 = 35 + 7\sin\frac{2\pi x}{365}$$

$$-5 = 7\sin\frac{2\pi x}{365}$$

$$-\frac{5}{7} = \sin\frac{2\pi x}{365}$$

$$-.71428571 = \sin\left(\frac{2\pi x}{365}\right)$$

In quadrant III and IV, sine is negative.
In quadrant III,

$$\frac{2\pi x}{365} = \pi + .79560295$$

$$= 3.9371956$$

$$x = \frac{365}{2\pi}(3.9371956)$$

$$= 228.7.$$

$x = 228.7$ means 228.7 days after March 21, on November 4.
In quadrant IV,

$$\frac{2\pi x}{365} = 2\pi - .79560295$$

$$= 5.4875823$$

$$x = \frac{365}{2\pi}(5.4875823)$$

$$= 318.8$$

$x = 318.8$ means about 318.8 days after March 21, on February 2.

85. $i = I_{\max}\sin 2\pi ft$

Let $i = 50$, $I_{\max} = 100$, $f = 120$.

$$50 = 100\sin 240\pi t$$

$$\sin 240\pi t = \frac{1}{2}$$

$$240\pi t = \frac{\pi}{6}$$

$$t = \frac{1}{1440}$$

$$t \approx .0007 \text{ sec}$$

87. $i = I_{\max}\sin 2\pi ft$

Let $i = \frac{1}{2}I_{\max}$, $f = 60$.

$$\frac{1}{2}I_{\max} = I_{\max}\sin 2\pi(60)t$$

$$\frac{1}{2} = \sin 120\pi t$$

$$120\pi t = \frac{\pi}{6}$$

$$t = \frac{1}{720}$$

$$t \approx .0014 \text{ sec}$$

89. $V = \cos 2\pi t, \; 0 \le t \le \dfrac{1}{2}$

(a) $V = 0$, $\cos 2\pi t = 0$

$$2\pi t = \cos^{-1} 0$$

$$2\pi t = \frac{\pi}{2}$$

$$t = \frac{\frac{\pi}{2}}{2\pi}$$

$$= \frac{1}{4}\text{ sec}$$

(b) $V = .5, \cos 2\pi t = .5$

$2\pi t = \cos^{-1}(.5)$

$2\pi t = \dfrac{\pi}{3}$

$t = \dfrac{\frac{\pi}{3}}{2\pi}$

$= \dfrac{1}{6} \sec$

(c) $V = .25, \cos 2\pi t = .25$

$2\pi t = \cos^{-1}(.25)$

$2\pi t = 1.3181161$

$t = \dfrac{1.3181161}{2\pi}$

$= .21 \sec$

91. $s(t) = \sin t + 2 \cos t$

(a) $\dfrac{2 + \sqrt{3}}{2} = \dfrac{2}{2} + \dfrac{\sqrt{3}}{2}$

$= 2 \cdot \dfrac{1}{2} + \dfrac{\sqrt{3}}{2}$

$= 2 \cos\left(\dfrac{\pi}{3}\right) + \sin\left(\dfrac{\pi}{3}\right)$

One such value is $\dfrac{\pi}{3}$.

(b) $\dfrac{3\sqrt{2}}{2} = \dfrac{2\sqrt{2}}{2} + \dfrac{\sqrt{2}}{2}$

$= 2\left(\dfrac{\sqrt{2}}{2}\right) + \dfrac{\sqrt{2}}{2}$

$= 2 \cos\left(\dfrac{\pi}{4}\right) + \sin\left(\dfrac{\pi}{4}\right)$

One such value is $\dfrac{\pi}{4}$.

Section 6.7

Exercises

1. C; $\arcsin 0 = 0$

3. C; $\arccos\left(-\dfrac{\sqrt{2}}{2}\right) = \dfrac{3\pi}{4}$

5. $y = 5 \cos x$

$\dfrac{y}{5} = \cos x$

$x = \arccos \dfrac{y}{5}$

7. $2y = \cot 3x$

$3x = \operatorname{arccot} 2y$

$x = \dfrac{1}{3} \operatorname{arccot} 2y$

9. $y = 3 \tan 2x$

$\dfrac{y}{3} = \tan 2x$

$2x = \arctan \dfrac{y}{3}$

$x = \dfrac{1}{2} \arctan \dfrac{y}{3}$

11. $y = 6 \cos \dfrac{x}{4}$

$\dfrac{y}{6} = \cos \dfrac{x}{4}$

$\dfrac{x}{4} = \arccos \dfrac{y}{6}$

$x = 4 \arccos \dfrac{y}{6}$

13. $y = -2 \cos 5x$

$-\dfrac{y}{2} = \cos 5x$

$5x = \arccos\left(-\dfrac{y}{2}\right)$

$x = \dfrac{1}{5} \arccos\left(-\dfrac{y}{2}\right)$

15. $y = \cos(x + 3)$

$x + 3 = \arccos y$

$x = -3 + \arccos y$

17. $y = \sin x - 2$

$y + 2 = \sin x$

$x = \arcsin(y + 2)$

19. $y = 2 \sin x - 4$

$y + 4 = 2 \sin x$

$\dfrac{y + 4}{2} = \sin x$

$x = \arcsin\left(\dfrac{y + 4}{2}\right)$

23. $\dfrac{4}{3}\cos^{-1}\dfrac{y}{4}=\pi$

$$\cos^{-1}\dfrac{y}{4}=\dfrac{3\pi}{4}$$

$$\dfrac{y}{4}=\cos\dfrac{3\pi}{4}$$

$$\dfrac{y}{4}=-\dfrac{\sqrt{2}}{2}$$

$$y=-2\sqrt{2}$$

25. $2\arccos\left(\dfrac{y-\pi}{3}\right)=2\pi$

$$\arccos\left(\dfrac{y-\pi}{3}\right)=\pi$$

$$\dfrac{y-\pi}{3}=\cos\pi$$

$$\dfrac{y-\pi}{3}=-1$$

$$y-\pi=-3$$

$$y=\pi-3$$

27. $\arcsin x=\arctan\dfrac{3}{4}$

Let $\arctan\dfrac{3}{4}=u$, so $\tan u=\dfrac{3}{4}$, u is in quadrant I.

Sketch a triangle and label it. The hypotenuse is $\sqrt{3^2+4^2}=5$.

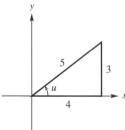

$\sin u=\dfrac{3}{r}=\dfrac{3}{5}$

This equation becomes $\arcsin x=u$, or $x=\sin u$.

$$x=\dfrac{3}{5}$$

29. $\cos^{-1}x=\sin^{-1}\dfrac{3}{5}$

Let $\sin^{-1}\dfrac{3}{5}=u$, so $\sin u=\dfrac{3}{5}$.

u is in quadrant I.

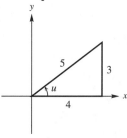

$\cos u=\dfrac{4}{5}$

The equation becomes

$\cos^{-1}x=u,$ or $x=\cos u.$

$$x=\dfrac{4}{5}$$

31. $\sin^{-1}x-\tan^{-1}1=-\dfrac{\pi}{4}$

$$\sin^{-1}x=\tan^{-1}1-\dfrac{\pi}{4}$$

$$\sin^{-1}x=\dfrac{\pi}{4}-\dfrac{\pi}{4}$$

$$\sin^{-1}x=0$$

$$\sin 0=x$$

$$x=0$$

33. $\arccos x+2\arcsin\dfrac{\sqrt{3}}{2}=\pi$

$$\arccos x=\pi-2\arcsin\dfrac{\sqrt{3}}{2}$$

$$\arccos x=\pi-2\left(\dfrac{\pi}{3}\right)$$

$$\arccos x=\pi-\dfrac{2\pi}{3}$$

$$\arccos x=\dfrac{\pi}{3}$$

$$x=\cos\dfrac{\pi}{3}$$

$$x=\dfrac{1}{2}$$

35. $\arcsin 2x + \arccos x = \dfrac{\pi}{6}$

$$\arcsin 2x = \dfrac{\pi}{6} - \arccos x$$

$$2x = \sin\left(\dfrac{\pi}{6} - \arccos x\right)$$

Use the identity
$\sin(A - B)\sin A \cos B - \cos A \sin B.$

$$2x = \sin\dfrac{\pi}{6}\cos(\arccos x) - \cos\dfrac{\pi}{6}\sin(\arccos x)$$

Let $u = \arccos x$.

$\cos u = x = \dfrac{x}{1}$

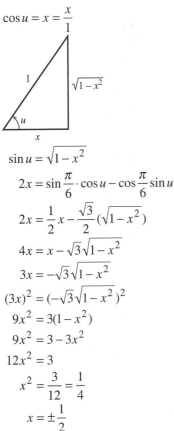

$\sin u = \sqrt{1 - x^2}$

$$2x = \sin\dfrac{\pi}{6}\cdot\cos u - \cos\dfrac{\pi}{6}\sin u$$

$$2x = \dfrac{1}{2}x - \dfrac{\sqrt{3}}{2}\left(\sqrt{1 - x^2}\right)$$

$$4x = x - \sqrt{3}\sqrt{1 - x^2}$$

$$3x = -\sqrt{3}\sqrt{1 - x^2}$$

$$(3x)^2 = \left(-\sqrt{3}\sqrt{1 - x^2}\right)^2$$

$$9x^2 = 3(1 - x^2)$$

$$9x^2 = 3 - 3x^2$$

$$12x^2 = 3$$

$$x^2 = \dfrac{3}{12} = \dfrac{1}{4}$$

$$x = \pm\dfrac{1}{2}$$

Check these proposed solutions since they were found by squaring an equation.

$x = \dfrac{1}{2}$:

$$\arcsin\left(2 \cdot \dfrac{1}{2}\right) + \arccos\left(\dfrac{1}{2}\right) = \dfrac{\pi}{2} + \dfrac{\pi}{3} \neq \dfrac{\pi}{6}$$

$x = -\dfrac{1}{2}$:

$$\arcsin\left(2\left(-\dfrac{1}{2}\right)\right) + \arccos\left(-\dfrac{1}{2}\right) = -\dfrac{\pi}{2} + \dfrac{2\pi}{3} = \dfrac{\pi}{6}$$

The only solution is $-\dfrac{1}{2}$.

37. $\cos^{-1} x + \tan^{-1} x = \dfrac{\pi}{2}$

$$\cos^{-1} x = \dfrac{\pi}{2} - \tan^{-1} x$$

$$x = \cos\left(\dfrac{\pi}{2} - \tan^{-1} x\right)$$

Use the identity
$\cos(A - B) = \cos A \cos B + \sin A \sin B.$

$$x = \cos\dfrac{\pi}{2}\cos\,(\tan^{-1} x) + \sin\dfrac{\pi}{2}\sin\,(\tan^{-1} x)$$

Let $u = \tan^{-1} x$ so $\tan u = x$.

$\cos u = \dfrac{1}{\sqrt{1 + x^2}}$

$\sin u = \dfrac{x}{\sqrt{1 + x^2}}$

$$x = \cos\dfrac{\pi}{2}\cdot\cos u + \sin\dfrac{\pi}{2}\cdot\sin u$$

$$x = 0\left(\dfrac{1}{\sqrt{1 + x^2}}\right) + 1\cdot\dfrac{x}{\sqrt{1 + x^2}}$$

$$x = \dfrac{x}{\sqrt{1 + x^2}}$$

$$x - \dfrac{x}{\sqrt{1 + x^2}} = 0$$

$$x\left(1 - \dfrac{1}{\sqrt{1 + x^2}}\right) = 0$$

$x = 0$ or $1 - \dfrac{1}{\sqrt{1 + x^2}} = 0$

$$\dfrac{1}{\sqrt{1 + x^2}} = 1$$

$$\sqrt{1 + x^2} = 1$$

$$1 + x^2 = 1$$

$$x^2 = 0$$

$$x = 0$$

39.

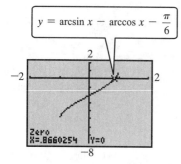

$$y = \arcsin x - \arccos x - \frac{\pi}{6}$$

41.

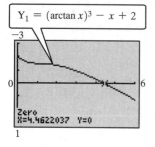

$$Y_1 = (\arctan x)^3 - x + 2$$

$x = 4.4622037$

43. $A = \sqrt{(A_1 \cos \phi_1 + A_2 \cos \phi_2)^2 + (A_1 \sin \phi_1 + A_2 \sin \phi_2)^2}$

and $\phi = \arctan \left(\dfrac{A_1 \sin \phi_1 + A_2 \sin \phi_2}{A_1 \cos \phi + A_2 \cos \phi_2} \right)$

Make sure your calculator is in radian mode.

(a) Let $A_1 = .0012$, $\phi_1 = .052$, $A_2 = .004$, and $\phi_2 = .61$.

$A = \sqrt{(.0012 \cos .052 + .004 \cos .61)^2 + (.0012 \sin .052 + .004 \sin .61)^2}$

$\quad \approx .00506$

$\phi = \arctan \left(\dfrac{.0012 \sin .052 + .004 \sin .61}{.0012 \cos .052 + .004 \cos .61} \right)$

$\quad \approx .484$

$P = A \sin(2\pi f t + \phi)$, let $f = 220$.

$P = .00506 \sin(440\pi t + .484)$

(b)

For $x = t$,
$P(t) = .00506 \sin(440\pi t + .484)$
$P_1(t) + P_2(t) = .0012 \sin(440\pi t + .052) +$
$\qquad\qquad .004 \sin(440\pi t + .61)$

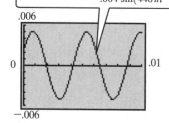

The two graphs are the same.

45. **(a)** $\tan\alpha = \dfrac{x}{z}$

$\tan\beta = \dfrac{x+y}{z}$

(b) $\tan\alpha = \dfrac{x}{z}$ $\qquad \tan\beta = \dfrac{x+y}{z}$

$z\tan\alpha = x \qquad z\tan\beta = x+y$

$z = \dfrac{x}{\tan\alpha} \qquad z = \dfrac{x+y}{\tan\beta}$

$\dfrac{x}{\tan\alpha} = \dfrac{x+y}{\tan\beta}$

(c) $(x+y)\tan\alpha = x\tan\beta$

$\tan\alpha = \dfrac{x\tan\beta}{x+y}$

$\alpha = \arctan\left(\dfrac{x\tan\beta}{x+y}\right)$

(d) $x\tan\beta = (x+y)\tan\alpha$

$\tan\beta = \dfrac{(x+y)\tan\alpha}{x}$

$\beta = \arctan\left[\dfrac{(x+y)\tan\alpha}{x}\right]$

47. **(a)** $e = E_{max}\sin 2\pi ft$

$\dfrac{e}{E_{max}} = \sin 2\pi ft$

$2\pi ft = \arcsin\dfrac{e}{E_{max}}$

$t = \dfrac{1}{2\pi f}\arcsin\dfrac{e}{E_{max}}$

(b) Let $E_{max} = 12$, $e = 5$, and $f = 100$.

$t = \dfrac{1}{2\pi(100)}\arcsin\dfrac{5}{12}$

$t = \dfrac{1}{200\pi}\arcsin .4166667 = .00068\,\text{sec}$

49. $y = \dfrac{1}{3}\sin\dfrac{4\pi t}{3}$

(a) $3y = \sin\dfrac{4\pi t}{3}$

$\dfrac{4\pi t}{3} = \arcsin 3y$

$4\pi t = 3\arcsin 3y$

$t = \dfrac{3}{4\pi}\arcsin 3y$

(b) If $y = .3$ radian,

$t = \dfrac{3}{4\pi}\arcsin .9$

$t = .27\,\text{sec}.$

Chapter 6 Review Exercises

1. $\sec x = \dfrac{1}{\cos x}$
The answer is B.

3. $\tan x = \dfrac{\sin x}{\cos x}$
The answer is C.

5. $\tan^2 x = \dfrac{1}{\cot^2 x}$
The answer is D.

7. $\dfrac{\cot\theta}{\sec\theta} = \dfrac{\frac{\cos\theta}{\sin\theta}}{\frac{1}{\cos\theta}} = \dfrac{\cos^2\theta}{\sin\theta}$

9. $\csc\theta + \cot\theta = \dfrac{1}{\sin\theta} + \dfrac{\cos\theta}{\sin\theta} = \dfrac{1+\cos\theta}{\sin\theta}$

11. $\tan x = -\dfrac{5}{4}$, $\dfrac{\pi}{2} < x < \pi$

$\sec^2 x = \tan^2 x + 1 = \left(-\dfrac{5}{4}\right)^2 + 1 = \dfrac{41}{16}$

Since x is in quadrant II, $\sec x < 0$, so
$\sec x = -\dfrac{\sqrt{41}}{4}$.

$\cos x = \dfrac{1}{\sec x} = -\dfrac{4}{\sqrt{41}} = -\dfrac{4\sqrt{41}}{41}$

$\sin x = \cos x\tan x = -\dfrac{4\sqrt{41}}{41}\left(-\dfrac{5}{4}\right) = \dfrac{5\sqrt{41}}{41}$

$\cot x = \dfrac{1}{\tan x} = -\dfrac{4}{5}$

$\csc x = \dfrac{1}{\sin x} = \dfrac{41}{5\sqrt{41}} = \dfrac{\sqrt{41}}{5}$

13. $\sin 35° = \cos(90° - 35°)$
$= \cos 55°$
The answer is B.

15. $-\sin 35° = \sin(-35°)$
The answer is A.

17. $\cos 75° = \cos \dfrac{150°}{2}$

$\qquad = \sqrt{\dfrac{1 + \cos 150°}{2}}$

The answer is C.

19. $\sin 300° = \sin 2(150°)$

$\qquad\qquad = 2 \sin 150° \cos 150°$

The answer is D.

21. Find sin $(x + y)$, cos $(x - y)$, and tan $(x + y)$, given $\sin x = -\dfrac{1}{4}$, $\cos y = -\dfrac{4}{5}$, x and y are in quadrant III.

Since x and y are in quadrant III, cos x and cos y are negative.

$\cos x = -\sqrt{1 - \sin^2 x}$

$\qquad = -\sqrt{1 - \dfrac{1}{16}}$

$\qquad = -\sqrt{\dfrac{15}{16}}$

$\qquad = -\dfrac{\sqrt{15}}{4}$

$\sin y = -\sqrt{1 - \cos^2 y}$

$\qquad = -\sqrt{1 - \left(-\dfrac{4}{5}\right)^2}$

$\qquad = -\sqrt{\dfrac{25 - 16}{25}}$

$\qquad = -\dfrac{3}{5}$

$\sin(x + y) = \sin x \cos y + \cos x \sin y$

$\qquad = \left(-\dfrac{1}{4}\right)\left(-\dfrac{4}{5}\right) + \left(-\dfrac{\sqrt{15}}{4}\right)\left(-\dfrac{3}{5}\right)$

$\qquad = \dfrac{4}{20} + \dfrac{3\sqrt{15}}{20}$

$\qquad = \dfrac{4 + 3\sqrt{15}}{20}$

$\cos(x - y) = \cos x \cos y + \sin x \sin y$

$\qquad = \left(-\dfrac{\sqrt{15}}{4}\right)\left(-\dfrac{4}{5}\right) + \left(-\dfrac{1}{4}\right)\left(-\dfrac{3}{5}\right)$

$\qquad = \dfrac{\sqrt{15}}{5} + \dfrac{3}{20}$

$\qquad = \dfrac{4\sqrt{15}}{20} + \dfrac{3}{20}$

$\qquad = \dfrac{4\sqrt{15} + 3}{20}$

$\tan(x + y) = \dfrac{\sin(x + y)}{\cos(x + y)}$

$\qquad = \dfrac{\dfrac{4 + 3\sqrt{15}}{20}}{\dfrac{4\sqrt{15} - 3}{20}}$

$\qquad = \dfrac{4 + 3\sqrt{15}}{4\sqrt{15} - 3}$

To find the quadrant of $x + y$, notice that $\sin(x + y) > 0$, which implies $x + y$ is in quadrant I or II. Also $\tan(x + y) > 0$, which implies that $x + y$ is in quadrant I or III. Therefore, $x + y$ is in quadrant I.

23. Find $\cos \dfrac{\theta}{2}$, given $\cos \theta = -\dfrac{1}{2}$, $90° < \theta < 180°$.

Since θ is in quadrant II, $\dfrac{\theta}{2}$ is in quadrant I, so $\cos \dfrac{\theta}{2} > 0$.

$\cos \dfrac{\theta}{2} = \sqrt{\dfrac{1 + \left(-\dfrac{1}{2}\right)}{2}} = \sqrt{\dfrac{\dfrac{1}{2}}{2}} = \sqrt{\dfrac{1}{4}} = \dfrac{1}{2}$

25.

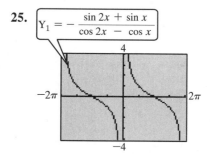

$Y_1 = -\dfrac{\sin 2x + \sin x}{\cos 2x - \cos x}$

The graph of $y = -\dfrac{\sin 2x + \sin x}{\cos 2x - \cos x}$ appears to be the same as the graph of $y = \cot \dfrac{x}{2}$.

$$-\frac{\sin 2x + \sin x}{\cos 2x - \cos x} = -\frac{2\sin x \cos x + \sin x}{2\cos^2 x - 1 - \cos x}$$

$$= -\frac{\sin x(2\cos x + 1)}{(2\cos x + 1)(\cos x - 1)}$$

$$= -\frac{\sin x}{\cos x - 1}$$

$$= \frac{\sin x}{1 - \cos x}$$

$$= \frac{1}{\frac{1 - \cos x}{\sin x}}$$

$$= \frac{1}{\tan \frac{x}{2}}$$

$$= \cot \frac{x}{2}$$

27. Verify $\sin^2 x - \sin^2 y = \cos^2 y - \cos^2 x$.

$$\sin^2 x - \sin^2 y = \left(1 - \cos^2 x\right) - \left(1 - \cos^2 y\right)$$

$$= 1 - \cos^2 x - 1 + \cos^2 y$$

$$= \cos^2 y - \cos^2 x$$

29. Verify $\dfrac{\sin^2 x}{2 - 2\cos x} = \cos^2 \dfrac{x}{2}$.
Work with the left side.

$$\frac{\sin^2 x}{2 - 2\cos x} = \frac{1 - \cos^2 x}{2(1 - \cos x)}$$

$$= \frac{(1 - \cos x)(1 + \cos x)}{2(1 - \cos x)}$$

$$= \frac{1 + \cos x}{2}$$

Work with the right side.

$$\cos^2 \frac{x}{2} = \frac{1 + \cos x}{2}$$

31. Verify $2\cos A - \sec A = \cos A - \dfrac{\tan A}{\csc A}$.
Work with the right side.

$$\cos A - \frac{\tan A}{\csc A} = \cos A - \frac{\frac{\sin A}{\cos A}}{\frac{1}{\sin A}}$$

$$= \cos A - \frac{\sin^2 A}{\cos A}$$

$$= \frac{\cos^2 A - \left(1 - \cos^2 A\right)}{\cos A}$$

$$= \frac{2\cos^2 A - 1}{\cos A}$$

$$= 2\cos A - \frac{1}{\cos A}$$

$$= 2\cos A - \sec A$$

33. Verify $1 + \tan^2 \alpha = 2\tan \alpha \csc 2\alpha$.

$$2\tan \alpha \csc 2\alpha = \frac{2\tan \alpha}{\sin 2\alpha}$$

$$= \frac{2\frac{\sin \alpha}{\cos \alpha}}{2\sin \alpha \cos \alpha}$$

$$= \frac{2\sin \alpha}{2\sin \alpha \cos^2 \alpha}$$

$$= \frac{1}{\cos^2 \alpha} = \sec^2 \alpha$$

$$= 1 + \tan^2 \alpha$$

35. Verify $\tan \theta \sin 2\theta = 2 - 2\cos^2 \theta$

$$\tan \theta \sin 2\theta = \tan \theta(2\sin \theta \cos \theta)$$

$$= \frac{\sin \theta}{\cos \theta}(2\sin \theta \cos \theta)$$

$$= 2\sin^2 \theta$$

$$= 2\left(1 - \cos^2 \theta\right)$$

$$= 2 - 2\cos^2 \theta$$

37. Verify $2\tan x \csc 2x - \tan^2 x = 1$.

$$2\tan x \csc 2x - \tan^2 x$$

$$= 2\tan x \frac{1}{\sin 2x} - \tan^2 x$$

$$= 2\tan x \frac{1}{2\sin x \cos x} - \tan^2 x$$

$$= \frac{\sin x}{\sin x \cos^2 x} - \frac{\sin^2 x}{\cos^2 x}$$

$$= \frac{1}{\cos^2 x} - \frac{\sin^2 x}{\cos^2 x}$$

$$= \frac{1 - \sin^2 x}{\cos^2 x}$$

$$= \frac{\cos^2 x}{\cos^2 x}$$

$$= 1$$

39. Verify $\tan \theta \cos^2 \theta = \dfrac{2\tan \theta \cos^2 \theta - \tan \theta}{1 - \tan^2 \theta}$.
Work with the right side.

$$\frac{2\tan \theta \cos^2 \theta - \tan \theta}{1 - \tan^2 \theta} = \frac{\tan \theta\left(2\cos^2 \theta - 1\right)}{1 - \tan^2 \theta}$$

$$= \frac{\tan \theta\left(2\cos^2 \theta - 1\right)}{\frac{\cos^2 \theta - \sin^2 \theta}{\cos^2 \theta}}$$

$$= \frac{\cos^2 \theta \tan \theta\left(2\cos^2 \theta - 1\right)}{2\cos^2 \theta - 1}$$

$$= \cos^2 \theta \tan \theta$$

$$= \tan \theta \cos^2 \theta$$

41. Verify $2\cos^3 x - \cos x = \dfrac{\cos^2 x - \sin^2 x}{\sec x}$.

Work with the right side.

$$\dfrac{\cos^2 x - \sin^2 x}{\sec x} = \dfrac{2\cos^2 x - 1}{\frac{1}{\cos x}}$$

$$= \left(2\cos^2 x - 1\right)\cos x$$

$$= 2\cos^3 x - \cos x$$

43. Verify $\sec^2 \alpha - 1 = \dfrac{\sec 2\alpha - 1}{\sec 2\alpha + 1}$.

Work with the right side.

$$\dfrac{\sec 2\alpha - 1}{\sec 2\alpha + 1} = \dfrac{\frac{1}{\cos 2\alpha} - 1}{\frac{1}{\cos 2\alpha} + 1}$$

$$= \dfrac{\frac{1}{\cos^2 \alpha - \sin^2 \alpha} - 1}{\frac{1}{\cos^2 \alpha - \sin^2 \alpha} + 1}$$

$$= \dfrac{1 - \cos^2 \alpha + \sin^2 \alpha}{1 + \cos^2 \alpha - \sin^2 \alpha}$$

$$= \dfrac{2\sin^2 \alpha}{2\cos^2 \alpha} = \tan^2 \alpha$$

$$= \sec^2 \alpha - 1$$

45. $y = \sin^{-1}\left(\dfrac{\sqrt{2}}{2}\right)$

$\sin y = \dfrac{\sqrt{2}}{2}, \ -\dfrac{\pi}{2} \le y \le \dfrac{\pi}{2}$

$y = \dfrac{\pi}{4}$

47. $y = \tan^{-1}(-\sqrt{3})$

$\tan y = -\sqrt{3}, \ -\dfrac{\pi}{2} < y < \dfrac{\pi}{2}$

$y = -\dfrac{\pi}{3}$

49. $y = \cos^{-1}\left(-\dfrac{\sqrt{2}}{2}\right)$

$\cos y = -\dfrac{\sqrt{2}}{2}, \ 0 \le y \le \pi$

$y = \dfrac{3\pi}{4}$

51. $y = \sec^{-1}(-2)$

$\sec y = -2, \ 0 \le y \le \pi, \ y \neq \dfrac{\pi}{2}$

$y = \dfrac{2\pi}{3}$

53. $y = \text{arccot}(-1)$

$\cot y = -1, \ 0 < y < \pi$

$y = \dfrac{3\pi}{4}$

55. $\theta = \arcsin\left(-\dfrac{\sqrt{3}}{2}\right)$

$\sin \theta = -\dfrac{\sqrt{3}}{2}, \ -90° \le \theta \le 90°$

$\theta = -60°$

For Exercises 57–61, be sure that your calculator is in degree mode. Keystroke sequences may vary based on the type and/or model of calculator being used.

57. $\theta = \arctan 1.7804675$

Enter 1.7804675 [INV] [TAN]

or [2nd] [TAN] 1.7804675 [ENTER]

Display: 60.67924514

$\theta = 60.67924514°$

59. $\theta = \cos^{-1} .80396577$

Enter .80396577 [INV] [COS]

or [2nd] [COS] .80396577 [ENTER]

Display: 36.4895081

$\theta = 36.4895081°$

61. $\theta = \text{arc sec } 3.4723155$

Enter: 3.4723155 [1/x] [INV] [COS]

or [2nd] [COS] 3.4723155 [x⁻¹] [ENTER]

Display: 73.26220613

$\theta = 73.26220613°$

63. $\cos\,(\arccos\,(-1))$

Let $\omega = \arccos\,(-1)$

Then, $\cos \omega = 1, \ 0 \le x \le \pi$.

$\cos(\arccos(-1)) = \cos \omega = -1$

65. $\arccos\left(\cos \dfrac{3\pi}{4}\right) = x$

$\cos x = \cos \dfrac{3\pi}{4}, \ 0 \le x \le \pi$,

so $x = \dfrac{3\pi}{4}$.

$\arccos\left(\cos \dfrac{3\pi}{4}\right) = \dfrac{3\pi}{4}$

67. $\tan^{-1}\left(\tan\dfrac{\pi}{4}\right) = x$

$\tan x = \tan\dfrac{\pi}{4}, \ -\dfrac{\pi}{2} < x < \dfrac{\pi}{2},$

so $x = \dfrac{\pi}{4}$.

$\tan^{-1}\left(\tan\dfrac{\pi}{4}\right) = \dfrac{\pi}{4}$

69. $\sin\left(\arccos\dfrac{3}{4}\right)$

Let $\omega = \arccos\dfrac{3}{4}$, so $\cos\omega = \dfrac{3}{4}, \ 0 \le \omega \le \pi$.

Sketch a triangle and label it using $\cos\omega = \dfrac{3}{4}$.

The side opposite $\omega = \sqrt{4^2 - 3^2} = \sqrt{7}$.

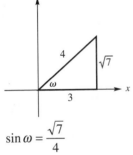

$\sin\omega = \dfrac{\sqrt{7}}{4}$

$\sin\left(\arccos\dfrac{3}{4}\right) = \sin\omega = \dfrac{\sqrt{7}}{4}$

71. $\cos(\csc^{-1}(-2))$

Let $\omega = \csc^{-1}(-2), \ -\dfrac{\pi}{2} \le \omega \le \dfrac{\pi}{2},$

$\omega \ne 0, \ \csc\omega = -2, \ \omega$ is in quadrant IV.

The side adjacent to ω is $\sqrt{2^2 - (-1)^2} = \sqrt{3}$.

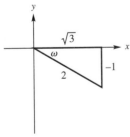

$\cos(\csc^{-1}(-2)) = \cos\omega = \dfrac{\sqrt{3}}{2}$

73. $\tan\left(\arcsin\dfrac{3}{5} + \arccos\dfrac{5}{7}\right)$

Let $\omega_1 = \arcsin\dfrac{3}{5}, \ -\dfrac{\pi}{2} \le \omega_1 \le \dfrac{\pi}{2}$.

$\sin\omega_1 = \dfrac{3}{5}$. The side adjacent to ω_1 is

$\sqrt{5^2 - 3^2} = 4$.

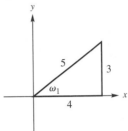

$\tan\omega_1 = \dfrac{3}{4}$

Let $\omega_2 = \arccos\dfrac{5}{7}, \ 0 \le \omega_2 \le \pi$.

$\cos\omega_2 = \dfrac{5}{7}$.

The side opposite ω_2 is

$\sqrt{7^2 - 5^2} = \sqrt{24} = 2\sqrt{6}$.

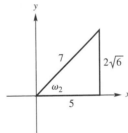

$\tan\omega_2 = \dfrac{2\sqrt{6}}{5}$

Use $\tan(\omega_1 + \omega_2) = \dfrac{\tan\omega_1 + \tan\omega_2}{1 - \tan\omega_1 \tan\omega_2}$.

$\tan\left(\arcsin\dfrac{3}{5} + \arccos\dfrac{5}{7}\right) = \dfrac{\dfrac{3}{4} + \dfrac{2\sqrt{6}}{5}}{1 - \left(\dfrac{3}{4}\right)\left(\dfrac{2\sqrt{6}}{5}\right)}$

$= \dfrac{\dfrac{15 + 8\sqrt{6}}{20}}{\dfrac{20 - 6\sqrt{6}}{20}}$

$= \dfrac{15 + 8\sqrt{6}}{20 - 6\sqrt{6}} \cdot \dfrac{20 + 6\sqrt{6}}{20 + 6\sqrt{6}}$

$= \dfrac{588 + 250\sqrt{6}}{184}$

$= \dfrac{294 + 125\sqrt{6}}{92}$

75. $\tan\left(\text{arcsec}\dfrac{\sqrt{u^2+1}}{u}\right)$

Let $s = \text{arcsec}\dfrac{\sqrt{u^2+1}}{u}$,

$0 < s < \pi, \; s \neq \dfrac{\pi}{2}$.

Then $\sec s = \dfrac{\sqrt{u^2+1}}{u}$.

If $u > 0$, s is in quadrant I.
If $u < 0$, s is in quadrant II.
The side opposite s, which is positive in both

quadrants, is $\sqrt{(u^2+1)-u^2} = 1$.

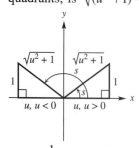

$\tan s = \dfrac{1}{u}$

$\tan\left(\text{arcsec}\dfrac{\sqrt{u^2+1}}{u}\right) = \tan s = \dfrac{1}{u}$

77. $2\tan x - 1 = 0$

$2\tan x = 1$

$\tan x = \dfrac{1}{2}$

$x = .463647609 \text{ or } x = 3.605240263$

79. $\tan x = \cot x, \; 0 \le x < 2\pi$

Use the identity $\cot x = \dfrac{1}{\tan x}$.

$\tan x = \dfrac{1}{\tan x}, \; \tan \neq 0$

$\tan^2 x = 1$

$\tan x = \pm 1$

If $\tan x = 1$, $x = \dfrac{\pi}{4}, \dfrac{5\pi}{4}$.

If $\tan x = -1$, $x = \dfrac{3\pi}{4}, \dfrac{7\pi}{4}$.

$x = \dfrac{\pi}{4}, \dfrac{3\pi}{4}, \dfrac{5\pi}{4}, \dfrac{7\pi}{4}$

81. $\tan^2 2x - 1 = 0, \; 0 \le 2x < 4\pi$

$\tan^2 2x = 1$

$\tan 2x = \pm 1$

If $\tan 2x = 1$, $2x = \dfrac{\pi}{4}, \dfrac{5\pi}{4}, \dfrac{9\pi}{4}, \dfrac{13\pi}{4}$

$x = \dfrac{\pi}{8}, \dfrac{5\pi}{8}, \dfrac{9\pi}{8}, \dfrac{13\pi}{8}$.

If $\tan 2x = -1$, $2x = \dfrac{3\pi}{4}, \dfrac{7\pi}{4}, \dfrac{11\pi}{4}, \dfrac{15\pi}{4}$

$x = \dfrac{3\pi}{8}, \dfrac{7\pi}{8}, \dfrac{11\pi}{8}, \dfrac{15\pi}{8}$.

$x = \dfrac{\pi}{8}, \dfrac{3\pi}{8}, \dfrac{5\pi}{8}, \dfrac{7\pi}{8}, \dfrac{9\pi}{8}, \dfrac{11\pi}{8}, \dfrac{13\pi}{8}, \dfrac{15\pi}{8}$

83. $\cos 2x + \cos x = 0, \; 0 \le x < 2\pi$

$2\cos^2 x - 1 + \cos x = 0$

$2\cos^2 x + \cos x - 1 = 0$

$(2\cos x - 1)(\cos x + 1) = 0$

$2\cos x - 1 = 0 \quad \text{or} \quad \cos x + 1 = 0$

$\cos x = \dfrac{1}{2} \qquad\qquad \cos x = -1$

$x = \dfrac{\pi}{3}, \dfrac{5\pi}{3} \qquad\qquad x = \pi$

$x = \dfrac{\pi}{3}, \pi, \dfrac{5\pi}{3}$

85. $\sin^2 \theta + 3\sin \theta + 2 = 0, \; 0° \le \theta < 360°$

$(\sin \theta + 2)(\sin \theta + 1) = 0$

$\sin \theta + 2 = 0 \quad \text{or} \quad \sin \theta + 1 = 0$

$\sin \theta = -2 \qquad\qquad \sin \theta = -1$

No solution $\qquad\qquad \theta = 270°$

$\theta = 270°$

87. $\sin 2\theta = \cos 2\theta + 1, \; 0° \le 2\theta < 720°$

$(\sin 2\theta)^2 = (\cos 2\theta + 1)^2$

$\sin^2 2\theta = \cos^2 2\theta + 2\cos 2\theta + 1$

$1 - \cos^2 2\theta = \cos^2 2\theta + 2\cos 2\theta + 1$

$2\cos^2 2\theta + 2\cos 2\theta = 0$

$\cos^2 2\theta + \cos 2\theta = 0$

$\cos 2\theta(\cos 2\theta + 1) = 0$

$\cos 2\theta = 0 \qquad\qquad \text{or} \quad \cos 2\theta + 1 = 0$

$2\theta = 90°, 270°, 450°, 630° \qquad \cos 2\theta = -1$

$2\theta = 180°, 540°$

Possible values for θ are
$\theta = 45°, \; 135°, \; 225°, \; 315°, \; 90°, \; 270°$.
All proposed solutions must be checked since the
solutions were found by squaring an equation.

A value for θ will be a solution if
$\sin 2\theta - \cos 2\theta = 1$.
$\theta = 45°, \quad 2\theta = 90°$
$\sin 90° - \cos 90° = 1 - 0 = 1$
$\theta = 90°, \quad 2\theta = 180°$
$\sin 180° - \cos 180° = 0 - (-1) = 1$
$\theta = 135°, \quad 2\theta = 270°$
$\sin 270° - \cos 270° = -1 - 0 \neq 1$
$\theta = 225°, \quad 2\theta = 450°$
$\sin 450° - \cos 450° = 1 - 0 = 1$
$\theta = 270°, \quad 2\theta = 540°$
$\sin 540° - \cos 540° = 0 - (-1) = 1$
$\theta = 315°, \quad 2\theta = 630°$
$\sin 630° - \cos 630° = -1 - 0 \neq 1$
$\theta = 45°, 90°, 225°, 270°$

89. $3\cos^2\theta + 2\cos\theta - 1 = 0$
$(3\cos\theta - 1)(\cos\theta + 1) = 0$
$3\cos\theta - 1 = 0 \quad$ or $\quad \cos\theta + 1 = 0$
$\cos\theta = \dfrac{1}{3} \qquad\qquad \cos\theta = -1$
$\theta = 70.5°, \ 289.5° \qquad \theta = 180°$
$\theta = 70.5°, 180°, 289.5°$

91. $4y = 2\sin x$
$2y = \sin x$
$x = \arcsin 2y$

93. $2y = \tan(3x + 2)$
$3x + 2 = \arctan 2y$
$3x = \arctan 2y - 2$
$x = \dfrac{1}{3}(\arctan 2y - 2)$
$x = \left(\dfrac{1}{3}\arctan 2y\right) - \dfrac{2}{3}$

95. $\dfrac{4}{3}\arctan\dfrac{x}{2} = \pi$
$\arctan\dfrac{x}{2} = \dfrac{3\pi}{4}$
But, by definition, the range of arctan is $\left(-\dfrac{\pi}{2}, \dfrac{\pi}{2}\right)$. So, this equation has no solution.

97. $\arccos x + \arctan 1 = \dfrac{11\pi}{12}$
$\arccos x = \dfrac{11\pi}{12} - \arctan 1$
$\arccos x = \dfrac{11\pi}{12} - \dfrac{\pi}{4}$
$\arccos x = \dfrac{11\pi}{12} - \dfrac{3\pi}{12} = \dfrac{8\pi}{12}$
$\arccos x = \dfrac{2\pi}{3}$
$\cos\dfrac{2\pi}{3} = x$
$x = -\dfrac{1}{2}$

99. a. Let α be the angle to the left of θ.
Then $\tan(\alpha + \theta) = \dfrac{5 + 10}{x}$
$\alpha + \theta = \arctan\left(\dfrac{15}{x}\right)$
$\theta = \arctan\left(\dfrac{15}{x}\right) - \alpha$
$\theta = \arctan\left(\dfrac{15}{x}\right) - \arctan\left(\dfrac{5}{x}\right)$

b.

The maximum occurs at $x = 8.6602567$.

c. $x = \sqrt{5 \cdot 15} = \sqrt{75} = 5\sqrt{3}$

101. If $\theta_1 > 48.8°$, then $\theta_2 > 90°$ and the light beam is completely underwater.

103. To see the graph, enter the function
$$Y_1 = ((x > 0) - (x < 0)) \cdot \left(\dfrac{\pi}{2} - \tan^{-1}\sqrt{x^2 - 1}\right).$$

Radian mode

Chapter 6 Test Exercises

1. Since $\dfrac{3\pi}{2} < x < 2\pi$, $\sin x < 0$ and $\cos x > 0$.
Then

$$\sec^2 x = \tan^2 x + 1 = \left(-\dfrac{5}{6}\right)^2 + 1$$
$$= \dfrac{25}{36} + 1$$
$$= \dfrac{61}{36}$$

So, $\sec x = \dfrac{\sqrt{61}}{6}$, taking the positive square

root. Thus, $\cos x = \dfrac{6}{\sqrt{61}} = \dfrac{6\sqrt{61}}{61}$.

$$\sin x = \tan x \cos x = -\dfrac{5}{6} \cdot \dfrac{6\sqrt{61}}{61} = -\dfrac{5\sqrt{61}}{61}$$

2. $\tan^2 x - \sec^2 x = \left(\dfrac{\sin x}{\cos x}\right)^2 - \left(\dfrac{1}{\cos x}\right)^2$

$$= \dfrac{\sin^2 x - 1}{\cos^2 x}$$
$$= -\dfrac{\cos^2 x}{\cos^2 x}$$
$$= -1$$

3. Since x is in quadrant III, $\cos x < 0$. Then
$$\sin^2 x + \cos^2 x = 1$$
$$\cos^2 x = 1 - \sin^2 x$$
$$= 1 - \left(-\dfrac{1}{3}\right)^2$$
$$= 1 - \dfrac{1}{9}$$
$$= \dfrac{8}{9}$$
$$\cos x = -\sqrt{\dfrac{8}{9}} = \dfrac{-2\sqrt{2}}{3}$$

Since y is in quadrant II, $\sin y > 0$. Then
$$\sin^2 y + \cos^2 y = 1$$
$$\sin^2 y = 1 - \cos^2 y$$
$$= 1 - \left(-\dfrac{2}{5}\right)^2$$
$$= 1 - \dfrac{4}{25}$$
$$= \dfrac{21}{25}$$
$$\sin y = \sqrt{\dfrac{21}{25}} = \dfrac{\sqrt{21}}{5}$$

$$\sin(x + y) = \sin x \cos y + \cos x \sin y$$
$$= \left(-\dfrac{1}{3}\right)\left(-\dfrac{2}{5}\right) + \left(-\dfrac{2\sqrt{2}}{3}\right)\left(\dfrac{\sqrt{21}}{5}\right)$$
$$= \dfrac{2}{15} - \dfrac{2\sqrt{42}}{15}$$
$$= \dfrac{2 - 2\sqrt{42}}{15}$$

$$\cos(x - y) = \cos x \cos y + \sin x \sin y$$
$$= \left(-\dfrac{2\sqrt{2}}{3}\right)\left(-\dfrac{2}{5}\right) + \left(-\dfrac{1}{3}\right)\left(\dfrac{\sqrt{21}}{5}\right)$$
$$= \dfrac{4\sqrt{2}}{15} - \dfrac{\sqrt{21}}{15}$$
$$= \dfrac{4\sqrt{2} - \sqrt{21}}{15}$$

$$\tan(x + y) = \dfrac{\tan x + \tan y}{1 - \tan x \tan y}$$
$$= \dfrac{\dfrac{\sqrt{2}}{4} + \left(-\dfrac{\sqrt{21}}{2}\right)}{1 - \left(\dfrac{\sqrt{2}}{4}\right)\left(-\dfrac{\sqrt{21}}{2}\right)}$$
$$= \dfrac{2\sqrt{2} - 4\sqrt{21}}{8 + \sqrt{42}}$$

4. $\sin(-22.5°) = \pm\sqrt{\dfrac{1 - \cos(-45°)}{2}}$
$$= \pm\sqrt{\dfrac{1 - \dfrac{\sqrt{2}}{2}}{2}}$$
$$= \pm\sqrt{\dfrac{2 - \sqrt{2}}{4}}$$
$$= \pm\dfrac{\sqrt{2 - \sqrt{2}}}{2}$$

Since $-22.5°$ is in quadrant IV, $\sin(-22.5°)$ is

negative. $\sin(-22.5°) = \dfrac{-\sqrt{2 - \sqrt{2}}}{2}$

5.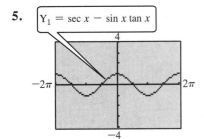

$Y_1 = \sec x - \sin x \tan x$

The graph of $\sec x - \sin x \tan x$ appears to be the same as the graph of $\cos x$.

$$\sec x - \sin x \tan x = \frac{1}{\cos x} - \sin x \left(\frac{\sin x}{\cos x}\right)$$
$$= \frac{1 - \sin^2 x}{\cos x}$$
$$= \frac{\cos^2 x}{\cos x}$$
$$= \cos x$$

6.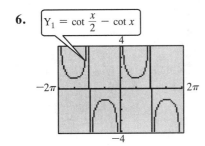

$Y_1 = \cot \frac{x}{2} - \cot x$

The graph of $\cot \frac{x}{2} - \cot x$ appears to be the same as the graph of $\csc x$.

$$\cot \frac{x}{2} - \cot x = \frac{1 + \cos x}{\sin x} - \frac{\cos x}{\sin x}$$
$$= \frac{1 + \cos x - \cos x}{\sin x}$$
$$= \frac{1}{\sin x}$$
$$= \csc x$$

7. Verify $\sec^2 B = \dfrac{1}{1 - \sin^2 B}$.

Work with the right side.

$$\frac{1}{1 - \sin^2 B} = \frac{1}{\cos^2 B} = \sec^2 B$$

8. Verify $\cos 2A = \dfrac{\cot A - \tan A}{\csc A \sec A}$.

Work with the right side.

$$\frac{\cot A - \tan A}{\csc A \sec A} = \frac{\frac{\cos A}{\sin A} - \frac{\sin A}{\cos A}}{\left(\frac{1}{\sin A}\right)\left(\frac{1}{\cos A}\right)}$$

$$= \frac{\frac{\cos^2 A - \sin^2 A}{\sin A \cos A}}{\frac{1}{\sin A \cos A}}$$

$$= \frac{\cos^2 A - \sin^2 A}{\sin A \cos A} \cdot \frac{\sin A \cos A}{1}$$

$$= \cos^2 A - \sin^2 A$$

$$= \cos^2 2A$$

9. (a) $\cos(270° - \theta) = \cos 270° \cos \theta + \sin 270° \sin \theta$
$$= 0 \cdot \cos \theta + (-1)\sin \theta$$
$$= -\sin \theta$$

(b) $\sin(\pi - \theta) = \sin \pi \cos \theta + \cos \pi \sin \theta$
$$= 0 \cdot \cos \theta + (-1)\sin \theta$$
$$= -\sin \theta$$

10. (a) $V = 163 \sin \omega t$. Since $\sin x = \cos\left(\dfrac{\pi}{2} - x\right)$,

$$V = 163 \cos\left(\frac{\pi}{2} - \omega t\right).$$

(b) If $V = 163 \cos\left(\dfrac{\pi}{2} - 120\pi t\right)$, the maximum

voltage occurs when $\cos\left(\dfrac{\pi}{2} - 120\pi t\right) = 1$.

Thus, the maximum voltagae is
$V = 163$ volts.

$\cos\left(\dfrac{\pi}{2} - 120\pi t\right) = 1$ when

$\dfrac{\pi}{2} - 120\pi t = 2k\pi$, where k is any integer.

The first maximum occurs when

$$\frac{\pi}{2} - 120\pi t = 0$$
$$\frac{\pi}{2} = 120\pi t$$
$$\frac{1}{120\pi} \cdot \frac{\pi}{2} = t$$
$$\frac{1}{240} = t$$

The maximum voltage will first occur at $\dfrac{1}{240}$ sec.

11.

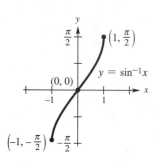

$y = \sin^{-1}x$

$(0, 0)$

$\left(1, \dfrac{\pi}{2}\right)$

$\left(-1, -\dfrac{\pi}{2}\right)$

Domain: $[-1, 1]$

Range: $\left[-\dfrac{\pi}{2}, \dfrac{\pi}{2}\right]$

12. (a)
$$y = \arccos\left(-\dfrac{1}{2}\right)$$
$$y = \cos^{-1}\left(-\dfrac{1}{2}\right)$$
$$\cos y = -\dfrac{1}{2}, \ 0 \le y \le \pi$$
$$y = \dfrac{2\pi}{3}$$

(b)
$$y = \sin^{-1}\left(-\dfrac{\sqrt{3}}{2}\right)$$
$$\sin y = -\dfrac{\sqrt{3}}{2}, -\dfrac{\pi}{2} \le y \le \dfrac{\pi}{2}$$
$$y = -\dfrac{\pi}{3}$$

(c)
$$y = \tan^{-1}(0)$$
$$\tan y = 0, \ -\dfrac{\pi}{2} < y < \dfrac{\pi}{2}$$
$$y = 0$$

(d)
$$y = \text{arcsec}(-2)$$
$$y = \sec^{-1}(-2)$$
$$\sec y = -2, 0 \le y \le \pi, y \ne \dfrac{\pi}{2}$$
$$y = \dfrac{2\pi}{3}$$

(e)
$$y = \csc^{-1}\left(\dfrac{2\sqrt{3}}{3}\right)$$
$$\csc y = \dfrac{2\sqrt{3}}{3}, -\dfrac{\pi}{2} \le y \le \dfrac{\pi}{2}, y \ne 0$$
$$y = \dfrac{\pi}{3}$$

(f)
$$y = \cot^{-1}(\sqrt{3})$$
$$\cot y = \sqrt{3}, -\dfrac{\pi}{2} \le y \le \dfrac{\pi}{2}, \ y \ne 0$$
$$y = \dfrac{\pi}{6}$$

13. (a) Let $\arcsin\dfrac{2}{3} = u$, so $\sin u = \dfrac{2}{3}$.

Then, $\cos\left(\arcsin\dfrac{2}{3}\right) = \cos u = \dfrac{\sqrt{5}}{3}$

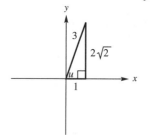

(b) Let $\arccos\left(\dfrac{1}{3}\right) = u$, so $\cos u = \dfrac{1}{3}$.

Then $\sin\left(2\cos^{-1}\dfrac{1}{3}\right) = \sin 2u$
$$= 2\sin u \cos u$$
$$= 2\left(\dfrac{2\sqrt{2}}{3}\right)\left(\dfrac{1}{3}\right)$$
$$= \dfrac{4\sqrt{2}}{9}$$

14. Let $x = \arcsin u$, then $\sin x = \dfrac{u}{1}$

$\tan(\arcsin u) = \tan x$

$$= \frac{u}{\sqrt{1-u^2}} \cdot \frac{\sqrt{1-u^2}}{\sqrt{1-u^2}}$$

$$= \frac{u\sqrt{1-u^2}}{1-u^2}$$

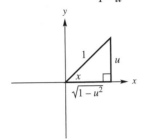

15.
$$\sin^2 \theta = \cos^2 \theta + 1$$
$$\sin^2 \theta - \cos^2 \theta = 1$$
$$-\cos 2\theta = 1$$
$$\cos 2\theta = -1$$
$$2\theta = 180° + n360°$$
$$\theta = 90° + 180°n$$
$$\theta = 90°, \ 270°$$
(since θ must be in the interval $[0, 360°)$)

16.
$$\csc^2 \theta - 2\cot \theta = 4$$
$$1 + \cot^2 \theta - 2\cot \theta = 4$$
$$\cot^2 \theta - 2\cot - 3 = 0$$
$$(\cot \theta - 3)(\cot \theta + 1) = 0$$
$$\cot \theta - 3 = 0 \qquad \text{or} \quad \cot \theta + 1 = 0$$
$$\cot \theta = 3 \qquad\qquad\qquad \cot \theta = -1$$
$$\theta = \tan^{-1}\left(\frac{1}{3}\right) \qquad\qquad \theta = \tan^{-1}(-1)$$
$$\theta = 18.4°, \ 198.4° \qquad \theta = 135°, \ 315°$$
$$\theta = 18.4°, \ 135°, \ 198.4°, \ 315°$$

17.
$$\cos x = \cos 2x$$
$$\cos x = 2\cos^2 x - 1$$
$$2\cos^2 x - \cos x - 1 = 0$$
$$(2\cos x + 1)(\cos x - 1) = 0$$
$$2\cos x + 1 = 0 \quad \text{or} \quad \cos x - 1 = 0$$
$$2\cos x = -1 \qquad\qquad \cos x = 1$$
$$\cos x = -\frac{1}{2} \qquad\qquad x = 0$$
$$x = \frac{2\pi}{3}, \ \frac{4\pi}{3}$$
$$x = 0, \ \frac{2\pi}{3}, \ \frac{4\pi}{3}$$

18. $2\sqrt{3}\sin\left(\dfrac{\theta}{2}\right) = 3$

$$\sin\left(\frac{\theta}{2}\right) = \frac{3}{2\sqrt{3}}$$
$$\frac{\theta}{2} = \arcsin\left(\frac{3}{2\sqrt{3}}\right)$$
$$\frac{\theta}{2} = 60°, \ 120°$$
$$\theta = 120°, \ 240°$$

19. (a)
$$y = \cos(3x)$$
$$3x = \arccos y$$
$$x = \frac{\arccos y}{3}$$

(b) Let $\omega = \arctan\left(\dfrac{4}{3}\right)$. Then $\tan \omega = \dfrac{4}{3}$.

$$\arcsin x = \arctan\left(\frac{4}{3}\right)$$
$$\arcsin x = \omega$$
$$x = \sin \omega = \frac{4}{5}$$

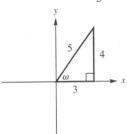

20.
$$y = \frac{\pi}{8}\cos\left[\pi\left(t - \frac{1}{3}\right)\right]$$
$$0 = \frac{\pi}{8}\cos\left[\pi\left(t - \frac{1}{3}\right)\right]$$
$$0 = \cos\left[\pi\left(t - \frac{1}{3}\right)\right]$$
$$\pi\left(t - \frac{1}{3}\right) = \arccos(0)$$
$$\pi\left(t - \frac{1}{3}\right) = \frac{\pi}{2} + n\pi, \ \text{where } n \text{ is an integer}$$
$$t - \frac{1}{3} = \frac{1}{2} + n$$
$$t = \frac{1}{2} + \frac{1}{3} + n$$
$$t = \frac{5}{6} + n$$

In the interval $[0, \pi)$, $n = 0, 1$, and 2 provide
valid values for t.

$$t = \frac{5}{6}, \frac{5}{6}+1, \frac{5}{6}+2$$

$$t = \frac{5}{6}\sec, \frac{11}{6}\sec, \frac{17}{6}\sec$$

CHAPTER 7 APPLICATIONS OF TRIGONOMETRY

Section 7.1

Exercises

1. C

3. The measure of angle C is
    $180° - (60° + 75°) = 45°$.

    $$\frac{a}{\sin A} = \frac{c}{\sin C}$$
    $$\frac{a}{\sin 60°} = \frac{\sqrt{2}}{\sin 45°}$$
    $$a = \frac{\sqrt{2}\sin 60°}{\sin 45°}$$
    $$a = \frac{\sqrt{2}\left(\frac{\sqrt{3}}{2}\right)}{\frac{\sqrt{2}}{2}}$$
    $$a = \sqrt{3}$$

5. $A = 37°$, $B = 48°$, $c = 18$ m
    $$C = 180° - A - B$$
    $$C = 180° - 37° - 48°$$
    $$C = 95°$$
    $$\frac{b}{\sin B} = \frac{c}{\sin C}$$
    $$b = \frac{18\sin 48°}{\sin 95°}$$
    $$b = 13 \text{ m}$$
    $$\frac{a}{\sin A} = \frac{c}{\sin C}$$
    $$a = \frac{18\sin 37°}{\sin 95°}$$
    $$a = 11 \text{ m}$$

7. $A = 27.2°$, $C = 115.5°$, $c = 76.0$ ft
    $$B = 180° - A - C$$
    $$B = 180° - 27.2° - 115.5°$$
    $$B = 37.3°$$
    $$\frac{a}{\sin A} = \frac{c}{\sin C}$$
    $$a = \frac{76.0\sin 27.2°}{\sin 115.5°}$$
    $$a = 38.5 \text{ ft}$$
    $$\frac{b}{\sin B} = \frac{c}{\sin C}$$
    $$b = \frac{76.0\sin 37.3°}{\sin 115.5°}$$
    $$b = 51.0 \text{ ft}$$

9. $A = 68.41°$, $B = 54.23°$, $a = 12.75$ ft
    $$C = 180° - A - B$$
    $$C = 180° - 68.41° - 54.23°$$
    $$C = 57.36°$$
    $$\frac{a}{\sin A} = \frac{b}{\sin B}$$
    $$b = \frac{12.75\sin 54.23°}{\sin 68.41°}$$
    $$b = 11.13 \text{ ft}$$
    $$\frac{a}{\sin A} = \frac{c}{\sin C}$$
    $$c = \frac{12.75\sin 57.36°}{\sin 68.41°}$$
    $$c = 11.55 \text{ ft}$$

11. $B = 20°50'$, $AC = 132$ ft, $C = 103°10'$
    $$A = 180° - B - C$$
    $$A = 180° - 20°50' - 103°10'$$
    $$A = 56°00'$$
    $$\frac{AC}{\sin B} = \frac{AB}{\sin C}$$
    $$AB = \frac{132\sin 103°10'}{\sin 20°50'}$$
    $$AB = 361 \text{ ft}$$
    $$\frac{BC}{\sin A} = \frac{AC}{\sin B}$$
    $$BC = \frac{132\sin 56°00'}{\sin 20°50'}$$
    $$BC = 308 \text{ ft}$$

13. $A = 39.70°$, $C = 30.35°$, $b = 39.74$ m
    $$B = 180° - A - C$$
    $$B = 180° - 39.70° - 30.35°$$
    $$B = 110.0° \text{ (rounded)}$$
    $$\frac{a}{\sin A} = \frac{b}{\sin B}$$
    $$a = \frac{39.74\sin 39.70°}{\sin 109.95°}$$
    $$a = 27.01 \text{ m}$$
    $$\frac{b}{\sin B} = \frac{c}{\sin C}$$
    $$c = \frac{39.74\sin 30.35°}{\sin 109.95°}$$
    $$c = 21.36 \text{ m}$$

15. $B = 42.88°, C = 102.40°, b = 3974$ ft

$A = 180° - B - C$

$A = 180° - 42.88° - 102.40°$

$A = 34.72°$

$$\frac{a}{\sin A} = \frac{b}{\sin B}$$

$$a = \frac{3974 \sin 34.72°}{\sin 42.88°}$$

$$a = 3326 \text{ ft}$$

$$\frac{b}{\sin B} = \frac{c}{\sin C}$$

$$c = \frac{3974 \sin 102.40°}{\sin 42.88°}$$

$$c = 5704 \text{ ft}$$

17. A

19. The vertical distance from the point $(3, 4)$ to the x-axis is 4.

(a) If h is more than 4, two triangles can be drawn. But h must be less than 5 for both triangles to be on the positive x-axis. So, $4 < h < 5$.

(b) If $h = 4$, then exactly one triangle is possible. If $h > 5$, then only one triangle is possible on the positive x-axis.

(c) If $h < 4$, then no triangle is possible, since the side of length h would not reach the x-axis.

21. $a = 31, b = 26, B = 48°$

$$\frac{a}{\sin A} = \frac{b}{\sin B}$$

$$\frac{31}{\sin A} = \frac{26}{\sin 48°}$$

$$\sin A = \frac{31 \sin 48°}{26}$$

$$\sin A \approx .886$$

$$A \approx 62.4°$$

Another possible value for A is $180° - 62.4° = 117.6°$. Therefore, two triangles are possible.

23. $a = 50, b = 61, A = 58°$

$$\frac{a}{\sin A} = \frac{b}{\sin B}$$

$$\frac{50}{\sin 58°} = \frac{61}{\sin B}$$

$$\sin B = \frac{61 \sin 58°}{50}$$

$$\sin B \approx 1.03$$

$\sin B > 1$ is impossible. Therefore, no triangle is possible for the given parts.

25.

$$\frac{b}{\sin B} = \frac{a}{\sin A}$$

$$\frac{2}{\sin B} = \frac{\sqrt{6}}{\sin 60°}$$

$$\sin B = \frac{2 \sin 60°}{\sqrt{6}}$$

$$= \frac{2\left(\frac{\sqrt{3}}{2}\right)}{\sqrt{6}}$$

$$= \frac{\sqrt{2}}{2}$$

$$B = 45°$$

Another possible value for B is $180° - 45 = 135°$, but this is too large since $A = 60°$. Therefore, $B = 45°$.

In Exercises 27–39, the number of possible triangles is found based on the given conditions. Remember that, for example, if angle B and sides a and b are given such that $a > b > a \sin B$, then two triangles are possible.

27. $A = 29.7°, b = 41.5$ ft, $a = 27.2$ ft

$b > a > b \sin A$ tells us that there are two possible triangles.

$$\frac{\sin B}{b} = \frac{\sin A}{a}$$

$$\sin B = \frac{41.5 \sin 29.7°}{27.2}$$

$$\sin B = .75593878$$

$$B_1 = 49.1°$$

$$C_1 = 180° - A - B_1$$

$$= 180° - 29.7 - 49.1°$$

$$= 101.2°$$

$$B_2 = 180° - B_1 = 130.9°$$

$$C_2 = 19.4°$$

29. $B = 74.3°, a = 859$ m, $b = 783$ m

$$\frac{\sin A}{a} = \frac{\sin B}{b}$$

$$\sin A = \frac{859 \sin 74.3°}{783}$$

$$\sin A = 1.0561331$$

$\sin A > 1$ is impossible.

Note that $b < a \sin B$.

No such triangle exists.

31. $A = 142.13°, b = 5.432$ ft, $a = 7.297$ ft
$a > b$ tells us that there is one triangle.
$$\frac{\sin B}{b} = \frac{\sin A}{a}$$
$$\sin B = \frac{5.432 \sin 142.13°}{7.297}$$
$$\sin B = .45697580$$
$$B = 27.19°$$
B must be acute since A is obtuse.
$$C = 180° - 142.13° - 27.19°$$
$$C = 10.68°$$

33. $A = 42.5°, a = 15.6$ ft, $b = 8.14$ ft
$a > b$ tells us that there is only one triangle.
$$\frac{\sin B}{b} = \frac{\sin A}{a}$$
$$\sin B = \frac{b \sin A}{a}$$
$$= \frac{8.14 \sin 42.5°}{15.6}$$
$$\sin B = .35251951$$
$$B = 20.6°$$
$B \neq 159.4°$ since $159.4° + A > 180°$.
$$C = 180° - 42.5° - 20.6°$$
$$= 116.9°$$
$$\frac{c}{\sin C} = \frac{a}{\sin A}$$
$$c = \frac{a \sin C}{\sin A}$$
$$= \frac{15.6 \sin 116.9°}{\sin 42.5°}$$
$$c = 20.6 \text{ ft}$$

35. $B = 72.2°, b = 78.3$ m, $c = 145$ m
$$\frac{\sin C}{c} = \frac{\sin B}{b}$$
$$\sin C = \frac{c \sin B}{b}$$
$$= \frac{145 \sin 72.2°}{78.3}$$
$$\sin C = 1.7632026$$
$\sin C > 1$ is impossible. Note that $c \sin B > b$.
No such triangle exists.

37. $a = 38°40', a = 9.72$ km, $b = 11.8$ km
$b > a > b \sin A$ tells us that there are two possible triangles.
$$\frac{\sin B}{b} = \frac{\sin A}{a}$$
$$\sin B = \frac{b \sin A}{a}$$
$$= \frac{11.8 \sin 38°40'}{9.72}$$
$$\sin B = .75848811$$

$$B_1 = 49°20'$$
$$C_1 = 180° - 38°40' - 49°20'$$
$$C_1 = 92°00'$$
$$\frac{c_1}{\sin C_1} = \frac{a}{\sin A}$$
$$c_1 = \frac{a \sin C_1}{\sin A}$$
$$= \frac{9.72 \sin 92°00'}{\sin 38°40'}$$
$$c_1 = 15.5 \text{ km}$$
$$B_2 = 130°40'$$
$$C_2 = 180° - 38°40' - 130°40'$$
$$C_2 = 10°40'$$
$$\frac{c_2}{\sin C_2} = \frac{a}{\sin A}$$
$$c_2 = \frac{a \sin C_2}{\sin A}$$
$$= \frac{9.72 \sin 10°40'}{\sin 38°40'}$$
$$c_2 = 2.88 \text{ km}$$

39. $B = 39.68°, a = 29.81$ m, $b = 23.76$ m
$a > b > a \sin B$ tells us that there are two possible triangles.
$$\frac{\sin A}{a} = \frac{\sin B}{b}$$
$$\sin A = \frac{a \sin B}{b}$$
$$= \frac{29.81 \sin 39.68°}{23.76}$$
$$\sin A = .80108002$$
$$A_1 = 53.23°$$
$$C_1 = 180° - 53.23° - 39.68°$$
$$C_1 = 87.09°$$
$$\frac{b}{\sin B} = \frac{c_1}{\sin C_1}$$
$$c_1 = \frac{b \sin C_1}{\sin B}$$
$$= \frac{23.76 \sin 87.09°}{\sin 39.68°}$$
$$c_1 = 37.16 \text{ m}$$
$$A_2 = 126.77°$$
$$C_2 = 180° - 126.77° - 39.68°$$
$$C_2 = 13.55°$$
$$\frac{b}{\sin B} = \frac{c_2}{\sin C_2}$$
$$c_2 = \frac{b \sin C_2}{\sin B}$$
$$= \frac{23.76 \sin 13.55°}{\sin 39.68°}$$
$$c_2 = 8.719 \text{ m}$$

41. $a = \sqrt{5}, c = 2\sqrt{5}, A = 30°$

$$\frac{a}{\sin A} = \frac{c}{\sin C}$$

$$\sin C = \frac{2\sqrt{5}\sin 30°}{\sqrt{5}}$$

$$\sin C = 1$$
$$C = 90°$$

This is a right triangle.

45. Let $A = 38°\,50'$, $a = 21.9$, $b = 78.3$.

$b\sin A = 78.3\sin 38°\,50'$
$\qquad\quad = 49.1$

Thus, $21.9 < 49.1$. That is, $a < b\sin A$.
The piece of property cannot exist with the given data.

47.

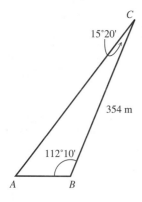

$A = 180° - B - C$
$A = 180° - 112°\,10' - 15°\,20'$
$A = 52°\,30'$

$$\frac{BC}{\sin A} = \frac{AB}{\sin C}$$

$$AB = \frac{354\sin 15°\,20'}{\sin 52°\,30'}$$

$$AB = 118\text{ m}$$

49. Let C = the transmitter.

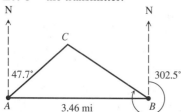

Since side AB is on an east-west line, the angle between it and any north-south line is 90°.
$A = 90° - 47.7° = 42.3°$
$B = 302.5° - 270° = 32.5°$
$C = 180° - A - B$
$\quad = 180° - 42.3° - 32.5°$
$C = 105.2°$

$$\frac{AC}{\sin 32.5°} = \frac{3.46}{\sin 105.2°}$$

$$AC = \frac{3.46\sin 32.5°}{\sin 105.2°}$$

$$AC = 1.93\text{ mi}$$

51.

$$\frac{x}{\sin 54.8°} = \frac{12.0}{\sin 70.4°}$$

$$x = \frac{12.0\sin 54.8°}{\sin 70.4°}$$

$$x = 10.4\text{ in.}$$

53. Label α in the triangle as shown.

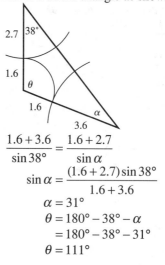

$$\frac{1.6 + 3.6}{\sin 38°} = \frac{1.6 + 2.7}{\sin \alpha}$$

$$\sin \alpha = \frac{(1.6 + 2.7)\sin 38°}{1.6 + 3.6}$$

$$\alpha = 31°$$
$$\theta = 180° - 38° - \alpha$$
$$\quad = 180° - 38° - 31°$$
$$\theta = 111°$$

55. Let x = the distance to the lighthouse at bearing N 37° E.
y = the distance to the lighthouse at bearing N 25° E.

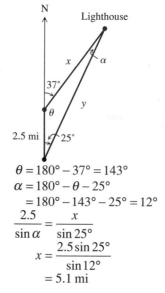

$\theta = 180° - 37° = 143°$
$\alpha = 180° - \theta - 25°$
$\quad = 180° - 143° - 25° = 12°$

$$\frac{2.5}{\sin \alpha} = \frac{x}{\sin 25°}$$

$$x = \frac{2.5\sin 25°}{\sin 12°}$$

$$\quad = 5.1\text{ mi}$$

$$\frac{2.5}{\sin\alpha} = \frac{y}{\sin\theta}$$
$$y = \frac{2.5\sin 143°}{\sin 12°}$$
$$= 7.2 \text{ mi}$$

57.

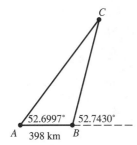

Angle C is equal to the difference between the angles of elevation.
$C = B - A = 52.7430° - 52.6997° = .0433°$
The distance BC to the moon can be determined using the law of sines.
$$\frac{BC}{\sin A} = \frac{AB}{\sin C}$$
$$BC = \frac{AB\sin A}{\sin C}$$
$$= \frac{398\sin 52.6997°}{\sin .0433°}$$
$$\approx 418,930 \text{ km}$$
If one finds distance AC, then
$$AC = \frac{AB\sin B}{\sin C}$$
$$= \frac{398\sin(180° - 52.7430°)}{\sin .0433°}$$
$$\approx 419,171 \text{ km.}$$
In either case the distance is approximately 419,000 km compared to the actual value of 406,000 km.

59. Using $K = \frac{1}{2}bh$,
$$K = \frac{1}{2}(1)(\sqrt{2})$$
$$= \frac{\sqrt{2}}{2}.$$
Using $K = \frac{1}{2}ab\sin C$,
$$K = \frac{1}{2}(2)(1)\sin 45°$$
$$= \frac{1}{2}(2)(1)\left(\frac{\sqrt{2}}{2}\right)$$
$$= \frac{\sqrt{2}}{2}.$$

61. $C = 72.2°, b = 43.8$ ft, $a = 35.1$ ft
Angle C is included between sides a and b.
$$\text{Area} = \frac{1}{2}ab\sin C$$
$$= \frac{1}{2}(35.1)(43.8)\sin 72.2°$$
$$= 732 \text{ ft}^2$$

63. $C = 142.7°, a = 21.9$ km, $b = 24.6$ km
Angle C is included between sides a and b.
$$\text{Area} = \frac{1}{2}ab\sin C$$
$$= \frac{1}{2}(21.9)(24.6)\sin 142.7°$$
$$= 163 \text{ km}^2$$

65. A $= 34.97°, b = 35.29$ m, $c = 28.67$ m
Angle A is included between sides b and c.
$$\text{Area} = \frac{1}{2}bc\sin A$$
$$= \frac{1}{2}(35.29)(28.67)\sin 34.97°$$
$$= 289.9 \text{ m}^2$$

67. $\text{Area} = \frac{1}{2}(52.1)(21.3)\sin 42.2°$
$$= 373 \text{ m}^2$$

68. The function $y = \sin x$ is increasing from $y = 0$ to $y = 1$ on the interval $0 \le x \le \frac{\pi}{2}$.

70. $\dfrac{a}{\sin A} = \dfrac{b}{\sin B}$
Solve for b.
$$\frac{a\sin B}{\sin A} = b$$
$$b = \frac{a\sin B}{\sin A}$$

71. From Exercise 70, $b = \dfrac{a\sin B}{\sin A}$.
If $\dfrac{\sin B}{\sin A} < 1$, then $b = a \cdot \dfrac{\sin B}{\sin A} < a \cdot 1$ or a.
So, $b < a$.

73. **(a)** Since $\dfrac{a}{\sin A} = \dfrac{b}{\sin B} = \dfrac{c}{\sin C} = 2r$

and $r = \dfrac{1}{2}$ (since the diameter is 1),

$$\dfrac{a}{\sin A} = \dfrac{b}{\sin B} = \dfrac{c}{\sin C} = 2\left(\dfrac{1}{2}\right) = 1.$$

Then, $a = \sin A$

$b = \sin B$

$c = \sin C$

74. **(b)** If $A = 18°$ and $B = 36°$

$$\text{Area} = \left[\dfrac{5\sin 18° \sin 36°}{\sin(18+36)°}\right] R^2$$

$$\approx 1.12257 R^2$$

(c) **i.** $11.4 \text{ in.} \times (10 \div 13) \text{ in.} = 8.77 \text{ in.}^2$

ii. $A = 50\left[5\dfrac{\sin 18° \sin 36°}{\sin(18° + 36°)}\right](.308)^2$

$A = 5.32 \text{ in.}^2$

iii. red

Section 7.2

Connections *(page 556)*

1. $A = \dfrac{1}{2}\left|(x_1 y_2 - y_1 x_2 + x_2 y_3 - y_2 x_3 + x_3 y_1 - y_3 x_1)\right|$

$= \dfrac{1}{2}\left|(2 \cdot 3 - 5(-1) + (-1)(0) - 3 \cdot 4 + 4 \cdot 5 - 0 \cdot 2)\right|$

$= \dfrac{1}{2}\left|(6 + 5 - 12 + 20)\right|$

$= \dfrac{1}{2}|19|$

$= 9.5$ square units

2. $a = \sqrt{(2 - (-1))^2 + (5 - 3)^2}$

$= \sqrt{3^2 + 2^2}$

$= \sqrt{13} \approx 3.60555$

$b = \sqrt{(2 - 4)^2 + (5 - 0)^2}$

$= \sqrt{(-2)^2 + 5^2}$

$= \sqrt{29} \approx 5.38516$

$c = \sqrt{(-1 - 4)^2 + (3 - 0)^2}$

$= \sqrt{(-5)^2 + 3^2}$

$= \sqrt{34} \approx 5.83095$

$s = \dfrac{1}{2}(a + b + c)$

$= \dfrac{1}{2}(\sqrt{13} + \sqrt{29} + \sqrt{34}) \approx 7.41083$

$A = \sqrt{s(s-a)(s-b)(s-c)}$

$\approx \sqrt{(7.41083)(3.80528)(2.02567)(1.57988)}$

≈ 9.5 square units

3. By the law of cosines,

$c^2 = a^2 + b^2 - 2ab\cos C$

$2ab\cos C = a^2 + b^2 - c^2$

$\cos C = \dfrac{a^2 + b^2 - c^2}{2ab}$

Using the lengths from part 2, we have:

$\cos C = \dfrac{13 + 29 - 34}{2\sqrt{13} \cdot \sqrt{29}}$

≈ 0.20601

$C \approx 78.1°$

$A = \dfrac{1}{2}ab\sin C$

$= \dfrac{1}{2}\sqrt{13} \cdot \sqrt{29}\sin 78.1°$

≈ 9.5 square units

Exercises

1. **(a)** law of cosines

$c^2 = a^2 + b^2 - 2ab\cos C$

$2ab\cos C = a^2 + b^2 - c^2$

$\cos C = \dfrac{a^2 + b^2 - c^2}{2ab}$

$= \dfrac{(342)^2 + (116)^2 - (401)^2}{2(342)(116)}$

$\approx -.38290$

$C \approx 112.5°$

(b) law of cosines

$c^2 = a^2 + b^2 - 2ab\cos C$

$= (12.2)^2 + (13.1)^2 - 2(12.2)(13.1)\cos 20.2°$

≈ 20.47

$c \approx 4.52$

(c) law of sines

$\dfrac{b}{\sin B} = \dfrac{a}{\sin A}$

$\dfrac{b}{\sin B} = \dfrac{a}{\sin(180 - (B + C))}$

$\dfrac{b}{\sin B} = \dfrac{a}{\sin(B + C)}$

$b = \dfrac{a\sin B}{\sin(B + C)}$

$= \dfrac{(21.13)\sin(48°13')}{\sin(48°13' + 81°42')}$

≈ 20.54

(d) Neither is applicable.

3. $a^2 = 3^2 + 8^2 - 2(3)(8)\cos 60°$

$\qquad = 9 + 64 - 48\left(\dfrac{1}{2}\right)$

$\qquad = 73 - 24$

$\qquad = 49$

$\qquad a = 7$

5. $\cos\theta = \dfrac{b^2 + c^2 - a^2}{2bc}$

$\qquad\quad = \dfrac{1^2 + (\sqrt{3})^2 - 1^2}{2(1)(\sqrt{3})}$

$\qquad\quad = \dfrac{1 + 3 - 1}{2\sqrt{3}}$

$\qquad\quad = \dfrac{3}{2\sqrt{3}}$

$\qquad\quad = \dfrac{\sqrt{3}}{2}$

$\qquad\quad \theta = 30°$

7. $C = 28.3°, b = 5.71$ in., $a = 4.21$ in.

$\quad c^2 = a^2 + b^2 - 2ab\cos C$

$\quad c = \sqrt{(4.21)^2 + (5.71)^2 - 2(4.21)(5.71)\cos 28.3°}$

$\quad c \approx 2.83$ in.

Keep all digits of $\sqrt{c^2}$ in the calculator for use in the next calculation. If 2.83 is used, the answer will vary slightly due to round-off error. Find angle A next, since it is the smaller angle and must be acute.

$\quad \sin A = \dfrac{a\sin C}{c} = \dfrac{4.21\sin 28.3°}{\sqrt{c^2}}$

$\quad \sin A = .70581857$

$\qquad A = 44.9°$

$\qquad B = 180° - 44.9° - 28.3°$

$\qquad B = 106.8°$

9. $C = 45.6°, b = 8.94$ m, $a = 7.23$ m

$\quad c^2 = a^2 + b^2 - 2ab\cos C$

$\quad c = \sqrt{(7.23)^2 + (8.94)^2 - 2(7.23)(8.94)\cos 45.6°}$

$\quad c = 6.46$ m

Find angle A next, since it is the smaller angle and must be acute.

$\quad \sin A = \dfrac{a\sin C}{c} = \dfrac{7.23\sin 45.6°}{\sqrt{c^2}}$

$\quad \sin A = .79946437$

$\qquad A = 53.1°$

$\qquad B = 180° - 53.1° - 45.6°$

$\qquad B = 81.3°$

11. $A = 80°40'\ b = 143$ cm, $c = 89.6$ cm

$\quad a^2 = b^2 + c^2 - 2bc\cos A$

$\quad a = \sqrt{143^2 + (89.6)^2 - 2(143)(89.6)\cos 80°40'}$

$\quad a = 156$ cm

Find angle C next, since it is the smaller angle and must be acute.

$\quad \sin C = \dfrac{c\sin A}{a} = \dfrac{89.6\sin 80°40'}{\sqrt{a^2}}$

$\quad \sin C = .56692713$

$\qquad C = 34°30'$

$\qquad B = 180° - 80°40' - 34°30'$

$\qquad B = 64°50'$

13. $B = 74.80°, a = 8.919$ in., $c = 6.427$ in.

$\quad b^2 = a^2 + c^2 - 2ac\cos B$

$\quad b = \sqrt{(8.919)^2 + (6.427)^2 - 2(8.919)(6.427)\cos 74.80°}$

$\quad b = 9.529$ in.

Find angle C next, since it is the smaller angle and must be acute.

$\quad \sin C = \dfrac{c\sin B}{b} = \dfrac{6.427\sin 74.80°}{\sqrt{b^2}}$

$\quad \sin C = .65089219$

$\qquad C = 40.61°$

$\qquad A = 180° - 74.80° - 40.61°$

$\qquad A = 64.59°$

15. $A = 112.8°, b = 6.28$ m, $c = 12.2$ m

$\quad a^2 = b^2 + c^2 - 2bc\cos A$

$\quad a = \sqrt{(6.28)^2 + (12.2)^2 - 2(6.28)(12.2)\cos 112.8°}$

$\quad a = 15.7$ m

Angle A is obtuse, so both B and C are acute. Find either angle next.

$\quad \sin B = \dfrac{b\sin A}{a} = \dfrac{6.28\sin 112.8°}{\sqrt{a^2}}$

$\quad \sin B = .36787456$

$\qquad B = 21.6°$

$\qquad C = 180° - 112.8° - 21.6°$

$\qquad C = 45.6°$

17. $a = 3.0$ ft, $b = 5.0$ ft, $c = 6.0$ ft
Angle C is the largest, so find it first.
$$c^2 = a^2 + b^2 - 2ab\cos C$$
$$\cos C = \frac{3.0^2 + 5.0^2 - 6.0^2}{2(3.0)(5.0)}$$
$$\cos C = -.06666667$$
$$C = 94°$$
$$\sin B = \frac{b\sin C}{c}$$
$$\sin B = .83147942$$
$$B = 56°$$
$$A = 180° - 56° - 94°$$
$$A = 30°$$

19. $a = 9.3$ cm, $b = 5.7$ cm, $c = 8.2$ cm
Angle A is the largest, so find it first.
$$a^2 = b^2 + c^2 - 2bc\cos A$$
$$\cos A = \frac{5.7^2 + 8.2^2 - 9.3^2}{2(5.7)(8.2)}$$
$$\cos A = .14163457$$
$$A = 82°$$

$$\sin B = \frac{b\sin A}{a}$$
$$\sin B = .60672455$$
$$B = 37°$$
$$C = 180° - 82° - 37°$$
$$C = 61°$$

21. $a = 42.9$ m, $b = 37.6$ m, $c = 62.7$ m
Angle C is the largest, so find it first.
$$c^2 = a^2 + b^2 - 2ab\cos C$$
$$\cos C = \frac{42.9^2 + 37.6^2 - 62.7^2}{2(42.9)(37.6)}$$
$$\cos C = -.20988940$$
$$C = 102.1°$$
$$\sin B = \frac{b\sin C}{c}$$
$$\sin B = .58632321$$
$$B = 35.9°$$
$$A = 180° - 35.9° - 102.1°$$
$$A = 42.0°$$

23. $AB = 1240$ ft, $AC = 876$ ft, $BC = 918$ ft
$AB = c$, $AC = b$, $BC = a$
Angle C is the largest, so find it first.
$$c^2 = a^2 + b^2 - 2ab\cos C$$
$$\cos C = \frac{a^2 + b^2 - c^2}{2ab}$$
$$\cos C = .04507765$$
$$C = 87.4°$$

$$\sin B = \frac{b\sin C}{c}$$
$$\sin B = .70573350$$
$$B = 44.9°$$
$$A = 180° - 44.9° - 87.4°$$
$$A = 47.7°$$

25. Find AB, or c, in the following triangle.

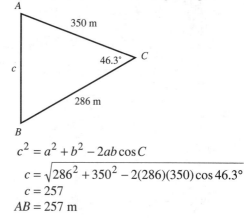

$$c^2 = a^2 + b^2 - 2ab\cos C$$
$$c = \sqrt{286^2 + 350^2 - 2(286)(350)\cos 46.3°}$$
$$c = 257$$
$$AB = 257 \text{ m}$$

27. Find x.
$$x^2 = 25^2 + 25^2 - 2(25)(25)\cos 52°$$
$$= 480$$
$$x = 22 \text{ ft}$$

29. Find AC, or b, in the following triangle.

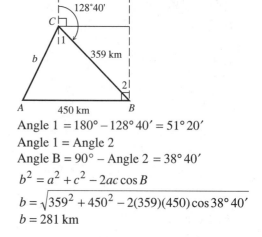

Angle $1 = 180° - 128°\,40' = 51°\,20'$
Angle 1 = Angle 2
Angle $B = 90° -$ Angle $2 = 38°\,40'$
$$b^2 = a^2 + c^2 - 2ac\cos B$$
$$b = \sqrt{359^2 + 450^2 - 2(359)(450)\cos 38°\,40'}$$
$$b = 281 \text{ km}$$

31. $AB^2 = 10^2 + 10^2 - 2(10)(10)\cos 128°$
$$AB^2 = 323$$
$$AB = 18 \text{ ft}$$

33. Let x = the distance from the tracking station to the satellite at 12:03 P.M.

Notice that the distance from the center of the earth to the satellite is $6400 + 1600 = 8000$ km. Let θ = the angle made by the movement of the satellite from noon to 12:03 P.M.

$$\frac{2\pi \text{ radians}}{2 \text{ hours}} = \frac{\theta \text{ radians}}{3 \text{ minutes}}$$

$$\frac{2\pi}{2(60)} = \frac{\theta}{3}$$

$$\theta = \frac{6\pi}{120} = \frac{\pi}{20} \text{ radian}$$

$$x^2 = 6400^2 + 8000^2 - 2(6400)(8000)\cos\frac{\pi}{20}$$

$$x = 2000$$

The distance between the satellite and the tracking station is 2000 km.

35. Let A = the man's location;
B = the factory whistle heard at 3 sec after 5:00;
C = the factory whistle heard at 6 sec after 5:00.

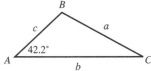

Since sound travels at 344 m per sec, and the man hears the whistles in 3 sec and 6 sec, the factories are

$$c = 3(344) = 1032 \text{ m}$$

and $b = 6(344) = 2064$ m

from the man.

$$a^2 = 1032^2 + 2064^2 - 2(1032)(2064)\cos 42.2°$$

$$a = 1470$$

The factories are 1470 m apart.

37. Let a be the length of the segment from $(0, 0)$ to $(6, 8)$. Use the distance formula.

$$a = \sqrt{(6-0)^2 + (8-0)^2}$$

$$= \sqrt{6^2 + 8^2}$$

$$= \sqrt{36 + 64}$$

$$= \sqrt{100} = 10$$

Let b be the length of the segment from $(0, 0)$ to $(4, 3)$.

$$b = \sqrt{(4-0)^2 + (3-0)^2}$$

$$= \sqrt{4^2 + 3^2}$$

$$= \sqrt{16 + 9}$$

$$= \sqrt{25} = 5$$

Let c be the length of the segment from $(4, 3)$ to $(6, 8)$.

$$c = \sqrt{(6-4)^2 + (8-3)^2}$$

$$= \sqrt{2^2 + 5^2}$$

$$= \sqrt{4 + 25} = \sqrt{29}$$

$$\cos\theta = \frac{a^2 + b^2 - c^2}{2ab}$$

$$\cos\theta = \frac{10^2 + 5^2 - (\sqrt{29})^2}{2(10)(5)}$$

$$\cos\theta = \frac{100 + 25 - 29}{100}$$

$$\cos\theta = .96$$

$$\theta \approx 16.26°$$

39. Using $K = \frac{1}{2}bh$,

$$K = \frac{1}{2}(16)(3\sqrt{3})$$

$$= 24\sqrt{3} \approx 41.57.$$

To use Heron's Formula, first find the semiperimeter.

$$s = \frac{1}{2}(a + b + c)$$

$$= \frac{1}{2}(6 + 14 + 16)$$

$$= \frac{1}{2}(36) = 18$$

Now find the area of the triangle.

$$K = \sqrt{s(s-a)(s-b)(s-c)}$$

$$= \sqrt{18(18-6)(18-14)(18-16)}$$

$$= \sqrt{18(12)(4)(2)}$$

$$= \sqrt{1728} \approx 41.57$$

Both formulas give the same area.

41. $a = 12$ m, $b = 16$ m, $c = 25$ m

$$s = \frac{1}{2}(12 + 16 + 25)$$

$$s = 26.5$$

$$\text{area} = \sqrt{s(s-a)(s-b)(s-c)}$$

$$= \sqrt{(26.5)(14.5)(10.5)(1.5)}$$

$$= 78 \text{ m}^2$$

43. $a = 154$ cm, $b = 179$ cm, $c = 183$ cm

$$s = \frac{1}{2}(154 + 179 + 183)$$

$$s = 258$$

$$\text{area} = \sqrt{s(s-a)(s-b)(s-c)}$$

$$= \sqrt{(258)(104)(79)(75)}$$

$$= 12,600 \text{ cm}^2$$

45. $a = 76.3$ ft, $b = 109$ ft, $c = 98.8$ ft

$$s = \frac{1}{2}(76.3 + 109 + 98.8)$$

$$s = 142.05$$

$$\text{area} = \sqrt{s(s-a)(s-b)(s-c)}$$

$$= \sqrt{(142.05)(65.75)(33.05)(43.25)}$$

$$= 3650 \text{ ft}^2$$

47. $AB = 22.47928$ mi, $AC = 28.14276$ mi,
$A = 58.56989°$
$BC^2 = AC^2 + AB^2 - 2(AC)(AB)\cos A$
Use a calculator and substitute.
$$BC^2 = 637.5539346$$
$$BC = 25.24983 \text{ mi}$$

49. Find the area of the region.

$$s = \frac{1}{2}(75 + 68 + 85)$$

$$s = 114$$

$$\text{area} = \sqrt{(114)(39)(46)(29)}$$

$$= 2435.3571 \text{ m}^2$$

$$\text{Number of cans needed} = \frac{(\text{area in m}^2)}{(\text{m}^2 \text{per can})}$$

$$\frac{2435.3571}{75} = 32.471428 \text{ cans}$$

She will need to open 33 cans.

51. Perimeter: $9 + 10 + 17 = 36$ feet, so the semi-perimeter is $\frac{1}{2} \cdot 36 = 18$ feet.

Use Heron's Formula to find the area.

$$\text{Area:} = \sqrt{s(s-a)(s-b)(s-c)}$$

$$= \sqrt{18(18-9)(18-10)(18-17)}$$

$$= \sqrt{18(9)(8)(1)}$$

$$= \sqrt{1296} = 36 \text{ ft}$$

Since the perimeter and area both equal 36 feet, the triangle is a *perfect triangle*.

53. Applying the law of cosines when $a = 3$, $b = 4$, and $c = 10$ gives

$$c^2 = a^2 + b^2 - 2ab\cos C$$

$$10^2 = 3^2 + 4^2 - 2(3)(4)\cos C$$

$$75 = -24\cos C$$

$$-3.125 = \cos C.$$

Since $-1 \le \cos C \le 1$, a triangle cannot have sides 3, 4, and 10.

55. **(a)** Using the law of sines

$$\frac{\sin A}{a} = \frac{\sin C}{c}$$

$$\sin C = \frac{c}{a}\sin A$$

$$= \frac{15}{13}\sin 60°$$

$$\approx 0.99926$$

$$c \approx 87.8° \text{ or } 92.2°$$

(b) By the law of cosines,

$$c^2 = a^2 + b^2 - 2ab\cos C$$

$$2ab\cos C = a^2 + b^2 - c^2$$

$$\cos C = \frac{a^2 + b^2 - c^2}{2ab}$$

$$= \frac{(13)^2 + (7)^2 - (15)^2}{2(13)(7)}$$

$$\approx -.03846$$

$$C = 92.2°$$

(c) With the law of cosines, we are required to find the inverse cosine of a negative number therefore, we know angle C is greater than $90°$.

57. Using the law of cosines,

$$a^2 = b^2 + c^2 - 2bc\cos A$$

$$c^2 - 2bc\cos A + (b^2 - a^2) = 0$$

$$c^2 - 2(24.9)(\cos 55.3°)c + (24.9^2 - 22.8^2) = 0$$

$$c^2 - 28.35c + 100.17 = 0$$

Apply the quadratic formula

$$c = \frac{28.35 \pm \sqrt{(-28.35)^2 - 4(1)(100.17)}}{2(1)}$$

$$= \frac{28.35 \pm \sqrt{803.72 - 400.68}}{2}$$

$$= \frac{28.35 \pm 20.08}{2}$$

$$c_1 = \frac{28.35 + 20.08}{2}$$

$$= 24.2 \text{ ft}$$

$$c_2 = \frac{28.35 - 20.08}{2}$$

$$= 4.14 \text{ ft}$$

61. Since A is obtuse, $90° < A < 180°$. The cosine of a quadrant II angle is negative.

62. In $a^2 = b^2 + c^2 - 2bc\cos A$, $\cos A$ is negative, so $a^2 = b^2 + c^2$ plus a positive quantity. Thus, $a^2 > b^2 + c^2$.

63. $b^2 + c^2 > b^2$ and $b^2 + c^2 > c^2$. If $a^2 > b^2 + c^2$, then $a^2 > b^2$ from which $a > b$ and $a > c$ because a, b, and c are all nonnegative.

64. Because A is obtuse it is the largest angle, so the longest side should be a, not c.

Section 7.3

Exercises

3. Equal vectors have the same magnitude and direction: $\mathbf{m} = \mathbf{p}$, $\mathbf{n} = \mathbf{r}$.

5. One vector is a positive scalar multiple of another if the two vectors point in the same direction; they may have different magnitudes.
$\mathbf{m} = 1\mathbf{p}$, $\mathbf{m} = 2\mathbf{t}$, $\mathbf{n} = 1\mathbf{r}$, $\mathbf{p} = 2\mathbf{t}$ or
$\mathbf{p} = 1\mathbf{m}$, $\mathbf{t} = \dfrac{1}{2}\mathbf{m}$, $\mathbf{r} = 1\mathbf{n}$, $\mathbf{t} = \dfrac{1}{2}\mathbf{p}$

7.

9.

11.

13.

15.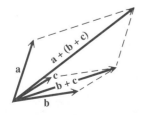

17.

19. $\mathbf{a} + (\mathbf{b} + \mathbf{c}) = (\mathbf{a} + \mathbf{b}) + \mathbf{c}$
Yes, vector addition is associative.

21. $|\mathbf{u}| = 12$, $|\mathbf{w}| = 20$, $\theta = 27°$

23. $|\mathbf{u}| = 20$, $|\mathbf{w}| = 30$, $\theta = 30°$
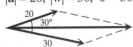

In Exercises 25–29, $\mathbf{x}$ is the horizontal component of $\mathbf{v}$, and $\mathbf{y}$ is the vertical component of $\mathbf{v}$.

25. $\alpha = 20°$, $|\mathbf{v}| = 50$
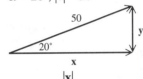

$$\cos 20° = \frac{|\mathbf{x}|}{50}$$
$$|\mathbf{x}| = 50 \cos 20° = 47$$
$$\sin 20° = \frac{|\mathbf{y}|}{50}$$
$$|\mathbf{y}| = 50 \sin 20° = 17$$

27. $\alpha = 35°\,50'$, $|\mathbf{v}| = 47.8$
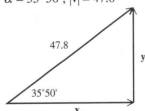

$|\mathbf{x}| = 47.8 \cos 35°\,50' = 38.8$
$|\mathbf{y}| = 47.8 \sin 35°\,50' = 28.0$

29. $\alpha = 128.5°$, $|\mathbf{v}| = 198$

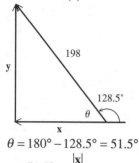

$\theta = 180° - 128.5° = 51.5°$

$\cos 51.5° = \dfrac{|\mathbf{x}|}{198}$

$|\mathbf{x}| = 198 \cos 51.5°$

$\qquad = 123$

$\sin 51.5° = \dfrac{|\mathbf{y}|}{198}$

$|\mathbf{y}| = 198 \sin 51.5°$

$\qquad = 155$

31. $360° - 131° = 229°$

33. Forces of 19 newtons and 32 newtons, forming an angle of 118°

$180° - 118° = 62°$

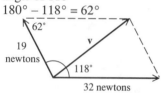

$|\mathbf{v}|^2 = 19^2 + 32^2 - 2(19)(32)\cos 62°$

$\qquad = 814.1226$

$|\mathbf{v}| = 29$ newtons

35. Forces of 37.8 lb and 53.7 lb, forming an angle of 68.5°

$180° - 68.5° = 111.5°$

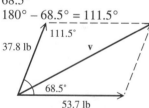

$|\mathbf{v}|^2 = (37.8)^2 + (53.7)^2 - 2(37.8)(53.7)\cos 111.5°$

$\qquad = 5800.422$

$|\mathbf{v}| = 76.2$ lb

37. Magnitude: $\sqrt{\left(8\sqrt{2}\right)^2 + \left(-8\sqrt{2}\right)^2} = \sqrt{256} = 16$

Angle: $\theta = \arctan\left(\dfrac{-8\sqrt{2}}{8\sqrt{2}}\right)$

$\qquad = \arctan(-1)$ (in quadrant IV

$\qquad\qquad\qquad$ since $x > 0$ and $y < 0$)

$\qquad = 315°$

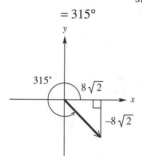

39. Magnitude: $\sqrt{(-7)^2 + (24)^2} = \sqrt{625} = 25$

Angle: $\theta = \arctan\left(\dfrac{24}{-7}\right)$ (in quadrant II

$\qquad\qquad\qquad$ since $x < 0$ and $y > 0$)

$\qquad \approx 106.3°$

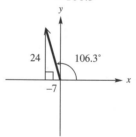

41.

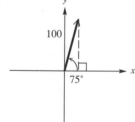

$a = |\mathbf{v}|\cos\theta \qquad\qquad b = |\mathbf{v}|\sin\theta$

$\quad = 100\cos 75° \qquad\quad = 100\sin 75°$

$\quad \approx 25.882 \qquad\qquad\quad \approx 96.593$

$\mathbf{v} = \langle 25.882,\ 96.593 \rangle$

43.

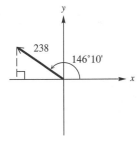

$$a = |\mathbf{v}|\cos\theta \qquad b = |\mathbf{v}|\sin\theta$$
$$\quad = 238\cos 146°10' \qquad = 238\sin 146°10'$$
$$\quad = 238\cos 146.167° \qquad = 238\sin 146.167°$$
$$\quad \approx -197.697 \qquad\qquad \approx 132.513$$
$$\mathbf{v} = \langle -197.697, 132.513\rangle$$

45. $\mathbf{u} - \mathbf{v} = \langle -2, 5\rangle - \langle 4, 3\rangle$
$$= \langle -2 - 4, 5 - 3\rangle$$
$$= \langle -6, 2\rangle$$

47. $5\mathbf{v} = 5\langle 4, 3\rangle$
$$= \langle 5\cdot 4, 5\cdot 3\rangle$$
$$= \langle 20, 15\rangle$$

49. $3\mathbf{u} + 6\mathbf{v} = 3\langle -2, 5\rangle + 6\langle 4, 3\rangle$
$$= \langle 3\cdot -2, 3\cdot 5\rangle + \langle 6\cdot 4, 6\cdot 3\rangle$$
$$= \langle -6, 15\rangle + \langle 24, 18\rangle$$
$$= \langle -6 + 24, 15 + 18\rangle$$
$$= \langle 18, 33\rangle$$

51. $\langle 6, -3\rangle = 6\mathbf{i} - 3\mathbf{j}$

53. $\langle 0, -4\rangle = 0\mathbf{i} - 4\mathbf{j} = -4\mathbf{j}$

55. $a = .6\cos 115° \quad b = .6\sin 115°$
$$\quad \approx -.254 \qquad\quad \approx .544$$
$$\langle -.254, .544\rangle = -.254\mathbf{i} + .544\mathbf{j}$$

57. $\langle -3, 8\rangle \cdot \langle 7, -5\rangle = -21 - 40 = -61$

59. $\langle 1, 2\rangle \cdot \langle 3, -1\rangle = 3 - 2 = 1$

61. $\langle 2, 4\rangle \cdot \langle 0, -1\rangle = 0 - 4 = -4$

For Exercises 63–67, use the formula $\theta = \arccos\left(\dfrac{\mathbf{u}\cdot\mathbf{v}}{|\mathbf{u}||\mathbf{v}|}\right)$.

63. $\theta = \arccos\left(\dfrac{\langle 1, 7\rangle \cdot \langle 1, 1\rangle}{\sqrt{1^2 + 7^2}\cdot\sqrt{1^2 + 1^2}}\right)$
$$= \arccos\left(\dfrac{1 + 7}{\sqrt{50}\cdot\sqrt{2}}\right)$$
$$= \arccos\left(\dfrac{8}{10}\right)$$
$$\approx 36.87°$$

65. $\theta = \arccos\left(\dfrac{\langle 4, 0\rangle \cdot \langle 2, 2\rangle}{\sqrt{4^2 + 0^2}\cdot\sqrt{2^2 + 2^2}}\right)$
$$= \arccos\left(\dfrac{8 + 0}{\sqrt{16}\cdot\sqrt{8}}\right)$$
$$= \arccos\left(\dfrac{8}{8\sqrt{2}}\right)$$
$$= \arccos\left(\dfrac{1}{\sqrt{2}}\right)$$
$$= \arccos\left(\dfrac{\sqrt{2}}{2}\right)$$
$$= 45°$$

67. $\theta = \arccos\left(\dfrac{\langle -5, 12\rangle \cdot \langle 3, 2\rangle}{\sqrt{(-5)^2 + 12^2}\cdot\sqrt{3^2 + 2^2}}\right)$
$$= \arccos\left(\dfrac{-15 + 24}{\sqrt{169}\sqrt{13}}\right)$$
$$= \arccos\left(\dfrac{9}{13\sqrt{13}}\right)$$
$$= \arccos\left(\dfrac{9\sqrt{13}}{169}\right)$$
$$\approx 78.93°$$

69. $\mathbf{u}\cdot\mathbf{v} - \mathbf{u}\cdot\mathbf{w} = \langle -2, 1\rangle \cdot \langle 3, 4\rangle - \langle -2, 1\rangle \cdot \langle -5, 12\rangle$
$$= (-6 + 4) - (10 + 12)$$
$$= -2 - 22$$
$$= -24$$

71. $\langle 1, 0\rangle \cdot \langle \sqrt{2}, 0\rangle = \sqrt{2} + 0$
$$= \sqrt{2}$$
The vectors are not orthogonal.

73. $\langle \sqrt{5}, -2\rangle \cdot \langle -5, 2\sqrt{5}\rangle = -5\sqrt{5} - 4\sqrt{5}$
$$= -9\sqrt{5}$$
The vectors are not orthogonal.

74. Draw a line parallel to the x-axis and the vector **u** + **v** (shown as a dashed line).

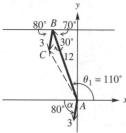

Since $\theta_1 = 110°$, its supplementary angle is 70°. Further since $\theta_2 = 260°$, $\alpha = 260° - 180° = 80°$. Then the angle CBA becomes $180 - (80 + 70) = 180 - 150 = 30°$. Using the law of cosines, the magnitude of **u** + **v** is

$$|\mathbf{u} + \mathbf{v}|^2 = a^2 + c^2 - 2ac\cos B$$
$$= (3)^2 + (12)^2 - 2(3)(12)\cos 30°$$
$$\approx 90.65$$
$$|\mathbf{u} + \mathbf{v}| = \sqrt{90.6461709}$$
$$\approx 9.52082827.$$

Using the law of sines,
$$\frac{\sin A}{a} = \frac{\sin B}{b}$$
$$\sin A = \frac{a\sin B}{b}$$
$$A = \arcsin\left(\frac{a\sin B}{b}\right)$$
$$A = \arcsin\left(\frac{3\sin 30°}{9.52}\right)$$
$$= 9.0646784°$$
The direction angle of **u** + **v** is
$$110 + 9.0646784 = 119.0646784°.$$

75. $a_1 = |\mathbf{u}|\cos\theta_1 \qquad b_1 = |\mathbf{u}|\sin\theta_1$
$\quad = 12\cos 110° \qquad = 12\sin 110°$
$\quad \approx -4.10424172 \qquad \approx 11.27631145$
$\langle -4.10424172, 11.27631145 \rangle$

76. $a_2 = |\mathbf{v}|\cos\theta_2 \qquad b_2 = |\mathbf{v}|\sin\theta_2$
$\quad = 3\cos 260° \qquad = 3\sin 260°$
$\quad \approx -5.20944533 \qquad \approx -2.954423259$
$\langle -.520944533, -2.954423259 \rangle$

77. $a = a_1 + a_2$
$\quad = -4.10424172 - .520944533$
$\quad = -4.625186253$
$b = b_1 + b_2$
$\quad = 11.27631145 - 2.954423259$
$\quad = 8.321888191$
$\langle -4.625186253, 8.321888191 \rangle$

78. Magnitude: $\sqrt{(-4.625186253)^2 + (8.321888191)^2}$
$\qquad \approx 9.52082827$
Angle: $\theta = \arccos\left(\dfrac{8.321888191}{-4.625186253}\right)$
$\qquad \approx 119.0646784°$
(in quadrant II since $y > 0$ and $x < 0$)

79. (a) They are the same.

Section 7.4

Exercises

1. Let α = the angle between the forces.

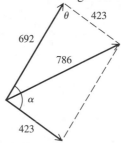

To find α, use the law of cosines to find θ.
$$786^2 = 692^2 + 423^2 - 2(692)(423)\cos\theta$$
$$\cos\theta = \frac{786^2 - 692^2 - 423^2}{-2(692)(423)}$$
$$\theta = 86.1°$$
$$\alpha = 180° - 86.1° = 93.9°$$

3. Let θ = the angle that the hill makes with the horizontal.

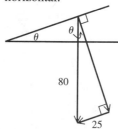

The 80-lb downward force has a 25-lb component parallel to the hill. The two right triangles are similar and have congruent angles.
$$\sin\theta = \frac{25}{80}$$
$$\theta = 18°$$

5. Find the force needed to pull a 60-ton monolith along the causeway.

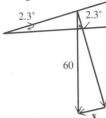

The force needed to pull 60 tons is equal to the magnitude of x, the component parallel to the causeway.

$$\sin 2.3° = \frac{|\mathbf{x}|}{60}$$
$$|\mathbf{x}| = 60 \sin 2.3°$$
$$= 2.4$$

The force needed is 2.4 tons.

7. Let **r** = the vertical component of the person exerting a 114-lb force and **s** = the vertical component of the person exerting a 150-lb force.

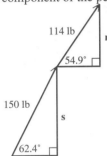

The weight of the box is the sum of the magnitudes of the vertical components of the two vectors representing the forces exerted by the two people.

$$|\mathbf{r}| = 114 \sin 54.9° = 93.27$$
$$|\mathbf{s}| = 150 \sin 62.4° = 132.93$$
$$\text{Weight of box} = |\mathbf{r}| + |\mathbf{s}|$$
$$= 226 \text{ lb}$$

9. Find the weight of the crate and the tension on the horizontal rope.

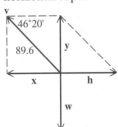

v has horizontal component **x** and vertical component **y**. The resultant **v** + **h** also has vertical component **y**. The resultant balances the weight of the crate, so its vertical component is the equilibrant of the crate's weight.

$$|\mathbf{w}| = |\mathbf{y}| = 89.6 \sin 46° 20'$$
$$|\mathbf{w}| = 64.8 \text{ lb}$$

Since the crate is not moving side-to-side, **h**, the horizontal tension on the rope, is the opposite of *x*.

$$|\mathbf{h}| = |\mathbf{x}| = 89.6 \cos 46° 20'$$
$$|\mathbf{h}| = 61.9 \text{ lb}$$

The weight of the crate is 64.8 lb; the tension is 61.9 lb.

11. Find the magnitude of the second force and of the resultant. Use the parallelogram rule; **v** is the resultant and **x** is the second force.

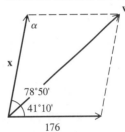

$$\alpha = 180° - 78° 50' = 101° 10'$$

the angle between the second force and the resultant is $\beta = 78° 50' - 41° 10' = 37° 40'$.

Use the law of sines to find $|\mathbf{v}|$.

$$\frac{|\mathbf{v}|}{\sin \alpha} = \frac{176}{\sin \beta}$$
$$|\mathbf{v}| = \frac{176 \sin 101° 10'}{\sin 37° 40'}$$
$$|\mathbf{v}| = 283 \text{ lb}$$

Use the law of sines to find $|\mathbf{x}|$.

$$\frac{|\mathbf{x}|}{\sin 41° 10'} = \frac{176}{\sin 37° 40'}$$
$$|\mathbf{x}| = \frac{176 \sin 41° 10'}{\sin 37° 40'}$$
$$|\mathbf{x}| = 190 \text{ lb}$$

13. Let **v** = the ground speed vector of the plane. Find the actual bearing of the plane.

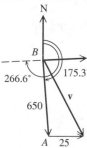

Angle $A = 266.6° - 175.3° = 91.3°$
Use the law of cosines to find $|\mathbf{v}|$.

$$|\mathbf{v}|^2 = 25^2 + 650^2 - 2(25)(650)\cos 91.3°$$
$$= 423,862$$
$$|\mathbf{v}| = 651$$

Use the law of sines to find the drift angle, B, the angle that **v** makes with the airspeed vector of the plane.

$$\frac{\sin B}{25} = \frac{\sin A}{651}$$
$$\sin B = .038392573$$
$$B = 2.2°$$

The bearing is $175.3° - 2.2° = 173.1°$.

15. Find the distance of the ship from point A.

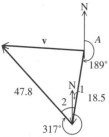

Angle $1 = 189° - 180° = 9°$
Angle $2 = 360° - 317° = 43°$
Angle 1 + Angle $2 = 9° + 43° = 52°$
Use the law of cosines to find $|\mathbf{v}|$.

$$|\mathbf{v}|^2 = (47.8)^2 + (18.5)^2 - 2(47.8)(18.5)\cos 52°$$
$$|\mathbf{v}|^2 = 1538.2311$$
$$|\mathbf{v}| = 39.2 \text{ km}$$

17. Let **v** = the ground speed vector. Find the bearing and ground speed of the plane.

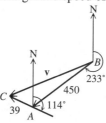

Angle $A = 233° - 114° = 119°$
Use the law of cosines to find $|\mathbf{v}|$.

$$|\mathbf{v}|^2 = 39^2 + 450^2 - 2(39)(450)\cos 119°$$
$$|\mathbf{v}|^2 = 221,038$$
$$|\mathbf{v}| = 470$$

The ground speed is 470 mph.
Use the law of sines to find angle B, the drift angle.

$$\frac{\sin B}{39} = \frac{\sin 119°}{470}$$
$$\sin B = .0726$$
$$B = 4°$$

The bearing is $4° + 233° = 237°$.

19. Let **v** = the airspeed vector.
The ground speed must be
$$\frac{400}{2.5} = 160 \text{ mph.}$$

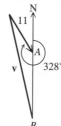

Angle $A = 328° - 180° = 148°$
Use the law of cosines to find $|\mathbf{v}|$.

$$|\mathbf{v}|^2 = 11^2 + 160^2 - 2(11)(160)\cos 148°$$
$$|\mathbf{v}|^2 = 28,706$$
$$|\mathbf{v}| = 170$$

The airspeed must be 170 mph.
Use the law of sines to find B, the drift angle.

$$\frac{\sin B}{11} = \frac{\sin 148°}{170}$$
$$\sin B = \frac{11\sin 148°}{170}$$
$$B = 2.0°$$

The bearing must be $360° - 2.0° = 358°$.

21. Find the ground speed and resulting bearing.

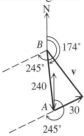

Angle $A = 245° - 174° = 71°$

Use the law of cosines to find $|\mathbf{v}|$.

$|\mathbf{v}|^2 = 30^2 + 240^2 - 2(30)(240)\cos 71°$

$|\mathbf{v}|^2 \approx 53,812$

$|\mathbf{v}| \approx 230$

The ground speed is 230 km per hr.
Use the law of sines to find angle B.

$\dfrac{\sin B}{30} = \dfrac{\sin 71°}{230}$

$\sin B = .1233$

$B = 7°$

The resulting bearing is $174° - 7° = 167°$.

23. At what time did the pilot turn? The plane will fly 2.6 hr before it runs out of fuel. In 2.6 hr, the carrier will travel $(2.6)(32) = 83.2$ mi and the plane will travel a total of $(2.6)(520) = 1352$ mi. Suppose it travels x mi on its initial bearing; then it travels $1352 - x$ mi after having turned.

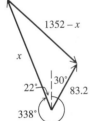

Use the law of cosines to get an equation in x.

$(1352 - x)^2 = x^2 + (83.2)^2$
$\qquad\qquad\qquad\quad - 2(x)(83.2)\cos 52°$

$1,827,904 - 2704x + x^2 = x^2 + 6922.24 - 102.45x$

$1,820,982 = 2601.55x$

$700 = x$

To travel 700 mi at 520 mph requires

$\dfrac{700}{520} = 1.35$ hr, or 1 hr and 21 min.

The pilot turned at 1 hr 21 min after 2 P.M., or at 3:21 P.M.

25. (a) First change $10.34''$ to radians in order to use the length of arc formula.

$10.34'' \cdot \dfrac{1°}{3600''} \cdot \dfrac{\pi}{180°} \approx 5.013 \times 10^{-5}$ radian.

In one year Barnard's Star will move in the tangential direction a distance of

$s = r\theta = (35 \times 10^{12})(5.013 \times 10^{-5})$

$\qquad = 1,754,550,000$ mi.

In one second Barnard's Star moves

$\dfrac{1,754,550,000}{60 \cdot 60 \cdot 24 \cdot 365} \approx 56$ mi tangentially. Thus,

$\mathbf{v}_t \approx 56$ mi/sec tangential to $\mathbf{v}_r$.

(b) The magnitude of $\mathbf{v}$ is given by

$|\mathbf{v}|^2 = |\mathbf{v}_r|^2 + |\mathbf{v}_t|^2 - 2|\mathbf{v}_r||\mathbf{v}_t|\cos 90°$.

Since $|\mathbf{v}_r| = 67$ and $|\mathbf{v}_t| = 56$, we have

$|\mathbf{v}|^2 = 67^2 + 56^2 - 2(67)(56)(0)$

$|\mathbf{v}| = \sqrt{67^2 + 56^2} \approx 87$

Since the magnitude or length of $\mathbf{v}$ is 87, $\mathbf{v}$ represents a velocity of 87 mi/sec.

26. $m = -\cot\theta$

From the figure, we see that L passes through the point $(b\cos\theta, b\sin\theta)$.

Using this information and the general form of the line: $y - b\sin\theta = -\cot\theta(x - b\cos\theta)$.

(Other answers are possible.)

27. At the end point of $\mathbf{v}$, $x = a$. Using the formula from Exercise 26:

$y - b\sin\theta = -\cot\theta(x - b\cos\theta)$

$y - b\sin\theta = -\cot\theta(a - b\cos\theta)$

$\qquad y = -a\cot\theta + b\cos\theta\cot\theta + b\sin\theta$

The coordinates are
$(a, -a\cot\theta + b\cos\theta\cot\theta + b\sin\theta)$.

28. $|\mathbf{v}| = \sqrt{(x_1 - 0)^2 + (y_1 - 0)^2}$

$= \sqrt{(a-0)^2 + (-a\cot\theta + b\cos\theta\cot\theta + b\sin\theta - 0)^2}$

$= \sqrt{a^2 + a^2\cot^2\theta - 2ab\cot^2\theta\cos\theta - 2ab\cot\theta\sin\theta + b^2\cos^2\theta\cot^2\theta + 2b^2\cos\theta\sin\theta\cot\theta + b^2\sin^2\theta}$

$= \sqrt{a^2 + a^2\cot^2\theta - 2ab\cot^2\theta\cos\theta - 2ab\cos\theta + b^2\cos^2\theta\cot^2\theta + 2b^2\cos^2\theta + b^2\sin^2\theta}$

$= \sqrt{\dfrac{a^2\sin^2\theta + a^2\cos^2\theta - 2ab\cos^3\theta - 2ab\cos\theta\sin^2\theta + b^2\cos^4\theta + 2b^2\cos^2\theta\sin^2\theta + b^2\sin^4\theta}{\sin^2\theta}}$

$= \dfrac{\sqrt{a^2(\sin^2\theta + \cos^2\theta) - 2ab\cos\theta(\cos^2\theta + \sin^2\theta) + b^2(\cos^4\theta + \cos^2\theta\sin^2\theta + \sin^2\theta)}}{\sin\theta}$

$= \dfrac{\sqrt{a^2 \cdot 1 - 2ab\cos\theta \cdot 1 + b^2(\cos^2\theta + \sin^2\theta)^2}}{\sin\theta}$

$= \dfrac{\sqrt{a^2 - 2ab\cos\theta + b^2 \cdot 1^2}}{\sin\theta}$

$= \dfrac{\sqrt{a^2 - 2ab\cos\theta + b^2}}{\sin\theta}$

$= \dfrac{\sqrt{a^2 + b^2 - 2ab\cos\theta}}{\sin\theta}$

29. Applying the law of cosines, we see that the quantity $a^2 + b^2 - 2ab\cos\theta$ is exactly the segment connecting the endpoint of **a** to the endpoint of **b**.

Section 7.5

Exercises

1. The plane determined by the x-axis and the z-axis is called the x-z plane.

3. The component form of the position vector with terminal point $(5, 3, -2)$ is $\langle 5, 3, -2 \rangle$.

5. $P = (0, 0, 0), \; Q = (2, -2, 5)$

$d(P, \; Q) = \sqrt{(2-0)^2 + (-2-0)^2 + (5-0)^2}$

$= \sqrt{2^2 + (-2)^2 + 5^2}$

$= \sqrt{4 + 4 + 25}$

$= \sqrt{33}$

7. $P = (10, 15, 9), \; Q = (8, 3, -4)$

$d(P, \; Q) = \sqrt{(8-10)^2 + (3-15)^2 + (-4-9)^2}$

$= \sqrt{(-2)^2 + (-12)^2 + (-13)^2}$

$= \sqrt{4 + 144 + 169}$

$= \sqrt{317}$

9. $P = (20, 25, 16), \; Q = (5, 5, 6)$

$d(P, \; Q) = \sqrt{(5-20)^2 + (5-25)^2 + (6-16)^2}$

$= \sqrt{(-15)^2 + (-20)^2 + (-10)^2}$

$= \sqrt{225 + 400 + 100}$

$= \sqrt{725}$

$= 5\sqrt{29}$

11. $P = (0, 0, 0), \; Q = (2, -2, 5)$
The two forms of the position vetor that corresponds to **PQ** are
component form:
$\langle 2-0, -2-0, 5-0 \rangle = \langle 2, -2, 5 \rangle$
i, j, k form:
$(2-0)\mathbf{i} + (-2-0)\mathbf{j} + (5-0)\mathbf{k} = 2\mathbf{i} - 2\mathbf{j} + 5\mathbf{k}.$

13. $P = (10, 15, 0), \; Q = (8, 3, -4)$
The two forms of the position vetor that corresponds to **PQ** are
component form:
$\langle 8-10, 3-15, -4-0 \rangle = \langle -2, -12, -4 \rangle$
i, j, k form:
$(8-10)\mathbf{i} + (3-15)\mathbf{j} + (-4-0)\mathbf{k} = -2\mathbf{i} - 12\mathbf{j} - 4\mathbf{k}.$

15. $P = (20,\ 25,\ 6),\ \ Q = (5,\ 5,\ 16)$
The two forms of the position vetor that
corresponds to **PQ** are
component form:
$\langle 5 - 20,\ 5 - 25,\ 16 - 6 \rangle = \langle -15,\ -20,\ 10 \rangle$
i, j, k form:
$(5 - 20)\mathbf{i} + (5 - 25)\mathbf{j} + (16 - 6)\mathbf{k}$
$= -15\mathbf{i} - 20\mathbf{j} + 10\mathbf{k}.$

19. $\mathbf{u} = 2\mathbf{i} + 4\mathbf{j} + 7\mathbf{k}$
$\mathbf{w} = 4\mathbf{i} - 3\mathbf{j} - 6\mathbf{k}$
$\mathbf{u} - \mathbf{w} = (2\mathbf{i} + 4\mathbf{j} + 7\mathbf{k}) - (4\mathbf{i} - 3\mathbf{j} - 6\mathbf{k})$
$\qquad = (2 - 4)\mathbf{i} + (4 - (-3))\mathbf{j} + (7 - (-6))\mathbf{k}$
$\qquad = -2\mathbf{i} + 7\mathbf{j} + 13\mathbf{k}$

21. $\mathbf{u} = 2\mathbf{i} + 4\mathbf{j} + 7\mathbf{k}$
$\mathbf{v} = -3\mathbf{i} + 5\mathbf{j} + 2\mathbf{k}$
$4\mathbf{u} + 5\mathbf{v} = 4(2\mathbf{i} + 4\mathbf{j} + 7\mathbf{k}) + 5(-3\mathbf{i} + 5\mathbf{j} + 2\mathbf{k})$
$\qquad = (8\mathbf{i} + 16\mathbf{j} + 28\mathbf{k}) + (-15\mathbf{i} + 25\mathbf{j} + 10\mathbf{k})$
$\qquad = (8 - 15)\mathbf{i} + (16 + 25)\mathbf{j} + (28 + 10)\mathbf{k}$
$\qquad = -7\mathbf{i} + 41\mathbf{j} + 38\mathbf{k}$

23. $\mathbf{u} = 2\mathbf{i} + 4\mathbf{j} + 7\mathbf{k}$
$|\mathbf{u}| = |2\mathbf{i} + 4\mathbf{j} + 7\mathbf{k}|$
$\qquad = \sqrt{2^2 + 4^2 + 7^2}$
$\qquad = \sqrt{4 + 16 + 49}$
$\qquad = \sqrt{69}$

25. $\mathbf{w} = 4\mathbf{i} - 3\mathbf{j} - 6\mathbf{k}$
$\mathbf{u} = 2\mathbf{i} + 4\mathbf{j} + 7\mathbf{k}$
$|\mathbf{w} + \mathbf{u}| = |(4\mathbf{i} - 3\mathbf{j} - 6\mathbf{k}) + (2\mathbf{i} + 4\mathbf{j} + 7\mathbf{k})|$
$\qquad = |(4 + 2)\mathbf{i} + (-3 + 4)\mathbf{j} + (-6 + 7)\mathbf{k}|$
$\qquad = |6\mathbf{i} + \mathbf{j} + \mathbf{k}|$
$\qquad = \sqrt{6^2 + 1^2 + 1^2}$
$\qquad = \sqrt{36 + 1 + 1}$
$\qquad = \sqrt{38}$

27. $\mathbf{v} = -3\mathbf{i} + 5\mathbf{j} + 2\mathbf{k}$
$\mathbf{w} = 4\mathbf{i} - 3\mathbf{j} - 6\mathbf{k}$
$\mathbf{v} \cdot \mathbf{w} = (-3\mathbf{i} + 5\mathbf{j} + 2\mathbf{k}) \cdot (4\mathbf{i} - 3\mathbf{j} - 6\mathbf{k})$
$\qquad = -3(4) + 5(-3) + 2(-6)$
$\qquad = -12 - 15 - 12$
$\qquad = -39$

29. $\mathbf{v} = -3\mathbf{i} + 5\mathbf{j} + 2\mathbf{k}$
$\mathbf{v} \cdot \mathbf{v} = (-3\mathbf{i} + 5\mathbf{j} + 2\mathbf{k}) \cdot (-3\mathbf{i} + 5\mathbf{j} + 2\mathbf{k})$
$\qquad = -3(-3) + 5(5) + 2(2)$
$\qquad = 9 + 25 + 4$
$\qquad = 38$

31. The angle between $\langle 2,\ -2,\ 0 \rangle$ and $\langle 5,\ -2,\ -1 \rangle$
is θ where
$$\cos\theta = \frac{\langle 2,\ -2,\ 0 \rangle \cdot \langle 5,\ -2,\ -1 \rangle}{|\langle 2,\ -2,\ 0 \rangle|\,|\langle 5,\ -2,\ -1 \rangle|}$$
$$= \frac{2(5) - 2(-2) + 0(-1)}{\sqrt{2^2 + (-2)^2 + 0^2}\,\sqrt{5^2 + (-2)^2 + (-1)^2}}$$
$$= \frac{10 + 4 + 0}{\sqrt{4 + 4 + 0}\sqrt{25 + 4 + 1}}$$
$$= \frac{14}{\sqrt{18}\sqrt{30}}$$
$$= \frac{14}{4\sqrt{15}}$$
$$= \frac{7}{2\sqrt{15}}.$$
Thus, $\theta = \cos^{-1}\left(\dfrac{7}{2\sqrt{15}}\right) \approx 25.4°.$

33. The angle between $\langle 6,\ 0,\ 0 \rangle$ and $\langle 8,\ 3,\ -4 \rangle$ is
θ where
$$\cos\theta = \frac{\langle 6,\ 0,\ 0 \rangle \cdot \langle 8,\ 3,\ -4 \rangle}{|\langle 6,\ 0,\ 0 \rangle|\,|\langle 8,\ 3,\ -4 \rangle|}$$
$$= \frac{6(8) + 0(3) + 0(-4)}{\sqrt{6^2 + 0^2 + 0^2}\,\sqrt{8^2 + 3^2 + (-4)^2}}$$
$$= \frac{48 + 0 + 0}{\sqrt{36 + 0 + 0}\sqrt{64 + 9 + 16}}$$
$$= \frac{48}{\sqrt{36}\sqrt{89}}$$
$$= \frac{48}{6\sqrt{89}}$$
$$= \frac{8}{\sqrt{89}}.$$
Thus, $\theta = \cos^{-1}\left(\dfrac{8}{\sqrt{89}}\right) \approx 32.0°.$

35. The angle between $\langle 1,\ 0,\ 0 \rangle$ and $\langle 0,\ 1,\ 0 \rangle$ is θ
where
$$\cos\theta = \frac{\langle 1,\ 0,\ 0 \rangle \cdot \langle 0,\ 1,\ 0 \rangle}{|\langle 1,\ 0,\ 0 \rangle|\,|\langle 0,\ 1,\ 0 \rangle|}$$
$$= \frac{1(0) + 0(1) - 0(0)}{\sqrt{1^2 + 0^2 + 0^2}\,\sqrt{0^2 + 1^2 + 0^2}}$$
$$= 0.$$
Thus, $\theta = \cos^{-1} 0 = 90°.$

37. $\mathbf{u} = 2\mathbf{i} + 4\mathbf{j} + 7\mathbf{k}$ so $a = 2$, $b = 4$, and $c = 7$.

$$|\mathbf{u}| = \sqrt{2^2 + 4^2 + 7^2}$$
$$= \sqrt{4 + 16 + 49}$$
$$= \sqrt{69}$$

$$\cos\alpha = \frac{a}{|\mathbf{u}|} = \frac{2}{\sqrt{69}}$$

$$\cos\beta = \frac{b}{|\mathbf{u}|} = \frac{4}{\sqrt{69}}$$

$$\cos\gamma = \frac{c}{|\mathbf{u}|} = \frac{7}{\sqrt{69}}$$

Thus,

$$\alpha = \cos^{-1}\left(\frac{2}{\sqrt{69}}\right) \approx 76.1°,$$

$$\beta = \cos^{-1}\left(\frac{4}{\sqrt{69}}\right) \approx 61.2°, \text{ and}$$

$$\gamma = \cos^{-1}\left(\frac{7}{\sqrt{69}}\right) \approx 32.6°.$$

39. $\mathbf{w} = 4\mathbf{i} - 3\mathbf{j} - 6\mathbf{k}$ so $a = 4$, $b = -3$, and $c = -6$.

$$|\mathbf{w}| = \sqrt{4^2 + (-3)^2 + (-6)^2}$$
$$= \sqrt{16 + 9 + 36}$$
$$= \sqrt{61}$$

$$\cos\alpha = \frac{a}{|\mathbf{w}|} = \frac{4}{\sqrt{61}}$$

$$\cos\beta = \frac{b}{|\mathbf{w}|} = \frac{-3}{\sqrt{61}}$$

$$\cos\gamma = \frac{c}{|\mathbf{w}|} = \frac{-6}{\sqrt{61}}$$

Thus,

$$\alpha = \cos^{-1}\left(\frac{4}{\sqrt{61}}\right) \approx 59.2°,$$

$$\beta = \cos^{-1}\left(\frac{-3}{\sqrt{61}}\right) \approx 112.6°, \text{ and}$$

$$\gamma = \cos^{-1}\left(\frac{-6}{\sqrt{61}}\right) \approx 140.2°.$$

41. $\cos\alpha = \cos 45° = \dfrac{\sqrt{2}}{2}$

$$\cos\beta = \cos 120° = -\frac{1}{2}$$

$$\cos^2\alpha + \cos^2\beta + \cos^2\gamma = 1$$

$$\left(\frac{\sqrt{2}}{2}\right)^2 + \left(-\frac{1}{2}\right)^2 + \cos^2\gamma = 1$$

$$\frac{1}{2} + \frac{1}{4} + \cos^2\gamma = 1$$

$$\cos^2\gamma = \frac{1}{4}$$

$$\cos\gamma = \frac{1}{2}$$

$$\gamma = 60°$$

43. The angle between $\mathbf{u} = 3\mathbf{i} - 2\mathbf{j} + \mathbf{k}$ and $\mathbf{v} = 4\mathbf{i} + 5\mathbf{j} - 2\mathbf{k}$ is θ where

$$\cos\theta = \frac{\mathbf{u} \cdot \mathbf{v}}{|\mathbf{u}|\,|\mathbf{v}|}$$

$$= \frac{3(4) - 2(5) + 1(-2)}{\sqrt{3^2 + (-2)^2 + 1^2}\sqrt{4^2 + 5^2 + (-2)^2}}$$

$$= \frac{12 - 10 - 2}{\sqrt{9 + 4 + 1}\sqrt{16 + 25 + 4}}$$

$$= \frac{0}{\sqrt{14}\sqrt{45}}$$

$$= 0$$

Thus $\theta = \cos^{-1} 0 = 90°$ and the vectors are orthogonal.

47. $\mathbf{F} = \langle 2, 0, 5\rangle$, $P = (0, 0, 0)$, $Q = (1, 3, 2)$
$\mathbf{PQ} = \langle 1 - 0, 3 - 0, 2 - 0\rangle = \langle 1, 3, 2\rangle$
The work done is
$$\mathbf{F} \cdot \mathbf{PQ} = \langle 2, 0, 5\rangle \cdot \langle 1, 3, 2\rangle$$
$$= 2(1) + 0(3) + 5(2)$$
$$= 2 + 0 + 10$$
$$= 12 \text{ work units.}$$

49. $\mathbf{F} = \mathbf{i} + 2\mathbf{j} - \mathbf{k}$, $P = (2, -1, 2)$, $Q = (5, 7, 8)$
$$\mathbf{PQ} = (5 - 2)\mathbf{i} + (7 - (-1))\mathbf{j} + (8 - 2)\mathbf{k}$$
$$= 3\mathbf{i} + 8\mathbf{j} + 6\mathbf{k}$$
The work done is
$$\mathbf{F} \cdot \mathbf{PQ} = (\mathbf{i} + 2\mathbf{j} - \mathbf{k}) \cdot (3\mathbf{i} + 8\mathbf{j} + 6\mathbf{k})$$
$$= 1(3) + 2(8) - 1(6)$$
$$= 3 + 16 - 6$$
$$= 13 \text{ work units.}$$

Section 7.6

Connections *(page 582)*

1. $\langle 6, -2 \rangle - \langle -4, -3 \rangle = \langle 6 - (-4), -2 - (-3) \rangle$
$$= \langle 10, 1 \rangle \text{ or } 10 + i$$

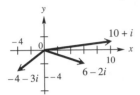

2. Answers will vary.

Exercises

1. The modulus of a complex number represents the magnitude (or length) of the vector representing it in the complex plane.

3.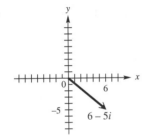

5.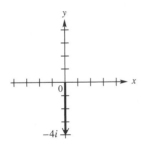

7.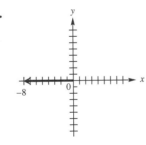

9. $1 - 4i$

11. $5 - 6i, \; -2 + 3i$
$$(5 - 6i) + (-2 + 3i) = 3 - 3i$$

13. $-3, \; 3i$
$$(-3 + 0i) + (0 + 3i) = -3 + 3i$$

15. $7 + 6i, \; 3i$
$$(7 + 6i) + (0 + 3i) = 7 + 9i$$

17. $10(\cos 90° + i \sin 90°)$
$$= 10(0 + i)$$
$$= 0 + 10i = 10i$$

19. $4(\cos 240° + i \sin 240°)$
$$= 4\left(-\frac{1}{2} - i\frac{\sqrt{3}}{2} \right)$$
$$= -2 - 2i\sqrt{3}$$

21.
$3 \operatorname{cis} 150°$
$$= 3(\cos 150° + i \sin 150°)$$
$$= 3\left(-\frac{\sqrt{3}}{2} + \frac{1}{2}i \right)$$
$$= -\frac{3\sqrt{3}}{2} + \frac{3}{2}i$$

23. $\sqrt{2} \operatorname{cis} 180°$
$$= \sqrt{2}(\cos 180° + i \sin 180°)$$
$$= \sqrt{2}(-1 + i \cdot 0)$$
$$= -\sqrt{2} + 0i$$
$$= -\sqrt{2}$$

25. $\sqrt{3} - i$
$$x = \sqrt{3}, \; y = -1$$
$$r = \sqrt{(\sqrt{3})^2 + (-1)^2} = 2$$
$$\tan \theta = \frac{-1}{\sqrt{3}} = -\frac{\sqrt{3}}{3}$$
$\sqrt{3} - i$ is in quadrant IV, so $\theta = 330°$.
$\sqrt{3} - i = 2(\cos 330° + i \sin 330°)$

27. $-5 - 5i$
$$x = -5, y = -5$$
$$r = \sqrt{(-5)^2 + (-5)^2}$$
$$= \sqrt{50} = 5\sqrt{2}$$
$$\tan \theta = \frac{-5}{-5} = 1$$
$-5 - 5i$ is in quadrant III, so $\theta = 225°$.
$-5 - 5i = 5\sqrt{2}(\cos 225° + i \sin 225°)$

29. $2 + 2i$

$x = 2, y = 2$

$r = \sqrt{2^2 + 2^2} = \sqrt{8} = 2\sqrt{2}$

$\tan \theta = \dfrac{2}{2} = 1$

$2 + 2i$ is in the quadrant I, so $\theta = 45°$.

$2 + 2i = 2\sqrt{2}(\cos 45° + i \sin 45°)$

31. $-4 = -4 + 0i$

$x = -4, y = 0$

$r = \sqrt{(-4)^2 + 0^2} = 4$

$-4 + 0i$ is on the negative x-axis, so $\theta = 180°$.

$-4 = 4(\cos 180° + i \sin 180°)$

33. $3(\cos 250° + i \sin 250°)$

$= 3[-.34202014 + (-.93969262)i]$

$= -1.0260604 - 2.8190779i$

35. $12i = 0 + 12i$

$x = 0, y = 12$

$r = \sqrt{0^2 + 12^2} = 12$

$0 + 12i$ is on the positive y-axis, so $0 = 90°$.

$12i = 12(\cos 90° + i \sin 90°)$

37. $3 + 5i$

$x = 3, y = 5$

$r = \sqrt{3^2 + 5^2} = \sqrt{34}$

$\tan \theta = \dfrac{5}{3}$

$3 + 5i$ is in the quadrant I, so $\theta = 59.04°$.

$3 + 5i = \sqrt{34}(\cos 59.04° + i \sin 59.04°)$

39. Since the modulus represents the magnitude of the vector in the complex plane, $r = 1$ would represent a circle of radius one centered at the origin.

41. Since the real part of $z = x + yi$ is 1, the graph of $1 + yi$ would be the vertical line $x = 1$.

43. $z = -.2i$

$z^2 - 1 = (-.2i)^2 - 1$

$= -.04 - 1$

$= -1.04$

The modulus is 1.04.

$(z^2 - 1)^2 - 1 = (-1.04)^2 - 1 = .0816$

The modulus is .0816.

$[(z^2 - 1)^2 - 1]^2 - 1 = (.0816)^2 - 1$

$\approx -.9933$

The modulus is about .9933.

The moduli do not exceed 2. Therefore, z is in the Julia set.

45. $[2(\cos 45° + i \sin 45°)] \cdot 2[(\cos 225 + i \sin 225°)]$

$= 4(\cos 270° + i \sin 270°)$

$= 4(0 - i)$

$= 0 - 4i$ or $-4i$

47. $[4(\cos 60° + i \sin 60°)] \cdot [6(\cos 330° + i \sin 330°)]$

$= 24(\cos 390° + i \sin 390°)]$

$= 24(\cos 30° + i \sin 30°)$

$= 24\left(\dfrac{\sqrt{3}}{2} + i\dfrac{1}{2}\right)$

$= 12\sqrt{3} + 12i$

49. $[5 \text{ cis } 90°][3 \text{ cis } 45°] = 15 \text{ cis } 135°$

$= 15(\cos 135° + i \sin 135°)$

$= 15\left(-\dfrac{\sqrt{2}}{2} + \dfrac{\sqrt{2}}{2}i\right)$

$= -\dfrac{15\sqrt{2}}{2} + \dfrac{15\sqrt{2}}{2}i$

51. $[\sqrt{3} \text{ cis } 45°][\sqrt{3} \text{ cis } 225°]$

$= 3 \text{ cis } 270°$

$= 3(\cos 270° + i \sin 270°)$

$= 3(0 - i)$

$= 0 - 3i$ or $-3i$

53. $\dfrac{10(\cos 225° + i \sin 225°)}{5(\cos 45° + i \sin 45°)}$

$= 2(\cos 180° + i \sin 180°)$

$= 2(-1 + 0 \cdot i)$

$= -2 + 0i$ or -2

55. $\dfrac{3 \text{ cis } 305°}{9 \text{ cis } 65°}$

$= \dfrac{1}{3} \text{ cis } 240°$

$= \dfrac{1}{3}(\cos 240° + i \sin 240°)$

$= \dfrac{1}{3}\left(-\dfrac{1}{2} - \dfrac{\sqrt{3}}{2}i\right)$

$= -\dfrac{1}{6} - \dfrac{\sqrt{3}}{6}i$

57. numerator: $r = \sqrt{0^2 + (-1)^2} = 1$

$\tan\theta = \dfrac{-1}{0}$ is undefined.

$\theta = 90° + 180° = 270°$

denominator: $r = \sqrt{1^2 + 1^2} = \sqrt{2}$

$\tan\theta = \dfrac{1}{1}$

$\theta = 45°$

$\dfrac{-i}{1+i} = \dfrac{\text{cis } 270°}{\sqrt{2}\,\text{cis } 45°}$

$= \dfrac{\sqrt{2}}{2}\,\text{cis } 225°$

$= \dfrac{\sqrt{2}}{2}(\cos 225° + i\sin 225°)$

$= \dfrac{\sqrt{2}}{2}\left(-\dfrac{\sqrt{2}}{2} - i\dfrac{\sqrt{2}}{2}\right)$

$= -\dfrac{1}{2} - \dfrac{1}{2}i$

59. numerator: $r = \sqrt{(2\sqrt{6})^2 + (-2\sqrt{2})^2} = 4\sqrt{2}$

$\tan\theta = \dfrac{-2\sqrt{2}}{2\sqrt{6}} = -\dfrac{1}{\sqrt{3}}$

$\theta = -30°$

denominator: $r = \sqrt{(\sqrt{2})^2 + (-\sqrt{6})^2} = 2\sqrt{2}$

$\tan\theta = \dfrac{-\sqrt{6}}{\sqrt{2}} = -\sqrt{3}$

$\theta = -60°$

$\dfrac{2\sqrt{6} - 2i\sqrt{2}}{\sqrt{2} - i\sqrt{6}} = \dfrac{4\sqrt{2}\,\text{cis}\,(-30°)}{2\sqrt{2}\,\text{cis}\,(-60°)}$

$= 2\,\text{cis}\,30°$

$= 2(\cos 30° + i\sin 30°)$

$= 2\left(\dfrac{\sqrt{3}}{2} + i\dfrac{1}{2}\right)$

$= \sqrt{3} + i$

61. $[2.5(\cos 35° + i\sin 35°)] \cdot [3.0(\cos 50° + i\sin 50°)]$

$= 7.5(\cos 85° + i\sin 85°)$

$= .65366807 + 7.4714602i$

63. $(12\,\text{cis}\,18.5°)(3\,\text{cis}\,12.5°)$

$= 36\,\text{cis}\,31°$

$= 36(\cos 31° + i\sin 31°)$

$= 30.858023 + 18.541371i$

65. $\dfrac{45(\cos 127° + i\sin 127°)}{22.5(\cos 43° + i\sin 43°)}$

$= 2(\cos 84° + i\sin 84°)$

$= .20905693 + 1.9890438i$

In Exercises 67–73, $w = -1 + i$ and $z = -1 - i$.

67. $w \cdot z = (-1 + i)(-1 - i)$

$= (-1)(-1) + (-1)(-i) + (i)(-1) + (i)(-i)$

$= 1 + i - i - i^2$

$= 1 - (-1)$

$= 2$

68. $w = -1 + i$

$r = \sqrt{(-1)^2 + 1^2} = \sqrt{2}$

$\tan\theta = \dfrac{1}{-1} = -1$

$\theta = 135°$

$w = \sqrt{2}\,\text{cis}\,135°$

$z = -1 - i$

$r = \sqrt{(-1)^2 + (-1)^2} = \sqrt{2}$

$\tan\theta = \dfrac{-1}{-1} = 1$

$\theta = 225°$

$z = \sqrt{2}\,\text{cis}\,225°$

69. $w \cdot z = (\sqrt{2}\,\text{cis}\,135°)(\sqrt{2}\,\text{cis}\,225°)$

$= (\sqrt{2})(\sqrt{2})\,\text{cis}\,(135° + 225°)$

$= 2\,\text{cis}\,360°$

$= 2\,\text{cis}\,0°$

70. $2\,\text{cis}\,0° = 2(\cos 0° + i\sin 0°)$

$= 2(1 + i(0))$

$= 2(1)$

$= 2$

The result here is the same as the result in Exercise 67.

71. $\dfrac{w}{z} = \dfrac{-1 + i}{-1 - i}$

$= \dfrac{-1 + i}{-1 - i} \cdot \dfrac{-1 + i}{-1 + i}$

$= \dfrac{1 - i - i + i^2}{1 - i^2}$

$= \dfrac{-2i}{2}$

$= -i$

72. $\dfrac{w}{z} = \dfrac{\sqrt{2}\,\text{cis}\,135°}{\sqrt{2}\,\text{cis}\,225°}$

$= \dfrac{\sqrt{2}}{\sqrt{2}}\,\text{cis}\,(135° - 225°)$

$= \text{cis}\,(-90°)$

73. cis $(-90°)$

$= \cos(-90°) + i\sin(-90°)$

$= 0 + i(-1)$

$= -i$

The result here is the same as the result in Exercise 71.

75. $E = 8(\cos 20° + i\sin 20°), \ R = 6,$

$X_L = 3$

$I = \dfrac{E}{Z}, \ Z = R + X_L i$

Write $Z = 6 + 3i$ in trigonometric form.

$x = 6, y = 3,$ so $r = \sqrt{6^2 + 3^2} = \sqrt{45}$.

$\tan\theta = \dfrac{3}{6} = \dfrac{1}{2},$ so $\theta = 26.6°$

$Z = \sqrt{45} \text{ cis } 26.6°$

$I = \dfrac{8 \text{ cis } 20°}{\sqrt{45} \text{ cis } 26.6°}$

$= 1.19 \text{ cis } (-6.6°)$

$\approx 1.18 - .14i$

77. Since $z_1 = 50 + 25i$ and $Z_2 = 60 + 20i$, it follows that

$\dfrac{1}{Z_1} = \dfrac{1}{50 + 25i} \cdot \dfrac{50 - 25i}{50 - 25i} = \dfrac{50 - 25i}{3125}$

$= \dfrac{2}{125} - \dfrac{1}{125}i;$

$\dfrac{1}{Z_2} = \dfrac{1}{60 + 20i} \cdot \dfrac{60 - 20i}{60 - 20i} = \dfrac{60 - 20i}{4000}$

$= \dfrac{3}{200} - \dfrac{1}{200}i.$

$\dfrac{1}{Z_1} + \dfrac{1}{Z_2} = \left[\dfrac{2}{125} - \dfrac{1}{125}i\right] + \left[\dfrac{3}{200} - \dfrac{1}{200}i\right]$

$= \dfrac{31}{1000} - \dfrac{13}{1000}i$

$Z = \dfrac{1}{\dfrac{1}{Z_1} + \dfrac{1}{Z_2}}$

$= \dfrac{1}{\dfrac{31}{1000} - \dfrac{13}{1000}i}$

$= \dfrac{1000}{31 - 13i} \cdot \dfrac{31 + 13i}{31 + 13i}$

$= \dfrac{31,000 + 13,000i}{1130}$

$= \dfrac{3100}{113} + \dfrac{1300}{113}i$

$\approx 27.43 + 11.5i$

Section 7.7

Exercises

1. $[3(\cos 30° + i\sin 30°)]^3$

$= 3^3[\cos(3)(30°) + i\sin(3)(30°)]$

$= 27(\cos 90° + i\sin 90°)$

$= 0 + 27i \text{ or } 27i$

3. $(\cos 45° + i\sin 45°)^8$

$= [\cos(45°)(8) + i\sin(8)(45°)]$

$= 1 + 0i \text{ or } 1$

5. $[3 \text{ cis } 100°]^3$

$= 3^3 \text{ cis } (3 \cdot 100°)$

$= 27 \text{ cis } 300°$

$= 27(\cos 300° + i\sin 300°)$

$= 27\left(\dfrac{1}{2} - \dfrac{\sqrt{3}}{2}i\right)$

$= \dfrac{27}{2} - \dfrac{27\sqrt{3}}{2}i$

7. $(\sqrt{3} + i)^5$

$x = \sqrt{3}, \ y = 1$

$r = \sqrt{(\sqrt{3})^2 + 1^2} = 2$

$\tan\theta = \dfrac{1}{\sqrt{3}}$ so $\theta = 30°$.

$(\sqrt{3} + i)^5$

$= [2(\cos 30° + i\sin 30°)]^5$

$= 2^5(\cos 150° + i\sin 150°)$

$= 32\left(-\dfrac{\sqrt{3}}{2} + i\dfrac{1}{2}\right)$

$= -16\sqrt{3} + 16i$

9. $(2 - 2i\sqrt{3})^4$

$r = \sqrt{2^2 + (-2\sqrt{3})^2} = 4$

$\tan\theta = \dfrac{-2\sqrt{3}}{2} = -\sqrt{3}$ so $\theta = 300°$.

$(2 - 2i\sqrt{3})^4$

$= [4(\cos 300° + i\sin 300°)]^4$

$= 4^4(\cos 1200° + i\sin 1200°)$

$= 256\left(-\dfrac{1}{2} + \dfrac{i\sqrt{3}}{2}\right)$

$= -128 + 128i\sqrt{3}$

11. $(-2-2i)^5$

$r = \sqrt{(-2)^2 + (-2)^2}$

$\quad = \sqrt{8} = 2\sqrt{2}$

$\tan\theta = \dfrac{-2}{-2} = 1$ so $\theta = 225°$.

$(-2-2i)^5$

$= (2\sqrt{2})^5(\cos 225° + i\sin 225°)^5$

$= 32\sqrt{32}(\cos 1125° + i\sin 1125°)$

$= 128\sqrt{2}(\cos 45° + i\sin 45°)$

$= 128\sqrt{2}\left(\dfrac{\sqrt{2}}{2} + \dfrac{\sqrt{2}}{2}i\right)$

$= 128 + 128i$

13. $(\cos 0° + i\sin 0°)$

$= 1(\cos 0° + i\sin 0°)$

$r = 1, \ \theta = 0°, \ n = 3$

$r^{1/3} = 1^{1/3} = 1$

$\alpha = \dfrac{\theta + 360° \cdot k}{n}$

$\quad = \dfrac{0° + 360° \cdot k}{3}$

If $k = 0$, $\alpha = \dfrac{0° + 360° \cdot 0}{3} = 0°$.

If $k = 1$, $\alpha = \dfrac{0° + 360° \cdot 1}{3} = 120°$.

If $k = 2$, $\alpha = \dfrac{0° + 360° \cdot 2}{3} = 240°$.

So the cube roots are
$(\cos 0° + i\sin 0°)$,
$(\cos 120° + i\sin 120°)$,
$(\cos 240° + i\sin 240°)$.

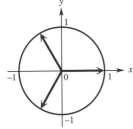

15. 8 cis 60°

$r = 8, \ \theta = 60°, \ n = 3$

$r^{1/3} = 8^{1/3} = 2$

$\alpha = \dfrac{60° + 360° \cdot k}{3}; \ k = 0, \ 1, \ 2$

$\alpha = 20°, \ 140°, \ 260°$

So the cube roots are
2 cis 20°,
2 cis 140°,
2 cis 260°.

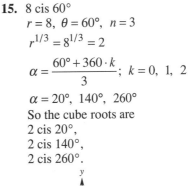

17. $-8i = 8(\cos 270° + i\sin 270°)$

$r = 8, \ \theta = 270°, \ n = 3$

$r^{1/3} = 8^{1/3} = 2$

$\alpha = \dfrac{270° + 360° \cdot k}{3}; \ k = 0, \ 1, \ 2$

$\alpha = 90°, \ 210°, \ 330°$

So the cube roots are
$2(\cos 90° + i\sin 90°)$,
$2(\cos 210° + i\sin 210°)$,
$2(\cos 330° + i\sin 330°)$.

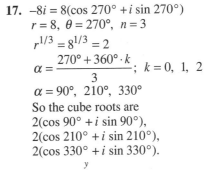

19. $-64 = 64(\cos 180° + i\sin 180°)$

$r = 64, \ \theta = 180°, \ n = 3$

$r^{1/3} = 64^{1/3} = 4$

$\alpha = \dfrac{180° + 360° \cdot k}{3}; \ k = 0, \ 1, \ 2$

$\alpha = 60°, \ 180°, \ 300°$

So the cube roots are
$4(\cos 60° + i\sin 60°)$,
$4(\cos 180° + i\sin 180°)$,
$4(\cos 300° + i\sin 300°)$.

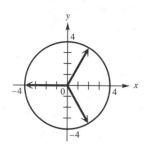

21. $1 + i\sqrt{3}$

$r = \sqrt{1^2 + (\sqrt{3})^2} = 2$

$\tan \theta = \dfrac{\sqrt{3}}{1}$ so $\theta = 60°$.

$1 + i\sqrt{3} = 2(\cos 60° + i \sin 60°)$

$r^{1/3} = 2^{1/3} = \sqrt[3]{2}$

$\alpha = \dfrac{60° + 360° \cdot k}{3}$; $k = 0,\ 1,\ 2$

$\alpha = 20°,\ 140°,\ 260°$

The cube roots are

$\sqrt[3]{2}(\cos 20° + i \sin 20°)$

$\sqrt[3]{2}(\cos 140° + i \sin 140°)$

$\sqrt[3]{2}(\cos 260° + i \sin 260°)$

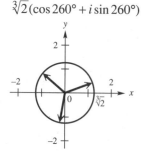

23. $-2\sqrt{3} + 2i$

$r = \sqrt{(-2\sqrt{3})^2 + 2^2} = 4$

$\tan \theta = \dfrac{2}{-2\sqrt{3}}$ so $\theta = 150°$.

$-2\sqrt{3} + 2i = 4(\cos 150° + i \sin 150°)$

$r^{1/3} = 4^{1/3} = \sqrt[3]{4}$

$\alpha = \dfrac{150° + 360° \cdot k}{3}$; $k = 0,\ 1,\ 2$

$\alpha = 50°,\ 170°,\ 290°$

The cube roots are

$\sqrt[3]{4}(\cos 50° + i \sin 50°)$,

$\sqrt[3]{4}(\cos 170° + i \sin 170°)$,

$\sqrt[3]{4}(\cos 290° + i \sin 290°)$.

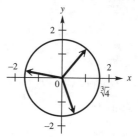

25. Find all the second (or square) roots of 1.

$1 = 1(\cos 0° + i \sin 0°)$

$r = 1,\ \theta = 0°,\ n = 2$

$r^{1/2} = 1^{1/2} = 1$

$\alpha = \dfrac{0° + 360° \cdot k}{2}$; $k = 0,\ 1$

$\alpha = 0°,\ 180°$

The second roots of 1 are

$(\cos 0° + i \sin 0°)$,

$(\cos 180° + i \sin 180°)$.

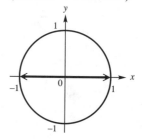

27. Find all the sixth roots of 1.

$1 = 1(\cos 0° + i \sin 0°)$

$r = 1,\ \theta = 0°,\ n = 6$

$r^{1/6} = 1^{1/6} = 1$

$\alpha = \dfrac{0° + 360° \cdot k}{6}$;

$k = 0, 1, 2, 3, 4, 5$

$\alpha = 0°,\ 60°,\ 120°,\ 180°,\ 240°,\ 300°$

The sixth roots of 1 are

$(\cos 0° + i \sin 0°)$,

$(\cos 60° + i \sin 60°)$,

$(\cos 120° + i \sin 120°)$,

$(\cos 180° + i \sin 180°)$,

$(\cos 240° + i \sin 240°)$,

$(\cos 300° + i \sin 300°)$.

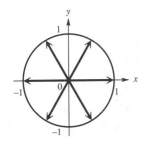

29. Find all the second (square) roots of i.
$i = \cos 90° + i \sin 90°$
$r = 1, \ \theta = 90°, \ n = 2$

$r^{1/2} = 1^{1/2} = 1$

$\alpha = \dfrac{90° + 360° \cdot k}{2}; \ k = 0, \ 1$

$\alpha = 45°, \ 225°$
The second roots of i are
$(\cos 45° + i \sin 45°)$,
$(\cos 225° + i \sin 225°)$.

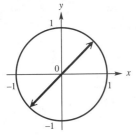

31. $x^3 - 1 = 0$
$\quad x^3 = 1$
$\qquad = 1 + 0i$
$\qquad = 1(\cos 0° + i \sin 0°)$
The modulus of the solutions is
$1^{1/3} = 1$.
The arguments of the solutions are
$\alpha = \dfrac{0° + 360° \cdot k}{3}; \ k = 0, \ 1, \ 2$.

If $k = 0$, $\dfrac{0° + 360° \cdot 0}{3} = 0°$.

If $k = 1$, $\dfrac{0° + 360° \cdot 1}{3} = 120°$.

If $k = 2$, $\dfrac{0° + 360° \cdot 2}{3} = 240°$.

$x = (\cos 0° + i \sin 0°)$,
$\quad (\cos 120° + i \sin 120°)$,
$\quad (\cos 240° + i \sin 240°)$

33. $x^3 + i = 0$
$\quad x^3 = -i$
$\qquad = 0 - i$
$\qquad = 1(\cos 270° + i \sin 270°)$
$1^{1/3} = 1$

$\alpha = \dfrac{270° + 360° \cdot k}{3}; \ k = 0, \ 1, \ 2$

$\alpha = 90°, \ 210°, \ 330°$
$x = (\cos 90° + i \sin 90°)$,
$\quad (\cos 210° + i \sin 210°)$,
$\quad (\cos 330° + i \sin 330°)$

35. $x^3 - 8 = 0$
$\quad x^3 = 8$
$\qquad = 8 + 0i$
$\qquad = 8(\cos 0° + i \sin 0°)$
$8^{1/3} = 2$

$\alpha = \dfrac{0° + 360° \cdot k}{3}; \ k = 0, \ 1, \ 2$

$\alpha = 0°, \ 120°, \ 240°$
$x = 2(\cos 0° + i \sin 0°)$,
$\quad 2(\cos 120° + i \sin 120°)$,
$\quad 2(\cos 240° + i \sin 240°)$

37. $x^4 + 1 = 0$
$\quad x^4 = -1$
$\qquad = -1 + 0i$
$\qquad = 1(\cos 180° + i \sin 180°)$
$1^{1/4} = 1$

$\alpha = \dfrac{180° + 360° \cdot k}{4}; \ k = 0, \ 1, \ 2, \ 3$

$\alpha = 45°, \ 135°, \ 225°, \ 315°$
$x = (\cos 45° + i \sin 45°)$,
$\quad (\cos 135° + i \sin 135°)$,
$\quad (\cos 225° + i \sin 225°)$,
$\quad (\cos 315° + i \sin 315°)$

39. $x^4 - i = 0$
$\quad x^4 = i$
$\qquad = 0 + i$
$\qquad = 1(\cos 90° + i \sin 90°)$
$1^{1/4} = 1$

$\alpha = \dfrac{90° + 360° \cdot k}{4}; \ k = 0, \ 1, \ 2, \ 3$

$\alpha = 22.5°, \ 112.5°, \ 202.5°, \ 292.5°$
$x = (\cos 22.5° + i \sin 22.5°)$,
$\quad (\cos 112.5° + i \sin 112.5°)$,
$\quad (\cos 202.5° + i \sin 202.5°)$,
$\quad (\cos 292.5° + i \sin 292.5°)$

41. $x^3 - (4 + 4i\sqrt{3}) = 0$

$$x^3 = 4 + 4i\sqrt{3}$$

$$r = \sqrt{(4)^2 + (4\sqrt{3})^2} = 8$$

$$\tan\theta = \frac{4\sqrt{3}}{4}, \quad \theta = 60°$$

$$x^3 = 8(\cos 60° + i\sin 60°)$$

$$8^{1/3} = 2$$

$$\alpha = \frac{60° + 360° \cdot k}{3}; \quad k = 0, \ 1, \ 2$$

$$\alpha = 20°, \ 140°, \ 260°$$

$$x = 2(\cos 20° + i\sin 20°),$$
$$2(\cos 140° + i\sin 140°),$$
$$2(\cos 260° + i\sin 260°)$$

43.
$$x^3 - 1 = 0$$
$$(x-1)(x^2 + x + 1) = 0$$
$$x - 1 = 0$$
$$x = 1$$
or
$$x^2 + x + 1 = 0$$
Use the quadratic formula with $a = 1$, $b = 1$, and $c = 1$.

$$x = \frac{-1 \pm \sqrt{1^2 - 4 \cdot 1 \cdot 1}}{2 \cdot 1}$$

$$x = \frac{-1 \pm \sqrt{-3}}{2}$$

$$x = \frac{-1 \pm i\sqrt{3}}{2}$$

$$x = -\frac{1}{2} \pm \frac{\sqrt{3}}{2}i$$

$$x = 1, \ -\frac{1}{2} + \frac{\sqrt{3}}{2}i, \ -\frac{1}{2} - \frac{\sqrt{3}}{2}i$$

We see that the solutions are the same as Exercise 31.
For Exercise 31, the solutions are
$(\cos 0° + i\sin 0°)$
$(\cos 120° + i\sin 120°)$
$(\cos 240° + i\sin 240°)$.
In standard form, these are

$$1, \ -\frac{1}{2} + \frac{\sqrt{3}}{2}i, \ -\frac{1}{2} - \frac{\sqrt{3}}{2}i.$$

45. $(\cos\theta + i\sin\theta)^2 = 1^2(\cos 2\theta + i\sin 2\theta)$
$$= \cos 2\theta + i\sin 2\theta$$

46. $(\cos\theta + i\sin\theta)^2$
$$= \cos^2\theta + 2i\sin\theta\cos\theta + i^2\sin^2\theta$$
$$= \cos^2\theta + 2i\sin\theta\cos\theta - \sin^2\theta$$
$$= (\cos^2\theta - \sin^2\theta) + i(2\sin\theta\cos\theta)$$
$$= \cos 2\theta + i\sin 2\theta$$

47. Two complex numbers $a + bi$ and $c + di$ are equal only if $a = c$ and $b = d$. Therefore,
$$\cos^2\theta - \sin^2\theta = \cos 2\theta \text{ and}$$
$$2\sin\theta\cos\theta = \sin 2\theta.$$

48. $\cos 2\theta + i\sin 2\theta$
$$= (\cos^2\theta - \sin^2\theta) + i(2\cos\theta\sin\theta)$$
Since $a + bi = c + di$ only if $a = c$ and $b = d$,
$i\sin 2\theta = i(2\cos\theta\sin\theta)$ and $\sin 2\theta = 2\cos\theta\sin\theta$.

49. (a) If $z = 0 + 0i$, then $z = 0$, $0^2 + 0 = 0$,
$0^2 + 0 = 0$, and so on. The calculations repeat as $0, 0, 0, \dots$, and will never exceed a modulus of 2. The point $(0, 0)$ is part of the Mandelbrot set. The pixel at the origin should be turned on.

(b) If $z = 1 - 1i$,
$$(1-i)^2 + (1-i) = 1 - 3i.$$
The modulus of $1 - 3i$ is $\sqrt{10}$, which is greater than 2. Therefore, $1 - 1i$ is not part of the Mandelbrot set, and the pixel at $(1, -1)$ should be left off.

(c) If $z = -.5i$,
$$(-.5i)^2 - .5i = -.25 - .5i;$$
$$(-.25) - .5i)^2 + (-.25 - .5i) = -.4375 - .25i;$$
$$(-.4375 - .25i)^2 + (-.4375 - .25i)$$
$$= -.308593 - .03125i;$$
$$(-.308593 - .03125i)^2$$
$$+ (-.308593 - .03125i)$$
$$= -.214339 - .0119629i;$$
$$(-.214339 - .0119629i)^2$$
$$+ (-.214339 - .0119629i)$$
$$= -.16854 - .00683466i.$$
This sequence appears to be approaching the origin, and no number has a modulus greater than 2. Thus, $-.5i$ is part of the Mandelbrot set, and the pixel at $(0, -.5)$ should be turned on.

51. Using the trace function, we find that the other four fifth roots of 1 are: $.30901699 + .95105652i$, $-.809017 + .58778525i$, $-.809017 - .5877853i$, $.30901699 - .9510565i$

53. $2 + 2\sqrt{3}i$ is one cube root.

$$r = \sqrt{2^2 + (2\sqrt{3})^2} = \sqrt{4 + 12} = 4$$

$$\tan\theta = \frac{2\sqrt{3}}{2} = \sqrt{3}; \ \theta = 60°$$

This root is 4 cis 60° = 4 cis (60° · 1).
Since the graphs of the other roots must be equally spaced around a circle and the graphs of these roots are all on a circle that has center at the origin and radius 4, the other roots are
4 cis (60° + 120°) = 4 cis 180° and
4 cis (60° + 2 · 120°) = 4 cis 300°.

4 cis 180° = 4(cos 180° + i sin 180°)
$$= 4(-1 + i \cdot 0) = -4$$

4 cis 300° = 4(cos 300° + i sin 300°)

$$= 4\left(\frac{1}{2} + i\left(-\frac{\sqrt{3}}{2}\right)\right)$$

$$= 2 - 2i\sqrt{3}$$

The roots are $2 - 2i\sqrt{3}, \ -4$ and $2 + 2i\sqrt{3}$.

55. $x^5 + 2 + 3i = 0$

$$x^5 = -2 - 3i$$
$$r = \sqrt{4 + 9} = \sqrt{13}$$
$$r^{1/n} = (\sqrt{13})^{1/5} = 13^{1/10} = 1.292$$

$$\tan\theta = \frac{-3}{-2} = 1.5$$

θ is in quadrant III.
$\theta = 236.30993°$

$$\alpha = \frac{236.30993° + 360° \cdot k}{5};$$

$k = 0, 1, 2, 3, 4$
$\alpha = 47.26°, \ 119.26°, \ 191.62°,$
    $263.26°, \ 335.26°$

$x \approx 1.292(\cos 47.26° + i \sin 47.26°),$
    $1.292(\cos 119.26° + i \sin 119.26°),$
    $1.292(\cos 191.26° + i \sin 191.26°),$
    $1.292(\cos 263.26° + i \sin 263.26°),$
    $1.292(\cos 335.26° + i \sin 335.26°)$
In standard form, $x \approx .87708 + .94922i$
$-.63173 + 1.1275i, \ -1.2675 - .25240i,$
$-.15164 - 1.28347i, \ 1.1738 - .54083i.$

57. The statement, "Every real number must have two real square roots," is false. Consider, for example, the real number –4. Its two square roots are $2i$ and $-2i$ which are not real.

Section 7.8

Connections *(page 599)*

1. $y = x - 3$
    $-x + y = -3$
    $x - y = 3$

2. $y = \pm\sqrt{4 - x^2}$
    $y^2 = 4 - x^2$
$x^2 + y^2 = 4$

Exercises

1. (a) II (since $r > 0$ and $90° < \theta < 135°$)

(b) I (since $r > 0$ and $0° < \theta < 90°$)

(c) IV (since $r > 0$ and $-90° < \theta < 0°$)

(d) III (since $r > 0$ and $180° < \theta < 270°$)

For Exercises 3–11, answers may vary.

3. Two other pairs of polar coordinates for (1, 45°) are (1, 405°) and (–1, 225°).

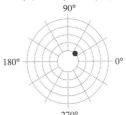

5. Two other pairs of polar coordinates for (–2, 135°) are (–2, 495°) and (2, 315°).

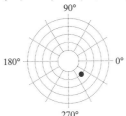

7. Two other pairs of polar coordinates for (5, –60°) are (5, 300°) and (–5, 120°).

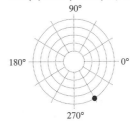

9. Two other pairs of polar coordinates for
    (−3, −210°) are (−3, 150°) and (3, −30°).

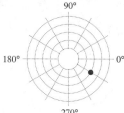

11. Two other pairs of polar coordinates for (3, 300°)
    are (3, 660°) and (−3, 120°).

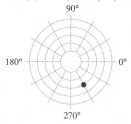

For Exercises 13–21, answers may vary.

13. $r = \sqrt{(-1)^2 + 1^2} = \sqrt{1+1} = \sqrt{2}$

    $\theta = \arctan\left(\dfrac{1}{-1}\right) = 135°$

    (since $x < 0$ and $y > 0$)
    So one possibility is $(\sqrt{2},\ 135°)$
    Alternatively if $r = -\sqrt{2},\ \theta = 135 + 180 = 315°$
    A second possibility is $(-\sqrt{2},\ 315°)$
    Two pairs:
    $(\sqrt{2},\ 135°),\ (-\sqrt{2},\ 315°)$

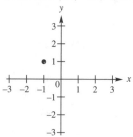

15. $r = \sqrt{0^2 + 3^2} = \sqrt{9} = 3$
    The point $(0, 3)$ is on the positive y-axis. Thus,
    $\theta = 90°$.
    One possibility is $(3, 90°)$.
    Alternatively, if $r = -3,\ \theta = 90 + 180 = 270°$
    A second possibility is: $(-3, 270°)$
    Two pairs:
    $(3, 90°),\ (-3, 270°)$

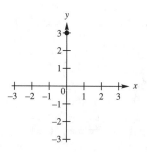

17. $r = \sqrt{(\sqrt{2})^2 + (\sqrt{2})^2} = \sqrt{2+2} = \sqrt{4} = 2$

    $\theta = \arctan\left(\dfrac{\sqrt{2}}{\sqrt{2}}\right) = \arctan(1) = 45°$

    (since $x > 0$ and $y > 0$)
    One possibility is: $(2, 45°)$
    Alternatively, if $r = -2$,
    $\theta = 45° + 180 = 225°$
    A second possibility is: $(-2, 225°)$
    Two pairs:
    $(2, 45°),\ (-2, 225°)$

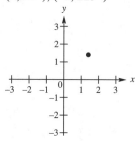

19. $r = \sqrt{\left(\dfrac{\sqrt{3}}{2}\right)^2 + \left(\dfrac{3}{2}\right)^2} = \sqrt{\dfrac{3}{4} + \dfrac{9}{4}} = \sqrt{3}$

    $\theta = \arctan\left(\dfrac{3}{2} \cdot \dfrac{2}{\sqrt{3}}\right) = \arctan(\sqrt{3}) = 60°$

    (since $x > 0$ and $y > 0$)
    One possibility is: $(\sqrt{3},\ 60°)$
    Alternatively, if $r = -\sqrt{3},\ \theta = 60 + 180 = 240°$.
    Two pairs:
    $(\sqrt{3},\ 60°),\ (-\sqrt{3},\ 240°)$.

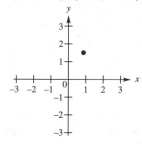

21. $r = \sqrt{3^2 + 0^2} = \sqrt{9} = 3$

$\theta = \arctan\left(\dfrac{0}{3}\right) = 0°$

(since $\tan \theta = 0$ and $x > 0$).
One possibility is: $(3, 0°)$
Alternatively, if $r = -3$, $\theta = 0 + 180 = 180°$
A second possibility is $(-3, 180°)$
Two pairs:
$(3, 0°), (-3, 180°)$

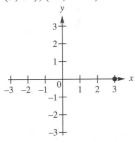

23. $r = 2 + 2\cos\theta$ (cardioid)

θ	0°	30°	60°	90°	120°	150°
$\cos\theta$	1	.9	.5	0	−.5	−.9
r	4	3.8	3	2	1	.2

θ	180°	210°	240°	270°	300°	330°
$\cos\theta$	−1	−.9	−.5	0	.5	.9
r	0	.3	1	2	3	3.7

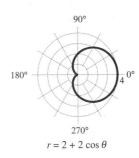

$r = 2 + 2\cos\theta$

25. $r = 3 + \cos\theta$ (limaçon)

θ	0°	30°	60°	90°	120°	150°
r	4	3.9	3.5	3	2.5	2.1

θ	180°	210°	240°	270°	300°	330°
r	2	2.1	2.5	3	3.5	3.9

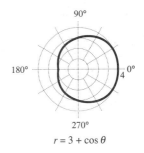

$r = 3 + \cos\theta$

27. $r = 4\cos 2\theta$ (four-leaved rose)

θ	0°	30°	45°	60°	90°	120°	135°	150°
r	4	2	0	−2	−4	−2	0	2

θ	180°	210°	225°	240°	270°	300°	315°	330°
r	4	2	0	−2	−4	−2	0	2

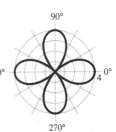

$r = 4\cos 2\theta$

29. $r^2 = 4\cos 2\theta$ (lemniscate)

$r = \pm 2\sqrt{\cos 2\theta}$

Graph only exists for $[0°, 45°]$, $[135°, 225°]$, and $[315°, 360°]$ because $\cos 2\theta$ must be positive.

θ	0°	30°	45°	135°	150°
r	±2	±1.4	0	0	±1.4

θ	180°	210°	225°	315°	330°
r	±2	±1.4	0	0	±1.4

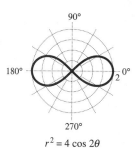

$r^2 = 4\cos 2\theta$

31. $r = 4(1 - \cos\theta)$ (cardioid)

θ	0°	30°	60°	90°	120°	150°
r	0	.5	2	4	6	7.5

θ	180°	210°	240°	270°	300°	330°
r	8	7.5	6	4	2	.5

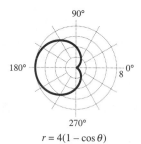

$r = 4(1 - \cos\theta)$

33. $r = 2\sin\theta\tan\theta$ (cissoid)

r is undefined at $\theta = 90°$ and $\theta = 270°$.

θ	0°	30°	45°	60°	90°	120°	135°	150°	180°
r	0	.6	1.4	3	–	−3	−1.4	−.6	0

Notice that for $[180°, 360°)$, the graph retraces the path traced for $[0°, 180°)$.

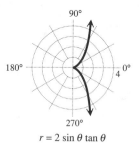

$r = 2\sin\theta\tan\theta$

35. **(a)** $(r, -\theta)$

(b) $(r, \pi - \theta)$ or $(-r, -\theta)$

(c) $(r, \pi + \theta)$ or $(-r, \theta)$

36. $-\theta$

37. $\pi - \theta$

38. $-r; -\theta$

39. $-r$

40. $\pi + \theta$

41. the polar axis

42. the line $\theta = \dfrac{\pi}{2}$

43. $r = 4 \cos 2\theta$, $0° \le \theta < 360°$
Since the largest value of $\cos 2\theta$ is 1 (the range of the cosine function is $[-1, 1]$), the largest value of r is $4 \cdot 1 = 4$.
$4 \cos 2\theta = 0$
$\cos 2\theta = 0$
Since $0° \le \theta < 360°$, $0° \le 2\theta < 720°$.
The cosine is 0 at $90°$, $270°$, $450°$, $630°$. Thus,
$2\theta = 90°$ or $2\theta = 270°$
$\theta = 45°$ or $\theta = 135°$
$2\theta = 450°$ or $2\theta = 630°$
$\theta = 225°$ or $\theta = 315°$.

47. $r = 2 + \sin\theta$, $r = 2 + \cos\theta$,
$0 \le \theta < 2\pi$
$2 + \sin\theta = 2 + \cos\theta$
$\sin\theta = \cos\theta$
$\theta = \dfrac{\pi}{4}$ or $\dfrac{5\pi}{4}$
$r = 2 + \sin\dfrac{\pi}{4} = 2 + \dfrac{\sqrt{2}}{2} = \dfrac{4 + \sqrt{2}}{2}$
$r = 2 + \sin\dfrac{5\pi}{4} = 2 - \dfrac{\sqrt{2}}{2} = \dfrac{4 - \sqrt{2}}{2}$
The points of intersection are
$\left(\dfrac{4 + \sqrt{2}}{2}, \dfrac{\pi}{4}\right)$, $\left(\dfrac{4 - \sqrt{2}}{2}, \dfrac{5\pi}{4}\right)$.

51. $r = 2 \sin\theta$
Multiply both sides by r.
$r^2 = 2r\sin\theta$
Since $r^2 = x^2 + y^2$ and $y = r\sin\theta$,
$x^2 + y^2 = 2y$.
Complete the square on y.
$x^2 + y^2 - 2y + 1 = 1$
$x^2 + (y - 1)^2 = 1$
The graph is a circle with center at $(0, 1)$ and radius 1.

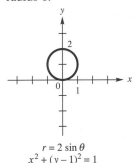

$r = 2 \sin\theta$
$x^2 + (y - 1)^2 = 1$

53. $r = \dfrac{2}{1 - \cos\theta}$
Multiply both sides by $1 - \cos\theta$.
$r - r\cos\theta = 2$
$\sqrt{x^2 + y^2} - x = 2$
$\sqrt{x^2 + y^2} = 2 + x$
$x^2 + y^2 = (2 + x)^2$
$x^2 + y^2 = 4 + 4x + x^2$
$y^2 = 4(1 + x)$
The graph is a parabola with vertex at $(-1, 0)$ and axis $y = 0$.

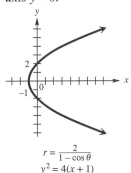

$r = \dfrac{2}{1 - \cos\theta}$
$y^2 = 4(x + 1)$

55.
$r + 2\cos\theta = -2\sin\theta$
$r^2 = -2r\sin\theta - 2r\cos\theta$
$x^2 + y^2 = -2y - 2x$
$x^2 + y^2 + 2y + 2x = 0$
$(x + 1)^2 + (y + 1)^2 = 2$
The graph is a circle with center $(-1, -1)$ and radius $\sqrt{2}$.

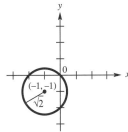

$r + 2\cos\theta = -2\sin\theta$
$(x + 1)^2 + (y + 1)^2 = 2$

57.
$$r = 2 \sec \theta$$
$$r = \frac{2}{\cos \theta}$$
$$r \cos \theta = 2$$
$$x = 2$$
The graph is a vertical line.

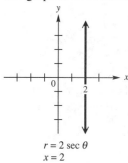

$r = 2 \sec \theta$
$x = 2$

59.
$$r(\cos \theta + \sin \theta) = 2$$
$$r \cos \theta + r \sin \theta = 2$$
$$x + y = 2$$
The graph is the line with intercepts $(0, 2)$ and $(2, 0)$.

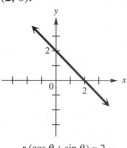

$r (\cos \theta + \sin \theta) = 2$
$x + y = 2$

61.
$$x + y = 4$$
$$r \cos \theta + r \sin \theta = 4$$
$$r(\cos \theta + \sin \theta) = 4$$
$$r = \frac{4}{\cos \theta + \sin \theta}$$

63.
$$x^2 + y^2 = 16$$
$$r^2 = 16$$
$$r = 4$$

65.
$$y = 2$$
$$r \sin \theta = 2 \text{ or}$$
$$r = \frac{2}{\sin \theta} = 2 \csc \theta$$

67. Graph $r = \theta$, a spiral of Archimedes.

θ	−360°	−270°	−180°	−90°
θ (radians)	−6.3	−4.7	−3.1	−1.6
r	−6.3	−4.7	−3.1	−1.6

θ	0°	90°	180°	270°	360°
θ (radians)	0	1.6	3.1	4.7	6.3
r	0	1.6	3.1	4.7	6.3

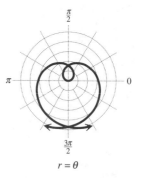

$r = \theta$

69. In rectangular coordinates, the line passes through $(1, 0)$ and $(0, 2)$. So
$$m = \frac{2 - 0}{0 - 1} = \frac{2}{-1} = -2 \text{ and}$$
$$(y - 0) = -2(x - 1)$$
$$y = -2x + 2$$
$$2x + y = 2$$

Converting to polar form $r = \dfrac{c}{a \cos \theta + b \sin \theta}$,

we have: $r = \dfrac{2}{2 \cos \theta + \sin \theta}$.

Section 7.9

Exercises

1. C; at $t = 2$, $x = 3(2) + 6 = 12$
$$y = -2(2) + 4 = 0$$

3. A; at $t = 5$, $x = 5$
$$y = 5^2 = 25$$

5. $x = 2t$, $y = t + 1$, for t in $[-2, 3]$

t	$x = 2t$	$y = t + 1$
-2	$2(-2) = -4$	$-2 + 1 = -1$
-1	$2(-1) = -2$	$-1 + 1 = 0$
0	$2(0) = 0$	$0 + 1 = 1$
1	$2(1) = 2$	$1 + 1 = 2$
2	$2(2) = 4$	$2 + 1 = 3$
3	$2(3) = 6$	$3 + 1 = 4$

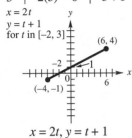

$$x = 2t, \ y = t + 1$$

Since $\dfrac{x}{2} = t, \ y = \dfrac{x}{2} + 1$.

Since t is in $[-2, 3]$, x is in $[2(-2), 2(3)]$ or $[-4, 6]$.

7. $x = \sqrt{t}, \ y = 3t - 4$, for t in $[0, 4]$.

t	$x = \sqrt{t}$	$y = 3t - 4$
0	$\sqrt{0} = 0$	$3(0) - 4 = -4$
1	$\sqrt{1} = 1$	$3(1) - 4 = -1$
2	$\sqrt{2} = 1.4$	$3(2) - 4 = 2$
3	$\sqrt{3} = 1.7$	$3(3) - 4 = 5$
4	$\sqrt{4} = 2$	$3(4) - 4 = 8$

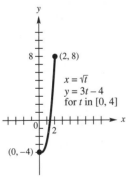

$$x = \sqrt{t} \quad y = 3t - 4$$

Since $x^2 = t, \ y = 3x^2 - 4$.

Since t is in $[0, 4]$, x is in $[\sqrt{0}, \ \sqrt{4}]$ or $[0, 2]$.

9. $x = t^3 + 1, \ y = t^3 - 1$, for t in $(-\infty, \infty)$

t	$x = t^3 + 1$	$y = t^3 - 1$
-2	$(-2)^3 + 1 = -7$	$(-2)^3 - 1 = -9$
-1	$(-1)^3 + 1 = 0$	$(-1)^3 - 1 = -2$
0	$0^3 + 1 = 1$	$0^3 - 1 = -1$
1	$1^3 + 1 = 2$	$1^3 - 1 = 0$
2	$2^3 + 1 = 9$	$2^3 - 1 = 7$
3	$3^3 + 1 = 28$	$3^3 - 1 = 26$

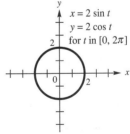

Since $x = t^3 + 1$,

$$x - 1 = t^3.$$

Since $y = t^3 - 1$,

$$y = (x - 1) - 1 = x - 2.$$

Since t is in $(-\infty, \infty)$, x is in $(-\infty, \infty)$.

11. $x = 2 \sin t, \ y = 2 \cos t$, for t in $[0, 2\pi]$

t	$x = 2 \sin t$	$y = 2 \cos t$
0	$2 \sin 0 = 0$	$2 \cos \theta = 2$
$\frac{\pi}{6}$	$2 \sin \frac{\pi}{6} = 1$	$2 \cos \frac{\pi}{6} = \sqrt{3}$
$\frac{\pi}{4}$	$2 \sin \frac{\pi}{4} = \sqrt{2}$	$2 \cos \frac{\pi}{4} = \sqrt{2}$
$\frac{\pi}{3}$	$2 \sin \frac{\pi}{3} = \sqrt{3}$	$2 \cos \frac{\pi}{3} = 1$
$\frac{\pi}{2}$	$2 \sin \frac{\pi}{2} = 2$	$2 \cos \frac{\pi}{2} = 0$

Since $x = 2 \sin t$ and $y = 2 \cos t$,

$$\frac{x}{2} = \sin t \text{ and } \frac{y}{2} = \cos t.$$

Since $\sin^2 t + \cos^2 t = 1$,

$$\left(\frac{x}{2}\right)^2 + \left(\frac{y}{2}\right)^2 = 1$$

$$\frac{x^2}{4} + \frac{y^2}{4} = 1$$

$$x^2 + y^2 = 4.$$

Since t is in $[0, 2\pi]$, x is in $[-2, 2]$ because the graph is a circle, centered at the origin, with radius 2.

13. $x = 3 \tan t$, $y = 2 \sec t$, for t in $\left(-\dfrac{\pi}{2}, \dfrac{\pi}{2}\right)$

t	$x = 3 \tan t$	$y = 2 \sec t$
$-\dfrac{\pi}{3}$	$3\tan\left(-\dfrac{\pi}{3}\right) = -3\sqrt{3}$	$2\sec\left(-\dfrac{\pi}{3}\right) = 4$
$-\dfrac{\pi}{6}$	$3\tan\left(-\dfrac{\pi}{6}\right) = -\sqrt{3}$	$2\sec\left(-\dfrac{\pi}{6}\right) = \dfrac{4\sqrt{3}}{3}$
0	$3 \tan 0 = 0$	$2 \sec 0 = 2$
$\dfrac{\pi}{6}$	$3\tan\dfrac{\pi}{6} = \sqrt{3}$	$2\sec\dfrac{\pi}{6} = \dfrac{4\sqrt{3}}{3}$
$\dfrac{\pi}{3}$	$3\tan\dfrac{\pi}{3} = 3\sqrt{3}$	$2\sec\dfrac{\pi}{3} = 4$

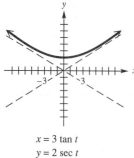

$x = 3 \tan t$
$y = 2 \sec t$
for t in $\left(-\dfrac{\pi}{2}, \dfrac{\pi}{2}\right)$

Since

$\dfrac{x}{3} = \tan t$ and $\dfrac{y}{2} = \sec t$,

and $1 + \tan^2 t = \left(\dfrac{y}{2}\right)^2 = \sec^2 t$,

$$1 + \left(\dfrac{x}{3}\right)^2 = \left(\dfrac{y}{2}\right)^2$$

$$1 + \dfrac{x^2}{9} = \dfrac{y^2}{4}$$

$$y^2 = 4\left(1 + \dfrac{x^2}{9}\right)$$

$$y = 2\sqrt{1 + \dfrac{x^2}{9}}.$$

Since this graph is the top half of a hyperbola, x is in $(-\infty, \infty)$.

15. $x = \sin t$, $y = \csc t = \dfrac{1}{\sin t}$

Therefore, $y = \dfrac{1}{x}$.

Since t is in $(0, \pi)$ and $x = \sin t$, x is in $(0, 1]$.

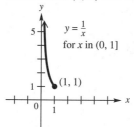

17. Since $x = t$ and $y = \sqrt{t^2 + 2}$, $y = \sqrt{x^2 + 2}$.

Since t is in $(-\infty, \infty)$ and $x = t$, x is in $(-\infty, \infty)$.

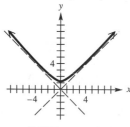

$y = \sqrt{x^2 + 2}$ for x in $(-\infty, \infty)$

19. Since $x = 2 + \sin t$ and $y = 1 + \cos t$,

$x - 2 = \sin t$ and $y - 1 = \cos t$.

Since $\sin^2 t + \cos^2 t = 1$,

$(x - 2)^2 + (y - 1)^2 = 1$.

Since this is a circle centered at $(2, 1)$ with radius 1, and t is in $[0, 2\pi]$, x is in $[1, 3]$.

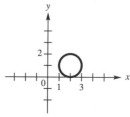

$(x - 2)^2 + (y - 1)^2 = 1$
for x in $[1, 3]$

21. Since $x = t + 2$ and $y = \dfrac{1}{t+2}$, $y = \dfrac{1}{x}$.

Since $t \neq -2$, $x \neq -2 + 2$, $x \neq 0$.

Therefore, x is in $(-\infty, 0) \cup (0, \infty)$.

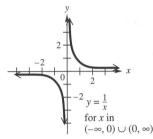

$y = \dfrac{1}{x}$
for x in
$(-\infty, 0) \cup (0, \infty)$

23. $x = \sin t$, $y = \cos t$

This graph is a circle centered at the origin with radius 1.

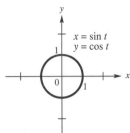

$x = \sin t$
$y = \cos t$

25. $x = t + 2$, $y = t - 4$

This graph is a line through $(6, 0)$ and $(0, -6)$.

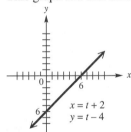

$x = t + 2$
$y = t - 4$

27.

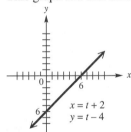

$x = t - \sin t$
$y = 1 - \cos t$ for t in $[0, 4\pi]$

For Exercises 29–31, recall that the motion of a projectile (neglecting air resistance) can be modeled by:
$x = (v_0 \cos\theta)t$, $y = (v_0 \sin\theta)t - 16t^2$ for t in $[0, k]$.

29. **(a)**
$$x = (v_0 \cos\theta)t \qquad y = (v_0 \sin\theta)t - 16t^2$$
$$= (48 \cos 60°)t \qquad = (48 \sin 60°)t - 16t^2$$
$$= 48\left(\frac{1}{2}\right)t \qquad = 48 \cdot \frac{\sqrt{3}}{2}t - 16t^2$$
$$= 24t \qquad = -16t^2 + 24\sqrt{3}t$$

(b) $t = \dfrac{x}{24}$, so

$$y = -16\left(\frac{x}{24}\right)^2 + 24\sqrt{3}\left(\frac{x}{24}\right)$$
$$= -\frac{x^2}{36} + \sqrt{3}x$$

(c) $y = -16t^2 + 24\sqrt{3}t$

When the rocket is no longer in flight, $y = 0$.
$$0 = -16t^2 + 24\sqrt{3}t$$
$$0 = t(-16t + 24\sqrt{3})$$
$$t = 0 \text{ or } -16t + 24\sqrt{3} = 0$$
$$-16t = -24\sqrt{3}$$
$$t = \frac{24\sqrt{3}}{16}$$
$$t = \frac{3\sqrt{3}}{2}$$
$$t \approx 2.6$$

The flight time is about 2.6 seconds.

The horizontal distance at $t = \dfrac{3\sqrt{3}}{2}$ is

$$x = 24t = 24\left(\frac{3\sqrt{3}}{2}\right) \approx 62 \text{ ft.}$$

31. **(a)**
$$x = (v_0 \cos\theta)t$$
$$= (88 \cos 20°)t$$
$$y = (v_0 \sin\theta)t - 16t^2 + 2$$
$$= (88 \sin 20°)t - 16t^2 + 2$$

(b) $t = \dfrac{x}{88\cos 20°}$

$y = 88\sin 20°\left(\dfrac{x}{88\cos 20°}\right)$

$\qquad -16\left(\dfrac{x}{88\cos 20°}\right)^2 + 2$

$\qquad = (\tan 20°)x - \dfrac{x^2}{484\cos^2 20°} + 2$

(c) $0 = -16t^2 + (88\sin 20°)t + 2$

$t = \dfrac{-88\sin 20° \pm \sqrt{(88\sin 20°)^2 - 4(-16)(2)}}{(-16)(2)}$

(Using the quadratic formula)

$\qquad = \dfrac{-30.098 \pm \sqrt{905.8759 + 128}}{-32}$

$\qquad \approx -0.064,\ 1.9$

Discard $t = -0.064$ since it is an unacceptable answer.

At $t \approx 1.9\,\text{sec}$, $x = (88\cos 20°)t \approx 161\,\text{ft}$. The softball traveled 1.9 sec and 161 feet.

33. (a)

$x = 82.69265063t$
$y = -16t^2 + 30.09777261t$

30

0

0   200

(b) $x = 82.69265063t = v_0(\cos\theta)t$

$\qquad 82.69265063 = v_0\cos\theta$

$y = -16t^2 + 30.09777261t$

$\qquad = v_0(\sin\theta)t - 16t^2$

$30.09777261 = v_0\sin\theta$

$\dfrac{30.09777261}{82.69265063} = \dfrac{v_0\sin\theta}{v_0\cos\theta}$

$0.3697 = \tan\theta$

$\qquad \theta = 20.0°$

(c) $30.09777261 = v_0\sin 20.0°$

$\qquad\qquad\quad v_0 = 88.0\ \text{ft/sec}$

$x = 88(\cos 20°)t$

$y = -16t^2 + 88(\sin 20°)t$

For Exercises 35 and 37, many answers are possible.

35. The equation of a line with slope m through $(x_1,\ y_1)$ is

$y - y_1 = m(x - x_1)$.

To find two parametric representations, let $x = t$. Then

$y - y_1 = m(t - x_1)$

$\qquad y = m(t - x_1) + y_1$.

Or, let $x = t^2$. Then

$y - y_1 = m(t^2 - x_1)$

$\qquad y = m(t^2 - x_1) + y_1$.

37. $\dfrac{x^2}{a^2} - \dfrac{y^2}{b^2} = 1$

To find a parametric representation, let $x = a\sec\theta$. Then

$\dfrac{(a\sec\theta)^2}{a^2} - \dfrac{y^2}{b^2} = 1$

$\sec^2\theta - \dfrac{y^2}{b^2} = 1$

$\sec^2\theta - 1 = \dfrac{y^2}{b^2}$

$\tan^2\theta = \dfrac{y^2}{b^2}$

$b^2\tan^2\theta = y^2$

$b\tan\theta = y$.

41. The second set of equations $x = \cos t$, $y = -\sin t$, t in $[0, 2\pi]$ trace the circle out clockwise. A table of values confirms this.

t	$x = \cos t$	$y = -\sin t$
0	$\cos 0 = 1$	$-\sin 0 = 0$
$\frac{\pi}{6}$	$\cos\frac{\pi}{6} = \frac{\sqrt{3}}{2}$	$-\sin\frac{\pi}{6} = -\frac{1}{2}$
$\frac{\pi}{4}$	$\cos\frac{\pi}{4} = \frac{\sqrt{2}}{2}$	$-\sin\frac{\pi}{4} = -\frac{\sqrt{2}}{2}$
$\frac{\pi}{3}$	$\cos\frac{\pi}{3} = \frac{1}{2}$	$-\sin\frac{\pi}{3} = -\frac{\sqrt{3}}{2}$
$\frac{\pi}{2}$	$\cos\frac{\pi}{2} = 0$	$-\sin\frac{\pi}{2} = -1$

Chapter 7 Review Exercises

1. Find b, given $C = 74.2°, c = 96.3$ m, $B = 39.5°$.
 Use the law of sines to find b.
 $$\frac{b}{\sin B} = \frac{c}{\sin C}$$
 $$b = \frac{c \sin B}{\sin C}$$
 $$= \frac{96.3 \sin 39.5°}{\sin 74.2°}$$
 $$= 63.7 \text{ m}$$

3. Find B, given $C = 51.3°, c = 68.3$ m, $b = 58.2$ m.
 Use the law of sines to find B.
 $$\frac{\sin B}{b} = \frac{\sin C}{c}$$
 $$\sin B = \frac{b \sin C}{c}$$
 $$= \frac{58.2 \sin 51.3°}{68.3}$$
 $$\sin B = .66502269$$
 $$B = 41.7°$$
 Angle B cannot be obtuse, since $b < c$, $B < C$, and C is acute.

5. Find A, given $B = 39° 50', b = 268$ m, $a = 340$ m.
 $a > b > a \sin B$ tells us that two triangles are possible and A can have two values.
 Use the law of sines to find A.
 $$\frac{\sin A}{a} = \frac{\sin B}{b}$$
 $$\sin A = \frac{a \sin B}{b}$$
 $$= \frac{340 \sin 39° 50'}{268}$$
 $$\sin A = .81264638$$
 $$A = 54° 20' \text{ or } A = 125° 40'$$

9. $a = 10, B = 30°$

 (a) The value of b that forms a right triangle would yield exactly one value for A. That is, $b = 10 \sin 30° = 5$. Also, any value of b greater than or equal to 10 would yield a unique value for A.

 (b) Any value of b between 5 and 10, would yield two possible values for A.

 (c) If b is less than 5, then no value for A is possible.

11. Find A, given $a = 86.14$ in., $b = 253.2$ in., $c = 241.9$ in.
 Use the law of cosines to find A.
 $$a^2 = b^2 + c^2 - 2bc \cos A$$
 $$\cos A = \frac{b^2 + c^2 - a^2}{2bc}$$
 $$= \frac{253.2^2 + 241.9^2 - 86.14^2}{2(253.2)(241.9)}$$
 $$\cos A = .94046923$$
 $$A = 19.87° \text{ or } 19° 52'$$

13. Find a, given $A = 51° 20', c = 68.3$ m, $b = 58.2$ m;
 Use the law of cosines to find a.
 $$a^2 = b^2 + c^2 - 2bc \cos A$$
 $$a = \sqrt{(58.2)^2 + (68.3)^2 - 2(58.2)(68.3) \cos 51° 20'}$$
 $$a = 55.5 \text{ m}$$

15. Find a, given $A = 60°, b = 5$cm, $c = 21$ cm.
 Use the law of cosines to find a.
 $$a^2 = b^2 + c^2 - 2bc \cos A$$
 $$a = \sqrt{(5)^2 + (21)^2 - 2(5)(21) \cos 60°}$$
 $$a = 19 \text{ cm}$$

17. Solve the triangle, given $A = 25.2°, a = 6.92$ yd, $b = 4.82$ yd.
 $a > b$ tells us that only one triangle is possible.
 Use the law of sines to find B.
 $$\frac{\sin B}{b} = \frac{\sin A}{a}$$
 $$\sin B = \frac{b \sin A}{a}$$
 $$\sin B = \frac{4.82 \sin 25.2°}{6.92}$$
 $$B = 17.3°$$
 (Angle B cannot be obtuse, since $b < a$, $B < A$, and A is acute.)
 $$C = 180° - A - B = 137.5°$$

 Use the law of sines to find c.
 $$\frac{c}{\sin C} = \frac{a}{\sin A}$$
 $$c = \frac{a \sin C}{\sin A}$$
 $$= \frac{6.92 \sin 137.5°}{\sin 25.2°}$$
 $$= 11.0 \text{ yd}$$

19. Solve the triangle, given $a = 27.6$ cm, $b = 19.8$ cm, $C = 42° \, 30'$.

Using the law of cosines, we have

$$c^2 = a^2 + b^2 - 2ab \cos C$$
$$c^2 = 27.6^2 + 19.8^2 - 2(27.6)(19.8)\cos 42° \, 30'$$
$$c = 18.7 \text{ cm}.$$

Note: Keep all values of $\sqrt{c^2}$ in your calculator for use in the next calculation. If 18.7 is used, the answer will vary slightly due to round-off error. Now use the law of sines to find B so there is no ambiguity.

$$\frac{c}{\sin C} = \frac{b}{\sin B}$$
$$\frac{18.65436576}{\sin 42° \, 30'} = \frac{19.8}{\sin B}$$
$$\sin B = \frac{19.8 \sin 42° \, 30'}{18.65436576}$$
$$B = 45° \, 50'.$$

Since the sum of the angles of a triangle is $180°$,

$$A = 180° - B - C$$
$$= 180° - 45° \, 50' - 42° \, 30'$$
$$A = 91° \, 40'.$$

21. Given $b = 840.6$ m, $c = 715.9$ m, $A = 149.3°$, find the area.

Angle A is included between sides b and c.

$$\text{area} = \frac{1}{2} bc \sin A$$
$$= \frac{1}{2}(840.6)(715.9)\sin 149.3°$$
$$\text{area} = 153,600 \text{ m}^2$$

23. Given $a = .913$ km, $b = .816$ km, $c = .582$ km, find the area.

$$s = \frac{1}{2}(a + b + c)$$
$$= \frac{1}{2}(.913 + .816 + .582)$$
$$= 1.1555$$
$$\text{area} = \sqrt{(1.1555)(.2425)(.3395)(.5735)}$$
$$\text{area} = .234 \text{ km}^2$$

25. Since $B = 58.4°$ and $C = 27.9°$,

$$A = 180 - (58.4 + 27.9) = 93.7°$$

Using the law of sines:

$$\frac{125}{\sin A} = \frac{AB}{\sin C}$$
$$AB = \frac{(125)\sin C}{\sin A}$$
$$= \frac{(125)(\sin 27.9°)}{\sin(93.7°)}$$
$$= 58.6$$

The canyon is 58.6 feet across.

27. Let AC = the height of the tree.

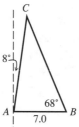

Angle $A = 90° - 8.0° = 82°$
Angle $C = 180° - B - A = 30°$
Use the law of sines to find $AC = b$.

$$\frac{b}{\sin B} = \frac{c}{\sin C}$$
$$b = \frac{c \sin B}{\sin C}$$
$$= \frac{7.0 \sin 68°}{\sin 30°}$$
$$= 13$$

The tree is 13 meters tall.

29. Let h = the height of tree.

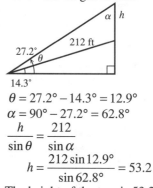

$$\theta = 27.2° - 14.3° = 12.9°$$
$$\alpha = 90° - 27.2° = 62.8°$$
$$\frac{h}{\sin \theta} = \frac{212}{\sin \alpha}$$
$$h = \frac{212 \sin 12.9°}{\sin 62.8°} = 53.2$$

The height of the tree is 53.2 ft.

31. Let x = the distance between the boats.

In 3 hours, the first boat travels $3(36.2) = 108.6$ km and the second travels $3(45.6) = 136.8$ km.

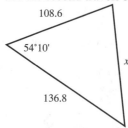

Use the law of cosines to find x.

$$x^2 = (108.6)^2 + (136.8)^2$$
$$- 2(108.6)(136.8)\cos 54° \, 10'$$
$$= 13,113.359$$
$$x = 115 \text{ km}$$

They are 115 km apart.

33. To find the angles of the triangle formed by the ship's positions with the lighthouse, we find the supplementary angle to 55°:

$180° - 55° = 125°$

and the third angle in the triangle:

$180° - (125° + 30°) = 25°$

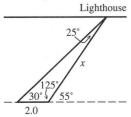

Using the law of sines,

$$\frac{2}{\sin 25°} = \frac{x}{\sin 30°}$$

$$x = \frac{2 \sin 30°}{\sin 25°}$$

$$\approx 2.4 \text{ mi}$$

The ship is 2.4 miles from the lighthouse.

35. Use the distance formula to find the distances between the points.

Distance between $(-8, 6)$ and $(0, 0)$:

$$\sqrt{(-8-0)^2 + (6-0)^2} = 10$$

Distance between $(-8, 6)$ and $(3, 4)$:

$$\sqrt{(-8-3)^2 + (6-4)^2} = \sqrt{125} = 11.2$$

Distance between $(3, 4)$ and $(0, 0)$:

$$\sqrt{(3-0)^2 + (4-0)^2} = 5$$

$$s = \frac{1}{2}(10 + 11.2 + 5)$$

$$s = 13.1$$

Area $= \sqrt{(13.1)(3.1)(1.9)(8.1)} = 25$

The area of the triangle is 25 square units.

37. $\mathbf{a} - \mathbf{b}$

39. **(a)** true

   (b) false

41. Forces of 475 lb and 586 lb, forming an angle of 78° 20′

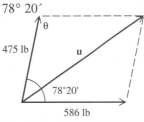

$\theta = 180° - 78° \ 20' = 101° \ 40'$

$|\mathbf{u}|^2 = 475^2 + 586^2 - 2(475)(586)\cos 101° \ 40'$

$|\mathbf{u}| = 826 \text{ lb}$

43. horizontal:

$x = |\mathbf{v}| \cos \theta = 964 \cos 154° \ 20'$

$\approx 964 \cos 154.333° \approx 869$

vertical:

$y = |\mathbf{v}| \sin \theta = 964 \sin 154° \ 20'$

$\approx 964 \sin 154.333° \approx 418$

45. $\mathbf{u} = \langle -9, 12 \rangle$

$$|\mathbf{u}| = \sqrt{(-9)^2 + 12^2}$$

$$= \sqrt{225} = 15$$

$$\cos \theta = \frac{a}{|\mathbf{u}|} = -\frac{9}{15}$$

$$\theta \approx 126.9°$$

47. **(a)** $\mathbf{u} \cdot \mathbf{v} = \langle 2\sqrt{3}, 2 \rangle \cdot \langle 5, 5\sqrt{3} \rangle$

$= 10\sqrt{3} + 10\sqrt{3}$

$= 20\sqrt{3}$

   (b) $|\mathbf{u}| = \sqrt{\left(2\sqrt{3}\right)^2 + 2^2} = \sqrt{16} = 4$

$|\mathbf{v}| = \sqrt{5^2 + \left(5\sqrt{3}\right)^2} = \sqrt{100} = 10$

$\cos \theta = \dfrac{\mathbf{u} \cdot \mathbf{v}}{|\mathbf{u}||\mathbf{v}|}$

$\theta = \arccos\left(\dfrac{20\sqrt{3}}{40}\right)$

$= \cos^{-1}\left(\dfrac{\sqrt{3}}{2}\right)$

$= 30°$

49. $|\mathbf{u}| = \sqrt{5^2 + 12^2} = \sqrt{169} = 13$

$\mathbf{u} = \dfrac{\mathbf{u}}{|\mathbf{u}|} = \dfrac{\langle 5, 12 \rangle}{13} = \left\langle \dfrac{5}{13}, \dfrac{12}{13} \right\rangle$

51. Let $|\mathbf{x}|$ = the resultant force.

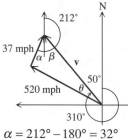

$$\theta = 180° - 15° - 10° = 155°$$
$$|\mathbf{x}|^2 = 12^2 + 18^2 - 2(12)(18)\cos 155°$$
$$|\mathbf{x}| = 29$$

The magnitude of the resultant force on Jessie and the sled is 29 lb.

53. Let $\mathbf{v}$ = the ground speed vector.

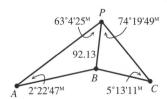

$$\alpha = 212° - 180° = 32°$$
$$\beta = 50°$$

because they are alternate interior angles.
Angle opposite $520 = \alpha + \beta = 82°$
$$\frac{\sin \theta}{37} = \frac{\sin 82°}{520}$$
$$\theta = 4°$$
Bearing $= 360° - 50° - \theta = 306°$
Angle opposite $\mathbf{v} = 180° - 82° - 4° = 94°$
$$\frac{|\mathbf{v}|}{\sin 94°} = \frac{520}{\sin 82°}$$
$$|\mathbf{v}| = 524 \text{ mph}$$

The pilot should fly on a bearing of 306°. Her actual speed is 524 mph.

55.

In each of the triangles ABP and PBC we know two angles and one side. Solve each triangle using the law of sines.

$$AB = \frac{92.13 \sin 63° \ 4' \ 25''}{\sin 2° \ 22' \ 47''}$$
$$\approx 1978.28 \text{ ft}$$
$$BC = \frac{92.13 \sin 74° \ 19' \ 49''}{\sin 5° \ 13' \ 11''}$$
$$\approx 975.05 \text{ ft}$$

57. $P = (-1, \ 2, \ 4), \ Q = (2, \ -2, \ 6)$

(a) $d(PQ) = \sqrt{(2 - (-1))^2 + (-2 - 2)^2 + (6 - 4)^2}$
$$= \sqrt{3^2 + (-4)^2 + 2^2}$$
$$= \sqrt{9 + 16 + 4}$$
$$= \sqrt{29}$$

(b) $\mathbf{PQ} = \langle 2 - (-1), \ -2 - 2, \ 6 - 4 \rangle = \langle 3, \ -4, \ 2 \rangle$

(c) $\mathbf{QP} = (-1 - 2)\mathbf{i} + (2 - (-2))\mathbf{j} + (4 - 6)\mathbf{k}$
$$= -3\mathbf{i} + 4\mathbf{j} - 2\mathbf{k}$$

59. $\mathbf{u} = -\mathbf{i} + 2\mathbf{j} + 4\mathbf{k}, \ \mathbf{v} = 3\mathbf{i} - \mathbf{j} + \mathbf{k}$

(a) $3\mathbf{u} - \mathbf{v} = 3(-\mathbf{i} + 2\mathbf{j} + 4\mathbf{k}) - (3\mathbf{i} - \mathbf{j} + \mathbf{k})$
$$= (-3\mathbf{i} + 6\mathbf{j} + 12\mathbf{k}) - (3\mathbf{i} - \mathbf{j} + \mathbf{k})$$
$$= (-3 - 3)\mathbf{i} + (6 - (-1))\mathbf{j} + (12 - 1)\mathbf{k}$$
$$= -6\mathbf{i} + 7\mathbf{j} + 11\mathbf{k}$$

(b) $\mathbf{u} + 2\mathbf{v} = (-\mathbf{i} + 2\mathbf{j} + 4\mathbf{k}) + 2(3\mathbf{i} - \mathbf{j} + \mathbf{k})$
$$= (-\mathbf{i} + 2\mathbf{j} + 4\mathbf{k}) + (6\mathbf{i} - 2\mathbf{j} + 2\mathbf{k})$$
$$= (-1 + 6)\mathbf{i} + (2 - 2)\mathbf{j} + (4 + 2)\mathbf{k}$$
$$= 5\mathbf{i} + 0\mathbf{j} + 6\mathbf{k}$$
$$= 5\mathbf{i} + 6\mathbf{k}$$

(c) $|\mathbf{u} + \mathbf{v}| = |(-\mathbf{i} + 2\mathbf{j} + 4\mathbf{k}) + (3\mathbf{i} - \mathbf{j} + \mathbf{k})|$
$$= |(-1 + 3)\mathbf{i} + (2 - 1)\mathbf{j} + (4 + 1)\mathbf{k}|$$
$$= |2\mathbf{i} + \mathbf{j} + 5\mathbf{k}|$$
$$= \sqrt{2^2 + 1^2 + 5^2}$$
$$= \sqrt{4 + 1 + 25}$$
$$= \sqrt{30}$$

(d) $\mathbf{u} \cdot \mathbf{v} = (-\mathbf{i} + 2\mathbf{j} + 4\mathbf{k}) \cdot (3\mathbf{i} - \mathbf{j} + \mathbf{k})$
$$= -1(3) + 2(-1) + 4(1)$$
$$= -3 - 2 + 4$$
$$= -1$$

(e) The angle between $(-\mathbf{i} + 2\mathbf{j} + 4\mathbf{k})$ and $(3\mathbf{i} - \mathbf{j} + \mathbf{k})$ is θ where
$$\cos \theta = \frac{(-\mathbf{i} + 2\mathbf{j} + 4\mathbf{k}) \cdot (3\mathbf{i} - \mathbf{j} + \mathbf{k})}{|-\mathbf{i} + 2\mathbf{j} + 4\mathbf{k}| \cdot |3\mathbf{i} - \mathbf{j} + \mathbf{k}|}$$
$$= \frac{-1}{\sqrt{(-1)^2 + 2^2 + 4^2}\sqrt{3^2 + (-1)^2 + 1^2}}$$
$$= \frac{-1}{\sqrt{1 + 4 + 16}\sqrt{9 + 1 + 1}}$$
$$= \frac{-1}{\sqrt{21}\sqrt{11}}$$
$$= \frac{-1}{\sqrt{231}}$$

Thus, $\theta = \cos^{-1}\left(\frac{-1}{\sqrt{231}}\right) \approx 93.8°$.

61. The sum of the squares of the three directional angle cosines is 1.

63. $\mathbf{F} = \langle 2, 1, 1 \rangle$
Let $P = (2, -1, -1)$ and $Q = (1, 1, 2)$.
$\mathbf{PQ} = \langle 1-2, 1-(-1), 2-(-1) \rangle = \langle -1, 2, 3 \rangle$
The work done by $\mathbf{F}$ in moving a particle from P to Q is
$\mathbf{F} \cdot \mathbf{PQ} = \langle 2, 1, 1 \rangle \cdot \langle -1, 2, 3 \rangle$
$= 2(-1) + 1(2) + 1(3)$
$= -2 + 2 + 3$
$= 3$ work units

65. $[3 \operatorname{cis} 135°][2 \operatorname{cis} 105°]$
$= 3 \cdot 2 \operatorname{cis}(135° + 105°)$
$= 6 \operatorname{cis} 240°$
$= 6(\cos 240° + i \sin 240°)$
$= 6\left(-\dfrac{1}{2} - \dfrac{\sqrt{3}}{2} i \right)$
$= -3 - 3\sqrt{3} i$

67. $\dfrac{4 \operatorname{cis} 270°}{2 \operatorname{cis} 90°}$
$= \dfrac{4}{2} \operatorname{cis}(270° - 90°)$
$= 2 \operatorname{cis} 180°$
$= 2(\cos 180° + i \sin 180°)$
$= 2(-1 + 0i)$
$= -2 + 0i$ or -2

69. $(\cos 100° + i \sin 100°)^6$
$= \cos 600° + i \sin 600°$
$= -\dfrac{1}{2} - \dfrac{\sqrt{3}}{2} i$

71.

73. $-2 + 2i$
$r = \sqrt{(-2)^2 + 2^2}$
$= \sqrt{8} = 2\sqrt{2}$
$\tan \theta = \dfrac{2}{-2} = -1$
θ is in quadrant II so $\theta = 135°$.
$-2 + 2r$
$= 2\sqrt{2}(\cos 135° + i \sin 135°)$

75. $2(\cos 225° + i \sin 225°)$
$= 2\left(-\dfrac{\sqrt{2}}{2} - \dfrac{i\sqrt{2}}{2} \right)$
$= -\sqrt{2} - i\sqrt{2}$

77. $1 - i$
$r = \sqrt{1^2 + (-1)^2} = \sqrt{2}$
$\tan \theta = \dfrac{-1}{1} = -1$
θ is in quadrant IV so $\theta = 315°$.
$1 - i = \sqrt{2}(\cos 315° + i \sin 315°)$

79. $-4i$
$r = 4$
$\theta = 270°$
$-4i = 4(\cos 270° + i \sin 270°)$

81. $z = x + yi$
Since the imaginary part of z is the negative of the real part of z, we are saying $y = -x$. This is a straight line.

83. Convert $1 - i$ to polar form
$r = \sqrt{1^2 + (-1)^2} = \sqrt{1+1} = \sqrt{2}$
$\theta = \arctan\left(\dfrac{-1}{1}\right) = \arctan(-1) = 315°$
(since $x > 0$ and $y < 0$)
then $1 - i = \sqrt{2}(\cos 315° + i \sin 315°)$ and the cube roots of $\sqrt{2}(\cos 315° + i \sin 315°)$ are:
$\sqrt[6]{2}(\cos \alpha + i \sin \alpha)$ where
$\alpha = \dfrac{\theta + 360° \cdot k}{n}$ for $k = 0, 1, 2$
$k = 0$: $\alpha = \dfrac{315 + (360)(0)}{3} = \dfrac{315}{3} = 105°$
$k = 1$: $\alpha = \dfrac{315 + (360)(1)}{3} = \dfrac{675}{3} = 225°$
$k = 2$: $\alpha = \dfrac{315 + (360)(2)}{3} = \dfrac{1035}{3} = 345°$

So the cube roots of $1 - i$ are:

$\sqrt[6]{2}(\cos 105° + i \sin 105°)$

$\sqrt[6]{2}(\cos 225° + i \sin 225°)$

$\sqrt[6]{2}(\cos 345° + i \sin 345°)$

85. The number –64 has no real sixth roots because a real number raised to the sixth power will never be negative.

87. $x^4 + 16 = 0$

$$x^4 = -16$$
$$= 16(\cos 180° + i \sin 180°)$$

$r = 16, \quad r^{1/4} = 2$

$\alpha = \dfrac{180° + 360° \cdot k}{4}; \quad k = 0,\ 1,\ 2,\ 3$

$\alpha = 45°,\ 135°,\ 225°,\ 315°$

$x = 2(\cos 45° + i \sin 45°),$

$\quad 2(\cos 135° + i \sin 135°),$

$\quad 2(\cos 225° + i \sin 225°),$

$\quad 2(\cos 315° + i \sin 315°)$

89.

$x = r \cos \theta \qquad y = r \sin \theta$

$\quad = 5 \cos 315° \qquad = 5 \sin 315°$

$\quad = \dfrac{5\sqrt{2}}{2} \qquad\quad = 5 - \dfrac{\sqrt{2}}{2}$

$\qquad\qquad\qquad\quad = -\dfrac{5\sqrt{2}}{2}$

the rectangular coordinates are:

$\left(\dfrac{5\sqrt{2}}{2},\ -\dfrac{5\sqrt{2}}{2} \right)$

91. $r = 4 \cos \theta$ is a circle.

θ	0°	30°	45°	60°	90°
r	4	3.5	2.8	2	0

θ	120°	135°	150°	180°
r	–2	–2.8	–3.5	–4

Graph is retraced in the interval $(180°, 360°)$

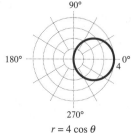

$r = 4 \cos \theta$

93. $r = 2 \sin 4\theta$ is an eight-leaved rose.

θ	0°	7.5°	15°	22.5°	0°	37.5°	45°
r	0	1	$\sqrt{3}$	2	$\sqrt{3}$	1	0

θ	52.5°	60°	67.5°	75°	82.5°	90°
r	–1	$-\sqrt{3}$	–2	$-\sqrt{3}$	–1	0

The graph continues to form eight petals for the interval $[0°, 360°)$.

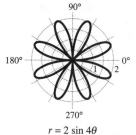

$r = 2 \sin 4\theta$

95.

$r = \sin \theta + \cos \theta$

$r^2 = r \sin \theta + r \cos \theta$

$x^2 + y^2 = x + y$

$x^2 + y^2 - x - y = 0$

or

$(x^2 - x) + (y^2 - y) = 0$

$\left(x^2 - x + \dfrac{1}{4} \right) + \left(y^2 - y + \dfrac{1}{4} \right) = \dfrac{1}{4} + \dfrac{1}{4}$

$\left(x - \dfrac{1}{2} \right)^2 + \left(y - \dfrac{1}{2} \right)^2 = \dfrac{1}{2}$

97.

$y = x$

$r \sin \theta = r \cos \theta$

$\sin \theta = \cos \theta$

or $\tan \theta = 1$

99. This is the line $y = 2$. Since $y = r \sin \theta$,

$r \sin \theta = 2$

$r = 2 \cdot \dfrac{1}{\sin \theta}$

$r = 2 \csc \theta.$

101. This is a circle centered at the origin with radius 2. Its equation is $x^2 + y^2 = 4$.

Since $r = \sqrt{x^2 + y^2}$,

$r^2 = x^2 + y^2$

$r^2 = 4$

$r = 2.$

103. $x = 3t + 2$, $y = t - 1$, for t in $[-5, 5]$
Solve for t in terms of y.
$$y + 1 = t$$
Substitute $y + 1$ for t in the equation for x.
$$x = 3(y + 1) + 2$$
$$x = 3y + 3 + 2$$
$$x = 3y + 5$$
$$x - 3y = 5$$
Since t is in $[-5, 5]$, x is in $[3(-5) + 2, 3(5) + 2]$ or $[-13, 17]$.

105. $x = t^2 + 5$, $y = \dfrac{1}{t^2 + 1}$, for t in $(-\infty, \infty)$
Then $x - 5 = t^2$. Substitute $x - 5$ for t^2 in the equation for y.
$$y = \frac{1}{t^2 + 1}$$
$$y = \frac{1}{x - 5 + 1}$$
$$y = \frac{1}{x - 4}$$
Since $x = t^2 + 5$ and $t^2 \geq 0$, $x \geq 0 + 5 = 5$.
Therefore, x is in $[5, \infty)$.

107. $x = \cos 2t$, $y = \sin t$ for t in $(-\pi, \pi)$
$$\cos 2t = \cos^2 t - \sin^2 t \quad \text{(double angle formula)}$$
Pythagorean Theorem:
$$\cos^2 t + \sin^2 t = 1$$
$$\cos^2 t - \sin^2 t + 2\sin^2 t = 1$$
$$x + 2y^2 = 1$$
$$2y^2 = 1 - x$$
$$y^2 = \frac{1}{2}(1 - x)$$
or $2y^2 + x - 1 = 0$
Since t is in $(-\pi, \pi)$, and $\cos 2t$ is in $[-1, 1]$, x is in $[-1, 1]$.

Chapter 7 Test Exercises

1. Using the law of sines:
$$\frac{\sin 25.2°}{6.92} = \frac{\sin B}{4.82}$$
$$\sin B = \frac{(\sin 25.2°)(4.82)}{6.92}$$
$$B = \sin^{-1}\left(\frac{(\sin 25.2°)(4.82)}{6.92}\right)$$
$$\approx 17.3°$$
Using the fact that the angles of a triangle sum to $180°$:
$$C = 180 - (A + B)$$
$$= 180 - (25.2 + 17.3)$$
$$= 137.5°$$
The angle C is $137.5°$.

2. Using the law of cosines:
$$c^2 = a^2 + b^2 - 2ab \cos C$$
$$= (75)^2 + (130)^2 - 2(75)(130)\cos 118°$$
$$\approx 31679$$
$$c = \sqrt{31679}$$
$$\approx 180 \text{ km}$$
c is approximately 180 km.

3. Using the law of cosines:
$$b^2 = a^2 + c^2 - 2ac \cos B$$
$$2ac \cos B = a^2 + c^2 - b^2$$
$$\cos B = \frac{a^2 + c^2 - b^2}{2ac}$$
$$B = \cos^{-1}\left(\frac{a^2 + c^2 - b^2}{2ac}\right)$$
$$= \cos^{-1}\left(\frac{(17.3)^2 + (29.8)^2 - (22.6)^2}{2(17.3)(29.8)}\right)$$
$$\approx 49.0°$$
B is approximately $49.0°$.

4. $A = \dfrac{1}{2}ab\sin c$
$$= \frac{1}{2}(75)(130)\sin 118°$$
$$\approx 4300 \text{ km}^2$$
(*Note*: Since c was found in Exercise 2, Heron's formula can also be used.)
The area of the triangle is approximately 4300 km^2.

5. Since $B > 90°$, b must be the longest side of the triangle.

  (a) $b > 10$

  (b) none

  (c) $b \leq 10$

6. The semi-perimeter s is:
$$s = \frac{1}{2}(a + b + c)$$
$$= \frac{1}{2}(22 + 26 + 40)$$
$$= 44$$
Using Heron's formula
$$A = \sqrt{s(s - a)(s - b)(s - c)}$$
$$= \sqrt{44(44 - 22)(44 - 26)(44 - 40)}$$
$$= \sqrt{69696}$$
$$= 264 \text{ square units}$$
The area of the triangle is 264 square units.

7. $|\mathbf{v}| = \sqrt{(-6)^2 + 8^2} = \sqrt{100} = 10$

$$\tan\theta = \frac{y}{x}$$

$$\theta = \tan^{-1}\left(\frac{y}{x}\right)$$

$$= \tan^{-1}\left(\frac{8}{-6}\right)$$

$$\approx 126.9°$$

The magnitude $|\mathbf{v}|$ is 10 and $\theta = 126.9°$.

8. (a) $\mathbf{u} + \mathbf{v} = \langle -1, 3 \rangle + \langle 2, -6 \rangle$

$$= \langle (-1+2), (3+(-6)) \rangle$$

$$= \langle 1, -3 \rangle$$

(b) $-3\mathbf{v} = -3\langle 2, -6 \rangle$

$$= \langle -6, 18 \rangle$$

(c) $\mathbf{u} \cdot \mathbf{v} = \langle -1, 3 \rangle \cdot \langle 2, -6 \rangle$

$$= -2 - 18$$

$$= -20$$

9. Find angle C:

$$C = 180 - (47° \ 20' + 24° \ 50')$$

$$= 180 - (72° \ 10')$$

$$= 107° \ 50'$$

Use this information and the law of sines to find AC:

$$\frac{8.4}{\sin 107° \ 50'} = \frac{AC}{\sin 47° \ 20'}$$

$$AC = \frac{8.4 \sin 47.333°}{\sin 107.833°}$$

$$\approx 6.5 \text{ mi}$$

Drop a perpendicular line from C to segment AB:

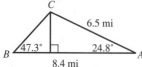

then $\sin 24.833° = \dfrac{h}{6.5}$

$h = (6.5)(\sin 24.833°)$

$$\approx 2.7 \text{ mi}$$

The balloon is 2.7 miles off the ground.

10. horizontal: $x = |\mathbf{v}|\cos\theta = 569\cos 127.5° \approx -346$

vertical: $y = |\mathbf{v}|\sin\theta = 569\sin 127.5° \approx 451$

The vector is $\langle -346, 451 \rangle$.

11.

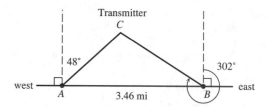

Consider the figure.

Since the bearing is 48° from A, the angle A in $\triangle ABC$ must be $90° - 48° = 42°$. Since the bearing is 302° from B, the angle B in $\triangle ABC$ must be $302° - 270° = 32°$. The angles of a triangle sum to 180°, so

$$C = 180° - (A + B)$$

$$= 180° - (42° + 32°)$$

$$= 106°$$

Using the law of sines:

$$\frac{b}{\sin B} = \frac{c}{\sin C}$$

$$\frac{b}{\sin 32°} = \frac{3.46}{\sin 106°}$$

$$b = \frac{(3.46)(\sin 32°)}{\sin 106°}$$

$$= 1.91 \text{ mi}$$

The distance from A to the transmitter is 1.91 miles.

12. $P = (3, 4, 6), \ Q = (10, 8, 9)$

$\mathbf{PQ} = (10-3)\mathbf{i} + (8-4)\mathbf{j} + (9-6)\mathbf{k} = 7\mathbf{i} + 4\mathbf{j} + 3\mathbf{k}$

13. $\mathbf{u} = 3\mathbf{i} + 4\mathbf{j} + 6\mathbf{k}$

Let $\mathbf{B}$ be the direction angle between the y-axis a $\mathbf{u}$.

$$\cos\beta = \frac{4}{|\mathbf{u}|}$$

$$= \frac{4}{\sqrt{3^2 + 4^2 + 6^2}}$$

$$= \frac{4}{\sqrt{9 + 16 + 36}}$$

$$= \frac{4}{\sqrt{61}}$$

Thus $\beta = \cos^{-1}\left(\dfrac{4}{\sqrt{61}}\right) \approx 59.2°$

14. (a) $r = \sqrt{0^2 + 3^2} = \sqrt{9} = 3$

The point $(0, 3)$ is on the positive y-axis. Thus, $\theta = 90°$.

$3i = 3(\cos 90° + i\sin 90°)$

(b) $r = \sqrt{1^2 + 2^2} = \sqrt{5}$

$\theta = \arctan\left(\dfrac{2}{1}\right) = \arctan(2) \approx 63.43°$

(since $x > 0$ and $y > 0$)

$1 + 2i = \sqrt{5}(\cos 63.43° + i \sin 63.43°)$

(c) $r = \sqrt{(-1)^2 + (-\sqrt{3})^2} = \sqrt{1+3} = \sqrt{4} = 2$

$\theta = \arctan\left(\dfrac{-\sqrt{3}}{-1}\right) = \arctan(\sqrt{3}) = 240°$

(since $(x < 0$ and $y < 0)$

$-1 - \sqrt{3}i = 2(\cos 240° + i \sin 240°)$

15. (a) $a = r\cos\theta \qquad b = r\sin\theta$

$\quad = 3\cos 30° \qquad = 3\sin 30°$

$\quad = 3\left(\dfrac{\sqrt{3}}{2}\right) \qquad = 3\left(\dfrac{1}{2}\right)$

$\quad = \dfrac{3\sqrt{3}}{2} \qquad\quad = \dfrac{3}{2}$

$3(\cos 30° + i \sin 30°) = \dfrac{3\sqrt{3}}{2} + \dfrac{3}{2}i$

(b) $a = r\cos\theta \qquad\qquad b = r\sin\theta$

$\quad = 4\cos 40° \qquad\qquad = 4\sin 40°$

$\quad \approx 3.06 \qquad\qquad\quad \approx 2.57$

$4 \text{ cis } 4° = 3.06 + 2.57i$

(c) $a = r\cos\theta \qquad\qquad b = r\sin\theta$

$\quad = 3\cos 90° \qquad\qquad = 3\sin 90°$

$\quad = 0 \qquad\qquad\qquad\quad = 3$

$3(\cos 90° + i \sin 90°) = 3i$

16. (a) $wz = 8 \cdot 2[\cos(40° + 10°) + i\sin(40° + 10°)]$

$\qquad\quad = 16(\cos 50° + i \sin 50°)$

(b) $\dfrac{w}{z} = \dfrac{8}{2}[\cos(40° - 10°) + i\sin(40° - 10°)]$

$\qquad\quad = 4(\cos 30° + i \sin 30°)$

$a = r\cos\theta \qquad\qquad b = r\sin\theta$

$\quad = 4\cos 30° \qquad\qquad = 4\sin 30°$

$\quad = 4 \cdot \dfrac{\sqrt{3}}{2} \qquad\qquad = 4 \cdot \dfrac{1}{2}$

$\quad = 2\sqrt{3} \qquad\qquad\quad = 2$

$a + bi = 2\sqrt{3} + 2i$

(c) $z^3 = [2(\cos 10° + i \sin 10°)]^3$

$\qquad = 2^3(\cos 3\cdot 10° + i \sin 3\cdot 10°)$

$\qquad = 8(\cos 30° + i \sin 30°)$

$a = 8\cos 30° \qquad\qquad b = 8\sin 30°$

$\quad = 8 \cdot \dfrac{\sqrt{3}}{2} \qquad\qquad = 8 \cdot \dfrac{1}{2}$

$\quad = 4\sqrt{3} \qquad\qquad\quad = 4$

$a + bi = 4\sqrt{3} + 4i$

17. Put $-16i$ into polar form

$r = \sqrt{0^2 + (-16)^2} = \sqrt{256} = 16$

$\theta = \arctan\left(\dfrac{-16}{0}\right) = 270°$

(since $\tan (\theta)$ is undefined and $y < 0$)

then $-16i = 16(\cos 270° + i \sin 270°)$.

The fourth roots of $-16i$ have the form

$\sqrt[n]{r}(\cos\alpha + i \sin\alpha)$ where

$\alpha = \dfrac{\theta + 360°k}{n}, \quad k = 0,\ 1,\ 2,\ 3$

$k = 0: \ \alpha = \dfrac{270° + 360(0)}{4} = 67.5$

$k = 1: \ \alpha = \dfrac{270 \pm 360(1)}{4} = 157.5$

$k = 2: \ \alpha = \dfrac{270 + 360(2)}{4} = 247.5$

$k = 3: \ \alpha = \dfrac{270 + 360(3)}{4} = 337.5$

The fourth roots of $-16i$ are:

$2(\cos 67.5° + \sin 67.5)$

$2(\cos 157.5° + i \sin 157.5°)$

$2(\cos 247.5° + i \sin 247.5°)$

$2(\cos 337.5° + i \sin 337.5°)$

For Exercise 18, answers may vary.

18. (a) $r = \sqrt{0^2 + 5^2} = \sqrt{25} = 5$

The point $(0, 5)$ is on the positive y-axis.
Thus, $\theta = 90°$.
One possibility is $(5, 90°)$.
Alternatively, if $\theta = 90° - 360° = -270°$,
a second possibility is $(5, -270°)$.
Two pairs: $(5, 90°)$, $(5, -270°)$.

(b) $r = \sqrt{(-2)^2 + (-2)^2} = \sqrt{4+4} = \sqrt{8} = 2\sqrt{2}$

$\theta = \arctan\left(\dfrac{-2}{-2}\right) = \arctan(1) = 225°$

(since $x < 0$ and $y < 0$)
One possibility is $(2\sqrt{2},\ 225°)$.
Alternatively, if $\theta = 225° - 360° = -135°$,
a second possibility is $(2\sqrt{2},\ -135°)$.
Two pairs: $(2\sqrt{2},\ 225°)$, $(2\sqrt{2},\ -135°)$

19. (a)
$$x = r\cos\theta \qquad y = r\sin\theta$$
$$= 3\cos 315° \qquad = 3\sin 315°$$
$$= 3 \cdot \frac{\sqrt{2}}{2} \qquad = 3\left(-\frac{\sqrt{2}}{2}\right)$$
$$= \frac{3\sqrt{2}}{2} \qquad = -\frac{3\sqrt{2}}{2}$$

The rectangular coordinates are:
$$\left(\frac{3\sqrt{2}}{2},\ -\frac{3\sqrt{2}}{2}\right).$$

(b)
$$x = r\cos\theta \qquad y = r\sin\theta$$
$$= -4\cos 90° \qquad = -4\sin 90°$$
$$= 0 \qquad = -4$$
The rectangular coordinates are: $(0, -4)$.

20. $r = 1 - \cos\theta$ is a cardioid.

θ	0°	30°	45°	60°	90°	135°
r	0	.1	.3	.5	1	1.7

θ	180°	225°	270°	315°	360°
r	2	1.7	1	.3	0

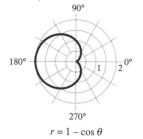
$r = 1 - \cos\theta$

21. $r = 3\cos 3\theta$ is a three-leaved rose.

θ	0°	30°	45°	60°	90°	120°
r	3	0	-2.1	-3	0	3

θ	135°	150°	180°
r	2.1	0	-3

Graph is retraced in the interval $(180°, 360°)$.

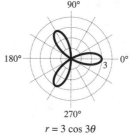
$r = 3\cos 3\theta$

22. This is the line where $a = -1$, $b = 2$, and $c = 4$
The rectangular form is:
$$-x + 2y = 4, \text{ so}$$
$$x - 2y = -4$$

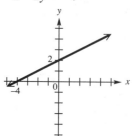

23. $x = 4t - 3$, $y = t^2$ for t in $[-3, 4]$

t	x	y
-3	-15	9
-1	-7	1
0	-3	0
1	1	1
2	5	4
4	13	16

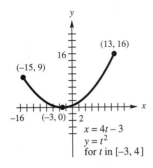

$x = 4t - 3$
$y = t^2$
for t in $[-3, 4]$

24. $x = \cos 2t$, $y = \sin 2t$ for t in $[0, 2\pi]$

t	x	y
0	1	0
$\frac{\pi}{8}$	$\frac{\sqrt{2}}{2}$	$\frac{\sqrt{2}}{2}$
$\frac{\pi}{4}$	0	1
$\frac{3\pi}{8}$	$-\frac{\sqrt{2}}{2}$	$\frac{\sqrt{2}}{2}$
$\frac{\pi}{2}$	-1	0
$\frac{5\pi}{8}$	$-\frac{\sqrt{2}}{2}$	$-\frac{\sqrt{2}}{2}$
$\frac{3\pi}{4}$	0	-1
π	1	0
$\frac{5\pi}{4}$	0	1
$\frac{3\pi}{2}$	-1	0
$\frac{7\pi}{4}$	0	-1
2π	1	0

$x = 2 \cos 2t$
$y = 2 \sin 2t$
for t in $[0, 2\pi]$

CHAPTER 8 SYSTEMS OF EQUATIONS AND INEQUALITIES

Section 8.1

Exercises

1. The two graphs meet at the approximate point (2002, 3.3). Therefore, in approximately 2002 both projections produce the same level of migration.

3. The point where the graphs meet, (2002, 3.3 million), is the solution of the system.

5. t would represent time in years and y would represent number of migrants.

7. $x - 5y = 8$ (1)
   $x = 6y$ (2)
   Substitute $6y$ for x in equation (1).
   $6y - 5y = 8$
   $\quad\quad y = 8$
   To find x, substitute 8 for y in equation (2).
   $x = 6(8) = 48$
   Solution set: $\{(48, 8)\}$

9. $6x - y = 5$ (1)
   $y = 11x$ (2)
   Substitute $11x$ for y in equation (1).
   $6x - 11x = 5$
   $\quad -5x = 5$
   $\quad\quad x = -1$
   To find x, substitute -1 for x in equation (2).
   $y = 11(-1) = -11$
   Solution set: $\{(-1, -11)\}$

11. $7x - y = -10$ (1)
    $3y - x = 10$ (2)
    Solve equation (1) for y.
    $y = 7x + 10$ (3)
    Substitute $7x + 10$ for y in equation (2) and solve for x.
    $3(7x + 10) - x = 10$
    $\quad 21x + 30 - x = 10$
    $\quad\quad\quad 20x = -20$
    $\quad\quad\quad\quad x = -1$
    To find y, substitute -1 for x in equation (3).
    $y = 7(-1) + 10 = 3$
    Solution set: $\{(-1, 3)\}$

13. $-2x = 6y + 18$ (1)
    $-29 = 5y - 3x$ (2)
    Solve equation (1) for x by dividing both sides by -2.
    $x = -3y - 9$
    Substitute this expression for x in equation (2).

$-29 = 5y - 3(-3y - 9)$
$-29 = 5y + 9y + 27$
$-56 = 14y$
$\quad y = -4$
If $y = -4$, $x = -3(-4) - 9 = 3$.
Solution set: $\{(3, -4)\}$

15. $3y = 5x + 6$ (1)
    $x + y = 2$ (2)
    Solve equation (2) for y by subtracting x from both sides.
    $y = 2 - x$
    Substitute this expression for y in equation (1).
    $3(2 - x) = 5x + 6$
    $\quad 6 - 3x = 5x + 6$
    $\quad\quad -3x = 5x$
    $\quad\quad\quad 0 = 8x$
    $\quad\quad\quad 0 = x$
    If $x = 0$, $y = 2 - 0 = 2$.
    Solution set: $\{(0, 2)\}$

17. $3x - y = -4$ (1)
    $x + 3y = 12$ (2)
    Multiply equation (2) by -3 and add the result to equation (1).
    $\quad 3x - y = -4$
    $\underline{-3x - 9y = -36}$
    $\quad -10y = -40$
    $\quad\quad y = 4$
    $x + 3(4) = 12$ Let $y = 4$ in (2)
    $\quad x = 0$
    Solution set: $\{(0, 4)\}$

19. $4x + 3y = -1$ (1)
    $2x + 5y = 3$ (2)
    Multiply equation (2) by -2 and add to equation (1).
    $\quad 4x + 3y = -1$
    $\underline{-4x - 10y = -6}$
    $\quad -7y = -7$
    $\quad\quad y = 1$
    $2x + 5(1) = 3$ Let $y = 1$ in (2)
    $\quad x = -1$
    Solution set: $\{(-1, 1)\}$

21. $12x - 5y = 9$ (1)
    $3x - 8y = -18$ (2)
    $\quad 12x - 5y = 9$
    $\underline{-12x + 32y = 72}$
    $\quad 27y = 81$ (3) Add (1) to -4 times (2)
    $\quad y = 3$ Solve (3) for y
    $3x - 8(3) = -18$ Let $y = 3$ in (2)
    $\quad 3x = 6$
    $\quad\quad x = 2$
    Solution set: $\{(2, 3)\}$

23. $\dfrac{x}{2} + \dfrac{y}{3} = 4$ (1)

$\dfrac{3x}{2} + \dfrac{3y}{2} = 15$ (2)

To clear denominators, multiply equation (1) by
-6 and equation (2) by 2. Add the resulting
equations.

$-3x - 2y = -24$

$\underline{\quad 3x + 3y = 30 \quad}$

$\qquad\qquad y = 6$

Substitute 6 for y in equation (1).

$\dfrac{x}{2} + \dfrac{6}{3} = 4$

$\dfrac{x}{2} + 2 = 4$

$\dfrac{x}{2} = 2$

$\qquad x = 4$

Solution set: $\{(4, 6)\}$

25. $\dfrac{2x-1}{3} + \dfrac{y+2}{4} = 4$ (1)

$\dfrac{x+3}{2} - \dfrac{x-y}{3} = 3$ (2)

Multiply equation (1) by 12 and equation (2) by 6
to clear denominators.

$4(2x - 1) + 3(y + 2) = 48$

$3(x + 3) - 2(x - y) = 18$

Remove parentheses and combine like terms.

$8x + 3y = 46$ (3)

$x + 2y = 9$ (4)

Multiply equation (4) by -8 and then add the
result to equation (3).

$8x + 3y = 46$

$\underline{-8x - 16y = -72}$

$\qquad -13y = -26$

$\qquad\qquad y = 2$

Substitute this value into equation (4).

$x + 2(2) = 9$

$\qquad x = 5$

Solution set: $\{(5, 2)\}$

27. $\sqrt{3}x - y = 5$ (1)

$100x - y = 9$ (2)

We solve each equation for y and use

$Y_1 = \sqrt{3}x - 5$

$Y_2 = -100x + 9$.

Graph these two functions on the same screen.
One suitable choice for the viewing window is
$[-1, 3]$ by $[-10, 5]$. Using the "intersect" option in
the CALC menu, we find that the coordinates of
the intersection point are approximately

$(.138, -4.762)$.
Solution set: $\{(.138, -4.762)\}$

29. $.2x + \sqrt{2}y = 1$ (1)

$\sqrt{5}x + .7y = 1$ (2)

We solve each equation for y and use

$Y_1 = \dfrac{1 - .2x}{\sqrt{2}}$

$Y_2 = \dfrac{1 - \sqrt{5}x}{.7}$.

Graph these two functions on the same screen.
One suitable choice for the viewing window is
$[-2, 2]$ by $[-2, 2]$. Using the "intersect" option in
the CALC menu, we find that the coordinates of
intersection point are approximately $(.236, .674)$.
Solution set: $\{(.236, .674)\}$

31. $9x - 5y = 1$ (1)

$-18x + 10y = 1$ (2)

Multiply equation (1) by 2 and add the result to
equation (2).

$18x - 10y = 2$

$\underline{-18x + 10y = 1}$

$\qquad\qquad 0 = 3$

This is a false statement.
The solution set is $\emptyset$, and the system is
inconsistent.

33. $4x - y = 9$ (1)

$-8x + 2y = -18$ (2)

Multiply equation (1) by 2 and add the result to
equation (2).

$8x - 2y = 18$

$\underline{-8x + 2y = -18}$

$\qquad\qquad 0 = 0$

This is a true statement. The equations are
dependent. We will express the solution set with y
as the arbitrary variable. Solve equation (1) for x.

$4x - y = 9$

$x = \dfrac{y+9}{4}$

Solution set: $\left\{ \left(\dfrac{y+9}{4},\ y \right) \right\}$

35. $x - 2y = 3$

$-2x + 4y = k$

Multiply the first equation by -2.

$-2x + 4y = -6$

$-2x + 4y = k$

The system will have no solution when $k \ne -6$.
The system will have infinitely many solutions
when $k = -6$.

37.
$$x + y + z = 2 \quad (1)$$
$$2x + y - z = 5 \quad (2)$$
$$x - y + z = -2 \quad (3)$$
Eliminate z first.
Add equations (1) and (2) to get
$3x + 2y = 7.$ (4)
Add equations (2) and (3) to get
$3x = 3$
$x = 1.$
$3(1) + 2y = 7$ Let $x = 1$ in (4)
$\quad\quad 2y = 4$
$\quad\quad\quad y = 2$
$1 + 2 + z = 2$ Let $x = 1$, $y = 2$ in (1)
$\quad\quad\quad z = -1$
Check by substituting $x = 1$, $y = 2$, and $z = -1$ in the three original equations.
Solution set: $\{(1, 2, -1)\}$

39.
$$x + 3y + 4z = 14 \quad (1)$$
$$2x - 3y + 2z = 10 \quad (2)$$
$$3x - y + z = 9 \quad (3)$$
Eliminate y first. Add equations (1) and (2) to get
$3x + 6z = 24.$ (4)
Multiply equation (3) by 3 and add the result to equation (1).
$$x + 3y + 4z = 14$$
$$\underline{9x - 3y + 3z = 27}$$
$$10x + \quad 7z = 41$$
This gives the new system
$3x + 6z = 24$ (4)
$10x + 7z = 41$ (5)
Multiply equation (4) by 10 and equation (5) by -3 and add.
$$30x + 60z = 240$$
$$\underline{-30x - 21z = -123}$$
$$\quad\quad 39z = 117$$
$$\quad\quad\quad z = 3$$
$3x + 6(3) = 24$ Let $z = 3$ in (4)
$\quad\quad 3x = 6$
$\quad\quad\quad x = 2$
$2 + 3y + 4(3) = 14$ Let $x = 2$, $z = 3$ in (1)
$\quad\quad\quad 3y = 0$
$\quad\quad\quad\quad y = 0$
Solution set: $\{(2, 0, 3)\}$

41.
$$x + 4y - z = 6 \quad (1)$$
$$2x - y + z = 3 \quad (2)$$
$$3x + 2y + 3z = 16 \quad (3)$$
Eliminate z first. Add equations (1) and (2) to get
$3x + 3y = 9$ or   (4)
$x + y = 3.$
Multiply equation (1) by 3 and add the result to equation (3).

$$3x + 12y - 3z = 18$$
$$\underline{3x + 2y + 3z = 16}$$
$$6x + 14y \quad\quad = 34 \quad (5)$$
Multiply equation (4) by -6 and add to (5).
$$-6x - 6y = -18$$
$$\underline{6x + 14y = 34}$$
$$\quad\quad 8y = 16$$
$$\quad\quad\quad y = 2$$
$x + 2 = 3$ Let $y = 2$ in (4)
$\quad x = 1$
$1 + 4(2) - z = 6$ Let $x = 1$, $y = 2$ in (1)
$\quad\quad z = 3$
Solution set: $\{(1, 2, 3)\}$

43.
$$x - 3y - 2z = -3 \quad (1)$$
$$3x + 2y - z = 12 \quad (2)$$
$$-x - y + 4z = 3 \quad (3)$$
Eliminate x first. Add equations (1) and (3).
$-4y + 2z = 0$ (4)
Multiply equation (3) by 3 and add to equation (2).
$$-3x - 3y + 12z = 9$$
$$\underline{3x + 2y - \quad z = 12} \quad (2)$$
$$\quad -y + 11z = 21 \quad (5)$$
This gives the new system
$-4y + 2z = 0$ (4)
$-y + 11z = 21.$ (5)
Multiply equation (5) by -4 and add to equation (4).
$$-4y + 2z = 0$$
$$\underline{4y - 44z = -84}$$
$$\quad -42z = -84$$
$$\quad\quad z = 2$$
$-4y + 2(2) = 0$ Let $z = 2$ in (4)
$\quad\quad -4y = -4$
$\quad\quad\quad y = 1$
$x - 3(1) - 2(2) = -3$ Let $y = 1$, $z = 2$ in (1)
$\quad x - 3 - 4 = -3$
$\quad\quad\quad x = 4$
Solution set: $\{(4, 1, 2)\}$

45.
$$2x + 6y - z = 6 \quad (1)$$
$$4x - 3y + 5z = -5 \quad (2)$$
$$6x + 9y - 2z = 11 \quad (3)$$
Eliminate y first. Add equation (1) to 2 times equation (2).
$$2x + 6y - z = 6 \quad (1)$$
$$\underline{8x - 6y + 10z = -10}$$
$$10x \quad + 9z = -4 \quad (4)$$
Add equation (3) to 3 times equation (2).
$$6x + 9y - 2z = 11$$
$$\underline{12x - 9y + 15z = -15}$$
$$18x \quad + 13z = -4 \quad (5)$$
This gives the new system

$10x + 9z = -4$ (4)
$18x + 13z = -4$ (5)
Multiply equation (4) by 9 and equation (5) by -5 and add the results.

$$90x + 81z = -36$$
$$\underline{-90x - 65z = 20}$$
$$16z = -16$$
$$z = -1$$

$10x + 9(-1) = -4$ Let $z = -1$ in (4)
$$10x = 5$$
$$x = \frac{1}{2}$$

$2\left(\dfrac{1}{2}\right) + 6y - (-1) = 6$ Let $x = \dfrac{1}{2}$,
$$z = -1 \text{ in (1)}$$
$$6y + 2 = 6$$
$$6y = 4$$
$$y = \frac{2}{3}$$

Solution set: $\left\{\left(\dfrac{1}{2}, \dfrac{2}{3}, -1\right)\right\}$

47. $x + y + z = 4$ $\qquad$ (1)

(a) $x + 2y + z = 5$ (2)
$2x - y + 3z = 4$ (3)
Equations (1), (2), and (3) form a system having exactly one solution, namely $(4, 1, -1)$. (There are other equations that would do the same.)

(b) $x + y + z = 5$ (4)
$2x - y + 3z = 4$ (5)
Equations (1), (4), and (5) form a system having no solution, since no ordered triple can satisfy equations (1) and (4) simultaneously. (There are other equations that would do the same.)

(c) $2x + 2y + 2z = 8$ (6)
$2x - y + 3z = 4$ (7)
Equations (1), (6), and (7) form a system having infinitely many solutions, since all the ordered triples that satisfy equation (1) will also satisfy equation (6). (There are other equations that would do the same.)

49. $3x + 5y - z = -2$ (1)
$4x - y + 2z = 1$ (2)
$-6x - 10y + 2x = 0$ (3)
We first eliminate z. Multiply equation (1) by 2 and add the result to equation (2).

$6x + 10y - 2z = -4$ (1)
$\underline{4x - y + 2z = 1}$ (2)
$\overline{10x + 9y \qquad = -3}$ (4)
Multiply equation (2) by -1 and add the result to equation (3).

$-4x + y - 2z = -1$ (2)
$\underline{-6x - 10y + 2z = 0}$ (3)
$\overline{-10x - 9y \qquad = -1}$ (5)
We now have the system
$10x + 9y = -3$ (4)
$-10x - 9y = -1$ (5)
Adding these equations, we obtain
$0 = -4$, which is a false statement.
The solution set is $\emptyset$, and the system is inconsistent.

51. $x - 8y + z = 4$ (1)
$3x - y + 2z = -1$ (2)
The equations are dependent.
There will be infinitely many ordered triples in the solution set.
To describe these ordered triples with z as the arbitrary variable, we proceed as follows.
We first eliminate x. Multiply equation (1) by -3 and add the result to equation (2).

$-3x + 24y - 3z = -12$
$\underline{3x - y + 2z = -1}$
$\overline{23y - z = -13}$
$$23y = z - 13$$
$$y = \frac{1}{23}z - \frac{13}{23}$$

Substitute this expression for y into equation (2) and solve for x in terms of z.

$$3x - \left(\frac{1}{23}z - \frac{13}{23}\right) + 2z = -1$$
$$3x - \frac{1}{23}z + \frac{13}{23} + 2z = -1$$
$$3x = -1 + \frac{1}{23}z - \frac{13}{23} - 2z$$
$$= -\frac{23}{23} + \frac{1}{23}z - \frac{13}{23} - \frac{46}{23}z$$
$$= -\frac{45}{23}z - \frac{36}{23}$$
$$x = -\frac{15}{23}z - \frac{12}{23}$$

Solution set: $\left\{-\dfrac{15}{23}z - \dfrac{12}{23}, \dfrac{1}{23}z - \dfrac{13}{23}, z\right\}$

53. Since $y = ax + b$ and the line passes through $(-2, 1)$ and $(-1, -2)$, we have the following equations.
$1 = a(-2) + b$
$-2 = a(-1) + b$

This becomes the following system:
$-2a + b = 1$ (1)
$-a + b = -2$ (2)
Multiply equation (1) by -1 and add the result to equation (2).

$$2a - b = -1$$
$$\underline{-a + b = -2}$$
$$a \quad = -3$$

Substitute this value into equation (1).
$$-2(-3) + b = 1$$
$$6 + b = 1$$
$$b = -5$$
The equation is $y = -3x - 5$.

55. Since $y = ax^2 + b + c$ and the parabola passes through the points $(2, 3)$, $(-1, 0)$, and $(-2, 2)$, we have the equations
$$3 = a(2)^2 + b(2) + c$$
$$0 = a(-1)^2 + b(-1) + c$$
$$2 = a(-2)^2 + b(-2) + c$$
This becomes the following system.
$4a + 2b + c = 3$ (1)
$a - b + c = 0$ (2)
$4a - 2b + c = 2$ (3)
First, we will eliminate c. Multiply equation (2) by -1 and add the result to equation (1).

$$4a + 2b + c = 3$$
$$\underline{-a + b - c = 0}$$
$$3a + 3b \quad = 3 \ \ (4)$$

Multiply equation (2) by -1 and add the result to equation (3).

$$-a + b - c = 0$$
$$\underline{4a - 2b + c = 2}$$
$$3a - b \quad = 2 \ \ (5)$$

We solve the system
$3a + 3b = 3$ (4)
$3a - b = 2$ (5)
by multiplying equation (4) by -1 and then adding the result to equation (5).

$$-3a - 3b = -3$$
$$\underline{3a - b = 2}$$
$$-4b = -1$$
$$b = \frac{1}{4}$$

Substitute this value into equation (5).
$$3a - \left(\frac{1}{4}\right) = 2$$
$$3a = \frac{9}{4}$$
$$a = \frac{3}{4}$$
Substitute this value into equation (1).

$$4\left(\frac{3}{4}\right) + 2\left(\frac{1}{4}\right) + c = 3$$
$$3 + \frac{1}{2} + c = 3$$
$$c = -\frac{1}{2}$$

The equation of the parabola is
$$y = \frac{3}{4}x^2 + \frac{1}{4}x - \frac{1}{2}.$$

57. Since $y = ax^2 + bx + c$ and the parabola passes through the points $(-2, -3.75)$, $(4, -3.75)$, and $(-1, -1.25)$, we have the equations
$$-3.75 = a(-2)^2 + b(-2) + c$$
$$-3.75 = a(4)^2 + b(4) + c$$
$$-1.25 = a(-1)^2 + b(-1) + c.$$
This becomes the following system.
$4a - 2b + c = -3.75$ (1)
$16a + 4b + c = -3.75$ (2)
$a - b + c = -1.25$ (3)
First, we will eliminate c. Multiply equation (2) by -1 and add the result to equation (1).

$$4a - 2b + c = -3.75$$
$$\underline{-16a - 4b - c = 3.75}$$
$$-12a - 6b \quad = 0 \ \ (4)$$

Multiply equation (2) by -1 and add the result to equation (3).

$$16a - 4b - c = 3.75$$
$$\underline{a - b + c = -1.25}$$
$$-15a - 5b \quad = 2.50 \ \ (5)$$

We now solve the system
$-12a - 6b = 0$ (4)
$-15a - 5b = 2.50$. (5)
Solve equation (4) for b.
$$-6b = 12a$$
$$b = -2a$$
Substitute this expression into equation (5).
$$-15a - 5(-2a) = 2.50$$
$$-5a = 2.50$$
$$a = -.5$$
Since $b = -2a$, $b = -2(-.5) = 1$.
Substitute into equation (1).
$$4(-.5) - 2(1) + c = -3.75$$
$$-4 + c = -3.75$$
$$c = .25$$
The equation of the parabola is
$$y = -.5x^2 + x + .25$$
or $y = -\dfrac{1}{2}x^2 + x + \dfrac{1}{4}.$

59. Since $x^2 + y^2 + ax + by + c = 0$ and the circle passes through the points

(2, 1), (–1, 0), and (3, 3), we have the equations
$$(2)^2 + (1)^2 + a(2) + b(1) + c = 0$$
$$(-1)^2 + (0)^2 + a(-1) + b(0) + c = 0$$
$$(3)^2 + (3)^2 + a(3) + b(3) + c = 0.$$
This becomes the following system.
$$2a + b + c = -5 \quad (1)$$
$$-a + c = -1 \quad (2)$$
$$3a + 3b + c = -18 \quad (3)$$
First, we eliminate b by multiplying equation (1) by –3 and adding the result to equation (3).
$$-6a - 3b - 3c = 15$$
$$\underline{3a + 3b \ + c = -18}$$
$$-3a - \quad 2c = -3 \quad (4)$$
We use this equation with equation (2) to form the system
$$-a + c = -1 \quad (2)$$
$$-3a - 2c = -3 \quad (4)$$
We eliminate c by multiplying equation (2) by 2 and adding the result to equation (4).
$$-2a + 2c = -2$$
$$\underline{-3a - 2c = -3}$$
$$-5a \quad = -5$$
$$a = 1$$
We substitute this value into equation (2).
$$-(1) + c = -1$$
$$c = 0$$
Substitute into equation (1).
$$2(1) + b + (0) = -5$$
$$b = -7$$
The equation of the circle is
$$x^2 + y^2 + x - 7y = 0.$$

61. $p = 16 - \dfrac{5}{4}q$

(a) $p = 16 - \dfrac{5}{4} \cdot 0$
$$= 16$$
The price is \$16.

(b) $p = 16 - \dfrac{5}{4} \cdot 4$
$$= 16 - 5$$
$$= 11$$
The price is \$11.

(c) $p = 16 - \dfrac{5}{4} \cdot 8$
$$= 16 - 10$$
$$= 6$$
The price is \$6.

(d) $6 = 16 - \dfrac{5}{4}q$
$$-10 = -\dfrac{5}{4}q$$
$$-40 = -5q$$
$$8 = q$$
The demand is 8 units.

(e) $11 = 16 - \dfrac{5}{4}q$
$$-5 = -\dfrac{5}{4}q$$
$$-20 = -5q$$
$$4 = q$$
The demand is 4 units.

(f) $16 = 16 - \dfrac{5}{4}q$
$$0 = -\dfrac{5}{4}q$$
$$0 = q$$
The demand is 0 units.

(g)

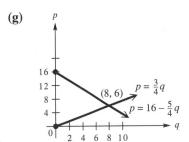

(h) $p = \dfrac{3}{4}q$
$$0 = \dfrac{3}{4}q$$
$$0 = q$$

(i) $10 = \dfrac{3}{4}q$
$$\dfrac{4}{3}(10) = q$$
$$\dfrac{40}{3} = q$$

(j) $20 = \dfrac{3}{4}q$
$$\dfrac{4}{3}(2) = q$$
$$\dfrac{80}{3} = q$$

(k) See part (g).

(l) To find the equilibrium supply, solve the system

$$p = 16 - \frac{5}{4}q \quad (1)$$

$$p = \frac{3}{4}q. \quad (2)$$

The value of q will give the equilibrium supply.

$$\frac{3}{4}q = 16 - \frac{5}{4}q$$

$$4\left(\frac{3}{4}q\right) = 4(16) - 4\left(\frac{5}{4}q\right)$$

$$3q = 64 - 5q$$

$$8q = 64$$

$$q = 8$$

The equilibrium supply is 8.

(m) To find p, substitute $q = 8$ into equation (2).

$$p = \frac{3}{4}(8)$$

$$= 6$$

The equilibrium price is $6.

63. (a) $f(x) = -6.393x + 894.9$
$g(x) = 19.14x + 746.9$
Set the two equations equal to each other and solve for x.
$-6.393x + 894.9 = 19.14x + 746.9$
$-6.393x - 19.14x = 746.9 - 894.9$
$-25.533x = -148$
$x \approx 5.8$
Substitute $x = 5.8$ into either equation and solve.
$f(5.8) = -6.393(5.8) + 894.9 \approx 857.8$
Solution set: $\{(5.8, 857.8)\}$

(b) $1990 + 5.8 = 1995.8$
During 1995, 857.8 million pounds of both canned tuna and fresh shrimp were available.

(c)

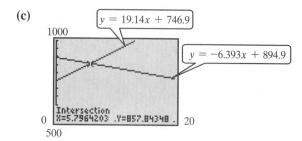

65. Let x = the number of $3.00 gallons;
y = the number of $4.50 gallons;
z = the number of $9.00 gallons.
One equation is $y = 2x$, or
$2x - y = 0$.

$$x + y + z = 300 \quad (1)$$
$$2x - y = 0 \quad (2)$$
$$3.00x + 4.50y + 9.00z = 6.00(300) \quad (3)$$

Eliminate z.

$-9x - 9y - 9z = -2700$ Multiply
                                   (1) by -9
$\underline{3x + 4.50y + 9z = 1800}$ (3)
$-6x - 4.50y = -900$ (4)

Use equations (2) and (4) to solve for y.
$6x - 3y = 0$ Multiply (2) by 3
$\underline{-6x - 4.50y = -900}$ (4)
$-7.50y = -900$

$$y = 120$$

Now solve for x and z.
$2x - 120 = 0$ Let $y = 120$ in (2)
$2x = 120$
$x = 60$
$60 + 120 + z = 300$ Let $x = 60$ and
                                   $y = 120$ in (1)
$z = 120$

She should use 60 gal of the $3.00 water, 120 gal of the $4.50 water, and 120 gal of the $9.00 water.

67. Let x = the length of the shortest side;
y = the length of the medium side;
z = the length of the longest side.
$z = y + 11$
$y = x + 3$
$x + y + z = 59$
Rewrite these equations.
$-y + z = 11$ (1)
$-x + y = 3$ (2)
$x + y + z = 59$ (3)
First eliminate x.
$-x + y = 3$ (2)
$\underline{x + y + z = 59}$ (3)
$2y + z = 62$ (4)
Use equations (1) and (4) to solve for z.
$-2y + 2z = 22$ Multiply (1) by 2
$\underline{2y + z = 62}$ (4)
$3z = 84$
$z = 28$
Now solve for x and y.
$-y + 28 = 11$ Let $z = 28$ in (1)
$-y = -17$
$y = 17$
$-x + 17 = 3$ Let $y = 17$ in (2)
$-x = -14$
$x = 14$
The lengths of the sides of the triangle are 14 inches, 17 inches, and 28 inches.

69. Let x = the amount invested at 5%;
$\quad\quad y$ = the amount invested at 4.5%;
$\quad\quad z$ = the amount invested at 3.75%.
$z = x + y - 20{,}000$ may be rewritten as
$x + y - z = 20{,}000.$

$$x + y - z = 20{,}000 \quad (1)$$
$$x + y + z = 100{,}000 \quad (2)$$
$$.05x + .45y + .0375z = 4450 \quad (3)$$

First eliminate z. Add equations (1) and (2).

$$x + \;\; y - z = 20{,}000 \quad (1)$$
$$\underline{x + \;\; y + z = 100{,}000 \quad (2)}$$
$$2x + 2y \quad\quad = 120{,}000$$

or $x + y = 60{,}000 \quad (4)$

Multiply equation (1) by .0375 and add the result to equation (3).

$$.0375x + .0375y - .0375z = 750$$
$$\underline{.05x + \;\; .045y + .0375z = 4450}$$
$$.0875x + .0825y \quad\quad\quad = 5200 \quad (5)$$

Use equations (4) and (5) to solve for x.
Multiply equation (4) by $-.0825$ and add the result to equation (5).

$$-.0825x - .0825y = -4950$$
$$\underline{.0875x + .0825y = 5200}$$
$$.005x \quad\quad\quad = 250$$
$$x = 50{,}000$$

Now solve for y and z.

$$50{,}000 + y = 60{,}000 \quad \text{Let } x = 50{,}000$$
$$\text{in (4)}$$
$$y = 10{,}000$$
$$50{,}000 + 10{,}000 + z = 100{,}000$$
$$\text{Let } x = 50{,}000$$
$$\text{and } y = 10{,}000$$
$$\text{in (2)}$$
$$z = 40{,}000$$

The amounts invested were $50,000 at 5%,
$10,000 at 4.5%, and $40,00 at 3.75%.

71. (a) Since $C = at^2 + bt + c$ and we have the ordered pairs (0, 315), (20, 335), and (40, 367), we have the equations

$$315 = a(0)^2 + b(0) + c$$
$$335 = a(20)^2 + b(20) + c$$
$$367 = a(40)^2 + b(40) + c.$$

This becomes the following system:

$$c = 315 \quad (1)$$
$$400a + 20b + c = 335 \quad (2)$$
$$1600a + 40b + c = 367 \quad (3)$$

Since $c = 315$, we substitute this value into equations (2) and (3) to obtain

$$400a + 20b + 315 = 335$$
$$1600a + 40b + 315 = 367$$

This leads to the following system:

$$400a + 20b = 20 \quad (4)$$
$$1600a + 40b = 52 \quad (5)$$

We eliminate b by multiplying equation (4) by -2 and adding the result to equation (5).

$$-800a - 40b = -40$$
$$\underline{1600a + 40b = 52}$$
$$800a = 12$$
$$a = \frac{12}{800}$$
$$= \frac{3}{200}$$
$$= .015$$

Substitute this value into equation (5).

$$1600\left(\frac{12}{800}\right) + 40b = 52$$
$$24 + 40b = 52$$
$$40b = 28$$
$$b = \frac{7}{10}$$
$$= .7$$

The constants are $a = \dfrac{3}{200} = .015,$

$b = \dfrac{7}{10} = .7$, and $c = 315.$

The relationship is

$$C = \frac{3}{200}t^2 + \frac{7}{10}t + 315 \text{ or}$$
$$C = .015t^2 + .7t + 315$$

(b) Since $t = 0$ corresponds to 1958, the amount of carbon dioxide will be double its 1958 level when

$$\frac{3}{200}t^2 + \frac{7}{10}t + 315 = 2(315).$$

Solve this equation.

$$\frac{3}{200}t^2 + \frac{7}{10}t - 315 = 0$$
$$3t^2 + 140t - 63{,}000 = 0$$
$$t = \frac{-140 \pm \sqrt{(140)^2 - 4(3)(6300)}}{2(3)}$$

$t \approx -170$ or $t \approx 123$

We reject the first proposed solution because time cannot be negative.
If $t = 123$, the year is $1958 + 123$ or 2081.

73. $\dfrac{5}{x} + \dfrac{15}{y} = 16$

$\dfrac{5}{x} + \dfrac{4}{y} = 5$

Let $t = 1/x$ and $y = 1/y$.
The system becomes

$$5t + 15u = 16$$
$$5t + 4u = \;\; 5.$$

74. $5t + 15u = 16$ (1)

$5t + 4u = 5$ (2)

We eliminate t by multiplying equation (2) by -1 and adding the result to equation (1).

$5t + 15u = 16$

$\underline{-5t - 4u = -5}$

$11u = 11$

$u = 1$

Substitute this value into equation (1).

$5t + 15(1) = 16$

$5t = 1$

$t = \dfrac{1}{5}$

Thus, $t = \dfrac{1}{5}$ and $u = 1$.

75. Since $t = \dfrac{1}{5}$, $\dfrac{1}{x} = \dfrac{1}{5}$ and $x = 5$.

Since $u = 1$, $\dfrac{1}{y} = 1$ and $y = 1$.

The solution for the given system is $x = 5$, $y = 1$.

76. $\dfrac{5}{x} + \dfrac{15}{y} = 16$

Multiply both sides by the LCD, xy.

$xy\left(\dfrac{5}{x}\right) + xy\left(\dfrac{15}{y}\right) = xy(16)$

$5y + 15x = 16xy$

$5y - 16xy = -15x$

Factor out x on the left.

$y(5 - 16x) = -15x$

$y = \dfrac{-15x}{5 - 16x}$

77. $\dfrac{5}{x} + \dfrac{4}{y} = 5$

Multiply both sides by xy.

$xy\left(\dfrac{5}{x}\right) + xy\left(\dfrac{4}{y}\right) = xy(5)$

$5y + 4x = 5xy$

$5y - 5xy = -4x$

Factor out y on the left.

$y(5 - 5x) = -4x$

$y = \dfrac{-4x}{5 - 5x}$

78. Use $Y_1 = \dfrac{-15x}{5 - 16x}$ and $Y_2 = \dfrac{-4x}{5 - 5x}$ in the viewing window [0, 10] by [0, 2]. The point of intersection is (5, 1).

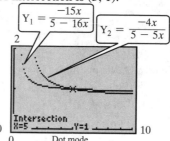

79. $\dfrac{2}{x} + \dfrac{1}{y} = \dfrac{3}{2}$

$\dfrac{3}{x} - \dfrac{1}{y} = 1$

Let $t = \dfrac{1}{x}$ and $u = \dfrac{1}{y}$. The system becomes

$2t + u = \dfrac{3}{2}$ (1)

$3t - u = 1$. (2)

Add the equations to eliminate u.

$5t = \dfrac{5}{2}$

$t = \dfrac{1}{2}$

Substitute this value into equation (1).

$2\left(\dfrac{1}{2}\right) + u = \dfrac{3}{2}$

$1 + u = \dfrac{3}{2}$

$u = \dfrac{1}{2}$

Since $t = \dfrac{1}{2}$, $\dfrac{1}{x} = \dfrac{1}{2}$ and $x = 2$.

Since $u = \dfrac{1}{2}$, $\dfrac{1}{y} = \dfrac{1}{2}$ and $y = 2$.

Solution set: $\{(2, 2)\}$

81.
$$\frac{1}{x}+\frac{1}{y}-\frac{1}{z}=\frac{1}{4}$$
$$\frac{2}{x}-\frac{1}{y}+\frac{3}{z}=\frac{9}{4}$$
$$-\frac{1}{x}-\frac{2}{y}+\frac{4}{z}=1$$

Let $r=\frac{1}{x}$ $s=\frac{1}{y}$, and $t=\frac{1}{z}$.

The system becomes
$$r+s-t=\frac{1}{4} \quad (1)$$
$$2r-s+3t=\frac{9}{4} \quad (2)$$
$$-r-2s+4t=1. \quad (3)$$

Eliminate s by adding equations (1) and (2).
$$r+s-t=\frac{1}{4}$$
$$2r-s+3t=\frac{9}{4}$$
$$\overline{}$$
$$3r+2t=\frac{5}{2} \quad (4)$$

Eliminate s again by multiplying equation (2) by -2 and adding the result to equation (3).
$$-4r+2s-6t=-\frac{9}{2}$$
$$-r-2s+4t=1$$
$$\overline{}$$
$$-5r-2t=-\frac{7}{2} \quad (5)$$

We now solve the system
$$3r+2t=\frac{10}{4} \quad (4)$$
$$-5r-2t=-\frac{7}{2}. \quad (5)$$

Adding equations (4) and (5), we obtain
$$-2r=-1$$
$$r=\frac{1}{2}.$$

Substitute this value into equation (4).
$$3\left(\frac{1}{2}\right)+2t=\frac{5}{2}$$
$$2t=1$$
$$t=\frac{1}{2}$$

Substitute these values into equation (1).
$$\left(\frac{1}{2}\right)+s-\left(\frac{1}{2}\right)=\frac{1}{4}$$
$$s=\frac{1}{4}.$$

Since $r=\frac{1}{2}$, $\frac{1}{x}=\frac{1}{2}$ and $x=2$.

Since $s=\frac{1}{4}$, $\frac{1}{y}=\frac{1}{4}$ and $y=4$.

Since $t=\frac{1}{2}$, $\frac{1}{z}=\frac{1}{2}$ and $z=2$.

Solution set: $\{(2,4,2)\}$

83. The solutions to this system of two equations in two variables occur at the intersection points of the two graphs: 1978, 1981, 1987, 1991.

84. (a) $y=800+25x$
$y=700=85x$
$800+25x=700+85x$
$100=60x$
$x=\frac{100}{60}=\frac{5}{3}=1\frac{2}{3}$ years

(b) \$1400 = lump sum payment after one year.
\$1000 + .06(\$1000) = \$1060 = principal plus one year's interest.
The \$1400 lump sum payment in one year is the better deal, by \$1400 − \$1060 = \$340.

Section 8.2

Connections *(page 653)*

1. For $n=3$
$$T(3)=\frac{2}{3}(3)^3+\frac{3}{2}(3)^2-\frac{7}{6}(3)=28$$
For $n=6$
$$T(6)=\frac{2}{3}(6)^3+\frac{3}{2}(6)^2-\frac{7}{6}(6)=191$$
Continuing in this manner we have:

n	T
3	28
6	191
10	805
29	17,487
100	681,550
200	5,393,100
400	42,906,200
1000	668,165,500
5000	8.3×10^{10}
10,000	6.7×10^{11}
100,000	6.7×10^{14}

2. Using the tables he would have to do 17,487 operations, which is too many to do by hand.

3. If the number of variables doubles, the number of operations increases by a factor of 8. 100

variables requires 681,550 operations and 200 variables requires 5,393,100 operations. The ratio $\dfrac{5,393,100}{681,550} = 7.91 \approx 8$.

4. A system of 100,000 variables has 6.7×10^{14} operations. If a Cray-T90 does 60 billion = 60×10^{9} operations per second, then the system would take $\dfrac{6.7 \times 10^{14}}{60 \times 10^{9}} = 11,166.67$ seconds or 3.1 hours.

Exercises

1. $\begin{bmatrix} 2 & 4 \\ 4 & 7 \end{bmatrix}$; $\begin{array}{l} -2 \text{ times row 1} \\ \text{added to row 2} \end{array}$

Using the third row transformation, the matrix is changed to

$\begin{bmatrix} 2 & 4 \\ 4+(-2)(2) & 7+(-2)(4) \end{bmatrix}$

$= \begin{bmatrix} 2 & 4 \\ 0 & -1 \end{bmatrix}$.

3. $\begin{bmatrix} 1 & 5 & 6 \\ -2 & 3 & -1 \\ 4 & 7 & 0 \end{bmatrix}$; $\begin{array}{l} 2 \text{ times row 1} \\ \text{added to row 2} \end{array}$

Using the row transformation, the matrix is changed to

$\begin{bmatrix} 1 & 5 & 6 \\ -2+2(1) & 3+2(5) & -1+2(6) \\ 4 & 7 & 0 \end{bmatrix}$

$= \begin{bmatrix} 1 & 5 & 6 \\ 0 & 13 & 11 \\ 4 & 7 & 0 \end{bmatrix}$.

5. $2x + 3y = 11$
   $x + 2y = 8$
   The augmented matrix is
   $\begin{bmatrix} 2 & 3 & | & 11 \\ 1 & 2 & | & 8 \end{bmatrix}$.
   Size is 2 × 3.

7. $\begin{array}{r} 2x + y + z = 3 \\ 3x - 4y + 2z = -7 \\ x + y + z = 2 \end{array}$
   has the augmented matrix
   $\begin{bmatrix} 2 & 1 & 1 & | & 3 \\ 3 & -4 & 2 & | & -7 \\ 1 & 1 & 1 & | & 2 \end{bmatrix}$.
   Size is 3 × 4.

9. $\begin{bmatrix} 3 & 2 & 1 & | & 1 \\ 0 & 2 & 4 & | & 22 \\ -1 & -2 & 3 & | & 15 \end{bmatrix}$
   is associated with the system
   $\begin{array}{r} 3x + 2y + z = 1 \\ 2y + 4z = 22 \\ -x - 2y + 3z = 15. \end{array}$

11. $\begin{bmatrix} 1 & 0 & 0 & | & 2 \\ 0 & 1 & 0 & | & 3 \\ 0 & 0 & 1 & | & -2 \end{bmatrix}$
    Is associated with the system
    $\begin{array}{r} x = 2 \\ y = 3 \\ z = -2. \end{array}$

13. The augmented matrix $\begin{bmatrix} 1 & 1 & 0 & | & 3 \\ 0 & 2 & 1 & | & -4 \\ 1 & 0 & -1 & | & 5 \end{bmatrix}$
    is associated with the following system of equations:
    $\begin{array}{r} x + y = 3 \\ 2y + z = -4 \\ x - z = 5. \end{array}$

15. $x + y = 5$
    $x - y = -1$
    has the augmented matrix
    $\begin{bmatrix} 1 & 1 & | & 5 \\ 1 & -1 & | & -1 \end{bmatrix}$.
    $\begin{bmatrix} 1 & 1 & | & 5 \\ 0 & -2 & | & -6 \end{bmatrix} -1R1 + R2$
    $\begin{bmatrix} 1 & 1 & | & 5 \\ 0 & 1 & | & 3 \end{bmatrix} -\frac{1}{2}R2$
    $\begin{bmatrix} 1 & 0 & | & 2 \\ 0 & 1 & | & 3 \end{bmatrix} -1R2 + R1$
    Solution set: {(2, 3)}.

17. $x + y = -3$
$2x - 5y = -6$

$$\begin{bmatrix} 1 & 1 & | & -3 \\ 2 & -5 & | & -6 \end{bmatrix}$$

$$\begin{bmatrix} 1 & 1 & | & -3 \\ 0 & -7 & | & 0 \end{bmatrix} -2R1 + R2$$

$$\begin{bmatrix} 1 & 1 & | & -3 \\ 0 & 1 & | & 0 \end{bmatrix} -\frac{1}{7}R2$$

$$\begin{bmatrix} 1 & 0 & | & -3 \\ 0 & 1 & | & 0 \end{bmatrix} -1R2 + R1$$

Solution set: $\{(-3, 0)\}$

19. $6x + y - 5 = 0$
$5x + y - 3 = 0$

Rewrite the system as
$6x + y = 5$
$5x + y = 3.$

$$\begin{bmatrix} 6 & 1 & | & 5 \\ 5 & 1 & | & 3 \end{bmatrix}$$

$$\begin{bmatrix} 1 & \frac{1}{6} & | & \frac{5}{6} \\ 5 & 1 & | & 3 \end{bmatrix} \frac{1}{6}R1$$

$$\begin{bmatrix} 1 & \frac{1}{6} & | & \frac{5}{6} \\ 0 & \frac{1}{6} & | & -\frac{7}{6} \end{bmatrix} -5R1 + R2$$

$$\begin{bmatrix} 1 & \frac{1}{6} & | & \frac{5}{6} \\ 0 & 1 & | & -7 \end{bmatrix} 6R2$$

$$\begin{bmatrix} 1 & 0 & | & 2 \\ 0 & 1 & | & -7 \end{bmatrix} -\frac{1}{6}R2 + R1$$

Solution set: $\{(2, -7)\}$

21. $4x - y - 3 = 0$
$-2x + 3y - 1 = 0$

Rewrite the system as
$4x - y = 3$
$-2x + 3y = 1.$

$$\begin{bmatrix} 4 & -1 & | & 3 \\ -2 & 3 & | & 1 \end{bmatrix}$$

$$\begin{bmatrix} 1 & -\frac{1}{4} & | & \frac{3}{4} \\ -2 & 3 & | & 1 \end{bmatrix} \frac{1}{4}R1$$

$$\begin{bmatrix} 1 & -\frac{1}{4} & | & \frac{3}{4} \\ 0 & \frac{5}{2} & | & \frac{5}{2} \end{bmatrix} 2R1 + R2$$

$$\begin{bmatrix} 1 & -\frac{1}{4} & | & \frac{3}{4} \\ 0 & 1 & | & 1 \end{bmatrix} \frac{2}{5}R2$$

$$\begin{bmatrix} 1 & 0 & | & 1 \\ 0 & 1 & | & 1 \end{bmatrix} \frac{1}{4}R2 + R1$$

Solution set: $\{(1, 1)\}$

23. $x + y - z = 6$
$2x - y + z = -9$
$x - 2y + 3z = 1$

$$\begin{bmatrix} 1 & 1 & -1 & | & 6 \\ 2 & -1 & 1 & | & -9 \\ 1 & -2 & 3 & | & 1 \end{bmatrix}$$

$$\begin{bmatrix} 1 & 1 & -1 & | & 6 \\ 0 & -3 & 3 & | & -21 \\ 0 & -3 & 4 & | & -5 \end{bmatrix} \begin{matrix} \\ -2R1 + R2 \\ -1R1 + R3 \end{matrix}$$

$$\begin{bmatrix} 1 & 1 & -1 & | & 6 \\ 0 & -3 & 3 & | & -21 \\ 0 & 0 & 1 & | & 16 \end{bmatrix} \begin{matrix} \\ \\ -1R2 + R3 \end{matrix}$$

$$\begin{bmatrix} 1 & 1 & -1 & | & 6 \\ 0 & 1 & -1 & | & 7 \\ 0 & 0 & 1 & | & 16 \end{bmatrix} \begin{matrix} \\ -\frac{1}{3}R2 \\ \\ \end{matrix}$$

$$\begin{bmatrix} 1 & 1 & 0 & | & 22 \\ 0 & 1 & 0 & | & 23 \\ 0 & 0 & 1 & | & 16 \end{bmatrix} \begin{matrix} R3 + R1 \\ R3 + R2 \\ \end{matrix}$$

$$\begin{bmatrix} 1 & 0 & 0 & | & -1 \\ 0 & 1 & 0 & | & 23 \\ 0 & 0 & 1 & | & 16 \end{bmatrix} -1R2 + R1$$

Solution set: $\{(-1, 23, 16)\}$

25. $x - z = -3$
$y + z = 9$
$x + z = 7$

$$\begin{bmatrix} 1 & 0 & -1 & | & -3 \\ 0 & 1 & 1 & | & 9 \\ 1 & 0 & 1 & | & 7 \end{bmatrix}$$

$$\begin{bmatrix} 1 & 0 & -1 & | & -3 \\ 0 & 1 & 1 & | & 9 \\ 0 & 0 & 2 & | & 10 \end{bmatrix} -1R1 + R3$$

$$\begin{bmatrix} 1 & 0 & -1 & | & -3 \\ 0 & 1 & 1 & | & 9 \\ 0 & 0 & 1 & | & 5 \end{bmatrix} \frac{1}{2}R3$$

$$\begin{bmatrix} 1 & 0 & -1 & | & -3 \\ 0 & 1 & 0 & | & 4 \\ 0 & 0 & 1 & | & 5 \end{bmatrix} -1R3 + R2$$

$$\begin{bmatrix} 1 & 0 & 0 & | & 2 \\ 0 & 1 & 0 & | & 4 \\ 0 & 0 & 1 & | & 5 \end{bmatrix} R3 + R1$$

Solution set: $\{(2, 4, 5)\}$

27. $y = -2x - 2z + 1$
$\quad x = -2y - z + 2$
$\quad z = x - y$

Rewrite the system as
$2x + y + 2z = 1$
$\quad x + 2y + z = 2$
$\quad x - y - z = 0.$

$\begin{bmatrix} 2 & 1 & 2 & | & 1 \\ 1 & 2 & 1 & | & 2 \\ 1 & -1 & -1 & | & 0 \end{bmatrix}$

$\begin{bmatrix} 1 & 2 & 1 & | & 2 \\ 2 & 1 & 2 & | & 1 \\ 1 & -1 & -1 & | & 0 \end{bmatrix}$ R1 ↔ R2

$\begin{bmatrix} 1 & 2 & 1 & | & 2 \\ 0 & -3 & 0 & | & -3 \\ 0 & -3 & -2 & | & -2 \end{bmatrix}$ $-2R1 + R2$
$\qquad\qquad\qquad\qquad -1R1 + R3$

$\begin{bmatrix} 1 & 2 & 1 & | & 2 \\ 0 & 1 & 0 & | & 1 \\ 0 & -3 & -2 & | & -2 \end{bmatrix}$ $-\frac{1}{3}R2$

$\begin{bmatrix} 1 & 0 & 1 & | & 0 \\ 0 & 1 & 0 & | & 1 \\ 0 & 0 & -2 & | & 1 \end{bmatrix}$ $-2R2 + R1$
$\qquad\qquad\qquad\qquad 3R2 + R3$

$\begin{bmatrix} 1 & 0 & 1 & | & 0 \\ 0 & 1 & 0 & | & 1 \\ 0 & 0 & 1 & | & -\frac{1}{2} \end{bmatrix}$ $-\frac{1}{2}R3$

$\begin{bmatrix} 1 & 0 & 0 & | & \frac{1}{2} \\ 0 & 1 & 0 & | & 1 \\ 0 & 0 & 1 & | & -\frac{1}{2} \end{bmatrix}$ $-1R3 + R1$

Solution set: $\left\{ \left(\frac{1}{2},\ 1,\ -\frac{1}{2} \right) \right\}$

29. $2x - y + 3z = 0$
$\quad x + 2y - z = 5$
$\qquad\quad 2y + z = 1$

$\begin{bmatrix} 2 & -1 & 3 & | & 0 \\ 1 & 2 & -1 & | & 5 \\ 0 & 2 & 1 & | & 1 \end{bmatrix}$

$\begin{bmatrix} 1 & -\frac{1}{2} & \frac{3}{2} & | & 0 \\ 1 & 2 & -1 & | & 5 \\ 0 & 2 & 1 & | & 1 \end{bmatrix}$ $\frac{1}{2}R1$

$\begin{bmatrix} 1 & -\frac{1}{2} & \frac{3}{2} & | & 0 \\ 0 & \frac{5}{2} & -\frac{5}{2} & | & 5 \\ 0 & 2 & 1 & | & 1 \end{bmatrix}$ $-1R1 + R2$

$\begin{bmatrix} 1 & -\frac{1}{2} & \frac{3}{2} & | & 0 \\ 0 & 1 & -1 & | & 2 \\ 0 & 2 & 1 & | & 1 \end{bmatrix}$ $\frac{2}{5}R2$

$\begin{bmatrix} 1 & -\frac{1}{2} & \frac{3}{2} & | & 0 \\ 0 & 1 & -1 & | & 2 \\ 0 & 0 & 3 & | & -3 \end{bmatrix}$ $-2R2 + R3$

$\begin{bmatrix} 1 & -\frac{1}{2} & \frac{3}{2} & | & 0 \\ 0 & 1 & -1 & | & 2 \\ 0 & 0 & 1 & | & -1 \end{bmatrix}$ $\frac{1}{3}R3$

$\begin{bmatrix} 1 & 0 & 1 & | & 1 \\ 0 & 1 & -1 & | & 2 \\ 0 & 0 & 1 & | & -1 \end{bmatrix}$ $\frac{1}{2}R2 + R1$

$\begin{bmatrix} 1 & 0 & 0 & | & 2 \\ 0 & 1 & 0 & | & 1 \\ 0 & 0 & 1 & | & -1 \end{bmatrix}$ $-1R3 + R1$
$\qquad\qquad\qquad\qquad R3 + R2$

Solution set: $\{(2, 1, -1)\}$

31. $3x + 5y - z + 2 = 0$
$\quad 4x - y + 2z - 1 = 0$
$\quad -6x - 10y + 2z = 0$

Rewrite the system as
$3x + 5y - z = -2$
$\quad 4x - y + 2z = 1$
$\quad -6x - 10y + 2z = 0.$

$\begin{bmatrix} 3 & 5 & -1 & | & -2 \\ 4 & -1 & 2 & | & 1 \\ -6 & -10 & 2 & | & 0 \end{bmatrix}$

$\begin{bmatrix} 1 & \frac{5}{3} & -\frac{1}{3} & | & -\frac{2}{3} \\ 4 & -1 & 2 & | & 1 \\ -6 & -10 & 2 & | & 0 \end{bmatrix}$ $\frac{1}{3}R1$

$\begin{bmatrix} 1 & \frac{5}{3} & -\frac{1}{3} & | & -\frac{2}{3} \\ 0 & -\frac{23}{3} & \frac{10}{3} & | & \frac{11}{3} \\ 0 & 0 & 0 & | & -4 \end{bmatrix}$ $-4R1 + R2$
$\qquad\qquad\qquad\qquad\quad 6R1 + R3$

The last row indicates that there is no solution.
The solution set is $\emptyset$.

33. $x - 8y + z = 4$
$\quad 3x - y + 2z = -1$

$\begin{bmatrix} 1 & -8 & 1 & | & 4 \\ 3 & -1 & 2 & | & -1 \end{bmatrix}$

$\begin{bmatrix} 1 & -8 & 1 & | & 4 \\ 0 & 23 & -1 & | & -13 \end{bmatrix}$ $-3R1 + R2$

$\begin{bmatrix} 1 & -8 & 1 & | & 4 \\ 0 & 1 & -\frac{1}{23} & | & -\frac{13}{23} \end{bmatrix}$ $\frac{1}{23}R2$

$$\begin{bmatrix} 1 & 0 & \frac{15}{23} & -\frac{12}{23} \\ 0 & 1 & -\frac{1}{23} & -\frac{13}{23} \end{bmatrix} \quad 8R2 + R1$$

This matrix is equivalent to the following system:

$$x + \frac{15}{23}z = -\frac{12}{23}$$

$$y - \frac{1}{23}z = -\frac{13}{23}.$$

This system has infinitely many solutions. We will express the solution set with z as the arbitrary variable.

Therefore,

$$x = -\frac{15}{23}z - \frac{12}{23}$$

and $y = \frac{1}{23}z - \frac{13}{23}.$

Solution set:

$$\left\{ \left(-\frac{15}{23}z - \frac{12}{23}, \frac{1}{23}z - \frac{13}{23}, z \right) \right\}$$

35. $x - y + 2z + w = 4$
$y + z = 3$
$z - w = 2$

$$\begin{bmatrix} 1 & -2 & 2 & 1 & 4 \\ 0 & 1 & 1 & 0 & 3 \\ 0 & 0 & 1 & -1 & 2 \end{bmatrix}$$

$$\begin{bmatrix} 1 & 0 & 3 & 1 & 7 \\ 0 & 1 & 1 & 0 & 3 \\ 0 & 0 & 1 & -1 & 2 \end{bmatrix} \quad 1R2 + R1$$

$$\begin{bmatrix} 1 & 0 & 0 & 4 & 1 \\ 0 & 1 & 0 & 1 & 1 \\ 0 & 0 & 1 & -1 & 2 \end{bmatrix} \quad \begin{matrix} -3R3 + R1 \\ -1R3 + R2 \end{matrix}$$

This gives the following system:
$x + 4w = 1$
$y + w = 1$
$z - w = 2.$

This system has an infinite number of solutions. We will write the solution set with w as the arbitrary variable.

$x = 1 - 4w$
$y = 1 - w$
$z = 2 + w$

Solution set:
$\{(1 - 4w, 1 - w, 2 + w, w)\}$

37. Answers may vary.

39. $\sqrt{5}x - 1.2y + z = -3$

$$\frac{1}{2}x - 3y + 4z = \frac{4}{3}$$

$$4x + 7y - 9z = \sqrt{2}$$

Write the augmented matrix.

$$\begin{bmatrix} \sqrt{5} & -1.2 & 1 & -3 \\ \frac{1}{2} & -3 & 4 & \frac{4}{3} \\ 4 & 7 & -9 & \sqrt{2} \end{bmatrix}$$

Use a graphing calculator to perform the required row operations.
Solution set; $\{(.407, 9.316, 7.270)\}$

41. $3x - 2y = 3$ or $y = \dfrac{3x}{2} - \dfrac{3}{2}$

$-2x + 4 = 14$ or $y = \dfrac{2x + 14}{4}$ or $y = \dfrac{x}{2} + \dfrac{7}{2}$

$x + y = 11$ or $y = -x + 11$

There is exactly one solution since the three lines intersect at exactly one point.
The solution set is $\{(5, 6)\}$.
Confirm answer by solving the system with the Gauss-Jordan method. Start with equations 2 and 3.

$$\begin{bmatrix} -2 & 4 & 14 \\ 1 & 1 & 11 \end{bmatrix}$$

$$\begin{bmatrix} 1 & 1 & 11 \\ -2 & 4 & 14 \end{bmatrix} \quad R_1 \leftrightarrow R_2$$

$$\begin{bmatrix} 1 & 1 & 11 \\ 0 & 6 & 36 \end{bmatrix} \quad 2R_1 + R_2$$

$$\begin{bmatrix} 1 & 1 & 11 \\ 0 & 1 & 6 \end{bmatrix} \quad \frac{1}{6}R_2$$

$$\begin{bmatrix} 1 & 0 & 5 \\ 0 & 1 & 6 \end{bmatrix} \quad -1R_2 + R_1$$

Solution set: $\{(5, 6)\}$
Check $x = 5$, $y = 6$ in the first equation.
$$3x - 2y = 3$$
$$3(5) - 2(6) = 3$$
$$15 - 12 = 3$$
$$3 = 3 \quad \text{True}$$

43. $\dfrac{1}{(x-1)(x+1)} = \dfrac{A}{x-1} + \dfrac{B}{x+1}$

Add the rational expression on the right.

$\dfrac{1}{(x-1)(x+1)} = \dfrac{A(x+1)+B(x-1)}{(x-1)(x+1)}$

Since the denominators are equal, the numerators must be equal.

$1 = A(x+1)+B(x-1)$

$1 = Ax+A+Bx-B$

Collect like terms.

$1 = (A+B)x+(A-B)$

Equating the coefficients of like powers of x gives the following system of equations.

$A+B=0$ (1)

$A-B=1$ (2)

This system can be solved by any of the methods studied so far. We use the elimination method.

$A+B=0$

$\underline{A-B=1}$

$2A=1$

$A=\dfrac{1}{2}$

$B=-\dfrac{1}{2}$

45. $\dfrac{x}{(x-a)(x+a)} = \dfrac{A}{x-a} + \dfrac{B}{x+a}$

$\dfrac{x}{(x-a)(x+a)} = \dfrac{A(x+a)+B(x-a)}{(x-a)(x+a)}$

Since the denominators are equal, the numerators must be equal.

$x = A(x+a)+B(x-a)$

$x = Ax+Aa+Bx-Ba$

$x = (A+B)x+(A-B)a$

$A+B=1$

$\underline{A-B=0}$

$2A=1$

$A=\dfrac{1}{2}$

$B=\dfrac{1}{2}$

47. (a) Let $x=95$ represent 1995 and $x=150$ represent 2050

65 and over: (95, 12.8), (150, 20.0)

$m = \dfrac{20.0-12.8}{150-95} = \dfrac{7.2}{55} \approx .1309 \approx .131$

$y-12.8 = .13091(x-95)$

$y-12.8 = .13091x-12.43645$

$\ y = .131x+.364$

25–34: (95, 15.5), (150, 12.5)

$m = \dfrac{12.5-15.5}{150-05} = \dfrac{-3}{55} \approx -.054545 \approx -.055$

$y-15.5 = -.054545(x-95)$

$y-15.5 = -.054545x+5.181818$

$\ y = -.055x+20.7$

(b) $.131x+.364 = -.055x+20.7$

$.186x = 20.336$

$x \approx 109.33$

$y = .131x+.364$

$y = .131(109.33)+.364$

$y \approx 14.7$

Solution set: $\{(109, 14.7)\}$

$x=109$ represents the year 2009.

In 2009, the two age groups will each include 14.7% of the population.

49. Let x = number of cubic centimeters of the 2% solution;

y = number of cubic centimeters of the 7% solution.

$x+y = 40$

$.02x+.07y = .032(40)$

$\begin{bmatrix} 1 & 1 & | & 40 \\ .02 & .07 & | & 1.28 \end{bmatrix}$

$\begin{bmatrix} 1 & 1 & | & 40 \\ 0 & .05 & | & .48 \end{bmatrix} \ -.02R1+R2$

$\begin{bmatrix} 1 & 1 & | & 40 \\ 0 & 1 & | & 9.6 \end{bmatrix} \ \tfrac{1}{.05}R2$

$\begin{bmatrix} 1 & 0 & | & 30.4 \\ 0 & 1 & | & 9.6 \end{bmatrix} \ -1R2+R1$

Solution set: $\{(30.4, 9.6)\}$

The chemist should mix 30.4 cm^3 of the 2% solution with 9.6 cm^3 of the 7% solution.

53. Let x = number of grams of food A;

y = number of grams of food B;

z = number of grams of food C.

From the given information, we have

$x+y+z=400$

$x=\dfrac{1}{3}y$

$x+z=2y.$

The system becomes

$x+y+z=400$

$3x-y=0$

$x-2y+z=0.$

$\begin{bmatrix} 1 & 1 & 1 & | & 400 \\ 3 & -1 & 0 & | & 0 \\ 1 & -2 & 1 & | & 0 \end{bmatrix}$

$$\left[\begin{array}{ccc|c} 1 & 1 & 1 & 400 \\ 0 & -4 & -3 & -1200 \\ 0 & -3 & 0 & -400 \end{array}\right] \begin{array}{l} \\ -3R1+R2 \\ -1R1+R3 \end{array}$$

$$\left[\begin{array}{ccc|c} 1 & 1 & 1 & 400 \\ 0 & 1 & \frac{3}{4} & 300 \\ 0 & -3 & 0 & -400 \end{array}\right] \begin{array}{l} \\ -\frac{1}{4}R2 \\ \\ \end{array}$$

$$\left[\begin{array}{ccc|c} 1 & 1 & 1 & 400 \\ 0 & 1 & \frac{3}{4} & 300 \\ 0 & 0 & \frac{9}{4} & 500 \end{array}\right] \begin{array}{l} -1R2+R1 \\ \\ 3R2+R3 \end{array}$$

$$\left[\begin{array}{ccc|c} 1 & 0 & \frac{1}{4} & 100 \\ 0 & 1 & \frac{3}{4} & 300 \\ 0 & 0 & 1 & \frac{2000}{9} \end{array}\right] \begin{array}{l} \\ \\ \frac{4}{9}R3 \end{array}$$

$$\left[\begin{array}{ccc|c} 1 & 0 & 0 & \frac{400}{9} \\ 0 & 1 & 0 & \frac{400}{3} \\ 0 & 0 & 1 & \frac{2000}{9} \end{array}\right] \begin{array}{l} -\frac{1}{4}R3+R1 \\ -\frac{3}{4}R3+R2 \\ \\ \end{array}$$

From the last matrix, we have $x = 400/9 \approx 44.4$, $y = 400/3 \approx 133.3$, and $z = 2000/9 \approx 222.2$. The diet should include 44.4 g of food A, 133.3 of food B, and 222.2 g of food C.

55. **(a)** A height of $6'11''$ is $83''$.
If $W = 7.46H - 374$,
$W = 7.46(83) - 374$
$W = 245.18$.
Using the first equation, the predicted weight is approximately 245 pounds.
If $W = 7.93H - 405$,
$W = 7.93(83) - 405$
$W = 253.19$.
Using the second equation, the predicted weight is approximately 253 pounds.

(b) For the first model $W = 7.46H - 374$, a 1-inch increase in height results in a 7.46-pound increase in weight.
For the second model $W = 7.93H - 405$, a 1-inch increase in height results in a 7.93-pound increase in weight.
In each case, the change is given by the slope of the line that is the graph of the given equation.

(c) $W - 7.46H = -374$
$W - 7.93H = -405$
Solve this system by the Gauss-Jordan method.

$$\left[\begin{array}{cc|c} 1 & -7.46 & -374 \\ 1 & -7.93 & -405 \end{array}\right]$$

$$\left[\begin{array}{cc|c} 1 & -7.46 & -374 \\ 0 & -.47 & -31 \end{array}\right] \begin{array}{l} \\ -1R1+R2 \end{array}$$

$$\left[\begin{array}{cc|c} 1 & -7.46 & -374 \\ 0 & 1 & 65.957 \end{array}\right] -\frac{1}{.47}R2$$

$$\left[\begin{array}{cc|c} 1 & 0 & 118.043 \\ 0 & 1 & 65.957 \end{array}\right] 7.46R2+R1$$

From the last matrix, we have $W \approx 118$ and $H \approx 66$.
The two models agree at a height of 66 inches and a weight of 118 pounds.

57. $F = a + bA + cP + dW$
Substituting the values, we have the following system of equations:
$a + 871b + 11.5c + 3d = 239$
$a + 847b + 12.2c + 2d = 234$
$a + 685b + 10.6c + 5d = 192$
$a + 969b + 14.2c + 1d = 343$.

58. The augmented matrix is

$$\left[\begin{array}{cccc|c} 1 & 871 & 11.5 & 3 & 239 \\ 1 & 847 & 12.2 & 2 & 234 \\ 1 & 685 & 10.6 & 5 & 192 \\ 1 & 969 & 14.2 & 1 & 343 \end{array}\right]$$

Using a graphing calculator capable of performing row operations, the solution we obtain is
$a \approx -715.457$, $b \approx .34756$,
$c \approx 48.6585$, and $d \approx 30.71951$.

59. Using these values,
$F = -714.457 + .34756A + 48.6585P$
$\quad + 30.71951W$

60. Using $A = 960$, $P = 12.6$, and $W = 3$ we obtain
$F = -715.457 + .34756(960) + 48.6585(12.6)$
$\quad + 30.71951(3)$
$F = 323.45623 \approx 323$
Therefore, the predicted fawn count is approximately 323, which is just slightly higher than the actual value of 320.

61. **(a)** Slope $m = \dfrac{620 - 660}{1992 - 1988} = -\dfrac{40}{4} = -10$
Use point-slope form to find an equation.
$y - y_1 = m(x - x_1)$
$y - 660 = -10(x - 1988)$
$y - 660 = -10x + 19880$
$\quad\quad\quad y = -10x + 20,540$

(b) Slope $m = \dfrac{780 - 520}{1992 - 1990} = \dfrac{260}{2} = 130$
Use point-slope form to find an equation.
$y - y_1 = m(x - x_1)$
$y - 520 = 130(x - 1990)$
$y - 520 = 130x - 258,700$
$\quad\quad\quad y = 130x - 258,180$

(c) The system can be written as
$$10x + y = 20,540$$
$$130x - y = 258,180$$
The augmented matrix is
$$\begin{bmatrix} 10 & 1 & | & 20,540 \\ 130 & -1 & | & 258,180 \end{bmatrix}.$$
Using a graphing calculator, to the nearest whole number, the reduced-row echelon form is
$$\begin{bmatrix} 1 & 0 & | & 1991 \\ 0 & 1 & | & 631 \end{bmatrix}.$$
To the nearest whole number, the solution is (1991, 631), which indicates that in 1991, both total presidential campaigns and congressional campaigns spent approximately $631 million.

Section 8.3

Exercises

1. $\begin{vmatrix} 2 & 5 \\ 4 & -7 \end{vmatrix} = 2(-7) - 4(5) = -34$

3. $\begin{vmatrix} -9 & 7 \\ 2 & 6 \end{vmatrix} = -9(6) - 2(7) = -68$

5. $\begin{vmatrix} y & 3 \\ -2 & x \end{vmatrix} = yx - (-2)(3) = yx + 6$

7. $\begin{vmatrix} -2 & 0 & 1 \\ 1 & 2 & 0 \\ 4 & 2 & 1 \end{vmatrix}$

Cofactor of 1: $(-1)\begin{vmatrix} 0 & 1 \\ 2 & 1 \end{vmatrix} = -1(-2) = 2$

Cofactor of 2: $1\begin{vmatrix} -2 & 1 \\ 4 & 1 \end{vmatrix} = 1(-6) = -6$

Cofactor of 0: $(-1)\begin{vmatrix} -2 & 0 \\ 4 & 2 \end{vmatrix} = -1(-4) = 4$

9. $\begin{vmatrix} 1 & 2 & -1 \\ 2 & 3 & -2 \\ -1 & 4 & 1 \end{vmatrix}$

Cofactor of 2: $(-1)\begin{vmatrix} 2 & -1 \\ 4 & 1 \end{vmatrix} = (-1)(6) = -6$

Cofactor of 3: $1\begin{vmatrix} 1 & -1 \\ -1 & 1 \end{vmatrix} = 1(0) = 0$

Cofactor of –2: $(-1)\begin{vmatrix} 1 & 2 \\ -1 & 4 \end{vmatrix} = (-1)(6) = -6$

11. $\begin{vmatrix} 1 & 0 & 0 \\ 0 & 1 & 0 \\ 0 & 0 & 1 \end{vmatrix}$

Expand by minors about row 1.
$$\begin{vmatrix} 1 & 0 & 0 \\ 0 & 1 & 0 \\ 0 & 0 & 1 \end{vmatrix} = 1\begin{vmatrix} 1 & 0 \\ 0 & 1 \end{vmatrix} - 0\begin{vmatrix} 0 & 0 \\ 0 & 1 \end{vmatrix} + 0\begin{vmatrix} 0 & 1 \\ 0 & 0 \end{vmatrix}$$
$$= 1(1) - 0 + 0$$
$$= 1$$

13. $\begin{vmatrix} -2 & 0 & 1 \\ 0 & 1 & 0 \\ 0 & 0 & -1 \end{vmatrix}$

Expand by minors about row 3 since row 3 has two zeros.
$$\begin{vmatrix} -2 & 0 & 1 \\ 0 & 1 & 0 \\ 0 & 0 & -1 \end{vmatrix}$$
$$= 0\begin{vmatrix} 0 & 1 \\ 1 & 0 \end{vmatrix} - 0\begin{vmatrix} -2 & 1 \\ 0 & 0 \end{vmatrix} + (-1)\begin{vmatrix} -2 & 0 \\ 0 & 1 \end{vmatrix}$$
$$= 0 - 0 - 1(-2 - 0)$$
$$= 2$$

15. $\begin{vmatrix} 0 & 5 & 2 \\ 0 & 3 & -1 \\ 0 & -4 & 7 \end{vmatrix}$

Expand by minors about column 1.
$$\begin{vmatrix} 0 & 5 & 2 \\ 0 & 3 & -1 \\ 0 & -4 & 7 \end{vmatrix}$$
$$= 0\begin{vmatrix} 3 & -1 \\ -4 & 7 \end{vmatrix} - 0\begin{vmatrix} 5 & 2 \\ -4 & 7 \end{vmatrix} + 0\begin{vmatrix} 5 & 2 \\ 3 & -1 \end{vmatrix}$$
$$= 0 + 0 + 0$$
$$= 0$$

17. $\begin{vmatrix} 0 & 3 & y \\ 0 & 4 & 2 \\ 1 & 0 & 1 \end{vmatrix}$

Expand by minors about column 1 since it has two zeros.
$$= 0\begin{vmatrix} 4 & 2 \\ 0 & 1 \end{vmatrix} - 0\begin{vmatrix} 3 & y \\ 0 & 1 \end{vmatrix} + 1\begin{vmatrix} 3 & y \\ 4 & 2 \end{vmatrix}$$
$$= 0 - 0 + 1(6 - 4y)$$
$$= 6 - 4y$$

19.
$$\begin{vmatrix} .4 & -.8 & .6 \\ .3 & .9 & .7 \\ 3.1 & 4.1 & -2.8 \end{vmatrix}$$

Expand by minors about the first row.

$$= .4 \begin{vmatrix} .9 & .7 \\ 4.1 & -2.8 \end{vmatrix} - (-.8) \begin{vmatrix} .3 & .7 \\ 3.1 & -2.8 \end{vmatrix}$$
$$+ .6 \begin{vmatrix} .3 & .9 \\ 3.1 & 4.1 \end{vmatrix}$$
$$= (.4)(-5.39) + (.8)(-3.01)$$
$$+ (.6)(-1.56)$$
$$= -5.5$$

21.
$$\begin{vmatrix} x & 2 & 1 \\ -1 & x & 4 \\ -2 & 0 & 5 \end{vmatrix}$$

Expand by minors about row 3.
$$\begin{vmatrix} x & 2 & 1 \\ -1 & x & 4 \\ -2 & 0 & 5 \end{vmatrix}$$
$$= -2 \begin{vmatrix} 2 & 1 \\ x & 4 \end{vmatrix} - 0 \begin{vmatrix} x & 1 \\ -1 & 4 \end{vmatrix} + 5 \begin{vmatrix} x & 2 \\ -1 & x \end{vmatrix}$$
$$= -2(8 - x) - 0 + 5(x^2 + 2)$$
$$= -16 + 2x + 5x^2 + 10$$
$$= 5x^2 + 2x - 6$$

22. The equation is
$5x^2 + 2x - 6 = 45$, which is a quadratic equation.

23. $5x^2 + 2x - 6 = 45$
Rewrite the equation in standard form.
$5x^2 + 2x - 51 = 0$
Solve this equation by factoring.
$(5x + 17)(x - 3) = 0$
$5x + 17 = 0 \quad$ or $\quad x - 3 = 0$
$$5x = -17$$
$$x = -\frac{17}{5}$$
$$x = -3.4 \quad \text{or} \quad x = 3$$
Solution set: $\{-3.4, 3\}$

24. If $x = 3$, the determinant becomes
$$\begin{vmatrix} 3 & 2 & 1 \\ -1 & 3 & 4 \\ -2 & 0 & 5 \end{vmatrix}$$
$$= -2 \begin{vmatrix} 2 & 1 \\ 3 & 4 \end{vmatrix} - 0 \begin{vmatrix} 3 & 1 \\ -1 & 4 \end{vmatrix} + 5 \begin{vmatrix} 3 & 2 \\ -1 & 3 \end{vmatrix}$$
$$= -2(5) - 0 + 5(11)$$
$$= -10 + 55$$
$$= 45$$

If $x = 3.4$, the determinant becomes
$$\begin{vmatrix} -3.4 & 2 & 1 \\ -1 & -3.4 & 4 \\ -2 & 0 & 5 \end{vmatrix}$$
$$= -2 \begin{vmatrix} 2 & 1 \\ -3.4 & 4 \end{vmatrix} - 0 \begin{vmatrix} -3.4 & 1 \\ -1 & 4 \end{vmatrix}$$
$$+ 5 \begin{vmatrix} -3.4 & 2 \\ -1 & -3.4 \end{vmatrix}$$
$$= -2(11.4) - 0 + 5(13.56)$$
$$= -22.8 + 67.8$$
$$= 45$$

25. To solve the equation
$$\begin{vmatrix} -2 & 0 & 1 \\ -1 & 3 & x \\ 5 & -2 & 0 \end{vmatrix} = 3,$$

expand by minors about the first row.
$$-2 \begin{vmatrix} 3 & x \\ -2 & 0 \end{vmatrix} - 0 \begin{vmatrix} -1 & x \\ 5 & 0 \end{vmatrix} + 1 \begin{vmatrix} -1 & 3 \\ 5 & -2 \end{vmatrix} = 3$$
$$-2(0 + 2x) - 0 + 1(2 - 15) = 3$$
$$-4x - 13 = 3$$
$$-4x = 16$$
$$x = -4$$
Solution set: $\{-4\}$

27.
$$\begin{vmatrix} 5 & 3x & -3 \\ 0 & 2 & -1 \\ 4 & -1 & x \end{vmatrix} = -7$$

Expand about the second row.
$$-0 \begin{vmatrix} 3x & -3 \\ -1 & x \end{vmatrix} + 2 \begin{vmatrix} 5 & -3 \\ 4 & x \end{vmatrix} - (-1) \begin{vmatrix} 5 & 3x \\ 4 & -1 \end{vmatrix} = -7$$
$$2(5x + 12) + (-5 - 12x) = -7$$
$$10x + 24 - 5 - 12x = -7$$
$$-2x + 19 = 2x$$
$$26 = 2x$$
$$13 = x$$

Solution set: $\{13\}$

29. $P(0, 0), Q(0, 2), R(1, 4)$
Find
$$D = \frac{1}{2} \begin{vmatrix} x_1 & y_1 & 1 \\ x_2 & y_2 & 1 \\ x_3 & y_3 & 1 \end{vmatrix},$$
where $P = (x_1, y_1) = (0, 0)$,
$$Q(x_2, y_2) = (0, 2), \text{ and}$$
$$R = (x_3, y_3) = (1, 4).$$

$$\frac{1}{2}\begin{vmatrix} 0 & 0 & 1 \\ 0 & 2 & 1 \\ 1 & 4 & 1 \end{vmatrix}$$

$$=\frac{1}{2}\left[0\begin{vmatrix} 2 & 1 \\ 4 & 1 \end{vmatrix}-0\begin{vmatrix} 0 & 1 \\ 1 & 1 \end{vmatrix}+1\begin{vmatrix} 0 & 2 \\ 1 & 4 \end{vmatrix}\right]$$

$$=\frac{1}{2}[0-0+1(-2)]$$

$$=-1$$

Area of triangle of $|D|=|-1|=1$

31. $P(2, 5)$, $Q(-1, 3)$, $R(4, 0)$

$$\frac{1}{2}\begin{vmatrix} 2 & 5 & 1 \\ -1 & 3 & 1 \\ 4 & 0 & 1 \end{vmatrix}$$

$$=\frac{1}{2}\left[4\begin{vmatrix} 5 & 1 \\ 3 & 1 \end{vmatrix}-0\begin{vmatrix} 2 & 1 \\ -1 & 1 \end{vmatrix}+1\begin{vmatrix} 2 & 5 \\ -1 & 3 \end{vmatrix}\right]$$

$$=\frac{1}{2}[4(2)-0+1(11)]$$

$$=\frac{1}{2}(8+11)$$

$$=\frac{19}{2}=9.5$$

Area of triangle $=|9.5|=9.5$

33. $P(101.3, 52.7)$, $Q(117.2, 253.9)$,
$R(313.1, 301.6)$

$$D=\frac{1}{2}\begin{vmatrix} 101.3 & 52.7 & 1 \\ 117.2 & 253.9 & 1 \\ 313.1 & 301.6 & 1 \end{vmatrix}$$

$$=\frac{1}{2}\begin{vmatrix} 101.3 & 52.7 & 1 \\ 15.9 & 201.2 & 0 \\ 211.8 & 47.7 & 0 \end{vmatrix}\begin{matrix} \\ -1R1+R2 \\ -1R1+R3 \end{matrix}$$

$$=\frac{1}{2}\left(1\begin{vmatrix} 15.9 & 201.2 \\ 211.8 & 248.9 \end{vmatrix}-0\begin{vmatrix} 101.3 & 52.7 \\ 211.8 & 248.9 \end{vmatrix}\right.$$

$$\left.+0\begin{vmatrix} 101.3 & 52.7 \\ 15.9 & 201.2 \end{vmatrix}\right)$$

$$=\frac{1}{2}(3957.51-42,614.16-0+0)$$

$$=\frac{1}{2}(-38,656.65)$$

$$=-19,328.325$$

Area of triangular lot =
$|-19,328.325|$ square feet or approximately
19,328 square feet.

37. $\begin{vmatrix} -1 & 2 & 4 \\ 4 & -8 & -16 \\ 3 & 0 & 5 \end{vmatrix}$

Row 1 of the matrix for this determinant equals
row 2 multiplied by $-\frac{1}{4}$, so, by Determinant
Theorem 4, we have

$$\begin{vmatrix} -1 & 2 & 4 \\ 4 & -8 & -16 \\ 3 & 0 & 5 \end{vmatrix}=-\frac{1}{4}\begin{vmatrix} 4 & -8 & -16 \\ 4 & -8 & -16 \\ 3 & 0 & 5 \end{vmatrix}.$$

By Theorem 5, the determinant of a matrix with
two identical rows equals 0, so the value of the
original determinant is

$$-\frac{1}{4}(0)=0.$$

39. $\begin{vmatrix} 4 & 8 & 0 \\ -1 & -2 & 1 \\ 2 & 4 & 3 \end{vmatrix}$

Multiply column 1 of the corresponding matrix by
-2, and add the result to column 2.
In the new matrix, all elements in column 2 are 0.
Thus,

$$\begin{vmatrix} 4 & 8 & 0 \\ -1 & -2 & 1 \\ 2 & 4 & 3 \end{vmatrix}=\begin{vmatrix} 4 & 0 & 0 \\ -1 & 0 & 1 \\ 2 & 0 & 3 \end{vmatrix}=0.$$

41. $\begin{vmatrix} 6 & 3 & 2 \\ 1 & 0 & 2 \\ 5 & 7 & 3 \end{vmatrix}$

Multiply column 1 of the corresponding matrix
column 1 by -2 and add the result to column 3.

$$=\begin{vmatrix} 6 & 3 & -10 \\ 1 & 0 & 0 \\ 5 & 7 & -7 \end{vmatrix}$$

Expand about row 2 since every element but one
is 0.

$$=-\begin{vmatrix} 3 & -10 \\ 7 & -7 \end{vmatrix}$$

$$=-1[-21-(-70)]$$

$$=-1(49)=-49$$

43. $x=\dfrac{Dx}{D}=\dfrac{-43}{-43}=1$

$y=\dfrac{Dy}{D}=\dfrac{0}{-43}=0$

$z=\dfrac{Dz}{D}=\dfrac{43}{-43}=-1$

Solution set: $\{(1, 0, -1)\}$

45. $3x + 2y = -4$
$2x - y = -5$

$$D = \begin{vmatrix} 3 & 2 \\ 2 & -1 \end{vmatrix} = -3 - 4 = -7$$

$$D_x = \begin{vmatrix} -4 & 2 \\ -5 & -1 \end{vmatrix} = 4 + 10 = 14$$

$$D_y = \begin{vmatrix} 3 & -4 \\ 2 & -5 \end{vmatrix} = -15 + 8 = -7$$

$$x = \frac{D_x}{D} = \frac{14}{-7} = -2$$

$$y = \frac{D_y}{D} = \frac{-7}{-7} = 1$$

47. $4x - y = 0$
$2x + 3y = 14$

$$D = \begin{vmatrix} 4 & -1 \\ 2 & 3 \end{vmatrix} = 12 + 2 = 14$$

$$D_x = \begin{vmatrix} 0 & -1 \\ 14 & 3 \end{vmatrix} = 0 + 14 = 14$$

$$D_y = \begin{vmatrix} 4 & 0 \\ 2 & 14 \end{vmatrix} = 56 - 0 = 56$$

$$x = \frac{D_x}{D} = \frac{14}{14} = 1$$

$$y = \frac{D_y}{D} = \frac{56}{14} = 4$$

Solution set: $\{(1, 4)\}$

49. $3x + 2y = -4$
$5x - y = 2$

$$D = \begin{vmatrix} 3 & 2 \\ 5 & -1 \end{vmatrix} = -3 - 10 = -13$$

$$D_x = \begin{vmatrix} -4 & 2 \\ 2 & -1 \end{vmatrix} = 4 - 4 = 0$$

$$D_y = \begin{vmatrix} 3 & -4 \\ 5 & 2 \end{vmatrix} = 6 + 20 = 26$$

$$x = \frac{D_x}{D} = \frac{0}{-13} = 0$$

$$y = \frac{D_y}{D} = \frac{26}{-13} = -2$$

Solution set: $\{(0, -2)\}$

51. $12x + 8y = 3$ (1)
$15x + 10 = 9$ (2)

$$D = \begin{vmatrix} 12 & 8 \\ 15 & 10 \end{vmatrix} = 0$$

Since $D = 0$, Cramer's Rule does not apply. Use the elimination method. Multiply equation (1) by 5 and equation (2) by -4, and then add the resulting equations.

$60x + 40y = 15$ (1)
$\underline{-60x - 40y = -36}$ (2)
$0 = -21$ False
The system is inconsistent.
Solution set: $\emptyset$

53. $4x + 3y = 9$
$12x + 9y = 27$

$$D = \begin{vmatrix} 4 & 3 \\ 12 & 9 \end{vmatrix} = 0$$

Cramer's rule cannot be used.
Use the Gauss-Jordan method.
$$\begin{bmatrix} 4 & 3 & | & 9 \\ 12 & 9 & | & 27 \end{bmatrix} = \begin{bmatrix} 4 & 3 & | & 9 \\ 0 & 0 & | & 0 \end{bmatrix} -3R1 + R2$$
The second row shows that the system contains dependent equations. We will use y as the arbitrary variable. Solve for x in terms of y.
$4x + 3y = 9$
$4x = 9 - 3y$
$$x = \frac{9 - 3y}{4}$$

Solution set: $\left\{ \left(\dfrac{9 - 3y}{4}, \ y \right) \right\}$

55. $x + y + z = 4$
$2x - y + 3z = 4$
$4x + 2y - z = -15$

$$D = \begin{vmatrix} 1 & 1 & 1 \\ 2 & -1 & 3 \\ 4 & 2 & -1 \end{vmatrix} = 17$$

$$D_x = \begin{vmatrix} 4 & 1 & 1 \\ 4 & -1 & 3 \\ -15 & 2 & -1 \end{vmatrix} = -68$$

$$D_y = \begin{vmatrix} 1 & 4 & 1 \\ 2 & 4 & 3 \\ 4 & -15 & -1 \end{vmatrix} = 51$$

$$D_z = \begin{vmatrix} 1 & 1 & 4 \\ 2 & -1 & 4 \\ 4 & 2 & -15 \end{vmatrix} = 85$$

$$x = \frac{D_x}{D} = \frac{-68}{17} = -4$$

$$y = \frac{D_y}{D} = \frac{51}{17} = 3$$

$$z = \frac{D_z}{D} = \frac{85}{17} = 5$$

Solution set: $\{(-4, 3, 5)\}$

57. $2x - 3y + z = 8$
$-x - 5y + z = -4$
$3x - 5y + 2x = 12$

$$D = \begin{vmatrix} 2 & -3 & 1 \\ -1 & -5 & 1 \\ 3 & -5 & 2 \end{vmatrix} = -5$$

$$D_x = \begin{vmatrix} 8 & -3 & 1 \\ -4 & -5 & 1 \\ 12 & -5 & 2 \end{vmatrix} = -20$$

$$D_y = \begin{vmatrix} 2 & 8 & 1 \\ -1 & -4 & 1 \\ 3 & 12 & 2 \end{vmatrix} = 0$$

$$D_z = \begin{vmatrix} 2 & -3 & 8 \\ -1 & -5 & -4 \\ 3 & -5 & 12 \end{vmatrix} = 0$$

$$x = \frac{D_x}{D} = \frac{-20}{-5} = 4$$

$$y = \frac{D_y}{D} = \frac{0}{-5} = 0$$

$$z = \frac{D_z}{D} = \frac{0}{-5} = 0$$

Solution set: $\{(4, 0, 0)\}$

59. $2x - y + 3z - 1 = 0$
$-2x + y - 3z - 2 = 0$
$5x - y + z - 2 = 0$

Rewrite the system.
$2x - y + 3z = 1$ (1)
$-2x + y - 3z = 2$ (2)
$5x - y + z = 2$ (3)

$$D = \begin{vmatrix} 2 & -1 & 3 \\ -2 & 1 & -3 \\ 5 & -1 & 1 \end{vmatrix} = 0$$

Since $D = 0$, Cramer's rule does not apply. Use the elimination method to complete the solution.
Add equations (1) and (2).
$2x - y + 3z = 1$
$\underline{-2x + y - 3z = 2}$
$ 0 = 3$ False
The system is inconsistent.
Solution set: $\emptyset$

61. $3x - 2y + 4z = 1$
$4x + y - 5z = 2$
$-6x + 4y - 8z = -2$

$$D = \begin{vmatrix} 3 & -2 & 4 \\ 4 & 1 & -5 \\ -6 & 4 & -8 \end{vmatrix} = 0$$

Cramer's rule cannot be used.

Use the Gauss-Jordan method.

$$\left[\begin{array}{ccc|c} 3 & -2 & 4 & 1 \\ 4 & 1 & -5 & 2 \\ -6 & 4 & -8 & -2 \end{array}\right]$$

$$\left[\begin{array}{ccc|c} 1 & -\frac{2}{3} & \frac{4}{3} & \frac{1}{3} \\ 4 & 1 & -5 & 2 \\ -6 & 4 & -8 & -2 \end{array}\right] \quad \frac{1}{3}\text{R1}$$

$$\left[\begin{array}{ccc|c} 1 & -\frac{2}{3} & \frac{4}{3} & \frac{1}{3} \\ 0 & \frac{11}{3} & -\frac{31}{3} & \frac{2}{3} \\ 0 & 0 & 0 & 0 \end{array}\right] \quad \begin{array}{l} -4\text{R1} + \text{R2} \\ 6\text{R1} + \text{R3} \end{array}$$

$$\left[\begin{array}{ccc|c} 1 & -\frac{2}{3} & \frac{4}{3} & \frac{1}{3} \\ 0 & 1 & \frac{-31}{11} & \frac{2}{11} \\ 0 & 0 & 0 & 0 \end{array}\right] \quad \frac{3}{11}\text{R2}$$

$$\left[\begin{array}{ccc|c} 1 & 0 & -\frac{6}{11} & \frac{5}{11} \\ 0 & 1 & \frac{-31}{11} & \frac{2}{11} \\ 0 & 0 & 0 & 0 \end{array}\right] \quad \frac{2}{3}\text{R2} + \text{R1}$$

The third row of the last matrix shows that the system has dependent equations.
We will give the solution set with z as the arbitrary variable. From the first two rows of the final matrix, we obtain the equations
$$x - \frac{6}{11}z = \frac{5}{11} \quad (1)$$
$$y - \frac{31}{11}z = \frac{2}{11}. \quad (2)$$
Equation (1) gives us
$$x = \frac{6}{11}z + \frac{5}{11},$$
and equation (2) gives us
$$y = \frac{31}{11}z + \frac{2}{11}.$$
Solution set:
$$\left\{\left(\frac{6z + 5}{11}, \ \frac{31z + 2}{11}, \ z\right)\right\}$$

63. $3x + 5y = -7$
$2x + 7z = 2$
$4y + 3z = -8$

$$D = \begin{vmatrix} 3 & 5 & 0 \\ 2 & 0 & 7 \\ 0 & 4 & 3 \end{vmatrix} = -114$$

$$D_x = \begin{vmatrix} -7 & 5 & 0 \\ 2 & 0 & 7 \\ -8 & 4 & 3 \end{vmatrix} = -114$$

$D_y = \begin{vmatrix} 3 & -7 & 0 \\ 2 & 2 & 7 \\ 0 & -8 & 3 \end{vmatrix} = 228$

$D_z = \begin{vmatrix} 3 & 5 & -7 \\ 2 & 0 & 2 \\ 0 & 4 & -8 \end{vmatrix} = 0$

$x = \dfrac{D_x}{D} = \dfrac{-114}{-114} = 1$

$y = \dfrac{D_y}{D} = \dfrac{228}{-114} = -2$

$z = \dfrac{D_z}{D} = \dfrac{0}{-114} = 0$

Solution set: $\{(1, -2, 0)\}$

65. $5x - 2y = 3$
$\quad\;\; 4y + z = 8$
$\quad\; x + 2z = 4$

$D = \begin{vmatrix} 5 & -2 & 0 \\ 0 & 4 & 1 \\ 1 & 0 & 2 \end{vmatrix} = 38$

$D_x = \begin{vmatrix} 3 & -2 & 0 \\ 8 & 4 & 1 \\ 4 & 0 & 2 \end{vmatrix} = 48$

$D_y = \begin{vmatrix} 5 & 3 & 0 \\ 0 & 8 & 1 \\ 1 & 4 & 2 \end{vmatrix} = 63$

$D_z = \begin{vmatrix} 5 & -2 & 3 \\ 0 & 4 & 8 \\ 1 & 0 & 4 \end{vmatrix} = 52$

$x = \dfrac{D_x}{D} = \dfrac{48}{38} = \dfrac{24}{19}$

$y = \dfrac{D_y}{D} = \dfrac{63}{38}$

$z = \dfrac{D_z}{D} = \dfrac{52}{38} = \dfrac{26}{19}$

Solution set: $\left\{\left(\dfrac{24}{19}, \dfrac{63}{38}, \dfrac{26}{19}\right)\right\}$

67. $\dfrac{\sqrt{3}}{2}(W_1 + W_2) = 100$
$\qquad W_1 - W_2 = 0$

Use the distributive property to rewrite the first equation; then use Cramer's rule.

$\dfrac{\sqrt{3}}{2}W_1 + \dfrac{\sqrt{3}}{2}W_2 = 100$
$\qquad\quad W_1 - W_2 = 0$

$D = \begin{vmatrix} \frac{\sqrt{3}}{2} & \frac{\sqrt{3}}{2} \\ 1 & -1 \end{vmatrix} = -\sqrt{3}$

$D_{W_1} = \begin{vmatrix} 100 & \frac{\sqrt{3}}{2} \\ 0 & -1 \end{vmatrix} = -100$

$D_{W_2} = \begin{vmatrix} \frac{\sqrt{3}}{2} & 100 \\ 1 & 0 \end{vmatrix} = -100$

$W_1 = \dfrac{D_{W_1}}{D} = \dfrac{-100}{-\sqrt{3}} = \dfrac{100}{\sqrt{3}} = \dfrac{100\sqrt{3}}{3} \approx 58$

$W_2 = \dfrac{D_{W_2}}{D} = \dfrac{-100}{-\sqrt{3}} \approx 58$

Both W_1 and W_2 are approximately 58 lb.

69. $bx + y = a^2$
$\quad\; ax + y = b^2$

$D = \begin{vmatrix} b & 1 \\ a & 1 \end{vmatrix} = b - a$

$D_x = \begin{vmatrix} a^2 & 1 \\ b^2 & 1 \end{vmatrix} = a^2 - b^2$

$D_y = \begin{vmatrix} b & a^2 \\ a & b^2 \end{vmatrix} = b^3 - a^3$

$x = \dfrac{D_x}{D} = \dfrac{a^2 - b^2}{b - a}$

$\quad = \dfrac{(a + b)(a - b)}{(b - a)}$

Factor numerator as difference of two squares

$\quad = -(a + b) = -a - b$

$y = \dfrac{D_y}{D} = \dfrac{a^3 - a^3}{b - a}$

$\quad = \dfrac{(b - a)(b^2 + ab + a^2)}{b - a}$

Factor numerator as difference of two cubes

$\quad = b^2 + ab + a^2$

Solution set:
$\{(-a - b,\; a^2 + ab + b^2)\}$

71. $b^2x + a^2y = b^2$
$\quad\; ax + by = a$

$D = \begin{vmatrix} b^2 & a^2 \\ a & b \end{vmatrix} = b^3 - a^3$

Note that for Cramer's rule to apply, $b^3 \neq a^3$, which is equivalent to $b \neq a$ or $b - a \neq 0$.

$$D_x = \begin{vmatrix} b^2 & a^2 \\ a & b \end{vmatrix} = b^3 - a^3$$

$$D_y = \begin{vmatrix} b^2 & b^2 \\ a & a \end{vmatrix} = ab^2 - ab^2 = 0$$

$$x = \frac{D_x}{D} = \frac{b^3 - a^3}{b^3 - a^3} = 1$$

$$y = \frac{D_y}{D} = \frac{0}{b^3 - a^3} = 0$$

Solution set: $\{(1, 0)\}$

73. One estimate might be $(1987, 610)$.

From Cramer's rule, $x = \dfrac{D_x}{D}$ and $y = \dfrac{D_y}{D}$.

$$D = \begin{vmatrix} 40 & -1 \\ 30 & 1 \end{vmatrix} = 40(1) - 30(-1) = 70$$

$$D_x = \begin{vmatrix} 78,860 & -1 \\ 60,227 & 1 \end{vmatrix} = 78,860(1) - 60,227(-1)$$

$$= 139,087$$

$$D_y = \begin{vmatrix} 40 & 78,860 \\ 30 & 60,227 \end{vmatrix} = 40(60,227) - 30(78,860)$$

$$= 43,280$$

$$x = \frac{139,087}{70} \approx 1987 \text{ and } y = \frac{43,280}{70} \approx 618$$

The solution of the system of equations is $(1987, 618)$.

Section 8.4

Exercises

1. $\dfrac{5}{3x(2x+1)} = \dfrac{A}{3x} + \dfrac{B}{2x+1}$

$$5 = A(2x+1) + B(3x)$$

Substitute $-\dfrac{1}{2}$ and 0 for x:

$$5 = A\left[(2)\left(-\frac{1}{2}\right) + 1\right] + B\left[(3)\left(-\frac{1}{2}\right)\right]$$

$$5 = -\frac{3}{2}B$$

$$-\frac{10}{3} = B$$

$$5 = A(2 \cdot 0 + 1) + B(3 \cdot 0)$$

$$5 = A$$

$$\frac{5}{3x(2x+1)} = \frac{5}{3x} + \frac{\left(-\frac{10}{3}\right)}{2x+1}$$

$$\frac{5}{3x(2x+1)} = \frac{5}{3x} + \frac{-10}{3(2x+1)}$$

3. $\dfrac{4x+2}{(x+2)(2x-1)} = \dfrac{A}{x+2} + \dfrac{B}{2x-1}$

$$4x + 2 = A(2x-1) + B(x+2)$$

Substitute $\dfrac{1}{2}$ and -2 for x:

$$4\left(\frac{1}{2}\right) + 2 = A\left(2 \cdot \frac{1}{2} - 1\right) + B\left(\frac{1}{2} + 2\right)$$

$$4 = \frac{5}{2}B$$

$$\frac{8}{5} = B$$

$$4(-2) + 2 = A[2(-2) - 1] + B(-2 + 2)$$

$$-6 = -5A$$

$$\frac{6}{5} = A$$

$$\frac{4x+2}{(x+2)(2x-1)} = \frac{6}{5(x+2)} + \frac{8}{5(2x-1)}$$

5. $\dfrac{x}{x^2 + 4x - 5} = \dfrac{x}{(x+5)(x-1)}$

$$\frac{x}{(x+5)(x-1)} = \frac{A}{x+5} + \frac{B}{x-1}$$

$$x = A(x-1) + B(x+5)$$

Substitute 1 and -5 for x:

$$1 = A(1-1) + B(1+5)$$

$$1 = 6B$$

$$\frac{1}{6} = B$$

$$-5 = A(-5-1) + B(-5+5)$$

$$-5 = -6A$$

$$\frac{5}{6} = A$$

$$\frac{x}{(x+5)(x-1)} = \frac{5}{6(x+5)} + \frac{1}{6(x-1)}$$

7. $\dfrac{2x}{(x+1)(x+2)^2} = \dfrac{A}{x+1} + \dfrac{B}{x+2} + \dfrac{C}{(x+2)^2}$

$$2x = A(x+2)^2 + B(x+1)(x+2) + C(x+1)$$

Substitute -2 and -1 for x:

$$2(-2) = A(-2+2)^2 + B(-2+1)(-2+2) + C(-2+1)$$

$$-4 = -C$$

$$4 = C$$

$$2(-1) = A(-1+2)^2 + B(-1+1)(-1+2) + C(-1+1)$$

$$-2 = A$$

Substitute any other number for x and use $A = -2$, $C = 4$ to find B. Let $x = 0$:

$2(0) = (-2)(0+2)^2 + B(0+1)(0+2) + 4(0+1)$

$0 = -8 + 2B + 4$

$4 = 2B$

$2 = B$

$$\frac{2x}{(x+1)(x+2)^2} = \frac{-2}{x+1} + \frac{2}{x+2} + \frac{4}{(x+2)^2}$$

9. $\dfrac{4}{x(1-x)} = \dfrac{A}{x} + \dfrac{B}{1-x}$

$4 = A(1-x) + Bx$

Substitute 1 and 0 for x:

$4 = A(1-1) + B(1)$

$4 = B$

$4 = A(1-0) + B(0)$

$4 = A$

$$\frac{4}{x(1-x)} = \frac{4}{x} + \frac{4}{1-x}$$

11. $\dfrac{4x^2 - x - 15}{x(x+1)(x-1)} = \dfrac{A}{x} + \dfrac{B}{x+1} + \dfrac{C}{x-1}$

$4x^2 - x - 15 = A(x+1)(x-1) + Bx(x-1)$
$\qquad\qquad\qquad + C(x)(x+1)$

Substitute 0, −1, and 1 for x:

$4(0)^2 - 0 - 15 = A(0+1)(0-1) + B(0)(0-1)$
$\qquad\qquad\qquad\qquad + C(0)(0+1)$

$15 = A$

$4(-1)^2 - (-1) - 15 = A(-1+1)(-1-1)$
$\qquad\qquad\qquad + B(-1)(-1-1) + C(-1)(-1+1)$

$-10 = 2B$

$-5 = B$

$4(1)^2 - 1 - 15 = A(1+1)(1-1) + B(1)(1-1)$
$\qquad\qquad\qquad\qquad + C(1)(1+1)$

$-12 = 2C$

$-6 = C$

$$\frac{4x^2 - x - 15}{x(x+1)(x-1)} = \frac{15}{x} + \frac{-5}{x+1} + \frac{-6}{x-1}$$

13. $\dfrac{x^2}{x^2 + 2x + 1}$

First find the quotient since the numerator and denominator have the same degree.

$$
\begin{array}{r}
1 \\
x^2 + 2x + 1 \overline{)\ x^2 } \\
\underline{x^2 + 2x + 1} \\
-2x - 1
\end{array}
$$

Find the partial fraction decomposition for the remainder.

$\dfrac{-2x-1}{(x+1)^2} = \dfrac{A}{x+1} + \dfrac{B}{(x+1)^2}$

$-2x - 1 = A(x+1) + B$

Substitute −1 for x.

$-2(-1) - 1 = A(-1+1) + B$

$1 = B$

To find A substitute any other value for x and use $B = 1$. Let $x = 2$.

$-2(2) - 1 = A(2+1) + 1$

$-5 = 3A + 1$

$-6 = 3A$

$-2 = A$

$$\frac{x^2}{x^2 + 2x + 1} = 1 + \frac{-2}{x+1} + \frac{1}{(x+1)^2}$$

15. $\dfrac{2x^5 + 3x^4 - 3x^3 - 2x^2 + x}{2x^2 + 5x + 2}$

The degree of the numerator is greater than the degree of the denominator, so first find the quotient.

$$
\begin{array}{r}
x^3 - x^2 \\
2x^2 + 5x + 2 \overline{)\ 2x^5 + 3x^4 - 3x^3 - 2x^2 + x} \\
\underline{2x^5 + 5x^4 + 2x^3} \\
-2x^4 - 5x^3 - 2x^2 + x \\
\underline{-2x^4 - 5x^3 - 2x^2} \\
x
\end{array}
$$

Find the partial fraction decomposition for the remainder.

$\dfrac{x}{(2x+1)(x+2)} = \dfrac{A}{2x+1} + \dfrac{B}{x+2}$

$x = A(x+2) + B(2x+1)$

Substitute −2 and $-\dfrac{1}{2}$ for x.

$-2 = A(-2+2) + B[2(-2)+1]$

$-2 = -3B$

$\dfrac{2}{3} = B$

$-\dfrac{1}{2} = A\left(-\dfrac{1}{2}+2\right) + B\left[2\left(-\dfrac{1}{2}\right)+1\right]$

$-\dfrac{1}{2} = A\left(\dfrac{3}{2}\right)$

$-\dfrac{1}{3} = A$

$\dfrac{2x^5 + 3x^4 - 3x^3 - 2x^2 + x}{2x^2 + 5x + 2}$

$\qquad = x^3 - x^2 + \dfrac{-1}{3(2x+1)} + \dfrac{2}{3(x+2)}$

17. $\dfrac{x^3+4}{9x^3-4x}$

Find the quotient since the degrees of the numerator and denominator are the same.

$$9x^3-4x\overline{)\,x^3+0x^2+0x+4\,}$$

quotient $\dfrac{1}{9}$

$$\underline{x^3\quad\ -\tfrac{4}{9}x}$$
$$\tfrac{4}{9}x+4$$

Find the partial fraction decomposition for the remainder.

$$\dfrac{\tfrac{4}{9}x+4}{x(3x+2)(3x-2)}=\dfrac{A}{x}+\dfrac{B}{3x+2}+\dfrac{C}{3x-2}$$

$$\dfrac{4}{9}x+4=A(3x+2)(3x-2)$$
$$+\,Bx(3x-2)+Cx(3x+2)$$

Substitute $-\dfrac{2}{3},\dfrac{2}{3}$, and 0 for x.

$$\dfrac{4}{9}\left(-\dfrac{2}{3}\right)+4=A\left[3\left(-\dfrac{2}{3}\right)+2\right]\left[3\left(-\dfrac{2}{3}\right)-2\right]$$
$$+\,B\left(-\dfrac{2}{3}\right)\left[3\left(-\dfrac{2}{3}\right)-2\right]$$
$$+\,C\left(-\dfrac{2}{3}\right)\left[3\left(-\dfrac{2}{3}\right)+2\right]$$

$$\dfrac{100}{27}=\dfrac{8}{3}B$$
$$\dfrac{25}{18}=B$$

$$\dfrac{4}{9}\left(\dfrac{2}{3}\right)+4=C\left(\dfrac{2}{3}\right)\left[3\left(\dfrac{2}{3}\right)+2\right]$$
$$\dfrac{116}{27}=\dfrac{8}{3}C$$
$$\dfrac{29}{18}=C$$

$$\dfrac{4}{9}(0)+4=A(3\cdot 0+2)(3\cdot 0-2)$$
$$4=-4A$$
$$-1=A$$

$$\dfrac{x^3+4}{9x^3-4x}=\dfrac{1}{9}+\dfrac{-1}{x}+\dfrac{25}{18(3x+2)}+\dfrac{29}{18(3x-2)}$$

19. $\dfrac{-3}{x^2(x^2+5)}=\dfrac{A}{x}+\dfrac{B}{x^2}+\dfrac{Cx+D}{x^2+5}$

$$-3=Ax(x^2+5)+B(x^2+5)$$
$$+(Cx+D)x^2$$

Combine like terms on the right side of the equation (Method 2).

$$-3=Ax^3+5Ax+Bx^2+5B+Cx^3+Dx^2$$
$$-3=(A+C)x^3+(B+D)x^2+(5A)x+5B$$

Equate the coefficients of like powers of x on the two sides of the equation.

$$0x^3=(A+C)x^3$$
$$0=A+C$$
$$0x^2=(B+D)x^2$$
$$0=B+D$$
$$0x=5Ax$$
$$0=5A$$
$$0=A$$
$$0=C$$
$$-3=5B$$
$$-\dfrac{3}{5}=B$$
$$\dfrac{3}{5}=D$$

$$\dfrac{-3}{x^2(x^2+5)}=\dfrac{-3}{5x^2}+\dfrac{3}{5(x^2+5)}$$

21. $\dfrac{3x-2}{(x+4)(3x^2+1)}=\dfrac{A}{x+4}+\dfrac{Bx+C}{3x^2+1}$

$$3x-2=A(3x^2+1)+(Bx+C)(x+4)$$

Substitute -4 for x to solve for A.

$$3(-4)-2=A[3(-4)^2+1]$$
$$-14=49A$$
$$-\dfrac{2}{7}=-\dfrac{14}{49}=A$$

Now substitute any other two values for x to find B and C, use $A=-\dfrac{2}{7}$. Let $x=0$ and 1.

$$3(0)-2=-\dfrac{2}{7}(3\cdot 0^2+1)+(B\cdot 0+C)(0+4)$$
$$-2=-\dfrac{2}{7}+4C$$
$$-\dfrac{12}{7}=4C$$
$$-\dfrac{3}{7}=C$$

$$3(1)-2=-\dfrac{2}{7}(3\cdot 1^2+1)+\left[B\cdot 1+\left(-\dfrac{3}{7}\right)\right](1+4)$$
$$1=-\dfrac{8}{7}+5B-\dfrac{15}{7}$$
$$\dfrac{30}{7}=5B$$
$$\dfrac{6}{7}=B$$

$$\dfrac{3x-2}{(x+4)(3x^2+1)}=\dfrac{-2}{7(x+4)}+\dfrac{6x-3}{7(3x^2+1)}$$

23. $\dfrac{1}{x(2x+1)(3x^2+4)} = \dfrac{A}{x} + \dfrac{B}{2x+1} + \dfrac{Cx+D}{3x^2+4}$

$1 = A(2x+1)(3x^2+4) + Bx(3x^2+4)$
$\qquad + (Cx+D)(x)(2x+1)$

Substitute 0 and $-\dfrac{1}{2}$ for x to solve for A and B.

$1 = A(2\cdot 0 + 1)(3\cdot 0^2 + 4)$

$1 = 4A$

$\dfrac{1}{4} = A$

$1 = B\left(-\dfrac{1}{2}\right)\left[3\left(-\dfrac{1}{2}\right)^2 + 4\right]$

$1 = -\dfrac{19}{8}B$

$-\dfrac{8}{19} = B$

Choose two other values for x to solve for C and D. Let $x = 1$ and -1.

$1 = \left(\dfrac{1}{4}\right)(2\cdot 1 + 1)(3\cdot 1^2 + 4)$

$\qquad + \left(-\dfrac{8}{19}\right)(1)(3\cdot 1^2 + 4)$

$\qquad + (C\cdot 1 + D)(1)(2\cdot 1 + 1)$

$1 = \dfrac{21}{4} + \dfrac{-56}{19} + 3C + 3D$

$1 = \dfrac{175}{76} + 3C + 3D$

$-\dfrac{99}{76} = 3C + 3D$

$-\dfrac{33}{76} = C + D$

$1 = \left(\dfrac{1}{4}\right)[2(-1)+1][3(-1)^2 + 4]$

$\qquad + \left(-\dfrac{8}{19}\right)(-1)[3(-1)^2 + 4]$

$\qquad + [C(-1)+D](-1)[2(-1)+1]$

$1 = -\dfrac{7}{4} + \dfrac{56}{19} + (-C) + D$

$-\dfrac{15}{76} = -C + D$

Solve the equation by elimination.

$-\dfrac{33}{76} = C + D$

$-\dfrac{15}{76} = -C + 3D$

$-\dfrac{48}{76} = 2D$

$-\dfrac{24}{76} = D$

$-\dfrac{15}{76} = -C + \left(-\dfrac{24}{76}\right)$

$-\dfrac{9}{76} = C$

$\dfrac{1}{x(2x+1)(3x^2+4)} = \dfrac{1}{4x} + \dfrac{-8}{19(2x+1)}$

$\qquad\qquad + \dfrac{-9x-24}{76(3x^2+4)}$

25. $\dfrac{3x-1}{x(2x^2+1)^2} = \dfrac{A}{x} + \dfrac{Bx+C}{2x^2+1} + \dfrac{Dx+F}{(2x^2+1)^2}$

$3x - 1 = A(2x^2+1)^2 + (Bx+C)(x)(2x^2+1)$
$\qquad\qquad + (Dx+F)x$

Let $x = 0$ and solve for A.

$3(0) - 1 = A(2\cdot 0^2 + 1)^2$

$-1 = A$

Combine like terms on the right side of the equation.

$3x - 1 = (-1)(4x^4 + 4x^2 + 1)$
$\qquad\quad + (Bx+C)(2x^3 + x) + Dx^2 + Fx$

$3x - 1 = -4x^4 - 4x^2 - 1 + 2Bx^4 + Bx^2 + 2Cx^3$
$\qquad\quad + Cx + Dx^2 + Fx$

$3x - 1 = (-4+2B)x^4 + (2C)x^3 + (-4+B+D)x^2$
$\qquad\quad + (C+F)x - 1 \qquad\qquad\qquad (1)$

Equate the coefficients of like powers of x on the two sides of equation **(1)**.

$0 = -4 + 2B$

$4 = 2B$

$2 = B$

$0 = 2C$

$0 = C$

$0 = -4 + B + D$

$4 = 2 + D$

$2 = D$

$3 = C + F$

$3 = 0 + F$

$3 = F$

$\dfrac{3x-1}{x(2x^2+1)^2} = \dfrac{-1}{x} + \dfrac{2x}{2x^2+1} + \dfrac{2x+3}{(2x^2+1)^2}$

27.

$$\frac{-x^4 - 8x^2 + 3x - 10}{(x+2)(x^2+4)^2}$$

$$= \frac{A}{x+2} + \frac{Bx+C}{x^2+4} + \frac{Dx+E}{(x^2+4)^2}$$

$$-x^4 - 8x^2 + 3x - 10$$

$$= A(x^2+4)^2 + (Bx+C)(x+2)(x^2+4)$$

$$+ (Dx+E)(x+2)$$

Let $x = -2$ and solve for A.

$$-(-2)^4 - 8(-2)^2 + 3(-2) - 10 = A[(-2)^2+4]^2$$

$$-16 - 32 - 6 - 10 = 64A$$

$$-64 = 64A$$

$$-1 = A$$

Combine like terms on the right side of the equation:

$$= (-1)(x^4 + 8x^2 + 16) + (Bx+C)(x^3 + 4x + 2x^2$$

$$+ 8) + Dx^2 + 2Dx + Ex + 2E$$

$$= -x^4 - 8x^2 - 16 + Bx^4 + 4Bx^2 + 2Bx^3 + 8Bx$$

$$+ Cx^3 + 4Cx + 2Cx^2 + 8C + Dx^2 + 2Dx + Ex$$

$$+ 2E$$

$$= (-1+B)x^4 + (2B+C)x^3 + (-8+4B+2C+D)x^2$$

$$+ (8B+4C+2D+E)x + (-16+8C+2E)$$

Equate the coefficients of like powers of x on the two sides of the equation.

$$-x^4 = (-1+B)x^4$$

$$-1 = -1 + B$$

$$0 = B$$

$$0x^3 = (2B+C)x^3$$

$$0 = 2B + C$$

$$0 = 2(0) + C$$

$$0 = C$$

$$-8x^2 = (-8+4B+2C+D)x^2$$

$$-8 = -8 + 4(0) + 2(0) + D$$

$$-8 = -8 + D$$

$$0 = D$$

$$-10 = -16 + 8C + 2E$$

$$-10 = -16 + 8(0) + 2E$$

$$6 = 2E$$

$$3 = E$$

$$\frac{-x^4 - 8x^2 + 3x - 10}{(x+2)(x^2+4)^2} = \frac{-1}{x+2} + \frac{3}{(x^2+4)^2}$$

29.

$$\frac{5x^5 + 10x^4 - 15x^3 + 4x^2 + 13x - 9}{x^3 + 2x^2 - 3x}$$

Since the degree of the numerator is higher than the degree of the denominator, first find the quotient.

$$\begin{array}{r} 5x^2 \\ x^3 + 2x^2 - 3x \overline{\smash{\big)}\, 5x^5 + 10x^4 - 15x^3 + 4x^2 + 13x - 9} \\ \underline{5x^5 + 10x^4 - 15x^3 } \\ 4x^2 + 13x - 9 \end{array}$$

Find the partial fraction decomposition of the remainder.

$$\frac{4x^2 + 13x - 9}{x^3 + 2x^2 - 3x} = \frac{4x^2 + 13x - 9}{x(x^2 + 2x - 3)}$$

$$= \frac{4x^2 + 13x - 9}{x(x+3)(x-1)}$$

$$= \frac{A}{x} + \frac{B}{x+3} + \frac{C}{x-1}$$

$$4x^2 + 13x - 9 = A(x+3)(x-1) + Bx(x-1)$$

$$+ Cx(x+3)$$

Let $x = -3$, 1, and 0 to solve for A, B, and C.

$$4(-3)^2 + 13(-3) - 9 = B(-3)(-3-1)$$

$$-12 = 12B$$

$$-1 = B$$

$$4(1)^2 + 13(1) - 9 = C(1)(1+3)$$

$$8 = 4C$$

$$2 = C$$

$$4(0)^2 + 13(0) - 9 = A(0+3)(0-1)$$

$$-9 = -3A$$

$$3 = A$$

$$\frac{5x^5 + 10x^4 - 15x^3 + 4x^2 + 13x - 9}{x^3 + 2x^2 - 3x}$$

$$= 5x^2 + \frac{3}{x} + \frac{-1}{x+3} + \frac{2}{x-1}$$

31.

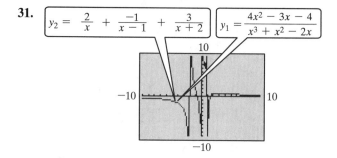

The graphs coincide; correct.

33.

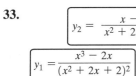

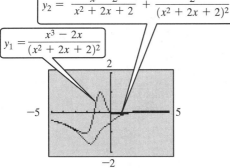

The graphs do not coincide; not correct.

Section 8.5

Connections *(page 676)*

1. A circle and a line can intersect in 0, 1, or 2 points.

2. A circle and a parabola can intersect in 0, 1, 2, 3 or 4 points.

3. Two circles can intersect in 0, 1, 2, or an infinite number of points.

Exercises

7. The system $x^2 - y = 4$
$$x + y = -2$$
cannot have more than two solutions because a parabola and a line cannot intersect in more than two points.

9. $y = x^2$ (1)
$$x + y = 2 \quad (2)$$
Use the substitution method.
Solve equation (2) for y.
$y = 2 - x$
Substitute this result into equation (1).
$$2 - x = x^2$$
$$x^2 + x - 2 = 0$$
$$(x + 2)(x - 1) = 0$$
$$x = -2 \text{ or } x = 1$$
If $x = -2$, then $y = (-2)^2 = 4$.

If $x = 1$, then $y = 1^2 = 1$.
Solution set: $\{(-2, 4), (1, 1)\}$

11. $y = (x - 1)^2$ (1)
$$x - 3y = -1 \qquad (2)$$
Substitute $(x - 1)^2$ for y in equation (2).
$$x - 3(x - 1)^2 = -1$$
$$x - 3(x^2 - 2x + 1) = -1$$
$$x - 3x^2 + 6x - 3 = -1$$
$$-3x^2 + 7x - 2 = 0$$
$$3x^2 - 7x + 2 = 0$$
$$(3x - 1)(x - 2) = 0$$
$$x = \frac{1}{3} \text{ or } x = 2$$
If $x = \frac{1}{3}$, then
$$y = \left(\frac{1}{3} - 1\right)^2$$
$$= \left(-\frac{2}{3}\right)^2$$
$$= \frac{4}{9}.$$
If $x = 2$, then $y = (2 - 1)^2$
$$= 1^2$$
$$= 1.$$
Solution set: $\left\{\left(\frac{1}{3}, \frac{4}{9}\right), (2, 1)\right\}$

13. $y = x^2 + 4x$ (1)
$$2x - y = -8 \qquad (2)$$
Substitute $x^2 + 4x$ for y in equation (2).
$$2x - (x^2 + 4x) = -8$$
$$2x - x^2 - 4x = -8$$
$$x^2 + 2x - 8 = 0$$
$$(x - 2)(x + 4) = 0$$
$$x = 2 \text{ or } x = -4$$
If $x = 2$, then
$$y = 2^2 + 4(2)$$
$$= 4 + 8$$
$$= 12.$$
If $x = -4$, then $y = (-4)^2 + 4(-4) = 0$.
Solution set: $\{(2, 12), (-4, 0)\}$

15. $3x^2 + 2y^2 = 5$ (1)

$\qquad x - y = -2$ (2)

Solve equation (2) for x.

$x = y - 2$

Substitute $y - 2$ for x in equation (1).

$$3(y-2)^2 + 2y^2 = 5$$

$$3(y^2 - 4y + 4) + 2y^2 = 5$$

$$2y^2 - 12y + 12 + 2y^2 = 5$$

$$5y^2 - 12y + 7 = 0$$

$$(5y - 7)(y - 1) = 0$$

$$y = \frac{7}{5} \text{ or } y = 1$$

If $y = \frac{7}{5}$, then,

$$x = y - 2$$

$$= \frac{7}{5} - 2$$

$$= -\frac{3}{5}.$$

If $y = 1$, then $x = 1 - 2 = -1$.

Solution set: $\left\{ \left(-\frac{3}{5}, \frac{7}{5} \right), (-1, \ 1) \right\}$

17. $x^2 + y^2 = 8$ (1)

$\quad x^2 - y^2 = 0$ (2)

Use the addition method.

Add equations (1) and (2).

$$\begin{array}{r} x^2 + y^2 = 8 \\ \underline{x^2 - y^2 = 0} \\ 2x^2 \qquad = 8 \\ x^2 \qquad = 4 \end{array}$$

$$x = \pm 2$$

If $x = 2$, then

$$2^2 - y^2 = 0$$

$$4 - y^2 = 0$$

$$y^2 = 4$$

$$y = \pm 2.$$

If $x = -2$, then

$$(-2)^2 - y^2 = 0$$

$$4 - y^2 = 0$$

$$y^2 = 4$$

$$y = \pm 2.$$

Solution set: $\{(2, 2), (2, -2), (-2, 2), (-2, -2)\}$

19. $5x^2 - y^2 = 0$ (1)

$\quad 3x^2 + 4y^2 = 0$ (2)

Multiply equation (1) by 4 and add to equation (2).

$$\begin{array}{r} 20x^2 - 4y^2 = 0 \\ \underline{3x^2 + 4y^2 = 0} \\ 23x^2 \qquad = 0 \\ x = 0 \end{array}$$

If $x = 0$,

$$5(0)^2 - y^2 = 0,$$

$$y = 0$$

Solution set: $\{(0, 0)\}$

21. $3x^2 + y^2 = 3$ (1)

$\quad 4x^2 + 5y^2 = 26$ (2)

Multiply equation (1) by -5 and add to equation (2).

$$\begin{array}{r} -15x^2 - 5y^2 = -15 \\ \underline{4x^2 + 5y^2 = 26} \\ -11x^2 \qquad\quad = 11 \\ x^2 = -1 \\ x = \pm i \end{array}$$

If $x = \pm i$,

$$3(\pm i)^2 + y^2 = 3$$

$$-3 + y^2 = 3$$

$$y^2 = 6$$

$$y = \pm\sqrt{6}.$$

Solution set:

$\{(i, \ \sqrt{6}), (-i, \ \sqrt{6}), (i, \ -\sqrt{6}), (-i, \ -\sqrt{6})\}$

23. $2x^2 + 3y^2 = 5$ (1)

$\quad 3x^2 - 4y^2 = -1$ (2)

Multiply equation (1) by 4 and equation (2) by 3 and add.

$$\begin{array}{r} 8x^2 + 12y^2 = 20 \\ \underline{9x^2 - 12y^2 = -3} \\ 17x^2 \qquad\quad = 17 \\ x^2 = 1 \\ x = \pm 1 \end{array}$$

If $x = \pm 1$,

$$2(\pm 1)^2 + 3y^2 = 5$$

$$3y^2 = 3$$

$$y^2 = 1$$

$$y = \pm 1.$$

Solution set:

$\{(1, 1), (1, -1), (-1, 1), (-1, -1)\}$

25. $2x^2 + 2y^2 = 20$ (1)

$4x^2 + 4y^2 = 30$ (2)

We eliminate x^2 by multiplying equation (1) by -2 and adding the result to equation (2).

$-4x^2 - 4y^2 = -40$

$\underline{4x^2 + 4y^2 = 30}$

$0 = -10$

This is a false statement.

The solution set is $\emptyset$.

27. $2x^2 - 3y^2 = 8$ (1)

$6x^2 + 5y^2 = 24$ (2)

$-6x^2 + 9y^2 = -24$

$\underline{6x^2 + 9y^2 = 24}$ Multiply (1) by -3.

$18y^2 = 0$

$y^2 = 0$

$y = 0$

If $y = 0$, then

$2x^2 - 3(0) = 8$

$2x^2 = 8$

$x^2 = 4$

$x = \pm 2.$

Solution set: $\{(2, 0), (-2, 0)\}$

29. $xy = 8$ (1)

$3x + 2y = -16$ (2)

Use the substitution method.

Solve equation (1) for y.

$y = \dfrac{8}{x}$ (3)

Substitute $\dfrac{8}{x}$ for y in equation (2) and solve for x.

$3x + 2\left(\dfrac{8}{x}\right) = -16$

$3x^2 + 16 = -16x$ Multiply by x.

$3x^2 + 16x + 16 = 0$

$(x + 4)(3x + 4) = 0$

$x = -4$ or $x = -\dfrac{4}{3}$

If $x = -4$, then

$-4(y) = 8$

$y = -2.$

If $x = -\dfrac{4}{3}$, then

$-\dfrac{4}{3}(y) = 8$

$y = -6.$

Solution set: $\left\{(-4, -2), \left(-\dfrac{4}{3}, -6\right)\right\}$

31. $-5xy + 2 = 0$ (1)

$x - 15y = 5$ (2)

Solve equation (1) for y.

$-5xy + 2 = 0$

$-5xy = -2$

$y = \dfrac{2}{5x}$ (3)

Substitute $\dfrac{2}{5x}$ for y in equation (2) and solve for x.

$x - 15\left(\dfrac{2}{5x}\right) = 5$

$x - \dfrac{6}{x} = 5$

$x^2 - 6 = 5x$ Multiply by x.

$x^2 - 5x - 6 = 0$

$(x - 6)(x + 1) = 0$

$x = 6$ or $x = -1$

Substitute $x = 6$ and $x = -1$ into equation (3) to find the corresponding value of y.

If $x = 6$, then

$y = \dfrac{2}{5 \cdot 6}$

$= \dfrac{1}{15}.$

If $x = -1$, then

$y = \dfrac{2}{5(-1)}$

$= -\dfrac{2}{5}.$

Solution set: $\left\{\left(6, \dfrac{1}{15}\right), \left(-1, -\dfrac{2}{5}\right)\right\}$

33. $5x^2 - 2y^2 = 6$ (1)

$xy = 2$ (2)

Solve equation (2) for y.

$y = \dfrac{2}{x}$ (3)

Substitute $\dfrac{2}{x}$ for y in equation (1) and solve for x.

$5x^2 - 2\left(\dfrac{2}{x}\right)^2 = 6$

$5x^2 - \dfrac{8}{x^2} = 6$

$5x^4 - 8 = 6x^2$ Multiply by x^2.

$5x^4 - 6x^2 - 8 = 0$

$(5x^2 + 4)(x^2 - 2) = 0$

$$5x^2 + 4 = 0$$
$$x^2 = -\frac{4}{5}$$
$$x = \pm\frac{2}{\sqrt{5}}i$$
$$= \pm\frac{2\sqrt{5}}{5}i$$
$$x^2 - 2 = 0$$
$$x^2 = 0$$
$$x = \pm\sqrt{2}.$$

Substitute each value of x into equation (3) to find the corresponding value of y.

$$x = \frac{2}{\sqrt{5}}i,$$
$$y = \frac{2\sqrt{5}}{2i}$$
$$= \frac{\sqrt{5}}{i} \cdot \frac{i}{i}$$
$$= -i\sqrt{5}.$$

If $x = -\frac{2}{\sqrt{5}}i,$
$$y = -\frac{2\sqrt{5}}{2i}$$
$$= -\frac{\sqrt{5}}{i} \cdot \frac{i}{i}$$
$$= i\sqrt{5}.$$

If $x = \sqrt{2},$
$$y = \frac{2}{\sqrt{2}}$$
$$= \sqrt{2}.$$

If $x = -\sqrt{2}$, $y = -\sqrt{2}.$
Solution set:

$$\left\{ \left(\frac{2\sqrt{5}}{5}i, -i\sqrt{5} \right), \left(-\frac{2\sqrt{5}}{5}i, i\sqrt{5} \right), \right.$$
$$\left. (\sqrt{2}, \sqrt{2}), (-\sqrt{2}, -\sqrt{2}) \right\}$$

35. $3x^2 + xy + 3y^2 = 7$ (1)
$\qquad x^2 + y^2 = 2$ (2)
$$3x^2 + xy + 3y^2 = 7$$
$$\underline{-3x^2 \qquad -3y^2 = -6} \quad \text{Multiply (2)}$$
$$xy = 1 \quad \text{by } -3.$$
$$y = \frac{1}{x} \quad (3)$$

Substitute $\frac{1}{x}$ for y in equation (2) and solve for x.

$$x^2 + \frac{1}{x^2} = 2$$
$$x^4 + 1 = 2x^2 \quad \text{Multiply by } x^2.$$
$$x^4 - 2x^2 + 1 = 0$$
$$(x^2 - 1)(x^2 - 1) = 0$$
$$x^2 - 1 = 0$$
$$x^2 = 1$$
$$x = \pm 1$$

Substitute each value of x into equation (3) to find the corresponding value of y.
If $x = 1,$
$$y = \frac{1}{1}$$
$$y = 1.$$
If $x = -1$
$$y = \frac{1}{-1}$$
$$y = -1.$$
Solution set: $\{(1, 1), (-1, -1)\}$

37. $3x^2 + 2xy - y^2 = 9$ (1)
$\qquad x^2 - xy + y^2 = 9$ (2)
This system can be solved using a combination of the addition and substitution methods.
First add equations (1) and (2).
$$3x^2 + 2xy - y^2 = 9 \quad (1)$$
$$\underline{x^2 - xy + y^2 = 9} \quad (2)$$
$$4x^2 + xy \qquad = 18 \quad (3)$$
Solve equation (3) for y.
$$xy = 18 - 4x^2$$
$$y = \frac{18 - 4x^2}{x} \quad (4)$$

Substitute $\frac{18 - 4x^2}{x}$ for y in equation (2) and solve for x.

$$x^2 - x\left(\frac{18 - 4x^2}{x} \right) + \left(\frac{18 - 4x^2}{x} \right) = 9$$
$$x^2 - 18 + 4x^2 + \frac{324 - 144x^2 + 16x^4}{x^2} = 9$$
$$x^4 - 18x^2 + 4x^4 + 324 - 144x^2 + 16x^4 = 9x^2$$
$$\text{Multiply by } x^2.$$
$$21x^4 - 171x^2 + 324 = 0$$
$$\text{Combine terms.}$$
$$7x^4 - 57x^2 + 108 = 0$$

Divide by 3.

$$(7x^2 - 36)(x^2 - 3) = 0$$
$$7x^2 - 36 = 0$$
$$7x^2 = 36$$
$$x^2 = \frac{36}{7}$$

$x = \pm\dfrac{6}{\sqrt{7}}$ $\qquad$ $x^2 - 3 = 0$

$ = \pm\dfrac{6\sqrt{7}}{7}$ $\qquad$ $x^2 = 3$

$\qquad\qquad\qquad x = \pm\sqrt{3}$

Substitute each value of x into equation (4) to find the corresponding value of y.

If $x = \dfrac{6\sqrt{7}}{7}$,

$$y = \frac{18 - 4\left(\dfrac{36}{7}\right)}{\dfrac{6\sqrt{7}}{7}}$$

$$ = -\frac{3\sqrt{7}}{7}.$$

If $x = -\dfrac{6\sqrt{7}}{7}$, $\ y = \dfrac{3\sqrt{7}}{7}$.

If $x = \sqrt{3}$,

$$y = \frac{18 - 4\cdot 3}{\sqrt{3}}$$

$$ = 2\sqrt{3}.$$

If $x = -\sqrt{3}$, $\ y = -2\sqrt{3}$.

Solution set:

$$\left\{ \left(\frac{6\sqrt{7}}{7}, -\frac{3\sqrt{7}}{7}\right), \left(-\frac{6\sqrt{7}}{7}, \frac{3\sqrt{7}}{7}\right), \right.$$
$$\left. (\sqrt{3},\ 2\sqrt{3}),\ (-\sqrt{3},\ -2\sqrt{3}) \right\}$$

39. $2x + |y| = 4 \qquad$ (1)

$x^2 + y^2 = 5 \qquad$ (2)

Solve equation (1) for y.

$|y| = -2x + 4$

$y = -2x + 4 \qquad$ (3) or

$y = 2x - 4 \qquad$ (4)

Substitute $-2x + 4$ for y in equation (2) and solve for x.

$$x^2 + (-2x + 4)^2 = 5$$
$$x^2 + 4x^2 - 16x + 16 = 5$$
$$5x^2 - 16x + 11 = 0$$
$$(5x - 11)(x - 1) = 0$$

$x = \dfrac{11}{5}$ or $x = 1$

Substituting $2x - 4$ for y in equation (2) leads to the same solutions.

Solve equation (2) for y.

$x^2 + y^2 = 5$

$\qquad y = \pm\sqrt{5 - x^2} \qquad$ (5)

Substitute each value of x into equation (5) to find the corresponding values of y.

If $x = 1$,

$y = \pm\sqrt{5 - 1}$

$ = \pm 2.$

If $x = \dfrac{11}{5}$,

$$y = \pm\sqrt{5 - \left(\frac{11}{5}\right)^2}$$

$$ = \sqrt{\frac{125 - 121}{25}}$$

$$ = \pm\frac{2}{5}.$$

Check $\left(\dfrac{11}{5},\ \pm\dfrac{2}{5}\right)$ in equation (2).

$$2\left(\frac{11}{5}\right) + \left|\pm\frac{2}{5}\right| = \frac{22}{5} + \frac{2}{5}$$

$$\phantom{2\left(\frac{11}{5}\right) + \left|\pm\frac{2}{5}\right|} = \frac{24}{5} \neq 4$$

$\left(\dfrac{11}{5},\ \pm\dfrac{2}{5}\right)$ does not check, but $(1, \pm 2)$ does check because

$2(1) + |\pm 2| = 2 + 2 = 4$.

Solution set: $\{(1, 2), (1, -2)\}$

41. Shift the graph of $y = |x|$ one unit to the right to obtain the graph of $y = |x - 1|$.

42. Shift the graph of $y = x^2$ four units down to obtain the graph of $y = x^2 - 4$.

43. If $x - 1 \geq 0$, $|x - 1| = x - 1$.

Thus, if $x \geq 1$, $|x - 1| = x - 1$.

If $x - 1 < 0$, $|x - 1| = -(x - 1)$.

Thus, if $x < 1$, $|x - 1| = 1 - x$.

Therefore,

$$y = \begin{cases} x - 1 \text{ if } x \geq 1 \\ 1 - x \text{ if } x < 1. \end{cases}$$

44. $x^2 - 4 = x - 1$ if $x \geq 1$.

$x^2 - 4 = 1 - x$ if $x < 1$.

45. $x^2 - 4 = x - 1$ if $x \geq 1$

$x^2 - x - 3 = 0$

$$x = \frac{-(-1) \pm \sqrt{(-1)^2 - 4(1)(-3)}}{2(1)}$$

$$x = \frac{1 \pm \sqrt{13}}{2}$$

$\dfrac{1 + \sqrt{13}}{2} \approx 2.3 \geq 1$

but $\dfrac{1 - \sqrt{13}}{2} \approx -1.3 \not\geq 1.$

Therefore,

$x = \dfrac{1 + \sqrt{13}}{2}.$

$x^2 - 4 = 1 - x$ if $x < 1$

$x^2 + x - 5 = 0$

$$x = \frac{-1 \pm \sqrt{(1)^2 - 4(1)(-5)}}{2(1)}$$

$$x = \frac{-1 \pm \sqrt{21}}{2}$$

$\dfrac{-1 - \sqrt{21}}{2} \approx -2.8 < 1$

but $\dfrac{-1 + \sqrt{21}}{2} \approx 1.8 \not< 1.$

Therefore, $x = \dfrac{-1 - \sqrt{21}}{2}.$

46. If $y = |x - 1|$ and $x = \dfrac{1 + \sqrt{13}}{2},$

$$y = \left| \frac{1 + \sqrt{13}}{2} - 1 \right|$$

$$y = \left| \frac{1 + \sqrt{13}}{2} - \frac{2}{2} \right|$$

$$y = \left| \frac{-1 + \sqrt{13}}{2} \right|$$

$$y = \frac{-1 + \sqrt{13}}{2},$$

since $\dfrac{-1 + \sqrt{13}}{2} \geq 0.$

One solution of the system is

$\left(\dfrac{1 + \sqrt{13}}{2},\ \dfrac{-1 + \sqrt{13}}{2} \right).$

If $y = 1 - x$ and $x = \dfrac{-1 - \sqrt{21}}{2},$

$$y = 1 - \left(\frac{-1 - \sqrt{21}}{2} \right)$$

$$y = \frac{2}{2} + \frac{1 + \sqrt{21}}{2}$$

$$y = \frac{3 + \sqrt{21}}{2}$$

The other solution of the system is

$\left(\dfrac{-1 - \sqrt{21}}{2},\ \dfrac{3 + \sqrt{21}}{2} \right).$

47. $y = \log(x + 5)$

$y = x^2$

Use $y_1 = \log(x + 5)$ and $y_2 = x^2$.

Using a graphing calculator, we find that the two curves intersect in two points whose coordinates are approximately $(-.79, .62)$ and $(.88, .77)$.

Solution set:

$\{(-.79, .62), (.88, .77)\}$

49. $y = e^{x+1}$

$2x + y = 3$

Use $y_1 = e^{x+1}$ and $y_2 = 3 - 2x$.

Using a graphing calculator, find that the curve and the line intersect in one point whose coordinates are approximately $(.06, 2.88)$.

Solution set: $\{(.06, 2.88)\}$

51. Let $x = $ one number;

$y = $ the other number.

$x + y = 17$ (1)

$xy = 42$ (2)

Solve equation (1) for y.

$y = 17 - x$

Substitute this into equation (2).

$x(17 - x) = 42$

$17x - x^2 = 42$

$0 = x^2 - 17x + 42$

$0 = (x - 3)(x - 14)$

$x = 3$ or $x = 14$

Using equation (1), if $x = 3$

$3 + y = 17$

$y = 14.$

If $x = 14,$

$14 + y = 17$

$y = 3.$

The two numbers are 3 and 14.

53. Let $x =$ one number;

$y =$ the other number.

$x^2 + y^2 = 100$ (1)

$x^2 - y^2 = 28$ (2)

We add the equations to eliminate y^2.

$2x^2 = 128$

$x^2 = 64$

$x = \pm 8$

Substitute -8 for x in equation (1).

$(-8)^2 + y^2 = 100$

$64 + y^2 = 100$

$y^2 = 36$

$y = \pm 6$

Similarly, if we substitute 8 for x in equation (1), we obtain $y = \pm 6$. The two numbers are -8 and 6, -8 and -6, 8 and 6, or 8 and -6.

55. Let x and y represent the numbers.

$\dfrac{x}{y} = \dfrac{9}{2}$ (1)

$xy = 162$ (2)

Rewrite (1) as $x = \dfrac{9}{2} y$, substitute $\dfrac{9}{2} y$ for x in (2).

$\left(\dfrac{9}{2} y \right) y = 162$

$\dfrac{9}{2} y^2 = 162$

$y^2 = 36$

$y = \pm 6$

If $y = 6$, $x = \dfrac{9}{2}(6) = 27$.

If $y = -6$, $x = \dfrac{9}{2}(-6) = -27$.

The two numbers are either 6 and 27, or -6 and -27.

57. If the system

$3x - 2y = 9$ (1)

$x^2 + y^2 = 25$ (2)

has a solution, the line and the circle intersect.

Solve equation (1) for x.

$3x = 9 + 2y$

$x = 3 + \dfrac{2}{3} y$ (3)

Substitute into equation (2).

$\left(3 + \dfrac{2}{3} y \right)^2 + y^2 = 25$

$9 + 4y + \dfrac{4}{9} y^2 + y^2 = 25$

$\dfrac{13}{9} y^2 + 4y - 16 = 0$

$13y^2 + 36y - 144 = 0$

Use the quadratic formula.

$y = \dfrac{-36 \pm \sqrt{(36)^2 - 4(13)(144)}}{2(13)}$

$= \dfrac{-36 \pm \sqrt{8784}}{26}$

$y \approx 2.2$ or $y \approx -4.989$

Substitute into equation (3) to find x.

If $y = 2.22$,

$x = 3 + \dfrac{2}{3}(2.22)$

$= 4.48$.

If $y = -4.989$,

$x = 3 + \dfrac{2}{3}(-4.989)$

$= -.326$.

Thus, the circle and the line do intersect, in fact twice, at $(4.48, 2.22)$ and at $(-3.26, -4.99)$.

59. $x + 2y = b$ (1)

$x^2 + y^2 = 9$ (2)

Solve equation (1) for x.

$x = b - 2y$

Substitute $b - 2y$ for x in equation (2).

$(b - 2y)^2 + y^2 = 9$

$b^2 - 4by + 4y^2 + y^2 = 9$

$b^2 - 4by + 5y^2 - 9 = 0$

$5y^2 - 4b \cdot y + (b^2 - 9) = 0$

This equation will have a unique solution when the discriminant is 0.

$(-4b)^2 - 4(5)(b^2 - 9) = 0$

$16b^2 - 20b^2 + 180 = 0$

$-4b^2 = -180$

$b^2 = 45$

$b = \pm \sqrt{45}$ or $\pm 3\sqrt{5}$

The line $x + 2y = b$ will touch the circle $x^2 + y^2 = 9$ in only one point if $b = \pm 3\sqrt{5}$.

61. (a) $p = \dfrac{2000}{2000 - q}$

$p = \dfrac{7000 - 3q}{2q}$

Set the equations equal to each other and solve for q.

$\dfrac{2000}{2000 - q} = \dfrac{7000 - 3q}{2q}$

$2q(2000) = (2000 - q)(7000 - 3q)$

$4000q = 14{,}000{,}000 - 13{,}000q + 3q^2$

$0 = 3q^2 - 17{,}000q + 14{,}000{,}000$

$0 = (3q - 14{,}000)(q - 1000)$

$3q - 14{,}000 = 0$ or $q - 1000 = 0$

$q \approx 4667$ $\qquad\qquad$ $q = 1000$

Reject $q \approx 4667$ since it would yield a negative supply. The equilibrium demand is 1000 units.

(b) Substitute 1000 for q in either equation and solve for p.

$p = \dfrac{2000}{2000 - 1000}$

$p = 2$

The equilibrium price is \$2.

63. $y_1 = -6.63x^2 + 177x - 885$

$y_2 = -1.61x^2 + 41.5x - 104$

Set the equations equal to each other and solve for x.

$-6.63x^2 + 177x - 885 = -1.61x^2 + 41.5x - 104$

$-5.02x^2 + 135.5 - 781 = 0$

$x = \dfrac{-135.5 \pm \sqrt{(135.5)^2 - 4(-5.02)(-781)}}{2(-5.02)}$

$x \approx \dfrac{-135.5 \pm 51.75}{-10.04}$

When $x \approx 8.34$,

$y = -6.63(8.34)^2 + 177(8.34) - 8.85$

$y \approx 130.2$.

When $x \approx 18.65$,

$y = -6.63(18.65)2 + 177(18.65) - 885$

$y \approx 110.0$.

The approximate solutions are (8.3, 130.2) and (18.7, 110.0).

The first solution indicates that during 1988, there were approximately 130 homicides by both firearms and other weapons. The second solution indicates that during 1998, there were approximately 110 homicides by both firearms and other weapons.

65. (a) The emission of carbon is increasing with time. The carbon emissions from the former USSR and Eastern Europe have surpassed the emissions of Western Europe.

(b) They were equal in 1962 or 1963 when the levels were approximately 400 million metric tons.

(c) $W = E$

$375(1.008)^{(t-1950)}$

$\quad = 260(1.038)^{(t-1950)}$

$\log[375(1.008)^{(t-1950)}]$

$\quad = \log[260(1.038)^{(t-1950)}]$

$\log 375 + (t - 1950)\log 1.008$

$\quad = \log 260 + (t - 1950)\log 1.038$

$\log 375 - \log 260$

$\quad = (t - 1950)\log 1.038$

$\quad\quad - (t - 1950)\log 1.008$

$\log 375 - \log 260$

$\quad = (\log 1.038 - \log 1.008)$

$\quad\quad \cdot (t - 1950)$

$\dfrac{\log 375 - \log 260}{\log 1.038 - \log 1.008}$

$\quad = t - 1950$

$t = 1950 + \dfrac{\log 375 - \log 260}{\log 1.038 - \log 1.008}$

$t \approx 1962.49$

If $t = 1962.49$,

$W = 375(1.008)^{(1962.49-1950)} \approx 414.24$.

In 1962, the emission levels were equal and were approximately 414 million metric tons.

Section 8.6

Exercises

1. $x \le 3$

The boundary is the vertical line $x = 3$. Because of the = portion of $\le$, the boundary is included in the graph, so draw a solid line. Select any test point not on the line, such as (0, 0). Since $0 \le 3$ is a true statement, shade the side of the line containing (0, 0).

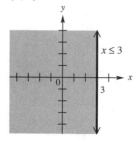

3. $x + 2y \leq 6$

The boundary is the line $x = 2y = 6$, which can be graphed using the x-intercept 6 and y-intercept 3. The boundary is included in the graph, so draw a solid line.
Use $(0, 0)$ as a test point.
Since $0 + 2(0) \leq 6$ is a true statement, shade the line of the graph containing $(0, 0)$.

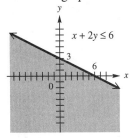

5. $2x + 3y \geq 4$

The boundary is the line $2x + 3y = 4$.
The boundary is included in the graph, so draw a solid line.
Use $(0, 0)$ as a test point.
Since $2(0) + 3(0) \geq 4$ is false, shade the side of the line that does not contain $(0, 0)$.

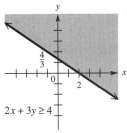

7. $3x - 5y > 6$

The boundary is the line $3x - 5y = 6$.
Since the inequality symbol is $>$, not $\geq$, the boundary is not included in the graph, so draw a dashed line.
Use $(0, 0)$ as a test point.
Since $3(0) - 5(0) > 6$ is false, shade the side of the line that does not include $(0, 0)$.

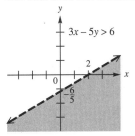

9. $5x \leq 4y - 2$

The boundary is the line $5x = 4y - 2$.
Draw a solid line.
Use $(0, 0)$ as a test point.
Since $5(0) \leq 4(0) - 2$ is false, shade the side of the line that does not include $(0, 0)$.

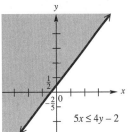

11. $y = 3x^2 + 2$

The boundary is the parabola $y = 3x^2 + 2$. Since the inequality symbol is $<$, draw a dashed curve.
Use $(0, 0)$ as a test point.
Since $0 < 3(0)^2 + 2$ is true, shade the region that includes $(0, 0)$.

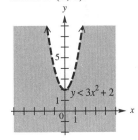

13. $y > (x - 1)^2 + 2$

The boundary is the parabola $y = (x - 1)^2 + 2$, with vertex $(1, 2)$. Since the inequality symbol is $>$, draw a dashed curve.
Use $(0, 0)$ as a test point.
Since $0 > (0 - 1)^2 + 2$ is false, shade the region that does not include $(0, 0)$.

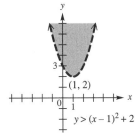

15. $x^2 + (y+3)^2 \leq 16$

The boundary is a circle with center $(0, -3)$ and radius 4. Draw a solid circle to show that the boundary is included in the graph.
Use $(0, 0)$ as a test point.

Since $0^2 + (0+3)^2 \leq 16$ is true, shade the region that includes $(0, 0)$, that is, the interior of the circle.

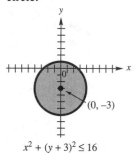

$x^2 + (y+3)^2 \leq 16$

19. $Ax + By \geq C, B > 0$

Solve this inequality for y.
$By \geq -Ax + C$
Since $B > 0$, the inequality symbol is not reversed when both sides are divided by B.
$$y \geq -\frac{A}{B}x + \frac{C}{B}$$
You would shade above the line.

21. The graph of $(x-5)^2 + (y-2)^2 = 4$
is a circle with center $(5, 2)$ and radius
$r = \sqrt{4} = 2$. The graph of $(x-5)^2 + (y-2)^2 < 4$
is the region inside this circle.
The correct response is B.

23. The graph of $y \leq 3x - 6$ is the region below the line with slope 3 and y-intercept -6. This is graph C.

25. The graph of $y \leq -3x - 6$ is the region below the line with slope -3 and y-intercept -6. This is graph A.

27. $x + y \geq 0$

$2x - y \geq 3$

Graph $x + y = 0$ as a solid line through the origin with a slope of -1. Shade the region above this line.
Graph $2x - y = 3$ as a solid line with x-intercept $\frac{3}{2}$ and y-intercept -3. Shade the region below this line.
The solution set is the common region, which is shaded in the final graph.

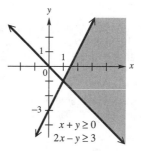

$x + y \geq 0$
$2x - y \geq 3$

29. $2x + y > 2$

$x - 3y < 6$

Graph $2x + y = 2$ as a dashed line with y-intercept 2 and x-intercept 1. Shade the region above this line.
Graph $x - 3y = 6$ as a dashed line with y-intercept -2 and x-intercept 6. Shade the region above this line.
The solution set is the common region, which is shaded in the final graph.

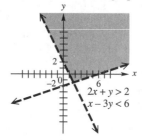

$2x + y > 2$
$x - 3y < 6$

31. $3x + 5y \leq 15$

$x - 3y \geq 9$

Graph $3x + 5y = 15$ as a solid line with y-intercept 3 and x-intercept 5. Shade the region below this line.
Graph $x - 3y = 9$ as a solid line with y-intercept -3 and x-intercept 9. Shade the region below this line.
The solution set is the common region, which is shaded in the final graph.

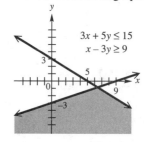

$3x + 5y \leq 15$
$x - 3y \geq 9$

33. $4x - 3y \le 12$

$y \le x^2$

Graph $4x - 3y = 12$ as a solid line with y-intercept -4 and x-intercept 3. Shade the region above this line.

Graph the solid parabola $y = x^2$. Shade the region outside of this parabola.

The solution set is the intersection of these two regions, which is shaded in the final graph.

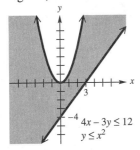

35. $x + y \le 9$

$x \le -y^2$

Graph $x + y = 9$ as a solid line with y-intercept 9 and x-intercept 9. Shade the region below this line.

Graph the solid horizontal parabola $x = -y^2$. Shade the region inside of this parabola.

The solution set is the intersection of these two regions, which is shaded in the final graph.

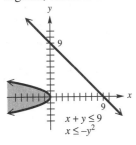

37. $y \le (x + 2)^2$

$y \ge -2x^2$

Graph $y = (x + 2)^2$ as a solid parabola opening up with a vertex at (–2, 0). Shade the region below the parabola.

Graph $y = -2x^2$ as a solid parabola opening down with a vertex at the origin. Shade the region above the parabola.

The solution set is the intersection of these two regions, which is shaded in the final graph.

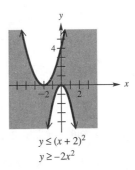

$y \le (x + 2)^2$
$y \ge -2x^2$

39. $x + y \le 36$

$-4 \le x \le 4$

Graph $x + y = 36$ as a solid line with y-intercept 36 and x-intercept 36. Shade the region below this line.

Graph the vertical lines $x = -4$ and $x = 4$ as solid lines. Shade the region between these lines.

The solution set is the intersection of these two regions, which is shaded in the final graph.

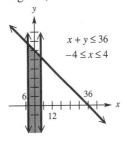

41. $y > (x - 2)^2 + 3$

$y \le -(x - 1)^2 + 6$

Graph $y = (x - 2)^2 + 3$ as a solid parabola opening up with a vertex at (2, 3). Shade the region above the parabola.

Graph $y = -(x - 1)^2 + 6$ as a solid parabola opening down with a vertex at (1, 6). Shade the region below the parabola.

The solution set is the intersection of these two regions, which is shaded in the final graph.

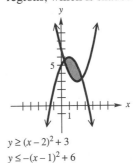

$y \ge (x - 2)^2 + 3$
$y \le -(x - 1)^2 + 6$

43. $3x - 2y \geq 6$

$x + y \leq -5$

$y \leq 4$

Graph $3x - 2y = 6$ as a solid line and shade the region below it.

Graph $x + y = -5$ as a solid line and shade the region below it.

Graph $y = 4$ as a solid horizontal line and shade the region below it.

The solution set is the intersection of these three regions, which is shaded in the final graph.

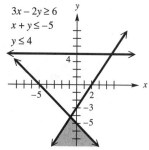

45. $-2 < x < 2$

$y > 1$

$x - y > 0$

Graph the vertical lines $x = -2$ and $x = 2$ as a dashed line. Shade the region between the two lines.

Graph the horizontal line $y = 1$ as a dashed line. Shade the region above the line.

Graph the line $x - y = 0$ as a dashed line through the origin with a slope of 1. Shade the region below this line.

The solution set is the intersection of these three regions, which is shaded in the final graph.

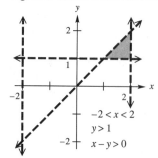

47. $x \leq 4$

$x \geq 0$

$y \geq 0$

$x + 2y \geq 2$

Graph $x = 4$ as a solid vertical line. Shade the region to the left of this line.

Graph $x = 0$ as a solid vertical line. (This is the y-axis.) Shade the region to the right of this line.

Graph $y = 0$ as a solid horizontal line. (This is the x-axis.) Shade the region above the line.

Graph $x + 2y = 2$ as a solid line with x-intercept 2 and y-intercept 1. Shade the region above the line. The solution set is the intersection of these four regions, which is shaded in the final graph.

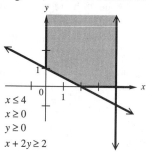

49. $2x + 3y \leq 12$

$2x + 3y > -6$

$3x + y < 4$

$x \geq 0$

$y \geq 0$

Graph $2x + 3y = 12$ as a solid line and shade the region below it.

Graph $2x + 3y = 6$ as a dashed line and shade the region above it.

Graph $3x + y = 4$ as a dashed line and shade the region below it.

$x = 0$ is the y-axis. Shade the region to the right of it.

$y = 0$ is the x-axis. Shade the region above it.

The solution set is the intersection of these five regions, which is shaded in the final graph. The open circles at $(0, 4)$ and $\left(\dfrac{4}{3},\ 0\right)$ indicate that those points are not included in the solution (due to the fact that the boundary line on which they lie, $3x + y = 4$, is not included).

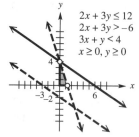

51. $y \leq \left(\dfrac{1}{2}\right)^{x}$

$y \leq 4$

Graph $y = \left(\dfrac{1}{2}\right)^{x}$ using a solid curve passing through the points $(-2, 4)$, $(-1, 2)$, $(0, 1)$, $\left(1, \dfrac{1}{2}\right)$, and $\left(2, \dfrac{1}{4}\right)$. Shade the region below this curve.

Graph the solid horizontal line $y = 4$ and shade the region above it.

The solution set consists of the intersection of these two regions, which is shaded in the final graph.

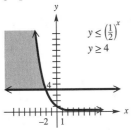

53. $y \le \log x$

$y \ge |x - 2|$

Graph $y = \log x$ using a solid curve passing through the points $\left(\dfrac{1}{10},\ 1\right)$, $(1,\ 0)$, and $(10,\ 1)$.

Shade the region below the curve.

Graph $y = |x - 2|$ using a solid curve. This is the same as the graph of $y = |x|$, but translated 2 units to the right. Shade the region above.

The solution set is the intersection of the two regions, which is shaded in the final graph.

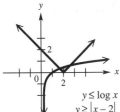

55. $y \ge x$

$y \le 2x - 3$

The graph is the region above the line $y = x$ and below the line $y = 2x - 2$. This is graph A.

57. $x^2 + y^2 \le 16$

$y \ge 0$

The graph is the region inside the circle $x^2 + y^2 = 16$ and above the horizontal line $y = 0$. This is graph B.

59. $3x + 2y \ge 6$

Solve the inequality for y.

$2y \le -3x + 6$

$y \le -\dfrac{3}{2}x + 3$

Enter $y_1 = (-3/2)x + 3$ and use a graphing calculator to shade the region above the line.

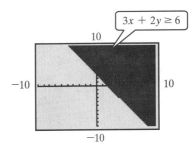

61. $x + y \ge 2$

$x + y \le 6$

Solve each inequality for y.

Enter $y_1 = -x + 2$ and $y_2 = -x + 6$.

Use a graphing calculator to shade the region above the graph of $y_1 = -x + 2$ and below the graph of $y_2 = -x + 6$.

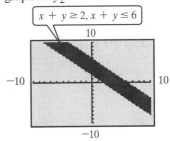

63. $y \ge 2^x$

$y \le 8$

Enter $y_1 = 2^x$ and $y_2 = 8$. Use a graphing calculator to shade the region above the graph of $y_1 = 2x$ and below the graph of $y_2 = 8$.

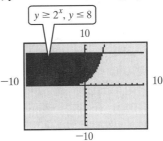

65.   Since we are in the first quadrant, $x \ge 0$ and $y \ge 0$.

The lines $x + 2y - 8 = 0$ and $x + 2y = 12$ are parallel, with $x + 2y = 12$ having the greater y-intercept.

Therefore, we must shade below $x + 2y = 12$ and above $x + 2y - 8 = 0$

The system is

$x + 2y - 8 \ge 0$

$x + 2y \le 12$

$x \ge 0,\ \ y \le 0$.

67.

Point	Value of $3x + 5y$
(1, 1)	$3(1) + 5(1) = 8 \leftarrow$ Minimum
(2, 7)	$3(2) + 5(7) = 41$
(5, 10)	$3(5) + 5(10) = 65 \leftarrow$ Maximum
(6, 3)	$3(6) + 5(3) = 33$

The maximum value is 65 at (5, 10).
The minimum value is 8 at (1, 1).

69.

Point	Value of $3x + 5y$
(1, 0)	$3(1) + 5(0) = 8 \leftarrow$ Minimum
(1, 10)	$3(1) + 5(10) = 53$
(7, 9)	$3(7) + 5(9) = 66 \leftarrow$ Maximum
(7, 6)	$3(7) + 5(6) = 51$

The maximum value is 66 at (7, 9).
The minimum value is 3 at (1, 0).

71.

Point	Value of $10y$
(1, 0)	$10(0) = 0 \quad \leftarrow$ Minimum
(1, 10)	$10(10) = 100 \leftarrow$ Maximum
(7, 9)	$10(9) = 90$
(7, 6)	$10(6) = 60$

The maximum value is 100 at (1, 10).
The minimum value is 0 at (1, 0).

73. Let $x =$ the number of Brand X pills;
$y =$ the number of Brand Y pills.
Then
$$3000x + 1000y \geq 6000$$
$$45x + 50y \geq 195$$
$$75x + 200y \geq 600$$
$$x \geq 0, \quad y \geq 0.$$
Graph $3000x + 1000y = 6000$ as a solid line with
x-intercept 2 and y-intercept 6. Shade the region
above the line.
Graph $45x + 50y = 195$ as a solid line with
x-intercept $4.\overline{3}$ and y-intercept 3.9. Shade the
region above the line.
Graph $75x + 200y = 600$ as a solid line with
x-intercept 8 and y-intercept 3. Shade the region
above the line.
Graph $x = 0$(the y-axis) as a solid line and shade
the region to the right of it.
Graph $y = 0$(the x-axis) as a solid line and shade
the region above it.
The region of feasible solutions is the intersection
of these five regions.

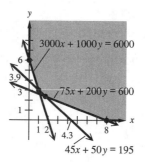

75. (a) Let $x =$ number of cartons of food;
$y =$ number of cartons of clothing.
$$40x + 10y \leq 16,000 \quad \text{Total weight}$$
$$20x + 30y < 18,000 \quad \text{Total volume}$$
$$x \geq 0$$
$$y \geq 0$$
Maximize $10x + 8y$.
First, graph the solution of the system.

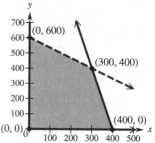

Evaluate $10x + 8y$ at each vertex.

Point	Number of people helped $10x + 8y$
(0, 0)	$10(0) + 8(0) = 0$
(0, 600)	$10(0) + 8(600) = 4800$
(300, 400)	$10(300) + 8(400) = 6200$
	$\uparrow$ Maximum
(400, 0)	$10(400) + 8(0) = 4000$

Send 300 cartons of food and 400 cartons of
clothes to maximize the number of people
helped.

(b) The maximum number of people helped is
6200.

77. Let $x =$ number of cabinet #1
$y =$ number of cabinet #2.
The cost constraint is $10x + 20y \leq 140$.
The space constraint is $6x + 8y \leq 72$.
Since the numbers of cabinets cannot be negative,
we also have $x \geq 0$, $y \geq 0$.
We want to maximize the volume of files, given
by $8x + 12y$.
Find the region of feasible solutions by graphing.

$20x + 40y = 280$ (shade below)

$6x + 8y = 72$ (shade below)

$x = 0$ (shade right)

$y = 0$ (shade above)

The vertices are at $(0, 7)$, $(0, 0)$, $(12, 0)$, and the intersection of $20x + 40y = 280$ and $6x + 8y = 72$, which is the point $(8, 3)$.

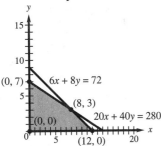

Find the value of $8x + 12y$ at each vertex.

Point	Value = $8x + 12y$
$(0, 7)$	84
$(0, 0)$	0
$(12, 0)$	96
$(8, 3)$	100 ← Maximum

$8x + 12y$ is maximized at $(8, 3)$.
She should get 8 #1 cabinets and 3 #2 cabinets. This will correspond to maximum storage capacity of 100 cu ft.

79. Let x = number of gallons of gasoline;
    y = number of gallons of fuel oil.
The constraints are

$x \geq 0, \ y \geq 0$

$x \geq 2y$

$y \geq 3{,}000{,}000$

$x \leq 6{,}400{,}000.$

Maximize revenue, given by $1.9x + 1.5y$.

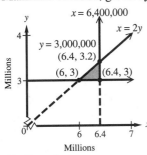

The boundaries are

$x = 0$

$y = 0$

$x = 2y$

$y = 3{,}000{,}000$

$x = 6{,}400{,}000.$

The vertices of the region of feasible solutions are $(6.4, 3)$, $(6, 3)$ and $(6.4, 3.2)$.
Testing these points in the expression to be maximized will show that $(6.4, 3.2)$ will maximize revenue.
6.4 million gallons of gasoline and 3.2 million gallons of fuel oil should be produced for maximum revenue of
$1.9 (6.4) + 1.5(3.2) = 16.96$
or $16,960,000.

81. Look for places where the graph of total presidential campaign spending lies above or intersects the graphs of congressional campaigns spending: 1972–1981 and 1987–1991. The intervals are [1972, 1981] and [1987, 1991].

Section 8.7

Exercises

1. If $\begin{bmatrix} w & x \\ y & z \end{bmatrix} = \begin{bmatrix} 3 & 2 \\ -1 & 4 \end{bmatrix}$,
then $w = 3$, $x = 2$, $y = -1$, and $z = 4$.

3. If $\begin{bmatrix} 2 & 5 & 6 \\ 1 & m & n \end{bmatrix} = \begin{bmatrix} z & y & 2 \\ 1 & 8 & -2 \end{bmatrix}$,
then $2 = z$, $5 = y$, $6 = w$, $m = 8$, and $n = -2$.

5. $\begin{bmatrix} a+2 & 3z+1 & 5m \\ 8k & 0 & 3 \end{bmatrix} + \begin{bmatrix} 3a & 2z & 5m \\ 2k & 5 & 6 \end{bmatrix}$

$= \begin{bmatrix} 10 & -14 & 80 \\ 10 & 5 & 9 \end{bmatrix}$

Add the matrices on the left.

$\begin{bmatrix} 4a+2 & 5z+1 & 10m \\ 10k & 5 & 9 \end{bmatrix} = \begin{bmatrix} 10 & -14 & 80 \\ 10 & 5 & 9 \end{bmatrix}$

For these two matrices to be equal, corresponding elements must be equal, so we have

$4a + 2 = 10 \quad 5z+1 = -14 \quad 10m = 80$

$ 4a = 8 \qquad 5z = -15 \qquad m = 8$

$ a = 2 \qquad\ \ z = -3$

$10k = 10$

$ k = 1.$

Thus, $a = 2$, $z = -3$, $m = 8$, and $k = 1$.

7. $\begin{bmatrix} -4 & 8 \\ 2 & 3 \end{bmatrix}$

This matrix has 2 rows and 2 columns, so it is a 2×2 square matrix.

9. $\begin{bmatrix} -6 & 8 & 0 & 0 \\ 4 & 1 & 9 & 2 \\ 3 & -5 & 7 & 1 \end{bmatrix}$

This matrix has 3 rows and 4 columns, so it is a 3×4 matrix.

11. $\begin{bmatrix} 2 \\ 4 \end{bmatrix}$

This matrix has 2 rows and 1 column, so it is a 2×1 column matrix.

15. $\begin{bmatrix} 6 & -9 & 2 \\ 4 & 1 & 3 \end{bmatrix} + \begin{bmatrix} -8 & 2 & 5 \\ 6 & -3 & 4 \end{bmatrix}$

$= \begin{bmatrix} 6+(-8) & -9+2 & 2+5 \\ 4+6 & 1+(-3) & 3+4 \end{bmatrix}$

$= \begin{bmatrix} -2 & -7 & 7 \\ 10 & -2 & 7 \end{bmatrix}$

17. $\begin{bmatrix} -6 & 8 \\ 0 & 0 \end{bmatrix} - \begin{bmatrix} 0 & 0 \\ -4 & -2 \end{bmatrix}$

$= \begin{bmatrix} -6 & 8 \\ 0 & 0 \end{bmatrix} + \begin{bmatrix} 0 & 0 \\ 4 & 2 \end{bmatrix}$

$= \begin{bmatrix} -6 & 8 \\ 4 & 2 \end{bmatrix}$

19. $\begin{bmatrix} 3x+y & x-2y & 2x \\ 5x & 3y & x+y \end{bmatrix}$

$+ \begin{bmatrix} 2x & 3y & 5x+y \\ 3x+2y & x & 2x \end{bmatrix}$

$= \begin{bmatrix} 5x+y & x+y & 7x+y \\ 8x+2y & x+3y & 3x+y \end{bmatrix}$

21. $\begin{bmatrix} 3 \\ 2 \end{bmatrix} + \begin{bmatrix} 2 & 3 \end{bmatrix}$

These two matrices are not the same size, so they cannot be added.

In Exercises 23–27, $A = \begin{bmatrix} -2 & 4 \\ 0 & 3 \end{bmatrix}$ and $B = \begin{bmatrix} -6 & 2 \\ 4 & 0 \end{bmatrix}$.

23. $2A - B = 2\begin{bmatrix} -2 & 4 \\ 0 & 3 \end{bmatrix} = \begin{bmatrix} -4 & 8 \\ 0 & 6 \end{bmatrix}$.

25. $2A - B = 2\begin{bmatrix} -2 & 4 \\ 0 & 3 \end{bmatrix} - \begin{bmatrix} -6 & 2 \\ 4 & 0 \end{bmatrix}$

$= \begin{bmatrix} -4 & 8 \\ 0 & 6 \end{bmatrix} + \begin{bmatrix} 6 & -2 \\ -4 & 0 \end{bmatrix}$

$= \begin{bmatrix} 2 & 6 \\ -4 & 6 \end{bmatrix}$

27. $-A + \dfrac{1}{2}B = -\begin{bmatrix} -2 & 4 \\ 0 & 3 \end{bmatrix} + \dfrac{1}{2}\begin{bmatrix} -6 & 2 \\ 4 & 0 \end{bmatrix}$

$= \begin{bmatrix} 2 & -4 \\ 0 & -3 \end{bmatrix} + \begin{bmatrix} -3 & 1 \\ 2 & 0 \end{bmatrix}$

$= \begin{bmatrix} -1 & -3 \\ 2 & -3 \end{bmatrix}$

29. $\begin{bmatrix} 1 & 2 \\ 3 & 4 \end{bmatrix}\begin{bmatrix} -1 \\ 7 \end{bmatrix}$

$= \begin{bmatrix} 1(-1) + 2(7) \\ 3(-1) + 4(7) \end{bmatrix}$

$= \begin{bmatrix} 13 \\ 25 \end{bmatrix}$

31. $\begin{bmatrix} 3 & -4 & 1 \\ 5 & 0 & 2 \end{bmatrix}\begin{bmatrix} -1 \\ 4 \\ 2 \end{bmatrix}$

$= \begin{bmatrix} 3(-1) + (-4)(4) + 1(2) \\ 5(-1) + 0(4) + 2(2) \end{bmatrix}$

$= \begin{bmatrix} -17 \\ -1 \end{bmatrix}$

33. $\begin{bmatrix} 5 & 2 \\ -1 & 4 \end{bmatrix}\begin{bmatrix} 3 & -2 \\ 1 & 0 \end{bmatrix} = \begin{bmatrix} 5(3) + 2(1) & 5(-2) + 2(0) \\ -1(3) + 4(1) & -1(-2) + 4(0) \end{bmatrix}$

$= \begin{bmatrix} 17 & -10 \\ 1 & 2 \end{bmatrix}$

35. $\begin{bmatrix} 2 & 2 & -1 \\ 3 & 0 & 1 \end{bmatrix}\begin{bmatrix} 0 & 2 \\ -1 & 4 \\ 0 & 2 \end{bmatrix}$

$= \begin{bmatrix} 2(0) + 2(-1) + (-1)(0) & 2(2) + 2(4) + (-1)(2) \\ 3(0) + 0(-1) + 1(0) & 3(2) + 0(4) + 1(2) \end{bmatrix}$

$= \begin{bmatrix} -2 & 10 \\ 0 & 8 \end{bmatrix}$

37. $\begin{bmatrix} -3 & 0 & 2 & 1 \\ 4 & 0 & 2 & 6 \end{bmatrix}\begin{bmatrix} -4 & 2 \\ 0 & 1 \end{bmatrix}$

It is not possible to find this product because the number of columns of the first matrix (four) is not equal to the number of rows of the second matrix (two).

39. $\begin{bmatrix} -2 & -3 & -4 \\ 2 & -1 & 0 \\ 4 & -2 & 3 \end{bmatrix}\begin{bmatrix} 0 & 1 & 4 \\ 1 & 2 & -1 \\ 3 & 2 & -2 \end{bmatrix} = \begin{bmatrix} -2(0)+(-3)(1)+(-4)(3) & -2(1)+(-3)(2)+(-4)(2) & -2(4)+(-3)(-1)+(-4)(-2) \\ 2(0)+(-1)(1)+0(3) & 2(1)+(-1)(2)+0(2) & 2(4)+(-1)(-1)+0(-2) \\ 4(0)+(-2)(1)+3(3) & 4(1)+(-2)(2)+3(2) & 4(4)+(-2)(-1)+3(-2) \end{bmatrix}$

$= \begin{bmatrix} -15 & -16 & 3 \\ -1 & 0 & 9 \\ 7 & 6 & 12 \end{bmatrix}$

41. $\begin{bmatrix} -2 & 4 & 1 \end{bmatrix}\begin{bmatrix} 3 & -2 & 4 \\ 2 & 1 & 0 \\ 0 & -1 & 4 \end{bmatrix}$

$= \begin{bmatrix} -2(3)+4(2)+1(0) & (-2)(-2)+4(1)+1(-1) & (-2)(4)+4(0)+1(4) \end{bmatrix}$

$= \begin{bmatrix} 2 & 7 & -4 \end{bmatrix}$

In Exercises 43–49, $A = \begin{bmatrix} 4 & -2 \\ 3 & 1 \end{bmatrix}$, $B = \begin{bmatrix} 5 & 1 \\ 0 & -2 \\ 3 & 7 \end{bmatrix}$ and $C = \begin{bmatrix} -5 & 4 & 1 \\ 0 & 3 & 6 \end{bmatrix}$.

43. $BA = \begin{bmatrix} 5 & 1 \\ 0 & -2 \\ 3 & 7 \end{bmatrix}\begin{bmatrix} 4 & -2 \\ 3 & 1 \end{bmatrix}$

$= \begin{bmatrix} 5(4)+1(3) & 5(-2)+1(1) \\ 0(4)+(-2)(3) & 0(-2)+(-2)(1) \\ 3(4)+7(3) & 3(-2)+7(1) \end{bmatrix}$

$= \begin{bmatrix} 23 & -9 \\ -6 & -2 \\ 33 & 1 \end{bmatrix}$

45. $BC = \begin{bmatrix} 5 & 1 \\ 0 & -2 \\ 3 & 7 \end{bmatrix}\begin{bmatrix} -5 & 4 & 1 \\ 0 & 3 & 6 \end{bmatrix}$

$= \begin{bmatrix} 5(-5)+1(0) & 5(4)+1(3) & 5(1)+1(6) \\ 0(-5)+(-2)(0) & 0(4)+(-2)(3) & 0(1)+(-2)(6) \\ 3(-5)+7(0) & 3(4)+7(3) & 3(1)+7(6) \end{bmatrix}$

$= \begin{bmatrix} -25 & 23 & 11 \\ 0 & -6 & -12 \\ -15 & 33 & 45 \end{bmatrix}$

47. $AB = \begin{bmatrix} 4 & -2 \\ 3 & 1 \end{bmatrix}\begin{bmatrix} 5 & 1 \\ 0 & -2 \\ 3 & 7 \end{bmatrix}$ is not possible.

49. $A^2 = AA = \begin{bmatrix} 4 & -2 \\ 3 & 1 \end{bmatrix}\begin{bmatrix} 4 & -2 \\ 3 & 1 \end{bmatrix}$

$= \begin{bmatrix} 4(4)+(-2)(3) & 4(-2)+(-2)(1) \\ 3(4)+1(3) & 3(-2)+1(1) \end{bmatrix}$

$= \begin{bmatrix} 10 & -10 \\ 15 & -5 \end{bmatrix}$

51. Since the answers to 43 and 47 are not equal, $BA \neq AB$.

Since the answers to 45 and 46 are not equal, $BC \neq CB$.

Since the answers to 44 and 48 are not equal, $AC \neq CA$.

No, matrix multiplication is not commutative.

53. For the Rite Aid Corporation, the matrix is:

$\begin{bmatrix} 11375 & 316 & 83000 \\ 6970 & 115 & 73000 \\ 5446 & 159 & 35700 \\ 4534 & 141 & 36700 \\ 4059 & 9 & 27364 \end{bmatrix}$

For the Walgreen Company, the matrix is:

$\begin{bmatrix} 15307 & 511 & 90000 \\ 13363 & 436 & 85000 \\ 11778 & 372 & 77000 \\ 10395 & 321 & 68000 \\ 9235 & 282 & 61900 \end{bmatrix}$

55. (a) The sales figure information may be written as the 3×3 matrix

$\begin{bmatrix} 50 & 100 & 30 \\ 10 & 90 & 50 \\ 60 & 120 & 40 \end{bmatrix}$.

(b) The income per gallon information may be written as the 3×1 matrix

$\begin{bmatrix} 12 \\ 10 \\ 15 \end{bmatrix}$.

(If the matrix in part (a) had been written with its rows and columns interchanged, then this income per gallon information would be written instead as a 1×3 matrix.)

(c) $\begin{bmatrix} 50 & 100 & 30 \\ 10 & 90 & 50 \\ 60 & 120 & 40 \end{bmatrix}\begin{bmatrix} 12 \\ 10 \\ 15 \end{bmatrix} = \begin{bmatrix} 2050 \\ 1770 \\ 2520 \end{bmatrix}$

(This result may be written as a 1×3 matrix instead.)

(d) $2050 + 1770 + 2520 = 6340$
The total daily income from the three locations is $6340.

57. (a) $j_1 = 690$, $s_p = 210$, $a_1 = 2100$

1st year:
$j_2 = .33a_1 = .33(2100) = 693$
$s_2 = .18j_1 = .18(690) \approx 124$
$a_2 = .71s_1 + .94a_1$
$\qquad = .71(210) + .94(2100) \approx 2123$
$j_2 + s_2 + a_2 = 693 + 124 + 2123$
$\qquad\qquad = 2940$

2nd year:
$j_3 = .33a_2 = .33(2123) \approx 700$
$s_3 = .18j_2 = .18(693) \approx 125$
$a_3 = .71s_2 + .94a_2$
$\qquad = .71(124)$
$\qquad = .94(2123) \approx 2084$
$j_3 + s_3 + a_3 = 700 + 125 + 2084$
$\qquad\qquad = 2909$

3rd year:
$j_4 = .33a_3 = .33(2084) \approx 687$
$s_4 = .18j_3 = .18(700) = 126$
$a_4 = .72s_3 + .94a_3$
$\qquad = .71(125) + .94(2084)$
$\qquad = 2048$
$j_3 + s_3 + a_3 = 687 + 126 + 2048$
$\qquad\qquad = 2861$

4th year:
$j_5 = .33a_4 = .33(2048) \approx 676$
$s_5 = .18j_4 = .18(687) \approx 124$
$a_5 = .72s_4 + .94a_4$
$\qquad = .71(126) + .94(2048)$
$\qquad = 2014$
$j_5 + s_5 + a_5 = 686 + 124 + 2048$
$\qquad\qquad = 2814$

5th year:
$j_6 = .33a_5 = .33(2014) \approx 664$
$s_6 = .18j_5 = .18(676) \approx 122$
$a_6 = .72s_5 + .94a_4$
$\qquad = .71(124) + .94(2014)$
$\qquad \approx 1981$
$j_6 + s_6 + a_6 = 664 + 122 + 1981$
$\qquad\qquad = 2767$

(b) There will be extinction of the northern spotted owl.

(c) $j_1 = 690,\ s_1 = 210,\ a_1 = 2100$

1st year:
$j_2 = .33a_1 = .33(2100) = 693$
$s_2 = .3j_1 = .3(690) = 207$
$a_2 = .71s_1 + .94a_1$
$\quad = .71(210) + .94(2100) \approx 2123$
$j_2 + s_2 + a_2 = 693 + 207 + 2123$
$\quad\quad\quad\quad = 3023$

2nd year:
$j_3 = .33a_2 = .33(2123) \approx 701$
$s_3 = .3j_2 = .3(693) \approx 208$
$a_3 = .71s_2 + .94a_2$
$\quad = .71(207)$
$\quad = .94(2123) \approx 2143$
$j_3 + s_3 + a_3 = 701 + 208 + 2143$
$\quad\quad\quad\quad = 3052$

3rd year:
$j_4 = .33a_3 = .33(2143) \approx 707$
$s_4 = .3j_3 = .3(701) = 210$
$a_4 = .71s_3 + .94a_3$
$\quad = .71(208) + .94(2143)$
$\quad \approx 2162$
$j_4 + s_4 + a_4 = 707 + 210 + 2162$
$\quad\quad\quad\quad = 3079$

4th year:
$j_5 = .33a_4 = .33(2162) \approx 714$
$s_5 = .3j_4 = .3(707) \approx 212$
$a_5 = .72s_4 + .94a_4$
$\quad = .71(210) + .94(2162)$
$\quad \approx 2181$
$j_5 + s_5 + a_5 = 714 + 212 + 2181$
$\quad\quad\quad\quad = 3107$

5th year:
$j_6 = .71sl_5 = .33a_5 = .33(2181) \approx 720$
$s_6 = .3j_5 = .3(714) \approx 214$
$a_6 = .71s_5 + .94a_5$
$\quad = .71(212) + .94(2181)$
$\quad = 2201$
$j_6 + s_6 + a_6 = 720 + 214 + 2201$
$\quad\quad\quad\quad = 3135$

Section 8.8

Exercises

1. $\begin{bmatrix} 5 & 7 \\ 2 & 3 \end{bmatrix} \begin{bmatrix} 3 & -7 \\ -2 & 5 \end{bmatrix}$

$= \begin{bmatrix} 5(3) + 7(-2) & 5(-7) + 7(5) \\ 2(3) + 3(-2) & 2(-7) + 3(5) \end{bmatrix}$

$= \begin{bmatrix} 1 & 0 \\ 0 & 1 \end{bmatrix}$

$\begin{bmatrix} 3 & -7 \\ -2 & 5 \end{bmatrix} \begin{bmatrix} 5 & 7 \\ 2 & 3 \end{bmatrix}$

$= \begin{bmatrix} 3(5) + (-7)(2) & 3(7) + (-7)(3) \\ (-2)(5) + 5(2) & (-2)(7) + 5(3) \end{bmatrix}$

$= \begin{bmatrix} 1 & 0 \\ 0 & 1 \end{bmatrix}$

Since the products obtained by multiplying the matrices in either order are both the 2×2 identity matrix, the given matrices are inverses of each other.

3. $\begin{bmatrix} -1 & 2 \\ 3 & -5 \end{bmatrix} \begin{bmatrix} -5 & -2 \\ -3 & -1 \end{bmatrix} = \begin{bmatrix} -1 & 0 \\ 0 & -1 \end{bmatrix}$

Since this product is not the 2×2 identity matrix, the given matrices are not inverses of each other.

5. $\begin{bmatrix} 0 & 1 & 0 \\ 0 & 0 & -2 \\ 1 & -1 & 0 \end{bmatrix} \begin{bmatrix} 1 & 0 & 1 \\ 1 & 0 & 0 \\ 0 & -1 & 0 \end{bmatrix} = \begin{bmatrix} 1 & 0 & 0 \\ 0 & 2 & 0 \\ 0 & 0 & 1 \end{bmatrix}$

Since this product is not the 3×3 identity matrix, the given matrices are not inverses of each other.

7. $\begin{bmatrix} -1 & -2 & -1 \\ 4 & 5 & 0 \\ 0 & 1 & -3 \end{bmatrix} \begin{bmatrix} 15 & 4 & -5 & -12 \\ -3 & 4 & -4 & -1 \\ -4 & -1 & & -1 \end{bmatrix}$

$= \begin{bmatrix} 1 & 0 & 0 \\ 0 & 1 & 0 \\ 0 & 0 & 1 \end{bmatrix} = I_3$

$\begin{bmatrix} 15 & 4 & -5 \\ -12 & -3 & 4 \\ -4 & -1 & 1 \end{bmatrix} \begin{bmatrix} -1 & -1 & -1 \\ 4 & 5 & 0 \\ 0 & 1 & -3 \end{bmatrix}$

$= \begin{bmatrix} 1 & 0 & 0 \\ 0 & 1 & 0 \\ 0 & 0 & 1 \end{bmatrix} = I_3$

The given matrices are inverses of each other.

9. Find the inverse of $A = \begin{bmatrix} -1 & 2 \\ -2 & -1 \end{bmatrix}$,

if it exists.

$$[A \mid I_2] = \begin{bmatrix} -1 & 2 & | & -1 & 0 \\ -2 & -1 & | & 0 & 1 \end{bmatrix}$$

$$\begin{bmatrix} 1 & -2 & | & -1 & 0 \\ -2 & -1 & | & 0 & 1 \end{bmatrix} -1R1$$

$$\begin{bmatrix} 1 & -2 & | & -1 & 0 \\ 0 & -5 & | & -2 & 1 \end{bmatrix} 2R1 + R2$$

$$\begin{bmatrix} 1 & -2 & | & -1 & 0 \\ 0 & 1 & | & \frac{2}{5} & -\frac{1}{5} \end{bmatrix} -\frac{1}{5}R2$$

$$\begin{bmatrix} 1 & 0 & | & -\frac{1}{5} & -\frac{2}{5} \\ 0 & 1 & | & \frac{2}{5} & -\frac{1}{5} \end{bmatrix} 2R2 + R1$$

$$A^{-1} = \begin{bmatrix} -\frac{1}{5} & -\frac{2}{5} \\ \frac{2}{5} & -\frac{1}{5} \end{bmatrix}$$

11. Find the inverse of $A = \begin{bmatrix} -1 & -2 \\ 3 & 4 \end{bmatrix}$, if it exists.

$$[A \mid I_2] = \begin{bmatrix} -1 & -2 & | & 1 & 0 \\ 3 & 4 & | & 0 & 1 \end{bmatrix}$$

$$\begin{bmatrix} -1 & -2 & | & 1 & 0 \\ 0 & -2 & | & 3 & 1 \end{bmatrix} 3R1 + R2$$

$$\begin{bmatrix} 1 & 2 & | & -1 & 0 \\ 0 & -2 & | & 3 & 1 \end{bmatrix} -1R1$$

$$\begin{bmatrix} 1 & 0 & | & 2 & 1 \\ 0 & -2 & | & 3 & 1 \end{bmatrix} R2 + R1$$

$$\begin{bmatrix} 1 & 0 & | & 2 & 1 \\ 0 & 1 & | & -\frac{3}{2} & -\frac{1}{2} \end{bmatrix} -\frac{1}{2}R2$$

$$A^{-1} = \begin{bmatrix} 2 & 1 \\ -\frac{3}{2} & -\frac{1}{2} \end{bmatrix}$$

13. Find the inverse of $\begin{bmatrix} 5 & 10 \\ -3 & -6 \end{bmatrix}$, if it exists.

$$[A \mid I_2] = \begin{bmatrix} 5 & 10 & | & 1 & 0 \\ -3 & -6 & | & 0 & 1 \end{bmatrix}$$

$$\begin{bmatrix} 1 & 2 & | & \frac{1}{5} & 0 \\ -3 & -6 & | & 0 & 1 \end{bmatrix} \frac{1}{5}R1$$

$$\begin{bmatrix} 1 & 2 & | & \frac{1}{5} & 0 \\ 0 & 0 & | & \frac{3}{5} & 1 \end{bmatrix} 3R1 + R2$$

At this point, the matrix should be changed so that the second-row, second-column element will be 1. Since that element is now 0, the desired transformation cannot be completed. Therefore, the inverse of the given matrix does not exist.

15. $A = \begin{bmatrix} 1 & 0 & 1 \\ 0 & -1 & 0 \\ 2 & 1 & 1 \end{bmatrix}$

$$[A \mid I_3] = \begin{bmatrix} 1 & 0 & 1 & | & 1 & 0 & 0 \\ 0 & -1 & 0 & | & 0 & 1 & 0 \\ 2 & 1 & 1 & | & 0 & 0 & 1 \end{bmatrix}$$

$$\begin{bmatrix} 1 & 0 & 1 & | & 1 & 0 & 0 \\ 0 & 1 & 0 & | & 0 & -1 & 0 \\ 0 & 1 & -1 & | & -2 & 0 & 1 \end{bmatrix} -2R1 + R3$$

$$\begin{bmatrix} 1 & 0 & 1 & | & 1 & 0 & 0 \\ 0 & 1 & 0 & | & 0 & -1 & 0 \\ 0 & 0 & -1 & | & -2 & 1 & 1 \end{bmatrix} \begin{array}{l} -1R2 \\ -1R2 + R3 \end{array}$$

$$\begin{bmatrix} 1 & 0 & 1 & | & 1 & 0 & 0 \\ 0 & 1 & 0 & | & 0 & -1 & 0 \\ 0 & 0 & 1 & | & 2 & -1 & -1 \end{bmatrix} -1R3$$

$$\begin{bmatrix} 1 & 0 & 0 & | & -1 & 1 & 1 \\ 0 & 1 & 0 & | & 0 & -1 & 0 \\ 0 & 0 & 1 & | & 2 & -1 & -1 \end{bmatrix} -1R3 + R1$$

$$A^{-1} = \begin{bmatrix} -1 & 1 & 1 \\ 0 & -1 & 0 \\ 2 & -1 & -1 \end{bmatrix}$$

17. $A = \begin{bmatrix} 1 & 3 & 3 \\ 1 & 4 & 3 \\ 1 & 3 & 4 \end{bmatrix}$

$$[A \mid I_3] = \begin{bmatrix} 1 & 3 & 3 & | & 1 & 0 & 0 \\ 1 & 4 & 3 & | & 0 & 1 & 0 \\ 1 & 3 & 4 & | & 0 & 0 & 1 \end{bmatrix}$$

$$\begin{bmatrix} 1 & 3 & 3 & | & 1 & 0 & 0 \\ 0 & 1 & 0 & | & -1 & 1 & 0 \\ 0 & 0 & 1 & | & -1 & 0 & 1 \end{bmatrix} \begin{array}{l} -1R1 + R2 \\ -1R1 + R3 \end{array}$$

$$\begin{bmatrix} 1 & 0 & 3 & | & 4 & -3 & 0 \\ 0 & 1 & 0 & | & -1 & 1 & 0 \\ 0 & 0 & 1 & | & -1 & 0 & 1 \end{bmatrix} -3R2 + R1$$

$$\begin{bmatrix} 1 & 0 & 0 & | & 7 & -3 & -3 \\ 0 & 1 & 0 & | & -1 & 1 & 0 \\ 0 & 0 & 1 & | & -1 & 0 & 1 \end{bmatrix} -3R3 + R1$$

$$A^{-1} = \begin{bmatrix} 7 & -3 & -3 \\ -1 & 1 & 0 \\ -1 & 0 & 1 \end{bmatrix}$$

19. $A = \begin{bmatrix} 2 & 2 & -4 \\ 2 & 6 & 0 \\ -3 & -3 & 5 \end{bmatrix}$

$[A \mid I_3] = \begin{bmatrix} 2 & 2 & -4 & 1 & 0 & 0 \\ 2 & 6 & 0 & 0 & 1 & 0 \\ -3 & -3 & 5 & 0 & 0 & 1 \end{bmatrix}$

$\begin{bmatrix} 1 & 1 & -2 & \frac{1}{2} & 0 & 0 \\ 2 & 6 & 0 & 0 & 1 & 0 \\ -3 & -3 & 5 & 0 & 0 & 1 \end{bmatrix}$ $\frac{1}{2}$R1

$\begin{bmatrix} 1 & 1 & -2 & \frac{1}{2} & 0 & 0 \\ 0 & 4 & 4 & -1 & 1 & 0 \\ 0 & 0 & -1 & \frac{3}{2} & 0 & 1 \end{bmatrix}$ $\begin{matrix} \\ -2\text{R1}+\text{R2} \\ 3\text{R1}+\text{R3} \end{matrix}$

$\begin{bmatrix} 1 & 1 & -2 & \frac{1}{2} & 0 & 0 \\ 0 & 1 & 1 & -\frac{1}{4} & \frac{1}{4} & 0 \\ 0 & 0 & -1 & \frac{3}{2} & 0 & 1 \end{bmatrix}$ $\frac{1}{4}$R2

$\begin{bmatrix} 1 & 0 & -3 & \frac{3}{4} & -\frac{1}{4} & 0 \\ 0 & 1 & 1 & -\frac{1}{4} & \frac{1}{4} & 0 \\ 0 & 0 & -1 & \frac{3}{2} & 0 & 1 \end{bmatrix}$ -1R2$+$R1

$\begin{bmatrix} 1 & 0 & -3 & \frac{3}{4} & -\frac{1}{4} & 0 \\ 0 & 1 & 1 & -\frac{1}{4} & \frac{1}{4} & 0 \\ 0 & 0 & 1 & -\frac{3}{2} & 0 & -1 \end{bmatrix}$ -1R3

$\begin{bmatrix} 1 & 0 & 0 & -\frac{15}{4} & -\frac{1}{4} & -3 \\ 0 & 1 & 0 & \frac{5}{4} & \frac{1}{4} & 1 \\ 0 & 0 & 1 & -\frac{3}{2} & 0 & -1 \end{bmatrix}$ $\begin{matrix} 3\text{R3}+\text{R1} \\ -1\text{R3}+\text{R2} \\ \\ \end{matrix}$

$A^{-1} = \begin{bmatrix} -\frac{15}{4} & -\frac{1}{4} & -3 \\ \frac{5}{4} & \frac{1}{4} & 1 \\ -\frac{3}{2} & 0 & -1 \end{bmatrix}$

21. $A = \begin{bmatrix} 1 & 1 & 0 & 2 \\ 2 & -1 & 1 & -1 \\ 3 & 3 & 2 & -2 \\ 1 & 2 & 1 & 0 \end{bmatrix}$

$[A \mid I_4] = \begin{bmatrix} 1 & 1 & 0 & 2 & 1 & 0 & 0 & 0 \\ 2 & -1 & 1 & -1 & 0 & 1 & 0 & 0 \\ 3 & 3 & 2 & -2 & 0 & 0 & 1 & 0 \\ 1 & 2 & 1 & 0 & 0 & 0 & 0 & 1 \end{bmatrix}$

$\begin{bmatrix} 1 & 1 & 0 & 2 & 1 & 0 & 0 & 0 \\ 0 & -3 & 1 & -5 & -2 & 1 & 0 & 0 \\ 0 & 0 & 2 & -8 & -3 & 0 & 1 & 0 \\ 0 & 1 & 1 & -2 & -1 & 0 & 0 & 1 \end{bmatrix}$ $\begin{matrix} \\ -2\text{R1}+\text{R2} \\ -3\text{R1}+\text{R3} \\ -1\text{R1}+\text{R4} \end{matrix}$

$\begin{bmatrix} 1 & 1 & 0 & 2 & 1 & 0 & 0 & 0 \\ 0 & 1 & -\frac{1}{3} & \frac{5}{3} & \frac{2}{3} & -\frac{1}{3} & 0 & 0 \\ 0 & 0 & 2 & -8 & -3 & 0 & 1 & 0 \\ 0 & 1 & 1 & -2 & -1 & 0 & 0 & 1 \end{bmatrix}$ $-\frac{1}{3}$R2

$\begin{bmatrix} 1 & 0 & \frac{1}{3} & \frac{1}{3} & \frac{1}{3} & \frac{1}{3} & 0 & 0 \\ 0 & 1 & -\frac{1}{3} & \frac{5}{3} & \frac{2}{3} & -\frac{1}{3} & 0 & 0 \\ 0 & 0 & 2 & -8 & -3 & 0 & 1 & 0 \\ 0 & 0 & \frac{4}{3} & -\frac{11}{3} & -\frac{5}{3} & \frac{1}{3} & 0 & 1 \end{bmatrix}$ $\begin{matrix} -1\text{R2}+\text{R1} \\ \\ \\ -1\text{R2}+\text{R4} \end{matrix}$

$\begin{bmatrix} 1 & 0 & \frac{1}{3} & \frac{1}{3} & \frac{1}{3} & \frac{1}{3} & 0 & 0 \\ 0 & 1 & -\frac{1}{3} & \frac{5}{3} & \frac{2}{3} & -\frac{1}{3} & 0 & 0 \\ 0 & 0 & 1 & -4 & -\frac{3}{2} & 0 & \frac{1}{2} & 0 \\ 0 & 0 & \frac{4}{3} & -\frac{11}{3} & -\frac{5}{3} & \frac{1}{3} & 0 & 1 \end{bmatrix}$ $\begin{matrix} \\ \\ \frac{1}{2}\text{R3} \\ \\ \end{matrix}$

$\begin{bmatrix} 1 & 0 & 0 & \frac{5}{3} & \frac{5}{6} & \frac{1}{3} & -\frac{1}{6} & 0 \\ 0 & 1 & 0 & \frac{1}{3} & \frac{1}{6} & -\frac{1}{3} & \frac{1}{6} & 0 \\ 0 & 0 & 1 & -4 & -\frac{3}{2} & 0 & \frac{1}{2} & 0 \\ 0 & 0 & 0 & \frac{5}{3} & \frac{1}{3} & \frac{1}{3} & -\frac{2}{3} & 1 \end{bmatrix}$ $\begin{matrix} -\frac{1}{3}\text{R3}+\text{R1} \\ \frac{1}{3}\text{R3}+\text{R2} \\ \\ -\frac{4}{3}\text{R3}+\text{R4} \end{matrix}$

$\begin{bmatrix} 1 & 0 & 0 & \frac{5}{3} & \frac{5}{6} & \frac{1}{3} & -\frac{1}{6} & 0 \\ 0 & 1 & 0 & \frac{1}{3} & \frac{1}{6} & -\frac{1}{3} & \frac{1}{6} & 0 \\ 0 & 0 & 1 & -4 & -\frac{3}{2} & 0 & \frac{1}{2} & 0 \\ 0 & 0 & 0 & 1 & \frac{1}{5} & \frac{1}{5} & -\frac{2}{5} & \frac{3}{5} \end{bmatrix}$ $\frac{3}{5}$R4

$\begin{bmatrix} 1 & 0 & 0 & 0 & \frac{1}{2} & 0 & \frac{1}{2} & -1 \\ 0 & 1 & 0 & 0 & \frac{1}{10} & -\frac{2}{5} & -\frac{3}{10} & -\frac{1}{5} \\ 0 & 0 & 1 & 0 & -\frac{7}{10} & \frac{4}{5} & -\frac{11}{10} & \frac{12}{5} \\ 0 & 0 & 0 & 1 & \frac{1}{5} & \frac{1}{5} & -\frac{2}{5} & \frac{3}{5} \end{bmatrix}$ $\begin{matrix} -\frac{5}{3}\text{R4}+\text{R1} \\ -\frac{1}{3}\text{R4}+\text{R2} \\ 4\text{R4}+\text{R3} \\ \\ \end{matrix}$

$A^{-1} = \begin{bmatrix} \frac{1}{2} & 0 & \frac{1}{2} & -1 \\ \frac{1}{10} & -\frac{2}{5} & \frac{3}{10} & -\frac{1}{5} \\ -\frac{7}{10} & \frac{4}{5} & -\frac{11}{10} & \frac{12}{5} \\ \frac{1}{5} & \frac{1}{5} & -\frac{2}{5} & \frac{3}{5} \end{bmatrix}$

23. $A^{-1} = \begin{bmatrix} 5 & -9 \\ -1 & 2 \end{bmatrix}$

Find $A = (A^{-1})^{-1}$.

$\begin{bmatrix} 5 & -9 & 1 & 0 \\ -1 & 2 & 0 & 1 \end{bmatrix}$

$\begin{bmatrix} 1 & -\frac{9}{5} & \frac{1}{5} & 0 \\ -1 & 2 & 0 & 1 \end{bmatrix}$ $\frac{1}{5}$R1

$\begin{bmatrix} 1 & -\frac{9}{5} & \frac{1}{5} & 0 \\ 0 & \frac{1}{5} & \frac{1}{5} & 1 \end{bmatrix}$ 1R1$+$R2

$\begin{bmatrix} 1 & -\frac{9}{5} & \frac{1}{5} & 0 \\ 0 & 1 & 1 & 5 \end{bmatrix}$ 5R2

$$\begin{bmatrix} 1 & 0 & | & 2 & 9 \\ 0 & 1 & | & 1 & 5 \end{bmatrix} \quad \tfrac{9}{5}R2 + R1$$

$$A = (A^{-1})^{-1} = \begin{bmatrix} 2 & 9 \\ 1 & 5 \end{bmatrix}$$

25. $A^{-1} = \begin{bmatrix} \frac{2}{3} & -\frac{1}{3} & 0 \\ \frac{1}{3} & -\frac{5}{3} & 1 \\ \frac{1}{3} & \frac{1}{3} & 0 \end{bmatrix}$

Find $A = (A^{-1})^{-1}$.

$$\begin{bmatrix} \frac{2}{3} & -\frac{1}{3} & 0 & | & 1 & 0 & 0 \\ \frac{1}{3} & -\frac{5}{3} & 1 & | & 0 & 1 & 0 \\ \frac{1}{3} & \frac{1}{3} & 0 & | & 0 & 0 & 1 \end{bmatrix}$$

$$\begin{bmatrix} 1 & -\frac{1}{2} & 0 & | & \frac{3}{2} & 0 & 0 \\ \frac{1}{3} & -\frac{5}{3} & 1 & | & 0 & 1 & 0 \\ \frac{1}{3} & \frac{1}{3} & 0 & | & 0 & 0 & 1 \end{bmatrix} \quad \tfrac{3}{2}R1$$

$$\begin{bmatrix} 1 & -\frac{1}{2} & 0 & | & \frac{3}{2} & 0 & 0 \\ 0 & -\frac{3}{2} & 1 & | & -\frac{1}{2} & 1 & 0 \\ 0 & \frac{1}{2} & 0 & | & -\frac{1}{2} & 0 & 1 \end{bmatrix} \quad \begin{matrix} -\tfrac{1}{3}R1 + R2 \\ -\tfrac{1}{3}R1 + R3 \end{matrix}$$

$$\begin{bmatrix} 1 & -\frac{1}{2} & 0 & | & \frac{3}{2} & 0 & 0 \\ 0 & 1 & -\frac{2}{3} & | & \frac{1}{3} & -\frac{2}{3} & 0 \\ 0 & \frac{1}{2} & 0 & | & -\frac{1}{2} & 0 & 1 \end{bmatrix} \quad -\tfrac{2}{3}R2$$

$$\begin{bmatrix} 1 & 0 & -\frac{1}{3} & | & \frac{5}{3} & -\frac{1}{3} & 0 \\ 0 & 1 & -\frac{2}{3} & | & \frac{1}{3} & -\frac{2}{3} & 0 \\ 0 & 0 & \frac{1}{3} & | & -\frac{2}{3} & \frac{1}{3} & 1 \end{bmatrix} \quad \begin{matrix} \tfrac{1}{2}R2 + R1 \\ \\ -\tfrac{1}{2}R2 + R3 \end{matrix}$$

$$\begin{bmatrix} 1 & 0 & -\frac{1}{3} & | & \frac{5}{3} & -\frac{1}{3} & 0 \\ 0 & 1 & -\frac{2}{3} & | & \frac{1}{3} & -\frac{2}{3} & 0 \\ 0 & 0 & 1 & | & -2 & 1 & 3 \end{bmatrix} \quad 3R3$$

$$\begin{bmatrix} 1 & 0 & 0 & | & 1 & 0 & 1 \\ 0 & 1 & 0 & | & -1 & 0 & 2 \\ 0 & 0 & 1 & | & -2 & 1 & 3 \end{bmatrix} \quad \begin{matrix} \tfrac{1}{3}R3 + R1 \\ \tfrac{2}{3}R3 + R2 \end{matrix}$$

$$A = (A^{-1}) = \begin{bmatrix} 1 & 0 & 1 \\ -1 & 0 & 2 \\ -2 & 1 & 3 \end{bmatrix}$$

27. If $A = \begin{bmatrix} a & b \\ c & d \end{bmatrix}$, then $ad - bc$ is the determinant of matrix A.

28. If

$$A^{-1} = \begin{bmatrix} \frac{d}{ad-bc} & \frac{-b}{ad-bc} \\ \frac{-c}{ad-bc} & \frac{a}{ad-bc} \end{bmatrix},$$

then

$$A^{-1} = \begin{bmatrix} \frac{d}{|A|} & \frac{-b}{|A|} \\ \frac{-c}{|A|} & \frac{a}{|A|} \end{bmatrix}.$$

29. $A^{-1} = \begin{bmatrix} \frac{d}{|A|} & \frac{-b}{|A|} \\ \frac{-c}{|A|} & \frac{a}{|A|} \end{bmatrix}$

$$= \begin{bmatrix} \frac{1}{|A|}d & \frac{1}{|A|}(-b) \\ \frac{1}{|A|}(-c) & \frac{1}{|A|}a \end{bmatrix}$$

$$= \frac{1}{|A|}\begin{bmatrix} d & -b \\ -c & a \end{bmatrix}$$

31. $A = \begin{bmatrix} 4 & 2 \\ 7 & 3 \end{bmatrix}$

$|A| = 12 - 14 = -2$

$$A^{-1} = \frac{1}{-2}\begin{bmatrix} 3 & -2 \\ -7 & 4 \end{bmatrix} = \begin{bmatrix} -\frac{3}{2} & 1 \\ \frac{7}{2} & -2 \end{bmatrix}$$

32. The inverse of a 2×2 matrix A does not exist if the determinant of A has the value zero.

33. $-x + y = 1$

$2x - y = 1$

$A = \begin{bmatrix} -1 & 1 \\ 2 & -1 \end{bmatrix}$, $X = \begin{bmatrix} x \\ y \end{bmatrix}$, $B = \begin{bmatrix} 1 \\ 1 \end{bmatrix}$

Find A^{-1}.

$$[A | I_2] = \begin{bmatrix} -1 & 1 & | & 1 & 0 \\ 2 & -1 & | & 0 & 1 \end{bmatrix}$$

$$\begin{bmatrix} -1 & 1 & | & 1 & 0 \\ 0 & 1 & | & 2 & 1 \end{bmatrix} \quad 2R1 + R2$$

$$\begin{bmatrix} -1 & 0 & | & -1 & -1 \\ 0 & 1 & | & 2 & 1 \end{bmatrix} \quad -1R2 + R1$$

$$\begin{bmatrix} 1 & 0 & | & 1 & 1 \\ 0 & 1 & | & 2 & 1 \end{bmatrix} \quad -1R1$$

$$A^{-1} = \begin{bmatrix} 1 & 1 \\ 2 & 1 \end{bmatrix}$$

$$X = A^{-1}B = \begin{bmatrix} 1 & 1 \\ 2 & 1 \end{bmatrix}\begin{bmatrix} 1 \\ 1 \end{bmatrix} = \begin{bmatrix} 2 \\ 3 \end{bmatrix}$$

Solution set: $\{(2, 3)\}$

35. $2x - y = -8$

$3x + y = -2$

$A = \begin{bmatrix} 2 & -1 \\ 3 & 1 \end{bmatrix}$, $X = \begin{bmatrix} x \\ y \end{bmatrix}$, $B = \begin{bmatrix} -8 \\ -2 \end{bmatrix}$

Find A^{-1}.

$[A | I_2] = \begin{bmatrix} 2 & -1 & | & 1 & 0 \\ 3 & 1 & | & 0 & 1 \end{bmatrix}$

$\begin{bmatrix} 1 & -\frac{1}{2} & | & \frac{1}{2} & 0 \\ 3 & 1 & | & 0 & 1 \end{bmatrix}$ $\frac{1}{2}$R1

$\begin{bmatrix} 1 & -\frac{1}{2} & | & \frac{1}{2} & 0 \\ 0 & \frac{5}{2} & | & -\frac{3}{2} & 1 \end{bmatrix}$ -3R1$+$R2

$\begin{bmatrix} 1 & -\frac{1}{2} & | & \frac{1}{2} & 0 \\ 0 & 1 & | & -\frac{3}{5} & \frac{2}{5} \end{bmatrix}$ $\frac{2}{5}$R2

$\begin{bmatrix} 1 & 0 & | & \frac{1}{5} & \frac{1}{5} \\ 0 & 1 & | & -\frac{3}{5} & \frac{2}{5} \end{bmatrix}$ $\frac{1}{2}$R2$+$R1

$A^{-1} = \begin{bmatrix} \frac{1}{5} & \frac{1}{5} \\ -\frac{3}{5} & \frac{2}{5} \end{bmatrix}$

$X = A^{-1}B = \begin{bmatrix} \frac{1}{5} & \frac{1}{5} \\ -\frac{3}{5} & \frac{2}{5} \end{bmatrix} \begin{bmatrix} -8 \\ -2 \end{bmatrix}$

$= \begin{bmatrix} -2 \\ 4 \end{bmatrix}$

Solution set: $\{(-2, 4)\}$

37. $2x + 3y = -10$

$3x + 4y = -12$

$A = \begin{bmatrix} 2 & 3 \\ 3 & 4 \end{bmatrix}$, $X = \begin{bmatrix} x \\ y \end{bmatrix}$, $B = \begin{bmatrix} -10 \\ -12 \end{bmatrix}$

Find A^{-1}.

$[A | I_2] = \begin{bmatrix} 2 & 3 & | & 1 & 0 \\ 3 & 4 & | & 0 & 1 \end{bmatrix}$

$\begin{bmatrix} 1 & \frac{3}{2} & | & \frac{1}{2} & 0 \\ 3 & 4 & | & 0 & 1 \end{bmatrix}$ $\frac{1}{2}$R1

$\begin{bmatrix} 1 & \frac{3}{2} & | & \frac{1}{2} & 0 \\ 0 & -\frac{1}{2} & | & -\frac{3}{2} & 1 \end{bmatrix}$ -3R1$+$R2

$\begin{bmatrix} 1 & \frac{3}{2} & | & \frac{1}{2} & 0 \\ 0 & 1 & | & 3 & -2 \end{bmatrix}$ -2R2

$\begin{bmatrix} 1 & 0 & | & -4 & 3 \\ 0 & 1 & | & 3 & -2 \end{bmatrix}$ $-\frac{3}{2}$R2$+$R1

$A^{-1} = \begin{bmatrix} -4 & 3 \\ 3 & -2 \end{bmatrix}$

$X = A^{-1}B = \begin{bmatrix} -4 & 3 \\ 3 & -2 \end{bmatrix} \begin{bmatrix} -10 \\ -12 \end{bmatrix}$

$= \begin{bmatrix} 4 \\ -6 \end{bmatrix}$

Solution set: $\{(4, -6)\}$

39. $x + 3y + 3z = 1$

$x + 4y + 3z = 0$

$x + 3y + 4z = -1$

$A = \begin{bmatrix} 1 & 3 & 3 \\ 1 & 4 & 3 \\ 1 & 3 & 4 \end{bmatrix}$, $X = \begin{bmatrix} x \\ y \\ z \end{bmatrix}$, $B = \begin{bmatrix} 1 \\ 0 \\ -1 \end{bmatrix}$

From Exercise 17,

$A^{-1} = \begin{bmatrix} 7 & -3 & -3 \\ -1 & 1 & 0 \\ -1 & 0 & 1 \end{bmatrix}$.

$X = A^{-1}B = \begin{bmatrix} 7 & -3 & -3 \\ -1 & 1 & 0 \\ -1 & 0 & 1 \end{bmatrix} \begin{bmatrix} 1 \\ 0 \\ -1 \end{bmatrix} = \begin{bmatrix} 10 \\ -1 \\ -2 \end{bmatrix}$

Solution set: $\{(10, -1, -2)\}$

41. $2x + 2y - 4z = 12$

$2x + 6y = 16$

$-3x - 3y + 5z = -20$

$A = \begin{bmatrix} 2 & 2 & -4 \\ 2 & 6 & 0 \\ -3 & -3 & 5 \end{bmatrix}$, $X = \begin{bmatrix} x \\ y \\ z \end{bmatrix}$, $B = \begin{bmatrix} 12 \\ 16 \\ -20 \end{bmatrix}$

From Exercise 19,

$A^{-1} = \begin{bmatrix} -\frac{15}{4} & -\frac{1}{4} & -3 \\ \frac{5}{4} & \frac{1}{4} & 1 \\ -\frac{3}{2} & 0 & -1 \end{bmatrix}$.

$X = A^{-1}B = \begin{bmatrix} -\frac{15}{4} & -\frac{1}{4} & -3 \\ \frac{5}{4} & \frac{1}{4} & 1 \\ -\frac{3}{2} & 0 & -1 \end{bmatrix} \begin{bmatrix} 12 \\ 16 \\ -20 \end{bmatrix}$

$= \begin{bmatrix} 11 \\ -1 \\ 2 \end{bmatrix}$

Solution set: $\{(11, -1, 2)\}$

43.
$$x + y + 2w = 3$$
$$2x - y + z - w = 3$$
$$3x + 3y + 2z - 2w = 5$$
$$x + 2y + z = 3$$

$$A = \begin{bmatrix} 1 & 1 & 0 & 2 \\ 2 & -1 & 1 & -1 \\ 3 & 3 & 2 & -2 \\ 1 & 2 & 1 & 0 \end{bmatrix}, \quad X = \begin{bmatrix} x \\ y \\ z \\ w \end{bmatrix},$$

$$B = \begin{bmatrix} 3 \\ 3 \\ 5 \\ 3 \end{bmatrix}$$

From Exercise 21,

$$A^{-1} = \begin{bmatrix} \frac{1}{2} & 0 & \frac{1}{2} & -1 \\ \frac{1}{10} & -\frac{2}{5} & \frac{3}{10} & -\frac{1}{5} \\ -\frac{7}{10} & \frac{4}{5} & -\frac{11}{10} & \frac{12}{5} \\ \frac{1}{5} & \frac{1}{5} & -\frac{2}{5} & \frac{3}{5} \end{bmatrix}.$$

$$X = A^{-1}B = \begin{bmatrix} \frac{1}{2} & 0 & \frac{1}{2} & -1 \\ \frac{1}{10} & -\frac{2}{5} & \frac{3}{10} & -\frac{1}{5} \\ -\frac{7}{10} & \frac{4}{5} & -\frac{11}{10} & \frac{12}{5} \\ \frac{1}{5} & \frac{1}{5} & -\frac{2}{5} & \frac{3}{5} \end{bmatrix} \begin{bmatrix} 3 \\ 3 \\ 5 \\ 3 \end{bmatrix}$$

$$= \begin{bmatrix} 1 \\ 0 \\ 2 \\ 1 \end{bmatrix}$$

Solution set: $\{(1, 0, 2, 1)\}$

45. (a)
$$602.7 = a + 5.543b + 37.14c$$
$$656.7 = a + 6.933b + 41.30c$$
$$778.5 = a + 7.638b + 45.62c$$

(b)
$$A = \begin{bmatrix} 1 & 5.543 & 37.14 \\ 1 & 6.933 & 41.30 \\ 1 & 7.638 & 45.62 \end{bmatrix}, \quad X = \begin{bmatrix} a \\ b \\ c \end{bmatrix}$$

$$B = \begin{bmatrix} 602.7 \\ 656.7 \\ 778.5 \end{bmatrix}$$

$$X = A^{-1}B$$

Using a graphing calculator with matrix capabilities, we obtain

$$\begin{bmatrix} a \\ b \\ c \end{bmatrix} = \begin{bmatrix} -490.547375 \\ -89 \\ 42.71875 \end{bmatrix}.$$

Thus, $a \approx -490.547$, $b \approx -89$, $c \approx 42.71875$.

(c) $S = -490.547 - 89A + 42.71875B$

(d) If $A = 7.752$ and $B = 47.38$, the predicted value of S is given by
$$S = -490.547 - 89(7.752)$$
$$+ 42.71875(47.38)$$
$$= 843.539375 \approx 843.5.$$
The predicted value is approximately 843.5.

(e) If $A = 8.9$ and $B = 66.25$, the predicted value of S is given by
$$S = -490.547 - 89(8.9)$$
$$+ 42.71875(66.25)$$
$$= 1547.470188 \approx 1547.5.$$
The predicted value is approximately 1547.5. Using only three consecutive years to forecast six years into the future, it is probably not very accurate.

47. $A = \begin{bmatrix} \sqrt{2} & .5 \\ -17 & \frac{1}{2} \end{bmatrix}$

Using a graphing calculator with matrix capabilities, we obtain

$$A^{-1} = \begin{bmatrix} .0543058761 & -.0543058761 \\ 1.846399787 & .153600213 \end{bmatrix}.$$

49. $A = \begin{bmatrix} 1.4 & .5 & .59 \\ .84 & 1.36 & .62 \\ .56 & .47 & 1.3 \end{bmatrix}$

Using a graphing calculator with matrix capabilities, we obtain

$$A^{-1}$$
$$= \begin{bmatrix} .9987635516 & -.252092087 & -.33056462 \\ -.50327783375 & 1.0077556675 & -.2518891688 \\ -.2481013617 & -.2556769758 & 1.003768868 \end{bmatrix}.$$

51. $x - \sqrt{2y} = 2.6$
$$.75x + y = -7$$

$$A = \begin{bmatrix} 1 & -\sqrt{2} \\ .75 & 1 \end{bmatrix}, \quad X = \begin{bmatrix} x \\ y \end{bmatrix}, \quad B = \begin{bmatrix} 2.6 \\ -7 \end{bmatrix}$$

$$X = A^{-1}B$$

Using a graphing calculator with matrix capabilities, we obtain

$$X = \begin{bmatrix} -3.542308934 \\ -4.343268299 \end{bmatrix}.$$

Solution set:
$\{(-3.542308934, -4.343268299)\}$

53. $\pi x + ey + \sqrt{2}z = 1$
$ex + \pi y + \sqrt{2}z = 2$
$\sqrt{2}x + ey + \pi z = 3$

$$A = \begin{bmatrix} \pi & e & \sqrt{2} \\ e & \pi & \sqrt{2} \\ \sqrt{2} & e & \pi \end{bmatrix}, \quad X = \begin{bmatrix} x \\ y \\ z \end{bmatrix}, \text{ and }$$

$$B = \begin{bmatrix} 1 \\ 2 \\ 3 \end{bmatrix}$$

$X = A^{-1}B$

Using a graphing calculator with matrix capabilities, we obtain

$$X = \begin{bmatrix} -.9704156959 \\ 1.391914631 \\ .1874077432 \end{bmatrix}.$$

Solution set:
$\{(-.9704156959, 1.391914631, .1874077432)\}$

61. $A = \begin{bmatrix} 1 & 0 & 0 \\ 0 & 0 & -1 \\ 0 & 1 & -1 \end{bmatrix}$

$$A^2 = AA = \begin{bmatrix} 1 & 0 & 0 \\ 0 & 0 & -1 \\ 0 & 1 & -1 \end{bmatrix} \begin{bmatrix} 1 & 0 & 0 \\ 0 & 0 & -1 \\ 0 & 1 & -1 \end{bmatrix}$$

$$= \begin{bmatrix} 1 & 0 & 0 \\ 0 & -1 & 1 \\ 0 & -1 & 0 \end{bmatrix}$$

$$A^3 = AA^2 = \begin{bmatrix} 1 & 0 & 0 \\ 0 & 0 & -1 \\ 0 & 1 & -1 \end{bmatrix} \begin{bmatrix} 1 & 0 & 0 \\ 0 & -1 & 1 \\ 0 & -1 & 0 \end{bmatrix}$$

$$= \begin{bmatrix} 1 & 0 & 0 \\ 0 & 1 & 0 \\ 0 & 0 & 1 \end{bmatrix}$$

Since $AA^2 = I$, $A^2 = A^{-1}$. Therefore,

$$A^{-1} = \begin{bmatrix} 1 & 0 & 0 \\ 0 & -1 & 1 \\ 0 & -1 & 0 \end{bmatrix}.$$

65. (a) $y = 85x - 167,650$
$y = 2.25x - 44,030$
Rewrite the system.
$85x - y = 167,650$
$22.5x - y = 44,030$

$$A = \begin{bmatrix} 85 & -1 \\ 22.5 & -1 \end{bmatrix}, \quad X = \begin{bmatrix} x \\ y \end{bmatrix}, \quad B = \begin{bmatrix} 167,650 \\ 44,030 \end{bmatrix}$$

The matrix equation is
$$\begin{bmatrix} 85 & -1 \\ 22.5 & -1 \end{bmatrix} \begin{bmatrix} x \\ y \end{bmatrix} = \begin{bmatrix} 167,650 \\ 44,030 \end{bmatrix}.$$

(b) Use a graphing calculator.
$$A^{-1} = \begin{bmatrix} .016 & -.016 \\ .36 & -1.36 \end{bmatrix}$$

(c) $X = A^{-1}B = \begin{bmatrix} .016 & -.016 \\ .36 & -1.36 \end{bmatrix} \begin{bmatrix} 167,650 \\ 44,030 \end{bmatrix}$

$$= \begin{bmatrix} 1977.92 \\ 473.2 \end{bmatrix}$$

The final matrix shows that the solution set of the system is (1978, 473). The solution indicates that total presidential campaigns and congressional campaigns both spent approximately $473 million in 1978.

Chapter 8 Review Exercises

1. $3x - 5y = 7$ (1)
$2x + 3y = 30$ (2)
Multiply equation (1) by 3, and multiply equation (2) by 5; then add the resulting equations.
$9x - 15y = 21$
$\underline{10x + 15y = 150}$
$19x = 171$
$x = \dfrac{171}{19}$
$x = 9$
Substitute this value into equation (2).
$2(9) + 3y = 30$
$18 + 3y = 30$
$3y = 12$
$y = 4$
Solution set: $\{(9, 4)\}$

3. $.2x + .5y = 6$ (1)
$.4x + y = 9$ (2)
Multiply equation (1) by -2 and add the result to equation (2).
$-.4x - y = -12$
$\underline{.4x + y = \quad 9}$
$0 = -3$
Since this is a false statement, the system is inconsistent.
Solution set: $\emptyset$

5. $2x - 5y + 3z = -1$ (1)

$\quad x + 4y - 2z = 9$ (2)

$\quad -x + 2y + 4z = 5$ (3)

First, we eliminate x. Multiply equation (2) by -2 and add the result to equation (1).

$\quad 2x - 5y + 3z = -1$

$\underline{-2x - 8y + 4z = -18}$

$\quad\quad -13y + 7z = -19$ (4)

Next, add equations (2) and (3).

$\quad x + 4y - 2z = 9$ (2)

$\underline{-x + 2y + 4z = 5}$ (3)

$\quad\quad 6y + 2z = 14$ (5)

Now, we solve the system

$-13y + 7z = -19$ (4)

$\quad 6y + 2z = 14.$ (5)

Multiply equation (4) by 2, multiply equation (5) by -7, and add the resulting equations.

$-26y + 14z = -38$

$\underline{-42y - 14z = -98}$

$-68y = -136$

$\quad\quad y = 2$

Substitute this value into equation (4).

$-13(2) + 7z = -19$

$\quad -26 + 7z = -19$

$\quad\quad 7z = 7$

$\quad\quad z = 1$

Substitute these values into equation (2).

$x + 4(2) - 2(1) = 9$

$\quad x + 8 - 2 = 9$

$\quad\quad x = 3$

Solution set: $\{(3, 2, 1)\}$

7. One possible answer is

$x + y = 2$

$x + y = 3.$

9. Let x = amount of rice

and y = amount of soybeans.

$\quad 15x + 22.5y = 9.5$ (1)

$810x + 270y = 324$ (2)

Multiply equation (1) by -12 and add the result to equation (2).

$-180x - 270y = -114$

$\underline{810x + 270y = 324}$

$630x = 210$

$\quad\quad x = \dfrac{1}{3}$

Substitute 1/3 for x in equation (1) and solve for y.

$15\left(\dfrac{1}{3}\right) + 22.5y = 9.5$

$\quad 5 + 22.5y = 9.5$

$\quad\quad 22.5y = 4.5$

$\quad\quad\quad y = .20$

$\quad\quad\quad = \dfrac{1}{5}$

1/3 cup of rice and 1/5 cup of soybeans should be used.

11. $y = 106x - 1070$

$y = 173x - 7630$

$106x - 1070 = 173x - 7630$

$\quad\quad -67x = -6560$

$\quad\quad\quad x \approx 97.9104$

$x \approx 97.9$ corresponds to late in 1997.

$y = 106(97.9104) - 1070$

$y \approx 9309$ thousand or $9,309,000.$

Late in 1997, both populations will number 9,309,000.

13. Since $y = ax^2 + bx + c$ and the points $(1, -2.3)$, $(2, -1.3)$, and $(3, 4.5)$ are on the parabola, we have the following equations:

$-2.3 = a(1)^2 + b(1) + c$

$-1.3 = a(2)^2 + b(2) + c$

$4.5 = a(3)^2 + b(3) + c.$

This becomes the following system:

$\quad a + b + c = -2.3$ (1)

$4a + 2b + c = -1.3$ (2)

$9a + 3b + c = 4.5$ (3)

First, eliminate c. Multiply equation (1) by -1 and the result to equation (2).

$-a - b - c = 2.3$ (1)

$\underline{4a + 2b + c = -1.3}$ (2)

$3a + b = 1$ (4)

Next, multiply equation (2) by -1 and add to equation (3).

$-4a - 2b - c = 1.3$ (2)

$\underline{9a + 3b + c = 4.5}$ (3)

$5a + b = 5.8$ (5)

We now solve the system

$3a + b = 1$ (4)

$5a + b = 5.8.$ (5)

Next, eliminate b. Multiply equation (4) by -1 and add the result to equation (5).

$$-3a - b = -1$$
$$\underline{5a + b = 5.8}$$
$$2a \quad\;\; = 4.8$$
$$a = 2.4$$

Substitute this value into equation (4).
$$3(2.4) + b = 1$$
$$7.2 + b = 1$$
$$b = -6.2$$

Substitute these values into equation (1).
$$(2.4) + (-6.2) + c = -2.3$$
$$-3.8 + c = -2.3$$
$$c = 1.5$$

The equation of the parabola is
$$y = 2.4x^2 - 6.2x + 1.5.$$

15. $3x - 4y + z = 2$ (1)
$\quad\;\; 2x + y = 1$ (2)

Solve equation (2) for y.
$$y = 1 - 2x$$

Substitute $1 - 2x$ for y in equation (1) and solve for z.
$$3x - 4(1 - 2x) + z = 2$$
$$3x - 4 + 8z + z = 2$$
$$11x + z = 6$$
$$z = 6 - 11x$$

Solution set: $\{(x, 1 - 2x, 6 - 11x)\}$

17. $5x + 2y = -10$
$\quad\;\; 3x - 5y = -6$

$$\begin{bmatrix} 1 & \frac{2}{5} & | & -2 \\ 3 & -5 & | & -6 \end{bmatrix} \;\; \frac{1}{5}R1$$

$$\begin{bmatrix} 1 & \frac{2}{5} & | & -2 \\ 0 & -\frac{31}{5} & | & 0 \end{bmatrix} \;\; -3R1 + R2$$

$$\begin{bmatrix} 1 & \frac{2}{5} & | & -2 \\ 0 & 1 & | & 0 \end{bmatrix} \;\; -\frac{5}{31}R2$$

$$\begin{bmatrix} 1 & 0 & | & -2 \\ 0 & 1 & | & 0 \end{bmatrix} \;\; -\frac{2}{5}R2 + R1$$

Solution set: $\{(-2, 0)\}$

19. $\quad x - z = -3$
$\quad\quad\;\; y + z = 6$
$\quad 2x - 3z = -9$

$$\begin{bmatrix} 1 & 0 & -1 & | & -3 \\ 0 & 1 & 1 & | & 6 \\ 2 & 0 & -3 & | & -9 \end{bmatrix}$$

$$\begin{bmatrix} 1 & 0 & -1 & | & -3 \\ 0 & 1 & 1 & | & 6 \\ 0 & 0 & -1 & | & -3 \end{bmatrix} \;\; -2R1 + R3$$

$$\begin{bmatrix} 1 & 0 & -1 & | & -3 \\ 0 & 1 & 0 & | & 3 \\ 0 & 0 & 1 & | & 3 \end{bmatrix} \begin{matrix} \\ R3 + R2 \\ -1R3 \end{matrix}$$

$$\begin{bmatrix} 1 & 0 & 0 & | & 0 \\ 0 & 1 & 0 & | & 3 \\ 0 & 0 & 1 & | & 3 \end{bmatrix} \;\; R3 + R1$$

Solution set: $\{0, 3, 3)\}$

21. Let $x =$ number of pounds of \$4.60 tea;
$\quad\quad y =$ the number of pounds of \$5.75 tea;
$\quad\quad z =$ the number of pound of \$6.50 tea.

$$x + y + z = 20 \quad \text{(1) Total pounds}$$
$$4.6x + 5.75y + 6.5z = 20(5.25) \quad \text{(2) Total value}$$
$$x = y + z \quad \begin{matrix}\text{(3) Amount of \$4.60}\\ \text{tea equals sum of}\\ \text{other two}\end{matrix}$$

Rewrite the system so that each equation is in standard form.
$$x + \quad y + \quad z = 20$$
$$4.6x + 5.75y + 6.5z = 105$$
$$x - \quad y - \quad z = 0$$

Write the augmented matrix; then solve by the Gauss-Jordan method.

$$\begin{bmatrix} 1 & 1 & 1 & | & 20 \\ 4.6 & 5.75 & 6.5 & | & 105 \\ 1 & -1 & -1 & | & 0 \end{bmatrix}$$

$$\begin{bmatrix} 1 & 1 & 1 & | & 20 \\ 0 & 1.15 & 1.9 & | & 13 \\ 0 & -2 & -2 & | & -20 \end{bmatrix} \begin{matrix} \\ -4.6R1 + R2 \\ -1R1 + R3 \end{matrix}$$

$$\begin{bmatrix} 1 & 1 & 1 & | & 20 \\ 0 & 1 & \frac{1.9}{1.15} & | & \frac{13}{1.15} \\ 0 & -2 & -2 & | & -20 \end{bmatrix} \;\; \frac{1}{1.15}R2$$

$$\begin{bmatrix} 1 & 1 & 1 & | & 20 \\ 0 & 1 & \frac{1.9}{1.15} & | & \frac{13}{1.15} \\ 0 & 0 & \frac{1.5}{1.15} & | & \frac{3}{1.15} \end{bmatrix} \;\; 2R2 + R3$$

$$\begin{bmatrix} 1 & 1 & 1 & | & 20 \\ 0 & 1 & \frac{1.9}{1.15} & | & \frac{13}{1.15} \\ 0 & 0 & 1 & | & 2 \end{bmatrix} \;\; \frac{1.15}{1.5}R3$$

$$\begin{bmatrix} 1 & 1 & 0 & | & 18 \\ 0 & 1 & 0 & | & 8 \\ 0 & 0 & 1 & | & 2 \end{bmatrix} \begin{matrix} -R3 + R1 \\ -\frac{1.9}{1.15}R3 + R2 \\ \\ \end{matrix}$$

$$\begin{bmatrix} 1 & 0 & 0 & | & 10 \\ 0 & 1 & 0 & | & 8 \\ 0 & 0 & 1 & | & 2 \end{bmatrix} \;\; -1R2 + R1$$

From the final matrix, we have $x = 10$, $y = 8$, $z = 2$. Therefore, 10 lb of $4.60 tea, 8 lb of $5.75 tea, and 2 lb of $6.50 tea should be used.

23. $y = -.5x + 7$
$y = x + 3.5$

$-.5x + 7 = x + 3.5$
$-1.5x = -3.5$
$x \approx 2.3$ corresponds to 1997.

$y = -.5(2.3) + 7$
$y \approx 5.8$

In 1997 (when $x = 2.3$), both companies had a market share of 5.8%.

25. $\begin{vmatrix} -2 & 4 \\ 0 & 3 \end{vmatrix} = -2(3) - (0)(4) = -6$

27. $\begin{vmatrix} -2 & 4 & 1 \\ 3 & 0 & 2 \\ -1 & 0 & 3 \end{vmatrix}$

Expand by minors about the second column.

$= -4 \begin{vmatrix} 3 & 2 \\ -1 & 3 \end{vmatrix} + 0 \begin{vmatrix} -2 & 1 \\ -1 & 3 \end{vmatrix} - 0 \begin{vmatrix} -2 & 1 \\ 3 & 2 \end{vmatrix}$

$= -4(9 + 2) + 0 - 0$
$= -4(11) = -44$

29. $\begin{vmatrix} 3x & 7 \\ -x & 4 \end{vmatrix} = 8$

$12x - (-7x) = 8$
$19x = 8$
$x = \dfrac{8}{19}$

Solution set: $\left\{ \dfrac{8}{19} \right\}$

31. $3x + 7y = 2$
$5x - y = -22$

$D = \begin{vmatrix} 3 & 7 \\ 5 & -1 \end{vmatrix} = -38$

$D_x = \begin{vmatrix} 2 & 7 \\ -22 & -1 \end{vmatrix} = 152$

$D_y = \begin{vmatrix} 3 & 2 \\ 5 & -22 \end{vmatrix} = -76$

$x = \dfrac{152}{-38} = -4$

$y = \dfrac{-76}{-38} = 2$

Solution set: $\{(-4, 2)\}$

33. $5x - 2y - z = 8$ (1)
$-5x + 2y + z = -8$ (2)
$x - 4y - 2z = 0$ (3)

$D = \begin{vmatrix} 5 & -2 & -1 \\ -5 & 2 & 1 \\ 1 & -4 & -2 \end{vmatrix} = 0$

Cramer's rule cannot be used since $D = 0$. Adding the first and second equations results in the equality $0 = 0$.
The system has dependent equations.
We can use the elimination method to complete the solution. We will write the solution set with z as the arbitrary variable. Multiply equation (1) by -2 and add the result to equation (3).

$-10x + 4y + 2z = -16$

$\underline{x - 4y - 2z = 0}$

$-9x = -16$
$x = \dfrac{16}{9}$

Substitute this value of x in equation (1). Solve the resulting equation for y in terms of z.

$5\left(\dfrac{16}{9} \right) - 2y - z = 8$

$\dfrac{80}{9} - 2y - z = 8$

$-2y - z = \dfrac{72}{9} - \dfrac{80}{9}$

$-2y - z = -\dfrac{8}{9}$

$-2y = -\dfrac{8}{9} + z$

$= \dfrac{-8 + 9z}{9}$

$y = -\dfrac{1}{2} \left(\dfrac{-8 + 9z}{9} \right)$

$= \dfrac{8 - 9z}{18}$

Solution set: $\left\{ \left(\dfrac{16}{9}, \dfrac{8 - 9z}{18}, z \right) \right\}$

35. $\dfrac{5x - 2}{x^3 - 4x} = \dfrac{5x - 2}{x(x - 2)(x + 2)}$

So we seek A, B, and C so that
$\dfrac{5x - 2}{x^3 - 4x} = \dfrac{A}{x} + \dfrac{B}{x - 2} + \dfrac{C}{x + 2}.$

Multiply both sides by $x^3 - 4x$ to get

$5x - 2 = A(x^2 - 4) + B(x^2 + 2x) + C(x^2 - 2x)$

$5x - 2 = (A + B + C)x^2 + (2B - 2C)x - 4A$

then equating like terms we have

$$A + B + C = 0 \quad (1)$$
$$2B - 2C = 5 \quad (2)$$
$$-4A = -2. \quad (3)$$

From (3) we have $A = \dfrac{1}{2}$; substitute into (1),

$B + C = -\dfrac{1}{2}$. Add 2 times (1) + (2) to

eliminate C.

$$2B + 2C = -1$$
$$2B - 2C = 5$$
$$4B = 4$$
$$B = 1$$

Finally let $B = 1$ in (2) and solve for C.

$$2 - 2C = 5$$
$$C = -\dfrac{3}{2}$$

Thus the decomposition is

$$\frac{5x - 2}{x^3 - 4x} = \frac{1}{2x} + \frac{1}{x - 2} - \frac{3}{2(x + 2)}.$$

37. $\quad x^2 = 2y - 3 \quad (1)$
$\quad\quad x + y = 3 \quad\quad (2)$

Solve equation (2) for y.
$y = 3 - x \quad (3)$
Substitute this expression into equation (1).

$$x^2 = 2(3 - x) - 3$$
$$x^2 = 6 - 2x - 3$$
$$x^2 + 2x - 3 = 0$$
$$(x + 1)(x - 1) = 0$$
$$x = -3 \text{ or } x = 1$$

For each value of x, use equation (3) to find the corresponding value of y.
If $x = -3$, $y = 3 - (-3) = 6$.
If $x = 1$, $y = 3 - 1 = 2$.
Solution set: $\{(-3, 6), (1, 2)\}$

39. $\quad xy = -2 \quad (1)$
$\quad\quad y - x = 3 \quad (2)$

Solve equation (2) for y.
$y = x + 3 \quad (3)$
Substitute this expression into equation (1).

$$x(x + 3) = -2$$
$$x^2 + 3x + 2 = 0$$
$$(x + 1)(x + 2) = 0$$
$$x = -1 \text{ or } x = -2$$

For each value of x, use equation (3) to find the corresponding value of y.
If $x = -1$, $y = (-1) + 3 = 2$.
If $x = -2$, $y = (-2) + 3 = 1$.
Solution set: $\{(-1, 2), (-2, 1)\}$

41. $\quad 3x - y = b \quad (1)$
$\quad\quad x^2 + y^2 = 25 \quad (2)$

Solve equation (1) for y.
$y = 3x - b$
Substitute this expression into equation (2).

$$x^2 + (3x - b)^2 = 25$$
$$x^2 + 9x^2 - 6bx + b^2 = 25$$
$$10x^2 - 6bx + (b^2 - 25) = 0$$

We solve this quadratic equation by using the quadratic formula.

$$x = \frac{-(-6b) \pm \sqrt{(-6b)^2 - 4(10)(b^2 - 25)}}{2(10)}$$

$$= \frac{6b \pm \sqrt{36b^2 - 40b^2 + 1000}}{20}$$

$$= \frac{6b \pm \sqrt{36b^2 - 40b^2 + 1000}}{20}$$

$$= \frac{6b \pm 2\sqrt{250 - b^2}}{20}$$

In order for there to be only one solution (the line touches the circle in one point),

$$250 - b^2 = 0$$
$$b^2 = 250$$
$$b = \pm\sqrt{250}$$
$$b = \pm 5\sqrt{10}.$$

43. $\quad x + y \le 6$
$\quad\quad 2x - y \ge 3$

Graph the solid line $x + y = 6$, which has x-intercept 6 and y-intercept 6. Shade the region below this line.
Graph the solid line $2x - y = 3$, which has x-intercept $\dfrac{3}{2}$ and y-intercept -3. Shade the region below this line.
The solution set is the intersection of these two regions, which is shaded in the final graph.

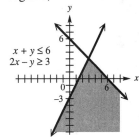

45. Find $x \geq 0$ and $y \geq 0$ such that
$$3x + 2y \leq 12$$
$$5x + y \geq 5$$
and $2x + 4y$ is maximized.
Graph the solid lines $x = 0$, $y = 0$, $3x + 2y = 12$, and $5x + y = 5$.

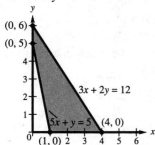

The vertices are $(1, 0)$, $(4, 0)$, $(0, 5)$ and $(0, 6)$.

Point	Value = $2x + 4y$
$(1, 0)$	$2(1) + 4(0) = 2$
$(4, 0)$	$2(4) + 4(0) = 8$
$(0, 5)$	$2(0) + 4(5) = 20$
$(0, 6)$	$2(0) + 4(6) = 24 \leftarrow$ Maximum

The maximum value is 24, which occurs at $(0, 6)$.

47. Let $x =$ number of units of food A;
    $y =$ number of units of food B.
$$2x + 6y \geq 30$$
$$4x + 2y \geq 20$$
$$x \geq 0$$
$$y \geq 2$$
Minimize $18x + 12y$.
First, graph the solution of the system.

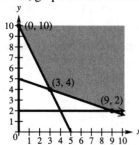

Evaluate $18x + 12y$ at each vertex.

Point	Cost = $18x + 12y$
$(0, 10)$	$18(0) + 12(10) = 120$
$(3, 4)$	$18(3) + 12(4) = 102 \leftarrow$ Minimum
$(9, 2)$	$18(9) + 12(2) = 186$

The minimum cost of $1.02 will be produced by 3 units of food A and 4 units of food B.

49.
$$\begin{bmatrix} 5 & x+2 \\ -6y & z \end{bmatrix} = \begin{bmatrix} a & 3x-1 \\ 5y & 9 \end{bmatrix}$$
$$a = 5 \quad x + 2 = 3x - 1$$
$$3 = 2x$$
$$\frac{3}{2} = x$$
$$-6y = 5y \quad z = 9$$
$$0 = 11y$$
$$0 = y$$
Thus, $a = 5$, $x = 3/2$, $y = 0$, and $z = 9$.

51.
$$\begin{bmatrix} 3 \\ 2 \\ 5 \end{bmatrix} - \begin{bmatrix} 8 \\ -4 \\ 6 \end{bmatrix} + \begin{bmatrix} 1 \\ 0 \\ 2 \end{bmatrix}$$
$$= \begin{bmatrix} -5 \\ 6 \\ -1 \end{bmatrix} + \begin{bmatrix} 1 \\ 0 \\ 2 \end{bmatrix} = \begin{bmatrix} -4 \\ 6 \\ 1 \end{bmatrix}$$

53.
$$\begin{bmatrix} -3 & 4 \\ 2 & 8 \end{bmatrix} \begin{bmatrix} -1 & 0 \\ 2 & 5 \end{bmatrix}$$
$$= \begin{bmatrix} -3(-1) + 4(2) & -3(0) + 4(5) \\ 2(-1) + 8(2) & 2(0) + 8(5) \end{bmatrix}$$
$$= \begin{bmatrix} 11 & 20 \\ 14 & 40 \end{bmatrix}$$

55.
$$\begin{bmatrix} 1 & -2 & 4 & 2 \\ 0 & 1 & -1 & 8 \end{bmatrix} \begin{bmatrix} -1 \\ 2 \\ 0 \\ 1 \end{bmatrix}$$
$$= \begin{bmatrix} 1(-1) + (-2)(2) + 4(0) + 2(1) \\ 0(-1) + 1(2) + (-1)(0) + 8(1) \end{bmatrix}$$
$$= \begin{bmatrix} -3 \\ 10 \end{bmatrix}$$

57. $[A] + [B] - [B] = [A]$
$$= \begin{bmatrix} 6 & 12 & 0 \\ -10 & -4 & 11 \end{bmatrix} - \begin{bmatrix} 4 & 6 & -5 \\ -6 & 3 & 2 \end{bmatrix}$$
$$= \begin{bmatrix} 6-4 & 12-6 & 0-(-5) \\ -10-(-6) & -4-3 & 11-2 \end{bmatrix} = \begin{bmatrix} 2 & 6 & 5 \\ -4 & -7 & 9 \end{bmatrix}$$

59. Find the inverse of $A = \begin{bmatrix} -4 & 2 \\ 0 & 3 \end{bmatrix}$ if it exists.

$[A|I_2] = \begin{bmatrix} -4 & 2 & | & 1 & 0 \\ 0 & 3 & | & 0 & 1 \end{bmatrix}$

$\begin{bmatrix} 1 & -\frac{1}{2} & | & -\frac{1}{4} & 0 \\ 0 & 3 & | & 0 & 1 \end{bmatrix} \; -\frac{1}{4}R1$

$\begin{bmatrix} 1 & -\frac{1}{2} & | & -\frac{1}{4} & 0 \\ 0 & 1 & | & 0 & \frac{1}{3} \end{bmatrix} \; \frac{1}{3}R2$

$\begin{bmatrix} 1 & 0 & | & -\frac{1}{4} & \frac{1}{6} \\ 0 & 1 & | & 0 & \frac{1}{3} \end{bmatrix} \; \frac{1}{2}R2 + R1$

$A^{-1} = \begin{bmatrix} -\frac{1}{4} & \frac{1}{6} \\ 0 & \frac{1}{3} \end{bmatrix}$

61. Find the inverses of

$A = \begin{bmatrix} 2 & 3 & 5 \\ -2 & -3 & -5 \\ 1 & 4 & 2 \end{bmatrix}$, if it exists.

$[A|I_3] = \begin{bmatrix} 2 & 3 & 5 & | & 1 & 0 & 0 \\ -2 & -3 & -5 & | & 0 & 1 & 0 \\ 1 & 4 & 2 & | & 0 & 0 & 1 \end{bmatrix}$

$\begin{bmatrix} 2 & 3 & 5 & | & 1 & 0 & 0 \\ 0 & 0 & 0 & | & 1 & 1 & 0 \\ 1 & 4 & 2 & | & 0 & 0 & 1 \end{bmatrix} \; R1 + R2$

Because all the elements of the second row are 0, it will not be possible to complete the required transformations. Therefore, the inverse of the given matrix does not exist.

63. $2x + y = 5$
$3x - 2y = 4$

$A = \begin{bmatrix} 2 & 1 \\ 3 & -2 \end{bmatrix}$, $X = \begin{bmatrix} x \\ y \end{bmatrix}$, $B = \begin{bmatrix} 5 \\ 4 \end{bmatrix}$

Find A^{-1}.

$[A|I] = \begin{bmatrix} 2 & 1 & | & 1 & 0 \\ 3 & -2 & | & 0 & 1 \end{bmatrix}$

$\begin{bmatrix} -1 & 3 & | & 1 & -1 \\ 3 & -2 & | & 0 & 1 \end{bmatrix} \; -1R2 + R1$

$\begin{bmatrix} 1 & -3 & | & -1 & 1 \\ 3 & -2 & | & 0 & 1 \end{bmatrix} \; -1R1$

$\begin{bmatrix} 1 & -3 & | & -1 & 1 \\ 0 & 7 & | & 3 & -2 \end{bmatrix} \; -3R1 + R2$

$\begin{bmatrix} 1 & -3 & | & -1 & 1 \\ 0 & 1 & | & \frac{3}{7} & -\frac{2}{7} \end{bmatrix} \; \frac{1}{7}R2$

$\begin{bmatrix} 1 & 0 & | & \frac{2}{7} & \frac{1}{7} \\ 0 & 1 & | & \frac{3}{7} & -\frac{2}{7} \end{bmatrix} \; 3R2 + R1$

$A^{-1} = \begin{bmatrix} \frac{2}{7} & \frac{1}{7} \\ \frac{3}{7} & -\frac{2}{7} \end{bmatrix}$

$X = A^{-1}B = \begin{bmatrix} \frac{2}{7} & \frac{1}{7} \\ \frac{3}{7} & -\frac{2}{7} \end{bmatrix} \begin{bmatrix} 5 \\ 4 \end{bmatrix} = \begin{bmatrix} 2 \\ 1 \end{bmatrix}$

Solution set: $\{(2, 1)\}$

65.
$$x = -3$$
$$y + z = 6$$
$$2x - 3z = -9$$

$$A = \begin{bmatrix} 1 & 0 & 0 \\ 0 & 1 & 1 \\ 2 & 0 & -3 \end{bmatrix}, X = \begin{bmatrix} x \\ y \\ z \end{bmatrix}, B = \begin{bmatrix} -3 \\ 6 \\ -9 \end{bmatrix}$$

Find A^{-1}.

$$[A \mid I] = \begin{bmatrix} 1 & 0 & 0 & | & 1 & 0 & 0 \\ 0 & 1 & 1 & | & 0 & 1 & 0 \\ 2 & 0 & -3 & | & 0 & 0 & 1 \end{bmatrix}$$

$$\begin{bmatrix} 1 & 0 & 0 & | & 1 & 0 & 0 \\ 0 & 1 & 1 & | & 0 & 1 & 0 \\ 0 & 0 & -3 & | & -2 & 0 & 1 \end{bmatrix} -2R1 + R3$$

$$\begin{bmatrix} 1 & 0 & 0 & | & 1 & 0 & 0 \\ 0 & 1 & 1 & | & 0 & 1 & 0 \\ 0 & 0 & 1 & | & \frac{2}{3} & 0 & -\frac{1}{3} \end{bmatrix} \frac{1}{3}R3$$

$$\begin{bmatrix} 1 & 0 & 0 & | & 1 & 0 & 0 \\ 0 & 1 & 0 & | & -\frac{2}{3} & 1 & \frac{1}{3} \\ 0 & 0 & 1 & | & \frac{2}{3} & 0 & -\frac{1}{3} \end{bmatrix} -1R3 + R2$$

$$A^{-1} = \begin{bmatrix} 1 & 0 & 0 \\ -\frac{2}{3} & 1 & \frac{1}{3} \\ \frac{2}{3} & 0 & -\frac{1}{3} \end{bmatrix}$$

$$X = A^{-1}B = \begin{bmatrix} 1 & 0 & 0 \\ -\frac{2}{3} & 1 & \frac{1}{3} \\ \frac{2}{3} & 0 & -\frac{1}{3} \end{bmatrix} \begin{bmatrix} -3 \\ 6 \\ -9 \end{bmatrix} = \begin{bmatrix} -3 \\ 5 \\ 1 \end{bmatrix}$$

Solution set: $\{(-3, 5, 1)\}$

Chapter 8 Test Exercises

1.
$$3x - y = 9 \quad (1)$$
$$x + 2y = 10 \quad (2)$$
Solve equation (2) for x.
$$x = 10 - 2y \quad (3)$$
Substitute this result into equation (1) and solve for y.
$$3(10 - 2y) - y = 9$$
$$30 - 6y - y = 9$$
$$-7y = -21$$
$$y = 3$$
Substitute $y = 3$ back into equation (3) to find x.
$$x = 10 - 2(3)$$
$$x = 4$$
Solution set: $\{(4, 3)\}$

2.
$$6x + 9y = -21 \quad (1)$$
$$4x + 6y = -14 \quad (2)$$
Solve equation (1) for x.
$$6x = -9y - 21$$
$$x = \frac{-9y - 21}{6}$$
$$x = \frac{-3y - 7}{2} \quad (3)$$
Substitute this result into equation (2).
$$4\left(\frac{-3y - 7}{2}\right) + 6y = -14$$
$$2(-3y - 7) + 6y = -14$$
$$-6y - 14 + 6y = -14$$
$$-14 = -14$$
The equations are dependent.
We express the solution set with y as the arbitrary variable.

Solution set: $\left\{ \left(\dfrac{-3y - 7}{2}, y \right) \right\}$

3.
$$\frac{1}{4}x - \frac{1}{3}y = -\frac{5}{12} \quad (1)$$
$$\frac{1}{10}x + \frac{1}{5}y = \frac{1}{2} \quad (2)$$
To eliminate fractions, multiply equation (1) by 12 and equation (2) by 10.
$$3x - 4y = -5 \quad (3)$$
$$x + 2y = 5 \quad (4)$$
Multiply equation (4) by 2 and add the result to equation (3).
$$3x - 4y = -5$$
$$\underline{2x + 4y = 10}$$
$$5x \qquad = 5$$
$$x = 1$$
Substitute $x = 1$ in equation (4) to find y.
$$1 + 2y = 5$$
$$2y = 4$$
$$y = 2$$
Solution set: $\{(1, 2)\}$

4.
$$x - 2y = 4 \quad (1)$$
$$-2x + 4y = 6 \quad (2)$$
Multiply equation (1) by 2 and add the result to equation (2).
$$2x - 4y = 8$$
$$\underline{-2x + 4y = 6}$$
$$0 = 14$$
The system is inconsistent.
Solution set: $\emptyset$

5. $2x + y + z = 3$ (1)
$x + 2y - z = 3$ (2)
$3x - y + z = 5$ (3)
Eliminate z first. Add equations (1) and (2).
$3x + 3y = 6$ (4)
Add equations (2) and (3).
$4x + y = 8$ (5)
Multiply equation (5) by -3 and add the results to equation (4).

$$\begin{array}{r} 3x + 3y = 6 \\ \underline{-12x - 3y = -24} \\ -9x = -18 \\ x = 2 \end{array}$$

Substitute $x = 2$ in equation (5) to find y.
$4(2) + y = 8$
$ y = 0$
Substitute $x = 2$ in equation (5) to find y.
$2(2) + 0 + z = 3$
$ z = -1$
Solution set: $\{(2, 0, -1)\}$

6. $3a - 2b = 13$
$4a - b = 19$
Write the augmented matrix.

$$\begin{bmatrix} 3 & -2 & | & 13 \\ 4 & -1 & | & 19 \end{bmatrix}$$

$$\begin{bmatrix} 1 & -\frac{2}{3} & | & \frac{13}{3} \\ 4 & -1 & | & 19 \end{bmatrix} \frac{1}{3}R1$$

$$\begin{bmatrix} 1 & -\frac{2}{3} & | & \frac{13}{3} \\ 0 & \frac{5}{3} & | & \frac{5}{3} \end{bmatrix} -4R1 + R2$$

$$\begin{bmatrix} 1 & -\frac{2}{3} & | & \frac{13}{3} \\ 0 & 1 & | & 1 \end{bmatrix} \frac{3}{5}R2$$

$$\begin{bmatrix} 1 & 0 & | & 5 \\ 0 & 1 & | & 1 \end{bmatrix} \frac{2}{3}R2 + R1$$

Solution set $\{(5, 1)\}$

7. $3a - 4b + 2c = 15$ (1)
$2a - b + c = 13$ (2)
$a + 2b - c = 5$ (3)
Write the augmented matrix.

$$\begin{bmatrix} 3 & -4 & 2 & | & 15 \\ 2 & -1 & 1 & | & 13 \\ 1 & 2 & -1 & | & 5 \end{bmatrix}$$

$$\begin{bmatrix} 1 & 2 & -1 & | & 5 \\ 2 & -1 & 1 & | & 13 \\ 3 & -4 & 2 & | & 15 \end{bmatrix} R1 \leftrightarrow R3$$

$$\begin{bmatrix} 1 & 2 & -1 & | & 5 \\ 0 & -5 & 3 & | & 3 \\ 0 & -10 & 5 & | & 0 \end{bmatrix} \begin{matrix} \\ -2R1 + R2 \\ -3R1 + R3 \end{matrix}$$

$$\begin{bmatrix} 1 & 2 & -1 & | & 5 \\ 0 & 1 & -\frac{3}{5} & | & -\frac{3}{5} \\ 0 & -10 & 5 & | & 0 \end{bmatrix} -\frac{1}{5}R2$$

$$\begin{bmatrix} 1 & 2 & -1 & | & 5 \\ 0 & 1 & -\frac{3}{5} & | & -\frac{3}{5} \\ 0 & 0 & -1 & | & -6 \end{bmatrix} 10R2 + R3$$

$$\begin{bmatrix} 1 & 2 & -1 & | & 5 \\ 0 & 1 & -\frac{3}{5} & | & -\frac{3}{5} \\ 0 & 0 & 1 & | & 6 \end{bmatrix} -1R3$$

$$\begin{bmatrix} 1 & 2 & 0 & | & 11 \\ 0 & 1 & 0 & | & 3 \\ 0 & 0 & 1 & | & 6 \end{bmatrix} \begin{matrix} R3 + R1 \\ \frac{3}{5}R3 + R2 \\ \end{matrix}$$

$$\begin{bmatrix} 1 & 0 & 0 & | & 5 \\ 0 & 1 & 0 & | & 3 \\ 0 & 0 & 1 & | & 6 \end{bmatrix} -2R2 + R1$$

Solution set: $\{(5, 3, 6)\}$

8. Since $y = ax^2 + bx + c$, and the points $(-1, -.95)$, $(1, -.35)$, and $(2, -.8)$ are on the graph, we have the following equations:

$-.95 = a(-1)^2 + b(-1) + c$

$-.35 = a(1)^2 + b(1) + c$

$-.8 = a(2)^2 + b(2) + c.$

This becomes the following system
$a - b + c = -.95$ (1)
$a + b + c = -.35$ (2)
$4x + 2b + c = -.8$ (3)

First, eliminate b by adding equations (1) and (2).

$$\begin{array}{r} a - b + c = -.95 (1) \\ \underline{a + b + c = -.35 (2)} \\ 2a + c = -1.3 (4) \end{array}$$

Next, multiply equation (2) by -2 and add result to equation (3).

$$-2a - 2b - 2c = .7$$
$$\underline{4a + 2b + c = -.8}$$
$$2a - c = -.1 \quad (5)$$

We now solve the system

$$2a + 2c = -1.3 \quad (4)$$
$$2a - c = -.1. \quad (5)$$

Multiply equation (5) by -1 and add the result to equation (1).

$$2a + 2c = -1.3$$
$$\underline{-2a + c = .1}$$
$$ 3c = -1.2$$
$$ c = -.4$$

Substitute this value into equation (5).

$$2a - (-.4) = -.1$$
$$2a + .4 = -.1$$
$$2a = -.5$$
$$a = -.25$$

Substitute these values into equation (2).

$$(-.25) + b + (-.4) = -.35$$
$$b - .65 = -.35$$
$$b = .3$$

The equation of the parabola is

$$y = -.25x^2 + .3x - .4.$$

9. Let x = number of units from Toronto;
   y = number of units from Montreal;
   z = number of units from Ottawa.

$$x + y + z = 100 \quad \text{Total units}$$

$$80x + 50y + 65z = 5990 \quad \text{Total cost}$$
$$\text{Toronto units}$$
$$x = z \quad\quad = \text{Ottawa units}$$

Multiply the first equation by -50 and add to the second equation.

$$-50x - 50y - 50z = -5000$$
$$\underline{80x + 50y + 65z = 5990}$$
$$30x + 15z = 990$$

Substitute x for z in this equation.

$$30x + 15x = 990$$
$$45x = 990$$
$$x = 22$$

If $x = 22$, then $z = 22$. Substitute 22 for x and for z in the first equation and solve for y.

$$22 + y + 22 = 100$$
$$y = 56$$

The number of units ordered is:
22 units from Toronto, 56 units from Montreal, and 22 units from Ottawa.

10. $\begin{vmatrix} 6 & 8 \\ 2 & -7 \end{vmatrix} = 6(-7) - 2(8) = -58$

11. $\begin{vmatrix} 2 & 0 & 8 \\ -1 & 7 & 9 \\ 12 & 5 & -3 \end{vmatrix}$

This determinant may be evaluated by expanding about any row or any column. Choose the first row or second column because they contain a 0. We will expand by minors about the first row.

$$\begin{vmatrix} 2 & 0 & 8 \\ -1 & 7 & 9 \\ 12 & 5 & -3 \end{vmatrix}$$

$$= 2\begin{vmatrix} 7 & 9 \\ 5 & -3 \end{vmatrix} - 0\begin{vmatrix} -1 & 9 \\ 12 & -3 \end{vmatrix} + 8\begin{vmatrix} -1 & 7 \\ 12 & 5 \end{vmatrix}$$
$$= 2[7(-3) - 5(9)] - 0 + 8[(-1)(5) - 12(7)]$$
$$= 2(-21 - 45) + 8(-5 - 84)$$
$$= 2(-66) + 8(-89)$$
$$= -132 - 712$$
$$= -844$$

12. $2x - 3y = -33$
$4x + 5y = 11$

$$D = \begin{vmatrix} 2 & -3 \\ 4 & 5 \end{vmatrix} = 2(5) - 4(-3) = 22$$

$$D_x = \begin{vmatrix} -33 & -3 \\ 11 & 5 \end{vmatrix} = -33(5) - 11(-3) = -132$$

$$D_y = \begin{vmatrix} 2 & -33 \\ 4 & 11 \end{vmatrix} = 2(11) - 4(-33) = 154$$

$$x = \frac{D_x}{D} = \frac{-132}{22} = -6$$

$$y = \frac{D_y}{D} = \frac{154}{22} = 7$$

Solution set: $\{(-6, 7)\}$

13. $x + y - z = -4$
$2x - 3y - z = 5$
$x + 2y + 2z = 3$

Expand about row 1.

$$D = \begin{vmatrix} 1 & 1 & -1 \\ 2 & -3 & -1 \\ 1 & 2 & 2 \end{vmatrix}$$

$$= 1\begin{vmatrix} -3 & -1 \\ 2 & 2 \end{vmatrix} - 1\begin{vmatrix} 2 & -1 \\ 1 & 2 \end{vmatrix} + (-1)\begin{vmatrix} 2 & -3 \\ 1 & 2 \end{vmatrix}$$
$$= -4 - 1(5) - 1(7)$$
$$= -16$$

Expand about row 1.

$$D_x = \begin{vmatrix} -4 & 1 & -1 \\ 5 & -3 & -1 \\ 3 & 2 & 2 \end{vmatrix}$$

$$= -4\begin{vmatrix} -3 & -1 \\ 2 & 2 \end{vmatrix} - 1\begin{vmatrix} 5 & -1 \\ 3 & 2 \end{vmatrix} + (-1)\begin{vmatrix} 5 & -3 \\ 3 & 2 \end{vmatrix}$$

$$= -4(-4) - 1(13) - 1(19)$$

$$= -16$$

Expand about row 1.

$$D_y = \begin{vmatrix} 1 & -4 & -1 \\ 2 & 5 & -1 \\ 1 & 3 & 2 \end{vmatrix}$$

$$= 1\begin{vmatrix} 5 & -1 \\ 3 & 2 \end{vmatrix} - (-4)\begin{vmatrix} 2 & -1 \\ 1 & 2 \end{vmatrix} + (-1)\begin{vmatrix} 2 & 5 \\ 1 & 3 \end{vmatrix}$$

$$= 13 + 4(5) - 1(1)$$

$$= 32$$

Expand about row 1.

$$D_z = \begin{vmatrix} 1 & 1 & -4 \\ 2 & -3 & 5 \\ 1 & 2 & 3 \end{vmatrix}$$

$$= 1\begin{vmatrix} -3 & 5 \\ 2 & 3 \end{vmatrix} - 1\begin{vmatrix} 2 & 5 \\ 1 & 3 \end{vmatrix} + (-4)\begin{vmatrix} 2 & -3 \\ 1 & 2 \end{vmatrix}$$

$$= 1(-19) - 1(1) - 4(7)$$

$$= -48$$

$$x = \frac{D_x}{D} = \frac{-16}{-16} = 1$$

$$x = \frac{D_y}{D} = \frac{32}{-16} = -2$$

$$z = \frac{D_z}{D} = \frac{-48}{-16} = 3$$

Solution set: $\{(1, -2, 3)\}$

14. $\dfrac{x+2}{x^3 - x^2 + 4x} = \dfrac{x+2}{x(x^2 - x + 4)}$

Find A, B, and C so that

$$\frac{x+2}{x^3 - x^2 + 4x} = \frac{A}{x} + \frac{Bx + C}{x^2 - x + 4}.$$

Multiply both sides by $x(x^2 - x + 4)$ to get

$$x + 2 = A(x^2 - x + 4) + (Bx + C)(x)$$

$$x + 2 = (A + B)x^2 + (C - A)x + 4A$$

equating like terms we have

$A + B = 0$ (1)
$C - A = 1$ (2)
$4A = 2$ (3)

$A = \dfrac{1}{2}$, substitute into (1) and (2) and solve.

$$C = \frac{3}{2}$$

$$B = -\frac{1}{2}$$

$$\frac{x+2}{x^3 - x^2 + 4x} = \frac{1}{2x} + \frac{-x+3}{2(x^2 - x + 4)}.$$

15. Yes: the system will have exactly one solution if the line is tangent to the circle.

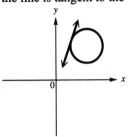

16. $2x^2 + y^2 = 6$ (1)
$x^2 - 4y^2 = -15$ (2)

$8x^2 + 4y^2 = 24$ Multiply (1) by 4.
$\underline{x^2 - 4y^2 = -15}$ (2)
$9x^2 \qquad = 9$
$\overline{\qquad x^2 = 1}$
$\qquad x = \pm 1$

Substitute these values into equation (1) and solve for y.

If $x = 1$, $2(1)^2 + y^2 = 6$
$\qquad\qquad 2 + y^2 = 6$
$\qquad\qquad\quad y^2 = 4$
$\qquad\qquad\quad\ y = \pm 2$.

Thus $(1, 2)$ and $(1, -2)$ are solutions.

If $x = -1$, $2(-1)^2 + y^2 = 6$
$\qquad\qquad\quad 2 + y^2 = 6$
$\qquad\qquad\qquad y^2 = 4$
$\qquad\qquad\qquad\ y = \pm 2$.

Thus, $(-1, 2)$ and $(-1, -2)$ are solutions.
Solution set: $\{(1, 2), (-1, 2), (1, -2), (-1, -2)\}$

17. $x^2 + y^2 = 25$ (1)
$x + y = 7$ (2)

Solve equation (2) for x:
$x = 7 - y$

Substitute this result into equation (1).

$$(7 - y)^2 + y^2 = 25$$

$$49 - 14y + y^2 + y^2 = 25$$

$$2y^2 - 14y + 24 = 0$$

$$y^2 - 7y + 12 = 0$$

$$(y - 3)(y - 4) = 0$$

$y = 3$ or $y = 4$
If $y = 3$, $x = y - 3 = 4$.
If $y = 4$, $x = 7 - 4 = 3$.
Solution set: $\{(3, 4), (4, 3)\}$

18. Let x and y represent the numbers.
$$x + y = -1 \quad (1)$$
$$x^2 + y^2 = 61 \quad (2)$$
Rewrite equation (1) as $y = -x - 1$ and substitute $-x - 1$ for y in (2).
$$x^2 + (-x - 1)^2 = 61$$
$$x^2 + x^2 + 2x + 1 = 61$$
$$2x^2 + 2x - 60 = 0$$
$$x^2 + x - 30 = 0$$
$$(x + 6)(x - 5) = 0$$
$$x = -6 \text{ or } x = 5$$
Substitute these values in equation (1) to find the corresponding values of y.
If $x = -6, -6 + y = -1$ or $y = 5$.
If $x = 5, 5 + y = -1$ or $y = -6$.
The same pair of numbers results from both cases.
The numbers are 5 and -6.

19. $x - 3y \geq 6$
$$y^2 \leq 16 - x^2$$
Graph $x - 3y = 6$ as a solid line with x-intercept 6 and y-intercept of -2. Shade the region below the line.
Graph $y^2 = 16 - x^2$ or $x^2 + y^2 = 16$ as a solid circle with a center at the origin and radius 4. Shade the region which is the interior of the circle.
The solution set is the intersection at these two regions, which is the region shaded in the final graph.

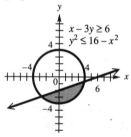

20. Find $x \geq 0$ and $y \geq 0$ such that
$$x + 2y \leq 24$$
$$3x + 4y \leq 60$$
and $2x + 3y$ is maximized.
Graph the equation $x + 2y = 24$ as a solid line with x-intercept 24 and y-intercept 12.
Graph the equation $3x + 4y = 60$ as a solid line with x-intercept 20 and y-intercept 15.
Graph the equation $x = 0$ (the y-axis).
Graph the equation $y = 0$ (the x-axis).
The region of feasible solutions is the intersection of the four regions.

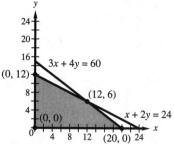

Three vertices are (0, 0), (0, 12), and (20, 0). To find the fourth vertex, we must solve the system
$$x + 2y = 24 \quad (1)$$
$$3x + 4y = 60 \quad (2)$$
To eliminate x, multiply equation (1) by -3 and add the result to equation (2).
$$-3x - 6y = -72$$
$$\underline{3x + 4y = 60}$$
$$-2y = -12$$
$$y = 6$$
Substitute this value into equation (1).
$$x + 2(6) = 24$$
$$x + 12 = 24$$
$$x = 24$$
The fourth vertex is (12, 6).
Find the value of $2x + 3y$ at each vertex.

Point	Value of $2x + 3y$
(0, 0)	$2(0) + 3(0) = 0$
(0, 12)	$2(0) + 3(12) = 36$
(12, 6)	$2(12) + 3(6) = 42 \leftarrow$ Maximum
(20, 0)	$2(20) + 3(0) = 40$

The maximum value is 42 at (12, 6).

21. Let x = number of VIP rings;
y = number of SST rings.
We translate the given information into the following linear programming problem.
Maximize $30x + 40y$ if
$$x + y \leq 24$$
$$3x + 2y \leq 60$$
$$x \geq 0, y \geq 0.$$
Graph $x + y = 24$ as a solid line with x-intercept 24 and y-intercept 24.
Graph $3x + 2y \leq 60$ as a solid line with x-intercept 20 and y-intercept 30.
Graph $x = 0$ (y-axis) as a solid line.
Graph $y = 0$ (x-axis) as a solid line.
The region of feasible solutions is the intersection of the four regions.

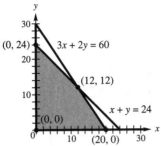

Three vertices are $(0, 0)$, $(0, 24)$, and $(20, 0)$. To find the fourth vertex, we must solve the system

$$x + y = 24 \quad (1)$$
$$3x + 2y = 60. \quad (2)$$

To eliminate x, multiply equation (1) by -3 and add the result to equation (2).

$$\begin{aligned} -3x - 3y &= -72 \\ 3x + 2y &= 60 \\ \hline -y &= -12 \\ y &= 12 \end{aligned}$$

Substitute this value into equation (1).

$$x + 12 = 24$$
$$x = 12$$

The fourth vertex is $(12, 12)$.

Point	Value of $30x + 40y$
$(0, 0)$	$30(0) + 40(0) = 0$
$(0, 24)$	$30(0) + 40(24) = 960 \leftarrow$ Minimum
$(12, 12)$	$30(12) + 40(12) = 840$
$(20, 0)$	$30(20) + 40(0) = 600$

The maximum profit is \$960 when no VIP rings are made and 24 SST rings are made.

22. $\begin{bmatrix} 5 & x+6 \\ 0 & 4 \end{bmatrix} = \begin{bmatrix} y-2 & 4-x \\ 0 & w+7 \end{bmatrix}$

All corresponding elements, position by position, of the two matrices must be equal.

$$5 = y - 2 \quad x + 6 = 4 \quad 4 = w + 7$$
$$7 = y \qquad 2x = -2 \quad -3 = w$$
$$\qquad\qquad x = -1$$

Thus, $x = -1$, $y = 7$, and $w = -3$.

23. $3\begin{bmatrix} 2 & 3 \\ 1 & -4 \\ 5 & 9 \end{bmatrix} - \begin{bmatrix} -2 & 6 \\ 3 & -1 \\ 0 & 8 \end{bmatrix} = \begin{bmatrix} 6 & 9 \\ 3 & -12 \\ 15 & 27 \end{bmatrix} + \begin{bmatrix} 2 & -6 \\ -3 & 1 \\ 0 & -8 \end{bmatrix}$

$$= \begin{bmatrix} 8 & 3 \\ 0 & -11 \\ 15 & 19 \end{bmatrix}$$

24. $\begin{bmatrix} 1 \\ 2 \end{bmatrix} + \begin{bmatrix} 4 \\ -6 \end{bmatrix} + \begin{bmatrix} 2 & 8 \\ -7 & 5 \end{bmatrix}$

The first two matrices are 2×1 and the third is 2×2. Only matrices of the same size can be added, so it is not possible to find this sum.

25. $\begin{bmatrix} 2 & 1 & -3 \\ 4 & 0 & 5 \end{bmatrix} \begin{bmatrix} 1 & 3 \\ 2 & 4 \\ 3 & -2 \end{bmatrix}$

$$= \begin{bmatrix} 2(1)+1(2)+(-3)(3) & 2(3)+1(4)+(-3)(-2) \\ 4(1)+0(2)+5(3) & 4(3)+0(4)+5(-2) \end{bmatrix}$$

$$= \begin{bmatrix} -5 & 16 \\ 19 & 2 \end{bmatrix}$$

26. $\begin{bmatrix} 2 & -4 \\ 3 & 5 \end{bmatrix} \begin{bmatrix} 4 \\ 2 \\ 7 \end{bmatrix}$

The first matrix is 2×2 and the second is 1×3. The product of two matrices can be found only if the number of columns of the first matrix is the same as the number of rows of the second matrix. The first matrix has two columns and the second has one row, so it is not possible to find this product.

27. There are associative, distributive, and identity properties that apply to multiplication of matrixes, but matrix multiplication is not commutative. The correct choice is A.

28. Find the inverse of $A = \begin{bmatrix} -8 & 5 \\ 3 & -2 \end{bmatrix}$, if it exists.

Form the augmented matrix $\begin{bmatrix} A | I_2 \end{bmatrix}$.

$$\begin{bmatrix} A | I_2 \end{bmatrix} = \begin{bmatrix} -8 & 5 & | & 1 & 0 \\ 3 & -2 & | & 0 & 1 \end{bmatrix}$$

Perform row transformations on $\begin{bmatrix} A | I_2 \end{bmatrix}$ until a matrix of the form $\begin{bmatrix} I_2 | B \end{bmatrix}$ is obtained.

$$\begin{bmatrix} A | I_2 \end{bmatrix} = \begin{bmatrix} 1 & -\frac{5}{8} & | & -\frac{1}{8} & 0 \\ 3 & -2 & | & 0 & 1 \end{bmatrix} -\frac{1}{8}R1$$

$$\begin{bmatrix} 1 & -\frac{5}{8} & | & -\frac{1}{8} & 0 \\ 0 & -\frac{1}{8} & | & \frac{3}{8} & 1 \end{bmatrix} -3R1 + R2$$

$$\begin{bmatrix} 1 & 0 & | & -2 & -5 \\ 0 & -\frac{1}{8} & | & \frac{3}{8} & 1 \end{bmatrix} -5R2 + R1$$

$$\begin{bmatrix} I_2 | B \end{bmatrix} = \begin{bmatrix} 1 & 0 & | & -2 & -5 \\ 0 & 1 & | & -3 & -8 \end{bmatrix} -8R2$$

$$A^{-1} = B = \begin{bmatrix} -2 & -5 \\ -3 & -8 \end{bmatrix}$$

29. Find the inverse of $A = \begin{bmatrix} 4 & 12 \\ 2 & 6 \end{bmatrix}$, if it exists.

$$[A|I_2] = \begin{bmatrix} 4 & 12 & | & 1 & 0 \\ 2 & 6 & | & 0 & 1 \end{bmatrix}$$

$$\begin{bmatrix} 1 & 3 & | & \frac{1}{4} & 0 \\ 2 & 6 & | & 0 & 1 \end{bmatrix} \frac{1}{4}R1$$

$$\begin{bmatrix} 1 & 3 & | & \frac{1}{4} & 0 \\ 0 & 0 & | & -\frac{1}{2} & 1 \end{bmatrix} -2R1+R2$$

The second row, second column element is now 0, so the desired transformation cannot be completed. Therefore, the inverse of the given matrix does not exist.

30. Find the inverse of $A = \begin{bmatrix} 1 & 3 & 4 \\ 2 & 7 & 8 \\ -2 & -5 & -7 \end{bmatrix}$, if it exists.

$$[A|I_3] = \begin{bmatrix} 1 & 3 & 4 & | & 1 & 0 & 0 \\ 2 & 7 & 8 & | & 0 & 1 & 0 \\ -2 & -5 & -7 & | & 0 & 0 & 1 \end{bmatrix}$$

$$\begin{bmatrix} 1 & 3 & 4 & | & 1 & 0 & 0 \\ 0 & 1 & 0 & | & -2 & 1 & 0 \\ 0 & 1 & 1 & | & 2 & 0 & 1 \end{bmatrix} \begin{matrix} -2R1+R2 \\ 2R1+R3 \end{matrix}$$

$$\begin{bmatrix} 1 & 0 & 1 & | & -5 & 0 & -3 \\ 0 & 1 & 0 & | & -2 & 1 & 0 \\ 0 & 1 & 1 & | & 2 & 0 & 1 \end{bmatrix} -3R3+R1$$

$$\begin{bmatrix} 1 & 0 & 1 & | & -5 & 0 & -3 \\ 0 & 1 & 0 & | & -2 & 1 & 0 \\ 0 & 0 & 1 & | & 4 & -1 & 1 \end{bmatrix} -1R2+R3$$

$$\begin{bmatrix} 1 & 0 & 0 & | & -9 & 1 & -4 \\ 0 & 1 & 0 & | & -2 & 1 & 0 \\ 0 & 0 & 1 & | & 4 & -1 & 1 \end{bmatrix} -1R3+R1$$

$$A^{-1} = \begin{bmatrix} -9 & 1 & -4 \\ -2 & 1 & 0 \\ 4 & -1 & 1 \end{bmatrix}$$

31. $2x + y = -6$
$3x - y = -29$

Represent the system as a matrix equation as follows.

Let $A = \begin{bmatrix} 2 & 1 \\ 3 & -1 \end{bmatrix}$, $X = \begin{bmatrix} x \\ y \end{bmatrix}$, $B = \begin{bmatrix} -6 \\ -29 \end{bmatrix}$,

then $AX = B$.

Find A^{-1}.

$$\begin{bmatrix} 2 & 1 & | & 1 & 0 \\ 3 & -1 & | & 0 & 1 \end{bmatrix}$$

$$\begin{bmatrix} 1 & \frac{1}{2} & | & \frac{1}{2} & 0 \\ 3 & -1 & | & 0 & 1 \end{bmatrix} \frac{1}{2}R1$$

$$\begin{bmatrix} 1 & \frac{1}{2} & | & \frac{1}{2} & 0 \\ 0 & -\frac{5}{2} & | & -\frac{3}{2} & 1 \end{bmatrix} -3R1+R2$$

$$\begin{bmatrix} 1 & 0 & | & \frac{1}{5} & \frac{1}{5} \\ 0 & -\frac{5}{2} & | & -\frac{3}{2} & 1 \end{bmatrix} \frac{1}{5}R2+R1$$

$$\begin{bmatrix} 1 & 0 & | & \frac{1}{5} & \frac{1}{5} \\ 0 & 1 & | & \frac{3}{5} & -\frac{2}{5} \end{bmatrix} -\frac{2}{5}R2$$

Thus,

$$A^{-1} = \begin{bmatrix} \frac{1}{5} & \frac{1}{5} \\ \frac{3}{5} & -\frac{2}{5} \end{bmatrix}.$$

$$A^{-1}B = \begin{bmatrix} \frac{1}{5} & \frac{1}{5} \\ \frac{3}{5} & -\frac{2}{5} \end{bmatrix} \begin{bmatrix} -6 \\ -29 \end{bmatrix}$$

$$= \begin{bmatrix} -\frac{6}{5} + \left(-\frac{29}{5}\right) \\ -\frac{18}{5} + \frac{58}{5} \end{bmatrix} = \begin{bmatrix} -\frac{35}{5} \\ \frac{40}{5} \end{bmatrix}$$

$$= \begin{bmatrix} -7 \\ 8 \end{bmatrix}$$

Since $X = A^{-1}B$, $X = \begin{bmatrix} -7 \\ 8 \end{bmatrix}$.

Solution set: $\{(-7, 8)\}$

32. $x + y = 5$
$y - 2z = 23$
$x + 3z = -27$

Let $A = \begin{bmatrix} 1 & 1 & 0 \\ 0 & 1 & -2 \\ 1 & 0 & 3 \end{bmatrix}$, $B = \begin{bmatrix} 5 \\ 23 \\ -27 \end{bmatrix}$, $X = \begin{bmatrix} x \\ y \\ z \end{bmatrix}$.

Then $AX = B$.

Find A^{-1}.

$$\left[\begin{array}{ccc|ccc} 1 & 1 & 0 & 1 & 0 & 0 \\ 0 & 1 & -2 & 0 & 1 & 0 \\ 1 & 0 & 3 & 0 & 0 & 1 \end{array}\right]$$

$$\left[\begin{array}{ccc|ccc} 1 & 1 & 0 & 1 & 0 & 0 \\ 0 & 1 & -2 & 0 & 1 & 0 \\ 0 & -1 & 3 & -1 & 0 & 1 \end{array}\right] -R1 + R3$$

$$\left[\begin{array}{ccc|ccc} 1 & 0 & 3 & 0 & 0 & 1 \\ 0 & 1 & -2 & 0 & 1 & 0 \\ 0 & -1 & 3 & -1 & 0 & 1 \end{array}\right] R3 + R1$$

$$\left[\begin{array}{ccc|ccc} 1 & 0 & 3 & 0 & 0 & 1 \\ 0 & 1 & -2 & 0 & 1 & 0 \\ 0 & 0 & 1 & -1 & 1 & 1 \end{array}\right] R2 + R3$$

$$\left[\begin{array}{ccc|ccc} 1 & 0 & 0 & 3 & -3 & -2 \\ 0 & 1 & -2 & 0 & 1 & 0 \\ 0 & 0 & 1 & -1 & 1 & 1 \end{array}\right] -3R3 + R1$$

$$\left[\begin{array}{ccc|ccc} 1 & 0 & 0 & 3 & -3 & -2 \\ 0 & 1 & 0 & -2 & 3 & 2 \\ 0 & 0 & 1 & -1 & 1 & 1 \end{array}\right] 2R3 + R2$$

Thus,

$A^{-1} = \begin{bmatrix} 3 & -3 & -2 \\ -2 & 3 & 2 \\ -1 & 1 & 1 \end{bmatrix}$.

$A^{-1}B = \begin{bmatrix} 3 & -3 & -2 \\ -2 & 3 & 2 \\ -1 & 1 & 1 \end{bmatrix} \begin{bmatrix} 5 \\ 23 \\ -27 \end{bmatrix}$

$= \begin{bmatrix} 0 \\ 5 \\ -9 \end{bmatrix} = X$

Solution set: $\{(0, 5, -9)\}$

CHAPTER 9 ANALYTIC GEOMETRY

Section 9.1

Exercises

1. **(a)** B

   (b) D

   (c) A

   (d) C

3. $x = -y^2$

   $\quad = -1(y-0)^2 + 0$

   $x - 0 = -1(y-0)^2$

   The vertex is (0, 0). The graph opens to the left and has the same shape as $y = x^2$. The domain is $(-\infty, 0]$. The range is $(-\infty, \infty)$. The axis is the horizontal line $y = 0$ (the x-axis). Use the vertex and axis and plot a few additional points.

x	-4	-1	0	-1	-4
y	-2	-1	0	1	2

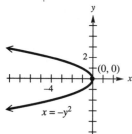

5. $x = (y-3)^2$

   $x - 0 = (y-3)^2$

   The vertex is (0, 3). The graph opens to the right and has the same shape as $x = y^2$. It is a translation 3 units up of the graph of $x = y^2$. The domain is $[0, \infty)$. The range is $(-\infty, \infty)$.

x	4	1	0	1	4
y	1	2	3	4	5

7. $x = (y-4)^2 + 2$

   $x - 2 = (y-4)^2$

   The vertex is (2, 4). The graph opens to the right and has the same shape as $x = y^2$. It is a translation 2 units to the right and 4 units up of the graph of $x = y^2$. The domain is $[2, \infty)$. The range is $(-\infty, \infty)$. The axis is the horizontal line $y = 4$.

x	6	3	2	3	6
y	2	3	4	5	6

9. $x = -3(y-1)^2 + 2$

   $x - 2 = -3(y-1)^2$

   The vertex is (2, 1). The graph opens to the left and has the same shape as $x = -3y^2$. It is a translation 1 unit up and 2 units to the right of the graph of $x = -3y^2$. The domain is $(-\infty, 2]$. The range is $(-\infty, \infty)$.

x	-10	-1	2	-1	-10
y	-1	0	1	2	3

11. $x = \dfrac{1}{2}(y-1)^2 + 4$

   $x - 4 = \dfrac{1}{2}(y-1)^2$

   The vertex is (4, 1). The graph opens to the right and has the same shape as $x = \dfrac{1}{2}y^2$. It is a translation 4 units to the right and 1 unit up of the graph of $x = \frac{1}{2}y^2$. The domain is $[4, \infty)$. The range is $(-\infty, \infty)$. The axis is the horizontal line $y = 1$.

x	6	4.5	4	4.5	6
y	−1	0	1	2	3

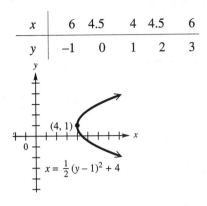

13. $x = y^2 + 4y + 2$

Complete the square on y to find the vertex and the axis.

$$x = (y^2 + 4y) + 2$$
$$= (y^2 + 4y + 4 - 4) + 2$$
$$= (y^2 + 4y + 4) - 4 + 2$$
$$= (y + 2)^2 - 2$$
$$x - (-2) = (y - (-2))^2$$

The vertex is (−2, −2) and the axis is the horizontal line $y = -2$. The domain is $[-2, \infty)$. The range is $(-\infty, \infty)$. The graph opens to the right and has the same shape as $x = y^2$. It is a translation 2 units to the left and 2 units down of the graph of $x = y^2$.

x	2	−1	−2	−1	2
y	−4	−3	−2	−1	0

(−2, −2)

$x = y^2 + 4y + 2$

15. $x = -4y^2 - 4y + 3$

Complete the square on y to find the vertex and the axis.

$$x = -4(y^2 + y) + 3$$
$$= -4\left(y^2 + y + \frac{1}{4} - \frac{1}{4}\right) + 3$$
$$= -4\left(y^2 + y + \frac{1}{4}\right) - 4\left(-\frac{1}{4}\right) + 3$$
$$= -4\left(y^2 + y + \frac{1}{4}\right) + 1 + 3$$
$$= -4\left(y + \frac{1}{2}\right)^2 + 4$$
$$x - 4 = -4\left(y - \left(-\frac{1}{2}\right)\right)^2$$

The vertex is $\left(4, -\frac{1}{2}\right)$ and the axis is the horizontal line $y = -\frac{1}{2}$. The domain is $(-\infty, 4]$. The range is $(-\infty, \infty)$. The graph opens to the left and has the same shape as $x = -4y^2$. It is a translation 4 units to the right and $\frac{1}{2}$ unit down of the graph of $x = -4y^2$.

x	−5	0	4	0	−5
y	$-2\frac{1}{2}$	$-1\frac{1}{2}$	$-\frac{1}{2}$	$\frac{1}{2}$	1

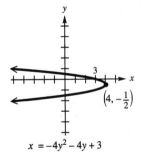

$\left(4, -\frac{1}{2}\right)$

$x = -4y^2 - 4y + 3$

17. $2x = y^2 - 4y + 6$

$$x = \frac{1}{2}y^2 - 2y + 3$$

Complete the square on y to find the vertex and the axis.

$$x = \frac{1}{2}(y^2 - 4y + 4 - 4) + 3$$

$$= \frac{1}{2}(y^2 - 4y + 4) - 2 + 3$$

$$= \frac{1}{2}(y - 2)^2 + 1$$

$$x - 1 = \frac{1}{2}(y - 2)^2$$

The vertex is (1, 2), and the axis is the horizontal line $y = 2$. The domain is $[1, \infty)$. The range is $(-\infty, \infty)$. The graph opens to the right and has the same shape as $x = \frac{1}{2}y^2$. It is a translation 1 unit to the right and 2 units up of the graph of $x = \frac{1}{2}y^2$.

x	3	1.5	1	1.5	3
y	0	1	2	3	4

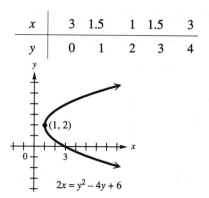

$2x = y^2 - 4y + 6$

19. $x^2 = 24y$

The equation has the form $x^2 = 4py$, with $4p = 24$, so $p = 6$. The parabola is vertical, with focus (0, 6), directrix $y = -6$, and the y-axis as axis of the parabola.

21. $y = -4x^2$

$$-\frac{1}{4}y = x^2$$

$$-\frac{1}{4} = 4p$$

$$-\frac{1}{16} = p$$

Focus: $\left(0, -\frac{1}{16}\right)$

Directrix: $y = \frac{1}{16}$

Axis: y-axis

23. $x = -32y^2$

$$-\frac{1}{32}x = y^2$$

This equation has the form $y^2 = 4px$, with $4p = -\frac{1}{32}$, so $p = -\frac{1}{128}$. The parabola is horizontal, with focus $\left(-\frac{1}{128}, 0\right)$, directrix $x = \frac{1}{128}$, and the x-axis as axis of the parabola.

25. $x = -\frac{1}{4}y^2$

$$-4x = y^2$$

$$4p = -4$$

$$p = -1$$

Focus: (-1, 0)

Directrix: $x = 1$

Axis: x-axis

27. $(y - 3)^2 = 12(x - 1)$

$$4p = 12$$

$$p = 3$$

The vertex is (1, 3).
The parabola opens to the right, so the focus is 3 units to the right of the vertex.

Focus: (4, 3)

Directrix: $x = -2$

Axis: $y = 3$

29. $(x - 7)^2 = 16(y + 5)$

$$4p = 16$$

$$p = 4$$

The vertex is (7, -5).
The parabola opens upward, so the focus is 4 units above the vertex and the directrix is 5 units below the vertex.

Focus: (7, -1)

Directrix: $y = -9$

Axis: $x = 7$

31. Focus is (5, 0), and vertex is at the origin.
Since the focus (5, 0) is on the x-axis, the parabola is horizontal. It opens to the right because $p = 5$ is positive. The equation has the form $y^2 = 4px$.

Substituting 5 for p, we find that an equation for this parabola is

$$y^2 = 4(5)x$$

$$y^2 = 20x.$$

33. Focus is $\left(0, \frac{1}{4}\right)$, and vertex is at the origin.

Since the focus $\left(0, \frac{1}{4}\right)$ is on the y-axis, the parabola is vertical. It opens up because p is positive. The equation has the form $x^2 = 4py$.

Substituting $\frac{1}{4}$ for p, we find that an equation for this parabola is

$$x^2 = 4\left(\frac{1}{4}\right)y$$
$$x^2 = y.$$

35. Through $(\sqrt{3}, 3)$, opening upward, vertex is at the origin.
Since the parabola opens upward, it is vertical, so the equation is of the form

$$x^2 = 4py.$$

Substitute $\sqrt{3}$ for x and 3 for y and solve for p.

$$(\sqrt{3})^2 = 4p(3)$$
$$3 = 12p$$
$$\frac{1}{4} = p$$

Thus, an equation of the parabola is

$$x^2 = 4\left(\frac{1}{4}\right)y$$
$$x^2 = y.$$

37. Through $(3, 2)$, symmetric with respect to the x-axis, vertex is at the origin.
Since the parabola is symmetric with respect to the x-axis, it is horizontal, so the equation is of the form

$$y^2 = 4px.$$

Substitute 3 for x and 2 for y and solve for p.

$$2^2 = 4p(3)$$
$$4 = 12p$$
$$\frac{1}{3} = p$$

Thus, an equation for the parabola is

$$y^2 = 4\left(\frac{1}{3}\right)x$$
$$y^2 = \frac{4}{3}x.$$

39. Vertex is $(4, 3)$, and focus is $(4, 5)$.
Since the focus is above the vertex, the axis is vertical and the parabola opens upward. The distance between the vertex and the focus is $5 - 3 = 2$. Since the parabola opens upward, choose $p = 2$. The equation will have the form

$$(x - h)^2 = 4p(y - k).$$

Substitute $p = 2$, $h = 4$, and $k = 3$ to find the required equation.

$$(x - 4)^2 = 4(2)(y - 3)$$
$$(x - 4)^2 = 8(y - 3)$$

41. Vertex is $(-5, 6)$, and focus is $(2, 6)$.
Since the focus is to the right of the vertex, the axis is horizontal and the parabola opens to the right. The distance between the vertex and the focus is $2 - (-5) = 7$. Since the parabola opens to the right, choose $p = 7$. The equation will have the form

$$(y - k)^2 = 4p(x - h).$$

Substitute $p = 7$, $h = -5$, and $k = 6$.

$$(y - 6)^2 = 4(7)[x - (-5)]$$
$$(y - 6)^2 = 28(x + 5)$$

43. Complete the square on y.

$$3y^2 + 6y - 4 = x$$
$$3y^2 + 6y = x + 4$$
$$3(y^2 + 2y) = x + 4$$
$$y^2 + 2y = \frac{x + 4}{3}$$
$$y^2 + 2y + 1 = \frac{x + 4}{3} + 1$$
$$(y + 1)^2 = \frac{x + 7}{3}$$
$$y + 1 = \pm\sqrt{\frac{x + 7}{3}}$$
$$y = -1 \pm\sqrt{\frac{x + 7}{3}}$$

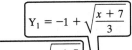

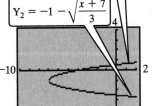

45. $-(y+1)^2 = x+2$

$(y+1)^2 = -x-2$

$y+1 = \pm\sqrt{-x-2}$

$y = -1 \pm \sqrt{-x-2}$

$\boxed{Y_1 = -1 + \sqrt{-x-2}}$

$\boxed{Y_2 = -1 - \sqrt{-x-2}}$

47. The equation is of the form

$x = ay^2 + by + c$

Substituting $x = -5$, $y = 1$, we get

$-5 = a(1)^2 + b(1) + c$

$-5 = a + b + c.$ (1)

Substituting $x = -14$, $y = -2$, we get

$-14 = a(-2)^2 + b(-2) + c$

$-14 = 4a - 2b + c.$ (2)

Substituting $x = -10$, $y = 2$, we get

$-10 = a(2)^2 + b(2) + c$

$-10 = 4a + 2b + c.$ (3)

48. The system of three equations is

$a + b + c = -5$ (1)

$4a - 2b + c = -14$ (2)

$4a + 2b + c = -10.$ (3)

Add equations (2) and (3).

$4a - 2b + c = -14$

$4a + 2b + c = -10$

$\overline{8a \qquad + 2c = -24}$ (4)

Add 2 times equation (1) to equation (2).

$2a + 2b + 2c = -10$

$4a - 2b + c = -14$

$\overline{6a \qquad + 3c = -24}$ (5)

Add −3 times equation (4) to 2 times equation (5).

$-24a - 6c = 72$

$12a + 6c = -48$

$\overline{-12a \qquad = 24}$

$a = -2$

Substitute $a = -2$ into equation (4).

$8(-2) + 2c = -24$

$2c = -8$

$c = -4$

Substitute $a = -2$ and $c = -4$ into equation (1).

$-2 + b - 4 = -5$

$b = 1$

Solution set: $\{(-2, 1, -4)\}$

49. Since $a = -2 < 0$, the parabola opens to the left.

50. Substituting $a = -2$, $b = 1$, and $c = -4$, the equation of the parabola is $x = -2y^2 + y - 4$.

51. **(a)** Locate the cannon at the origin. With $v = 252.982$, the equation becomes

$y = x - \dfrac{32}{v^2}x^2$

$y = x - \dfrac{32}{252.982^2}x^2$

$y = x - \dfrac{1}{2000}x^2$

Complete the square on x.

$y = -\dfrac{1}{2000}(x^2 - 2000x)$

$y = -\dfrac{1}{2000}(x^2 - 2000x + 1,000,000)$

$\qquad + \dfrac{1,000,000}{2000}$

$y = -\dfrac{1}{2000}(x - 1000)^2 + 500$

$y - 500 = -\dfrac{1}{2000}(x - 1000)^2$

Thus, the vertex of the parabola is located at $(1000, 500)$. The shell then travels an additional 1000 feet for a maximum distance of 2000 feet.

(b) The envelope parabola has x-intercepts located at $(-2000, 0)$ and $(2000, 0)$. The vertex is easily found to be located at $(0, 1000)$.

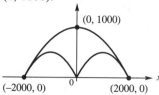

Because the axis of the parabola is the y-axis and it opens down, the equation is of the form $y = ax^2 + b$.

Since $(0, 1000)$ is on the parabola, we substitute $x = 0$ and $y = 1000$ into this equation to find the value of b.

$y = ax^2 + b$

$1000 = a \cdot 0^2 + b$

$b = 1000$

So the equation of the parabola becomes $y = ax^2 + 1000$.

Now substitute $x = 2000$ and $y = 0$ into this equation find the value of a.

$$y = ax^2 + 1000$$

$$0 = a \cdot 2000^2 + 1000$$

$$a \cdot 2000^2 = -1000$$

$$a = -\frac{1000}{2000^2}$$

$$a = -.00025$$

Thus, the equation of the envelope parabola is $y = 1000 - .00025x^2$.

(c) Using the equation of the envelope parabola in part (b), we calculate the maximum possible height of a shell when x is 1500 feet.

$$y = 1000 - .00025x^2$$

$$y = 1000 - .00025 \cdot 1500^2$$

$$y = 437.5$$

If the helicopter flies at a height of 450 feet, a shell fired by the canon would never reach the helicopter.

53. $y = \dfrac{19}{11}x - \dfrac{g}{3872}x^2$

(a) Using $g = 5.2$ for the moon and $g = 12.6$ for Mars, we obtain the equations

$$Y_1 = \frac{19}{11}x - \frac{5.2}{3872}x^2$$

$$\text{and } Y_2 = \frac{19}{11}x - \frac{12.6}{3872}x^2$$

Graph these two functions on the same screen using the simultaneous mode.

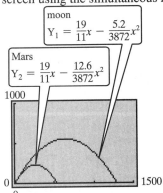

(b) Using TRACE, or the "maximum" option in the CALC menu, we see that the ball reaches a maximum height of $y \approx 229$ ft on Mars and $y \approx 555$ ft on the moon.

55. Place the parabola that represents the arch on a coordinate system with the center of the bottom of the arch at the origin.

Because the axis of the parabola is the y-axis, the equation of the parabola is of the form

$$y = ax^2 + b.$$

Since the y-intercept is 12, the equation becomes

$$y = ax^2 + 12.$$

Since $(6, 0)$ is on the parabola, we substitute $x = 6$ and $y = 0$ into this equation to find the value of a.

$$y = ax^2 + 12$$

$$0 = a \cdot 6^2 + 12$$

$$0 = 36a + 12$$

$$-12 = 36a$$

$$a = -\frac{1}{3}$$

Thus, the equation of the parabola is

$$y = -\frac{1}{3}x^2 + 12.$$

Next, we find the x-coordinate of point P, whose y-coordinate is 9 and whose x-coordinate is positive.

$$9 = -\frac{1}{3}x^2 + 12$$

$$-3 = -\frac{1}{3}x^2$$

$$9 = x^2$$

$$x = \sqrt{9} = 3$$

From the symmetry of the parabola, we see that the width of the arch 9 ft up is 2 (3 ft) = 6 ft.

57. $y = -\dfrac{k}{2v_0}x^2$

When $x = .4$,

$$y = \left(-\frac{5 \times 10^{-9}}{2 \times 10^7}\right)(.4)^2$$

$$= \left(-2.5 \times 10^{-16}\right)(.16)$$

$$= -4 \times 10^{-17}.$$

The alpha particle is deflected 4×10^{-17} m downward.

Section 9.2

Exercises

1. (a) A

(b) C

(c) D

(d) B

3. $\dfrac{x^2}{25} + \dfrac{y^2}{9} = 1$

The graph is an ellipse with center $(0, 0)$. Rewrite the given equation as

$\dfrac{x^2}{5^2} + \dfrac{y^2}{3^2} = 1.$

Since $5 > 3$, we have $a = 5$ and $b = 3$, and the major axis is horizontal. Thus, the vertices are $(-5, 0)$ and $(5, 0)$. The endpoints of the minor axis are $(0, -3)$ and $(0, 3)$. The domain is $[-5, 5]$. The range is $[-3, 3]$. Find the foci.

$c^2 = a^2 - b^2$
$\qquad = 25 - 9 = 16$
$\quad c = 4$

Since the major axis lies on the x-axis, the foci are $(-4, 0)$ and $(4, 0)$.

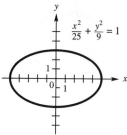

5. $\dfrac{x^2}{9} + y^2 = 1$

Rewrite the equation as $\dfrac{x^2}{3^2} + \dfrac{y^2}{1^2} = 1.$

The center is $(0, 0)$. The vertices are $(-3, 0)$ and $(3, 0)$. The endpoints of the minor axis are $(0, -1)$ and $(0, 1)$. The domain is $[-3, 3]$. The range is $[-1, 1]$. Find the foci.

$c^2 = a^2 - b^2$
$\qquad = 9 - 1 = 8$
$\quad c = \sqrt{8} = 2\sqrt{2}$

Since the major axis lies on the x-axis, the foci are $(-2\sqrt{2}, 0)$ and $(2\sqrt{2}, 0)$.

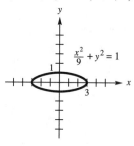

7. $9x^2 + y^2 = 81$

Divide both sides by 81.

$\dfrac{x^2}{9} + \dfrac{y^2}{81} = 1$ or $\dfrac{x^2}{3^2} + \dfrac{y^2}{9^2} = 1$

The center is $(0, 0)$. The vertices are $(0, -9)$ and $(0, 9)$. The endpoints of the minor axis are $(-3, 0)$ and $(3, 0)$. The domain is $[-3, 3]$. The range is $[-9, 9]$. Find the foci.

$c^2 = a^2 - b^2$
$\qquad = 81 - 9 = 72$
$\quad c = \sqrt{72} = 6\sqrt{2}$

Since the major axis lies on the y-axis, the foci are $\left(0, -6\sqrt{2}\right)$ and $\left(0, 6\sqrt{2}\right)$.

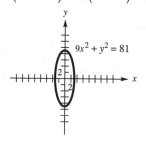

9. $4x^2 + 25y^2 = 100$

Divide both sides by 100.

$\dfrac{x^2}{25} + \dfrac{y^2}{4} = 1$ or $\dfrac{x^2}{5^2} + \dfrac{y^2}{2^2} = 1$

The center is $(0, 0)$. The vertices are $(-5, 0)$ and $(5, 0)$. The endpoints of the minor axis are $(0, -2)$ and $(0, 2)$. The domain is $[-5, 5]$. The range is $[-2, 2]$. Find the foci.

$c^2 = a^2 - b^2$
$\qquad = 25 - 4 = 21$
$\quad c = \sqrt{21}$

Since the major axis lies on the x-axis, the foci are $(-\sqrt{21}, 0)$ and $(\sqrt{21}, 0)$.

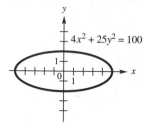

11. $\dfrac{(x-2)^2}{25} + \dfrac{(y-1)^2}{4} = 1$ or $\dfrac{(x-2)^2}{5^2} + \dfrac{(y-1)^2}{2^2} = 1$

The center is (2, 1). Since $a = 5$ is associated with x^2, the major axis of the ellipse is horizontal. The vertices are on a horizontal line through (2, 1), while the endpoints of the minor axis are on the vertical line through (2, 1). The vertices are 5 units to the left and right of the center at (–3, 1) and (7, 1). The endpoints of the minor axis are 2 units below and 2 units above the center at (2, –1) and (2, 3). The domain is [–3, 7]. The range is [–1, 3]. Find the foci.

$c^2 = a^2 - b^2$
$\quad = 25 - 4 = 21$
$\quad c = \sqrt{21}$

Since the major axis lies on $y = 1$, the foci are $(2 - \sqrt{21}, 1)$ and $(2 + \sqrt{21}, 1)$.

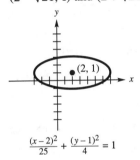

$\dfrac{(x-2)^2}{25} + \dfrac{(y-1)^2}{4} = 1$

13. $\dfrac{(x+3)^2}{16} + \dfrac{(y-2)^2}{36} = 1$ or $\dfrac{(x+3)^2}{4^2} + \dfrac{(y-2)^2}{6^2} = 1$

The center is (–3, 2). We have $a = 6$ and $b = 4$. Since $a = 6$ is associated with y^2, the major axis of the ellipse is vertical. The vertices are on the vertical line through (–3, 2), and the endpoints of the minor axis are on the horizontal line through (–3, 2). The vertices are 6 units below and 6 units above the center at (–3, –4) and (–3, 8). The endpoints of the minor axis are 4 units to the left and 4 units to the right of the center at (–7, 2) and (1, 2). The domain is [–7, 1]. The range is [–4, 8]. Find the foci.

$c^2 = a^2 - b^2$
$\quad = 36 - 16 = 20$
$\quad c = \sqrt{20} = 2\sqrt{5}$

Since the major axis lies on $x = -3$, the foci are $(-3, 2 - 2\sqrt{5})$ and $(-3, 2 + 2\sqrt{5})$.

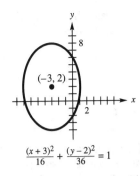

$\dfrac{(x+3)^2}{16} + \dfrac{(y-2)^2}{36} = 1$

15. x-intercepts ± 5; foci at (–3, 0), (3, 0)

From the given information, $a = 5$ and $c = 3$. Find b^2.

$c^2 = a^2 - b^2$
$9 = 25 - b^2$
$b^2 = 16$

Since the foci are on the x-axis and the ellipse is centered at the origin, the equation has the form

$\dfrac{x^2}{a^2} + \dfrac{y^2}{b^2} = 1.$

Since $a^2 = 25$ and $b^2 = 16$, the equation of the ellipse is

$\dfrac{x^2}{25} + \dfrac{y^2}{16} = 1.$

17. Major axis with length 6, foci at (0, 2), (0, –2).

The length of the major axes is $2a$, so we have

$2a = 6$
$\quad a = 3.$

From the foci, we have $c = 2$. Solve for b^2.

$c^2 = a^2 - b^2$
$4 = 9 - b^2$
$b^2 = 5$

Since the foci are on the y-axis and the ellipse is centered at the origin, the equation has the form

$\dfrac{x^2}{b^2} + \dfrac{y^2}{a^2} = 1.$

Thus, the equation is

$\dfrac{x^2}{5} + \dfrac{y^2}{9} = 1.$

19. Center at (5, 2); minor axis vertical, with length 8; $c = 3$.

The length of the minor axis is $2b$, so $b = 4$.

Find a^2.

$c^2 = a^2 - b^2$
$9 = a^2 - 16$
$a^2 = 25$

Since the center is (5, 2) and the minor axis is vertical, the equation has the form
$$\frac{(x-5)^2}{a^2}+\frac{(y-2)^2}{b^2}=1.$$
Thus, the equation is
$$\frac{(x-5)^2}{25}+\frac{(y-2)^2}{16}=1.$$

21. Vertices at (4, 9), (4, 1); minor axis with length 6.
The length of the minor axis is $2b$ so $b = 3$.
The distance between the vertices is $9 - 1 = 8$, so $2a = 8$ and thus $a = 4$. The center is halfway between the vertices and lies on the vertical line $x = 4$. The major axis is vertical, so the equation is of the form
$$\frac{(x-4)^2}{b^2}+\frac{(y-5)^2}{a^2}=1.$$
Thus, the equation is
$$\frac{(x-4)^2}{9}+\frac{(y-5)^2}{16}=1.$$

23. Foci at (0, –3), (0, 3); (8, 3) on the ellipse.
The distance between the foci is $3 - (-3) = 6$, so $2c = 6$ and thus $c = 3$. The center is halfway between the foci, so the center is (0, 0). Since the foci lie on the y-axis, the major axis is vertical, so the equation is of the form
$$\frac{x^2}{b^2}+\frac{y^2}{a^2}=1.$$
Let $P(8,3)$, $F'(0,-3)$, and $F(0,3)$ represent the point on the ellipse and the foci, respectively. Recall that for the point P on an ellipse, $PF' + PF = 2a$.
Then
$$PF' + PF = \sqrt{(8-0)^2+(3+3)^2}$$
$$+\sqrt{(8-0)^2+(3-3)^2}$$
$$=10+8$$
$$=18$$
$$2a = 18$$
$$a = 9.$$
Solve for b^2.
$$c^2 = a^2 - b^2$$
$$9 = 81 - b^2$$
$$b^2 = 72$$
Thus the equation is
$$\frac{x^2}{72}+\frac{y^2}{81}=1.$$

25. Foci at (0, 4), (0, –4); sum of distances from foci to point on ellipse is 10.
The distance between the foci is $4 - (-4) = 8$, so $2c = 8$ and thus $c = 4$. The center is halfway between the foci, so the center is (0, 0). Since the foci lie on the y-axis, the equation is of the form
$$\frac{x^2}{b^2}+\frac{y^2}{a^2}=1.$$
The sum of the distances from the foci to any point on the ellipse is 10, so
$$2a = 10$$
$$a = 5.$$
Solve for b^2.
$$c^2 = a^2 - b^2$$
$$16 = 25 - b^2$$
$$b^2 = 9$$
Thus, the equation is $\dfrac{x^2}{9}+\dfrac{y^2}{25}=1.$

27. Eccentricity $\dfrac{3}{4}$, foci at (0, –2), (0, 2).
The foci are on the y-axis, so the equation has the form $\dfrac{x^2}{b^2}+\dfrac{y^2}{a^2}=1.$
From the foci, we have $c = 2$. Use the eccentricity to find a.
$$e = \frac{c}{a}$$
$$\frac{3}{4} = \frac{2}{a}$$
$$a = \frac{8}{3}$$
Now, solve for b^2.
$$c^2 = a^2 - b^2$$
$$4 = \frac{64}{9} - b^2$$
$$b^2 = \frac{28}{9}$$
Thus, the equation is
$$\frac{x^2}{\frac{28}{9}}+\frac{y^2}{\frac{64}{9}}=1 \text{ or } \frac{9x^2}{28}+\frac{9y^2}{64}=1.$$

29. $\dfrac{y}{2} = \sqrt{1 - \dfrac{x^2}{25}}$

Square both sides to get

$$\dfrac{y^2}{4} = 1 - \dfrac{x^2}{25}$$

$$\dfrac{x^2}{25} + \dfrac{y^2}{4} = 1,$$

which is the equation of an ellipse with x-intercepts ± 5 and y-intercepts ± 2. Since

$$\sqrt{1 - \dfrac{x^2}{25}} \ge 0,$$

the only possible values of y are those making

$\dfrac{y}{2} \ge 0$ or $y \ge 0$.

The domain is $[-5, 5]$. The range is $[0, 2]$. The graph of the original equation is the upper half of the ellipse. By applying the vertical line test, we see that this is the graph of a function.

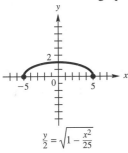

$\dfrac{y}{2} = \sqrt{1 - \dfrac{x^2}{25}}$

31. $x = -\sqrt{1 - \dfrac{y^2}{64}}$

Square both sides to get

$$x^2 = 1 - \dfrac{y^2}{64}$$

$$x^2 + \dfrac{y^2}{64} = 1,$$

the equation of an ellipse centered at $(0, 0)$, with vertices $(0, 8)$ and $(0, -8)$ and minor axis endpoints at $(-1, 0)$ and $(1, 0)$.
Since

$$-\sqrt{1 - \dfrac{y^2}{64}} \le 0,$$

we must have $x \le 0$, so the graph of the original equation is the left half of the ellipse. The domain is $[-1, 0]$. The range is $[-8, 8]$. The vertical line test shows that this is not the graph of a function.

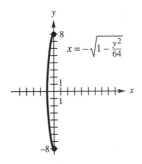

$x = -\sqrt{1 - \dfrac{y^2}{64}}$

33. Solve for y in the equation of the ellipse.

$$\dfrac{x^2}{16} + \dfrac{y^2}{4} = 1$$

$$\dfrac{y^2}{4} = 1 - \dfrac{x^2}{16}$$

$$y^2 = 4\left(1 - \dfrac{x^2}{16}\right)$$

$$y = \pm\sqrt{4\left(1 - \dfrac{x^2}{16}\right)}$$

$$y = \pm 2\sqrt{1 - \dfrac{x^2}{16}}$$

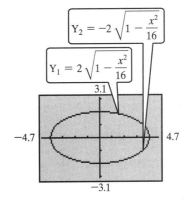

$Y_2 = -2\sqrt{1 - \dfrac{x^2}{16}}$

$Y_1 = 2\sqrt{1 - \dfrac{x^2}{16}}$

35. Solve for y in the equation of the ellipse.

$$\frac{(x-3)^2}{25} + \frac{y^2}{9} = 1$$

$$\frac{y^2}{9} = 1 - \frac{(x-3)^2}{25}$$

$$y^2 = 9\left(1 - \frac{(x-3)^2}{25}\right)$$

$$y = \pm\sqrt{9\left(1 - \frac{(x-3)^2}{25}\right)}$$

$$y = \pm 3\sqrt{1 - \frac{(x-3)^2}{25}}$$

$$Y_1 = 3\sqrt{1 - \frac{(x-3)^2}{25}}$$

$$Y_2 = -3\sqrt{1 - \frac{(x-3)^2}{25}}$$

37. $[-1, 5]$

38. Examining the graphing calculator solution

$$y = -1 \pm 4\sqrt{1 - \frac{(x-2)^2}{9}}$$

the expression under the radical $1 - \frac{(x-2)^2}{9}$

must be greater than or equal to 0.

39. $1 - \frac{(x-2)^2}{9} \geq 0$

40.

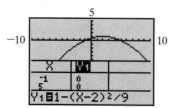

The graph lies *above* or *on* the x-axis on the interval $[-1, 5]$. This does agree with the answer in Exercise 37.

43. (a) An ellipse with major axis 620 ft and minor axis 513 ft has $2a = 620$ and $2b = 513$, or $a = 310$ and $b = 256.5$. The distance between the center and a focus is c, where

$$c^2 = a^2 - b^2$$

$$c^2 = 310^2 - (256.5)^2$$

$$c^2 = 96,100 - 65,792.25$$

$$c^2 = 30,307.75$$

$$c \approx 174.1$$

(The negative value of c is rejected.) The distance between the two foci of the ellipse is $2c = 2(174.1) = 348.2$. There are 348.2 ft between the foci of the Roman Coliseum.

(b) $C \approx 2\pi\sqrt{\dfrac{a^2 + b^2}{2}}$

Let $a = \dfrac{620}{2} = 310$,

and $b = \dfrac{513}{2} = 256.5$.

$$C \approx 2\pi\sqrt{\frac{310^2 + (256.5)^2}{2}}$$

$$\approx 1787.6$$

The circumference of the Roman Coliseum is about 1787.6 ft.

45. The stone and the wave source must be placed at the foci, $(c, 0)$ and $(-c, 0)$. Here $a^2 = 36$ and $b^2 = 9$, so $c = \sqrt{a^2 - b^2} = \sqrt{36 - 9} = \sqrt{27} = 3\sqrt{3}$. Thus, the kidney stone and source of the beam must be placed $3\sqrt{3} \approx 5.20$ units from the center.

47. If the height is 15 feet at the center, $a^2 = 15^2 = 225$. If the width is 20 feet, each half is 10 feet, so $b^2 = 10^2 = 100$.

Thus, the equation of the ellipse is

$$\frac{x^2}{10^2} + \frac{y^2}{15^2} = 1$$

$$\frac{x^2}{100} + \frac{y^2}{225} = 1.$$

Find the height of the truck, that is, the height y of the overpass.

Since the truck is 12 feet wide, it falls 6 feet to the right and 6 feet to the left of the center as it goes under the overpass, that is $x = \pm 6$.

$$\frac{(\pm 6)^2}{100} + \frac{y^2}{225} = 1$$

$$\frac{36}{100} + \frac{y^2}{225} = 1$$

Multiply by 22,500.

$$8100 + 100y^2 = 22,500$$
$$100y^2 = 14,400$$
$$y^2 = 144$$
$$y = \pm 12$$

Discard -12, since height cannot be negative. The tallest truck can be 12 feet tall.

49. (a) v_{max}

$$= \frac{2\pi a}{P}\sqrt{\frac{1+e}{1-e}}$$

$$= \frac{2\pi \times 1.496 \times 10^8}{60 \times 60 \times 24 \times 365.25} \times \sqrt{\frac{1 + .0167}{1 - .0167}}$$

$$\approx 30.3 \text{ km/sec}$$

v_{min}

$$= \frac{2\pi a}{P}\sqrt{\frac{1-e}{1+e}}$$

$$= \frac{2\pi \times 1.496 \times 10^8}{60 \times 60 \times 24 \times 365.25} \times \sqrt{\frac{1 - .0167}{1 + .0167}}$$

$$\approx 29.3 \text{ km/sec}$$

(b) For a circle $e = 0$, so $v_{max} = v_{min} = \frac{2\pi}{P}$.

The minimum and maximum velocities are equal. Therefore, the planet's velocity is constant.

(c) A planet is at its maximum and minimum distance from a focus when it is located at the vertices of the ellipse. Thus, the minimum and maximum velocities of a planet will occur at the vertices of the elliptical orbit.

51. (a) Use the given values of e and a to find the value of c for each planet. Then use the values of a and c to find the value of b.
Neptune:

$$e = \frac{c}{a}$$
$$c = ea$$
$$= (.009)(30.1)$$
$$= .2709$$
$$b^2 = a^2 - c^2$$
$$= (30.1)^2 - (.2709)^2$$
$$\approx 905.9366$$
$$b \approx 30.1$$

Since $c = .2709$, the graph should be translated .2709 units to the right so that the sun will be located at the origin. It's essentially circular with equation

$$\frac{(x - .2709)^2}{30.1^2} + \frac{y^2}{30.1^2} = 1.$$

Pluto:

$$c = ea$$
$$= (.249)(39.4)$$
$$= 9.8106$$
$$b^2 = a^2 - c^2$$
$$= (39.4)^2 - (9.8106)^2$$
$$\approx 1456.1121$$
$$b \approx 38.16$$

As with Neptune, we translate the graph by c units to the right so that the sun will be located at the origin. The equation is

$$\frac{(x - 9.8106)^2}{39.4^2} + \frac{y^2}{38.16^2} = 1.$$

(b) In order to graph these equations on a graphing calculator, we must solve each equation for y. Each equation will be broken down into two functions, so we will need to graph four functions.
Neptune:

$$\frac{(x - .2709)^2}{30.1^2} + \frac{y^2}{30.1^2} = 1.$$
$$(x - .2709)^2 + y^2 = 30.1^2$$
$$y = \pm\sqrt{30.1^2 - (x - .2709)^2}$$

Pluto:

$$\frac{(x - 9.8106)^2}{39.4^2} + \frac{y^2}{38.16^2} = 1$$

$$\frac{y^2}{38.16^2} = 1 - \frac{(x - 9.8106)^2}{39.4^2}$$

$$y^2 = 38.16^2\left(1 - \frac{(x - 9.8106)^2}{39.4^2}\right)$$

$$y = \pm\sqrt{38.16^2\left(1 - \frac{(x - 9.8106)^2}{39.4^2}\right)}$$

$$y = \pm 38.16\sqrt{1 - \frac{(x - 9.8106)^2}{39.4^2}}$$

Graph the four functions

$$Y_1 = \sqrt{30.1^2 - (x - .2709)^2}$$

$$Y_2 = -\sqrt{30.1^2 - (x - .2709)^2} = -Y_1$$

$$Y_3 = 38.16\sqrt{1 - \frac{(x - 9.8106)^2}{39.4^2}}$$

$$Y_4 = -38.16\sqrt{1 - \frac{(x - 9.8106)^2}{39.4^2}} = -Y_3$$

on the same screen.

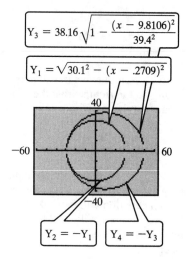

53. Replace the number 1 by 4. Next, to obtain the standard equation for an ellipse, multiply both sides by $\frac{1}{4}$ and simplify.

$$\frac{x^2}{25} + \frac{y^2}{9} = 4$$

$$\frac{1}{4}\left(\frac{x^2}{25} + \frac{y^2}{9}\right) = \frac{1}{4} \cdot 4$$

$$\frac{x^2}{100} + \frac{y^2}{36} = 1$$

$$\frac{x^2}{10^2} + \frac{y^2}{6^2} = 1$$

The original ellipse had $a = 5$ and $b = 3$. The new ellipse has $a = 10$ and $b = 6$. Thus, the original is enlarged by a factor of 2.

Section 9.3

Connections (*page 760*)

Locate the center of the hyperbola at the origin and label as illustrated.

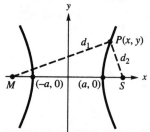

From the definition of a hyperbola, we know the difference of the distances equals the constant $2a$. And, substituting the given values, we have

$$d_1 - d_2 = 2a$$

$$80 - 30 = 2a$$

$$50 = 2a$$

$$a = 25.$$

Since the distance between foci is $2c$, we have

$$2c = 100$$

$$c = 50.$$

Using these values, we solve for b^2.

$$b^2 = c^2 - a^2$$

$$b^2 = 50^2 - 25^2$$

$$b^2 = 1875$$

Substituting these values into the general equation of a hyperbola, we get

$$\frac{x^2}{a^2} - \frac{y^2}{b^2} = 1$$

$$\frac{x^2}{625} - \frac{y^2}{1875} = 1.$$

Exercises

1. $\dfrac{x^2}{25} + \dfrac{y^2}{9} = 1$

This is an equation of an ellipse with x-intercepts ± 5 and y-intercepts ± 3. The correct graph is C.

3. $\dfrac{x^2}{9} - \dfrac{y^2}{25} = 1$

This is the graph of a hyperbola with x-intercepts ± 3 and no y-intercepts. The correct graph is D.

5. $\dfrac{x^2}{16} - \dfrac{y^2}{9} = 1$

This equation may be written as

$\dfrac{x^2}{4^2} - \dfrac{y^2}{3^2} = 1$, which has the form $\dfrac{x^2}{a^2} - \dfrac{y^2}{b^2} = 1$.

The hyperbola is centered at (0, 0) with branches opening to the left and right. The graph has x-intercepts ± 4, so the vertices are $(-4, 0)$ and $(4, 0)$. There are no y-intercepts. The domain is $(-\infty, -4] \cup [4, \infty)$. The range is $(-\infty, \infty)$. The foci are on the x-axis.

$c^2 = a^2 + b^2$
$\quad = 16 + 9 = 25$
$\quad c = 5$

The foci are $(-5, 0)$ and $(5, 0)$. The asymptotes are

$y = \pm \dfrac{b}{a} x = \pm \dfrac{3}{4} x.$

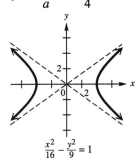

$\dfrac{x^2}{16} - \dfrac{y^2}{9} = 1$

7. $\dfrac{y^2}{25} - \dfrac{x^2}{49} = 1$

This equation may be written as $\dfrac{y^2}{5^2} - \dfrac{x^2}{7^2} = 1$

which has the form $\dfrac{y^2}{a^2} - \dfrac{x^2}{b^2} = 1.$

The hyperbola is centered at (0, 0) with branches opening upward and downward. The graph has y-intercepts ± 5, so the vertices are $(0, -5)$ and $(0, 5)$. There are no x-intercepts. The domain is $(-\infty, \infty)$. The range is $(-\infty, -5] \cup [5, \infty)$. The foci are on the y-axis.

$c^2 = a^2 + b^2$
$\quad = 25 + 49 = 74$
$\quad c = \sqrt{74}$

The foci are $(0, -\sqrt{74})$ and $(0, \sqrt{74})$. The asymptotes are $y = \pm \dfrac{a}{b} x = \pm \dfrac{5}{7} x.$

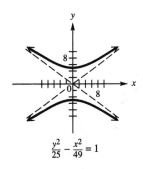

$\dfrac{y^2}{25} - \dfrac{x^2}{49} = 1$

9. $x^2 - y^2 = 9$

Divide both sides by 9.

$\dfrac{x^2}{9} - \dfrac{y^2}{9} = 1$

Thus, $a = 3$ and $b = 3$.

The center is (0, 0), and the vertices are $(-3, 0)$ and $(3, 0)$. The domain is $(-\infty, -3] \cup [3, \infty)$. The range is $(-\infty, \infty)$.

$c^2 = a^2 + b^2$
$\quad = 9 + 9 = 18$
$\quad c = \sqrt{18} = 3\sqrt{2}$

The foci are $(-3\sqrt{2}, 0)$ and $(3\sqrt{2}, 0)$. The asymptotes are $y = \pm \dfrac{b}{a} x = \pm \dfrac{3}{3} x = \pm x.$

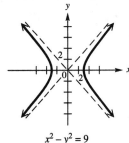

$x^2 - y^2 = 9$

11. $9x^2 - 25y^2 = 225$

Divide both sides by 225.

$\dfrac{9x^2}{225} - \dfrac{25y^2}{225} = \dfrac{225}{225}$

$\dfrac{x^2}{25} - \dfrac{y^2}{9} = 1$

Thus, $a = 5$ and $b = 3$.

The center is (0, 0), and the vertices are $(-5, 0)$ and $(5, 0)$. The domain is $(-\infty, -5] \cup [5, \infty)$. The range is $(-\infty, \infty)$.

$c^2 = a^2 + b^2$
$\quad = 25 + 9 = 34$
$\quad c = \sqrt{34}$

The foci are $(-\sqrt{34}, 0)$ and $(\sqrt{34}, 0)$. The asymptotes are $y = \pm \dfrac{b}{a} x = \pm \dfrac{3}{5} x.$

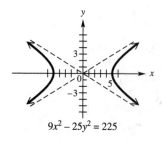

$$9x^2 - 25y^2 = 225$$

13. $4x^2 - y^2 = -16$

Divide both sides by -16 and rearrange.

$$\frac{4x^2}{-16} - \frac{y^2}{-16} = \frac{-16}{-16}$$

$$-\frac{x^2}{4} + \frac{y^2}{16} = 1$$

$$\frac{y^2}{16} - \frac{x^2}{4} = 1$$

Thus, $a = 4$ and $b = 2$.
The center is $(0, 0)$, and the vertices are $(0, -4)$ and $(0, 4)$. The domain is $(-\infty, \infty)$. The range is $(-\infty, -4] \cup [4, \infty)$.

$$c^2 = a^2 + b^2$$

$$= 16 + 4 = 20$$

$$c = \sqrt{20} = 2\sqrt{5}$$

The foci are $(0, -2\sqrt{5})$ and $(0, 2\sqrt{5})$. The asymptotes are $y = \pm\dfrac{a}{b}x = \pm\dfrac{4}{2}x = \pm 2x$.

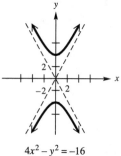

$$4x^2 - y^2 = -16$$

15. $9x^2 - 4y^2 = 1$

Rewrite in standard form.

$$\frac{x^2}{\frac{1}{9}} - \frac{y^2}{\frac{1}{4}} = 1$$

Thus, $a = \dfrac{1}{3}$ and $b = \dfrac{1}{2}$.
The center is $(0, 0)$, and the vertices are $\left(-\dfrac{1}{3}, 0\right)$ and $\left(\dfrac{1}{3}, 0\right)$. The domain is $\left(-\infty, -\dfrac{1}{3}\right] \cup \left[\dfrac{1}{3}, \infty\right)$. The range is $(-\infty, \infty)$.

$$c^2 = a^2 + b^2$$

$$= \frac{1}{9} + \frac{1}{4} = \frac{13}{36}$$

$$c = \sqrt{\frac{13}{36}} = \frac{\sqrt{13}}{6}$$

The foci are $\left(-\dfrac{\sqrt{13}}{6}, 0\right)$ and $\left(\dfrac{\sqrt{13}}{6}, 0\right)$. The asymptotes are $y = \pm\dfrac{b}{a}x = \pm\dfrac{\frac{1}{2}}{\frac{1}{3}}x = \pm\dfrac{3}{2}x.$

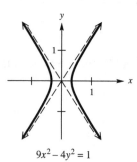

$$9x^2 - 4y^2 = 1$$

17. $\dfrac{(y-7)^2}{36} - \dfrac{(x-4)^2}{64} = 1$

Here, $a = 6$ and $b = 8$.
The center is $(4, 7)$. The vertices are 6 units above and below the center $(4, 7)$. These points are $(4, 1)$ and $(4, 13)$. The domain is $(-\infty, \infty)$. The range is $(-\infty, 1] \cup [13, \infty)$.

$$c^2 = a^2 + b^2$$

$$= 36 + 64 = 100$$

$$c = \sqrt{100} = 10$$

The foci are 10 units below and above the center $(4, 7)$. The foci are $(4, -3)$ and $(4, 17)$. The asymptotes are

$$y - k = \pm\frac{a}{b}(x - h)$$

$$y - 7 = \pm\frac{6}{8}(x - 4)$$

$$y = 7 \pm \frac{3}{4}(x - 4).$$

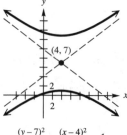

$$\frac{(y-7)^2}{36} - \frac{(x-4)^2}{64} = 1$$

19. $\dfrac{(x+3)^2}{16} - \dfrac{(y-2)^2}{9} = 1$

Here, $a = 4$ and $b = 3$.

The center is $(-3, 2)$. The vertices are 4 units to the left and right of the center $(-3, 2)$. These points are $(-7, 2)$ and $(1, 2)$. The domain is $(-\infty, -7] \cup [1, \infty)$. The range is $(-\infty, \infty)$.

$$c^2 = a^2 + b^2$$
$$= 16 + 9 = 25$$
$$x = \sqrt{25} = 5$$

The foci are 5 units to the left and right of the center $(-3, 2)$. These points are $(-8, 2)$ and $(2, 2)$. The asymptotes are

$$y - k = \pm\frac{b}{a}(x - h)$$
$$y - 2 = \pm\frac{3}{4}(x + 3)$$
$$y = 2 \pm\frac{3}{4}(x + 3).$$

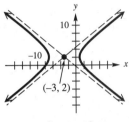

$$\dfrac{(x+3)^2}{16} - \dfrac{(y-2)^2}{9} = 1$$

21. $16(x + 5)^2 - (y - 3)^2 = 1$

Rewrite in standard form.

$$\dfrac{(x+5)^2}{\frac{1}{16}} - \dfrac{(y-3)^2}{1} = 1$$

Thus, $a = \dfrac{1}{4}$ and $b = 1$.

The center is $(-5, 3)$. The vertices are $\dfrac{1}{4}$ unit to the left and right of $(-5, 3)$. These points are $\left(-\dfrac{21}{4}, 3\right)$ and $\left(-\dfrac{19}{4}, 3\right)$. The domain is $\left(-\infty, -\dfrac{21}{4}\right] \cup \left[-\dfrac{19}{4}, \infty\right)$. The range is $(-\infty, \infty)$.

$$c^2 = a^2 + b^2$$
$$= \dfrac{1}{16} + 1 = \dfrac{17}{16}$$
$$c = \sqrt{\dfrac{17}{16}} = \dfrac{\sqrt{17}}{4}$$

The foci are $\dfrac{\sqrt{17}}{4}$ units to the left and right of the center $(-5, 3)$. These points are $\left(-5 - \dfrac{\sqrt{17}}{4}, 3\right)$ and $\left(-5 + \dfrac{\sqrt{17}}{4}, 3\right)$. The asymptotes are

$$y - k = \pm\frac{b}{a}(x - h)$$
$$y - 3 = \pm\frac{1}{\frac{1}{4}}(x + 5)$$
$$y = 3 \pm 4(x + 5).$$

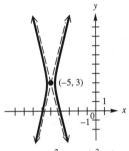

$$16(x + 5)^2 - (y - 3)^2 = 1$$

23. $\dfrac{y}{3} = \sqrt{1 + \dfrac{x^2}{16}}$

Square both sides and write in standard form.

$$\dfrac{y^2}{9} = 1 + \dfrac{x^2}{16}$$
$$\dfrac{y^2}{9} - \dfrac{x^2}{16} = 1$$

This is the equation of a hyperbola centered at $(0, 0)$, with vertices $(0, \pm 3)$ and asymptotes $y = \pm\dfrac{3}{4}x$. The original equation is the top half of the hyperbola. The domain is $(-\infty, \infty)$. The range is $[3, \infty)$. The vertical line test shows this is a graph of a function.

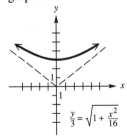

$$\dfrac{y}{3} = \sqrt{1 + \dfrac{x^2}{16}}$$

25. $5x = -\sqrt{1 + 4y^2}$

Square both sides and write in standard form.
$$25x^2 = 1 + 4y^2$$
$$25x^2 - 4y^2 = 1$$
$$\frac{x^2}{\frac{1}{25}} - \frac{y^2}{\frac{1}{4}} = 1$$

This is the equation of a hyperbola centered at $(0, 0)$, with vertices $\left(\pm\frac{1}{5}, 0\right)$ and asymptotes $y = \pm\frac{25}{4}x$. The original equation is the left half of the hyperbola. The domain is $(-\infty, -.2]$. The range is $(-\infty, \infty)$. The vertical line test shows this is not the graph of a function.

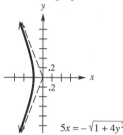

27. x-intercepts ± 4; foci at $(-5, 0)$, $(5, 0)$.
Since the x-intercepts are ± 4, the equation has the form $\frac{x^2}{a^2} - \frac{y^2}{b^2} = 1$. $a = 4$, so $a^2 = 16$.
The foci are at $(\pm 5, 0)$, so $c = 5$.
$$c^2 = a^2 + b^2$$
$$25 = 16 + b^2$$
$$9 = b^2$$
The equation is $\frac{x^2}{16} - \frac{y^2}{9} = 1$.

29. Vertices at $(0, 6)$, $(0, -6)$; asymptotes $y = \pm\frac{1}{2}x$.
Since the vertices are at $(0, \pm 6)$, the equation has the form $\frac{y^2}{a^2} - \frac{x^2}{b^2} = 1$. $a = 6$, so $a^2 = 36$.

The slopes of the asymptotes are $\pm\frac{1}{2}$, so
$$\frac{a}{b} = \frac{1}{2}$$
$$\frac{6}{b} = \frac{1}{2}$$
$$b = 12$$
$$b^2 = 144.$$

The equation is $\frac{y^2}{36} - \frac{x^2}{144} = 1$.

31. Vertices at $(-3, 0)$, $(3, 0)$; passing through $(6, 1)$.
Since the vertices are at $(\pm 3, 0)$, the equation has the form $\frac{x^2}{9} - \frac{y^2}{b^2} = 1$.
The hyperbola goes through the point $(6, 1)$, so the substitute $x = 6$ and $y = 1$ into the equation and solve for b^2.
$$\frac{36}{9} - \frac{1}{b^2} = 1$$
$$4 - \frac{1}{b^2} = 1$$
$$-\frac{1}{b^2} = -3$$
$$b^2 = \frac{1}{3}$$
The equation is $\frac{x^2}{9} - \frac{y^2}{\frac{1}{3}} = 1$ or $\frac{x^2}{9} - 3y^2 = 1$.

33. Foci at $(0, \sqrt{13})$, $(0, -\sqrt{13})$; asymptotes $y = \pm 5x$.
Since the foci are on the y-axis, the equation has the form $\frac{y^2}{a^2} - \frac{x^2}{b^2} = 1$. $c = \sqrt{13}$, so
$$c^2 = a^2 + b^2$$
$$13 = a^2 + b^2. \quad (1)$$
The slopes of the asymptotes are ± 5. Use the positive slope to find a in terms of b and a^2 in terms of b^2.
$$\frac{a}{b} = 5$$
$$a = 5b$$
$$a^2 = 25b^2$$
Substitute $a^2 = 25b^2$ into equation (1).
$$13 = 25b^2 + b^2$$
$$13 = 26b^2$$
$$b^2 = \frac{1}{2}$$
$$a^2 = 25\left(\frac{1}{2}\right) = \frac{25}{2}$$

The equation is $\frac{y^2}{\frac{25}{2}} - \frac{x^2}{\frac{1}{2}} = 1$ or $\frac{2y^2}{25} - 2x^2 = 1$.

35. Vertices at $(4, 5)$, $(4, 1)$; asymptotes $y = \pm 7(x - 4) + 3$.
The center is halfway between the vertices at $(4, 3)$. Since the distance between the vertices is 4, we have $2a = 4$, and thus $a = 2$.
The equation has the form
$$\frac{(y - 3)^2}{4} - \frac{(x - 4)^2}{b^2} = 1.$$

The slopes of the asymptotes are ± 7. Use the positive slope to find b and b^2.

$$\frac{a}{b} = 7$$

$$\frac{2}{b} = 7$$

$$b = \frac{2}{7}$$

$$b^2 = \frac{4}{49}$$

The equation is $\dfrac{(y-3)^2}{4} - \dfrac{(x-4)^2}{\frac{4}{49}} = 1$ or

$$\frac{(y-3)^2}{4} - \frac{49(x-4)^2}{4} = 1.$$

37. Center at $(1, -2)$; focus at $(4, -2)$; vertex at $(3, -2)$.
The center is halfway between the vertices. Since one vertex is $(3, -2)$, the other vertex must be $(-1, -2)$, and $a = 2$.
The equation has the form

$$\frac{(x-1)^2}{4} - \frac{(y+2)^2}{b^2} = 1.$$

One focus is at $(4, -2)$, 3 units from the center, so $c = 3$.

$$c^2 = a^2 + b^2$$
$$9 = 4 + b^2$$
$$b^2 = 5$$

The equation is $\dfrac{(x-1)^2}{4} - \dfrac{(y+2)^2}{5} = 1.$

39. Eccentricity 3; center at $(0, 0)$; vertex at $(0, 7)$.
Since the center and vertex lie on a vertical line, the equation is of the form $\dfrac{y^2}{a^2} - \dfrac{x^2}{b^2} = 1$.
The distance between the center and a vertex is 7 so $a = 7$. Use the eccentricity to find c.

$$e = \frac{c}{a}$$

$$3 = \frac{c}{7}$$

$$c = 21$$

Now solve for b^2.

$$c^2 = a^2 + b^2$$
$$441 = 49 + b^2$$
$$392 = b^2$$

The equation is $\dfrac{y^2}{49} - \dfrac{x^2}{392} = 1.$

41. Vertices at $(-2, 10)$, $(-2, 2)$; eccentricity $\dfrac{5}{4}$.
The center is halfway between the vertices at $(-2, 6)$. The distance from the center to each vertex is 4, so $a = 4$. Use the eccentricity to find c.

$$e = \frac{c}{a}$$

$$\frac{5}{4} = \frac{c}{4}$$

$$c = 5$$

Now solve for b^2.

$$c^2 = a^2 + b^2$$
$$25 = 16 + b^2$$
$$b^2 = 9$$

The equation is $\dfrac{(y-6)^2}{16} - \dfrac{(x+2)^2}{9} = 1.$

43. We solve the equation for y.

$$\frac{x^2}{4} - \frac{y^2}{16} = 1$$

$$\frac{x^2}{4} - 1 = \frac{y^2}{16}$$

$$y^2 = 16\left(\frac{x^2}{4} - 1\right)$$

$$y = \pm 4\sqrt{\frac{x^2}{4} - 1}$$

$$y = \pm 2\sqrt{x^2 - 4}$$

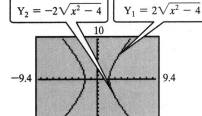

$$Y_2 = -2\sqrt{x^2 - 4} \qquad Y_1 = 2\sqrt{x^2 - 4}$$

45. We solve the equation for y.

$$4y^2 - 36x^2 = 144$$
$$4y^2 = 36x^2 + 144$$
$$4y^2 - 36x^2 = 144$$
$$4y^2 = 36x^2 + 144$$
$$y^2 = 9x^2 + 36$$
$$y = \pm\sqrt{9x^2 + 36}$$
$$y = \pm 3\sqrt{x^2 + 4}$$

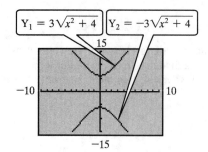

$Y_1 = 3\sqrt{x^2+4}$ $Y_2 = -3\sqrt{x^2+4}$

47. $\dfrac{x^2}{4} - y^2 = 1$

Solve the equation for y.

$$\frac{x^2}{4} - 1 = y^2$$

$$y = \pm\sqrt{\frac{x^2}{4} - 1}$$

The positive square root is

$$y = \sqrt{\frac{x^2}{4} - 1} \ \text{ or } \ y = \frac{1}{2}\sqrt{x^2 - 4}.$$

48. Write the equation in the standard form.

$$\frac{x^2}{4} - y^2 = 1$$

$$\frac{x^2}{4} - \frac{y^2}{1} = 1$$

Here, $a = 2$ and $b = 1$. The slopes of the asymptotes are $\pm\dfrac{b}{a} = \pm\dfrac{1}{2}$. The equation of the asymptote with positive slope is $y = \dfrac{1}{2}x$.

49. $y = \dfrac{1}{2}\sqrt{x^2 - 4}$

At $x = 50$, $y = \dfrac{1}{2}\sqrt{50^2 - 4} \approx 24.98$.

50. On the asymptote $y = \dfrac{1}{2}x$, when $x = 50$,

$$y = \frac{1}{2} \cdot 50 = 25.$$

51. Because $24.98 < 25$, the graph of $y = \dfrac{1}{2}\sqrt{x^2 - 4}$

lies below the graph of $y = \dfrac{1}{2}x$ when $x = 50$.

52. If we choose x-values larger than 50, the y-values on the hyperbola will be even closer to the y-values on the asymptote.

53. **(a)** We must determine a and b in the equation

$$\frac{x^2}{a^2} - \frac{y^2}{b^2} = 1.$$

The asymptotes are $y = x$ and $y = -x$, which have slopes of 1 and -1, respectively, so $a = b$. Look at the small right triangle that is shown in quadrant III.

The line $y = x$ intersects quadrants I and III at a 45º angle. Since the right angle vertex of the triangle lies on the line $y = x$, we know that this triangle is a 45º–45º–90º triangle (an isosceles right triangle). Thus, both legs of the triangle have length d, and by the Pythagorean theorem,

$$c^2 = d^2 + d^2$$
$$c^2 = 2d^2$$
$$c = d\sqrt{2}. \qquad (1)$$

Thus, the coordinates of N are $\left(-d\sqrt{2}, 0\right)$.

Since N is a focus of the hyperbola, c represents the center of the hyperbola, which is $(0, 0)$, and either focus. Since $a = b$, we have

$$c^2 = a^2 + b^2$$
$$c^2 = 2a^2$$
$$c = a\sqrt{2}. \qquad (2)$$

From equations (1) and (2), we have

$$d\sqrt{2} = a\sqrt{2}$$
$$d = a.$$

Thus, $a = b = d = 5 \times 10^{-14}$.

The equation of the trajectory of A is given by

$$\frac{x^2}{a^2} - \frac{y^2}{b^2} = 1$$

$$\frac{x^2}{(5\times10^{-14})^2} - \frac{y^2}{(5\times10^{-14})^2} = 1$$

$$x^2 - y^2 = (5\times10^{-14})^2$$
$$= 25\times10^{-28}$$
$$= 2.5\times10^{-27}$$
$$x^2 = y^2 + (2.5\times10^{-27})$$
$$x = \sqrt{y^2 + (2.5\times10^{-27})}.$$

(We choose the positive square root since the trajectory occurs only where $x > 0$. This equation represents the right half of the hyperbola, as shown in the figure in the textbook.)

(b) The minimum distance between their centers is

$$c + a = d\sqrt{2} + d$$
$$= (5 \times 10^{-14})\sqrt{2} + (5 \times 10^{-14})$$
$$\approx 12.07 \times 10^{-14}$$
$$\approx 1.2 \times 10^{-13}\,\text{m}.$$

57. (a) Locate the goal posts and point $P\,(x, y)$ as in the figure on the left in the exercise. Label the distances A, B and x as illustrated.

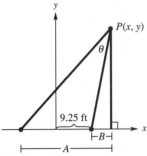

(Here, A corresponds to a and B to b in the above figure. These have been changed to, hopefully, avoid confusion with the same letters in the standard equation for a hyperbola.) From the illustration, we can see that $A = x + 9.25$ and $B = x - 9.25$. Using Regiomatanus' result with the reorientation of axes we have the angle θ is greatest when

$$y = \sqrt{AB}$$
$$y = \sqrt{(x + 9.25)(x - 9.25)}$$
$$y^2 = x^2 - 9.25^2$$
$$x^2 - y^2 = 9.25^2.$$

(b) If the ball is placed on the line 10 feet to the right of the goal post, then $B = 10$ and $x = 10 + 9.25 = 19.25$. Thus,

$$x^2 - y^2 = 9.25^2$$
$$19.25^2 - y^2 = 9.25^2$$
$$y^2 = 19.25^2 - 9.25^2$$
$$y^2 = \sqrt{285} \approx 16.88.$$

The ball should be placed about 16.88 feet from the goal.

(c) The equations for the asymptotes of the hyperbola $x^2 - y^2 = 9.25^2$ are $y = \pm x$. For the ball located 10 feet to the right of the goal post, $x = 19.25$ and we use the asymptote equation with positive slope, $y = x$, to obtain $y = 19.25$. Thus, the difference between the point on the asymptote and the point on the hyperbola is $19.25 - 16.88 = 2.37$, or about 2.4 feet.

Section 9.4

Exercises

1. C

3. F

5. G

7. J

9. B

11.
$$x^2 + y^2 = 144$$
$$(x - 0)^2 + (y - 0)^2 = 12^2$$
The graph of this equation is a circle.

13. $y = 2x^2 + 3x - 4$
The graph of this equation is a parabola.

15. $x - 1 = -3(y - 4)^2$
The graph of this equation is a parabola.

17.
$$\frac{x^2}{49} + \frac{y^2}{100} = 1$$
$$\frac{x^2}{7^2} + \frac{y^2}{10^2} = 1$$
The graph of this equation is an ellipse.

19.
$$\frac{x^2}{4} - \frac{y^2}{16} = 1$$
$$\frac{x^2}{2^2} - \frac{y^2}{4^2} = 1$$
The graph of this equation is a hyperbola.

21.
$$\frac{x^2}{25} - \frac{y^2}{25} = 1$$
$$\frac{x^2}{5^2} - \frac{y^2}{5^2} = 1$$
The graph of this equation is a hyperbola.

23. E

25. H

27. A

29. I

31. D

33.
$$\frac{x^2}{4} = 1 - \frac{y^2}{9}$$
$$\frac{x^2}{4} + \frac{y^2}{9} = 1$$
The graph of this equation is an ellipse.

35.
$$\frac{x^2}{4} + \frac{y^2}{4} = 1$$
$$x^2 + y^2 = 4$$
The graph of this equation is a circle.

37.
$$x^2 = 25 + y^2$$
$$x^2 - y^2 = 25$$
$$\frac{x^2}{25} - \frac{y^2}{25} = 1$$
The graph is a hyperbola.

39. $9x^2 + 36y^2 = 36$
$$\frac{x^2}{4} + \frac{y^2}{1} = 1$$
The graph is an ellipse.

41.
$$\frac{(x+3)^2}{16} + \frac{(y-2)^2}{16} = 1$$
$$(x+3)^2 + (y-2)^2 = 16$$
The graph is a circle.

43.
$$y^2 - 4y = x + 4$$
$$y^2 - 4y - 4 = x$$
The graph is a parabola.

45. $(x+7)^2 + (y-5)^2 + 4 = 0$
$$(x+y)^2 + (y-5)^2 = -4$$
A sum of squares can never be negative. This equation has no graph.

47.
$$3x^2 + 6x + 3y^2 - 12y = 12$$
$$x^2 + 2x + y^2 - 4y = 4$$
$$(x^2 + 2x + 1) + (y^2 - 4y + 4) = 4 + 1 + 4$$
$$(x+1)^2 + (y-2)^2 = 9$$
The graph is a circle.

49. $x^2 - 6x + y = 0$
$$y = -x^2 + 6x$$
The graph is a parabola.

51.
$$4x^2 - 8x - y^2 - 6y = 6$$
$$4(x^2 - 2x + 1) - 1(y^2 + 6y + 9) = 6 + 4 - 9$$
$$4(x-1)^2 - 1(y+3)^2 = 1$$
$$\frac{(x-1)^2}{\frac{1}{4}} - \frac{(y+3)^2}{1} = 1$$
The graph is a hyperbola.

53.
$$4x^2 - 8x + 9y^2 + 54y = -84$$
$$4(x^2 - 2x + 1) + 9(y^2 + 6y + 9) = -84 + 4 + 81$$
$$4(x-1)^2 + 9(y+3)^2 = 1$$
$$\frac{(x-1)^2}{\frac{1}{4}} + \frac{(y+3)^2}{\frac{1}{9}} = 1$$
The graph is an ellipse.

55.
$$6x^2 - 12x + 6y^2 - 18y + 25 = 0$$
$$6(x^2 - 2x + 1) + 6\left(y^2 - 3y + \frac{9}{4}\right) = -25 + 6 + \frac{27}{2}$$
$$6(x-1)^2 + 6\left(y - \frac{3}{2}\right)^2 = -\frac{50}{2} + \frac{12}{2} + \frac{27}{2}$$
$$6(x-1)^2 + 6\left(y - \frac{3}{2}\right)^2 = -\frac{11}{2}$$
$$(x-1)^2 + \left(y - \frac{3}{2}\right)^2 = -\frac{11}{12}$$
A sum of squares can never be negative. This equation has no graph.

57. The definition of an ellipse states that "an ellipse is the set of all points in a plane the sum of whose distances from two fixed points is constant." Therefore, the set of all points in a plane for which the sum of the distances from the points (5, 0) and (–5, 0) is 14 is an ellipse with foci (5, 0) and (–5, 0).

59. Refer to the "Geometric Characterization of Conic Sections" box in the textbook. We see that [Distance of P from F] = $e \cdot$[Distance of P from L], so this conic section has eccentricity $1\frac{1}{2} = \frac{3}{2}$. Since $e > 1$, this is a hyperbola.

61. From the graph, we see that $P = (-3, 8)$, $F = (3, 0)$ and L is the vertical line $x = 27$. By the distance formula, we have
$$\text{Distance of } P \text{ from } F = \sqrt{(-6)^2 + 8^2}$$
$$= \sqrt{36 + 64}$$
$$= \sqrt{100} = 10.$$
The distance from a point to a line is defined as the perpendicular distance, so

Distance of P from $L = |27 - (-3)|$
$$= 30$$
Then $e = \dfrac{\text{Distance of } P \text{ from } F}{\text{Distance of } P \text{ from } L} = \dfrac{10}{30} = \dfrac{1}{3}$.

63. From the graph, we see that $F = (\sqrt{2},\, 0)$ and L is
the vertical line $x = -\sqrt{2}$.
Choose $(0, 0)$, the vertex of the parabola, as P.
Distance of P from $F = \sqrt{2}$
Distance of P from $L = \sqrt{2}$
Then $e = \dfrac{\text{Distance of } P \text{ from } F}{\text{Distance of } P \text{ from } L} = \dfrac{\sqrt{2}}{\sqrt{2}} = 1$.

65. From the graph, we see that $P = (9, -7.5)$,
$F = (9, 0)$ and L is the vertical line $x = 4$.
Distance of P from $F = 7.5$
Distance of P from $L = 5$
Then $e = \dfrac{\text{Distance of } P \text{ from } F}{\text{Distance of } P \text{ from } L} = \dfrac{7.5}{5} = \dfrac{3}{2}$.

67. $\dfrac{k}{\sqrt{D}} = \dfrac{2.82 \times 10^7}{\sqrt{42.5 \times 10^6}}$

$= \dfrac{2.82 \times 10^7}{\sqrt{42.5} \times 10^3}$

$\approx .432568 \times 10^4$

≈ 4326

Since $V = 2090$, we have

$V < \dfrac{k}{\sqrt{D}}$,

so the shape of the satellite's trajectory was
elliptic.

73.

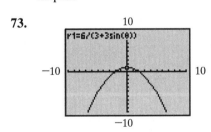

75.

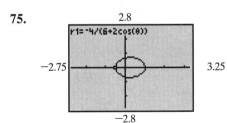

77.

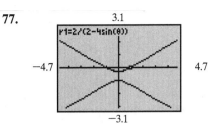

79.

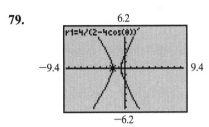

81.

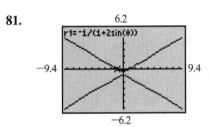

83.

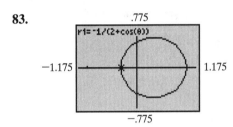

85. Since a parabola with vertical directrix 3 units to
the right of the pole has the equation

$r = \dfrac{ep}{1 + e\cos\theta}$ where $e = 1$ and $p = 3$,

$r = \dfrac{1 \cdot 3}{1 + 1\cos\theta} = \dfrac{3}{1 + \cos\theta}$.

87. Since a parabola with a horizontal directrix 5 units
below the pole has the equation $r = \dfrac{ep}{1 - e\sin\theta}$
where $e = 1$ and $p = 5$, $r = \dfrac{1 \cdot 5}{1 - 1\sin\theta} = \dfrac{5}{1 - \sin\theta}$.

89. A conic section with vertical directrix 5 units to
the right of the pole has a polar equation of the
form $r = \dfrac{ep}{1 + e\cos\theta}$ where $p = 5$. When $e = \dfrac{4}{5}$,
we get

$$r = \frac{\frac{4}{5} \cdot 5}{1 + \frac{4}{5}\cos\theta}$$

$$r = \frac{4}{\frac{5 + 4\cos\theta}{5}}$$

$$r = \frac{20}{5 + 4\cos\theta}.$$

Since $e < 1$, the graph of the equation is an ellipse.

91. A conic section with horizontal directrix 8 units below the pole has a polar equation of the form

$$r = \frac{ep}{1 - e\sin\theta}$$ where $p = 8$. When $e = \frac{5}{4}$, we get

$$r = \frac{\frac{5}{4} \cdot 8}{1 - \frac{5}{4}\sin\theta}$$

$$r = \frac{10}{\frac{4 - 5\sin\theta}{4}}$$

$$r = \frac{40}{4 - 5\sin\theta}.$$

Since $e > 1$, the graph of the equation is a hyperbola.

93. To identify the type of conic, rewrite the equation in standard form to find e.

$$r = \frac{6}{3 - \cos\theta}$$

$$r = \frac{3 \cdot 2}{3\left(1 - \frac{1}{3}\cos\theta\right)}$$

$$r = \frac{2}{1 - \frac{1}{3}\cos\theta}$$

Thus, $e = \frac{1}{3}$. Since $e < 1$, the graph of the equation is an ellipse. To convert to rectangular form, start with the given equation.

$$r = \frac{6}{3 - \cos\theta}$$

$$r(3 - \cos\theta) = 6$$

$$3r - r\cos\theta = 6$$

$$3r = r\cos\theta + 6$$

$$(3r)^2 = (r\cos\theta + 6)^2$$

$$(3r)^2 = (x + 6)^2$$

$$9r^2 = x^2 + 12x + 36$$

$$9(x^2 + y^2) = x^2 + 12x + 36$$

$$9x^2 + 9y^2 = x^2 + 12x + 36$$

$$8x^2 + 9y^2 - 12x - 36 = 0$$

95. To identify the type of conic, rewrite the equation in standard form to find e. $r = \frac{-2}{1 + 2\cos\theta}$ is in standard form. Thus, $e = 2$. Since $e > 1$, the graph of the equation is a hyperbola. To convert to rectangular form, start with the given equation.

$$r = \frac{-2}{1 + 2\cos\theta}$$

$$r(1 + 2\cos\theta) = -2$$

$$r + 2r\cos\theta = -2$$

$$r = -2r\cos\theta - 2$$

$$r^2 = (-2r\cos\theta - 2)^2$$

$$r^2 = (-2x - 2)^2$$

$$x^2 + y^2 = 4x^2 + 8x + 4$$

$$0 = 3x^2 - y^2 + 8x + 4$$

97. To identify the type of conic, rewrite the equation in standard form to find e.

$$r = \frac{-6}{4 + 2\sin\theta}$$

$$r = \frac{4 \cdot \frac{-6}{4}}{4\left(1 + \frac{1}{2}\sin\theta\right)}$$

$$r = \frac{\frac{-3}{2}}{1 + \frac{1}{2}\sin\theta}$$

Thus, $e = \frac{1}{2}$. Since $e < 1$, the graph of the equation is an ellipse. To convert to rectangular form, start with the given equation.

$$r = \frac{-6}{4 + 2\sin\theta}$$

$$r(4 + 2\sin\theta) = -6$$

$$4r + 2r\sin\theta = -6$$

$$4r = -2r\sin\theta - 6$$

$$(4r)^2 = (-2r\sin\theta - 6)^2$$

$$(4r)^2 = (-2y - 6)^2$$

$$16r^2 = 4y^2 + 24y + 36$$

$$16(x^2 + y^2) = 4y^2 + 24y + 36$$

$$16x^2 + 16y^2 = 4y^2 + 24y + 36$$

$$16x^2 + 12y^2 - 24y - 36 = 0$$

$$4x^2 + 3y^2 - 6y - 9 = 0$$

99. To identify the type of conic, rewrite the equation in standard form to find e.

$$r = \frac{10}{2 - 2\sin\theta}$$

$$r = \frac{2 \cdot 5}{2(1 - \sin\theta)}$$

$$r = \frac{5}{1 - \sin\theta}$$

Thus, $e = 1$ and the graph of the equation is a parabola. To convert to rectangular form, start with the given equation.

$$r = \frac{10}{2 - 2\sin\theta}$$
$$r(2 - 2\sin\theta) = 10$$
$$2r - 2r\sin\theta = 10$$
$$2r = 2r\sin\theta + 10$$
$$(2r)^2 = (2r\sin\theta + 10)^2$$
$$(2r)^2 = (2y + 10)^2$$
$$4r^2 = 4y^2 + 40y + 100$$
$$4(x^2 + y^2) = 4y^2 + 40y + 100$$
$$4x^2 + 4y^2 = 4y^2 + 40y + 100$$
$$4x^2 - 40y - 100 = 0$$
$$x^2 - 10y - 25 = 0$$

Section 9.5

Exercises

1. $4x^2 + 3y^2 + 2xy - 5x = 8$
$A = 4$, $B = 2$, $C = 3$
$B^2 - 4AC = 2^2 - 4(4)(3)$
$\quad = 4 - 48$
$\quad = -44$
Since $B^2 - 4AC < 0$, the graph will be a circle or ellipse or a point.

3. $2x^2 + 3xy - 4y^2 = 0$
$A = 2$, $B = 3$, $C = -4$
$B^2 - 4AC = 3^2 - 4(2)(-4)$
$\quad = 9 + 32$
$\quad = 41$
Since $B^2 - 4AC > 0$, the graph will be a hyperbola or two intersecting lines.

5. $4x^2 + 4xy + y^2 + 15 = 0$
$A = 4$, $B = 4$, $C = 1$
$B^2 - 4AC = 4^2 - 4(4)(1)$
$\quad = 16 - 16$
$\quad = 0$
Since $B^2 - 4AC = 0$, the graph will be a parabola or one line or two parallel lines.

7. The xy-term is removed from $2x^2 + \sqrt{3}xy + y^2 + x = 5$ by a rotation of the axes through an angle θ satisfying $\cot 2\theta = \dfrac{A - C}{B}$ where $A = 2$, $B = \sqrt{3}$, and $C = 1$.
$\cot 2\theta = \dfrac{2 - 1}{\sqrt{3}}$
$\cot 2\theta = \dfrac{1}{\sqrt{3}}$
$2\theta = \cot^{-1}\dfrac{1}{\sqrt{3}}$
$2\theta = 60°$
$\theta = 30°$

9. The xy-term is removed from $3x^2 + \sqrt{3}xy + 4y^2 + 2x - 3y = 12$ by a rotation of the axes through an angle θ satisfying $\cot 2\theta = \dfrac{A - C}{B}$ where $A = 3$, $B = \sqrt{3}$, and $C = 4$.
$\cot 2\theta = \dfrac{3 - 4}{\sqrt{3}}$
$\cot 2\theta = \dfrac{-1}{\sqrt{3}}$
$2\theta = \cot^{-1}\dfrac{-1}{\sqrt{3}}$
$2\theta = -60°$
Since the angle θ must satisfy $0° < \theta < 90°$, the angle 2θ must satisfy $0° < 2\theta < 180°$. We add $180°$ to get 2θ between $0°$ and $180°$. This does not change the value of $\cot 2\theta$ since the period of cotangent is $180°$.
$2\theta = -60° + 180°$
$2\theta = 120°$
$\theta = 60°$

11. The xy-term is removed from $x^2 - 4xy + 5y^2 = 18$ by a rotation of the axes through $\cot 2\theta = \dfrac{A - C}{B}$ where $A = 1$, $B = -4$, and $C = 5$.
$\cot 2\theta = \dfrac{1 - 5}{-4}$
$\cot 2\theta = \dfrac{-4}{-4}$
$\cot 2\theta = 1$
$2\theta = \cot^{-1} 1$
$2\theta = 45°$
$\theta = 22.5°$

13. Since $\theta = 45°$, then $\sin\theta = \dfrac{\sqrt{2}}{2}$ and $\cos\theta = \dfrac{\sqrt{2}}{2}$, and the rotation equations are $x = \dfrac{\sqrt{2}}{2}x' - \dfrac{\sqrt{2}}{2}y'$ and

$y = \dfrac{\sqrt{2}}{2}x' + \dfrac{\sqrt{2}}{2}y'$. Substituting these values into the given equation yields

$$x^2 - xy + y^2 = 6$$

$$\left(\frac{\sqrt{2}}{2}x' - \frac{\sqrt{2}}{2}y'\right)^2 - \left(\frac{\sqrt{2}}{2}x' - \frac{\sqrt{2}}{2}y'\right)\left(\frac{\sqrt{2}}{2}x' + \frac{\sqrt{2}}{2}y'\right) + \left(\frac{\sqrt{2}}{2}x' + \frac{\sqrt{2}}{2}y'\right)^2 = 6$$

$$\frac{1}{2}x'^2 - x'y' + \frac{1}{2}y'^2 - \frac{1}{2}x'^2 + \frac{1}{2}y'^2 + \frac{1}{2}x'^2 + x'y' + \frac{1}{2}y'^2 = 6$$

$$\frac{1}{2}x'^2 + \frac{3}{2}y'^2 = 6$$

$$\frac{x'^2}{12} + \frac{y'^2}{4} = 1$$

The graph of the equation is an ellipse.

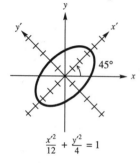

$$\frac{x'^2}{12} + \frac{y'^2}{4} = 1$$

15. Since $\sin\theta = \dfrac{2}{\sqrt{5}}$, $\cos\theta = \dfrac{1}{\sqrt{5}}$, and the rotation equations are $x = \dfrac{1}{\sqrt{5}}x' - \dfrac{2}{\sqrt{5}}y'$ and $y = \dfrac{2}{\sqrt{5}}x' + \dfrac{1}{\sqrt{5}}y'$.

Substituting these values into the given equation yields

$$8x^2 - 4xy + 5y^2 = 36$$

$$8\left(\frac{1}{\sqrt{5}}x' - \frac{2}{\sqrt{5}}y'\right)^2 - 4\left(\frac{1}{\sqrt{5}}x' - \frac{2}{\sqrt{5}}y'\right)\left(\frac{2}{\sqrt{5}}x' + \frac{1}{\sqrt{5}}y'\right) + 5\left(\frac{2}{\sqrt{5}}x' + \frac{1}{\sqrt{5}}y'\right)^2 = 36$$

$$\frac{8}{5}x'^2 - \frac{32}{5}x'y' + \frac{32}{5}y'^2 - \frac{8}{5}x'^2 + \frac{12}{5}x'y' + \frac{8}{5}y'^2 + \frac{20}{5}x'^2 + \frac{20}{5}x'y' + \frac{5}{5}y'^2 = 36$$

$$4x'^2 + 9y'^2 = 36$$

$$\frac{x'^2}{9} + \frac{y'^2}{4} = 1.$$

The graph of the equation is an ellipse.

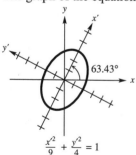

$$\frac{x'^2}{9} + \frac{y'^2}{4} = 1$$

17. $3x^2 - 2xy + 3y^2 = 8$

$A = 3, \ B = -2, \ C = 3$

$\cot 2\theta = \dfrac{A - C}{B} = \dfrac{3 - 3}{-2} = 0$

$\cos 2\theta = 0$

$\sin \theta = \sqrt{\dfrac{1 - \cos 2\theta}{2}} = \sqrt{\dfrac{1 - 0}{2}} = \sqrt{\dfrac{1}{2}} = \dfrac{\sqrt{2}}{2}, \quad \cos \theta = \sqrt{\dfrac{1 + \cos 2\theta}{2}} = \sqrt{\dfrac{1 + 0}{2}} = \sqrt{\dfrac{1}{2}} = \dfrac{\sqrt{2}}{2}$

Thus, $\theta = 45°$ and the rotation equations are $x = \dfrac{\sqrt{2}}{2} x' - \dfrac{\sqrt{2}}{2} y'$ and $y = \dfrac{\sqrt{2}}{2} x' + \dfrac{\sqrt{2}}{2} y'$. Substituting these values into the given equation yields

$$3x^2 - 2xy + 3y^2 = 8$$

$$3\left(\dfrac{\sqrt{2}}{2} x' - \dfrac{\sqrt{2}}{2} y'\right)^2 - 2\left(\dfrac{\sqrt{2}}{2} x' - \dfrac{\sqrt{2}}{2} y'\right)\left(\dfrac{\sqrt{2}}{2} x' + \dfrac{\sqrt{2}}{2} y'\right) + 3\left(\dfrac{\sqrt{2}}{2} x' + \dfrac{\sqrt{2}}{2} y'\right)^2 = 8$$

$$\dfrac{3}{2} x'^2 - 3x'y' + \dfrac{3}{2} y'^2 - x'^2 + y'^2 + \dfrac{3}{2} x'^2 + 3x'y' + \dfrac{3}{2} y'^2 = 8$$

$$2x'^2 + 4y'^2 = 8$$

$$\dfrac{x'^2}{4} + \dfrac{y'^2}{2} = 1.$$

The graph of the equation is an ellipse.

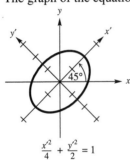

$$\dfrac{x'^2}{4} + \dfrac{y'^2}{2} = 1$$

19. $x^2 - 4xy + y^2 = -5$

$A = 1, \ B = -4, \ C = 1$

$\cot 2\theta = \dfrac{A - C}{B} = \dfrac{1 - 1}{-4} = 0$

$\cos 2\theta = 0$

$\sin\theta = \sqrt{\dfrac{1 - \cos 2\theta}{2}} = \sqrt{\dfrac{1 - 0}{2}} = \sqrt{\dfrac{1}{2}} = \dfrac{\sqrt{2}}{2}, \quad \cos\theta = \sqrt{\dfrac{1 + \cos 2\theta}{2}} = \sqrt{\dfrac{1 + 0}{2}} = \sqrt{\dfrac{1}{2}} = \dfrac{\sqrt{2}}{2}$

Thus, $\theta = 45°$ and the rotation equations are $x = \dfrac{\sqrt{2}}{2}x' - \dfrac{\sqrt{2}}{2}y'$ and $y = \dfrac{\sqrt{2}}{2}x' + \dfrac{\sqrt{2}}{2}y'$. Substituting these values into the given equation yields

$$x^2 - 4xy + y^2 = -5$$

$$\left(\dfrac{\sqrt{2}}{2}x' - \dfrac{\sqrt{2}}{2}y'\right)^2 - 4\left(\dfrac{\sqrt{2}}{2}x' - \dfrac{\sqrt{2}}{2}y'\right)\left(\dfrac{\sqrt{2}}{2}x' + \dfrac{\sqrt{2}}{2}y'\right) + \left(\dfrac{\sqrt{2}}{2}x' + \dfrac{\sqrt{2}}{2}y'\right)^2 = -5$$

$$\dfrac{1}{2}x'^2 - x'y' + \dfrac{1}{2}y'^2 - 2x'^2 + 2y'^2 + \dfrac{1}{2}x'^2 + x'y' + \dfrac{1}{2}y'^2 = -5$$

$$-x'^2 + 3y'^2 = -5$$

$$\dfrac{x'^2}{5} - \dfrac{3y'^2}{5} = 1.$$

The graph of the equation is a hyperbola.

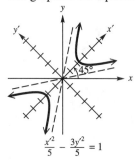

$\dfrac{x'^2}{5} - \dfrac{3y'^2}{5} = 1$

21. $7x^2 + 6\sqrt{3}xy + 13y^2 = 64$

$A = 7, \ B = 6\sqrt{3}, \ C = 13$

$\cot 2\theta = \dfrac{A - C}{B} = \dfrac{7 - 13}{6\sqrt{3}} = -\dfrac{1}{\sqrt{3}}$

$\cos 2\theta = -\dfrac{1}{\sqrt{1^2 + (\sqrt{3})^2}} = -\dfrac{1}{\sqrt{1 + 3}} = -\dfrac{1}{\sqrt{4}} = -\dfrac{1}{2}$

$\sin\theta = \sqrt{\dfrac{1 - \cos 2\theta}{2}} = \sqrt{\dfrac{1 - \left(-\frac{1}{2}\right)}{2}} = \sqrt{\dfrac{3}{4}} = \dfrac{\sqrt{3}}{2}, \quad \cos\theta = \sqrt{\dfrac{1 + \cos 2\theta}{2}} = \sqrt{\dfrac{1 + \left(-\frac{1}{2}\right)}{2}} = \sqrt{\dfrac{1}{4}} = \dfrac{1}{2}$

Thus, $\theta = 60°$ and the rotation equations are $x = \dfrac{1}{2}x' - \dfrac{\sqrt{3}}{2}y'$ and $y = \dfrac{\sqrt{3}}{2}x' + \dfrac{1}{2}y'$. Substituting these values into the given equation yields

$$7x^2 + 6\sqrt{3}xy + 13y^2 = 64$$

$$7\left(\dfrac{1}{2}x' - \dfrac{\sqrt{3}}{2}y'\right)^2 + 6\sqrt{3}\left(\dfrac{1}{2}x' - \dfrac{\sqrt{3}}{2}y'\right)\left(\dfrac{\sqrt{3}}{2}x' + \dfrac{1}{2}y'\right) + 13\left(\dfrac{\sqrt{3}}{2}x' + \dfrac{1}{2}y'\right)^2 = 64$$

$$\dfrac{7}{4}x'^2 - \dfrac{7\sqrt{3}}{2}x'y' + \dfrac{21}{4}y'^2 + \dfrac{18}{4}x'^2 - \dfrac{6\sqrt{3}}{2}x'y' - \dfrac{18}{4}y'^2 + \dfrac{39}{4}x'^2 + \dfrac{13\sqrt{3}}{2}x'y' + \dfrac{13}{4}y'^2 = 64$$

$$\dfrac{64}{4}x'^2 + \dfrac{16}{4}y'^2 = 64$$

$$\dfrac{x'^2}{4} + \dfrac{y'^2}{16} = 1.$$

The graph of the equation is an ellipse.

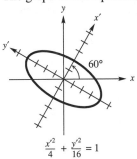

$\dfrac{x'^2}{4} + \dfrac{y'^2}{16} = 1$

23. $3x^2 - 2\sqrt{3}xy + y^2 - 2x - 2\sqrt{3}y = 0$

$A = 3, \ B = -2\sqrt{3}, \ C = 1$

$\cot 2\theta = \dfrac{A-C}{B} = \dfrac{3-1}{-2\sqrt{3}} = -\dfrac{1}{\sqrt{3}}$

$\cos 2\theta = -\dfrac{1}{\sqrt{1^2 + (\sqrt{3})^2}} = -\dfrac{1}{\sqrt{1+3}} = -\dfrac{1}{\sqrt{4}} = -\dfrac{1}{2}$

$\sin\theta = \sqrt{\dfrac{1-\cos 2\theta}{2}} = \sqrt{\dfrac{1-\left(-\frac{1}{2}\right)}{2}} = \sqrt{\dfrac{3}{4}} = \dfrac{\sqrt{3}}{2}, \ \cos\theta = \sqrt{\dfrac{1+\cos 2\theta}{2}} = \sqrt{\dfrac{1+\left(-\frac{1}{2}\right)}{2}} = \sqrt{\dfrac{1}{4}} = \dfrac{1}{2}$

Thus, $\theta = 60°$ and the rotation equations are $x = \dfrac{1}{2}x' - \dfrac{\sqrt{3}}{2}y'$ and $y = \dfrac{\sqrt{3}}{2}x' + \dfrac{1}{2}y'$. Substituting these values into the given equation yields

$$3x^2 - 2\sqrt{3}xy + y^2 - 2x - 2\sqrt{3}y = 0$$

$$3\left(\dfrac{1}{2}x' - \dfrac{\sqrt{3}}{2}y'\right)^2 - 2\sqrt{3}\left(\dfrac{1}{2}x' - \dfrac{\sqrt{3}}{2}y'\right)\left(\dfrac{\sqrt{3}}{2}x' + \dfrac{1}{2}y'\right)$$

$$+\left(\dfrac{\sqrt{3}}{2}x' + \dfrac{1}{2}y'\right)^2 - 2\left(\dfrac{1}{2}x' - \dfrac{\sqrt{3}}{2}y'\right) - 2\sqrt{3}\left(\dfrac{\sqrt{3}}{2}x' + \dfrac{1}{2}y'\right) = 0$$

$$\dfrac{3}{4}x'^2 - \dfrac{3\sqrt{3}}{2}x'y' + \dfrac{9}{4}y'^2 - \dfrac{6}{4}x'^2 + \sqrt{3}x'y' + \dfrac{6}{4}y'^2 + \dfrac{3}{4}x'^2 + \dfrac{\sqrt{3}}{2}x'y' + \dfrac{1}{4}y'^2 - x' + \sqrt{3}y' - 3x' - \sqrt{3}y' = 0$$

$$\dfrac{16}{4}y'^2 - 4x' = 0$$

$$4y'^2 = 4x'$$

$$y'^2 = x'.$$

The graph of the equation is a parabola.

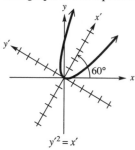

$y'^2 = x'$

25. $x^2 + 3xy + y^2 - 5\sqrt{2}\,y = 15$

$A = 1, \ B = 3, \ C = 1$

$\cot 2\theta = \dfrac{A - C}{B} = \dfrac{1 - 1}{3} = 0$

$\cos 2\theta = 0$

$\sin\theta = \sqrt{\dfrac{1 - \cos 2\theta}{2}} = \sqrt{\dfrac{1 - 0}{2}} = \sqrt{\dfrac{1}{2}} = \dfrac{\sqrt{2}}{2}, \quad \cos\theta = \sqrt{\dfrac{1 + \cos 2\theta}{2}} = \sqrt{\dfrac{1 + 0}{2}} = \sqrt{\dfrac{1}{2}} = \dfrac{\sqrt{2}}{2}$

Thus, $\theta = 45°$ and the rotation equations are $x = \dfrac{\sqrt{2}}{2}\,x' - \dfrac{\sqrt{2}}{2}\,y'$ and $y = \dfrac{\sqrt{2}}{2}\,x' + \dfrac{\sqrt{2}}{2}\,y'$. Substituting these values into the given equation yields

$$x^2 + 3xy + y^2 - 5\sqrt{2}\,y = 15$$

$$\left(\frac{\sqrt{2}}{2}\,x' - \frac{\sqrt{2}}{2}\,y'\right)^2 + 3\left(\frac{\sqrt{2}}{2}\,x' - \frac{\sqrt{2}}{2}\,y'\right)\left(\frac{\sqrt{2}}{2}\,x' + \frac{\sqrt{2}}{2}\,y'\right)$$

$$+ \left(\frac{\sqrt{2}}{2}\,x' + \frac{\sqrt{2}}{2}\,y'\right)^2 - 5\sqrt{2}\left(\frac{\sqrt{2}}{2}\,x' + \frac{\sqrt{2}}{2}\,y'\right) = 15$$

$$\frac{1}{2}x'^2 - x'y' + \frac{1}{2}y'^2 + \frac{3}{2}x'^2 - \frac{3}{2}y'^2 + \frac{1}{2}x'^2 + x'y' + \frac{1}{2}y'^2 - 5x' - 5y' = 15$$

$$\frac{5}{2}x'^2 - \frac{1}{2}y'^2 - 5x' - 5y' = 15$$

$$5x'^2 - y'^2 - 10x' - 10y' = 30$$

$$5x'^2 - 10x' - y'^2 - 10y' = 30$$

$$5(x'^2 - 2x' + 1) - (y'^2 + 10y' + 25) = 30 + 5 - 25$$

$$5(x' - 1)^2 - (y'^2 + 5)^2 = 10$$

$$\frac{(x' - 1)^2}{2} - \frac{(y'^2 + 5)^2}{10} = 1.$$

The graph of the equation is a hyperbola with its center at $x' = 1$ and $y' = -5$. By translating the axes of the $x'\,y'$ system down 5 units and right 1 unit, we get an $x''\,y''$–coordinate system, in which the hyperbola is centered at the origin.

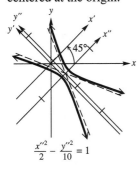

$$\frac{x''^2}{2} - \frac{y''^2}{10} = 1$$

27. $4x^2 + 4xy + y^2 - 24x + 38y - 19 = 0$

$A = 4, \quad B = 4, \quad C = 1$

$\cot 2\theta = \dfrac{A - C}{B} = \dfrac{4 - 1}{4} = \dfrac{3}{4}$

$\cos 2\theta = \dfrac{3}{\sqrt{3^2 + 4^2}} = \dfrac{3}{\sqrt{9 + 16}} = \dfrac{3}{\sqrt{25}} = \dfrac{3}{5}$

$\sin\theta = \sqrt{\dfrac{1 - \cos 2\theta}{2}} = \sqrt{\dfrac{1 - \frac{3}{5}}{2}} = \sqrt{\dfrac{2}{10}} = \dfrac{\sqrt{5}}{5}, \quad \sin\theta = \sqrt{\dfrac{1 + \cos 2\theta}{2}} = \sqrt{\dfrac{1 + \frac{3}{5}}{2}} = \sqrt{\dfrac{8}{10}} = \dfrac{2\sqrt{5}}{5}$

Thus, $\theta = \sin^{-1}\left(\dfrac{\sqrt{5}}{5}\right) \approx 26.57°$ and the rotation equations are $x = \dfrac{2\sqrt{5}}{5}x' - \dfrac{\sqrt{5}}{5}y'$ and $y = \dfrac{\sqrt{5}}{5}x' + \dfrac{2\sqrt{5}}{5}y'$.

Substituting these values into the given equation yields

$$4x^2 + 4xy + y^2 - 24x + 38y - 19 = 0$$

$$4\left(\frac{2\sqrt{5}}{5}x' - \frac{\sqrt{5}}{5}y'\right)^2 + 4\left(\frac{2\sqrt{5}}{5}x' - \frac{\sqrt{5}}{5}y'\right)\left(\frac{\sqrt{5}}{5}x' + \frac{2\sqrt{5}}{5}y'\right) + \left(\frac{\sqrt{5}}{5}x' + \frac{2\sqrt{5}}{5}y'\right)^2$$

$$-24\left(\frac{2\sqrt{5}}{5}x' - \frac{\sqrt{5}}{5}y'\right) + 38\left(\frac{\sqrt{5}}{5}x' + \frac{2\sqrt{5}}{5}y'\right) - 19 = 0$$

$$\frac{16}{5}x'^2 - \frac{16}{5}x'y' + \frac{4}{5}y'^2 + \frac{8}{5}x'^2 + \frac{12}{5}x'y' - \frac{8}{5}y'^2 + \frac{1}{5}x'^2 + \frac{4}{5}x'y' + \frac{4}{5}y'^2$$

$$-\frac{48\sqrt{5}}{5}x' + \frac{24\sqrt{5}}{5}y' + \frac{38\sqrt{5}}{5}x' + \frac{76\sqrt{5}}{5}y' - 19 = 0$$

$$5x'^2 - 2\sqrt{5}x' + 20\sqrt{5}y' - 19 = 0$$

$$5\left(x'^2 - \frac{2\sqrt{5}}{5}x' + \frac{1}{5}\right) + 20\sqrt{5}y' - 19 = 1$$

$$5\left(x' - \frac{\sqrt{5}}{5}\right)^2 = 20 - 20\sqrt{5}y'$$

$$\left(x' - \frac{\sqrt{5}}{5}\right)^2 = 4 - 4\sqrt{5}y'$$

$$\left(x' - \frac{\sqrt{5}}{5}\right)^2 = -4\sqrt{5}\left(y' - \frac{\sqrt{5}}{5}\right).$$

The graph of the equation is a parabola with its vertex at $x' = -\dfrac{\sqrt{5}}{5}$ and $y' = \dfrac{\sqrt{5}}{5}$. By translating the axes of the

$x'\,y'$ system up $\dfrac{3}{2}$ and left $\dfrac{\sqrt{3}}{2}$ units, we get an $x''\,y''$–coordinate system, in which the vertex of the parabola is at the origin.

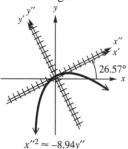

$x''^2 \approx -8.94y''$

29. $16x^2 + 24xy + 9y^2 - 130x + 90y = 0$

$A = 16, \ B = 24, \ C = 9$

$\cot 2\theta = \dfrac{A-C}{B} = \dfrac{16-9}{24} = \dfrac{7}{24}$

$\cos 2\theta = \dfrac{7}{\sqrt{7^2 + 24^2}} = \dfrac{7}{\sqrt{49+576}} = \dfrac{7}{\sqrt{625}} = \dfrac{7}{25}$

$\sin\theta = \sqrt{\dfrac{1-\cos 2\theta}{2}} = \sqrt{\dfrac{1-\frac{7}{25}}{2}} = \sqrt{\dfrac{9}{25}} = \dfrac{3}{5}, \ \cos\theta = \sqrt{\dfrac{1+\cos 2\theta}{2}} = \sqrt{\dfrac{1+\frac{7}{25}}{2}} = \sqrt{\dfrac{16}{25}} = \dfrac{4}{5}$

Thus, $\theta = \sin^{-1}\!\left(\dfrac{3}{5}\right) \approx 36.87°$ and the rotation equations are $x = \dfrac{4}{5}x' - \dfrac{3}{5}y'$ and $y = \dfrac{3}{5}x' + \dfrac{4}{5}y'$. Substituting these values into the given equation yields

$$16x^2 + 24xy + 9y^2 - 130x + 90y = 0$$

$$16\!\left(\dfrac{4}{5}x' - \dfrac{3}{5}y'\right)^2 + 24\!\left(\dfrac{4}{5}x' - \dfrac{3}{5}y'\right)\!\left(\dfrac{3}{5}x' + \dfrac{4}{5}y'\right)$$

$$+9\!\left(\dfrac{3}{5}x' + \dfrac{4}{5}y'\right)^2 - 130\!\left(\dfrac{4}{5}x' - \dfrac{3}{5}y'\right) + 90\!\left(\dfrac{3}{5}x' + \dfrac{4}{5}y'\right) = 0$$

$$\dfrac{256}{25}x'^2 - \dfrac{384}{25}x'y' + \dfrac{144}{25}y'^2 + \dfrac{288}{25}x'^2 + \dfrac{168}{25}x'y' - \dfrac{288}{25}y'^2$$

$$+\dfrac{81}{25}x'^2 + \dfrac{216}{25}x'y' + \dfrac{144}{25}y'^2 - 104x' + 78y' + 54x' + 72y' = 0$$

$$25x'^2 - 50x' + 150y' = 0$$

$$25(x'^2 - 2x') = -150y'$$

$$25(x'^2 - 2x' + 1) = -150y' + 25$$

$$25(x'-1)^2 = -150\!\left(y' - \dfrac{1}{6}\right)$$

$$(x'-1)^2 = -6\!\left(y' - \dfrac{1}{6}\right).$$

The graph of the equation is a parabola with its vertex at $x' = 1$ and $y' = \dfrac{1}{6}$. By translating the axes of the $x' y'$ system up $\dfrac{1}{6}$ unit and right 1 unit, we get $x'' y''$–coordinate system in which the vertex of the parabola is at the origin.

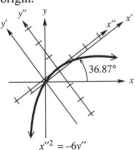

$x''^2 = -6y''$

Chapter 9 Review Exercises

1. $x = 4(y-5)^2 + 2$

The graph is a parabola opening to the right. The domain is $[2, \infty)$. The range is $(-\infty, \infty)$. The vertex is $(2, 5)$, and the axis is the horizontal line $y = 5$.

x	18	6	2	6	18
y	3	4	5	6	7

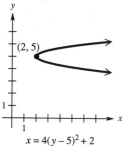

$x = 4(y-5)^2 + 2$

3. $x = 5y^2 - 5y + 3$

Complete the square on y to find the vertex and axis of this parabola.

$$x = 5\left(y^2 - y + \frac{1}{4} - \frac{1}{4}\right) + 3$$
$$= 5\left(y - \frac{1}{2}\right)^2 + 5\left(-\frac{1}{4}\right) + 3$$
$$= 5\left(y - \frac{1}{2}\right)^2 + \frac{7}{4}$$

The parabola opens to the right. The domain is $\left[\frac{7}{4}, \infty\right)$. The range is $(-\infty, \infty)$. The vertex is $\left(\frac{7}{4}, \frac{1}{2}\right)$ and the axis is the horizontal line $y = \frac{1}{2}$.

x	$\frac{27}{4}$	3	$\frac{7}{4}$	3	$\frac{27}{4}$
y	$-\frac{1}{2}$	0	$\frac{1}{2}$	1	$\frac{3}{2}$

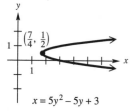

$x = 5y^2 - 5y + 3$

5. $y^2 = -\frac{2}{3}x$

The equation has the form $y^2 = 4px$, with $4p = -\frac{2}{3}$, so $p = -\frac{1}{6}$. The parabola is horizontal, with domain $(-\infty, 0]$, range $(-\infty, \infty)$, focus $\left(-\frac{1}{6}, 0\right)$, directrix $x = \frac{1}{6}$, and axis the horizontal line $y = 0$ (the x-axis).

x	-6	$-\frac{3}{2}$	0
y	± 2	± 1	0

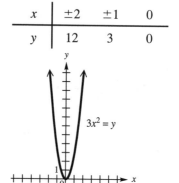

$y^2 = -\frac{2}{3}x$

7. $3x^2 = y$

$$x^2 = \frac{1}{3}y$$

The equation has the form $x^2 = 4py$, with $4p = \frac{1}{3}$, so $p = \frac{1}{12}$. The parabola is vertical, with domain $(-\infty, \infty)$, range $[0, \infty)$, focus $\left(0, \frac{1}{12}\right)$, directrix $y = -\frac{1}{12}$, and axis the vertical line $x = 0$ (the y-axis).

x	± 2	± 1	0
y	12	3	0

$3x^2 = y$

9. Focus $(4, 0)$, vertex at the origin.

Since the focus is on the x-axis, the parabola is horizontal. It opens to the right since $p = 4$ is positive. The equation has the form $y^2 = 4px$.

Substituting 4 for p, we get $y^2 = 16x$ or

$x = \dfrac{1}{16}y^2$.

11. Through $(-3, 4)$, opening upward, vertex at the origin.

The form of the equation is $x^2 = 4py$.

Substitute $x = -3$ and $y = 4$, and solve for p.

$(-3)^2 = 4p(4)$

$9 = 16p$

$p = \dfrac{9}{16}$

The equation is $x^2 = 4\left(\dfrac{9}{16}\right)y = \dfrac{9}{4}y$ or $y = \dfrac{4}{9}x^2$.

13. $y^2 + 9x^2 = 9$

$x^2 + \dfrac{y^2}{9} = 1$

The graph of this equation is an ellipse.

15. $3y^2 - 5x^2 = 30$

$\dfrac{y^2}{10} - \dfrac{x^2}{6} = 1$

The graph of this equation is a hyperbola.

17. $4x^2 - y = 0$

$y = 4x^2$

The graph of this equation is a parabola.

19.

$4x^2 - 8x + 9y^2 + 36y = -4$

$4(x^2 - 2x) + 9(y^2 + 4y) = -4$

$4(x^2 - 2x + 1) + 9(y^2 + 4y + 4) = -4 + 4 + 36$

$4(x - 1)^2 + 9(y + 2)^2 = 36$

$\dfrac{(x - 1)^2}{9} + \dfrac{(y + 2)^2}{4} = 1$

The graph of this equation is an ellipse.

21. $4x^2 + y^2 = 36$

$\dfrac{4x^2}{36} + \dfrac{y^2}{36} = \dfrac{36}{36}$

$\dfrac{x^2}{9} + \dfrac{y^2}{36} = 1$

This is an ellipse centered at $(0, 0)$, with vertices at $(0, -6)$ and $(0, 6)$ and endpoints of the minor axis at $(-3, 0)$ and $(3, 0)$. The correct graph is F.

23. $(x - 2)^2 + (y + 3)^2 = 36$

This is a circle centered at $(2, -3)$, with a radius of 6. The correct graph is A.

25. $(y - 1)^2 - (x - 2)^2 = 36$

$\dfrac{(y - 1)^2}{36} - \dfrac{(x - 2)^2}{36} = 1$

This is a hyperbola centered at $(2, 1)$, opening upward and downward, with vertices at $(2, -5)$ and $(2, 7)$. The correct graph is B.

27. $\dfrac{x^2}{4} + \dfrac{y^2}{9} = 1$

The graph is an ellipse with domain $[-2, 2]$, range $[-3, 3]$, and vertices at $(0, -3)$ and $(0, 3)$. The endpoints of the minor axis are $(-2, 0)$ and $(2, 0)$.

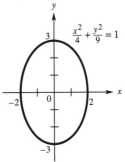

29. $\dfrac{x^2}{64} - \dfrac{y^2}{36} = 1$

The graph is a hyperbola with domain $(-\infty, -8] \cup [8, \infty)$, range $(-\infty, \infty)$, and vertices $(-8, 0)$ and $(8, 0)$. The asymptotes are the lines

$y = \pm\dfrac{3}{4}x$.

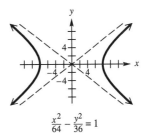

31. $\dfrac{(x+1)^2}{16} + \dfrac{(y-1)^2}{16} = 1$

Rewrite in standard form.

$(x+1)^2 + (y-1)^2 = 16$

The graph is a circle with domain $[-5, 3]$, range $[-3, 5]$, center $(-1, 1)$ and radius 4.

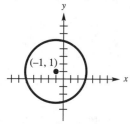

$\dfrac{(x+1)^2}{16} + \dfrac{(y-1)^2}{16} = 1$

33. $4x^2 + 9y^2 = 36$

$\dfrac{x^2}{9} + \dfrac{y^2}{4} = 1$

The graph is an ellipse with domain $[-3, 3]$, range $[-2, 2]$, vertices at $(-3, 0)$ and $(3, 0)$. The endpoints of the minor axis at $(0, -2)$ and $(0, 2)$.

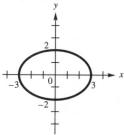

$4x^2 + 9y^2 = 36$

35. $\dfrac{(x-3)^2}{4} + (y+1)^2 = 1$

The graph is an ellipse centered at $(3, -1)$. Since $a = 2$, the vertices are $(3 - 2, -1) = (1, -1)$ and $(3 + 2, -1) = (5, -1)$. Since $b = 1$, the endpoints of the minor axis are $(3, -1-1) = (3, -2)$ and $(3, -1+1) = (3, 0)$. The domain is $[1, 5]$ and the range is $[-2, 0]$.

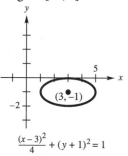

$\dfrac{(x-3)^2}{4} + (y+1)^2 = 1$

37. $\dfrac{(y+2)^2}{4} - \dfrac{(x+3)^2}{9} = 1$

The graph is a hyperbola centered at $(-3, -2)$. Since $a = 2$, the vertices are at $(-3, -2-2) = (-3, -4)$ and $(-3, -2+2) = (-3, 0)$. The domain is $(-\infty, \infty)$ and the range is $(-\infty, -4] \cup [0, \infty)$. The asymptotes are the lines

$y + 2 = \pm \dfrac{2}{3}(x+3)$

$y = \pm \dfrac{2}{3}(x+3) - 2.$

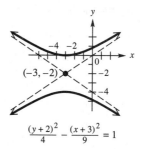

$\dfrac{(y+2)^2}{4} - \dfrac{(x+3)^2}{9} = 1$

39. $\dfrac{x}{3} = -\sqrt{1 - \dfrac{y^2}{16}}$ (1)

Square both sides.

$\dfrac{x^2}{9} = 1 - \dfrac{y^2}{16}$

$\dfrac{x^2}{9} + \dfrac{y^2}{16} = 1$ (2)

The graph of equation (2) is ellipse with vertices at $(0, -4)$ and $(0, 4)$. The graph of equation (1) is the left half of this ellipse. The domain is $[-3, 0]$ and the range is $[-4, 4]$. The vertical line test shows that this relation is not a function.

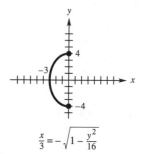

$\dfrac{x}{3} = -\sqrt{1 - \dfrac{y^2}{16}}$

41. $y = -\sqrt{1 + x^2}$ (1)

Square both sides.

$$y^2 = 1 + x^2$$

$$y^2 - x^2 = 1$$

$$\frac{y^2}{1} - \frac{x^2}{1} = 1 \qquad (2)$$

The graph of equation (2) is a hyperbola with vertices at $(0, -1)$ and $(0, 1)$. The graph of equation (1) is the bottom half of the hyperbola. The domain is $(-\infty, \infty)$ and the range is $(-\infty, -1]$. The vertical line test shows that the relation is a function.

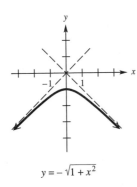

$$y = -\sqrt{1 + x^2}$$

43. Ellipse; vertex at $(0, 4)$, focus at $(0, 2)$, center at the origin.

Since the vertex is at $(0, 4)$, we have $a = 4$, so the equation is of the form $\dfrac{x^2}{b^2} + \dfrac{y^2}{16} = 1$.

Since there is a focus at $(0, 2)$, we have $c = 2$.

$$c^2 = a^2 - b^2$$

$$4 = 16 - b^2$$

$$b^2 = 12$$

The equation is $\dfrac{x^2}{12} + \dfrac{y^2}{16} = 1$.

45. Hyperbola; focus at $(0, -5)$, transverse axis of length 8, center at the origin.

Since the focus is at $(0, -5)$, $c = 5$, the hyperbola opens up and down, and the equation has the form $\dfrac{y^2}{a^2} - \dfrac{x^2}{b^2} = 1$.

Since the transverse axis has length 8, $2a = 8$, so $a = 4$.

$$c^2 = a^2 + b^2$$

$$25 = 16 + b^2$$

$$9 = b^2$$

The equation is $\dfrac{y^2}{16} - \dfrac{x^2}{9} = 1$.

47. Parabola with focus at $(3, 2)$ and directrix $x = -3$.

Since the directrix is $x = -3$ and the focus is $(3, 2)$, the vertex must be $(0, 2)$, and $p = 3$. The parabola opens to the right and the equation is

$$4px = (y - 2)^2$$

$$12x = (y - 2)^2$$

$$x = \frac{1}{12}(y - 2)^2.$$

49. Ellipse with foci at $(-2, 0)$ and $(2, 0)$ and major axis of length 10.

Since the foci are at $(-2, 0)$ and $(2, 0)$, we know that $c = 2$ and the equation is of the form

$$\frac{x^2}{a^2} + \frac{y^2}{b^2} = 1.$$

Since the major axis is of length 10, $2a = 10$, so $a = 5$.

$$c^2 = a^2 - b^2$$

$$4 = 25 - b^2$$

$$b^2 = 21$$

The equation is $\dfrac{x^2}{25} + \dfrac{y^2}{21} = 1$.

51. Hyperbola with x-intercepts ± 3; foci at $(-5, 0)$, $(5, 0)$.

The foci are $(-5, 0)$ and $(5, 0)$, so $c = 5$. The x-intercepts are ± 3, so $a = 3$.

$$c^2 = a^2 + b^2$$

$$25 = 9 + b^2$$

$$16 = b^2$$

The equation is $\dfrac{x^2}{9} - \dfrac{y^2}{16} = 1$.

53. The points $F'(0, 0)$ and $F(4, 0)$ are the foci, so the center of the ellipse is $(2, 0)$. For any point P on the ellipse, $PF' + PF = 2a = 8$, so $a = 4$.

Solve for b^2.

$$c^2 = a^2 - b^2$$

$$4 = 16 - b^2$$

$$b^2 = 12$$

The equation is $\dfrac{(x - 2)^2}{16} + \dfrac{y^2}{12} = 1$.

55. Graph A is an ellipse, so $e < 1$.

Graph B is a parabola, so $e = 1$.

Graph C is a circle, so $e = 0$.

Graph D is a hyperbola, so $e > 1$.

In increasing order of eccentricity, the graphs are C, A, B, D.

57. Since the eccentricity is .964,

$$e = \frac{c}{a} = .964$$

$$c = .964a$$

The closest distance to the sun is 89, so

$$a - c = 89$$

$$a - .964a = 89$$

$$.036a = 89$$

$$a = 2472.\overline{2}$$

$$c = 2383.\overline{2}.$$

Solve for b^2.

$$c^2 = a^2 - b^2$$

$$5,679,748 = 6,111,883 - b^2$$

$$b^2 = 432,135$$

The equation is $\dfrac{x^2}{6,111,883} + \dfrac{y^2}{432,135} = 1.$

59.

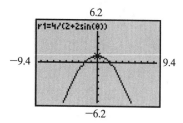

61.

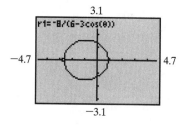

63. The polar equation of the parabola with focus at the pole, having a horizontal directrix 3 units above the pole has the form

$$r = \frac{ep}{1 + e\sin\theta} \quad \text{where } e = 1 \text{ and } p = 3.$$

$$r = \frac{1 \cdot 3}{1 + 1\sin\theta}$$

$$= \frac{3}{1 + \sin\theta}$$

65. To identify the type of conic, convert to a standard polar form to find e.

$$r = \frac{-6}{3 + \sin\theta}$$

$$= \frac{3(-2)}{3\left(1 + \frac{1}{3}\sin\theta\right)}$$

$$= \frac{-2}{1 + \frac{1}{3}\sin\theta}.$$

Thus $e = \dfrac{1}{3}$. Since $e < 1$, the graph of the equation is an ellipse to convert to rectangular form, start with the given equation.

$$r = \frac{-6}{3 + \sin\theta}$$

$$r(3 + \sin\theta) = -6$$

$$3r + r\sin\theta = -6$$

$$3r = -r\sin\theta - 6$$

$$3r = -y - 6$$

$$(3r)^2 = (-y - 6)^2$$

$$9r^2 = y^2 + 12y + 36$$

$$9(x^2 + y^2) = y^2 + 12y + 36$$

$$9x^2 + 9y^2 = y^2 + 12y + 36$$

$$9x^2 + 8y^2 - 12y - 36 = 0$$

67. $3xy - y^2 - 5 = 0$

$$A = 0, \ B = 3, \ C = -1$$

$$B^2 - 4AC = 3^2 - 4(0)(-1)$$

$$= 9$$

Since $B^2 - 4AC > 0$, the graph of the equation is a hyperbola or two intersecting lines.

69. $x^2 - xy + 2x - 3y = 0$

$$A = 1, \ B = -1, \ C = 0$$

$$B^2 - 4AC = (-1)^2 - 4(1)(0)$$

$$= 1$$

Since $B^2 - 4AC > 0$, the graph of the equation is a hyperbola or two intersecting lines.

71. $2\sqrt{3}x^2 + xy + \sqrt{3}y^2 + y = 2$

$$A = 2\sqrt{3}, \ B = 1, \ C = \sqrt{3}$$

$$\cot 2\theta = \frac{A - C}{B}$$

$$\cot 2\theta = \frac{2\sqrt{3} - \sqrt{3}}{1}$$

$$\cot 2\theta = \sqrt{3}$$

$$2\theta = \cot^{-1}(\sqrt{3})$$

$$2\theta = 30°$$

$$\theta = 15°$$

73. $-3xy + 9\sqrt{2}x = 15$

$A = 0, \ B = -3, \ C = 0$

$\cot 2\theta = \dfrac{A-C}{B} = \dfrac{0-0}{-3} = 0$

$\cos 2\theta = 0$

$\sin\theta = \sqrt{\dfrac{1-\cos 2\theta}{2}} = \sqrt{\dfrac{1-0}{2}} = \sqrt{\dfrac{1}{2}} = \dfrac{\sqrt{2}}{2}$

$\cos\theta = \sqrt{\dfrac{1+\cos 2\theta}{2}} = \sqrt{\dfrac{1+0}{2}} = \sqrt{\dfrac{1}{2}} = \dfrac{\sqrt{2}}{2}$

Thus $\theta = 45°$ and the rotation equations are $x = \dfrac{\sqrt{2}}{2}x' - \dfrac{\sqrt{2}}{2}y'$ and $y = \dfrac{\sqrt{2}}{2}x' + \dfrac{\sqrt{2}}{2}y'$. Substituting these values into the given equation yields

$$-3xy + 9\sqrt{2}x = 15$$

$$-3\left(\dfrac{\sqrt{2}}{2}x' - \dfrac{\sqrt{2}}{2}y'\right)\left(\dfrac{\sqrt{2}}{2}x' + \dfrac{\sqrt{2}}{2}y'\right) + 9\sqrt{2}\left(\dfrac{\sqrt{2}}{2}x' - \dfrac{\sqrt{2}}{2}y'\right) = 15$$

$$\dfrac{-3}{2}x'^2 + \dfrac{3}{2}y'^2 + 9x' - 9y' = 15$$

$$-3x'^2 + 3y'^2 + 18x' - 18y' = 30$$

$$-3(x'^2 - 6x') + 3(y'^2 - 6y') = 30$$

$$3(y'^2 - 6y' + 9) - 3(x'^2 - 6x' + 9) = 30 + 27 - 27$$

$$3(y' - 3)^2 - 3(x' - 3)^2 = 30$$

$$\dfrac{(y'-3)^2}{10} - \dfrac{(x'-3)^2}{10} = 1$$

The graph of the equation is a hyperbola with its center at $x' = 3$ and $y' = 3$. By translating the axes of the $x'\,y'$ system up 3 units and right 3 units, we get an $x''\,y''$–coordinate system in which the hyperbola is centered at the origin.

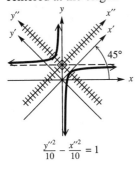

$\dfrac{y''^2}{10} - \dfrac{x''^2}{10} = 1$

Chapter 9 Test Exercises

1. $y = -x^2 + 6x$

Complete the square on x to find the vertex and axis.

$y = -(x^2 - 6x + 9 - 9)$

$\quad = -(x - 3)^2 + 9$

The parabola opens downward. The vertex is $(3, 9)$ and the axis is the vertical line $x = 3$. The domain is $(-\infty, \infty)$. The range is $(-\infty, 9]$.

x	1	2	3	4	5
y	5	8	9	8	5

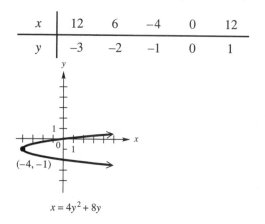

$y = -x^2 + 6x$

2. $x = 4y^2 + 8y$

Complete the square on y to find the vertex and axis.

$x = 4(y^2 + 2y + 1 - 1)$

$\quad = 4(y + 1)^2 - 4$

The parabola opens to the right. The vertex is $(-4, -1)$ and the axis is the horizontal line $y = -1$. The domain is $[-4, \infty)$. The range is $(-\infty, \infty)$.

x	12	6	−4	0	12
y	−3	−2	−1	0	1

$x = 4y^2 + 8y$

3. $x = 8y^2$

$\dfrac{1}{8}x = y^2$

The parabola is of the form $4px = y^2$,

so $4p = \dfrac{1}{8}$, $p = \dfrac{1}{32}$.

The focus is $\left(\dfrac{1}{32}, 0\right)$ and the directrix is the line

$x = -\dfrac{1}{32}$.

4. Parabola; vertex at $(2, 3)$, passing through $(-18, 1)$, opening to the left.

The equation is of the form $(y - 3)^2 = 4p(x - 2)$. Substitute $x = -18$ and $y = 1$, and solve for p.

$(1 - 3)^2 = 4p(-18 - 2)$

$-80p = 4$

$p = -\dfrac{1}{20}$

The equation is

$(y - 3)^2 = -\dfrac{1}{5}(x - 2)$

$x = -5(y - 3)^2 + 2.$

6. $\dfrac{(x - 8)^2}{100} + \dfrac{(y - 5)^2}{49} = 1$

The graph is an ellipse centered at $(8, 5)$. Since $a = 10$, the vertices are $(8 - 10, 5) = (-2, 5)$ and $(8 + 10, 5) = (18, 5)$. Since $b = 7$, the endpoints of the minor axis are $(8, 5 - 7) = (8, -2)$ and $(8, 5 + 7) = (8, 12)$. The domain is $[-2, 18]$. The range is $[-2, 12]$.

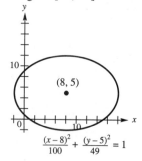

$\dfrac{(x - 8)^2}{100} + \dfrac{(y - 5)^2}{49} = 1$

7. $16x^2 + 4y^2 = 64$

$$\frac{x^2}{4} + \frac{y^2}{16} = 1$$

The graph is an ellipse with vertices $(0, -4)$ and $(0, 4)$. The endpoints of the minor axis are $(-2, 0)$ and $(2, 0)$. The domain is $[-2, 2]$. The range is $[-4, 4]$.

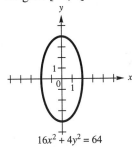

$16x^2 + 4y^2 = 64$

8. $y = -\sqrt{1 - \dfrac{x^2}{36}}$

Square both sides.

$$y^2 = 1 - \frac{x^2}{36}$$

$$\frac{x^2}{36} + y^2 = 1$$

This is the equation of an ellipse with vertices $(-6, 0)$ and $(6, 0)$. The endpoints of the minor axis are at $(0, -1)$ and $(0, 1)$. The graph of the original equation is the bottom half of the ellipse. The vertical line test shows that this relation is a function.

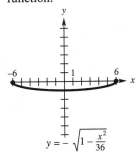

$y = -\sqrt{1 - \dfrac{x^2}{36}}$

9. Ellipse; centered at the origin, horizontal major axis with length 6, minor axis with length 4. Since the major axis is horizontal and has length 6, $2a = 6$. Thus, $a = 3$. Since the minor axis has length 4, $2b = 4$, so $b = 2$. The equation is

$$\frac{x^2}{9} + \frac{y^2}{4} = 1.$$

10. Place the arch on a coordinate system with the center of the ellipse at the origin.

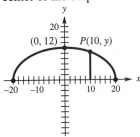

Since the arch is 40 ft wide, $2a = 40$, so $a = 20$. Since the arch is 12 ft high at the center, $b = 12$.

The equation is $\dfrac{x^2}{400} + \dfrac{y^2}{144} = 1$.

At a distance of 10 ft from the center of the bottom, $x = 10$. Find the y-coordinate of the point P on the hyperbola whose x-coordinate is 10.

$$\frac{x^2}{400} + \frac{y^2}{144} = 1$$

$$\frac{100}{400} + \frac{y^2}{144} = 1 \qquad \text{Let } x = 10$$

$$\frac{y^2}{144} = \frac{3}{4}$$

$$y^2 = 108$$

$$y = \sqrt{108} \qquad y \ge 0$$

$$y \approx 10.39$$

The arch is approximately 10.39 ft high 10 ft from the center of the bottom.

11. $\dfrac{x^2}{4} - \dfrac{y^2}{4} = 1$

The graph is a hyperbola with vertices $(-2, 0)$ and $(2, 0)$. The domain is $(-\infty, -2] \cup [2, \infty)$. The range is $(-\infty, \infty)$. The asymptotes are the lines

$$y = \pm\left(\frac{4}{4}\right)x = \pm x.$$

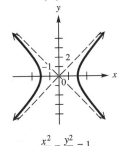

$\dfrac{x^2}{4} - \dfrac{y^2}{4} = 1$

12. $9x^2 - 4y^2 = 36$

$$\frac{x^2}{4} - \frac{y^2}{9} = 1$$

The graph is a hyperbola with vertices $(-2, 0)$ and $(2, 0)$. The domain is $(-\infty, -2] \cup [2, \infty)$. The range is

$(-\infty, \infty)$. The asymptotes are the lines $y = \pm\frac{3}{2}x$.

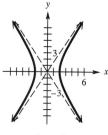

$9x^2 - 4y^2 = 36$

13. Hyperbola; x-intercepts ± 5, foci at $(-6, 0)$ and $(6, 0)$.

The x-intercepts are ± 5, so $a = 5$. The foci are $(-6, 0)$ and $(6, 0)$, so $c = 6$. Solve for b^2.

$c^2 = a^2 + b^2$

$36 = 25 + b^2$

$11 = b^2$

The equation is $\dfrac{x^2}{25} - \dfrac{y^2}{11} = 1$.

14. $x^2 + 8x + y^2 - 4y + 2 = 0$

Since the x^2 and y^2 terms have coefficients of the same positive coefficients, the graph of this equation is a circle.

15. $5x^2 + 10x - 2y^2 - 12y - 23 = 0$

Since the x^2 and y^2 terms have coefficients of different sign, the graph of this equation is a hyperbola.

16. $3x^2 + 10y^2 - 30 = 0$

Since the x^2 and y^2 terms have different positive coefficients, the graph of this equation is an ellipse.

17. $x^2 - 4y = 0$

Since only the x term is squared, the graph of this equation is a parabola.

18. $(x + 9)^2 + (y - 3)^2 = 0$

This is the equation of a "circle" with radius 0. The graph of this equation is a point.

19. $x^2 + 4x + y^2 - 6y + 30 = 0$

$(x^2 + 4x + 4) + (y^2 - 6y + 9) = -30 + 4 + 9$

$(x + 2)^2 + (y - 3)^2 = -17$

This equation has the form of the equation of a circle. However, since r^2 cannot be negative, there is no graph of this equation.

20. $\dfrac{x^2}{25} - \dfrac{y^2}{49} = 1$

Solve the equation for y.

$$\frac{x^2}{25} - 1 = \frac{y^2}{49}$$

$$\pm\sqrt{\frac{x^2}{25} - 1} = \frac{y}{7}$$

$$\pm 7\sqrt{\frac{x^2}{25} - 1} = y$$

Thus, the functions

$Y_1 = 7\sqrt{\dfrac{x^2}{25} - 1}$ and $Y_2 = -7\sqrt{\dfrac{x^2}{25} - 1}$ were used

to obtain the graph.

21.

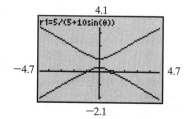

22. The polar equation of the conic with focus at the pole and having horizontal directrix 6 units above

the pole has the form $r = \dfrac{ep}{1 + e\sin\theta}$ where $p = 6$.

When $e = \dfrac{1}{2}$, we get

$$r = \frac{\frac{1}{2} \cdot 6}{1 + \frac{1}{2}\sin\theta}$$

$$= \frac{3}{\frac{2 + \sin\theta}{2}}$$

$$= \frac{6}{2 + \sin\theta}.$$

23.
$$r = \frac{1}{1+\cos\theta}$$
$$r(1+\cos\theta) = 1$$
$$r + r\cos\theta = 1$$
$$r = -r\cos\theta + 1$$
$$r = -x + 1$$
$$r^2 = (-x+1)^2$$
$$r^2 = x^2 - 2x + 1$$
$$x^2 + y^2 = x^2 - 2x + 1$$
$$y^2 + 2x - 1 = 0$$

Since this equation can be written as

$y^2 = -2x+1$ or $y^2 = -2\left(x - \frac{1}{2}\right)$, we know that

the graph of this equation is a parabola.

24. $5x^2 + 4xy + y^2 + 2x = 5$
$$A = 5,\ B = 4,\ C = 1$$
$$\cot 2\theta = \frac{A-C}{B}$$
$$\cot 2\theta = \frac{5-1}{4}$$
$$\cot 2\theta = 1$$
$$2\theta = 45°$$
$$\theta = 22.5°$$

25. $5x^2 + 8xy + 5y^2 = 9$
$$A = 5,\ B = 8,\ C = 5$$
$$\cot 2\theta = \frac{A-C}{B}$$
$$\cot 2\theta = \frac{5-5}{8} = 0$$
$$\cos 2\theta = 0$$
$$\sin\theta = \sqrt{\frac{1-\cos 2\theta}{2}} = \sqrt{\frac{1-0}{2}} = \sqrt{\frac{1}{2}} = \frac{\sqrt{2}}{2}$$
$$\cos\theta = \sqrt{\frac{1+\cos 2\theta}{2}} = \sqrt{\frac{1+0}{2}} = \sqrt{\frac{1}{2}} = \frac{\sqrt{2}}{2}$$

Thus $\theta = 45°$ and the rotation equations are $x = \frac{\sqrt{2}}{2}x' - \frac{\sqrt{2}}{2}y'$ and $y = \frac{\sqrt{2}}{2}x' + \frac{\sqrt{2}}{2}y'$. Substituting these

values into the given equation yields

$$5x^2 + 8xy + 5y^2 = 9$$
$$5\left(\frac{\sqrt{2}}{2}x' - \frac{\sqrt{2}}{2}y'\right)^2 + 8\left(\frac{\sqrt{2}}{2}x' - \frac{\sqrt{2}}{2}y'\right)\left(\frac{\sqrt{2}}{2}x' + \frac{\sqrt{2}}{2}y'\right) + 5\left(\frac{\sqrt{2}}{2}x' + \frac{\sqrt{2}}{2}y'\right)^2 = 9$$
$$\frac{5}{2}x'^2 - 5x'y' + \frac{5}{2}y'^2 + 4x'^2 - 4y'^2 + \frac{5}{2}x'^2 + 5x'y' + \frac{5}{2}y'^2 = 9$$
$$9x'^2 + y'^2 = 9$$
$$x'^2 + \frac{y'^2}{9} = 1.$$

The graph of the equation is an ellipse.

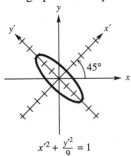

$x'^2 + \dfrac{y'^2}{9} = 1$

CHAPTER 10 FURTHER TOPICS IN ALGEBRA

Section 10.1

Connections *(page 788)*

1. Before the withdrawal, the balance at the end of the year is given by $B_n = 1.06B_{n-1}$. Since the withdrawal is simple and does not change from year to year, the balance after the withdrawal is found by subtraction: $B_n = 1.06_{n-1} - 127$.

   $B_2 = 1.06(1000) - 127 = 933$

   $B_3 = 1.06(933) - 127 = 861.98$

   \$933 and \$861.98

2. The account will be depleted sometime in the eleventh year.

   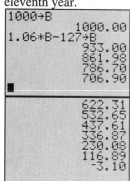

3.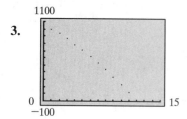

4. We use $B_n = 1.06B_{n-1} - 45$ and find the balance will exceed \$2000 sometime in the twenty-eighth year.

   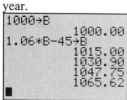

Exercises

1. $a_n = 4n + 10$

   Replace n with 1, 2, 3, 4, and 5.

   $n = 1$: $a_1 = 4(1) + 10 = 14$

   $n = 2$: $a_2 = 4(2) + 10 = 18$

   $n = 3$: $a_3 = 4(3) + 10 = 22$

   $n = 4$: $a_4 = 4(4) + 10 = 26$

   $n = 5$: $a_5 = 4(5) + 10 = 30$

   The first five terms are 14, 18, 22, 26, and 30.

3. $a_n = 2^{n-1}$

   Replace n with 1, 2, 3, 4, and 5.

   $n = 1$: $a_1 = 2^{1-1} = 2^0 = 1$

   $n = 2$: $a_2 = 2^{2-1} = 2^1 = 2$

   $n = 3$: $a_3 = 2^{3-1} = 2^2 = 4$

   $n = 4$: $a_4 = 2^{4-1} = 2^3 = 8$

   $n = 5$: $a_5 = 2^{5-1} = 2^4 = 16$

   The first five terms are 1, 2, 4, 8, and 16.

5. $a_n = (-1)^n(2n)$

   Replace n with 1, 2, 3, 4, and 5.

   $n = 1$: $a_1 = (-1)^1[2(1)] = -1(2) = -2$

   $n = 2$: $a_2 = (-1)^2[2(2)] = 1(4) = 4$

   $n = 3$: $a_3 = (-1)^3[2(3)] = -1(6) = -6$

   $n = 4$: $a_4 = (-1)^4[2(4)] = 1(8) = 8$

   $n = 5$: $a_5 = (-1)^5[2(5)] = -1(10) = -10$

   The first five terms are $-2, 4, -6, 8,$ and -10.

7. $a_n = \dfrac{4n-1}{n^2+2}$

   Replace n with 1, 2, 3, 4, and 5.

   $n = 1$: $a_1 = \dfrac{4(1)-1}{(1)^2+2} = \dfrac{4-1}{1+2} = \dfrac{3}{3} = 1$

   $n = 2$: $a_2 = \dfrac{4(2)-1}{(2)^2+2} = \dfrac{8-1}{4+2} = \dfrac{7}{6}$

   $n = 3$: $a_3 = \dfrac{4(3)-1}{(3)^2+2} = \dfrac{12-1}{9+2} = \dfrac{11}{11} = 1$

   $n = 4$: $a_4 = \dfrac{4(4)-1}{(4)^2+2} = \dfrac{16-1}{16+2} = \dfrac{15}{18} = \dfrac{5}{6}$

   $n = 5$: $a_5 = \dfrac{4(5)-1}{(5)^2+2} = \dfrac{20-1}{25+2} = \dfrac{19}{27}$

   The first five terms are $1, \dfrac{7}{6}, 1, \dfrac{5}{6},$ and $\dfrac{19}{27}$.

9. $a_1 = -2, a_2 = 4, a_3 = -8, a_4 = 16, a_5 = -32$

11. $a_1 = 0, a_2 = 1, a_3 = 8, a_4 = 81, a_5 = 1024$

15. The sequence of the days of the week has as its domain $\{1, 2, 3, 4, 5, 6, 7\}$. Therefore, it is a finite sequence.

17. The sequence 1, 2, 3, 4, has as its domain $\{1, 2, 3, 4\}$. Therefore, it is a finite sequence.

19. The sequence 1, 2, 3, 4, …has as its domain $\{1, 2, 3, 4, …\}$. Therefore, the sequence is infinite.

21. The sequence $a_1 = 3$ and for $2 \leq n \leq 10$,
$a_n = 3 \cdot a_{n-1}$ has as its domain $\{1, 2, 3, \ldots, 10\}$.
Therefore, the sequence is finite.

23. $a_1 = -2$, $a_n = a_{n-1} + 3$, for $n > 1$
$n = 2$: $a_2 = a_1 + 3 = (-2) + 3 = 1$
$n = 3$: $a_3 = a_2 + 3 = (1) + 3 = 4$
$n = 4$: $a_4 = a_3 + 3 = (4) + 3 = 7$
The first four terms are -2, 1, 4, and 7.

25. $a_1 = 1$, $a_2 = 1$, $a_n = a_{n-1} + a_{n-2}$, for $n \geq 3$
$n = 3$: $a_3 = a_2 + a_1 = 1 + 1 = 2$
$n = 4$: $a_4 = a_3 + a_2 = 2 + 1 = 3$
The first four terms are 1, 1, 2, and 3.

27. $\displaystyle\sum_{i=1}^{4} \frac{1}{j} = \frac{1}{1} + \frac{1}{2} + \frac{1}{3} + \frac{1}{4}$
$= \dfrac{12}{12} + \dfrac{6}{12} + \dfrac{4}{12} + \dfrac{3}{12}$
$= \dfrac{25}{12}$

29. $\displaystyle\sum_{i=1}^{4} i^i = 1^1 + 2^2 + 3^3 + 4^4$
$= 1 + 4 + 27 + 256$
$= 288$

31. $\displaystyle\sum_{k=1}^{6} (-1)^k \cdot k$
$= (-1)^1 \cdot 1 + (-1)^2 \cdot 2 + (-1)^3 \cdot 3$
$\quad + (-1)^4 \cdot 4 + (-1)^5 \cdot 5 + (-1)^6 \cdot 6$
$= -1 \cdot 1 + 1 \cdot 2 + (-1) \cdot 3 + 1 \cdot 4 + (-1) \cdot 5 + 1 \cdot 6$
$= -1 + 2 - 3 + 4 - 5 + 6$
$= 3$

33. $\displaystyle\sum_{i=1}^{10} (4i^2 - 5) = 1490$

```
seq(4I²-5,I,1,10
)→L₁
{-1 11 31 59 95…
sum(L₁)
            1490
```

35. $\displaystyle\sum_{j=3}^{9} (3j - j^2) = -154$

```
seq(3J-J²,J,3,9)
→L₁
{0 -4 -10 -18 -…
sum(L₁)
            -154
■
```

37. $\displaystyle\sum_{i=1}^{5} (2x_i + 3)$
$= (2x_1 + 3) + (2x_2 + 3) + (2x_3 + 3)$
$\quad + (2x_4 + 3) + (2x_5 + 3)$
$= [2(-2) + 3] + [2(-1) + 3] + [2(0) + 3]$
$\quad + [2(1) + 3] + [2(2) + 3]$
$= -1 + 1 + 3 + 5 + 7$

39. $\displaystyle\sum_{i=2}^{5} \frac{x_i + 1}{x_i + 2}$
$= \dfrac{x_2 + 1}{x_2 + 2} + \dfrac{x_3 + 1}{x_3 + 2} + \dfrac{x_4 + 1}{x_4 + 2} + \dfrac{x_5 + 1}{x_5 + 2}$
$= \dfrac{(-1) + 1}{(-1) + 2} + \dfrac{(0) + 1}{(0) + 2} + \dfrac{(1) + 1}{(1) + 2} + \dfrac{(2) + 1}{(2) + 2}$
$= 0 + \dfrac{1}{2} + \dfrac{2}{3} + \dfrac{3}{4}$

41. $f(x) = 2x^2$, $\Delta x = .5$
$\displaystyle\sum_{i=1}^{4} f(x_i) \Delta x$
$= f(x_1)\Delta x + f(x_2)\Delta x + f(x_3)\Delta x + f(x_4)\Delta x$
$= 2(x_1)^2(.5) + 2(x_2)^2(.5) + 2(x_3)^2(.5) + 2(x_4)^2(.5)$
$= 2(0)^2(.5) + 2(2)^2(.5) + 2(4)^2(.5) + 2(6)^2(.5)$
$= 0 + (8)(.5) + (32)(.5) + (72)(.5)$
$= 0 + 4 + 16 + 36$

43. $f(x) = \dfrac{-2}{x+1}$, $\Delta x = .5$

$\displaystyle\sum_{i=1}^{4} f(x_i)\Delta x$

$= f(x_1)\Delta x + f(x_2)\Delta x + f(x_3)\Delta x + f(x_4)\Delta x$

$= \dfrac{-2}{x_1+1}(.5) + \dfrac{-2}{x_2+1}(.5) + \dfrac{-2}{x_3+1}(.5) + \dfrac{-2}{x_4+1}(.5)$

$= \dfrac{-2}{(0)+1}(.5) + \dfrac{-2}{(2)+1}(.5) + \dfrac{-2}{(4)+1}(.5)$

$\quad + \dfrac{-2}{(6)+1}(.5)$

$= (-2)(.5) + \left(-\dfrac{2}{3}\right)(.5) + \left(-\dfrac{2}{5}\right)(.5) + \left(-\dfrac{2}{7}\right)(.5)$

$= -1 - \dfrac{1}{3} - \dfrac{1}{5} - \dfrac{1}{7}$

45. $\displaystyle\sum_{i=1}^{5}(5i+3) = \sum_{i=1}^{5} 5i + \sum_{i=1}^{5} 3$

$\qquad = 5\displaystyle\sum_{i=1}^{5} i + 5(3)$

$\qquad = 5\left[\dfrac{5(5+1)}{2}\right] + 15$

$\qquad = 5(15) + 15$

$\qquad = 90$

47. $\displaystyle\sum_{i=1}^{5}(4i^2 - 2i + 6)$

$= \displaystyle\sum_{i=1}^{5} 4i^2 - \sum_{i=1}^{5} 2i + \sum_{i=1}^{5} 6$

$= 4\displaystyle\sum_{i=1}^{5} i^2 - 2\sum_{i=1}^{5} i + 5(6)$

$= 4\left[\dfrac{5(5+1)(10+1)}{6}\right] - 2\left[\dfrac{5(5+1)}{2}\right] + 30$

$= 220 - 30 + 30$

$= 220$

49. $\displaystyle\sum_{i=1}^{4}(3i^3 + 2i - 4)$

$= \displaystyle\sum_{i=1}^{4} 3i^3 + \sum_{i=1}^{4} 2i - \sum_{i=1}^{4} 4$

$= 3\displaystyle\sum_{i=1}^{4} i^3 + 2\sum_{i=1}^{4} i - 4(4)$

$= 3\left[\dfrac{4^2(4+1)^2}{4}\right] + 2\left[\dfrac{4(4+1)}{2}\right] - 16$

$= 300 + 20 - 16$

$= 304$

51. $\dfrac{1}{3(1)} + \dfrac{1}{3(2)} + \dfrac{1}{3(3)} + \ldots + \dfrac{1}{3(9)} = \displaystyle\sum_{i=1}^{9}\dfrac{1}{3i}$

53. $1 - \dfrac{1}{2} + \dfrac{1}{4} - \dfrac{1}{8} + \ldots - \dfrac{1}{128}$

$= \dfrac{1}{2^0} - \dfrac{1}{2^1} + \dfrac{1}{2^2} - \dfrac{1}{2^3} + \ldots - \dfrac{1}{2^7}$

$= \displaystyle\sum_{k=1}^{8}(-1)^{k-1}\dfrac{1}{2^{k-1}}$

55. $a_n = \dfrac{n+4}{2n}$

Using the sequence graphing capability of a graphing calculator, the given sequence appears to converge to $\dfrac{1}{2}$.

57. $a_n = 2e^n$

Using the sequence graphing capability of a graphing calculator, the given sequence appears to diverge.

59. $a_n = \left(1 + \dfrac{1}{n}\right)^n$

Using the sequence graphing capability of a graphing calculator, the given sequence appears to converge to $e \approx 2.71828$.

61. $a_1 \approx 760$, $a_2 \approx 785$, $a_3 \approx 861$, $a_4 \approx 966$, $a_5 \approx 1083$, $a_6 \approx 1192$

63. (a) At the beginning, $A_0 = 563$. After the first payment, $A_1 = 1.01 \cdot 563 - 116$. Thus, $A_n = 1.01A_{n-1} - 116$.

(b) $A_1 = 452.63$,
$A_2 = 1.01(452.63) - 116 = 341.16$,

$A_3 = 1.01(341.16) - 116 = 228.57$
$341.16 and $228.57

(c) $A_4 \approx 114.85$, $A_5 \approx 0$
The loan will be paid off in 5 months (4 payments).

65. (a) Since the number of bacteria doubles every 40 minutes, it follows that
$$N_{j+1} = 2N_j \text{ for } j \geq 1.$$

(b) Two hours is 120 minutes. If
$$120 = 40(j-1),$$
then $\quad 3 = j - 1$
$\qquad\qquad j = 4.$
$N_1 = 230$, $N_2 = 460$, $N_3 = 920$, and
$N_4 = 1840$.
If there are initially 230 bacteria, then there will be 1840 bacteria after two hours.

(c) We must graph the sequence
$N_{j+1} = 2N_j$ for $j = 1, 2, 3, \ldots, 7$ if
$N_1 = 230$.

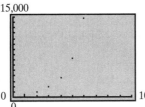

(d) The growth is very rapid. Since there is a doubling of the bacteria at equal intervals, their growth is exponential.

Section 10.2

Exercises

1. $2, 5, 8, 11, \ldots$
$d = a_2 - a_1 = 5 - 2 = 3$

3. $3, -2, -7, -12, \ldots$
$d = -2 - 3 = -5$

5. $x + 3y, 2x + 5y, 3x + 7y, \ldots$
$d = (2x + 5y) - (x + 3y)$
$\quad = 2x + 5y - x - 3y$
$\quad = x + 2y$

7. $a_1 = 8$ and $d = 6$
Starting with $a_1 = 8$, add $d = 6$ to each term to get the next term.

$a_2 = 8 + 6 = 14$
$a_3 = 14 + 6 = 20$
$a_4 = 20 + 6 = 26$
$a_5 = 26 + 6 = 32$
The first five terms are 8, 14, 20, 26, and 32.

9. $a_1 = 5$, $d = -2$
$a_2 = 5 + (-2) = 3$
$a_3 = 3 + (-2) = 1$
$a_4 = 1 + (-2) = -1$
$a_5 = -1 + (-2) = -3$
The first five terms are 5, 3, 1, -1, and -3.

11. $a_3 = 10$, $d = -2$
$a_4 = 10 + d = 10 + (-2) = 8$
$a_5 = 8 + d = 8 + (-2) = 6$
Subtract the common difference -2 to find the earlier terms.
$a_2 = a_3 - d = 10 - (-2) = 12$
$a_1 = a_2 - d = 12 - (-2) = 14$
The first five terms are 14, 12, 10, 8, and 6.

13. $a_1 = 5$, $d = 2$
$a_8 = a_1 + 7d$
$\quad = 5 + 7(2)$
$a_8 = 19$
$a_n = a_1 + (n-1)d$
$\quad = 5 + (n-1)(2)$
$a_n = 3 + 2n$

15. $a_1 = 5$, $a_4 = 15$
$a_4 = a_1 + 3d$
$15 = 5 + 3d$
$d = \dfrac{10}{3}$
$a_8 = a_1 + 7d$
$\quad = 5 + 7\left(\dfrac{10}{3}\right)$
$a_8 = \dfrac{85}{3}$
$a_n = a_1 + (n-1)d$
$a_n = 5 + (n-1)\left(\dfrac{10}{3}\right)$
$\quad = 5 + \dfrac{10}{3}n - \dfrac{10}{3}$
$a_n = \dfrac{5}{3} + \dfrac{10}{3}n$

17. $a_{10} = 6$, $a_{12} = 15$
First find a_1 and d.

$a_n = a_1 + (n-1)d$

$a_{10} = a_1 + 9d$

$6 = a_1 + 9d$ (1)

$a_{12} = a_1 + 11d$

$15 = a_1 + 11d$ (2)

Solve the system formed by equations (1) and (2) by the substitution method. Solve equation (1) for a_1.

$a_1 = 6 - 9d$ (3)

Substitute $6 - 9d$ for a_1 in equation (2).

$15 = (6 - 9d) + 11d$

$15 = 6 + 2d$

$9 = 2d$

$\dfrac{9}{2} = d$

Now substitute $d = \dfrac{9}{2}$ into equation (3) to find a_1.

$a_1 = 6 - 9\left(\dfrac{9}{2}\right)$

$= \dfrac{12}{2} - \dfrac{81}{2}$

$a_1 = -\dfrac{69}{2}$

Now find a_8 and a_n.

$a_8 = a_1 + 7d$

$= -\dfrac{69}{2} + 7\left(\dfrac{9}{2}\right)$

$= -\dfrac{69}{2} + \dfrac{63}{2}$

$a_8 = -\dfrac{6}{2} = -3$

$a_n = a_1 + (n-1)(d)$

$= -\dfrac{69}{2} + (n-1)\left(\dfrac{9}{2}\right)$

$= -\dfrac{69}{2} + \dfrac{9}{2}n - \dfrac{9}{2}$

$= -\dfrac{78}{2} + \dfrac{9}{2}n$

$a_n = -39 + \dfrac{9}{2}n$

19. $a_1 = x,\ a_2 = x + 3$

$d = (x + 3) - x = 3$

$a_8 = a_1 + 7d$

$= x + 7(3)$

$a_8 = x + 21$

$a_n = a_1 + (n-1)d$

$= x + (n-1)(3)$

$a_n = x + 3n - 3$

21. $a_5 = 27$ and $a_{15} = 87$

$27 = a_1 + 4d$ or $a_1 = 27 - 4d$

$87 = a_1 + 14d$ or $a_1 = 87 - 14d$

By substitution,

$27 - 4d = 87 - 14d$

$10d = 60$

$d = 6.$

Then,

$a_1 = 27 - 4d$

$= 27 - 4(6)$

$= 27 - 24$

$= 3.$

23. $S_{16} = -160$ and $a_{16} = -25$

$S_n = \dfrac{n}{2}(a_1 + a_n)$

$S_{16} = \dfrac{16}{2}(a_1 + a_{16})$

$-160 = 8(a_1 - 25)$

$-160 = 8a_1 - 200$

$40 = 8a_1$

$a_1 = 5$

25. Find S_{10} if $a_1 = 8$ and $d = 3$.

S_{10} represents the sum of the first ten terms of a sequence.

To find S_{10}, substitute $n = 10$, $a_1 = 8$, and $d = 3$ into the formula

$S_n = \dfrac{n}{2}[2a_1 + (n-1)d].$

$S_{10} = \dfrac{10}{2}[2(8) + (9)(3)]$

$= 5(16 + 27) = 5(43)$

$= 215$

27. Find S_{10} if $a_3 = 5$ and $a_4 = 8$. Find a_1 and d first.

$d = a_4 - a_3 = 8 - 5 = 3$

$a_3 = a_1 + 2d$

$5 = a_1 + 2 \cdot 3$

$-1 = a_1$

$S_n = \dfrac{n}{2}[2a_1 + (n-1)d]$

$S_{10} = \dfrac{10}{2}[2(-1) + (9)(3)]$

$= 5(-2 + 27) = 5(25)$

$= 125$

29. To find S_{10} for the sequence 5, 9, 13, …, substitute $n = 10$, $a_1 = 5$, and $d = 4$ into the formula.

$$S_n = \frac{n}{2}[2a_1 + (n-1)d].$$

$$S_{10} = \frac{10}{2}[2(5) + (9)(4)]$$

$$= 5(10 + 36) = 230$$

31. $a_1 = 10$, $a_{10} = 5.5$

Use the formula $S_n = \frac{n}{2}(a_1 + a_n)$ since a_1 and

a_{10} are given.

$$S_{10} = \frac{10}{2}(10 + 5.5)$$

$$= 5(15.5)$$

$$= 77.5$$

33. $S_{20} = 1090$, $a_{20} = 102$

The formula for the sum is

$$S_n = \frac{n}{2}(a_1 + a_n), \text{ so}$$

$$S_{20} = \frac{20}{2}(a_1 + a_{20}).$$

$$1090 = 10(a_1 + 102)$$

Solve for a_1.

$$109 = a_1 + 102$$

$$7 = a_1$$

Solve for d.

$$a_n = a_1 + (n-1)d$$

$$a_{20} = a_1 + (20-1)d$$

$$102 = 7 + 19d$$

$$95 = 19d$$

$$5 = d$$

35. $S_{12} = -108$, $a_{12} = -19$

The formula for the sum is

$$S_n = \frac{n}{2}(a_1 + a_n), \text{ so}$$

$$S_{12} = \frac{12}{2}(a_1 + a_{12}).$$

$$-108 = 6(a_1 - 19)$$

$$-108 = 6a_1 - 114$$

$$6 = 6a_1$$

$$1 = a_1$$

Solve for d.

$$a_n = a_1 + (n-1)d$$

$$a_{12} = a_1 + (12-1)d$$

$$-19 = 1 + 11d$$

$$-20 = 11d$$

$$-\frac{20}{11} = d$$

37. $\sum_{i=1}^{3}(i+4)$

This is a sum of three terms having a common difference of 1, so it is the sum of the first three terms of the arithmetic sequence having $a_1 = 1 + 4 = 5$, $n = 3$, and $a_n = a_3 = 3 + 4 = 7$.
Thus,

$$\sum_{i=1}^{3}(i+4) = S_3 = \frac{n}{2}(a_1 + a_3)$$

$$= \frac{3}{2}(5 + 7)$$

$$= 18.$$

39. $\sum_{j=1}^{10}(2j+3)$

There is a common difference of $2 \cdot 1$ or 2, so this is the sum of an arithmetic sequence with $a_1 = 2(1) + 3 = 5$, $n = 10$, and $a_n = a_{10} = 2(10) + 3 = 23$.
Thus,

$$\sum_{j=1}^{10}(2j+3) = S_{10} = \frac{10}{2}(a_1 + a_{10})$$

$$= 5(5 + 23)$$

$$= 140.$$

41. $\sum_{i=1}^{12}(-5-8i)$

This is the sum of an arithmetic sum sequence with $d = -8$, $a_1 = -5 - 8(1) = -13$, $n = 12$, and $a_n = a_{12} = -5 - 8(12) = -101$.

$$\sum_{i=1}^{12}(-5-8i) = S_{12} = \frac{12}{2}[(-13) + (-101)]$$

$$= 6(-114)$$

$$= -684$$

43. $\sum_{i=1}^{1000} i$

This is the sum of an arithmetic sequence with $d = 1$, $a_1 = 1$, $n = 1000$, and $a_n = a_{1000} = 1000$.

$$\sum_{i=1}^{1000} i = S_{1000} = \frac{1000}{2}(1 + 1000)$$

$$= 500(1001)$$

$$= 500,500$$

45. $f(x) = mx + b$

$$f(1) = m(1) + b = m + b$$

$$f(2) = m(2) + b = 2m + b$$

$$f(3) = m(3) + b = 3m + b$$

46. The sequence $f(1), f(2), f(3)$ is an arithmetic sequence since the difference between any two adjacent terms is m.

47. The common difference is the difference between any two adjacent terms.
$$d = (3m + b) - (2m + b) = m$$

48. From Exercise 45, we know that $a_1 = m + b$.
From Exercise 47, we know that $d = m$.
Therefore,
$$\begin{aligned} a_n &= a_1 + (n-1)d \\ &= (m+b) + (n-1)m \\ &= m + b + nm - m \\ a_n &= mn + b. \end{aligned}$$

49. $a_n = 4.2n + 9.73$
Using the sequence feature of a graphing calculator, we obtain $S_{10} = 328.3$.

51. $a_n = \sqrt{8}n + \sqrt{3}$
Using the sequence feature of a graphing calculator, we obtain $S_{10} \approx 172.884$.

53. Find the sum of all the integers from 51 to 71.
$$\begin{aligned} \sum_{i=51}^{71} i &= \sum_{i=1}^{71} i - \sum_{i=1}^{50} i \\ &= S_{71} - S_{50} \end{aligned}$$
We know $a_1 = 1$, $d = 1$, $a_{50} = 50$, and $a_{71} = 71$.
Thus,
$$S_{71} = \frac{71}{2}(1 + 71) = 71(36) = 2556,$$
$$S_{50} = \frac{50}{2}(1 + 50) = 25(51) = 1275.$$
Thus, the sum is
$$S_{71} - S_{50} = 2556 - 1275 = 1281.$$

55. In every 12-hour cycle, the clock will chime $1 + 2 + 3 + \ldots + 12$ times.
$a_1 = 1$, $n = 12$, $a_{12} = 12$
$$S_{12} = \frac{12}{2}(1 + 12) = 6(13) = 78$$
Since there are two 12-hour cycles in 1 day, every day the clock will chime $2(78) = 156$ times.
Since there are 30 days in this month, the clock will chime $156 \cdot 30 = 4680$ times.

57. At the end of the first year, Keon's balance is
$1120 + .05(1120) = 1176$.
At the end of the second year, Keon's balance is
$$\begin{aligned} 1176 + .05(1120) &= [1120 + .05(1120)] + .05(1120) \\ &= 1120 + .05(1120)(2) \\ &= 1232. \end{aligned}$$
Thus, $a_n = 1120(1 + .05n)$.

$$\begin{aligned} a_1 &= 1120[1 + .05(1)] = 1176 \\ a_2 &= 1120[1 + .05(2)] = 1232 \\ a_3 &= 1120[1 + .05(3)] = 1288 \\ a_4 &= 1120[1 + .05(4)] = 1344 \end{aligned}$$
The accumulated amounts after each of the four years are $1176, $1232, $1288, and $1344.
The amount of interest after the first four years is $1344 - 1120 = 224$ or $224.

59. (a) The balance at the end of each month is given by
$$b_n = b_{n-1} - 150 - .01b_{n-1} = .99n_{n-1} - 150$$
with $b_1 = 1800$. The interest payments are thus given by $a_n = .01[1800 - 150(n-1)]$.

(b) We find $b_{11} = 41.68$ and $b_{12} = -108.73$. It will take Maria 12 payments to pay off the loan.

(c)
$$\begin{aligned} a_1 &= .01[1800 - 150(1 - 1)] = 18 \\ a_{12} &= .01[1800 - 150(12 - 1)] = 1.5 \\ S_{12} &= \frac{12}{2}(18 + 1.5) = 117 \end{aligned}$$
The total interest is $117.

61. $a_1 = 18$
$a_{31} = 28$
$n = 31$
Find S_{31}.
$$\begin{aligned} S_{31} &= \frac{31}{2}(18 + 28) \\ &= \frac{31}{2}(46) \\ &= 713 \end{aligned}$$
713 inches of material would be needed.

66. (a) For the median person who joins the work force immediately after high school,
$$\begin{aligned} a_1 &= 23{,}972 \\ a_2 &= 23{,}972 + 534 \\ a_3 &= 23{,}972 + 534(2) \end{aligned}$$
so that $a_n = 23{,}972 + 534(n-1)$
The person will work for $65 - 18 = 47$ years after entering the work force and the sum of his/her earnings will be
$$\sum_{i=1}^{47}[23{,}972 + 534(n-1)] = 1{,}703{,}938$$
or $1,703,938.

(b) For the median person who attends four years of college before joining the work force.

$b_1 = 40,508$

$b_2 = 40,508 + 994$

$b_3 = 40,508 + 994(2)$

so that $b_n = 40,508 + 994(n-1)$

The person will work for $65 - 22 = 43$ years after college and after entering the work force and the sum of his/her earnings will be

$$\sum_{i=1}^{43} [40,508 + 994(n-1)] = 2,639,426$$

or $\$2,639,426$.

(c) $2,639,426 - 1,703,938 = 935,488$.
The difference is $\$935,488$, which is much greater than $\$130,000$.

Section 10.3

Connections *(page 809)*

1. Using the recursive definition of the balances $S_n = 1.06S_{n-1} + 1000$ with a graphing calculator, we find $S_6 = 6975.32$ and $S_7 = 8393.84$.

2. Using the techniques from the Connections Box in Section 10.1, we have $S_n = \dfrac{100\left[1 - (1.06)^n\right]}{1 - 1.06}$.
We find $S_8 = 9897.47$ and $S_9 = 11,491.32$. Thus, it takes about 8 years for the amount of the annuity to reach $\$10,000$.

Exercises

1. $a_1 = \dfrac{5}{3}, r = 3, n = 4$

$a_2 = a_1 r = \left(\dfrac{5}{3}\right)(3) = 5$

$a_3 = a_2 r = 5(3) = 15$

$a_4 = a_3 r = 15(3) = 45$

The first four terms of the sequence are $\dfrac{5}{3}$, 5, 15, and 45.

3. $a_4 = 5, a_5 = 10, n = 5$
First find r.

$r = \dfrac{a_5}{a_4} = \dfrac{10}{5} = 2$

$a_3 = \dfrac{a_4}{r} = \dfrac{5}{2}$

$a_2 = \dfrac{a_3}{r} = \dfrac{\frac{5}{2}}{2} = \dfrac{5}{4}$

$a_1 = \dfrac{a_2}{r} = \dfrac{\frac{5}{4}}{2} = \dfrac{5}{8}$

The first five terms are

$\dfrac{5}{8}, \dfrac{5}{4}, \dfrac{5}{2}$, 5, and 10.

5. $a_1 = 5, r = -2$

$a_5 = a_1 r^{5-1}$

$a_5 = 5(-2)^4 = 80$

$a_n = a_1 r^{n-1}$

$a_n = 5(-2)^{n-1}$

7. $a_4 = 243, r = -3$
First find a_1.

$a_4 = a_1 r^{4-1}$

$243 = a_1(-3)^3$

$-27a_1 = 243$

$a_1 = -9$

Now find a_5 and a_n.

$a_5 = a_1 r^{5-1}$

$a_5 = (-9)(-3)^4$

$a_5 = -729$

$a_n = a_1 r^{n-1}$

$a_n = (-9)(-3)^{n-1}$

Note that

$(-9)(-3)^{n-1} = -(-3)^2(-3)^{n-1}$

$= -(-3)^{n+1}$,

so $a_n = -(-3)^{n+1}$ is an equivalent formula for the nth term of this sequence.

9. $-4, -12, -36, -108, \ldots$
First find r.

$r = \dfrac{-12}{-4} = 3$

Now find a_5 and a_n.

$a_5 = a_1 r^{5-1}$

$a_5 = (-4)(3)^4 = -324$

$a_n = a_1 r^{n-1}$

$a_n = -4(3)^{n-1}$

11. $\dfrac{4}{5}, 2, 5, \dfrac{25}{2}, \ldots$

$$r = \dfrac{2}{\dfrac{4}{5}} = \dfrac{5}{2}$$

$$a_5 = a_1 r^{5-1}$$

$$a_5 = \left(\dfrac{4}{5}\right)\left(\dfrac{5}{2}\right)^4 = \dfrac{125}{4}$$

$$a_n = a_1 r^{n-1}$$

$$a_n = \left(\dfrac{4}{5}\right)\left(\dfrac{5}{2}\right)^{n-1}$$

Note that

$$\left(\dfrac{4}{5}\right)\left(\dfrac{5}{2}\right)^{n-1} = \dfrac{2^2}{5^1} \cdot \dfrac{5^{n-1}}{2^{n-1}}$$

$$= \dfrac{5^{n-2}}{2^{n-3}},$$

so $a_n = \dfrac{5^{n-2}}{2^{n-3}}$ is an equivalent formula for the nth term of this sequence.

13. $a_3 = 5$ and $a_8 = \dfrac{1}{625}$

Using $a_n = a_1 r^{n-1}$, we write the following system of equations:

$$a_3 = a_1 r^2 \qquad (1)$$

$$a_8 = a_1 r^7. \qquad (2)$$

Substituting the given values for a_3 and a_8, we have

$$a_1 r^2 = 5 \qquad (1)$$

$$a_1 r^7 = \dfrac{1}{625}. \qquad (2)$$

Dividing equation (2) by equation (1), we obtain

$$\dfrac{a_1 r^7}{a_1 r^2} = \dfrac{\frac{1}{625}}{5} = \dfrac{1}{625} \cdot \dfrac{1}{5}$$

$$r^5 = \dfrac{1}{3125}$$

$$r = \dfrac{1}{5}.$$

Substituting this value into equation (1), we obtain

$$a_1\left(\dfrac{1}{5}\right)^2 = 5$$

$$\dfrac{a_1}{25} = 5$$

$$a_1 = 125.$$

15. $a_4 = -\dfrac{1}{4}$ and $a_9 = -\dfrac{1}{128}$

Using $a_n = a_1 r^{n-1}$, we write the following system of equations:

$$a_4 = a_1 r^3 \qquad (1)$$

$$a_9 = a_1 r^8. \qquad (2)$$

Substituting the given values for a_4 and a_9, we have

$$a_1 r^3 = -\dfrac{1}{4} \qquad (1)$$

$$a_1 r^8 = -\dfrac{1}{128}. \qquad (2)$$

Dividing equation (2) by equation (1), we obtain

$$\dfrac{a_1 r^8}{a_1 r^3} = \dfrac{-\frac{1}{128}}{-\frac{1}{4}} = \left(-\dfrac{1}{128}\right)\left(-\dfrac{4}{1}\right)$$

$$r^5 = \dfrac{1}{32}$$

$$r = \dfrac{1}{2}.$$

Substituting this value into equation (1), we obtain

$$a_1\left(\dfrac{1}{2}\right)^3 = -\dfrac{1}{4}$$

$$\dfrac{a_1}{8} = -\dfrac{1}{4}$$

$$a_1 = -2.$$

17. $2, 8, 32, 128, \ldots$

This geometric sequence has

$$r = \dfrac{8}{2} = 4 \text{ and } a_1 = 2.$$

Use the formula $S_n = \dfrac{a_1(1-r^n)}{1-r}$ with $n = 5$, $a_1 = 2$, and $r = 4$.

$$S_5 = \dfrac{2[1-4^5]}{1-4}$$

$$= \dfrac{2(1-1024)}{-3}$$

$$= 682$$

19. $18, -9, \dfrac{9}{2}, -\dfrac{9}{4}, \ldots$

This geometric sequence has

$$r = \dfrac{-9}{18} = -\dfrac{1}{2} \text{ and } a_1 = 18.$$

$$S_n = \frac{a_1(1 - r^n)}{1 - r}$$

$$S_5 = \frac{18\left[1 - \left(-\frac{1}{2}\right)^5\right]}{1 - \left(-\frac{1}{2}\right)}$$

$$= \frac{18\left(1 + \frac{1}{32}\right)}{\frac{3}{2}}$$

$$= 18\left(\frac{33}{32}\right)\left(\frac{2}{3}\right)$$

$$= \frac{99}{8}$$

21. $a_1 = 8.423,\ r = 2.859$

$$S_n = \frac{a_1(1 - r^n)}{1 - r}$$

$$S_5 = \frac{8.423\left[1 - (2.859)^5\right]}{1 - 2.859}$$

$$\approx \frac{8.423(-190.016)}{-1.859}$$

$$\approx 860.95$$

23. $\sum\limits_{i=1}^{5} 3^i$

For this geometric series, $a_1 = 3$, $r = 3$, and $n = 5$.

$$S_n = \frac{a_1(1 - r^n)}{1 - r}$$

$$S_5 = \frac{3[1 - 3^5]}{1 - 3}$$

$$= \frac{3(1 - 243)}{-2}$$

$$= 363$$

25. $\sum\limits_{j=1}^{6} 48\left(\frac{1}{2}\right)^j$

For this geometric series, $a_1 = 24$, $r = \frac{1}{2}$, and $n = 6$.

$$S_n = \frac{a_1(1 - r^n)}{1 - r}$$

$$S_6 = \frac{24\left[1 - \left(\frac{1}{2}\right)^6\right]}{1 - \frac{1}{2}}$$

$$= \frac{24\left(1 - \frac{1}{64}\right)}{\frac{1}{2}}$$

$$= 24\left(\frac{63}{64}\right)\left(\frac{2}{1}\right)$$

$$= \frac{189}{4}$$

27. $\sum\limits_{k=4}^{10} 2^k$

For this geometric series, $a_1 = 2^4 = 16$ and $r = 2$. The number of terms is $n = 10 - 4 + 1 = 7$.

$$S_n = \frac{a_1(1 - r^n)}{1 - r}$$

$$S_7 = \frac{16[1 - 2^7]}{1 - 2}$$

$$= \frac{16(1 - 128)}{-1}$$

$$= 2032$$

29. The sum of an infinite geometric series exists if $|r| < 1$.

31. 12, 24, 48, 96, …

$$r = \frac{24}{12} = 2$$

The sum of the terms of this infinite geometric sequence would not converge since $r = 2$ is not between -1 and 1.

33. $-48, -24, -12, -6, \ldots$

$$r = \frac{-24}{-48} = \frac{1}{2}$$

Since $|r| < 1$, the sum converges.

35. $18 + 6 + 2 + \dfrac{2}{3} + \ldots$

For this infinite geometric series, $a_1 = 18$ and

$$r = \frac{6}{18} = \frac{1}{3}.$$

$$S_\infty = \frac{a_1}{1 - r}$$

$$= \frac{18}{1 - \frac{1}{3}}$$

$$= \frac{18}{\frac{2}{3}}$$

$$= 27$$

37. $\dfrac{1}{4} - \dfrac{1}{6} + \dfrac{1}{9} - \dfrac{2}{27} + \ldots$

For this geometric series, $a_1 = \dfrac{1}{4}$ and

$r = \dfrac{-\frac{1}{6}}{\frac{1}{4}} = -\dfrac{2}{3}.$

$\begin{aligned} S_\infty &= \dfrac{a_1}{1-r} \\[4pt] &= \dfrac{\frac{1}{4}}{1-\left(-\frac{2}{3}\right)} \\[4pt] &= \dfrac{\frac{1}{4}}{\frac{5}{3}} \\[4pt] &= \dfrac{3}{20} \end{aligned}$

39. $\displaystyle\sum_{i=1}^{\infty} 3\left(\dfrac{1}{4}\right)^{i-1}$

This series has

$a_1 = 3\left(\dfrac{1}{4}\right)^{1-1} = 3\left(\dfrac{1}{4}\right)^{0} = 3 \cdot 1 = 3$ and $r = \dfrac{1}{4}.$

The sum is

$\begin{aligned} \sum_{i=1}^{\infty} 3\left(\dfrac{1}{4}\right)^{i-1} &= S_\infty = \dfrac{a_1}{1-r} \\[4pt] &= \dfrac{3}{1-\frac{1}{4}} \\[4pt] &= \dfrac{3}{\frac{3}{4}} \\[4pt] &= 3 \cdot \dfrac{4}{3} \\[4pt] &= 4. \end{aligned}$

41. $\displaystyle\sum_{k=1}^{\infty} (.3)^{k}$

This series has $a_1 = (.3)^1 = .3$ and $r = .3.$
The sum is

$\begin{aligned} \sum_{k=1}^{\infty} (.3)^{k} &= S_\infty = \dfrac{a_1}{1-r} \\[4pt] &= \dfrac{.3}{1-.3} \\[4pt] &= \dfrac{.3}{.7} \\[4pt] &= \dfrac{3}{7}. \end{aligned}$

43. $g(x) = ab^{x}$

$g(1) = ab^{1} = ab$

$g(2) = ab^{2}$

$g(3) = ab^{3}$

44. The sequence $g(1)$, $g(2)$, $g(3)$ is a geometric sequence because each term after the first is a constant multiple of the preceding term. The common ration is $\dfrac{ab^{2}}{ab} = b.$

45. From Exercise 43, $a_1 = ab$. From Exercise 44, $r = b$. Therefore,

$\begin{aligned} a_n &= a_1 r^{n-1} \\ &= ab(b)^{n-1} \\ &= ab^{n}. \end{aligned}$

47. $\displaystyle\sum_{i=1}^{10} (1.4)^{i}$

Using the sequence feature of a graphing calculator, we obtain $S_{10} \approx 97.739.$

49. $\displaystyle\sum_{j=3}^{8} 2(.4)^{j}$

Using the sequence feature of a graphing calculator, the sum is approximately .212.

51. $S_n = R\left[\dfrac{(1+i)^{n}-1}{i}\right]$

$S_{25} = 2000\left[\dfrac{(1.06)^{25}-1}{.06}\right]$

$S_{25} = 109,729.02$

The total amount in Michael's IRA will be $109,729.02.

53. **(a)** $a_n = 1276(.916)^{n}$

$a_1 = 1276(.916)^{1} \approx 1169$

$r = .916$

(b) $a_n = 1276(.916)^{n}$

$a_{10} = 1276(.916)^{10} \approx 531$

$a_{20} = 1276(.916)^{20} \approx 221$

This means that a person who is 10 years from retirement should have savings of 531% of his or her annual salary; a person 20 years from retirement should have savings of 221% of his or her annual salary.

55. **(a)** $a_n = a_1 \cdot 2^{n-1}$

(b) If $a_1 = 100$, we have
$$a_n = 100 \cdot 2^{n-1}.$$
Since $100 = 10^2$ and $1,000,000 = 10^6$, we need to solve the equation $10^2 \cdot 2^{n-1} = 10^6$. Divide both sides by 10^2.
$$2^{n-1} = 10^4.$$
Take common logs (base 10) on both sides.
$$\log 2^{n-1} = \log 10^4$$
$$(n-1)\log 2 = 4$$
$$n - 1 = \frac{4}{\log 2}$$
$$n = \frac{4}{\log 2} + 1 \approx 14.28$$
Since the number of bacteria is increasing, the first value of n where $a_n > 1,000,000$ is 15.

(c) Since a_n represents the number of bacteria after $40(n - 1)$ minutes, a_{15} represents the number after
$$40(15 - 1) = 40 \cdot 14$$
$$= 560 \text{ minutes}$$
or 9 hours, 20 minutes.

57. This situation may be represented as a geometric sequence with $a_1 = 100$. Also, $r = .80$, since the strength of the mixture after each draining and replacing is $\frac{100 - 20}{100} = \frac{80}{100} = 80\%$ of the previous strength.
Initially the percentage of chemical in the mixture is $100(.80)^0 = 100 \cdot 1 = 100$.
After 1 draining, the percentage will be
$$100(.80)^1 = 100(.80) = 80.$$
After 9 drainings, the percentage will be
$$100(.80)^9 \approx 100(.134) = 13.4.$$
That is, after 9 drainings, the strength of the mixture will be about 13.4%.

59. Use the formula for the sum of an infinite geometric sequence with $a_1 = 1000$ and $r = .1$.
$$S_\infty = \frac{a_1}{1-r}$$
$$= \frac{1000}{1 - .1}$$
$$= \frac{1000}{.9}$$
$$= \frac{10,000}{9}$$

The manager should have ordered $\frac{10,000}{9}$ units of sugar.

61. Use the formula for the sum of the first n terms of a geometric sequence with $a_1 = 2$, $r = 2$, and $n = 5$.
$$S_n = \frac{a_1(1 - r^n)}{1 - r}$$
$$S_5 = \frac{2[1 - 2^5]}{1 - 2}$$
$$= \frac{2(1 - 32)}{-1}$$
$$= 62$$
Going back five generations, the total number of ancestors is 62. Next, use the same formula with $a_1 = 2$, $r = 2$, and $n = 10$.
$$S_{10} = \frac{2[1 - 2^{10}]}{1 - 2}$$
$$= \frac{2(1 - 1024)}{-1}$$
$$= 2046$$
Going back ten generations, the total number of ancestors is 2046.

63. When the midpoints of the sides of an equilateral triangle are connected, the length of a side of the new triangle is one-half the length of a side of the original triangle. Use the formula for the nth term of a geometric sequence with $a_1 = 2$, $r = \frac{1}{2}$, and $n = 8$.
$$a_n = a_1 r^{n-1}$$
$$a_8 = (2)\left(\frac{1}{2}\right)^{8-1}$$
$$= 2\left(\frac{1}{128}\right)$$
$$= \frac{1}{64}$$

The eighth triangle has sides of length $\frac{1}{64}$ m.

65. The future value of an annuity uses the formula
$$S_n = \frac{a_1(1 - r^n)}{1 - r}, \text{ where } r = 1 + \text{interest rate.}$$
The payments are \$1000 for 9 yr at 8% compounded annually, so $a_1 = 1000$, $r = 1.08$, and $n = 9$.
$$S_9 = \frac{1000[1 - (1.08)^9]}{1 - 1.08}$$
$$\approx 12,487.56$$
The future value is \$12,487.56.

67. The future value of an annuity uses the formula
$$S_n = \frac{a_1(1 - r_n)}{1 - r}, r = 1 + \text{interest rate.}$$
The payments are \$2430 for 10 yr at 6%

compounded annually, so $a_1 = 2430$, $r = 1.06$, $n = 10$.

$$S_{10} = \frac{2430[1 - (1.06)^{10}]}{1 - 1.06}$$
$$\approx 32,029.33.$$

The future value is \$32,029.33.

69. $S_n = R\left[\frac{(1 + i)^n - 1}{i}\right]$

$S_{11} = 2430\left[\frac{(1.06)^{11} - 1}{.06}\right] \approx 36,381.09$

The balance after 11 years is \$36,381.09.

71. The first option is modeled by the sequence $a_n = 5000 + 10,000n$ with sum

$$S_n = \sum_{i=1}^{n} a_i$$
$$S_{30} = \sum_{i=1}^{30} (5000 + 10,000i) = 4,800,000$$

Thus, the first option will pay you \$4,800,000 for the month's work. The second option is modeled by the sequence $a_n = .01(2)^{n-1}$ with sum

$$S_n = \sum_{i=1}^{n} a_i$$
$$S_{30} = \sum_{i=1}^{30} .01(2)^{i-1} = 10,737,418.23$$

The second will pay you \$10,737,418.23. Option 2 pays better.

Section 10.4

Connections *(page 814)*

1. $1 + 6 + 10 + 4 = 21$
$1 + 7 + 15 + 10 + 1 = 34$
$1 + 8 + 21 + 20 + 5 = 55$

2. Answers may vary. One example is 1, 2, 3, 4, 5, 6; another is 1, 3, 6, 10, 15; and another is 1, 4, 10, 20, 35. The first sequence is arithmetic; the others are neither arithmetic nor geometric.

Exercises

1. $\dfrac{6!}{3!\,3!} = \dfrac{6 \cdot 5 \cdot 4 \cdot 3 \cdot 2 \cdot 1}{3 \cdot 2 \cdot 1 \cdot 3 \cdot 2 \cdot 1}$
$= \dfrac{6 \cdot 5 \cdot 4}{3 \cdot 2 \cdot 1}$
$= 20$

3. $\dfrac{7!}{3!\,4!} = \dfrac{7 \cdot 6 \cdot 5 \cdot 4 \cdot 3 \cdot 2 \cdot 1}{3 \cdot 2 \cdot 1 \cdot 4 \cdot 3 \cdot 2 \cdot 1}$
$= \dfrac{7 \cdot 6 \cdot 5}{3 \cdot 2 \cdot 1}$
$= 35$

5. $\dbinom{8}{3} = \dfrac{8!}{3!\,5!}$
$= \dfrac{8 \cdot 7 \cdot 6 \cdot 5 \cdot 4 \cdot 3 \cdot 2 \cdot 1}{3 \cdot 2 \cdot 1 \cdot 5 \cdot 4 \cdot 3 \cdot 2 \cdot 1}$
$= \dfrac{8 \cdot 7 \cdot 6}{3 \cdot 2 \cdot 1}$
$= 56$

7. $\dbinom{10}{8} = \dfrac{10!}{8!\,2!}$
$= \dfrac{10 \cdot 9 \cdot 8!}{8! \cdot 2 \cdot 1}$
$= \dfrac{10 \cdot 9}{2 \cdot 1}$
$= 45$

9. $\dbinom{13}{13} = \dfrac{13!}{13!\,0!}$
$= \dfrac{13!}{13! \cdot 1}$
$= 1$

11. $_{100}C_2 = \dfrac{100!}{2!(100 - 2)!}$
$= \dfrac{100!}{2!\,98!}$
$= \dfrac{100 \cdot 99}{2 \cdot 1}$
$= 4950$

15. $(x + y)^6$
$= x^6 + \dbinom{6}{1}x^5y + \dbinom{6}{2}x^4y^2 + \dbinom{6}{3}x^3y^3$
$\quad + \dbinom{6}{4}x^2y^4 + \dbinom{6}{5}xy^5 + y^6$
$= x^6 + \dfrac{6!}{1!\,5!}x^5y + \dfrac{6!}{2!\,4!}x^4y^2 + \dfrac{6!}{3!\,3!}x^3y^3$
$\quad + \dfrac{6!}{4!\,2!}x^2y^4 + \dfrac{6!}{5!\,1!}xy^5 + y^6$
$= x^6 + 6x^5y + 15x^4y^2 + 20x^3y^3 + 15x^2y^4$
$\quad + 6xy^5 + y^6$

17. $(p-q)^5$

$$= p^5 + \binom{5}{1}p^4(-q) + \binom{5}{2}p^3(-q)^2 + \binom{5}{3}p^2(-q)^3$$

$$+ \binom{5}{4}p(-q)^4 + (-q)^5$$

$$= p^5 + \frac{5!}{1!\,4!}p^4(-q) + \frac{5!}{2!\,3!}p^3q^2 + \frac{5!}{3!\,2!}p^2(-q)^3$$

$$+ \frac{5!}{4!\,1!}pq^4 - q^5$$

$$= p^5 - 5p^4q + 10p^3q^2 - 10p^2q^3 + 5pq^4 - q^5$$

19. $(r^2+s)^5$

$$= (r^2)^5 + \binom{5}{1}(r^2)^4 s + \binom{5}{2}(r^2)^3 s^2 + \binom{5}{3}(r^2)^2 s^3$$

$$+ \binom{5}{4}(r^2)s^4 + s^5$$

$$= r^{10} + 5r^8 s + 10r^6 s^2 + 10r^4 s^3 + 5r^2 s^4 + s^5$$

21. $(p+2q)^4$

$$= p^4 + \binom{4}{1}p^3(2q) + \binom{4}{2}p^2(2q)^2 + \binom{4}{3}p(2q)^3$$

$$+ (2q)^4$$

$$= p^4 + 4p^3(2q) + 6p^2(4q^2) + 4p(8q^3) + 16q^4$$

$$= p^4 + 8p^3q + 24p^2q^2 + 32pq^3 + 16q^4$$

23. $(7p+2q)^4$

$$= (7p)^4 + \binom{4}{1}(7p)^3(2q) + \binom{4}{2}(7p)^2(2q)^2$$

$$+ \binom{4}{3}(7p)(2q)^3 + (2q)^4$$

$$= 2401p^4 + 4(686p^3q) + 6(49p^2)(4q^2)$$

$$+ 4(7p)(2q)^3 + 16q^4$$

$$= 2401p^4 + 2744p^3q + 1176p^2q^2 + 224pq^3$$

$$+ 16q^4$$

25. $(3x-2y)^6$

$$= (3x)^6 + \binom{6}{1}(3x)^5(-2y)$$

$$+ \binom{6}{2}(3x)^4(-2y)^2 + \binom{6}{3}(3x)^3(-2y)^3$$

$$+ \binom{6}{4}(3x)^2(-2y)^4 + \binom{6}{5}(3x)(-2y)^5 + (-2y)^6$$

$$= 729x^6 + 6(243x^5)(-2y)$$

$$+ 15(81x^4)(4y^2) + 20(27x^3)(-8y^3)$$

$$+ 15(9x^2)(16y^4) + 6(3x)(-32y^5) + 64y^6$$

$$= 729x^6 - 2916x^5y + 4860x^4y^2 - 4320x^3y^3$$

$$+ 2160x^2y^4 - 576xy^5 + 64y^6$$

27. $\left(\dfrac{m}{2} - 1\right)^6$

$$= \left(\frac{m}{2}\right)^6 + \binom{6}{1}\left(\frac{m}{2}\right)^5(-1) + \binom{6}{2}\left(\frac{m}{2}\right)^4(-1)^2$$

$$+ \binom{6}{3}\left(\frac{m}{2}\right)^3(-1)^3 + \binom{6}{4}\left(\frac{m}{2}\right)^2(-1)^4$$

$$+ \binom{6}{5}\left(\frac{m}{2}\right)(-1)^5 + (-1)^6$$

$$= \frac{m^6}{64} - 6\left(\frac{m^5}{32}\right) + 15\left(\frac{m^4}{16}\right) - 20\left(\frac{m^3}{8}\right)$$

$$+ 15\left(\frac{m^2}{4}\right) - 6\left(\frac{m}{2}\right) + 1$$

$$= \frac{m^6}{64} - \frac{3m^5}{16} + \frac{15m^4}{16} - \frac{5m^3}{2} + \frac{15m^2}{4} - 3m + 1$$

29. $\left(\sqrt{2}r + \dfrac{1}{m}\right)^4$

$$= (\sqrt{2}r)^4 + \binom{4}{1}(\sqrt{2}r)^3\left(\frac{1}{m}\right) + \binom{4}{2}(\sqrt{2}r)^2\left(\frac{1}{m}\right)^2$$

$$+ \binom{4}{3}(\sqrt{2}r)\left(\frac{1}{m}\right)^3 + \left(\frac{1}{m}\right)^4$$

$$= (\sqrt{2}r)^4 r^4 + 4\left[(\sqrt{2}r)^3 r^3\left(\frac{1}{m}\right)\right]$$

$$+ 6\left[(\sqrt{2}r)^2 r^2\left(\frac{1}{m}\right)^2\right] + 4(\sqrt{2}r)\left(\frac{1}{m}\right)^3 + \left(\frac{1}{m}\right)^4$$

$$= 4r^4 + \frac{8\sqrt{2}r^3}{m} + \frac{12r^2}{m^2} + \frac{4\sqrt{2}r}{m^3} + \frac{1}{m^4}$$

31. $(4h-j)^8$

Use the formula $\binom{n}{k-1}x^{n-(k-1)}y^{k-1}$ with $n = 8$,

$k - 1 = 5$, and $n - (k-1) = 3$.
The sixth term of the expansion is

$$\binom{8}{5}(4h)^3(-j)^5$$

$$= \frac{8!}{5!\,3!}(64h^3)(-j^5)$$

$$= 56(-64h^3j^5)$$

$$= -3584h^3j^5.$$

33. $(a^2+b)^{22}$

Here $n = 22$, $k = 15$, $k - 1 = 14$, and
$n - (k-1) = 8$.
The fifteenth term of the expansion is

$\dbinom{22}{14}(a^2)^8(b)^{14}$

$= \dfrac{22!}{14!\,8!}(a^{16})(b^{14})$

$= 319{,}770a^{16}b^{14}.$

35. $(x - y^3)^{20}$

Here $n = 20$, $k = 15$, $k - 1 = 14$, and
$n - (k - 1) = 6$.
The fifteenth term of the expansion is

$\dbinom{20}{14}(x)^6(-y^3)^{14}$

$= \dfrac{20!}{14!\,6!}(x^6)(y^{42})$

$= 38{,}760x^6y^{42}.$

37. x^4y^5 appears in the sixth term of $(3x - 2y)^9$.

$\dbinom{9}{5}(3x)^4(-2y)^5 = -326{,}592x^4y^5$

The coefficient is $-326{,}592$.

39. $(3x^7 + 2y^3)^8$

This expansion has 9 terms, so the middle term is
the fifth term, which is

$\dbinom{8}{4}(3x^7)^4(2y^3)^4$

$= (70)(81x^{28})(16y^{12})$

$= 90{,}720x^{28}y^{12}.$

41. If the coefficients of the fifth and eighth terms in
the expansion of $(x + y)^n$ are the same, then the
symmetry of the expansion can be used to
determine n. There are four terms before the fifth
term, so there must be four terms after the eighth
term. This means that the last term of the
expansion is the twelfth term. This in turn means
that $n = 11$, since $(x + y)^{11}$ is the expansion that
has twelve terms.

47. Using a calculator, we obtain the exact value
$10! = 3{,}628{,}800$.
Using Stirling's formula, we obtain the
approximate value

$10! \approx \sqrt{2\pi(10)} \cdot 10^{10} \cdot e^{-10}$
$\approx 3{,}598{,}695.619.$

48. $\dfrac{3{,}628{,}800 - 3{,}598{,}695.619}{3{,}628{,}800} \approx .00830$

As a percent, this is .830%.

49. Using a calculator, we obtain the exact value
$12! = 479{,}001{,}600$.

Using Stirling's formula, we obtain the
approximate value

$12! \approx \sqrt{2\pi(12)} \cdot 12^{12} \cdot e^{-12}$
$\approx 475{,}687{,}486.5.$

Find the percent error.

$\dfrac{479{,}001{,}600 - 475{,}687{,}486.5}{479{,}001{,}600} \approx .00692$

As a percent, this is .692%.

50. Using a calculator, we obtain the exact value $13!$
$= 6{,}227{,}020{,}800$.
Using Stirling's formula, we obtain the
approximate value

$13! \approx \sqrt{2\pi(13)} \cdot 13^{13} \cdot e^{-13}$
$\approx 6{,}187{,}239{,}475.$

Find the percent error.

$\dfrac{6{,}227{,}020{,}800 - 6{,}187{,}239{,}475}{6{,}227{,}020{,}800} \approx .00639$

As a percent, this is .639%.
As n gets larger, the percent decreases.

Section 10.5

Connections *(page 823)*

1. $f(n) = 3n + 1$
$f(1) = 3(1) + 1 = 4$
$f(2) = 3(2) + 1 = 7$
$f(3) = 3(3) + 1 = 10$

2. $g(k) = \dfrac{k(3k + 5)}{2}$

3. $g(k) + f(k + 1) = \dfrac{k(3k + 5)}{2} + [3(k + 1) + 1]$

$= \dfrac{3k^2 + 5k}{2} + 3k + 4$

$= \dfrac{3k^2 + 5k + 2(3k + 4)}{2}$

$= \dfrac{3k^2 + 11k + 8}{2}$

$= \dfrac{(k + 1)(3k + 8)}{2}$

$= \dfrac{(k + 1)[3(k + 1) + 5]}{2}$

$= g(k + 1)$

Exercises

1. Let S_n be the statement
$2 + 4 + 6 + \ldots + 2n = n(n + 1)$.
S_1: $2 = 1(1 + 1)$
$2 = 2$

S_2: $2 + 4 = 2(2 + 1)$
$6 = 6$
S_3: $2 + 4 + 6 = 3(3 + 1)$
$12 = 12$
S_4: $2 + 4 + 6 + 8 = 4(4 + 1)$
$20 = 20$
S_5: $2 + 4 + 6 + 8 + 10 = 5(5 + 1)$
$30 = 30$
Prove that S_n is true for every positive integer n.
Step 1: Show that the statement is true for $n = 1$. S_1 is the statement $2 = 1(1 + 1)$, which is true.
Step 2: Show that if S_k is true, S_{k+1} is also true. S_k is the statement
$$2 + 4 + 6 + \ldots + 2k = k(k + 1)$$
and S_{k+1} is the statement
$$2 + 4 + 6 + \ldots + 2k + 2(k + 1) = (k + 1)(k + 2).$$
Start with S_k:
$$2 + 4 + 6 + \ldots + 2k = k(k + 1).$$
Add the $(k + 1)$st term, $2(k + 1)$, to both sides:
$$2 + 4 + 6 + \ldots + 2k + 2(k + 1) = k(k + 1) + 2(k + 1).$$
Now factor out the common factor on the right to get
$$2 + 4 + 6 + \ldots + 2k + 2(k + 1) = (k + 1)(k + 2).$$
This result is the statement S_{k+1}. Thus, we have shown that if S_k is true, S_{k+1} is also true. The two steps required for a proof by mathematical induction have been completed, so the statement
$$2 + 4 + 6 + \ldots + 2n = n(n + 1)$$
is true for every positive integer n.

3. Let S_n be the statement
$$3 + 6 + 9 + \ldots + 3n = \frac{3n(n + 1)}{2}.$$
Prove that S_n is true for every positive integer n.
Step 1: S_1 is the statement
$$3 = \frac{3 \cdot 1(1 + 1)}{2}$$
$$3 = \frac{6}{2},$$
which is true.
Step 2: Show that if S_k is true, S_{k+1} is also true. S_k is the statement
$$3 + 6 + 9 + \ldots + 3k = \frac{3k(k + 1)}{2}.$$
Add the $(k + 1)$st term, $3(k + 1)$, to both sides:
$$3 + 6 + 9 + \ldots + 3k + 3(k + 1)$$

$$= \frac{3k(k + 1)}{2} + 3(k + 1)$$
$$= \frac{3k(k + 1)}{2} + \frac{6(k + 1)}{2}$$
$$= \frac{(k + 1)(3k + 6)}{2}$$
$$3 + 6 + 9 + \ldots + 3k + 3(k + 1)$$
$$= \frac{3(k + 1)(k + 2)}{2}$$
The final equation is the statement S_{k+1}. Thus, if S_k is true, S_{k+1} is also true.
Steps 1 and *2* have been completed, so S_n is true for all positive integers n.

5. Let S_n be the statement
$$2 + 4 + 8 + \ldots + 2^n = 2^{n+1} - 2.$$
Prove that S_n is true for every positive integer n.
Step 1: S_1 is the statement
$$2 = 2^{1+1} - 2$$
$$2 = 4 - 2,$$
which is true.
Step 2: Show that if S_k is true, then S_{k+1} is also true. S_k is the statement
$$2 + 4 + 8 + \ldots + 2^k = 2^{k+1} - 2.$$
Add the $(k + 1)$st term, 2^{k+1}, to both sides:
$$2 + 4 + 8 + \ldots + 2^k + 2^{k+1}$$
$$= (2^{k+1} - 2) + 2^{k+1}$$
$$= 2 \cdot 2^{k+1} - 2$$
$$= 2^{k+2} - 2$$
$$2 + 4 + 8 + \ldots + 2^k + 2^{k+1}$$
$$= 2^{(k+1)+1} - 2$$
The final equation is the statement S_{k+1}. Thus, if S_k is true, S_{k+1} is also true.
Therefore, by mathematical induction, S_n is true for every positive integer n.

7. Let S_n be the statement
$$1^2 + 2^2 + 3^2 + \ldots + n^2 = \frac{n(n + 1)(2n + 1)}{6}.$$
Prove that S_n is true for every positive integer n.
Step 1: S_1 is the statement
$$1^2 = \frac{1(2)(3)}{6}$$
$$1 = \frac{6}{6},$$
which is true.
Step 2: Show that if S_k is true, S_{k+1} is also true. S_k is the statement
$$1^2 + 2^2 + 3^2 + \ldots + k^2 = \frac{k(k + 1)(2k + 1)}{6}.$$
Add the $(k + 1)$st term, $(k + 1)^2$, to both sides:
$$1^2 + 2^2 + 3^2 + \ldots + k^2 + (k + 1)^2$$

$$= \frac{k(k+1)(2k+1)}{6} + (k+1)^2$$

$$= \frac{k(2k^2 + 3k + 1)}{6} + k^2 + 2k + 1$$

$$= \frac{k(2k^2 + 3k + 1)}{6} + \frac{6(k^2 + 2k + 1)}{6}$$

$$= \frac{2k^3 + 3k^2 + k + 6k^2 + 12k + 6}{6}$$

$$= \frac{2k^3 + 9k^2 + 13k + 6}{6}$$

$$= \frac{(k+1)(2k^2 + 7k + 6)}{6}$$

$$= \frac{(k+1)(k+2)(2k+3)}{6}$$

$$= \frac{(k+1)(k+2)[2(k+1)+1]}{6}$$

The final equation is the statement S_{k+1}. Thus, if S_k is true, S_{k+1} is also true. Therefore, by mathematical induction, S_n is true for every positive integer n.

9. Let S_n be the statement
$$5 \cdot 6 + 5 \cdot 6^2 + 5 \cdot 6^3 + \ldots + 5 \cdot 6^n = 6(6^n - 1).$$
Prove that S_n is true for every positive integer n.
Step 1: S_1 is the statement
$$5 \cdot 6 = 6(6^1 - 1)$$
$$30 = 6 \cdot 5,$$
which is true.
Step 2: Show that if S_k is true, S_{k+1} is also true.
S_k is the statement
$$5 \cdot 6 + 5 \cdot 6^2 + 5 \cdot 6^3 + \ldots + 5 \cdot 6^k = 6(6^k - 1).$$
Add the $(k+1)$st term, $5 \cdot 6^{k+1}$, to both sides:
$$5 \cdot 6 + 5 \cdot 6^2 + \ldots + 5 \cdot 6^k + 5 \cdot 6^{k+1}$$
$$= 6(6^k - 1) + 5 \cdot 6^{k+1}$$
$$= 6 \cdot 6^k - 6 + 5 \cdot 6^{k+1}$$
$$= 6^{k+1} + 5 \cdot 6^{k+1} - 6$$
$$= 1 \cdot 6^{k+1} + 5 \cdot 6^{k+1} - 6$$
$$= 6 \cdot 6^{k+1} - 6$$
$$= 6(6^{k+1} - 1)$$
The final result is the statement S_{k+1}. Thus, if S_k is true, S_{k+1} is also true. Therefore, by mathematical induction, S_n is true for every positive integer n.

11. Let S_n be the statement
$$\frac{1}{1 \cdot 2} + \frac{1}{2 \cdot 3} + \frac{1}{3 \cdot 4} + \ldots + \frac{1}{n(n+1)} = \frac{n}{n+1}.$$

Prove that S_n is true for every positive integer n.
Step 1: S_1 is the statement
$$\frac{1}{1 \cdot 2} = \frac{1}{1+1}$$
$$\frac{1}{2} = \frac{1}{2},$$
which is true.
Step 2: Show that if S_k is true, S_{k+1} is also true.
S_k is the statement
$$\frac{1}{1 \cdot 2} + \frac{1}{2 \cdot 3} + \frac{1}{3 \cdot 4} + \ldots + \frac{1}{k(k+1)} = \frac{k}{k+1}.$$
Add the $(k+1)$st term, $\dfrac{1}{(k+1)(k+2)}$, to both sides:
$$\frac{1}{1 \cdot 2} + \frac{1}{2 \cdot 3} + \ldots + \frac{1}{k(k+1)} + \frac{1}{(k+1)(k+2)}$$
$$= \frac{k}{k+1} + \frac{1}{(k+1)(k+2)}$$
$$= \frac{k(k+2) + 1}{(k+1)(k+2)}$$
$$= \frac{k^2 + 2k + 1}{(k+1)(k+2)}$$
$$= \frac{(k+1)^2}{(k+1)(k+2)}$$
$$= \frac{k+1}{k+2}$$
The final result is the statement S_{k+1}. Thus, if S_k is true, S_{k+1} is also true. Therefore, by mathematical induction, S_n is true for every positive integer n.

13. Let S_n be the statement
$$\frac{1}{2} + \frac{1}{2^2} + \frac{1}{2^3} + \ldots + \frac{1}{2^n} = 1 - \frac{1}{2^n}.$$
Prove that S_n is true for every positive integer n.
Step 1: S_1 is the statement
$$\frac{1}{2} = 1 - \frac{1}{2},$$
which is true.
Step 2: Show that if S_k is true, S_{k+1} is also true.
S_k is the statement
$$\frac{1}{2} + \frac{1}{2^2} + \frac{1}{2^3} + \ldots + \frac{1}{2^k} = 1 - \frac{1}{2^k}$$
Add the $(k+1)$st term, $\dfrac{1}{2^{k+1}}$, to both sides:

$$\frac{1}{2}+\frac{1}{2^2}+\frac{1}{2^3}+\ldots+\frac{1}{2^k}+\frac{1}{2^{k+1}}$$

$$=1-\frac{1}{2^k}+\frac{1}{2^{k+1}}$$

$$=1-\frac{1}{2^k}+\frac{1}{2^1 2^k}$$

$$=1-\frac{1}{2^k}+\frac{1}{2}\left(\frac{1}{2^k}\right)$$

$$=1-\frac{1}{2}\left(\frac{1}{2^k}\right)$$

$$=1-\frac{1}{2^{k+1}}$$

The final result is the statement S_{k+1}. Thus, if S_k is true, S_{k+1} is also true. Therefore, by mathematical induction, S_n is true for every positive integer n.

15. $2^n > 2n$

If $n = 1$, we have $2^1 > 2(1)$ or $2 > 2$, which is false.
If $n = 2$, we have $2^2 > 2(2)$ or $4 > 4$, which is false.
If $n = 3$, we have $2^3 > 2(3)$ or $8 > 6$, which is true.
For $n \geq 3$, the statement is true. The statement is false for $n = 1$ or 2.

17. $2^n > n^2$

If $n = 1$, we have $2^1 > 1^2$ or $2 > 1$, which is true.
If $n = 2$, we have $2^2 > 2^2$ or $4 > 4$, which is false.
If $n = 3$, we have $2^3 > 3^2$ or $8 > 9$, which is false.
If $n = 4$, we have $2^4 > 4^2$ or $16 > 16$, which is false.
If $n = 5$, we have $2^5 > 5^2$ or $32 > 25$, which is true.
For $n \geq 5$, the statement is true. The statement is false for $n = 2$, 3, or 4.

19. Let S_n be the statement
$$(a^m)^n = a^{mn}. \quad \text{(Assume that } a \text{ and } m \text{ are constant.)}$$
Step 1: S_1 is the statement
$$(a^m)^1 = a^{m \cdot 1}$$
$$a^m = a^m.$$
Thus, S_1 is true.
Step 2: Show that if S_k is true, then S_{k+1} is also true. S_k is the statement
$$(a^m)^k = a^{mk},$$
and S_{k+1} is the statement

$$(a^m)^{k+1} = a^{m(k+1)}.$$
$$(a^m)^{k+1} = (a^m)^k(a^m)^1 \quad \text{Using the property}$$
$$a^m \cdot a^n = a^{m+n}$$
$$= a^{mk} \cdot a^m \quad \text{Using the assumption}$$
$$\text{that } S_k \text{ is true}$$
$$= a^{mk+m} \quad \text{Using the property}$$
$$a^m \cdot a^n = a^{m+n}$$
$$= a^{m(k+1)} \quad \text{Factor } mk + m$$
Thus, we have shown that S_1 is true, and that if S_k is true, S_{k+1} is also true. Therefore, by mathematical induction, S_n is true for every positive integer n.

21. Let S_n be the following statement:
If $n \geq 3$, $2^n > 2n$.
Step 1: S_3 is the statement
$$2^3 > 2(3)$$
$$8 > 6,$$
which is true.
Step 2: Show that if S_k is true, then S_{k+1} is also true. Since S_k is true, $2^k > 2k$.
Multiply both sides by 2.
$$2(2^k) > 2(2k)$$
$$2^{k+1} > 2k + 2k$$
However, since $k \geq 3$, $2k > 2$.
$$2^{k+1} > 2k + 2k > 2k + 2$$
$$2^{k+1} > 2(k + 1)$$
Therefore, S_{k+1} is true. By STEPS 1 and 2, S_n is true for every positive integer $n \geq 3$.

23. Let S_n be the following statement:
If $a > 1$, then $a^n > 1$.
Step 1: S_1 is the statement
If $a > 1$, then $a^n > 1$, which is obviously true for every positive integer n.
Step 2: Show that if S_k is true, then S_{k+1} is also true. Since S_k is true, S_k is the statement:
If $a > 1$, then $a^k > 1$.
Multiply both sides of the inequality $a^k > 1$ by a.
Since $a > 1 > 0$, the direction of the inequality symbol will not be changed.
$$a \cdot a^k > a \cdot 1$$
$$a^1 \cdot a^k > a$$
$$a^{k+1} > a \quad \text{Using the property}$$
$$a^m \cdot a^n = a^{m+n}$$
Since $a > 1$, we have $a^{k+1} > a > 1$.
Therefore, if $a > 1$, $a^{k+1} > 1$, and S_{k+1} is true.
By *Steps 1* and *2*, S_n is true for every positive integer n.

25. Let S_n be the statement:

If $0 < a < 1$, then $a^n < a^{n-1}$.

Step 1: S_1 is the statement

If $0 < a < 1$, then $a < a^0$.

Since $a^0 = 1$, this is equivalent to:

If $0 < a < 1$, then $a < 1$, which is obviously true.

Step 2: Show that S_k if true, then S_{k+1} is also true. S_k is the statement:

If $0 < a < 1$, then $a^k < a^{k-1}$.

S_{k+1} is the statement:

If $0 < a < 1$, then

$$a^{k+1} < a^{(k+1)-1}$$

or $\quad a^{k+1} < a^k$.

Multiply both sides of the inequality $a^k < a^{k-1}$ by a.

Since $a > 0$, the direction of the inequality symbol will not change.

$$a \cdot a^k < a \cdot a^{k-1}$$

$$a^{k+1} < a^{1+(k-1)} \qquad \text{Using the property}$$
$$a^m \cdot a^n = a^{m+n}$$

$$a^{k+1} < a^{(k+1)-1}$$

$$a^{k+1} < a^k$$

The final result is the statement S_{k+1}. Thus, if S_k is true, S_{k+1} is also true. By *Steps 1* and *2*, S_n is true for every positive integer n.

27. Let S_n be the following statement:

If $n \geq 4$, then $n! > 2^n$.

Step 1: S_4 is the statement

$$4! > 2^4$$
$$24 > 16$$

which is true.

Step 2: Show that S_k if true, then S_{k+1} is also true. S_k is the statement: $k! > 2^k$.

Multiply both sides by $k + 1$. (Since $k + 1 > 0$, the direction of the inequality symbol will not change.)

$$(k+1)k! > (k+1)2^k$$

By the definition of $n!$, we have

$(k + 1) \cdot k! = (k + 1)!$.

$$(k+1)! > (k+1)2^k$$

Since $k + 1 > 2$, $(k+1)2^k \geq 2 \cdot 2^k = 2^{1+k}$

$$(k+1)! > 2^{1+k}$$

$$(k+1)! > 2^{k+1}$$

Therefore, S_{k+1} is true. By *Steps 1* and *2*, S_n is true for every positive integer $n \geq 4$.

29. Let S_n be the number of handshakes of the n people is $\dfrac{n^2 - n}{2}$.

Since 2 is the smallest number of people who can

shake hands, we need to prove this statement for every positive integer $n \geq 2$.

Step 1: S_2 is the statement that 2 people can shake hands in 1 way, since

$$\frac{2^2 - 2}{2} = \frac{2}{2} = 1.$$

Step 2: Show that if S_k is true, S_{k+1} is also true. S_k is the statement:

k people shake hands in $\dfrac{k^2 - k}{2}$ ways.

If one more person joins the k people, this $(k + 1)$st person will shake hands with the previous k people one time each. Thus, there will be k additional handshakes. Thus, the number of handshakes for $k + 1$ people is

$$\frac{k^2 - k}{2} + k = \frac{k^2 - k}{2} + \frac{2k}{2}$$

$$= \frac{k^2 + k}{2}$$

$$= \frac{(k^2 + 2k + 1) - (k + 1)}{2}$$

$$= \frac{(k+1)^2 - (k+1)}{2}$$

This result is the statement S_{k+1}. By *Steps 1* and *2*, S_n is true for every positive integer $n \geq 2$.

31. The number of sides of the nth figure is $3 \cdot 4^{n-1}$ (from Exercise 30). To see this, let a^n = the number of sides of the nth figure.

$$a_1 = 3$$
$$a_2 = 3 \cdot 4 \qquad \text{since each side of the}$$
$$\text{first figure will develop}$$
$$\text{into 4 sides}$$
$$a_3 = 3 \cdot 4^2, \text{ and so on.}$$

This gives a geometric sequence with $a_1 = 3$ and $r = 4$, so $a_n = 3 \cdot 4^{n-1}$.

To find the perimeter of each figure, multiply the number of sides by the length of each side. In each figure, the lengths of the sides are $\dfrac{1}{3}$ the lengths of the sides in the preceding figure. Thus, if P_n = perimeter of nth figure,

$$P_1 = 3(1) = 3$$

$$P_2 = 3 \cdot 4\left(\frac{1}{3}\right) = 4$$

$$P_3 = 3 \cdot 4^2\left(\frac{1}{9}\right) = \frac{16}{3}, \text{ and so on.}$$

This gives a geometric sequence with

$$P_1 = 3 \text{ and } r = \frac{4}{3}.$$

Thus, $P_n = a_1 r^{n-1}$

$$P_n = 3\left(\frac{4}{3}\right)^{n-1}.$$

The result may also be written as

$$P_n = \frac{3^1 \cdot 4^{n-1}}{3^{n-1}}$$

$$= \frac{4^{n-1}}{3^{-1} \cdot 3^{n-1}}$$

$$P_n = \frac{4^{n-1}}{3^{n-2}}.$$

33. With 1 ring, 1 move is required. With 2 rings, 3 moves are required. Note that $3 = 2 + 1$.
With 3 rings, 7 moves are required. Note that $7 = 2^2 + 2 + 1$.
With n rings,
$$2^{n-1} + 2^{n-2} + \ldots + 2^1 + 1 = 2^n - 1$$
moves are required.
Let S_n be the following statement:
For n rings, the number of required moves is $2^n - 1$.
We will prove that S_n is true for every positive integer n.
Step 1: S_1 is the following statement:
For 1 ring, the number of required moves is $2^1 - 1$ or $2 - 1$ which is 1. The statement is true.
Step 2: Show that if S_k is true then S_{k+1} is also true. Assume $k + 1$ rings are on the first peg. since S_k is true, the top k rings can be moved to the second peg in $2^k - 1$ moves.
Now move the bottom ring to the third peg. Since S_k is true, move the k rings on the second peg on top of the largest ring on the third peg in $2^k - 1$ moves.
The total number of moves is
$$2^k - 1 + 1 + 2^k - 1 = 2 \cdot 2^k - 1$$
$$= 2^{k+1} - 1$$
Therefore, S_{k+1} is true. By *Steps 1* and *2*, S_n is true for every positive integer n.

Section 10.6

Exercises

1. $P(12, 8)$
$$= \frac{12!}{(12 - 8)!}$$
$$= \frac{12!}{4!}$$
$$= \frac{12 \cdot 11 \cdot 10 \cdot 9 \cdot 8 \cdot 7 \cdot 6 \cdot 5 \cdot 4 \cdot 3 \cdot 2 \cdot 1}{4!}$$
$$= 12 \cdot 11 \cdot 10 \cdot 9 \cdot 8 \cdot 7 \cdot 6 \cdot 5$$
$$= 19,958,400$$

3. $P(9, 2) = \frac{9!}{(9 - 2)!} = \frac{9!}{7!} = \frac{9 \cdot 8 \cdot 7!}{7!}$
$$= 9 \cdot 8 = 72$$

5. $P(5, 1) = \frac{5!}{(5 - 1)!} = \frac{5!}{4!} = \frac{5 \cdot 4!}{4!} = 5$

7. $\binom{4}{2} = \frac{4!}{(4 - 2)!\,2!} = \frac{4!}{2!\,2!} = \frac{4 \cdot 3 \cdot 2!}{2!\,2!} = 6$

9. $\binom{6}{0} = \frac{6!}{(6 - 0)!\,0!} = \frac{6!}{6! \cdot 1} = 1$

11. $\binom{12}{4} = \frac{12!}{(12 - 4)!\,4!} = \frac{12!}{8!\,4!} = \frac{12 \cdot 11 \cdot 10 \cdot 9 \cdot 8!}{8!\,4 \cdot 3 \cdot 2 \cdot 1}$
$$= \frac{12 \cdot 11 \cdot 10 \cdot 9}{4 \cdot 3 \cdot 2 \cdot 1} = 495$$

13. $_{20}P_5 = \frac{20!}{(20 - 5)!}$
$$= \frac{20!}{15!} = \frac{20 \cdot 19 \cdot 18 \cdot 17 \cdot 16 \cdot 15!}{15!}$$
$$= 1,860,480$$

15. $_{15}P_8 = \frac{15!}{(15 - 8)!}$
$$= \frac{15!}{7!} = \frac{15 \cdot 14 \cdot 13 \cdot 12 \cdot 11 \cdot 10 \cdot 9 \cdot 8 \cdot 7!}{7!}$$
$$= 15 \cdot 14 \cdot 13 \cdot 12 \cdot 11 \cdot 10 \cdot 9 \cdot 8$$
$$= 259,459,200$$

17. $_{20}C_5 = \frac{20!}{(20 - 5)!\,5!}$
$$= \frac{20!}{15!\,5!} = \frac{20 \cdot 19 \cdot 18 \cdot 17 \cdot 16 \cdot 15!}{5 \cdot 4 \cdot 3 \cdot 2 \cdot 1 \cdot 15!}$$
$$= 15,504$$

19. $_{15}C_8 = \frac{15!}{(15 - 8)!\,8!}$
$$= \frac{15!}{7!\,8!} = \frac{15 \cdot 14 \cdot 13 \cdot 12 \cdot 11 \cdot 10 \cdot 9 \cdot 8!}{7 \cdot 6 \cdot 5 \cdot 4 \cdot 3 \cdot 2 \cdot 1 \cdot 8!}$$
$$= 6435$$

21. **(a)** Since the order of digits in a telephone number does matter, this involves a permutation.

(b) Since the order of digits in a social security number does matter, this involves a permutation.

(c) Since the order of the cards in a poker hand does not matter, this involves a combination.

(d) Since the order of members on a committee of politicians does not matter, this involves a combination.

(e) Since the order of numbers of the "combination" on a combination lock does matter, this involves a permutation.

(f) Since the order does not matter, the lottery choice of six numbers involves a combination.

(g) Since the order of digits and/or letters on a license plate does matter, this involves a permutation.

23. $5 \cdot 3 \cdot 2 = 30$
There are 30 different homes available if a builder offers a choice of 5 basic plans, 3 roof styles, and 2 exterior finishes.

25. (a) The first letter can be one of 2.
The second letter can be one of 25.
The third letter can be one of 24.
The fourth letter can be one of 23.
Since $2 \cdot 25 \cdot 24 \cdot 23 = 27,600$, there are 27,600 different call letters without repeats.

(b) With repeats, the count is
$2 \cdot 26 \cdot 26 \cdot 26 = 35,152$.

(c) The first letter can one of 2.
The second letter can be one of 24, since it cannot repeat the first letter or be R.
The third letter can be one of 23, since it cannot repeat either of the first two letters or be R.
The fourth letter can be one of 1, since it must be R.
Since $2 \cdot 24 \cdot 23 \cdot 1 = 1104$, there are 1104 different such call letters.

26. Use the multiplication principle of counting.
$3 \cdot 8 \cdot 5 = 120$
There are 120 different possible meals.

27. Use the multiplication principle of counting.
$3 \cdot 5 = 15$
There are 15 different first- and middle-name arrangements.

29. (a) The first three positions could each be any one of 26 letters, and the second three positions could each be any one of 10 numbers.
$26 \cdot 26 \cdot 26 \cdot 10 \cdot 10 \cdot 10 \cdot = 17,576,000$
17,576,000 license plates were possible.

(b) $10 \cdot 10 \cdot 10 \cdot 26 \cdot 26 \cdot 26 = 17,576,000$
17,576,000 additional license plates were made possible by the reversal.

(c) $26 \cdot 10 \cdot 10 \cdot 10 \cdot 26 \cdot 26 \cdot 26 = 456,976,000$
456,976,000 plates were provided by prefixing the previous pattern with an additional letter.

31. $P(4, 4) = \dfrac{4!}{(4-4)!}$
$= \dfrac{4!}{0!}$
$= \dfrac{4 \cdot 3 \cdot 2 \cdot 1}{1}$
$= 24$

33. He has 6 choices for the first course, 5 choices for the second, and 4 choices for the third.
$6 \cdot 5 \cdot 4 = 120$

35. The number of ways in which the 3 officers can be chosen from the 15 members is given by
$P(15,3) = \dfrac{15!}{(15-3)!}$
$= \dfrac{15!}{12!}$
$= \dfrac{15 \cdot 14 \cdot 13 \cdot 12!}{12!}$
$= 15 \cdot 14 \cdot 13$
$= 2730.$

37. 5 players can be assigned the 5 positions in $P(5, 5) = 5! = 120$ ways.
10 players can be assigned 5 positions in
$P(10,5) = \dfrac{10!}{(10-5)!}$
$= \dfrac{10!}{5!}$
$= 10 \cdot 9 \cdot 8 \cdot 7 \cdot 6$
$= 30,240$ ways.

39. We want to choose 4 group members out of 30 and the order is not important. The number of possible groups is
$\dbinom{30}{4} = \dfrac{30!}{(30-4)!\,4!}$
$= \dfrac{30!}{26!\,4!}$
$= \dfrac{30 \cdot 29 \cdot 28 \cdot 27 \cdot 26!}{4!\,26!}$
$= \dfrac{30 \cdot 29 \cdot 28 \cdot 27}{24}$
$= 27,405.$

41. $\binom{6}{3} = \dfrac{6!}{(6-3)!\,3!}$

$= \dfrac{6!}{3!\,3!}$

$= \dfrac{6 \cdot 5 \cdot 4 \cdot 3!}{3! \cdot 3 \cdot 2 \cdot 1}$

$= 20$

20 different kinds of hamburgers can be made.

43. This problem involves choosing 2 members from a set of 5 members. There are $\binom{5}{2}$ such subsets.

$\binom{5}{2} = \dfrac{5!}{3!\,2!}$

$= \dfrac{5 \cdot 4 \cdot 3!}{3! \cdot 2}$

$= \dfrac{5 \cdot 4}{2}$

$= 10$

There are 10 different 2-card combinations.

45. Since 2 blue marbles are to be chosen and there are 8 blue marbles, this problem involves choosing 2 members from a set of 8 members. There are $\binom{8}{2}$ ways of doing this.

$\binom{8}{2} = \dfrac{8!}{(8-2)!\,2!}$

$= \dfrac{8!}{6!\,2!}$

$= \dfrac{8 \cdot 7 \cdot 6!}{6!\,2!}$

$= \dfrac{8 \cdot 7}{2}$

$= 28$

47. There are 5 liberal and 4 conservatives, giving a total of 9 members. Three members are chosen as delegates to a convention.

(a) There are $\binom{9}{3}$ ways of doing this.

$\binom{9}{3} = \dfrac{9!}{(9-3)!\,3!}$

$= \dfrac{9!}{6!\,3!}$

$= \dfrac{9 \cdot 8 \cdot 7 \cdot 6!}{6!\,3!}$

$= \dfrac{9 \cdot 8 \cdot 7}{6}$

$= 84$

84 delegations are possible.

(b) To get all liberals, we must choose 3 members from a set of 5, which can be done $\binom{5}{3}$ ways.

$\binom{5}{3} = \dfrac{5!}{(5-3)!\,3!}$

$= \dfrac{5!}{2!\,3!}$

$= \dfrac{5 \cdot 4 \cdot 3!}{2!\,3!}$

$= \dfrac{5 \cdot 4}{2}$

$= 10$

10 delegations could have all liberals.

(c) To get 2 liberals and 1 conservative involves two independent events. First select the liberals. The number of ways to do this is

$\binom{5}{2} = \dfrac{5!}{3!\,2!}$

$= \dfrac{5 \cdot 4 \cdot 3!}{3! \cdot 2 \cdot 1}$

$= 10.$

Now select the conservative. The number of ways to do this is

$\binom{4}{1} = \dfrac{4!}{(4-1)!\,1!}$

$= \dfrac{4!}{3!}$

$= 4.$

To find the number of delegations, use the fundamental principle of counting. The number of delegations with 2 liberals and 1 conservative is $10 \cdot 4 = 40$.

(d) If one particular person must be on the delegation, then there are 2 people left to choose from a set consisting of 8 members.

$\binom{8}{2} = \dfrac{8!}{(8-2)!\,2!}$

$= \dfrac{8!}{6!\,2!}$

$= \dfrac{8 \cdot 7 \cdot 6!}{6!\,2!}$

$= \dfrac{8 \cdot 7}{2}$

$= 28$

28 delegations are possible which includes the mayor.

49. The problem asks how many ways can Matthew arrange his schedule. Therefore, order is important, and this is a permutation problem.

There are $P(8,4) = \dfrac{8!}{(8-4)!} = \dfrac{8!}{4!} = 1680$ ways to arrange his schedule.

51. The order of the vegetables in the soup is not important, so this is a combination problem.

There are $\dbinom{6}{4} = \dfrac{6!}{(6-4)!\,4!} = \dfrac{6!}{2!\,4!} = 15$ different soups she can make.

53. Order is important in seatings, so this is a permutation problem. All twelve children will have a specific location; the first eleven will sit down and twelfth will be left standing.

$$P(12, 12) = \dfrac{12!}{(12-12)!}$$
$$= \dfrac{12!}{0!}$$
$$= 12!$$
$$= 479{,}001{,}600$$

There are 479,001,600 seatings possible.

55. A club has 8 men and 11 women members. There are a total of $8 + 11 = 19$ members, and 5 of them are to be chosen. Order is not important, so this is a combination problem.

   (a) Choose all men.
   That is, of the 8 men, choose 5.
   $$\dbinom{8}{5} = \dfrac{8!}{(8-5)!\,5!}$$
   $$= \dfrac{8!}{3!\,5!}$$
   $$= \dfrac{8\cdot 7 \cdot 6 \cdot 5!}{3!\,5!}$$
   $$= \dfrac{8\cdot 7 \cdot 6}{6}$$
   $$= 56$$
   56 committees having 5 men can be chosen.

   (b) Choose all women.
   That is, of the 11 women, choose 5.
   $$\dbinom{11}{5} = \dfrac{11!}{(11-5)!\,5!}$$
   $$= \dfrac{11!}{6!\,5!}$$
   $$= \dfrac{11\cdot 10 \cdot 9 \cdot 8 \cdot 7 \cdot 6!}{6!\,5!}$$
   $$= \dfrac{11\cdot 10 \cdot 9 \cdot 8 \cdot 7}{5\cdot 4 \cdot 3 \cdot 2 \cdot 1}$$
   $$= 462$$
   462 committees having 5 women can be chosen.

   (c) Choose 3 men and 2 women.
   Since choosing the men and choosing the women are independent events, we can use the multiplication principle of counting to find the number of committees with 3 men and 2 women.
   $$\dbinom{8}{3}\cdot \dbinom{11}{2}$$
   $$\dfrac{8!}{(8-3)!\,3!} \cdot \dfrac{11!}{(11-2)!\,2!}$$
   $$= \dfrac{8!}{5!\,3!} \cdot \dfrac{11!}{9!\,2!}$$
   $$= \dfrac{8\cdot 7 \cdot 6 \cdot 5!}{5!\,3!} \cdot \dfrac{11\cdot 10 \cdot 9!}{9!\,2!}$$
   $$= \dfrac{8\cdot 7 \cdot 6}{6} \cdot \dfrac{11\cdot 10}{2}$$
   $$= 56 \cdot 55$$
   $$= 3080$$
   3080 committees having 3 men and 2 women can be chosen.

   (d) Choose no more than 3 women.
   This means choose
   0 women (and 5 men) or choose
   1 woman (and 4 men) or choose
   2 women (and 3 men) or choose
   3 women (and 2 men).
   Thus, the number of possible committees with no more than 3 women is
   $$\dbinom{11}{0}\cdot\dbinom{8}{5}+\dbinom{11}{1}\cdot\dbinom{8}{4}+\dbinom{11}{2}\cdot\dbinom{8}{3}+\dbinom{11}{3}\cdot\dbinom{8}{2}$$
   $$= 1\cdot 56 + 11\cdot 70 + 55\cdot 56 + 165\cdot 28$$
   $$= 56 + 770 + 3080 + 4620$$
   $$= 8526.$$
   8526 committees having no more than 3 women can be chosen.

57. For an exacta, order counts. So there are $_9P_2 = 72$ different exacta bets that can be placed.
   For a quinella, order doesn't count. So there are $_9C_2 = 36$ different quinella bets that can be placed.

67. (a) $\log 50! = \log 1 + \log 2 + \log 3 + \dots + \log 50$
   Using a sum and sequence utility on a calculator, we obtain
   $$\log 50! \approx 64.48307487$$
   $$50! \approx 10^{64.48307487}$$
   $$50! \approx 10^{.48307487} \times 10^{64}$$
   $$50! \approx 3.04140932 \times 10^{64}.$$
   Computing the value directly, we obtain
   $50! \approx 3.04140932 \times 10^{64}$.

   (b) $\log 60! = \log 1 + \log 2 + \log 3 + \dots + \log 60$
   Using a sum and sequence utility on a

calculator, we obtain

$\log 60! \approx 81.92017485$

$60! \approx 10^{81.92017485}$

$60! \approx 10^{.92017485} \times 10^{81}$

$60! \approx 8.320987113 \times 10^{81}$.

Computing the value directly, we obtain
$60! \approx 8.320987113 \times 10^{81}$.

(c) $\log 65! = \log 1 + \log 2 + \log 3 + \dots + \log 65$
Using a sum and sequence utility on a calculator, we obtain

$\log 65! \approx 90.91633025$

$65! \approx 10^{90.91633025}$

$65! \approx 10^{.91633025} \times 10^{90}$

$65! \approx 8.247650592 \times 10^{90}$.

Computing the value directly, we obtain
$65! \approx 8.247650592 \times 10^{90}$.

68. (a) $P(47, 13) = \dfrac{47!}{34!}$

$P(47, 13) = 47 \cdot 46 \cdot 45 \cdot \dots \cdot 35$

$\log P(47, 13) = \log 47 + \log 46 + \log 45$
$\qquad\qquad\qquad + \dots + \log 35$

$\log P(47, 13) \approx 20.94250295$

$P(47, 13) \approx 10^{20.94250295}$

$P(47, 13) \approx 10^{.94250295} \times 10^{20}$

$P(47, 13) \approx 8.759976613 \times 10^{20}$

(b) $P(50, 4) = \dfrac{50!}{46!}$

$P(50, 4) = 50 \cdot 49 \cdot 48 \cdot 47$

$\log P(50, 4) = \log 50 + \log 49 + \log 48$
$\qquad\qquad\qquad + \log 47$

$P(50, 4) \approx 6.74250518$

$P(50, 4) \approx 10^{6.74250518}$

$P(50, 4) \approx 5,527,200$

(This is in fact the exact value
of $P(50, 4)$.)

(c) $P(29, 21) = \dfrac{29!}{8!}$

$P(29, 21) = 29 \cdot 28 \cdot 27 \cdot \dots \cdot 9$

$\log P(29, 21) = \log 29 + \log 28 + \log 27$
$\qquad\qquad\qquad + \dots + \log 9$

$\log P(29, 21) \approx 26.34101830$

$P(29, 21) \approx 10^{26.34101830}$

$P(29, 21) \approx 10^{.34101830} \times 10^{26}$

$P(29, 21) \approx 2.19289732 \times 10^{26}$

Section 10.7

Exercises

1. Let H = heads, T = tails.
The only possible outcome is a head. Hence, the sample space is $S = \{H\}$.

3. Since each coin can be a head or a tail and there are 3 coins, the sample space is
$S = \{(H, H, H), (H, H, T), (H, T, H),$
$\quad (T, H, H), (H, T, T), (T, H, T),$
$\quad (T, T, H), (T, T, T)\}$.

5. The sample space is
$S = \{(1, 1), (1, 2), (1, 3),$
$\quad (2, 1), (2, 2), (2, 3),$
$\quad (3, 1), (3, 2), (3, 3)\}$

7. (a) "The result is heads" is the event $E_1 = \{H\}$.
This event is certain to occur, $P(E_1) = 1$.

(b) "The result is tails" is the event $E_2 = \emptyset$ This event is an impossible event, so
$P(E_2) = 0$.

9. (a) The result is a repeated number" is the event
$E = \{(1, 1), (2, 2), (3, 3)\}$
$n(E) = 3$
$P(E) = \dfrac{n(E)}{n(S)} = \dfrac{3}{9} = \dfrac{1}{3}$

(b) "The second number is 1 or 3" is the event
$E = \{(1, 1), (1, 3), (2, 1), (2, 3), (3, 1), (3, 3)\}$
$n(E) = 6$
$P(E) = \dfrac{n(E)}{n(S)} = \dfrac{6}{9} = \dfrac{2}{3}$

(c) "The first number is even and the second number is odd" is the event
$E = \{(2, 1), (2, 3)\}$
$n(E) = 2$
$P(E) = \dfrac{n(E)}{n(S)} = \dfrac{2}{9}$

13. (a) vi

(b) iv

(c) i

(d) vi

(e) iii

(f) ii

(g) v

15. A batting average of .300 means for every 10 times at bat (the sample space), the batter will get 3 hits. If the event E is "getting a hit," $P(E) = .300$. Thus $P(E') = 1 - .300 = .700$. The odds in favor of his getting a hit are

$$\frac{P(E)}{P(E')} = \frac{.300}{.700} = \frac{3}{7} \text{ or 3 to 7.}$$

17. Let E be the event "English is spoken." This corresponds to $100\% - 20.4\% = 79.6\%$ of the households so $P(E) = .796$. Thus, $P(E') = .204$. The odds that English is spoken is

$$\frac{P(E)}{P(E')} = \frac{.796}{.204} = \frac{199}{51} \text{ or about 39 to 10.}$$

19. The total of all types is 335,050.

    (a) $P(\text{of Hispanic origin}) = \dfrac{58,930}{335,050} \approx .176$

    (b) $P(\text{not white}) = 1 - P(\text{White})$
    $$= 1 - \frac{209,117}{335,050}$$
    $$\approx .376$$

    (c) $P\begin{pmatrix} \text{non - Hispanic} \\ \text{Indian} \\ \text{or Black} \end{pmatrix} = \dfrac{2,744 + 43,511}{335,050} \approx .138$

    (d) Let E be "selected resident was Asian." Then
    $$P(E) = \frac{20,748}{335,050}$$
    and $P(E') = 1 - P(E)$
    $$= 1 - \frac{20,748}{335,050}$$
    $$= \frac{314,302}{335,050}$$
    The odds that a randomly selected U.S. resident was a non-Hispanic Asian is
    $$\frac{P(E)}{P(E')} = \frac{\frac{20,748}{335,050}}{\frac{314,302}{335,050}} = \frac{10,374}{157,151} \text{ or about}$$
    1 to 15.

21. Each suit has thirteen cards, and the probability of choosing the correct card in that suit is $\dfrac{1}{13}$.

    $$P(4 \text{ correct choices}) = \frac{1}{13} \cdot \frac{1}{13} \cdot \frac{1}{13} \cdot \frac{1}{13} = \frac{1}{28,561}$$

    The probability of getting all four picks correct and winning \$5000 is $\dfrac{1}{28,561} \approx .000035$.

23. **(a)** A 40-year old man who lives thirty more years would be a 70-year old man. Let E be "selected man will live to be 70." Then $n(E) = 66,172$.
    Let S be "selected man is 40." Then $n(S) = 94,558$.
    Thus, $P(E) = \dfrac{n(E)}{n(S)} = \dfrac{66,172}{94,558} \approx .6998$.

    (b) Using the notation and results from part (a), $P(E') = 1 - P(E) = 1 - .6998 = .3002$.

    (c) Use the notation and results from part (a). In this binomial experiment, we call "a 40-year old man survives to age 70" a success. Then $n = 5$, $r = 3$, and $p = P(E) = .6998$.
    $$P(\text{exactly 3}) = \binom{5}{3}(.6998)^3(1 - .6998)^2$$
    $$= 10(.6998)^3(.3002)^2$$
    $$\approx .3088$$

    (d) Let F be the event "both men survive to the age 70." Then we are to find $P(F)$. Consider the complementary event F': "neither man survives to age 70." From the hint, we know that the probability that neither man survives to age 70 is the product of the probabilities that each man does not survive to age 70. Using the results of part (b), this probability is
    $$P(E') \cdot P(E') = (.3002)^2 \approx .0901.$$
    Thus, $P(F) = 1 - P(F') \approx 1 - .0901 = .9099$.

25. The amount of growth would be $11,400 - 10,000 = 1400$ so the percent growth would be $\dfrac{1400}{10,000} = .14$. Let E be the event "worth at least \$11,400 by the end of the year." This is equivalent to "at least 14 percent growth" which is equivalent to "14 or 18 percent growth." Thus,
    $$P(E) = P(14 \text{ percent growth or } 18 \text{ percent growth})$$
    $$= P(14 \text{ percent growth})$$
    $$+ P(18 \text{ percent growth})$$
    $$= .20 + .10$$
    $$P(E) = .30$$

27. In this binomial experiment, we call "smoked less than 10" a success. Then $n = 10$, $r = 4$, and $p = .45 + .24 = .69$.
    $P(4 \text{ smoked less than 10})$
    $$= \binom{10}{4}(.69)^4(1 - .69)^6$$
    $$= 210(.69)^4(.31)^6 = .042246$$

29. In this binomial experiment, we call "smoked between 1 and 19" a success. Then
P(smoked between 1 and 19)
= P(smoked 1 to 9 or smoked 10 to 19)
= P(smoked 1 to 9) + P(smoked 10 to 19)
= .24 + .20
= .44
Also, "fewer than 2" corresponds to "0 or 1." thus, $n = 10$, $r = 0$ or 1, and $p = .44$.
P(fewer than 2 smoked between 1 and 19)
= P(0 smoked between 1 and 19)
  + P(1 smoked between 1 and 19)

$= \binom{10}{0}(.44)^0(1-.44)^{10} + \binom{10}{1}(.44)^1(1-.44)^9$

$= 1(.44)^0(.56)^{10} + 10(.44)^1(.56)^9$

$= .003033 + .023831$

$= .026864$

31. In these binomial experiments, we call "the man is color-blind" a success.

(a) For "exactly 5 are color-blind", we have $n = 53$, $r = 5$, and $p = .042$.
P(exactly 5 are color-blind)

$= \binom{53}{5}(.042)^5(1-.042)^{53-5}$

$= 2,869,685(.042)^5(.958)^{48}$

$= .047822$

(b) "No more than 5 are color-blind" corresponds to "0, 1, 2, 3, 4, or 5 are color-blind." Then $n = 53$, $r = 0, 1, 2, 3, 4,$ or 5, and $p = .042$.
P(no more than 5 are color-blind)
= P(0 are color-blind)
  + P(1 are color-blind)
  + P(2 are color-blind)
  + P(3 are color-blind)
  + P(4 are color-blind)
  + P(5 are color-blind)

$= \binom{53}{0}(.042)^0(1-.042)^{53}$

$\quad + \binom{53}{1}(.042)^1(1-.042)^{52}$

$\quad + \binom{53}{2}(.042)^2(1-.042)^{51}$

$\quad + \binom{53}{3}(.042)^3(1-.042)^{50}$

$\quad + \binom{53}{4}(.042)^4(1-.042)^{49}$

$\quad + \binom{53}{5}(.042)^5(1-.042)^{48}$

$= 1(.042)^0(.958)^{53}$

$\quad + 53(.042)^1(.958)^{52}$

$\quad + 1378(.042)^2(.958)^{51}$

$\quad + 23,426(.042)^3(.958)^{50}$

$\quad + 292,825(.042)^4(.958)^{49}$

$\quad + 2,869,685(.042)^5(.958)^{48}$

$= .102890 + .239074 + .272514 + .203105$

$\quad + .111305 + .047822$

$= .976710$

(c) Let E be "at least 1 is color-blind." Consider the complementary event E': "0 are color-blind." Thus,
$P(E) = 1 - P(E')$

$= 1 - \binom{53}{0}(.042)^0(1-.042)^{53}$

$= 1 - .102890$ (from part (b))

$= .897110$

33. (a) First compute $q = (1-p)^I = (1-.1)^2 = .81$. Then, with $S = 4$, $k = 3$, and $q = .81$,

$P = \binom{S}{k}q^k(1-q)^{S-k}$

$= \binom{4}{3}.81^3(1-.81)^{4-3}$

$= 4 \times .81^3 \times .19^1 \approx .404$.
There is about a 40.4% chance of exactly 3 people not becoming infected.

(b) Compute $q = (1-p)^I = (1-.5)^2 = .25$. Then,

$P = \binom{S}{k}q^k(1-q)^{S-k}$

$= \binom{4}{3}.25^3(1-.25)^{4-3}$

$= 4 \times .25^3 \times .75^1 \approx .047$.
There is about 4.7 % chance of this occurring when the disease is highly infectious.

(c) Compute $q = (1-p)^I = (1-.5)^1 = .5$. Then, with $S = 9$, $k = 0$, and $p = .5$,

$P\binom{S}{k}q^k(1-q)^{S-k}$

$= \binom{9}{0}.5^0(1-.5)^9$

$= 1 \times 1 \times .5^9 \approx .002$.
There is about a .2% chance of everyone becoming infected. This means that in a large family or group of people, it is highly

unlikely that everyone will become sick even though the disease is highly infectious.

Chapter 10 Review Exercises

1. $a_n = \dfrac{n}{n+1}$

$a_1 = \dfrac{1}{1+1} = \dfrac{1}{2}$

$a_2 = \dfrac{2}{2+1} = \dfrac{2}{3}$

$a_3 = \dfrac{3}{3+1} = \dfrac{3}{4}$

$a_4 = \dfrac{4}{4+1} = \dfrac{4}{5}$

$a_5 = \dfrac{5}{5+1} = \dfrac{5}{6}$

The first five terms are $\dfrac{1}{2}, \dfrac{2}{3}, \dfrac{3}{4}, \dfrac{4}{5},$ and $\dfrac{5}{6}$.
This sequence does not have a common difference or a common ratio, so the sequence is neither arithmetic nor geometric.

3. $a_n = 2(n+3)$

$a_1 = 2(1+3) = 8$

$a_2 = 2(2+3) = 10$

$a_3 = 2(3+3) = 12$

$a_4 = 2(4+3) = 14$

$a_5 = 2(5+3) = 16$

The first five terms are 8, 10, 12, 14, and 16. There is a common difference, $d = 2$, so the sequence is arithmetic.

5. $a_1 = 5$; for $n \geq 2$, $a_n = a_{n-1} - 3$

$a_2 = a_{2-1} - 3 = a_1 - 3 = 5 - 3 = 2$

$a_3 = a_{2-1} - 3 = 2 - 3 = -1$

$a_4 = a_{3-1} - 3 = -1 - 3 = -4$

$a_5 = a_{4-1} - 3 = -4 - 3 = -7$

The first five terms are 5, 2, -1, -4, and -7. There is a common difference, $d = -3$, so the sequence is arithmetic.

7. Arithmetic, $a_3 = \pi$, $a_4 = 1$

$d = a_4 - a_3 = 1 - \pi$

$a_3 = a_1 + 2d$

$\pi = a_1 + 2(1 - \pi)$

$\pi = a_1 + 2 - 2\pi$

$3\pi - 2 = a_1$

$a_2 = a_1 + d = (3\pi - 2) + (1 - \pi) = 2\pi - 1$

$a_5 = a_1 + 4d = (3\pi - 2) + 4(1 - \pi)$

$= 3\pi - 2 + 4 - 4\pi$

$= -\pi + 2$

The first five terms are $3\pi - 2$, $2\pi - 1$, π, 1, $-\pi + 2$.

9. Geometric, $a_1 = -5$, $a_2 = -1$

$r = \dfrac{a_2}{a_1} = \dfrac{-1}{-5} = \dfrac{1}{5}$

$a_3 = a_1 r^2 = -5\left(\dfrac{1}{5}\right)^2 = -5 \cdot \dfrac{1}{25} = -\dfrac{1}{5}$

$a_4 = a_1 r^3 = -5\left(\dfrac{1}{5}\right)^3 = -5 \cdot \dfrac{1}{125} = -\dfrac{1}{25}$

$a_5 = a_1 r^4 = -5\left(\dfrac{1}{5}\right)^4 = -5 \cdot \dfrac{1}{625} = -\dfrac{1}{125}$

The first five terms are

$-5, -1, -\dfrac{1}{5}, -\dfrac{1}{25},$ and $-\dfrac{1}{125}$.

11. Geometric, $a_1 = -8$ and $a_7 = -\dfrac{1}{8}$

Use the formula for the nth term of a geometric sequence to solve for r.

$a_7 = a_1 r^{7-1}$

$-\dfrac{1}{8} = -8r^6$

$r^6 = \dfrac{1}{64}$

$r = \pm\dfrac{1}{2}$

There are two geometric sequences that satisfy the given conditions. If $r = \dfrac{1}{2}$,

$a_4 = (-8)\left(\dfrac{1}{2}\right)^3 = -1$ and $a_n = -8\left(\dfrac{1}{2}\right)^{n-1}$

or $a_n = -2^3\left(\dfrac{1}{2}\right)^{n-1} = -\left(\dfrac{1}{2}\right)^{n-4}$.

If $r = -\dfrac{1}{2}$, $a_4 = (-8)\left(-\dfrac{1}{2}\right)^3 = 1$ and

$a_n = -8\left(-\dfrac{1}{2}\right)^{n-1}$ or

$a_n = (-2)^3\left(-\dfrac{1}{2}\right)^{n-1} = \left(-\dfrac{1}{2}\right)^{n-4}$.

13. $a_1 = 6x - 9$, $a_2 = 5x + 1$

$d = a_2 - a_1 = (5x + 1) - (6x - 9) = -x + 10$

$a_n = a_1 + (n-1)d$

$a_8 = a_1 + (8-1)d$

$= (6x - 9) + 7(-x + 10)$

$= 6x - 9 - 7x + 70$

$= -x + 61$

15. $a_2 = 6$, $d = 10$

First, find a_1.

$$a_2 = a_1 + d$$
$$6 = a_1 + 10$$
$$a_1 = -4$$

Now we can find S_{12}.

$$S_n = \frac{n}{2}[2a_1 + (n-1)d]$$
$$S_{12} = \frac{12}{2}[2(-4) + (12-1)(10)]$$
$$= 6[-8 + 110]$$
$$= 612$$

17. $a_3 = 4$, $r = \frac{1}{5}$

$$a_4 = a_3 r = 4 \cdot \frac{1}{5} = \frac{4}{5}$$
$$a_5 = a_4 r = \frac{4}{5} \cdot \frac{1}{5} = \frac{4}{25}$$

19. $a_1 = -1$, $r = 3$

Use the formula $S_n = \dfrac{a_1(1-r^n)}{1-r}$, with $n = 4$.

$$S_4 = \frac{-1(1-3^4)}{1-3}$$
$$= \frac{-1(1-81)}{-2}$$
$$= \frac{-1(-80)}{-2}$$
$$= -40$$

21. $\displaystyle\sum_{i=1}^{7} (-1)^{i-1}$

This is a geometric series with $a_1 = 1$ and $r = -1$.

$$S_n = \frac{a_1(1-r^n)}{1-r}$$
$$S_7 = \frac{a_1(1-r^7)}{1-r}$$
$$= \frac{1[1-(-1)^7]}{1-(-1)}$$
$$= \frac{1 \cdot 2}{2} = 1$$

23. $\displaystyle\sum_{i=1}^{4} \frac{i+1}{i} = \frac{2}{1} + \frac{3}{2} + \frac{4}{3} + \frac{5}{4}$

$$= \frac{24}{12} + \frac{18}{12} + \frac{16}{12} + \frac{15}{12}$$
$$= \frac{73}{12}$$

25. $\displaystyle\sum_{j=1}^{2500} j = \frac{2500(2500+1)}{2}$

$$= 1250(2501)$$
$$= 3,126,250$$

27. $\displaystyle\sum_{i=1}^{\infty} \left(\frac{4}{7}\right)^i$

This is an infinite geometric series with $a_1 = \frac{4}{7}$

and $r = \frac{4}{7}$.

$$S_\infty = \frac{a_1}{1-r}$$
$$= \frac{\frac{4}{7}}{1-\frac{4}{7}}$$
$$= \frac{\frac{4}{7}}{\frac{3}{7}}$$
$$= \frac{4}{3}$$

29. $24 + 8 + \dfrac{8}{3} + \dfrac{8}{9} + \dots$

This is an infinite geometric series with $a_1 = 24$

and $r = \dfrac{8}{24} = \dfrac{1}{3}$.

$$S_\infty = \frac{a_1}{1-r}$$
$$= \frac{24}{1-\frac{1}{3}}$$
$$= \frac{24}{\frac{2}{3}}$$
$$= 36$$

31. $\dfrac{1}{12} + \dfrac{1}{6} + \dfrac{1}{3} + \dfrac{2}{3} + \dots$

This is an infinite geometric series with $a_1 = \dfrac{1}{12}$

and $r = \dfrac{\frac{1}{6}}{\frac{1}{12}} = 2$.

Since $|r| > 1$, the series diverges.

33. $\displaystyle\sum_{i=1}^{4} (x_i^2 - 6)$

$$= (x_1^2 - 6) + (x_2^2 - 6) + (x_3^2 - 6) + (x_4^2 - 6)$$
$$= (0^2 - 6) + (1^2 - 6) + (2^2 - 6) + (3^2 - 6)$$
$$= -6 + (-5) + (-2) + 3$$
$$= -10$$

35. $4 - 1 - 6 - \ldots - 66$

This series is the sum of an arithmetic sequence with $a_1 = 4$ and $d = -1 - 4 = -5$. Therefore, the nth term is

$$a_n = a_1 + (n-1)d$$
$$= 4 + (n-1)(-5)$$
$$= 4 - 5n + 5$$
$$= -5n + 9,$$

or, equivalently, $a_i = -5i + 9$.

The last term of the series is -66, so $a_i = -5i + 9$. becomes

$$-66 = -5i + 9$$
$$-75 = -5i$$
$$i = 15.$$

This indicates that the series consists of 15 terms.

$$4 - 1 - 6 - \ldots - 66 = \sum_{i=1}^{15}(-5i + 9)$$

37. $4 + 12 + 36 + \ldots + 972$

This series is the sum of a geometric sequence with $a_1 = 4$ and $r = \dfrac{12}{4} = 3$.

Find the nth term.

$$a_n = a_1 r^{n-1}$$
$$a_n = 4(3)^{n-1},$$

or, equivalently, $a_i = 4(3)^{i-1}$.

Now find the number of terms.

$$972 = 4(3)^{i-1}$$
$$243 = 3^{i-1}$$
$$3^5 = 3^{i-1}$$
$$5 = i - 1$$
$$i = 6$$

Therefore, $4 + 12 + 36 + \ldots + 972 = \displaystyle\sum_{i=1}^{6} 4(3)^{i-1}$.

39. $(x + 2y)^4$

$$= x^4 + \binom{4}{3}x^{4-1}(2y)^1 + \binom{4}{2}x^{4-2}(2y)^2$$
$$+ \binom{4}{1}x^{4-3}(2y)^3 + (2y)^4$$
$$= x^4 + \frac{4!}{3!\,1!}x^3(2y) + \frac{4!}{2!\,2!}x^2(2y)^2$$
$$+ 4x(8y^3) + 16y^4$$
$$= x^4 + 8x^3y + 24x^2y^2 + 32xy^3 + 16y^4$$

41. $\left(3\sqrt{x} - \dfrac{1}{\sqrt{x}}\right)^5$

$$= [3x^{1/2} + (-x^{-1/2})]^5$$
$$= (3x^{1/2})^5 + \binom{5}{1}(3x^{1/2})^4(-x^{-1/2})$$
$$+ \binom{5}{2}(3x^{1/2})^3(-x^{-1/2})^2$$
$$+ \binom{5}{3}(3x^{1/2})^2(-x^{-1/2})^3$$
$$+ \binom{5}{4}(3x^{1/2})(-x^{-1/2})^4 + (-x^{-1/2})^5$$
$$= 243x^{5/2} + (5)(81x^2)(-x^{-1/2})$$
$$+ (10)(27x^{3/2})(x^{-1}) + (10)(9x)(-x^{-3/2})$$
$$+ (5)(3x^{1/2})(x^{-2}) + (-x^{-5/2})$$
$$= 243x^{5/2} - 405x^{3/2} + 270x^{1/2} - 90x^{-1/2}$$
$$+ 15x^{-3/2} - x^{-5/2}$$

43. $(4x - y)^8$

The sixth term of the expansion is $\binom{8}{5}(4x)^3(-y)^5$

$$= \frac{8!}{3!\,5!}(64x^3)(-y^5)$$
$$= 56(-64x^3y^5)$$
$$= -3584x^3y^5.$$

45. $(x + 2)^{12}$

The first four terms of this expansion are as follows.

$$(x)^{12} + \binom{12}{1}(x)^{11}(2)^1 + \binom{12}{2}(x)^{10}(2)^2$$
$$+ \binom{12}{3}(x)^9(2)^3$$

$$= x^{12} + \frac{12!}{11!\,1!}(x^{11})(2) + \frac{12!}{10!\,2!}(x^{10})(4)$$
$$+ \frac{12!}{9!\,3!}(x^9)(8)$$
$$= x^{12} + 12(2x^{11}) + 66(4x^{10}) + 220(8x^9)$$
$$= x^{12} + 24x^{11} + 264x^{10} + 1760x^9$$

49. Let S_n be the statement

$$1 + 3 + 5 + 7 + \ldots + (2n - 1) = n^2.$$

Step 1　　S_1 is $1 = 1^2$ or
$$1 = 1.$$
The statement is true for $n = 1$.

Step 2　　Show that S_k implies S_{k+1}, where S_k is the statement $1 + 3 + 5 + 7 + \ldots + (2k - 1) = k^2$ and S_{k+1} is the statement

$1+3+5+7+\ldots+[2(k+1)-1]=(k+1)^2$.
Adding $[2(k+1)-1]$ to both sides of S_k gives
$1+3+5+7+\ldots+[2(k+1)-1]$
$= k^2+[2(k+1)-1]$
$= k^2+2k+2-1$
$= k^2+2k+1$
$= (k+1)^2$.
The final result is the statement for
$n=k+1$; it has been shown that S_k implies
S_{k+1}. Therefore, by mathematical induction,
S_n is true for every positive integer n.

51. Let S_n be the statement
$$2+2^2+2^3+\ldots+2^n=2(2^n-1).$$
Step 1 S_1 is the statement
$$2=2(2^1-1)$$
$$2=2\cdot1, \quad \text{which is true.}$$
Step 2   Show that if S_k is true, then S_{k+1} is
also true, where S_k is the statement
$$2+2^2+2^3+\ldots+2^k=2(2^k-1),$$
and S_{k+1} is the statement
$$2+2^2+2^3+\ldots+2^k+2^{k+1}=2(2^{k+1}-1).$$
Start with S_k. Add 2^{k+1} to both sides.
$$2+2^2+2^3+\ldots+2^k=2(2^k-1)$$
$$2+2^2+2^3+\ldots+2^k+2^{k+1}=2(2^k-1)+2^{k+1}$$
$$=2^{k+1}-2+2^{k+1}$$
$$=2\cdot2^{k+1}-2\cdot1$$
$$=2(2^{k+1}-1)$$
Thus, $2+2^2+2^3+\ldots+2^n=2(2^n-1)$ is true for
every positive integer n.

55. $P(6,0)=\dfrac{6!}{(6-0)!}$
$=\dfrac{6!}{6!}=1$

57. $9!=9\cdot8\cdot7\cdot6\cdot5\cdot4\cdot3\cdot2\cdot1=362,880$

59. $2\cdot4\cdot3\cdot2=48$
48 different wedding arrangements are possible.

61. There are 4 choices for the first job,
3 choices for the second job, and so on.
$4\cdot3\cdot2\cdot1=24$
There are 24 ways in which the jobs can be
assigned.

63. Order is important, so this is a permutation
problem.

$P(9,3)=\dfrac{9!}{6!}$
$=9\cdot8\cdot7$
$=504$
The winners can be determined 504 ways.

65. The total number of students polled is
$n(S)=1640$.

(a) Let E be "selected student us conservative
politically."
$$P(E)=\frac{n(E)}{n(S)}=\frac{303.4}{1640}=\frac{37}{200}=.185$$

(b) Let E be "selected student is on the far left or
the far right."
$$P(E)=P\left(\begin{matrix}\text{selected student}\\\text{is on the far left}\end{matrix}\right)$$
$$+P\left(\begin{matrix}\text{selected student}\\\text{is on the far right}\end{matrix}\right)$$
$$=\frac{n(\text{far left})}{n(S)}+\frac{n(\text{far right})}{n(S)}$$
$$=\frac{44.28}{1640}+\frac{24.6}{1640}$$
$$=\frac{68.88}{1640}$$
$$=.042$$

(c) Let E be "selected student is middle of the
road." Then
$n(E)=926.6$
$n(E')=1640-926.6=713.4$
Thus, the odds against E are
$\dfrac{n(E')}{n(E)}=\dfrac{713.4}{926.6}=\dfrac{87}{113}$ or 87 to 113 or about
1 to 1.3.

67. (a) $P(\text{black king})=\dfrac{n(\text{black kings})}{n(\text{black cards in deck})}$
$$=\frac{2}{52}=\frac{1}{26}$$

(b) There are 52 cards, so $n(S)=52$. Consider
the events
F: face card is drawn
A: ace is drawn.
There are 12 face cards, so
$$n(F)=12 \text{ and } P(F)=\frac{12}{52}=\frac{3}{13}.$$
There are 4 aces, so
$$n(A)=4 \text{ and } P(A)=\frac{4}{52}=\frac{1}{13}.$$
There are no cards which are both face cards
and aces, so

$n(F \cap A) = 0$ and $P(F \cap A) = 0$.

$P(F \text{ or } A) = P(F) + P(A) - P(F \cap A)$

$\qquad = \dfrac{3}{13} + \dfrac{1}{13} - 0$

$\qquad = \dfrac{4}{13}$

(c) $P(\text{ace or diamond})$

$= P(\text{ace}) + P(\text{diamond}) - P(\text{diamond and ace})$

$= \dfrac{4}{52} + \dfrac{13}{52} - \dfrac{1}{52}$

$= \dfrac{16}{52} = \dfrac{4}{13}$

(d) There are 52 cards, so $n(S) = 52$. Consider the event D: diamond is drawn.
There are 13 diamonds, so $n(D) = 13$ and

$P(D) = \dfrac{13}{52} = \dfrac{1}{4}$. The probability that the card drawn is not a diamond is

$P(D') = 1 - P(D)$

$\qquad = 1 - \dfrac{1}{4}$

$\qquad = \dfrac{3}{4}$.

69. In this binomial experiment, we call rolling a five a success.

Then $n = 12$, $r = 2$, and $p = \dfrac{1}{6}$.

$P(2 \text{ fives}) = \dbinom{12}{2}\left(\dfrac{1}{6}\right)^2\left(1 - \dfrac{1}{6}\right)^{10}$

$\qquad\qquad = 66 \cdot \dfrac{1}{6^2} \cdot \dfrac{5^{10}}{6^{10}}$

$\qquad\qquad \approx .296$

Chapter 10 Test Exercises

1. $a_n = (-1)^n(n^2 + 2)$

$n = 1\text{: } a_1 = (-1)^1(1^2 + 2) = -3$

$n = 2\text{: } a_2 = (-1)^2(2^2 + 2) = 6$

$n = 3\text{: } a_3 = (-1)^3(3^2 + 2) = -11$

$n = 4\text{: } a_4 = (-1)^4(4^2 + 2) = 18$

$n = 5\text{: } a_5 = (-1)^5(5^2 + 2) = -27$

The first five terms are $-3, 6, -11, 18$, and -27.
This sequence does not have either a common difference or a common ration, so the sequence is neither arithmetic nor geometric.

2. $a_n = -3 \cdot \left(\dfrac{1}{2}\right)^n$

$n = 1\text{: } a_1 = -3\left(\dfrac{1}{2}\right)^1 = -\dfrac{3}{2}$

$n = 2\text{: } a_2 = -3\left(\dfrac{1}{2}\right)^2 = -\dfrac{3}{4}$

$n = 3\text{: } a_3 = -3\left(\dfrac{1}{2}\right)^3 = -\dfrac{3}{8}$

$n = 4\text{: } a_4 = -3\left(\dfrac{1}{2}\right)^4 = -\dfrac{3}{16}$

$n = 5\text{: } a_5 = -3\left(\dfrac{1}{2}\right)^5 = -\dfrac{3}{32}$

The first five terms are

$-\dfrac{3}{2}, -\dfrac{3}{4}, -\dfrac{3}{8}, -\dfrac{3}{16}$, and $-\dfrac{3}{32}$.

This sequence has a common ration, $r = \dfrac{1}{2}$, so the sequence is geometric.

3. $a_1 = 2$, $a_2 = 3$, $a_n = a_{n-1} + 2a_{n-2}$, for $n \geq 3$

$n = 3\text{: } a_3 = a_2 + 2a_1 = 3 + 2(2) = 7$

$n = 4\text{: } a_4 = a_3 + 2a_2 = 7 + 2(3) = 13$

$n = 5\text{: } a_5 = a_4 + 2a_3 = 13 + 2(7) = 27$

The first five terms are $2, 3, 7, 13$, and 27.
There is no common difference or common ratio, so the sequence is neither arithmetic nor geometric.

4. $a_1 = 1$ and $a_3 = 25$

$a_n = a_1 + (n - 1)d$

$a_3 = a_1 + 2d$

$25 = 1 + 2d$

$2d = 24$

$d = 12$

$a_5 = a_1 + 4d$

$\quad = 1 + 4(12)$

$\quad = 1 + 48$

$\quad = 49$

5. $a_1 = 81$ and $r = -\dfrac{2}{3}$

$a_n = a_1 r^{n-1}$

$a_6 = 81\left(-\dfrac{2}{3}\right)^5$

$\quad = 81\left(-\dfrac{32}{243}\right)$

$\quad = -\dfrac{32}{3}$

6. Arithmetic, with $a_1 = -43$ and $d = 12$

$$S_n = \frac{n}{2}[2a_1 + (n-1)d]$$

$$S_{10} = \frac{10}{2}[2(-43) + 9(12)]$$

$$= 5(-86 + 108)$$

$$= 5(22)$$

$$= 110$$

7. Geometric, with $a_1 = 5$ and $r = -2$

$$S_n = \frac{a_1(1 - r^n)}{1 - r}$$

$$S_{10} = \frac{5[1 - (-2)^{10}]}{1 - (-2)}$$

$$= \frac{5(1 - 1024)}{3}$$

$$= \frac{5(-1023)}{3}$$

$$= -1705$$

8. $\displaystyle\sum_{i=1}^{30}(5i + 2)$

This sum represents the sum of the first 30 terms of the arithmetic sequence having
$a_1 = 5 \cdot 1 + 2 = 7$ and
$a_n = a_{30} = 5 \cdot 30 + 2 = 152.$

$$\sum_{i=1}^{30}(5i + 2) = S_{30}$$

$$= \frac{n}{2}(a_1 + a_n)$$

$$= \frac{30}{2}(a_1 + a_{30})$$

$$= 15(7 + 152)$$

$$= 2385$$

9. $\displaystyle\sum_{i=1}^{5}(-3 \cdot 2^i)$

This sum represents the sum of the first five terms of the geometric sequence having
$a_1 = -3 \cdot 2^1 = -6$ and $r = 2.$

$$\sum_{i=1}^{5} -3 \cdot 2^1 = S_5$$

$$= \frac{a_1(1 - r^n)}{1 - r}$$

$$= \frac{-6(1 - 2^5)}{1 - 2}$$

$$= \frac{-6(1 - 32)}{-1}$$

$$= 6(-31)$$

$$= -186$$

10. $\displaystyle\sum_{i=1}^{\infty}(2^i) \cdot 4$

This is the sum of an infinite geometric sequence with $r = 2$. Since $|r| > 1$, the sum does not exist.

11. $\displaystyle\sum_{i=1}^{\infty} 54\left(\frac{2}{9}\right)^i$

This is the sum of the infinite geometric sequence with

$$a_1 = 54\left(\frac{2}{9}\right)^1 = 12 \text{ and } r = \frac{2}{9}.$$

$$\sum_{i=1}^{\infty} 54\left(\frac{2}{9}\right)^i = S_\infty = \frac{a_1}{1 - r}$$

$$= \frac{12}{1 - \frac{2}{9}}$$

$$= \frac{12}{\frac{7}{9}}$$

$$= \frac{9 \cdot 12}{7}$$

$$= \frac{108}{7}$$

12. $(x + y)^6$

$$= x^6 + \binom{6}{1}x^5 y + \binom{6}{2}x^4 y^2 + \binom{6}{3}x^3 y^3 + \binom{6}{4}x^2 y^4$$

$$+ \binom{6}{5}xy^5 + y^6$$

$$= x^6 + \frac{6!}{1! \, 5!}x^5 y + \frac{6!}{2! \, 4!}x^4 y^2 + \frac{6!}{3! \, 3!}x^3 y^3$$

$$+ \frac{6!}{4! \, 2!}x^2 y^4 + \frac{6!}{5! \, 1!}xy^5 + y^6$$

$$= x^6 + 6x^5 y + 15x^4 y^2 + 20x^3 y^3 + 15x^2 y^4$$

$$+ 6xy^5 + y^6$$

13.　$(2x - 3y)^4$

$$= (2x)^4 + \binom{4}{1}(2x)^3(-3y) + \binom{4}{2}(2x)^2(-3y)^2$$

$$+ \binom{4}{3}(2x)(-3y)^3 + (-3y)^4$$

$$= 16x^4 + 4(8x^3)(-3y) + 6(4x^2)(9x^2)$$

$$+ 4(2x)(-27y^3) + 81y^4$$

$$= 16x^4 - 96x^3y + 216x^2y^2 - 216xy^3 + 81y^4$$

14.　To find the third term in the expansion of

$(w - 2y)^6$, use the formula $\binom{n}{k-1}x^{n-(k-1)}y^{k-1}$

with $n = 6$ and $k = 3$.
Then $k - 1 = 2$ and $n - (k - 1) = 4$. Thus, the third term is

$$\binom{6}{2}w^4(-2y)^2 = 15w^4(4y^2)$$

$$= 60w^4y^2.$$

15.　$C(10, 2) = \dfrac{10!}{(10 - 2)!\,2!}$

$$= \dfrac{10 \cdot 9 \cdot 8!}{8! \cdot 2 \cdot 1}$$

$$= 45$$

16.　$\binom{7}{3} = \dfrac{7!}{(7 - 3)!\,3!}$

$$= \dfrac{7 \cdot 6 \cdot 5 \cdot 4!}{4! \cdot 3 \cdot 2 \cdot 1}$$

$$= 35$$

17.　$P(11, 3) = \dfrac{11!}{(11 - 3)!}$

$$= \dfrac{11!}{8!}$$

$$= \dfrac{11 \cdot 10 \cdot 9 \cdot 8!}{8!}$$

$$= 990$$

18.　$8! = 8 \cdot 7 \cdot 6 \cdot 5 \cdot 4 \cdot 3 \cdot 2 \cdot 1 = 40{,}320$

19.　Prove that
　　$8 + 14 + 20 + 26 + \ldots + (6n + 2) = 3n^2 + 5n$ is true for every positive integer n.
　　Step 1　S_1 is the statement

　　　　$8 = 3(1^2) + 5(1)$, which is true.

　　Step 2　Show that if S_k is true, then S_{k+1} is also true. S_k is the statement

　　$8 + 14 + 20 + 26 + \ldots + (6k + 2) = 3k^2 + 5k$,
　　and S_{k+1} is the statement

$$8 + 14 + 20 + 26 + \ldots + (6k + 2) + [6(k + 1) + 2]$$
$$= 3(k + 1)^2 + 5(k + 1).$$
Start with S_k.

$8 + 14 + 20 + 26 + \ldots + (6k + 2) = 3k^2 + 5k$
Add the $(k + 1)$st term, $6(k + 1) + 2$, to both sides.
$8 + 14 + 20 + 26 + \ldots + (6k + 2) + [6(k + 1) + 2]$

$$= (3k^2 + 5k) + [6(k + 1) + 2]$$

$$= 3k^2 + 5k + 5(k + 1) + (k + 1) + 2$$

$$= (3k^2 + 6k + 3) + 5(k + 1)$$

$$= 3(k^2 + 2k + 1) + 5(k + 1)$$

$$= 3(k + 1)^2 + 5(k + 1)$$

The final equation is the statement S_{k+1}. Thus we have shown that if S_k is true, then S_{k+1} is also true. The two steps required for a proof by mathematical induction have been completed, so the statement

$8 + 14 + 20 + 26 + \ldots + (6n + 2) = 3n^2 + 5n$
is true for every positive integer n.

20.　Using the fundamental principle of counting, the number of different types of shoes is
　　$4 \cdot 3 \cdot 2 = 24$.

21.　We are choosing three people from a group of ten without regard to order so there are
　　$C(10, 3) = 120$ or 120 ways to do this.
　　If one black and exactly one Asian officer must be included, we have 1 way to select the black officer, 2 ways to select the Asian officer, and 7 ways to select the remaining officer. Altogether, then, we have $1 \cdot 2 \cdot 7 = 14$
　　or 14 ways to do this.

22.　The two women can be selected from the four women in $C(4, 2) = 6$ or 6 ways. The two women can be selected from the six men in
　　$C(6, 2) = 15$ or 15 ways. Altogether, then, we have $6 \cdot 15 = 90$ or 90 ways to do this.

24.　(a)　Consider the event E: "drawing red three." There are 2 red threes in a deck, so
　　　　$n(E) = 2$.

$$P(E) = \frac{n(E)}{n(S)}$$

$$= \frac{2}{52}$$

$$= \frac{1}{26}$$

　　The probability of drawing a red three is $\dfrac{1}{26}$.

(b) Consider the event E: "draw a face card." Each suit contains 3 face cards (jack, queen, and king), so the deck contains 12 face cards.

Thus $n(E) = 12$

and $P(E) = \dfrac{12}{52} = \dfrac{3}{13}$.

The probability of drawing a card that is not a face card is

$P(E') = 1 - P(E)$

$= 1 - \dfrac{3}{13} = \dfrac{10}{13}$.

(c) The events E: "draw a king" and F: "draw a spade" are not mutually exclusive, since it is possible to draw the king of spades, an outcome satisfying both events.

$P(E \text{ or } F) = P(E \cup F)$

$\quad\quad\quad\quad = P(E) + P(F) - P(E \cap F)$

$P(\text{king or spade})$

$= P(\text{king}) + P(\text{spade}) - P(\text{king and spade})$

$= \dfrac{4}{52} + \dfrac{13}{52} - \dfrac{1}{52}$

$= \dfrac{16}{52} = \dfrac{4}{13}$

The probability of drawing a king or a spade is $\dfrac{4}{13}$.

(d) Consider the event E: "draw a face card." As shown in the solution to part (b),

$P(E) = \dfrac{3}{13}$ and $P(E') = \dfrac{10}{13}$.

The odds in favor of drawing a face card are

$\dfrac{P(E)}{P(E')} = \dfrac{\frac{3}{13}}{\frac{10}{13}} = \dfrac{3}{10}$ or 3 to 10.

25. "At most 2" means "0 or 1 or 2."

$P(\text{at most 2})$

$= P(0 \text{ or } 1 \text{ or } 2)$

$= P(0) + P(1) + P(2) \left(\begin{array}{c}\text{since the events are}\\ \text{mutually exclusive}\end{array}\right)$

$= .19 + .43 + .30$

$= .92$

The probability that at most 2 filters are defective is .92.

CHAPTER 11   AN INTRODUCTION TO CALCULUS: LIMITS AND DERIVATIVES

Section 11.1

Connections (page 860)

1. The distance between $f(x)$ and 11 is given by $|f(x)-11|$, and the distance between x and 4 is given by $|x-4|$. Thus, we are looking for a value of $\delta > 0$ such that $|f(x)-11| < .1$ whenever $|x-4| < \delta$. Now

$$|f(x)-11| < .1$$
$$|(2x+3)-11| < .1$$
$$|2x-8| < .1$$
$$2|x-4| < .1$$
$$|x-4| < .05.$$

Since $|f(x)-11| < .1$ whenever $|x-4| < .05$, $\delta = .05$.

Exercises

1. False; consider $\lim_{x \to 0} f(x)$, where

$$f(x) = \begin{cases} x & \text{if } x \neq 0 \\ 2 & \text{if } x = 0 \end{cases}.$$

$\lim_{x \to 0} f(x) = 0$, but $f(0) = 2$.

3. False; the existence of $\lim_{x \to 1} f(x)$ only requires that $f(x)$ be defined *near* 1 not *at* 1.

5. True

7. $\lim_{x \to 2} F(x) = 4$

9. $\lim_{x \to 3} f(x)$ does not exist.

11. $\lim_{x \to 1} h(x) = 1$

13. $\lim_{x \to 2} f(x)$ does not exist.

15. $\lim_{x \to -2} g(x)$ does not exist.

17. $\lim_{x \to 2} f(x) = 1.5$

19. $\lim_{x \to 2} f(x) = -1$

21.

x	1.9	1.99	1.999	2.001	2.01	2.1
$k(x)$	9.41	9.9401	9.9940	10.0060	10.0601	10.61

$\lim_{x \to 2} k(x) = 10$

23.

x	.9	.99	.999	1.001	1.01	1.1
$h(x)$	10.5132	100.501	1000.5	−999.5	−99.5012	−9.51191

$\lim_{x \to 1} h(x)$ does not exist.

25.

x	−3.1	−3.01	−3.001	−2.999	−2.99	−2.9
$f(x)$	10.61	10.0601	10.006	9.994	9.9401	9.41

$\lim_{x \to -3} f(x) = 10$

27.

x	4.9	4.99	4.999	5.001	5.01	5.1
$f(x)$	5.8	5.98	5.998	6.002	6.02	6.2

$\lim_{x \to 5} |2x-4| = 6$

29.

x	4.9	4.99	4.999	5.001	5.01	5.1
$f(x)$	6.9	6.99	6.999	7.001	7.01	7.1

$$\lim_{x \to 5} \frac{x^2 - 3x - 10}{x - 5} = 7$$

31.

x	−2.1	−2.01	−2.001	−1.999	−1.99	−1.9
$f(x)$	− 64.1	− 604.01	− 6004.001	5996.001	596.01	56.1

$$\lim_{x \to -2} \frac{x^2 + 2}{x + 2} \text{ does not exist.}$$

33.

x	1.9	1.99	1.999	2.001	2.01	2.1
$f(x)$	2.9	2.99	2.999	3.001	3.01	3.1

$$\lim_{x \to 2} \frac{x^2 - x - 2}{x - 2} = 3$$

35.

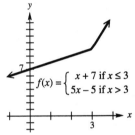

$$f(x) = \begin{cases} x + 7 & \text{if } x \le 3 \\ 5x - 5 & \text{if } x > 3 \end{cases}$$

x	2.9	2.99	2.999	3.001	3.01	3.1
$f(x)$	9.9	9.99	9.999	10.005	10.05	10.5

$$\lim_{x \to 3} f(x) = 10$$

37.

x	.9	.99	.999	1.001	1.01	1.1
$f(x)$	.5132	.5013	.5001	.4999	.4988	.4881

$$\lim_{x \to 1} \frac{\sqrt{x} - 1}{x - 1} = .5$$

39.

x	− .1	− .01	− .001	.001	.01	.1
$f(x)$	.50251	.50003	.5000003	.5000003	.50003	.50251

$$\lim_{x \to 0} \frac{\sin x}{\sin 2x} = .5$$

41.

x	3	3.1	3.14	3.15	3.2	4
$f(x)$	−2.0101087	−2.0008656	−2.0000012	−2.00000353	−2.0017081	−2.5298857

$$\lim_{x \to \pi} \frac{\tan^2 x}{1 + \sec x} = -2$$

43.

x	.9	.99	.999	1.001	1.01	1.1
$f(x)$	1.0536	1.005	1.0005	.9995	.995	.9531

$$\lim_{x \to 1} \frac{\ln x}{x - 1} = 1$$

45.

x	$-.1$	$-.01$	$-.001$	.001	.01	.1
$f(x)$	-1.0517	-1.005	-1.0005	$-.9995$	$-.9950$	$-.9516$

$$\lim_{x \to 0} \frac{e^{-x} - 1}{x} = -1$$

47.

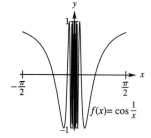

$$\lim_{x \to 0} \cos \frac{1}{x} \text{ does not exist.}$$

Section 11.2

Exercises

1. $\lim_{x \to 4}[f(x) - g(x)] = \lim_{x \to 4} f(x) - \lim_{x \to 4} g(x)$
$$= 16 - 8 = 8$$

3. $\lim_{x \to 4} \dfrac{f(x)}{g(x)} = \dfrac{\lim_{x \to 4} f(x)}{\lim_{x \to 4} g(x)} = \dfrac{16}{8} = 2$

5. $\lim_{x \to 4} \sqrt{f(x)} = \lim_{x \to 4}[f(x)]^{1/2} = \left[\lim_{x \to 4} f(x)\right]^{1/2}$
$$= 16^{1/2} = 4$$

7. $\lim_{x \to 4} 2^{g(x)} = 2^{\lim_{x \to 4} g(x)} = 2^8 = 256$

9. $\lim_{x \to 4} \dfrac{f(x) + g(x)}{2g(x)} = \dfrac{\lim_{x \to 4}[f(x) + g(x)]}{\lim_{x \to 4} 2g(x)}$
$$= \dfrac{\lim_{x \to 4} f(x) + \lim_{x \to 4} g(x)}{\lim_{x \to 4} 2 \cdot \lim_{x \to 4} g(x)}$$
$$= \dfrac{16 + 8}{2 \cdot 8}$$
$$= \dfrac{24}{16}$$
$$= \dfrac{3}{2}$$

11. $\lim_{x \to -3} 7 = 7$

13. $\lim_{x \to \pi} x = \pi$

15. $\lim_{x \to 1}(5x^8 - 3x^2 + 2) = 5(1)^8 - 3(1)^2 + 2$
$$= 5 - 3 + 2$$
$$= 4$$

17. $\displaystyle\lim_{x\to 3}\frac{x^3-1}{x^2+1}=\frac{\displaystyle\lim_{x\to 3}(x^3-1)}{\displaystyle\lim_{x\to 3}(x^2+1)}$

$\displaystyle=\frac{3^3-1}{3^2+1}$

$\displaystyle=\frac{27-1}{9+1}$

$\displaystyle=\frac{26}{10}$

$\displaystyle=\frac{13}{5}$

19. $\displaystyle\lim_{x\to 0}\frac{x^2+2x}{x}=\lim_{x\to 0}\frac{x(x+2)}{x}$

$\displaystyle=\lim_{x\to 0}(x+2)$

$=0+2$

$=2$

21. $\displaystyle\lim_{x\to -2}\frac{x^2-4}{x+2}=\lim_{x\to -2}\frac{(x+2)(x-2)}{x+2}$

$\displaystyle=\lim_{x\to -2}(x-2)$

$=-2-2$

$=-4$

23. $\displaystyle\lim_{x\to 5}\frac{x^2-3x-10}{x-5}=\lim_{x\to 5}\frac{(x-5)(x+2)}{x-5}$

$\displaystyle=\lim_{x\to 5}(x+2)$

$=5+2$

$=7$

25. $\displaystyle\lim_{x\to 5}\frac{x^2-7x+10}{x^2-25}=\lim_{x\to 5}\frac{(x-2)(x-5)}{(x+5)(x-5)}$

$\displaystyle=\lim_{x\to 5}\frac{x-2}{x+5}$

$\displaystyle=\frac{5-2}{5+5}$

$\displaystyle=\frac{3}{10}$

27. $\displaystyle\lim_{x\to -4}(1-6x)^{3/2}=\left[\lim_{x\to -4}(1-6x)\right]^{3/2}$

$=[1-6(-4)]^{3/2}$

$=25^{3/2}$

$=125$

29. $\displaystyle\lim_{x\to 3}5^{\sqrt{x+1}}=5^{\lim_{x\to 3}\sqrt{x+1}}$

$\displaystyle=5^{\lim_{x\to 3}(x+1)^{1/2}}$

$\displaystyle=5^{\left[\lim_{x\to 3}(x+1)\right]^{1/2}}$

$=5^{[3+1]^{1/2}}$

$=5^{4^{1/2}}$

$=5^2$

$=25$

31. $\displaystyle\lim_{x\to 4}[\log_2(14+\sqrt{x})]=\log_2\left[\lim_{x\to 4}\left(14+\sqrt{x}\right)\right]$

$\displaystyle=\log_2\left[\lim_{x\to 4}14+\lim_{x\to 4}\sqrt{x}\right]$

$\displaystyle=\log_2\left[14+\sqrt{\lim_{x\to 4}x}\right]$

$=\log_2[14+\sqrt{4}]$

$=\log_2 16$

$=4$

33. $\displaystyle\lim_{x\to 0}[2^{3x}-\ln(x+1)]=2^{\lim_{x\to 0}3x}-\ln\left[\lim_{x\to 0}(x+1)\right]$

$=2^{3(0)}-\ln(0+1)$

$=2^0-\ln 1$

$=1-0$

$=1$

35. $\displaystyle\lim_{x\to 0}\frac{\sin x-3x}{x}=\lim_{x\to 0}\frac{\sin x}{x}-\lim_{x\to 0}\frac{3x}{x}$

$\displaystyle=1-\lim_{x\to 0}3$

$=1-3$

$=-2$

37. $\displaystyle\lim_{x\to 0}x\cot x=\lim_{x\to 0}\frac{x\cos x}{\sin x}$

$\displaystyle=\lim_{x\to 0}\frac{x}{\sin x}\cdot\lim_{x\to 0}\cos x$

$=1\cdot 1$

$=1$

39. $\displaystyle\lim_{x\to 0}\frac{\cos x-1}{3x}=\lim_{x\to 0}\frac{1}{3}\cdot\lim_{x\to 0}\frac{\cos x-1}{x}$

$\displaystyle=\frac{1}{3}\cdot 0$

$=0$

Section 11.3

Exercises

1. a) $\displaystyle\lim_{x\to2^+} f(x) = \lim_{x\to2^+} 4 = 4$

   b) $\displaystyle\lim_{x\to2^-} f(x) = \lim_{x\to2^-} x = 2$

3. a)

x	3.1	3.01	3.001
$f(x)$	-620	$-602,000$	$-600,200,000$

   $\displaystyle\lim_{x\to3^+} f(x) = \lim_{x\to3^+} \frac{x}{5(3-x)^3} = -\infty$

   b)

x	2.9	2.99	2.999
$f(x)$	580	598,000	599,800,000

   $\displaystyle\lim_{x\to3^-} f(x) = \lim_{x\to3^-} \frac{x}{5(3-x)^3} = \infty$

5. a)

x	$-.9$	$-.99$	$-.999$	$-.9999$
$f(x)$	-90	-9900	$-999,000$	$-99,990,000$

   $\displaystyle\lim_{x\to-1^+} f(x) = \lim_{x\to-1^+} \frac{x}{(x+1)^2} = -\infty$

   b)

x	-1.1	-1.01	-1.001	-1.0001
$f(x)$	-110	$-10,100$	$-1,001,000$	$-100,010,000$

   $\displaystyle\lim_{x\to-1^-} f(x) = \lim_{x\to-1^-} \frac{x}{(x+1)^2} = -\infty$

7. $\displaystyle\lim_{x\to-\infty} \frac{6x^2+1}{2x^2+3} = \lim_{x\to-\infty} \frac{6+\frac{1}{x^2}}{2+\frac{3}{x^2}} = \frac{\displaystyle\lim_{x\to-\infty}\left(6+\frac{1}{x^2}\right)}{\displaystyle\lim_{x\to-\infty}\left(2+\frac{3}{x^2}\right)}$

   $= \dfrac{\displaystyle\lim_{x\to-\infty} 6 + \lim_{x\to-\infty}\frac{1}{x^2}}{\displaystyle\lim_{x\to-\infty} 2 + 3\cdot \lim_{x\to-\infty}\frac{1}{x^2}}$

   $= \dfrac{6+0}{2+0} = \dfrac{6}{2} = 3$

9. The graph indicates that $\displaystyle\lim_{x\to\infty} x\sin x$ does not exist.

11.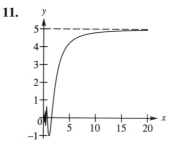

The graph indicates that $\displaystyle\lim_{x\to\infty} x\sin\frac{5}{x} = 5$.

13.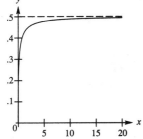

The graph indicates that $\lim_{x \to \infty} \sqrt{x^2 + x} - x = .5$.

15.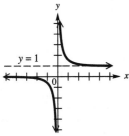

$x = 0, y = 1, y = 0$

17.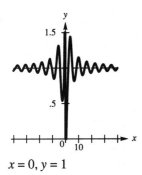

$x = 0, y = 1$

19. a) $\lim_{x \to 1^+} f(x) = \lim_{x \to 1^+} x^2 = 1^2 = 1$

b) $\lim_{x \to 1^-} f(x) = \lim_{x \to 1^-} (2x + 3) = 2(1) + 3 = 5$

21.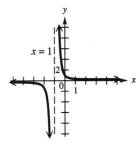

a) $\lim_{x \to -1^+} \dfrac{1}{(1+x)^3} = \infty$

b) $\lim_{x \to -1^+} \dfrac{1}{(1+x)^3} = -\infty$

23.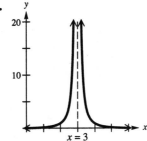

a) $\lim_{x \to 3^+} \dfrac{1}{(x-3)^2} = \infty$

b) $\lim_{x \to 3^-} \dfrac{1}{(x-3)^2} = \infty$

25. $\lim_{x \to \infty} \dfrac{3x}{5x - 1} = \lim_{x \to \infty} \dfrac{3}{5 - \frac{1}{x}}$

$= \dfrac{\lim_{x \to \infty} 3}{\lim_{x \to \infty} 5 - \lim_{x \to \infty} \frac{1}{x}}$

$= \dfrac{3}{5}$

27. $\lim_{x \to -\infty} \dfrac{2x + 3}{4x - 7} = \lim_{x \to -\infty} \dfrac{2 + \frac{3}{x}}{4 - \frac{7}{x}}$

$= \dfrac{\lim_{x \to -\infty} 2 + 3 \lim_{x \to -\infty} \frac{1}{x}}{\lim_{x \to -\infty} 4 - 7 \lim_{x \to -\infty} \frac{1}{x}}$

$= \dfrac{2}{4}$

$= \dfrac{1}{2}$

29. $\lim_{x \to \infty} \dfrac{x^2 + 2x}{2x^3 - 2x + 1} = \lim_{x \to \infty} \dfrac{\frac{1}{x} + \frac{2}{x^2}}{2 - \frac{2}{x^2} + \frac{1}{x^3}}$

$= \dfrac{\lim_{x \to \infty} \frac{1}{x} + 2 \lim_{x \to \infty} \frac{1}{x^2}}{\lim_{x \to \infty} 2 - 2\lim_{x \to \infty} \frac{1}{x^2} + \lim_{x \to \infty} \frac{1}{x^3}}$

$= \dfrac{0}{2}$

$= 0$

31. $\lim\limits_{x \to \infty} \dfrac{3x^3 + 2x - 1}{2x^4 - 3x^3 - 2}$

$= \lim\limits_{x \to \infty} \dfrac{\dfrac{3}{x} + \dfrac{2}{x^3} - \dfrac{1}{x^4}}{2 - \dfrac{3}{x} - \dfrac{2}{x^4}}$

$= \dfrac{3 \lim\limits_{x \to \infty} \dfrac{1}{x} + 2 \lim\limits_{x \to \infty} \dfrac{1}{x^3} - \lim\limits_{x \to \infty} \dfrac{1}{x^4}}{\lim\limits_{x \to \infty} 2 - 3 \lim\limits_{x \to \infty} \dfrac{1}{x} - 2 \lim\limits_{x \to \infty} \dfrac{1}{x^4}}$

$= \dfrac{0}{2}$

$= 0$

33.

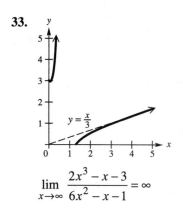

$\lim\limits_{x \to \infty} \dfrac{2x^3 - x - 3}{6x^2 - x - 1} = \infty$

In Exercises 35–41, other correct answers are possible.

35. The function $f(x) = \dfrac{1}{x}$ shifted 5 units to the right,

giving $f(x) = \dfrac{1}{x - 5}$.

37. Any polynomial with a negative leading coefficient has this behavior, for example, $f(x) = -x^3$.

39. Pick $g(x)$ to be any function that satisfies $\lim\limits_{x \to \infty} g(x) = \infty$, and let $f(x) = 2g(x)$, for example, $f(x) = 2x$ and $g(x) = x$.

41. Pick functions $f(x) = \dfrac{1}{x^n}$ and $g(x) = x^m$ such

that $m > n$, for example, $f(x) = \dfrac{1}{x}$, $g(x) = x^2$.

43. $\lim\limits_{x \to \infty} \left(\dfrac{1}{2}x + 3 \right) = \infty$, so, $\lim\limits_{x \to \infty} f(x) = \infty$.

45. (a)

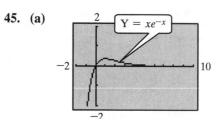

$\lim\limits_{x \to \infty} xe^{-x} = 0$

x	5	10	15
y	.03368974	.000454	.00000459

(b)

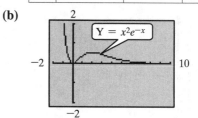

$\lim\limits_{x \to \infty} x^2 e^{-x} = 0$

x	5	10	15
y	.16844868	.00453999	.00006883

(c) For any positive integer n, $\lim\limits_{x \to \infty} x^n e^{-x} = 0$.

47. $\lim\limits_{t \to \infty} [176(1 - e^{-.2t})] = \lim\limits_{t \to \infty} [176 - 176e^{-.2t}]$

$\qquad = \lim\limits_{t \to \infty} 176 - 176 \lim\limits_{t \to \infty} e^{-.2t}$

$\qquad = 176 - 0$

$\qquad = 176$

The terminal speed of the skydiver is 176 feet per second.

49. $\lim\limits_{t \to \infty} [12 - 4e^{-.5t}] = \lim\limits_{t \to \infty} 12 - 4 \lim\limits_{t \to \infty} e^{-.5t}$

$\qquad = 12 - 0$

$\qquad = 12$

In the long run, the price will level off near $12.

Section 11.4

Exercises

1. The tangent line passes through the point (5, 3) and appears to pass through (6, 5). Thus, a reasonable estimate of the slope of the tangent line is $m = \dfrac{5-3}{6-5} = \dfrac{2}{1} = 2$.

3. The tangent line passes through the point (−2, 2) and appears to pass through (3, 3). Thus, a reasonable estimate of the slope of the tangent line is $m = \dfrac{3-2}{3-(-2)} = \dfrac{1}{5}$.

5. $\begin{aligned} m &= \lim_{x\to 4} \frac{f(x)-f(4)}{x-4} = \lim_{x\to 4} \frac{x^2-4^2}{x-4} \\ &= \lim_{x\to 4} \frac{(x+4)(x-4)}{x-4} \\ &= \lim_{x\to 4} (x+4) \\ &= 4+4 \\ &= 8 \end{aligned}$

7. $\begin{aligned} m &= \lim_{x\to -2} \frac{f(x)-f(-2)}{x-(-2)} \\ &= \lim_{x\to -2} \frac{[-4x^2+11x]-[-4(-2)^2+11(-2)]}{x+2} \\ &= \lim_{x\to -2} \frac{-4x^2+11x+38}{x+2} \\ &= \lim_{x\to -2} \frac{(x+2)(-4x+19)}{x+2} \\ &= \lim_{x\to -2} (-4x+19) = -4(-2)+19 = 27 \end{aligned}$

9. $\begin{aligned} m &= \lim_{x\to 4} \frac{f(x)-f(4)}{x-4} = \lim_{x\to 4} \frac{\left[-\frac{2}{x}\right]-\left[-\frac{2}{4}\right]}{x-4} \\ &= \lim_{x\to 4} \frac{\frac{-4+x}{2x}}{x-4} \\ &= \lim_{x\to 4} \frac{1}{2x} \\ &= \frac{1}{2(4)} \\ &= \frac{1}{8} \end{aligned}$

11. $\begin{aligned} m &= \lim_{x\to 1} \frac{f(x)-f(1)}{x-1} = \lim_{x\to 1} \frac{[-3\sqrt{x}]-[-3\sqrt{1}]}{x-1} \\ &= \lim_{x\to 1} \frac{-3\sqrt{x}+3}{x-1} \\ &= \lim_{x\to 1} \frac{-3(\sqrt{x}-1)}{(\sqrt{x}+1)(\sqrt{x}-1)} \\ &= \lim_{x\to 1} \frac{-3}{\sqrt{x}+1} \\ &= \frac{-3}{\sqrt{1}+1} \\ &= -\frac{3}{2} \end{aligned}$

13. $f(3) = (3)^2 + 2(3) = 15$, so (3, 15) is a point on the tangent line. The slope of the tangent line is

$\begin{aligned} m &= \lim_{x\to 3} \frac{f(x)-f(3)}{x-3} = \lim_{x\to 3} \frac{x^2+2x-15}{x-3} \\ &= \lim_{x\to 3} (x+5) \\ &= 8. \end{aligned}$

The equation of the tangent line is
$y - y_1 = m(x - x_1)$
$y - 15 = 8(x - 3)$
$\quad y = 8x - 9.$

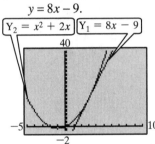

15. $f(2) = \dfrac{5}{2}$, so $\left(2, \dfrac{5}{2}\right)$ is a point on the tangent line. The slope of the tangent line is

$\begin{aligned} m &= \lim_{x\to 2} \frac{f(x)-f(2)}{x-2} = \lim_{x\to 2} \frac{\frac{5}{x}-\frac{5}{2}}{x-2} \\ &= \lim_{x\to 2} \frac{\frac{10-5x}{2x}}{x-2} \\ &= \lim_{x\to 2} \frac{\frac{5(2-x)}{2x}}{x-2} \\ &= \lim_{x\to 2} \left(-\frac{5}{2x}\right) \\ &= -\frac{5}{4}. \end{aligned}$

The equation of the tangent line is
$$y - y_1 = m(x - x_1)$$
$$y - \frac{5}{2} = -\frac{5}{4}(x - 2)$$
$$y = -\frac{5}{4}x + 5.$$

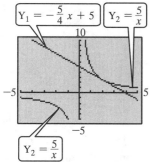

17. $f(9) = 4\sqrt{9} = 12$, so $(9, 12)$ is a point on the tangent line. The slope of the tangent line is

$$m = \lim_{x \to 9} \frac{f(x) - f(9)}{x - 9} = \lim_{x \to 9} \frac{4\sqrt{x} - 12}{x - 9}$$

$$= \lim_{x \to 9} \frac{4(\sqrt{x} - 3)}{(\sqrt{x} + 3)(\sqrt{x} - 3)}$$

$$= \lim_{x \to 9} \frac{4}{\sqrt{x} + 3}$$

$$= \frac{4}{\sqrt{9} + 3}$$

$$= \frac{2}{3}.$$

The equation of the tangent line is
$$y - y_1 = m(x - x_1)$$
$$y - 12 = \frac{2}{3}(x - 9)$$
$$y = \frac{2}{3}x + 6.$$

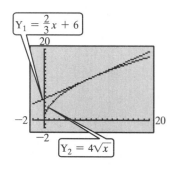

In Exercises 19 and 21, each function $f(x)$ is linear. Since $f'(2)$ represents the *slope* of the curve $y = f(x)$ at $x = 2$, $f'(2)$ is the slope of the line.

19.

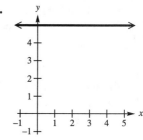

$f'(2) = 0$

21.

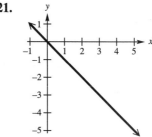

$f'(2) = -1$

23.

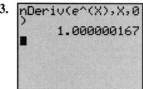

A reasonable estimate of $f'(0)$ is 1.

25.

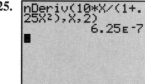

A reasonable estimate of $f'(2)$ is 0.

27.

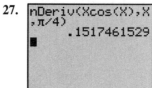

A reasonable estimate of $f'\left(\dfrac{\pi}{4}\right)$ is .1517.

29. $f'(0) =$ the slope of the tangent line $= \dfrac{1}{3}$.

31. Since $(a, f(a))$ is a point common to all three secant lines, we can find its coordinates by finding the intersection point of any two of the three lines. Using the first two lines listed and substitution, we have
$$2.03x - .53 = 2.02x - .52$$
$$.01x = .01$$
$$x = 1$$

$$y = 2.03(1) - .53 = 1.5.$$

Thus, $a = 1$ and $f(a) = 1.5$.
Based on the trend in the slopes of the secant lines, a reasonable estimate of $f'(a)$ is 2. [Note: The graph is not drawn to scale.]

33. The tangent line appears to pass through the points $(7, 6)$ and $(13, 11)$. Thus, its slope is
$$f'(10) = \frac{11 - 6}{13 - 7} = \frac{5}{6}.$$
On January 1, 1989, the interest rate was rising at a rate of $\frac{5}{6}\%$ per year.

35.
$$W'(4) = \lim_{t \to 4} \frac{W(t) - W(4)}{t - 4}$$
$$= \lim_{t \to 4} \frac{.1t^2 - .1(4)^2}{t - 4}$$
$$= \lim_{t \to 4} \frac{.1(t^2 - 16)}{t - 4}$$
$$= \lim_{t \to 4} \frac{.1(t + 4)(t - 4)}{t - 4}$$
$$= \lim_{t \to 4} .1(t + 4) = .1(4 + 4) = .8$$
At time $t = 4$, the tumor is growing at a rate of .8 gram per week.

37. a) When the helicopter is at a height of 20 feet, $s(t) = 20$. Thus, by substitution,
$$20 = t^2 + t$$
$$0 = t^2 + t - 20$$
$$0 = (t + 5)(t - 4)$$
$$t = -5 \text{ or } t = 4.$$
Since a negative number is not a valid time in this application, $t = 4$. It will take 4 seconds for the helicopter to rise 20 feet.

b) The vertical velocity of the helicopter when it is 20 feet above the ground is $s'(t)$ when $t = 4$.
$$s'(4) = \lim_{t \to 4} \frac{s(t) - s(4)}{t - 4}$$
$$= \lim_{t \to 4} \frac{[t^2 + t] - [4^2 + 4]}{t - 4}$$
$$= \lim_{t \to 4} \frac{t^2 + t - 20}{t - 4}$$
$$= \lim_{t \to 4} (t + 5)$$
$$= 9$$
When the helicopter is 20 feet above the ground, it is rising at a rate of 9 feet per second.

39. The marginal profit at $x = 1000$ is given by $R'(1000)$
$$= \lim_{x \to 1000} \frac{R(x) - R(1000)}{x - 1000}$$
$$= \lim_{x \to 1000} \frac{[10x - .002x^2] - [10(1000) - .002(1000)^2]}{x - 1000}$$
$$= \lim_{x \to 1000} \frac{.002x^2 + 10x - 8000}{x - 1000}$$
$$= \lim_{x \to 1000} \frac{(-.002x + 8)(x - 1000)}{x - 1000}$$
$$= \lim_{x \to 1000} (-.002x + 8)$$
$$= 6.$$
When 1000 units are produced, the marginal revenue is $6000 per unit.

41.

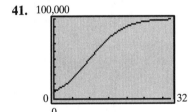

After 8 days, the rumor is spreading at a rate of about 5332 people per day.
From the calculator, $f'(8) \approx 5332$ people per day.

43. We can use the equation of the tangent line to find the value $f(x)$ of the Dow Jones average in 1981 $(x = 11)$, since their graphs intersect at that point. Thus, $f(11) = 35(11) + 615 = 1000$. At the beginning of 1981, the Dow Jones average was 1000 points. The slope of the tangent line represents the rate of change of the Dow Jones average at $x = 11$. Thus, in 1981, the Dow Jones average was rising at a rate of 35 points per year.

44. (a) The monthly payment on a 30-year mortgage of $100,000 at 8% interest is

$$f(8) = \frac{100,000\left(\frac{8}{1200}\right)\left(1+\frac{8}{1200}\right)^{360}}{\left(1+\frac{8}{1200}\right)^{360}-1}$$

$$\approx \$733.76.$$

(b)

From the calculator, $f'(8) \approx \$69.71$ per percent change in interest rate. This is the marginal monthly mortgage payment per percent change in interest rate.

(c) We want the equation of the line passing through the point $(8, 733.36)$ with slope $m = 69.71$.

$$y - 733.36 = 69.71(x - 8)$$
$$y = 69.71x + 176.08$$

(d) (i) If the interest rate rises to 8.25%, your new monthly payment will be about

$y = 69.71(8.25) + 176.08 = \$751.19.$ This is an increase of

$\$751.19 - \$733.76 = \$17.43.$

(ii) If the interest rate falls to 7.5%, your new monthly payment will be about

$y = 69.71(7.5) + 176.08 = \$698.91.$ This is a decrease of $\$733.76 - \$698.91 = \$34.85.$

Chapter 11 Review Exercises

1. (a) $\lim_{x \to 1^-} f(x) = 2$

(b) $\lim_{x \to 1^+} f(x) = 2$

(c) $\lim_{x \to 1} f(x) = 2$

3. (a) $\lim_{x \to 4^-} f(x) = \infty$

(b) $\lim_{x \to 4^+} f(x) = -\infty$

(c) $\lim_{x \to 4} f(x)$ does not exist.

5. $\lim_{x \to 1}(2x^2 - 3x) = 2(1)^2 - 3(1) = -1$

7. $\lim_{x \to 2} \dfrac{3x+4}{x+3} = \dfrac{3(2)+4}{2+3} = \dfrac{10}{5} = 2$

9. $\lim_{x \to -1} \sqrt{5x+21} = \sqrt{5(-1)+21} = 4$

11. $\lim_{x \to 1}[\log_2(5x+3)] = \log_2[5(1)+3]$
$$= \log_2 8$$
$$= 3$$

13. $\lim_{x \to 5} \dfrac{2x-10}{5-x} = \lim_{x \to 5} \dfrac{2(x-5)}{5-x}$
$$= \lim_{x \to 5}(-2)$$
$$= -2$$

15. $\lim_{x \to -3} \dfrac{x^2+2x-3}{x+3} = \lim_{x \to -3} \dfrac{(x+3)(x-1)}{x+3}$
$$= \lim_{x \to -3}(x-1)$$
$$= -3-1$$
$$= -4$$

17. $\lim_{x \to 2} \dfrac{x^2-x-2}{x^2-5x+6} = \lim_{x \to 2} \dfrac{(x-2)(x+1)}{(x-2)(x-3)}$
$$= \lim_{x \to 2} \dfrac{x+1}{x-3}$$
$$= \dfrac{2+1}{2-3}$$
$$= -3$$

19.

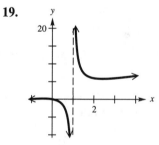

$\lim_{x \to 1} \dfrac{x^2+x}{x-1}$ does not exist.

21. $\lim_{x \to 0} \dfrac{\sin x}{3x} = \dfrac{\lim_{x \to 0} \dfrac{\sin x}{x}}{\lim_{x \to 0} 3} = \dfrac{1}{3}$

23.

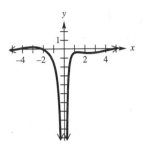

$$\lim_{x\to 0}\frac{x\cos x-1}{x^2}=-\infty$$

25. $\lim_{x\to 2^-}f(x)=\lim_{x\to 2^-}(3x-1)=3(2)-1=5$
$\lim_{x\to 2^+}f(x)=\lim_{x\to 2^+}(x+3)=2+3=5$
Therefore, $\lim_{x\to 2}f(x)=5.$

27. $\lim_{x\to 2^-}f(x)=\lim_{x\to 2^-}(x^2-1)=(2)^2-1=3$

29.

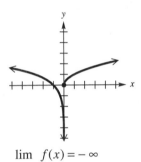

$$\lim_{x\to 0^-}f(x)=-\infty$$

31.

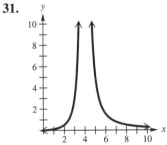

(a) $\lim_{x\to 4^+}\dfrac{x}{(x-4)^2}=\infty$

(b) $\lim_{x\to 4^-}\dfrac{x}{(x-4)^2}=\infty$

33. $\lim_{x\to\infty}\dfrac{5x+1}{2x-7}=\lim_{x\to\infty}\dfrac{5+\frac{1}{x}}{2-\frac{7}{x}}=\dfrac{5}{2}$

35.

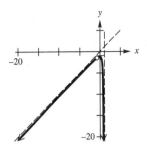

$$\lim_{x\to-\infty}\frac{x^3+1}{x^2-1}=-\infty$$

37. $\lim_{x\to\infty}\left(5+\dfrac{x}{1+x^2}\right)=\lim_{x\to\infty}5+\lim_{x\to\infty}\dfrac{x}{1+x^2}$

$$=5+\lim_{x\to\infty}\frac{\frac{1}{x}}{\frac{1}{x^2}+1}$$

$$=5+\frac{0}{1}$$

$$=5$$

39.

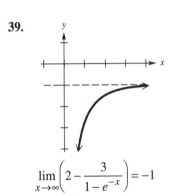

$$\lim_{x\to\infty}\left(2-\frac{3}{1-e^{-x}}\right)=-1$$

In Exercise 41, other correct answers are possible.

41. $f(x)=\dfrac{1}{x-2},\ g(x)=\dfrac{-1}{x-2}$

43.

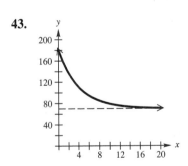

$$\lim_{t\to\infty}(70+110e^{-.25t})=70$$

The coffee cools to $70°$ F.

45. The slope of the tangent line is

$$m = \lim_{x \to 1} \frac{f(x) - f(1)}{x - 1} = \lim_{x \to 1} \frac{\frac{3}{x} - \frac{3}{1}}{x - 1}$$

$$= \lim_{x \to 1} \frac{\frac{3 - 3x}{x}}{x - 1}$$

$$= \lim_{x \to 1} \frac{\frac{-3(x-1)}{x}}{x - 1}$$

$$= \lim_{x \to 1} \frac{-3}{x}$$

$$= -\frac{3}{1}$$

$$= -3.$$

47. The value of $f(x)$ at $x = 2$ is $f(2) = 2^2 - 2 = 2$.
Thus, the tangent line passes through the point $(2, 2)$. Furthermore, the slope of the tangent line is

$$m = \lim_{x \to 2} \frac{f(x) - f(2)}{x - 2}$$

$$= \lim_{x \to 2} \frac{x^2 - x - 2}{x - 2}$$

$$= \lim_{x \to 2} \frac{(x - 2)(x + 1)}{x - 2}$$

$$= \lim_{x \to 2} (x + 1)$$

$$= 2 + 1$$

$$= 3.$$

Therefore, the equation of the tangent line is

$$y - y_1 = m(x - x_1)$$
$$y - 2 = 3(x - 2)$$
$$y = 3x - 4.$$

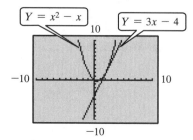

49. Since $f'\left(\dfrac{\pi}{2}\right)$ is the slope of the tangent line to the graph of $f(x) = \sin x$ at the point $\left(\dfrac{\pi}{2},\ 1\right)$ and the tangent line is horizontal (slope = 0), $f'\left(\dfrac{\pi}{2}\right) = 0$.

51. `nDeriv(e^(X),X,0`
`)`
`       1.000000167`

A reasonable estimate of $f'(0)$ is 1.

53. The equation for the height of the ball after t seconds is $s(t) = -16t^2 + 100t + 4$.
The velocity of the ball after 3 seconds is $s'(3)$

$$= \lim_{t \to 3} \frac{s(t) - s(3)}{t - 3}$$

$$= \lim_{t \to 3} \frac{[-16t^2 + 100t + 4] - [-16(3)^2 + 100(3) + 4]}{t - 3}$$

$$= \lim_{t \to 3} \frac{-16t^2 + 100t - 156}{t - 3}$$

$$= \lim_{t \to 3} \frac{(-16t + 52)(t - 3)}{t - 3}$$

$$= \lim_{t \to 3} (-16t + 52)$$

$$= -16(3) + 52$$

$$= 4.$$

After 3 seconds, the ball is moving upward at a rate of 4 feet per second.

Chapter 11 Test Exercises

1. $\displaystyle \lim_{x \to 4^-} f(x) = 5$

2. $\displaystyle \lim_{x \to \infty} f(x) = 0$

3. (a) $\displaystyle \lim_{x \to 3^+} f(x) = \infty$

   (b) $\displaystyle \lim_{x \to 3^-} f(x) = 4$

4. $\displaystyle \lim_{x \to 1} \frac{x^2 + x + 1}{x^2 + 1} = \frac{1^2 + 1 + 1}{1^2 + 1} = \frac{3}{2}$

5. $\displaystyle \lim_{x \to -2} \frac{x^2 + 2x}{x + 2} = \lim_{x \to -2} \frac{x(x + 2)}{x + 2} = \lim_{x \to -2} x = -2$

6. $\displaystyle \lim_{x \to 3} \frac{x^2 - 6x + 9}{x - 3} = \lim_{x \to 3} \frac{(x - 3)^2}{x - 3}$

$$= \lim_{x \to 3} (x - 3)$$
$$= 3 - 3$$
$$= 0$$

7. $\lim\limits_{x\to 2}\dfrac{x^2+x-6}{x^2-4}=\lim\limits_{x\to 2}\dfrac{(x+3)(x-2)}{(x+2)(x-2)}$

$=\lim\limits_{x\to 2}\dfrac{x+3}{x+2}$

$=\dfrac{2+3}{2+2}$

$=\dfrac{5}{4}$

8. $\lim\limits_{x\to -1}\dfrac{x^2+3x+2}{x^2+x}=\lim\limits_{x\to -1}\dfrac{(x+1)(x+2)}{x(x+1)}$

$=\lim\limits_{x\to -1}\dfrac{x+2}{x}$

$=\dfrac{-1+2}{-1}$

$=-1$

9. $\lim\limits_{x\to 3}\sqrt{x^2+7}=\sqrt{(3)^2+7}=4$

10. $\lim\limits_{x\to \infty}\dfrac{2x^2-3}{5x^2+x+1}=\lim\limits_{x\to \infty}\dfrac{2-\frac{3}{x^2}}{5+\frac{1}{x}+\frac{1}{x^2}}$

$=\dfrac{2-0}{5+0+0}$

$=\dfrac{2}{5}$

11. $\lim\limits_{x\to -\infty}\dfrac{3x-4}{4x-3}=\lim\limits_{x\to -\infty}\dfrac{3-\frac{4}{x}}{4-\frac{3}{x}}=\dfrac{3-0}{4-0}=\dfrac{3}{4}$

12. $\lim\limits_{x\to 0}\dfrac{\sin x}{x\cos x}=\dfrac{\lim\limits_{x\to 0}\frac{\sin x}{x}}{\lim\limits_{x\to 0}\cos x}=\dfrac{1}{1}=1$

13. $\lim\limits_{x\to 0}\dfrac{x^2-10}{x^3+1}=\dfrac{0^2-10}{0^3+1}=-10$

14. $\lim\limits_{x\to 1^+}f(x)=\lim\limits_{x\to 1^+}(1-2x^2)=1-2(1)^2=-1$

15. The slope of the tangent line is

$m=\lim\limits_{x\to 1}\dfrac{f(x)-f(1)}{x-1}=\lim\limits_{x\to 1}\dfrac{[2x^2-1]-[2(1)^2-1]}{x-1}$

$=\lim\limits_{x\to 1}\dfrac{2x^2-2}{x-1}$

$=\lim\limits_{x\to 1}\dfrac{2(x+1)(x-1)}{x-1}$

$=\lim\limits_{x\to 1}2(x+1)$

$=2(1+1)$

$=4.$

16. The tangent line passes through the point $(1,-3)$ and has slope

$m=\lim\limits_{x\to 1}\dfrac{f(x)-f(1)}{x-1}=\lim\limits_{x\to 1}\dfrac{\frac{-3}{x}-(-3)}{x-1}$

$=\lim\limits_{x\to 1}\dfrac{\frac{3x-3}{x}}{x-1}$

$=\lim\limits_{x\to 1}\dfrac{\frac{3(x-1)}{x}}{x-1}$

$=\lim\limits_{x\to 1}\dfrac{3}{x}$

$=\dfrac{3}{1}$

$=3.$

Thus, the equation of the tangent line is

$y-y_1=m(x-x_1)$

$y-(-3)=3(x-1)$

$y=3x-6.$

17.
```
nDeriv((1+e^(X))
/X,X,4)
        10.17465434
```

A reasonable estimate of $f'(4)$ is 10.1747.

18. The tangent line appears to pass through the points $(6, 1.6)$ and $(22, 0)$. Thus, the slope of the tangent line is $m=\dfrac{0-1.6}{22-6}=-\dfrac{1}{10}$.

After 14 years, the cobalt is disintegrating at a rate of $\dfrac{1}{10}$ gram per year.

19. When 1800 units are produced, the marginal revenue is

$R'(1800)$

$=\lim\limits_{x\to 1800}\dfrac{R(x)-R(1800)}{x-1800}$

$=\lim\limits_{x\to 1800}\dfrac{[-.0012x^2+3x]-[-.0012(1800)^2+3(1800)]}{x-1800}$

$=\lim\limits_{x\to 1800}\dfrac{-.0012x^2+3x-1512}{x-1800}$

$=\lim\limits_{x\to 1800}\dfrac{(-.0012x+.84)(x-1800)}{x-1800}$

$=\lim\limits_{x\to 1800}(-.0012x+.84)$

$=-.0012(1800)+.84$

$=\$-1.32$ per unit.

20.

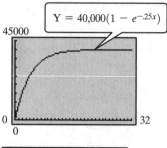

$$Y = 40{,}000(1 - e^{-.25x})$$

```
nDeriv(40000(1-e
^(-.25X)),X,3)
       4723.665577
```

$f'(3) \approx 4723.67$

After 3 days the information is spreading at the
rate of about 4724 people per day.

**CHAPTER R REFERENCE: ALGEBRAIC
EXPRESSIONS**

Section R.1

Exercises

3. $(2^2)^5 = 2^{2 \cdot 5}$ Power rule
$\qquad = 2^{10}$

5. $(2x^5 y^4)^3$
$\quad = 2^3 (x^5)^3 (y^4)^3$ Power rule
$\quad = 2^3 x^{5 \cdot 3} y^{4 \cdot 3}$ Power rule
$\quad = 2^3 x^{15} y^{12}$
$\quad = 8 x^{15} y^{12}$

7. $-\left(\dfrac{p^4}{q}\right)^2 = -\dfrac{(p^4)^2}{q^2}$ Power rule
$\qquad\qquad = -\dfrac{p^{4 \cdot 2}}{q^2}$ Power rule
$\qquad\qquad = -\dfrac{p^8}{q^2}$

9. $-5x^{11}$ is a polynomial. It is a monomial since it has one term. It has degree 11 since 11 is the highest exponent.

11. $18p^5 q + 6pq$ is a polynomial. It is a binomial since it has two terms. It has degree 6 because 6 is the sum of the exponents in the term $18p^5 q$, and this term has a higher degree than the term $6pq$.

13. $\sqrt{2}x^2 + \sqrt{3}x^6$ is a polynomial. It is a binomial since it has two terms. It has degree 6 since 6 is the highest exponent.

15. $\dfrac{1}{3}r^2 s^2 - \dfrac{3}{5}r^4 s^2 + rs^3$ is a polynomial. It is a trinomial since it has three terms. It has degree 6 because the sum of the exponents in the term $-\dfrac{3}{5}r^4 s^2$ is 6, and this term has the highest degree.

17. $\dfrac{5}{p} + \dfrac{2}{p^2} + \dfrac{5}{p^3}$ is not a polynomial since positive exponents in the denominator are equivalent to negative exponents in the numerator.

19. $(3x^2 - 4x + 5) + (-2x^2 + 3x - 2)$
$= (3x^2 - 2x^2) + (-4x + 3x) + (5 - 2)$
Remove parentheses and group like terms.
$= x^2 - x + 3$ Combine like terms.

21. $(12y^2 - 8y + 6) - (3y^2 - 4y + 2)$
$= 12y^2 - 8y + 6 - 3y^2 + 4y - 2$
Remove parentheses.
$= (12y^2 - 3y^2) + (4y - 8y) + (6 - 2)$
Group like terms.
$= 9y^2 - 4y + 4$
Combine like terms.

23. $(6m^4 - 3m^2 + m) - (2m^3 + 5m^2 + 4m)$
$\quad + (m^2 - m)$
$= (6m^4 - 3m^2 + m) + (-2m^3 - 5m^2 - 4m)$
$\quad + (m^2 - m)$
$= 6m^4 - 2m^3 - 3m^2 - 5m^2 + m^2$
$\quad + m - 4m - m$
$= 6m^4 - 2m^3 + (-3 - 5 + 1)m^2$
$\quad + (1 - 4 - 1)m$
$= 6m^4 - 2m^3 - 7m^2 - 4m$

25. $(4r - 1)(7r + 2)$
$= 4r(7r) + 4r(2) - 1(7r) - 1(2)$ FOIL
$= 28r^2 + 8r - 7r - 2$
$= 28r^2 + r - 2$ Combine like terms.

27. $\left(3x - \dfrac{2}{3}\right)\left(5x + \dfrac{1}{3}\right)$
$= 3x(5x) + 3x\left(\dfrac{1}{3}\right) + \left(-\dfrac{2}{3}\right)(5x) + \left(-\dfrac{2}{3}\right)\left(\dfrac{1}{3}\right)$
$= 15x^2 + \dfrac{3}{3}x - \dfrac{10}{3}x - \dfrac{2}{9}$
$= 15x^2 - \dfrac{7}{3}x - \dfrac{2}{9}$

29. $4x^2(3x^3 + 2x^2 - 5x + 1)$
$= (4x^2)(3x^3) + (4x^2)(2x^2) - (4x^2)(5x)$
$\quad + (4x^2)(1)$
Distributive property
$= 12x^5 + 8x^4 - 20x^3 + 4x^2$

31. $(2z-1)(-z^2+3z-4)$

$= 2z(-z^2+3z-4)-1(-z^2+3z-4)$
Distributive property

$= -2z^3+6z^2-8z+z^2-3z+4$

$= -2z^3+(6z^2+z^2)+(-8z-3z)+4$

$= -2z^3+7z^2-11z+4$

We may also multiply vertically.

$$
\begin{array}{r}
-z^2+3z-4 \\
2z-1 \\
\hline
z^2-3z+4 \\
-2z^3+6z^2-8z \\
\hline
-2z^3+7z^2-11z+4
\end{array}
$$

33. $(m-n+k)(m+2n-3k)$

$= m(m+2n-3k)-n(m+2n-3k)$
$\quad +k(m+2n-3k)$
Distributive property

$= m^2+2mn-3km-mn-2n^2+3kn$
$\quad +km+2kn-3k^2$
Distributive property

$= m^2+(2mn-mn)-2n^2+(-3km+km)$
$\quad +(3kn+2kn)-3k^2$

$= m^2+mn-2n^2-2km+5kn-3k^2$

35. $(2m+3)(2m-3)$

$= (2m)^2-3^2$ Product of sum and difference

$= 4m^2-9$

37. $(4m+2n)^2$

$= (4m)^2+2(4m)(2n)+(2n)^2$
Square of a binomial

$= 16m^2+16mn+4n^2$

39. $(5r+3t^2)^2$

$= (5r)^2+2(5r)(3t^2)+(3t^2)^2$
Square of a binomial

$= 25r^2+30rt^2+9t^4$

41. $[(2p-3)+q]^2$

$= (2p-3)^2+2(2p-3)(q)+q^2$
Square of a binomial, treating
$(2p-3)$ as one term

$= (2p)^2-2(2p)(3)+3^2+2(2p-3)q+q^2$
Square the binomial $(2p-3)$

$= 4p^2-12p+9+4pq-6q+q^2$

43. $[(3q+5)-p][(3q+5)+p]$

$= (3q+5)^2-p^2$
Difference of two squares

$= [(3q)^2+2(3q)(5)+5^2]-p^2$
Square of a binomial

$= 9q^2+30q+25-p^2$

45. $[(3a+b)-1]^2$

$= (3a+b)^2-2(3a+b)(1)+1^2$
Square of a binomial

$= (9a^2+6ab+b^2)-2(3a+b)+1$
Square of a binomial

$= 9a^2+6ab+b^2-6a-2b+1$
Distributive property

47. $(p^3-4p^2+p)-(3p^2+2p+7)$

$= p^3-4p^2+p-3p^2-2p-7$

$= p^3-7p^2-p-7$

49. $(7m+2n)(7m-2n)$

$= (7m)^2-(2n)^2$ Difference of two squares

$= 49m^2-4n^2$

51. $-3(4q^2-3q+2)+2(-q^2+q-4)$

$= -12q^2+9q-6-2q^2+2q-8$
Distributive property

$= (-12q^2-2q^2)+(9q+2q)+(-6-8)$
Group like terms

$= -14q^2+11q-14$ Combine like terms

53. $p(4p-6)+2(3p-8)$

$= 4p^2-6p+6p-16$
Distributive property

$= 4p^2-16$ Combine like terms

55. $-y(y^2-4)+6y^2(2y-3)$

$= -y^3+4y+12y^3-18y^2$
Distributive property

$= (-y^3+12y^3)-18y^2+4y$
Group like terms

$= 11y^3-18y^2+4y$
Group like terms

1. **(a)** Since $(x + 5y)^2 = x^2 + 10xy + 25y^2$,
 a matches B.

 (b) Since $(x - 5y)^2 = x^2 - 10xy + 25y^2$,
 b matches C.

 (c) Since $(x + 5y)(x - 5y) = x^2 - 25y^2$,
 c matches A.

 (d) Since $(5y + x)(5y - x) = 25y^2 - x^2$,
 d matches D.

3. $4k^2 m^3 + 8k^4 m^3 - 12k^2 m^4$

 The greatest common factor is $4k^2 m^3$.
$$4k^2 m^3 + 8k^4 m^3 - 12k^2 m^4$$
$$= 4k^2 m^3 (1) + 4k^2 m^3 (2k^2) + 4k^2 m^3 (-3m)$$
$$= 4k^2 m^3 (1 + 2k^2 - 3m)$$

5. $2(a + b) + 4m(a + b) = 2(a + b)(1 + 2m)$
 $2(a + b)$ is the greatest common factor.

7. $(5r - 6)(r + 3) - (2r - 1)(r + 3)$
$$= (r + 3)[(5r - 6) - (2r - 1)]$$
    $r + 3$ is a common factor.
$$= (r + 3)[5r - 6 - 2r + 1]$$
$$= (r + 3)(3r - 5)$$

9. $2(m - 1) - 3(m - 1)^2 + 2(m - 1)^3$
$$= (m - 1)[2 - 3(m - 1) + 2(m - 1)^2]$$
    $m - 1$ is a common factor.
$$= (m - 1)[2 - 3m + 3] + 2(m^2 - 2m + 1)$$
$$= (m - 1)(2 - 3m + 3 + 2m^2 - 4m + 2)$$
$$= (m - 1)(2m^2 - 7m + 7)$$

11. $6st + 9t - 10s - 15$
$$= (6st + 9t) + (-10s - 15) \quad \text{Group the terms.}$$
$$= 3t(2s + 3) - 5(2s + 3) \quad \text{Factor each group.}$$
$$= (2s + 3)(3t - 5) \quad \text{Factor out } 2s + 3.$$

13. $2m^4 + 6 - am^4 - 3a$
$$= (2m^4 + 6) + (-am^4 - 3a) \quad \text{Group the terms.}$$
$$= 2(m^4 + 3) - a(m^4 + 3) \quad \text{Factor each group.}$$
$$= (m^4 + 3)(2 - a) \quad \text{Factor out } m^4 + 3.$$

15. $20z^2 + 18z^2 - 8zx - 45zx$
 Rearrange the terms in order to factor by grouping.
$$20z^2 - 8zx - 45zx + 18x^2$$
$$= (20z^2 - 8zx) + (-45zx + 18x^2)$$
    Group the terms.
$$= 4z(5z - 2x) - 9x(5z - 2x)$$
    Factor each group.
$$= (5z - 2x)(4z - 9x)$$
    Factor out $5z - 2x$.

17. $6a^2 - 48a - 120 = 6(a^2 - 8a - 20)$
 Factor out the greatest common factor, 6.
 To factor $a^2 - 8a - 20$, we look for two numbers whose sum is -8 and whose product is -20.
 2 and -10 are such numbers.
 Thus,
$$6a^2 - 48a - 120 = 6(a^2 - 8a - 20)$$
$$= 6(a - 10)(a + 2).$$

19. $3m^2 + 12m^2 + 9m = 3m(m^2 + 4m + 3)$
 Factor out the greatest common factor, $3m$.
 To factor $m^2 + 4m + 3$, look for two numbers whose sum is 4 and whose product is 3. 1 and 3 are such numbers.
 Thus,
$$3m(m^2 + 4m + 3) = 3m(m^2 + 4m + 3)$$
$$= 3m(m + 1)(m + 3).$$

21. $6k^2 + 5kp - 6p^2$
 The positive factors of 6 could be 2 and 3, or 1 and 6. As factors of -6, we could have -1 and 6, -6 and 1, -2 and 3, or -3 and 2. Try different combinations of these factors until the correct one is found.
$$6k^2 + 5kp - 6p^2 = (2k + 3p)(3k - 2p)$$

23. $5a^2 - 7ab - 6b^2$
 The positive factors of 5 can only be 1 and 5. As factors of -6, we could have -1 and 6, -6 and 1, -2 and 3, or -3 and 2. Try different combinations of these factors until the correct one is found.
$$5a^2 - 7ab - 6b^2 = (5a + 3b)(a - 2b)$$

25. $9x^2 - 6x^3 + x^4$
$$= x^2(9 - 6x + x^2)$$
    x^2 is the greatest common factor.
$$= x^2(3 - x)^2$$
    Perfect square trinomial

27. $24a^4 + 10a^3b - 4a^2b^2$

First, factor out the greatest common factor, $2a^2$.
$24a^4 + 10a^3b - 4a^2b^2 = 2a^2(12a^2 + 5ab - 2b^2)$
Now factor the trinomial by trial and error.
$12a^2 + 5ab - 2b^2 = (4a - b)(3a + 2b)$
Thus,
$$24a^4 + 10a^3b - 4a^2b^2 = 2a^2(12a^2 + 5ab - 2b^2)$$
$$= 2a^2(4a - b)(3a + 2b).$$

29. $9m^2 - 12m + 4$
$= (3m)^2 - 12m + 2^2$
$= (3m)^2 - 2(3m)(2) + 2^2$
                Perfect square trinomial
$= (3m - 2)^2$

31. $32a^2 + 48ab + 18b^2$
$= 2(16a^2 + 24ab + 9b^2)$
        2 is the greatest common factor.
$= 2[(4a)^2 + 24ab + (3b)^2]$
$= 2[(4a)^2 + 2(4a)(3b) + (3b)^2]$
        Perfect square trinomial
$= 2(4a + 3b)^2$

33. $4x^2y^2 + 28xy + 49$
$= (2xy)^2 + 28xy + 7^2$
$= (2xy)^2 + 2(2xy)(7) + 7^2$
                Perfect square trinomial
$= (2xy + 7)^2$

35. $(a - 3b)^2 - 6(a - 3b) + 9$
Let $x = a - 3b$.
$(a - 3b)^2 - 6(a - 3b) + 9$
$= x^2 - 6x + 9$
$= x^2 - 2(x)(3) + 3^2$
                Perfect square trinomial
$= (x - 3)^2$
Replacing x with $a - 3b$ gives
$(a - 3b)^2 - 6(a - 3b) + 9 = (a - 3b - 3)^2.$

37. $9a^2 - 16 = (3a)^2 - 4^2$
                Difference of two squares
$= (3a + 4)(3a - 4)$

39. $25s^4 - 9t^2 = (5s^2)^2 - (3t)^2$
                Difference of two squares
$= (5s^2 + 3t)(5s^2 - 3t)$

41. $(a + b)^2 - 16$
$= (a + b)^2 - 4^2$
                Difference of two squares
$= [(a + b) + 4][(a + b) - 4]$
$= (a + b + 4)(a + b - 4)$

43. $p^4 - 625$
$= (p^2)^2 - 25^2$
                Difference of two squares
$= (p^2 + 25)(p^2 - 25)$
$= (p^2 + 25)(p^2 - 5^2)$
                Difference of two squares
$= (p^2 + 25)(p + 5)(p - 5)$
Note that $p^2 + 25$ is a prime factor.

45. The correct complete factorization of $x^4 - 1$ is B:
$(x^2 + 1)(x + 1) \cdot (x - 1)$. Choice A is not a
complete factorization, since $x^2 - 1$ can be
factored as $(x + 1)(x - 1)$.
The other choices are not correct factorizations
of $x^4 - 1$.

47. $8 - a^3$
$= 2^3 - a^3$ Difference of two cubes
$= (2 - a)(a^2 + 2 \cdot a + a^2)$
$= (2 - a)(4 + 2a + a^2)$

49. $125x^3 - 27$
$= (5x)^3 - 3^3$ Difference of two cubes
$= (5x - 3)\left[(5x)^2 + 5x \cdot 3 + 3^2\right]$
$= (5x - 3)(25x^2 + 15x + 9)$

51. $27y^9 + 125z^6$
$= (3y^3)^3 + (5z^2)^3$ Sum of two cubes
$= (3y^3 + 5z^2) \cdot \left[(3y^3)^2 - (3y^3)(5z^2) + (5z^2)^2\right]$
$= (3y^3 + 5z^2)(9y^6 - 15y^3z^2 + 25z^4)$

53. $(r + 6)^3 - 216$
Let $x = r + 6$. Then
$(r + 6)^3 - 216$
$= x^3 - 216$
$= x^3 - 6^3$ Difference of two cubes
$= (x - 6)(x^2 + 6x + 6^2)$
$= (x - 6)(x^2 + 6x + 36).$

Replacing x with $(r + 6)$ gives

$(r+6)^3 - 216$

$= ((r+6)-6) \cdot \left[(r+6)^2 + 6(r+6) + 36 \right]$

$= r(r^2 + 12r + 36 + 6r + 36 + 36)$

$= r(r^2 + 18r + 108).$

55. $27 - (m + 2n)^3$

Let $x = m + 2n$. Then

$27 - (m + 2n)^3$

$= 27 - x^3$

$= 3^3 - x^3$ Difference of two cubes

$= (3 - x)(3^2 + 3x + x^2)$

$= (3 - x)(9 + 3x + x^2).$

Replacing x with $m + 2n$ gives

$27 - (m + 2n)^3$

$= [3 - (m + 2n)] \cdot \left[3^2 + 3(m + 2n) + (m + 2n)^2 \right]$

$= (3 - m - 2n) \cdot (9 + 3m + 6n + m^2 + 4mn + 4n^2).$

57. $m^4 - 3m^2 - 10$

Let $x = m^2$.

Substituting x for m^2, we have

$x^2 - 3x - 10.$

Factor this trinomial as

$x^2 - 3x - 10 = (x - 5)(x + 2).$

Replacing x with m^2 gives

$m^4 - 3m^2 - 10 = (m^2 - 5)(m^2 + 2).$

59. $7(3k - 1)^2 + 26(3k - 1) - 8$

Let $x = 3k - 1$. This substitution gives

$7(3k - 1)^2 + 26(3k - 1) - 8$

$= 7x^2 + 26x - 8$

$= (7x - 2)(x + 4).$

Replacing x with $3k - 1$ gives

$7(3k - 1)^2 + 26(3k - 1) - 8$

$= [7(3k - 1) - 2][(3k - 1) + 4]$

$= (21k - 7 - 2)(3k - 1 + 4)$

$= (21k - 9)(3k + 3)$

$= 3(7k - 3)(3)(k + 1)$

$= 9(7k - 3)(k + 1).$

61. $9(a - 4)^2 + 30(a - 4) + 25$

Let $x = a - 4$.

With this substitution, we have

$9(a - 4)^2 + 30(a - 4) + 25$

$= 9x^2 + 30x + 25$

$= (3x + 5)^2.$ Perfect square trinomial

Replacing x by $a - 4$ gives

$[3(a - 4) + 5]^2 = (3a - 12 + 5)^2$

$= (3a - 7)^2.$

63. $4b^2 + 4bc + c^2 - 16$

$= (4b^2 + 4bc + c^2) - 16$

$= (2b + c)^2 - 4^2$ Difference of two squares

$= [(2b + c) + 4][(2b + c) - 4]$

$= (2b + c + 4)(2b + c - 4)$

65. $x^2 + xy - 5x - 5y$

$= (x^2 + xy) + (-5x - 5y)$

      Group the terms.

$= x(x + y) - 5(x + y)$

      Factor each group.

$= (x + y)(x - 5)$ Factor out $x + y$.

67. $p^4(m - 2n) + q(m - 2n)$

$= (m - 2n)(p^4 + q)$ Factor out $m - 2n$.

69. $4z^2 + 28z + 49$

$= (2z)^2 + 2(2z)(7) + 7^2$

      Perfect square trinomial

$= (2z + 7)^2$

71. $1000x^3 + 343y^3$

$= (10x)^3 + (7y)^3$ Sum of two cubes

$= (10x + 7y) \cdot \left[(10x^2)^2 - (10x)(7y) + (7y)^2 \right]$

$= (10x + 7y)(100x^2 - 70xy + 49y^2)$

73. $125m^6 - 216$

$= (5m^2)^3 - 6^3$ Difference of two cubes

$= (5m^2 - 6)\left[(5m^2)^2 + 5m^2 \cdot 6 + 6^2 \right]$

$= (5m^2 - 6)(25m^4 + 30m^2 + 36)$

75. $12m^2 + 16mn - 35n^2$

Try different combinations of the factors of 12 and −35 until the correct one is found.

$12m^2 + 16mn - 35n^2 = (6m - 7n)(2m + 5n)$

77. $4p^2 + 3p - 1$

The positive factors of 4 could be 2 and 2 or 1 and 4. The factors of -1 can only be 1 and -1. Try different combinations of these factors until the correct one is found.

$4p^2 + 3p - 1 = (4p - 1)(p + 1)$

79. $144z^2 + 121$

The sum of two squares cannot be factored.

$144z^2 + 121$ is prime.

81. $(x + y)^2 - (x - y)^2$

Factor this expression as the difference of two squares.

$$= [(x + y) - (x - y)] \cdot [(x + y) + (x - y)]$$
$$= (x + y - x + y)(x + y + x - y)$$
$$= (2y)(2x)$$
$$= 4xy$$

85. $9p^2 + bp + 25$

In order for the trinomial to be a perfect square, it must have the form

$(3p)^2 + 2(3p)(5) + 5^2$ or

$(3p)^2 - 2(3p)(5) + 5^2$.

Therefore, $\quad b = 2 \cdot 3 \cdot 5 = 30$

$\qquad$ or $b = -(2 \cdot 3 \cdot 5) = -30$.

Thus, we will have a perfect square trinomial if $b = \pm 30$.

87. $49x^2 + 70x + c$

The perfect square form is

$(7x)^2 + \underbrace{2(7x)(5)}_{70x} + 5^2$.

Therefore, $c = 25$.

Section R.3

Exercises

1. In the rational expression $\dfrac{x + 3}{x - 6}$, the solution to the equation $x - 6 = 0$ is excluded from the domain.

$x - 6 = 0$

$\qquad x = 6$

The domain is $\{x \mid x \neq 6\}$.

3. In the rational expression $\dfrac{3x + 7}{(4x + 2)(x - 1)}$, the solution to the equation $(4x + 2)(x - 1) = 0$ is excluded from the domain.

$(4x + 2)(x - 1) = 0$

$4x + 2 = 0 \quad$ or $\quad x - 1 = 0$

$\quad 4x = -2 \qquad\qquad x = 1$

$\qquad x = -\tfrac{1}{2}$

The domain is $\left\{ x \mid x \neq -\dfrac{1}{2}, 1 \right\}$.

5. In the rational expression $\dfrac{12}{x^2 + 5x + 6}$, the solution to the equation $x^2 + 5x + 6 = 0$ is excluded from the domain.

$x^2 + 5x + 6 = 0$

$(x + 3)(x + 2) = 0$

$x + 3 = 0 \quad$ or $\quad x + 2 = 0$

$\quad x = -3 \qquad\qquad x = -2$

The domain is $\{x \mid x \neq -3, -2\}$.

7. $\dfrac{8k + 16}{9k + 18} = \dfrac{8(k + 2)}{9(k + 2)}$ $\quad$ Factor numerator and denominator.

$\qquad\qquad = \dfrac{8}{9}$ $\quad$ Fundamental principle

9. $\dfrac{3(t + 5)}{(t + 5)(t - 3)} = \dfrac{3}{t - 3}$ $\quad$ Fundamental principle

11. $\dfrac{8x^2 + 16x}{4x^2}$

$= \dfrac{8x(x + 2)}{4x^2}$ $\quad$ Factor.

$= \dfrac{2 \cdot 4x(x + 2)}{x \cdot 4x}$ $\quad$ Factor.

$= \dfrac{2(x + 2)}{x}$ $\quad$ Fundamental principle

$= \dfrac{2x + 4}{x}$

13. $\dfrac{m^2 - 4m + 4}{m^2 + m - 6}$

$= \dfrac{(m - 2)(m - 2)}{(m - 2)(m + 3)}$ $\quad$ Factor.

$= \dfrac{m - 2}{m + 3}$ $\quad$ Use the fundamental principle to write the expression in lowest terms.

15. $\dfrac{8m^2+6m-9}{16m^2-9}$

$= \dfrac{(2m+3)(4m-3)}{(4m+3)(4m-3)}$ Factor.

$= \dfrac{2m+3}{4m+3}$ Use the fundamental principle to write the expression in lowest terms.

17. $\dfrac{15p^3}{9p^2} \div \dfrac{6p}{10p^2}$

$= \dfrac{15p^3}{9p^2} \cdot \dfrac{10p^2}{6p}$ Definition of division

$= \dfrac{150p^5}{54p^3}$ Multiply.

$= \dfrac{25 \cdot 6p^5}{9 \cdot 6p^3}$ Factor.

$= \dfrac{25p^2}{9}$ Fundamental principle

19. $\dfrac{2k+8}{6} \div \dfrac{3k+12}{2}$

$= \dfrac{2k+8}{6} \cdot \dfrac{2}{3k+12}$ Definition of division

$= \dfrac{2(k+4)(2)}{6(3)(k+4)}$ Multiply and factor.

$= \dfrac{4}{18}$

$= \dfrac{2}{9}$ Fundamental principle

21. $\dfrac{x^2+x}{5} \cdot \dfrac{25}{xy+y}$

$= \dfrac{x(x+1)}{5} \cdot \dfrac{25}{y(x+1)}$ Factor.

$= \dfrac{25x(x+1)}{5y(x+1)}$ Multiply.

$= \dfrac{5x}{y}$ Fundamental principle

23. $\dfrac{4a-12}{2a-10} \div \dfrac{a^2-9}{a^2-a-20}$

$= \dfrac{4a+12}{2a-10} \cdot \dfrac{a^2-a-20}{a^2-9}$ Definition of division

$= \dfrac{4(a+3)(a-5)(a+4)}{2(a-5)(a+3)(a-3)}$ Multiply and factor.

$= \dfrac{2(a+4)}{(a-3)}$ Fundamental principle

or $\dfrac{2a+8}{a-3}$

25. $\dfrac{p^2-p-12}{p^2-2p-15} \cdot \dfrac{p^2-9p+20}{p^2-8p+16}$

$= \dfrac{(p-4)(p+3)(p-5)(p-4)}{(p-5)(p+3)(p-4)(p-4)}$ Multiply and factor.

$= 1$ Fundamental principle

27. $\dfrac{m^2+3m+2}{m^2+5m+4} \div \dfrac{m^2+5m+6}{m^2+10m+24}$

$= \dfrac{m^2+3m+2}{m^2+5m+4} \cdot \dfrac{m^2+10m+24}{m^2+5m+6}$ Definition of division

$= \dfrac{(m+2)(m+1)(m+6)(m+4)}{(m+4)(m+1)(m+3)(m+2)}$ Multiply and factor.

$= \dfrac{m+6}{m+3}$ Fundamental principle

29. $\dfrac{xz-xw+2yz-2yw}{z^2-w^2} \cdot \dfrac{4z+4w+xz+wx}{16-x^2}$

$= \dfrac{(x+2y)(z-w)(4+x)(z+w)}{(z-w)(z+w)(4-x)(4+x)}$ Multiply and factor.

$= \dfrac{x+2y}{4-x}$ Fundamental principal

31. $\dfrac{x^3+y^3}{x^3-y^3} \cdot \dfrac{x^2-y^2}{x^2+2xy+y^2}$

$= \dfrac{(x+y)(x^2-xy+y^2)(x-y)(x+y)}{(x-y)(x^2+xy+y^2)(x+y)(x+y)}$ Factor, using sum of two cubes and difference of two squares.

$= \dfrac{x^2-xy+y^2}{x^2+xy+y^2}$ Fundamental principle

33. Expressions (B) and (C) are both equal to -1, since the numerator and denominator are additive inverses.

B. $\dfrac{-x-4}{x+4} = \dfrac{-1(x+4)}{x+4} = -1$

C. $\dfrac{x-4}{4-x} = \dfrac{-1(4-x)}{4-x} = -1$

35. $\dfrac{3}{2k} + \dfrac{5}{3k} = \dfrac{3 \cdot 3}{2k \cdot 3} + \dfrac{5 \cdot 2}{3k \cdot 2}$ Fundamental principle Common denominator

$= \dfrac{9}{6k} + \dfrac{10}{6k}$

$= \dfrac{19}{6k}$ Add numerators.

37. $\dfrac{a+1}{2} - \dfrac{a-1}{2}$

$= \dfrac{(a+1)-(a-1)}{2}$ Subtract numerators.

$= \dfrac{a+1-a+1}{2}$ Remove parentheses.

$= \dfrac{2}{2}$

$= 1$

39. $\dfrac{3}{p} + \dfrac{1}{2} = \dfrac{3\cdot 2}{p\cdot 2} + \dfrac{1\cdot p}{2\cdot p}$ Fundamental principle

       $= \dfrac{6}{2p} + \dfrac{p}{2p}$ Common denominator

       $= \dfrac{6+p}{2p}$ Add numerators.

41. $\dfrac{1}{6m} + \dfrac{2}{5m} + \dfrac{4}{m}$

$= \dfrac{1\cdot 5}{6m\cdot 5} + \dfrac{2\cdot 6}{5m\cdot 6} + \dfrac{4\cdot 6\cdot 5}{m\cdot 6\cdot 5}$ Fundamental principle

$= \dfrac{5}{30m} + \dfrac{12}{30m} + \dfrac{120}{30m}$ Common denominator

$= \dfrac{137}{30m}$ Add numerators.

43. $\dfrac{1}{a} - \dfrac{b}{a^2} = \dfrac{1\cdot a}{a\cdot a} - \dfrac{b}{a^2}$ Fundamental principle

       $= \dfrac{a}{a^2} - \dfrac{b}{a^2}$ Common denominators

       $= \dfrac{a-b}{a^2}$ Subtract denominators.

45. $\dfrac{1}{x+z} + \dfrac{1}{x-z}$

$= \dfrac{1(x-z)}{(x+z)(x-z)} + \dfrac{1(x+z)}{(x-z)(x+z)}$ Fundamental principle

$= \dfrac{x-z}{(x-z)(x+z)} + \dfrac{x+z}{(x+z)(x-z)}$ Common denominator

$= \dfrac{2x}{(x+z)(x-z)}$ Add numerators.

47. $\dfrac{3}{a-2} - \dfrac{1}{2-a}$

$= \dfrac{3}{a-2} - \dfrac{1(-1)}{(2-a)(-1)}$

           $a-2 = (-1)(2-a)$

$= \dfrac{3}{a-2} - \dfrac{-1}{a-2}$

$= \dfrac{3+1}{a-2}$

$= \dfrac{4}{a-2}$

We may also use $2-a$ as the common denominator.

$\dfrac{3(-1)}{(a-2)(-1)} - \dfrac{1}{2-a}$

$= \dfrac{-3}{2-a} - \dfrac{1}{2-a}$

$= \dfrac{-4}{2-a}$

The two results, $\dfrac{4}{a-2}$ and $\dfrac{-4}{2-a}$, are equivalent rational expressions.

49. $\dfrac{x+y}{2x-y} - \dfrac{2x}{y-2x}$

$= \dfrac{x+y}{2x-y} - \dfrac{2x(-1)}{(y-2x)(-1)}$

           $2x-y = (-1)(y-2x)$

$= \dfrac{x+y}{2x-y} - \dfrac{-2x}{2x-y}$

$= \dfrac{x+y+2x}{2x-y}$

$= \dfrac{3x+y}{2x-y}$

We may also use $y-2x$ as the common denominator. In this case, our result will be $\dfrac{-3x-y}{y-2x}$.

The two results are equivalent rational expressions.

51. $\dfrac{1}{x^2+x-12} - \dfrac{1}{x^2-7x+12} + \dfrac{1}{x^2-16}$

$= \dfrac{1}{(x+4)(x-3)} - \dfrac{1}{(x-4)(x-3)} + \dfrac{1}{(x-4)(x+4)}$ Factor denominators.

The least common denominator is $(x+4)(x-3)(x-4)$.

$= \dfrac{1(x-4)}{(x+4)(x-3)(x-4)} - \dfrac{1(x+4)}{(x-4)(x-3)(x+4)} + \dfrac{1(x-3)}{(x-4)(x+4)(x-3)}$ Fundamental principle

$= \dfrac{(x-4)-(x+4)+(x-3)}{(x-4)(x+4)(x-3)}$ Subtract and add numerators.

$= \dfrac{x-4-x-4+x-3}{(x-4)(x+4)(x-3)}$ Remove parentheses.

$= \dfrac{x-11}{(x-4)(x+4)(x-3)}$

53. $\dfrac{1+\frac{1}{x}}{1-\frac{1}{x}}$

Multiply both numerator and denominator by the least common denominator of all the factions, x.

$\dfrac{1+\frac{1}{x}}{1-\frac{1}{x}} = \dfrac{x\left(1+\frac{1}{x}\right)}{x\left(1-\frac{1}{x}\right)}$

$\qquad = \dfrac{x\cdot 1 + x\left(\frac{1}{x}\right)}{x\cdot 1 - x\left(\frac{1}{x}\right)}$

$\qquad = \dfrac{x+1}{x-1}$

55. $\dfrac{\frac{1}{x+1}-\frac{1}{x}}{\frac{1}{x}}$

Multiply both numerator and denominator by the least common denominator of all the fractions, $x(x+1)$.

$\dfrac{\frac{1}{x+1}-\frac{1}{x}}{\frac{1}{x}}$

$= \dfrac{x(x+1)\left(\frac{1}{x+1}-\frac{1}{x}\right)}{x(x+1)\left(\frac{1}{x}\right)}$

$= \dfrac{x(x+1)\left(\frac{1}{x+1}\right) - x(x+1)\left(\frac{1}{x}\right)}{x(x+1)\left(\frac{1}{x}\right)}$

$= \dfrac{x-(x+1)}{x+1}$

$= \dfrac{x-x-1}{x+1}$

$= \dfrac{-1}{x+1}$

57. $\dfrac{1+\frac{1}{1-b}}{1-\frac{1}{1+b}}$

Multiply both numerator and denominator by the least common denominator of all the fractions, $(1-b)(1+b)$.

$\dfrac{1+\frac{1}{1-b}}{1-\frac{1}{1+b}}$

$= \dfrac{(1-b)(1+b)\left(1+\frac{1}{1-b}\right)}{(1-b)(1+b)\left(1-\frac{1}{1+b}\right)}$

$= \dfrac{(1-b)(1+b)+(1+b)}{(1-b)(1+b)-(1-b)}$

$= \dfrac{(1+b)[(1-b)+1]}{(1-b)[(1+b)-1]}$

Factor out common factors in numerator and denominator.

$= \dfrac{(1+b)(2-b)}{(1-b)b}$ or $\dfrac{(2-b)(1+b)}{b(1-b)}$

59. $\dfrac{m-\frac{1}{m^2-4}}{\frac{1}{m+2}} = \dfrac{m-\frac{1}{(m+2)(m-2)}}{\frac{1}{m+2}}$

Multiply both numerator and denominator by the least common denominator of all the fractions, $(m+2)(m-2)$.

$\dfrac{m-\frac{1}{m^2-4}}{\frac{1}{m+2}} = \dfrac{(m+2)(m-2)\left(m-\frac{1}{(m+2)(m-2)}\right)}{(m+2)(m-2)\left(\frac{1}{m+2}\right)}$

$= \dfrac{(m+2)(m-2)(m)-(m+2)(m-2)\left(\frac{1}{(m+2)(m-2)}\right)}{(m+2)(m-2)\left(\frac{1}{m+2}\right)}$

$= \dfrac{m(m^2-4)-1}{m-2}$

$= \dfrac{m^3-4m-1}{m-2}$

61. $\dfrac{\frac{1}{x+h}-\frac{1}{x}}{h}$

To simplify this complex fraction, multiply both numerator and denominator by the least common denominator of all the fractions, $x(x+h)$.

$$\dfrac{\frac{1}{x+h}-\frac{1}{x}}{h}$$

$$=\dfrac{x(x+h)\left(\frac{1}{x+h}-\frac{1}{x}\right)}{x(x+h)(h)}$$

$$=\dfrac{x(x+h)\left(\frac{1}{x+h}\right)-x(x+h)\left(\frac{1}{x}\right)}{x(x+h)(h)}$$

$$=\dfrac{x-(x+h)}{xh(x+h)}$$

$$=\dfrac{-h}{xh(x+h)}$$

$$=\dfrac{-1}{x(x+h)}$$

Section R.4

Exercises

1. $\left(\dfrac{4}{9}\right)^{3/2}=\left[\left(\dfrac{4}{9}\right)^{1/2}\right]^{3}=\left(\dfrac{2}{3}\right)^{3}=\dfrac{2^{3}}{3^{3}}=\dfrac{8}{27}$; E

3. $-\left(\dfrac{9}{4}\right)^{3/2}=-\left[\left(\dfrac{9}{4}\right)^{1/2}\right]^{3}=-\left(\dfrac{3}{2}\right)^{3}$

$$=-\dfrac{3^{3}}{2^{3}}=-\dfrac{27}{8}$$; F

5. $\left(\dfrac{8}{27}\right)^{2/3}=\left[\left(\dfrac{8}{27}\right)^{1/3}\right]^{2}=\left(\dfrac{2}{3}\right)^{2}=\dfrac{2^{2}}{3^{2}}=\dfrac{4}{9}$; D

7. $-\left(\dfrac{27}{8}\right)^{2/3}=-\left[\left(\dfrac{27}{8}\right)^{1/3}\right]^{2}=-\left(\dfrac{3}{2}\right)^{2}$

$$=-\dfrac{3^{2}}{2^{2}}=-\dfrac{9}{4}$$; B

9. $(-4)^{-3}=\dfrac{1}{(-4)^{3}}=\dfrac{1}{-64}=-\dfrac{1}{64}$

11. $8^{2/3}=(8^{1/3})^{2}=2^{2}=4$

13. $-81^{3/4}=-[(81)^{1/4}]^{3}=-(3)^{3}=-27$

15. $\left(\dfrac{27}{64}\right)^{-4/3}$

$$=\left(\dfrac{64}{27}\right)^{4/3}=\left[\left(\dfrac{64}{27}\right)^{1/3}\right]^{4}=\left(\dfrac{4}{3}\right)^{4}=\dfrac{4^{4}}{3^{4}}=\dfrac{256}{81}$$

19. $\dfrac{4^{-2}\cdot4^{-1}}{4^{-3}}=\dfrac{4^{-3}}{4^{-3}}=1$

21. $(m^{2/3})(m^{5/3})$

$$=m^{2/3+5/3}$$ Product rule

$$=m^{7/3}$$

23. $(1+n)^{1/2}(1+n)^{3/4}$

$$=(1+n)^{1/2+3/4}$$

$$=(1+n)^{5/4}$$ Add exponents.

25. $(2y^{3/4}z)(3y^{-2}z^{-1/3})$

$$=6y^{3/4+(-2)}z^{1+(-1/3)}$$

$$=6y^{3/4-8/4}z^{3/3-1/3}$$

$$=6y^{-5/4}z^{2/3}$$

$$=\dfrac{6z^{2/3}}{y^{5/4}}$$

27. $(4a^{-2}b^{7})^{1/2}\cdot(2a^{1/4}b^{3})^{5}$

$$=(4^{1/2}a^{-1}b^{7/2})(2^{5}a^{5/4}b^{15})$$

$$=2\cdot2^{5}\cdot a^{-1}\cdot a^{5/4}\cdot b^{7/2}\cdot b^{15}$$

$$=2^{6}a^{-4/4+5/4}b^{7/2+30/2}$$

$$=2^{6}a^{1/4}b^{37/2}$$

29. $\left(\dfrac{r^{-2}}{s^{-5}}\right)^{-3}=\dfrac{(r^{-2})^{-3}}{(s^{-5})^{-3}}$

$$=\dfrac{r^{(-2)(-3)}}{s^{(-5)(-3)}}$$

$$=\dfrac{r^{6}}{s^{15}}$$

31. $\left(\dfrac{-a}{b^{-3}}\right)^{-1}=\dfrac{(-a)^{-1}}{(b^{-3})^{-1}}$

$$=\dfrac{1}{-ab^{3}}$$

$$=-\dfrac{1}{ab^{3}}$$

33. $\dfrac{12^{5/4}y^{-2}}{12^{-1}y^{-3}} = 12^{5/4-(-4/4)}y^{-2-(-3)}$

$\qquad\qquad\qquad$ Quotient rule

$\qquad = 12^{9/4}y$

35. $\dfrac{8p^{-3}(4p^2)^{-2}}{p^{-5}} = \dfrac{8p^{-3}\cdot 4^{-2}p^{-4}}{p^{-5}}$

$\qquad = \dfrac{8\cdot 4^{-2}\cdot p^{-7}}{p^{-5}}$

$\qquad = \dfrac{8}{4^2 p^{-5}p^7}$

$\qquad = \dfrac{8}{16p^2}$

$\qquad = \dfrac{1}{2p^2}$

37. $\dfrac{m^{7/3}n^{-2/5}p^{3/8}}{m^{-2/3}n^{3/5}p^{-5/8}} = \dfrac{m^{7/3}m^{2/3}p^{3/8}p^{5/8}}{n^{3/5}n^{2/5}}$

$\qquad = \dfrac{m^{9/3}p^{8/8}}{n^{5/5}}$

$\qquad = \dfrac{m^3 p}{n}$

39. $\dfrac{-4a^{-1}a^{2/3}}{a^{-2}} = \dfrac{-4a^{-3/3}a^{-2/3}}{a^{-2}}$

$\qquad = \dfrac{-4a^{-1/3}}{a^{-2}}$

$\qquad = \dfrac{-4a^{-1/3}a^2}{1}$

$\qquad = -4a^{5/3}$

41. $\dfrac{(k+5)^{1/2}(k+5)^{-1/4}}{(k+5)^{3/4}} = (k+5)^{1/2-1/4-3/4}$

$\qquad = (k+5)^{-1/2}$

$\qquad = \dfrac{1}{(k+5)^{1/2}}$

43. $y^{5/8}(y^{3/8} - 10y^{11/8})$

$\qquad = y^{5/8}y^{3/8} - 10y^{5/8}y^{11/8}$

$\qquad = y^{5/8+3/8} - 10y^{5/8+11/8}$

$\qquad = y - 10y^2$

45. $-4k(k^{7/3} - 6k^{1/3}) = -4k^1 k^{7/3} + 24k^1 k^{1/3}$

$\qquad\qquad = -4k^{10/3} + 24k^{4/3}$

47. $(x + x^{1/2})(x - x^{1/2})$

$\qquad = x^2 - (x^{1/2})^2$ Difference of two squares

$\qquad = x^2 - x$

49. $(r^{1/2} - r^{-1/2})^2$

$\qquad = (r^{1/2})^2 - 2(r^{1/2})(r^{-1/2}) + (r^{-1/2})^2$

$\qquad = r - 2r^0 + r^{-1}$

$\qquad = r - 2 + r^{-1}$ or $r - 2 + \dfrac{1}{r}$

51. Factor $4k^{-1} + k^{-2}$, using the common factor k^{-2}.

$\qquad 4k^{-1} + k^{-2} = k^{-2}(4k+1)$ or $\dfrac{4k+1}{k^2}$

53. Factor $9z^{-1/2} + 2z^{1/2}$, using the common factor $z^{-1/2}$.

$\qquad 9z^{-1/2} + 2z^{1/2} = z^{-1/2}(9+2z)$ or $\dfrac{9+2z}{z^{1/2}}$

55. Factor $p^{-3/4} - 2p^{-7/4}$, using the common factor $p^{-7/4}$.

$\qquad p^{-3/4} - 2p^{-7/4} = p^{-7/4}(p^{4/4} - 2)$

$\qquad\qquad\qquad = p^{-7/4}(p - 2)$ or $\dfrac{p-2}{p^{7/4}}$

57. Factor $(p+4)^{-3/2} + (p+4)^{-1/2} + (p+4)^{1/2}$ using the common factor $(p+4)^{-3/2}$.

$\qquad = (p+4)^{-3/2}\cdot[1 + (p+4) + (p+4)^2]$

$\qquad = (p+4)^{-3/2}\cdot(1 + p + 4 + p^2 + 8p + 16)$

$\qquad = (p+4)^{-3/2}(p^2 + 9p + 21)$ or $\dfrac{p^2+9p+21}{(p+4)^{3/2}}$

59. $\dfrac{a^{-1} + b^{-1}}{(ab)^{-1}}$

$\qquad = \dfrac{\frac{1}{a} + \frac{1}{b}}{\frac{1}{ab}}$ Definition of negative integer exponent

$\qquad = \dfrac{\frac{1\cdot b}{a\cdot b} + \frac{1\cdot a}{b\cdot a}}{\frac{1}{ab}}$

$\qquad = \dfrac{\frac{b+a}{ab}}{\frac{1}{ab}}$

$\qquad = \dfrac{b+a}{ab}\cdot\dfrac{ab}{1}$ Definition of division

$\qquad = b + a$

61. $\dfrac{r^{-1}+q^{-1}}{r^{-1}-q^{-1}}\cdot\dfrac{r-q}{r+q}$

$=\dfrac{\frac{1}{r}+\frac{1}{q}}{\frac{1}{r}-\frac{1}{q}}\cdot\dfrac{r-q}{r+q}$

$=\dfrac{rq\left(\frac{1}{r}+\frac{1}{q}\right)}{rq\left(\frac{1}{r}-\frac{1}{q}\right)}\cdot\dfrac{r-q}{r+q}$

Multiply numerator and denominator of first fraction by common denonominator, rq.

$=\dfrac{q+r}{q-r}\cdot\dfrac{r-q}{r+q}$

$=\dfrac{r-q}{q-r}$

$=\dfrac{-1(r-q)}{-1(q-r)}$

$=\dfrac{-1(r-q)}{r-q}$

$=-1$

63. $\dfrac{x-9y^{-1}}{(x-3y^{-1})(x+3y^{-1})}$

$=\dfrac{x-\frac{9}{y}}{\left(x-\frac{3}{y}\right)\left(x+\frac{3}{y}\right)}$ Definition of negative integer exponent

$=\dfrac{x-\frac{9}{y}}{x^2-\frac{9}{y^2}}$ Multiply in denominator.

$=\dfrac{y^2\left(x-\frac{9}{y}\right)}{y^2\left(x^2-\frac{9}{y^2}\right)}$

Multiply numerator and denominator by least common denominator, y^2.

$=\dfrac{y^2 x-9y}{y^2 x^2-9}$ Distributive property

$=\dfrac{y(xy-9)}{x^2 y^2-9}$ Factor numerator.

Section R.5

Exercises

1. $(-3x)^{1/3}=\sqrt[3]{-3x}$ (F)

3. $(-3x)^{-1/3}=\dfrac{1}{(-3x)^{1/3}}=\dfrac{1}{\sqrt[3]{-3x}}$ (H)

5. $(3x)^{1/3}=\sqrt[3]{3x}$ (G)

7. $(3x)^{-1/3}=\dfrac{1}{\sqrt[3]{3x}}$ (C)

9. $(-m)^{2/3}=\sqrt[3]{(-m)^2}$ or $\left(\sqrt[3]{-m}\right)^2$

11. $(2m+p)^{2/3}=\sqrt[3]{(2m+p)^2}$ or $\left(\sqrt[3]{2m+p}\right)^2$

13. $\sqrt[5]{k^2}=k^{2/5}$

15. $-3\sqrt{5p^3}=-3(5p^3)^{1/2}=-3\cdot 5^{1/2}p^{3/2}$

17. A is true.

19. It is true for all $x\geq 0$.

21. $\sqrt[3]{125}=5$

23. $\sqrt[5]{-3125}=-5$

25. $\sqrt{50}=\sqrt{25\cdot 2}=\sqrt{25}\cdot\sqrt{2}=5\sqrt{2}$

27. $\sqrt[3]{81}=\sqrt[3]{27\cdot 3}=\sqrt[3]{27}\cdot\sqrt[3]{3}=3\sqrt[3]{3}$

29. $-\sqrt[4]{32}=-\sqrt[4]{16\cdot 2}=-\sqrt[4]{16}\cdot\sqrt[4]{2}=-2\sqrt[4]{2}$

31. $-\sqrt{\dfrac{9}{5}}=\dfrac{-3}{\sqrt{5}}\cdot\dfrac{\sqrt{5}}{\sqrt{5}}=-\dfrac{3\sqrt{5}}{5}$

33. $-\sqrt[3]{\dfrac{4}{5}}=-\dfrac{\sqrt[3]{4}}{\sqrt[3]{5}}\cdot\dfrac{\sqrt[3]{5^2}}{\sqrt[3]{5^2}}$

$=-\dfrac{\sqrt[3]{4}\cdot\sqrt[3]{5^2}}{\sqrt[3]{5^3}}$

$=-\dfrac{\sqrt[3]{4\cdot 25}}{5}$

$=-\dfrac{\sqrt[3]{100}}{5}$

35. $\sqrt[3]{16(-2)^4(2)^8}=\sqrt[3]{2^4\cdot(-2)^4 2^8}$

$=\sqrt[3]{2^4\cdot 2^4\cdot 2^8}$

$=\sqrt[3]{2^{16}}$

$=\sqrt[3]{2^{15}\cdot 2}$

$=\sqrt[3]{2^{15}}\cdot\sqrt[3]{2}$

$=32\sqrt[3]{2}$

37. $\sqrt{8x^5z^8} = \sqrt{2 \cdot 4 \cdot x^4 \cdot x \cdot z^8}$
$= \sqrt{4x^4z^8} \cdot \sqrt{2x}$
$= 2x^2z^4\sqrt{2x}$

39. $\sqrt[3]{16z^5x^8y^4} = \sqrt[3]{8 \cdot 2 \cdot z^3z^2x^6x^2y^3y}$
$= \sqrt[3]{(8z^3x^6y^3)(2z^2x^2y)}$
Group all perfect cubes
$= \sqrt[3]{8z^3x^6y^3} \cdot \sqrt[3]{2z^2x^2y}$
$= 2zx^2y\sqrt[3]{2z^2x^2y}$

41. $\sqrt[4]{m^2n^7p^8} = \sqrt[4]{m^2n^4n^3p^8}$
$= \sqrt[4]{n^4p^8} \cdot \sqrt[4]{m^2n^3}$
$= np^2\sqrt[4]{m^2n^3}$

43. $\sqrt[4]{x^4 + y^4}$ cannot be simplified further.

45. $\sqrt{\dfrac{2}{3x}} = \dfrac{\sqrt{2}}{\sqrt{3x}} = \dfrac{\sqrt{2}}{\sqrt{3x}} \cdot \dfrac{\sqrt{3x}}{\sqrt{3x}} = \dfrac{\sqrt{6x}}{3x}$

47. $\sqrt{\dfrac{x^5y^3}{z^2}} = \dfrac{\sqrt{x^5y^3}}{\sqrt{z^2}}$
$= \dfrac{\sqrt{x^4xy^2y}}{z}$
$= \dfrac{\sqrt{x^4y^2} \cdot \sqrt{xy}}{z}$
$= \dfrac{x^2y\sqrt{xy}}{z}$

49. $\sqrt[3]{\dfrac{8}{x^2}} = \dfrac{\sqrt[3]{8}}{\sqrt[3]{x^2}}$
$= \dfrac{2}{\sqrt[3]{x^2}} \cdot \dfrac{\sqrt[3]{x}}{\sqrt[3]{x}}$
$= \dfrac{2\sqrt[3]{x}}{x}$

51. $\sqrt[4]{\dfrac{g^3h^5}{9r^6}} = \dfrac{\sqrt[4]{g^3h^5}}{\sqrt[4]{9r^6}}$
$= \dfrac{h\sqrt[4]{g^3h}}{\sqrt[4]{9r^6}} \cdot \dfrac{\sqrt[4]{9r^2}}{\sqrt[4]{9r^2}}$
$= \dfrac{h\sqrt[4]{9g^3hr^2}}{\sqrt[4]{81r^8}}$
$= \dfrac{h\sqrt[4]{9g^3hr^2}}{3r^2}$

53. $\dfrac{\sqrt[3]{mn} \cdot \sqrt[3]{m^2}}{\sqrt[3]{n^2}} = \sqrt[3]{\dfrac{mnm^2}{n^2}}$
$= \sqrt[3]{\dfrac{m^3}{n}}$
$= \dfrac{\sqrt[3]{m^3}}{\sqrt[3]{n}} \cdot \dfrac{\sqrt[3]{n^2}}{\sqrt[3]{n^2}}$
$= \dfrac{m\sqrt[3]{n^2}}{n}$

55. $\dfrac{\sqrt[4]{32x^5y} \cdot \sqrt[4]{2xy^4}}{\sqrt[4]{4x^3y^2}} = \sqrt[4]{\dfrac{64x^6y^5}{4x^3y^2}}$
$= \sqrt[4]{16x^3y^3}$
$= 2\sqrt[4]{x^3y^3}$

57. $\sqrt[3]{\sqrt{4}} = \sqrt[3]{4^{1/2}}$
$= (4^{1/2})^{1/3}$
$= 4^{1/6}$
$= (2^2)^{1/6}$
$= 2^{2/6}$
$= 2^{1/3}$
$= \sqrt[3]{2}$

59. $2\sqrt[3]{3} + 4\sqrt[3]{24} - \sqrt[3]{81}$
$= 2\sqrt[3]{3} + 4\sqrt[3]{8 \cdot 3} - \sqrt[3]{27 \cdot 3}$
$= 2\sqrt[3]{3} + 4\left(2\sqrt[3]{3}\right) - 3\sqrt[3]{3}$
$= 2\sqrt[3]{3} + 8\sqrt[3]{3} - 3\sqrt[3]{3}$
$= 7\sqrt[3]{3}$ Combine like radicals.

61. $\dfrac{1}{\sqrt{2}}+\dfrac{3}{\sqrt{8}}+\dfrac{1}{\sqrt{32}}$

$=\dfrac{1}{\sqrt{2}}+\dfrac{3}{2\sqrt{2}}+\dfrac{1}{4\sqrt{2}}$

$=\dfrac{4}{4\sqrt{2}}+\dfrac{6}{4\sqrt{2}}+\dfrac{1}{4\sqrt{2}}$

$=\dfrac{11}{4\sqrt{2}}$

$=\dfrac{11}{4\sqrt{2}}\cdot\dfrac{\sqrt{2}}{\sqrt{2}}$ Rationalize denominator.

$=\dfrac{11\sqrt{2}}{8}$

63. $\dfrac{-4}{\sqrt[3]{3}}+\dfrac{1}{\sqrt[3]{24}}-\dfrac{2}{\sqrt[3]{81}}$

$=\dfrac{-4}{\sqrt[3]{3}}+\dfrac{1}{2\sqrt[3]{3}}-\dfrac{2}{3\sqrt[3]{3}}$

$=\dfrac{-24}{6\sqrt[3]{3}}+\dfrac{3}{6\sqrt[3]{3}}-\dfrac{4}{6\sqrt[3]{3}}$

$=\dfrac{-25}{6\sqrt[3]{3}}$

$=\dfrac{-25}{6\sqrt[3]{3}}\cdot\dfrac{\sqrt[3]{3^2}}{\sqrt[3]{3^2}}$ Rationalize denominator.

$=-\dfrac{25\sqrt[3]{9}}{18}$

65. $\left(\sqrt{5}+\sqrt{2}\right)\left(\sqrt{5}-\sqrt{2}\right)=\left(\sqrt{5}\right)^2-\left(\sqrt{2}\right)^2$

$=5-2$

$=3$

67. $\left(\sqrt[3]{7}+3\right)\left(\sqrt[3]{7^2}-3\sqrt[3]{7}+9\right)$

This product has the pattern
$(a+b)(a^2-ab+b^2)=a^3+b^3$, the sum of two cubes. Thus,

$\left(\sqrt[3]{7}+3\right)\left(\sqrt[3]{7^2}-3\sqrt[3]{7}+9\right)=\left(\sqrt[3]{7}\right)^3+3^3$

$=7+27$

$=34.$

69. $\left(\sqrt{2}-1\right)^2=\left(\sqrt{2}\right)^2-2\left(\sqrt{2}\right)+1^2$

Square of a binomial

$=2-2\sqrt{2}+1$

$=3-2\sqrt{2}$

71. $\left(4\sqrt{5}-1\right)\left(3\sqrt{5}+2\right)$

$=12\cdot5+8\sqrt{5}-3\sqrt{5}-2$

$=60+5\sqrt{5}-2$

$=58+5\sqrt{5}$

73. $\dfrac{\sqrt{3}}{\sqrt{5}+\sqrt{3}}=\dfrac{\sqrt{3}}{\sqrt{5}+\sqrt{3}}\cdot\dfrac{\sqrt{5}-\sqrt{3}}{\sqrt{5}-\sqrt{3}}$

Multiply numerator and denominator by conjugate of denominator.

$=\dfrac{\sqrt{3}\left(\sqrt{5}-\sqrt{3}\right)}{\left(\sqrt{5}\right)^2-\left(\sqrt{3}\right)^2}$ Difference of two squares

$=\dfrac{\sqrt{3}\sqrt{5}-\sqrt{3}\sqrt{3}}{5-3}$ Distributive property

$=\dfrac{\sqrt{15}-3}{2}$

75. $\dfrac{1+\sqrt{3}}{3\sqrt{5}+2\sqrt{3}}=\dfrac{1+\sqrt{3}}{3\sqrt{5}+2\sqrt{3}}\cdot\dfrac{3\sqrt{5}-2\sqrt{3}}{3\sqrt{5}-2\sqrt{3}}$

Multiply numerator and denominator by conjugate of denominator.

$=\dfrac{\left(1+\sqrt{3}\right)\left(3\sqrt{5}-2\sqrt{3}\right)}{\left(3\sqrt{5}\right)^2-\left(2\sqrt{3}\right)^2}$

Difference of two squares

$=\dfrac{3\sqrt{5}-2\sqrt{3}+3\sqrt{15}-6}{45-12}$

$=\dfrac{3\sqrt{5}-2\sqrt{3}+3\sqrt{15}-6}{33}$

77. $\dfrac{p}{\sqrt{p}+2}=\dfrac{p}{\sqrt{p}+2}\cdot\dfrac{\sqrt{p}-2}{\sqrt{p}-2}$

Multiply numerator and denominator by conjugate of denominator.

$=\dfrac{p\left(\sqrt{p}-2\right)}{\left(\sqrt{p}\right)^2-2^2}$ Difference of two squares

$=\dfrac{p\left(\sqrt{p}-2\right)}{p-4}$

79.
$$\frac{a}{\sqrt{a+b}-1} = \frac{a}{\sqrt{a+b}-1} \cdot \frac{\sqrt{a+b}+1}{\sqrt{a+b}+1}$$

$$= \frac{a\left(\sqrt{a+b}+1\right)}{\left(\sqrt{a+b}\right)^2 - 1^2}$$

$$= \frac{a\left(\sqrt{a+b}+1\right)}{a+b-1}$$